Title 11 & 11A, United States Code

Bankruptcy
Plus
Federal Rules
of
Bankruptcy Procedure
with
Official Bankruptcy Forms

Iron Press Publishing

TITLE 11—BANKRUPTCY

This title was enacted by Pub. L. 95–598, title I, § 101, Nov. 6, 1978, 92 Stat. 2549

AMENDMENTS

2005—Pub. L. 109–8, title VIII, § 801(b), title X, § 1007(d), Apr. 20, 2005, 119 Stat. 145, 188, substituted "Adjustments of Debts of a Family Farmer or Family Fisherman with Regular Annual Income" for "Adjustment of Debts of Family Farmers with Regular Annual Income" in item for chapter 12 and added item for chapter 15.

1994—Pub. L. 103–394, title V, § 501(d)(39), Oct. 22, 1994, 108 Stat. 4147, struck out item for chapter 15, "United States Trustees".

1986—Pub. L. 99–554, title II, § 257(a), Oct. 27, 1986, 100 Stat. 3114, added item for chapter 12.

TABLE I

*ERR82*This Table lists the sections of former Title 11, *ERR82*Bankruptcy, and indicates the sections of Title 11, *ERR82*as revised by Pub. L. 95–598 which cover similar *ERR82*and related subject matter.

Title 11 Former Sections	*Title 11 New Sections*
1(1)–(3)	Rep.
1(4)	101(12)
1(5)–(7)	Rep.
1(8)	101(8)
1(9), (10)	Rep.
1(11)	101(9)
1(12), (13)	Rep.
1(14)	101(11)
1(15), (16)	Rep.
1(17)	101(17), (18)
1(18)	Rep.
1(19)	101(26)
1(20)–(22)	Rep.
1(23)	101(30)
1(24)	101(31)
1(25), (26)	Rep.
1(27)	101(34)
1(28), (29)	Rep.
1(29a)	101(38)
1(30)	101(40)
1(31)	Rep.
1(32)	101(24)
1(33), (34)	Rep.
1(35)	102(7)
11(a)(1)	109(a)
11(a)(2)	502(j)

[1] So in original. Does not conform to chapter heading.

TABLE I—CONTINUED

Title 11 Former Sections	*Title 11 New Sections*
11(a)(2A)	505(a), (b)
11(a)(3), (4)	Rep.
11(a)(5)	721
11(a)(6)	Rep.
11(a)(7)	363
11(a)(8)	350
11(a)(9)–(14)	Rep.
11(a)(15)	105
11(a)(16)	Rep.
11(a)(17)	324
11(a)(18)	303(i)
11(a)(19), (20)	Rep.
11(a)(21)	543(b), (c)
11(a)(22)	305(a)(2)
11(b)	Rep.
21	303(h)
22	109(b)
22(a)	301
22(b)	303(a)
23(a)	Rep.
23(b)	303(b)
23(c)–(f)	Rep.
23(g)	723
23(h)–(k)	Rep.
24	522
25(a)(1)	343, 521(4)
25(a)(2)	Rep.
25(a)(3)	521(2)
25(a)(4)	521(3)
25(a)(5)	521(3)
25(a)(6)	521(2)
25(a)(7)	521(2)
25(a)(8), (9)	521(1)
25(a)(10)	343, 344
25(a)(11)	521(3)
25(b)	Rep.
26	541(a)
27, 28	Rep.
29(a)	362
29(b)–(d)	Rep.
29(e)	108(a), (b)
29(f)	108(c)
30, 31	(See former 501–1103)
32(a)	727(a)(10), 1141(d)(4)
32(b)	727(c)
32(c)(1)	727(a)(2), (4)
32(c)(2)	727(a)(3)
32(c)(3)	727(a)(4)
32(c)(4)	727(a)(2)
32(c)(5)	727(a)(8), (9)
32(c)(6)	727(a)(6)
32(c)(7)	727(a)(5)
32(c)(8)	Rep.
32(d), (e)	Rep.
32(f)	524(a)
32(g), (h)	Rep.
33	727(d), (e), 1328(e)
34	524(e)
35(a)(1)	523(a)(1)
35(a)(2)	523(a)(2)
35(a)(3)	523(a)(3)
35(a)(4)	523(a)(4)
35(a)(5), (6)	Rep.
35(a)(7)	523(a)(5)
35(a)(8)	523(a)(6)
35(b)	523(b), 349(a)
35(c)	523(c)
35(c)(4)	362
41(a)	Rep.
41(b)	303(d)
41(c)–(e)	Rep.
41(f)	301
42	T. 28 § 1480
43	Rep.
44(a)	343
44(b)–(f)	Rep.
44(g)	549(c)
44(h)–(*l*)	Rep.
45–51	Rep.
52, 53	Rep.

TABLE I—CONTINUED

Title 11 *Former Sections*	*Title 11* *New Sections*
54	Rep.
55	T. 28 § 1475
61–71	Rep.
72(a)	702
72(b)	705
72(c)	327(c)
73	321
74	325, 703(a)
75(a)(1)	704(1)
75(a)(2)	345
75(a)(3)	704(2)
75(a)(4)	Rep.
75(a)(5)	704(2)
75(a)(6)	Rep.
75(a)(7)	704(3)
75(a)(8)	704(4)
75(a)(9)	704(5)
75(a)(10)	704(6)
75(a)(11), (12)	Rep.
75(a)(13)	704(8)
75(a)(14)	Rep.
75(b), (c)	Rep.
76(a), (b)	Rep.
76(c)	326(a), 330
76(d)	Rep.
76(e)	326(d)
76(f), (g)	Rep.
76a	330
77	107
78(a)	Rep.
78(b)	322(a)
78(c)	322(b)(1)
78(d)	322(b)(2)
78(e)	Rep.
78(f), (g)	322(b)(2)
78(h)	Rep.
78(i)	322(c)
78(j)–(*l*)	Rep.
78(m)	322(d)
78(n)	Rep.
79–82	Rep.
91, 92	341
93(a)–(c)	Rep.
93(d)	502(a), (c)
93(e)	Rep.
93(f)	502(b)
93(g)	502(d)
93(h)	506(a), (b)
93(i)	501(b), 509
93(j)	724(a)
93(k)	502(j)
93(*l*), (m)	Rep.
93(n)	501(a), 726(a)(3)
93a	Rep.
94	342
95(a)	301
95(b)	303(b)
95(c), (d)	Rep.
95(e)	303(b)
95(f)	303(c)
95(g)	303(j), 707
95(h)	Rep.
96	547
96(a)(4)	547(e)(1)(B)
96(b)	550, 551
96(c)	547(c)(4), 553
96(d)	329
96(e)(1)	741
96(e)(2)	745, 751, 752
96(e)(3)	753
96(e)(5)	749
101	345
101a	Rep.
102(a)(1)	503(b)(2)
102(a)(2)–(4)	Rep.
102(b)	Rep.
102(c)	504
102(d)	Rep.
103	101(4)
103(a)(9)	502(b)(7)
103(c)	365
103a	Rep.
104(a)	507
104(a)(1)	503(b)
104(a)(2)	507(a)(3)
104(a)(4)	502(b)(4), 505(a), (b)
104(b)	Rep.
105(a)–(c)	Rep.
105(d)	508
105(e)	Rep.
106(a)	347(a)
106(b)	Rep.
107(a)	349(b), 547(b), (d), 551
107(b), (c)	545
107(c)(1)(A)	545(1)
107(c)(1)(B)	545(2), 546(b)
107(c)(1)(C)	545(3), (4)
107(c)(2)	551
107(c)(3)	724(b)
107(d)(1)(a)–(c)	Rep.
107(d)(1)(d)	101(26)
107(d)(1)(e)	Rep.
107(d)(2)	548(a)
107(d)(3)	550
107(d)(4)	548(b)
107(d)(5)	548(d)(1)
107(d)(6)	548(c), 550, 551
107(d)(7)	Rep.
107(e), (f)	Rep.
108	502(b)(3), 553
109(a)	303(e)
109(b)	303(i)
109(c)	Rep.
109(d)	303(g), 543(b), (c)
110(a)	541(a)
110(a)(3)	541(b)
110(a)(5)	522(d)(7), (8)
110(b)	365
110(c)	541(e), 544(a)
110(d)(1)	549(a)
110(d)(2), (3)	542(c)
110(d)(4), (5)	Rep.
110(e)	544(b)
110(f)	363
110(g)–(i)	Rep.
111, 112	Rep.
201, 202	(See former 501–1103)
202a–204	Rep.
205(a)	Rep.
205(b)	1171(b), 1172
205(c)(1)	1163
205(c)(2)	1166
205(c)(3)–(5)	Rep.
205(c)(6)	1169
205(c)(7)–(13)	Rep.
205(d)	Rep.
205(e)	1173
205(f)–(i)	Rep.
205(j)	1168
205(k), (*l*)	Rep.
205(m)	101(33)
205(n)	1167, 1171(a)
205(*o*)	1170
205(p)–(s)	Rep.
205a	Rep.
206, 207	(See former 501–1103)
208	Rep.
301–303	Rep.
401(1)	101(4)
401(2)	Rep.
401(3)	101(9)
401(4)	Rep.
401(5)	101(11)
401(6)	101(28)
401(7)	101(30)
401(8)	101(12)
401(9)	Rep.
401(10)	902(2)
401(11)	903(3)
402(a)	Rep.
402(b)(1), (2)	901
402(b)(3)	Rep.
402(c)	904
402(d)	921(b)
403	903
404	101(29), 109(c)
405(a)	921(a), (c)–(f)
405(b)	901, 924
405(c)	Rep.
405(d)	923
405(e)	901
405(e)(1)	922(a)
405(f), (g)	Rep.
405(h)	901, 926
406, 407	Rep.
408(a)	925
408(b)	901
408(c)	Rep.
409	901
410(a)	941, 942
410(b)	942
411, 412	901
413	901, 943(a)
414(a)	901
414(b)(1)	943(b)(5), (6)
414(b)(2)	943(b)(2)
414(b)(3)	Rep.
414(b)(4)	943(b)(3)
414(b)(5)	Rep.
414(b)(6)	943(b)(4)
415(a)	944(a)
415(b)(1)	944(b)
415(b)(2)	944(c)
416(a)	Rep.
416(b)	901
416(c)	Rep.
416(d)	347(b), 901
416(e)	945(a)
416(f)	Rep.
417	946

TABLE I—CONTINUED

Title 11 Former Sections	*Title 11 New Sections*
418	927
501, 502	Rep.
506(1)	101(4)
506(2), (3)	Rep.
506(4)	101(9)
506(5)	101(12)
506(6)	101(11)
506(7)	Rep.
506(8)	101(23)
506(9)	101(31)
506(10)	Rep.
506(11)	101(35)
506(12), (13)	Rep.
507	1124
511, 512	Rep.
513	362
514, 515	Rep.
516(1)	365
516(2)	364
516(3)	363
516(4)	362
516(5), (6)	1110
517–521	Rep.
526	303(b)
527	Rep.
528	T. 28 §1472
529–533	Rep.
536, 537	303(d)
541–549	Rep.
556	1104(a)
557	327
558	101(13)
559	1105
560	324, 1104(c)
561, 562	Rep.
563	1107(a)
564	1106(a)(2)
565	Rep.
566	107
567(1)	1106(a)(3)
567(2)	Rep.
567(3)	1106(a)(4)(A)
567(4)	Rep.
567(5)	1106(a)(4)
567(6)	Rep.
568	1104(b), 1106(b)
569	1106(a)(5)
570	1121
571–574	Rep.
575	1125(d)
576	1125(b)
577, 578	Rep.
579	1126, 1128(a)
580	1128(b)
586	541(a)
587	1106
588	1107(a)
589	1108
590	Rep.
591	327
596	501(a), 1111
597	1122
598	501(a)
599	1126(a)
600, 601	Rep.
602	502(b)(7)
603	1126(e)
604	1143
605	347(b)
606	1109(b)
607	1109
608	1109(a)
609–613	Rep.
616(1)	1123(b)(1)
616(2)	1123(a)(5), (b)(4)
616(3)	Rep.
616(4)	1123(b)(2)
616(5)	1123(a)(3)
616(6)	1123(a)(2)
616(7)–(9)	Rep.
616(10)	1123(a)(5)
616(11)	1123(a)(7)
616(12)(a)	1123(a)(6)
616(12)(b)	Rep.
616(13)	1123(b)(3)
616(14)	1123(b)(5)
621(1)	1100(a)(1)
621(2)	1129(a)(7), (11)
621(3)	1129(a)(3)
621(4)	1129(a)(4)
621(5)	1129(a)(5)
622	1127
623	1127(d)
624(1)	1141(a)
624(2)	1129(a)(6), 1142(a)
624(3), (4)	Rep.
625	Rep.
626	1141(c)
627	1142(b)
628(1)	1141(d)(1)–(3)

TABLE I—CONTINUED

Title 11 Former Sections	*Title 11 New Sections*
628(2)–(4)	Rep.
629(a)	1101(2)
629(b)	Rep.
629(c)	1127(b)
636	1112(b)
637	Rep.
638	348
641(1), (2)	Rep.
641(3), (4)	330
641(5)	503(b)(4)
642(1)	503(b)(3), (5)
642(2)	Rep.
642(3)	503(b)(4)
643	503(b)(3), (4)
644(1)	330
644(2)	503(b)(4)
644(3)	330
644(4)	503(b)(3), (4)
645–650	Rep.
656–659	Rep.
661	108(c)
662	Rep.
663	362
664(a)	1145(a)
664(b)	1145(b)
665, 666	Rep.
667	1146(c)
668	346(j)(1)
669	1129(d)
670	346(j)(5)
671, 672	Rep.
676	Rep.
701, 702	Rep.
706(1), (2)	Rep.
706(3)	101(12), 109(d)
706(4)	Rep.
706(5)	101(31)
707(1)	101(9)
707(2)	101(4), (11)
708	1124
711, 712	Rep.
713(1)	365
713(2)	363
713(3)	Rep.
714	362
715, 716	Rep.
721–728	Rep.
731–733	Rep.
734	341
735	341
735(3)	1128(a)
736	341
736(2)	501(a)
736(3)	343
737(1)	Rep.
737(2)	1129(a)(9)
737(3)	1128(a)
738	1102
739(1)(a)	1103(c)(2)
739(1)(b)–(e)	1103(c)(3)
739(1)(f)	1104(c)(5)
739(2)	503(b)(4), 1103(a)
741	Rep.
742	1107(a)
743	1108
744	364
751	1122
752	Rep.
753	502(b)(7)
754, 755	Rep.
755a	501(a)
756	Rep.
757(1)	Rep.
757(2)	1123(b)(2)
757(3)–(7)	Rep.
757(8)	1123(b)(5)
761	1129(a)(3)
762	Rep.
763	1127
764	1127(d)
765	1127(c)
766(1)	1129(a)(1)
766(2)	1129(a)(7), (11)
766(3)	1129(a)(2)
766(4)	1129(a)(3)
767(1)	1141(a)
767(2)–(4)	Rep.
768–770	Rep.
771	1141(d)(1)–(3)
772	Rep.
776, 777	1112(b)
778	348
779–781	Rep.
786	1144
787(1)	1127(b)
787(2)	1127(c)
787(3)	1127(d)
787(4)	Rep.
791	108(c)
792	Rep.

TABLE I—CONTINUED

Title 11 Former Sections	Title 11 New Sections
793(a)	1145(a)
793(b)	1145(b)
794	Rep.
795	346(j)(1)
796	346(j)(5)
797	Rep.
799	Rep.
801, 802	Rep.
806(1)	Rep.
806(2)	101(4)
806(3), (4)	Rep.
806(5)	101(9)
806(6)	101(12), 109(d)
806(7)	101(11)
806(8)	101(23)
806(9)	101(31)
807	1124
811, 812	Rep.
813(1)	365
813(2)	363
813(3)	Rep.
814	362
815, 816	Rep.
821–827	Rep.
828	362
831	Rep.
832	1104(a)
833	Rep.
834	341
835	341, 1128(a)
836	341
836(2)	501(a)
836(3)	343
837(1)	1104(a)
837(2)	Rep.
837(3)	1128(a)
841	Rep.
842	1106
843	348
844	1107(a)
845	1108
846	364
851	501(a), 1111
852	1122
853	Rep.
854	501(a)
855–857	Rep.
858	502(b)(7)
859	Rep.
861(1)–(3)	Rep.
861(4)	1123(b)(2)
861(5), (6)	Rep.
861(7)	1123(b)(4)
861(8)	Rep.
861(9)	1123(a)(3)
861(10)	1123(a)(2)
861(11)	Rep.
861(12)	1123(a)(5)
861(13)	1123(b)(5)
866	Rep.
867	1129(a)(3)
868	Rep.
869	1127(a), (b)
870	1127(d)
871	1127(c)
872(1)	1129(a)(1)
872(2)	1129(a)(7), (11)
872(3)	1129(a)(2)
872(4)	1129(a)(3)
872(5)	1129(a)(4)
873(1)	1141(a)
873(2)	1142(a)
873(3)	Rep.
874	1141(c)
875	1142(b)
876	1141(d)(1)–(3)
877	Rep.
881, 882	1112(b)
883	348
884–886	Rep.
891(1)	Rep.
891(2), (3)	330
892(1)	503(b)(3)
892(2)	Rep.
892(3)	503(b)(4)
893(1)	Rep.
893(2)	503(b)(4)
893(3)	330
893(4)	503(b)(4)
894–898	Rep.
906–909	Rep.
911	1144
916	108(c)
917	362
918(a)	1145(a)
918(b)	1145(b)
919	Rep.
920	346(j)(1)
921	1129(d)
922	346(j)(5)
923	Rep.
926	Rep.
1001, 1002	Rep.
1006(1)	101(4)
1006(2)	101(9)
1006(3)	101(12), 109(e)
1006(4)	101(11)
1006(5)	Rep.
1006(6)	101(31)
1006(7)	Rep.
1006(8)	101(24), 109(e)
1007	Rep.
1011, 1012	Rep.
1013(1)	365
1013(2)	Rep.
1014	362
1015, 1016	Rep.
1021–1026	Rep.
1031	Rep.
1032, 1033	341
1033(1)	343, 501(a)
1033(2)	1321
1033(5)	1324
1036	1303
1037	Rep.
1041–1044	Rep.
1046(1)	1322(b)(1)
1046(2)	1322(b)(2)
1046(3)	1322(a)(2)
1046(4)	1322(a)(1)
1046(5)	1329(a)
1046(6)	1322(b)(7)
1046(7)	1322(b)(10)
1051	1325(a)(3)
1052	Rep.
1053	1323(a)
1054	1323(c)
1055	Rep.
1056(a)(1)	1325(a)(1)
1056(a)(2)	1325(a)(6)
1056(a)(3)	Rep.
1056(a)(4)	1325(a)(3)
1056(b)	502(b)
1057	1327(a)
1058	Rep.
1059	1326(a)
1060	1328(a), (c), (d)
1061	1328(b)
1062	Rep.
1066	348, 1307
1067	348
1068, 1069	Rep.
1071	1330
1076	108(c)
1077–1079	Rep.
1080	1305(a)(1)
1086	Rep.
1101–1103	Rep.
1200–1255	Rep.

TABLE II

*ERR82*This Table lists the sections of revised Title 11,
*ERR82*Bankruptcy, and indicates the sections of former
*ERR82*Title 11, which covered similar and related subject
*ERR82*matter.

Title 11 New Sections	Title 11 Former Sections
101(1)–(3)	
101(4)	103, 401(1), 506(1), 707(2), 806(2), 1006(1)
101(5)–(7)	
101(8)	1(8)
101(9)	1(11), 401(3), 506(4), 707(1), 806(5), 1062(2)
101(10)	
101(11)	1(14), 401(5), 506(6), 707(2), 806(7), 1006(4)
101(12)	1(4), 401(8), 506(5), 706(3), 806(6), 1006(3)
101(13)	558
101(14)–(16)	
101(17), (18)	1(17)
101(19)–(21)	
101(22)	T. 15 §77ccc(7)
101(23)	506(8), 806(8)
101(24)	1(32), 1006(8)
101(25)	
101(26)	1(19), 107(d)(1)(d)
101(27)	
101(28)	401(6)
101(29)	404
101(30)	1(23), 401(7)

TABLE II—CONTINUED

Title 11 New Sections	Title 11 Former Sections
101(31)	1(24), 506(9), 706(5), 806(9), 1006(6)
101(32)	
101(33)	205(m)
101(34)	1(27)
101(35)	506(11)
101(36), (37)	
101(38)	1(29a)
101(39)	T. 15 §78c(a)(4), (5)
101(40)	1(30)
102(1)–(6)	
102(7)	1(35)
102(8)	
103, 104	
105	11(a)(15)
106	
107	77, 566
108(a), (b)	29(e)
108(c)	29(f), 661, 791, 1076
109(a)	11(a)(1)
109(b)	22
109(c)	404
109(d)	706(3), 806(6)
109(e)	1006(3), (8)
301	22(a), 41(f), 95(a)
302	
303(a)	22(b)
303(b)	23(b), 95(b), (e), 526
303(c)	95(f)
303(d)	41(b), 536, 537
303(e)	109(a)
303(f)	
303(g)	109(d)
303(h)	21
303(i)	11(a)(18), 19(b)
303(j)	95(g)
303(k)	
304	
305(a)(1)	
305(a)(2)	11(a)(22)
305(b), (c)	
306	
321	73
322(a)	78(b)
322(b)(1)	78(c)
322(b)(2)	78(d), (f), (g)
322(c)	78(i)
322(d)	78(m)
323	
324	11(a)(17), 560
325	74
326(a)	76(c)
326(b), (c)	
326(d)	76(e)
327	557, 591
327(c)	72(c)
328	
329	96(d)
330	76(c), 76a, 641(3), (4), 644(1), (3), 891(2), (3), 893(3)
331	
341	91, 92, 734–736, 834–836, 1032, 1033
342	94
343	44(a), 25(a)(1), (10), 736(3), 836(3), 1033(1)
344	25(a)(10)
345	101, 75(a)(2)
346(a)–(i)	
346(j)(1)	668, 795, 920
346(j)(2)–(4)	
346(j)(5)	670, 796, 922
346(j)(6), (7)	
347(a)	106(a)
347(b)	416(d), 605
348	638, 778, 843, 1066, 1067
349(a)	35(b)
349(b)	107(a)
350	11(a)(8)
361	
362	29(a), 35(c)(4), 513, 516(4), 663, 714, 814, 828, 917, 1014
363	11(a)(7), 110(f), 516(3), 713(2), 813(2)
364	516(2), 744, 846
365	103(c), 110(b), 516(1), 713(1), 813(1), 1013(1)
366	
501(a)	93(n), 596, 598, 736(2), 755a, 836(2), 851, 854, 1030(1)
501(b)	93(i)
501(c), (d)	
502(a)	93(d)
502(b)	93(f), 1056(b)
502(b)(3)	108
502(b)(4)	104(a)(4)
502(b)(7)	103(a)(9), 602, 753, 858
502(c)	93(d)
502(d)	93(g)
502(e)–(i)	
502(j)	93(k), 11(a)(2)
503(a)	

TABLE II—CONTINUED

Title 11 New Sections	Title 11 Former Sections
503(b)	104(a)(1)
503(b)(2)	102(a)(1)
503(b)(3)	642(1), 643, 644(4), 892(1)
503(b)(4)	641(5), 642(3), 643, 644(2), (4), 739(2), 892(3), 893(2), (4)
503(b)(5)	642(1)
504	102(c)
505(a), (b)	11(a)(2A), 104(a)(4)
505(c)	
506(a), (b)	93(h)
506(c), (d)	
507	104(a)
507(a)(3)	104(a)(2)
508	105(d)
509	93(i)
510	
521(1)	25(a)(8), (9)
521(2)	25(a)(3), (6), (7)
521(3)	25(a)(4), (5), (11)
521(4)	25(a)(1)
522	24
523(a)(1)	35(a)(1)
523(a)(2)	35(a)(2)
523(a)(3)	35(a)(3)
523(a)(4)	35(a)(4)
523(a)(5)	35(a)(7)
523(a)(6)	35(a)(8)
523(a)(7)–(9)	
523(b)	35(b)
523(c)	35(c)
523(d)	
524(a)	32(f)
524(b)–(d)	
524(e)	34
525	
541(a)	26, 110(a), 586
541(b)	110(a)(3)
541(c), (d)	
541(e)	110(c)
542(a), (b)	
542(c)	110(d)(2), (3)
542(d), (e)	
543(a)	
543(b), (c)	11(a)(21), 109(d)
543(d)	
544(a)	110(c)
544(b)	110(e)
545	107(b), (c)
545(1)	107(c)(1)(A)
545(2)	107(c)(1)(B)
545(3), (4)	107(c)(1)(C)
546(a)	
546(b)	107(c)(1)(B)
546(c)	
547	96
547(b)	107(a)
547(c)(4)	96(c)
547(d)	107(a)
547(e)(1)(B)	96(a)(4)
548(a)	107(d)(2)
548(b)	107(d)(4)
548(c)	107(d)(6)
548(d)(1)	107(d)(5)
548(d)(2)	
549(a)	110(d)(1)
549(b)	
549(c)	44(g)
549(d)	
550	96(b), 107(d)(3), (6)
551	96(b), 107(a)(3), (c)(2), (d)(6), 110(e)(2)
552	
553	96(c), 108
554	
701	
702	72(a)
703(a)	74
703(b), (c)	
704(1)	75(a)(1)
704(2)	75(a)(3), (5)
704(3)	75(a)(7)
704(4)	75(a)(8)
704(5)	75(a)(9)
704(6)	75(a)(10)
704(7)	
704(8)	75(a)(13)
705	72(b)
706	
707	95(g)
721	11(a)(5)
722	
723	23(g)
724(a)	93(j)
724(b)	107(c)(3)
724(c), (d)	
725	
726(a)(1), (2)	
726(a)(3)	93(n)
726(a)(4)–(6), (b), (c)	
727(a)(1)	

TABLE II—CONTINUED

Title 11 New Sections	*Title 11 Former Sections*
727(a)(2)	32(c)(1), (4)
727(a)(3)	32(c)(2)
727(a)(4)	32(c)(1), (3)
727(a)(5)	32(c)(7)
727(a)(6)	32(c)(6)
727(a)(7)	
727(a)(8), (9)	32(c)(5)
727(a)(10)	32(a)
727(b)	
727(c)	32(b)
727(d), (e)	33
728	
741	96(e)(1)
742–744	
745	96(e)(2)
746–748	
749	96(e)(5)
750	
751	96(e)(2)
752	96(e)(2), (3)
761–766	
901	402(b)(1), (2), 405(b), (e), (h), 408(b), 409, 411, 412, 413, 414(a), 416(b), (d)
902(1)	
902(2)	401(10)
902(3)	401(11)
902(4)	
903	403
904	402(c)
921(a)	405(a)
921(b)	402(d)
921(c)–(f)	405(a)
922(a)	405(e)(1)
922(b)	
923	405(d)
924	405(b)
925	408(a)
926	405(h)
927	418
941	410(a)
942	410(a), (b)
943(a)	413
943(b)(1)	
943(b)(2)	414(b)(2)
943(b)(3)	414(b)(4)
943(b)(4)	414(b)(6)
943(b)(5), (6)	414(b)(1)
944(a)	415(a)
944(b)	415(b)(1)
944(c)	415(b)(2)
945(a)	416(e)
945(b)	
946	417
1101(1)	
1101(2)	629(a)
1102	738
1103(a)	739(2)
1103(b), (c)(1)	
1103(c)(2)	739(1)(a)
1103(c)(3)	739(1)(b)–(e)
1103(c)(4)	
1103(c)(5)	739(1)(f)
1103(d)	
1104(a)	556, 832, 837(1)
1104(b)	568
1104(c)	560
1105	559
1106	587, 842
1106(a)(2)	564
1106(a)(3)	567(1)
1106(a)(4)	567(5)
1106(a)(4)(A)	567(3)
1106(a)(5)	569
1106(b)	568
1107(a)	563, 588, 742, 844
1107(b)	
1108	589, 743, 845
1109	607
1109(a)	608
1109(b)	606
1110	516(5), (6)
1111	596, 851
1112(a)	
1112(b)	636, 776, 777, 881, 882
1112(c)–(e)	
1121	570
1122	597, 751, 852
1123(a)(1)	
1123(a)(2)	616(6), 861(10)
1123(a)(3)	616(5), 861(9)
1123(a)(4)	
1123(a)(5)	616(2), (10), 861(12)
1123(a)(6)	616(12)(a)
1123(a)(7)	616(11)
1123(b)(1)	616(1)
1123(b)(2)	616(4), 757(2), 861(4)
1123(b)(3)	616(13)
1123(b)(4)	616(2), 861(7)
1123(b)(5)	616(14), 757(8), 861(13)
1123(c)	
1124	507, 708, 807
1125(a)	
1125(b)	576
1125(c)	
1125(d)	575
1125(e)	
1126	579
1126(a)	599
1126(e)	603
1127	622, 763
1127(a)	869
1127(b)	629(c), 787(1), 869
1127(c)	765, 787(2), (3), 871
1127(d)	623, 764, 870
1128(a)	579, 735(3), 737(3), 835, 837(3)
1128(b)	580
1129(a)(1)	621(1), 766(1), 872(1)
1129(a)(2)	766(3), 872(3)
1129(a)(3)	621(3), 761, 766(4), 867, 872(4)
1129(a)(4)	621(4), 872(5)
1129(a)(5)	621(5)
1129(a)(6)	624(2)
1129(a)(7)	621(2), 766(2), 872(2)
1129(a)(8)	
1129(a)(9)	737(2)
1129(a)(10)	
1129(a)(11)	621(2), 766(2), 872(2)
1129(b), (c)	
1129(d)	669, 921
1141(a)	624(1), 767(1), 873(1)
1141(b)	
1141(c)	626, 874
1141(d)(1)–(3)	628(1), 771, 876
1141(d)(4)	32(a)
1142(a)	624(2), 873(2)
1142(b)	627, 875
1143	604
1144	786, 911
1145(a)	664(a), 793(a), 918(a)
1145(b)	664(b), 793(b), 918(b)
1145(c), (d)	
1146(a), (b)	
1146(c)	667
1146(d)	
1161, 1162	
1163	205(c)(1)
1164, 1165	
1166	205(c)(2)
1167	205(n)
1168	205(j)
1169	205(c)(6)
1170	205(*o*)
1171(a)	205(n)
1171(b)	205(b)
1172	205(b)
1173	205(e)
1174	
1301, 1302	
1303	1036
1304	
1305(a)(1)	1080
1305(a)(2), (b), (c)	
1306	
1307	1066
1321	1033(2)
1322(a)(1)	1046(4)
1322(a)(2)	1046(3)
1322(a)(3)	
1322(b)(1)	1046(1)
1322(b)(2)	1046(2)
1322(b)(3)–(6)	
1322(b)(7)	1046(6)
1322(b)(8), (9)	
1322(b)(10)	1046(7)
1322(c)	
1323(a)	1053
1323(b)	
1323(c)	1054
1324	1033(5)
1325(a)(1)	1056(a)(1)
1325(a)(2)	
1325(a)(3)	1051, 1056(a)(4)
1325(a)(4), (5)	
1325(a)(6)	1056(a)(2)
1325(b)	
1326(a)	1059
1326(b)	
1327(a)	1057
1327(b), (c)	
1328(a)	1060
1328(b)	1061
1328(c), (d)	1060
1328(e)	33
1329(a)	1046(5)
1329(b), (c)	
1330	1071
1501–151326	

ENACTING CLAUSE

Pub. L. 95-598, title I, §101, Nov. 6, 1978, 92 Stat. 2549, provided in part: "The law relating to bankruptcy is codified and enacted as title 11 of the United States Code, entitled 'Bankruptcy', and may be cited as 11 U.S.C. §—."

REPEALS

Pub. L. 95-598, title IV, §401(a), Nov. 6, 1978, 92 Stat. 2682, provided that: "The Bankruptcy Act [act July 1, 1898, ch. 541, 30 Stat. 544, as amended] is repealed."

EFFECTIVE DATE

Pub. L. 95-598, title IV, §402, Nov. 6, 1978, 92 Stat. 2682, as amended by Pub. L. 98-249, §1(a), Mar. 31, 1984, 98 Stat. 116; Pub. L. 98-271, §1(a), Apr. 30, 1984, 98 Stat. 163; Pub. L. 98-299, §1(a), May 25, 1984, 98 Stat. 214; Pub. L. 98-325, §1(a), June 20, 1984, 98 Stat. 268; Pub. L. 98-353, title I, §§113, 121(a), July 10, 1984, 98 Stat. 343, 345; Pub. L. 98-454, title X, §1001, Oct. 5, 1984, 98 Stat. 1745, provided that:

"(a) Except as otherwise provided in this title [sections 401 to 411], this Act [for classification to the Code, see Tables] shall take effect on October 1, 1979.

"(b) Except as provided in subsections (c) and (d) of this section, the amendments made by title II [sections 201 to 252] of this Act shall not be effective.

"(c) The amendments made by sections 210, 214, 219, 220, 222, 224, 225, 228, 229, 235, 244, 245, 246, 249, and 251 of this Act shall take effect on October 1, 1979.

"(d) The amendments made by sections 217, 218, 230, 247, 302, 314(j), 317, 327, 328, 338, and 411 of this Act shall take effect on the date of enactment of this Act [Nov. 6, 1978].

"(e) [Repealed. Pub. L. 98-454, title X, §1001, Oct. 5, 1984, 98 Stat. 1745]."

[Amendment of section 402(b) of Pub. L. 95-598, set out above, by section 113 of Pub. L. 98-353 effective June 27, 1984, see section 122(c) of Pub. L. 98-353, set out as an Effective Date note under section 151 of Title 28, Judiciary and Judicial Procedure.]

SAVINGS PROVISION

Pub. L. 95-598, title IV, §403, Nov. 6, 1978, 92 Stat. 2683, as amended by Pub. L. 98-353, title III, §382, July 10, 1984, 98 Stat. 364, provided that:

"(a) A case commenced under the Bankruptcy Act, [act July 1, 1898, ch. 541, 30 Stat. 544, as amended], and all matters and proceedings in or relating to any such case, shall be conducted and determined under such Act as if this Act had not been enacted, and the substantive rights of parties in connection with any such bankruptcy case, matter, or proceeding shall continue to be governed by the law applicable to such case, matter, or proceeding as if the [this] Act had not been enacted.

"(b) Notwithstanding subsection (a) of this section, sections 1165, 1167, 1168, 1169, and 1171 of title 11 of the United States Code, as enacted by section 101 of this Act, apply to cases pending under section 77 of the Bankruptcy Act ([former] 11 U.S.C. 205) on the date of enactment of this Act [Nov. 6, 1978] in which the trustee has not filed a plan of reorganization.

"(c) The repeal [of the Bankruptcy Act] made by section 401(a) of this Act does not affect any right of a referee in bankruptcy, United States bankruptcy judge, or survivor of a referee in bankruptcy or United States bankruptcy judge to receive any annuity or other payment under the civil service retirement laws.

"(d) The amendments made by section 314 of this Act [for classification to the Code, see Tables] do not affect the application of chapter 9, chapter 96, section 2516, section 3057, or section 3284 of title 18 of the United States Code to any act of any person—

"(1) committed before October 1, 1979; or

"(2) committed after October 1, 1979, in connection with a case commenced before such date.

"(e) Notwithstanding subsection (a) of this section—

"(1) a fee may not be charged under section 40c(2)(a) of the Bankruptcy Act [former 11 U.S.C. 68(c)(2)(a)] in a case pending under such Act after September 30, 1979, to the extent that such fee exceeds $200,000;

"(2) a fee may not be charged under section 40c(2)(b) of the Bankruptcy Act in a case in which the plan is confirmed after September 30, 1978, or in which the final determination as to the amount of such fee is made after September 30, 1979, notwithstanding an earlier confirmation date, to the extent that such fee exceeds $100,000;

"(3) after September 30, 1979, all moneys collected for payment into the referees' salary and expense fund in cases filed under the Bankruptcy Act shall be collected and paid into the general fund of the Treasury; and

"(4) any balance in the referees' salary and expense fund in the Treasury on October 1, 1979, shall be transferred to the general fund of the Treasury and the referees' salary and expense fund account shall be closed."

Pub. L. 98-353, title III, §381, July 10, 1984, 98 Stat. 364, provided that: "This subtitle [(§§381, 382) amending section 403(e) of Pub. L. 95-598, set out above] may be cited as the 'Referees Salary and Expense Fund Act of 1984'."

HISTORY OF BANKRUPTCY ACTS

The bankruptcy laws were revised generally and enacted as Title 11, Bankruptcy, by Pub. L. 95-598, Nov. 6, 1978, 92 Stat. 2549.

Earlier bankruptcy laws included the following acts:

Apr. 4, 1800, ch. 19, 2 Stat. 19, repealed Dec. 19, 1803, ch. 6, 2 Stat. 248.

Aug. 19, 1841, ch. 9, 5 Stat. 440, repealed Mar. 3, 1843, ch. 82, 5 Stat. 614.

Mar. 2, 1867, ch. 176, 14 Stat. 517, the provisions of which were incorporated in Rev. Stat. Title LXI, §§4972 to 5132, were materially amended June 22, 1874, ch. 390, 18 Stat. 178, and were repealed June 7, 1878, ch. 160, 20 Stat. 99.

The Bankruptcy Act of July 1, 1898, ch. 541, 30 Stat. 544, as amended, sometimes called the Nelson Act, repealed by Pub. L. 95-598.

The Chandler Act of July 22, 1938, ch. 575, 52 Stat. 883, which revised the Bankruptcy Act generally and materially amended the provisions covering corporate reorganizations, repealed by Pub. L. 95-598.

NATIONAL BANKRUPTCY REVIEW COMMISSION

Pub. L. 103-394, title VI, Oct. 22, 1994, 108 Stat. 4147, established the National Bankruptcy Review Commission to (1) investigate and study issues and problems relating to title 11, United States Code, (2) evaluate the advisability of proposals and current arrangements with respect to such issues and problems, (3) solicit divergent views of all parties concerned with the operation of the bankruptcy system, and (4) prepare and submit to the Congress, the Chief Justice, and the President a report not later than 2 years after the date of its first meeting, and provided for termination of the Commission 30 days after submission of the report which was submitted on Oct. 20, 1997.

COMMISSION ON THE BANKRUPTCY LAWS OF THE UNITED STATES

Pub. L. 91-354, §§1-6, July 24, 1970, 84 Stat. 468, as amended by Pub. L. 92-251, Mar. 17, 1972, 86 Stat. 63; Pub. L. 93-56, §1, July 1, 1973, 87 Stat. 140, established the Commission on the Bankruptcy Laws of the United States, to study and recommend changes to this title, which ceased to exist 30 days after the date of submission of its final report which was required prior to July 31, 1973.

CHAPTER 1—GENERAL PROVISIONS

AMENDMENTS

2005—Pub. L. 109-8, title I, §106(e)(2), title II, §233(b), Apr. 20, 2005, 119 Stat. 41, 74, added items 111 and 112.

1994—Pub. L. 103-394, title III, §308(b), Oct. 22, 1994, 108 Stat. 4137, added item 110.

§ 101. Definitions

In this title the following definitions shall apply:

(1) The term "accountant" means accountant authorized under applicable law to practice public accounting, and includes professional accounting association, corporation, or partnership, if so authorized.

(2) The term "affiliate" means—

(A) entity that directly or indirectly owns, controls, or holds with power to vote, 20 percent or more of the outstanding voting securities of the debtor, other than an entity that holds such securities—

(i) in a fiduciary or agency capacity without sole discretionary power to vote such securities; or

(ii) solely to secure a debt, if such entity has not in fact exercised such power to vote;

(B) corporation 20 percent or more of whose outstanding voting securities are directly or indirectly owned, controlled, or held with power to vote, by the debtor, or by an entity that directly or indirectly owns, controls, or holds with power to vote, 20 percent or more of the outstanding voting securities of the debtor, other than an entity that holds such securities—

(i) in a fiduciary or agency capacity without sole discretionary power to vote such securities; or

(ii) solely to secure a debt, if such entity has not in fact exercised such power to vote;

(C) person whose business is operated under a lease or operating agreement by a debtor, or person substantially all of whose property is operated under an operating agreement with the debtor; or

(D) entity that operates the business or substantially all of the property of the debtor under a lease or operating agreement.

(3) The term "assisted person" means any person whose debts consist primarily of consumer debts and the value of whose nonexempt property is less than $150,000.

(4) The term "attorney" means attorney, professional law association, corporation, or partnership, authorized under applicable law to practice law.

(4A) The term "bankruptcy assistance" means any goods or services sold or otherwise provided to an assisted person with the express or implied purpose of providing information, advice, counsel, document preparation, or filing, or attendance at a creditors' meeting or appearing in a case or proceeding on behalf of another or providing legal representation with respect to a case or proceeding under this title.

(5) The term "claim" means—

(A) right to payment, whether or not such right is reduced to judgment, liquidated, unliquidated, fixed, contingent, matured, unmatured, disputed, undisputed, legal, equitable, secured, or unsecured; or

(B) right to an equitable remedy for breach of performance if such breach gives rise to a right to payment, whether or not such right to an equitable remedy is reduced to judgment, fixed, contingent, matured, unmatured, disputed, undisputed, secured, or unsecured.

(6) The term "commodity broker" means futures commission merchant, foreign futures commission merchant, clearing organization, leverage transaction merchant, or commodity options dealer, as defined in section 761 of this title, with respect to which there is a customer, as defined in section 761 of this title.

(7) The term "community claim" means claim that arose before the commencement of the case concerning the debtor for which property of the kind specified in section 541(a)(2) of this title is liable, whether or not there is any such property at the time of the commencement of the case.

(7A) The term "commercial fishing operation" means—

(A) the catching or harvesting of fish, shrimp, lobsters, urchins, seaweed, shellfish, or other aquatic species or products of such species; or

(B) for purposes of section 109 and chapter 12, aquaculture activities consisting of raising for market any species or product described in subparagraph (A).

(7B) The term "commercial fishing vessel" means a vessel used by a family fisherman to carry out a commercial fishing operation.

(8) The term "consumer debt" means debt incurred by an individual primarily for a personal, family, or household purpose.

(9) The term "corporation"—

(A) includes—

(i) association having a power or privilege that a private corporation, but not an individual or a partnership, possesses;

(ii) partnership association organized under a law that makes only the capital subscribed responsible for the debts of such association;

(iii) joint-stock company;

(iv) unincorporated company or association; or

(v) business trust; but

(B) does not include limited partnership.

(10) The term "creditor" means—

(A) entity that has a claim against the debtor that arose at the time of or before the order for relief concerning the debtor;

(B) entity that has a claim against the estate of a kind specified in section 348(d), 502(f), 502(g), 502(h) or 502(i) of this title; or

(C) entity that has a community claim.

(10A) The term "current monthly income"—

(A) means the average monthly income from all sources that the debtor receives (or in a joint case the debtor and the debtor's spouse receive) without regard to whether such income is taxable income, derived during the 6-month period ending on—

(i) the last day of the calendar month immediately preceding the date of the commencement of the case if the debtor files the schedule of current income required by section 521(a)(1)(B)(ii); or

(ii) the date on which current income is determined by the court for purposes of this title if the debtor does not file the schedule of current income required by section 521(a)(1)(B)(ii); and

(B) includes any amount paid by any entity other than the debtor (or in a joint case the debtor and the debtor's spouse), on a regular basis for the household expenses of the debtor or the debtor's dependents (and in a joint case the debtor's spouse if not otherwise a dependent), but excludes benefits received under the Social Security Act, payments to victims of war crimes or crimes against humanity on account of their status as victims of such crimes, and payments to victims of international terrorism (as defined in section 2331 of title 18) or domestic terrorism (as defined in section 2331 of title 18) on account of their status as victims of such terrorism.

(11) The term "custodian" means—

(A) receiver or trustee of any of the property of the debtor, appointed in a case or proceeding not under this title;

(B) assignee under a general assignment for the benefit of the debtor's creditors; or

(C) trustee, receiver, or agent under applicable law, or under a contract, that is appointed or authorized to take charge of property of the debtor for the purpose of enforcing a lien against such property, or for the purpose of general administration of such property for the benefit of the debtor's creditors.

(12) The term "debt" means liability on a claim.

(12A) The term "debt relief agency" means any person who provides any bankruptcy assistance to an assisted person in return for the payment of money or other valuable consideration, or who is a bankruptcy petition preparer under section 110, but does not include—

(A) any person who is an officer, director, employee, or agent of a person who provides such assistance or of the bankruptcy petition preparer;

(B) a nonprofit organization that is exempt from taxation under section 501(c)(3) of the Internal Revenue Code of 1986;

(C) a creditor of such assisted person, to the extent that the creditor is assisting such assisted person to restructure any debt owed by such assisted person to the creditor;

(D) a depository institution (as defined in section 3 of the Federal Deposit Insurance Act) or any Federal credit union or State credit union (as those terms are defined in section 101 of the Federal Credit Union Act), or any affiliate or subsidiary of such depository institution or credit union; or

(E) an author, publisher, distributor, or seller of works subject to copyright protection under title 17, when acting in such capacity.

(13) The term "debtor" means person or municipality concerning which a case under this title has been commenced.

(13A) The term "debtor's principal residence"—

(A) means a residential structure, including incidental property, without regard to whether that structure is attached to real property; and

(B) includes an individual condominium or cooperative unit, a mobile or manufactured home, or trailer.

(14) The term "disinterested person" means a person that—

(A) is not a creditor, an equity security holder, or an insider;

(B) is not and was not, within 2 years before the date of the filing of the petition, a director, officer, or employee of the debtor; and

(C) does not have an interest materially adverse to the interest of the estate or of any class of creditors or equity security holders, by reason of any direct or indirect relationship to, connection with, or interest in, the debtor, or for any other reason.

(14A) The term "domestic support obligation" means a debt that accrues before, on, or after the date of the order for relief in a case under this title, including interest that accrues on that debt as provided under applicable nonbankruptcy law notwithstanding any other provision of this title, that is—

(A) owed to or recoverable by—

(i) a spouse, former spouse, or child of the debtor or such child's parent, legal guardian, or responsible relative; or

(ii) a governmental unit;

(B) in the nature of alimony, maintenance, or support (including assistance provided by a governmental unit) of such spouse, former spouse, or child of the debtor or such child's parent, without regard to whether such debt is expressly so designated;

(C) established or subject to establishment before, on, or after the date of the order for relief in a case under this title, by reason of applicable provisions of—

(i) a separation agreement, divorce decree, or property settlement agreement;

(ii) an order of a court of record; or

(iii) a determination made in accordance with applicable nonbankruptcy law by a governmental unit; and

(D) not assigned to a nongovernmental entity, unless that obligation is assigned voluntarily by the spouse, former spouse, child of the debtor, or such child's parent, legal guardian, or responsible relative for the purpose of collecting the debt.

(15) The term "entity" includes person, estate, trust, governmental unit, and United States trustee.

(16) The term "equity security" means—

(A) share in a corporation, whether or not transferable or denominated "stock", or similar security;

(B) interest of a limited partner in a limited partnership; or

(C) warrant or right, other than a right to convert, to purchase, sell, or subscribe to a share, security, or interest of a kind specified in subparagraph (A) or (B) of this paragraph.

(17) The term "equity security holder" means holder of an equity security of the debtor.

(18) The term "family farmer" means—

(A) individual or individual and spouse engaged in a farming operation whose aggregate debts do not exceed $3,237,000 and not less than 50 percent of whose aggregate noncontingent, liquidated debts (excluding a debt for the principal residence of such individual or such individual and spouse unless such debt arises out of a farming operation), on the date the case is filed, arise out of a farming operation owned or operated by such individual or such individual and spouse, and such individual or such individual and spouse receive from such farming operation more than 50 percent of such individual's or such individual and spouse's gross income for—

(i) the taxable year preceding; or

(ii) each of the 2d and 3d taxable years preceding;

the taxable year in which the case concerning such individual or such individual and spouse was filed; or

(B) corporation or partnership in which more than 50 percent of the outstanding stock or equity is held by one family, or by one family and the relatives of the members of such family, and such family or such relatives conduct the farming operation, and

(i) more than 80 percent of the value of its assets consists of assets related to the farming operation;

(ii) its aggregate debts do not exceed $3,237,000 and not less than 50 percent of its aggregate noncontingent, liquidated debts (excluding a debt for one dwelling which is owned by such corporation or partnership and which a shareholder or partner maintains as a principal residence, unless such debt arises out of a farming operation), on the date the case is filed, arise out of the farming operation owned or operated by such corporation or such partnership; and

(iii) if such corporation issues stock, such stock is not publicly traded.

(19) The term "family farmer with regular annual income" means family farmer whose annual income is sufficiently stable and regular to enable such family farmer to make payments under a plan under chapter 12 of this title.

(19A) The term "family fisherman" means—

(A) an individual or individual and spouse engaged in a commercial fishing operation—

(i) whose aggregate debts do not exceed $1,500,000 and not less than 80 percent of whose aggregate noncontingent, liquidated debts (excluding a debt for the principal residence of such individual or such individual and spouse, unless such debt arises out of a commercial fishing operation), on the date the case is filed, arise out of a commercial fishing operation owned or operated by such individual or such individual and spouse; and

(ii) who receive from such commercial fishing operation more than 50 percent of such individual's or such individual's and spouse's gross income for the taxable year preceding the taxable year in which the case concerning such individual or such individual and spouse was filed; or

(B) a corporation or partnership—

(i) in which more than 50 percent of the outstanding stock or equity is held by—

(I) 1 family that conducts the commercial fishing operation; or

(II) 1 family and the relatives of the members of such family, and such family or such relatives conduct the commercial fishing operation; and

(ii)(I) more than 80 percent of the value of its assets consists of assets related to the commercial fishing operation;

(II) its aggregate debts do not exceed $1,500,000 and not less than 80 percent of its aggregate noncontingent, liquidated debts (excluding a debt for 1 dwelling which is owned by such corporation or partnership and which a shareholder or partner maintains as a principal residence, unless such debt arises out of a commercial fishing operation), on the date the case is filed, arise out of a commercial fishing operation owned or operated by such corporation or such partnership; and

(III) if such corporation issues stock, such stock is not publicly traded.

(19B) The term "family fisherman with regular annual income" means a family fisherman whose annual income is sufficiently stable and regular to enable such family fisherman to make payments under a plan under chapter 12 of this title.

(20) The term "farmer" means (except when such term appears in the term "family farmer") person that received more than 80 percent of such person's gross income during the taxable year of such person immediately preceding the taxable year of such person during which the case under this title concerning such person was commenced from a farming operation owned or operated by such person.

(21) The term "farming operation" includes farming, tillage of the soil, dairy farming, ranching, production or raising of crops, poultry, or livestock, and production of poultry or livestock products in an unmanufactured state.

(21A) The term "farmout agreement" means a written agreement in which—

(A) the owner of a right to drill, produce, or operate liquid or gaseous hydrocarbons on property agrees or has agreed to transfer or assign all or a part of such right to another entity; and

(B) such other entity (either directly or through its agents or its assigns), as consideration, agrees to perform drilling, reworking, recompleting, testing, or similar or related operations, to develop or produce liquid or gaseous hydrocarbons on the property.

(21B) The term "Federal depository institutions regulatory agency" means—

(A) with respect to an insured depository institution (as defined in section 3(c)(2) of the Federal Deposit Insurance Act) for which no conservator or receiver has been appointed, the appropriate Federal banking agency (as defined in section 3(q) of such Act);

(B) with respect to an insured credit union (including an insured credit union for which the National Credit Union Administration has been appointed conservator or liquidating agent), the National Credit Union Administration;

(C) with respect to any insured depository institution for which the Resolution Trust Corporation has been appointed conservator or receiver, the Resolution Trust Corporation; and

(D) with respect to any insured depository institution for which the Federal Deposit Insurance Corporation has been appointed conservator or receiver, the Federal Deposit Insurance Corporation.

(22) The term "financial institution" means—

(A) a Federal reserve bank, or an entity that is a commercial or savings bank, industrial savings bank, savings and loan association, trust company, federally-insured credit union, or receiver, liquidating agent, or conservator for such entity and, when any such Federal reserve bank, receiver, liquidating agent, conservator or entity is acting as agent or custodian for a customer (whether or not a "customer", as defined in section 741) in connection with a securities contract (as defined in section 741) such customer; or

(B) in connection with a securities contract (as defined in section 741) an investment company registered under the Investment Company Act of 1940.

(22A) The term "financial participant" means—

(A) an entity that, at the time it enters into a securities contract, commodity contract, swap agreement, repurchase agreement, or forward contract, or at the time of the date of the filing of the petition, has one or more agreements or transactions described in paragraph (1), (2), (3), (4), (5), or (6) of section 561(a) with the debtor or any other entity (other than an affiliate) of a total gross dollar value of not less than $1,000,000,000 in notional or actual principal amount outstanding (aggregated across counterparties) at such time or on any day during the 15-month period preceding the date of the filing of the petition, or has gross mark-to-market positions of not less than $100,000,000 (aggregated across counterparties) in one or more such agreements or transactions with the debtor or any other entity (other than an affiliate) at such time or on any day during the 15-month period preceding the date of the filing of the petition; or

(B) a clearing organization (as defined in section 402 of the Federal Deposit Insurance Corporation Improvement Act of 1991).

(23) The term "foreign proceeding" means a collective judicial or administrative proceeding in a foreign country, including an interim proceeding, under a law relating to insolvency or adjustment of debt in which proceeding the assets and affairs of the debtor are subject to control or supervision by a foreign court, for the purpose of reorganization or liquidation.

(24) The term "foreign representative" means a person or body, including a person or body appointed on an interim basis, authorized in a foreign proceeding to administer the reorganization or the liquidation of the debtor's assets or affairs or to act as a representative of such foreign proceeding.

(25) The term "forward contract" means—

(A) a contract (other than a commodity contract, as defined in section 761) for the purchase, sale, or transfer of a commodity, as defined in section 761(8) of this title, or any similar good, article, service, right, or interest which is presently or in the future becomes the subject of dealing in the forward contract trade, or product or byproduct thereof, with a maturity date more than two days after the date the contract is entered into, including, but not limited to, a repurchase or reverse repurchase transaction (whether or not such repurchase or reverse repurchase transaction is a "repurchase agreement", as defined in this section)[1] consignment, lease, swap, hedge transaction, deposit, loan, option, allocated transaction, unallocated transaction, or any other similar agreement;

(B) any combination of agreements or transactions referred to in subparagraphs (A) and (C);

(C) any option to enter into an agreement or transaction referred to in subparagraph (A) or (B);

(D) a master agreement that provides for an agreement or transaction referred to in subparagraph (A), (B), or (C), together with all supplements to any such master agreement, without regard to whether such master agreement provides for an agreement or transaction that is not a forward contract under this paragraph, except that such master agreement shall be considered to be a forward contract under this paragraph only with respect to each agreement or transaction under such master agreement that is referred to in subparagraph (A), (B), or (C); or

[1] So in original. Probably should be followed by a comma.

(E) any security agreement or arrangement, or other credit enhancement related to any agreement or transaction referred to in subparagraph (A), (B), (C), or (D), including any guarantee or reimbursement obligation by or to a forward contract merchant or financial participant in connection with any agreement or transaction referred to in any such subparagraph, but not to exceed the damages in connection with any such agreement or transaction, measured in accordance with section 562.

(26) The term "forward contract merchant" means a Federal reserve bank, or an entity the business of which consists in whole or in part of entering into forward contracts as or with merchants in a commodity (as defined in section 761) or any similar good, article, service, right, or interest which is presently or in the future becomes the subject of dealing in the forward contract trade.

(27) The term "governmental unit" means United States; State; Commonwealth; District; Territory; municipality; foreign state; department, agency, or instrumentality of the United States (but not a United States trustee while serving as a trustee in a case under this title), a State, a Commonwealth, a District, a Territory, a municipality, or a foreign state; or other foreign or domestic government.

(27A) The term "health care business"—

(A) means any public or private entity (without regard to whether that entity is organized for profit or not for profit) that is primarily engaged in offering to the general public facilities and services for—

(i) the diagnosis or treatment of injury, deformity, or disease; and

(ii) surgical, drug treatment, psychiatric, or obstetric care; and

(B) includes—

(i) any—

(I) general or specialized hospital;

(II) ancillary ambulatory, emergency, or surgical treatment facility;

(III) hospice;

(IV) home health agency; and

(V) other health care institution that is similar to an entity referred to in subclause (I), (II), (III), or (IV); and

(ii) any long-term care facility, including any—

(I) skilled nursing facility;

(II) intermediate care facility;

(III) assisted living facility;

(IV) home for the aged;

(V) domiciliary care facility; and

(VI) health care institution that is related to a facility referred to in subclause (I), (II), (III), (IV), or (V), if that institution is primarily engaged in offering room, board, laundry, or personal assistance with activities of daily living and incidentals to activities of daily living.

(27B) The term "incidental property" means, with respect to a debtor's principal residence—

(A) property commonly conveyed with a principal residence in the area where the real property is located;

(B) all easements, rights, appurtenances, fixtures, rents, royalties, mineral rights, oil or gas rights or profits, water rights, escrow funds, or insurance proceeds; and

(C) all replacements or additions.

(28) The term "indenture" means mortgage, deed of trust, or indenture, under which there is outstanding a security, other than a voting-trust certificate, constituting a claim against the debtor, a claim secured by a lien on any of the debtor's property, or an equity security of the debtor.

(29) The term "indenture trustee" means trustee under an indenture.

(30) The term "individual with regular income" means individual whose income is sufficiently stable and regular to enable such individual to make payments under a plan under chapter 13 of this title, other than a stockbroker or a commodity broker.

(31) The term "insider" includes—

(A) if the debtor is an individual—

(i) relative of the debtor or of a general partner of the debtor;

(ii) partnership in which the debtor is a general partner;

(iii) general partner of the debtor; or

(iv) corporation of which the debtor is a director, officer, or person in control;

(B) if the debtor is a corporation—

(i) director of the debtor;

(ii) officer of the debtor;

(iii) person in control of the debtor;

(iv) partnership in which the debtor is a general partner;

(v) general partner of the debtor; or

(vi) relative of a general partner, director, officer, or person in control of the debtor;

(C) if the debtor is a partnership—

(i) general partner in the debtor;

(ii) relative of a general partner in, general partner of, or person in control of the debtor;

(iii) partnership in which the debtor is a general partner;

(iv) general partner of the debtor; or

(v) person in control of the debtor;

(D) if the debtor is a municipality, elected official of the debtor or relative of an elected official of the debtor;

(E) affiliate, or insider of an affiliate as if such affiliate were the debtor; and

(F) managing agent of the debtor.

(32) The term "insolvent" means—

(A) with reference to an entity other than a partnership and a municipality, financial condition such that the sum of such entity's debts is greater than all of such entity's property, at a fair valuation, exclusive of—

(i) property transferred, concealed, or removed with intent to hinder, delay, or defraud such entity's creditors; and

(ii) property that may be exempted from property of the estate under section 522 of this title;

(B) with reference to a partnership, financial condition such that the sum of such partnership's debts is greater than the aggregate of, at a fair valuation—

(i) all of such partnership's property, exclusive of property of the kind specified in subparagraph (A)(i) of this paragraph; and

(ii) the sum of the excess of the value of each general partner's nonpartnership property, exclusive of property of the kind specified in subparagraph (A) of this paragraph, over such partner's nonpartnership debts; and

(C) with reference to a municipality, financial condition such that the municipality is—

(i) generally not paying its debts as they become due unless such debts are the subject of a bona fide dispute; or

(ii) unable to pay its debts as they become due.

(33) The term "institution-affiliated party"—

(A) with respect to an insured depository institution (as defined in section 3(c)(2) of the Federal Deposit Insurance Act), has the meaning given it in section 3(u) of the Federal Deposit Insurance Act; and

(B) with respect to an insured credit union, has the meaning given it in section 206(r) of the Federal Credit Union Act.

(34) The term "insured credit union" has the meaning given it in section 101(7) of the Federal Credit Union Act.

(35) The term "insured depository institution"—

(A) has the meaning given it in section 3(c)(2) of the Federal Deposit Insurance Act; and

(B) includes an insured credit union (except in the case of paragraphs (23) and (35) of this subsection).

(35A) The term "intellectual property" means—

(A) trade secret;

(B) invention, process, design, or plant protected under title 35;

(C) patent application;

(D) plant variety;

(E) work of authorship protected under title 17; or

(F) mask work protected under chapter 9 of title 17;

to the extent protected by applicable nonbankruptcy law.

(36) The term "judicial lien" means lien obtained by judgment, levy, sequestration, or other legal or equitable process or proceeding.

(37) The term "lien" means charge against or interest in property to secure payment of a debt or performance of an obligation.

(38) The term "margin payment" means, for purposes of the forward contract provisions of this title, payment or deposit of cash, a security or other property, that is commonly known in the forward contract trade as original margin, initial margin, maintenance margin, or variation margin, including mark-to-market payments, or variation payments.

(38A) The term "master netting agreement"—

(A) means an agreement providing for the exercise of rights, including rights of netting, setoff, liquidation, termination, acceleration, or close out, under or in connection with one or more contracts that are described in any one or more of paragraphs (1) through (5) of section 561(a), or any security agreement or arrangement or other credit enhancement related to one or more of the foregoing, including any guarantee or reimbursement obligation related to 1 or more of the foregoing; and

(B) if the agreement contains provisions relating to agreements or transactions that are not contracts described in paragraphs (1) through (5) of section 561(a), shall be deemed to be a master netting agreement only with respect to those agreements or transactions that are described in any one or more of paragraphs (1) through (5) of section 561(a).

(38B) The term "master netting agreement participant" means an entity that, at any time before the date of the filing of the petition, is a party to an outstanding master netting agreement with the debtor.

(39) The term "mask work" has the meaning given it in section 901(a)(2) of title 17.

(39A) The term "median family income" means for any year—

(A) the median family income both calculated and reported by the Bureau of the Census in the then most recent year; and

(B) if not so calculated and reported in the then current year, adjusted annually after such most recent year until the next year in which median family income is both calculated and reported by the Bureau of the Census, to reflect the percentage change in the Consumer Price Index for All Urban Consumers during the period of years occurring after such most recent year and before such current year.

(40) The term "municipality" means political subdivision or public agency or instrumentality of a State.

(40A) The term "patient" means any individual who obtains or receives services from a health care business.

(40B) The term "patient records" means any written document relating to a patient or a record recorded in a magnetic, optical, or other form of electronic medium.

(41) The term "person" includes individual, partnership, and corporation, but does not include governmental unit, except that a governmental unit that—

(A) acquires an asset from a person—

(i) as a result of the operation of a loan guarantee agreement; or

(ii) as receiver or liquidating agent of a person;

(B) is a guarantor of a pension benefit payable by or on behalf of the debtor or an affiliate of the debtor; or

(C) is the legal or beneficial owner of an asset of—

(i) an employee pension benefit plan that is a governmental plan, as defined in section 414(d) of the Internal Revenue Code of 1986; or

(ii) an eligible deferred compensation plan, as defined in section 457(b) of the Internal Revenue Code of 1986;

shall be considered, for purposes of section 1102 of this title, to be a person with respect to such asset or such benefit.

(41A) The term "personally identifiable information" means—

(A) if provided by an individual to the debtor in connection with obtaining a product or a service from the debtor primarily for personal, family, or household purposes—

(i) the first name (or initial) and last name of such individual, whether given at birth or time of adoption, or resulting from a lawful change of name;

(ii) the geographical address of a physical place of residence of such individual;

(iii) an electronic address (including an e-mail address) of such individual;

(iv) a telephone number dedicated to contacting such individual at such physical place of residence;

(v) a social security account number issued to such individual; or

(vi) the account number of a credit card issued to such individual; or

(B) if identified in connection with 1 or more of the items of information specified in subparagraph (A)—

(i) a birth date, the number of a certificate of birth or adoption, or a place of birth; or

(ii) any other information concerning an identified individual that, if disclosed, will result in contacting or identifying such individual physically or electronically.

(42) The term "petition" means petition filed under section 301, 302, 303, or 304[2] of this title, as the case may be, commencing a case under this title.

(42A) The term "production payment" means a term overriding royalty satisfiable in cash or in kind—

(A) contingent on the production of a liquid or gaseous hydrocarbon from particular real property; and

(B) from a specified volume, or a specified value, from the liquid or gaseous hydrocarbon produced from such property, and determined without regard to production costs.

(43) The term "purchaser" means transferee of a voluntary transfer, and includes immediate or mediate transferee of such a transferee.

(44) The term "railroad" means common carrier by railroad engaged in the transportation of individuals or property or owner of trackage facilities leased by such a common carrier.

(45) The term "relative" means individual related by affinity or consanguinity within the third degree as determined by the common law, or individual in a step or adoptive relationship within such third degree.

(46) The term "repo participant" means an entity that, at any time before the filing of the petition, has an outstanding repurchase agreement with the debtor.

(47) The term "repurchase agreement" (which definition also applies to a reverse repurchase agreement)—

(A) means—

(i) an agreement, including related terms, which provides for the transfer of one or more certificates of deposit, mortgage related securities (as defined in section 3 of the Securities Exchange Act of 1934), mortgage loans, interests in mortgage related securities or mortgage loans, eligible bankers' acceptances, qualified foreign government securities (defined as a security that is a direct obligation of, or that is fully guaranteed by, the central government of a member of the Organization for Economic Cooperation and Development), or securities that are direct obligations of, or that are fully guaranteed by, the United States or any agency of the United States against the transfer of funds by the transferee of such certificates of deposit, eligible bankers' acceptances, securities, mortgage loans, or interests, with a simultaneous agreement by such transferee to transfer to the transferor thereof certificates of deposit, eligible bankers' acceptance, securities, mortgage loans, or interests of the kind described in this clause, at a date certain not later than 1 year after such transfer or on demand, against the transfer of funds;

(ii) any combination of agreements or transactions referred to in clauses (i) and (iii);

(iii) an option to enter into an agreement or transaction referred to in clause (i) or (ii);

(iv) a master agreement that provides for an agreement or transaction referred to in clause (i), (ii), or (iii), together with all supplements to any such master agreement, without regard to whether such master agreement provides for an agreement or transaction that is not a repurchase agreement under this paragraph, except that such master agreement shall be considered to be a repurchase agreement under this paragraph only with respect to each agreement or transaction under the master agreement that is referred to in clause (i), (ii), or (iii); or

(v) any security agreement or arrangement or other credit enhancement related to any agreement or transaction referred to in clause (i), (ii), (iii), or (iv), including any guarantee or reimbursement obligation by or to a repo participant or financial participant in connection with any agreement or transaction referred to in any such clause, but not to exceed the damages in connection with any such agreement or transaction, measured in accordance with section 562 of this title; and

(B) does not include a repurchase obligation under a participation in a commercial mortgage loan.

(48) The term "securities clearing agency" means person that is registered as a clearing

[2] See References in Text note below.

agency under section 17A of the Securities Exchange Act of 1934, or exempt from such registration under such section pursuant to an order of the Securities and Exchange Commission, or whose business is confined to the performance of functions of a clearing agency with respect to exempted securities, as defined in section 3(a)(12) of such Act for the purposes of such section 17A.

(48A) The term "securities self regulatory organization" means either a securities association registered with the Securities and Exchange Commission under section 15A of the Securities Exchange Act of 1934 or a national securities exchange registered with the Securities and Exchange Commission under section 6 of the Securities Exchange Act of 1934.

(49) The term "security"—

(A) includes—

(i) note;

(ii) stock;

(iii) treasury stock;

(iv) bond;

(v) debenture;

(vi) collateral trust certificate;

(vii) pre-organization certificate or subscription;

(viii) transferable share;

(ix) voting-trust certificate;

(x) certificate of deposit;

(xi) certificate of deposit for security;

(xii) investment contract or certificate of interest or participation in a profit-sharing agreement or in an oil, gas, or mineral royalty or lease, if such contract or interest is required to be the subject of a registration statement filed with the Securities and Exchange Commission under the provisions of the Securities Act of 1933, or is exempt under section 3(b) of such Act from the requirement to file such a statement;

(xiii) interest of a limited partner in a limited partnership;

(xiv) other claim or interest commonly known as "security"; and

(xv) certificate of interest or participation in, temporary or interim certificate for, receipt for, or warrant or right to subscribe to or purchase or sell, a security; but

(B) does not include—

(i) currency, check, draft, bill of exchange, or bank letter of credit;

(ii) leverage transaction, as defined in section 761 of this title;

(iii) commodity futures contract or forward contract;

(iv) option, warrant, or right to subscribe to or purchase or sell a commodity futures contract;

(v) option to purchase or sell a commodity;

(vi) contract or certificate of a kind specified in subparagraph (A)(xii) of this paragraph that is not required to be the subject of a registration statement filed with the Securities and Exchange Commission and is not exempt under section 3(b) of the Securities Act of 1933 from the requirement to file such a statement; or

(vii) debt or evidence of indebtedness for goods sold and delivered or services rendered.

(50) The term "security agreement" means agreement that creates or provides for a security interest.

(51) The term "security interest" means lien created by an agreement.

(51A) The term "settlement payment" means, for purposes of the forward contract provisions of this title, a preliminary settlement payment, a partial settlement payment, an interim settlement payment, a settlement payment on account, a final settlement payment, a net settlement payment, or any other similar payment commonly used in the forward contract trade.

(51B) The term "single asset real estate" means real property constituting a single property or project, other than residential real property with fewer than 4 residential units, which generates substantially all of the gross income of a debtor who is not a family farmer and on which no substantial business is being conducted by a debtor other than the business of operating the real property and activities incidental.

(51C) The term "small business case" means a case filed under chapter 11 of this title in which the debtor is a small business debtor.

(51D) The term "small business debtor"—

(A) subject to subparagraph (B), means a person engaged in commercial or business activities (including any affiliate of such person that is also a debtor under this title and excluding a person whose primary activity is the business of owning or operating real property or activities incidental thereto) that has aggregate noncontingent liquidated secured and unsecured debts as of the date of the petition or the date of the order for relief in an amount not more than $2,000,000 (excluding debts owed to 1 or more affiliates or insiders) for a case in which the United States trustee has not appointed under section 1102(a)(1) a committee of unsecured creditors or where the court has determined that the committee of unsecured creditors is not sufficiently active and representative to provide effective oversight of the debtor; and

(B) does not include any member of a group of affiliated debtors that has aggregate noncontingent liquidated secured and unsecured debts in an amount greater than $2,000,000 (excluding debt owed to 1 or more affiliates or insiders).

(52) The term "State" includes the District of Columbia and Puerto Rico, except for the purpose of defining who may be a debtor under chapter 9 of this title.

(53) The term "statutory lien" means lien arising solely by force of a statute on specified circumstances or conditions, or lien of distress for rent, whether or not statutory, but does not include security interest or judicial lien, whether or not such interest or lien is provided by or is dependent on a statute and whether or not such interest or lien is made fully effective by statute.

(53A) The term "stockbroker" means person—

(A) with respect to which there is a customer, as defined in section 741 of this title; and

(B) that is engaged in the business of effecting transactions in securities—

(i) for the account of others; or

(ii) with members of the general public, from or for such person's own account.

(53B) The term "swap agreement"—

(A) means—

(i) any agreement, including the terms and conditions incorporated by reference in such agreement, which is—

(I) an interest rate swap, option, future, or forward agreement, including a rate floor, rate cap, rate collar, cross-currency rate swap, and basis swap;

(II) a spot, same day-tomorrow, tomorrow-next, forward, or other foreign exchange, precious metals, or other commodity agreement;

(III) a currency swap, option, future, or forward agreement;

(IV) an equity index or equity swap, option, future, or forward agreement;

(V) a debt index or debt swap, option, future, or forward agreement;

(VI) a total return, credit spread or credit swap, option, future, or forward agreement;

(VII) a commodity index or a commodity swap, option, future, or forward agreement;

(VIII) a weather swap, option, future, or forward agreement;

(IX) an emissions swap, option, future, or forward agreement; or

(X) an inflation swap, option, future, or forward agreement;

(ii) any agreement or transaction that is similar to any other agreement or transaction referred to in this paragraph and that—

(I) is of a type that has been, is presently, or in the future becomes, the subject of recurrent dealings in the swap or other derivatives markets (including terms and conditions incorporated by reference therein); and

(II) is a forward, swap, future, option, or spot transaction on one or more rates, currencies, commodities, equity securities, or other equity instruments, debt securities or other debt instruments, quantitative measures associated with an occurrence, extent of an occurrence, or contingency associated with a financial, commercial, or economic consequence, or economic or financial indices or measures of economic or financial risk or value;

(iii) any combination of agreements or transactions referred to in this subparagraph;

(iv) any option to enter into an agreement or transaction referred to in this subparagraph;

(v) a master agreement that provides for an agreement or transaction referred to in clause (i), (ii), (iii), or (iv), together with all supplements to any such master agreement, and without regard to whether the master agreement contains an agreement or transaction that is not a swap agreement under this paragraph, except that the master agreement shall be considered to be a swap agreement under this paragraph only with respect to each agreement or transaction under the master agreement that is referred to in clause (i), (ii), (iii), or (iv); or

(vi) any security agreement or arrangement or other credit enhancement related to any agreements or transactions referred to in clause (i) through (v), including any guarantee or reimbursement obligation by or to a swap participant or financial participant in connection with any agreement or transaction referred to in any such clause, but not to exceed the damages in connection with any such agreement or transaction, measured in accordance with section 562; and

(B) is applicable for purposes of this title only, and shall not be construed or applied so as to challenge or affect the characterization, definition, or treatment of any swap agreement under any other statute, regulation, or rule, including the Gramm-Leach-Bliley Act, the Legal Certainty for Bank Products Act of 2000, the securities laws (as such term is defined in section 3(a)(47) of the Securities Exchange Act of 1934) and the Commodity Exchange Act.

(53C) The term "swap participant" means an entity that, at any time before the filing of the petition, has an outstanding swap agreement with the debtor.

(56A)[3] The term "term overriding royalty" means an interest in liquid or gaseous hydrocarbons in place or to be produced from particular real property that entitles the owner thereof to a share of production, or the value thereof, for a term limited by time, quantity, or value realized.

(53D) The term "timeshare plan" means and shall include that interest purchased in any arrangement, plan, scheme, or similar device, but not including exchange programs, whether by membership, agreement, tenancy in common, sale, lease, deed, rental agreement, license, right to use agreement, or by any other means, whereby a purchaser, in exchange for consideration, receives a right to use accommodations, facilities, or recreational sites, whether improved or unimproved, for a specific period of time less than a full year during any given year, but not necessarily for consecutive years, and which extends for a period of more than three years. A "timeshare interest" is that interest purchased in a timeshare plan which grants the purchaser the right to use and occupy accommodations, facilities, or recreational sites, whether improved or unimproved, pursuant to a timeshare plan.

(54) The term "transfer" means—

(A) the creation of a lien;

[3] So in original.

(B) the retention of title as a security interest;

(C) the foreclosure of a debtor's equity of redemption; or

(D) each mode, direct or indirect, absolute or conditional, voluntary or involuntary, of disposing of or parting with—

(i) property; or

(ii) an interest in property.

(54A) The term "uninsured State member bank" means a State member bank (as defined in section 3 of the Federal Deposit Insurance Act) the deposits of which are not insured by the Federal Deposit Insurance Corporation.

(55) The term "United States", when used in a geographical sense, includes all locations where the judicial jurisdiction of the United States extends, including territories and possessions of the United States.

(Pub. L. 95-598, Nov. 6, 1978, 92 Stat. 2549; Pub. L. 97-222, §1, July 27, 1982, 96 Stat. 235; Pub. L. 98-353, title III, §§391, 401, 421, July 10, 1984, 98 Stat. 364, 366, 367; Pub. L. 99-554, title II, §§201, 251, 283(a), Oct. 27, 1986, 100 Stat. 3097, 3104, 3116; Pub. L. 100-506, §1(a), Oct. 18, 1988, 102 Stat. 2538; Pub. L. 100-597, §1, Nov. 3, 1988, 102 Stat. 3028; Pub. L. 101-311, title I, §101, title II, §201, June 25, 1990, 104 Stat. 267, 268; Pub. L. 101-647, title XXV, §2522(e), Nov. 29, 1990, 104 Stat. 4867; Pub. L. 102-486, title XXX, §3017(a), Oct. 24, 1992, 106 Stat. 3130; Pub. L. 103-394, title I, §106, title II, §§208(a), 215, 217(a), 218(a), title III, §304(a), title V, §501(a), (b)(1), (d)(1), Oct. 22, 1994, 108 Stat. 4111, 4124, 4126-4128, 4132, 4141-4143; Pub. L. 106-554, §1(a)(5) [title I, §112(c)(3), (4)], Dec. 21, 2000, 114 Stat. 2763, 2763A-393, 2763A-394; Pub. L. 109-8, title I, §102(b), (k), title II, §§211, 226(a), 231(b), title III, §306(c), title IV, §§401(a), 414, 432(a), title VIII, §802(b), title IX, §907(a)(1), (b), (c), title X, §§1004, 1005, 1007(a), title XI, §1101(a), (b), title XII, §1201, Apr. 20, 2005, 119 Stat. 32, 35, 50, 66, 73, 80, 104, 107, 110, 145, 170, 175, 186, 187, 189, 192; Pub. L. 109-390, §5(a)(1), Dec. 12, 2006, 120 Stat. 2695.)

HISTORICAL AND REVISION NOTES

LEGISLATIVE STATEMENTS

Section 101(2) defines "affiliate." The House amendment contains a provision that is a compromise between the definition in the House-passed version of H.R. 8200 and the Senate amendment in the nature of a substitute to H.R. 8200. Subparagraphs (A) and (B) are derived from the Senate amendment and subparagraph (D) is taken from the House bill, while subparagraph (C) represents a compromise, taking the House position with respect to a person whose business is operated under a lease or an operating agreement by the debtor and with respect to a person substantially all of whose property is operated under an operating agreement by the debtor and with respect to a person substantially all of whose property is operated under an operating agreement by the debtor and the Senate position on leased property. Thus, the definition of "affiliate" excludes persons substantially all of whose property is operated under a lease agreement by a debtor, such as a small company which owns equipment all of which is leased to a larger nonrelated company.

Section 101(4)(B) represents a modification of the House-passed bill to include the definition of "claim" a right to an equitable remedy for breach of performance if such breach gives rise to a right to payment. This is intended to cause the liquidation or estimation of contingent rights of payment for which there may be an alternative equitable remedy with the result that the equitable remedy will be susceptible to being discharged in bankruptcy. For example, in some States, a judgment for specific performance may be satisfied by an alternative right to payment, in the event performance is refused; in that event, the creditor entitled to specific performance would have a "claim" for purposes of a proceeding under title 11.

On the other hand, rights to an equitable remedy for a breach of performance with respect to which such breach does not give rise to a right to payment are not "claims" and would therefore not be susceptible to discharge in bankruptcy.

In a case under chapter 9 to title 11, "claim" does not include a right to payment under an industrial development bond issued by a municipality as a matter of convenience for a third party.

Municipalities are authorized, under section 103(c) of the Internal Revenue Code of 1954, as amended [title 26], to issue tax-exempt industrial development revenue bonds to provide for the financing of certain projects for privately owned companies. The bonds are sold on the basis of the credit of the company on whose behalf they are issued, and the principal, interest, and premium, if any, are payable solely from payments made by the company to the trustee under the bond indenture and do not constitute claims on the tax revenues or other funds of the issuing municipalities. The municipality merely acts as the vehicle to enable the bonds to be issued on a tax-exempt basis. Claims that arise by virtue of these bonds are not among the claims defined by this paragraph and amounts owed by private companies to the holders of industrial development revenue bonds are not to be included among the assets of the municipality that would be affected by the plan.

Section 101(6) defines "community claim" as provided by the Senate amendment in order to indicate that a community claim exists whether or not there is community property in the estate as of the commencement of the case.

Section 101(7) of the House amendment contains a definition of consumer debt identical to the definition in the House bill and Senate amendment. A consumer debt does not include a debt to any extent the debt is secured by real property.

Section 101(9) of the Senate amendment contained a definition of "court." The House amendment deletes the provision as unnecessary in light of the pervasive jurisdiction of a bankruptcy court under all chapters of title 11 as indicated in title II of the House amendment to H.R. 8200.

Section 101(11) defines "debt" to mean liability on a claim, as was contained in the House-passed version of H.R. 8200. The Senate amendment contained language indicating that "debt" does not include a policy loan made by a life insurance company to the debtor. That language is deleted in the House amendment as unnecessary since a life insurance company clearly has no right to have a policy loan repaid by the debtor, although such company does have a right of offset with respect to such policy loan. Clearly, then, a "debt" does not include a policy loan made by a life insurance company. Inclusion of the language contained in the Senate amendment would have required elaboration of other legal relationships not arising by a liability on a claim. Further the language would have required clarification that interest on a policy loan made by a life insurance company is a debt, and that the insurance company does have right to payment to that interest.

Section 101(14) adopts the definition of "entity" contained in the Senate-passed version of H.R. 8200. Since the Senate amendment to H.R. 8200 deleted the U.S. trustee, a corresponding definitional change is made in chapter 15 of the House amendment for U.S. trustees under the pilot program. Adoption by the House amendment of a pilot program for U.S. trustees under chapter 15 requires insertion of "United States trustee" in many sections. Several provisions in chapter 15 of the House amendment that relate to the U.S. trustee were not contained in the Senate amendment in the nature of a substitute.

Section 101(17) defines "farmer," as in the Senate amendment with an income limitation percentage of 80 percent instead of 75 percent.

Section 101(18) contains a new definition of "farming operation" derived from present law and the definition of "farmer" in the Senate amendment. This definition gives a broad construction to the term "farming operation".

Section 101(20) contains a definition of "foreign representative". It clarifies the House bill and Senate amendment by indicating that a foreign representative must be duly selected in a foreign proceeding.

Section 101(35) defines "security" as contained in the Senate amendment. H.R. 8200 as adopted by the House excluded certain commercial notes from the definition of "security", and that exclusion is deleted.

Section 101(40) defines "transfer" as in the Senate amendment. The definition contained in H.R. 8200 as passed by the House included "setoff" in the definition of "transfer". Inclusion of "setoff" is deleted. The effect is that a "setoff" is not subject to being set aside as a preferential "transfer" but will be subject to special rules.

SENATE REPORT NO. 95–989

Section 101 of title 11 contains 40 definitions:

Paragraph (1) defines "accountant" as an accountant authorized under applicable law to practice accounting. The term includes a professional accounting association, corporation, or partnership if applicable law authorizes such a unit to practice accounting.

Paragraph (2) defines "affiliate." An affiliate is an entity with a close relationship to the debtor. It includes a 20 percent parent or subsidiary of the debtor, whether a corporate, partnership, individual, or estate parent.

The use of "directly or indirectly" in subparagraphs (A) and (B) is intended to cover situations in which there is an opportunity to control, and where the existence of that opportunity operates as indirect control.

"Affiliate" is defined primarily for use in the definition of insider, infra, and for use in the chapter 11 reorganization cases. The definition of "affiliate" does not include an entity acting in a fiduciary or agency capacity if the entity does not have the sole discretionary power to vote 20 percent of the voting securities but hold them solely as security and have not exercised the power to vote. This restriction applies to a corporate affiliate under subparagraph (B) of paragraph (2).

Subsections (C) and (D) of paragraph (2) define affiliate also as those persons and entities whose business or substantially all of whose property is operated under a lease or operating agreement by a debtor and whose business or property is more than 50 percent under the control of the debtor.

The definition of "attorney" in paragraph (3) is similar to the definition of accountant.

Paragraph (4) defines "claim." The effect of the definition is a significant departure from present law. Under present law, "claim" is not defined in straight bankruptcy. Instead it is simply used, along with the concept of provability in section 63 of the Bankruptcy Act [section 103 of former title 11], to limit the kinds of obligations that are payable in a bankruptcy case. The term is defined in the debtor rehabilitation chapters of present law far more broadly. The definition in paragraph (4) adopts an even broader definition of claim than is found in the present debtor rehabilitation chapters. The definition is any right to payment, whether or not reduced to judgment, liquidated, unliquidated, fixed, contingent, matured, unmatured, disputed, undisputed, legal, equitable, secured, or unsecured. The definition also includes as a claim an equitable right to performance that does not give rise to a right to payment. By this broadest possible definition and by the use of the term throughout the title 11, especially in subchapter I of chapter 5, the bill contemplates that all legal obligations of the debtor, no matter how remote or contingent, will be able to be dealt with in the bankruptcy case. It permits the broadest possible relief in the bankruptcy court.

Paragraph (5) defines "commodity broker" by reference to various terms used and defined in subchapter IV of chapter 7, Commodity Broker Liquidation. The terms are described in connection with section 761, infra.

Paragraph (6) defines "community claim" for those eight States that have community property laws. The definition is keyed to the liability of the debtor's property for a claim against either the debtor or the debtor's spouse. If the debtor's property is liable for a claim against either, that claim is a community claim.

Paragraph (7) defines "consumer debt". The definition is adapted from the definition used in various consumer protection laws. It encompasses only a debt incurred by an individual primarily for a personal, family, or household purpose.

The definition of "corporation" in paragraph (8) is similar to the definition in current law, section 1(8) [section 1(8) of former title 11]. The term encompasses any association having the power or privilege that a private corporation, but not an individual or partnership, has; partnership associations organized under a law that makes only the capital subscribed responsible for the debts of the partnership; joint-stock company; unincorporated company or association; and business trust. "Unincorporated association" is intended specifically to include a labor union, as well as other bodies that come under that phrase as used under current law. The exclusion of limited partnerships is explicit, and not left to the case law.

Paragraph (9) defines "court" as the bankruptcy judge in the district in which the case is pending except in municipal adjustment and railroad reorganization cases, where "court" means the Federal district judge.

Paragraph (10) [enacted as (9)] defines "creditor" to include holders of prepetition claims against the debtor. However, it also encompasses certain holders of claims that are deemed to arise before the date of the filing of the petition, such as those injured by the rejection of an executory contract or unexpired lease, certain investment tax credit recapture claim holders, "involuntary gap" creditors, and certain holders of the right of setoff. The term also includes the holder of a prepetition community claim. A guarantor of or surety for a claim against the debtor is also a creditor, because he holds a contingent claim against the debtor that becomes fixed when he pays the creditor whose claim he has guaranteed or insured.

Paragraph (11) [enacted as (10)] defines "custodian." There is no similar definition in current law. It is defined to facilitate drafting, and means a prepetition liquidator of the debtor's property, such as an assignee for the benefit of creditors, a receiver of the debtor's property, or administrator of the debtor's property. The definition of custodian to include a receiver or trustee is descriptive, and not meant to be limited to court officers with those titles. The definition is intended to include other officers of the court if their functions are substantially similar to those of a receiver or trustee.

"Debt" is defined in paragraph (12) [enacted as (11)] as a liability on a claim. The terms "debt" and "claim" are coextensive: a creditor has a "claim" against the debtor; the debtor owes a "debt" to the creditor. This definition of "debt" and the definition of "claim" on which it is based, proposed 11 U.S.C. 101(4), does not include a transaction such as a policy loan on an insurance policy. Under that kind of transaction, the debtor is not liable to the insurance company for repayment; the amount owed is merely available to the company for setoff against any benefits that become payable under the policy. As such, the loan is not a claim (it is not a right to payment) that the company can assert against the estate; nor is the debtor's obligation a debt (a liability on a claim) that will be discharged under proposed 11 U.S.C. 523 or 524.

Paragraph (13) [enacted as (12)] defines "debtor." Debtor means person or municipality concerning which a case under title 11 has been commenced. This is a change in terminology from present law, which identifies the person by or against whom a petition is filed in a straight bankruptcy liquidation case as the "bankrupt", and a person or municipality that is proceeding under a debtor rehabilitation chapter (chapters VIII through XIII of the Bankruptcy Act) [chapters 8 through 13 of former title 11] as a "debtor." The term "debtor" is used for both kinds of cases in this bill, for ease of reference in chapters 1, 3, and 5 (which apply to straight bankruptcy and reorganization cases).

Paragraph (14) [enacted as (13)] defines "disinterested person." The definition is adapted from section 158 of chapter X of current law [section 558 of former title 11], though it is expanded and modified in some respects. A person is a disinterested person if the person is not a creditor, equity security holder, or insider; is not and was not an investment banker of the debtor for any outstanding security of the debtor (the change from underwriter in current law to investment banker is to make the term more descriptive and to avoid conflict with the definition of underwriter in section 2(11) of the Securities Act of 1933 (15 U.S.C. 77b(11)); has not been an investment banker for a security of the debtor within 3 years before the date of the filing of the petition (the change from five years to three years here conforms the definition with the statute of limitations in the Securities Act of 1933) [15 U.S.C. 77m], or an attorney for such an investment banker; is not an insider of the debtor or of such an investment banker; and does not have an interest materially adverse to the estate.

"Entity" is defined, for convenience, in paragraph (15) [enacted as (14)], to include person, estate, trust, and governmental unit. It is the most inclusive of the various defined terms relating to bodies or units.

Paragraph (16) defines "equity security." The term includes a share or stock in a corporation, a limited partner's interest in a limited partnership, and a warrant or right to subscribe to an equity security. The term does not include a security, such as a convertible debenture, that is convertible into equity security, but has not been converted.

Paragraph (17) [enacted as (15)] defines "equity security holder" for convenience as the holder of an equity securing of the debtor.

Paragraph (18) [enacted as (17)] defines "farmer". It encompasses only those persons for whom farming operations contribute 75 percent or more of their total income.

Paragraphs (19) and (20) define "foreign proceeding" and "foreign representative". A foreign proceeding is a proceeding in another country in which the debtor has some substantial connection for the purpose of liquidating the estate of the debtor or the purpose of financial rehabilitation of the debtor. A foreign representative is the representative of the estate in a foreign proceeding, such as a trustee or administrator.

Paragraph (21) defines "governmental unit" in the broadest sense. The definition encompasses the United States, a State, Commonwealth, District, Territory, municipality, or foreign state, and a department, agency, or instrumentality of any of those entities. "Department, agency, or instrumentality" does not include an entity that owes its existence to State action, such as the granting of a charter or a license but that has no other connection with a State or local government or the Federal Government. The relationship must be an active one in which the department, agency, or instrumentality is actually carrying out some governmental function.

Paragraph (22) defines "indenture." It is similar to the definition of indenture in the Trust Indenture Act of 1939 [15 U.S.C. 77ccc(7)]. An indenture is the instrument under which securities, either debt or equity, of the debtor are outstanding.

Paragraph (23) defines "indenture trustee" as the trustee under an indenture.

Paragraph (24) defines "individual with regular income." The effect of this definition, and of its use in section 109(e), is to expand substantially the kinds of individuals that are eligible for relief under chapter 13, Adjustment of Debts of an Individual with Regular Income. Chapter XIII [chapter 13 of former title 11] is now available only for wage earners. The definition encompasses all individuals with incomes that are sufficiently stable and regular to enable them to make payments under a chapter 13 plan. Thus, individuals on welfare, social security, fixed pension incomes, or who live on investment incomes, will be able to work out repayment plans with their creditors rather than being forced into straight bankruptcy. Also, self-employed individuals will be eligible to use chapter 13 if they have regular incomes.

However, the definition excludes certain stockbrokers and commodity brokers, in order to prohibit them from proceeding under chapter 13 and avoiding the customer protection provisions of chapter 7.

"Insider", defined in paragraph (25), is a new term. An insider is one who has a sufficiently close relationship with the debtor that his conduct is made subject to closer scrutiny than those dealing at arms length with the debtor. If the debtor is an individual, then a relative of the debtor, a partnership in which the debtor is a general partner, a general partner of the debtor, and a corporation controlled by the debtor are all insiders. If the debtor is a corporation, then a controlling person, a relative of a controlling person, a partnership in which the debtor is a general partner, and a general partner of the debtor are all insiders. If the debtor is a partnership, then a general partner of or in the debtor, a relative of a general partner in the debtor, and a person in control are all insiders. If the debtor is a municipality, then an elected official of the debtor is an insider. In addition, affiliates of the debtor and managing agents are insiders.

The definition of "insolvent" in paragraph (26) is adopted from section 1(19) of current law [section 1(19) of former title 11]. An entity is insolvent if its debts are greater than its assets, at a fair valuation, exclusive of property exempted or fraudulently transferred. It is the traditional bankruptcy balance sheet test of insolvency. For a partnership, the definition is modified to account for the liability of a general partner for the partnership's debts. The difference in this definition from that in current law is in the exclusion of exempt property for all purposes in the definition of insolvent.

Paragraph (27) defines "judicial lien." It is one of three kinds of liens defined in this section. A judicial lien is a lien obtained by judgment, levy, sequestration, or other legal or equitable process or proceeding.

Paragraph (28) defines "lien." The definition is new and is very broad. A lien is defined as a charge against or interest in property to secure payment of a debt or performance of an obligation. It includes inchoate liens. In general, the concept of lien is divided into three kinds of liens: judicial liens, security interests, and statutory liens. Those three categories are mutually exclusive and are exhaustive except for certain common law liens.

Paragraph (29) defines "municipality." The definition is adapted from the terms used in the chapter IX (municipal bankruptcy) [chapter 9 of former title 11] amendment to the Bankruptcy Act enacted in 1976 (Pub. L. 94-260). That amendment spoke in terms of "political subdivision or public agency or instrumentality of a State". Bankruptcy Act Sec. 84 [section 404 of former title 11]. The term municipality is defined by those three terms for convenience. It does not include the District of Columbia or any territories of the United States.

"Person" is defined in paragraph (30). The definition is a change in wording, but not in substance, from the definition in section 1(23) of the Bankruptcy Act [section 1(23) of former title 11]. The definition is also similar to the one contained in 1 U.S.C. sec. 1, but is repeated here for convenience and ease of reference. Person includes individual partnership, and corporation. The exclusion of governmental units is made explicit in order to avoid any confusion that may arise if, for example, a municipality is incorporated and thus is legally a corporation as well as governmental unit. The definition does not include an estate or a trust, which are included only in the definition of "entity" in proposed 11 U.S.C. 101(14).

"Petition" is defined for convenience in paragraph (31). Petition is a petition under section 301, 302, 303, or 304 of the bankruptcy code—that is, a petition that commences a case under title 11.

Paragraph (32) defines purchaser as a transferee of a voluntary transfer, such as a sale or gift, and includes an immediate or mediate transferee of a purchaser.

The definition of "railroad" in paragraph (33) is derived from section 77 of the Bankruptcy Act [section 205 of former title 11]. A railroad is a common carrier by railroad engaged in the transportation of individuals or property, or an owner of trackage facilities leased by such a common carrier. The effect of the definition and the use of the term in section 109(d) is to eliminate the limitation now found in section 77 of the Bankruptcy Act that only railroads engaged in interstate commerce may proceed under the railroad reorganization provisions. The limitation may have been inserted because of a doubt that the commerce power could not reach intrastate railroads. Be that as it may, this bill is enacted under the bankruptcy power.

Paragraph (34) defines "relative" as an individual related by affinity or consanguinity within the third degree as determined by the common law, and includes individuals in a step or adoptive relationship. The definition is similar to current law, but adds the latter phrase. This definition should be applied as of the time when the transaction that it concerns took place. Thus, a former spouse is not a relative, but if, for example, for purposes of the preference section, proposed 11 U.S.C. 547(b)(4)(B), the transferee was a spouse of the debtor at the time of the transfer sought to be avoided, then the transferee would be relative and subject to the insider rules, even if the transferee was no longer married to the debtor at the time of the commencement of the case or at the time of the commencement of the preference recovery proceeding.

Paragraph (35) defines "security." The definition is new and is modeled on the most recent draft of the American Law Institute's proposed securities code, with some exceptions. The interest of a limited partner in a limited partnership is included in order to make sure that everything that is defined as an equity security is also a "security." The definition, as with the definition of "entity", "insider", and "person", is open-ended because the term is not susceptible of precise specification. Thus the courts will be able to use the characterization provided in this definition to treat with new kinds of documents on a flexible basis.

Paragraphs (36) and (37) defined "security agreement" and "security interest." A security interest is one of the kinds of liens. It is a lien created by an agreement. Security agreement is defined as the agreement creating the security interest. Though these terms are similar to the same terms in the Uniform Commercial Code, article IX, they are broader. For example, the U.C.C. does not cover real property mortgages. Under this definition, such a mortgage is included, as are all other liens created by agreement, even though not covered by the U.C.C. All U.C.C. security interests and security agreements are, however, security interests and security agreements under this definition. Whether a consignment or a lease constitutes a security interest under the bankruptcy code will depend on whether it constitutes a security interest under applicable State or local law.

Paragraph (38) defines another kind of lien, "statutory lien." The definition, derived from current law, states that a statutory lien is a lien arising solely by force of statute on specified circumstances or conditions and includes a lien of distress for rent (whether statutory, common law, or otherwise). The definition excludes judicial liens and security interests, whether or not they are provided for or are dependent on a statute, and whether or not they are made fully effective by statute. A statutory lien is only one that arises automatically, and is not based on an agreement to give a lien or on judicial action. Mechanics', materialmen's, and warehousemen's liens are examples. Tax liens are also included in the definition of statutory lien.

"Stockbroker" is defined in paragraph (39) as a person engaged in the business of effecting transactions in securities for the account of others or with members of the general public from or for such person's own account, if the person has a customer, as defined. Thus, the definition, derived from a combination of the definitions of "broker" and "dealer" in the Securities Exchange Act of 1934 [15 U.S.C. 78c], encompasses both brokers and dealers. The definition is used in section 109 and in subchapter III of chapter 7, Stockholder Liquidation. The term does not encompass an employee who acts for a principal that "effects" transaction or deals with the public, because such an employee will not have a "customer".

Paragraph (40) defines "transfer." It is derived and adapted, with stylistic changes, from section 1(30) of the Bankruptcy Act [section 1(30) of former title 11]. A transfer is a disposition of an interest in property. The definition of transfer is as broad as possible. Many of the potentially limiting words in current law are deleted, and the language is simplified. Under this definition, any transfer of an interest in property is a transfer, including a transfer of possession, custody, or control even if there is no transfer of title, because possession, custody, and control are interests in property. A deposit in a bank account or similar account is a transfer.

REFERENCES IN TEXT

The Social Security Act, referred to in par. (10A)(B), is act Aug. 14, 1935, ch. 531, 49 Stat. 620, as amended, which is classified generally to chapter 7 (§301 et seq.) of Title 42, The Public Health and Welfare. For complete classification of this Act to the Code, see section 1305 of Title 42 and Tables.

The Internal Revenue Code of 1986, referred to in pars. (12A)(B) and (41)(C), is classified generally to Title 26, Internal Revenue Code.

Section 3 of the Federal Deposit Insurance Act, referred to in pars. (12A)(D), (21B)(A), (33)(A), (35)(A), and (54A), is classified to section 1813 of Title 12, Banks and Banking.

Sections 101 and 206(r) of the Federal Credit Union Act, referred to in pars. (12A)(D), (33)(B), and (34), are classified to sections 1752 and 1786(r), respectively, of Title 12, Banks and Banking.

The Investment Company Act of 1940, referred to in par. (22)(B), is title I of act Aug. 22, 1940, ch. 686, 54 Stat. 789, as amended, which is classified generally to subchapter I (§80a–1 et seq.) of chapter 2D of Title 15, Commerce and Trade. For complete classification of this Act to the Code, see section 80a–51 of Title 15 and Tables.

Section 402 of the Federal Deposit Insurance Corporation Improvement Act of 1991, referred to in par. (22A)(B), is classified to section 4402 of Title 12, Banks and Banking.

Section 304 of this title, referred to in par. (42), was repealed by Pub. L. 109–8, title VIII, §802(d)(3), Apr. 20, 2005, 119 Stat. 146.

The Securities Exchange Act of 1934, referred to in pars. (47)(A)(i), (48), (48A), and (53B)(B), is act June 6, 1934, ch. 404, 48 Stat. 881, as amended, which is classified principally to chapter 2B (§78a et seq.) of Title 15, Commerce and Trade. Sections 3, 6, 15A, and 17A of the Act are classified to sections 78c, 78f, 78*o*–3 and 78q–1, respectively, of Title 15. For complete classification of this Act to the Code, see section 78a of Title 15 and Tables.

The Securities Act of 1933, referred to in par. (49)(A)(xii), is act May 27, 1933, ch. 38, title I, 48 Stat. 74, as amended, which is classified generally to subchapter I (§77a et seq.) of chapter 2A of Title 15, Commerce and Trade. Section 3(b) of the Act is classified to section 77c(b) of Title 15. For complete classification of this Act to the Code, see section 77a of Title 15 and Tables.

The Gramm-Leach-Bliley Act, referred to in par. (53B)(B), is Pub. L. 106–102, Nov. 12, 1999, 113 Stat. 1338, as amended. For complete classification of this Act to the Code, see Short Title of 1999 Amendment note set out under section 1811 of Title 12, Banks and Banking, and Tables.

The Legal Certainty for Bank Products Act of 2000, referred to in par. (53B)(B), is title IV of H.R. 5660, as enacted by Pub. L. 106–554, §1(a)(5), Dec. 21, 2000, 114 Stat. 2763, 2763A–457, which is classified to sections 27 to 27f of Title 7, Agriculture. For complete classification of this Act to the Code, see Short Title of 2000 Amendment note set out under section 1 of Title 7 and Tables.

The Commodity Exchange Act, referred to in par. (53B)(B), is act Sept. 21, 1922, ch. 369, 42 Stat. 998, as amended, which is classified generally to chapter 1 (§1 et seq.) of Title 7, Agriculture. For complete classification of this Act to the Code, see section 1 of Title 7 and Tables.

AMENDMENTS

2006—Par. (22)(A). Pub. L. 109–390, §5(a)(1)(A), struck out "(domestic or foreign)" after "an entity" and inserted "(whether or not a 'customer', as defined in section 741)" after "custodian for a customer".

Par. (22A)(A). Pub. L. 109–390, §5(a)(1)(B), inserted "(aggregated across counterparties)" after "principal amount outstanding" and substituted "at such time or on any day during the 15-month period preceding the date of the filing of the petition" for "on any day during the previous 15-month period" in two places.

Par. (25)(A). Pub. L. 109–390, §5(a)(1)(C), inserted ", as defined in section 761" after "commodity contract" and substituted "repurchase or reverse repurchase transaction (whether or not such repurchase or reverse repurchase transaction is a 'repurchase agreement', as defined in this section)" for "repurchase transaction, reverse repurchase transaction,".

Par. (53B)(A)(i)(II). Pub. L. 109–390, §5(a)(1)(D)(i)(I), substituted ", precious metals, or other commodity" for "or precious metals".

Par. (53B)(A)(i)(VIII). Pub. L. 109–390, §5(a)(1)(D)(i)(III), substituted "option, future, or forward agreement" for "weather derivative, or weather option".

Par. (53B)(A)(i)(IX), (X). Pub. L. 109–390, §5(a)(1)(D)(i)(II), (IV), added subcls. (IX) and (X).

Par. (53B)(A)(ii). Pub. L. 109–390, §5(a)(1)(D)(ii), inserted "or other derivatives" after "dealings in the swap" in subcl. (I) and substituted "future, option, or spot transaction" for "future, or option" in subcl. (II).

Par. (53B)(B). Pub. L. 109–390, §5(a)(1)(E), substituted "the Gramm-Leach-Bliley Act, the Legal Certainty for Bank Products Act of 2000, the securities laws (as such term is defined in section 3(a)(47) of the Securities Exchange Act of 1934) and the Commodity Exchange Act" for "the Securities Act of 1933, the Securities Exchange Act of 1934, the Public Utility Holding Company Act of 1935, the Trust Indenture Act of 1939, the Investment Company Act of 1940, the Investment Advisers Act of 1940, the Securities Investor Protection Act of 1970, the Commodity Exchange Act, the Gramm-Leach-Bliley Act, and the Legal Certainty for Bank Products Act of 2000".

2005—Pub. L. 109–8, §1201(1), substituted "In this title the following definitions shall apply:" for "In this title—" in introductory provisions.

Pars. (1), (2). Pub. L. 109–8, §1201(2), (8), inserted "The term" after par. designation and substituted a period for semicolon at end.

Par. (3). Pub. L. 109–8, §1201(2), (8), inserted "The term" after par. designation and substituted a period for semicolon at end.

Pub. L. 109–8, §226(a)(1), added par. (3).

Par. (4). Pub. L. 109–8, §1201(2), (8), inserted "The term" after par. designation and substituted a period for semicolon at end.

Par. (4A). Pub. L. 109–8, §1201(2), (8), inserted "The term" after par. designation and substituted a period for semicolon at end.

Pub. L. 109–8, §226(a)(2), added par. (4A).

Pars. (5) to (7). Pub. L. 109–8, §1201(2), (8), inserted "The term" after par. designation and substituted a period for semicolon at end.

Pars. (7A), (7B). Pub. L. 109–8, §1201(2), (8), inserted "The term" after par. designation and substituted a period for semicolon at end.

Pub. L. 109–8, §1007(a)(1), added pars. (7A) and (7B).

Pars. (8) to (10). Pub. L. 109–8, §1201(2), (8), inserted "The term" after par. designation and substituted a period for semicolon at end.

Par. (10A). Pub. L. 109–8, §1201(2), (8), inserted "The term" after par. designation and substituted a period for semicolon at end.

Pub. L. 109–8, §102(b), added par. (10A).

Pars. (11), (12). Pub. L. 109–8, §1201(2), (8), inserted "The term" after par. designation and substituted a period for semicolon at end.

Par. (12A). Pub. L. 109–8, §1201(8), which directed the substitution of a period for a semicolon at end, could not be executed because par. (12A) ended in a period after amendment by Pub. L. 109–8, §226(a)(3). See below.

Pub. L. 109–8, §1201(2), inserted "The term" after par. designation.

Pub. L. 109–8, §§211(1), 226(a)(3), added par. (12A) and struck out former par. (12A) which read as follows: "'debt for child support' means a debt of a kind specified in section 523(a)(5) of this title for maintenance or support of a child of the debtor;".

Par. (13). Pub. L. 109–8, §1201(2), (8), inserted "The term" after par. designation and substituted a period for semicolon at end.

Par. (13A). Pub. L. 109–8, §1201(2), (8), inserted "The term" after par. designation and substituted a period for semicolon at end.

Pub. L. 109–8, §306(c)(1), added par. (13A).

Par. (14). Pub. L. 109–8, §1201(2), (8), inserted "The term" after par. designation and substituted a period for semicolon at end.

Pub. L. 109–8, §414, amended par. (14) generally. Prior to amendment, par. (14) consisted of subpars. (A) to (E) defining "disinterested person".

Par. (14A). Pub. L. 109–8, §1201(2), (8), inserted "The term" after par. designation and substituted a period for semicolon at end.

Pub. L. 109–8, §211(2), added par. (14A).

Pars. (15) to (17). Pub. L. 109–8, §1201(2), (8), inserted "The term" after par. designation and substituted a period for semicolon at end.

Par. (18). Pub. L. 109–8, §1201(2), (8), inserted "The term" after par. designation and substituted a period for semicolon at end.

Par. (18)(A). Pub. L. 109–8, §1005, substituted "for—

"(i) the taxable year preceding; or

"(ii) each of the 2d and 3d taxable years preceding; the taxable year" for "for the taxable year preceding the taxable year".

Pub. L. 109–8, §1004(1), substituted "$3,237,000" for "$1,500,000" and "not less than 50 percent" for "not less than 80 percent".

Par. (18)(B)(ii). Pub. L. 109–8, §1004(2), substituted "$3,237,000" for "$1,500,000" and "50 percent" for "80 percent".

Par. (19). Pub. L. 109–8, §1201(2), (8), inserted "The term" after par. designation and substituted a period for semicolon at end.

Pars. (19A), (19B). Pub. L. 109–8, §1201(2), (8), inserted "The term" after par. designation and substituted a period for semicolon at end.

Pub. L. 109–8, §1007(a)(2), added pars. (19A) and (19B).

Pars. (20) to (21B). Pub. L. 109–8, §1201(2), (8), inserted "The term" after par. designation and substituted a period for semicolon at end.

Par. (22). Pub. L. 109–8, §1201(2), (8), inserted "The term" after par. designation and substituted a period for semicolon at end.

Pub. L. 109–8, §907(b)(1), added par. (22) and struck out former par. (22) which consisted of introductory provisions and subpars. (A) and (B) defining "financial institution".

Par. (22A). Pub. L. 109–8, §1201(2), (8), inserted "The term" after par. designation and substituted a period for semicolon at end.

Pub. L. 109–8, §907(b)(2), added par. (22A).

Pars. (23), (24). Pub. L. 109–8, §1201(2), (8), inserted "The term" after par. designation and substituted a period for semicolon at end.

Pub. L. 109–8, §802(b), added pars. (23) and (24) and struck out former pars. (23) and (24) which read as follows:

"(23) 'foreign proceeding' means proceeding, whether judicial or administrative and whether or not under bankruptcy law, in a foreign country in which the debtor's domicile, residence, principal place of business, or principal assets were located at the commencement of such proceeding, for the purpose of liquidating an estate, adjusting debts by composition, extension, or discharge, or effecting a reorganization;

"(24) 'foreign representative' means duly selected trustee, administrator, or other representative of an estate in a foreign proceeding;".

Par. (25). Pub. L. 109–8, §1201(2), (8), inserted "The term" after par. designation and substituted a period for semicolon at end.

Pub. L. 109–8, §907(a)(1)(A), substituted "means—" for "means", designated subsequent provisions as subpar. (A), substituted ", or any other similar agreement" for ", or any combination thereof or option thereon", and added subpars. (B) to (E).

Par. (26). Pub. L. 109–8, §1201(2), (8), inserted "The term" after par. designation and substituted a period for semicolon at end.

Pub. L. 109–8, §907(b)(3), added par. (26) and struck out former par. (26) which read as follows: "'forward contract merchant' means a person whose business consists in whole or in part of entering into forward contracts as or with merchants in a commodity, as defined in section 761(8) of this title, or any similar good, article, service, right, or interest which is presently or in the future becomes the subject of dealing in the forward contract trade;".

Par. (27). Pub. L. 109–8, §1201(2), (8), inserted "The term" after par. designation and substituted a period for semicolon at end.

Par. (27A). Pub. L. 109–8, §1201(2), (8), inserted "The term" after par. designation and substituted a period for semicolon at end.

Pub. L. 109–8, §1101(a)(2), added par. (27A). Former par. (27A) redesignated (27B).

Pub. L. 109–8, §306(c)(2), added par. (27A).

Par. (27B). Pub. L. 109–8, §1201(2), (8), inserted "The term" after par. designation and substituted a period for semicolon at end.

Pub. L. 109–8, §1101(a)(1), redesignated par. (27A) as (27B).

Pars. (28) to (34). Pub. L. 109–8, §1201(2), (8), inserted "The term" after par. designation and substituted a period for semicolon at end.

Par. (35). Pub. L. 109–8, §1201(2), (8), inserted "The term" after par. designation and substituted a period for semicolon at end.

Par. (35)(B). Pub. L. 109–8, §1201(3), substituted "paragraphs (23) and (35)" for "paragraphs (21B) and (33)(A)".

Par. (35A). Pub. L. 109–8, §1201(2), (4), inserted "The term" after par. designation and substituted a period for "; and" at end.

Pars. (36), (37). Pub. L. 109–8, §1201(2), (8), inserted "The term" after par. designation and substituted a period for semicolon at end.

Par. (38). Pub. L. 109–8, §1201(2), (4), inserted "The term" after par. designation and substituted a period for "; and" at end.

Pars. (38A), (38B). Pub. L. 109–8, §1201(2), (8), inserted "The term" after par. designation and substituted a period for semicolon at end.

Pub. L. 109–8, §907(c), added pars. (38A) and (38B).

Par. (39). Pub. L. 109–8, §1201(2), inserted "The term" after par. designation.

Par. (39A). Pub. L. 109–8, §1201(2), (8), inserted "The term" after par. designation and substituted a period for semicolon at end.

Pub. L. 109–8, §102(k), added par. (39A).

Par. (40). Pub. L. 109–8, §1201(2), (8), inserted "The term" after par. designation and substituted a period for semicolon at end.

Pars. (40A), (40B). Pub. L. 109–8, §1201(2), (8), inserted "The term" after par. designation and substituted a period for semicolon at end.

Pub. L. 109–8, §1101(b), added pars. (40A) and (40B).

Par. (41). Pub. L. 109–8, §1201(2), (8), inserted "The term" after par. designation and substituted a period for semicolon at end.

Par. (41A). Pub. L. 109–8, §1201(2), (8), inserted "The term" after par. designation and substituted a period for semicolon at end.

Pub. L. 109–8, §231(b), added par. (41A).

Pars. (42) to (45). Pub. L. 109–8, §1201(2), (8), inserted "The term" after par. designation and substituted a period for semicolon at end.

Par. (46). Pub. L. 109–8, §1201(2), (8), inserted "The term" after par. designation and substituted a period for semicolon at end.

Pub. L. 109–8, §907(a)(1)(B), substituted "at any time before" for "on any day during the period beginning 90 days before the date of".

Par. (47). Pub. L. 109–8, §1201(2), (8), inserted "The term" after par. designation and substituted a period for semicolon at end.

Pub. L. 109–8, §907(a)(1)(C), amended par. (47) generally. Prior to amendment, par. (47) read as follows: "'repurchase agreement' (which definition also applies to a reverse repurchase agreement) means an agreement, including related terms, which provides for the transfer of certificates of deposit, eligible bankers' acceptances, or securities that are direct obligations of, or that are fully guaranteed as to principal and interest by, the United States or any agency of the United States against the transfer of funds by the transferee of such certificates of deposit, eligible bankers' acceptances, or securities with a simultaneous agreement by such transferee to transfer to the transferor thereof certificates of deposit, eligible bankers' acceptances, or securities as described above, at a date certain not later than one year after such transfers or on demand, against the transfer of funds;".

Par. (48). Pub. L. 109–8, §1201(2), (8), inserted "The term" after par. designation and substituted a period for semicolon at end.

Pub. L. 109–8, §907(a)(1)(D), inserted ", or exempt from such registration under such section pursuant to an order of the Securities and Exchange Commission," after "1934".

Par. (48A). Pub. L. 109–8, §1201(2), (8), inserted "The term" after par. designation and substituted a period for semicolon at end.

Pub. L. 109–8, §401(a), added par. (48A).

Pars. (49) to (51A). Pub. L. 109–8, §1201(2), (8), inserted "The term" after par. designation and substituted a period for semicolon at end.

Par. (51B). Pub. L. 109–8, §1201(2), (5), (8), inserted "The term" after par. designation and "who is not a family farmer" after "income of a debtor" and substituted a period for "thereto having aggregate noncontingent, liquidated secured debts in an amount no more than $4,000,000;".

Pars. (51C), (51D). Pub. L. 109–8, §1201(2), (8), inserted "The term" after par. designation and substituted a period for semicolon at end.

Pub. L. 109–8, §432(a), added pars. (51C) and (51D) and struck out former par. (51C) which read as follows: "'small business' means a person engaged in commercial or business activities (but does not include a person whose primary activity is the business of owning or operating real property and activities incidental thereto) whose aggregate noncontingent liquidated secured and unsecured debts as of the date of the petition do not exceed $2,000,000;".

Pars. (52) to (53A). Pub. L. 109–8, §1201(2), (8), inserted "The term" after par. designation and substituted a period for semicolon at end.

Par. (53B). Pub. L. 109–8, §1201(2), (8), inserted "The term" after par. designation and substituted a period for semicolon at end.

Pub. L. 109–8, §907(a)(1)(E), amended par. (53B) generally. Prior to amendment, par. (53B) consisted of introductory provisions and subpars. (A) to (C) defining "swap agreement".

Par. (53C). Pub. L. 109–8, §1201(2), (8), inserted "The term" after par. designation and substituted a period for semicolon at end.

Par. (53D). Pub. L. 109–8, §1201(2), (8), inserted "The term" after par. designation and substituted a period for semicolon at end.

Par. (54). Pub. L. 109–8, §1201(8), substituted a period for semicolon at end.

Pub. L. 109–8, §1201(6), added par. (54) and struck out former par. (54) which read as follows: "The term 'transfer' means every mode, direct or indirect, absolute or conditional, voluntary or involuntary, of disposing of or parting with property or with an interest in property, including retention of title as a security interest and foreclosure of the debtor's equity of redemption;".

Pub. L. 109–8, §1201(2), inserted "The term" after par. designation.

Par. (54A). Pub. L. 109–8, §1201(8), which directed the substitution of a period for semicolon at end, could not be executed because par. (54A) ended in a period after amendment by Pub. L. 109–8, §1201(4). See below.

Pub. L. 109–8, §1201(4), (7), substituted "The term" for "the term", realigned left margin, and substituted a period for "; and" at end.

Par. (55). Pub. L. 109–8, §1201(2), (8), inserted "The term" after par. designation and substituted a period for semicolon at end.

Par. (56A). Pub. L. 109–8, §1201(8), which directed the substitution of a period for semicolon "in each of paragraphs (40) through (55)" at end, was executed to par. (56A), to reflect the probable intent of Congress, because par. (56A) follows par. (53C) in text.

Pub. L. 109–8, §1201(2), inserted "The term" after par. designation.

2000—Par. (22). Pub. L. 106–554, §1(a)(5) [title I, §112(c)(3)], amended par. (22) generally. Prior to amendment par. (22) read as follows: "'financial institution' means a person that is a commercial or savings bank, industrial savings bank, savings and loan association, or trust company and, when any such person is acting as agent or custodian for a customer in connection with a securities contract, as defined in section 741 of this title, such customer;".

Par. (54A). Pub. L. 106–554, §1(a)(5) [title I, §112(c)(4)], added par. (54A).

1994—Par. (3). Pub. L. 103–394, §501(a)(1), redesignated par. (3) as (21B) and inserted it after par. (21A).

Par. (6). Pub. L. 103–394, §501(b)(1)(A), substituted "section 761" for "section 761(9)" after "customer, as defined in".

Par. (12A). Pub. L. 103–394, §304(a), added par. (12A).

Par. (21B). Pub. L. 103–394, §501(a)(1), redesignated par. (3) as (21B).

Par. (22). Pub. L. 103–394, §501(b)(1)(B), substituted "section 741" for "section 741(7)".

Par. (33)(A). Pub. L. 103–394, §501(d)(1)(A)(i), struck out "(12 U.S.C. 1813(u))" after "section 3(u) of the Federal Deposit Insurance Act".

Par. (33)(B). Pub. L. 103–394, §501(d)(1)(A)(ii), struck out "(12 U.S.C. 1786(r))" after "Act".

Par. (34). Pub. L. 103–394, §501(d)(1)(B), struck out "(12 U.S.C. 1752(7))" after "Act".

Par. (35). Pub. L. 103–394, §501(b)(1)(C), (d)(1)(C), struck out "(12 U.S.C. 1813(c)(2))" after "Act" in subpar. (A) and substituted "paragraphs (21B)" for "paragraphs (3)" in subpar. (B).

Par. (35A). Pub. L. 103–394, §501(a)(4), redesignated par. (56) defining "intellectual property" as (35A) and inserted it after par. (35).

Par. (39). Pub. L. 103–394, §501(a)(5), redesignated par. (57) defining "mask work" as (39) and inserted it after par. (38). Former par. (39) redesignated (51A).

Par. (41). Pub. L. 103–394, §106, amended par. (41) generally. Prior to amendment, par. (41) read as follows: "'person' includes individual, partnership, and corporation, but does not include governmental unit, *Provided, however*, That any governmental unit that acquires an asset from a person as a result of operation of a loan guarantee agreement, or as receiver or liquidating agent of a person, will be considered a person for purposes of section 1102 of this title."

Par. (42A). Pub. L. 103–394, §208(a)(1), added par. (42A).

Par. (48). Pub. L. 103–394, §501(d)(1)(D), struck out "(15 U.S.C. 78q–1)" after "Act of 1934" and "(15 U.S.C. 78c(12))" after "such Act".

Par. (49)(A)(xii). Pub. L. 103–394, §501(d)(1)(E)(i), struck out "(15 U.S.C. 77a et seq.)" after "Act of 1933" and "(15 U.S.C. 77c(b))" after "such Act".

Par. (49)(B). Pub. L. 103–394, §501(b)(1)(D), (d)(1)(E)(ii), substituted "section 761" for "section 761(13)" in cl. (ii) and struck out "(15 U.S.C. 77c(b))" after "Act of 1933" in cl. (vi).

Par. (51A). Pub. L. 103–394, §501(a)(2), redesignated par. (39) as (51A) and inserted it after par. (51).

Par. (51B). Pub. L. 103–394, §218(a), added par. (51B).

Par. (51C). Pub. L. 103–394, §217(a), added par. (51C).

Par. (53A). Pub. L. 103–394, §501(a)(3), (b)(1)(E), redesignated par. (54) defining "stockbroker" as (53A) and substituted "section 741" for "section 741(2)" in subpar. (A).

Par. (53B). Pub. L. 103–394, §501(a)(3), redesignated par. (55) defining "swap agreement" as (53B).

Par. (53C). Pub. L. 103–394, §501(a)(3), redesignated par. (56) defining "swap participant" as (53C).

Par. (53D). Pub. L. 103–394, §501(a)(3), (d)(1)(F), redesignated par. (57) defining "timeshare plan" as (53D) and substituted semicolon for period at end.

Par. (54). Pub. L. 103–394, §501(a)(3), redesignated par. (54) defining "stockbroker" as (53A).

Par. (55). Pub. L. 103–394, §501(a)(3), redesignated par. (55) defining "swap agreement" as (53B).

Pub. L. 103–394, §215, inserted "spot foreign exchange agreement," after "forward foreign exchange agreement,".

Par. (56). Pub. L. 103–394, §501(a)(3), redesignated par. (56) defining "swap participant" as (53C).

Pub. L. 103–394, §501(a)(4), redesignated par. (56) defining "intellectual property" as (35A) and inserted it after par. (35).

Par. (56A). Pub. L. 103–394, §208(a)(2), added par. (56A) and inserted it after par. defining "swap participant".

Par. (57). Pub. L. 103–394, §501(a)(3), redesignated par. (57) defining "timeshare plan" as (53D).

Pub. L. 103–394, §501(a)(5), redesignated par. (57) defining "mask work" as (39) and inserted it after par. (38).

1992—Par. (21A). Pub. L. 102–486 added par. (21A).

1990—Par. (3). Pub. L. 101–647, §2522(e)(4), added par. (3). Former par. (3) redesignated (4).

Pars. (4) to (23). Pub. L. 101–647, §2522(e)(3), redesignated pars. (3) to (22) as (4) to (23), respectively. Former par. (23) redesignated (24).

Par. (24). Pub. L. 101–647, §2522(e)(3), redesignated par. (23) as (24). Former par. (24) redesignated (25).

Pub. L. 101–311, §201(1), inserted "as defined in section 761(8) of this title, or any similar good, article, service, right, or interest which is presently or in the future becomes the subject of dealing in the forward contract trade," after "transfer of commodity," and ", including, but not limited to, a repurchase transaction, reverse repurchase transaction, consignment, lease, swap, hedge transaction, deposit, loan, option, allocated transaction, unallocated transaction, or any combination thereof or option thereon" after "entered into".

Par. (25). Pub. L. 101–647, §2522(e)(3), redesignated par. (24) as (25). Former par. (25) redesignated (26).

Pub. L. 101–311, §201(2), substituted "a commodity, as defined in section 761(8) of this title, or any similar good, article, service, right, or interest which is presently or in the future becomes the subject of dealing in the forward contract trade" for "commodities".

Pars. (26) to (32). Pub. L. 101–647, §2522(e)(3), redesignated pars. (25) to (31) as (26) to (32), respectively. Former par. (32) redesignated (36).

Par. (33). Pub. L. 101–647, §2522(e)(2), added par. (33). Former par. (33) redesignated (37).
Par. (34). Pub. L. 101–647, §2522(e)(2), added par. (34). Former par. (34) redesignated (38).
Pub. L. 101–311, §201(4), added par. (34). Former par. (34) redesignated (36).
Par. (35). Pub. L. 101–647, §2522(e)(2), added par. (35). Former par. (35) redesignated (39).
Pub. L. 101–311, §201(4), added par. (35). Former par. (35) redesignated (37).
Par. (36). Pub. L. 101–647, §2522(e)(1), redesignated par. (32) as (36). Former par. (36) redesignated (40).
Pub. L. 101–311, §201(3), redesignated par. (34) as (36). Former par. (36) redesignated (38).
Pars. (37) to (48). Pub. L. 101–647, §2522(e)(1), redesignated pars. (33) to (44) as (37) to (48), respectively. Former pars. (45) to (48) redesignated (49) to (52), respectively.
Pub. L. 101–311, §201(3), redesignated pars. (35) to (46) as (37) to (48), respectively. Former pars. (47) and (48) redesignated (49) and (50), respectively.
Pars. (49), (50). Pub. L. 101–647, §2522(e)(1), redesignated pars. (45) and (46) as (49) and (50), respectively. Former pars. (49) and (50) redesignated (53) and (54) defining "stockbroker", respectively.
Pub. L. 101–311, §201(3), redesignated pars. (47) and (48) as (49) and (50), respectively. Former pars. (49) and (50) redesignated (51) and (52), respectively.
Pub. L. 101–311, §101(2), added pars. (49) and (50). Former pars. (49) and (50) redesignated (51) and (52), respectively.
Par. (51). Pub. L. 101–647, §2522(e)(1), redesignated par. (47) as (51). Former par. (51) redesignated (55) defining "swap agreement".
Pub. L. 101–311, §201(3), redesignated par. (49) as (51). Former par. (51) redesignated (53).
Pub. L. 101–311, §101(1), redesignated par. (49) as (51). Former par. (51) redesignated (53).
Par. (52). Pub. L. 101–647, §2522(e)(1), redesignated par. (48) as (52). Former par. (52) redesignated (56) defining "swap participant".
Pub. L. 101–311, §201(3), redesignated par. (50) as (52). Former par. (52) redesignated (54) defining "transfer".
Pub. L. 101–311, §101(1), redesignated par. (50) as (52). Former par. (52) redesignated (54).
Par. (53). Pub. L. 101–647, §2522(e)(1), redesignated par. (49) as (53). Former par. (53) redesignated (57) defining "timeshare plan".
Pub. L. 101–311, §201(3), redesignated par. (51) as (53). Former par. (53) redesignated (55) defining "United States".
Pub. L. 101–311, §101(1), redesignated par. (51) as (53). Former par. (53) redesignated (55).
Par. (54). Pub. L. 101–647, §2522(e)(1), redesignated par. (50) as (54) defining "stockbroker".
Pub. L. 101–311, §201(3), redesignated par. (52) as (54) defining "transfer". Former par. (54) redesignated (56) defining "intellectual property".
Pub. L. 101–311, §101(1), redesignated par. (52) as (54).
Par. (55). Pub. L. 101–647, §2522(e)(1), redesignated par. (51) as (55) defining "swap agreement".
Pub. L. 101–311, §201(3), redesignated par. (53) as (55) defining "United States". Former par. (55) redesignated (57) defining "mask work".
Pub. L. 101–311, §101(1), redesignated par. (53) as (55).
Par. (56). Pub. L. 101–647, §2522(e)(1), redesignated par. (52) as (56) defining "swap participant".
Pub. L. 101–311, §201(3), redesignated par. (54) as (56) defining "intellectual property".
Par. (57). Pub. L. 101–647, §2522(e)(1), redesignated par. (53) as (57) defining "timeshare plan".
Pub. L. 101–311, §201(3), redesignated par. (55) as (57) defining "mask work".
1988—Par. (31). Pub. L. 100–597 inserted "and a municipality" after "partnership" in subpar. (A) and added subpar. (C).
Pars. (52), (53). Pub. L. 100–506 added pars. (52) and (53).
1986—Par. (14). Pub. L. 99–554, §201(1), substituted "governmental unit, and United States trustee" for "and governmental unit".
Pars. (17), (18). Pub. L. 99–554, §251(2), (3), added pars. (17) and (18) and redesignated former pars. (17) and (18) as (19) and (20), respectively.
Par. (19). Pub. L. 99–554, §251(1), (2), redesignated former par. (17) as (19) and inserted "(except when such term appears in the term 'family farmer')". Former par. (19) redesignated (21).
Pars. (20) to (25). Pub. L. 99–554, §251(2), redesignated former pars. (18) to (23) as (20) to (25), respectively. Former pars. (24) and (25) redesignated (26) and (27), respectively.
Par. (26). Pub. L. 99–554, §201(2), inserted "(but not a United States trustee while serving as a trustee in a case under this title)".
Pub. L. 99–554, §251(2), redesignated former par. (24) as (26). Former par. (26) redesignated (28).
Pars. (27) to (42). Pub. L. 99–554, §251(2), redesignated former pars. (25) to (40) as (27) to (42), respectively. Former pars. (41) and (42) redesignated (43) and (44), respectively.
Par. (43). Pub. L. 99–554, §251(2), redesignated former par. (41) as (43). Former par. (43) redesignated (45).
Par. (43)(A)(xv). Pub. L. 99–554, §283(a)(1), substituted "security" for "secuity".
Pars. (44) to (50). Pub. L. 99–554, §251(2), redesignated former pars. (42) to (48) as (44) to (50), respectively. Former par. (49) redesignated (51).
Par. (51). Pub. L. 99–554, §283(a)(2), substituted a period for the semicolon at the end thereof.
Pub. L. 99–554, §251(2), redesignated former par. (49) as (51).
1984—Par. (2)(D). Pub. L. 98–353, §421(a), struck out "or all" after "business".
Par. (8)(B). Pub. L. 98–353, §421(b), substituted a semicolon for the colon at end of subpar. (B).
Par. (9)(B). Pub. L. 98–353, §421(c), inserted reference to section 348(d).
Par. (14). Pub. L. 98–353, §421(d), inserted "and" after "trust,".
Pars. (19) to (21). Pub. L. 98–353, §421(j)(3), (4), added par. (19) and redesignated former pars. (19), (20), and (21) as (20), (21), and (24), respectively.
Pars. (22), (23). Pub. L. 98–353, §421(j)(2), (5), added pars. (22) and (23) and redesignated former pars. (22) and (23) as (25) and (26), respectively.
Pars. (24) to (26). Pub. L. 98–353, §421(j)(2), redesignated former pars. (21) to (23) as (24) to (26), respectively. Former pars. (24) to (26) redesignated (27) to (29), respectively.
Par. (27). Pub. L. 98–353, §421(e), (j)(2), redesignated former par. (24) as (27) and substituted "stockbroker" for "stock broker". Former par. (27) redesignated (30).
Par. (28). Pub. L. 98–353, §421(j)(2), redesignated former par. (25) as (28). Former par. (28) redesignated (31).
Par. (29). Pub. L. 98–353, §421(f), (j)(2), redesignated former par. (26) as (29) and, in subpar. (B)(ii), substituted "nonpartnership" and "(A)" for "separate" and "(A)(ii)", respectively, wherever appearing. Former par. (29) redesignated (32).
Pars. (30) to (32). Pub. L. 98–353, §421(j)(2), redesignated former pars. (27) to (29) as (30) to (32), respectively. Former pars. (30) to (32) redesignated (33) to (35), respectively.
Par. (33). Pub. L. 98–353, §421(g), (j)(2), redesignated former par. (30) as (33) and amended definition of "person" generally, thereby inserting proviso relating to consideration of certain governmental units as persons for purposes of section 1102 of this title. Former par. (33) redesignated (36).
Par. (34). Pub. L. 98–353, §421(j)(2), redesignated former par. (31) as (34). Former par. (34) redesignated (37).
Pars. (35), (36). Pub. L. 98–353, §421(j)(2), redesignated former pars. (32) and (33) as (35) and (36), respectively. Former pars. (35) and (36), as added by Pub. L. 98–353, §391(2), redesignated (38) and (39), respectively.
Pub. L. 98–353, §391, added pars. (35) and (36), and redesignated former pars. (35) and (36) as (37) and (38) which were again redesignated as (40) and (41), respectively.

Par. (37). Pub. L. 98-353, §421(j)(2), redesignated former par. (34) as (37). Former par. (37) redesignated successively as (39) and again as (42).

Par. (38). Pub. L. 98-353, §§391(2), 421(j)(2), added par. (35) and redesignated such par. (35) as (38). Former par. (38) redesignated successively as (40) and again as (43).

Par. (39). Pub. L. 98-353, §§391(2), 421(j)(2), added par. (36) and redesignated such par. (36) as (39). Former par. (39) redesignated successively as (41) and again as (45).

Par. (40). Pub. L. 98-353, §§391(1), 421(j)(2), redesignated successively former par. (35) as (37) and again as (40). Former par. (40) redesignated successively as (42) and again as (46).

Par. (41). Pub. L. 98-353, §§391(1), 401(1), 421(h), (j)(2), redesignated successively former par. (36) as (38) and again as (41), and, in subpar. (B)(vi), substituted "certificate of a kind specified in subparagraph (A)(xii)" for "certificate specified in clause (xii) of subparagraph (A)" and substituted "required to be the subject of a registration statement" for "the subject of such registration statement". Former par. (41) redesignated successively as (43), again as (44), and again as (48).

Par. (42). Pub. L. 98-353, §§391(1), 421(j)(2), redesignated successively former par. (37) as (39) and again as (42).

Par. (43). Pub. L. 98-353, §§391(1), 421(j)(2), redesignated successively former par. (38) as (40) and again as (43).

Pub. L. 98-353, §401, redesignated former par. (43), originally par. (41), as (44), and added another par. (43) which was redesignated (47).

Par. (44). Pub. L. 98-353, §421(j)(6), added par. (44). Former par. (44) originally was par. (41) and was redesignated successively as (43), again as (44), and again as (48).

Pars. (45), (46). Pub. L. 98-353, §§391(1), 421(j)(1), redesignated successively former pars. (39) and (40) as (41) and (42), and again as (45) and (46), respectively.

Par. (47). Pub. L. 98-353, §§401(2), 421(j)(1), added par. (43) and redesignated such par. (43) as (47).

Par. (48). Pub. L. 98-353, §§391(1), 401(1), 421(i), (j)(1), redesignated successively former par. (41) as (43), again as (44), and again as (48), and substituted "and foreclosure of the debtor's equity of redemption; and" for the period at the end.

Par. (49). Pub. L. 98-353, §421(j)(7), added par. (49).

1982—Par. (35). Pub. L. 97-222, §1(a)(2), added par. (35). Former par. (35) redesignated (36).

Par. (36). Pub. L. 97-222, §1(a)(1), (b), (c), redesignated par. (35) as (36) and substituted "is required to be the subject of a registration statement" for "is the subject of a registration statement" in subpar. (A)(xii) and substituted "forward contract" for "forward commodity contract" in subpar. (B)(iii). Former par. (36) redesignated (37).

Pars. (37) to (39). Pub. L. 97-222, §1(a)(1), redesignated pars. (36) to (38) as (37) to (39), respectively. Former par. (39) redesignated (40).

Pars. (40), (41). Pub. L. 97-222, §1(a)(1), (d), redesignated former par. (39) as (40) and restructured its provisions by dividing the former introductory provisions into subpars. (A) and (B) and by redesignating former subpars. (A) and (B) as cls. (i) and (ii), respectively, of subpar. (B). Former par. (40) redesignated (41).

EFFECTIVE DATE OF 2006 AMENDMENT

Pub. L. 109-390, §7, Dec. 12, 2006, 120 Stat. 2700, provided that: "The amendments made by this Act [see Short Title of 2006 Amendment note set out under this section] shall not apply to any cases commenced under title 11, United States Code, or appointments made under any Federal or State law, before the date of the enactment of this Act [Dec. 12, 2006]."

EFFECTIVE DATE OF 2005 AMENDMENT

Pub. L. 109-8, title XV, §1501, Apr. 20, 2005, 119 Stat. 216, provided that:

"(a) EFFECTIVE DATE.—Except as otherwise provided in this Act, this Act [see Tables for classification] and the amendments made by this Act shall take effect 180 days after the date of enactment of this Act [Apr. 20, 2005].

"(b) APPLICATION OF AMENDMENTS.—

"(1) IN GENERAL.—Except as otherwise provided in this Act and paragraph (2), the amendments made by this Act shall not apply with respect to cases commenced under title 11, United States Code, before the effective date of this Act.

"(2) CERTAIN LIMITATIONS APPLICABLE TO DEBTORS.—The amendments made by sections 308, 322, and 330 [amending sections 104, 522, 727, 1141, 1228, and 1328 of this title] shall apply with respect to cases commenced under title 11, United States Code, on or after the date of the enactment of this Act [Apr. 20, 2005]."

EFFECTIVE DATE OF 1994 AMENDMENT

Section 702 of Pub. L. 103-394 provided that:

"(a) EFFECTIVE DATE.—Except as provided in subsection (b), this Act [see Tables for classification] shall take effect on the date of the enactment of this Act [Oct. 22, 1994].

"(b) APPLICATION OF AMENDMENTS.—(1) Except as provided in paragraph (2), the amendments made by this Act shall not apply with respect to cases commenced under title 11 of the United States Code before the date of the enactment of this Act.

"(2)(A) Paragraph (1) shall not apply with respect to the amendment made by section 111 [amending section 524 of this title].

"(B) The amendments made by sections 113 and 117 [amending sections 106 and 330 of this title] shall apply with respect to cases commenced under title 11 of the United States Code before, on, and after the date of the enactment of this Act.

"(C) Section 1110 of title 11, United States Code, as amended by section 201 of this Act, shall apply with respect to any lease, as defined in such section 1110(c) as so amended, entered into in connection with a settlement of any proceeding in any case pending under title 11 of the United States Code on the date of the enactment of this Act.

"(D) The amendments made by section 305 [amending sections 1123, 1222, and 1322 of this title] shall apply only to agreements entered into after the date of enactment of this Act."

EFFECTIVE DATE OF 1992 AMENDMENT

Section 3017(c) of Pub. L. 102-486 provided that:

"(1) Except as provided in paragraph (2), the amendments made by this section [amending this section and section 541 of this title] shall take effect on the date of the enactment of this Act [Oct. 24, 1992].

"(2) The amendments made by this section shall not apply with respect to cases commenced under title 11 of the United States Code before the date of the enactment of this Act."

EFFECTIVE DATE OF 1988 AMENDMENTS

Section 12 of Pub. L. 100-597 provided that:

"(a) EFFECTIVE DATE.—Except as provided in subsection (b), this Act and the amendments made by this Act [enacting sections 927 to 929 of this title, amending this section and sections 109, 901, 902, 922, 926, and 943 of this title, and renumbering section 927 of this title as 930] shall take effect on the date of the enactment of this Act [Nov. 3, 1988].

"(b) APPLICATION OF AMENDMENTS.—The amendments made by this Act shall not apply with respect to cases commenced under title 11 of the United States Code before the date of the enactment of this Act [Nov. 3, 1988]."

Section 2 of Pub. L. 100-506 provided that:

"(a) EFFECTIVE DATE.—Except as provided in subsection (b), this Act and the amendments made by this Act [amending this section and section 365 of this title] shall take effect on the date of the enactment of this Act [Oct. 18, 1988].

"(b) APPLICATION OF AMENDMENTS.—The amendments made by this Act shall not apply with respect to any case commenced under title 11 of the United States Code before the date of the enactment of this Act [Oct. 18, 1988].''

EFFECTIVE DATE OF 1986 AMENDMENT

Effective date and applicability of amendment by section 201 of Pub. L. 99–554 dependent upon the judicial district involved, see section 302(d), (e) of Pub. L. 99–554, set out as a note under section 581 of Title 28, Judiciary and Judicial Procedure.

Amendment by section 251 of Pub. L. 99–554 effective 30 days after Oct. 27, 1986, but not applicable to cases commenced under this title before that date, see section 302(a), (c)(1) of Pub. L. 99–554.

Amendment by section 283 of Pub. L. 99–554 effective 30 days after Oct. 27, 1986, see section 302(a) of Pub. L. 99–554.

EFFECTIVE DATE OF 1984 AMENDMENT

Section 552, formerly §553, of title III (§§301–553) of Pub. L. 98–353, as renumbered by Pub. L. 98–531, §1(2), Oct. 19, 1984, 98 Stat. 2704, provided that:

''(a) Except as otherwise provided in this section the amendments made by this title [see Tables for classification] shall become effective to cases filed 90 days after the date of enactment of this Act [July 10, 1984].

''(b) The amendments made by section 426(b) [amending section 303 of this title] shall become effective upon the date of enactment of this Act.

''(c) The amendments made by subtitle J [enacting section 1113 of this title], shall become effective as provided in section 541(c) [set out as an Effective Date note under section 1113 of this title].''

SHORT TITLE OF 2009 AMENDMENT

Pub. L. 111–16, §1, May 7, 2009, 123 Stat. 1607, provided that: ''This Act [amending sections 109, 322, 332, 342, 521, 704, 749, and 764 of this title, sections 983, 1514, 1963, 2252A, 2339B, 3060, 3432, 3509, and 3771 of Title 18, Crimes and Criminal Procedure, section 7 of the Classified Information Procedures Act set out in the Appendix to Title 18, section 853 of Title 21, Food and Drugs, and sections 636, 1453, and 2107 of Title 28, Judiciary and Judicial Procedure, and enacting provisions set out as a note under section 109 of this title] may be cited as the 'Statutory Time-Periods Technical Amendments Act of 2009'.''

SHORT TITLE OF 2008 AMENDMENT

Pub. L. 110–438, §1, Oct. 20, 2008, 122 Stat. 5000, provided that: ''This Act [amending section 707 of this title and enacting provisions set out as a note under section 707 of this title] may be cited as the 'National Guard and Reservists Debt Relief Act of 2008'.''

SHORT TITLE OF 2006 AMENDMENT

Pub. L. 109–439, §1, Dec. 20, 2006, 120 Stat. 3285, provided that: ''This Act [amending section 1325 of this title] may be cited as the 'Religious Liberty and Charitable Donation Clarification Act of 2006'.''

Pub. L. 109–390, §1, Dec. 12, 2006, 120 Stat. 2692, provided that: ''This Act [amending this section, sections 362, 546, and 741 of this title, sections 1787, 1821, 4403, and 4404 of Title 12, Banks and Banking, and section 78eee of Title 15, Commerce and Trade, and enacting provisions set out as notes under this section] may be cited as the 'Financial Netting Improvements Act of 2006'.''

SHORT TITLE OF 2005 AMENDMENT

Pub. L. 109–8, §1(a), Apr. 20, 2005, 119 Stat. 23, provided that: ''This Act [see Tables for classification] may be cited as the 'Bankruptcy Abuse Prevention and Consumer Protection Act of 2005'.''

Pub. L. 109–8, title III, §332(a), Apr. 20, 2005, 119 Stat. 103, provided that: ''This section [amending section 303 of this title and section 157 of Title 18, Crimes and Criminal Procedure] may be cited as the 'Involuntary Bankruptcy Improvement Act of 2005'.''

SHORT TITLE OF 2004 AMENDMENT

Pub. L. 108–369, §1, Oct. 25, 2004, 118 Stat. 1749, provided that: ''This Act [amending sections 1201 to 1208 and 1221 to 1231 of this title and enacting and amending provisions set out as notes under section 1201 of this title] may be cited as the 'Family Farmer Bankruptcy Relief Act of 2004'.''

SHORT TITLE OF 2003 AMENDMENT

Pub. L. 108–73, §1, Aug. 15, 2003, 117 Stat. 891, provided that: ''This Act [amending sections 1201 to 1208 and 1221 to 1231 of this title and enacting and amending provisions set out as notes under section 1201 of this title] may be cited as the 'Family Farmer Bankruptcy Relief Act of 2003'.''

SHORT TITLE OF 2002 AMENDMENT

Pub. L. 107–377, §1, Dec. 19, 2002, 116 Stat. 3115, provided that: ''This Act [amending sections 1201 to 1208 and 1221 to 1231 of this title, and enacting and amending provisions set out as notes under section 1201 of this title] may be cited as the 'Protection of Family Farmers Act of 2002'.''

SHORT TITLE OF 1998 AMENDMENT

Pub. L. 105–183, §1, June 19, 1998, 112 Stat. 517, provided that: ''This Act [amending sections 544, 546, 548, 707, and 1325 of this title and enacting provisions set out as notes under section 544 of this title] may be cited as the 'Religious Liberty and Charitable Donation Protection Act of 1998'.''

SHORT TITLE OF 1994 AMENDMENT

Section 1(a) of Pub. L. 103–394 provided that: ''This Act [see Tables for classification] may be cited as the 'Bankruptcy Reform Act of 1994'.''

SHORT TITLE OF 1990 AMENDMENTS

Pub. L. 101–581, §1, Nov. 15, 1990, 104 Stat. 2865, and section 3101 of title XXXI of Pub. L. 101–647, provided respectively that such Act and such title [amending sections 523 and 1328 of this title and enacting provisions set out as a note under section 523 of this title] may be cited as the ''Criminal Victims Protection Act of 1990''.

SHORT TITLE OF 1988 AMENDMENT

Pub. L. 100–334, §1, June 16, 1988, 102 Stat. 610, provided that: ''This Act [enacting section 1114 of this title, amending section 1129 of this title, enacting provisions set out as a note under section 1114 of this title, and amending and repealing provisions set out as notes under section 1106 of this title] may be cited as the 'Retiree Benefits Bankruptcy Protection Act of 1988'.''

SHORT TITLE OF 1984 AMENDMENT

Section 361 of subtitle C (§§361–363) of title III of Pub. L. 98–353 provided that: ''This subtitle [amending sections 362, 365, and 541 of this title] may be cited as the 'Leasehold Management Bankruptcy Amendments Act of 1983'.''

SAVINGS PROVISION

Pub. L. 109–8, title IX, §912, as added Pub. L. 109–390, §5(d), Dec. 12, 2006, 120 Stat. 2698, provided that: ''The meanings of terms used in this title [see Tables for classification] are applicable for the purposes of this title only, and shall not be construed or applied so as to challenge or affect the characterization, definition, or treatment of any similar terms under any other statute, regulation, or rule, including the Gramm-Leach-Bliley Act [Pub. L. 106–102, see Short Title of 1999 Amendment note set out under section 1811 of Title 12, Banks and Banking], the Legal Certainty for Bank Products Act of 2000 [7 U.S.C. 27 to 27f], the securities laws (as such term is defined in section 3(a)(47) of the Securities Exchange Act of 1934 [15 U.S.C. 78c(a)(47)]), and the Commodity Exchange Act [7 U.S.C. 1 et seq.].''

SEPARABILITY

Section 701 of Pub. L. 103–394 provided that: "If any provision of this Act [see Tables for classification] or amendment made by this Act or the application of such provision or amendment to any person or circumstance is held to be unconstitutional, the remaining provisions of and amendments made by this Act and the application of such other provisions and amendments to any person or circumstance shall not be affected thereby."

Section 551 of title III (§§301–553) of Pub. L. 98–353 provided that: "If any provision of this title or any amendment made by this title [see Tables for classification], or the application thereof to any person or circumstance is held invalid, the provisions of every other part, and their application shall not be affected thereby."

CONSTRUCTION

Pub. L. 109–8, title X, §1007(e), Apr. 20, 2005, 119 Stat. 188, provided that: "Nothing in this section [amending this section and sections 109, 1203, and 1206 of this title] shall change, affect, or amend the Fishery Conservation and Management Act of 1976 (16 U.S.C. 1801 et seq.)."

Pub. L. 109–8, title XI, §1101(c), Apr. 20, 2005, 119 Stat. 189, provided that: "The amendments made by subsection (a) of this section [amending this section] shall not affect the interpretation of section 109(b) of title 11, United States Code."

NONLIMITATION OF INFORMATION

Pub. L. 109–8, title I, §102(e), Apr. 20, 2005, 119 Stat. 33, provided that: "Nothing in this title [see Tables for classification] shall limit the ability of a creditor to provide information to a judge (except for information communicated ex parte, unless otherwise permitted by applicable law), United States trustee (or bankruptcy administrator, if any), or trustee."

JUDICIAL EDUCATION

Pub. L. 109–8, title XII, §1226, Apr. 20, 2005, 119 Stat. 199, provided that: "The Director of the Federal Judicial Center, in consultation with the Director of the Executive Office for United States Trustees, shall develop materials and conduct such training as may be useful to courts in implementing this Act [see Short Title of 2005 Amendment note above] and the amendments made by this Act, including the requirements relating to the means test under section 707(b), and reaffirmation agreements under section 524, of title 11 of the United States Code, as amended by this Act."

ADJUSTMENT OF DOLLAR AMOUNTS

For adjustment of dollar amounts specified in pars. (3), (18), (19A), and (51D) of this section by the Judicial Conference of the United States, see notes set out under section 104 of this title.

§102. Rules of construction

In this title—

(1) "after notice and a hearing", or a similar phrase—

(A) means after such notice as is appropriate in the particular circumstances, and such opportunity for a hearing as is appropriate in the particular circumstances; but

(B) authorizes an act without an actual hearing if such notice is given properly and if—

(i) such a hearing is not requested timely by a party in interest; or

(ii) there is insufficient time for a hearing to be commenced before such act must be done, and the court authorizes such act;

(2) "claim against the debtor" includes claim against property of the debtor;

(3) "includes" and "including" are not limiting;

(4) "may not" is prohibitive, and not permissive;

(5) "or" is not exclusive;

(6) "order for relief" means entry of an order for relief;

(7) the singular includes the plural;

(8) a definition, contained in a section of this title that refers to another section of this title, does not, for the purpose of such reference, affect the meaning of a term used in such other section; and

(9) "United States trustee" includes a designee of the United States trustee.

(Pub. L. 95–598, Nov. 6, 1978, 92 Stat. 2554; Pub. L. 98–353, title III, §422, July 10, 1984, 98 Stat. 369; Pub. L. 99–554, title II, §202, Oct. 27, 1986, 100 Stat. 3097.)

HISTORICAL AND REVISION NOTES

LEGISLATIVE STATEMENTS

Section 102 specifies various rules of construction but is not exclusive. Other rules of construction that are not set out in title 11 are nevertheless intended to be followed in construing the bankruptcy code. For example, the phrase "on request of a party in interest" or a similar phrase, is used in connection with an action that the court may take in various sections of the Code. The phrase is intended to restrict the court from acting sua sponte. Rules of bankruptcy procedure or court decisions will determine who is a party in interest for the particular purposes of the provision in question, but the court will not be permitted to act on its own.

Although "property" is not construed in this section, it is used consistently throughout the code in its broadest sense, including cash, all interests in property, such as liens, and every kind of consideration including promises to act or forbear to act as in section 548(d).

Section 102(1) expands on a rule of construction contained in H.R. 8200 as passed by the House and in the Senate amendment. The phrase "after notice and a hearing", or a similar phrase, is intended to be construed according to the particular proceeding to mean after such notice as is appropriate in the particular circumstances, and such opportunity, if any, for a hearing as is appropriate in the particular circumstances. If a provision of title 11 authorizes an act to be taken "after notice and a hearing" this means that if appropriate notice is given and no party to whom such notice is sent timely requests a hearing, then the act sought to be taken may be taken without an actual hearing.

In very limited emergency circumstances, there will be insufficient time for a hearing to be commenced before an action must be taken. The action sought to be taken may be taken if authorized by the court at an ex parte hearing of which a record is made in open court. A full hearing after the fact will be available in such an instance.

In some circumstances, such as under section 1128, the bill requires a hearing and the court may act only after a hearing is held. In those circumstances the judge will receive evidence before ruling. In other circumstances, the court may take action "after notice and a hearing," if no party in interest requests a hearing. In that event a court order authorizing the action to be taken is not necessary as the ultimate action taken by the court implies such an authorization.

Section 102(8) is new. It contains a rule of construction indicating that a definition contained in a section in title 11 that refers to another section of title 11 does not, for the purposes of such reference, take the meaning of a term used in the other section. For example, section 522(a)(2) defines "value" for the purposes of section 522. Section 548(d)(2) defines "value" for purposes of section 548. When section 548 is incorporated by reference in section 522, this rule of construction makes clear that the definition of "value" in section 548 governs its meaning in section 522 notwithstanding a different definition of "value" in section 522(a)(2).

SENATE REPORT NO. 95–989

Section 102 provides seven rules of construction. Some are derived from current law; others are derived from 1 U.S.C. 1; a few are new. They apply generally throughout proposed title 11. These are terms that are not appropriate for definition, but that require an explanation.

Paragraph (1) defines the concept of "after notice and a hearing." The concept is central to the bill and to the separation of the administrative and judicial functions of bankruptcy judges. The phrase means after such notice as is appropriate in the particular circumstances (to be prescribed by either the Rules of Bankruptcy Procedure or by the court in individual circumstances that the Rules do not cover. In many cases, the Rules will provide for combined notice of several proceedings), and such opportunity for a hearing as is appropriate in the particular circumstances. Thus, a hearing will not be necessary in every instance. If there is no objection to the proposed action, the action may go ahead without court action. This is a significant change from present law, which requires the affirmative approval of the bankruptcy judge for almost every action. The change will permit the bankruptcy judge to stay removed from the administration of the bankruptcy or reorganization case, and to become involved only when there is a dispute about a proposed action, that is, only when there is an objection. The phrase "such opportunity for a hearing as is appropriate in the particular circumstances" is designed to permit the Rules and the courts to expedite or dispense with hearings when speed is essential. The language "or similar phrase" is intended to cover the few instances in the bill where "after notice and a hearing" is interrupted by another phrase, such as "after notice to the debtor and a hearing."

Paragraph (2) specifies that "claim against the debtor" includes claim against property of the debtor. This paragraph is intended to cover nonrecourse loan agreements where the creditor's only rights are against property of the debtor, and not against the debtor personally. Thus, such an agreement would give rise to a claim that would be treated as a claim against the debtor personally, for the purposes of the bankruptcy code.

Paragraph (3) is a codification of *American Surety Co. v. Marotta*, 287 U.S. 513 (1933). It specifies that "includes" and "including" are not limiting.

Paragraph (4) specifies that "may not" is prohibitive and not permissive (such as in "might not").

Paragraph (5) specifies that "or" is not exclusive. Thus, if a party "may do (a) or (b)", then the party may do either or both. The party is not limited to a mutually exclusive choice between the two alternatives.

Paragraph (6) makes clear that "order for relief" means entry of an order for relief. If the court orally orders relief, but the order is not entered until a later time, then any time measurements in the bill are from entry, not from the oral order. In a voluntary case, the entry of the order for relief is the filing of the petition commencing the voluntary case.

Paragraph (7) specifies that the singular includes the plural. The plural, however, generally does not include the singular. The bill uses only the singular, even when the item in question most often is found in plural quantities, in order to avoid the confusion possible if both rules of construction applied. When an item is specified in the plural, the plural is intended.

AMENDMENTS

1986—Par. (9). Pub. L. 99–554 added par. (9).

1984—Par. (8). Pub. L. 98–353 substituted "contained" for "continued".

EFFECTIVE DATE OF 1986 AMENDMENT

Effective date and applicability of amendment by Pub. L. 99–554 dependent upon the judicial district involved, see section 302(d), (e) of Pub. L. 99–554, set out as a note under section 581 of Title 28, Judiciary and Judicial Procedure.

EFFECTIVE DATE OF 1984 AMENDMENT

Amendment by Pub. L. 98–353 effective with respect to cases filed 90 days after July 10, 1984, see section 552(a) of Pub. L. 98–353, set out as a note under section 101 of this title.

§ 103. Applicability of chapters

(a) Except as provided in section 1161 of this title, chapters 1, 3, and 5 of this title apply in a case under chapter 7, 11, 12, or 13 of this title, and this chapter, sections 307, 362(n), 555 through 557, and 559 through 562 apply in a case under chapter 15.

(b) Subchapters I and II of chapter 7 of this title apply only in a case under such chapter.

(c) Subchapter III of chapter 7 of this title applies only in a case under such chapter concerning a stockbroker.

(d) Subchapter IV of chapter 7 of this title applies only in a case under such chapter concerning a commodity broker.

(e) SCOPE OF APPLICATION.—Subchapter V of chapter 7 of this title shall apply only in a case under such chapter concerning the liquidation of an uninsured State member bank, or a corporation organized under section 25A of the Federal Reserve Act, which operates, or operates as, a multilateral clearing organization pursuant to section 409 of the Federal Deposit Insurance Corporation Improvement Act of 1991.

(f) Except as provided in section 901 of this title, only chapters 1 and 9 of this title apply in a case under such chapter 9.

(g) Except as provided in section 901 of this title, subchapters I, II, and III of chapter 11 of this title apply only in a case under such chapter.

(h) Subchapter IV of chapter 11 of this title applies only in a case under such chapter concerning a railroad.

(i) Chapter 13 of this title applies only in a case under such chapter.

(j) Chapter 12 of this title applies only in a case under such chapter.

(k) Chapter 15 applies only in a case under such chapter, except that—

(1) sections 1505, 1513, and 1514 apply in all cases under this title; and

(2) section 1509 applies whether or not a case under this title is pending.

(Pub. L. 95–598, Nov. 6, 1978, 92 Stat. 2555; Pub. L. 97–222, §2, July 27, 1982, 96 Stat. 235; Pub. L. 98–353, title III, §423, July 10, 1984, 98 Stat. 369; Pub. L. 99–554, title II, §252, Oct. 27, 1986, 100 Stat. 3104; Pub. L. 106–554, §1(a)(5) [title I, §112(c)(5)(A)], Dec. 21, 2000, 114 Stat. 2763, 2763A–394; Pub. L. 109–8, title VIII, §802(a), Apr. 20, 2005, 119 Stat. 145.)

HISTORICAL AND REVISION NOTES

SENATE REPORT NO. 95–989

Section 103 prescribes which chapters of the proposed bankruptcy code apply in various cases. All cases, other than cases ancillary to foreign proceedings, are filed under chapter 7, 9, 11, or 13, the operative chapters of the proposed bankruptcy code. The general provisions that apply no matter which chapter a case is filed under are found in chapters 1, 3, and 5. Subsection (a) makes this explicit, with an exception for chapter 9. The other provisions, which are self-explanatory, provide the special rules for Stockbroker Liquidations, Commodity Broker Liquidations, Municipal Debt Adjustments, and Railroad Reorganizations.

REFERENCES IN TEXT

Section 25A of the Federal Reserve Act, referred to in subsec. (e), popularly known as the Edge Act, is classified to subchapter II (§611 et seq.) of chapter 6 of Title 12, Banks and Banking. For complete classification of this Act to the Code, see Short Title note set out under section 611 of Title 12 and Tables.

Section 409 of the Federal Deposit Insurance Corporation Improvement Act of 1991, referred to in subsec. (e), is classified to section 4422 of Title 12, Banks and Banking.

AMENDMENTS

2005—Subsec. (a). Pub. L. 109–8, §802(a)(1), inserted ", and this chapter, sections 307, 362(n), 555 through 557, and 559 through 562 apply in a case under chapter 15" before period.

Subsec. (k). Pub. L. 109–8, §802(a)(2), added subsec. (k).

2000—Subsecs. (e) to (j). Pub. L. 106–554 added subsec. (e) and redesignated former subsecs. (e) to (i) as (f) to (j), respectively.

1986—Subsec. (a). Pub. L. 99–554, §252(1), inserted reference to chapter 12.

Subsec. (i). Pub. L. 99–554, §252(2), added subsec. (i).

1984—Subsec. (c). Pub. L. 98–353 substituted "stockbroker" for "stockholder".

1982—Subsec. (d). Pub. L. 97–222 struck out "except with respect to section 746(c) which applies to margin payments made by any debtor to a commodity broker or forward contract merchant" after "concerning a commodity broker".

EFFECTIVE DATE OF 2005 AMENDMENT

Amendment by Pub. L. 109–8 effective 180 days after Apr. 20, 2005, and not applicable with respect to cases commenced under this title before such effective date, except as otherwise provided, see section 1501 of Pub. L. 109–8, set out as a note under section 101 of this title.

EFFECTIVE DATE OF 1986 AMENDMENT

Amendment by Pub. L. 99–554 effective 30 days after Oct. 27, 1986, but not applicable to cases commenced under this title before that date, see section 302(a), (c)(1) of Pub. L. 99–554, set out as a note under section 581 of Title 28, Judiciary and Judicial Procedure.

EFFECTIVE DATE OF 1984 AMENDMENT

Amendment by Pub. L. 98–353 effective with respect to cases filed 90 days after July 10, 1984, see section 552(a) of Pub. L. 98–353, set out as a note under section 101 of this title.

§104. Adjustment of dollar amounts

(a) On April 1, 1998, and at each 3-year interval ending on April 1 thereafter, each dollar amount in effect under sections 101(3), 101(18), 101(19A), 101(51D), 109(e), 303(b), 507(a), 522(d), 522(f)(3) and 522(f)(4), 522(n), 522(p), 522(q), 523(a)(2)(C), 541(b), 547(c)(9), 707(b), 1322(d), 1325(b), and 1326(b)(3) of this title and section 1409(b) of title 28 immediately before such April 1 shall be adjusted—

(1) to reflect the change in the Consumer Price Index for All Urban Consumers, published by the Department of Labor, for the most recent 3-year period ending immediately before January 1 preceding such April 1, and

(2) to round to the nearest $25 the dollar amount that represents such change.

(b) Not later than March 1, 1998, and at each 3-year interval ending on March 1 thereafter, the Judicial Conference of the United States shall publish in the Federal Register the dollar amounts that will become effective on such April 1 under sections 101(3), 101(18), 101(19A), 101(51D), 109(e), 303(b), 507(a), 522(d), 522(f)(3) and 522(f)(4), 522(n), 522(p), 522(q), 523(a)(2)(C), 541(b), 547(c)(9), 707(b), 1322(d), 1325(b), and 1326(b)(3) of this title and section 1409(b) of title 28.

(c) Adjustments made in accordance with subsection (a) shall not apply with respect to cases commenced before the date of such adjustments.

(Pub. L. 95–598, Nov. 6, 1978, 92 Stat. 2555; Pub. L. 103–394, title I, §108(e), Oct. 22, 1994, 108 Stat. 4112; Pub. L. 109–8, title I, §102(j), title II, §§224(e)(2), 226(b), title III, §322(b), title IV, §432(c), title X, §1002, title XII, §1202, Apr. 20, 2005, 119 Stat. 35, 65, 67, 97, 110, 186, 193; Pub. L. 110–406, §7, Oct. 13, 2008, 122 Stat. 4293.)

HISTORICAL AND REVISION NOTES

LEGISLATIVE STATEMENTS

Section 104 represents a compromise between the House bill and the Senate amendment with respect to the adjustment of dollar amounts in title 11. The House amendment authorizes the Judicial Conference of the United States to transmit a recommendation for the uniform percentage of adjustment for each dollar amount in title 11 and in 28 U.S.C. 1930 to the Congress and to the President before May 1, 1985, and before May 1 of every sixth year thereafter. The requirement in the House bill that each such recommendation be based only on any change in the cost-of-living increase during the period immediately preceding the recommendation is deleted.

SENATE REPORT NO. 95–989

This section requires that the Director of the Administrative Office of the U. S. Courts report to Congress and the President before Oct. 1, 1985, and before May 1 every 6 years thereafter a recommendation for adjustment in dollar amounts found in this title. The Committee feels that regular adjustment of the dollar amounts by the Director will conserve congressional time and yet assure that the relative dollar amounts used in the bill are maintained. Changes in the cost of living should be a significant, but not necessarily the only, factor considered by the Director. The fact that there has been an increase in the cost of living does not necessarily mean that an adjustment of dollar amounts would be needed or warranted.

HOUSE REPORT NO. 95–595

This section requires the Judicial Conference to report to the Congress every four years after the effective date of the bankruptcy code any changes that have occurred in the cost of living during the preceding four years, and the appropriate adjustments to the dollar amounts in the bill. The dollar amounts are found primarily in the exemption section (11 U.S.C. 522), the wage priority (11 U.S.C. 507), and the eligibility for chapter 13 (11 U.S.C. 109). This section requires that the Conference recommend uniform percentage changes in these amounts based solely on cost of living changes. The dollar amounts in the bill would not change on that recommendation, absent Congressional veto. Instead, Congress is required to take affirmative action, by passing a law amending the appropriate section, if it wishes to accomplish the change.

If the Judicial Conference has policy recommendations concerning the appropriate dollar amounts in the bankruptcy code based other than on cost of living considerations there are adequate channels through which it may communicate its views. This section is solely for the housekeeping function of maintaining the dollar amounts in the code at fairly constant real dollar levels.

Amendments

2008—Pub. L. 110–406 redesignated subsec. (b)(1) as (a), subpars. (A) and (B) of subsec. (b)(1) as pars. (1) and (2), respectively, of subsec. (a), and pars. (2) and (3) of subsec. (b) as subsecs. (b) and (c), respectively, substituted "subsection (a)" for "paragraph (1)" in subsec. (c), and struck out former subsec. (a) which read as follows: "The Judicial Conference of the United States shall transmit to the Congress and to the President before May 1, 1985, and before May 1 of every sixth year after May 1, 1985, a recommendation for the uniform percentage adjustment of each dollar amount in this title and in section 1930 of title 28."

2005—Subsec. (b)(1). Pub. L. 109–8, §1202(1)–(4), in introductory provisions, inserted "101(19A)," after "101(18),", "522(f)(3) and 522(f)(4)," after "522(d),", and "541(b), 547(c)(9)," after "523(a)(2)(C)," and substituted "1322(d), 1325(b), and 1326(b)(3) of this title and section 1409(b) of title 28" for "and 1325(b)(3)".

Pub. L. 109–8, §1002, inserted "101(18)," after "101(3)," in introductory provisions.

Pub. L. 109–8, §432(c), inserted "101(51D)," after "101(3)," in introductory provisions.

Pub. L. 109–8, §322(b), inserted "522(p), 522(q)," after "522(n)," in introductory provisions.

Pub. L. 109–8, §226(b), inserted "101(3)," after "sections" in introductory provisions.

Pub. L. 109–8, §224(e)(2), inserted "522(n)," after "522(d)," in introductory provisions.

Pub. L. 109–8, §102(j), substituted "523(a)(2)(C), 707(b), and 1325(b)(3)" for "and 523(a)(2)(C)" in introductory provisions.

Subsec. (b)(2). Pub. L. 109–8, §1202(1)–(3), (5), inserted "101(19A)," after "101(18),", "522(f)(3) and 522(f)(4)," after "522(d),", and "541(b), 547(c)(9)," after "523(a)(2)(C)," and substituted "1322(d), 1325(b), and 1326(b)(3) of this title and section 1409(b) of title 28" for "and 1325(b)(3) of this title".

Pub. L. 109–8, §1002, inserted "101(18)," after "101(3),".

Pub. L. 109–8, §432(c), inserted "101(51D)," after "101(3),".

Pub. L. 109–8, §322(b), inserted "522(p), 522(q)," after "522(n),".

Pub. L. 109–8, §226(b), inserted "101(3)," after "sections".

Pub. L. 109–8, §224(e)(2), inserted "522(n)," after "522(d),".

Pub. L. 109–8, §102(j), substituted "523(a)(2)(C), 707(b), and 1325(b)(3)" for "and 523(a)(2)(C)".

1994—Pub. L. 103–394 designated existing provisions as subsec. (a) and added subsec. (b).

Effective Date of 2005 Amendment

Amendment by Pub. L. 109–8 effective 180 days after Apr. 20, 2005, with amendments by sections 102(j), 224(e)(2), 226(b), 432(c), 1002, and 1202 of Pub. L. 109–8 not applicable with respect to cases commenced under this title before such effective date, except as otherwise provided, and amendment by section 322(b) of Pub. L. 109–8 applicable with respect to cases commenced under this title on or after Apr. 20, 2005, see section 1501 of Pub. L. 109–8, set out as a note under section 101 of this title.

Effective Date of 1994 Amendment

Amendment by Pub. L. 103–394 effective Oct. 22, 1994, and not applicable with respect to cases commenced under this title before Oct. 22, 1994, see section 702 of Pub. L. 103–394, set out as a note under section 101 of this title.

Adjustment of Dollar Amounts

By notice dated Feb. 19, 2010, 75 F.R. 8747, the Judicial Conference of the United States adjusted the dollar amounts in provisions specified in subsec. (a) of this section, effective Apr. 1, 2010, as follows:

28 U.S.C.	Dollar amount to be adjusted	New (adjusted) dollar amount
1409(b)—a trustee may commence a proceeding arising in or related to a case to recover		
(1)—money judgment of or property worth less than.	$1,100	$1,175
(2)—a consumer debt less than	16,425	17,575
(3)—a non consumer debt against a non insider less than.	10,950	11.725

11 U.S.C.	Dollar amount to be adjusted	New (adjusted) dollar amount
101(3)—definition of assisted person	$164,250	$175,750
101(18)(A) & (B)(ii)—definition of family farmer.	3,544,525 (each time it appears).	3,792,650 (each time it appears).
101(19A)(A)(i) & (b)(ii)(II)—definition of family fisherman.	1,642,500 (each time it appears).	1,757,475 (each time it appears).
101(51D)(A) & (B)—definition of small business debtor.	2,190,000 (each time it appears).	2,343,300 (each time it appears).
109(e)—allowable debt limits for individual filing bankruptcy under chapter 13.	336,900 (each time it appears).	360,475 (each time it appears).
	1,010,650 (each time it appears).	1,081,400 (each time it appears).
303(b)—minimum aggregate claims needed for the commencement of involuntary chapter 7 or chapter 11 bankruptcy		
(1)—in paragraph (1)	13.475	14,425
(2)—in paragraph (2)	13.475	14,425
507(a)—priority expenses and claims		
(1)—in paragraph (4)	10,950	11.725
(2)—in paragraph (5)	10,950	11.725
(3)—in paragraph (6)	5,400	5,775
(4)—in paragraph (7)	2,425	2.600
522(d)—value of property exemptions allowed to the debtor		
(1)—in paragraph (1)	20,200	21,625
(2)—in paragraph (2)	3,225	3.450
(3)—in paragraph (3)	525	550
	10,775	11.525
(4)—in paragraph (4)	1,350	1,450
(5)—in paragraph (5)	1,075	1.150
	10,125	10.825
(6)—in paragraph (6)	2,025	2,175
(7)—in paragraph (8)	10,775	11,525
(8)—in paragraph (11)(D)	20.200	21,625
522(f)(3)(B)—exception to lien avoidance under certain state laws.	5,475	5,850
522(f)(4)(B)—items excluded from definition of household goods for lien avoidance purposes.	550 (each time it appears).	600 (each time it appears).
522(n)—maximum aggregate value of assets in individual retirement accounts exempted.	1,095,000	1,171,650
522(p)(1)—qualified homestead exemption.	136,875	146.450
522(q)(1)—state homestead exemption.	136.875	146,450
523(a)(2)(C)—exceptions to discharge		
in subclause (i)(I)—consumer debts, incurred < = 90 days before filing owed to a single creditor in the aggregate.	550	600
in subclause (i)(II)—cash advances incurred < = 70 days before filing in the aggregate.	825	875
541(b)—property of the estate exclusions		
(1)—in paragraph (5)(C)—education IRA funds in the aggregate.	5,475	5,850

11 U.S.C.	Dollar amount to be adjusted	New (adjusted) dollar amount
(2)—in paragraph (6)(C)—prepurchased tuition credits in the aggregate.	5.475	5.850
547(c)(9)—preferences. trustee may not avoid a transfer if. in a case filed by a debtor whose debts are not primarily consumer debts. the aggregate value of property is less than.	5.475	5.850
707(b)—dismissal of a case or conversion to a case under chapter 11 or 13 (means test)		
(1)—in paragraph (2)(A)(i)(I)	6.575	7.025
(2)—in paragraph (2)(A)(i)(II)	10.950	11.725
(3)—in paragraph (2)(A)(ii)(IV) ...	1.650	1.775
(4)—in paragraph (2)(B)(iv)(I)	6.575	7.025
(5)—in paragraph (2)(B)(iv)(II) ...	10.950	11.725
(6)—in paragraph (5)(B)	1.100	1.175
(7)—in paragraph 6(C)	575	625
(8)—in paragraph 7(A)(ii)	575	625
1322(d)(1)(c)[(C)] & (2)(c)[(C)]—contents of chapter 13 plan. monthly income.	575 (each time it appears).	625 (each time it appears).
1325(b)(3) & (b)(4)—chapter 13 confirmation of plan. disposable income.	575 (each time it appears).	625 (each time it appears).
1326(b)(3)(B)—payments to former chapter 7 trustee.	25	25

Similar notices by the Judicial Conference of the United States adjusting the dollar amounts in provisions specified in subsec. (a) of this section were contained in the following:

Feb. 14. 2007. 72 F.R. 7082. effective Apr. 1. 2007.
Feb. 18. 2004. 69 F.R. 8482. effective Apr. 1. 2004.
Feb. 13. 2001. 66 F.R. 10910. effective Apr. 1. 2001.
Feb. 3. 1998. 63 F.R. 7179. effective Apr. 1. 1998.

§ 105. Power of court

(a) The court may issue any order, process, or judgment that is necessary or appropriate to carry out the provisions of this title. No provision of this title providing for the raising of an issue by a party in interest shall be construed to preclude the court from, sua sponte, taking any action or making any determination necessary or appropriate to enforce or implement court orders or rules, or to prevent an abuse of process.

(b) Notwithstanding subsection (a) of this section, a court may not appoint a receiver in a case under this title.

(c) The ability of any district judge or other officer or employee of a district court to exercise any of the authority or responsibilities conferred upon the court under this title shall be determined by reference to the provisions relating to such judge, officer, or employee set forth in title 28. This subsection shall not be interpreted to exclude bankruptcy judges and other officers or employees appointed pursuant to chapter 6 of title 28 from its operation.

(d) The court, on its own motion or on the request of a party in interest—

(1) shall hold such status conferences as are necessary to further the expeditious and economical resolution of the case; and

(2) unless inconsistent with another provision of this title or with applicable Federal Rules of Bankruptcy Procedure, issue an order at any such conference prescribing such limitations and conditions as the court deems appropriate to ensure that the case is handled expeditiously and economically, including an order that—

(A) sets the date by which the trustee must assume or reject an executory contract or unexpired lease; or

(B) in a case under chapter 11 of this title—

(i) sets a date by which the debtor, or trustee if one has been appointed, shall file a disclosure statement and plan;

(ii) sets a date by which the debtor, or trustee if one has been appointed, shall solicit acceptances of a plan;

(iii) sets the date by which a party in interest other than a debtor may file a plan;

(iv) sets a date by which a proponent of a plan, other than the debtor, shall solicit acceptances of such plan;

(v) fixes the scope and format of the notice to be provided regarding the hearing on approval of the disclosure statement; or

(vi) provides that the hearing on approval of the disclosure statement may be combined with the hearing on confirmation of the plan.

(Pub. L. 95–598, Nov. 6, 1978, 92 Stat. 2555; Pub. L. 98–353, title I, § 118, July 10, 1984, 98 Stat. 344; Pub. L. 99–554, title II, § 203, Oct. 27, 1986, 100 Stat. 3097; Pub. L. 103–394, title I, § 104(a), Oct. 22, 1994, 108 Stat. 4108; Pub. L. 109–8, title IV, § 440, Apr. 20, 2005, 119 Stat. 114.)

Historical and Revision Notes

SENATE REPORT NO. 95–989

Section 105 is derived from section 2a (15) of present law [section 11(a)(15) of former title 11], with two changes. First, the limitation on the power of a bankruptcy judge (the power to enjoin a court being reserved to the district judge) is removed as inconsistent with the increased powers and jurisdiction of the new bankruptcy court. Second, the bankruptcy judge is prohibited from appointing a receiver in a case under title 11 under any circumstances. The bankruptcy code has ample provision for the appointment of a trustee when needed. Appointment of a receiver would simply circumvent the established procedures.

This section is also an authorization, as required under 28 U.S.C. 2283, for a court of the United States to stay the action of a State court. As such, *Toucey v. New York Life Insurance Company*, 314 U.S. 118 (1941), is overruled.

References in Text

The Federal Rules of Bankruptcy Procedure, referred to in subsec. (d)(2), are set out in the Appendix to this title.

Amendments

2005—Subsec. (d). Pub. L. 109–8, § 440(1), struck out ", may" after "party in interest" in introductory provisions.

Subsec. (d)(1). Pub. L. 109–8, § 440(2), added par. (1) and struck out former par. (1) which read as follows: "hold a status conference regarding any case or proceeding under this title after notice to the parties in interest; and".

1994—Subsec. (d). Pub. L. 103–394 added subsec. (d).

1986—Subsec. (a). Pub. L. 99–554 inserted at end "No provision of this title providing for the raising of an issue by a party in interest shall be construed to preclude the court from, sua sponte, taking any action or making any determination necessary or appropriate to enforce or implement court orders or rules, or to prevent an abuse of process."

1984—Subsecs. (a), (b). Pub. L. 98–353, § 118(1), struck out "bankruptcy" before "court".

Subsec. (c). Pub. L. 98-353, §118(2), added subsec. (c).

EFFECTIVE DATE OF 2005 AMENDMENT

Amendment by Pub. L. 109-8 effective 180 days after Apr. 20, 2005, and not applicable with respect to cases commenced under this title before such effective date, except as otherwise provided, see section 1501 of Pub. L. 109-8, set out as a note under section 101 of this title.

EFFECTIVE DATE OF 1994 AMENDMENT

Amendment by Pub. L. 103-394 effective Oct. 22, 1994, and not applicable with respect to cases commenced under this title before Oct. 22, 1994, see section 702 of Pub. L. 103-394, set out as a note under section 101 of this title.

EFFECTIVE DATE OF 1986 AMENDMENT

Effective date and applicability of amendment by Pub. L. 99-554 dependent upon the judicial district involved, see section 302(d), (e) of Pub. L. 99-554, set out as a note under section 581 of Title 28, Judiciary and Judicial Procedure.

EFFECTIVE DATE OF 1984 AMENDMENT

Amendment by Pub. L. 98-353 effective July 10, 1984, see section 122(a) of Pub. L. 98-353, set out as an Effective Date note under section 151 of Title 28, Judiciary and Judicial Procedure.

§ 106. Waiver of sovereign immunity

(a) Notwithstanding an assertion of sovereign immunity, sovereign immunity is abrogated as to a governmental unit to the extent set forth in this section with respect to the following:

(1) Sections 105, 106, 107, 108, 303, 346, 362, 363, 364, 365, 366, 502, 503, 505, 506, 510, 522, 523, 524, 525, 542, 543, 544, 545, 546, 547, 548, 549, 550, 551, 552, 553, 722, 724, 726, 728,[1] 744, 749, 764, 901, 922, 926, 928, 929, 944, 1107, 1141, 1142, 1143, 1146, 1201, 1203, 1205, 1206, 1227, 1231, 1301, 1303, 1305, and 1327 of this title.

(2) The court may hear and determine any issue arising with respect to the application of such sections to governmental units.

(3) The court may issue against a governmental unit an order, process, or judgment under such sections or the Federal Rules of Bankruptcy Procedure, including an order or judgment awarding a money recovery, but not including an award of punitive damages. Such order or judgment for costs or fees under this title or the Federal Rules of Bankruptcy Procedure against any governmental unit shall be consistent with the provisions and limitations of section 2412(d)(2)(A) of title 28.

(4) The enforcement of any such order, process, or judgment against any governmental unit shall be consistent with appropriate nonbankruptcy law applicable to such governmental unit and, in the case of a money judgment against the United States, shall be paid as if it is a judgment rendered by a district court of the United States.

(5) Nothing in this section shall create any substantive claim for relief or cause of action not otherwise existing under this title, the Federal Rules of Bankruptcy Procedure, or nonbankruptcy law.

(b) A governmental unit that has filed a proof of claim in the case is deemed to have waived sovereign immunity with respect to a claim against such governmental unit that is property of the estate and that arose out of the same transaction or occurrence out of which the claim of such governmental unit arose.

(c) Notwithstanding any assertion of sovereign immunity by a governmental unit, there shall be offset against a claim or interest of a governmental unit any claim against such governmental unit that is property of the estate.

(Pub. L. 95-598, Nov. 6, 1978, 92 Stat. 2555; Pub. L. 103-394, title I, §113, Oct. 22, 1994, 108 Stat. 4117.)

HISTORICAL AND REVISION NOTES

LEGISLATIVE STATEMENTS

Section 106(c) relating to sovereign immunity is new. The provision indicates that the use of the term "creditor," "entity," or "governmental unit" in title 11 applies to governmental units notwithstanding any assertion of sovereign immunity and that an order of the court binds governmental units. The provision is included to comply with the requirement in case law that an express waiver of sovereign immunity is required in order to be effective. Section 106(c) codifies *In re Gwilliam*, 519 F.2d 407 (9th Cir., 1975), and *In re Dolard*, 519 F.2d 282 (9th Cir., 1975), permitting the bankruptcy court to determine the amount and dischargeability of tax liabilities owing by the debtor or the estate prior to or during a bankruptcy case whether or not the governmental unit to which such taxes are owed files a proof of claim. Except as provided in sections 106(a) and (b), subsection (c) is not limited to those issues, but permits the bankruptcy court to bind governmental units on other matters as well. For example, section 106(c) permits a trustee or debtor in possession to assert avoiding powers under title 11 against a governmental unit; contrary language in the House report to H.R. 8200 is thereby overruled.

SENATE REPORT NO. 95-989

Section 106 provides for a limited waiver of sovereign immunity in bankruptcy cases. Though Congress has the power to waive sovereign immunity for the Federal government completely in bankruptcy cases, the policy followed here is designed to achieve approximately the same result that would prevail outside of bankruptcy. Congress does not, however, have the power to waive sovereign immunity completely with respect to claims of a bankrupt estate against a State, though it may exercise its bankruptcy power through the supremacy clause to prevent or prohibit State action that is contrary to bankruptcy policy.

There is, however, a limited change from the result that would prevail in the absence of bankruptcy; the change is two-fold and is within Congress' power vis-a-vis both the Federal Government and the States. First, the filing of a proof of claim against the estate by a governmental unit is a waiver by that governmental unit of sovereign immunity with respect to compulsory counterclaims, as defined in the Federal Rules of Civil Procedure [title 28, appendix], that is, counterclaims arising out of the same transaction or occurrence. The governmental unit cannot receive a distribution from the estate without subjecting itself to any liability it has to the estate within the confines of a compulsory counterclaim rule. Any other result would be one-sided. The counterclaim by the estate against the governmental unit is without limit.

Second, the estate may offset against the allowed claim of a governmental unit, up to the amount of the governmental unit's claim, any claim that the debtor, and thus the estate, has against the governmental unit, without regard to whether the estate's claim arose out of the same transaction or occurrence as the government's claim. Under this provision, the setoff permitted is only to the extent of the governmental unit's claim. No affirmative recovery is permitted. Subsection (a) governs affirmative recovery.

[1] See References in Text note below.

Though this subsection creates a partial waiver of immunity when the governmental unit files a proof of claim, it does not waive immunity if the debtor or trustee, and not the governmental unit, files proof of a governmental unit's claim under proposed 11 U.S.C. 501(c).

This section does not confer sovereign immunity on any governmental unit that does not already have immunity. It simply recognizes any immunity that exists and prescribes the proper treatment of claims by and against that sovereign.

REFERENCES IN TEXT

Section 728 of this title, referred to in subsec. (a)(1), was repealed by Pub. L. 109–8, title VII, §719(b)(1), Apr. 20, 2005, 119 Stat. 133.

The Federal Rules of Bankruptcy Procedure, referred to in subsec. (a)(3), (5), are set out in the Appendix to this title.

AMENDMENTS

1994—Pub. L. 103–394 amended section generally. Prior to amendment, section read as follows:

"(a) A governmental unit is deemed to have waived sovereign immunity with respect to any claim against such governmental unit that is property of the estate and that arose out of the same transaction or occurrence out of which such governmental unit's claim arose.

"(b) There shall be offset against an allowed claim or interest of a governmental unit any claim against such governmental unit that is property of the estate.

"(c) Except as provided in subsections (a) and (b) of this section and notwithstanding any assertion of sovereign immunity—

"(1) a provision of this title that contains 'creditor', 'entity', or 'governmental unit' applies to governmental units; and

"(2) a determination by the court of an issue arising under such a provision binds governmental units."

EFFECTIVE DATE OF 1994 AMENDMENT

Amendment by Pub. L. 103–394 effective Oct. 22, 1994, and applicable with respect to cases commenced under this title before, on, and after Oct. 22, 1994, see section 702(a), (b)(2)(B) of Pub. L. 103–394 set out as a note under section 101 of this title.

§ 107. Public access to papers

(a) Except as provided in subsections (b) and (c) of this section and subject to section 112, a paper filed in a case under this title and the dockets of a bankruptcy court are public records and open to examination by an entity at reasonable times without charge.

(b) On request of a party in interest, the bankruptcy court shall, and on the bankruptcy court's own motion, the bankruptcy court may—

(1) protect an entity with respect to a trade secret or confidential research, development, or commercial information; or

(2) protect a person with respect to scandalous or defamatory matter contained in a paper filed in a case under this title.

(c)(1) The bankruptcy court, for cause, may protect an individual, with respect to the following types of information to the extent the court finds that disclosure of such information would create undue risk of identity theft or other unlawful injury to the individual or the individual's property:

(A) Any means of identification (as defined in section 1028(d) of title 18) contained in a paper filed, or to be filed, in a case under this title.

(B) Other information contained in a paper described in subparagraph (A).

(2) Upon ex parte application demonstrating cause, the court shall provide access to information protected pursuant to paragraph (1) to an entity acting pursuant to the police or regulatory power of a domestic governmental unit.

(3) The United States trustee, bankruptcy administrator, trustee, and any auditor serving under section 586(f) of title 28—

(A) shall have full access to all information contained in any paper filed or submitted in a case under this title; and

(B) shall not disclose information specifically protected by the court under this title.

(Pub. L. 95–598, Nov. 6, 1978, 92 Stat. 2556; Pub. L. 109–8, title II, §§233(c), 234(a), (c), Apr. 20, 2005, 119 Stat. 74, 75.)

HISTORICAL AND REVISION NOTES

SENATE REPORT NO. 95–989

Subsection (a) of this section makes all papers filed in a bankruptcy case and the dockets of the bankruptcy court public and open to examination at reasonable times without charge. "Docket" includes the claims docket, the proceedings docket, and all papers filed in a case.

Subsection (b) permits the court, on its own motion, and requires the court, on the request of a party in interest, to protect trade secrets, confidential research, development, or commercial information, and to protect persons against scandalous or defamatory matter.

AMENDMENTS

2005—Subsec. (a). Pub. L. 109–8, §234(c), which directed the substitution of "subsections (b) and (c)," for "subsection (b),", was executed by substituting "subsections (b) and (c)" for "subsection (b)", to reflect the probable intent of Congress.

Pub. L. 109–8, §233(c), inserted "and subject to section 112" after "section".

Subsec. (c). Pub. L. 109–8, §234(a), added subsec. (c).

EFFECTIVE DATE OF 2005 AMENDMENT

Amendment by Pub. L. 109–8 effective 180 days after Apr. 20, 2005, and not applicable with respect to cases commenced under this title before such effective date, except as otherwise provided, see section 1501 of Pub. L. 109–8, set out as a note under section 101 of this title.

§ 108. Extension of time

(a) If applicable nonbankruptcy law, an order entered in a nonbankruptcy proceeding, or an agreement fixes a period within which the debtor may commence an action, and such period has not expired before the date of the filing of the petition, the trustee may commence such action only before the later of—

(1) the end of such period, including any suspension of such period occurring on or after the commencement of the case; or

(2) two years after the order for relief.

(b) Except as provided in subsection (a) of this section, if applicable nonbankruptcy law, an order entered in a nonbankruptcy proceeding, or an agreement fixes a period within which the debtor or an individual protected under section 1201 or 1301 of this title may file any pleading, demand, notice, or proof of claim or loss, cure a default, or perform any other similar act, and such period has not expired before the date of the filing of the petition, the trustee may only file, cure, or perform, as the case may be, before the later of—

(1) the end of such period, including any suspension of such period occurring on or after the commencement of the case; or

(2) 60 days after the order for relief.

(c) Except as provided in section 524 of this title, if applicable nonbankruptcy law, an order entered in a nonbankruptcy proceeding, or an agreement fixes a period for commencing or continuing a civil action in a court other than a bankruptcy court on a claim against the debtor, or against an individual with respect to which such individual is protected under section 1201 or 1301 of this title, and such period has not expired before the date of the filing of the petition, then such period does not expire until the later of—

(1) the end of such period, including any suspension of such period occurring on or after the commencement of the case; or

(2) 30 days after notice of the termination or expiration of the stay under section 362, 922, 1201, or 1301 of this title, as the case may be, with respect to such claim.

(Pub. L. 95–598, Nov. 6, 1978, 92 Stat. 2556; Pub. L. 98–353, title III, §424, July 10, 1984, 98 Stat. 369; Pub. L. 99–554, title II, §257(b), Oct. 27, 1986, 100 Stat. 3114; Pub. L. 109–8, title XII, §1203, Apr. 20, 2005, 119 Stat. 193.)

HISTORICAL AND REVISION NOTES

LEGISLATIVE STATEMENTS

Extension of time: The House amendment adopts section 108(c)(1) of the Senate amendment which expressly includes any special suspensions of statutes of limitation periods on collection outside bankruptcy when assets are under the authority of a court. For example, section 6503(b) of the Internal Revenue Code [title 26] suspends collection of tax liabilities while the debtor's assets are in the control or custody of a court, and for 6 months thereafter. By adopting the language of the Senate amendment, the House amendment insures not only that the period for collection of the taxes outside bankruptcy will not expire during the title 11 proceedings, but also that such period will not expire until at least 6 months thereafter, which is the minimum suspension period provided by the Internal Revenue Code [title 26].

SENATE REPORT NO. 95–989

Subsections (a) and (b), derived from Bankruptcy Act section 11 [section 29 of former title 11], permit the trustee, when he steps into the shoes of the debtor, an extension of time for filing an action or doing some other act that is required to preserve the debtor's rights. Subsection (a) extends any statute of limitation for commencing or continuing an action by the debtor for two years after the date of the order for relief, unless it would expire later. Subsection (b) gives the trustee 60 days to take other actions not covered under subsection (a), such as filing a pleading, demand, notice, or proof of claim or loss (such as an insurance claim), unless the period for doing the relevant act expires later than 60 days after the date of the order for relief.

Subsection (c) extends the statute of limitations for creditors. Thus, if a creditor is stayed from commencing or continuing an action against the debtor because of the bankruptcy case, then the creditor is permitted an additional 30 days after notice of the event by which the stay is terminated, whether that event be relief from the automatic stay under proposed 11 U.S.C. 362 or 1301, the closing of the bankruptcy case (which terminates the stay), or the exception from discharge of the debts on which the creditor claims.

In the case of Federal tax liabilities, the Internal Revenue Code [title 26] suspends the statute of limitations on a tax liability of a taxpayer from running while his assets are in the control or custody of a court and for 6 months thereafter (sec. 6503(b) of the Code [title 26]). The amendment applies this rule in a title 11 proceeding. Accordingly, the statute of limitations on collection of a nondischargeable Federal tax liability of a debtor will resume running after 6 months following the end of the period during which the debtor's assets are in the control or custody of the bankruptcy court. This rule will provide the Internal Revenue Service adequate time to collect nondischargeable taxes following the end of the title 11 proceedings.

AMENDMENTS

2005—Subsec. (c)(2). Pub. L. 109–8 substituted "922, 1201, or" for "922, or".

1986—Subsec. (b). Pub. L. 99–554, §257(b)(1), inserted reference to section 1201 of this title.

Subsec. (c). Pub. L. 99–554, §257(b)(2)(A), inserted reference to section 1201 of this title in provisions preceding par. (1).

Subsec. (c)(2). Pub. L. 99–554, §257(b)(2)(B), which directed the amendment of subsec. (c) by inserting "1201," after "722," could not be executed because "722," did not appear in text.

1984—Subsec. (a). Pub. L. 98–353, §424(b), inserted "nonbankruptcy" after "applicable" and "entered in a" in provisions preceding par. (1).

Subsec. (a)(1). Pub. L. 98–353, §424(a), substituted "or" for "and" after the semicolon.

Subsec. (b). Pub. L. 98–353, §424(b), inserted "nonbankruptcy" after "applicable" and "entered in a" in provisions preceding par. (1).

Subsec. (b)(1). Pub. L. 98–353, §424(a), substituted "or" for "and" after the semicolon.

Subsec. (c). Pub. L. 98–353, §424(b), inserted "nonbankruptcy" after "applicable" and "entered in a" in provisions preceding par. (1).

Subsec. (c)(1). Pub. L. 98–353, §424(a), substituted "or" for "and" after the semicolon.

EFFECTIVE DATE OF 2005 AMENDMENT

Amendment by Pub. L. 109–8 effective 180 days after Apr. 20, 2005, and not applicable with respect to cases commenced under this title before such effective date, except as otherwise provided, see section 1501 of Pub. L. 109–8, set out as a note under section 101 of this title.

EFFECTIVE DATE OF 1986 AMENDMENT

Amendment by Pub. L. 99–554 effective 30 days after Oct. 27, 1986, but not applicable to cases commenced under this title before that date, see section 302(a), (c)(1) of Pub. L. 99–554, set out as a note under section 581 of Title 28, Judiciary and Judicial Procedure.

EFFECTIVE DATE OF 1984 AMENDMENT

Amendment by Pub. L. 98–353 effective with respect to cases filed 90 days after July 10, 1984, see section 552(a) of Pub. L. 98–353, set out as a note under section 101 of this title.

§ 109. Who may be a debtor

(a) Notwithstanding any other provision of this section, only a person that resides or has a domicile, a place of business, or property in the United States, or a municipality, may be a debtor under this title.

(b) A person may be a debtor under chapter 7 of this title only if such person is not—

(1) a railroad;

(2) a domestic insurance company, bank, savings bank, cooperative bank, savings and loan association, building and loan association, homestead association, a New Markets Venture Capital company as defined in section 351 of the Small Business Investment Act of 1958, a small business investment company licensed by the Small Business Administration under section 301 of the Small Business Investment Act of 1958, credit union, or industrial bank or similar institution which is an insured bank as defined in section 3(h) of the Federal Deposit Insurance Act, except that an uninsured State member bank, or a corporation organized under section 25A of the Federal Reserve Act, which operates, or operates as, a multilateral clearing organization pursuant to section 409 of the Federal Deposit Insurance Corporation Improvement Act of 1991 may be a debtor if a petition is filed at the direction of the Board of Governors of the Federal Reserve System; or

(3)(A) a foreign insurance company, engaged in such business in the United States; or

(B) a foreign bank, savings bank, cooperative bank, savings and loan association, building and loan association, or credit union, that has a branch or agency (as defined in section 1(b) of the International Banking Act of 1978[1] in the United States.

(c) An entity may be a debtor under chapter 9 of this title if and only if such entity—

(1) is a municipality;

(2) is specifically authorized, in its capacity as a municipality or by name, to be a debtor under such chapter by State law, or by a governmental officer or organization empowered by State law to authorize such entity to be a debtor under such chapter;

(3) is insolvent;

(4) desires to effect a plan to adjust such debts; and

(5)(A) has obtained the agreement of creditors holding at least a majority in amount of the claims of each class that such entity intends to impair under a plan in a case under such chapter;

(B) has negotiated in good faith with creditors and has failed to obtain the agreement of creditors holding at least a majority in amount of the claims of each class that such entity intends to impair under a plan in a case under such chapter;

(C) is unable to negotiate with creditors because such negotiation is impracticable; or

(D) reasonably believes that a creditor may attempt to obtain a transfer that is avoidable under section 547 of this title.

(d) Only a railroad, a person that may be a debtor under chapter 7 of this title (except a stockbroker or a commodity broker), and an uninsured State member bank, or a corporation organized under section 25A of the Federal Reserve Act, which operates, or operates as, a multilateral clearing organization pursuant to section 409 of the Federal Deposit Insurance Corporation Improvement Act of 1991 may be a debtor under chapter 11 of this title.

(e) Only an individual with regular income that owes, on the date of the filing of the petition, noncontingent, liquidated, unsecured debts of less than $250,000 and noncontingent, liquidated, secured debts of less than $750,000, or an individual with regular income and such individual's spouse, except a stockbroker or a commodity broker, that owe, on the date of the filing of the petition, noncontingent, liquidated, unsecured debts that aggregate less than $250,000 and noncontingent, liquidated, secured debts of less than $750,000 may be a debtor under chapter 13 of this title.

(f) Only a family farmer or family fisherman with regular annual income may be a debtor under chapter 12 of this title.

(g) Notwithstanding any other provision of this section, no individual or family farmer may be a debtor under this title who has been a debtor in a case pending under this title at any time in the preceding 180 days if—

(1) the case was dismissed by the court for willful failure of the debtor to abide by orders of the court, or to appear before the court in proper prosecution of the case; or

(2) the debtor requested and obtained the voluntary dismissal of the case following the filing of a request for relief from the automatic stay provided by section 362 of this title.

(h)(1) Subject to paragraphs (2) and (3), and notwithstanding any other provision of this section, an individual may not be a debtor under this title unless such individual has, during the 180-day period preceding the date of filing of the petition by such individual, received from an approved nonprofit budget and credit counseling agency described in section 111(a) an individual or group briefing (including a briefing conducted by telephone or on the Internet) that outlined the opportunities for available credit counseling and assisted such individual in performing a related budget analysis.

(2)(A) Paragraph (1) shall not apply with respect to a debtor who resides in a district for which the United States trustee (or the bankruptcy administrator, if any) determines that the approved nonprofit budget and credit counseling agencies for such district are not reasonably able to provide adequate services to the additional individuals who would otherwise seek credit counseling from such agencies by reason of the requirements of paragraph (1).

(B) The United States trustee (or the bankruptcy administrator, if any) who makes a determination described in subparagraph (A) shall review such determination not later than 1 year after the date of such determination, and not less frequently than annually thereafter. Notwithstanding the preceding sentence, a nonprofit budget and credit counseling agency may be disapproved by the United States trustee (or the bankruptcy administrator, if any) at any time.

(3)(A) Subject to subparagraph (B), the requirements of paragraph (1) shall not apply with respect to a debtor who submits to the court a certification that—

(i) describes exigent circumstances that merit a waiver of the requirements of paragraph (1);

[1] So in original. Probably should be followed by a closing parenthesis.

(ii) states that the debtor requested credit counseling services from an approved nonprofit budget and credit counseling agency, but was unable to obtain the services referred to in paragraph (1) during the 7-day period beginning on the date on which the debtor made that request; and

(iii) is satisfactory to the court.

(B) With respect to a debtor, an exemption under subparagraph (A) shall cease to apply to that debtor on the date on which the debtor meets the requirements of paragraph (1), but in no case may the exemption apply to that debtor after the date that is 30 days after the debtor files a petition, except that the court, for cause, may order an additional 15 days.

(4) The requirements of paragraph (1) shall not apply with respect to a debtor whom the court determines, after notice and hearing, is unable to complete those requirements because of incapacity, disability, or active military duty in a military combat zone. For the purposes of this paragraph, incapacity means that the debtor is impaired by reason of mental illness or mental deficiency so that he is incapable of realizing and making rational decisions with respect to his financial responsibilities; and "disability" means that the debtor is so physically impaired as to be unable, after reasonable effort, to participate in an in person, telephone, or Internet briefing required under paragraph (1).

(Pub. L. 95–598, Nov. 6, 1978, 92 Stat. 2557; Pub. L. 97–320, title VII, §703(d), Oct. 15, 1982, 96 Stat. 1539; Pub. L. 98–353, title III, §§301, 425, July 10, 1984, 98 Stat. 352, 369; Pub. L. 99–554, title II, §253, Oct. 27, 1986, 100 Stat. 3105; Pub. L. 100–597, §2, Nov. 3, 1988, 102 Stat. 3028; Pub. L. 103–394, title I, §108(a), title II, §220, title IV, §402, title V, §501(d)(2), Oct. 22, 1994, 108 Stat. 4111, 4129, 4141, 4143; Pub. L. 106–554, §1(a)(5) [title I, §112(c)(1), (2)], §1(a)(8) [§1(e)], Dec. 21, 2000, 114 Stat. 2763, 2763A–393, 2763A–665; Pub. L. 109–8, title I, §106(a), title VIII, §802(d)(1), title X, §1007(b), title XII, §1204(1), Apr. 20, 2005, 119 Stat. 37, 146, 188, 193; Pub. L. 111–16, §2(1), May 7, 2009, 123 Stat. 1607.)

Historical and Revision Notes

Legislative Statements

Section 109(b) of the House amendment adopts a provision contained in H.R. 8200 as passed by the House. Railroad liquidations will occur under chapter 11, not chapter 7.

Section 109(c) contains a provision which tracks the Senate amendment as to when a municipality may be a debtor under chapter 11 of title 11. As under the Bankruptcy Act [former title 11], State law authorization and prepetition negotiation efforts are required.

Section 109(e) represents a compromise between H.R. 8200 as passed by the House and the Senate amendment relating to the dollar amounts restricting eligibility to be a debtor under chapter 13 of title 11. The House amendment adheres to the limit of $100,000 placed on unsecured debts in H.R. 8200 as passed by the House. It adopts a midpoint of $350,000 as a limit on secured claims, a compromise between the level of $500,000 in H.R. 8200 as passed by the House and $200,000 as contained in the Senate amendment.

Senate Report No. 95–989

This section specifies eligibility to be a debtor under the bankruptcy laws. The first criterion, found in the current Bankruptcy Act section 2a(1) [section 11(a)(1) of former title 11] requires that the debtor reside or have a domicile, a place of business, or property in the United States.

Subsection (b) defines eligibility for liquidation under chapter 7. All persons are eligible except insurance companies, and certain banking institutions. These exclusions are contained in current law. However, the banking institution exception is expanded in light of changes in various banking laws since the current law was last amended on this point. A change is also made to clarify that the bankruptcy laws cover foreign banks and insurance companies not engaged in the banking or insurance business in the United States but having assets in the United States. Banking institutions and insurance companies engaged in business in this country are excluded from liquidation under the bankruptcy laws because they are bodies for which alternate provision is made for their liquidation under various State or Federal regulatory laws. Conversely, when a foreign bank or insurance company is not engaged in the banking or insurance business in the United States, then those regulatory laws do not apply, and the bankruptcy laws are the only ones available for administration of any assets found in United States.

The first clause of subsection (b) provides that a railroad is not a debtor except where the requirements of section 1174 are met.

Subsection (c) [enacted as (d)] provides that only a person who may be a debtor under chapter 7 and a railroad may also be a debtor under chapter 11, but a stockbroker or commodity broker is eligible for relief only under chapter 7. Subsection (d) [enacted as (e)] establishes dollar limitations on the amount of indebtedness that an individual with regular income can incur and yet file under chapter 13.

House Report No. 95–595

Subsection (c) defines eligibility for chapter 9. Only a municipality that is unable to pay its debts as they mature, and that is not prohibited by State law from proceeding under chapter 9, is permitted to be a chapter 9 debtor. The subsection is derived from Bankruptcy Act §84 [section 404 of former title 11], with two changes. First, section 84 requires that the municipality be "generally authorized to file a petition under this chapter by the legislature, or by a governmental officer or organization empowered by State law to authorize the filing of a petition." The "generally authorized" language is unclear, and has generated a problem for a Colorado Metropolitan District that attempted to use chapter IX [chapter 9 of former title 11] in 1976. The "not prohibited" language provides flexibility for both the States and the municipalities involved, while protecting State sovereignty as required by *Ashton v. Cameron County Water District No. 1*, 298 U.S. 513 (1936) [56 S.Ct. 892, 80 L.Ed. 1309, 31 Am.Bankr.Rep.N.S. 96, rehearing denied 57 S.Ct. 5, 299 U.S. 619, 81 L.Ed. 457] and *Bekins v. United States*, 304 U.S. 27 (1938) [58 S.Ct. 811, 82 L.Ed. 1137, 36 Am.Bankr.Rep.N.S. 187, rehearing denied 58 S.Ct. 1043, 1044, 304 U.S. 589, 82 L.Ed. 1549].

The second change deletes the four prerequisites to filing found in section 84 [section 404 of former title 11]. The prerequisites require the municipality to have worked out a plan in advance, to have attempted to work out a plan without success, to fear that a creditor will attempt to obtain a preference, or to allege that prior negotiation is impracticable. The loopholes in those prerequisites are larger than the requirement itself. It was a compromise from pre-1976 chapter IX [chapter 9 of former title 11] under which a municipality could file only if it had worked out an adjustment plan in advance. In the meantime, chapter IX protection was unavailable. There was some controversy at the time of the enactment of current chapter IX concerning deletion of the pre-negotiation requirement. It was argued that deletion would lead to a rash of municipal bankruptcies. The prerequisites now contained in section 84 were inserted to assuage that fear. They are largely cosmetic and precatory, however, and do not offer any significant deterrent to use of chapter IX. Instead, other factors, such as a general reluctance on the part of any debtor, especially a municipality, to use the bankruptcy laws, operates as a much more effective deterrent against capricious use.

Subsection (d) permits a person that may proceed under chapter 7 to be a debtor under chapter 11, Reorganization, with two exceptions. Railroads, which are excluded from chapter 7, are permitted to proceed under chapter 11. Stockbrokers and commodity brokers, which are permitted to be debtors under chapter 7, are excluded from chapter 11. The special rules for treatment of customer accounts that are the essence of stockbroker and commodity broker liquidations are available only in chapter 7. Customers would be unprotected under chapter 11. The special protective rules are unavailable in chapter 11 because their complexity would make reorganization very difficult at best, and unintelligible at worst. The variety of options available in reorganization cases make it extremely difficult to reorganize and continue to provide the special customer protection necessary in these cases.

Subsection (e) specifies eligibility for chapter 13, Adjustment of Debts of an Individual with Regular Income. An individual with regular income, or an individual with regular income and the individual's spouse, may proceed under chapter 13. As noted in connection with the definition of the term "individual with regular income", this represents a significant departure from current law. The change might have been too great, however, without some limitation. Thus, the debtor (or the debtor and spouse) must have unsecured debts that aggregate less than $100,000, and secured debts that aggregate less than $500,000. These figures will permit the small sole proprietor, for whom a chapter 11 reorganization is too cumbersome a procedure, to proceed under chapter 13. It does not create a presumption that any sole proprietor within that range is better off in chapter 13 than chapter 11. The conversion rules found in section 1307 will govern the appropriateness of the two chapters for any particular individual. The figures merely set maximum limits.

Whether a small business operated by a husband and wife, the so-called "mom and pop grocery store," will be a partnership and thus excluded from chapter 13, or a business owned by an individual, will have to be determined on the facts of each case. Even if partnership papers have not been filed, for example, the issue will be whether the assets of the grocery store are for the benefit of all creditors of the debtor or only for business creditors, and whether such assets may be the subject of a chapter 13 proceeding. The intent of the section is to follow current law that a partnership by estoppel may be adjudicated in bankruptcy and therefore would not prevent a chapter 13 debtor from subjecting assets in such a partnership to the reach of all creditors in a chapter 13 case. However, if the partnership is found to be a partnership by agreement, even informal agreement, than a separate entity exists and the assets of that entity would be exempt from a case under chapter 13.

References in Text

Section 351 of the Small Business Investment Act of 1958, referred to in subsec. (b)(2), is classified to section 689 of Title 15, Commerce and Trade.

Section 301 of the Small Business Investment Act of 1958, referred to in subsec. (b)(2), is classified to section 681 of Title 15, Commerce and Trade.

Section 3(h) of the Federal Deposit Insurance Act, referred to in subsec. (b)(2), is classified to section 1813(h) of Title 12, Banks and Banking.

Section 25A of the Federal Reserve Act, referred to in subsecs. (b)(2) and (d), popularly known as the Edge Act, is classified to subchapter II (§611 et seq.) of chapter 6 of Title 12, Banks and Banking. For complete classification of this Act to the Code, see Short Title note set out under section 611 of Title 12 and Tables.

Section 409 of the Federal Deposit Insurance Corporation Improvement Act of 1991, referred to in subsecs. (b)(2) and (d), is classified to section 4422 of Title 12, Banks and Banking.

Section 1(b) of the International Banking Act of 1978, referred to in subsec. (b)(3)(B), is classified to section 3101 of Title 12, Banks and Banking.

Amendments

2009—Subsec. (h)(3)(A)(ii). Pub. L. 111–16 substituted "7-day" for "5-day".

2005—Subsec. (b)(2). Pub. L. 109–8, §1204(1), struck out "subsection (c) or (d) of" before "section 301".

Subsec. (b)(3). Pub. L. 109–8, §802(d)(1), added par. (3) and struck out former par. (3) which read as follows: "a foreign insurance company, bank, savings bank, cooperative bank, savings and loan association, building and loan association, homestead association, or credit union, engaged in such business in the United States."

Subsec. (f). Pub. L. 109–8, §1007(b), inserted "or family fisherman" after "family farmer".

Subsec. (h). Pub. L. 109–8, §106(a), added subsec. (h).

2000—Subsec. (b)(2). Pub. L. 106–554, §1(a)(8) [§1(e)], inserted "a New Markets Venture Capital company as defined in section 351 of the Small Business Investment Act of 1958," after "homestead association,".

Pub. L. 106–554, §1(a)(5) [title I, §112(c)(1)], substituted ", except that an uninsured State member bank, or a corporation organized under section 25A of the Federal Reserve Act, which operates, or operates as, a multilateral clearing organization pursuant to section 409 of the Federal Deposit Insurance Corporation Improvement Act of 1991 may be a debtor if a petition is filed at the direction of the Board of Governors of the Federal Reserve System; or" for "; or".

Subsec. (d). Pub. L. 106–554, §1(a)(5) [title I, §112(c)(2)], amended subsec. (d) generally. Prior to amendment, subsec. (d) read as follows: "Only a person that may be a debtor under chapter 7 of this title, except a stockbroker or a commodity broker, and a railroad may be a debtor under chapter 11 of this title."

1994—Subsec. (b)(2). Pub. L. 103–394, §§220, 501(d)(2), inserted "a small business investment company licensed by the Small Business Administration under subsection (c) or (d) of section 301 of the Small Business Investment Act of 1958," after "homestead association," and struck out "(12 U.S.C. 1813(h))" after "Insurance Act".

Subsec. (c)(2). Pub. L. 103–394, §402, substituted "specifically authorized, in its capacity as a municipality or by name," for "generally authorized".

Subsec. (e). Pub. L. 103–394, §108(a), substituted "$250,000" and "$750,000" for "$100,000" and "$350,000", respectively, in two places.

1988—Subsec. (c)(3). Pub. L. 100–597 struck out "or unable to meet such entity's debts as such debts mature" after "insolvent".

1986—Subsec. (f). Pub. L. 99–554, §253(1)(B), (2), added subsec. (f) and redesignated former subsec. (f) as (g).

Subsec. (g). Pub. L. 99–554, §253(1), redesignated former subsec. (f) as (g) and inserted reference to family farmer.

1984—Subsec. (a). Pub. L. 98–353, §425(a), struck out "in the United States," after "only a person that resides".

Subsec. (c)(5)(D). Pub. L. 98–353, §425(b), substituted "transfer that is avoidable under section 547 of this title" for "preference".

Subsec. (d). Pub. L. 98–353, §425(c), substituted "stockbroker" for "stockholder".

Subsec. (f). Pub. L. 98–353, §301, added subsec. (f).

1982—Subsec. (b)(2). Pub. L. 97–320 inserted reference to industrial banks or similar institutions which are insured banks as defined in section 3(h) of the Federal Deposit Insurance Act (12 U.S.C. 1813(h)).

Effective Date of 2009 Amendment

Pub. L. 111–16, §7, May 7, 2009, 123 Stat. 1609, provided that: "The amendments made by this Act [amending this section, sections 322, 332, 342, 521, 704, 749, and 764 of this title, sections 983, 1514, 1963, 2252A, 2339B, 3060, 3432, 3509, and 3771 of Title 18, Crimes and Criminal Procedure, section 7 of the Classified Information Procedures Act set out in the Appendix to Title 18, section 853 of Title 21, Food and Drugs, and sections 636, 1453, and 2107 of Title 28, Judiciary and Judicial Procedure] shall take effect on December 1, 2009."

EFFECTIVE DATE OF 2005 AMENDMENT

Amendment by Pub. L. 109-8 effective 180 days after Apr. 20, 2005, and not applicable with respect to cases commenced under this title before such effective date, except as otherwise provided, see section 1501 of Pub. L. 109-8, set out as a note under section 101 of this title.

EFFECTIVE DATE OF 1994 AMENDMENT

Amendment by Pub. L. 103-394 effective Oct. 22, 1994, and not applicable with respect to cases commenced under this title before Oct. 22, 1994, see section 702 of Pub. L. 103-394, set out as a note under section 101 of this title.

EFFECTIVE DATE OF 1988 AMENDMENT

Amendment by Pub. L. 100-597 effective Nov. 3, 1988, but not applicable to any case commenced under this title before that date, see section 12 of Pub. L. 100-597, set out as a note under section 101 of this title.

EFFECTIVE DATE OF 1986 AMENDMENT

Amendment by Pub. L. 99-554 effective 30 days after Oct. 27, 1986, but not applicable to cases commenced under this title before that date, see section 302(a), (c)(1) of Pub. L. 99-554, set out as a note under section 581 of Title 28, Judiciary and Judicial Procedure.

EFFECTIVE DATE OF 1984 AMENDMENT

Amendment by Pub. L. 98-353 effective with respect to cases filed 90 days after July 10, 1984, see section 552(a) of Pub. L. 98-353, set out as a note under section 101 of this title.

ADJUSTMENT OF DOLLAR AMOUNTS

For adjustment of dollar amounts specified in subsec. (e) of this section by the Judicial Conference of the United States, see note set out under section 104 of this title.

§ 110. Penalty for persons who negligently or fraudulently prepare bankruptcy petitions

(a) In this section—

(1) "bankruptcy petition preparer" means a person, other than an attorney for the debtor or an employee of such attorney under the direct supervision of such attorney, who prepares for compensation a document for filing; and

(2) "document for filing" means a petition or any other document prepared for filing by a debtor in a United States bankruptcy court or a United States district court in connection with a case under this title.

(b)(1) A bankruptcy petition preparer who prepares a document for filing shall sign the document and print on the document the preparer's name and address. If a bankruptcy petition preparer is not an individual, then an officer, principal, responsible person, or partner of the bankruptcy petition preparer shall be required to—

(A) sign the document for filing; and

(B) print on the document the name and address of that officer, principal, responsible person, or partner.

(2)(A) Before preparing any document for filing or accepting any fees from a debtor, the bankruptcy petition preparer shall provide to the debtor a written notice which shall be on an official form prescribed by the Judicial Conference of the United States in accordance with rule 9009 of the Federal Rules of Bankruptcy Procedure.

(B) The notice under subparagraph (A)—

(i) shall inform the debtor in simple language that a bankruptcy petition preparer is not an attorney and may not practice law or give legal advice;

(ii) may contain a description of examples of legal advice that a bankruptcy petition preparer is not authorized to give, in addition to any advice that the preparer may not give by reason of subsection (e)(2); and

(iii) shall—

(I) be signed by the debtor and, under penalty of perjury, by the bankruptcy petition preparer; and

(II) be filed with any document for filing.

(c)(1) A bankruptcy petition preparer who prepares a document for filing shall place on the document, after the preparer's signature, an identifying number that identifies individuals who prepared the document.

(2)(A) Subject to subparagraph (B), for purposes of this section, the identifying number of a bankruptcy petition preparer shall be the Social Security account number of each individual who prepared the document or assisted in its preparation.

(B) If a bankruptcy petition preparer is not an individual, the identifying number of the bankruptcy petition preparer shall be the Social Security account number of the officer, principal, responsible person, or partner of the bankruptcy petition preparer.

(d) A bankruptcy petition preparer shall, not later than the time at which a document for filing is presented for the debtor's signature, furnish to the debtor a copy of the document.

(e)(1) A bankruptcy petition preparer shall not execute any document on behalf of a debtor.

(2)(A) A bankruptcy petition preparer may not offer a potential bankruptcy debtor any legal advice, including any legal advice described in subparagraph (B).

(B) The legal advice referred to in subparagraph (A) includes advising the debtor—

(i) whether—

(I) to file a petition under this title; or

(II) commencing a case under chapter 7, 11, 12, or 13 is appropriate;

(ii) whether the debtor's debts will be discharged in a case under this title;

(iii) whether the debtor will be able to retain the debtor's home, car, or other property after commencing a case under this title;

(iv) concerning—

(I) the tax consequences of a case brought under this title; or

(II) the dischargeability of tax claims;

(v) whether the debtor may or should promise to repay debts to a creditor or enter into a reaffirmation agreement with a creditor to reaffirm a debt;

(vi) concerning how to characterize the nature of the debtor's interests in property or the debtor's debts; or

(vii) concerning bankruptcy procedures and rights.

(f) A bankruptcy petition preparer shall not use the word "legal" or any similar term in any advertisements, or advertise under any category that includes the word "legal" or any similar term.

(g) A bankruptcy petition preparer shall not collect or receive any payment from the debtor or on behalf of the debtor for the court fees in connection with filing the petition.

(h)(1) The Supreme Court may promulgate rules under section 2075 of title 28, or the Judicial Conference of the United States may prescribe guidelines, for setting a maximum allowable fee chargeable by a bankruptcy petition preparer. A bankruptcy petition preparer shall notify the debtor of any such maximum amount before preparing any document for filing for a debtor or accepting any fee from the debtor.

(2) A declaration under penalty of perjury by the bankruptcy petition preparer shall be filed together with the petition, disclosing any fee received from or on behalf of the debtor within 12 months immediately prior to the filing of the case, and any unpaid fee charged to the debtor. If rules or guidelines setting a maximum fee for services have been promulgated or prescribed under paragraph (1), the declaration under this paragraph shall include a certification that the bankruptcy petition preparer complied with the notification requirement under paragraph (1).

(3)(A) The court shall disallow and order the immediate turnover to the bankruptcy trustee any fee referred to in paragraph (2) found to be in excess of the value of any services—

(i) rendered by the bankruptcy petition preparer during the 12-month period immediately preceding the date of the filing of the petition; or

(ii) found to be in violation of any rule or guideline promulgated or prescribed under paragraph (1).

(B) All fees charged by a bankruptcy petition preparer may be forfeited in any case in which the bankruptcy petition preparer fails to comply with this subsection or subsection (b), (c), (d), (e), (f), or (g).

(C) An individual may exempt any funds recovered under this paragraph under section 522(b).

(4) The debtor, the trustee, a creditor, the United States trustee (or the bankruptcy administrator, if any) or the court, on the initiative of the court, may file a motion for an order under paragraph (2).[1]

(5) A bankruptcy petition preparer shall be fined not more than $500 for each failure to comply with a court order to turn over funds within 30 days of service of such order.

(i)(1) If a bankruptcy petition preparer violates this section or commits any act that the court finds to be fraudulent, unfair, or deceptive, on the motion of the debtor, trustee, United States trustee (or the bankruptcy administrator, if any), and after notice and a hearing, the court shall order the bankruptcy petition preparer to pay to the debtor—

(A) the debtor's actual damages;

(B) the greater of—

(i) $2,000; or

(ii) twice the amount paid by the debtor to the bankruptcy petition preparer for the preparer's services; and

(C) reasonable attorneys' fees and costs in moving for damages under this subsection.

(2) If the trustee or creditor moves for damages on behalf of the debtor under this subsection, the bankruptcy petition preparer shall be ordered to pay the movant the additional amount of $1,000 plus reasonable attorneys' fees and costs incurred.

(j)(1) A debtor for whom a bankruptcy petition preparer has prepared a document for filing, the trustee, a creditor, or the United States trustee in the district in which the bankruptcy petition preparer resides, has conducted business, or the United States trustee in any other district in which the debtor resides may bring a civil action to enjoin a bankruptcy petition preparer from engaging in any conduct in violation of this section or from further acting as a bankruptcy petition preparer.

(2)(A) In an action under paragraph (1), if the court finds that—

(i) a bankruptcy petition preparer has—

(I) engaged in conduct in violation of this section or of any provision of this title;

(II) misrepresented the preparer's experience or education as a bankruptcy petition preparer; or

(III) engaged in any other fraudulent, unfair, or deceptive conduct; and

(ii) injunctive relief is appropriate to prevent the recurrence of such conduct,

the court may enjoin the bankruptcy petition preparer from engaging in such conduct.

(B) If the court finds that a bankruptcy petition preparer has continually engaged in conduct described in subclause (I), (II), or (III) of clause (i) and that an injunction prohibiting such conduct would not be sufficient to prevent such person's interference with the proper administration of this title, has not paid a penalty imposed under this section, or failed to disgorge all fees ordered by the court the court may enjoin the person from acting as a bankruptcy petition preparer.

(3) The court, as part of its contempt power, may enjoin a bankruptcy petition preparer that has failed to comply with a previous order issued under this section. The injunction under this paragraph may be issued on the motion of the court, the trustee, or the United States trustee (or the bankruptcy administrator, if any).

(4) The court shall award to a debtor, trustee, or creditor that brings a successful action under this subsection reasonable attorneys' fees and costs of the action, to be paid by the bankruptcy petition preparer.

(k) Nothing in this section shall be construed to permit activities that are otherwise prohibited by law, including rules and laws that prohibit the unauthorized practice of law.

(*l*)(1) A bankruptcy petition preparer who fails to comply with any provision of subsection (b), (c), (d), (e), (f), (g), or (h) may be fined not more than $500 for each such failure.

[1] See References in Text note below.

(2) The court shall triple the amount of a fine assessed under paragraph (1) in any case in which the court finds that a bankruptcy petition preparer—

(A) advised the debtor to exclude assets or income that should have been included on applicable schedules;

(B) advised the debtor to use a false Social Security account number;

(C) failed to inform the debtor that the debtor was filing for relief under this title; or

(D) prepared a document for filing in a manner that failed to disclose the identity of the bankruptcy petition preparer.

(3) A debtor, trustee, creditor, or United States trustee (or the bankruptcy administrator, if any) may file a motion for an order imposing a fine on the bankruptcy petition preparer for any violation of this section.

(4)(A) Fines imposed under this subsection in judicial districts served by United States trustees shall be paid to the United States trustees, who shall deposit an amount equal to such fines in the United States Trustee Fund.

(B) Fines imposed under this subsection in judicial districts served by bankruptcy administrators shall be deposited as offsetting receipts to the fund established under section 1931 of title 28, and shall remain available until expended to reimburse any appropriation for the amount paid out of such appropriation for expenses of the operation and maintenance of the courts of the United States.

(Added Pub. L. 103–394, title III, §308(a), Oct. 22, 1994, 108 Stat. 4135; amended Pub. L. 109–8, title II, §221, title XII, §1205, Apr. 20, 2005, 119 Stat. 59, 194; Pub. L. 110–161, div. B, title II, §212(b), Dec. 26, 2007, 121 Stat. 1914.)

REFERENCES IN TEXT

The Federal Rules of Bankruptcy Procedure, referred to in subsec. (b)(2)(A), are set out in the Appendix to this title.

Paragraph (2), referred to in subsec. (h)(4), was redesignated as par. (3) and repealed and a new par. (3) was added by Pub. L. 109–8, title II, §221(8)(A), (D), Apr. 20, 2005, 119 Stat. 59. The new par. (3) provides for court orders similar to those provided for in former par. (2).

AMENDMENTS

2007—Subsec. (*l*)(4)(A). Pub. L. 110–161 amended subpar. (A) generally. Prior to amendment, subpar. (A) read as follows: "Fines imposed under this subsection in judicial districts served by United States trustees shall be paid to the United States trustee, who shall deposit an amount equal to such fines in a special account of the United States Trustee System Fund referred to in section 586(e)(2) of title 28. Amounts deposited under this subparagraph shall be available to fund the enforcement of this section on a national basis."

2005—Subsec. (a)(1). Pub. L. 109–8, §221(1), substituted "for the debtor or an employee of such attorney under the direct supervision of such attorney" for "or an employee of an attorney".

Subsec. (b)(1). Pub. L. 109–8, §221(2)(A), inserted at end "If a bankruptcy petition preparer is not an individual, then an officer, principal, responsible person, or partner of the bankruptcy petition preparer shall be required to—" and added subpars. (A) and (B).

Subsec. (b)(2). Pub. L. 109–8, §221(2)(B), added par. (2) and struck out former par. (2) which read as follows: "A bankruptcy petition preparer who fails to comply with paragraph (1) may be fined not more than $500 for each such failure unless the failure is due to reasonable cause."

Subsec. (c)(2). Pub. L. 109–8, §221(3)(A), designated existing provisions as subpar. (A), substituted "Subject to subparagraph (B), for purposes" for "For purposes", and added subpar. (B).

Subsec. (c)(3). Pub. L. 109–8, §221(3)(B), struck out par. (3) which read as follows: "A bankruptcy petition preparer who fails to comply with paragraph (1) may be fined not more than $500 for each such failure unless the failure is due to reasonable cause."

Subsec. (d). Pub. L. 109–8, §221(4), struck out par. (1) designation before "A bankruptcy petition preparer shall" and struck out par. (2) which read as follows: "A bankruptcy petition preparer who fails to comply with paragraph (1) may be fined not more than $500 for each such failure unless the failure is due to reasonable cause."

Subsec. (e)(2). Pub. L. 109–8, §221(5), added par. (2) and struck out former par. (2) which read as follows: "A bankruptcy petition preparer may be fined not more than $500 for each document executed in violation of paragraph (1)."

Subsec. (f). Pub. L. 109–8, §221(6), struck out par. (1) designation before "A bankruptcy petition preparer shall not" and struck out par. (2) which read as follows: "A bankruptcy petition preparer shall be fined not more than $500 for each violation of paragraph (1)."

Subsec. (g). Pub. L. 109–8, §221(7), struck out par. (1) designation before "A bankruptcy petition preparer shall not" and struck out par. (2) which read as follows: "A bankruptcy petition preparer shall be fined not more than $500 for each violation of paragraph (1)."

Subsec. (h)(1). Pub. L. 109–8, §221(8)(B), added par. (1). Former par. (1) redesignated (2).

Subsec. (h)(2). Pub. L. 109–8, §221(8)(A), (C), redesignated par. (1) as (2), substituted "A" for "Within 10 days after the date of the filing of a petition, a bankruptcy petition preparer shall file a", inserted "by the bankruptcy petition preparer shall be filed together with the petition," after "perjury", and inserted at end "If rules or guidelines setting a maximum fee for services have been promulgated or prescribed under paragraph (1), the declaration under this paragraph shall include a certification that the bankruptcy petition preparer complied with the notification requirement under paragraph (1)." Former par. (2) redesignated (3).

Subsec. (h)(3). Pub. L. 109–8, §221(8)(D), added par. (3) and struck out former par. (3) which read as follows: "The court shall disallow and order the immediate turnover to the bankruptcy trustee of any fee referred to in paragraph (1) found to be in excess of the value of services rendered for the documents prepared. An individual debtor may exempt any funds so recovered under section 522(b)."

Pub. L. 109–8, §221(8)(A) redesignated par. (2) as (3). Former par. (3) redesignated (4).

Subsec. (h)(4). Pub. L. 109–8, §221(8)(E), substituted "the United States trustee (or the bankruptcy administrator, if any) or the court, on the initiative of the court," for "or the United States trustee".

Pub. L. 109–8, §221(8)(A) redesignated par. (3) as (4). Former par. (4) redesignated (5).

Subsec. (h)(5). Pub. L. 109–8, §221(8)(A) redesignated par. (4) as (5).

Subsec. (i)(1). Pub. L. 109–8, §221(9), inserted introductory provisions and struck out former introductory provisions which read as follows: "If a bankruptcy case or related proceeding is dismissed because of the failure to file bankruptcy papers, including papers specified in section 521(1) of this title, the negligence or intentional disregard of this title or the Federal Rules of Bankruptcy Procedure by a bankruptcy petition preparer, or if a bankruptcy petition preparer violates this section or commits any fraudulent, unfair, or deceptive act, the bankruptcy court shall certify that fact to the district court, and the district court, on motion of the debtor, the trustee, or a creditor and after a hearing, shall order the bankruptcy petition preparer to pay to the debtor—".

Subsec. (j)(2)(A)(i)(I). Pub. L. 109–8, §221(10)(A)(i), struck out "a violation of which subjects a person to criminal penalty" after "any provision of this title".

Subsec. (j)(2)(B). Pub. L. 109–8, §221(10)(A)(ii), substituted "has not paid a penalty" for "or has not paid a penalty" and inserted "or failed to disgorge all fees ordered by the court" after "a penalty imposed under this section,".

Subsec. (j)(3). Pub. L. 109–8, §221(10)(C) added par. (3). Former par. (3) redesignated (4).

Subsec. (j)(4). Pub. L. 109–8, §1205, substituted "attorneys" for "attorney's".

Pub. L. 109–8, §221(10)(B), redesignated par. (3) as (4).

Subsec. (*l*). Pub. L. 109–8, §221(11), added subsec. (*l*).

EFFECTIVE DATE OF 2005 AMENDMENT

Amendment by Pub. L. 109–8 effective 180 days after Apr. 20, 2005, and not applicable with respect to cases commenced under this title before such effective date, except as otherwise provided, see section 1501 of Pub. L. 109–8, set out as a note under section 101 of this title.

EFFECTIVE DATE

Section effective Oct. 22, 1994, and not applicable with respect to cases commenced under this title before Oct. 22, 1994, see section 702 of Pub. L. 103–394, set out as an Effective Date of 1994 Amendment note under section 101 of this title.

§111. Nonprofit budget and credit counseling agencies; financial management instructional courses

(a) The clerk shall maintain a publicly available list of—

(1) nonprofit budget and credit counseling agencies that provide 1 or more services described in section 109(h) currently approved by the United States trustee (or the bankruptcy administrator, if any); and

(2) instructional courses concerning personal financial management currently approved by the United States trustee (or the bankruptcy administrator, if any), as applicable.

(b) The United States trustee (or bankruptcy administrator, if any) shall only approve a nonprofit budget and credit counseling agency or an instructional course concerning personal financial management as follows:

(1) The United States trustee (or bankruptcy administrator, if any) shall have thoroughly reviewed the qualifications of the nonprofit budget and credit counseling agency or of the provider of the instructional course under the standards set forth in this section, and the services or instructional courses that will be offered by such agency or such provider, and may require such agency or such provider that has sought approval to provide information with respect to such review.

(2) The United States trustee (or bankruptcy administrator, if any) shall have determined that such agency or such instructional course fully satisfies the applicable standards set forth in this section.

(3) If a nonprofit budget and credit counseling agency or instructional course did not appear on the approved list for the district under subsection (a) immediately before approval under this section, approval under this subsection of such agency or such instructional course shall be for a probationary period not to exceed 6 months.

(4) At the conclusion of the applicable probationary period under paragraph (3), the United States trustee (or bankruptcy administrator, if any) may only approve for an additional 1-year period, and for successive 1-year periods thereafter, an agency or instructional course that has demonstrated during the probationary or applicable subsequent period of approval that such agency or instructional course—

(A) has met the standards set forth under this section during such period; and

(B) can satisfy such standards in the future.

(5) Not later than 30 days after any final decision under paragraph (4), an interested person may seek judicial review of such decision in the appropriate district court of the United States.

(c)(1) The United States trustee (or the bankruptcy administrator, if any) shall only approve a nonprofit budget and credit counseling agency that demonstrates that it will provide qualified counselors, maintain adequate provision for safekeeping and payment of client funds, provide adequate counseling with respect to client credit problems, and deal responsibly and effectively with other matters relating to the quality, effectiveness, and financial security of the services it provides.

(2) To be approved by the United States trustee (or the bankruptcy administrator, if any), a nonprofit budget and credit counseling agency shall, at a minimum—

(A) have a board of directors the majority of which—

(i) are not employed by such agency; and

(ii) will not directly or indirectly benefit financially from the outcome of the counseling services provided by such agency;

(B) if a fee is charged for counseling services, charge a reasonable fee, and provide services without regard to ability to pay the fee;

(C) provide for safekeeping and payment of client funds, including an annual audit of the trust accounts and appropriate employee bonding;

(D) provide full disclosures to a client, including funding sources, counselor qualifications, possible impact on credit reports, and any costs of such program that will be paid by such client and how such costs will be paid;

(E) provide adequate counseling with respect to a client's credit problems that includes an analysis of such client's current financial condition, factors that caused such financial condition, and how such client can develop a plan to respond to the problems without incurring negative amortization of debt;

(F) provide trained counselors who receive no commissions or bonuses based on the outcome of the counseling services provided by such agency, and who have adequate experience, and have been adequately trained to provide counseling services to individuals in financial difficulty, including the matters described in subparagraph (E);

(G) demonstrate adequate experience and background in providing credit counseling; and

(H) have adequate financial resources to provide continuing support services for budgeting plans over the life of any repayment plan.

(d) The United States trustee (or the bankruptcy administrator, if any) shall only approve an instructional course concerning personal financial management—

(1) for an initial probationary period under subsection (b)(3) if the course will provide at a minimum—

(A) trained personnel with adequate experience and training in providing effective instruction and services;

(B) learning materials and teaching methodologies designed to assist debtors in understanding personal financial management and that are consistent with stated objectives directly related to the goals of such instructional course;

(C) adequate facilities situated in reasonably convenient locations at which such instructional course is offered, except that such facilities may include the provision of such instructional course by telephone or through the Internet, if such instructional course is effective;

(D) the preparation and retention of reasonable records (which shall include the debtor's bankruptcy case number) to permit evaluation of the effectiveness of such instructional course, including any evaluation of satisfaction of instructional course requirements for each debtor attending such instructional course, which shall be available for inspection and evaluation by the Executive Office for United States Trustees, the United States trustee (or the bankruptcy administrator, if any), or the chief bankruptcy judge for the district in which such instructional course is offered; and

(E) if a fee is charged for the instructional course, charge a reasonable fee, and provide services without regard to ability to pay the fee.

(2) for any 1-year period if the provider thereof has demonstrated that the course meets the standards of paragraph (1) and, in addition—

(A) has been effective in assisting a substantial number of debtors to understand personal financial management; and

(B) is otherwise likely to increase substantially the debtor's understanding of personal financial management.

(e) The district court may, at any time, investigate the qualifications of a nonprofit budget and credit counseling agency referred to in subsection (a), and request production of documents to ensure the integrity and effectiveness of such agency. The district court may, at any time, remove from the approved list under subsection (a) a nonprofit budget and credit counseling agency upon finding such agency does not meet the qualifications of subsection (b).

(f) The United States trustee (or the bankruptcy administrator, if any) shall notify the clerk that a nonprofit budget and credit counseling agency or an instructional course is no longer approved, in which case the clerk shall remove it from the list maintained under subsection (a).

(g)(1) No nonprofit budget and credit counseling agency may provide to a credit reporting agency information concerning whether a debtor has received or sought instruction concerning personal financial management from such agency.

(2) A nonprofit budget and credit counseling agency that willfully or negligently fails to comply with any requirement under this title with respect to a debtor shall be liable for damages in an amount equal to the sum of—

(A) any actual damages sustained by the debtor as a result of the violation; and

(B) any court costs or reasonable attorneys' fees (as determined by the court) incurred in an action to recover those damages.

(Added Pub. L. 109-8, title I, §106(e)(1), Apr. 20, 2005, 119 Stat. 38.)

Effective Date

Section effective 180 days after Apr. 20, 2005, and not applicable with respect to cases commenced under this title before such effective date, except as otherwise provided, see section 1501 of Pub. L. 109-8, set out as an Effective Date of 2005 Amendment note under section 101 of this title.

Debtor Financial Management Training Test Program

Pub. L. 109-8, title I, §105, Apr. 20, 2005, 119 Stat. 36, provided that:

"(a) Development of Financial Management and Training Curriculum and Materials.—The Director of the Executive Office for United States Trustees (in this section referred to as the 'Director') shall consult with a wide range of individuals who are experts in the field of debtor education, including trustees who serve in cases under chapter 13 of title 11, United States Code, and who operate financial management education programs for debtors, and shall develop a financial management training curriculum and materials that can be used to educate debtors who are individuals on how to better manage their finances.

"(b) Test.—

"(1) Selection of districts.—The Director shall select 6 judicial districts of the United States in which to test the effectiveness of the financial management training curriculum and materials developed under subsection (a).

"(2) Use.—For an 18-month period beginning not later than 270 days after the date of the enactment of this Act [Apr. 20, 2005], such curriculum and materials shall be, for the 6 judicial districts selected under paragraph (1), used as the instructional course concerning personal financial management for purposes of section 111 of title 11, United States Code.

"(c) Evaluation.—

"(1) In general.—During the 18-month period referred to in subsection (b), the Director shall evaluate the effectiveness of—

"(A) the financial management training curriculum and materials developed under subsection (a); and

"(B) a sample of existing consumer education programs such as those described in the Report of the National Bankruptcy Review Commission (October 20, 1997) that are representative of consumer education programs carried out by the credit industry, by trustees serving under chapter 13 of title 11, United States Code, and by consumer counseling groups.

"(2) Report.—Not later than 3 months after concluding such evaluation, the Director shall submit a report to the Speaker of the House of Representatives and the President pro tempore of the Senate, for referral to the appropriate committees of the Congress, containing the findings of the Director regarding the effectiveness of such curriculum, such materials, and such programs and their costs."

§ 112. Prohibition on disclosure of name of minor children

The debtor may be required to provide information regarding a minor child involved in matters under this title but may not be required to disclose in the public records in the case the name of such minor child. The debtor may be required to disclose the name of such minor child in a nonpublic record that is maintained by the court and made available by the court for examination by the United States trustee, the trustee, and the auditor (if any) serving under section 586(f) of title 28, in the case. The court, the United States trustee, the trustee, and such auditor shall not disclose the name of such minor child maintained in such nonpublic record.

(Added Pub. L. 109–8, title II, §233(a), Apr. 20, 2005, 119 Stat. 74.)

EFFECTIVE DATE

Section effective 180 days after Apr. 20, 2005, and not applicable with respect to cases commenced under this title before such effective date, except as otherwise provided, see section 1501 of Pub. L. 109–8, set out as an Effective Date of 2005 Amendment note under section 101 of this title.

CHAPTER 3—CASE ADMINISTRATION

SUBCHAPTER I—COMMENCEMENT OF A CASE

[1] So in original. Does not conform to section catchline.

AMENDMENTS

2005—Pub. L. 109–8, title II, §232(c), title IV, §434(a)(2), title VII, §719(a)(2), title VIII, §802(d)(4), title XI, §§1102(b), 1104(a)(2), Apr. 20, 2005, 119 Stat. 74, 111, 133, 146, 190, 192, added items 308, 332, 333, and 351, substituted "Special provisions related to the treatment of State and local taxes" for "Special tax provisions" in item 346, and struck out item 304 "Cases ancillary to foreign proceedings".

1986—Pub. L. 99–554, title II, §205(b), Oct. 27, 1986, 100 Stat. 3098, added item 307.

SUBCHAPTER I—COMMENCEMENT OF A CASE

§ 301. Voluntary cases

(a) A voluntary case under a chapter of this title is commenced by the filing with the bankruptcy court of a petition under such chapter by an entity that may be a debtor under such chapter.

(b) The commencement of a voluntary case under a chapter of this title constitutes an order for relief under such chapter.

(Pub. L. 95–598, Nov. 6, 1978, 92 Stat. 2558; Pub. L. 109–8, title V, §501(b), Apr. 20, 2005, 119 Stat. 118.)

HISTORICAL AND REVISION NOTES

LEGISLATIVE STATEMENTS

Sections 301, 302, 303, and 304 are all modified in the House amendment to adopt an idea contained in sections 301 and 303 of the Senate amendment requiring a petition commencing a case to be filed with the bankruptcy court. The exception contained in section 301 of the Senate bill relating to cases filed under chapter 9 is deleted. Chapter 9 cases will be handled by a bankruptcy court as are other title 11 cases.

SENATE REPORT NO. 95–989

Section 301 specifies the manner in which a voluntary bankruptcy case is commenced. The debtor files a petition under this section under the particular operative chapter of the bankruptcy code under which he wishes to proceed. The filing of the petition constitutes an order for relief in the case under that chapter. The section contains no change from current law, except for the use of the phrase "order for relief" instead of "adjudication." The term adjudication is replaced by a less pejorative phrase in light of the clear power of Congress to permit voluntary bankruptcy without the necessity for an adjudication, as under the 1898 act [former title 11], which was adopted when voluntary bankruptcy was a concept not thoroughly tested.

AMENDMENTS

2005—Pub. L. 109–8 designated existing provisions as subsec. (a), struck out "The commencement of a voluntary case under a chapter of this title constitutes an order for relief under such chapter." at end, and added subsec. (b).

EFFECTIVE DATE OF 2005 AMENDMENT

Amendment by Pub. L. 109–8 effective 180 days after Apr. 20, 2005, and not applicable with respect to cases commenced under this title before such effective date, except as otherwise provided, see section 1501 of Pub. L. 109–8, set out as a note under section 101 of this title.

§ 302. Joint cases

(a) A joint case under a chapter of this title is commenced by the filing with the bankruptcy court of a single petition under such chapter by an individual that may be a debtor under such chapter and such individual's spouse. The commencement of a joint case under a chapter of this title constitutes an order for relief under such chapter.

(b) After the commencement of a joint case, the court shall determine the extent, if any, to which the debtors' estates shall be consolidated.

(Pub. L. 95–598, Nov. 6, 1978, 92 Stat. 2558.)

HISTORICAL AND REVISION NOTES

SENATE REPORT NO. 95–989

A joint case is a voluntary bankruptcy case concerning a wife and husband. Under current law, there is no explicit provision for joint cases. Very often, however, in the consumer debtor context, a husband and wife are jointly liable on their debts, and jointly hold most of their property. A joint case will facilitate consolidation of their estates, to the benefit of both the debtors and their creditors, because the cost of administration will be reduced, and there will be only one filing fee.

Section 302 specifies that a joint case is commenced by the filing of a petition under an appropriate chapter by an individual and that individual's spouse. Thus, one spouse cannot take the other into bankruptcy without the other's knowledge or consent. The filing of the petition constitutes an order for relief under the chapter selected.

Subsection (b) requires the court to determine the extent, if any, to which the estates of the two debtors will be consolidated; that is, assets and liabilities combined in a single pool to pay creditors. Factors that will be relevant in the court's determination include the extent of jointly held property and the amount of jointly-owned debts. The section, of course, is not license to consolidate in order to avoid other provisions of the title to the detriment of either the debtors or their creditors. It is designed mainly for ease of administration.

§303. Involuntary cases

(a) An involuntary case may be commenced only under chapter 7 or 11 of this title, and only against a person, except a farmer, family farmer, or a corporation that is not a moneyed, business, or commercial corporation, that may be a debtor under the chapter under which such case is commenced.

(b) An involuntary case against a person is commenced by the filing with the bankruptcy court of a petition under chapter 7 or 11 of this title—

(1) by three or more entities, each of which is either a holder of a claim against such person that is not contingent as to liability or the subject of a bona fide dispute as to liability or amount, or an indenture trustee representing such a holder, if such noncontingent, undisputed claims aggregate at least $10,000 more than the value of any lien on property of the debtor securing such claims held by the holders of such claims;

(2) if there are fewer than 12 such holders, excluding any employee or insider of such person and any transferee of a transfer that is voidable under section 544, 545, 547, 548, 549, or 724(a) of this title, by one or more of such holders that hold in the aggregate at least $10,000 of such claims;

(3) if such person is a partnership—

(A) by fewer than all of the general partners in such partnership; or

(B) if relief has been ordered under this title with respect to all of the general partners in such partnership, by a general partner in such partnership, the trustee of such a general partner, or a holder of a claim against such partnership; or

(4) by a foreign representative of the estate in a foreign proceeding concerning such person.

(c) After the filing of a petition under this section but before the case is dismissed or relief is ordered, a creditor holding an unsecured claim that is not contingent, other than a creditor filing under subsection (b) of this section, may join in the petition with the same effect as if such joining creditor were a petitioning creditor under subsection (b) of this section.

(d) The debtor, or a general partner in a partnership debtor that did not join in the petition, may file an answer to a petition under this section.

(e) After notice and a hearing, and for cause, the court may require the petitioners under this section to file a bond to indemnify the debtor for such amounts as the court may later allow under subsection (i) of this section.

(f) Notwithstanding section 363 of this title, except to the extent that the court orders otherwise, and until an order for relief in the case, any business of the debtor may continue to operate, and the debtor may continue to use, acquire, or dispose of property as if an involuntary case concerning the debtor had not been commenced.

(g) At any time after the commencement of an involuntary case under chapter 7 of this title but before an order for relief in the case, the court, on request of a party in interest, after notice to the debtor and a hearing, and if necessary to preserve the property of the estate or to prevent loss to the estate, may order the United States trustee to appoint an interim trustee under section 701 of this title to take possession of the property of the estate and to operate any business of the debtor. Before an order for relief, the debtor may regain possession of property in the possession of a trustee ordered appointed under this subsection if the debtor files such bond as the court requires, conditioned on the debtor's accounting for and delivering to the trustee, if there is an order for relief in the case, such property, or the value, as of the date the debtor regains possession, of such property.

(h) If the petition is not timely controverted, the court shall order relief against the debtor in an involuntary case under the chapter under which the petition was filed. Otherwise, after trial, the court shall order relief against the debtor in an involuntary case under the chapter under which the petition was filed, only if—

(1) the debtor is generally not paying such debtor's debts as such debts become due unless such debts are the subject of a bona fide dispute as to liability or amount; or

(2) within 120 days before the date of the filing of the petition, a custodian, other than a trustee, receiver, or agent appointed or authorized to take charge of less than substantially all of the property of the debtor for the

purpose of enforcing a lien against such property, was appointed or took possession.

(i) If the court dismisses a petition under this section other than on consent of all petitioners and the debtor, and if the debtor does not waive the right to judgment under this subsection, the court may grant judgment—

(1) against the petitioners and in favor of the debtor for—

(A) costs; or

(B) a reasonable attorney's fee; or

(2) against any petitioner that filed the petition in bad faith, for—

(A) any damages proximately caused by such filing; or

(B) punitive damages.

(j) Only after notice to all creditors and a hearing may the court dismiss a petition filed under this section—

(1) on the motion of a petitioner;

(2) on consent of all petitioners and the debtor; or

(3) for want of prosecution.

[(k) Repealed. Pub. L. 109–8, title VIII, §802(d)(2), Apr. 20, 2005, 119 Stat. 146.]

(*l*)(1) If—

(A) the petition under this section is false or contains any materially false, fictitious, or fraudulent statement;

(B) the debtor is an individual; and

(C) the court dismisses such petition,

the court, upon the motion of the debtor, shall seal all the records of the court relating to such petition, and all references to such petition.

(2) If the debtor is an individual and the court dismisses a petition under this section, the court may enter an order prohibiting all consumer reporting agencies (as defined in section 603(f) of the Fair Credit Reporting Act (15 U.S.C. 1681a(f))) from making any consumer report (as defined in section 603(d) of that Act) that contains any information relating to such petition or to the case commenced by the filing of such petition.

(3) Upon the expiration of the statute of limitations described in section 3282 of title 18, for a violation of section 152 or 157 of such title, the court, upon the motion of the debtor and for good cause, may expunge any records relating to a petition filed under this section.

(Pub. L. 95–598, Nov. 6, 1978, 92 Stat. 2559; Pub. L. 98–353, title III, §§426, 427, July 10, 1984, 98 Stat. 369; Pub. L. 99–554, title II, §§204, 254, 283(b), Oct. 27, 1986, 100 Stat. 3097, 3105, 3116; Pub. L. 103–394, title I, §108(b), Oct. 22, 1994, 108 Stat. 4112; Pub. L. 109–8, title III, §332(b), title VIII, §802(d)(2), title XII, §1234(a), Apr. 20, 2005, 119 Stat. 103, 146, 204.)

Historical and Revision Notes

LEGISLATIVE STATEMENTS

Section 303(b)(1) is modified to make clear that unsecured claims against the debtor must be determined by taking into account liens securing property held by third parties.

Section 303(b)(3) adopts a provision contained in the Senate amendment indicating that an involuntary petition may be commenced against a partnership by fewer than all of the general partners in such partnership. Such action may be taken by fewer than all of the general partners notwithstanding a contrary agreement between the partners or State or local law.

Section 303(h)(1) in the House amendment is a compromise of standards found in H.R. 8200 as passed by the House and the Senate amendment pertaining to the standards that must be met in order to obtain an order for relief in an involuntary case under title 11. The language specifies that the court will order such relief only if the debtor is generally not paying debtor's debts as they become due.

Section 303(h)(2) reflects a compromise pertaining to section 543 of title 11 relating to turnover of property by a custodian. It provides an alternative test to support an order for relief in an involuntary case. If a custodian, other than a trustee, receiver, or agent appointed or authorized to take charge of less than substantially all of the property of the debtor for the purpose of enforcing a lien against such property, was appointed or took possession within 120 days before the date of the filing of the petition, then the court may order relief in the involuntary case. The test under section 303(h)(2) differs from section 3a(5) of the Bankruptcy Act [section 21(a)(5) of former title 11], which requires an involuntary case to be commenced before the earlier of time such custodian was appointed or took possession. The test in section 303(h)(2) authorizes an order for relief to be entered in an involuntary case from the later date on which the custodian was appointed or took possession.

SENATE REPORT NO. 95–989

Section 303 governs the commencement of involuntary cases under title 11. An involuntary case may be commenced only under chapter 7, Liquidation, or chapter 11, Reorganization. Involuntary cases are not permitted for municipalities, because to do so may constitute an invasion of State sovereignty contrary to the 10th amendment, and would constitute bad policy, by permitting the fate of a municipality, governed by officials elected by the people of the municipality, to be determined by a small number of creditors of the municipality. Involuntary chapter 13 cases are not permitted either. To do so would constitute bad policy, because chapter 13 only works when there is a willing debtor that wants to repay his creditors. Short of involuntary servitude, it is difficult to keep a debtor working for his creditors when he does not want to pay them back. See chapter 3, supra.

The exceptions contained in current law that prohibit involuntary cases against farmers, ranchers and eleemosynary institutions are continued. Farmers and ranchers are excepted because of the cyclical nature of their business. One drought year or one year of low prices, as a result of which a farmer is temporarily unable to pay his creditors, should not subject him to involuntary bankruptcy. Eleemosynary institutions, such as churches, schools, and charitable organizations and foundations, likewise are exempt from involuntary bankruptcy.

The provisions for involuntary chapter 11 cases is a slight change from present law, based on the proposed consolidation of the reorganization chapters. Currently, involuntary cases are permitted under chapters X and XII [chapters 10 and 12 of former title 11] but not under chapter XI [chapter 11 of former title 11]. The consolidation requires a single rule for all kinds of reorganization proceedings. Because the assets of an insolvent debtor belong equitably to his creditors, the bill permits involuntary cases in order that creditors may realize on their assets through reorganization as well as through liquidation.

Subsection (b) of the section specifies who may file an involuntary petition. As under current law, if the debtor has more than 12 creditors, three creditors must join in the involuntary petition. The dollar amount limitation is changed from current law to $5,000. The new amount applies both to liquidation and reorganization cases in order that there not be an artificial difference between the two chapters that would provide an incentive for one or the other. Subsection (b)(1) makes explicit the right of an indenture trustee to be one of the three petitioning creditors on behalf of the creditors the trustee represents under the indenture. If all of the general partners in a partnership are in bankruptcy, then the trustee of a single general partner may file an involuntary petition against the partnership. Finally, a foreign representative may file an involuntary case concerning the debtor in the foreign proceeding, in order to administer assets in this country. This subsection is not intended to overrule Bankruptcy Rule 104(d), which places certain restrictions on the transfer of claims for the purpose of commencing an involuntary case. That Rule will be continued under section 405(d) of this bill.

Subsection (c) permits creditors other than the original petitioning creditors to join in the petition with the same effect as if the joining creditor had been one of the original petitioning creditors. Thus, if the claim of one of the original petitioning creditors is disallowed, the case will not be dismissed for want of three creditors or want of $5,000 in petitioning claims if the joining creditor suffices to fulfill the statutory requirements.

Subsection (d) permits the debtor to file an answer to an involuntary petition. The subsection also permits a general partner in a partnership debtor to answer an involuntary petition against the partnership if he did not join in the petition. Thus, a partnership petition by less than all of the general partners is treated as an involuntary, not a voluntary, petition.

The court may, under subsection (e), require the petitioners to file a bond to indemnify the debtor for such amounts as the court may later allow under subsection (i). Subsection (i) provides for costs, attorneys fees, and damages in certain circumstances. The bonding requirement will discourage frivolous petitions as well as spiteful petitions based on a desire to embarrass the debtor (who may be a competitor of a petitioning creditor) or to put the debtor out of business without good cause. An involuntary petition may put a debtor out of business even if it is without foundation and is later dismissed.

Subsection (f) is both a clarification and a change from existing law. It permits the debtor to continue to operate any business of the debtor and to dispose of property as if the case had not been commenced. The court is permitted, however, to control the debtor's powers under this subsection by appropriate orders, such as where there is a fear that the debtor may attempt to abscond with assets, dispose of them at less than their fair value, or dismantle his business, all to the detriment of the debtor's creditors.

The court may also, under subsection (g), appoint an interim trustee to take possession of the debtor's property and to operate any business of the debtor, pending trial on the involuntary petition. The court may make such an order only on the request of a party in interest, and after notice to the debtor and a hearing. There must be a showing that a trustee is necessary to preserve the property of the estate or to prevent loss to the estate. The debtor may regain possession by posting a sufficient bond.

Subsection (h) provides the standard for an order for relief on an involuntary petition. If the petition is not timely controverted (the Rules of Bankruptcy Procedure will fix time limits), the court orders relief after a trial, only if the debtor is generally unable to pay its debts as they mature, or if the debtor has failed to pay a major portion of his debts as they become due, or if a custodian was appointed during the 90-day period preceding the filing of the petition. The first two tests are variations of the equity insolvency test. They represent the most significant departure from present law concerning the grounds for involuntary bankruptcy, which requires an act of bankruptcy. Proof of the commission of an act of bankruptcy has frequently required a showing that the debtor was insolvent on a "balance-sheet" test when the act was committed. This bill abolishes the concept of acts of bankruptcy.

The equity insolvency test has been in equity jurisprudence for hundreds of years, and though it is new in the bankruptcy context (except in chapter X [chapter 10 of former title 11]), the bankruptcy courts should have no difficulty in applying it. The third test, appointment of a custodian within ninety days before the petition, is provided for simplicity. It is not a partial re-enactment of acts of bankruptcy. If a custodian of all or substantially all of the property of the debtor has been appointed, this paragraph creates an irrebuttable presumption that the debtor is unable to pay its debts as they mature. Moreover, once a proceeding to liquidate assets has been commenced, the debtor's creditors have an absolute right to have the liquidation (or reorganization) proceed in the bankruptcy court and under the bankruptcy laws with all of the appropriate creditor and debtor protections that those laws provide. Ninety days gives creditors ample time in which to seek bankruptcy liquidation after the appointment of a custodian. If they wait beyond the ninety day period, they are not precluded from filing an involuntary petition. They are simply required to prove equity insolvency rather than the more easily provable custodian test.

Subsection (i) permits the court to award costs, reasonable attorney's fees, or damages if an involuntary petition is dismissed other than by consent of all petitioning creditors and the debtor. The damages that the court may award are those that may be caused by the taking of possession of the debtor's property under subsection (g) or section 1104 of the bankruptcy code. In addition, if a petitioning creditor filed the petition in bad faith, the court may award the debtor any damages proximately caused by the filing of the petition. These damages may include such items as loss of business during and after the pendency of the case, and so on. "Or" is not exclusive in this paragraph. The court may grant any or all of the damages provided for under the provision. Dismissal in the best interests of credits under section 305(a)(1) would not give rise to a damages claim.

Under subsection (j), the court may dismiss the petition by consent only after giving notice to all creditors. The purpose of the subsection is to prevent collusive settlements among the debtor and the petitioning creditors while other creditors, that wish to see relief ordered with respect to the debtor but that did not participate in the case, are left without sufficient protection.

Subsection (k) governs involuntary cases against foreign banks that are not engaged in business in the United States but that have assets located here. The subsection prevents a foreign bank from being placed into bankruptcy in this country unless a foreign proceeding against the bank is pending. The special protection afforded by this section is needed to prevent creditors from effectively closing down a foreign bank by the commencement of an involuntary bankruptcy case in this country unless that bank is involved in a proceeding under foreign law. An involuntary case commenced under this subsection gives the foreign representative an alternative to commencing a case ancillary to a foreign proceeding under section 304.

AMENDMENTS

2005—Subsec. (b)(1). Pub. L. 109–8, §1234(a)(1), inserted "as to liability or amount" after "bona fide dispute" and substituted "if such noncontingent, undisputed claims" for "if such claims".

Subsec. (h)(1). Pub. L. 109–8, §1234(a)(2), inserted "as to liability or amount" before semicolon.

Subsec. (k). Pub. L. 109–8, §802(d)(2), struck out subsec. (k) which read as follows: "Notwithstanding subsection (a) of this section, an involuntary case may be commenced against a foreign bank that is not engaged in such business in the United States only under chapter 7 of this title and only if a foreign proceeding concerning such bank is pending."

Subsec. (*l*). Pub. L. 109–8, §332(b), added subsec. (*l*).

1994—Subsec. (b). Pub. L. 103–394 substituted "$10,000" for "$5,000" in pars. (1) and (2).

1986—Subsec. (a). Pub. L. 99–554, §254, inserted reference to family farmer.

Subsec. (b). Pub. L. 99–554, §283(b)(1), substituted "subject of" for "subject on".

Subsec. (g). Pub. L. 99–554, §204(1), substituted "may order the United States trustee to appoint" for "may appoint".

Subsec. (h)(1). Pub. L. 99–554, §283(b)(2), substituted "are the" for "that are the".

Subsec. (i)(1). Pub. L. 99–554, §204(2), inserted "or" at end of subpar. (A) and struck out subpar. (C) which read as follows: "any damages proximately caused by the taking of possession of the debtor's property by a trustee appointed under subsection (g) of this section or section 1104 of this title; or".

1984—Subsec. (b). Pub. L. 98–353, §426(a), inserted "against a person" after "involuntary case".

Subsec. (b)(1). Pub. L. 98–353, §426(b)(1), inserted "or the subject on a bona fide dispute,".

Subsec. (h)(1). Pub. L. 98–353, §426(b)(2), inserted "unless such debts that are the subject of a bona fide dispute".

Subsec. (j)(2). Pub. L. 98–353, §427, substituted "debtor" for "debtors".

EFFECTIVE DATE OF 2005 AMENDMENT

Pub. L. 109–8, title XII, §1234(b), Apr. 20, 2005, 119 Stat. 204, provided that: "This section [amending this section] and the amendments made by this section shall take effect on the date of the enactment of this Act [Apr. 20, 2005] and shall apply with respect to cases commenced under title 11 of the United States Code before, on, and after such date."

Amendment by sections 332(b) and 802(d)(2) of Pub. L. 109–8 effective 180 days after Apr. 20, 2005, and not applicable with respect to cases commenced under this title before such effective date, except as otherwise provided, see section 1501 of Pub. L. 109–8, set out as a note under section 101 of this title.

EFFECTIVE DATE OF 1994 AMENDMENT

Amendment by Pub. L. 103–394 effective Oct. 22, 1994, and not applicable with respect to cases commenced under this title before Oct. 22, 1994, see section 702 of Pub. L. 103–394, set out as a note under section 101 of this title.

EFFECTIVE DATE OF 1986 AMENDMENT

Effective date and applicability of amendment by section 204 of Pub. L. 99–554 dependent upon the judicial district involved, see section 302(d), (e) of Pub. L. 99–554, set out as a note under section 581 of Title 28, Judiciary and Judicial Procedure.

Amendment by section 254 of Pub. L. 99–554 effective 30 days after Oct. 27, 1986, but not applicable to cases commenced under this title before that date, see section 302(a), (c)(1) of Pub. L. 99–554.

Amendment by section 283 of Pub. L. 99–554 effective 30 days after Oct. 27, 1986, see section 302(a) of Pub. L. 99–554.

EFFECTIVE DATE OF 1984 AMENDMENT

Amendment by sections 426(a) and 427 of Pub. L. 98–353 effective with respect to cases filed 90 days after July 10, 1984, and amendment by section 426(b) of Pub. L. 98–353 effective July 10, 1984, see section 552(a), (b) of Pub. L. 98–353, set out as a note under section 101 of this title.

ADJUSTMENT OF DOLLAR AMOUNTS

For adjustment of dollar amounts specified in subsec. (b)(1), (2) of this section by the Judicial Conference of the United States, see note set out under section 104 of this title.

[§304. Repealed. Pub. L. 109–8, title VIII, §802(d)(3), Apr. 20, 2005, 119 Stat. 146]

Section, Pub. L. 95–598, Nov. 6, 1978, 92 Stat. 2560, related to cases ancillary to foreign proceedings.

EFFECTIVE DATE OF REPEAL

Repeal effective 180 days after Apr. 20, 2005, and not applicable with respect to cases commenced under this title before such effective date, except as otherwise provided, see section 1501 of Pub. L. 109–8, set out as an Effective Date of 2005 Amendment note under section 101 of this title.

§305. Abstention

(a) The court, after notice and a hearing, may dismiss a case under this title, or may suspend all proceedings in a case under this title, at any time if—

(1) the interests of creditors and the debtor would be better served by such dismissal or suspension; or

(2)(A) a petition under section 1515 for recognition of a foreign proceeding has been granted; and

(B) the purposes of chapter 15 of this title would be best served by such dismissal or suspension.

(b) A foreign representative may seek dismissal or suspension under subsection (a)(2) of this section.

(c) An order under subsection (a) of this section dismissing a case or suspending all proceedings in a case, or a decision not so to dismiss or suspend, is not reviewable by appeal or otherwise by the court of appeals under section 158(d), 1291, or 1292 of title 28 or by the Supreme Court of the United States under section 1254 of title 28.

(Pub. L. 95–598, Nov. 6, 1978, 92 Stat. 2561; Pub. L. 101–650, title III, §309(a), Dec. 1, 1990, 104 Stat. 5113; Pub. L. 102–198, §5, Dec. 9, 1991, 105 Stat. 1623; Pub. L. 109–8, title VIII, §802(d)(6), Apr. 20, 2005, 119 Stat. 146.)

HISTORICAL AND REVISION NOTES

SENATE REPORT NO. 95–989

A principle of the common law requires a court with jurisdiction over a particular matter to take jurisdiction. This section recognizes that there are cases in which it would be appropriate for the court to decline jurisdiction. Abstention under this section, however, is of jurisdiction over the entire case. Abstention from jurisdiction over a particular proceeding in a case is governed by proposed 28 U.S.C. 1471(c). Thus, the court is permitted, if the interests of creditors and the debtor would be better served by dismissal of the case or suspension of all proceedings in the case, to so order. The court may dismiss or suspend under the first paragraph, for example, if an arrangement is being worked out by creditors and the debtor out of court, there is no prejudice to the results of creditors in that arrangement, and an involuntary case has been commenced by a few recalcitrant creditors to provide a basis for future threats to extract full payment. The less expensive out-of-court workout may better serve the interests in the case. Likewise, if there is pending a foreign proceeding concerning the debtor and the factors specified in proposed 11 U.S.C. 304(c) warrant dismissal or suspension, the court may so act.

Subsection (b) gives a foreign representative authority to appear in the bankruptcy court to request dismissal or suspension. Subsection (c) makes the dismissal or suspension order nonreviewable by appeal or otherwise. The bankruptcy court, based on its experience and discretion is vested with the power of decision.

AMENDMENTS

2005—Subsec. (a)(2). Pub. L. 109–8 added par. (2) and struck out former par. (2) which read as follows:

"(2)(A) there is pending a foreign proceeding; and

"(B) the factors specified in section 304(c) of this title warrant such dismissal or suspension."

1991—Subsec. (c). Pub. L. 102-198 substituted "title 28" for "this title" in two places.

1990—Subsec. (c). Pub. L. 101-650 inserted before period at end "by the court of appeals under section 158(d), 1291, or 1292 of this title or by the Supreme Court of the United States under section 1254 of this title".

EFFECTIVE DATE OF 2005 AMENDMENT

Amendment by Pub. L. 109-8 effective 180 days after Apr. 20, 2005, and not applicable with respect to cases commenced under this title before such effective date, except as otherwise provided, see section 1501 of Pub. L. 109-8, set out as a note under section 101 of this title.

§ 306. Limited appearance

An appearance in a bankruptcy court by a foreign representative in connection with a petition or request under section 303 or 305 of this title does not submit such foreign representative to the jurisdiction of any court in the United States for any other purpose, but the bankruptcy court may condition any order under section 303 or 305 of this title on compliance by such foreign representative with the orders of such bankruptcy court.

(Pub. L. 95-598, Nov. 6, 1978, 92 Stat. 2561; Pub. L. 109-8, title VIII, § 802(d)(5), Apr. 20, 2005, 119 Stat. 146.)

HISTORICAL AND REVISION NOTES

SENATE REPORT NO. 95-989

Section 306 permits a foreign representative that is seeking dismissal or suspension under section 305 of an ancillary case or that is appearing in connection with a petition under section 303 or 304 to appear without subjecting himself to the jurisdiction of any other court in the United States, including State courts. The protection is necessary to allow the foreign representative to present his case and the case of the foreign estate, without waiving the normal jurisdictional rules of the foreign country. That is, creditors in this country will still have to seek redress against the foreign estate according to the host country's jurisdictional rules. Any other result would permit local creditors to obtain unfair advantage by filing an involuntary case, thus requiring the foreign representative to appear, and then obtaining local jurisdiction over the representative in connection with his appearance in this country. That kind of bankruptcy law would legalize an ambush technique that has frequently been rejected by the common law in other contexts.

However, the bankruptcy court is permitted under section 306 to condition any relief under section 303, 304, or 305 on the compliance by the foreign representative with the orders of the bankruptcy court. The last provision is not carte blanche to the bankruptcy court to require the foreign representative to submit to jurisdiction in other courts contrary to the general policy of the section. It is designed to enable the bankruptcy court to enforce its own orders that are necessary to the appropriate relief granted under section 303, 304, or 305.

AMENDMENTS

2005—Pub. L. 109-8 struck out ", 304," after "section 303" in two places.

EFFECTIVE DATE OF 2005 AMENDMENT

Amendment by Pub. L. 109-8 effective 180 days after Apr. 20, 2005, and not applicable with respect to cases commenced under this title before such effective date, except as otherwise provided, see section 1501 of Pub. L. 109-8, set out as a note under section 101 of this title.

§ 307. United States trustee

The United States trustee may raise and may appear and be heard on any issue in any case or proceeding under this title but may not file a plan pursuant to section 1121(c) of this title.

(Added Pub. L. 99-554, title II, § 205(a), Oct. 27, 1986, 100 Stat. 3098.)

EFFECTIVE DATE

Effective date and applicability of section dependent upon the judicial district involved, see section 302(d), (e) of Pub. L. 99-554, set out as a note under section 581 of Title 28, Judiciary and Judicial Procedure.

STANDING AND AUTHORITY OF BANKRUPTCY ADMINISTRATOR

Pub. L. 101-650, title III, § 317(b), Dec. 1, 1990, 104 Stat. 5115, provided that: "A bankruptcy administrator may raise and may appear and be heard on any issue in any case under title 11, United States Code, but may not file a plan pursuant to section 1121(c) of such title."

§ 308. Debtor reporting requirements

(a) For purposes of this section, the term "profitability" means, with respect to a debtor, the amount of money that the debtor has earned or lost during current and recent fiscal periods.

(b) A small business debtor shall file periodic financial and other reports containing information including—

(1) the debtor's profitability;

(2) reasonable approximations of the debtor's projected cash receipts and cash disbursements over a reasonable period;

(3) comparisons of actual cash receipts and disbursements with projections in prior reports;

(4)(A) whether the debtor is—

(i) in compliance in all material respects with postpetition requirements imposed by this title and the Federal Rules of Bankruptcy Procedure; and

(ii) timely filing tax returns and other required government filings and paying taxes and other administrative expenses when due;

(B) if the debtor is not in compliance with the requirements referred to in subparagraph (A)(i) or filing tax returns and other required government filings and making the payments referred to in subparagraph (A)(ii), what the failures are and how, at what cost, and when the debtor intends to remedy such failures; and

(C) such other matters as are in the best interests of the debtor and creditors, and in the public interest in fair and efficient procedures under chapter 11 of this title.

(Added Pub. L. 109-8, title IV, § 434(a)(1), Apr. 20, 2005, 119 Stat. 111.)

REFERENCES IN TEXT

The Federal Rules of Bankruptcy Procedure, referred to in subsec. (b)(4)(A)(i), are set out in the Appendix to this title.

EFFECTIVE DATE

Pub. L. 109-8, title IV, § 434(b), Apr. 20, 2005, 119 Stat. 111, provided that: "The amendments made by subsection (a) [enacting this section] shall take effect 60 days after the date on which rules are prescribed under section 2075 of title 28, United States Code, to establish forms to be used to comply with section 308 of title 11, United States Code, as added by subsection (a) [See Bankruptcy Form No. 25C, eff. Dec. 1, 2008, set out in the Appendix to this title]."

SUBCHAPTER II—OFFICERS

§ 321. Eligibility to serve as trustee

(a) A person may serve as trustee in a case under this title only if such person is—

(1) an individual that is competent to perform the duties of trustee and, in a case under chapter 7, 12, or 13 of this title, resides or has an office in the judicial district within which the case is pending, or in any judicial district adjacent to such district; or

(2) a corporation authorized by such corporation's charter or bylaws to act as trustee, and, in a case under chapter 7, 12, or 13 of this title, having an office in at least one of such districts.

(b) A person that has served as an examiner in the case may not serve as trustee in the case.

(c) The United States trustee for the judicial district in which the case is pending is eligible to serve as trustee in the case if necessary.

(Pub. L. 95–598, Nov. 6, 1978, 92 Stat. 2561; Pub. L. 98–353, title III, § 428, July 10, 1984, 98 Stat. 369; Pub. L. 99–554, title II, §§ 206, 257(c), Oct. 27, 1986, 100 Stat. 3098, 3114.)

HISTORICAL AND REVISION NOTES

LEGISLATIVE STATEMENTS

Section 321 indicates that an examiner may not serve as a trustee in the case.

SENATE REPORT NO. 95–989

Section 321 is adapted from current Bankruptcy Act § 45 [section 73 of former title 11] and Bankruptcy Rule 209. Subsection (a) specifies that an individual may serve as trustee in a bankruptcy case only if he is competent to perform the duties of trustee and resides or has an office in the judicial district within which the case is pending, or in an adjacent judicial district. A corporation must be authorized by its charter or bylaws to act as trustee, and, for chapter 7 or 13 cases, must have an office in any of the above mentioned judicial districts.

AMENDMENTS

1986—Subsec. (a). Pub. L. 99–554, § 257(c), inserted reference to chapter 12 in two places.

Subsec. (c). Pub. L. 99–554, § 206, added subsec. (c).

1984—Subsec. (b). Pub. L. 98–353 substituted "the case" for "a case" after "an examiner in".

EFFECTIVE DATE OF 1986 AMENDMENT

Effective date and applicability of amendment by section 206 of Pub. L. 99–554 dependent upon the judicial district involved, see section 302(d), (e) of Pub. L. 99–554, set out as a note under section 581 of Title 28, Judiciary and Judicial Procedure.

Amendment by section 257 of Pub. L. 99–554 effective 30 days after Oct. 27, 1986, but not applicable to cases commenced under this title before that date, see section 302(a), (c)(1) of Pub. L. 99–554.

EFFECTIVE DATE OF 1984 AMENDMENT

Amendment by Pub. L. 98–353 effective with respect to cases filed 90 days after July 10, 1984, see section 552(a) of Pub. L. 98–353, set out as a note under section 101 of this title.

§ 322. Qualification of trustee

(a) Except as provided in subsection (b)(1), a person selected under section 701, 702, 703, 1104, 1163, 1202, or 1302 of this title to serve as trustee in a case under this title qualifies if before seven days after such selection, and before beginning official duties, such person has filed with the court a bond in favor of the United States conditioned on the faithful performance of such official duties.

(b)(1) The United States trustee qualifies wherever such trustee serves as trustee in a case under this title.

(2) The United States trustee shall determine—

(A) the amount of a bond required to be filed under subsection (a) of this section; and

(B) the sufficiency of the surety on such bond.

(c) A trustee is not liable personally or on such trustee's bond in favor of the United States for any penalty or forfeiture incurred by the debtor.

(d) A proceeding on a trustee's bond may not be commenced after two years after the date on which such trustee was discharged.

(Pub. L. 95–598, Nov. 6, 1978, 92 Stat. 2562; Pub. L. 98–353, title III, § 429, July 10, 1984, 98 Stat. 369; Pub. L. 99–554, title II, §§ 207, 257(d), Oct. 27, 1986, 100 Stat. 3098, 3114; Pub. L. 103–394, title V, § 501(d)(3), Oct. 22, 1994, 108 Stat. 4143; Pub. L. 111–16, § 2(2), May 7, 2009, 123 Stat. 1607.)

HISTORICAL AND REVISION NOTES

LEGISLATIVE STATEMENTS

Section 322(a) is modified to include a trustee serving in a railroad reorganization under subchapter IV of chapter 11.

SENATE REPORT NO. 95–989

A trustee qualifies in a case by filing, within five days after selection, a bond in favor of the United States, conditioned on the faithful performance of his official duties. This section is derived from the Bankruptcy Act section 50b [section 78(b) of former title 11]. The court is required to determine the amount of the bond and the sufficiency of the surety on the bond. Subsection (c), derived from Bankruptcy Act section 50i [section 78(i) of former title 11], relieves the trustee from personal liability and from liability on his bond for any penalty or forfeiture incurred by the debtor. Subsection (d), derived from section 50m [section 78(m) of former title 11], fixes a two-year statute of limitations on any action on a trustee's bond. Finally, subsection (e) dispenses with the bonding requirement for the United States trustee.

AMENDMENTS

2009—Subsec. (a). Pub. L. 111–16 substituted "seven days" for "five days".

1994—Subsec. (a). Pub. L. 103–394 substituted "1202, or 1302" for "1302, or 1202".

1986—Subsec. (a). Pub. L. 99–554, § 257(d), inserted reference to section 1202 of this title.

Pub. L. 99–554, § 207(1), substituted "Except as provided in subsection (b)(1), a person" for "A person".

Subsec. (b). Pub. L. 99–554, § 207(2), amended subsec. (b) generally, adding par. (1), designating existing provisions as par. (2), substituting "The United States trustee" for "The court", "(A) the amount" for "(1) the amount", and "(B) the sufficiency" for "(2) the sufficiency".

1984—Subsec. (b)(1). Pub. L. 98–353 inserted "required to be".

EFFECTIVE DATE OF 2009 AMENDMENT

Amendment by Pub. L. 111–16 effective Dec. 1, 2009, see section 7 of Pub. L. 111–16, set out as a note under section 109 of this title.

EFFECTIVE DATE OF 1994 AMENDMENT

Amendment by Pub. L. 103–394 effective Oct. 22, 1994, and not applicable with respect to cases commenced under this title before Oct. 22, 1994, see section 702 of Pub. L. 103–394, set out as a note under section 101 of this title.

EFFECTIVE DATE OF 1986 AMENDMENT

Effective date and applicability of amendment by section 207 of Pub. L. 99–554 dependent upon the judicial district involved, see section 302(d), (e) of Pub. L. 99–554, set out as a note under section 581 of Title 28, Judiciary and Judicial Procedure.

Amendment by section 257 of Pub. L. 99–554 effective 30 days after Oct. 27, 1986, but not applicable to cases commenced under this title before that date, see section 302(a), (c)(1) of Pub. L. 99–554.

EFFECTIVE DATE OF 1984 AMENDMENT

Amendment by Pub. L. 98–353 effective with respect to cases filed 90 days after July 10, 1984, see section 552(a) of Pub. L. 98–353, set out as a note under section 101 of this title.

§ 323. Role and capacity of trustee

(a) The trustee in a case under this title is the representative of the estate.

(b) The trustee in a case under this title has capacity to sue and be sued.

(Pub. L. 95–598, Nov. 6, 1978, 92 Stat. 2562.)

HISTORICAL AND REVISION NOTES

SENATE REPORT NO. 95–989

Subsection (a) of this section makes the trustee the representative of the estate. Subsection (b) grants the trustee the capacity to sue and to be sued. If the debtor remains in possession in a chapter 11 case, section 1107 gives the debtor in possession these rights of the trustee: the debtor in possession becomes the representative of the estate, and may sue and be sued. The same applies in a chapter 13 case.

§ 324. Removal of trustee or examiner

(a) The court, after notice and a hearing, may remove a trustee, other than the United States trustee, or an examiner, for cause.

(b) Whenever the court removes a trustee or examiner under subsection (a) in a case under this title, such trustee or examiner shall thereby be removed in all other cases under this title in which such trustee or examiner is then serving unless the court orders otherwise.

(Pub. L. 95–598, Nov. 6, 1978, 92 Stat. 2562; Pub. L. 99–554, title II, §208, Oct. 27, 1986, 100 Stat. 3098.)

HISTORICAL AND REVISION NOTES

SENATE REPORT NO. 95–989

This section permits the court, after notice and a hearing, to remove a trustee for cause.

AMENDMENTS

1986—Pub. L. 99–554 amended section generally, designating existing provisions as subsec. (a), substituting "a trustee, other than the United States trustee, or an examiner" for "a trustee or an examiner", and adding subsec. (b).

EFFECTIVE DATE OF 1986 AMENDMENT

Effective date and applicability of amendment by Pub. L. 99–554 dependent upon the judicial district involved, see section 302(d), (e) of Pub. L. 99–554, set out as a note under section 581 of Title 28, Judiciary and Judicial Procedure.

§ 325. Effect of vacancy

A vacancy in the office of trustee during a case does not abate any pending action or proceeding, and the successor trustee shall be substituted as a party in such action or proceeding.

(Pub. L. 95–598, Nov. 6, 1978, 92 Stat. 2562.)

HISTORICAL AND REVISION NOTES

SENATE REPORT NO. 95–989

Section 325, derived from Bankruptcy Act section 46 [section 74 of former title 11] and Bankruptcy Rule 221(b), specifies that a vacancy in the office of trustee during a case does not abate any pending action or proceeding. The successor trustee, when selected and qualified, is substituted as a party in any pending action or proceeding.

§ 326. Limitation on compensation of trustee

(a) In a case under chapter 7 or 11, the court may allow reasonable compensation under section 330 of this title of the trustee for the trustee's services, payable after the trustee renders such services, not to exceed 25 percent on the first $5,000 or less, 10 percent on any amount in excess of $5,000 but not in excess of $50,000, 5 percent on any amount in excess of $50,000 but not in excess of $1,000,000, and reasonable compensation not to exceed 3 percent of such moneys in excess of $1,000,000, upon all moneys disbursed or turned over in the case by the trustee to parties in interest, excluding the debtor, but including holders of secured claims.

(b) In a case under chapter 12 or 13 of this title, the court may not allow compensation for services or reimbursement of expenses of the United States trustee or of a standing trustee appointed under section 586(b) of title 28, but may allow reasonable compensation under section 330 of this title of a trustee appointed under section 1202(a) or 1302(a) of this title for the trustee's services, payable after the trustee renders such services, not to exceed five percent upon all payments under the plan.

(c) If more than one person serves as trustee in the case, the aggregate compensation of such persons for such service may not exceed the maximum compensation prescribed for a single trustee by subsection (a) or (b) of this section, as the case may be.

(d) The court may deny allowance of compensation for services or reimbursement of expenses of the trustee if the trustee failed to make diligent inquiry into facts that would permit denial of allowance under section 328(c) of this title or, with knowledge of such facts, employed a professional person under section 327 of this title.

(Pub. L. 95–598, Nov. 6, 1978, 92 Stat. 2562; Pub. L. 98–353, title III, §430(a), (b), July 10, 1984, 98 Stat. 369; Pub. L. 99–554, title II, §209, Oct. 27, 1986, 100 Stat. 3098; Pub. L. 103–394, title I, §107, Oct. 22, 1994, 108 Stat. 4111.)

HISTORICAL AND REVISION NOTES

LEGISLATIVE STATEMENTS

Section 326(a) of the House amendment modifies a provision as contained in H.R. 8200 as passed by the House. The percentage limitation on the fees of a trustee contained in the House bill is retained, but no additional percentage is specified for cases in which a trustee operates the business of the debtor. Section 326(b) of the Senate amendment is deleted as an unnecessary restatement of the limitation contained in section 326(a) as modified. The provision contained in section 326(a) of the Senate amendment authorizing a trustee to receive a maximum fee of $150 regardless of the availability of assets in the estate is deleted. It will not be necessary in view of the increase in section 326(a) and the doubling of the minimum fee as provided in section 330(b).

Section 326(b) of the House amendment derives from section 326(c) of H.R. 8200 as passed by the House. It is a conforming amendment to indicate a change with respect to the selection of a trustee in a chapter 13 case under section 1302(a) of title 11.

SENATE REPORT NO. 95-989

This section is derived in part from section 48c of the Bankruptcy Act [section 76(c) of former title 11]. It must be emphasized that this section does not authorize compensation of trustees. This section simply fixes the maximum compensation of a trustee. Proposed 11 U.S.C. 330 authorizes and fixes the standard of compensation. Under section 48c of current law, the maximum limits have tended to become minimums in many cases. This section is not intended to be so interpreted. The limits in this section, together with the limitations found in section 330, are to be applied as outer limits, and not as grants or entitlements to the maximum fees specified.

The maximum fee schedule is derived from section 48c(1) of the present act [section 76(c)(1) of former title 11], but with a change relating to the bases on which the percentage maxima are computed. The maximum fee schedule is based on decreasing percentages of increasing amounts. The amounts are the amounts of money distributed by the trustee to parties in interest, excluding the debtor, but including secured creditors. These amounts were last amended in 1952. Since then, the cost of living has approximately doubled. Thus, the bases were doubled.

It should be noted that the bases on which the maximum fee is computed includes moneys turned over to secured creditors, to cover the situation where the trustee liquidates property subject to a lien and distributes the proceeds. It does not cover cases in which the trustee simply turns over the property to the secured creditor, nor where the trustee abandons the property and the secured creditor is permitted to foreclose. The provision is also subject to the rights of the secured creditor generally under proposed section 506, especially 506(c). The $150 discretionary fee provision of current law is retained.

Subsection (b) of this section entitles an operating trustee to a reasonable fee, without any limitation based on the maximum provided for a liquidating trustee as in current law, Bankruptcy Act §48c(2) [section 76(c)(2) of former title 11].

Subsection (c) [enacted as (b)] permits a maximum fee of five percent on all payments to creditors under a chapter 13 plan to the trustee appointed in the case.

Subsection (d) [enacted as (c)] provides a limitation not found in current law. Even if more than one trustee serves in the case, the maximum fee payable to all trustees does not change. For example, if an interim trustee is appointed and an elected trustee replaces him, the combined total of the fees payable to the interim trustee and the permanent trustee may not exceed the amount specified in this section. Under current law, very often a receiver receives a full fee and a subsequent trustee also receives a full fee. The resultant "double-dipping", especially in cases in which the receiver and the trustee are the same individual, is detrimental to the interests of creditors, by needlessly increasing the cost of administering bankruptcy estates.

Subsection (e) [enacted as (d)] permits the court to deny compensation to a trustee if the trustee has been derelict in his duty by employing counsel, who is not disinterested.

AMENDMENTS

1994—Subsec. (a). Pub. L. 103-394 substituted "25 percent on the first $5,000 or less, 10 percent on any amount in excess of $5,000 but not in excess of $50,000, 5 percent on any amount in excess of $50,000 but not in excess of $1,000,000, and reasonable compensation not to exceed 3 percent of such moneys in excess of $1,000,000" for "fifteen percent on the first $1,000 or less, six percent on any amount in excess of $1,000 but not in excess of $3,000, and three percent on any amount in excess of $3,000".

1986—Subsec. (b). Pub. L. 99-554 amended subsec. (b) generally, substituting "under chapter 12 or 13 of this title" for "under chapter 13 of this title", "expenses of the United States trustee or of a standing trustee appointed under section 586(b) of title 28" for "expenses of a standing trustee appointed under section 1302(d) of this title", and "under section 1202(a) or 1302(a) of this title" for "under section 1302(a) of this title".

1984—Subsec. (a). Pub. L. 98-353, §430(a), substituted "and three percent on any amount in excess of $3000" for "three percent on any amount in excess of $3,000 but not in excess of $20,000, two percent on any amount in excess of $20,000 but not in excess of $50,000, and one percent on any amount in excess of $50,000".

Subsec. (d). Pub. L. 98-353, §430(b), amended subsec. (d) generally. Prior to amendment, subsec. (d) read as follows: "The court may deny allowance of compensation for services and reimbursement of expenses of the trustee if the trustee—

"(1) failed to make diligent inquiry into facts that would permit denial of allowance under section 328(c) of this title; or

"(2) with knowledge of such facts, employed a professional person under section 327 of this title."

EFFECTIVE DATE OF 1994 AMENDMENT

Amendment by Pub. L. 103-394 effective Oct. 22, 1994, and not applicable with respect to cases commenced under this title before Oct. 22, 1994, see section 702 of Pub. L. 103-394, set out as a note under section 101 of this title.

EFFECTIVE DATE OF 1986 AMENDMENT

Effective date and applicability of amendment by Pub. L. 99-554 dependent upon the judicial district involved, see section 302(d), (e) of Pub. L. 99-554, set out as a note under section 581 of Title 28, Judiciary and Judicial Procedure.

EFFECTIVE DATE OF 1984 AMENDMENT

Amendment by Pub. L. 98-353 effective with respect to cases filed 90 days after July 10, 1984, see section 552(a) of Pub. L. 98-353, set out as a note under section 101 of this title.

REFERENCES IN SUBSECTION (b) TEMPORARILY DEEMED TO INCLUDE ADDITIONAL REFERENCES

Until the amendments made by subtitle A (§§201 to 231) of title II of Pub. L. 99-554 become effective in a district and apply to a case, for purposes of such case any reference in subsec. (b) of this section—

(1) to chapter 13 of this title is deemed to be a reference to chapter 12 or 13 of this title,

(2) to section 1302(d) of this title is deemed to be a reference to section 1302(d) of this title or section 586(b) of Title 28, Judiciary and Judicial Procedure, and

(3) to section 1302(a) of this title is deemed to be a reference to section 1202(a) or 1302(a) of this title,

see section 302(c)(3)(A), (d), (e) of Pub. L. 99-554, set out as an Effective Date note under section 581 of Title 28.

§ 327. Employment of professional persons

(a) Except as otherwise provided in this section, the trustee, with the court's approval, may employ one or more attorneys, accountants, appraisers, auctioneers, or other professional persons, that do not hold or represent an interest adverse to the estate, and that are disinterested persons, to represent or assist the trustee in carrying out the trustee's duties under this title.

(b) If the trustee is authorized to operate the business of the debtor under section 721, 1202, or 1108 of this title, and if the debtor has regularly employed attorneys, accountants, or other professional persons on salary, the trustee may retain or replace such professional persons if necessary in the operation of such business.

(c) In a case under chapter 7, 12, or 11 of this title, a person is not disqualified for employment under this section solely because of such person's employment by or representation of a creditor, unless there is objection by another creditor or the United States trustee, in which case the court shall disapprove such employment if there is an actual conflict of interest.

(d) The court may authorize the trustee to act as attorney or accountant for the estate if such authorization is in the best interest of the estate.

(e) The trustee, with the court's approval, may employ, for a specified special purpose, other than to represent the trustee in conducting the case, an attorney that has represented the debtor, if in the best interest of the estate, and if such attorney does not represent or hold any interest adverse to the debtor or to the estate with respect to the matter on which such attorney is to be employed.

(f) The trustee may not employ a person that has served as an examiner in the case.

(Pub. L. 95-598, Nov. 6, 1978, 92 Stat. 2563; Pub. L. 98-353, title III, §430(c), July 10, 1984, 98 Stat. 370; Pub. L. 99-554, title II, §§210, 257(e), Oct. 27, 1986, 100 Stat. 3099, 3114.)

HISTORICAL AND REVISION NOTES

LEGISLATIVE STATEMENTS

Section 327(a) of the House amendment contains a technical amendment indicating that attorneys, and perhaps other officers enumerated therein, represent, rather than assist, the trustee in carrying out the trustee's duties.

Section 327(c) represents a compromise between H.R. 8200 as passed by the House and the Senate amendment. The provision states that former representation of a creditor, whether secured or unsecured, will not automatically disqualify a person from being employed by a trustee, but if such person is employed by the trustee, the person may no longer represent the creditor in connection with the case.

Section 327(f) prevents an examiner from being employed by the trustee.

SENATE REPORT NO. 95-989

This section authorizes the trustee, subject to the court's approval, to employ professional persons, such as attorneys, accountants, appraisers, and auctioneers, to represent or perform services for the estate. The trustee may employ only disinterested persons that do not hold or represent an interest adverse to the estate.

Subsection (b) is an exception, and authorizes the trustee to retain or replace professional persons that the debtor has employed if necessary in the operation of the debtor's business.

Subsection (c) provides a professional person is not disqualified for employment solely because of the person's prior employment by or representation of a secured or unsecured creditor.

Subsection (d) permits the court to authorize the trustee, if qualified to act as his own counsel or accountant.

Subsection (e) permits the trustee, subject to the court's approval, to employ for a specified special purpose an attorney that has represented the debtor, if such employment is in the best interest of the estate and if the attorney does not hold or represent an interest adverse to the debtor of the estate with respect to the matter on which he is to be employed. This subsection does not authorize the employment of the debtor's attorney to represent the estate generally or to represent the trustee in the conduct of the bankruptcy case. The subsection will most likely be used when the debtor is involved in complex litigation, and changing attorneys in the middle of the case after the bankruptcy case has commenced would be detrimental to the progress of that other litigation.

HOUSE REPORT NO. 95-595

Subsection (c) is an additional exception. The trustee may employ as his counsel a nondisinterested person if the only reason that the attorney is not disinterested is because of his representation of an unsecured creditor.

AMENDMENTS

1986—Subsec. (b). Pub. L. 99-554, §257(e)(1), which directed the insertion of ", 1202," after "section 721," was executed by making the insertion after "section 721" to reflect the probable intent of Congress.

Subsec. (c). Pub. L. 99-554, §257(e)(2), which directed the insertion of ", 12," after "section 7," was executed by making the insertion after "chapter 7" to reflect the probable intent of Congress.

Pub. L. 99-554, §210, inserted "or the United States trustee" after "another creditor".

1984—Subsec. (c). Pub. L. 98-353 substituted "In a case under chapter 7 or 11 of this title, a person is not disqualified for employment under this section solely because of such person's employment by or representation of a creditor, unless there is objection by another creditor, in which case the court shall disapprove such employment if there is an actual conflict of interest." for "In a case under chapter 7 or 11 of this title, a person is not disqualified for employment under this section solely because of such person's employment by or representation of a creditor, but may not, while employed by the trustee, represent, in connection with the case, a creditor."

EFFECTIVE DATE OF 1986 AMENDMENT

Effective date and applicability of amendment by section 210 of Pub. L. 99-554 dependent upon the judicial district involved, see section 302(d), (e) of Pub. L. 99-554, set out as a note under section 581 of Title 28, Judiciary and Judicial Procedure.

Amendment by section 257 of Pub. L. 99-554 effective 30 days after Oct. 27, 1986, but not applicable to cases commenced under this title before that date, see section 302(a), (c)(1) of Pub. L. 99-554.

EFFECTIVE DATE OF 1984 AMENDMENT

Amendment by Pub. L. 98-353 effective with respect to cases filed 90 days after July 10, 1984, see section 552(a) of Pub. L. 98-353, set out as a note under section 101 of this title.

§328. Limitation on compensation of professional persons

(a) The trustee, or a committee appointed under section 1102 of this title, with the court's approval, may employ or authorize the employment of a professional person under section 327 or 1103 of this title, as the case may be, on any reasonable terms and conditions of employment, including on a retainer, on an hourly basis, on a fixed or percentage fee basis, or on a contingent fee basis. Notwithstanding such terms and conditions, the court may allow compensation different from the compensation provided under such terms and conditions after the conclusion of such employment, if such terms and conditions prove to have been improvident in light of developments not capable of being anticipated at the time of the fixing of such terms and conditions.

(b) If the court has authorized a trustee to serve as an attorney or accountant for the estate under section 327(d) of this title, the court may allow compensation for the trustee's services as such attorney or accountant only to the extent that the trustee performed services as attorney or accountant for the estate and not for performance of any of the trustee's duties that are generally performed by a trustee without the assistance of an attorney or accountant for the estate.

(c) Except as provided in section 327(c), 327(e), or 1107(b) of this title, the court may deny allowance of compensation for services and reimbursement of expenses of a professional person employed under section 327 or 1103 of this title if, at any time during such professional person's employment under section 327 or 1103 of this title, such professional person is not a disinterested person, or represents or holds an interest adverse to the interest of the estate with respect to the matter on which such professional person is employed.

(Pub. L. 95-598, Nov. 6, 1978, 92 Stat. 2563; Pub. L. 98-353, title III, §431, July 10, 1984, 98 Stat. 370; Pub. L. 109-8, title XII, §1206, Apr. 20, 2005, 119 Stat. 194.)

HISTORICAL AND REVISION NOTES

LEGISLATIVE STATEMENTS

Section 328(c) adopts a technical amendment contained in the Senate amendment indicating that an attorney for the debtor in possession is not disqualified for compensation for services and reimbursement of expenses simply because of prior representation of the debtor.

SENATE REPORT NO. 95-989

This section, which is parallel to section 326, fixes the maximum compensation allowable to a professional person employed under section 327. It authorizes the trustee, with the court's approval, to employ professional persons on any reasonable terms, including on a retainer, on an hourly or on a contingent fee basis. Subsection (a) further permits the court to allow compensation different from the compensation provided under the trustee's agreement if the prior agreement proves to have been improvident in light of development unanticipatable at the time of the agreement. The court's power includes the power to increase as well as decrease the agreed upon compensation. This provision is permissive, not mandatory, and should not be used by the court if to do so would violate the code of ethics of the professional involved.

Subsection (b) limits a trustee that has been authorized to serve as his own counsel to only one fee for each service. The purpose of permitting the trustee to serve as his own counsel is to reduce costs. It is not included to provide the trustee with a bonus by permitting him to receive two fees for the same service or to avoid the maxima fixed in section 326. Thus, this subsection requires the court to differentiate between the trustee's services as trustee, and his services as trustee's counsel, and to fix compensation accordingly. Services that a trustee normally performs for an estate without assistance of counsel are to be compensated under the limits fixed in section 326. Only services that he performs that are normally performed by trustee's counsel may be compensated under the maxima imposed by this section.

Subsection (c) permits the court to deny compensation for services and reimbursement of expenses if the professional person is not disinterested or if he represents or holds an interest adverse to the estate on the matter on which he is employed. The subsection provides a penalty for conflicts of interest.

AMENDMENTS

2005—Subsec. (a). Pub. L. 109-8 inserted "on a fixed or percentage fee basis," after "hourly basis,".

1984—Subsec. (a). Pub. L. 98-353 substituted "not capable of being anticipated" for "unanticipatable".

EFFECTIVE DATE OF 2005 AMENDMENT

Amendment by Pub. L. 109-8 effective 180 days after Apr. 20, 2005, and not applicable with respect to cases commenced under this title before such effective date, except as otherwise provided, see section 1501 of Pub. L. 109-8, set out as a note under section 101 of this title.

EFFECTIVE DATE OF 1984 AMENDMENT

Amendment by Pub. L. 98-353 effective with respect to cases filed 90 days after July 10, 1984, see section 552(a) of Pub. L. 98-353, set out as a note under section 101 of this title.

§329. Debtor's transactions with attorneys

(a) Any attorney representing a debtor in a case under this title, or in connection with such a case, whether or not such attorney applies for compensation under this title, shall file with the court a statement of the compensation paid or agreed to be paid, if such payment or agreement was made after one year before the date of the filing of the petition, for services rendered or to be rendered in contemplation of or in connection with the case by such attorney, and the source of such compensation.

(b) If such compensation exceeds the reasonable value of any such services, the court may cancel any such agreement, or order the return of any such payment, to the extent excessive, to—

(1) the estate, if the property transferred—

(A) would have been property of the estate; or

(B) was to be paid by or on behalf of the debtor under a plan under chapter 11, 12, or 13 of this title; or

(2) the entity that made such payment.

(Pub. L. 95-598, Nov. 6, 1978, 92 Stat. 2564; Pub. L. 98-353, title III, §432, July 10, 1984, 98 Stat. 370; Pub. L. 99-554, title II, §257(c), Oct. 27, 1986, 100 Stat. 3114.)

HISTORICAL AND REVISION NOTES

SENATE REPORT NO. 95-989

This section, derived in large part from current Bankruptcy Act section 60d [section 96(d) of former title 11], requires the debtor's attorney to file with the court a statement of the compensation paid or agreed to be paid to the attorney for services in contemplation of and in connection with the case, and the source of the compensation. Payments to a debtor's attorney provide serious potential for evasion of creditor protection provisions of the bankruptcy laws, and serious potential for overreaching by the debtor's attorney, and should be subject to careful scrutiny.

Subsection (b) permits the court to deny compensation to the attorney, to cancel an agreement to pay compensation, or to order the return of compensation paid, if the compensation exceeds the reasonable value of the services provided. The return of payments already made are generally to the trustee for the benefit of the estate. However, if the property would not have come into the estate in any event, the court will order it returned to the entity that made the payment.

The Bankruptcy Commission recommended a provision similar to this that would have also permitted an examination of the debtor's transactions with insiders. S. 236, 94th Cong., 1st sess. sec. 4-311(b) (1975). Its exclusion here is to permit it to be dealt with by the Rules of Bankruptcy Procedure. It is not intended that the provision be deleted entirely, only that the flexibility of the rules is more appropriate for such evidentiary matters.

AMENDMENTS

1986—Subsec. (b)(1)(B). Pub. L. 99-554 inserted reference to chapter 12.

1984—Subsec. (a). Pub. L. 98-353, §432(a), substituted "or" for "and" after "in contemplation of".

Subsec. (b)(1). Pub. L. 98-353, §432(b), substituted "estate" for "trustee".

EFFECTIVE DATE OF 1986 AMENDMENT

Amendment by Pub. L. 99-554 effective 30 days after Oct. 27, 1986, but not applicable to cases commenced under this title before that date, see section 302(a), (c)(1) of Pub. L. 99-554, set out as a note under section 581 of Title 28, Judiciary and Judicial Procedure.

EFFECTIVE DATE OF 1984 AMENDMENT

Amendment by Pub. L. 98-353 effective with respect to cases filed 90 days after July 10, 1984, see section 552(a) of Pub. L. 98-353, set out as a note under section 101 of this title.

§ 330. Compensation of officers

(a)(1) After notice to the parties in interest and the United States Trustee and a hearing, and subject to sections 326, 328, and 329, the court may award to a trustee, a consumer privacy ombudsman appointed under section 332, an examiner, an ombudsman appointed under section 333, or a professional person employed under section 327 or 1103—

(A) reasonable compensation for actual, necessary services rendered by the trustee, examiner, ombudsman, professional person, or attorney and by any paraprofessional person employed by any such person; and

(B) reimbursement for actual, necessary expenses.

(2) The court may, on its own motion or on the motion of the United States Trustee, the United States Trustee for the District or Region, the trustee for the estate, or any other party in interest, award compensation that is less than the amount of compensation that is requested.

(3) In determining the amount of reasonable compensation to be awarded to an examiner, trustee under chapter 11, or professional person, the court shall consider the nature, the extent, and the value of such services, taking into account all relevant factors, including—

(A) the time spent on such services;

(B) the rates charged for such services;

(C) whether the services were necessary to the administration of, or beneficial at the time at which the service was rendered toward the completion of, a case under this title;

(D) whether the services were performed within a reasonable amount of time commensurate with the complexity, importance, and nature of the problem, issue, or task addressed;

(E) with respect to a professional person, whether the person is board certified or otherwise has demonstrated skill and experience in the bankruptcy field; and

(F) whether the compensation is reasonable based on the customary compensation charged by comparably skilled practitioners in cases other than cases under this title.

(4)(A) Except as provided in subparagraph (B), the court shall not allow compensation for—

(i) unnecessary duplication of services; or

(ii) services that were not—

(I) reasonably likely to benefit the debtor's estate; or

(II) necessary to the administration of the case.

(B) In a chapter 12 or chapter 13 case in which the debtor is an individual, the court may allow reasonable compensation to the debtor's attorney for representing the interests of the debtor in connection with the bankruptcy case based on a consideration of the benefit and necessity of such services to the debtor and the other factors set forth in this section.

(5) The court shall reduce the amount of compensation awarded under this section by the amount of any interim compensation awarded under section 331, and, if the amount of such interim compensation exceeds the amount of compensation awarded under this section, may order the return of the excess to the estate.

(6) Any compensation awarded for the preparation of a fee application shall be based on the level and skill reasonably required to prepare the application.

(7) In determining the amount of reasonable compensation to be awarded to a trustee, the court shall treat such compensation as a commission, based on section 326.

(b)(1) There shall be paid from the filing fee in a case under chapter 7 of this title $45 to the trustee serving in such case, after such trustee's services are rendered.

(2) The Judicial Conference of the United States—

(A) shall prescribe additional fees of the same kind as prescribed under section 1914(b) of title 28; and

(B) may prescribe notice of appearance fees and fees charged against distributions in cases under this title;

to pay $15 to trustees serving in cases after such trustees' services are rendered. Beginning 1 year after the date of the enactment of the Bankruptcy Reform Act of 1994, such $15 shall be paid in addition to the amount paid under paragraph (1).

(c) Unless the court orders otherwise, in a case under chapter 12 or 13 of this title the compensation paid to the trustee serving in the case shall not be less than $5 per month from any distribution under the plan during the administration of the plan.

(d) In a case in which the United States trustee serves as trustee, the compensation of the trustee under this section shall be paid to the clerk of the bankruptcy court and deposited by the clerk into the United States Trustee System Fund established by section 589a of title 28.

(Pub. L. 95–598, Nov. 6, 1978, 92 Stat. 2564; Pub. L. 98–353, title III, §§433, 434, July 10, 1984, 98 Stat. 370; Pub. L. 99–554, title II, §§211, 257(f), Oct. 27, 1986, 100 Stat. 3099, 3114; Pub. L. 103–394, title I, §117, title II, §224(b), Oct. 22, 1994, 108 Stat. 4119, 4130; Pub. L. 109–8, title II, §232(b), title IV, §§407, 415, title XI, §1104(b), Apr. 20, 2005, 119 Stat. 74, 106, 107, 192.)

Historical and Revision Notes

Legislative Statements

Section 330(a) contains the standard of compensation adopted in H.R. 8200 as passed by the House rather than the contrary standard contained in the Senate amendment. Attorneys' fees in bankruptcy cases can be quite large and should be closely examined by the court. However bankruptcy legal services are entitled to command the same competency of counsel as other cases. In that light, the policy of this section is to compensate attorneys and other professionals serving in a case under title 11 at the same rate as the attorney or other professional would be compensated for performing comparable services other than in a case under title 11. Contrary language in the Senate report accompanying S. 2266 is rejected, and *Massachusetts Mutual Life Insurance Company v. Brock*, 405 F.2d 429, 432 (5th Cir. 1968) is overruled. Notions of economy of the estate in fixing fees are outdated and have no place in a bankruptcy code.

Section 330(a)(2) of the Senate amendment is deleted although the Securities and Exchange Commission retains a right to file an advisory report under section 1109.

Section 330(b) of the Senate amendment is deleted as unnecessary, as the limitations contained therein are covered by section 328(c) of H.R. 8200 as passed by the House and contained in the House amendment.

Section 330(c) of the Senate amendment providing for a trustee to receive a fee of $20 for each estate from the filing fee paid to the clerk is retained as section 330(b) of the House amendment. The section will encourage private trustees to serve in cases under title 11 and in pilot districts will place less of a burden on the U.S. trustee to serve in no-asset cases.

Section 330(b) of H.R. 8200 as passed by the House is retained by the House amendment as section 330(c) [section 15330].

Senate Report No. 95–989

Section 330 authorizes the court to award compensation for services and reimbursement of expenses of officers of the estate, and other professionals. The compensation is to be reasonable, for economy in administration is the basic objective. Compensation is to be for actual necessary services, based on the time spent, the nature, the extent and the value of the services rendered, and the cost of comparable services in nonbankruptcy cases. There are the criteria that have been applied by the courts as analytic aids in defining "reasonable" compensation.

The reference to "the cost of comparable services" in a nonbankruptcy case is not intended as a change of existing law. In a bankruptcy case fees are not a matter for private agreement. There is inherent a "public interest" that "must be considered in awarding fees." *Massachusetts Mutual Life Insurance Co. v. Brock*, 405 F.2d 429, 432 (C.A.5, 1968), cert. denied, 395 U.S. 906 (1969). An allowance is the result of a balance struck between moderation in the interest of the estate and its security holders and the need to be "generous enough to encourage" lawyers and others to render the necessary and exacting services that bankruptcy cases often require. *In re Yale Express System, Inc.*, 366 F.Supp. 1376, 1381 (S.D.N.Y. 1973). The rates for similar kinds of services in private employment is one element, among others, in that balance. Compensation in private employment noted in subsection (a) is a point of reference, not a controlling determinant of what shall be allowed in bankruptcy cases.

One of the major reforms in 1938, especially for reorganization cases, was centralized control over fees in the bankruptcy courts. See *Brown v. Gerdes*, 321 U.S. 178, 182–184 (1944); *Leiman v. Guttman*, 336 U.S. 1, 4–9 (1949). It was intended to guard against a recurrence of "the many sordid chapters" in "the history of fees in corporate reorganizations." *Dickinson Industrial Site, Inc. v. Cowan*, 309 U.S. 382, 388 (1940). In the years since then the bankruptcy bar has flourished and prospered, and persons of merit and quality have not eschewed public service in bankruptcy cases merely because bankruptcy courts, in the interest of economy in administration, have not allowed them compensation that may be earned in the private economy of business or the professions. There is no reason to believe that, in generations to come, their successors will be less persuaded by the need to serve in the public interest because of stronger allures of private gain elsewhere.

Subsection (a) provides for compensation of paraprofessionals in order to reduce the cost of administering bankruptcy cases. Paraprofessionals can be employed to perform duties which do not require the full range of skills of a qualified professional. Some courts have not hesitated to recognize paraprofessional services as compensable under existing law. An explicit provision to that effect is useful and constructive.

The last sentence of subsection (a) provides that in the case of a public company—defined in section 1101(3)—the court shall refer, after a hearing, all applications to the Securities and Exchange Commission for a report, which shall be advisory only. In Chapter X cases in which the Commission has appeared, it generally filed reports on fee applications. Usually, courts have accorded the SEC's views substantial weight, as representing the opinion of a disinterested agency skilled and experienced in reorganization affairs. The last sentence intends for the advisory assistance of the Commission to be sought only in case of a public company in reorganization under chapter 11.

Subsection (b) reenacts section 249 of Chapter X of the Bankruptcy Act ([former] 11 U.S.C. 649). It is a codification of equitable principles designed to prevent fiduciaries in the case from engaging in the specified transactions since they are in a position to gain inside information or to shape or influence the course of the reorganization. *Wolf v. Weinstein*, 372 U.S. 633 (1963). The statutory bar of compensation and reimbursement is based on the principle that such transactions involve conflicts of interest. Private gain undoubtedly prompts the purchase or sale of claims or stock interests, while the fiduciary's obligation is to render loyal and disinterested service which his position of trust has imposed upon him. Subsection (b) extends to a trustee, his attorney, committees and their attorneys, or any other persons "acting in the case in a representative or fiduciary capacity." It bars compensation to any of the foregoing, who after assuming to act in such capacity has purchased or sold, directly or indirectly, claims against, or stock in the debtor. The bar is absolute. It makes no difference whether the transaction brought a gain or loss, or neither, and the court is not authorized to approve a purchase or sale, before or after the transaction. The exception is for an acquisition or transfer "otherwise" than by a voluntary purchase or sale, such as an acquisition by bequest. See *Otis & Co. v. Insurance Bldg. Corp.*, 110 F.2d 333, 335 (C.A.1, 1940).

Subsection (c) [enacted as (b)] is intended for no asset liquidation cases where minimal compensation for trustees is needed. The sum of $20 will be allowed in each case, which is double the amount provided under current law.

HOUSE REPORT NO. 95–595

Section 330 authorizes compensation for services and reimbursement of expenses of officers of the estate. It also prescribes the standards on which the amount of compensation is to be determined. As noted above, the compensation allowable under this section is subject to the maxima set out in sections 326, 328, and 329. The compensation is to be reasonable, for actual necessary services rendered, based on the time, the nature, the extent, and the value of the services rendered, and on the cost of comparable services other than in a case under the bankruptcy code. The effect of the last provision is to overrule *In re Beverly Crest Convalescent Hospital, Inc.*, 548 F.2d 817 (9th Cir. 1976, as amended 1977), which set an arbitrary limit on fees payable based on the amount of a district judge's salary, and other, similar cases that require fees to be determined based on notions of conservation of the estate and economy of administration. If that case were allowed to stand, attorneys that could earn much higher incomes in other fields would leave the bankruptcy arena. Bankruptcy specialists, who enable the system to operate smoothly, efficiently, and expeditiously, would be driven elsewhere, and the bankruptcy field would be occupied by those who could not find other work and those who practice bankruptcy law only occasionally almost as a public service. Bankruptcy fees that are lower than fees in other areas of the legal profession may operate properly when the attorneys appearing in bankruptcy cases do so intermittently, because a low fee in a small segment of a practice can be absorbed by other work. Bankruptcy specialists, however, if required to accept fees in all of their cases that are consistently lower than fees they could receive elsewhere, will not remain in the bankruptcy field.

This subsection provides for reimbursement of actual, necessary expenses. It further provides for compensation of paraprofessionals employed by professional persons employed by the estate of the debtor. The provision is included to reduce the cost of administering bankruptcy cases. In nonbankruptcy areas, attorneys are able to charge for a paraprofessional's time on an hourly basis, and not include it in overhead. If a similar practice does not pertain in bankruptcy cases then the attorney will be less inclined to use paraprofessionals even where the work involved could easily be handled by an attorney's assistant, at much lower cost to the estate. This provision is designed to encourage attorneys to use paraprofessional assistance where possible, and to insure that the estate, not the attorney, will bear the cost, to the benefit of both the estate and the attorneys involved.

REFERENCES IN TEXT

The date of the enactment of the Bankruptcy Reform Act of 1994, referred to in subsec. (b)(2), is the date of enactment of Pub. L. 103–394, which was approved Oct. 22, 1994.

AMENDMENTS

2005—Subsec. (a)(1). Pub. L. 109–8, §1104(b)(1), inserted "an ombudsman appointed under section 333, or" before "a professional person" in introductory provisions.

Pub. L. 109–8, §232(b), inserted "a consumer privacy ombudsman appointed under section 332," before "an examiner" in introductory provisions.

Subsec. (a)(1)(A). Pub. L. 109–8, §1104(b)(2), inserted "ombudsman," before "professional person".

Subsec. (a)(3). Pub. L. 109–8, §407(1), in introductory provisions, substituted "In" for "(A) In" and inserted "to an examiner, trustee under chapter 11, or professional person" after "awarded".

Subsec. (a)(3)(E), (F). Pub. L. 109–8, §415, added subpar. (E) and redesignated former subpar. (E) as (F).

Subsec. (a)(7). Pub. L. 109–8, §407(2), added par. (7).

1994—Subsec. (a). Pub. L. 103–394, §224(b), amended subsec. (a) generally. Prior to amendment, subsec. (a) read as follows: "After notice to any parties in interest and to the United States trustee and a hearing, and subject to sections 326, 328, and 329 of this title, the court may award to a trustee, to an examiner, to a professional person employed under section 327 or 1103 of this title, or to the debtor's attorney—

"(1) reasonable compensation for actual, necessary services rendered by such trustee, examiner, professional person, or attorney, as the case may be, and by any paraprofessional persons employed by such trustee, professional person, or attorney, as the case may be, based on the nature, the extent, and the value of such services, the time spent on such services, and the cost of comparable services other than in a case under this title; and

"(2) reimbursement for actual, necessary expenses."

Subsec. (b). Pub. L. 103–394, §117, designated existing provisions as par. (1) and added par. (2).

1986—Subsec. (a). Pub. L. 99–554, §211(1), inserted "to any parties in interest and to the United States trustee" after "notice".

Subsec. (c). Pub. L. 99–554, §257(f), inserted reference to chapter 12.

Subsec. (d). Pub. L. 99–554, §211(2), added subsec. (d).

1984—Subsec. (a). Pub. L. 98–353, §433(1), struck out "to any parties in interest and to the United States trustee" after "After notice".

Subsec. (a)(1). Pub. L. 98–353, §433(2), substituted "nature, the extent, and the value of such services, the time spent on such services" for "time, the nature, the extent, and the value of such services".

Subsec. (b). Pub. L. 98–353, §434(a), substituted "$45" for "$20".

Subsec. (c). Pub. L. 98–353, §434(b), added subsec. (c).

EFFECTIVE DATE OF 2005 AMENDMENT

Amendment by Pub. L. 109–8 effective 180 days after Apr. 20, 2005, and not applicable with respect to cases commenced under this title before such effective date, except as otherwise provided, see section 1501 of Pub. L. 109–8, set out as a note under section 101 of this title.

EFFECTIVE DATE OF 1994 AMENDMENT

Amendment by section 117 of Pub. L. 103–394 effective Oct. 22, 1994, and applicable with respect to cases commenced under this title before, on, and after Oct. 22, 1994, and amendment by section 224(b) of Pub. L. 103–394 effective Oct. 22, 1994, and not applicable with respect to cases commenced under this title before Oct. 22, 1994, see section 702 of Pub. L. 103–394, set out as a note under section 101 of this title.

EFFECTIVE DATE OF 1986 AMENDMENT

Effective date and applicability of amendment by section 211 of Pub. L. 99–554 dependent upon the judicial district involved, see section 302(d), (e) of Pub. L. 99–554, set out as a note under section 581 of Title 28, Judiciary and Judicial Procedure.

Amendment by section 257 of Pub. L. 99–554 effective 30 days after Oct. 27, 1986, but not applicable to cases commenced under this title before that date, see section 302(a), (c)(1) of Pub. L. 99–554.

EFFECTIVE DATE OF 1984 AMENDMENT

Amendment by Pub. L. 98–353 effective with respect to cases filed 90 days after July 10, 1984, see section 552(a) of Pub. L. 98–353, set out as a note under section 101 of this title.

§331. Interim compensation

A trustee, an examiner, a debtor's attorney, or any professional person employed under section 327 or 1103 of this title may apply to the court not more than once every 120 days after an order for relief in a case under this title, or more often if the court permits, for such compensation for services rendered before the date of such an application or reimbursement for expenses incurred before such date as is provided under section 330 of this title. After notice and a hearing, the court may allow and disburse to such applicant such compensation or reimbursement.

(Pub. L. 95-598, Nov. 6, 1978, 92 Stat. 2564.)

HISTORICAL AND REVISION NOTES

SENATE REPORT NO. 95-989

Section 331 permits trustees and professional persons to apply to the court not more than once every 120 days for interim compensation and reimbursement payments. The court may permit more frequent applications if the circumstances warrant, such as in very large cases where the legal work is extensive and merits more frequent payments. The court is authorized to allow and order disbursement to the applicant of compensation and reimbursement that is otherwise allowable under section 330. The only effect of this section is to remove any doubt that officers of the estate may apply for, and the court may approve, compensation and reimbursement during the case, instead of being required to wait until the end of the case, which in some instances, may be years. The practice of interim compensation is followed in some courts today, but has been subject to some question. This section explicitly authorizes it.

This section will apply to professionals such as auctioneers and appraisers only if they are not paid on a per job basis.

§332. Consumer privacy ombudsman

(a) If a hearing is required under section 363(b)(1)(B), the court shall order the United States trustee to appoint, not later than 7 days before the commencement of the hearing, 1 disinterested person (other than the United States trustee) to serve as the consumer privacy ombudsman in the case and shall require that notice of such hearing be timely given to such ombudsman.

(b) The consumer privacy ombudsman may appear and be heard at such hearing and shall provide to the court information to assist the court in its consideration of the facts, circumstances, and conditions of the proposed sale or lease of personally identifiable information under section 363(b)(1)(B). Such information may include presentation of—

(1) the debtor's privacy policy;

(2) the potential losses or gains of privacy to consumers if such sale or such lease is approved by the court;

(3) the potential costs or benefits to consumers if such sale or such lease is approved by the court; and

(4) the potential alternatives that would mitigate potential privacy losses or potential costs to consumers.

(c) A consumer privacy ombudsman shall not disclose any personally identifiable information obtained by the ombudsman under this title.

(Added Pub. L. 109-8, title II, §232(a), Apr. 20, 2005, 119 Stat. 73; amended Pub. L. 111-16, §2(3), May 7, 2009, 123 Stat. 1607.)

AMENDMENTS

2009—Subsec. (a). Pub. L. 111-16 substituted "7 days" for "5 days".

EFFECTIVE DATE OF 2009 AMENDMENT

Amendment by Pub. L. 111-16 effective Dec. 1, 2009, see section 7 of Pub. L. 111-16, set out as a note under section 109 of this title.

EFFECTIVE DATE

Section effective 180 days after Apr. 20, 2005, and not applicable with respect to cases commenced under this title before such effective date, except as otherwise provided, see section 1501 of Pub. L. 109-8, set out as an Effective Date of 2005 Amendment note under section 101 of this title.

§333. Appointment of patient care ombudsman

(a)(1) If the debtor in a case under chapter 7, 9, or 11 is a health care business, the court shall order, not later than 30 days after the commencement of the case, the appointment of an ombudsman to monitor the quality of patient care and to represent the interests of the patients of the health care business unless the court finds that the appointment of such ombudsman is not necessary for the protection of patients under the specific facts of the case.

(2)(A) If the court orders the appointment of an ombudsman under paragraph (1), the United States trustee shall appoint 1 disinterested person (other than the United States trustee) to serve as such ombudsman.

(B) If the debtor is a health care business that provides long-term care, then the United States trustee may appoint the State Long-Term Care Ombudsman appointed under the Older Americans Act of 1965 for the State in which the case is pending to serve as the ombudsman required by paragraph (1).

(C) If the United States trustee does not appoint a State Long-Term Care Ombudsman under subparagraph (B), the court shall notify the State Long-Term Care Ombudsman appointed under the Older Americans Act of 1965 for the State in which the case is pending, of the name and address of the person who is appointed under subparagraph (A).

(b) An ombudsman appointed under subsection (a) shall—

(1) monitor the quality of patient care provided to patients of the debtor, to the extent necessary under the circumstances, including interviewing patients and physicians;

(2) not later than 60 days after the date of appointment, and not less frequently than at 60-day intervals thereafter, report to the court after notice to the parties in interest, at a hearing or in writing, regarding the quality of patient care provided to patients of the debtor; and

(3) if such ombudsman determines that the quality of patient care provided to patients of the debtor is declining significantly or is otherwise being materially compromised, file with the court a motion or a written report, with notice to the parties in interest immediately upon making such determination.

(c)(1) An ombudsman appointed under subsection (a) shall maintain any information obtained by such ombudsman under this section that relates to patients (including information relating to patient records) as confidential information. Such ombudsman may not review confidential patient records unless the court approves such review in advance and imposes restrictions on such ombudsman to protect the confidentiality of such records.

(2) An ombudsman appointed under subsection (a)(2)(B) shall have access to patient records

consistent with authority of such ombudsman under the Older Americans Act of 1965 and under non-Federal laws governing the State Long-Term Care Ombudsman program.

(Added Pub. L. 109–8, title XI, §1104(a)(1), Apr. 20, 2005, 119 Stat. 191.)

REFERENCES IN TEXT

The Older Americans Act of 1965, referred to in subsecs. (a)(2)(B), (C) and (c)(2), is Pub. L. 89–73, July 14, 1965, 79 Stat. 218, as amended, which is classified generally to chapter 35 (§3001 et seq.) of Title 42, The Public Health and Welfare. For complete classification of this Act to the Code, see Short Title note set out under section 3001 of Title 42 and Tables.

EFFECTIVE DATE

Section effective 180 days after Apr. 20, 2005, and not applicable with respect to cases commenced under this title before such effective date, except as otherwise provided, see section 1501 of Pub. L. 109–8, set out as an Effective Date of 2005 Amendment note under section 101 of this title.

SUBCHAPTER III—ADMINISTRATION

§341. Meetings of creditors and equity security holders

(a) Within a reasonable time after the order for relief in a case under this title, the United States trustee shall convene and preside at a meeting of creditors.

(b) The United States trustee may convene a meeting of any equity security holders.

(c) The court may not preside at, and may not attend, any meeting under this section including any final meeting of creditors. Notwithstanding any local court rule, provision of a State constitution, any otherwise applicable nonbankruptcy law, or any other requirement that representation at the meeting of creditors under subsection (a) be by an attorney, a creditor holding a consumer debt or any representative of the creditor (which may include an entity or an employee of an entity and may be a representative for more than 1 creditor) shall be permitted to appear at and participate in the meeting of creditors in a case under chapter 7 or 13, either alone or in conjunction with an attorney for the creditor. Nothing in this subsection shall be construed to require any creditor to be represented by an attorney at any meeting of creditors.

(d) Prior to the conclusion of the meeting of creditors or equity security holders, the trustee shall orally examine the debtor to ensure that the debtor in a case under chapter 7 of this title is aware of—

(1) the potential consequences of seeking a discharge in bankruptcy, including the effects on credit history;

(2) the debtor's ability to file a petition under a different chapter of this title;

(3) the effect of receiving a discharge of debts under this title; and

(4) the effect of reaffirming a debt, including the debtor's knowledge of the provisions of section 524(d) of this title.

(e) Notwithstanding subsections (a) and (b), the court, on the request of a party in interest and after notice and a hearing, for cause may order that the United States trustee not convene a meeting of creditors or equity security holders if the debtor has filed a plan as to which the debtor solicited acceptances prior to the commencement of the case.

(Pub. L. 95–598, Nov. 6, 1978, 92 Stat. 2564; Pub. L. 99–554, title II, §212, Oct. 27, 1986, 100 Stat. 3099; Pub. L. 103–394, title I, §115, Oct. 22, 1994, 108 Stat. 4118; Pub. L. 109–8, title IV, §§402, 413, Apr. 20, 2005, 119 Stat. 104, 107.)

HISTORICAL AND REVISION NOTES

LEGISLATIVE STATEMENTS

Section 341(c) of the Senate amendment is deleted and a contrary provision is added indicating that the bankruptcy judge will not preside at or attend the first meeting of creditors or equity security holders but a discharge hearing for all individuals will be held at which the judge will preside.

SENATE REPORT NO. 95–989

Section [Subsection] (a) of this section requires that there be a meeting of creditors within a reasonable time after the order for relief in the case. The Bankruptcy Act [former title 11] and the current Rules of Bankruptcy Procedure provide for a meeting of creditors, and specify the time and manner of the meeting, and the business to be conducted. This bill leaves those matters to the rules. Under section 405(d) of the bill, the present rules will continue to govern until new rules are promulgated. Thus, pending the adoption of different rules, the present procedure for the meeting will continue.

Subsection (b) authorizes the court to order a meeting of equity security holders in cases where such a meeting would be beneficial or useful, for example, in a chapter 11 reorganization case where it may be necessary for the equity security holders to organize in order to be able to participate in the negotiation of a plan of reorganization.

Subsection (c) makes clear that the bankruptcy judge is to preside at the meeting of creditors.

AMENDMENTS

2005—Subsec. (c). Pub. L. 109–8, §413, inserted at end "Notwithstanding any local court rule, provision of a State constitution, any otherwise applicable nonbankruptcy law, or any other requirement that representation at the meeting of creditors under subsection (a) be by an attorney, a creditor holding a consumer debt or any representative of the creditor (which may include an entity or an employee of an entity and may be a representative for more than 1 creditor) shall be permitted to appear at and participate in the meeting of creditors in a case under chapter 7 or 13, either alone or in conjunction with an attorney for the creditor. Nothing in this subsection shall be construed to require any creditor to be represented by an attorney at any meeting of creditors."

Subsec. (e). Pub. L. 109–8, §402, added subsec. (e).

1994—Subsec. (d). Pub. L. 103–394 added subsec. (d).

1986—Subsec. (a). Pub. L. 99–554, §212(1), substituted "the United States trustee shall convene and preside at a meeting of creditors" for "there shall be a meeting of creditors".

Subsec. (b). Pub. L. 99–554, §212(2), substituted "United States trustee may convene" for "court may order".

Subsec. (c). Pub. L. 99–554, §212(3), inserted "including any final meeting of creditors".

EFFECTIVE DATE OF 2005 AMENDMENT

Amendment by Pub. L. 109–8 effective 180 days after Apr. 20, 2005, and not applicable with respect to cases commenced under this title before such effective date, except as otherwise provided, see section 1501 of Pub. L. 109–8, set out as a note under section 101 of this title.

EFFECTIVE DATE OF 1994 AMENDMENT

Amendment by Pub. L. 103-394 effective Oct. 22, 1994, and not applicable with respect to cases commenced under this title before Oct. 22, 1994, see section 702 of Pub. L. 103-394, set out as a note under section 101 of this title.

EFFECTIVE DATE OF 1986 AMENDMENT

Effective date and applicability of amendment by Pub. L. 99-554 dependent upon the judicial district involved, see section 302(d), (e) of Pub. L. 99-554, set out as a note under section 581 of Title 28, Judiciary and Judicial Procedure.

PARTICIPATION BY BANKRUPTCY ADMINISTRATOR AT MEETINGS OF CREDITORS AND EQUITY SECURITY HOLDERS

Section 105 of Pub. L. 103-394 provided that:

"(a) PRESIDING OFFICER.—A bankruptcy administrator appointed under section 302(d)(3)(I) of the Bankruptcy Judges, United States Trustees, and Family Farmer Bankruptcy Act of 1986 (28 U.S.C. 581 note; Public Law 99-554; 100 Stat. 3123), as amended by section 317(a) of the Federal Courts Study Committee Implementation Act of 1990 (Public Law 101-650; 104 Stat. 5115), or the bankruptcy administrator's designee may preside at the meeting of creditors convened under section 341(a) of title 11, United States Code. The bankruptcy administrator or the bankruptcy administrator's designee may preside at any meeting of equity security holders convened under section 341(b) of title 11, United States Code.

"(b) EXAMINATION OF THE DEBTOR.—The bankruptcy administrator or the bankruptcy administrator's designee may examine the debtor at the meeting of creditors and may administer the oath required under section 343 of title 11, United States Code."

§ 342. Notice

(a) There shall be given such notice as is appropriate, including notice to any holder of a community claim, of an order for relief in a case under this title.

(b) Before the commencement of a case under this title by an individual whose debts are primarily consumer debts, the clerk shall give to such individual written notice containing—

(1) a brief description of—

(A) chapters 7, 11, 12, and 13 and the general purpose, benefits, and costs of proceeding under each of those chapters; and

(B) the types of services available from credit counseling agencies; and

(2) statements specifying that—

(A) a person who knowingly and fraudulently conceals assets or makes a false oath or statement under penalty of perjury in connection with a case under this title shall be subject to fine, imprisonment, or both; and

(B) all information supplied by a debtor in connection with a case under this title is subject to examination by the Attorney General.

(c)(1) If notice is required to be given by the debtor to a creditor under this title, any rule, any applicable law, or any order of the court, such notice shall contain the name, address, and last 4 digits of the taxpayer identification number of the debtor. If the notice concerns an amendment that adds a creditor to the schedules of assets and liabilities, the debtor shall include the full taxpayer identification number in the notice sent to that creditor, but the debtor shall include only the last 4 digits of the taxpayer identification number in the copy of the notice filed with the court.

(2)(A) If, within the 90 days before the commencement of a voluntary case, a creditor supplies the debtor in at least 2 communications sent to the debtor with the current account number of the debtor and the address at which such creditor requests to receive correspondence, then any notice required by this title to be sent by the debtor to such creditor shall be sent to such address and shall include such account number.

(B) If a creditor would be in violation of applicable nonbankruptcy law by sending any such communication within such 90-day period and if such creditor supplies the debtor in the last 2 communications with the current account number of the debtor and the address at which such creditor requests to receive correspondence, then any notice required by this title to be sent by the debtor to such creditor shall be sent to such address and shall include such account number.

(d) In a case under chapter 7 of this title in which the debtor is an individual and in which the presumption of abuse arises under section 707(b), the clerk shall give written notice to all creditors not later than 10 days after the date of the filing of the petition that the presumption of abuse has arisen.

(e)(1) In a case under chapter 7 or 13 of this title of a debtor who is an individual, a creditor at any time may both file with the court and serve on the debtor a notice of address to be used to provide notice in such case to such creditor.

(2) Any notice in such case required to be provided to such creditor by the debtor or the court later than 7 days after the court and the debtor receive such creditor's notice of address, shall be provided to such address.

(f)(1) An entity may file with any bankruptcy court a notice of address to be used by all the bankruptcy courts or by particular bankruptcy courts, as so specified by such entity at the time such notice is filed, to provide notice to such entity in all cases under chapters 7 and 13 pending in the courts with respect to which such notice is filed, in which such entity is a creditor.

(2) In any case filed under chapter 7 or 13, any notice required to be provided by a court with respect to which a notice is filed under paragraph (1), to such entity later than 30 days after the filing of such notice under paragraph (1) shall be provided to such address unless with respect to a particular case a different address is specified in a notice filed and served in accordance with subsection (e).

(3) A notice filed under paragraph (1) may be withdrawn by such entity.

(g)(1) Notice provided to a creditor by the debtor or the court other than in accordance with this section (excluding this subsection) shall not be effective notice until such notice is brought to the attention of such creditor. If such creditor designates a person or an organizational subdivision of such creditor to be responsible for receiving notices under this title and establishes reasonable procedures so that such notices receivable by such creditor are to be delivered to such person or such subdivision, then a notice provided to such creditor other than in accordance with this section (excluding this subsection) shall not be considered to have been brought to the attention of such creditor until such notice is received by such person or such subdivision.

(2) A monetary penalty may not be imposed on a creditor for a violation of a stay in effect under section 362(a) (including a monetary penalty imposed under section 362(k)) or for failure to comply with section 542 or 543 unless the conduct that is the basis of such violation or of such failure occurs after such creditor receives notice effective under this section of the order for relief.

(Pub. L. 95–598, Nov. 6, 1978, 92 Stat. 2565; Pub. L. 98–353, title III, §§302, 435, July 10, 1984, 98 Stat. 352, 370; Pub. L. 103–394, title II, §225, Oct. 22, 1994, 108 Stat. 4131; Pub. L. 109–8, title I, §§102(d), 104, title II, §234(b), title III, §315(a), Apr. 20, 2005, 119 Stat. 33, 35, 75, 88; Pub. L. 111–16, §2(4), May 7, 2009, 123 Stat. 1607.)

HISTORICAL AND REVISION NOTES

LEGISLATIVE STATEMENTS

Section 342(b) and (c) of the Senate amendment are adopted in principle but moved to section 549(c), in lieu of section 342(b) of H.R. 8200 as passed by the House.

Section 342(c) of H.R. 8200 as passed by the House is deleted as a matter to be left to the Rules of Bankruptcy Procedure.

SENATE REPORT NO. 95–989

Subsection (a) of section 342 requires the clerk of the bankruptcy court to give notice of the order for relief. The rules will prescribe to whom the notice should be sent and in what manner notice will be given. The rules already prescribe such things, and they will continue to govern unless changed as provided in section 404(a) of the bill. Due process will certainly require notice to all creditors and equity security holders. State and Federal governmental representatives responsible for collecting taxes will also receive notice. In cases where the debtor is subject to regulation, the regulatory agency with jurisdiction will receive notice. In order to insure maximum notice to all parties in interest, the Rules will include notice by publication in appropriate cases and for appropriate issues. Other notices will be given as appropriate.

Subsections (b) and (c) [enacted as section 549(c)] are derived from section 21g of the Bankruptcy Act [section 44(g) of former title 11]. They specify that the trustee may file notice of the commencement of the case in land recording offices in order to give notice of the pendency of the case to potential transferees of the debtor's real property. Such filing is unnecessary in the county in which the bankruptcy case is commenced. If notice is properly filed, a subsequent purchaser of the property will not be a bona fide purchaser. Otherwise, a purchaser, including a purchaser at a judicial sale, that has no knowledge of the case, is not prevented from obtaining the status of a bona fide purchaser by the mere commencement of the case. "County" is defined in title 1 of the United States Code to include other political subdivisions where counties are not used.

AMENDMENTS

2009—Subsec. (e)(2). Pub. L. 111–16 substituted "7 days" for "5 days".

2005—Subsec. (b). Pub. L. 109–8, §104, amended subsec. (b) generally. Prior to amendment, subsec. (b) read as follows: "Prior to the commencement of a case under this title by an individual whose debts are primarily consumer debts, the clerk shall give written notice to such individual that indicates each chapter of this title under which such individual may proceed."

Subsec. (c). Pub. L. 109–8, §315(a)(1) designated existing provisions as par. (1), struck out ", but the failure of such notice to contain such information shall not invalidate the legal effect of such notice" after "number of the debtor", and added par. (2).

Pub. L. 109–8, §234(b), inserted "last 4 digits of the" before "taxpayer identification number" and "If the notice concerns an amendment that adds a creditor to the schedules of assets and liabilities, the debtor shall include the full taxpayer identification number in the notice sent to that creditor, but the debtor shall include only the last 4 digits of the taxpayer identification number in the copy of the notice filed with the court." at end.

Subsec. (d). Pub. L. 109–8, §102(d), added subsec. (d).

Subsecs. (e) to (g). Pub. L. 109–8, §315(a)(2), added subsecs. (e) to (g).

1994—Subsec. (c). Pub. L. 103–394 added subsec. (c).

1984—Subsec. (a). Pub. L. 98–353, §435, amended subsec. (a) generally, inserting requirement respecting notice to any holder of a community claim.

Pub. L. 98–353, §302(1), designated existing provisions as subsec. (a).

Subsec. (b). Pub. L. 98–353, §302(2), added subsec. (b).

EFFECTIVE DATE OF 2009 AMENDMENT

Amendment by Pub. L. 111–16 effective Dec. 1, 2009, see section 7 of Pub. L. 111–16, set out as a note under section 109 of this title.

EFFECTIVE DATE OF 2005 AMENDMENT

Amendment by Pub. L. 109–8 effective 180 days after Apr. 20, 2005, and not applicable with respect to cases commenced under this title before such effective date, except as otherwise provided, see section 1501 of Pub. L. 109–8, set out as a note under section 101 of this title.

EFFECTIVE DATE OF 1994 AMENDMENT

Amendment by Pub. L. 103–394 effective Oct. 22, 1994, and not applicable with respect to cases commenced under this title before Oct. 22, 1994, see section 702 of Pub. L. 103–394, set out as a note under section 101 of this title.

EFFECTIVE DATE OF 1984 AMENDMENT

Amendment by Pub. L. 98–353 effective with respect to cases filed 90 days after July 10, 1984, see section 552(a) of Pub. L. 98–353, set out as a note under section 101 of this title.

§ 343. Examination of the debtor

The debtor shall appear and submit to examination under oath at the meeting of creditors under section 341(a) of this title. Creditors, any indenture trustee, any trustee or examiner in the case, or the United States trustee may examine the debtor. The United States trustee may administer the oath required under this section.

(Pub. L. 95–598, Nov. 6, 1978, 92 Stat. 2565; Pub. L. 98–353, title III, §436, July 10, 1984, 98 Stat. 370; Pub. L. 99–554, title II, §213, Oct. 27, 1986, 100 Stat. 3099.)

HISTORICAL AND REVISION NOTES

SENATE REPORT NO. 95–989

This section, derived from section 21a of the Bankruptcy Act [section 44(a) of former title 11], requires the debtor to appear at the meeting of creditors and submit to examination under oath. The purpose of the examination is to enable creditors and the trustee to determine if assets have improperly been disposed of or concealed or if there are grounds for objection to discharge. The scope of the examination under this section will be governed by the Rules of Bankruptcy Procedure, as it is today. See rules 205(d), 10–213(c), and 11–26. It is expected that the scope prescribed by these rules for liquidation cases, that is, "only the debtor's acts, conduct, or property, or any matter that may affect the administration of the estate, or the debtor's right to discharge" will remain substantially unchanged. In reorganization cases, the examination would be broader, including inquiry into the liabilities and financial condition of the debtor, the operation of his business, and the desirability of the continuance thereof, and other matters relevant to the case and to the formulation of the plan. Examination of other persons in connection with the bankruptcy case is left completely to the rules, just as examination of witnesses in civil cases is governed by the Federal Rules of Civil Procedure.

AMENDMENTS

1986—Pub. L. 99–554 amended section generally. Prior to amendment, section read as follows: "The debtor shall appear and submit to examination under oath at the meeting of creditors under section 341(a) of this title. Creditors, any indenture trustee, or any trustee or examiner in the case may examine the debtor."

1984—Pub. L. 98–353 substituted "examine" for "examiner".

EFFECTIVE DATE OF 1986 AMENDMENT

Effective date and applicability of amendment by Pub. L. 99–554 dependent upon the judicial district involved, see section 302(d), (e) of Pub. L. 99–554, set out as a note under section 581 of Title 28, Judiciary and Judicial Procedure.

EFFECTIVE DATE OF 1984 AMENDMENT

Amendment by Pub. L. 98–353 effective with respect to cases filed 90 days after July 10, 1984, see section 552(a) of Pub. L. 98–353, set out as a note under section 101 of this title.

PARTICIPATION BY BANKRUPTCY ADMINISTRATOR AT MEETINGS OF CREDITORS AND EQUITY SECURITY HOLDERS

A bankruptcy administrator or the bankruptcy administrator's designee may examine debtor at meeting of creditors and may administer oath required by this section, see section 105 of Pub. L. 103–394, set out as a note under section 341 of this title.

§ 344. Self-incrimination; immunity

Immunity for persons required to submit to examination, to testify, or to provide information in a case under this title may be granted under part V of title 18.

(Pub. L. 95–598, Nov. 6, 1978, 92 Stat. 2565.)

HISTORICAL AND REVISION NOTES

SENATE REPORT NO. 95–989

Part V [§6001 et seq.] of title 18 of the United States Code governs the granting of immunity to witnesses before Federal tribunals. The immunity provided under part V is only use immunity, not transactional immunity. Part V applies to all proceedings before Federal courts, before Federal grand juries, before administrative agencies, and before Congressional committees. It requires the Attorney General or the U. S. attorney to request or to approve any grant of immunity, whether before a court, grand jury, agency, or congressional committee.

This section carries part V over into bankruptcy cases. Thus, for a witness to be ordered to testify before a bankruptcy court in spite of a claim of privilege, the U. S. attorney for the district in which the court sits would have to request from the district court for that district the immunity order. The rule would apply to both debtors, creditors, and any other witnesses in a bankruptcy case. If the immunity were granted, the witness would be required to testify. If not, he could claim the privilege against self-incrimination.

Part V is a significant departure from current law. Under section 7a(10) of the Bankruptcy Act [section 25(a)(10) of former title 11], a debtor is required to testify in all circumstances, but any testimony he gives may not be used against him in any criminal proceeding, except testimony given in any hearing on objections to discharge. With that exception, section 7a(10) amounts to a blanket grant of use immunity to all debtors. Immunity for other witnesses in bankruptcy courts today is governed by part V of title 18.

The consequences of a claim of privileges by a debtor under proposed law and under current law differ as well. Under section 14c(6) of current law [section 32(c)(6) of former title 11], any refusal to answer a material question approved by the court will result in the denial of a discharge, even if the refusal is based on the privilege against self incrimination. Thus, the debtor is confronted with the choice between losing his discharge and opening himself up to possible criminal prosecution.

Under section 727(a)(6) of the proposed title 11, a debtor is only denied a discharge if he refuses to testify after having been granted immunity. If the debtor claims the privilege and the U. S. attorney does not request immunity from the district courts, then the debtor may refuse to testify and still retain his right to a discharge. It removes the Scylla and Charibdis choice for debtors that exists under the Bankruptcy Act [former title 11].

§ 345. Money of estates

(a) A trustee in a case under this title may make such deposit or investment of the money of the estate for which such trustee serves as will yield the maximum reasonable net return on such money, taking into account the safety of such deposit or investment.

(b) Except with respect to a deposit or investment that is insured or guaranteed by the United States or by a department, agency, or instrumentality of the United States or backed by the full faith and credit of the United States, the trustee shall require from an entity with which such money is deposited or invested—

(1) a bond—

(A) in favor of the United States;

(B) secured by the undertaking of a corporate surety approved by the United States trustee for the district in which the case is pending; and

(C) conditioned on—

(i) a proper accounting for all money so deposited or invested and for any return on such money;

(ii) prompt repayment of such money and return; and

(iii) faithful performance of duties as a depository; or

(2) the deposit of securities of the kind specified in section 9303 of title 31;

unless the court for cause orders otherwise.

(c) An entity with which such moneys are deposited or invested is authorized to deposit or invest such moneys as may be required under this section.

(Pub. L. 95–598, Nov. 6, 1978, 92 Stat. 2565; Pub. L. 97–258, § 3(c), Sept. 13, 1982, 96 Stat. 1064; Pub. L.

98-353, title III, §437, July 10, 1984, 98 Stat. 370; Pub. L. 99-554, title II, §214, Oct. 27, 1986, 100 Stat. 3099; Pub. L. 103-394, title II, §210, Oct. 22, 1994, 108 Stat. 4125.)

HISTORICAL AND REVISION NOTES

LEGISLATIVE STATEMENTS

The House amendment moves section 345(c) of the House bill to chapter 15 as part of the pilot program for the U.S. trustees. The bond required by section 345(b) may be a blanket bond posted by the financial depository sufficient to cover deposits by trustees in several cases, as is done under current law.

SENATE REPORT NO. 95-989

This section is a significant departure from section 61 of the Bankruptcy Act [section 101 of former title 11]. It permits a trustee in a bankruptcy case to make such deposit of investment of the money of the estate for which he serves as will yield the maximum reasonable net return on the money, taking into account the safety of such deposit or investment. Under current law, the trustee is permitted to deposit money only with banking institutions. Thus, the trustee is generally unable to secure a high rate of return on money of estates pending distribution, to the detriment of creditors. Under this section, the trustee may make deposits in savings and loans, may purchase government bonds, or make such other deposit or investment as is appropriate. Under proposed 11 U.S.C. 541(a)(6), and except as provided in subsection (c) of this section, any interest or gain realized on the deposit or investment of funds under this section will become property of the estate, and will thus enhance the recovery of creditors.

In order to protect the creditors, subsection (b) requires certain precautions against loss of the money so deposited or invested. The trustee must require from a person with which he deposits or invests money of an estate a bond in favor of the United States secured by approved corporate surety and conditioned on a proper accounting for all money deposited or invested and for any return on such money. Alternately, the trustee may require the deposit of securities of the kind specified in section 15 of title 6 of the United States Code [31 U.S.C. 9303], which governs the posting of security by banks that receive public moneys on deposit. These bonding requirements do not apply to deposits or investments that are insured or guaranteed the United States or a department, agency, or instrumentality of the United States, or that are backed by the full faith and credit of the United States.

These provisions do not address the question of aggregation of funds by a private chapter 13 trustee and are not to be construed as excluding such possibility. The Rules of Bankruptcy Procedure may provide for aggregation under appropriate circumstances and adequate safeguards in cases where there is a significant need, such as in districts in which there is a standing chapter 13 trustee. In such case, the interest or return on the funds would help defray the cost of administering the cases in which the standing trustee serves.

AMENDMENTS

1994—Subsec. (b). Pub. L. 103-394 substituted semicolon for period at end of par. (2) and inserted concluding provisions after par. (2).

1986—Subsec. (b). Pub. L. 99-554 amended subsec. (b) generally, substituting "approved by the United States trustee for the district" for "approved by the court for the district" in par. (1)(B).

1984—Subsec. (c). Pub. L. 98-353 added subsec. (c).

1982—Subsec. (b)(2). Pub. L. 97-258 substituted "section 9303 of title 31" for "section 15 of title 6".

EFFECTIVE DATE OF 1994 AMENDMENT

Amendment by Pub. L. 103-394 effective Oct. 22, 1994, and not applicable with respect to cases commenced under this title before Oct. 22, 1994, see section 702 of Pub. L. 103-394, set out as a note under section 101 of this title.

EFFECTIVE DATE OF 1986 AMENDMENT

Effective date and applicability of amendment by Pub. L. 99-554 dependent upon the judicial district involved, see section 302(d), (e) of Pub. L. 99-554, set out as a note under section 581 of Title 28, Judiciary and Judicial Procedure.

EFFECTIVE DATE OF 1984 AMENDMENT

Amendment by Pub. L. 98-353 effective with respect to cases filed 90 days after July 10, 1984, see section 552(a) of Pub. L. 98-353, set out as a note under section 101 of this title.

§ 346. Special provisions related to the treatment of State and local taxes

(a) Whenever the Internal Revenue Code of 1986 provides that a separate taxable estate or entity is created in a case concerning a debtor under this title, and the income, gain, loss, deductions, and credits of such estate shall be taxed to or claimed by the estate, a separate taxable estate is also created for purposes of any State and local law imposing a tax on or measured by income and such income, gain, loss, deductions, and credits shall be taxed to or claimed by the estate and may not be taxed to or claimed by the debtor. The preceding sentence shall not apply if the case is dismissed. The trustee shall make tax returns of income required under any such State or local law.

(b) Whenever the Internal Revenue Code of 1986 provides that no separate taxable estate shall be created in a case concerning a debtor under this title, and the income, gain, loss, deductions, and credits of an estate shall be taxed to or claimed by the debtor, such income, gain, loss, deductions, and credits shall be taxed to or claimed by the debtor under a State or local law imposing a tax on or measured by income and may not be taxed to or claimed by the estate. The trustee shall make such tax returns of income of corporations and of partnerships as are required under any State or local law, but with respect to partnerships, shall make such returns only to the extent such returns are also required to be made under such Code. The estate shall be liable for any tax imposed on such corporation or partnership, but not for any tax imposed on partners or members.

(c) With respect to a partnership or any entity treated as a partnership under a State or local law imposing a tax on or measured by income that is a debtor in a case under this title, any gain or loss resulting from a distribution of property from such partnership, or any distributive share of any income, gain, loss, deduction, or credit of a partner or member that is distributed, or considered distributed, from such partnership, after the commencement of the case, is gain, loss, income, deduction, or credit, as the case may be, of the partner or member, and if such partner or member is a debtor in a case under this title, shall be subject to tax in accordance with subsection (a) or (b).

(d) For purposes of any State or local law imposing a tax on or measured by income, the taxable period of a debtor in a case under this title shall terminate only if and to the extent that the taxable period of such debtor terminates under the Internal Revenue Code of 1986.

(e) The estate in any case described in subsection (a) shall use the same accounting method as the debtor used immediately before the commencement of the case, if such method of accounting complies with applicable nonbankruptcy tax law.

(f) For purposes of any State or local law imposing a tax on or measured by income, a transfer of property from the debtor to the estate or from the estate to the debtor shall not be treated as a disposition for purposes of any provision assigning tax consequences to a disposition, except to the extent that such transfer is treated as a disposition under the Internal Revenue Code of 1986.

(g) Whenever a tax is imposed pursuant to a State or local law imposing a tax on or measured by income pursuant to subsection (a) or (b), such tax shall be imposed at rates generally applicable to the same types of entities under such State or local law.

(h) The trustee shall withhold from any payment of claims for wages, salaries, commissions, dividends, interest, or other payments, or collect, any amount required to be withheld or collected under applicable State or local tax law, and shall pay such withheld or collected amount to the appropriate governmental unit at the time and in the manner required by such tax law, and with the same priority as the claim from which such amount was withheld or collected was paid.

(i)(1) To the extent that any State or local law imposing a tax on or measured by income provides for the carryover of any tax attribute from one taxable period to a subsequent taxable period, the estate shall succeed to such tax attribute in any case in which such estate is subject to tax under subsection (a).

(2) After such a case is closed or dismissed, the debtor shall succeed to any tax attribute to which the estate succeeded under paragraph (1) to the extent consistent with the Internal Revenue Code of 1986.

(3) The estate may carry back any loss or tax attribute to a taxable period of the debtor that ended before the date of the order for relief under this title to the extent that—

(A) applicable State or local tax law provides for a carryback in the case of the debtor; and

(B) the same or a similar tax attribute may be carried back by the estate to such a taxable period of the debtor under the Internal Revenue Code of 1986.

(j)(1) For purposes of any State or local law imposing a tax on or measured by income, income is not realized by the estate, the debtor, or a successor to the debtor by reason of discharge of indebtedness in a case under this title, except to the extent, if any, that such income is subject to tax under the Internal Revenue Code of 1986.

(2) Whenever the Internal Revenue Code of 1986 provides that the amount excluded from gross income in respect of the discharge of indebtedness in a case under this title shall be applied to reduce the tax attributes of the debtor or the estate, a similar reduction shall be made under any State or local law imposing a tax on or measured by income to the extent such State or local law recognizes such attributes. Such State or local law may also provide for the reduction of other attributes to the extent that the full amount of income from the discharge of indebtedness has not been applied.

(k)(1) Except as provided in this section and section 505, the time and manner of filing tax returns and the items of income, gain, loss, deduction, and credit of any taxpayer shall be determined under applicable nonbankruptcy law.

(2) For Federal tax purposes, the provisions of this section are subject to the Internal Revenue Code of 1986 and other applicable Federal nonbankruptcy law.

(Pub. L. 95–598, Nov. 6, 1978, 92 Stat. 2565; Pub. L. 98–353, title III, §438, July 10, 1984, 98 Stat. 370; Pub. L. 99–554, title II, §§257(g), 283(c), Oct. 27, 1986, 100 Stat. 3114, 3116; Pub. L. 103–394, title V, §501(d)(4), Oct. 22, 1994, 108 Stat. 4143; Pub. L. 109–8, title VII, §719(a)(1), Apr. 20, 2005, 119 Stat. 131.)

Historical and Revision Notes

Legislative Statements

Section 346 of the House amendment, together with sections 728 and 1146, represent special tax provisions applicable in bankruptcy. The policy contained in those sections reflects the policy that should be applied in Federal, State, and local taxes in the view of the House Committee on the Judiciary. The House Ways and Means Committee and the Senate Finance Committee did not have time to process a bankruptcy tax bill during the 95th Congress. It is anticipated that early in the 96th Congress, and before the effective date of the bankruptcy code [Oct. 1, 1979], the tax committees of Congress will have an opportunity to consider action with respect to amendments to the Internal Revenue Code [title 26] and the special tax provisions in title 11. Since the special tax provisions are likely to be amended during the first part of the 96th Congress, it is anticipated that the bench and bar will also study and comment on these special tax provisions prior to their revision.

Special tax provisions: State and local rules. This section provides special tax provisions dealing with the treatment, under State or local, but not Federal, tax law, of the method of taxing bankruptcy estates of individuals, partnerships, and corporations; survival and allocation of tax attributes between the bankrupt and the estate; return filing requirements; and the tax treatment of income from discharge of indebtedness. The Senate bill removed these rules pending adoption of Federal rules on these issues in the next Congress. The House amendment returns the State and local tax rules to section 346 so that they may be studied by the bankruptcy and tax bars who may wish to submit comments to Congress.

Withholding rules: Both the House bill and Senate amendment provide that the trustee is required to comply with the normal withholding rules applicable to the payment of wages and other payments. The House amendment retains this rule for State and local taxes only. The treatment of withholding of Federal taxes will be considered in the next Congress.

Section 726 of the Senate amendment provides that the rule requiring pro rata payment of all expenses within a priority category does not apply to the payment of amounts withheld by a bankruptcy trustee. The purpose of this rule was to insure that the trustee pay the full amount of the withheld taxes to the appropriate governmental tax authority. The House amendment deletes this rule as unnecessary because the existing practice conforms essentially to that rule. If the trustee fails to pay over in full amounts that he withheld, it is a violation of his trustee's duties which would permit the taxing authority to sue the trustee on his bond.

When taxes considered "incurred": The Senate amendment contained rules of general application dealing with when a tax is "incurred" for purposes of the various tax collection rules affecting the debtor and the estate. The House amendment adopts the substance of these rules and transfers them to section 507 of title 11.

Penalty for failure to pay tax: The Senate amendment contains a rule which relieves the debtor and the trustee from certain tax penalties for failure to make timely payment of a tax to the extent that the bankruptcy rules prevent the trustee or the debtor from paying the tax on time. Since most of these penalties relate to Federal taxes, the House amendment deletes these rules pending consideration of Federal tax rules affecting bankruptcy in the next Congress.

SENATE REPORT NO. 95-989

Subsection (a) indicates that subsections (b), (c), (d), (e), (g), (h), (i), and (j) apply notwithstanding any State or local tax law, but are subject to Federal tax law.

Subsection (b)(1) provides that in a case concerning an individual under chapter 7 or 11 of title 11, income of the estate is taxable only to the estate and not to the debtor. The second sentence of the paragraph provides that if such individual is a partner, the tax attributes of the partnership are distributable to the partner's estate rather than to the partner, except to the extent that section 728 of title 11 provides otherwise.

Subsection (b)(2) states a general rule that the estate of an individual is to be taxed as an estate. The paragraph is made subject to the remainder of section 346 and section 728 of title 11.

Subsection (b)(3) requires the accounting method, but not necessarily the accounting period, of the estate to be the same as the method used by the individual debtor.

Subsection (c)(1) states a general rule that the estate of a partnership or a corporated debtor is not a separate entity for tax purposes. The income of the debtor is to be taxed as if the case were not commenced, except as provided in the remainder of section 346 and section 728.

Subsection (c)(2) requires the trustee, except as provided in section 728 of title 11, to file all tax returns on behalf of the partnership or corporation during the case.

Subsection (d) indicates that the estate in a chapter 13 case is not a separate taxable entity and that all income of the estate is to be taxed to the debtor.

Subsection (e) establishes a business deduction consisting of allowed expenses of administration except for tax or capital expenses that are not otherwise deductible. The deduction may be used by the estate when it is a separate taxable entity or by the entity to which the income of the estate is taxed when it is not.

Subsection (f) imposes a duty on the trustee to comply with any Federal, State, or local tax law requiring withholding or collection of taxes from any payment of wages, salaries, commissions, dividends, interest, or other payments. Any amount withheld is to be paid to the taxing authority at the same time and with the same priority as the claim from which such amount withheld was paid.

Subsection (g)(1)(A) indicates that neither gain nor loss is recognized on the transfer by law of property from the debtor or a creditor to the estate. Subparagraph (B) provides a similar policy if the property of the estate is returned from the estate to the debtor other than by a sale of property to debtor. Subparagraph (C) also provides for nonrecognition of gain or loss in a case under chapter 11 if a corporate debtor transfers property to a successor corporation or to an affiliate under a joint plan. An exception is made to enable a taxing authority to cause recognition of gain or loss to the extent provided in IRC [title 26] section 371 (as amended by section 109 of this bill).

Subsection (g)(2) provides that any of the three kinds of transferees specified in paragraph (1) take the property with the same character, holding period, and basis in the hands of the transferor at the time of such transfer. The transferor's basis may be adjusted under section 346(j)(5) even if the discharge of indebtedness occurs after the transfer of property. Of course, no adjustment will occur if the transfer is from the debtor to the estate or if the transfer is from an entity that is not discharged.

Subsection (h) provides that the creation of the estate of an individual under chapter 7 or 11 of title 11 as a separate taxable entity does not affect the number of taxable years for purposes of computing loss carryovers or carrybacks. The section applies with respect to carryovers or carrybacks of the debtor transferred into the estate under section 346(i)(1) of title 11 or back to the debtor under section 346(i)(2) of title 11.

Subsection (i)(1) states a general rule that an estate that is a separate taxable entity nevertheless succeeds to all tax attributes of the debtor. The six enumerated attributes are illustrative and not exhaustive.

Subsection (i)(2) indicates that attributes passing from the debtor into an estate that is a separate taxable entity will return to the debtor if unused by the estate. The debtor is permitted to use any such attribute as though the case had not been commenced.

Subsection (i)(3) permits an estate that is a separate taxable entity to carryback losses of the estate to a taxable period of the debtor that ended before the case was filed. The estate is treated as if it were the debtor with respect to time limitations and other restrictions. The section makes clear that the debtor may not carryback any loss of his own from a tax year during the pendency of the case to such a period until the case is closed. No tolling of any period of limitation is provided with respect to carrybacks by the debtor of postpetition losses.

Subsection (j) sets forth seven special rules treating with the tax effects of forgiveness or discharge of indebtedness. The terms "forgiveness" and "discharge" are redundant, but are used to clarify that "discharge" in the context of a special tax provision in title 11 includes forgiveness of indebtedness whether or not such indebtedness is "discharged" in the bankruptcy sense.

Paragraph (1) states the general rule that forgiveness of indebtedness is not taxable except as otherwise provided in paragraphs (2)-(7). The paragraph is patterned after sections 268, 395, and 520 of the Bankruptcy Act [sections 668, 795, and 920 of former title 11].

Paragraph (2) disallows deductions for liabilities of a deductible nature in any year during or after the year of cancellation of such liabilities. For the purposes of this paragraph, "a deduction with respect to a liability" includes a capital loss incurred on the disposition of a capital asset with respect to a liability that was incurred in connection with the acquisition of such asset.

Paragraph (3) causes any net operating loss of a debtor that is an individual or corporation to be reduced by any discharge of indebtedness except as provided in paragraphs (2) or (4). If a deduction is disallowed under paragraph (2), then no double counting occurs. Thus, paragraph (3) will reflect the reduction of losses by liabilities that have been forgiven, including deductible liabilities or nondeductible liabilities such as repayment of principal on borrowed funds.

Paragraph (4) specifically excludes two kinds of indebtedness from reduction of net operating losses under paragraph (3) or from reduction of basis under paragraph (5). Subparagraph (A) excludes items of a deductible nature that were not deducted or that could not be deducted such as gambling losses or liabilities for interest owed to a relative of the debtor. Subparagraph (B) excludes indebtedness of a debtor that is an individual or corporation that resulted in deductions which did not offset income and that did not contribute to an unexpired net operating loss or loss carryover. In these situations, the debtor has derived no tax benefit so there is no need to incur an offsetting reduction.

Paragraph (5) provides a two-point test for reduction of basis. The paragraph replaces sections 270, 396, and

522 of the Bankruptcy Act [sections 670, 796, and 922 of former title 11]. Subparagraph (A) sets out the maximum amount by which basis may be reduced—the total indebtedness forgiven less adjustments made under paragraphs (2) and (3). This avoids double counting. If a deduction is disallowed under paragraph (2) or a carryover is reduced under paragraph (3) then the tax benefit is neutralized, and there is no need to reduce basis. Subparagraph (B) reduces basis to the extent the debtor's total basis of assets before the discharge exceeds total preexisting liabilities still remaining after discharge of indebtedness. This is a "basis solvency" limitation which differs from the usual test of solvency because it measures against the remaining liabilities the benefit aspect of assets, their basis, rather than their value. Paragraph (5) applies so that any transferee of the debtor's property who is required to use the debtor's basis takes the debtor's basis reduced by the lesser of (A) and (B). Thus, basis will be reduced, but never below a level equal to undischarged liabilities.

Paragraph (6) specifies that basis need not be reduced under paragraph (5) to the extent the debtor treats discharged indebtedness as taxable income. This permits the debtor to elect whether to recognize income, which may be advantageous if the debtor anticipates subsequent net operating losses, rather than to reduce basis.

Paragraph (7) establishes two rules excluding from the category of discharged indebtedness certain indebtedness that is exchanged for an equity security issued under a plan or that is forgiven as a contribution to capital by an equity security holder. Subparagraph (A) creates the first exclusion to the extent indebtedness consisting of items not of a deductible nature is exchanged for an equity security, other than the interests of a limited partner in a limited partnership, issued by the debtor or is forgiven as a contribution to capital by an equity security holder. Subparagraph (B) excludes indebtedness consisting of items of a deductible nature, if the exchange of stock for debts has the same effect as a cash payment equal to the value of the equity security, in the amount of the fair market value of the equity security or, if less, the extent to which such exchange has such effect. The two provisions treat the debtor as if it had originally issued stock instead of debt. Subparagraph (B) rectifies the inequity under current law between a cash basis and accrual basis debtor concerning the issuance of stock in exchange for previous services rendered that were of a greater value than the stock. Subparagraph (B) also changes current law by taxing forgiveness of indebtedness to the extent that stock is exchanged for the accrued interest component of a security, because the recipient of such stock would not be regarded as having received money under the *Carman* doctrine.

REFERENCES IN TEXT

The Internal Revenue Code of 1986, referred to in text, is classified generally to Title 26, Internal Revenue Code.

AMENDMENTS

2005—Pub. L. 109–8 amended section catchline and text generally. Prior to amendment, text consisted of subsecs. (a) to (j) relating to special tax provisions.

1994—Subsec. (a). Pub. L. 103–394, §504(d)(4)(A), substituted "Internal Revenue Code of 1986" for "Internal Revenue Code of 1954 (26 U.S.C. 1 et seq.)".

Subsec. (g)(1)(C). Pub. L. 103–394, §501(d)(4)(B), substituted "Internal Revenue Code of 1986" for "Internal Revenue Code of 1954 (26 U.S.C. 371)".

1986—Subsec. (b)(1). Pub. L. 99–554, §257(g)(1), inserted reference to chapter 12.

Subsec. (g)(1)(C). Pub. L. 99–554, §257(g)(2), inserted reference to chapter 12.

Subsec. (i)(1). Pub. L. 99–554, §257(g)(3), inserted reference to chapter 12.

Subsec. (j)(7). Pub. L. 99–554, §283(c), substituted "owed" for "owned".

1984—Subsec. (c)(2). Pub. L. 98–353 substituted "corporation" for "operation".

EFFECTIVE DATE OF 2005 AMENDMENT

Amendment by Pub. L. 109–8 effective 180 days after Apr. 20, 2005, and not applicable with respect to cases commenced under this title before such effective date, except as otherwise provided, see section 1501 of Pub. L. 109–8, set out as a note under section 101 of this title.

EFFECTIVE DATE OF 1994 AMENDMENT

Amendment by Pub. L. 103–394 effective Oct. 22, 1994, and not applicable with respect to cases commenced under this title before Oct. 22, 1994, see section 702 of Pub. L. 103–394, set out as a note under section 101 of this title.

EFFECTIVE DATE OF 1986 AMENDMENT

Amendment by section 257 of Pub. L. 99–554 effective 30 days after Oct. 27, 1986, but not applicable to cases commenced under this title before that date, see section 302(a), (c)(1) of Pub. L. 99–554, set out as a note under section 581 of Title 28, Judiciary and Judicial Procedure.

Amendment by section 283 of Pub. L. 99–554 effective 30 days after Oct. 27, 1986, see section 302(a) of Pub. L. 99–554.

EFFECTIVE DATE OF 1984 AMENDMENT

Amendment by Pub. L. 98–353 effective with respect to cases filed 90 days after July 10, 1984, see section 552(a) of Pub. L. 98–353, set out as a note under section 101 of this title.

§347. Unclaimed property

(a) Ninety days after the final distribution under section 726, 1226, or 1326 of this title in a case under chapter 7, 12, or 13 of this title, as the case may be, the trustee shall stop payment on any check remaining unpaid, and any remaining property of the estate shall be paid into the court and disposed of under chapter 129 of title 28.

(b) Any security, money, or other property remaining unclaimed at the expiration of the time allowed in a case under chapter 9, 11, or 12 of this title for the presentation of a security or the performance of any other act as a condition to participation in the distribution under any plan confirmed under section 943(b), 1129, 1173, or 1225 of this title, as the case may be, becomes the property of the debtor or of the entity acquiring the assets of the debtor under the plan, as the case may be.

(Pub. L. 95–598, Nov. 6, 1978, 92 Stat. 2568; Pub. L. 99–554, title II, §257(h), Oct. 27, 1986, 100 Stat. 3114.)

HISTORICAL AND REVISION NOTES

LEGISLATIVE STATEMENTS

Section 347(a) of the House amendment adopts a comparable provision contained in the Senate amendment instructing the trustee to stop payment on any check remaining unpaid more than 90 days after the final distribution in a case under Chapter 7 or 13. Technical changes are made in section 347(b) to cover distributions in a railroad reorganization.

SENATE REPORT NO. 95–989

Section 347 is derived from Bankruptcy Act §66 [section 106 of former title 11]. Subsection (a) requires the trustee to stop payment on any distribution check that is unpaid 90 days after the final distribution in a case under chapter 7 or 13. The unclaimed funds, and any other property of the estate are paid into the court and disposed of under chapter 129 [§2041 et seq.] of title 28.

which requires the clerk of court to hold the funds for their owner for 5 years, after which they escheat to the Treasury.

Subsection (b) specifies that any property remaining unclaimed at the expiration of the time allowed in a chapter 9 or 11 case for presentation (exchange) of securities or the performance of any other act as a condition to participation in the plan reverts to the debtor or the entity acquiring the assets of the debtor under the plan. Conditions to participation under a plan include such acts as cashing a check, surrendering securities for cancellation, and so on. Similar provisions are found in sections 96(d) and 205 of current law [sections 416(d) and 605 of former title 11].

AMENDMENTS

1986—Subsec. (a). Pub. L. 99–554, §257(h)(1), inserted references to section 1226 and chapter 12 of this title.

Subsec. (b). Pub. L. 99–554, §257(h)(2), inserted references to chapter 12 and section 1225 of this title.

EFFECTIVE DATE OF 1986 AMENDMENT

Amendment by Pub. L. 99–554 effective 30 days after Oct. 27, 1986, but not applicable to cases commenced under this title before that date, see section 302(a), (c)(1) of Pub. L. 99–554, set out as a note under section 581 of Title 28, Judiciary and Judicial Procedure.

§348. Effect of conversion

(a) Conversion of a case from a case under one chapter of this title to a case under another chapter of this title constitutes an order for relief under the chapter to which the case is converted, but, except as provided in subsections (b) and (c) of this section, does not effect a change in the date of the filing of the petition, the commencement of the case, or the order for relief.

(b) Unless the court for cause orders otherwise, in sections 701(a), 727(a)(10), 727(b), 728(a), 728(b),[1] 1102(a), 1110(a)(1), 1121(b), 1121(c), 1141(d)(4), 1146(a), 1146(b), 1201(a), 1221, 1228(a), 1301(a), and 1305(a) of this title, "the order for relief under this chapter" in a chapter to which a case has been converted under section 706, 1112, 1208, or 1307 of this title means the conversion of such case to such chapter.

(c) Sections 342 and 365(d) of this title apply in a case that has been converted under section 706, 1112, 1208, or 1307 of this title, as if the conversion order were the order for relief.

(d) A claim against the estate or the debtor that arises after the order for relief but before conversion in a case that is converted under section 1112, 1208, or 1307 of this title, other than a claim specified in section 503(b) of this title, shall be treated for all purposes as if such claim had arisen immediately before the date of the filing of the petition.

(e) Conversion of a case under section 706, 1112, 1208, or 1307 of this title terminates the service of any trustee or examiner that is serving in the case before such conversion.

(f)(1) Except as provided in paragraph (2), when a case under chapter 13 of this title is converted to a case under another chapter under this title—

(A) property of the estate in the converted case shall consist of property of the estate, as of the date of filing of the petition, that remains in the possession of or is under the control of the debtor on the date of conversion;

(B) valuations of property and of allowed secured claims in the chapter 13 case shall apply only in a case converted to a case under chapter 11 or 12, but not in a case converted to a case under chapter 7, with allowed secured claims in cases under chapters 11 and 12 reduced to the extent that they have been paid in accordance with the chapter 13 plan; and

(C) with respect to cases converted from chapter 13—

(i) the claim of any creditor holding security as of the date of the petition shall continue to be secured by that security unless the full amount of such claim determined under applicable nonbankruptcy law has been paid in full as of the date of conversion, notwithstanding any valuation or determination of the amount of an allowed secured claim made for the purposes of the case under chapter 13; and

(ii) unless a prebankruptcy default has been fully cured under the plan at the time of conversion, in any proceeding under this title or otherwise, the default shall have the effect given under applicable nonbankruptcy law.

(2) If the debtor converts a case under chapter 13 of this title to a case under another chapter under this title in bad faith, the property of the estate in the converted case shall consist of the property of the estate as of the date of conversion.

(Pub. L. 95–598, Nov. 6, 1978, 92 Stat. 2568; Pub. L. 99–554, title II, §257(i), Oct. 27, 1986, 100 Stat. 3115; Pub. L. 103–394, title III, §311, title V, §501(d)(5), Oct. 22, 1994, 108 Stat. 4138, 4144; Pub. L. 109–8, title III, §309(a), title XII, §1207, Apr. 20, 2005, 119 Stat. 82, 194.)

HISTORICAL AND REVISION NOTES

LEGISLATIVE STATEMENTS

The House amendment adopts section 348(b) of the Senate amendment with slight modifications, as more accurately reflecting sections to which this particular effect of conversion should apply.

Section 348(e) of the House amendment is a stylistic revision of similar provisions contained in H.R. 8200 as passed by the House and in the Senate amendment. Termination of services is expanded to cover any examiner serving in the case before conversion, as done in H.R. 8200 as passed by the House.

SENATE REPORT NO. 95–989

This section governs the effect of the conversion of a case from one chapter of the bankruptcy code to another chapter. Subsection (a) specifies that the date of the filing of the petition, the commencement of the case, or the order for relief are unaffected by conversion, with some exceptions specified in subsections (b) and (c).

Subsection (b) lists certain sections in the operative chapters of the bankruptcy code in which there is a reference to "the order for relief under this chapter." In those sections, the reference is to be read as a reference to the conversion order if the case has been converted into the particular chapter. Subsection (c) specifies that notice is to be given of the conversion order the same as notice was given of the order for relief, and that the time the trustee (or debtor in possession) has for assuming or rejecting executory contracts recommences, thus giving an opportunity for a newly appointed trustee to familiarize himself with the case.

Subsection (d) provides for special treatment of claims that arise during chapter 11 or 13 cases before

[1] See References in Text note below.

the case is converted to a liquidation case. With the exception of claims specified in proposed 11 U.S.C. 503(b) (administrative expenses), preconversion claims are treated the same as prepetition claims.

Subsection (e) provides that conversion of a case terminates the service of any trustee serving in the case prior to conversion.

REFERENCES IN TEXT

Section 728 of this title, referred to in subsec. (b), was repealed by Pub. L. 109-8, title VII, §719(b)(1), Apr. 20, 2005, 119 Stat. 133.

AMENDMENTS

2005—Subsec. (f)(1)(B). Pub. L. 109-8, §309(a)(2)(A), substituted "only in a case converted to a case under chapter 11 or 12, but not in a case converted to a case under chapter 7, with allowed secured claims in cases under chapters 11 and 12" for "in the converted case, with allowed secured claims".

Subsec. (f)(1)(C). Pub. L. 109-8, §309(a)(1), (2)(B), (3), added subpar. (C).

Subsec. (f)(2). Pub. L. 109-8, §1207, inserted "of the estate" after "bad faith, the property".

1994—Subsec. (b). Pub. L. 103-394, §501(d)(5), substituted "1201(a), 1221, 1228(a), 1301(a), and 1305(a)" for "1301(a), 1305(a), 1201(a), 1221, and 1228(a)" and "1208, or 1307" for "1307, or 1208".

Subsecs. (c) to (e). Pub. L. 103-394, §501(d)(5)(B), substituted "1208, or 1307" for "1307, or 1208".

Subsec. (f). Pub. L. 103-394, §311, added subsec. (f).

1986—Subsec. (b). Pub. L. 99-554, §257(i)(1), substituted references to sections 1201(a), 1221, and 1228(a) of this title for reference to section 1328(a) of this title, and inserted reference to section 1208 of this title.

Subsecs. (c) to (e). Pub. L. 99-554, §257(i)(2), (3), inserted reference to section 1208 of this title.

EFFECTIVE DATE OF 2005 AMENDMENT

Amendment by Pub. L. 109-8 effective 180 days after Apr. 20, 2005, and not applicable with respect to cases commenced under this title before such effective date, except as otherwise provided, see section 1501 of Pub. L. 109-8, set out as a note under section 101 of this title.

EFFECTIVE DATE OF 1994 AMENDMENT

Amendment by Pub. L. 103-394 effective Oct. 22, 1994, and not applicable with respect to cases commenced under this title before Oct. 22, 1994, see section 702 of Pub. L. 103-394, set out as a note under section 101 of this title.

EFFECTIVE DATE OF 1986 AMENDMENT

Amendment by Pub. L. 99-554 effective 30 days after Oct. 27, 1986, but not applicable to cases commenced under this title before that date, see section 302(a), (c)(1) of Pub. L. 99-554, set out as a note under section 581 of Title 28, Judiciary and Judicial Procedure.

§ 349. Effect of dismissal

(a) Unless the court, for cause, orders otherwise, the dismissal of a case under this title does not bar the discharge, in a later case under this title, of debts that were dischargeable in the case dismissed; nor does the dismissal of a case under this title prejudice the debtor with regard to the filing of a subsequent petition under this title, except as provided in section 109(g) of this title.

(b) Unless the court, for cause, orders otherwise, a dismissal of a case other than under section 742 of this title—

(1) reinstates—

(A) any proceeding or custodianship superseded under section 543 of this title;

(B) any transfer avoided under section 522, 544, 545, 547, 548, 549, or 724(a) of this title, or preserved under section 510(c)(2), 522(i)(2), or 551 of this title; and

(C) any lien voided under section 506(d) of this title;

(2) vacates any order, judgment, or transfer ordered, under section 522(i)(1), 542, 550, or 553 of this title; and

(3) revests the property of the estate in the entity in which such property was vested immediately before the commencement of the case under this title.

(Pub. L. 95-598, Nov. 6, 1978, 92 Stat. 2569; Pub. L. 98-353, title III, §303, July 10, 1984, 98 Stat. 352; Pub. L. 103-394, title V, §501(d)(6), Oct. 22, 1994, 108 Stat. 4144.)

HISTORICAL AND REVISION NOTES

LEGISLATIVE STATEMENTS

Section 349(b)(2) of the House amendment adds a cross reference to section 553 to reflect the new right of recovery of setoffs created under that section. Corresponding changes are made throughout the House amendment.

SENATE REPORT NO. 95-989

Subsection (a) specifies that unless the court for cause orders otherwise, the dismissal of a case is without prejudice. The debtor is not barred from receiving a discharge in a later case of debts that were dischargeable in the case dismissed. Of course, this subsection refers only to pre-discharge dismissals. If the debtor has already received a discharge and it is not revoked, then the debtor would be barred under section 727(a) from receiving a discharge in a subsequent liquidation case for six years. Dismissal of an involuntary on the merits will generally not give rise to adequate cause so as to bar the debtor from further relief.

Subsection (b) specifies that the dismissal reinstates proceedings or custodianships that were superseded by the bankruptcy case, reinstates avoided transfers, reinstates voided liens, vacates any order, judgment, or transfer ordered as a result of the avoidance of a transfer and revests the property of the estate in the entity in which the property was vested at the commencement of the case. The court is permitted to order a different result for cause. The basic purpose of the subsection is to undo the bankruptcy case, as far as practicable, and to restore all property rights to the position in which they were found at the commencement of the case. This does not necessarily encompass undoing sales of property from the estate to a good faith purchaser. Where there is a question over the scope of the subsection, the court will make the appropriate orders to protect rights acquired in reliance on the bankruptcy case.

AMENDMENTS

1994—Subsec. (a). Pub. L. 103-394 substituted "109(g)" for "109(f)".

1984—Subsec. (a). Pub. L. 98-353 inserted "; nor does the dismissal of a case under this title prejudice the debtor with regard to the filing of a subsequent petition under this title, except as provided in section 109(f) of this title".

EFFECTIVE DATE OF 1994 AMENDMENT

Amendment by Pub. L. 103-394 effective Oct. 22, 1994, and not applicable with respect to cases commenced under this title before Oct. 22, 1994, see section 702 of Pub. L. 103-394, set out as a note under section 101 of this title.

EFFECTIVE DATE OF 1984 AMENDMENT

Amendment by Pub. L. 98-353 effective with respect to cases filed 90 days after July 10, 1984, see section 552(a) of Pub. L. 98-353, set out as a note under section 101 of this title.

§ 350. Closing and reopening cases

(a) After an estate is fully administered and the court has discharged the trustee, the court shall close the case.

(b) A case may be reopened in the court in which such case was closed to administer assets, to accord relief to the debtor, or for other cause.

(Pub. L. 95–598, Nov. 6, 1978, 92 Stat. 2569; Pub. L. 98–353, title III, § 439, July 10, 1984, 98 Stat. 370.)

HISTORICAL AND REVISION NOTES

SENATE REPORT NO. 95–989

Subsection (a) requires the court to close a bankruptcy case after the estate is fully administered and the trustee discharged. The Rules of Bankruptcy Procedure will provide the procedure for case closing. Subsection (b) permits reopening of the case to administer assets, to accord relief to the debtor, or for other cause. Though the court may permit reopening of a case so that the trustee may exercise an avoiding power, laches may constitute a bar to an action that has been delayed too long. The case may be reopened in the court in which it was closed. The rules will prescribe the procedure by which a case is reopened and how it will be conducted after reopening.

AMENDMENTS

1984—Subsec. (b). Pub. L. 98–353 substituted "A" for "a".

EFFECTIVE DATE OF 1984 AMENDMENT

Amendment by Pub. L. 98–353 effective with respect to cases filed 90 days after July 10, 1984, see section 552(a) of Pub. L. 98–353, set out as a note under section 101 of this title.

§ 351. Disposal of patient records

If a health care business commences a case under chapter 7, 9, or 11, and the trustee does not have a sufficient amount of funds to pay for the storage of patient records in the manner required under applicable Federal or State law, the following requirements shall apply:

(1) The trustee shall—

(A) promptly publish notice, in 1 or more appropriate newspapers, that if patient records are not claimed by the patient or an insurance provider (if applicable law permits the insurance provider to make that claim) by the date that is 365 days after the date of that notification, the trustee will destroy the patient records; and

(B) during the first 180 days of the 365-day period described in subparagraph (A), promptly attempt to notify directly each patient that is the subject of the patient records and appropriate insurance carrier concerning the patient records by mailing to the most recent known address of that patient, or a family member or contact person for that patient, and to the appropriate insurance carrier an appropriate notice regarding the claiming or disposing of patient records.

(2) If, after providing the notification under paragraph (1), patient records are not claimed during the 365-day period described under that paragraph, the trustee shall mail, by certified mail, at the end of such 365-day period a written request to each appropriate Federal agency to request permission from that agency to deposit the patient records with that agency, except that no Federal agency is required to accept patient records under this paragraph.

(3) If, following the 365-day period described in paragraph (2) and after providing the notification under paragraph (1), patient records are not claimed by a patient or insurance provider, or request is not granted by a Federal agency to deposit such records with that agency, the trustee shall destroy those records by—

(A) if the records are written, shredding or burning the records; or

(B) if the records are magnetic, optical, or other electronic records, by otherwise destroying those records so that those records cannot be retrieved.

(Added Pub. L. 109–8, title XI, § 1102(a), Apr. 20, 2005, 119 Stat. 189.)

EFFECTIVE DATE

Section effective 180 days after Apr. 20, 2005, and not applicable with respect to cases commenced under this title before such effective date, except as otherwise provided, see section 1501 of Pub. L. 109–8, set out as an Effective Date of 2005 Amendment note under section 101 of this title.

SUBCHAPTER IV—ADMINISTRATIVE POWERS

§ 361. Adequate protection

When adequate protection is required under section 362, 363, or 364 of this title of an interest of an entity in property, such adequate protection may be provided by—

(1) requiring the trustee to make a cash payment or periodic cash payments to such entity, to the extent that the stay under section 362 of this title, use, sale, or lease under section 363 of this title, or any grant of a lien under section 364 of this title results in a decrease in the value of such entity's interest in such property;

(2) providing to such entity an additional or replacement lien to the extent that such stay, use, sale, lease, or grant results in a decrease in the value of such entity's interest in such property; or

(3) granting such other relief, other than entitling such entity to compensation allowable under section 503(b)(1) of this title as an administrative expense, as will result in the realization by such entity of the indubitable equivalent of such entity's interest in such property.

(Pub. L. 95–598, Nov. 6, 1978, 92 Stat. 2569; Pub. L. 98–353, title III, § 440, July 10, 1984, 98 Stat. 370.)

HISTORICAL AND REVISION NOTES

LEGISLATIVE STATEMENTS

Section 361 of the House amendment represents a compromise between H.R. 8200 as passed by the House and the Senate amendment regarding the issue of "adequate protection" of a secured party. The House amendment deletes the provision found in section 361(3) of H.R. 8200 as passed by the House. It would have permitted adequate protection to be provided by giving the secured party an administrative expense regarding any decrease in the value of such party's collateral. In every case there is the uncertainty that the estate will have sufficient property to pay administrative expenses in full.

Section 361(4) of H.R. 8200 as passed by the House is modified in section 361(3) of the House amendment to indicate that the court may grant other forms of adequate protection, other than an administrative expense, which will result in the realization by the secured creditor of the indubitable equivalent of the creditor's interest in property. In the special instance where there is a reserve fund maintained under the security agreement, such as in the typical bondholder case, indubitable equivalent means that the bondholders would be entitled to be protected as to the reserve fund, in addition to the regular payments needed to service the debt. Adequate protection of an interest of an entity in property is intended to protect a creditor's allowed secured claim. To the extent the protection proves to be inadequate after the fact, the creditor is entitled to a first priority administrative expense under section 503(b).

In the special case of a creditor who has elected application of creditor making an election under section 1111(b)(2), that creditor is entitled to adequate protection of the creditor's interest in property to the extent of the value of the collateral not to the extent of the creditor's allowed secured claim, which is inflated to cover a deficiency as a result of such election.

SENATE REPORT NO. 95–989

Sections 362, 363, and 364 require, in certain circumstances, that the court determine in noticed hearings whether the interest of a secured creditor or co-owner of property with the debtor is adequately protected in connection with the sale or use of property. The interests of which the court may provide protection in the ways described in this section include equitable as well as legal interests. For example, a right to enforce a pledge and a right to recover property delivered to a debtor under a consignment agreement or an agreement of sale or return are interests that may be entitled to protection. This section specifies means by which adequate protection may be provided but, to avoid placing the court in an administrative role, does not require the court to provide it. Instead, the trustee or debtor in possession or the creditor will provide or propose a protection method. If the party that is affected by the proposed action objects, the court will determine whether the protection provided is adequate. The purpose of this section is to illustrate means by which it may be provided and to define the limits of the concept.

The concept of adequate protection is derived from the fifth amendment protection of property interests as enunciated by the Supreme Court. See *Wright v. Union Central Life Ins. Co.*, 311 U.S. 273 (1940); *Louisville Joint Stock Land Bank v. Radford*, 295 U.S. 555 (1935).

The automatic stay also provides creditor protection. Without it, certain creditors would be able to pursue their own remedies against the debtor's property. Those who acted first would obtain payment of the claims in preference to and to the detriment of other creditors. Bankruptcy is designed to provide an orderly liquidation procedure under which all creditors are treated equally. A race of diligence by creditors for the debtor's assets prevents that.

Subsection (a) defines the scope of the automatic stay, by listing the acts that are stayed by the commencement of the case. The commencement or continuation, including the issuance of process, of a judicial, administrative or other proceeding against the debtor that was or could have been commenced before the commencement of the bankruptcy case is stayed under paragraph (1). The scope of this paragraph is broad. All proceedings are stayed, including arbitration, administrative, and judicial proceedings. Proceeding in this sense encompasses civil actions and all proceedings even if they are not before governmental tribunals.

The stay is not permanent. There is adequate provision for relief from the stay elsewhere in the section. However, it is important that the trustee have an opportunity to inventory the debtor's position before proceeding with the administration of the case. Undoubtedly the court will lift the stay for proceedings before specialized or nongovernmental tribunals to allow those proceedings to come to a conclusion. Any party desiring to enforce an order in such a proceeding would thereafter have to come before the bankruptcy court to collect assets. Nevertheless, it will often be more appropriate to permit proceedings to continue in their place of origin, when no great prejudice to the bankruptcy estate would result, in order to leave the parties to their chosen forum and to relieve the bankruptcy court from many duties that may be handled elsewhere.

Paragraph (2) stays the enforcement, against the debtor or against property of the estate, of a judgment obtained before the commencement of the bankruptcy case. Thus, execution and levy against the debtors' prepetition property are stayed, and attempts to collect a judgment from the debtor personally are stayed.

Paragraph (3) stays any act to obtain possession of property of the estate (that is, property of the debtor as of the date of the filing of the petition) or property from the estate (property over which the estate has control or possession). The purpose of this provision is to prevent dismemberment of the estate. Liquidation must proceed in an orderly fashion. Any distribution of property must be by the trustee after he has had an opportunity to familiarize himself with the various rights and interests involved and with the property available for distribution.

Paragraph (4) stays lien creation against property of the estate. Thus, taking possession to perfect a lien or obtaining court process is prohibited. To permit lien creation after bankruptcy would give certain creditors preferential treatment by making them secured instead of unsecured.

Paragraph (5) stays any act to create or enforce a lien against property of the debtor, that is, most property that is acquired after the date of the filing of the petition, property that is exempted, or property that does not pass to the estate, to the extent that the lien secures a prepetition claim. Again, to permit postbankruptcy lien creation or enforcement would permit certain creditors to receive preferential treatment. It may also circumvent the debtors' discharge.

Paragraph (6) prevents creditors from attempting in any way to collect a prepetition debt. Creditors in consumer cases occasionally telephone debtors to encourage repayment in spite of bankruptcy. Inexperienced, frightened, or ill-counseled debtors may succumb to suggestions to repay notwithstanding their bankruptcy. This provision prevents evasion of the purpose of the bankruptcy laws by sophisticated creditors.

Paragraph (7) stays setoffs of mutual debts and credits between the debtor and creditors. As with all other paragraphs of subsection (a), this paragraph does not affect the right of creditors. It simply stays its enforcement pending an orderly examination of the debtor's and creditors' rights.

Subsection (b) lists seven exceptions to the automatic stay. The effect of an exception is not to make the action immune from injunction.

The court has ample other powers to stay actions not covered by the automatic stay. Section 105, of proposed title 11, derived from Bankruptcy Act §2a(15) [section 11(a)(15) of former title 11], grants the power to issue orders necessary or appropriate to carry out the provisions of title 11. The district court and the bankruptcy court as its adjunct have all the traditional injunctive powers of a court of equity, 28 U.S.C. §§151 and 164 as proposed in S. 2266, §201, and 28 U.S.C. §1334, as proposed in S. 2266, §216. Stays or injunctions issued under these other sections will not be automatic upon the commencement of the case, but will be granted or issued under the usual rules for the issuance of injunctions. By excepting an act or action from the automatic stay, the bill simply requires that the trustee move the court into action, rather than requiring the stayed party to request relief from the stay. There are some actions, enumerated in the exceptions, that generally should not be stayed automatically upon the commencement of the case, for reasons of either policy or practicality. Thus, the court will have to determine on a case-by-case basis whether a particular action which may be harming the estate should be stayed.

With respect to stays issued under other powers, or the application of the automatic stay, to governmental actions, this section and the other sections mentioned are intended to be an express waiver of sovereign immunity of the Federal Government, and an assertion of the bankruptcy power over State governments under the supremacy clause notwithstanding a State's sovereign immunity.

The first exception is of criminal proceedings against the debtor. The bankruptcy laws are not a haven for criminal offenders, but are designed to give relief from financial overextension. Thus, criminal actions and proceedings may proceed in spite of bankruptcy.

Paragraph (2) excepts from the stay the collection of alimony, maintenance or support from property that is not property of the estate. This will include property acquired after the commencement of the case, exempted property, and property that does not pass to the estate. The automatic stay is one means of protecting the debtor's discharge. Alimony, maintenance and support obligations are excepted from discharge. Staying collection of them, when not to the detriment of other creditors (because the collection effort is against property that is not property of the estate) does not further that goal. Moreover, it could lead to hardship on the part of the protected spouse or children.

Paragraph (3) excepts any act to perfect an interest in property to the extent that the trustee's rights and powers are limited under section 546(a) of the bankruptcy code. That section permits postpetition perfection of certain liens to be effective against the trustee. If the act of perfection, such as filing, were stayed, the section would be nullified.

Paragraph (4) excepts commencement or continuation of actions and proceedings by governmental units to enforce police or regulatory powers. Thus, where a governmental unit is suing a debtor to prevent or stop violation of fraud, environmental protection, consumer protection, safety, or similar police or regulatory laws, or attempting to fix damages for violation of such a law, the action or proceeding is not stayed under the automatic stay.

Paragraph (5) makes clear that the exception extends to permit an injunction and enforcement of an injunction, and to permit the entry of a money judgment, but does not extend to permit enforcement of a money judgment. Since the assets of the debtor are in the possession and control of the bankruptcy court, and since they constitute a fund out of which all creditors are entitled to share, enforcement by a governmental unit of a money judgment would give it preferential treatment to the detriment of all other creditors.

Paragraph (6) excepts the setoff of any mutual debt and claim for commodity transactions.

Paragraph (7) excepts actions by the Secretary of Housing and Urban Development to foreclose or take possession in a case of a loan insured under the National Housing Act [12 U.S.C. 1701 et seq.]. A general exception for such loans is found in current sections 263 and 517 [sections 663 and 917 of former title 11], the exception allowed by this paragraph is much more limited.

Subsection (c) of section 362 specifies the duration of the automatic stay. Paragraph (1) terminates a stay of an act against property of the estate when the property ceases to be property of the estate, such as by sale, abandonment, or exemption. It does not terminate the stay against property of the debtor if the property leaves the estate and goes to the debtor. Paragraph (2) terminates the stay of any other act on the earliest of the time the case is closed, the time the case is dismissed, or the time a discharge is granted or denied (unless the debtor is a corporation or partnership in a chapter 7 case).

Subsection (c) governs automatic termination of the stay. Subsections (d) through (g) govern termination of the stay by the court on the request of a party in interest.

Subsection (d) requires the court, upon motion of a party in interest, to grant relief from the stay for cause, such as by terminating, annulling, modifying, or conditioning the stay. The lack of adequate protection of an interest in property is one cause for relief, but is not the only cause. Other causes might include the lack of any connection with or interference with the pending bankruptcy case. Generally, proceedings in which the debtor is a fiduciary, or involving postpetition activities of the debtor, need not be stayed because they bear no relationship to the purpose of the automatic stay, which is protection of the debtor and his estate from his creditors.

Upon the court's finding that the debtor has no equity in the property subject to the stay and that the property is not necessary to an effective reorganization of the debtor, the subsection requires the court grant relief from the stay. To aid in this determination, guidelines are established where the property subject to the stay is real property. An exception to "the necessary to an effective reorganization" requirement is made for real property on which no business is being conducted other than operating the real property and activities incident thereto. The intent of this exception is to reach the single-asset apartment type cases which involve primarily tax-shelter investments and for which the bankruptcy laws have provided a too facile method to relay conditions, but not the operating shopping center and hotel cases where attempts at reorganization should be permitted. Property in which the debtor has equity but which is not necessary to an effective reorganization of the debtor should be sold under section 363. Hearings under this subsection are given calendar priority to ensure that court congestion will not unduly prejudice the rights of creditors who may be obviously entitled to relief from the operation of the automatic stay.

Subsection (e) provides protection that is not always available under present law. The subsection sets a time certain within which the bankruptcy court must rule on the adequacy of protection provided for the secured creditor's interest. If the court does not rule within 30 days from a request by motion for relief from the stay, the stay is automatically terminated with respect to the property in question. To accommodate more complex cases, the subsection permits the court to make a preliminary ruling after a preliminary hearing. After a preliminary hearing, the court may continue the stay only if there is a reasonable likelihood that the party opposing relief from the stay will prevail at the final hearing. Because the stay is essentially an injunction, the three stages of the stay may be analogized to the three stages of an injunction. The filing of the petition which gives rise to the automatic stay is similar to a temporary restraining order. The preliminary hearing is similar to the hearing on a preliminary injunction, and the final hearing and order are similar to the hearing and issuance or denial of a permanent injunction. The main difference lies in which party must bring the issue before the court. While in the injunction setting, the party seeking the injunction must prosecute the action, in proceeding for relief from the automatic stay, the enjoined party must move. The difference does not, however, shift the burden of proof. Subsection (g) leaves that burden on the party opposing relief from the stay (that is, on the party seeking continuance of the injunction) on the issue of adequate protection and existence of an equity. It is not, however, intended to be confined strictly to the constitutional requirement. This section and the concept of adequate protection are based as much on policy grounds as on constitutional grounds. Secured creditors should not be deprived of the benefit of their bargain. There may be situations in bankruptcy where giving a secured creditor an absolute right to his bargain may be impossible or seriously detrimental to the policy of the bankruptcy laws. Thus, this section recognizes the availability of alternate means of protecting a secured creditor's interest where such steps are a necessary part of the rehabilitative process. Though the creditor might not be able to retain his lien upon the specific collateral held at the time of filing, the purpose of the section is to insure that the secured creditor receives the value for which he bargained.

The section specifies two exclusive means of providing adequate protection, both of which may require an approximate determination of the value of the protected entity's interest in the property involved. The section does not specify how value is to be determined, nor does it specify when it is to be determined. These matters are left to case-by-case interpretation and development. In light of the restrictive approach of the section to the availability of means of providing adequate protection, this flexibility is important to permit the courts to adapt to varying circumstances and changing modes of financing.

Neither is it expected that the courts will construe the term value to mean, in every case, forced sale liquidation value or full going concern value. There is wide latitude between those two extremes although forced sale liquidation value will be a minimum.

In any particular case, especially a reorganization case, the determination of which entity should be entitled to the difference between the going concern value and the liquidation value must be based on equitable considerations arising from the facts of the case. Finally, the determination of value is binding only for the purposes of the specific hearing and is not to have a res judicata effect.

The first method of adequate protection outlined is the making of cash payments to compensate for the expected decrease in value of the opposing entity's interest. This provision is derived from *In re Bermec Corporation*, 445 F.2d 367 (2d Cir. 1971), though in that case it is not clear whether the payments offered were adequate to compensate the secured creditors for their loss. The use of periodic payments may be appropriate where, for example, the property in question is depreciating at a relatively fixed rate. The periodic payments would be to compensate for the depreciation and might, but need not necessarily, be in the same amount as payments due on the secured obligation.

The second method is the fixing of an additional or replacement lien on other property of the debtor to the extent of the decrease in value or actual consumption of the property involved. The purpose of this method is to provide the protected entity with an alternative means of realizing the value of the original property, if it should decline during the case, by granting an interest in additional property from whose value the entity may realize its loss. This is consistent with the view expressed in *Wright v. Union Central Life Ins. Co.*, 311 U.S. 273 (1940), where the Court suggested that it was the value of the secured creditor's collateral, and not necessarily his rights in specific collateral, that was entitled to protection.

The section makes no provision for the granting of an administrative priority as a method of providing adequate protection to an entity as was suggested in *In re Yale Express System, Inc.*, 384 F.2d 990 (2d Cir. 1967), because such protection is too uncertain to be meaningful.

HOUSE REPORT NO. 95–595

The section specifies four means of providing adequate protection. They are neither exclusive nor exhaustive. They all rely, however, on the value of the protected entity's interest in the property involved. The section does not specify how value is to be determined, nor does it specify when it is to be determined. These matters are left to case-by-case interpretation and development. It is expected that the courts will apply the concept in light of facts of each case and general equitable principles. It is not intended that the courts will develop a hard and fast rule that will apply in every case. The time and method of valuation is not specified precisely, in order to avoid that result. There are an infinite number of variations possible in dealings between debtors and creditors, the law is continually developing, and new ideas are continually being implemented in this field. The flexibility is important to permit the courts to adapt to varying circumstances and changing modes of financing.

Neither is it expected that the courts will construe the term value to mean, in every case, forced sale liquidation value or full going concern value. There is wide latitude between those two extremes. In any particular case, especially a reorganization case, the determination of which entity should be entitled to the difference between the going concern value and the liquidation value must be based on equitable considerations based on the facts of the case. It will frequently be based on negotiation between the parties. Only if they cannot agree will the court become involved.

The first method of adequate protection specified is periodic cash payments by the estate, to the extent of a decrease in value of the opposing entity's interest in the property involved. This provision is derived from *In re Yale Express, Inc.*, 384 F.2d 990 (2d Cir. 1967) (though in that case it is not clear whether the payments required were adequate to compensate the secured creditors for their loss). The use of periodic payments may be appropriate, where for example, the property in question is depreciating at a relatively fixed rate. The periodic payments would be to compensate for the depreciation.

The second method is the provision of an additional or replacement lien on other property to the extent of the decrease in value of the property involved. The purpose of this method is to provide the protected entity with a means of realizing the value of the original property, if it should decline during the case, by granting an interest in additional property from whose value the entity may realize its loss.

The third method is the granting of an administrative expense priority to the protected entity to the extent of his loss. This method, more than the others, requires a prediction as to whether the unencumbered assets that will remain if the case if converted from reorganization to liquidation will be sufficient to pay the protected entity in full. It is clearly the most risky, from the entity's perspective and should be used only when there is relative certainty that administrative expenses will be able to be paid in full in the event of liquidation.

The fourth [enacted as third] method gives the parties and the courts flexibility by allowing such other relief as will result in the realization by the protected entity of the value of its interest in the property involved. Under this provision, the courts will be able to adapt to new methods of financing and to formulate protection that is appropriate to the circumstances of the case if none of the other methods would accomplish the desired result. For example, another form of adequate protection might be the guarantee by a third party outside the judicial process of compensation for any loss incurred in the case. Adequate protection might also, in some circumstances, be provided by permitting a secured creditor to bid in his claim at the sale of the property and to offset the claim against the price bid in.

The paragraph also defines, more clearly than the others, the general concept of adequate protection, by requiring such relief as will result in the realization of value. It is the general category, and as such, is defined by the concept involved rather than any particular method of adequate protection.

AMENDMENTS

1984—Par. (1). Pub. L. 98–353 inserted "a cash payment or" after "make".

EFFECTIVE DATE OF 1984 AMENDMENT

Amendment by Pub. L. 98–353 effective with respect to cases filed 90 days after July 10, 1984, see section

552(a) of Pub. L. 98–353, set out as a note under section 101 of this title.

§ 362. Automatic stay

(a) Except as provided in subsection (b) of this section, a petition filed under section 301, 302, or 303 of this title, or an application filed under section 5(a)(3) of the Securities Investor Protection Act of 1970, operates as a stay, applicable to all entities, of—

(1) the commencement or continuation, including the issuance or employment of process, of a judicial, administrative, or other action or proceeding against the debtor that was or could have been commenced before the commencement of the case under this title, or to recover a claim against the debtor that arose before the commencement of the case under this title;

(2) the enforcement, against the debtor or against property of the estate, of a judgment obtained before the commencement of the case under this title;

(3) any act to obtain possession of property of the estate or of property from the estate or to exercise control over property of the estate;

(4) any act to create, perfect, or enforce any lien against property of the estate;

(5) any act to create, perfect, or enforce against property of the debtor any lien to the extent that such lien secures a claim that arose before the commencement of the case under this title;

(6) any act to collect, assess, or recover a claim against the debtor that arose before the commencement of the case under this title;

(7) the setoff of any debt owing to the debtor that arose before the commencement of the case under this title against any claim against the debtor; and

(8) the commencement or continuation of a proceeding before the United States Tax Court concerning a corporate debtor's tax liability for a taxable period the bankruptcy court may determine or concerning the tax liability of a debtor who is an individual for a taxable period ending before the date of the order for relief under this title.

(b) The filing of a petition under section 301, 302, or 303 of this title, or of an application under section 5(a)(3) of the Securities Investor Protection Act of 1970, does not operate as a stay—

(1) under subsection (a) of this section, of the commencement or continuation of a criminal action or proceeding against the debtor;

(2) under subsection (a)—

(A) of the commencement or continuation of a civil action or proceeding—

(i) for the establishment of paternity;

(ii) for the establishment or modification of an order for domestic support obligations;

(iii) concerning child custody or visitation;

(iv) for the dissolution of a marriage, except to the extent that such proceeding seeks to determine the division of property that is property of the estate; or

(v) regarding domestic violence;

(B) of the collection of a domestic support obligation from property that is not property of the estate;

(C) with respect to the withholding of income that is property of the estate or property of the debtor for payment of a domestic support obligation under a judicial or administrative order or a statute;

(D) of the withholding, suspension, or restriction of a driver's license, a professional or occupational license, or a recreational license, under State law, as specified in section 466(a)(16) of the Social Security Act;

(E) of the reporting of overdue support owed by a parent to any consumer reporting agency as specified in section 466(a)(7) of the Social Security Act;

(F) of the interception of a tax refund, as specified in sections 464 and 466(a)(3) of the Social Security Act or under an analogous State law; or

(G) of the enforcement of a medical obligation, as specified under title IV of the Social Security Act;

(3) under subsection (a) of this section, of any act to perfect, or to maintain or continue the perfection of, an interest in property to the extent that the trustee's rights and powers are subject to such perfection under section 546(b) of this title or to the extent that such act is accomplished within the period provided under section 547(e)(2)(A) of this title;

(4) under paragraph (1), (2), (3), or (6) of subsection (a) of this section, of the commencement or continuation of an action or proceeding by a governmental unit or any organization exercising authority under the Convention on the Prohibition of the Development, Production, Stockpiling and Use of Chemical Weapons and on Their Destruction, opened for signature on January 13, 1993, to enforce such governmental unit's or organization's police and regulatory power, including the enforcement of a judgment other than a money judgment, obtained in an action or proceeding by the governmental unit to enforce such governmental unit's or organization's police or regulatory power;

[(5) Repealed. Pub. L. 105–277, div. I, title VI, § 603(1), Oct. 21, 1998, 112 Stat. 2681–866;]

(6) under subsection (a) of this section, of the exercise by a commodity broker, forward contract merchant, stockbroker, financial institution, financial participant, or securities clearing agency of any contractual right (as defined in section 555 or 556) under any security agreement or arrangement or other credit enhancement forming a part of or related to any commodity contract, forward contract or securities contract, or of any contractual right (as defined in section 555 or 556) to offset or net out any termination value, payment amount, or other transfer obligation arising under or in connection with 1 or more such contracts, including any master agreement for such contracts;

(7) under subsection (a) of this section, of the exercise by a repo participant or financial participant of any contractual right (as defined in section 559) under any security agreement or arrangement or other credit enhance-

ment forming a part of or related to any repurchase agreement, or of any contractual right (as defined in section 559) to offset or net out any termination value, payment amount, or other transfer obligation arising under or in connection with 1 or more such agreements, including any master agreement for such agreements;

(8) under subsection (a) of this section, of the commencement of any action by the Secretary of Housing and Urban Development to foreclose a mortgage or deed of trust in any case in which the mortgage or deed of trust held by the Secretary is insured or was formerly insured under the National Housing Act and covers property, or combinations of property, consisting of five or more living units;

(9) under subsection (a), of—

(A) an audit by a governmental unit to determine tax liability;

(B) the issuance to the debtor by a governmental unit of a notice of tax deficiency;

(C) a demand for tax returns; or

(D) the making of an assessment for any tax and issuance of a notice and demand for payment of such an assessment (but any tax lien that would otherwise attach to property of the estate by reason of such an assessment shall not take effect unless such tax is a debt of the debtor that will not be discharged in the case and such property or its proceeds are transferred out of the estate to, or otherwise revested in, the debtor).

(10) under subsection (a) of this section, of any act by a lessor to the debtor under a lease of nonresidential real property that has terminated by the expiration of the stated term of the lease before the commencement of or during a case under this title to obtain possession of such property;

(11) under subsection (a) of this section, of the presentment of a negotiable instrument and the giving of notice of and protesting dishonor of such an instrument;

(12) under subsection (a) of this section, after the date which is 90 days after the filing of such petition, of the commencement or continuation, and conclusion to the entry of final judgment, of an action which involves a debtor subject to reorganization pursuant to chapter 11 of this title and which was brought by the Secretary of Transportation under section 31325 of title 46 (including distribution of any proceeds of sale) to foreclose a preferred ship or fleet mortgage, or a security interest in or relating to a vessel or vessel under construction, held by the Secretary of Transportation under chapter 537 of title 46 or section 109(h) of title 49, or under applicable State law;

(13) under subsection (a) of this section, after the date which is 90 days after the filing of such petition, of the commencement or continuation, and conclusion to the entry of final judgment, of an action which involves a debtor subject to reorganization pursuant to chapter 11 of this title and which was brought by the Secretary of Commerce under section 31325 of title 46 (including distribution of any proceeds of sale) to foreclose a preferred ship or fleet mortgage in a vessel or a mortgage, deed of trust, or other security interest in a fishing facility held by the Secretary of Commerce under chapter 537 of title 46;

(14) under subsection (a) of this section, of any action by an accrediting agency regarding the accreditation status of the debtor as an educational institution;

(15) under subsection (a) of this section, of any action by a State licensing body regarding the licensure of the debtor as an educational institution;

(16) under subsection (a) of this section, of any action by a guaranty agency, as defined in section 435(j) of the Higher Education Act of 1965 or the Secretary of Education regarding the eligibility of the debtor to participate in programs authorized under such Act;

(17) under subsection (a) of this section, of the exercise by a swap participant or financial participant of any contractual right (as defined in section 560) under any security agreement or arrangement or other credit enhancement forming a part of or related to any swap agreement, or of any contractual right (as defined in section 560) to offset or net out any termination value, payment amount, or other transfer obligation arising under or in connection with 1 or more such agreements, including any master agreement for such agreements;

(18) under subsection (a) of the creation or perfection of a statutory lien for an ad valorem property tax, or a special tax or special assessment on real property whether or not ad valorem, imposed by a governmental unit, if such tax or assessment comes due after the date of the filing of the petition;

(19) under subsection (a), of withholding of income from a debtor's wages and collection of amounts withheld, under the debtor's agreement authorizing that withholding and collection for the benefit of a pension, profit sharing, stock bonus, or other plan established under section 401, 403, 408, 408A, 414, 457, or 501(c) of the Internal Revenue Code of 1986, that is sponsored by the employer of the debtor, or an affiliate, successor, or predecessor of such employer—

(A) to the extent that the amounts withheld and collected are used solely for payments relating to a loan from a plan under section 408(b)(1) of the Employee Retirement Income Security Act of 1974 or is subject to section 72(p) of the Internal Revenue Code of 1986; or

(B) a loan from a thrift savings plan permitted under subchapter III of chapter 84 of title 5, that satisfies the requirements of section 8433(g) of such title;

but nothing in this paragraph may be construed to provide that any loan made under a governmental plan under section 414(d), or a contract or account under section 403(b), of the Internal Revenue Code of 1986 constitutes a claim or a debt under this title;

(20) under subsection (a), of any act to enforce any lien against or security interest in real property following entry of the order under subsection (d)(4) as to such real property in any prior case under this title, for a period of 2 years after the date of the entry of such an order, except that the debtor, in a subse-

quent case under this title, may move for relief from such order based upon changed circumstances or for other good cause shown, after notice and a hearing;

(21) under subsection (a), of any act to enforce any lien against or security interest in real property—

(A) if the debtor is ineligible under section 109(g) to be a debtor in a case under this title; or

(B) if the case under this title was filed in violation of a bankruptcy court order in a prior case under this title prohibiting the debtor from being a debtor in another case under this title;

(22) subject to subsection (*l*), under subsection (a)(3), of the continuation of any eviction, unlawful detainer action, or similar proceeding by a lessor against a debtor involving residential property in which the debtor resides as a tenant under a lease or rental agreement and with respect to which the lessor has obtained before the date of the filing of the bankruptcy petition, a judgment for possession of such property against the debtor;

(23) subject to subsection (m), under subsection (a)(3), of an eviction action that seeks possession of the residential property in which the debtor resides as a tenant under a lease or rental agreement based on endangerment of such property or the illegal use of controlled substances on such property, but only if the lessor files with the court, and serves upon the debtor, a certification under penalty of perjury that such an eviction action has been filed, or that the debtor, during the 30-day period preceding the date of the filing of the certification, has endangered property or illegally used or allowed to be used a controlled substance on the property;

(24) under subsection (a), of any transfer that is not avoidable under section 544 and that is not avoidable under section 549;

(25) under subsection (a), of—

(A) the commencement or continuation of an investigation or action by a securities self regulatory organization to enforce such organization's regulatory power;

(B) the enforcement of an order or decision, other than for monetary sanctions, obtained in an action by such securities self regulatory organization to enforce such organization's regulatory power; or

(C) any act taken by such securities self regulatory organization to delist, delete, or refuse to permit quotation of any stock that does not meet applicable regulatory requirements;

(26) under subsection (a), of the setoff under applicable nonbankruptcy law of an income tax refund, by a governmental unit, with respect to a taxable period that ended before the date of the order for relief against an income tax liability for a taxable period that also ended before the date of the order for relief, except that in any case in which the setoff of an income tax refund is not permitted under applicable nonbankruptcy law because of a pending action to determine the amount or legality of a tax liability, the governmental unit may hold the refund pending the resolution of the action, unless the court, on the motion of the trustee and after notice and a hearing, grants the taxing authority adequate protection (within the meaning of section 361) for the secured claim of such authority in the setoff under section 506(a);

(27) under subsection (a) of this section, of the exercise by a master netting agreement participant of any contractual right (as defined in section 555, 556, 559, or 560) under any security agreement or arrangement or other credit enhancement forming a part of or related to any master netting agreement, or of any contractual right (as defined in section 555, 556, 559, or 560) to offset or net out any termination value, payment amount, or other transfer obligation arising under or in connection with 1 or more such master netting agreements to the extent that such participant is eligible to exercise such rights under paragraph (6), (7), or (17) for each individual contract covered by the master netting agreement in issue; and

(28) under subsection (a), of the exclusion by the Secretary of Health and Human Services of the debtor from participation in the medicare program or any other Federal health care program (as defined in section 1128B(f) of the Social Security Act pursuant to title XI or XVIII of such Act).

The provisions of paragraphs (12) and (13) of this subsection shall apply with respect to any such petition filed on or before December 31, 1989.

(c) Except as provided in subsections (d), (e), (f), and (h) of this section—

(1) the stay of an act against property of the estate under subsection (a) of this section continues until such property is no longer property of the estate;

(2) the stay of any other act under subsection (a) of this section continues until the earliest of—

(A) the time the case is closed;

(B) the time the case is dismissed; or

(C) if the case is a case under chapter 7 of this title concerning an individual or a case under chapter 9, 11, 12, or 13 of this title, the time a discharge is granted or denied;

(3) if a single or joint case is filed by or against debtor who is an individual in a case under chapter 7, 11, or 13, and if a single or joint case of the debtor was pending within the preceding 1-year period but was dismissed, other than a case refiled under a chapter other than chapter 7 after dismissal under section 707(b)—

(A) the stay under subsection (a) with respect to any action taken with respect to a debt or property securing such debt or with respect to any lease shall terminate with respect to the debtor on the 30th day after the filing of the later case;

(B) on the motion of a party in interest for continuation of the automatic stay and upon notice and a hearing, the court may extend the stay in particular cases as to any or all creditors (subject to such conditions or limitations as the court may then impose) after notice and a hearing completed before the expiration of the 30-day period only if the party in interest demonstrates that the filing of the later case is in good faith as to the creditors to be stayed; and

(C) for purposes of subparagraph (B), a case is presumptively filed not in good faith (but such presumption may be rebutted by clear and convincing evidence to the contrary)—

(i) as to all creditors, if—

(I) more than 1 previous case under any of chapters 7, 11, and 13 in which the individual was a debtor was pending within the preceding 1-year period;

(II) a previous case under any of chapters 7, 11, and 13 in which the individual was a debtor was dismissed within such 1-year period, after the debtor failed to—

(aa) file or amend the petition or other documents as required by this title or the court without substantial excuse (but mere inadvertence or negligence shall not be a substantial excuse unless the dismissal was caused by the negligence of the debtor's attorney);

(bb) provide adequate protection as ordered by the court; or

(cc) perform the terms of a plan confirmed by the court; or

(III) there has not been a substantial change in the financial or personal affairs of the debtor since the dismissal of the next most previous case under chapter 7, 11, or 13 or any other reason to conclude that the later case will be concluded—

(aa) if a case under chapter 7, with a discharge; or

(bb) if a case under chapter 11 or 13, with a confirmed plan that will be fully performed; and

(ii) as to any creditor that commenced an action under subsection (d) in a previous case in which the individual was a debtor if, as of the date of dismissal of such case, that action was still pending or had been resolved by terminating, conditioning, or limiting the stay as to actions of such creditor; and

(4)(A)(i) if a single or joint case is filed by or against a debtor who is an individual under this title, and if 2 or more single or joint cases of the debtor were pending within the previous year but were dismissed, other than a case refiled under section 707(b), the stay under subsection (a) shall not go into effect upon the filing of the later case; and

(ii) on request of a party in interest, the court shall promptly enter an order confirming that no stay is in effect;

(B) if, within 30 days after the filing of the later case, a party in interest requests the court may order the stay to take effect in the case as to any or all creditors (subject to such conditions or limitations as the court may impose), after notice and a hearing, only if the party in interest demonstrates that the filing of the later case is in good faith as to the creditors to be stayed;

(C) a stay imposed under subparagraph (B) shall be effective on the date of the entry of the order allowing the stay to go into effect; and

(D) for purposes of subparagraph (B), a case is presumptively filed not in good faith (but such presumption may be rebutted by clear and convincing evidence to the contrary)—

(i) as to all creditors if—

(I) 2 or more previous cases under this title in which the individual was a debtor were pending within the 1-year period;

(II) a previous case under this title in which the individual was a debtor was dismissed within the time period stated in this paragraph after the debtor failed to file or amend the petition or other documents as required by this title or the court without substantial excuse (but mere inadvertence or negligence shall not be substantial excuse unless the dismissal was caused by the negligence of the debtor's attorney), failed to provide adequate protection as ordered by the court, or failed to perform the terms of a plan confirmed by the court; or

(III) there has not been a substantial change in the financial or personal affairs of the debtor since the dismissal of the next most previous case under this title, or any other reason to conclude that the later case will not be concluded, if a case under chapter 7, with a discharge, and if a case under chapter 11 or 13, with a confirmed plan that will be fully performed; or

(ii) as to any creditor that commenced an action under subsection (d) in a previous case in which the individual was a debtor if, as of the date of dismissal of such case, such action was still pending or had been resolved by terminating, conditioning, or limiting the stay as to such action of such creditor.

(d) On request of a party in interest and after notice and a hearing, the court shall grant relief from the stay provided under subsection (a) of this section, such as by terminating, annulling, modifying, or conditioning such stay—

(1) for cause, including the lack of adequate protection of an interest in property of such party in interest;

(2) with respect to a stay of an act against property under subsection (a) of this section, if—

(A) the debtor does not have an equity in such property; and

(B) such property is not necessary to an effective reorganization;

(3) with respect to a stay of an act against single asset real estate under subsection (a), by a creditor whose claim is secured by an interest in such real estate, unless, not later than the date that is 90 days after the entry of the order for relief (or such later date as the court may determine for cause by order entered within that 90-day period) or 30 days after the court determines that the debtor is subject to this paragraph, whichever is later—

(A) the debtor has filed a plan of reorganization that has a reasonable possibility of being confirmed within a reasonable time; or

(B) the debtor has commenced monthly payments that—

(i) may, in the debtor's sole discretion, notwithstanding section 363(c)(2), be made from rents or other income generated before, on, or after the date of the commencement of the case by or from the property to each creditor whose claim is secured by such real estate (other than a claim secured by a judgment lien or by an unmatured statutory lien); and

(ii) are in an amount equal to interest at the then applicable nondefault contract rate of interest on the value of the creditor's interest in the real estate; or

(4) with respect to a stay of an act against real property under subsection (a), by a creditor whose claim is secured by an interest in such real property, if the court finds that the filing of the petition was part of a scheme to delay, hinder, and defraud creditors that involved either—

(A) transfer of all or part ownership of, or other interest in, such real property without the consent of the secured creditor or court approval; or

(B) multiple bankruptcy filings affecting such real property.

If recorded in compliance with applicable State laws governing notices of interests or liens in real property, an order entered under paragraph (4) shall be binding in any other case under this title purporting to affect such real property filed not later than 2 years after the date of the entry of such order by the court, except that a debtor in a subsequent case under this title may move for relief from such order based upon changed circumstances or for good cause shown, after notice and a hearing. Any Federal, State, or local governmental unit that accepts notices of interests or liens in real property shall accept any certified copy of an order described in this subsection for indexing and recording.

(e)(1) Thirty days after a request under subsection (d) of this section for relief from the stay of any act against property of the estate under subsection (a) of this section, such stay is terminated with respect to the party in interest making such request, unless the court, after notice and a hearing, orders such stay continued in effect pending the conclusion of, or as a result of, a final hearing and determination under subsection (d) of this section. A hearing under this subsection may be a preliminary hearing, or may be consolidated with the final hearing under subsection (d) of this section. The court shall order such stay continued in effect pending the conclusion of the final hearing under subsection (d) of this section if there is a reasonable likelihood that the party opposing relief from such stay will prevail at the conclusion of such final hearing. If the hearing under this subsection is a preliminary hearing, then such final hearing shall be concluded not later than thirty days after the conclusion of such preliminary hearing, unless the 30-day period is extended with the consent of the parties in interest or for a specific time which the court finds is required by compelling circumstances.

(2) Notwithstanding paragraph (1), in a case under chapter 7, 11, or 13 in which the debtor is an individual, the stay under subsection (a) shall terminate on the date that is 60 days after a request is made by a party in interest under subsection (d), unless—

(A) a final decision is rendered by the court during the 60-day period beginning on the date of the request; or

(B) such 60-day period is extended—

(i) by agreement of all parties in interest; or

(ii) by the court for such specific period of time as the court finds is required for good cause, as described in findings made by the court.

(f) Upon request of a party in interest, the court, with or without a hearing, shall grant such relief from the stay provided under subsection (a) of this section as is necessary to prevent irreparable damage to the interest of an entity in property, if such interest will suffer such damage before there is an opportunity for notice and a hearing under subsection (d) or (e) of this section.

(g) In any hearing under subsection (d) or (e) of this section concerning relief from the stay of any act under subsection (a) of this section—

(1) the party requesting such relief has the burden of proof on the issue of the debtor's equity in property; and

(2) the party opposing such relief has the burden of proof on all other issues.

(h)(1) In a case in which the debtor is an individual, the stay provided by subsection (a) is terminated with respect to personal property of the estate or of the debtor securing in whole or in part a claim, or subject to an unexpired lease, and such personal property shall no longer be property of the estate if the debtor fails within the applicable time set by section 521(a)(2)—

(A) to file timely any statement of intention required under section 521(a)(2) with respect to such personal property or to indicate in such statement that the debtor will either surrender such personal property or retain it and, if retaining such personal property, either redeem such personal property pursuant to section 722, enter into an agreement of the kind specified in section 524(c) applicable to the debt secured by such personal property, or assume such unexpired lease pursuant to section 365(p) if the trustee does not do so, as applicable; and

(B) to take timely the action specified in such statement, as it may be amended before expiration of the period for taking action, unless such statement specifies the debtor's intention to reaffirm such debt on the original contract terms and the creditor refuses to agree to the reaffirmation on such terms.

(2) Paragraph (1) does not apply if the court determines, on the motion of the trustee filed before the expiration of the applicable time set by section 521(a)(2), after notice and a hearing, that such personal property is of consequential value or benefit to the estate, and orders appropriate adequate protection of the creditor's interest, and orders the debtor to deliver any collateral in the debtor's possession to the trustee. If the court does not so determine, the stay provided by subsection (a) shall terminate upon the conclusion of the hearing on the motion.

(i) If a case commenced under chapter 7, 11, or 13 is dismissed due to the creation of a debt repayment plan, for purposes of subsection (c)(3), any subsequent case commenced by the debtor under any such chapter shall not be presumed to be filed not in good faith.

(j) On request of a party in interest, the court shall issue an order under subsection (c) confirming that the automatic stay has been terminated.

(k)(1) Except as provided in paragraph (2), an individual injured by any willful violation of a stay provided by this section shall recover actual damages, including costs and attorneys' fees, and, in appropriate circumstances, may recover punitive damages.

(2) If such violation is based on an action taken by an entity in the good faith belief that subsection (h) applies to the debtor, the recovery under paragraph (1) of this subsection against such entity shall be limited to actual damages.

(*l*)(1) Except as otherwise provided in this subsection, subsection (b)(22) shall apply on the date that is 30 days after the date on which the bankruptcy petition is filed, if the debtor files with the petition and serves upon the lessor a certification under penalty of perjury that—

(A) under nonbankruptcy law applicable in the jurisdiction, there are circumstances under which the debtor would be permitted to cure the entire monetary default that gave rise to the judgment for possession, after that judgment for possession was entered; and

(B) the debtor (or an adult dependent of the debtor) has deposited with the clerk of the court, any rent that would become due during the 30-day period after the filing of the bankruptcy petition.

(2) If, within the 30-day period after the filing of the bankruptcy petition, the debtor (or an adult dependent of the debtor) complies with paragraph (1) and files with the court and serves upon the lessor a further certification under penalty of perjury that the debtor (or an adult dependent of the debtor) has cured, under nonbankrupcty[1] law applicable in the jurisdiction, the entire monetary default that gave rise to the judgment under which possession is sought by the lessor, subsection (b)(22) shall not apply, unless ordered to apply by the court under paragraph (3).

(3)(A) If the lessor files an objection to any certification filed by the debtor under paragraph (1) or (2), and serves such objection upon the debtor, the court shall hold a hearing within 10 days after the filing and service of such objection to determine if the certification filed by the debtor under paragraph (1) or (2) is true.

(B) If the court upholds the objection of the lessor filed under subparagraph (A)—

(i) subsection (b)(22) shall apply immediately and relief from the stay provided under subsection (a)(3) shall not be required to enable the lessor to complete the process to recover full possession of the property; and

(ii) the clerk of the court shall immediately serve upon the lessor and the debtor a certified copy of the court's order upholding the lessor's objection.

(4) If a debtor, in accordance with paragraph (5), indicates on the petition that there was a judgment for possession of the residential rental property in which the debtor resides and does not file a certification under paragraph (1) or (2)—

(A) subsection (b)(22) shall apply immediately upon failure to file such certification, and relief from the stay provided under subsection (a)(3) shall not be required to enable the lessor to complete the process to recover full possession of the property; and

(B) the clerk of the court shall immediately serve upon the lessor and the debtor a certified copy of the docket indicating the absence of a filed certification and the applicability of the exception to the stay under subsection (b)(22).

(5)(A) Where a judgment for possession of residential property in which the debtor resides as a tenant under a lease or rental agreement has been obtained by the lessor, the debtor shall so indicate on the bankruptcy petition and shall provide the name and address of the lessor that obtained that pre-petition judgment on the petition and on any certification filed under this subsection.

(B) The form of certification filed with the petition, as specified in this subsection, shall provide for the debtor to certify, and the debtor shall certify—

(i) whether a judgment for possession of residential rental housing in which the debtor resides has been obtained against the debtor before the date of the filing of the petition; and

(ii) whether the debtor is claiming under paragraph (1) that under nonbankruptcy law applicable in the jurisdiction, there are circumstances under which the debtor would be permitted to cure the entire monetary default that gave rise to the judgment for possession, after that judgment of possession was entered, and has made the appropriate deposit with the court.

(C) The standard forms (electronic and otherwise) used in a bankruptcy proceeding shall be amended to reflect the requirements of this subsection.

(D) The clerk of the court shall arrange for the prompt transmittal of the rent deposited in accordance with paragraph (1)(B) to the lessor.

(m)(1) Except as otherwise provided in this subsection, subsection (b)(23) shall apply on the date that is 15 days after the date on which the lessor files and serves a certification described in subsection (b)(23).

(2)(A) If the debtor files with the court an objection to the truth or legal sufficiency of the certification described in subsection (b)(23) and serves such objection upon the lessor, subsection (b)(23) shall not apply, unless ordered to apply by the court under this subsection.

(B) If the debtor files and serves the objection under subparagraph (A), the court shall hold a hearing within 10 days after the filing and service of such objection to determine if the situation giving rise to the lessor's certification under paragraph (1) existed or has been remedied.

[1] So in original. Probably should be "nonbankruptcy".

(C) If the debtor can demonstrate to the satisfaction of the court that the situation giving rise to the lessor's certification under paragraph (1) did not exist or has been remedied, the stay provided under subsection (a)(3) shall remain in effect until the termination of the stay under this section.

(D) If the debtor cannot demonstrate to the satisfaction of the court that the situation giving rise to the lessor's certification under paragraph (1) did not exist or has been remedied—

(i) relief from the stay provided under subsection (a)(3) shall not be required to enable the lessor to proceed with the eviction; and

(ii) the clerk of the court shall immediately serve upon the lessor and the debtor a certified copy of the court's order upholding the lessor's certification.

(3) If the debtor fails to file, within 15 days, an objection under paragraph (2)(A)—

(A) subsection (b)(23) shall apply immediately upon such failure and relief from the stay provided under subsection (a)(3) shall not be required to enable the lessor to complete the process to recover full possession of the property; and

(B) the clerk of the court shall immediately serve upon the lessor and the debtor a certified copy of the docket indicating such failure.

(n)(1) Except as provided in paragraph (2), subsection (a) does not apply in a case in which the debtor—

(A) is a debtor in a small business case pending at the time the petition is filed;

(B) was a debtor in a small business case that was dismissed for any reason by an order that became final in the 2-year period ending on the date of the order for relief entered with respect to the petition;

(C) was a debtor in a small business case in which a plan was confirmed in the 2-year period ending on the date of the order for relief entered with respect to the petition; or

(D) is an entity that has acquired substantially all of the assets or business of a small business debtor described in subparagraph (A), (B), or (C), unless such entity establishes by a preponderance of the evidence that such entity acquired substantially all of the assets or business of such small business debtor in good faith and not for the purpose of evading this paragraph.

(2) Paragraph (1) does not apply—

(A) to an involuntary case involving no collusion by the debtor with creditors; or

(B) to the filing of a petition if—

(i) the debtor proves by a preponderance of the evidence that the filing of the petition resulted from circumstances beyond the control of the debtor not foreseeable at the time the case then pending was filed; and

(ii) it is more likely than not that the court will confirm a feasible plan, but not a liquidating plan, within a reasonable period of time.

(*o*) The exercise of rights not subject to the stay arising under subsection (a) pursuant to paragraph (6), (7), (17), or (27) of subsection (b) shall not be stayed by any order of a court or administrative agency in any proceeding under this title.

(Pub. L. 95–598, Nov. 6, 1978, 92 Stat. 2570; Pub. L. 97–222, §3, July 27, 1982, 96 Stat. 235; Pub. L. 98–353, title III, §§304, 363(b), 392, 441, July 10, 1984, 98 Stat. 352, 363, 365, 371; Pub. L. 99–509, title V, §5001(a), Oct. 21, 1986, 100 Stat. 1911; Pub. L. 99–554, title II, §§257(j), 283(d), Oct. 27, 1986, 100 Stat. 3115, 3116; Pub. L. 101–311, title I, §102, title II, §202, June 25, 1990, 104 Stat. 267, 269; Pub. L. 101–508, title III, §3007(a)(1), Nov. 5, 1990, 104 Stat. 1388–28; Pub. L. 103–394, title I, §§101, 116, title II, §§204(a), 218(b), title III, §304(b), title IV, §401, title V, §501(b)(2), (d)(7), Oct. 22, 1994, 108 Stat. 4107, 4119, 4122, 4128, 4132, 4141, 4142, 4144; Pub. L. 105–277, div. I, title VI, §603, Oct. 21, 1998, 112 Stat. 2681–886; Pub. L. 109–8, title I, §106(f), title II, §§214, 224(b), title III, §§302, 303, 305(1), 311, 320, title IV, §§401(b), 441, 444, title VII, §§709, 718, title IX, §907(d), (*o*)(1), (2), title XI, §1106, title XII, §1225, Apr. 20, 2005, 119 Stat. 41, 54, 64, 75, 77, 79, 84, 94, 104, 114, 117, 127, 131, 176, 181, 182, 192, 199; Pub. L. 109–304, §17(b)(1), Oct. 6, 2006, 120 Stat. 1706; Pub. L. 109–390, §5(a)(2), Dec. 12, 2006, 120 Stat. 2696.)

Historical and Revision Notes

Legislative Statements

Section 362(a)(1) of the House amendment adopts the provision contained in the Senate amendment enjoining the commencement or continuation of a judicial, administrative, or other proceeding to recover a claim against the debtor that arose before the commencement of the case. The provision is beneficial and interacts with section 362(a)(6), which also covers assessment, to prevent harassment of the debtor with respect to pre-petition claims.

Section 362(a)(7) contains a provision contained in H.R. 8200 as passed by the House. The differing provision in the Senate amendment was rejected. It is not possible that a debt owing to the debtor may be offset against an interest in the debtor.

Section 362(a)(8) is new. The provision stays the commencement or continuation of any proceeding concerning the debtor before the U.S. Tax Court.

Section 362(b)(4) indicates that the stay under section 362(a)(1) does not apply to affect the commencement or continuation of an action or proceeding by a governmental unit to enforce the governmental unit's police or regulatory power. This section is intended to be given a narrow construction in order to permit governmental units to pursue actions to protect the public health and safety and not to apply to actions by a governmental unit to protect a pecuniary interest in property of the debtor or property of the estate.

Section 362(b)(6) of the House amendment adopts a provision contained in the Senate amendment restricting the exception to the automatic stay with respect to setoffs to permit only the setoff of mutual debts and claims. Traditionally, the right of setoff has been limited to mutual debts and claims and the lack of the clarifying term "mutual" in H.R. 8200 as passed by the House created an unintentional ambiguity. Section 362(b)(7) of the House amendment permits the issuance of a notice of tax deficiency. The House amendment rejects section 362(b)(7) in the Senate amendment. It would have permitted a particular governmental unit to obtain a pecuniary advantage without a hearing on the merits contrary to the exceptions contained in sections 362(b)(4) and (5).

Section 362(d) of the House amendment represents a compromise between comparable provisions in the House bill and Senate amendment. Under section 362(d)(1) of the House amendment, the court may terminate, annul, modify, or condition the automatic stay for cause, including lack of adequate protection of an interest in property of a secured party. It is anticipated that the Rules of Bankruptcy Procedure will provide that those hearings will receive priority on the calendar. Under section 362(d)(2) the court may alternatively terminate, annul, modify, or condition the automatic stay for cause including inadequate protection for the creditor. The court shall grant relief from the stay if there is no equity and it is not necessary to an effective reorganization of the debtor.

The latter requirement is contained in section 362(d)(2). This section is intended to solve the problem of real property mortgage foreclosures of property where the bankruptcy petition is filed on the eve of foreclosure. The section is not intended to apply if the business of the debtor is managing or leasing real property, such as a hotel operation, even though the debtor has no equity if the property is necessary to an effective reorganization of the debtor. Similarly, if the debtor does have an equity in the property, there is no requirement that the property be sold under section 363 of title 11 as would have been required by the Senate amendment.

Section 362(e) of the House amendment represents a modification of provisions in H.R. 8200 as passed by the House and the Senate amendment to make clear that a final hearing must be commenced within 30 days after a preliminary hearing is held to determine whether a creditor will be entitled to relief from the automatic stay. In order to insure that those hearings will in fact occur within such 30-day period, it is anticipated that the rules of bankruptcy procedure provide that such final hearings receive priority on the court calendar.

Section 362(g) places the burden of proof on the issue of the debtor's equity in collateral on the party requesting relief from the automatic stay and the burden on other issues on the debtor.

An amendment has been made to section 362(b) to permit the Secretary of the Department of Housing and Urban Development to commence an action to foreclose a mortgage or deed of trust. The commencement of such an action is necessary for tax purposes. The section is not intended to permit the continuation of such an action after it is commenced nor is the section to be construed to entitle the Secretary to take possession in lieu of foreclosure.

Automatic stay: Sections 362(b)(8) and (9) contained in the Senate amendment are largely deleted in the House amendment. Those provisions add to the list of actions not stayed (a) jeopardy assessments, (b) other assessments, and (c) the issuance of deficiency notices. In the House amendment, jeopardy assessments against property which ceases to be property of the estate is already authorized by section 362(c)(1). Other assessments are specifically stayed under section 362(a)(6), while the issuance of a deficiency notice is specifically permitted. Stay of the assessment and the permission to issue a statutory notice of a tax deficiency will permit the debtor to take his personal tax case to the Tax Court, if the bankruptcy judge authorizes him to do so (as explained more fully in the discussion of section 505).

SENATE REPORT NO. 95–989

The automatic stay is one of the fundamental debtor protections provided by the bankruptcy laws. It gives the debtor a breathing spell from his creditors. It stops all collection efforts, all harassment, and all foreclosure actions. It permits the debtor to attempt a repayment or reorganization plan, or simply to be relieved of the financial pressures that drove him into bankruptcy.

The action commenced by the party seeking relief from the stay is referred to as a motion to make it clear that at the expedited hearing under subsection (e), and at hearings on relief from the stay, the only issue will be the lack of adequate protection, the debtor's equity in the property, and the necessity of the property to an effective reorganization of the debtor, or the existence of other cause for relief from the stay. This hearing will not be the appropriate time at which to bring in other issues, such as counterclaims against the creditor, which, although relevant to the question of the amount of the debt, concern largely collateral or unrelated matters. This approach is consistent with that taken in cases such as *In re Essex Properties, Ltd.*, 430 F.Supp. 1112 (N.D.Cal.1977), that an action seeking relief from the stay is not the assertion of a claim which would give rise to the right or obligation to assert counterclaims. Those counterclaims are not to be handled in the summary fashion that the preliminary hearing under this provision will be. Rather, they will be the subject of more complete proceedings by the trustee to recover property of the estate or to object to the allowance of a claim. However, this would not preclude the party seeking continuance of the stay from presenting evidence on the existence of claims which the court may consider in exercising its discretion. What is precluded is a determination of such collateral claims on the merits at the hearing.

HOUSE REPORT NO. 95–595

Paragraph (7) [of subsec. (a)] stays setoffs of mutual debts and credits between the debtor and creditors. As with all other paragraphs of subsection (a), this paragraph does not affect the right of creditors. It simply stays its enforcement pending an orderly examination of the debtor's and creditors' rights.

Subsection (c) governs automatic termination of the stay. Subsections (d) through (g) govern termination of the stay by the court on the request of a party in interest. Subsection (d) requires the court, on request of a party in interest, to grant relief from the stay, such as by terminating, annulling, modifying, or conditioning the stay, for cause. The lack of adequate protection of an interest in property of the party requesting relief from the stay is one cause for relief, but is not the only cause. As noted above, a desire to permit an action to proceed to completion in another tribunal may provide another cause. Other causes might include the lack of any connection with or interference with the pending bankruptcy case. For example, a divorce or child custody proceeding involving the debtor may bear no relation to the bankruptcy case. In that case, it should not be stayed. A probate proceeding in which the debtor is the executor or administrator of another's estate usually will not be related to the bankruptcy case, and should not be stayed. Generally, proceedings in which the debtor is a fiduciary, or involving postpetition activities of the debtor, need not be stayed because they bear no relationship to the purpose of the automatic stay, which is debtor protection from his creditors. The facts of each request will determine whether relief is appropriate under the circumstances.

Subsection (e) provides a protection for secured creditors that is not available under present law. The subsection sets a time certain within which the bankruptcy court must rule on the adequacy of protection provided of the secured creditor's interest. If the court does not rule within 30 days from a request for relief from the stay, the stay is automatically terminated with respect to the property in question. In order to accommodate more complex cases, the subsection permits the court to make a preliminary ruling after a preliminary hearing. After a preliminary hearing, the court may continue the stay only if there is a reasonable likelihood that the party opposing relief from the stay will prevail at the final hearing. Because the stay is essentially an injunction, the three stages of the stay may be analogized to the three stages of an injunction. The filing of the petition which gives rise to the automatic stay is similar to a temporary restraining order. The preliminary hearing is similar to the hearing on a preliminary injunction, and the final hearing and order is similar to a permanent injunction. The main difference lies in which party must bring the issue before the court. While in the injunction setting, the party seeking the injunction must prosecute the action, in proceedings for relief from the automatic stay, the enjoined party must move. The difference does not, however, shift the burden of proof. Subsection (g) leaves that burden on the party opposing relief from the stay (that is, on the party seeking continuance of the injunction) on the issue of adequate protection.

At the expedited hearing under subsection (e), and at all hearings on relief from the stay, the only issue will be the claim of the creditor and the lack of adequate protection or existence of other cause for relief from the stay. This hearing will not be the appropriate time at which to bring in other issues, such as counterclaims against the creditor on largely unrelated matters. Those counterclaims are not to be handled in the summary fashion that the preliminary hearing under this provision will be. Rather, they will be the subject of more complete proceedings by the trustees to recover property of the estate or to object to the allowance of a claim.

REFERENCES IN TEXT

Section 5(a)(3) of the Securities Investor Protection Act of 1970, referred to in subsecs. (a) and (b), is classified to section 78eee(a)(3) of Title 15, Commerce and Trade.

The Social Security Act, referred to in subsec. (b)(2)(D) to (G), (28), is act Aug. 14, 1935, ch. 531, 49 Stat. 620, as amended. Titles IV, XI, and XVIII of the Act are classified generally to subchapters IV (§601 et seq.), XI (§1301 et seq.), and XVIII (§1395 et seq.), respectively, of chapter 7 of Title 42, The Public Health and Welfare. Sections 464, 466, and 1128B of the Act are classified to sections 664, 666, and 1320a–7b, respectively, of Title 42. For complete classification of this Act to the Code, see section 1305 of Title 42 and Tables.

The National Housing Act, referred in subsec. (b)(8), is act June 27, 1934, ch. 847, 48 Stat. 1246, as amended, which is classified principally to chapter 13 (§1701 et seq.) of Title 12, Banks and Banking. For complete classification of this Act to the Code, see section 1701 of Title 12 and Tables.

The Higher Education Act of 1965, referred to in subsec. (b)(16), is Pub. L. 89–329, Nov. 8, 1965, 79 Stat. 1219, as amended, which is classified principally to chapter 28 (§1001 et seq.) of Title 20, Education. Section 435(j) of the Act is classified to section 1085(j) of Title 20. For complete classification of this Act to the Code, see Short Title note set out under section 1001 of Title 20 and Tables.

The Internal Revenue Code of 1986, referred to in subsec. (b)(19), is classified generally to Title 26, Internal Revenue Code.

Section 408(b)(1) of the Employee Retirement Income Security Act of 1974, referred to in subsec. (b)(19)(A), is classified to section 1108(b)(1) of Title 29, Labor.

AMENDMENTS

2006—Subsec. (b)(6), (7). Pub. L. 109–390, §5(a)(2)(A), added pars. (6) and (7) and struck out former pars. (6) and (7) which read as follows:

"(6) under subsection (a) of this section, of the setoff by a commodity broker, forward contract merchant, stockbroker, financial institution, financial participant, or securities clearing agency of any mutual debt and claim under or in connection with commodity contracts, as defined in section 761 of this title, forward contracts, or securities contracts, as defined in section 741 of this title, that constitutes the setoff of a claim against the debtor for a margin payment, as defined in section 101, 741, or 761 of this title, or settlement payment, as defined in section 101 or 741 of this title, arising out of commodity contracts, forward contracts, or securities contracts against cash, securities, or other property held by, pledged to, under the control of, or due from such commodity broker, forward contract merchant, stockbroker, financial institution, financial participant, or securities clearing agency to margin, guarantee, secure, or settle commodity contracts, forward contracts, or securities contracts;

"(7) under subsection (a) of this section, of the setoff by a repo participant or financial participant, of any mutual debt and claim under or in connection with repurchase agreements that constitutes the setoff of a claim against the debtor for a margin payment, as defined in section 741 or 761 of this title, or settlement payment, as defined in section 741 of this title, arising out of repurchase agreements against cash, securities, or other property held by, pledged to, under the control of, or due from such repo participant or financial participant to margin, guarantee, secure or settle repurchase agreements;".

Subsec. (b)(12). Pub. L. 109–304, §17(b)(1)(A), substituted "chapter 537 of title 46 or section 109(h) of title 49" for "section 207 or title XI of the Merchant Marine Act, 1936".

Subsec. (b)(13). Pub. L. 109–304, §17(b)(1)(B), substituted "chapter 537 of title 46" for "section 207 or title XI of the Merchant Marine Act, 1936".

Subsec. (b)(17). Pub. L. 109–390, §5(a)(2)(B), added par. (17) and struck out former par. (17) which read as follows: "under subsection (a), of the setoff by a swap participant or financial participant of a mutual debt and claim under or in connection with one or more swap agreements that constitutes the setoff of a claim against the debtor for any payment or other transfer of property due from the debtor under or in connection with any swap agreement against any payment due to the debtor from the swap participant or financial participant under or in connection with any swap agreement or against cash, securities, or other property held by, pledged to, under the control of, or due from such swap participant or financial participant to margin, guarantee, secure, or settle any swap agreement;".

Subsec. (b)(27). Pub. L. 109–390, §5(a)(2)(C), added par. (27) and struck out former par. (27) which read as follows: "under subsection (a), of the setoff by a master netting agreement participant of a mutual debt and claim under or in connection with one or more master netting agreements or any contract or agreement subject to such agreements that constitutes the setoff of a claim against the debtor for any payment or other transfer of property due from the debtor under or in connection with such agreements or any contract or agreement subject to such agreements against any payment due to the debtor from such master netting agreement participant under or in connection with such agreements or any contract or agreement subject to such agreements or against cash, securities, or other property held by, pledged to, under the control of, or due from such master netting agreement participant to margin, guarantee, secure, or settle such agreements or any contract or agreement subject to such agreements, to the extent that such participant is eligible to exercise such offset rights under paragraph (6), (7), or (17) for each individual contract covered by the master netting agreement in issue; and".

2005—Subsec. (a)(8). Pub. L. 109–8, §709, substituted "a corporate debtor's tax liability for a taxable period the bankruptcy court may determine or concerning the tax liability of a debtor who is an individual for a taxable period ending before the date of the order for relief under this title" for "the debtor".

Subsec. (b)(2). Pub. L. 109–8, §214, added par. (2) and struck out former par. (2) which read as follows: "under subsection (a) of this section—

"(A) of the commencement or continuation of an action or proceeding for—

"(i) the establishment of paternity; or

"(ii) the establishment or modification of an order for alimony, maintenance, or support; or

"(B) of the collection of alimony, maintenance, or support from property that is not property of the estate;".

Subsec. (b)(6). Pub. L. 109–8, §907(d)(1)(A), (*o*)(1), substituted "financial institution, financial participant," for "financial institutions," in two places and inserted ", pledged to, under the control of," after "held by".

Subsec. (b)(7). Pub. L. 109–8, §907(d)(1)(B), (*o*)(2), inserted "or financial participant" after "repo participant" in two places and ", pledged to, under the control of," after "held by".

Subsec. (b)(17). Pub. L. 109–8, §907(d)(1)(C), added par. (17) and struck out former par. (17) which read as follows: "under subsection (a) of this section, of the setoff by a swap participant, of any mutual debt and claim under or in connection with any swap agreement that constitutes the setoff of a claim against the debtor for any payment due from the debtor under or in connection with any swap agreement against any payment due to the debtor from the swap participant under or in connection with any swap agreement or against cash, securities, or other property of the debtor held by or due from such swap participant to guarantee, secure or settle any swap agreement;".

Subsec. (b)(18). Pub. L. 109–8, §1225, amended par. (18) generally. Prior to amendment, par. (18) read as follows: "under subsection (a) of the creation or perfection of a statutory lien for an ad valorem property tax imposed by the District of Columbia, or a political subdivision of a State, if such tax comes due after the filing of the petition;".

Subsec. (b)(19). Pub. L. 109–8, §224(b), added par. (19).

Subsec. (b)(20), (21). Pub. L. 109–8, §303(b), added pars. (20) and (21).

Subsec. (b)(22) to (24). Pub. L. 109–8, §311(a), added pars. (22) to (24).

Subsec. (b)(25). Pub. L. 109–8, §401(b), added par. (25).

Subsec. (b)(26). Pub. L. 109–8, §718, added par. (26).

Subsec. (b)(27). Pub. L. 109–8, §907(d)(1)(D), added par. (27).

Subsec. (b)(28). Pub. L. 109–8, §1106, added par. (28).

Subsec. (c). Pub. L. 109–8, §305(1)(A), substituted "(e), (f), and (h)" for "(e), and (f)" in introductory provisions.

Subsec. (c)(3), (4). Pub. L. 109–8, §302, added pars. (3) and (4).

Subsec. (d). Pub. L. 109–8, §303(a), added par. (4) and concluding provisions.

Subsec. (d)(3). Pub. L. 109–8, §444(1), inserted "or 30 days after the court determines that the debtor is subject to this paragraph, whichever is later" after "90-day period)" in introductory provisions.

Subsec. (d)(3)(B). Pub. L. 109–8, §444(2), added subpar. (B) and struck out former subpar. (B) which read as follows: "the debtor has commenced monthly payments to each creditor whose claim is secured by such real estate (other than a claim secured by a judgment lien or by an unmatured statutory lien), which payments are in an amount equal to interest at a current fair market rate on the value of the creditor's interest in the real estate; or".

Subsec. (e). Pub. L. 109–8, §320, designated existing provisions as par. (1) and added par. (2).

Subsec. (h). Pub. L. 109–8, §305(1)(C), added subsec. (h). Former subsec. (h) redesignated (k).

Subsecs. (i), (j). Pub. L. 109–8, §106(f), added subsecs. (i) and (j).

Subsec. (k). Pub. L. 109–8, §441(1), designated existing provisions as par. (1), substituted "Except as provided in paragraph (2), an" for "An", and added par. (2).

Pub. L. 109–8, §305(1)(B), redesignated subsec. (h) as (k).

Subsecs. (*l*), (m). Pub. L. 109–8, §311(b), added subsecs. (*l*) and (m).

Subsec. (n). Pub. L. 109–8, §441(2), added subsec. (n).

Subsec. (*o*). Pub. L. 109–8, §907(d)(2), added subsec. (*o*).

1998—Subsec. (b)(4), (5). Pub. L. 105–277 added par. (4) and struck out former pars. (4) and (5) which read as follows:

"(4) under subsection (a)(1) of this section, of the commencement or continuation of an action or proceeding by a governmental unit to enforce such governmental unit's police or regulatory power;

"(5) under subsection (a)(2) of this section, of the enforcement of a judgment, other than a money judgment, obtained in an action or proceeding by a governmental unit to enforce such governmental unit's police or regulatory power;".

1994—Subsecs. (a), (b). Pub. L. 103–394, §501(d)(7)(A), (B)(i), struck out "(15 U.S.C. 78eee(a)(3))" after "Act of 1970" in introductory provisions.

Subsec. (b)(2). Pub. L. 103–394, §304(b), amended par. (2) generally. Prior to amendment, par. (2) read as follows: "under subsection (a) of this section, of the collection of alimony, maintenance, or support from property that is not property of the estate;".

Subsec. (b)(3). Pub. L. 103–394, §204(a), inserted ", or to maintain or continue the perfection of," after "to perfect".

Subsec. (b)(6). Pub. L. 103–394, §501(b)(2)(A), substituted "section 761" for "section 761(4)", "section 741" for "section 741(7)", "section 101, 741, or 761" for "section 101(34), 741(5), or 761(15)", and "section 101 or 741" for "section 101(35) or 741(8)".

Subsec. (b)(7). Pub. L. 103–394, §501(b)(2)(B), substituted "section 741 or 761" for "section 741(5) or 761(15)" and "section 741" for "section 741(8)".

Subsec. (b)(9). Pub. L. 103–394, §116, amended par. (9) generally. Prior to amendment, par. (9) read as follows: "under subsection (a) of this section, of the issuance to the debtor by a governmental unit of a notice of tax deficiency;".

Subsec. (b)(10). Pub. L. 103–394, §501(d)(7)(B)(ii), struck out "or" at end.

Subsec. (b)(12). Pub. L. 103–394, §501(d)(7)(B)(iii), substituted "section 31325 of title 46" for "the Ship Mortgage Act, 1920 (46 App. U.S.C. 911 et seq.)" and struck out "(46 App. U.S.C. 1117 and 1271 et seq., respectively)" after "Act, 1936".

Subsec. (b)(13). Pub. L. 103–394, §501(d)(7)(B)(iv), substituted "section 31325 of title 46" for "the Ship Mortgage Act, 1920 (46 App. U.S.C. 911 et seq.)" and struck out "(46 App. U.S.C. 1117 and 1271 et seq., respectively)" after "Act, 1936" and "or" at end.

Subsec. (b)(14). Pub. L. 103–394, §501(d)(7)(B)(vii), amended par. (14) relating to the setoff by a swap participant of any mutual debt and claim under or in connection with a swap agreement by substituting "; or" for period at end, redesignating par. (14) as (17), and inserting it after par. (16).

Subsec. (b)(15). Pub. L. 103–394, §501(d)(7)(B)(v), struck out "or" at end.

Subsec. (b)(16). Pub. L. 103–394, §501(d)(7)(B)(vi), struck out "(20 U.S.C. 1001 et seq.)" after "Act of 1965" and substituted semicolon for period at end.

Subsec. (b)(17). Pub. L. 103–394, §501(d)(7)(B)(vii)(II), (III), redesignated par. (14) relating to the setoff by a swap participant of any mutual debt and claim under or in connection with a swap agreement as (17) and inserted it after par. (16).

Subsec. (b)(18). Pub. L. 103–394, §401, added par. (18).

Subsec. (d)(3). Pub. L. 103–394, §218(b), added par. (3).

Subsec. (e). Pub. L. 103–394, §101, in last sentence substituted "concluded" for "commenced" and inserted before period at end ", unless the 30-day period is extended with the consent of the parties in interest or for a specific time which the court finds is required by compelling circumstances".

1990—Subsec. (b)(6). Pub. L. 101–311, §202, inserted reference to sections 101(34) and 101(35) of this title.

Subsec. (b)(12). Pub. L. 101–508, §3007(a)(1)(A), which directed the striking of "or" after "State law;", could not be executed because of a prior amendment by Pub. L. 101–311. See below.

Pub. L. 101–311, §102(1), struck out "or" after "State law;".

Subsec. (b)(13). Pub. L. 101–508, §3007(a)(1)(B), which directed the substitution of a semicolon for period at end, could not be executed because of a prior amendment by Pub. L. 101–311. See below.

Pub. L. 101–311, §102(2), substituted "; or" for period at end.

Subsec. (b)(14) to (16). Pub. L. 101–508, §3007(a)(1)(C), added pars. (14) to (16). Notwithstanding directory language adding pars. (14) to (16) immediately following par. (13), pars. (14) to (16) were added after par. (14), as added by Pub. L. 101–311, to reflect the probable intent of Congress.

Pub. L. 101–311, §102(3), added par. (14) relating to the setoff by a swap participant of any mutual debt and claim under or in connection with a swap agreement.

Notwithstanding directory language adding par. (14) at end of subsec. (b), par. (14) was added after par. (13) to reflect the probable intent of Congress.

1986—Subsec. (b). Pub. L. 99–509 inserted sentence at end.

Subsec. (b)(6). Pub. L. 99–554, §283(d)(1), substituted ", financial institutions" for "financial institution," in two places.

Subsec. (b)(9). Pub. L. 99–554, §283(d)(2), (3), struck out "or" at end of first par. (9) and redesignated as par. (10) the second par. (9) relating to leases of nonresidential property, which was added by section 363(b) of Pub. L. 98–353.

Subsec. (b)(10). Pub. L. 99–554, §283(d)(3), (4), redesignated as par. (10) the second par. (9) relating to leases of nonresidential property, added by section 363(b) of Pub. L. 99–353, and substituted "property; or" for "property.". Former par. (10) redesignated (11).

Subsec. (b)(11). Pub. L. 99–554, §283(d)(3), redesignated former par. (10) as (11).

Subsec. (b)(12), (13). Pub. L. 99–509 added pars. (12) and (13).

Subsec. (c)(2)(C). Pub. L. 99–554, §257(j), inserted reference to chapter 12 of this title.

1984—Subsec. (a)(1). Pub. L. 98–353, §441(a)(1), inserted "action or" after "other".

Subsec. (a)(3). Pub. L. 98–353, §441(a)(2), inserted "or to exercise control over property of the estate".

Subsec. (b)(3). Pub. L. 98–353, §441(b)(1), inserted "or to the extent that such act is accomplished within the period provided under section 547(e)(2)(A) of this title".

Subsec. (b)(6). Pub. L. 98–353, §441(b)(2), inserted "or due from" after "held by" and "financial institution," after "stockbroker" in two places, and substituted "secure, or settle commodity contracts" for "or secure commodity contracts".

Subsec. (b)(7) to (9). Pub. L. 98–353, §441(b)(3), (4), in par. (8) as redesignated by Pub. L. 98–353, §392, substituted "the" for "said" and struck out "or" the last place it appeared which probably meant "or" after "units;" that was struck out by Pub. L. 98–353, §363(b)(1); and, in par. (9), relating to notices of deficiencies, as redesignated by Pub. L. 98–353, §392, substituted a semicolon for the period.

Pub. L. 98–353, §392, added par. (7) and redesignated former pars. (7) and (8) as (8) and (9), respectively.

Pub. L. 98–353, §363(b), struck out "or" at end of par. (7), substituted "; or" for the period at end of par. (8), and added par. (9) relating to leases of nonresidential property.

Subsec. (b)(10). Pub. L. 98–353, §441(b)(5), added par. (10).

Subsec. (c)(2)(B). Pub. L. 98–353, §441(c), substituted "or" for "and".

Subsec. (d)(2). Pub. L. 98–353, §441(d), inserted "under subsection (a) of this section" after "property".

Subsec. (e). Pub. L. 98–353, §441(e), inserted "the conclusion of" after "pending" and substituted "The court shall order such stay continued in effect pending the conclusion of the final hearing under subsection (d) of this section if there is a reasonable likelihood that the party opposing relief from such stay will prevail at the conclusion of such final hearing. If the hearing under this subsection is a preliminary hearing, then such final hearing shall be commenced not later than thirty days after the conclusion of such preliminary hearing." for "If the hearing under this subsection is a preliminary hearing—

"(1) the court shall order such stay so continued if there is a reasonable likelihood that the party opposing relief from such stay will prevail at the final hearing under subsection (d) of this section; and

"(2) such final hearing shall be commenced within thirty days after such preliminary hearing."

Subsec. (f). Pub. L. 98–353, §441(f), substituted "Upon request of a party in interest, the court, with or" for "The court,".

Subsec. (h). Pub. L. 98–353, §304, added subsec. (h).

1982—Subsec. (a). Pub. L. 97–222, §3(a), inserted ", or an application filed under section 5(a)(3) of the Securities Investor Protection Act of 1970 (15 U.S.C. 78eee(a)(3))," after "this title" in provisions preceding par. (1).

Subsec. (b). Pub. L. 97–222, §3(b), inserted ", or of an application under section 5(a)(3) of the Securities Investor Protection Act of 1970 (15 U.S.C. 78eee(a)(3))," after "this title" in provisions preceding par. (1).

Subsec. (b)(6). Pub. L. 97–222, §3(c), substituted provisions that the filing of a bankruptcy petition would not operate as a stay, under subsec. (a) of this section, of the setoff by a commodity broker, forward contract merchant, stockbroker, or securities clearing agency of any mutual debt and claim under or in connection with commodity, forward, or securities contracts that constitutes the setoff of a claim against the debtor for a margin or settlement payment arising out of commodity, forward, or securities contracts against cash, securities, or other property held by any of the above agents to margin, guarantee, or secure commodity, forward, or securities contracts, for provisions that such filing would not operate as a stay under subsection (a)(7) of this section, of the setoff of any mutual debt and claim that are commodity futures contracts, forward commodity contracts, leverage transactions, options, warrants, rights to purchase or sell commodity futures contracts or securities, or options to purchase or sell commodities or securities.

Effective Date of 2006 Amendment

Amendment by Pub. L. 109–390 not applicable to any cases commenced under this title or to appointments made under any Federal or State law, before Dec. 12, 2006, see section 7 of Pub. L. 109–390, set out as a note under section 101 of this title.

Effective Date of 2005 Amendment

Amendment by Pub. L. 109–8 effective 180 days after Apr. 20, 2005, and not applicable with respect to cases commenced under this title before such effective date, except as otherwise provided, see section 1501 of Pub. L. 109–8, set out as a note under section 101 of this title.

Effective Date of 1994 Amendment

Amendment by Pub. L. 103–394 effective Oct. 22, 1994, and not applicable with respect to cases commenced under this title before Oct. 22, 1994, see section 702 of Pub. L. 103–394, set out as a note under section 101 of this title.

Effective Date of 1990 Amendment

Section 3007(a)(3) of Pub. L. 101–508 provided that: "The amendments made by this subsection [amending this section and section 541 of this title] shall be effective upon date of enactment of this Act [Nov. 5, 1990]."

Section 3008 of Pub. L. 101–508, provided that the amendments made by subtitle A (§§3001–3008) of title III of Pub. L. 101–508, amending this section, sections 541 and 1328 of this title, and sections 1078, 1078–1, 1078–7, 1085, 1088, and 1091 of Title 20, Education, and provisions set out as a note under section 1078–1 of Title 20, were to cease to be effective Oct. 1, 1996, prior to repeal by Pub. L. 102–325, title XV, §1558, July 23, 1992, 106 Stat. 841.

Effective Date of 1986 Amendments

Amendment by section 257 of Pub. L. 99–554 effective 30 days after Oct. 27, 1986, but not applicable to cases commenced under this title before that date, see section 302(a), (c)(1) of Pub. L. 99–554, set out as a note under section 581 of Title 28, Judiciary and Judicial Procedure.

Amendment by section 283 of Pub. L. 99–554 effective 30 days after Oct. 27, 1986, see section 302(a) of Pub. L. 99–554.

Section 5001(b) of Pub. L. 99–509 provided that: "The amendments made by subsection (a) of this section [amending this section] shall apply only to petitions filed under section 362 of title 11, United States Code, which are made after August 1, 1986."

EFFECTIVE DATE OF 1984 AMENDMENT

Amendment by Pub. L. 98–353 effective with respect to cases filed 90 days after July 10, 1984, see section 552(a) of Pub. L. 98–353, set out as a note under section 101 of this title.

REPORT TO CONGRESSIONAL COMMITTEES

Section 5001(a) of Pub. L. 99–509 directed Secretary of Transportation and Secretary of Commerce, before July 1, 1989, to submit reports to Congress on the effects of amendments to 11 U.S.C. 362 by this subsection.

§ 363. Use, sale, or lease of property

(a) In this section, "cash collateral" means cash, negotiable instruments, documents of title, securities, deposit accounts, or other cash equivalents whenever acquired in which the estate and an entity other than the estate have an interest and includes the proceeds, products, offspring, rents, or profits of property and the fees, charges, accounts or other payments for the use or occupancy of rooms and other public facilities in hotels, motels, or other lodging properties subject to a security interest as provided in section 552(b) of this title, whether existing before or after the commencement of a case under this title.

(b)(1) The trustee, after notice and a hearing, may use, sell, or lease, other than in the ordinary course of business, property of the estate, except that if the debtor in connection with offering a product or a service discloses to an individual a policy prohibiting the transfer of personally identifiable information about individuals to persons that are not affiliated with the debtor and if such policy is in effect on the date of the commencement of the case, then the trustee may not sell or lease personally identifiable information to any person unless—

(A) such sale or such lease is consistent with such policy; or

(B) after appointment of a consumer privacy ombudsman in accordance with section 332, and after notice and a hearing, the court approves such sale or such lease—

(i) giving due consideration to the facts, circumstances, and conditions of such sale or such lease; and

(ii) finding that no showing was made that such sale or such lease would violate applicable nonbankruptcy law.

(2) If notification is required under subsection (a) of section 7A of the Clayton Act in the case of a transaction under this subsection, then—

(A) notwithstanding subsection (a) of such section, the notification required by such subsection to be given by the debtor shall be given by the trustee; and

(B) notwithstanding subsection (b) of such section, the required waiting period shall end on the 15th day after the date of the receipt, by the Federal Trade Commission and the Assistant Attorney General in charge of the Antitrust Division of the Department of Justice, of the notification required under such subsection (a), unless such waiting period is extended—

(i) pursuant to subsection (e)(2) of such section, in the same manner as such subsection (e)(2) applies to a cash tender offer;

(ii) pursuant to subsection (g)(2) of such section; or

(iii) by the court after notice and a hearing.

(c)(1) If the business of the debtor is authorized to be operated under section 721, 1108, 1203, 1204, or 1304 of this title and unless the court orders otherwise, the trustee may enter into transactions, including the sale or lease of property of the estate, in the ordinary course of business, without notice or a hearing, and may use property of the estate in the ordinary course of business without notice or a hearing.

(2) The trustee may not use, sell, or lease cash collateral under paragraph (1) of this subsection unless—

(A) each entity that has an interest in such cash collateral consents; or

(B) the court, after notice and a hearing, authorizes such use, sale, or lease in accordance with the provisions of this section.

(3) Any hearing under paragraph (2)(B) of this subsection may be a preliminary hearing or may be consolidated with a hearing under subsection (e) of this section, but shall be scheduled in accordance with the needs of the debtor. If the hearing under paragraph (2)(B) of this subsection is a preliminary hearing, the court may authorize such use, sale, or lease only if there is a reasonable likelihood that the trustee will prevail at the final hearing under subsection (e) of this section. The court shall act promptly on any request for authorization under paragraph (2)(B) of this subsection.

(4) Except as provided in paragraph (2) of this subsection, the trustee shall segregate and account for any cash collateral in the trustee's possession, custody, or control.

(d) The trustee may use, sell, or lease property under subsection (b) or (c) of this section only—

(1) in accordance with applicable nonbankruptcy law that governs the transfer of property by a corporation or trust that is not a moneyed, business, or commercial corporation or trust; and

(2) to the extent not inconsistent with any relief granted under subsection (c), (d), (e), or (f) of section 362.

(e) Notwithstanding any other provision of this section, at any time, on request of an entity that has an interest in property used, sold, or leased, or proposed to be used, sold, or leased, by the trustee, the court, with or without a hearing, shall prohibit or condition such use, sale, or lease as is necessary to provide adequate protection of such interest. This subsection also applies to property that is subject to any unexpired lease of personal property (to the exclusion of such property being subject to an order to grant relief from the stay under section 362).

(f) The trustee may sell property under subsection (b) or (c) of this section free and clear of any interest in such property of an entity other than the estate, only if—

(1) applicable nonbankruptcy law permits sale of such property free and clear of such interest;

(2) such entity consents;

(3) such interest is a lien and the price at which such property is to be sold is greater than the aggregate value of all liens on such property;

(4) such interest is in bona fide dispute; or

(5) such entity could be compelled, in a legal or equitable proceeding, to accept a money satisfaction of such interest.

(g) Notwithstanding subsection (f) of this section, the trustee may sell property under subsection (b) or (c) of this section free and clear of any vested or contingent right in the nature of dower or curtesy.

(h) Notwithstanding subsection (f) of this section, the trustee may sell both the estate's interest, under subsection (b) or (c) of this section, and the interest of any co-owner in property in which the debtor had, at the time of the commencement of the case, an undivided interest as a tenant in common, joint tenant, or tenant by the entirety, only if—

(1) partition in kind of such property among the estate and such co-owners is impracticable;

(2) sale of the estate's undivided interest in such property would realize significantly less for the estate than sale of such property free of the interests of such co-owners;

(3) the benefit to the estate of a sale of such property free of the interests of co-owners outweighs the detriment, if any, to such co-owners; and

(4) such property is not used in the production, transmission, or distribution, for sale, of electric energy or of natural or synthetic gas for heat, light, or power.

(i) Before the consummation of a sale of property to which subsection (g) or (h) of this section applies, or of property of the estate that was community property of the debtor and the debtor's spouse immediately before the commencement of the case, the debtor's spouse, or a co-owner of such property, as the case may be, may purchase such property at the price at which such sale is to be consummated.

(j) After a sale of property to which subsection (g) or (h) of this section applies, the trustee shall distribute to the debtor's spouse or the co-owners of such property, as the case may be, and to the estate, the proceeds of such sale, less the costs and expenses, not including any compensation of the trustee, of such sale, according to the interests of such spouse or co-owners, and of the estate.

(k) At a sale under subsection (b) of this section of property that is subject to a lien that secures an allowed claim, unless the court for cause orders otherwise the holder of such claim may bid at such sale, and, if the holder of such claim purchases such property, such holder may offset such claim against the purchase price of such property.

(*l*) Subject to the provisions of section 365, the trustee may use, sell, or lease property under subsection (b) or (c) of this section, or a plan under chapter 11, 12, or 13 of this title may provide for the use, sale, or lease of property, notwithstanding any provision in a contract, a lease, or applicable law that is conditioned on the insolvency or financial condition of the debtor, on the commencement of a case under this title concerning the debtor, or on the appointment of or the taking possession by a trustee in a case under this title or a custodian, and that effects, or gives an option to effect, a forfeiture, modification, or termination of the debtor's interest in such property.

(m) The reversal or modification on appeal of an authorization under subsection (b) or (c) of this section of a sale or lease of property does not affect the validity of a sale or lease under such authorization to an entity that purchased or leased such property in good faith, whether or not such entity knew of the pendency of the appeal, unless such authorization and such sale or lease were stayed pending appeal.

(n) The trustee may avoid a sale under this section if the sale price was controlled by an agreement among potential bidders at such sale, or may recover from a party to such agreement any amount by which the value of the property sold exceeds the price at which such sale was consummated, and may recover any costs, attorneys' fees, or expenses incurred in avoiding such sale or recovering such amount. In addition to any recovery under the preceding sentence, the court may grant judgment for punitive damages in favor of the estate and against any such party that entered into such an agreement in willful disregard of this subsection.

(*o*) Notwithstanding subsection (f), if a person purchases any interest in a consumer credit transaction that is subject to the Truth in Lending Act or any interest in a consumer credit contract (as defined in section 433.1 of title 16 of the Code of Federal Regulations (January 1, 2004), as amended from time to time), and if such interest is purchased through a sale under this section, then such person shall remain subject to all claims and defenses that are related to such consumer credit transaction or such consumer credit contract, to the same extent as such person would be subject to such claims and defenses of the consumer had such interest been purchased at a sale not under this section.

(p) In any hearing under this section—

(1) the trustee has the burden of proof on the issue of adequate protection; and

(2) the entity asserting an interest in property has the burden of proof on the issue of the validity, priority, or extent of such interest.

(Pub. L. 95–598, Nov. 6, 1978, 92 Stat. 2572; Pub. L. 98–353, title III, §442, July 10, 1984, 98 Stat. 371; Pub. L. 99–554, title II, §257(k), Oct. 27, 1986, 100 Stat. 3115; Pub. L. 103–394, title I, §109, title II, §§214(b), 219(c), title V, §501(d)(8), Oct. 22, 1994, 108 Stat. 4113, 4126, 4129, 4144; Pub. L. 109–8, title II, §§204, 231(a), title XII, §1221(a), Apr. 20, 2005, 119 Stat. 49, 72, 195.)

Historical and Revision Notes

Legislative Statements

Section 363(a) of the House amendment defines "cash collateral" as defined in the Senate amendment. The broader definition of "soft collateral" contained in H.R. 8200 as passed by the House is deleted to remove limitations that were placed on the use, lease, or sale of inventory, accounts, contract rights, general intangibles, and chattel paper by the trustee or debtor in possession.

Section 363(c)(2) of the House amendment is derived from the Senate amendment. Similarly, sections 363(c)(3) and (4) are derived from comparable provisions in the Senate amendment in lieu of the contrary procedure contained in section 363(c) as passed by the House.

The policy of the House amendment will generally require the court to schedule a preliminary hearing in accordance with the needs of the debtor to authorize the trustee or debtor in possession to use, sell, or lease cash collateral. The trustee or debtor in possession may use, sell, or lease cash collateral in the ordinary course of business only "after notice and a hearing."

Section 363(f) of the House amendment adopts an identical provision contained in the House bill, as opposed to an alternative provision contained in the Senate amendment.

Section 363(h) of the House amendment adopts a new paragraph (4) representing a compromise between the House bill and Senate amendment. The provision adds a limitation indicating that a trustee or debtor in possession sell jointly owned property only if the property is not used in the production, transmission, or distribution for sale, of electric energy or of natural or synthetic gas for heat, light, or power. This limitation is intended to protect public utilities from being deprived of power sources because of the bankruptcy of a joint owner.

Section 363(k) of the House amendment is derived from the third sentence of section 363(e) of the Senate amendment. The provision indicates that a secured creditor may bid in the full amount of the creditor's allowed claim, including the secured portion and any unsecured portion thereof in the event the creditor is undersecured, with respect to property that is subject to a lien that secures the allowed claim of the sale of the property.

SENATE REPORT NO. 95–989

This section defines the right and powers of the trustee with respect to the use, sale or lease of property and the rights of other parties that have interests in the property involved. It applies in both liquidation and reorganization cases.

Subsection (a) defines "cash collateral" as cash, negotiable instruments, documents of title, securities, deposit accounts, or other cash equivalents in which the estate and an entity other than the estate have an interest, such as a lien or a co-ownership interest. The definition is not restricted to property of the estate that is cash collateral on the date of the filing of the petition. Thus, if "non-cash" collateral is disposed of and the proceeds come within the definition of "cash collateral" as set forth in this subsection, the proceeds would be cash collateral as long as they remain subject to the original lien on the "non-cash" collateral under section 552(b). To illustrate, rents received from real property before or after the commencement of the case would be cash collateral to the extent that they are subject to a lien.

Subsection (b) permits the trustees to use, sell, or lease, other than in the ordinary course of business, property of the estate upon notice and opportunity for objections and hearing thereon.

Subsection (c) governs use, sale, or lease in the ordinary course of business. If the business of the debtor is authorized to be operated under §721, 1108, or 1304 of the bankruptcy code, then the trustee may use, sell, or lease property in the ordinary course of business or enter into ordinary course transactions without need for notice and hearing. This power is subject to several limitations. First, the court may restrict the trustee's powers in the order authorizing operation of the business. Second, with respect to cash collateral, the trustee may not use, sell, or lease cash collateral except upon court authorization after notice and a hearing, or with the consent of each entity that has an interest in such cash collateral. The same preliminary hearing procedure in the automatic stay section applies to a hearing under this subsection. In addition, the trustee is required to segregate and account for any cash collateral in the trustee's possession, custody, or control.

Under subsections (d) and (e), the use, sale, or lease of property is further limited by the concept of adequate protection. Sale, use, or lease of property in which an entity other than the estate has an interest may be effected only to the extent not inconsistent with any relief from the stay granted to that interest's holder. Moreover, the court may prohibit or condition the use, sale, or lease as is necessary to provide adequate protection of that interest. Again, the trustee has the burden of proof on the issue of adequate protection. Subsection (e) also provides that where a sale of the property is proposed, an entity that has an interest in such property may bid at the sale thereof and set off against the purchase price up to the amount of such entity's claim. No prior valuation under section 506(a) would limit this bidding right, since the bid at the sale would be determinative of value.

Subsection (f) permits sale of property free and clear of any interest in the property of an entity other than the estate. The trustee may sell free and clear if applicable nonbankruptcy law permits it, if the other entity consents, if the interest is a lien and the sale price of the property is greater than the amount secured by the lien, if the interest is in bona fide dispute, or if the other entity could be compelled to accept a money satisfaction of the interest in a legal or equitable proceeding. Sale under this subsection is subject to the adequate protection requirement. Most often, adequate protection in connection with a sale free and clear of other interests will be to have those interests attach to the proceeds of the sale.

At a sale free and clear of other interests, any holder of any interest in the property being sold will be permitted to bid. If that holder is the high bidder, he will be permitted to offset the value of his interest against the purchase price of the property. Thus, in the most common situation, a holder of a lien on property being sold may bid at the sale and, if successful, may offset the amount owed to him that is secured by the lien on the property (but may not offset other amounts owed to him) against the purchase price, and be liable to the trustee for the balance of the sale price, if any.

Subsection (g) permits the trustee to sell free and clear of any vested or contingent right in the nature of dower or curtesy.

Subsection (h) permits sale of a co-owner's interest in property in which the debtor had an undivided ownership interest such as a joint tenancy, a tenancy in common, or a tenancy by the entirety. Such a sale is permissible only if partition is impracticable, if sale of the estate's interest would realize significantly less for the estate that sale of the property free of the interests of the co-owners, and if the benefit to the estate of such a sale outweighs any detriment to the co-owners. This subsection does not apply to a co-owner's interest in a public utility when a disruption of the utilities services could result.

Subsection (i) provides protections for co-owners and spouses with dower, curtesy, or community property rights. It gives a right of first refusal to the co-owner or spouse at the price at which the sale is to be consummated.

Subsection (j) requires the trustee to distribute to the spouse or co-owner the appropriate portion of the proceeds of the sale, less certain administrative expenses.

Subsection (k) [enacted as *(l)*] permits the trustee to use, sell, or lease property notwithstanding certain bankruptcy or ipso facto clauses that terminate the debtor's interest in the property or that work a forfeiture or modification of that interest. This subsection is not as broad as the anti-ipso facto provision in proposed 11 U.S.C. 541(c)(1).

Subsection *(l)* [enacted as (m)] protects good faith purchasers of property sold under this section from a reversal on appeal of the sale authorization, unless the authorization for the sale and the sale itself were stayed pending appeal. The purchaser's knowledge of the appeal is irrelevant to the issue of good faith.

Subsection (m) [enacted as (n)] is directed at collusive bidding on property sold under this section. It permits the trustee to void a sale if the price of the sale was controlled by an agreement among potential bidders. The trustees may also recover the excess of the value of the property over the purchase price, and may recover any costs, attorney's fees, or expenses incurred in voiding the sale or recovering the difference. In addition, the court is authorized to grant judgment in favor of the estate and against the collusive bidder if the agreement controlling the sale price was entered into in willful disregard of this subsection. The subsection does not specify the precise measure of damages, but simply provides for punitive damages, to be fixed in light of the circumstances.

REFERENCES IN TEXT

Section 7A of the Clayton Act, referred to in subsec. (b)(2), is classified to section 18a of Title 15, Commerce and Trade.

The Truth in Lending Act, referred to in subsec. (*o*), is title I of Pub. L. 90–321, May 29, 1968, 82 Stat. 146, as amended, which is classified generally to subchapter I (§1601 et seq.) of chapter 41 of Title 15, Commerce and Trade. For complete classification of this Act to the Code, see Short Title note set out under section 1601 of Title 15 and Tables.

AMENDMENTS

2005—Subsec. (b)(1). Pub. L. 109–8, §231(a), substituted ", except that if the debtor in connection with offering a product or a service discloses to an individual a policy prohibiting the transfer of personally identifiable information about individuals to persons that are not affiliated with the debtor and if such policy is in effect on the date of the commencement of the case, then the trustee may not sell or lease personally identifiable information to any person unless—" and subpars. (A) and (B) for period at end.

Subsec. (d). Pub. L. 109–8, §1221(a), substituted "only—" and pars. (1) and (2) for "only to the extent not inconsistent with any relief granted under section 362(c), 362(d), 362(e), or 362(f) of this title."

Subsecs. (*o*), (p). Pub. L. 109–8, §204, added subsec. (*o*) and redesignated former subsec. (*o*) as (p).

1994—Subsec. (a). Pub. L. 103–394, §214(b), inserted "and the fees, charges, accounts or other payments for the use or occupancy of rooms and other public facilities in hotels, motels, or other lodging properties" after "property".

Subsec. (b)(2). Pub. L. 103–394, §§109, 501(d)(8)(A), struck out "(15 U.S.C. 18a)" after "Clayton Act" and amended subpars. (A) and (B) generally. Prior to amendment, subpars. (A) and (B) read as follows:

"(A) notwithstanding subsection (a) of such section, such notification shall be given by the trustee; and

"(B) notwithstanding subsection (b) of such section, the required waiting period shall end on the tenth day after the date of the receipt of such notification, unless the court, after notice and hearing, orders otherwise."

Subsec. (c)(1). Pub. L. 103–394, §501(d)(8)(B), substituted "1203, 1204, or 1304" for "1304, 1203, or 1204".

Subsec. (e). Pub. L. 103–394, §219(c), inserted at end "This subsection also applies to property that is subject to any unexpired lease of personal property (to the exclusion of such property being subject to an order to grant relief from the stay under section 362)."

1986—Subsec. (c)(1). Pub. L. 99–554, §257(k)(1), inserted reference to sections 1203 and 1204 of this title.

Subsec. (*l*). Pub. L. 99–554, §257(k)(2), inserted reference to chapter 12.

1984—Subsec. (a). Pub. L. 98–353, §442(a), inserted "whenever acquired" after "equivalents" and "and includes the proceeds, products, offspring, rents, or profits of property subject to a security interest as provided in section 552(b) of this title, whether existing before or after the commencement of a case under this title" after "interest".

Subsec. (b). Pub. L. 98–353, §442(b), designated existing provisions as par. (1) and added par. (2).

Subsec. (e). Pub. L. 98–353, §442(c), inserted ", with or without a hearing," after "court" and struck out "In any hearing under this section, the trustee has the burden of proof on the issue of adequate protection".

Subsec. (f)(3). Pub. L. 98–353, §442(d), substituted "all liens on such property" for "such interest".

Subsec. (h). Pub. L. 98–353, §442(e), substituted "at the time of" for "immediately before".

Subsec. (j). Pub. L. 98–353, §442(f), substituted "compensation" for "compenation".

Subsec. (k). Pub. L. 98–353, §442(g), substituted "unless the court for cause orders otherwise the holder of such claim may bid at such sale, and, if the holder" for "if the holder".

Subsec. (*l*). Pub. L. 98–353, §442(h), substituted "Subject to the provisions of section 365, the trustee" for "The trustee", "condition" for "conditions", "or the taking" for "a taking", and "interest" for "interests".

Subsec. (n). Pub. L. 98–353, §442(i), substituted "avoid" for "void", "avoiding" for "voiding", and "In addition to any recovery under the preceding sentence, the court may grant judgment for punitive damages in favor of the estate and against any such party that entered into such an agreement in willful disregard of this subsection" for "The court may grant judgment in favor of the estate and against any such party that entered into such agreement in willful disregard of this subsection for punitive damages in addition to any recovery under the preceding sentence".

Subsec. (*o*). Pub. L. 98–353, §442(j), added subsec. (*o*).

EFFECTIVE DATE OF 2005 AMENDMENT

Pub. L. 109–8, title XII, §1221(d), Apr. 20, 2005, 119 Stat. 196, provided that: "The amendments made by this section [amending this section and sections 541 and 1129 of this title and enacting provisions set out as a note under this section] shall apply to a case pending under title 11, United States Code, on the date of enactment of this Act [Apr. 20, 2005], or filed under that title on or after that date of enactment, except that the court shall not confirm a plan under chapter 11 of title 11, United States Code, without considering whether this section would substantially affect the rights of a party in interest who first acquired rights with respect to the debtor after the date of the filing of the petition. The parties who may appear and be heard in a proceeding under this section include the attorney general of the State in which the debtor is incorporated, was formed, or does business."

Amendment by sections 204 and 231(a) of Pub. L. 109–8 effective 180 days after Apr. 20, 2005, and not applicable with respect to cases commenced under this title before such effective date, except as otherwise provided, see section 1501 of Pub. L. 109–8, set out as a note under section 101 of this title.

EFFECTIVE DATE OF 1994 AMENDMENT

Amendment by Pub. L. 103–394 effective Oct. 22, 1994, and not applicable with respect to cases commenced under this title before Oct. 22, 1994, see section 702 of Pub. L. 103–394, set out as a note under section 101 of this title.

EFFECTIVE DATE OF 1986 AMENDMENT

Amendment by Pub. L. 99–554 effective 30 days after Oct. 27, 1986, but not applicable to cases commenced under this title before that date, see section 302(a), (c)(1) of Pub. L. 99–554, set out as a note under section 581 of Title 28, Judiciary and Judicial Procedure.

EFFECTIVE DATE OF 1984 AMENDMENT

Amendment by Pub. L. 98–353 effective with respect to cases filed 90 days after July 10, 1984, see section 552(a) of Pub. L. 98–353, set out as a note under section 101 of this title.

CONSTRUCTION OF SECTION 1221 OF PUB. L. 109–8

Pub. L. 109–8, title XII, §1221(e), Apr. 20, 2005, 119 Stat. 196, provided that: "Nothing in this section [see Effective Date of 2005 Amendment note above] shall be construed to require the court in which a case under chapter 11 of title 11, United States Code, is pending to remand or refer any proceeding, issue, or controversy to any other court or to require the approval of any other court for the transfer of property."

§ 364. Obtaining credit

(a) If the trustee is authorized to operate the business of the debtor under section 721, 1108, 1203, 1204, or 1304 of this title, unless the court orders otherwise, the trustee may obtain unsecured credit and incur unsecured debt in the ordinary course of business allowable under section 503(b)(1) of this title as an administrative expense.

(b) The court, after notice and a hearing, may authorize the trustee to obtain unsecured credit or to incur unsecured debt other than under subsection (a) of this section, allowable under section 503(b)(1) of this title as an administrative expense.

(c) If the trustee is unable to obtain unsecured credit allowable under section 503(b)(1) of this title as an administrative expense, the court, after notice and a hearing, may authorize the obtaining of credit or the incurring of debt—

(1) with priority over any or all administrative expenses of the kind specified in section 503(b) or 507(b) of this title;

(2) secured by a lien on property of the estate that is not otherwise subject to a lien; or

(3) secured by a junior lien on property of the estate that is subject to a lien.

(d)(1) The court, after notice and a hearing, may authorize the obtaining of credit or the incurring of debt secured by a senior or equal lien on property of the estate that is subject to a lien only if—

(A) the trustee is unable to obtain such credit otherwise; and

(B) there is adequate protection of the interest of the holder of the lien on the property of the estate on which such senior or equal lien is proposed to be granted.

(2) In any hearing under this subsection, the trustee has the burden of proof on the issue of adequate protection.

(e) The reversal or modification on appeal of an authorization under this section to obtain credit or incur debt, or of a grant under this section of a priority or a lien, does not affect the validity of any debt so incurred, or any priority or lien so granted, to an entity that extended such credit in good faith, whether or not such entity knew of the pendency of the appeal, unless such authorization and the incurring of such debt, or the granting of such priority or lien, were stayed pending appeal.

(f) Except with respect to an entity that is an underwriter as defined in section 1145(b) of this title, section 5 of the Securities Act of 1933, the Trust Indenture Act of 1939, and any State or local law requiring registration for offer or sale of a security or registration or licensing of an issuer of, underwriter of, or broker or dealer in, a security does not apply to the offer or sale under this section of a security that is not an equity security.

(Pub. L. 95–598, Nov. 6, 1978, 92 Stat. 2574; Pub. L. 99–554, title II, § 257(*l*), Oct. 27, 1986, 100 Stat. 3115; Pub. L. 103–394, title V, § 501(d)(9), Oct. 22, 1994, 108 Stat. 4144.)

Historical and Revision Notes

Legislative Statements

Section 364(f) of the House amendment is new. This provision continues the exemption found in section 3(a)(7) of the Securities Act of 1933 [15 U.S.C. 77c(a)(7)] for certificates of indebtedness issued by a trustee in bankruptcy. The exemption applies to any debt security issued under section 364 of title 11. The section does not intend to change present law which exempts such securities from the Trust Indenture Act, 15 U.S.C. 77aaa, et seq. (1976).

Senate Report No. 95–989

This section is derived from provisions in current law governing certificates of indebtedness, but is much broader. It governs all obtaining of credit and incurring of debt by the estate.

Subsection (a) authorizes the obtaining of unsecured credit and the incurring of unsecured debt in the ordinary course of business if the business of the debtor is authorized to be operated under section 721, 1108, or 1304. The debts so incurred are allowable as administrative expenses under section 503(b)(1). The court may limit the estate's ability to incur debt under this subsection.

Subsection (b) permits the court to authorize the trustee to obtain unsecured credit and incur unsecured debts other than in the ordinary course of business, such as in order to wind up a liquidation case, or to obtain a substantial loan in an operating case. Debt incurred under this subsection is allowable as an administrative expense under section 503(b)(1).

Subsection (c) is closer to the concept of certificates of indebtedness in current law. It authorizes the obtaining of credit and the incurring of debt with some special priority, if the trustee is unable to obtain unsecured credit under subsection (a) or (b). The various priorities are (1) with priority over any or all administrative expenses; (2) secured by a lien on unencumbered property of the estate; or (3) secured by a junior lien on encumbered property. The priorities granted under this subsection do not interfere with existing property rights.

Subsection (d) grants the court the authority to authorize the obtaining of credit and the incurring of debt with a superiority, that is a lien on encumbered property that is senior or equal to the existing lien on the property. The court may authorize such a superpriority only if the trustee is otherwise unable to obtain credit, and if there is adequate protection of the original lien holder's interest. Again, the trustee has the burden of proof on the issue of adequate protection.

Subsection (e) provides the same protection for credit extenders pending an appeal of an authorization to incur debt as is provided under section 363(*l*) for purchasers: the credit is not affected on appeal by reversal of the authorization and the incurring of the debt were stayed pending appeal. The protection runs to a good faith lender, whether or not he knew of the pendency of the appeal.

A claim arising as a result of lending or borrowing under this section will be a priority claim, as defined in proposed section 507(a)(1), even if the claim is granted a super-priority over administrative expenses and is to be paid in advance of other first priority claims.

References in Text

Section 5 of the Securities Act of 1933, referred to in subsec. (f), is classified to section 77e of Title 15, Commerce and Trade.

The Trust Indenture Act of 1939, referred to in subsec. (f), is title III of act May 27, 1933, ch. 38, as added Aug. 3, 1939, ch. 411, 53 Stat. 1149, as amended, which is classified generally to subchapter III (§ 77aaa et seq.) of chapter 2A of Title 15. For complete classification of this Act to the Code, see section 77aaa of Title 15 and Tables.

AMENDMENTS

1994—Subsec. (a). Pub. L. 103-394, §501(d)(9)(A), substituted "1203, 1204, or 1304" for "1304, 1203, or 1204".

Subsec. (f). Pub. L. 103-394, §501(d)(9)(B), struck out "(15 U.S.C. 77e)" after "Act of 1933" and "(15 U.S.C. 77aaa et seq.)" after "Act of 1939".

1986—Subsec. (a). Pub. L. 99-554 inserted reference to sections 1203 and 1204 of this title.

EFFECTIVE DATE OF 1994 AMENDMENT

Amendment by Pub. L. 103-394 effective Oct. 22, 1994, and not applicable with respect to cases commenced under this title before Oct. 22, 1994, see section 702 of Pub. L. 103-394, set out as a note under section 101 of this title.

EFFECTIVE DATE OF 1986 AMENDMENT

Amendment by Pub. L. 99-554 effective 30 days after Oct. 27, 1986, but not applicable to cases commenced under this title before that date, see section 302(a), (c)(1) of Pub. L. 99-554, set out as a note under section 581 of Title 28, Judiciary and Judicial Procedure.

§ 365. Executory contracts and unexpired leases

(a) Except as provided in sections 765 and 766 of this title and in subsections (b), (c), and (d) of this section, the trustee, subject to the court's approval, may assume or reject any executory contract or unexpired lease of the debtor.

(b)(1) If there has been a default in an executory contract or unexpired lease of the debtor, the trustee may not assume such contract or lease unless, at the time of assumption of such contract or lease, the trustee—

(A) cures, or provides adequate assurance that the trustee will promptly cure, such default other than a default that is a breach of a provision relating to the satisfaction of any provision (other than a penalty rate or penalty provision) relating to a default arising from any failure to perform nonmonetary obligations under an unexpired lease of real property, if it is impossible for the trustee to cure such default by performing nonmonetary acts at and after the time of assumption, except that if such default arises from a failure to operate in accordance with a nonresidential real property lease, then such default shall be cured by performance at and after the time of assumption in accordance with such lease, and pecuniary losses resulting from such default shall be compensated in accordance with the provisions of this paragraph;

(B) compensates, or provides adequate assurance that the trustee will promptly compensate, a party other than the debtor to such contract or lease, for any actual pecuniary loss to such party resulting from such default; and

(C) provides adequate assurance of future performance under such contract or lease.

(2) Paragraph (1) of this subsection does not apply to a default that is a breach of a provision relating to—

(A) the insolvency or financial condition of the debtor at any time before the closing of the case;

(B) the commencement of a case under this title;

(C) the appointment of or taking possession by a trustee in a case under this title or a custodian before such commencement; or

(D) the satisfaction of any penalty rate or penalty provision relating to a default arising from any failure by the debtor to perform nonmonetary obligations under the executory contract or unexpired lease.

(3) For the purposes of paragraph (1) of this subsection and paragraph (2)(B) of subsection (f), adequate assurance of future performance of a lease of real property in a shopping center includes adequate assurance—

(A) of the source of rent and other consideration due under such lease, and in the case of an assignment, that the financial condition and operating performance of the proposed assignee and its guarantors, if any, shall be similar to the financial condition and operating performance of the debtor and its guarantors, if any, as of the time the debtor became the lessee under the lease;

(B) that any percentage rent due under such lease will not decline substantially;

(C) that assumption or assignment of such lease is subject to all the provisions thereof, including (but not limited to) provisions such as a radius, location, use, or exclusivity provision, and will not breach any such provision contained in any other lease, financing agreement, or master agreement relating to such shopping center; and

(D) that assumption or assignment of such lease will not disrupt any tenant mix or balance in such shopping center.

(4) Notwithstanding any other provision of this section, if there has been a default in an unexpired lease of the debtor, other than a default of a kind specified in paragraph (2) of this subsection, the trustee may not require a lessor to provide services or supplies incidental to such lease before assumption of such lease unless the lessor is compensated under the terms of such lease for any services and supplies provided under such lease before assumption of such lease.

(c) The trustee may not assume or assign any executory contract or unexpired lease of the debtor, whether or not such contract or lease prohibits or restricts assignment of rights or delegation of duties, if—

(1)(A) applicable law excuses a party, other than the debtor, to such contract or lease from accepting performance from or rendering performance to an entity other than the debtor or the debtor in possession, whether or not such contract or lease prohibits or restricts assignment of rights or delegation of duties; and

(B) such party does not consent to such assumption or assignment; or

(2) such contract is a contract to make a loan, or extend other debt financing or financial accommodations, to or for the benefit of the debtor, or to issue a security of the debtor; or

(3) such lease is of nonresidential real property and has been terminated under applicable nonbankruptcy law prior to the order for relief.

(d)(1) In a case under chapter 7 of this title, if the trustee does not assume or reject an executory contract or unexpired lease of residential real property or of personal property of the debtor within 60 days after the order for relief, or within such additional time as the court, for cause, within such 60-day period, fixes, then such contract or lease is deemed rejected.

(2) In a case under chapter 9, 11, 12, or 13 of this title, the trustee may assume or reject an executory contract or unexpired lease of residential real property or of personal property of the debtor at any time before the confirmation of a plan but the court, on the request of any party to such contract or lease, may order the trustee to determine within a specified period of time whether to assume or reject such contract or lease.

(3) The trustee shall timely perform all the obligations of the debtor, except those specified in section 365(b)(2), arising from and after the order for relief under any unexpired lease of nonresidential real property, until such lease is assumed or rejected, notwithstanding section 503(b)(1) of this title. The court may extend, for cause, the time for performance of any such obligation that arises within 60 days after the date of the order for relief, but the time for performance shall not be extended beyond such 60-day period. This subsection shall not be deemed to affect the trustee's obligations under the provisions of subsection (b) or (f) of this section. Acceptance of any such performance does not constitute waiver or relinquishment of the lessor's rights under such lease or under this title.

(4)(A) Subject to subparagraph (B), an unexpired lease of nonresidential real property under which the debtor is the lessee shall be deemed rejected, and the trustee shall immediately surrender that nonresidential real property to the lessor, if the trustee does not assume or reject the unexpired lease by the earlier of—

(i) the date that is 120 days after the date of the order for relief; or

(ii) the date of the entry of an order confirming a plan.

(B)(i) The court may extend the period determined under subparagraph (A), prior to the expiration of the 120-day period, for 90 days on the motion of the trustee or lessor for cause.

(ii) If the court grants an extension under clause (i), the court may grant a subsequent extension only upon prior written consent of the lessor in each instance.

(5) The trustee shall timely perform all of the obligations of the debtor, except those specified in section 365(b)(2), first arising from or after 60 days after the order for relief in a case under chapter 11 of this title under an unexpired lease of personal property (other than personal property leased to an individual primarily for personal, family, or household purposes), until such lease is assumed or rejected notwithstanding section 503(b)(1) of this title, unless the court, after notice and a hearing and based on the equities of the case, orders otherwise with respect to the obligations or timely performance thereof. This subsection shall not be deemed to affect the trustee's obligations under the provisions of subsection (b) or (f). Acceptance of any such performance does not constitute waiver or relinquishment of the lessor's rights under such lease or under this title.

(e)(1) Notwithstanding a provision in an executory contract or unexpired lease, or in applicable law, an executory contract or unexpired lease of the debtor may not be terminated or modified, and any right or obligation under such contract or lease may not be terminated or modified, at any time after the commencement of the case solely because of a provision in such contract or lease that is conditioned on—

(A) the insolvency or financial condition of the debtor at any time before the closing of the case;

(B) the commencement of a case under this title; or

(C) the appointment of or taking possession by a trustee in a case under this title or a custodian before such commencement.

(2) Paragraph (1) of this subsection does not apply to an executory contract or unexpired lease of the debtor, whether or not such contract or lease prohibits or restricts assignment of rights or delegation of duties, if—

(A)(i) applicable law excuses a party, other than the debtor, to such contract or lease from accepting performance from or rendering performance to the trustee or to an assignee of such contract or lease, whether or not such contract or lease prohibits or restricts assignment of rights or delegation of duties; and

(ii) such party does not consent to such assumption or assignment; or

(B) such contract is a contract to make a loan, or extend other debt financing or financial accommodations, to or for the benefit of the debtor, or to issue a security of the debtor.

(f)(1) Except as provided in subsections (b) and (c) of this section, notwithstanding a provision in an executory contract or unexpired lease of the debtor, or in applicable law, that prohibits, restricts, or conditions the assignment of such contract or lease, the trustee may assign such contract or lease under paragraph (2) of this subsection.

(2) The trustee may assign an executory contract or unexpired lease of the debtor only if—

(A) the trustee assumes such contract or lease in accordance with the provisions of this section; and

(B) adequate assurance of future performance by the assignee of such contract or lease is provided, whether or not there has been a default in such contract or lease.

(3) Notwithstanding a provision in an executory contract or unexpired lease of the debtor, or in applicable law that terminates or modifies, or permits a party other than the debtor to terminate or modify, such contract or lease or a right or obligation under such contract or lease on account of an assignment of such contract or lease, such contract, lease, right, or obligation may not be terminated or modified under such provision because of the assumption or assignment of such contract or lease by the trustee.

(g) Except as provided in subsections (h)(2) and (i)(2) of this section, the rejection of an executory contract or unexpired lease of the debtor constitutes a breach of such contract or lease—

(1) if such contract or lease has not been assumed under this section or under a plan confirmed under chapter 9, 11, 12, or 13 of this title, immediately before the date of the filing of the petition; or

(2) if such contract or lease has been assumed under this section or under a plan confirmed under chapter 9, 11, 12, or 13 of this title—

(A) if before such rejection the case has not been converted under section 1112, 1208, or 1307 of this title, at the time of such rejection; or

(B) if before such rejection the case has been converted under section 1112, 1208, or 1307 of this title—

(i) immediately before the date of such conversion, if such contract or lease was assumed before such conversion; or

(ii) at the time of such rejection, if such contract or lease was assumed after such conversion.

(h)(1)(A) If the trustee rejects an unexpired lease of real property under which the debtor is the lessor and—

(i) if the rejection by the trustee amounts to such a breach as would entitle the lessee to treat such lease as terminated by virtue of its terms, applicable nonbankruptcy law, or any agreement made by the lessee, then the lessee under such lease may treat such lease as terminated by the rejection; or

(ii) if the term of such lease has commenced, the lessee may retain its rights under such lease (including rights such as those relating to the amount and timing of payment of rent and other amounts payable by the lessee and any right of use, possession, quiet enjoyment, subletting, assignment, or hypothecation) that are in or appurtenant to the real property for the balance of the term of such lease and for any renewal or extension of such rights to the extent that such rights are enforceable under applicable nonbankruptcy law.

(B) If the lessee retains its rights under subparagraph (A)(ii), the lessee may offset against the rent reserved under such lease for the balance of the term after the date of the rejection of such lease and for the term of any renewal or extension of such lease, the value of any damage caused by the nonperformance after the date of such rejection, of any obligation of the debtor under such lease, but the lessee shall not have any other right against the estate or the debtor on account of any damage occurring after such date caused by such nonperformance.

(C) The rejection of a lease of real property in a shopping center with respect to which the lessee elects to retain its rights under subparagraph (A)(ii) does not affect the enforceability under applicable nonbankruptcy law of any provision in the lease pertaining to radius, location, use, exclusivity, or tenant mix or balance.

(D) In this paragraph, "lessee" includes any successor, assign, or mortgagee permitted under the terms of such lease.

(2)(A) If the trustee rejects a timeshare interest under a timeshare plan under which the debtor is the timeshare interest seller and—

(i) if the rejection amounts to such a breach as would entitle the timeshare interest purchaser to treat the timeshare plan as terminated under its terms, applicable nonbankruptcy law, or any agreement made by timeshare interest purchaser, the timeshare interest purchaser under the timeshare plan may treat the timeshare plan as terminated by such rejection; or

(ii) if the term of such timeshare interest has commenced, then the timeshare interest purchaser may retain its rights in such timeshare interest for the balance of such term and for any term of renewal or extension of such timeshare interest to the extent that such rights are enforceable under applicable nonbankruptcy law.

(B) If the timeshare interest purchaser retains its rights under subparagraph (A), such timeshare interest purchaser may offset against the moneys due for such timeshare interest for the balance of the term after the date of the rejection of such timeshare interest, and the term of any renewal or extension of such timeshare interest, the value of any damage caused by the nonperformance after the date of such rejection, of any obligation of the debtor under such timeshare plan, but the timeshare interest purchaser shall not have any right against the estate or the debtor on account of any damage occurring after such date caused by such nonperformance.

(i)(1) If the trustee rejects an executory contract of the debtor for the sale of real property or for the sale of a timeshare interest under a timeshare plan, under which the purchaser is in possession, such purchaser may treat such contract as terminated, or, in the alternative, may remain in possession of such real property or timeshare interest.

(2) If such purchaser remains in possession—

(A) such purchaser shall continue to make all payments due under such contract, but may, offset against such payments any damages occurring after the date of the rejection of such contract caused by the nonperformance of any obligation of the debtor after such date, but such purchaser does not have any rights against the estate on account of any damages arising after such date from such rejection, other than such offset; and

(B) the trustee shall deliver title to such purchaser in accordance with the provisions of such contract, but is relieved of all other obligations to perform under such contract.

(j) A purchaser that treats an executory contract as terminated under subsection (i) of this section, or a party whose executory contract to purchase real property from the debtor is rejected and under which such party is not in possession, has a lien on the interest of the debtor in such property for the recovery of any portion of the purchase price that such purchaser or party has paid.

(k) Assignment by the trustee to an entity of a contract or lease assumed under this section relieves the trustee and the estate from any liability for any breach of such contract or lease occurring after such assignment.

(*l*) If an unexpired lease under which the debtor is the lessee is assigned pursuant to this section, the lessor of the property may require a deposit or other security for the performance of the debtor's obligations under the lease substantially the same as would have been required by the landlord upon the initial leasing to a similar tenant.

(m) For purposes of this section 365 and sections 541(b)(2) and 362(b)(10), leases of real property shall include any rental agreement to use real property.

(n)(1) If the trustee rejects an executory contract under which the debtor is a licensor of a right to intellectual property, the licensee under such contract may elect—

(A) to treat such contract as terminated by such rejection if such rejection by the trustee amounts to such a breach as would entitle the licensee to treat such contract as terminated by virtue of its own terms, applicable nonbankruptcy law, or an agreement made by the licensee with another entity; or

(B) to retain its rights (including a right to enforce any exclusivity provision of such contract, but excluding any other right under applicable nonbankruptcy law to specific performance of such contract) under such contract and under any agreement supplementary to such contract, to such intellectual property (including any embodiment of such intellectual property to the extent protected by applicable nonbankruptcy law), as such rights existed immediately before the case commenced, for—

(i) the duration of such contract; and

(ii) any period for which such contract may be extended by the licensee as of right under applicable nonbankruptcy law.

(2) If the licensee elects to retain its rights, as described in paragraph (1)(B) of this subsection, under such contract—

(A) the trustee shall allow the licensee to exercise such rights;

(B) the licensee shall make all royalty payments due under such contract for the duration of such contract and for any period described in paragraph (1)(B) of this subsection for which the licensee extends such contract; and

(C) the licensee shall be deemed to waive—

(i) any right of setoff it may have with respect to such contract under this title or applicable nonbankruptcy law; and

(ii) any claim allowable under section 503(b) of this title arising from the performance of such contract.

(3) If the licensee elects to retain its rights, as described in paragraph (1)(B) of this subsection, then on the written request of the licensee the trustee shall—

(A) to the extent provided in such contract, or any agreement supplementary to such contract, provide to the licensee any intellectual property (including such embodiment) held by the trustee; and

(B) not interfere with the rights of the licensee as provided in such contract, or any agreement supplementary to such contract, to such intellectual property (including such embodiment) including any right to obtain such intellectual property (or such embodiment) from another entity.

(4) Unless and until the trustee rejects such contract, on the written request of the licensee the trustee shall—

(A) to the extent provided in such contract or any agreement supplementary to such contract—

(i) perform such contract; or

(ii) provide to the licensee such intellectual property (including any embodiment of such intellectual property to the extent protected by applicable nonbankruptcy law) held by the trustee; and

(B) not interfere with the rights of the licensee as provided in such contract, or any agreement supplementary to such contract, to such intellectual property (including such embodiment), including any right to obtain such intellectual property (or such embodiment) from another entity.

(*o*) In a case under chapter 11 of this title, the trustee shall be deemed to have assumed (consistent with the debtor's other obligations under section 507), and shall immediately cure any deficit under, any commitment by the debtor to a Federal depository institutions regulatory agency (or predecessor to such agency) to maintain the capital of an insured depository institution, and any claim for a subsequent breach of the obligations thereunder shall be entitled to priority under section 507. This subsection shall not extend any commitment that would otherwise be terminated by any act of such an agency.

(p)(1) If a lease of personal property is rejected or not timely assumed by the trustee under subsection (d), the leased property is no longer property of the estate and the stay under section 362(a) is automatically terminated.

(2)(A) If the debtor in a case under chapter 7 is an individual, the debtor may notify the creditor in writing that the debtor desires to assume the lease. Upon being so notified, the creditor may, at its option, notify the debtor that it is willing to have the lease assumed by the debtor and may condition such assumption on cure of any outstanding default on terms set by the contract.

(B) If, not later than 30 days after notice is provided under subparagraph (A), the debtor notifies the lessor in writing that the lease is assumed, the liability under the lease will be assumed by the debtor and not by the estate.

(C) The stay under section 362 and the injunction under section 524(a)(2) shall not be violated by notification of the debtor and negotiation of cure under this subsection.

(3) In a case under chapter 11 in which the debtor is an individual and in a case under chapter 13, if the debtor is the lessee with respect to personal property and the lease is not assumed in the plan confirmed by the court, the lease is deemed rejected as of the conclusion of the hearing on confirmation. If the lease is rejected, the stay under section 362 and any stay under section 1301 is automatically terminated with respect to the property subject to the lease.

(Pub. L. 95–598, Nov. 6, 1978, 92 Stat. 2574; Pub. L. 98–353, title III, §§362, 402–404, July 10, 1984, 98 Stat. 361, 367; Pub. L. 99–554, title II, §§257(j), (m), 283(e), Oct. 27, 1986, 100 Stat. 3115, 3117; Pub. L. 100–506, §1(b), Oct. 18, 1988, 102 Stat. 2538; Pub. L. 101–647, title XXV, §2522(c), Nov. 29, 1990, 104 Stat. 4866; Pub. L. 102–365, §19(b)–(e), Sept. 3, 1992, 106 Stat. 982–984; Pub. L. 103–394, title II, §§205(a), 219(a), (b), title V, §501(d)(10), Oct. 22, 1994, 108 Stat. 4122, 4128, 4145; Pub. L. 103–429, §1, Oct. 31, 1994, 108 Stat. 4377; Pub. L. 109–8, title

III, §§309(b), 328(a), title IV, §404, Apr. 20, 2005, 119 Stat. 82, 100, 104.)

Historical and Revision Notes

Legislative Statements

Section 365(b)(3) represents a compromise between H.R. 8200 as passed by the House and the Senate amendment. The provision adopts standards contained in section 365(b)(5) of the Senate amendment to define adequate assurance of future performance of a lease of real property in a shopping center.

Section 365(b)(4) of the House amendment indicates that after default the trustee may not require a lessor to supply services or materials without assumption unless the lessor is compensated as provided in the lease.

Section 365(c)(2) and (3) likewise represent a compromise between H.R. 8200 as passed by the House and the Senate amendment. Section 365(c)(2) is derived from section 365(b)(4) of the Senate amendment but does not apply to a contract to deliver equipment as provided in the Senate amendment. As contained in the House amendment, the provision prohibits a trustee or debtor in possession from assuming or assigning an executory contract of the debtor to make a loan, or extend other debt financing or financial accommodations, to or for the benefit of the debtor, or the issuance of a security of the debtor.

Section 365(e) is a refinement of comparable provisions contained in the House bill and Senate amendment. Sections 365(e)(1) and (2)(A) restate section 365(e) of H.R. 8200 as passed by the House. Sections 365(e)(2)(B) expands the section to permit termination of an executory contract or unexpired lease of the debtor if such contract is a contract to make a loan, or extend other debt financing or financial accommodations, to or for the benefit of the debtor, or for the issuance of a security of the debtor.

Characterization of contracts to make a loan, or extend other debt financing or financial accommodations, is limited to the extension of cash or a line of credit and is not intended to embrace ordinary leases or contracts to provide goods or services with payments to be made over time.

Section 365(f) is derived from H.R. 8200 as passed by the House. Deletion of language in section 365(f)(3) of the Senate amendment is done as a matter of style. Restrictions with respect to assignment of an executory contract or unexpired lease are superfluous since the debtor may assign an executory contract or unexpired lease of the debtor only if such contract is first assumed under section 364(f)(2)(A) of the House amendment.

Section 363(h) of the House amendment represents a modification of section 365(h) of the Senate amendment. The House amendment makes clear that in the case of a bankrupt lessor, a lessee may remain in possession for the balance of the term of a lease and any renewal or extension of the term only to the extent that such renewal or extension may be obtained by the lessee without the permission of the landlord or some third party under applicable non-bankruptcy law.

Senate Report No. 95-989

Subsection (a) of this section authorizes the trustee, subject to the court's approval, to assume or reject an executory contract or unexpired lease. Though there is no precise definition of what contracts are executory, it generally includes contracts on which performance remains due to some extent on both sides. A note is not usually an executory contract if the only performance that remains is repayment. Performance on one side of the contract would have been completed and the contract is no longer executory.

Because of the volatile nature of the commodities markets and the special provisions governing commodity broker liquidations in subchapter IV of chapter 7, the provisions governing distribution in section 765(a) will govern if any conflict between those provisions and the provisions of this section arise.

Subsections (b), (c), and (d) provide limitations on the trustee's powers. Subsection (b) requires the trustee to cure any default in the contract or lease and to provide adequate assurance of future performance if there has been a default, before he may assume. This provision does not apply to defaults under ipso facto or bankruptcy clauses, which is a significant departure from present law.

Subsection (b)(3) permits termination of leases entered into prior to the effective date of this title in liquidation cases if certain other conditions are met.

Subsection (b)(4) [enacted as (c)(2)] prohibits the trustee's assumption of an executory contract requiring the other party to make a loan or deliver equipment to or to issue a security of the debtor. The purpose of this subsection is to make it clear that a party to a transaction which is based upon the financial strength of a debtor should not be required to extend new credit to the debtor whether in the form of loans, lease financing, or the purchase or discount of notes.

Subsection (b)(5) provides that in lease situations common to shopping centers, protections must be provided for the lessor if the trustee assumes the lease, including protection against decline in percentage rents, breach of agreements with other tenants, and preservation of the tenant mix. Protection for tenant mix will not be required in the office building situation.

Subsection (c) prohibits the trustee from assuming or assigning a contract or lease if applicable nonbankruptcy law excuses the other party from performance to someone other than the debtor, unless the other party consents. This prohibition applies only in the situation in which applicable law excuses the other party from performance independent of any restrictive language in the contract or lease itself.

Subsection (d) places time limits on assumption and rejection. In a liquidation case, the trustee must assume within 60 days (or within an additional 60 days, if the court, for cause, extends the time). If not assumed, the contract or lease is deemed rejected. In a rehabilitation case, the time limit is not fixed in the bill. However, if the other party to the contract or lease requests the court to fix a time, the court may specify a time within which the trustee must act. This provision will prevent parties in contractual or lease relationships with the debtor from being left in doubt concerning their status vis-a-vis the estate.

Subsection (e) invalidates ipso facto or bankruptcy clauses. These clauses, protected under present law, automatically terminate the contract or lease, or permit the other contracting party to terminate the contract or lease, in the event of bankruptcy. This frequently hampers rehabilitation efforts. If the trustee may assume or assign the contract under the limitations imposed by the remainder of the section, the contract or lease may be utilized to assist in the debtor's rehabilitation or liquidation.

The unenforcibility [sic] of ipso facto or bankruptcy clauses proposed under this section will require the courts to be sensitive to the rights of the nondebtor party to executory contracts and unexpired leases. If the trustee is to assume a contract or lease, the court will have to insure that the trustee's performance under the contract or lease gives the other contracting party the full benefit of his bargain.

This subsection does not limit the application of an ipso facto or bankruptcy clause if a new insolvency or receivership occurs after the bankruptcy case is closed. That is, the clause is not invalidated in toto, but merely made inapplicable during the case for the purposes of disposition of the executory contract or unexpired lease.

Subsection (f) partially invalidates restrictions on assignment of contracts or leases by the trustee to a third party. The subsection imposes two restrictions on the trustee: he must first assume the contract or lease, subject to all the restrictions on assumption found in the section, and adequate assurance of future performance must be provided to the other contracting party. Paragraph (3) of the subsection invalidates contractual provisions that permit termination or modification in the event of an assignment, as contrary to the policy of this subsection.

Subsection (g) defines the time as of which a rejection of an executory contract or unexpired lease constitutes a breach of the contract or lease. Generally, the breach is as of the date immediately preceding the date of the petition. The purpose is to treat rejection claims as prepetition claims. The remainder of the subsection specifies different times for cases that are converted from one chapter to another. The provisions of this subsection are not a substantive authorization to breach or reject an assumed contract. Rather, they prescribe the rules for the allowance of claims in case an assumed contract is breached, or if a case under chapter 11 in which a contract has been assumed is converted to a case under chapter 7 in which the contract is rejected.

Subsection (h) protects real property lessees of the debtor if the trustee rejects an unexpired lease under which the debtor is the lessor (or sublessor). The subsection permits the lessee to remain in possession of the leased property or to treat the lease as terminated by the rejection. The balance of the term of the lease referred to in paragraph (1) will include any renewal terms that are enforceable by the tenant, but not renewal terms if the landlord had an option to terminate. Thus, the tenant will not be deprived of his estate for the term for which he bargained. If the lessee remains in possession, he may offset the rent reserved under the lease against damages caused by the rejection, but does not have any affirmative rights against the estate for any damages after the rejection that result from the rejection.

Subsection (i) gives a purchaser of real property under a land installment sales contract similar protection. The purchaser, if the contract is rejected, may remain in possession or may treat the contract as terminated. If the purchaser remains in possession, he is required to continue to make the payments due, but may offset damages that occur after rejection. The trustee is required to deliver title, but is relieved of all other obligations to perform.

A purchaser that treats the contract as terminated is granted a lien on the property to the extent of the purchase price paid. A party with a contract to purchase land from the debtor has a lien on the property to secure the price already paid, if the contract is rejected and the purchaser is not yet in possession.

Subsection (k) relieves the trustee and the estate of liability for a breach of an assigned contract or lease that occurs after the assignment.

HOUSE REPORT NO. 95–595

Subsection (c) prohibits the trustee from assuming or assigning a contract or lease if applicable nonbankruptcy law excuses the other party from performance to someone other than the debtor, unless the other party consents. This prohibition applies only in the situation in which applicable law excuses the other party from performance independent of any restrictive language in the contract or lease itself. The purpose of this subsection, at least in part, is to prevent the trustee from requiring new advances of money or other property. The section permits the trustee to continue to use and pay for property already advanced, but is not designed to permit the trustee to demand new loans or additional transfers of property under lease commitments.

Thus, under this provision, contracts such as loan commitments and letters of credit are nonassignable, and may not be assumed by the trustee.

Subsection (e) invalidates ipso facto or bankruptcy clauses. These clauses, protected under present law, automatically terminate the contract or lease, or permit the other contracting party to terminate the contract or lease, in the event of bankruptcy. This frequently hampers rehabilitation efforts. If the trustee may assume or assign the contract under the limitations imposed by the remainder of the section, then the contract or lease may be utilized to assist in the debtor's rehabilitation or liquidation.

The unenforceability of ipso facto or bankruptcy clauses proposed under this section will require the courts to be sensitive to the rights of the nondebtor party to executory contracts and unexpired leases. If the trustee is to assume a contract or lease, the courts will have to insure that the trustee's performance under the contract or lease gives the other contracting party the full benefit of his bargain. An example of the complexity that may arise in these situations and the need for a determination of all aspects of a particular executory contract or unexpired lease is the shopping center lease under which the debtor is a tenant in a shopping center.

A shopping center is often a carefully planned enterprise, and though it consists of numerous individual tenants, the center is planned as a single unit, often subject to a master lease or financing agreement. Under these agreements, the tenant mix in a shopping center may be as important to the lessor as the actual promised rental payments, because certain mixes will attract higher patronage of the stores in the center, and thus a higher rental for the landlord from those stores that are subject to a percentage of gross receipts rental agreement. Thus, in order to assure a landlord of his bargained for exchange, the court would have to consider such factors as the nature of the business to be conducted by the trustee or his assignee, whether that business complies with the requirements of any master agreement, whether the kind of business proposed will generate gross sales in an amount such that the percentage rent specified in the lease is substantially the same as what would have been provided by the debtor, and whether the business proposed to be conducted would result in a breach of other clauses in master agreements relating, for example, to tenant mix and location.

This subsection does not limit the application of an ipso facto or bankruptcy clause to a new insolvency or receivership after the bankruptcy case is closed. That is, the clause is not invalidated in toto, but merely made inapplicable during the case for the purpose of disposition of the executory contract or unexpired lease.

AMENDMENTS

2005—Subsec. (b)(1)(A). Pub. L. 109–8, §328(a)(1)(A), inserted before semicolon at end "other than a default that is a breach of a provision relating to the satisfaction of any provision (other than a penalty rate or penalty provision) relating to a default arising from any failure to perform nonmonetary obligations under an unexpired lease of real property, if it is impossible for the trustee to cure such default by performing nonmonetary acts at and after the time of assumption, except that if such default arises from a failure to operate in accordance with a nonresidential real property lease, then such default shall be cured by performance at and after the time of assumption in accordance with such lease, and pecuniary losses resulting from such default shall be compensated in accordance with the provisions of this paragraph".

Subsec. (b)(2)(D). Pub. L. 109–8, §328(a)(1)(B), substituted "penalty rate or penalty provision" for "penalty rate or provision".

Subsec. (c)(4). Pub. L. 109–8, §328(a)(2), struck out par. (4) which read as follows: "such lease is of nonresidential real property under which the debtor is the lessee of an aircraft terminal or aircraft gate at an airport at which the debtor is the lessee under one or more additional nonresidential leases of an aircraft terminal or aircraft gate and the trustee, in connection with such assumption or assignment, does not assume all such leases or does not assume and assign all of such leases to the same person, except that the trustee may assume or assign less than all of such leases with the airport operator's written consent."

Subsec. (d)(4). Pub. L. 109–8, §404(a), amended par. (4) generally. Prior to amendment, par. (4) read as follows:

"Notwithstanding paragraphs (1) and (2), in a case under any chapter of this title, if the trustee does not assume or reject an unexpired lease of nonresidential real property under which the debtor is the lessee within 60 days after the date of the order for relief, or within such additional time as the court, for cause, within such 60-day period, fixes, then such lease is deemed rejected, and the trustee shall immediately surrender such nonresidential real property to the lessor."

Subsec. (d)(5) to (10). Pub. L. 109–8, §328(a)(3), redesignated par. (10) as (5) and struck out former pars. (5) to (9) which related to rejection of leases under which the debtor is an affected air carrier that is the lessee of an aircraft terminal or aircraft gate.

Subsec. (f)(1). Pub. L. 109–8, §404(b), substituted "provided in subsections (b) and" for "provided in subsection".

Pub. L. 109–8, §328(a)(4), struck out "; except that the trustee may not assign an unexpired lease of nonresidential real property under which the debtor is an affected air carrier that is the lessee of an aircraft terminal or aircraft gate if there has occurred a termination event" before period at end.

Subsec. (p). Pub. L. 109–8, §309(b), added subsec. (p).

1994—Subsec. (b)(2)(D). Pub. L. 103–394, §219(a), added subpar. (D).

Subsec. (d)(6)(C). Pub. L. 103–429, §1(1), substituted "section 40102(a) of title 49" for "section 101 of the Federal Aviation Act of 1958 (49 App. U.S.C. 1301)".

Pub. L. 103–394, §501(d)(10)(A), which directed the substitution of "section 40102 of title 49" for "the Federal Aviation Act of 1958 (49 U.S.C. 1301)", could not be executed because the phrase "(49 U.S.C. 1301)" did not appear in text.

Subsec. (d)(10). Pub. L. 103–394, §219(b), added par. (10).

Subsec. (g)(2)(A), (B). Pub. L. 103–394, §501(d)(10)(B), substituted "1208, or 1307" for "1307, or 1208".

Subsec. (h). Pub. L. 103–394, §205(a), amended subsec. (h) generally. Prior to amendment, subsec. (h) read as follows:

"(h)(1) If the trustee rejects an unexpired lease of real property of the debtor under which the debtor is the lessor, or a timeshare interest under a timeshare plan under which the debtor is the timeshare interest seller, the lessee or timeshare interest purchaser under such lease or timeshare plan may treat such lease or timeshare plan as terminated by such rejection, where the disaffirmance by the trustee amounts to such a breach as would entitle the lessee or timeshare interest purchaser to treat such lease or timeshare plan as terminated by virtue of its own terms, applicable nonbankruptcy law, or other agreements the lessee or timeshare interest purchaser has made with other parties; or, in the alternative, the lessee or timeshare interest purchaser may remain in possession of the leasehold or timeshare interest under any lease or timeshare plan the term of which has commenced for the balance of such term and for any renewal or extension of such term that is enforceable by such lessee or timeshare interest purchaser under applicable nonbankruptcy law.

"(2) If such lessee or timeshare interest purchaser remains in possession as provided in paragraph (1) of this subsection, such lessee or timeshare interest purchaser may offset against the rent reserved under such lease or moneys due for such timeshare interest for the balance of the term after the date of the rejection of such lease or timeshare interest, and any such renewal or extension thereof, any damages occurring after such date caused by the nonperformance of any obligation of the debtor under such lease or timeshare plan after such date, but such lessee or timeshare interest purchaser does not have any rights against the estate on account of any damages arising after such date from such rejection, other than such offset."

Subsec. (n)(1)(B). Pub. L. 103–394, §501(d)(10)(C), substituted "a right to" for "a right to to".

Subsec. (*o*). Pub. L. 103–394, §501(d)(10)(D), substituted "a Federal depository institutions regulatory agency (or predecessor to such agency)" for "the Federal Deposit Insurance Corporation, the Resolution Trust Corporation, the Director of the Office of Thrift Supervision, the Comptroller of the Currency, or the Board of Governors of the Federal Reserve System, or its predecessors or successors,".

Subsec. (p). Pub. L. 103–429, §1(2), which directed the amendment of subsec. (p) by substituting "section 40102(a) of title 49" for "section 101(3) of the Federal Aviation Act of 1958", could not be executed because subsec. (p) was repealed by Pub. L. 103–394, §501(d)(10)(E). See below.

Pub. L. 103–394, §501(d)(10)(E), struck out subsec. (p), which read as follows: "In this section, 'affected air carrier' means an air carrier, as defined in section 101(3) of the Federal Aviation Act of 1958, that holds 65 percent or more in number of the aircraft gates at an airport—

"(1) which is a Large Air Traffic Hub as defined by the Federal Aviation Administration in Report FAA-AP 92-1, February 1992; and

"(2) all of whose remaining aircraft gates are leased or under contract on the date of enactment of this subsection."

1992—Subsec. (c)(4). Pub. L. 102–365, §19(c), added par. (4).

Subsec. (d)(5) to (9). Pub. L. 102–365, §19(b), added pars. (5) to (9).

Subsec. (f)(1). Pub. L. 102–365, §19(d), substituted for period at end "; except that the trustee may not assign an unexpired lease of nonresidential real property under which the debtor is an affected air carrier that is the lessee of an aircraft terminal or aircraft gate if there has occurred a termination event."

Subsec. (p). Pub. L. 102–365, §19(e), added subsec. (p).

1990—Subsec. (*o*). Pub. L. 101–647 added subsec. (*o*).

1988—Subsec. (n). Pub. L. 100–506 added subsec. (n).

1986—Subsec. (c)(1)(A). Pub. L. 99–554, §283(e)(1), struck out "or an assignee of such contract or lease" after "debtor in possession".

Subsec. (c)(3). Pub. L. 99–554, §283(e)(2), inserted "is" after "lease" and "and" after "property".

Subsecs. (d)(2), (g)(1). Pub. L. 99–554, §257(j), (m)(1), inserted reference to chapter 12.

Subsec. (g)(2). Pub. L. 99–554, §257(m)(2), inserted references to chapter 12 and section 1208 of this title.

Subsec. (h)(1). Pub. L. 99–554, §283(e)(2), inserted "or timeshare plan" after "to treat such lease".

Subsec. (m). Pub. L. 99–554, §283(e)(3), substituted "362(b)(10)" for "362(b)(9)".

1984—Subsec. (a). Pub. L. 98–353, §362(a), amended subsec. (a) generally, making minor changes.

Subsec. (b). Pub. L. 98–353, §362(a), amended subsec. (b) generally, inserting in par. (3) reference to par. (2)(B) of subsec. (f) of this section, in par. (3)(A) inserting provisions relating to financial condition and operating performance in the case of an assignment, and in par. (3)(C) substituting "that assumption or assignment of such lease is subject to all the provisions thereof, including (but not limited to) provisions such as a radius, location, use, or exclusivity provision, and will not breach any such provision contained in any other lease, financing agreement, or master agreement relating to such shopping center" for "that assumption or assignment of such lease will not breach substantially any provision, such as a radius, location, use, or exclusivity provision, in any other lease, financing agreement, or master agreement relating to such shopping center".

Subsec. (c). Pub. L. 98–353, §362(a), amended subsec. (c) generally, substituting in par. (1)(A) "applicable law excuses a party, other than the debtor, to such contract or lease from accepting performance from or rendering performance to an entity other than the debtor or the debtor in possession or an assignee of such contract or lease, whether or not such contract or lease prohibits or restricts assignment of rights or delegation of duties" for "applicable law excuses a party, other than the debtor, to such contract or lease from accepting performance from or rendering performance to the trustee or an assignee of such contract or lease, whether or not such contract or lease prohibits or restricts assignment of rights or delegation of duties" and adding par. (3).

Subsec. (d). Pub. L. 98–353, §362(a), amended subsec. (d) generally, inserting in par. (1) reference to residential real property or personal property of the debtor, inserting in par. (2) reference to residential real property or personal property of the debtor, and adding pars. (3) and (4).

Subsec. (h)(1). Pub. L. 98–353, §402, amended par. (1) generally. Prior to amendment, par. (1) read as follows: "If the trustee rejects an unexpired lease of real property of the debtor under which the debtor is the lessor, the lessee under such lease may treat the lease as terminated by such rejection, or, in the alternative, may remain in possession for the balance of the term of such lease and any renewal or extension of such term that is enforceable by such lessee under applicable nonbankruptcy law."

Subsec. (h)(2). Pub. L. 98–353, §403, amended par. (2) generally. Prior to amendment, par. (2) read as follows: "If such lessee remains in possession, such lessee may offset against the rent reserved under such lease for the balance of the term after the date of the rejection of such lease, and any such renewal or extension, any damages occurring after such date caused by the nonperformance of any obligation of the debtor after such date, but such lessee does not have any rights against the estate on account of any damages arising after such date from such rejection, other than such offset."

Subsec. (i)(1). Pub. L. 98–353, §404, amended par. (1) generally, inserting provisions relating to timeshare interests under timeshare plans.

Subsecs. (*l*), (m). Pub. L. 98–353, §362(b), added subsecs. (*l*) and (m).

EFFECTIVE DATE OF 2005 AMENDMENT

Amendment by Pub. L. 109–8 effective 180 days after Apr. 20, 2005, and not applicable with respect to cases commenced under this title before such effective date, except as otherwise provided, see section 1501 of Pub. L. 109–8, set out as a note under section 101 of this title.

EFFECTIVE DATE OF 1994 AMENDMENT

Amendment by Pub. L. 103–394 effective Oct. 22, 1994, and not applicable with respect to cases commenced under this title before Oct. 22, 1994, see section 702 of Pub. L. 103–394, set out as a note under section 101 of this title.

EFFECTIVE DATE OF 1992 AMENDMENT

Section 19(f) of Pub. L. 102–365 provided that: "The amendments made by this section [amending this section] shall be in effect for the 12-month period that begins on the date of enactment of this Act [Sept. 3, 1992] and shall apply in all proceedings involving an affected air carrier (as defined in section 365(p) of title 11, United States Code, as amended by this section) that are pending during such 12-month period. Not later than 9 months after the date of enactment, the Administrator of the Federal Aviation Administration shall report to the Committee on Commerce, Science, and Transportation and Committee on the Judiciary of the Senate and the Committee on the Judiciary and Committee on Public Works and Transportation of the House of Representatives on whether this section shall apply to proceedings that are commenced after such 12-month period."

EFFECTIVE DATE OF 1988 AMENDMENT

Amendment by Pub. L. 100–506 effective Oct. 18, 1988, but not applicable to any case commenced under this title before such date, see section 2 of Pub. L. 100–506, set out as a note under section 101 of this title.

EFFECTIVE DATE OF 1986 AMENDMENT

Amendment by section 257 of Pub. L. 99–554 effective 30 days after Oct. 27, 1986, but not applicable to cases commenced under this title before that date, see section 302(a), (c)(1) of Pub. L. 99–554, set out as a note under section 581 of Title 28, Judiciary and Judicial Procedure.

Amendment by section 283 of Pub. L. 99–554 effective 30 days after Oct. 27, 1986, see section 302(a) of Pub. L. 99–554.

EFFECTIVE DATE OF 1984 AMENDMENT

Amendment by Pub. L. 98–353 effective with respect to cases filed 90 days after July 10, 1984, see section 552(a) of Pub. L. 98–353, set out as a note under section 101 of this title.

AIRPORT LEASES

Section 19(a) of Pub. L. 102–365 provided that: "Congress finds that—

"(1) there are major airports served by an air carrier that has leased a substantial majority of the airport's gates;

"(2) the commerce in the region served by such a major airport can be disrupted if the air carrier that leases most of its gates enters bankruptcy and either discontinues or materially reduces service; and

"(3) it is important that such airports be empowered to continue service in the event of such a disruption."

§366. Utility service

(a) Except as provided in subsections (b) and (c) of this section, a utility may not alter, refuse, or discontinue service to, or discriminate against, the trustee or the debtor solely on the basis of the commencement of a case under this title or that a debt owed by the debtor to such utility for service rendered before the order for relief was not paid when due.

(b) Such utility may alter, refuse, or discontinue service if neither the trustee nor the debtor, within 20 days after the date of the order for relief, furnishes adequate assurance of payment, in the form of a deposit or other security, for service after such date. On request of a party in interest and after notice and a hearing, the court may order reasonable modification of the amount of the deposit or other security necessary to provide adequate assurance of payment.

(c)(1)(A) For purposes of this subsection, the term "assurance of payment" means—

(i) a cash deposit;

(ii) a letter of credit;

(iii) a certificate of deposit;

(iv) a surety bond;

(v) a prepayment of utility consumption; or

(vi) another form of security that is mutually agreed on between the utility and the debtor or the trustee.

(B) For purposes of this subsection an administrative expense priority shall not constitute an assurance of payment.

(2) Subject to paragraphs (3) and (4), with respect to a case filed under chapter 11, a utility referred to in subsection (a) may alter, refuse, or discontinue utility service, if during the 30-day period beginning on the date of the filing of the petition, the utility does not receive from the debtor or the trustee adequate assurance of payment for utility service that is satisfactory to the utility.

(3)(A) On request of a party in interest and after notice and a hearing, the court may order modification of the amount of an assurance of payment under paragraph (2).

(B) In making a determination under this paragraph whether an assurance of payment is adequate, the court may not consider—

(i) the absence of security before the date of the filing of the petition;

(ii) the payment by the debtor of charges for utility service in a timely manner before the date of the filing of the petition; or

(iii) the availability of an administrative expense priority.

(4) Notwithstanding any other provision of law, with respect to a case subject to this subsection, a utility may recover or set off against a security deposit provided to the utility by the debtor before the date of the filing of the petition without notice or order of the court.

(Pub. L. 95–598, Nov. 6, 1978, 92 Stat. 2578; Pub. L. 98–353, title III, §443, July 10, 1984, 98 Stat. 373; Pub. L. 109–8, title IV, §417, Apr. 20, 2005, 119 Stat. 108.)

Historical and Revision Notes

LEGISLATIVE STATEMENTS

Section 366 of the House amendment represents a compromise between comparable provisions contained in H.R. 8200 as passed by the House and the Senate amendment. Subsection (a) is modified so that the applicable date is the date of the order for relief rather than the date of the filing of the petition. Subsection (b) contains a similar change but is otherwise derived from section 366(b) of the Senate amendment, with the exception that a time period for continued service of 20 days rather than 10 days is adopted.

SENATE REPORT NO. 95–989

This section gives debtors protection from a cut-off of service by a utility because of the filing of a bankruptcy case. This section is intended to cover utilities that have some special position with respect to the debtor, such as an electric company, gas supplier, or telephone company that is a monopoly in the area so that the debtor cannot easily obtain comparable service from another utility. The utility may not alter, refuse, or discontinue service because of the nonpayment of a bill that would be discharged in the bankruptcy case. Subsection (b) protects the utility company by requiring the trustee or the debtor to provide, within ten days, adequate assurance of payment for service provided after the date of the petition.

Amendments

2005—Subsec. (a). Pub. L. 109–8, §417(1), substituted "subsections (b) and (c)" for "subsection (b)".

Subsec. (c). Pub. L. 109–8, §417(2), added subsec. (c).

1984—Subsec. (a). Pub. L. 98–353 inserted "of the commencement of a case under this title or" after "basis".

Effective Date of 2005 Amendment

Amendment by Pub. L. 109–8 effective 180 days after Apr. 20, 2005, and not applicable with respect to cases commenced under this title before such effective date, except as otherwise provided, see section 1501 of Pub. L. 109–8, set out as a note under section 101 of this title.

Effective Date of 1984 Amendment

Amendment by Pub. L. 98–353 effective with respect to cases filed 90 days after July 10, 1984, see section 552(a) of Pub. L. 98–353, set out as a note under section 101 of this title.

CHAPTER 5—CREDITORS, THE DEBTOR, AND THE ESTATE

SUBCHAPTER I—CREDITORS AND CLAIMS

SUBCHAPTER II—DEBTOR'S DUTIES AND BENEFITS

SUBCHAPTER III—THE ESTATE

Amendments

2005—Pub. L. 109–8, title II, §§227(b), 228(b), 229(b), title VII, §704(b), title IX, §§907(k)(2), (p)(1), 910(a)(2), Apr. 20, 2005, 119 Stat. 69, 71, 72, 126, 181, 182, 184, added items 511, 526 to 528, 561 and 562 and substituted "Contractual right to liquidate, terminate, or accelerate a securities contract" for "Contractual right to liquidate a securities contract" in item 555, "Contractual right to liquidate, terminate, or accelerate a commodities contract or forward contract" for "Contractual right to liquidate a commodity contract or forward contract" in item 556, "Contractual right to liquidate, terminate, or accelerate a repurchase agreement" for "Contractual right to liquidate a repurchase agreement" in item 559, and "Contractual right to liquidate, terminate, or

[1] So in original. Does not conform to section catchline.

accelerate a swap agreement" for "Contractual right to terminate a swap agreement" in item 560.

1990—Pub. L. 101–311, title I, §106(b), June 25, 1990, 104 Stat. 268, added item 560.

1986—Pub. L. 99–554, title II, §283(q), Oct. 27, 1986, 100 Stat. 3118, amended items 557 to 559 generally, substituting "interests in, and abandonment or other disposition of grain assets" for "in and disposition of grain" in item 557.

1984—Pub. L. 98–353, title III, §§352(b), 396(b), 470(b), July 10, 1984, 98 Stat. 361, 366, 380, added items 557, 558, and 559.

1982—Pub. L. 97–222, §6(b), July 27, 1982, 96 Stat. 237, added items 555 and 556.

SUBCHAPTER I—CREDITORS AND CLAIMS

§501. Filing of proofs of claims or interests

(a) A creditor or an indenture trustee may file a proof of claim. An equity security holder may file a proof of interest.

(b) If a creditor does not timely file a proof of such creditor's claim, an entity that is liable to such creditor with the debtor, or that has secured such creditor, may file a proof of such claim.

(c) If a creditor does not timely file a proof of such creditor's claim, the debtor or the trustee may file a proof of such claim.

(d) A claim of a kind specified in section 502(e)(2), 502(f), 502(g), 502(h) or 502(i) of this title may be filed under subsection (a), (b), or (c) of this section the same as if such claim were a claim against the debtor and had arisen before the date of the filing of the petition.

(e) A claim arising from the liability of a debtor for fuel use tax assessed consistent with the requirements of section 31705 of title 49 may be filed by the base jurisdiction designated pursuant to the International Fuel Tax Agreement (as defined in section 31701 of title 49) and, if so filed, shall be allowed as a single claim.

(Pub. L. 95–598, Nov. 6, 1978, 92 Stat. 2578; Pub. L. 98–353, title III, §444, July 10, 1984, 98 Stat. 373; Pub. L. 109–8, title VII, §702, Apr. 20, 2005, 119 Stat. 125.)

Historical and Revision Notes

LEGISLATIVE STATEMENTS

The House amendment adopts section 501(b) of the Senate amendment leaving the Rules of Bankruptcy Procedure free to determine where a proof of claim must be filed.

Section 501(c) expands language contained in section 501(c) of the House bill and Senate amendment to permit the debtor to file a proof of claim if a creditor does not timely file a proof of the creditor's claim in a case under title 11.

The House amendment deletes section 501(e) of the Senate amendment as a matter to be left to the rules of bankruptcy procedure. It is anticipated that the rules will enable governmental units, like other creditors, to have a reasonable time to file proofs of claim in bankruptcy cases.

For purposes of section 501, a proof of "interest" includes the interest of a general or limited partner in a partnership, the interest of a proprietor in a sole proprietorship, or the interest of a common or preferred stockholder in a corporation.

SENATE REPORT NO. 95–989

This section governs the means by which creditors and equity security holders present their claims or interests to the court. Subsection (a) permits a creditor to file a proof of claim or interest. An indenture trustee representing creditors may file a proof of claim on behalf of the creditors he represents.

This subsection is permissive only, and does not require filing of a proof of claim by any creditor. It permits filing where some purpose would be served, such as where a claim that appears on a list filed under proposed 11 U.S.C. 924 or 1111 was incorrectly stated or listed as disputed, contingent, or unliquidated, where a creditor with a lien is undersecured and asserts a claim for the balance of the debt owed him (his unsecured claim, as determined under proposed 11 U.S.C. 506(a)), or in a liquidation case where there will be a distribution of assets to the holders of allowed claims. In other instances, such as in no-asset liquidation cases, in situations where a secured creditor does not assert any claim against the estate and a determination of his claim is not made under proposed 11 U.S.C. 506, or in situations where the claim asserted would be subordinated and the creditor would not recover from the estate in any event, filing of a proof of claim may simply not be necessary. The Rules of Bankruptcy Procedure and practice under the law will guide creditors as to when filing is necessary and when it may be dispensed with. In general, however, unless a claim is listed in a chapter 9 or chapter 11 case and allowed as a result of the list, a proof of claim will be a prerequisite to allowance for unsecured claims, including priority claims and the unsecured portion of a claim asserted by the holder of a lien.

The Rules of Bankruptcy Procedure will set the time limits, the form, and the procedure for filing, which will determine whether claims are timely or tardily filed. The rules governing time limits for filing proofs of claims will continue to apply under section 405(d) of the bill. These provide a 6-month-bar date for the filing of tax claims.

Subsection (b) permits a codebtor, surety, or guarantor to file a proof of claim on behalf of the creditor to which he is liable if the creditor does not timely file a proof of claim.

In liquidation and individual repayment plan cases, the trustee or the debtor may file a proof of claim under subsection (c) if the creditor does not timely file. The purpose of this subsection is mainly to protect the debtor if the creditor's claim is nondischargeable. If the creditor does not file, there would be no distribution on the claim, and the debtor would have a greater debt to repay after the case is closed than if the claim were paid in part or in full in the case or under the plan.

Subsection (d) governs the filing of claims of the kind specified in subsections (f), (g), (h), (i), or (j) of proposed 11 U.S.C. 502. The separation of this provision from the other claim-filing provisions in this section is intended to indicate that claims of the kind specified, which do not become fixed or do not arise until after the commencement of the case, must be treated differently for filing purposes such as the bar date for filing claims. The rules will provide for later filing of claims of these kinds.

Subsection (e) gives governmental units (including tax authorities) at least six months following the date for the first meeting of creditors in a chapter 7 or chapter 13 case within which to file proof of claims.

Amendments

2005—Subsec. (e). Pub. L. 109–8 added subsec. (e).

1984—Subsec. (d). Pub. L. 98–353 inserted "502(e)(2),".

Effective Date of 2005 Amendment

Amendment by Pub. L. 109–8 effective 180 days after Apr. 20, 2005, and not applicable with respect to cases commenced under this title before such effective date, except as otherwise provided, see section 1501 of Pub. L. 109–8, set out as a note under section 101 of this title.

Effective Date of 1984 Amendment

Amendment by Pub. L. 98–353 effective with respect to cases filed 90 days after July 10, 1984, see section

552(a) of Pub. L. 98-353, set out as a note under section 101 of this title.

CHILD SUPPORT CREDITORS OR THEIR REPRESENTATIVES; APPEARANCE BEFORE COURT

Pub. L. 103-394, title III, §304(g), Oct. 22, 1994, 108 Stat. 4134, provided that: "Child support creditors or their representatives shall be permitted to appear and intervene without charge, and without meeting any special local court rule requirement for attorney appearances, in any bankruptcy case or proceeding in any bankruptcy court or district court of the United States if such creditors or representatives file a form in such court that contains information detailing the child support debt, its status, and other characteristics."

§ 502. Allowance of claims or interests

(a) A claim or interest, proof of which is filed under section 501 of this title, is deemed allowed, unless a party in interest, including a creditor of a general partner in a partnership that is a debtor in a case under chapter 7 of this title, objects.

(b) Except as provided in subsections (e)(2), (f), (g), (h) and (i) of this section, if such objection to a claim is made, the court, after notice and a hearing, shall determine the amount of such claim in lawful currency of the United States as of the date of the filing of the petition, and shall allow such claim in such amount, except to the extent that—

(1) such claim is unenforceable against the debtor and property of the debtor, under any agreement or applicable law for a reason other than because such claim is contingent or unmatured;

(2) such claim is for unmatured interest;

(3) if such claim is for a tax assessed against property of the estate, such claim exceeds the value of the interest of the estate in such property;

(4) if such claim is for services of an insider or attorney of the debtor, such claim exceeds the reasonable value of such services;

(5) such claim is for a debt that is unmatured on the date of the filing of the petition and that is excepted from discharge under section 523(a)(5) of this title;

(6) if such claim is the claim of a lessor for damages resulting from the termination of a lease of real property, such claim exceeds—

(A) the rent reserved by such lease, without acceleration, for the greater of one year, or 15 percent, not to exceed three years, of the remaining term of such lease, following the earlier of—

(i) the date of the filing of the petition; and

(ii) the date on which such lessor repossessed, or the lessee surrendered, the leased property; plus

(B) any unpaid rent due under such lease, without acceleration, on the earlier of such dates;

(7) if such claim is the claim of an employee for damages resulting from the termination of an employment contract, such claim exceeds—

(A) the compensation provided by such contract, without acceleration, for one year following the earlier of—

(i) the date of the filing of the petition; or

(ii) the date on which the employer directed the employee to terminate, or such employee terminated, performance under such contract; plus

(B) any unpaid compensation due under such contract, without acceleration, on the earlier of such dates;

(8) such claim results from a reduction, due to late payment, in the amount of an otherwise applicable credit available to the debtor in connection with an employment tax on wages, salaries, or commissions earned from the debtor; or

(9) proof of such claim is not timely filed, except to the extent tardily filed as permitted under paragraph (1), (2), or (3) of section 726(a) of this title or under the Federal Rules of Bankruptcy Procedure, except that a claim of a governmental unit shall be timely filed if it is filed before 180 days after the date of the order for relief or such later time as the Federal Rules of Bankruptcy Procedure may provide, and except that in a case under chapter 13, a claim of a governmental unit for a tax with respect to a return filed under section 1308 shall be timely if the claim is filed on or before the date that is 60 days after the date on which such return was filed as required.

(c) There shall be estimated for purpose of allowance under this section—

(1) any contingent or unliquidated claim, the fixing or liquidation of which, as the case may be, would unduly delay the administration of the case; or

(2) any right to payment arising from a right to an equitable remedy for breach of performance.

(d) Notwithstanding subsections (a) and (b) of this section, the court shall disallow any claim of any entity from which property is recoverable under section 542, 543, 550, or 553 of this title or that is a transferee of a transfer avoidable under section 522(f), 522(h), 544, 545, 547, 548, 549, or 724(a) of this title, unless such entity or transferee has paid the amount, or turned over any such property, for which such entity or transferee is liable under section 522(i), 542, 543, 550, or 553 of this title.

(e)(1) Notwithstanding subsections (a), (b), and (c) of this section and paragraph (2) of this subsection, the court shall disallow any claim for reimbursement or contribution of an entity that is liable with the debtor on or has secured the claim of a creditor, to the extent that—

(A) such creditor's claim against the estate is disallowed;

(B) such claim for reimbursement or contribution is contingent as of the time of allowance or disallowance of such claim for reimbursement or contribution; or

(C) such entity asserts a right of subrogation to the rights of such creditor under section 509 of this title.

(2) A claim for reimbursement or contribution of such an entity that becomes fixed after the commencement of the case shall be determined, and shall be allowed under subsection (a), (b), or (c) of this section, or disallowed under subsection (d) of this section, the same as if such

claim had become fixed before the date of the filing of the petition.

(f) In an involuntary case, a claim arising in the ordinary course of the debtor's business or financial affairs after the commencement of the case but before the earlier of the appointment of a trustee and the order for relief shall be determined as of the date such claim arises, and shall be allowed under subsection (a), (b), or (c) of this section or disallowed under subsection (d) or (e) of this section, the same as if such claim had arisen before the date of the filing of the petition.

(g)(1) A claim arising from the rejection, under section 365 of this title or under a plan under chapter 9, 11, 12, or 13 of this title, of an executory contract or unexpired lease of the debtor that has not been assumed shall be determined, and shall be allowed under subsection (a), (b), or (c) of this section or disallowed under subsection (d) or (e) of this section, the same as if such claim had arisen before the date of the filing of the petition.

(2) A claim for damages calculated in accordance with section 562 shall be allowed under subsection (a), (b), or (c), or disallowed under subsection (d) or (e), as if such claim had arisen before the date of the filing of the petition.

(h) A claim arising from the recovery of property under section 522, 550, or 553 of this title shall be determined, and shall be allowed under subsection (a), (b), or (c) of this section, or disallowed under subsection (d) or (e) of this section, the same as if such claim had arisen before the date of the filing of the petition.

(i) A claim that does not arise until after the commencement of the case for a tax entitled to priority under section 507(a)(8) of this title shall be determined, and shall be allowed under subsection (a), (b), or (c) of this section, or disallowed under subsection (d) or (e) of this section, the same as if such claim had arisen before the date of the filing of the petition.

(j) A claim that has been allowed or disallowed may be reconsidered for cause. A reconsidered claim may be allowed or disallowed according to the equities of the case. Reconsideration of a claim under this subsection does not affect the validity of any payment or transfer from the estate made to a holder of an allowed claim on account of such allowed claim that is not reconsidered, but if a reconsidered claim is allowed and is of the same class as such holder's claim, such holder may not receive any additional payment or transfer from the estate on account of such holder's allowed claim until the holder of such reconsidered and allowed claim receives payment on account of such claim proportionate in value to that already received by such other holder. This subsection does not alter or modify the trustee's right to recover from a creditor any excess payment or transfer made to such creditor.

(k)(1) The court, on the motion of the debtor and after a hearing, may reduce a claim filed under this section based in whole on an unsecured consumer debt by not more than 20 percent of the claim, if—

(A) the claim was filed by a creditor who unreasonably refused to negotiate a reasonable alternative repayment schedule proposed on behalf of the debtor by an approved nonprofit budget and credit counseling agency described in section 111;

(B) the offer of the debtor under subparagraph (A)—

(i) was made at least 60 days before the date of the filing of the petition; and

(ii) provided for payment of at least 60 percent of the amount of the debt over a period not to exceed the repayment period of the loan, or a reasonable extension thereof; and

(C) no part of the debt under the alternative repayment schedule is nondischargeable.

(2) The debtor shall have the burden of proving, by clear and convincing evidence, that—

(A) the creditor unreasonably refused to consider the debtor's proposal; and

(B) the proposed alternative repayment schedule was made prior to expiration of the 60-day period specified in paragraph (1)(B)(i).

(Pub. L. 95–598, Nov. 6, 1978, 92 Stat. 2579; Pub. L. 98–353, title III, §445, July 10, 1984, 98 Stat. 373; Pub. L. 99–554, title II, §§257(j), 283(f), Oct. 27, 1986, 100 Stat. 3115, 3117; Pub. L. 103–394, title II, §213(a), title III, §304(h)(1), Oct. 22, 1994, 108 Stat. 4125, 4134; Pub. L. 109–8, title II, §201(a), title VII, §716(d), title IX, §910(b), Apr. 20, 2005, 119 Stat. 42, 130, 184.)

Historical and Revision Notes

legislative statements

The House amendment adopts a compromise position in section 502(a) between H.R. 8200, as passed by the House, and the Senate amendment. Section 502(a) has been modified to make clear that a party in interest includes a creditor of a partner in a partnership that is a debtor under chapter 7. Since the trustee of the partnership is given an absolute claim against the estate of each general partner under section 723(c), creditors of the partner must have standing to object to claims against the partnership at the partnership level because no opportunity will be afforded at the partner's level for such objection.

The House amendment contains a provision in section 502(b)(1) that requires disallowance of a claim to the extent that such claim is unenforceable against the debtor and unenforceable against property of the debtor. This is intended to result in the disallowance of any claim for deficiency by an undersecured creditor on a non-recourse loan or under a State antideficiency law, special provision for which is made in section 1111, since neither the debtor personally, nor the property of the debtor is liable for such a deficiency. Similarly claims for usurious interest or which could be barred by an agreement between the creditor and the debtor would be disallowed.

Section 502(b)(7)(A) represents a compromise between the House bill and the Senate amendment. The House amendment takes the provision in H.R. 8200 as passed by the House of Representatives but increases the percentage from 10 to 15 percent.

As used in section 502(b)(7), the phrase "lease of real property" applies only to a "true" or "bona fide" lease and does not apply to financing leases of real property or interests therein, or to leases of such property which are intended as security.

Historically, the limitation on allowable claims of lessors of real property was based on two considerations. First, the amount of the lessor's damages on breach of a real estate lease was considered contingent and difficult to prove. Partly for this reason, claims of a lessor of real estate were not provable prior to the 1934 amendments, to the Bankruptcy Act [former title 11]. Second, in a true lease of real property, the lessor retains all risks and benefits as to the value of the real estate at the termination of the lease. Historically, it was, therefore, considered equitable to limit the claims of real estate lessor.

However, these considerations are not present in "lease financing" transactions where, in substance, the "lease" involves a sale of the real estate and the rental payments are in substance the payment of principal and interest on a secured loan or sale. In a financing lease the lessor is essentially a secured or unsecured creditor (depending upon whether his interest is perfected or not) of the debtor, and the lessor's claim should not be subject to the 502(b)(7) limitation. Financing "leases" are in substance installment sales or loans. The "lessors" are essentially sellers or lenders and should be treated as such for purposes of the bankruptcy law.

Whether a "lease" is true or bona fide lease or, in the alternative a financing "lease" or a lease intended as security, depends upon the circumstances of each case. The distinction between a true lease and a financing transaction is based upon the economic substance of the transaction and not, for example, upon the locus of title, the form of the transaction or the fact that the transaction is denominated as a "lease." The fact that the lessee, upon compliance with the terms of the lease, becomes or has the option to become the owner of the leased property for no additional consideration or for nominal consideration indicates that the transaction is a financing lease or lease intended as security. In such cases, the lessor has no substantial interest in the leased property at the expiration of the lease term. In addition, the fact that the lessee assumes and discharges substantially all the risks and obligations ordinarily attributed to the outright ownership of the property is more indicative of a financing transaction than of a true lease. The rental payments in such cases are in substance payments of principal and interest either on a loan secured by the leased real property or on the purchase of the leased real property. See, e.g., Financial Accounting Standards Board Statement No. 13 and SEC Reg. S-X, 17 C.F.R. sec. 210.3-16(q) (1977); *cf. First National Bank of Chicago v. Irving Trust Co.*, 74 F.2d 263 (2nd Cir. 1934); and Albenda and Lief, "Net Lease Financing Transactions Under the Proposed Bankruptcy Act of 1973," 30 Business Lawyer, 713 (1975).

Section 502(c) of the House amendment presents a compromise between similar provisions contained in the House bill and the Senate amendment. The compromise language is consistent with an amendment to the definition of "claim" in section 104(4)(B) of the House amendment and requires estimation of any right to an equitable remedy for breach of performance if such breach gives rise to a right to payment. To the extent language in the House and Senate reports indicate otherwise, such language is expressly overruled.

Section 502(e) of the House amendment contains language modifying a similar section in the House bill and Senate amendment. Section 502(e)(1) states the general rule requiring the court to disallow any claim for reimbursement or contribution of an entity that is liable with the debtor on, or that has secured, the claim of a creditor to any extent that the creditor's claim against the estate is disallowed. This adopts a policy that a surety's claim for reimbursement or contribution is entitled to no better status than the claim of the creditor assured by such surety. Section 502(e)(1)(B) alternatively disallows any claim for reimbursement or contribution by a surety to the extent such claim is contingent as of the time of allowance. Section 502(e)(2) is clear that to the extent a claim for reimbursement or contribution becomes fixed after the commencement of the case that it is to be considered a prepetition claim for purposes of allowance. The combined effect of sections 502(e)(1)(B) and 502(e)(2) is that a surety or codebtor is generally permitted a claim for reimbursement or contribution to the extent the surety or codebtor has paid the assured party at the time of allowance. Section 502(e)(1)(C) alternatively indicates that a claim for reimbursement or contribution of a surety or codebtor is disallowed to the extent the surety or codebtor requests subrogation under section 509 with respect to the rights of the assured party. Thus, the surety or codebtor has a choice; to the extent a claim for contribution or reimbursement would be advantageous, such as in the case where such a claim is secured, a surety or codebtor may opt for reimbursement or contribution under section 502(e). On the other hand, to the extent the claim for such surety or codebtor by way of subrogation is more advantageous, such as where such claim is secured, the surety may elect subrogation under section 509.

The section changes current law by making the election identical in all other respects. To the extent a creditor's claim is satisfied by a surety or codebtor, other creditors should not benefit by the surety's inability to file a claim against the estate merely because such surety or codebtor has failed to pay such creditor's claim in full. On the other hand, to the extent the creditor's claim against the estate is otherwise disallowed, the surety or codebtor should not be entitled to increased rights by way of reimbursement or contribution, to the detriment of competing claims of other unsecured creditors, than would be realized by way of subrogation.

While the foregoing scheme is equitable with respect to other unsecured creditors of the debtor, it is desirable to preserve present law to the extent that a surety or codebtor is not permitted to compete with the creditor he has assured until the assured party's claim has paid in full. Accordingly, section 509(c) of the House amendment subordinates both a claim by way of subrogation or a claim for reimbursement or contribution of a surety or codebtor to the claim of the assured party until the assured party's claim is paid in full.

Section 502(h) of the House amendment expands similar provisions contained in the House bill and the Senate amendment to indicate that any claim arising from the recovery of property under section 522(i), 550, or 553 shall be determined as though it were a prepetition claim.

Section 502(i) of the House amendment adopts a provision contained in section 502(j) of H.R. 8200 as passed by the House but that was not contained in the Senate amendment.

Section 502(i) of H.R. 8200 as passed by the House, but was not included in the Senate amendment, is deleted as a matter to be left to the bankruptcy tax bill next year.

The House amendment deletes section 502(i) of the Senate bill but adopts the policy of that section to a limited extent for confirmation of a plan of reorganization in section 1111(b) of the House amendment.

Section 502(j) of the House amendment is new. The provision codifies section 57k of the Bankruptcy Act [section 93(k) of former title 11].

Allowance of Claims or Interest: The House amendment adopts section 502(b)(9) of the House bill which disallows any tax claim resulting from a reduction of the Federal Unemployment Tax Act (FUTA) credit (sec. 3302 of the Internal Revenue Code [26 U.S.C. 3302]) on account of a tardy contribution to a State unemployment fund if the contribution is attributable to ways or other compensation paid by the debtor before bankruptcy. The Senate amendment allowed this reduction, but would have subordinated it to other claims in the distribution of the estate's assets by treating it as a punitive (nonpecuniary loss) penalty. The House amendment would also not bar reduction of the FUTA credit on account of a trustee's late payment of a contribution to a State unemployment fund if the contribution was attributable to a trustee's payment of compensation earned from the estate.

Section 511 of the Senate amendment is deleted. Its substance is adopted in section 502(b)(9) of the House amendment which reflects an identical provision contained in H.R. 8200 as passed by the House.

SENATE REPORT NO. 95-989

A proof of claim or interest is prima facie evidence of the claim or interest. Thus, it is allowed under subsection (a) unless a party in interest objects. The rules and case law will determine who is a party in interest for purposes of objection to allowance. The case law is well developed on this subject today. As a result of the change in the liability of a general partner's estate for the debts of this partnership, see proposed 11 U.S.C. 723, the category of persons that are parties in interest in the partnership case will be expanded to include a creditor of a partner against whose estate the trustee of the partnership estate may proceed under proposed 11 U.S.C. 723(c).

Subsection (b) prescribes the grounds on which a claim may be disallowed. The court will apply these standards if there is an objection to a proof of claim. The burden of proof on the issue of allowance is left to the Rules of Bankruptcy Procedure. Under the current chapter XIII rules, a creditor is required to prove that his claim is free from usury, rule 13-301. It is expected that the rules will make similar provision for both liquidation and individual repayment plan cases. See Bankruptcy Act §656(b) [section 1056(b) of former title 11]; H.R. 31, 94th Cong., 1st sess., sec. 6-104(a) (1975).

Paragraph (1) requires disallowance if the claim is unenforceable against the debtor for any reason (such as usury, unconscionability, or failure of consideration) other than because it is contingent or unmatured. All such contingent or unmatured claims are to be liquidated by the bankruptcy court in order to afford the debtor complete bankruptcy relief; these claims are generally not provable under present law.

Paragraph (2) requires disallowance to the extent that the claim is for unmatured interest as of the date of the petition. Whether interest is matured or unmatured on the date of bankruptcy is to be determined without reference to any ipso facto or bankruptcy clause in the agreement creating the claim. Interest disallowed under this paragraph includes postpetition interest that is not yet due and payable, and any portion of prepaid interest that represents an original discounting of the claim, yet that would not have been earned on the date of bankruptcy. For example, a claim on a $1,000 note issued the day before bankruptcy would only be allowed to the extent of the cash actually advanced. If the original discount was 10 percent so that the cash advanced was only $900, then notwithstanding the face amount of note, only $900 would be allowed. If $900 was advanced under the note some time before bankruptcy, the interest component of the note would have to be prorated and disallowed to the extent it was for interest after the commencement of the case.

Section 502(b) thus contains two principles of present law. First, interest stops accruing at the date of the filing of the petition, because any claim for unmatured interest is disallowed under this paragraph. Second, bankruptcy operates as the acceleration of the principal amount of all claims against the debtor. One unarticulated reason for this is that the discounting factor for claims after the commencement of the case is equivalent to contractual interest rate on the claim. Thus, this paragraph does not cause disallowance of claims that have not been discounted to a present value because of the irrebuttable presumption that the discounting rate and the contractual interest rate (even a zero interest rate) are equivalent.

Paragraph (3) requires disallowance of a claim to the extent that the creditor may offset the claim against a debt owing to the debtor. This will prevent double recovery, and permit the claim to be filed only for the balance due. This follows section 68 of the Bankruptcy Act [section 108 of former title 11].

Paragraph (4) requires disallowance of a property tax claim to the extent that the tax due exceeds the value of the property. This too follows current law to the extent the property tax is ad valorem.

Paragraph (5) prevents overreaching by the debtor's attorneys and concealing of assets by debtors. It permits the court to examine the claim of a debtor's attorney independently of any other provision of this subsection, and to disallow it to the extent that it exceeds the reasonable value of the attorneys' services.

Postpetition alimony, maintenance or support claims are disallowed under paragraph (6). They are to be paid from the debtor's postpetition property, because the claims are nondischargeable.

Paragraph (7), derived from current law, limits the damages allowable to a landlord of the debtor. The history of this provision is set out at length in *Oldden v. Tonto Realty Co.*, 143 F.2d 916 (2d Cir. 1944). It is designed to compensate the landlord for his loss while not permitting a claim so large (based on a long-term lease) as to prevent other general unsecured creditors from recovering a dividend from the estate. The damages a landlord may assert from termination of a lease are limited to the rent reserved for the greater of one year or ten percent of the remaining lease term, not to exceed three years, after the earlier of the date of the filing of the petition and the date of surrender or repossession in a chapter 7 case and 3 years lease payments in a chapter 9, 11, or 13 case. The sliding scale formula for chapter 7 cases is new and designed to protect the long-term lessor. This subsection does not apply to limit administrative expense claims for use of the leased premises to which the landlord is otherwise entitled.

This paragraph will not overrule *Oldden*, or the proposition for which it has been read to stand: To the extent that a landlord has a security deposit in excess of the amount of his claim allowed under this paragraph, the excess comes into the estate. Moreover, his allowed claim is for his total damages, as limited by this paragraph. By virtue of proposed 11 U.S.C. 506(a) and 506(d), the claim will be divided into a secured portion and an unsecured portion in those cases in which the deposit that the landlord holds is less than his damages. As under *Oldden*, he will not be permitted to offset his actual damages against his security deposit and then claim for the balance under this paragraph. Rather, his security deposit will be applied in satisfaction of the claim that is allowed under this paragraph.

As used in section 502(b)(7), the phrase "lease of real property" applies only to a "true" or "bona fide" lease and does not apply to financing leases of real property or interests therein, or to leases of such property which are intended as security.

Historically, the limitation on allowable claims of lessors of real property was based on two considerations. First, the amount of the lessor's damages on breach of a real estate lease was considered contingent and difficult to prove. Partly for this reason, claims of a lessor of real estate were not provable prior to the 1934 amendments to the Bankruptcy Act [former title 11]. Second, in a true lease of real property, the lessor retains all risk and benefits as to the value of the real estate at the termination of the lease. Historically, it was, therefore, considered equitable to limit the claims of a real estate lessor.

However, these considerations are not present in "lease financing" transactions where, in substance, the "lease" involves a sale of the real estate and the rental payments are in substance the payment of principal and interest on a secured loan or sale. In a financing lease the lessor is essentially a secured or unsecured creditor (depending upon whether his interest is perfected or not) of the debtor, and the lessor's claim should not be subject to the 502(b)(7) limitation. Financing "leases" are in substance installment sales or loans. The "lessors" are essentially sellers or lenders and should be treated as such for purposes of the bankruptcy law.

Whether a "lease" is true or bona fide lease or, in the alternative, a financing "lease" or a lease intended as security, depends upon the circumstances of each case. The distinction between a true lease and a financing transaction is based upon the economic substance of the transaction and not, for example, upon the locus of title, the form of the transaction or the fact that the transaction is denominated as a "lease". The fact that the lessee, upon compliance with the terms of the lease, becomes or has the option to become the owner of the leased property for no additional consideration or for nominal consideration indicates that the transaction is a financing lease or lease intended as security. In such cases, the lessor has no substantial interest in the leased property at the expiration of the lease term. In addition, the fact that the lessee assumes and discharges substantially all the risks and obligations ordinarily attributed to the outright ownership of the property is more indicative of a financing transaction than of a true lease. The rental payments in such cases are in substance payments of principal and interest either on a loan secured by the leased real property or on the purchase of the leased real property. See, e. g., Financial Accounting Standards Board Statement No. 13 and SEC Reg. S-X, 17 C.F.R. sec. 210.3-16(q) (1977); cf. *First National Bank of Chicago v. Irving Trust Co.*, 74 F.2d 263 (2nd Cir. 1934); and Albenda and Lief, "Net Lease Financing Transactions Under the Proposed Bankruptcy Act of 1973," 30 Business Lawyer, 713 (1975).

Paragraph (8) is new. It tracks the landlord limitation on damages provision in paragraph (7) for damages resulting from the breach by the debtor of an employment contract, but limits the recovery to the compensation reserved under an employment contract for the year following the earlier of the date of the petition and the termination of employment.

Subsection (c) requires the estimation of any claim liquidation of which would unduly delay the closing of the estate, such as a contingent claim, or any claim for which applicable law provides only an equitable remedy, such as specific performance. This subsection requires that all claims against the debtor be converted into dollar amounts.

Subsection (d) is derived from present law. It requires disallowance of a claim of a transferee of a voidable transfer in toto if the transferee has not paid the amount or turned over the property received as required under the sections under which the transferee's liability arises.

Subsection (e) also derived from present law, requires disallowance of the claim for reimbursement or contribution of a codebtor, surety or guarantor of an obligation of the debtor, unless the claim of the creditor on such obligation has been paid in full. The provision prevents competition between a creditor and his guarantor for the limited proceeds in the estate.

Subsection (f) specifies that "involuntary gap" creditors receive the same treatment as prepetition creditors. Under the allowance provisions of this subsection, knowledge of the commencement of the case will be irrelevant. The claim is to be allowed "the same as if such claim had arisen before the date of the filing of the petition." Under voluntary petition, proposed 11 U.S.C. 303(f), creditors must be permitted to deal with the debtor and be assured that their claims will be paid. For purposes of this subsection, "creditors" include governmental units holding claims for tax liabilities incurred during the period after the petition is filed and before the earlier of the order for relief or appointment of a trustee.

Subsection (g) gives entities injured by the rejection of an executory contract or unexpired lease, either under section 365 or under a plan or reorganization, a prepetition claim for any resulting damages, and requires that the injured entity be treated as a prepetition creditor with respect to that claim.

Subsection (h) gives a transferee of a setoff that is recovered by one trustee a prepetition claim for the amount recovered.

Subsection (i) answers the nonrecourse loan problem and gives the creditor an unsecured claim for the difference between the value of the collateral and the debt in response to the decision in *Great National Life Ins. Co. v. Pine Gate Associates, Ltd.*, Bankruptcy Case No. B75-4345A (N.D.Ga. Sept. 16, 1977).

The bill, as reported, deletes a provision in the bill as originally introduced (former sec. 502(i)) requiring a tax authority to file a proof of claim for recapture of an investment credit where, during title 11 proceedings, the trustee sells or otherwise disposes of property before the title 11 case began. The tax authority should not be required to submit a formal claim for a taxable event (a sale or other disposition of the asset) of whose occurrence the trustee necessarily knows better than the taxing authority. For procedural purposes, the recapture of investment credit is to be treated as an administrative expense, as to which only a request for payment is required.

HOUSE REPORT NO. 95-595

Paragraph (9) [of subsec. (b)] requires disallowance of certain employment tax claims. These relate to a Federal tax credit for State unemployment insurance taxes which is disallowed if the State tax is paid late. This paragraph disallows the Federal claim for the tax the same as if the credit had been allowed in full on the Federal return.

REFERENCES IN TEXT

The Federal Rules of Bankruptcy Procedure, referred to in subsec. (b)(9), are set out in the Appendix to this title.

AMENDMENTS

2005—Subsec. (b)(9). Pub. L. 109-8, §716(d), inserted ", and except that in a case under chapter 13, a claim of a governmental unit for a tax with respect to a return filed under section 1308 shall be timely if the claim is filed on or before the date that is 60 days after the date on which such return was filed as required" before period at end.

Subsec. (g). Pub. L. 109-8, §910(b), designated existing provisions as par. (1) and added par. (2).

Subsec. (k). Pub. L. 109-8, §201(a), added subsec. (k).

1994—Subsec. (b)(9). Pub. L. 103-394, §213(a), added par. (9).

Subsec. (i). Pub. L. 103-394, §304(h)(1), substituted "507(a)(8)" for "507(a)(7)".

1986—Subsec. (b)(6)(A)(ii). Pub. L. 99-554, §283(f)(1), substituted "repossessed" for "reposessed".

Subsec. (g). Pub. L. 99-554, §257(j), inserted reference to chapter 12.

Subsec. (i). Pub. L. 99-554, §283(f)(2), substituted "507(a)(7)" for "507(a)(6)".

1984—Subsec. (a). Pub. L. 98-353, §445(a), inserted "general" before "partner".

Subsec. (b). Pub. L. 98-353, §445(b)(1), (2), in provisions preceding par. (1), inserted "(e)(2)," after "subsections" and "in lawful currency of the United States" after "claim".

Subsec. (b)(1). Pub. L. 98-353, §445(b)(3), substituted "and" for ", and unenforceable against".

Subsec. (b)(3). Pub. L. 98-353, §445(b)(5), inserted "the" after "exceeds".

Pub. L. 98-353, §445(b)(4), struck out par. (3) "such claim may be offset under section 553 of this title against a debt owing to the debtor;", and redesignated par. (4) as (3).

Subsec. (b)(4). Pub. L. 98-353, §445(b)(4), redesignated par. (5) as (4). Former par. (4) redesignated (3).

Subsec. (b)(5). Pub. L. 98-353, §445(b)(6), substituted "such claim" for "the claim" and struck out the comma after "petition".

Pub. L. 98-353, §445(b)(4), redesignated par. (6) as (5). Former par. (5) redesignated (4).

Subsec. (b)(6). Pub. L. 98-353, §445(b)(4), redesignated par. (7) as (6). Former par. (6) redesignated (5).

Subsec. (b)(7). Pub. L. 98-353, §445(b)(7)(A), inserted "the claim of an employee" before "for damages".

Pub. L. 98-353, §445(b)(4), redesignated par. (8) as (7). Former par. (7) redesignated (6).

Subsec. (b)(7)(A)(i). Pub. L. 98-353, §445(b)(7)(B), substituted "or" for "and".

Subsec. (b)(7)(B). Pub. L. 98-353, §445(b)(7)(C), (D), substituted "any" for "the" and inserted a comma after "such contract".

Subsec. (b)(8), (9). Pub. L. 98-353, §445(b)(4), redesignated par. (9) as (8). Former par. (8) redesignated (7).

Subsec. (c)(1). Pub. L. 98-353, §445(c)(1), inserted "the" before "fixing" and substituted "administration" for "closing".

Subsec. (c)(2). Pub. L. 98–353, §445(c)(2), inserted "right to payment arising from a" after "any" and struck out "if such breach gives rise to a right to payment" after "breach of performance".

Subsec. (e)(1). Pub. L. 98–353, §445(d)(1), (2), in provisions preceding subpar. (A) substituted ", (b), and (c)" for "and (b)" and substituted "or has secured" for ", or has secured,".

Subsec. (e)(1)(B). Pub. L. 98–353, §445(d)(3), inserted "or disallowance" after "allowance".

Subsec. (e)(1)(C). Pub. L. 98–353, §445(d)(4), substituted "asserts a right of subrogation to the rights of such creditor" for "requests subrogation" and struck out "to the rights of such creditor" after "of this title".

Subsec. (h). Pub. L. 98–353, §445(e), substituted "522" for "522(i)".

Subsec. (j). Pub. L. 98–353, §445(f), amended subsec. (j) generally, inserting provisions relating to reconsideration of a disallowed claim, and provisions relating to reconsideration of a claim under this subsection.

EFFECTIVE DATE OF 2005 AMENDMENT

Amendment by Pub. L. 109–8 effective 180 days after Apr. 20, 2005, and not applicable with respect to cases commenced under this title before such effective date, except as otherwise provided, see section 1501 of Pub. L. 109–8, set out as a note under section 101 of this title.

EFFECTIVE DATE OF 1994 AMENDMENT

Amendment by Pub. L. 103–394 effective Oct. 22, 1994, and not applicable with respect to cases commenced under this title before Oct. 22, 1994, see section 702 of Pub. L. 103–394, set out as a note under section 101 of this title.

EFFECTIVE DATE OF 1986 AMENDMENT

Amendment by section 257 of Pub. L. 99–554 effective 30 days after Oct. 27, 1986, but not applicable to cases commenced under this title before that date, see section 302(a), (c)(1) of Pub. L. 99–554, set out as a note under section 581 of Title 28, Judiciary and Judicial Procedure.

Amendment by section 283 of Pub. L. 99–554 effective 30 days after Oct. 27, 1986, see section 302(a) of Pub. L. 99–554.

EFFECTIVE DATE OF 1984 AMENDMENT

Amendment by Pub. L. 98–353 effective with respect to cases filed 90 days after July 10, 1984, see section 552(a) of Pub. L. 98–353, set out as a note under section 101 of this title.

§503. Allowance of administrative expenses

(a) An entity may timely file a request for payment of an administrative expense, or may tardily file such request if permitted by the court for cause.

(b) After notice and a hearing, there shall be allowed administrative expenses, other than claims allowed under section 502(f) of this title, including—

(1)(A) the actual, necessary costs and expenses of preserving the estate including—

(i) wages, salaries, and commissions for services rendered after the commencement of the case; and

(ii) wages and benefits awarded pursuant to a judicial proceeding or a proceeding of the National Labor Relations Board as back pay attributable to any period of time occurring after commencement of the case under this title, as a result of a violation of Federal or State law by the debtor, without regard to the time of the occurrence of unlawful conduct on which such award is based or to whether any services were rendered, if the court determines that payment of wages and benefits by reason of the operation of this clause will not substantially increase the probability of layoff or termination of current employees, or of nonpayment of domestic support obligations, during the case under this title;

(B) any tax—

(i) incurred by the estate, whether secured or unsecured, including property taxes for which liability is in rem, in personam, or both, except a tax of a kind specified in section 507(a)(8) of this title; or

(ii) attributable to an excessive allowance of a tentative carryback adjustment that the estate received, whether the taxable year to which such adjustment relates ended before or after the commencement of the case;

(C) any fine, penalty, or reduction in credit relating to a tax of a kind specified in subparagraph (B) of this paragraph; and

(D) notwithstanding the requirements of subsection (a), a governmental unit shall not be required to file a request for the payment of an expense described in subparagraph (B) or (C), as a condition of its being an allowed administrative expense;

(2) compensation and reimbursement awarded under section 330(a) of this title;

(3) the actual, necessary expenses, other than compensation and reimbursement specified in paragraph (4) of this subsection, incurred by—

(A) a creditor that files a petition under section 303 of this title;

(B) a creditor that recovers, after the court's approval, for the benefit of the estate any property transferred or concealed by the debtor;

(C) a creditor in connection with the prosecution of a criminal offense relating to the case or to the business or property of the debtor;

(D) a creditor, an indenture trustee, an equity security holder, or a committee representing creditors or equity security holders other than a committee appointed under section 1102 of this title, in making a substantial contribution in a case under chapter 9 or 11 of this title;

(E) a custodian superseded under section 543 of this title, and compensation for the services of such custodian; or

(F) a member of a committee appointed under section 1102 of this title, if such expenses are incurred in the performance of the duties of such committee;

(4) reasonable compensation for professional services rendered by an attorney or an accountant of an entity whose expense is allowable under subparagraph (A), (B), (C), (D), or (E) of paragraph (3) of this subsection, based on the time, the nature, the extent, and the value of such services, and the cost of comparable services other than in a case under this title, and reimbursement for actual, necessary expenses incurred by such attorney or accountant;

(5) reasonable compensation for services rendered by an indenture trustee in making a substantial contribution in a case under chapter 9 or 11 of this title, based on the time, the nature, the extent, and the value of such services, and the cost of comparable services other than in a case under this title;

(6) the fees and mileage payable under chapter 119 of title 28;

(7) with respect to a nonresidential real property lease previously assumed under section 365, and subsequently rejected, a sum equal to all monetary obligations due, excluding those arising from or relating to a failure to operate or a penalty provision, for the period of 2 years following the later of the rejection date or the date of actual turnover of the premises, without reduction or setoff for any reason whatsoever except for sums actually received or to be received from an entity other than the debtor, and the claim for remaining sums due for the balance of the term of the lease shall be a claim under section 502(b)(6);

(8) the actual, necessary costs and expenses of closing a health care business incurred by a trustee or by a Federal agency (as defined in section 551(1) of title 5) or a department or agency of a State or political subdivision thereof, including any cost or expense incurred—

(A) in disposing of patient records in accordance with section 351; or

(B) in connection with transferring patients from the health care business that is in the process of being closed to another health care business; and

(9) the value of any goods received by the debtor within 20 days before the date of commencement of a case under this title in which the goods have been sold to the debtor in the ordinary course of such debtor's business.

(c) Notwithstanding subsection (b), there shall neither be allowed, nor paid—

(1) a transfer made to, or an obligation incurred for the benefit of, an insider of the debtor for the purpose of inducing such person to remain with the debtor's business, absent a finding by the court based on evidence in the record that—

(A) the transfer or obligation is essential to retention of the person because the individual has a bona fide job offer from another business at the same or greater rate of compensation;

(B) the services provided by the person are essential to the survival of the business; and

(C) either—

(i) the amount of the transfer made to, or obligation incurred for the benefit of, the person is not greater than an amount equal to 10 times the amount of the mean transfer or obligation of a similar kind given to nonmanagement employees for any purpose during the calendar year in which the transfer is made or the obligation is incurred; or

(ii) if no such similar transfers were made to, or obligations were incurred for the benefit of, such nonmanagement employees during such calendar year, the amount of the transfer or obligation is not greater than an amount equal to 25 percent of the amount of any similar transfer or obligation made to or incurred for the benefit of such insider for any purpose during the calendar year before the year in which such transfer is made or obligation is incurred;

(2) a severance payment to an insider of the debtor, unless—

(A) the payment is part of a program that is generally applicable to all full-time employees; and

(B) the amount of the payment is not greater than 10 times the amount of the mean severance pay given to nonmanagement employees during the calendar year in which the payment is made; or

(3) other transfers or obligations that are outside the ordinary course of business and not justified by the facts and circumstances of the case, including transfers made to, or obligations incurred for the benefit of, officers, managers, or consultants hired after the date of the filing of the petition.

(Pub. L. 95–598, Nov. 6, 1978, 92 Stat. 2581; Pub. L. 98–353, title III, §446, July 10, 1984, 98 Stat. 374; Pub. L. 99–554, title II, §283(g), Oct. 27, 1986, 100 Stat. 3117; Pub. L. 103–394, title I, §110, title II, §213(c), title III, §304(h)(2), Oct. 22, 1994, 108 Stat. 4113, 4126, 4134; Pub. L. 109–8, title III, §§329, 331, title IV, §445, title VII, §712(b), (c), title XI, §1103, title XII, §§1208, 1227(b), Apr. 20, 2005, 119 Stat. 101, 102, 117, 128, 190, 194, 200.)

Historical and Revision Notes

Legislative Statements

Section 503(a) of the House amendment represents a compromise between similar provisions in the House bill and the Senate amendment by leaving to the Rules of Bankruptcy Procedure the determination of the location at which a request for payment of an administrative expense may be filed. The preamble to section 503(b) of the House bill makes a similar change with respect to the allowance of administrative expenses.

Section 503(b)(1) adopts the approach taken in the House bill as modified by some provisions contained in the Senate amendment. The preamble to section 503(b) makes clear that none of the paragraphs of section 503(b) apply to claims or expenses of the kind specified in section 502(f) that arise in the ordinary course of the debtor's business or financial affairs and that arise during the gap between the commencement of an involuntary case and the appointment of a trustee or the order for relief, whichever first occurs. The remainder of section 503(b) represents a compromise between H.R. 8200 as passed by the House and the Senate amendments. Section 503(b)(3)(E) codifies present law in cases such as *Randolph v. Scruggs*, 190 U.S. 533, which accords administrative expense status to services rendered by a prepetition custodian or other party to the extent such services actually benefit the estate. Section 503(b)(4) of the House amendment conforms to the provision contained in H.R. 8200 as passed by the House and deletes language contained in the Senate amendment providing a different standard of compensation under section 330 of that amendment.

Senate Report No. 95–989

Subsection (a) of this section permits administrative expense claimants to file with the court a request for payment of an administrative expense. The Rules of Bankruptcy Procedure will specify the time, the form, and the method of such a filing.

Subsection (b) specifies the kinds of administrative expenses that are allowable in a case under the bankruptcy code. The subsection is derived mainly from section 64a(1) of the Bankruptcy Act [section 104(a)(1) of former title 11], with some changes. The actual, necessary costs and expenses of preserving the estate, including wages, salaries, or commissions for services rendered after the order for relief, and any taxes on, measured by, or withheld from such wages, salaries, or commissions, are allowable as administrative expenses.

In general, administrative expenses include taxes which the trustee incurs in administering the debtor's estate, including taxes on capital gains from sales of property by the trustee and taxes on income earned by the estate during the case. Interest on tax liabilities and certain tax penalties incurred by the trustee are also included in this first priority.

Taxes which the Internal Revenue Service may find due after giving the trustee a so-called "quickie" tax refund and later doing an audit of the refund are also payable as administrative expenses. The tax code [title 26] permits the trustee of an estate which suffers a net operating loss to carry back the loss against an earlier profit year of the estate or of the debtor and to obtain a tentative refund for the earlier year, subject, however, to a later full audit of the loss which led to the refund. The bill, in effect, requires the Internal Revenue Service to issue a tentative refund to the trustee (whether the refund was applied for by the debtor or by the trustee), but if the refund later proves to have been erroneous in amount, the Service can request that the tax attributable to the erroneous refund be payable by the estate as an administrative expense.

Postpetition payments to an individual debtor for services rendered to the estate are administrative expenses, and are not property of the estate when received by the debtor. This situation would most likely arise when the individual was a sole proprietor and was employed by the estate to run the business after the commencement of the case. An individual debtor in possession would be so employed, for example. See *Local Loan v. Hunt*, 292 U.S. 234, 243 (1943).

Compensation and reimbursement awarded officers of the estate under section 330 are allowable as administrative expenses. Actual, necessary expenses, other than compensation of a professional person, incurred by a creditor that files an involuntary petition, by a creditor that recovers property for the benefit of the estate, by a creditor that acts in connection with the prosecution of a criminal offense relating to the case, by a creditor, indenture, trustee, equity security holder, or committee of creditors or equity security holders (other than official committees) that makes a substantial contribution to a reorganization or municipal debt adjustment case, or by a superseded custodian, are all allowable administrative expenses. The phrase "substantial contribution in the case" is derived from Bankruptcy Act §§242 and 243 [sections 642 and 643 of former title 11]. It does not require a contribution that leads to confirmation of a plan, for in many cases, it will be a substantial contribution if the person involved uncovers facts that would lead to a denial of confirmation, such as fraud in connection with the case.

Paragraph (4) permits reasonable compensation for professional services rendered by an attorney or an accountant of an equity whose expense is compensable under the previous paragraph. Paragraph (5) permits reasonable compensation for an indenture trustee in making a substantial contribution in a reorganization or municipal debt adjustment case. Finally, paragraph (6) permits witness fees and mileage as prescribed under chapter 119 [§2041 et seq.] of title 28.

AMENDMENTS

2005—Subsec. (b)(1)(A). Pub. L. 109–8, §329, amended subpar. (A) generally. Prior to amendment, subpar. (A) read as follows: "the actual, necessary costs and expenses of preserving the estate, including wages, salaries, or commissions for services rendered after the commencement of the case;".

Subsec. (b)(1)(B)(i). Pub. L. 109–8, §712(b), inserted "whether secured or unsecured, including property taxes for which liability is in rem, in personam, or both," before "except".

Subsec. (b)(1)(D). Pub. L. 109–8, §712(c), added subpar. (D).

Subsec. (b)(4). Pub. L. 109–8, §1208, inserted "subparagraph (A), (B), (C), (D), or (E) of" before "paragraph (3)".

Subsec. (b)(7). Pub. L. 109–8, §445, added par. (7).

Subsec. (b)(8). Pub. L. 109–8, §1103, added par. (8).

Subsec. (b)(9). Pub. L. 109–8, §1227(b), added par. (9).

Subsec. (c). Pub. L. 109–8, §331, added subsec. (c).

1994—Subsec. (a). Pub. L. 103–394, §213(c), inserted "timely" after "may" and ", or may tardily file such request if permitted by the court for cause" before period at end.

Subsec. (b)(1)(B)(i). Pub. L. 103–394, §304(h)(2), substituted "507(a)(8)" for "507(a)(7)".

Subsec. (b)(3)(F). Pub. L. 103–394, §110, added subpar. (F).

1986—Subsec. (b)(1)(B)(i). Pub. L. 99–554, §283(g)(1), substituted "507(a)(7)" for "507(a)(6)".

Subsec. (b)(5). Pub. L. 99–554, §283(g)(2), inserted "and" after "title;".

Subsec. (b)(6). Pub. L. 99–554, §283(g)(3), substituted a period for "; and".

1984—Subsec. (b). Pub. L. 98–353, §446(1), struck out the comma after "be allowed" in provisions preceding par. (1).

Subsec. (b)(1)(C). Pub. L. 98–353, §446(2), struck out the comma after "credit".

Subsec. (b)(2). Pub. L. 98–353, §446(3), inserted "(a)" after "330".

Subsec. (b)(3). Pub. L. 98–353, §446(4), inserted a comma after "paragraph (4) of this subsection".

Subsec. (b)(3)(C). Pub. L. 98–353, §446(5), struck out the comma after "case".

Subsec. (b)(5). Pub. L. 98–353, §446(6), struck out "and" after "title;".

Subsec. (b)(6). Pub. L. 98–353, §446(7), substituted "; and" for period at end.

EFFECTIVE DATE OF 2005 AMENDMENT

Amendment by Pub. L. 109–8 effective 180 days after Apr. 20, 2005, and not applicable with respect to cases commenced under this title before such effective date, except as otherwise provided, see section 1501 of Pub. L. 109–8, set out as a note under section 101 of this title.

EFFECTIVE DATE OF 1994 AMENDMENT

Amendment by Pub. L. 103–394 effective Oct. 22, 1994, and not applicable with respect to cases commenced under this title before Oct. 22, 1994, see section 702 of Pub. L. 103–394, set out as a note under section 101 of this title.

EFFECTIVE DATE OF 1986 AMENDMENT

Amendment by Pub. L. 99–554 effective 30 days after Oct. 27, 1986, see section 302(a) of Pub. L. 99–554, set out as a note under section 581 of Title 28, Judiciary and Judicial Procedure.

EFFECTIVE DATE OF 1984 AMENDMENT

Amendment by Pub. L. 98–353 effective with respect to cases filed 90 days after July 10, 1984, see section 552(a) of Pub. L. 98–353, set out as a note under section 101 of this title.

§504. Sharing of compensation

(a) Except as provided in subsection (b) of this section, a person receiving compensation or reimbursement under section 503(b)(2) or 503(b)(4) of this title may not share or agree to share—

(1) any such compensation or reimbursement with another person; or

(2) any compensation or reimbursement received by another person under such sections.

(b)(1) A member, partner, or regular associate in a professional association, corporation, or partnership may share compensation or reimbursement received under section 503(b)(2) or 503(b)(4) of this title with another member, partner, or regular associate in such association, corporation, or partnership, and may share in any compensation or reimbursement received under such sections by another member, partner, or regular associate in such association, corporation, or partnership.

(2) An attorney for a creditor that files a petition under section 303 of this title may share compensation and reimbursement received under section 503(b)(4) of this title with any other attorney contributing to the services rendered or expenses incurred by such creditor's attorney.

(c) This section shall not apply with respect to sharing, or agreeing to share, compensation with a bona fide public service attorney referral program that operates in accordance with non-Federal law regulating attorney referral services and with rules of professional responsibility applicable to attorney acceptance of referrals.

(Pub. L. 95–598, Nov. 6, 1978, 92 Stat. 2582; Pub. L. 109–8, title III, §326, Apr. 20, 2005, 119 Stat. 99.)

HISTORICAL AND REVISION NOTES

SENATE REPORT NO. 95–989

Section 504 prohibits the sharing of compensation, or fee splitting, among attorneys, other professionals, or trustees. The section provides only two exceptions: partners or associates in the same professional association, partnership, or corporation may share compensation inter se; and attorneys for petitioning creditors that join in a petition commencing an involuntary case may share compensation.

AMENDMENTS

2005—Subsec. (c). Pub. L. 109–8 added subsec. (c).

EFFECTIVE DATE OF 2005 AMENDMENT

Amendment by Pub. L. 109–8 effective 180 days after Apr. 20, 2005, and not applicable with respect to cases commenced under this title before such effective date, except as otherwise provided, see section 1501 of Pub. L. 109–8, set out as a note under section 101 of this title.

§505. Determination of tax liability

(a)(1) Except as provided in paragraph (2) of this subsection, the court may determine the amount or legality of any tax, any fine or penalty relating to a tax, or any addition to tax, whether or not previously assessed, whether or not paid, and whether or not contested before and adjudicated by a judicial or administrative tribunal of competent jurisdiction.

(2) The court may not so determine—

(A) the amount or legality of a tax, fine, penalty, or addition to tax if such amount or legality was contested before and adjudicated by a judicial or administrative tribunal of competent jurisdiction before the commencement of the case under this title;

(B) any right of the estate to a tax refund, before the earlier of—

(i) 120 days after the trustee properly requests such refund from the governmental unit from which such refund is claimed; or

(ii) a determination by such governmental unit of such request; or

(C) the amount or legality of any amount arising in connection with an ad valorem tax on real or personal property of the estate, if the applicable period for contesting or redetermining that amount under any law (other than a bankruptcy law) has expired.

(b)(1)(A) The clerk shall maintain a list under which a Federal, State, or local governmental unit responsible for the collection of taxes within the district may—

(i) designate an address for service of requests under this subsection; and

(ii) describe where further information concerning additional requirements for filing such requests may be found.

(B) If such governmental unit does not designate an address and provide such address to the clerk under subparagraph (A), any request made under this subsection may be served at the address for the filing of a tax return or protest with the appropriate taxing authority of such governmental unit.

(2) A trustee may request a determination of any unpaid liability of the estate for any tax incurred during the administration of the case by submitting a tax return for such tax and a request for such a determination to the governmental unit charged with responsibility for collection or determination of such tax at the address and in the manner designated in paragraph (1). Unless such return is fraudulent, or contains a material misrepresentation, the estate, the trustee, the debtor, and any successor to the debtor are discharged from any liability for such tax—

(A) upon payment of the tax shown on such return, if—

(i) such governmental unit does not notify the trustee, within 60 days after such request, that such return has been selected for examination; or

(ii) such governmental unit does not complete such an examination and notify the trustee of any tax due, within 180 days after such request or within such additional time as the court, for cause, permits;

(B) upon payment of the tax determined by the court, after notice and a hearing, after completion by such governmental unit of such examination; or

(C) upon payment of the tax determined by such governmental unit to be due.

(c) Notwithstanding section 362 of this title, after determination by the court of a tax under this section, the governmental unit charged with responsibility for collection of such tax may assess such tax against the estate, the debtor, or a successor to the debtor, as the case may be, subject to any otherwise applicable law.

(Pub. L. 95–598, Nov. 6, 1978, 92 Stat. 2582; Pub. L. 98–353, title III, §447, July 10, 1984, 98 Stat. 374; Pub. L. 109–8, title VII, §§701(b), 703, 715, Apr. 20, 2005, 119 Stat. 124, 125, 129.)

HISTORICAL AND REVISION NOTES

LEGISLATIVE STATEMENTS

Section 505 of the House amendment adopts a compromise position with respect to the determination of tax liability from the position taken in H.R. 8200 as passed by the House and in the Senate amendment.

Determinations of tax liability: Authority of bankruptcy court to rule on merits of tax claims.—The House amendment authorizes the bankruptcy court to rule on the merits of any tax claim involving an unpaid tax, fine, or penalty relating to a tax, or any addition to a tax, of the debtor or the estate. This authority applies, in general, whether or not the tax, penalty, fine, or addition to tax had been previously assessed or paid. However, the bankruptcy court will not have jurisdiction to rule on the merits of any tax claim which has been previously adjudicated, in a contested proceeding, before a court of competent jurisdiction. For this purpose, a proceeding in the U.S. Tax Court is to be considered "contested" if the debtor filed a petition in the Tax Court by the commencement of the case and the Internal Revenue Service had filed an answer to the petition. Therefore, if a petition and answer were filed in the Tax Court before the title II petition was filed, and if the debtor later defaults in the Tax Court, then, under res judicata principles, the bankruptcy court could not then rule on the debtor's or the estate's liability for the same taxes.

The House amendment adopts the rule of the Senate bill that the bankruptcy court can, under certain conditions, determine the amount of tax refund claim by the trustee. Under the House amendment, if the refund results from an offset or counterclaim to a claim or request for payment by the Internal Revenue Service, or other tax authority, the trustee would not first have to file an administrative claim for refund with the tax authority.

However, if the trustee requests a refund in other situations, he would first have to submit an administrative claim for the refund. Under the House amendment, if the Internal Revenue Service, or other tax authority does not rule on the refund claim within 120 days, then the bankruptcy court may rule on the merits of the refund claim.

Under the Internal Revenue Code [title 26], a suit for refund of Federal taxes cannot be filed until 6 months after a claim for refund is filed with the Internal Revenue Service (sec. 6532(a) [title 26]). Because of the bankruptcy aim to close the estate as expeditiously as possible, the House amendment shortens to 120 days the period for the Internal Revenue Service to decide the refund claim.

The House amendment also adopts the substance of the Senate bill rule permitting the bankruptcy court to determine the amount of any penalty, whether punitive or pecuniary in nature, relating to taxes over which it has jurisdiction.

Jurisdiction of the tax court in bankruptcy cases: The Senate amendment provided a detailed series of rules concerning the jurisdiction of the U.S. Tax Court, or similar State or local administrative tribunal to determine personal tax liabilities of an individual debtor. The House amendment deletes these specific rules and relies on procedures to be derived from broad general powers of the bankruptcy court.

Under the House amendment, as under present law, a corporation seeking reorganization under chapter 11 is considered to be personally before the bankruptcy court for purposes of giving that court jurisdiction over the debtor's personal liability for a nondischargeable tax.

The rules are more complex where the debtor is an individual under chapter 7, 11, or 13. An individual debtor or the tax authority can, as under section 17c of the present Bankruptcy Act [section 35(c) of former title 11], file a request that the bankruptcy court determine the debtor's personal liability for the balance of any nondischargeable tax not satisfied from assets of the estate. The House amendment intends to retain these procedures and also adds a rule staying commencement or continuation of any proceeding in the Tax Court after the bankruptcy petition is filed, unless and until that stay is lifted by the bankruptcy judge under section 362(a)(8). The House amendment also stays assessment as well as collection of a prepetition claim against the debtor (sec. 362(a)(6)). A tax authority would not, however, be stayed from issuing a deficiency notice during the bankruptcy case (sec. (b)(7)) [sec. 362(b)(8)]. The Senate amendment repealed the existing authority of the Internal Revenue Service to make an immediate assessment of taxes upon bankruptcy (sec. 6871(a) of the code [title 26]. See section 321 of the Senate bill. As indicated, the substance of that provision, also affecting State and local taxes, is contained in section 362(a)(6) of the House amendment. The statute of limitations is tolled under the House amendment while the bankruptcy case is pending.

Where no proceeding in the Tax Court is pending at the commencement of the bankruptcy case, the tax authority can, under the House amendment, file a claim against the estate for a prepetition tax liability and may also file a request that the bankruptcy court hear arguments and decide the merits of an individual debtor's personal liability for the balance of any nondischargeable tax liability not satisfied from assets of the estate. Bankruptcy terminology refers to the latter type of request as a creditor's complaint to determine the dischargeability of a debt. Where such a complaint is filed, the bankruptcy court will have personal jurisdiction over an individual debtor, and the debtor himself would have no access to the Tax Court, or to any other court, to determine his personal liability for nondischargeable taxes.

If a tax authority decides not to file a claim for taxes which would typically occur where there are few, if any, assets in the estate, normally the tax authority would also not request the bankruptcy court to rule on the debtor's personal liability for a nondischargeable tax. Under the House amendment, the tax authority would then have to follow normal procedures in order to collect a nondischargeable tax. For example, in the case of nondischargeable Federal income taxes, the Internal Revenue Service would be required to issue a deficiency notice to an individual debtor, and the debtor could then file a petition in the Tax Court—or a refund suit in a district court—as the forum in which to litigate his personal liability for a nondischargeable tax.

Under the House amendment, as under present law, an individual debtor can also file a complaint to determine dischargeability. Consequently, where the tax authority does not file a claim or a request that the bankruptcy court determine dischargeability of a specific tax liability, the debtor could file such a request on his own behalf, so that the bankruptcy court would then determine both the validity of the claim against assets in the estate and also the personal liability of the debtor for any nondischargeable tax.

Where a proceeding is pending in the Tax Court at the commencement of the bankruptcy case, the commencement of the bankruptcy case automatically stays further action in the Tax Court case unless and until the stay is lifted by the bankruptcy court. The Senate amendment repealed a provision of the Internal Revenue case barring a debtor from filing a petition in the Tax Court after commencement of a bankruptcy case (sec. 6871(b) of the code [26 U.S.C. 6871(b)]). See section 321 of the Senate bill. As indicated earlier, the equivalent of the code amendment is embodied in section 362(a)(8) of the House amendment, which automatically stays commencement or continuation of any proceeding in the Tax Court until the stay is lifted or the case is terminated. The stay will permit sufficient time for the bankruptcy trustee to determine if he desires to join the Tax Court proceeding on behalf of the estate. Where the trustee chooses to join the Tax Court proceeding, it is expected that he will seek permission to intervene in the Tax Court case and then request that the stay on the Tax Court proceeding be lifted. In such a case, the merits of the tax liability will be determined by the Tax Court, and its decision will bind both the individual debtor as to any taxes which are nondischargeable and the trustee as to the tax claim against the estate.

Where the trustee does not want to intervene in the Tax Court, but an individual debtor wants to have the

Tax Court determine the amount of his personal liability for nondischargeable taxes, the debtor can request the bankruptcy court to lift the automatic stay on existing Tax Court proceedings. If the stay is lifted and the Tax Court reaches its decision before the bankruptcy court's decision on the tax claim against the estate, the decision of the Tax Court would bind the bankruptcy court under principles of res judicata because the decision of the Tax Court affected the personal liability of the debtor. If the trustee does not wish to subject the estate to the decision of the Tax Court if the latter court decides the issues before the bankruptcy court rules, the trustee could resist the lifting of the stay on the existing Tax Court proceeding. If the Internal Revenue Service had issued a deficiency notice to the debtor before the bankruptcy case began, but as of the filing of the bankruptcy petition the 90-day period for filing in the Tax Court was still running, the debtor would be automatically stayed from filing a petition in the Tax Court. If either the debtor or the Internal Revenue Service then files a complaint to determine dischargeability in the bankruptcy court, the decision of the bankruptcy court would bind both the debtor and the Internal Revenue Service.

The bankruptcy judge could, however, lift the stay on the debtor to allow him to petition the Tax Court, while reserving the right to rule on the tax authority's claim against assets of the estate. The bankruptcy court could also, upon request by the trustee, authorize the trustee to intervene in the Tax Court for purposes of having the estate also governed by the decision of the Tax Court.

In essence, under the House amendment, the bankruptcy judge will have authority to determine which court will determine the merits of the tax claim both as to claims against the estate and claims against the debtor concerning his personal liability for nondischargeable taxes. Thus, if the Internal Revenue Service, or a State or local tax authority, files a petition to determine dischargeability, the bankruptcy judge can either rule on the merits of the claim and continue the stay on any pending Tax Court proceeding or lift the stay on the Tax Court and hold the dischargeability complaint in abeyance. If he rules on the merits of the complaint before the decision of the Tax Court is reached, the bankruptcy court's decision would bind the debtor as to nondischargeable taxes and the Tax Court would be governed by that decision under principles of res judicata. If the bankruptcy judge does not rule on the merits of the complaint before the decision of the Tax Court is reached, the bankruptcy court will be bound by the decision of the Tax Court as it affects the amount of any claim against the debtor's estate.

If the Internal Revenue Service does not file a complaint to determine dischargeability and the automatic stay on a pending Tax Court proceeding is not lifted, the bankruptcy court could determine the merits of any tax claim against the estate. That decision will not bind the debtor personally because he would not have been personally before the bankruptcy court unless the debtor himself asks the bankruptcy court to rule on his personal liability. In any such situation where no party filed a dischargeability petition, the debtor would have access to the Tax Court to determine his personal liability for a nondischargeable tax debt. While the Tax Court in such a situation could take into account the ruling of the bankruptcy court on claims against the estate in deciding the debtor's personal liability, the bankruptcy court's ruling would not bind the Tax Court under principles of res judicata, because the debtor, in that situation, would not have been personally before the bankruptcy court.

If neither the debtor nor the Internal Revenue Service files a claim against the estate or a request to rule on the debtor's personal liability, any pending tax court proceeding would be stayed until the closing of the bankruptcy case, at which time the stay on the tax court would cease and the tax court case could continue for purposes of deciding the merits of the debtor's personal liability for nondischargeable taxes.

Audit of trustee's returns: Under both bills, the bankruptcy court could determine the amount of any administrative period taxes. The Senate amendment, however, provided for an expedited audit procedure, which was mandatory in some cases. The House amendment (sec. 505(b)), adopts the provision of the House bill allowing the trustee discretion in all cases whether to ask the Internal Revenue Service, or State or local tax authority for a prompt audit of his returns on behalf of the estate. The House amendment, however, adopts the provision of the Senate bill permitting a prompt audit only on the basis of tax returns filed by the trustee for completed taxable periods. Procedures for a prompt audit set forth in the Senate bill are also adopted in modified form.

Under the procedure, before the case can be closed, the trustee may request a tax audit by the local, State or Federal tax authority of all tax returns filed by the trustee. The taxing authority would have to notify the trustee and the bankruptcy court within 60 days whether it accepts returns or desires to audit the returns more fully. If an audit is conducted, the taxing authority would have to notify the trustee of tax deficiency within 180 days after the original request, subject to extensions of time if the bankruptcy court approves. If the trustee does not agree with the results of the audit, the trustee could ask the bankruptcy court to resolve the dispute. Once the trustee's tax liability for administration period taxes has thus been determined, the legal effect in a case under chapter 7 or 11 would be to discharge the trustee and any predecessor of the trustee, and also the debtor, from any further liability for these taxes.

The prompt audit procedure would not be available with respect to any tax liability as to which any return required to be filed on behalf of the estate is not filed with the proper tax authority. The House amendment also specifies that a discharge of the trustee or the debtor which would otherwise occur will not be granted, or will be void if the return filed on behalf of the estate reflects fraud or material misrepresentation of facts.

For purposes of the above prompt audit procedures, it is intended that the tax authority with which the request for audit is to be filed is, as the Federal taxes, the office of the District Director in the district where the bankruptcy case is pending.

Under the House amendment, if the trustee does not request a prompt audit, the debtor would not be discharged from possible transferee liability if any assets are returned to the debtor.

Assessment after decision: As indicated above, the commencement of a bankruptcy case automatically stays assessment of any tax (sec. 362(a)(6)). However, the House amendment provides (sec. 505(c)) that if the bankruptcy court renders a final judgment with regard to any tax (under the rules discussed above), the tax authority may then make an assessment (if permitted to do so under otherwise applicable tax law) without waiting for termination of the case or confirmation of a reorganization plan.

Trustee's authority to appeal tax cases: The equivalent provision in the House bill (sec. 505(b)) and in the Senate bill (sec. 362(h)) authorizing the trustee to prosecute an appeal or review of a tax case are deleted as unnecessary. Section 541(a) of the House amendment provides that property of the estate is to include all legal or equitable interests of the debtor. These interests include the debtor's causes of action, so that the specific provisions of the House and Senate bills are not needed.

SENATE REPORT NO. 95-989

Subsections (a) and (b) are derived, with only stylistic changes, from section 2a(2A) of the Bankruptcy Act [section 11(a)(2A) of former title 11]. They permit determination by the bankruptcy court of any unpaid tax liability of the debtor that has not been contested before or adjudicated by a judicial or administrative tribunal of competent jurisdiction before the bankruptcy case, and the prosecution by the trustee of an appeal from an order of such a body if the time for review or appeal has not expired before the commencement of the bankruptcy case. As under current Bankruptcy Act §2a (2A). *Arkansas Corporation Commissioner v. Thompson*, 313 U.S. 132 (1941), remains good law to permit abstention where uniformity of assessment is of significant importance.

Section (c) deals with procedures for obtaining a prompt audit of tax returns filed by the trustee in a liquidation or reorganization case. Under the bill as originally introduced, a trustee who is "in doubt" concerning tax liabilities of the estate incurred during a title 11 proceeding could obtain a discharge from personal liability for himself and the debtor (but not for the debtor or the debtor's successor in a reorganization), provided that certain administrative procedures were followed. The trustee could request a prompt tax audit by the local, State, or Federal governmental unit. The taxing authority would have to notify the trustee and the court within sixty days whether it accepted the return or desired to audit the returns more fully. If an audit were conducted, the tax office would have to notify the trustee of any tax deficiency within 4 months (subject to an extension of time if the court approved). These procedures would apply only to tax years completed on or before the case was closed and for which the trustee had filed a tax return.

The committee bill eliminates the "in doubt" rule and makes mandatory (rather than optional) the trustee's request for a prompt audit of the estate's tax returns. In many cases, the trustee could not be certain that his returns raised no doubt about possible tax issues. In addition, it is desirable not to create a situation where the taxing authority asserts a tax liability against the debtor (as transferee of surplus assets, if any, return to him) after the case is over; in any such situation, the debtor would be called on to defend a tax return which he did not prepare. Under the amendment, all disputes concerning these returns are to be resolved by the bankruptcy court, and both the trustee and the debtor himself do not then face potential post-bankruptcy tax liabilities based on these returns. This result would occur as to the debtor, however, only in a liquidation case.

In a reorganization in which the debtor or a successor to the debtor continues in existence, the trustee could obtain a discharge from personal liability through the prompt audit procedure, but the Treasury could still claim a deficiency against the debtor (or his successor) for additional taxes due on returns filed during the title 11 proceedings.

HOUSE REPORT NO. 95–595

Subsection (c) is new. It codifies in part the referee's decision in *In re Statmaster Corp.*, 465 F.2d 987 (5th Cir. 1972). Its purpose is to protect the trustee from personal liability for a tax falling on the estate that is not assessed until after the case is closed. If necessary to permit expeditious closing of the case, the court, on request of the trustee, must order the governmental unit charged with the responsibility for collection or determination of the tax to audit the trustee's return or be barred from attempting later collection. The court will be required to permit sufficient time to perform an audit, if the taxing authority requests it. The final order of the court and the payment of the tax determined in that order discharges the trustee, the debtor, and any successor to the debtor from any further liability for the tax. See Plumb, The Tax Recommendations of the Commission on the Bankruptcy Laws: Tax Procedures, 88 Harv. L. Rev. 1360, 1423–42 (1975).

AMENDMENTS

2005—Subsec. (a)(2)(C). Pub. L. 109–8, §701(b), added subpar. (C).

Subsec. (b). Pub. L. 109–8, §703, added par. (1), redesignated existing provisions of subsec. (b) as par. (2) and inserted "at the address and in the manner designated in paragraph (1)" after "determination of such tax" in introductory provisions, redesignated former pars. (1) to (3) of subsec. (b) as subpars. (A) to (C), respectively, of par. (2), and redesignated former subpars (A) and (B) of par. (1) as cls. (i) and (ii), respectively, of subpar. (A).

Subsec. (b)(2). Pub. L. 109–8, §715, inserted "the estate," after "misrepresentation," in introductory provisions.

1984—Subsec. (a)(2)(B)(i). Pub. L. 98–353 substituted "or" for "and".

EFFECTIVE DATE OF 2005 AMENDMENT

Amendment by Pub. L. 109–8 effective 180 days after Apr. 20, 2005, and not applicable with respect to cases commenced under this title before such effective date, except as otherwise provided, see section 1501 of Pub. L. 109–8, set out as a note under section 101 of this title.

EFFECTIVE DATE OF 1984 AMENDMENT

Amendment by Pub. L. 98–353 effective with respect to cases filed 90 days after July 10, 1984, see section 552(a) of Pub. L. 98–353, set out as a note under section 101 of this title.

§ 506. Determination of secured status

(a)(1) An allowed claim of a creditor secured by a lien on property in which the estate has an interest, or that is subject to setoff under section 553 of this title, is a secured claim to the extent of the value of such creditor's interest in the estate's interest in such property, or to the extent of the amount subject to setoff, as the case may be, and is an unsecured claim to the extent that the value of such creditor's interest or the amount so subject to setoff is less than the amount of such allowed claim. Such value shall be determined in light of the purpose of the valuation and of the proposed disposition or use of such property, and in conjunction with any hearing on such disposition or use or on a plan affecting such creditor's interest.

(2) If the debtor is an individual in a case under chapter 7 or 13, such value with respect to personal property securing an allowed claim shall be determined based on the replacement value of such property as of the date of the filing of the petition without deduction for costs of sale or marketing. With respect to property acquired for personal, family, or household purposes, replacement value shall mean the price a retail merchant would charge for property of that kind considering the age and condition of the property at the time value is determined.

(b) To the extent that an allowed secured claim is secured by property the value of which, after any recovery under subsection (c) of this section, is greater than the amount of such claim, there shall be allowed to the holder of such claim, interest on such claim, and any reasonable fees, costs, or charges provided for under the agreement or State statute under which such claim arose.

(c) The trustee may recover from property securing an allowed secured claim the reasonable, necessary costs and expenses of preserving, or disposing of, such property to the extent of any benefit to the holder of such claim, including the payment of all ad valorem property taxes with respect to the property.

(d) To the extent that a lien secures a claim against the debtor that is not an allowed secured claim, such lien is void, unless—

(1) such claim was disallowed only under section 502(b)(5) or 502(e) of this title; or

(2) such claim is not an allowed secured claim due only to the failure of any entity to file a proof of such claim under section 501 of this title.

(Pub. L. 95–598, Nov. 6, 1978, 92 Stat. 2583; Pub. L. 98–353, title III, § 448, July 10, 1984, 98 Stat. 374; Pub. L. 109–8, title III, § 327, title VII, § 712(d), Apr. 20, 2005, 119 Stat. 99, 128.)

HISTORICAL AND REVISION NOTES

LEGISLATIVE STATEMENTS

Section 506(a) of the House amendment adopts the provision contained in the Senate amendment and rejects a contrary provision as contained in H.R. 8200 as passed by the House. The provision contained in the Senate amendment and adopted by the House amendment recognizes that an amount subject to set-off is sufficient to recognize a secured status in the holder of such right. Additionally a determination of what portion of an allowed claim is secured and what portion is unsecured is binding only for the purpose for which the determination is made. Thus determinations for purposes of adequate protection is not binding for purposes of "cram down" on confirmation in a case under chapter 11.

Section 506(b) of the House amendment adopts language contained in the Senate amendment and rejects language contained in H.R. 8200 as passed by the House. If the security agreement between the parties provides for attorneys' fees, it will be enforceable under title 11, notwithstanding contrary law, and is recoverable from the collateral after any recovery under section 506(c).

Section 506(c) of the House amendment was contained in H.R. 8200 as passed by the House and adopted, verbatim, in the Senate amendment. Any time the trustee or debtor in possession expends money to provide for the reasonable and necessary cost and expenses of preserving or disposing of a secured creditor's collateral, the trustee or debtor in possession is entitled to recover such expenses from the secured party or from the property securing an allowed secured claim held by such party.

Section 506(d) of the House amendment is derived from H.R. 8200 as passed by the House and is adopted in lieu of the alternative test provided in section 506(d) of the Senate amendment. For purposes of section 506(d) of the House amendment, the debtor is a party in interest.

Determination of Secured Status: The House amendment deletes section 506(d)(3) of the Senate amendment, which insures that a tax lien securing a nondischargeable tax claim is not voided because a tax authority with notice or knowledge of the bankruptcy case fails to file a claim for the liability (as it may elect not to do, if it is clear there are insufficient assets to pay the liability). Since the House amendment retains section 506(d) of the House bill that a lien is not voided unless a party in interest has requested that the court determine and allow or disallow the claim, provision of the Senate amendment is not necessary.

SENATE REPORT NO. 95–989

Subsection (a) of this section separates an undersecured creditor's claim into two parts: He has a secured claim to the extent of the value of his collateral; and he has an unsecured claim for the balance of his claim. The subsection also provides for the valuation of claims which involve setoffs under section 553. While courts will have to determine value on a case-by-case basis, the subsection makes it clear that valuation is to be determined in light of the purpose of the valuation and the proposed disposition or use of the subject property. This determination shall be made in conjunction with any hearing on such disposition or use of property or on a plan affecting the creditor's interest. To illustrate, a valuation early in the case in a proceeding under sections 361–363 would not be binding upon the debtor or creditor at the time of confirmation of the plan. Throughout the bill, references to secured claims are only to the claim determined to be secured under this subsection, and not to the full amount of the creditor's claim. This provision abolishes the use of the terms "secured creditor" and "unsecured creditor" and substitutes in their places the terms "secured claim" and "unsecured claim."

Subsection (b) codifies current law by entitling a creditor with an oversecured claim to any reasonable fees (including attorney's fees), costs, or charges provided under the agreement under which the claim arose. These fees, costs, and charges are secured claims to the extent that the value of the collateral exceeds the amount of the underlying claim.

Subsection (c) also codifies current law by permitting the trustee to recover from property the value of which is greater than the sum of the claims secured by a lien on that property the reasonable, necessary costs and expenses of preserving, or disposing of, the property. The recovery is limited to the extent of any benefit to the holder of such claim.

Subsection (d) provides that to the extent a secured claim is not allowed, its lien is void unless the holder had neither actual notice nor knowledge of the case, the lien was not listed by the debtor in a chapter 9 or 11 case or such claim was disallowed only under section 502(e).

HOUSE REPORT NO. 95–595

Subsection (d) permits liens to pass through the bankruptcy case unaffected. However, if a party in interest requests the court to determine and allow or disallow the claim secured by the lien under section 502 and the claim is not allowed, then the lien is void to the extent that the claim is not allowed. The voiding provision does not apply to claims disallowed only under section 502(e), which requires disallowance of certain claims against the debtor by a codebtor, surety, or guarantor for contribution or reimbursement.

AMENDMENTS

2005—Subsec. (a). Pub. L. 109–8, § 327, designated existing provisions as par. (1) and added par. (2).

Subsec. (b). Pub. L. 109–8, § 712(d)(1), inserted "or State statute" after "agreement".

Subsec. (c). Pub. L. 109–8, § 712(d)(2), inserted ", including the payment of all ad valorem property taxes with respect to the property" before period at end.

1984—Subsec. (b). Pub. L. 98–353, § 448(a), inserted "for" after "provided".

Subsec. (d)(1). Pub. L. 98–353, § 448(b), substituted "such claim was disallowed only under section 502(b)(5) or 502(e) of this title" for "a party in interest has not requested that the court determine and allow or disallow such claim under section 502 of this title".

Subsec. (d)(2). Pub. L. 98–353, § 448(b), substituted "such claim is not an allowed secured claim due only to the failure of any entity to file a proof of such claim under section 501 of this title" for "such claim was disallowed only under section 502(e) of this title".

EFFECTIVE DATE OF 2005 AMENDMENT

Amendment by Pub. L. 109–8 effective 180 days after Apr. 20, 2005, and not applicable with respect to cases commenced under this title before such effective date, except as otherwise provided, see section 1501 of Pub. L. 109–8, set out as a note under section 101 of this title.

EFFECTIVE DATE OF 1984 AMENDMENT

Amendment by Pub. L. 98–353 effective with respect to cases filed 90 days after July 10, 1984, see section 552(a) of Pub. L. 98–353, set out as a note under section 101 of this title.

§ 507. Priorities

(a) The following expenses and claims have priority in the following order:

(1) First:

(A) Allowed unsecured claims for domestic support obligations that, as of the date of the filing of the petition in a case under this title, are owed to or recoverable by a spouse, former spouse, or child of the debtor, or such child's parent, legal guardian, or responsible relative, without regard to whether the claim is filed by such person or is filed by a governmental unit on behalf of such person, on the condition that funds received under this paragraph by a governmental unit under this title after the date of the filing of the petition shall be applied and distributed in accordance with applicable nonbankruptcy law.

(B) Subject to claims under subparagraph (A), allowed unsecured claims for domestic support obligations that, as of the date of the filing of the petition, are assigned by a spouse, former spouse, child of the debtor, or such child's parent, legal guardian, or responsible relative to a governmental unit (unless such obligation is assigned voluntarily by the spouse, former spouse, child, parent, legal guardian, or responsible relative of the child for the purpose of collecting the debt) or are owed directly to or recoverable by a governmental unit under applicable nonbankruptcy law, on the condition that funds received under this paragraph by a governmental unit under this title after the date of the filing of the petition be applied and distributed in accordance with applicable nonbankruptcy law.

(C) If a trustee is appointed or elected under section 701, 702, 703, 1104, 1202, or 1302, the administrative expenses of the trustee allowed under paragraphs (1)(A), (2), and (6) of section 503(b) shall be paid before payment of claims under subparagraphs (A) and (B), to the extent that the trustee administers assets that are otherwise available for the payment of such claims.

(2) Second, administrative expenses allowed under section 503(b) of this title, and any fees and charges assessed against the estate under chapter 123 of title 28.

(3) Third, unsecured claims allowed under section 502(f) of this title.

(4) Fourth, allowed unsecured claims, but only to the extent of $10,000 for each individual or corporation, as the case may be, earned within 180 days before the date of the filing of the petition or the date of the cessation of the debtor's business, whichever occurs first, for—

(A) wages, salaries, or commissions, including vacation, severance, and sick leave pay earned by an individual; or

(B) sales commissions earned by an individual or by a corporation with only 1 employee, acting as an independent contractor in the sale of goods or services for the debtor in the ordinary course of the debtor's business if, and only if, during the 12 months preceding that date, at least 75 percent of the amount that the individual or corporation earned by acting as an independent contractor in the sale of goods or services was earned from the debtor.

(5) Fifth, allowed unsecured claims for contributions to an employee benefit plan—

(A) arising from services rendered within 180 days before the date of the filing of the petition or the date of the cessation of the debtor's business, whichever occurs first; but only

(B) for each such plan, to the extent of—

(i) the number of employees covered by each such plan multiplied by $10,000; less

(ii) the aggregate amount paid to such employees under paragraph (4) of this subsection, plus the aggregate amount paid by the estate on behalf of such employees to any other employee benefit plan.

(6) Sixth, allowed unsecured claims of persons—

(A) engaged in the production or raising of grain, as defined in section 557(b) of this title, against a debtor who owns or operates a grain storage facility, as defined in section 557(b) of this title, for grain or the proceeds of grain, or

(B) engaged as a United States fisherman against a debtor who has acquired fish or fish produce from a fisherman through a sale or conversion, and who is engaged in operating a fish produce storage or processing facility—

but only to the extent of $4,000 for each such individual.

(7) Seventh, allowed unsecured claims of individuals, to the extent of $1,800 for each such individual, arising from the deposit, before the commencement of the case, of money in connection with the purchase, lease, or rental of property, or the purchase of services, for the personal, family, or household use of such individuals, that were not delivered or provided.

(8) Eighth, allowed unsecured claims of governmental units, only to the extent that such claims are for—

(A) a tax on or measured by income or gross receipts for a taxable year ending on or before the date of the filing of the petition—

(i) for which a return, if required, is last due, including extensions, after three years before the date of the filing of the petition;

(ii) assessed within 240 days before the date of the filing of the petition, exclusive of—

(I) any time during which an offer in compromise with respect to that tax was pending or in effect during that 240-day period, plus 30 days; and

(II) any time during which a stay of proceedings against collections was in effect in a prior case under this title during that 240-day period, plus 90 days.[1]

(iii) other than a tax of a kind specified in section 523(a)(1)(B) or 523(a)(1)(C) of this title, not assessed before, but assessable, under applicable law or by agreement, after, the commencement of the case;

(B) a property tax incurred before the commencement of the case and last payable

[1] So in original. The period probably should be "; or".

without penalty after one year before the date of the filing of the petition;

(C) a tax required to be collected or withheld and for which the debtor is liable in whatever capacity;

(D) an employment tax on a wage, salary, or commission of a kind specified in paragraph (4) of this subsection earned from the debtor before the date of the filing of the petition, whether or not actually paid before such date, for which a return is last due, under applicable law or under any extension, after three years before the date of the filing of the petition;

(E) an excise tax on—

(i) a transaction occurring before the date of the filing of the petition for which a return, if required, is last due, under applicable law or under any extension, after three years before the date of the filing of the petition; or

(ii) if a return is not required, a transaction occurring during the three years immediately preceding the date of the filing of the petition;

(F) a customs duty arising out of the importation of merchandise—

(i) entered for consumption within one year before the date of the filing of the petition;

(ii) covered by an entry liquidated or reliquidated within one year before the date of the filing of the petition; or

(iii) entered for consumption within four years before the date of the filing of the petition but unliquidated on such date, if the Secretary of the Treasury certifies that failure to liquidate such entry was due to an investigation pending on such date into assessment of antidumping or countervailing duties or fraud, or if information needed for the proper appraisement or classification of such merchandise was not available to the appropriate customs officer before such date; or

(G) a penalty related to a claim of a kind specified in this paragraph and in compensation for actual pecuniary loss.

An otherwise applicable time period specified in this paragraph shall be suspended for any period during which a governmental unit is prohibited under applicable nonbankruptcy law from collecting a tax as a result of a request by the debtor for a hearing and an appeal of any collection action taken or proposed against the debtor, plus 90 days; plus any time during which the stay of proceedings was in effect in a prior case under this title or during which collection was precluded by the existence of 1 or more confirmed plans under this title, plus 90 days.

(9) Ninth, allowed unsecured claims based upon any commitment by the debtor to a Federal depository institutions regulatory agency (or predecessor to such agency) to maintain the capital of an insured depository institution.

(10) Tenth, allowed claims for death or personal injury resulting from the operation of a motor vehicle or vessel if such operation was unlawful because the debtor was intoxicated from using alcohol, a drug, or another substance.

(b) If the trustee, under section 362, 363, or 364 of this title, provides adequate protection of the interest of a holder of a claim secured by a lien on property of the debtor and if, notwithstanding such protection, such creditor has a claim allowable under subsection (a)(2) of this section arising from the stay of action against such property under section 362 of this title, from the use, sale, or lease of such property under section 363 of this title, or from the granting of a lien under section 364(d) of this title, then such creditor's claim under such subsection shall have priority over every other claim allowable under such subsection.

(c) For the purpose of subsection (a) of this section, a claim of a governmental unit arising from an erroneous refund or credit of a tax has the same priority as a claim for the tax to which such refund or credit relates.

(d) An entity that is subrogated to the rights of a holder of a claim of a kind specified in subsection (a)(1), (a)(4), (a)(5), (a)(6), (a)(7), (a)(8), or (a)(9) of this section is not subrogated to the right of the holder of such claim to priority under such subsection.

(Pub. L. 95–598, Nov. 6, 1978, 92 Stat. 2583; Pub. L. 98–353, title III, §§350, 449, July 10, 1984, 98 Stat. 358, 374; Pub. L. 101–647, title XXV, §2522(d), Nov. 29, 1990, 104 Stat. 4867; Pub. L. 103–394, title I, §108(c), title II, §207, title III, §304(c), title V, §501(b)(3), (d)(11), Oct. 22, 1994, 108 Stat. 4112, 4123, 4132, 4142, 4145; Pub. L. 109–8, title II, §§212, 223, title VII, §§705, 706, title XIV, §1401, title XV, §1502(a)(1), Apr. 20, 2005, 119 Stat. 51, 62, 126, 214, 216.)

Historical and Revision Notes

LEGISLATIVE STATEMENTS

Section 507(a)(3) of the House amendment represents a compromise dollar amount and date for the priority between similar provisions contained in H.R. 8200 as passed by the House and the Senate amendments. A similar compromise is contained in section 507(a)(4).

Section 507(a)(5) represents a compromise on amount between the priority as contained in H.R. 8200 as passed by the House and the Senate amendment. The Senate provision for limiting the priority to consumers having less than a fixed gross income is deleted.

Section 507(a)(6) of the House amendment represents a compromise between similar provisions contained in H.R. 8200 as passed by the House and the Senate amendment.

Section 507(b) of the House amendment is new and is derived from the compromise contained in the House amendment with respect to adequate protection under section 361. Subsection (b) provides that to the extent adequate protection of the interest of a holder of a claim proves to be inadequate, then the creditor's claim is given priority over every other allowable claim entitled to distribution under section 507(a). Section 507(b) of the Senate amendment is deleted.

Section 507(c) of the House amendment is new. Section 507(d) of the House amendment prevents subrogation with respect to priority for certain priority claims. Subrogation with respect to priority is intended to be permitted for administrative claims and claims arising during the gap period.

Priorities: Under the House amendment, taxes receive priority as follows:

First. Administration expenses: The amendment generally follows the Senate amendment in providing expressly that taxes incurred during the administration of the estate share the first priority given to administrative expenses generally. Among the taxes which receives first priority, as defined in section 503, are the employees' and the employer's shares of employment taxes on wages earned and paid after the petition is filed. Section 503(b)(1) also includes in administration expenses a tax liability arising from an excessive allowance by a tax authority of a "quickie refund" to the estate. (In the case of Federal taxes, such refunds are allowed under special rules based on net operating loss carrybacks (sec. 6411 of the Internal Revenue Code [title 26]).

An exception is made to first priority treatment for taxes incurred by the estate with regard to the employer's share of employment taxes on wages earned from the debtor before the petition but paid from the estate after the petition has been filed. In this situation, the employer's tax receives either sixth priority or general claim treatment.

The House amendment also adopts the provisions of the Senate amendment which include in the definition of administrative expenses under section 503 any fine, penalty (including "additions to tax" under applicable tax laws) or reduction in credit imposed on the estate.

Second. "Involuntary gap" claims: "Involuntary gap" creditors are granted second priority by paragraph (2) of section 507(a). This priority includes tax claims arising in the ordinary course of the debtor's business or financial affairs after he has been placed involuntarily in bankruptcy but before a trustee is appointed or before the order for relief.

Third. Certain taxes on prepetition wages: Wage claims entitled to third priority are for compensation which does not exceed $2,000 and was earned during the 90 days before the filing of the bankruptcy petition or the cessation of the debtor's business. Certain employment taxes receive third priority in payment from the estate along with the payment of wages to which the taxes relate. In the case of wages earned before the filing of the petition, but paid by the trustee (rather than by the debtor) after the filing of the petition, claims or the employees' share of the employment taxes (withheld income taxes and the employees' share of the social security or railroad retirement tax) receive third priority to the extent the wage claims themselves are entitled to this priority.

In the case of wages earned from and paid by the debtor before the filing of the petition, the employer's share of the employment taxes on these wages paid by the debtor receives sixth priority or, if not entitled to that priority, are treated only as general claims. Under the House amendment, the employer's share of employment taxes on wages earned by employees of the debtor, but paid by the trustee after the filing of the bankruptcy petition, will also receive sixth priority to the extent that claims for the wages receive third priority. To the extent the claims for wages do not receive third priority, but instead are treated only as general claims, claims for the employer's share of the employment taxes attributable to those wages will also be treated as general claims. In calculating the amounts payable as general wage claims, the trustee must pay the employer's share of employment taxes on such wages.

Sixth priority. The House amendment modifies the provisions of both the House bill and Senate amendment in the case of sixth priority taxes. Under the amendment, the following Federal, State and local taxes are included in the sixth priority:

First. Income and gross receipts taxes incurred before the date of the petition for which the last due date of the return, including all extensions of time granted to file the return, occurred within 3 years before the date on which the petition was filed, or after the petition date. Under this rule, the due date of the return, rather than the date on which the taxes were assessed, determines the priority.

Second. Income and gross receipts taxes assessed at any time within 240 days before the petition date. Under this rule, the date on which the governmental unit assesses the tax, rather than the due date of the return, determines the priority.

If, following assessment of a tax, the debtor submits an offer in compromise to the governmental unit, the House amendment provides that the 240-day period is to be suspended for the duration of the offer and will resume running after the offer is withdrawn or rejected by the governmental unit, but the tax liability will receive priority if the title 11 petition is filed during the balance of the 240-day period or during a minimum of 30 days after the offer is withdrawn or rejected. This rule modifies a provision of the Senate amendment dealing specifically with offers in compromise. Under the modified rule, if, after the assessment, an offer in compromise is submitted by the debtor and is still pending (without having been accepted or rejected) at the date on which a title 11 petition is filed, the underlying liability will receive sixth priority. However, if an assessment of a tax liability is made but the tax is not collected within 240 days, the tax will not receive priority under section 507(a)(6)(A)(i) and the debtor cannot revive a priority for that tax by submitting an offer in compromise.

Third. Income and gross receipts taxes not assessed before the petition date but still permitted, under otherwise applicable tax laws, to be assessed. Thus, for example, a prepetition tax liability is to receive sixth priority under this rule if, under the applicable statute of limitations, the tax liability can still be assessed by the tax authority. This rule also covers situations referred to in section 507(a)(6)(B)(ii) of the Senate amendment where the assessment or collection of a tax was prohibited before the petition pending exhaustion of judicial or administrative remedies, except that the House amendment eliminates the 300-day limitation of the Senate bill. So, for example, if before the petition a debtor was engaged in litigation in the Tax Court, during which the Internal Revenue Code [title 26] bars the Internal Revenue Service from assessing or collecting the tax, and if the tax court decision is made in favor of the Service before the petition under title 11 is filed, thereby lifting the restrictions on assessment and collection, the tax liability will receive sixth priority even if the tax authority does not make an assessment within 300 days before the petition (provided, of course, that the statute of limitations on assessment has not expired by the petition date).

In light of the above categories of the sixth priority, and tax liability of the debtor (under the Internal Revenue Code [title 26] or State or local law) as a transferee of property from another person will receive sixth priority without the limitations contained in the Senate amendment so long as the transferee liability had not been assessed by the tax authority by the petition date but could still have been assessed by that date under the applicable tax statute of limitations or, if the transferee liability had been assessed before the petition, the assessment was made no more than 240 days before the petition date.

Also in light of the above categories, the treatment of prepetition tax liabilities arising from an excessive allowance to the debtor of a tentative carryback adjustment, such as a "quickie refund" under section 6411 of the Internal Revenue Code [title 26] is revised as follows: If the tax authority has assessed the additional tax before the petition, the tax liability will receive priority if the date of assessment was within 240 days before the petition date. If the tax authority had not assessed the additional tax by the petition, the tax liability will still receive priority so long as, on the petition date, assessment of the liability is not barred by the statute of limitations.

Fourth. Any property tax assessed before the commencement of the case and last payable without penalty within 1 year before the petition, or thereafter.

Fifth. Taxes which the debtor was required by law to withhold or collect from others and for which he is liable in any capacity, regardless of the age of the tax claims. This category covers the so-called "trust fund" taxes, that is, income taxes which an employer is required to withhold from the pay of his employees, and the employees' share of social security taxes.

In addition, this category includes the liability of a responsible officer under the Internal Revenue Code (sec. 6672) [title 26] for income taxes or for the employees' share of social security taxes which that officer was responsible for withholding from the wages of employees and paying to the Treasury, although he was not himself the employer. This priority will operate when a person found to be a responsible officer has himself filed in title 11, and the priority will cover the debtor's responsible officer liability regardless of the age of the tax year to which the tax relates. The U.S. Supreme Court has interpreted present law to require the same result as will be reached under this rule. *U.S. v. Sotelo*, 436 U.S. 268 (1978) [98 S.Ct. 1795, 56 L.Ed.2d 275, rehearing denied 98 S.Ct. 3126, 438 U.S. 907, 57 L.Ed.2d 1150].

This category also includes the liability under section 3505 of the Internal Revenue Code [26 U.S.C. 3505] of a taxpayer who loans money for the payment of wages or other compensation.

Sixth. The employer's share of employment taxes on wages paid before the petition and on third-priority wages paid postpetition by the estate. The priority rules under the House amendment governing employment taxes can thus be summarized as follows: Claims for the employees' shares of employment taxes attributable to wages both earned and paid before the filing of the petition are to receive sixth priority. In the case of employee wages earned, but not paid, before the filing of the bankruptcy petition, claims for the employees' share of employment taxes receive third priority to the extent the wages themselves receive third priority. Claims which relate to wages earned before the petition, but not paid before the petition (and which are not entitled to the third priority under the rule set out above), will be paid as general claims. Since the related wages will receive no priority, the related employment taxes would also be paid as nonpriority general claims.

The employer's share of the employment taxes on wages earned and paid before the bankruptcy petition will receive sixth priority to the extent the return for these taxes was last due (including extensions of time) within 3 years before the filing of the petition, or was due after the petition was filed. Older tax claims of this nature will be payable as general claims. In the case of wages earned by employees before the petition, but actually paid by the trustee (as claims against the estate) after the title 11 case commenced, the employer's share of the employment taxes on third priority wages will be payable as sixth priority claims and the employer's taxes on prepetition wages which are treated only as general claims will be payable only as general claims. In calculating the amounts payable as general wage claims, the trustee must pay the employer's share of employment taxes on such wages. The House amendment thus deletes the provision of the Senate amendment that certain employer taxes receive third priority and are to be paid immediately after payment of third priority wages and the employees' shares of employment taxes on those wages.

In the case of employment taxes relating to wages earned and paid after the petition, both the employees' shares and the employer's share will receive first priority as administration expenses of the estate.

Seventh. Excise taxes on transactions for which a return, if required, is last due, under otherwise applicable law or under any extension of time to file the return, within 3 years before the petition was filed, or thereafter. If a return is not required with regard to a particular excise tax, priority is given if the transaction or event itself occurred within 3 years before the date on which the title 11 petition was filed. All Federal, State or local taxes generally considered or expressly treated as excises are covered by this category, including sales taxes, estate and gift taxes, gasoline and special fuel taxes, and wagering and truck taxes.

Eighth. Certain unpaid customs duties. The House amendment covers in this category duties on imports entered for consumption within 1 year before the filing of the petition, but which are still unliquidated on the petition date; duties covered by an entry liquidated or reliquidated within 1 year before the petition date; and any duty on merchandise entered for consumption within 4 years before the petition but not liquidated on the petition date, if the Secretary of the Treasury or his delegate certifies that duties were not liquidated because of possible assessment of antidumping or countervailing duties or fraud penalties.

For purposes of the above priority rules, the House amendment adopts the provision of the Senate bill that any tax liability which, under otherwise applicable tax law, is collectible in the form of a "penalty," is to be treated in the same manner as a tax liability. In bankruptcy terminology, such tax liabilities are referred to as pecuniary loss penalties. Thus, any tax liability which under the Internal Revenue Code [title 26] or State or local tax law is payable as a "penalty," in addition to the liability of a responsible person under section 6672 of the Internal Revenue Code [26 U.S.C. 6672] will be entitled to the priority which the liability would receive if it were expressly labeled as a "tax" under the applicable tax law. However, a tax penalty which is punitive in nature is given subordinated treatment under section 726(a)(4).

The House amendment also adopts the provision of the Senate amendment that a claim arising from an erroneous refund or credit of tax, other than a "quickie refund," is to receive the same priority as the tax to which the refund or credit relates.

The House amendment deletes the express provision of the Senate amendment that a tax liability is to receive sixth priority if it satisfies any one of the subparagraphs of section 507(a)(6) even if the liability fails to satisfy the terms of one or more other subparagraphs. No change of substance is intended by the deletion, however, in light of section 102(5) of the House amendment, providing a rule of construction that the word "or" is not intended to be exclusive.

The House amendment deletes from the express priority categories of the Senate amendment the priority for a debtor's liability as a third party for failing to surrender property or to pay an obligation in response to a levy for taxes of another, and the priority for amounts provided for under deferred payment agreements between a debtor and the tax authority.

The House amendment also adopts the substance of the definition in section 346(a) the Senate amendment of when taxes are to be considered "incurred" except that the House amendment applies these definitions solely for purposes of determining which category of section 507 tests the priority of a particular tax liability. Thus, for example, the House amendment contains a special rule for the treatment of taxes under the 45-day exception to the preference rules under section 547 and the definitions of when a tax is incurred for priority purposes are not to apply to such preference rules. Under the House amendment, for purposes of the priority rules, a tax on income for a particular period is to be considered "incurred" on the last day of the period. A tax on or measured by some event, such as the payment of wages or a transfer by reason of death or gift, or an excise tax on a sale or other transaction, is to be considered "incurred" on the date of the transaction or event.

SENATE REPORT NO. 95–989

Section 507 specifies the kinds of claims that are entitled to priority in distribution, and the order of their priority. Paragraph (1) grants first priority to allowed administrative expenses and to fees and charges assessed against the estate under chapter 123 [§1911 et seq.] of title 28. Taxes included as administrative expenses under section 503(b)(1) of the bill generally receive the first priority, but the bill makes certain qualifications: Examples of these specially treated claims are the estate's liability for recapture of an investment tax credit claimed by the debtor before the title 11 case (this liability receives sixth priority) and the estate's employment tax liabilities on wages earned before, but paid after, the petition was filed (this liability generally receives the same priority as the wages).

"Involuntary gap" creditors, granted first priority under current law, are granted second priority by paragraph (2). This priority, covering claims arising in the ordinary course of the debtor's business or financial affairs after a title 11 case has begun but before a trustee is appointed or before the order for relief, includes taxes incurred during the conduct of such activities.

Paragraph (3) expands and increases the wage priority found in current section 64a(2) [section 104(a)(2) of former title 11]. The amount entitled to priority is raised from $600 to $1,800. The former figure was last adjusted in 1926. Inflation has made it nearly meaningless, and the bill brings it more than up to date. The three month limit of current law is retained, but is modified to run from the earlier of the date of the filing of the petition or the date of the cessation of the debtor's business. The priority is expanded to cover vacation, severance, and sick leave pay. The bill adds to the third priority so-called "trust fund" taxes, that is, withheld income taxes and the employees' share of the social security or railroad retirement taxes, but only to the extent that the wages on which taxes are imposed are themselves entitled to third priority.

The employer's share, the employment tax and the employer's share of the social security or railroad retirement tax on third priority compensation, is also included in the third priority category, but only if, and to the extent that the wages and related trust fund taxes have first been paid in full. Because of the claimants urgent need for their wages in the typical cases, the employer's taxes should not be paid before the wage claims entitled to priority, as well as the related trust fund taxes, are fully paid.

Paragraph (4) overrules *United States v. Embassy Restaurant*, 359 U.S. 29 (1958), which held that fringe benefits were not entitled to wage priority status. The bill recognizes the realities of labor contract negotiations, where fringe benefits may be substituted for wage demands. The priority granted is limited to claims for contributions to employee benefit plans such as pension plans, health or life insurance plans, and others, arising from services rendered within 120 days before the commencement of the case or the date of cessation of the debtor's business, whichever occurs first. The dollar limit placed on the total of all contributions payable under this paragraph is equal to the difference between the maximum allowable priority under paragraph (3), $1,800, times the number of employees covered by the plan less the actual distributions under paragraph (3) with respect to these employees.

Paragraph (5) is a new priority for consumer creditors—those who have deposited money in connection with the purchase, lease, or rental of property, or the purchase of services, for their personal, family, or household use, that were not delivered or provided. The priority amount is not to exceed $600. In order to reach only those persons most deserving of this special priority, it is limited to individuals whose adjustable gross income from all sources derived does not exceed $20,000. See Senate Hearings, testimony of Prof. Vern Countryman, at pp. 848–849. The income of the husband and wife should be aggregated for the purposes of the $20,000 limit if either or both spouses assert such a priority claim.

The sixth priority is for certain taxes. Priority is given to income taxes for a taxable year that ended on or before the date of the filing of the petition, if the last due date of the return for such year occurred not more than 3 years immediately before the date on which the petition was filed (§507(a)(6)(A)(i)). For the purposes of this rule, the last due date of the return is the last date under any extension of time to file the return which the taxing authority may have granted the debtor.

Employment taxes and transfer taxes (including gift, estate, sales, use and other excise taxes) are also given sixth priority if the transaction or event which gave rise to the tax occurred before the petition date, provided that the required return or report of such tax liabilities was last due within 3 years before the petition was filed or was last due after the petition date (§507(a)(6)(A)(ii)). The employment taxes covered under this rule are the employer's share of the social security and railroad retirement taxes and required employer payments toward unemployment insurance.

Priority is given to income taxes and other taxes of a kind described in section 507(a)(6)(A)(i) and (ii) which the Federal, State, or local tax authority had assessed within 3 years after the last due date of the return, that is, including any extension of time to file the return, if the debtor filed in title 11 within 240 days after the assessment was made (§507(a)(6)(B)(i)). This rule may bring into the sixth priority the debtor's tax liability for some taxable years which would not qualify for priority under the general three-year rule of section 507(a)(6)(A).

The sixth priority category also includes taxes which the tax authority was barred by law from assessing or collecting at any time during the 300 days before the petition under title 11 was filed (§507(a)(6)(B)(ii)). In the case of certain Federal taxes, this preserves a priority for tax liabilities for years more than three years before the filing of the petition where the debtor and the Internal Revenue Service were negotiating over an audit of the debtor's returns or were engaged in litigation in the Tax Court. In such situations, the tax law prohibits the service's right to assess a tax deficiency until ninety days after the service sends the taxpayer a deficiency letter or, if the taxpayer files a petition in the Tax Court during that 90-day period, until the outcome of the litigation. A similar priority exists in present law, except that the taxing authority is allowed no time to assess and collect the taxes after the restrictions on assessment (discussed above) are lifted. Some taxpayers have exploited this loophole by filing in bankruptcy immediately after the end of the 90-day period or immediately after the close of Tax Court proceedings. The bill remedies this defect by preserving a priority for taxes the assessment of which was barred by law by giving the tax authority 300 days within which to make the assessment after the lifting of the bar and then to collect or file public notice of its tax lien. Thus, if a taxpayer files a title 11 petition at any time during that 300-day period, the tax deficiency will be entitled to priority. If the petition is filed more than 300 days after the restriction on assessment was lifted, the taxing authority will not have priority for the tax deficiency.

Taxes for which an offer in compromise was withdrawn by the debtor, or rejected by a governmental unit, within 240 days before the petition date (§507(a)(6)(B)(iii)) will also receive sixth priority. This rule closes a loophole under present law under which, following an assessment of tax, some taxpayers have submitted a formal offer in compromise, dragged out negotiations with the taxing authority until the tax liability would lose priority under the three-year priority period of present law, and then filed in bankruptcy before the governmental unit could take collection steps.

Also included are certain taxes for which no return or report is required by law (§507(a)(6)(C)), if the taxable transaction occurred within three years before the petition was filed.

Taxes (not covered by the third priority) which the debtor was required by law to withhold or collect from others and for which he is liable in any capacity, regardless of the age of the tax claims (§507(a)(6)(D)) are included. This category covers the so-called "trust fund" taxes, that is, income taxes which an employer is required to withhold from the pay of his employees, the employees' shares of social security and railroad retirement taxes, and also Federal unemployment insurance. This category also includes excise taxes which a seller of goods or services is required to collect from a buyer and pay over to a taxing authority.

This category also covers the liability of a responsible corporate officer under the Internal Revenue Code [title 26] for income taxes or for the employees' share of employment taxes which, under the tax law, the employer was required to withhold from the wages of employees. This priority will operate where a person found to be a responsible officer has himself filed a petition under title 11, and the priority covers the debtor's liability as an officer under the Internal Revenue Code, regardless of the age of the tax year to which the tax relates.

The priority rules under the bill governing employment taxes can be summarized as follows: In the case of wages earned and actually paid before the petition under title 11 was filed, the liability for the employees' share of the employment taxes, regardless of the prepetition year in which the wages were earned and paid. The employer's share of the employment taxes on all wages earned and paid before the petition receive sixth priority; generally, these taxes will be those for which a return was due within three years before the petition. With respect to wages earned by employees before the petition but actually paid by the trustee after the title 11 case commenced, taxes required to be withheld receives the same priority as the wages themselves. Thus, the employees' share of taxes on third priority wages also receives third priority. Taxes on the balance of such wages receive no priority and are collectible only as general claims because the wages themselves are payable only as general claims and liability for the taxes arises only to the extent the wages are actually paid. The employer's share of employment taxes on third priority wages earned before the petition but paid after the petition was filed receives third priority, but only if the wages in this category have first been paid in full. Assuming there are sufficient funds to pay third priority wages and the related employer taxes in full, the employer's share of taxes on the balance of wage payments becomes a general claim (because the wages themselves are payable as general claims). Both the employees' and the employer's share of employment taxes on wages earned and paid after the petition was filed receive first priority as administrative expenses.

Also covered by this sixth priority are property taxes required to be assessed within 3 years before the filing of the petition (§507(a)(6)(E)).

Taxes attributable to a tentative carryback adjustment received by the debtor before the petition was filed, such as a "quickie refund" received under section 6411 of the Internal Revenue Code [title 26] (§507(a)(6)(F)) are included. However, the tax claim against the debtor will rein a prepetition loss year for which the tax return was last due, including extensions, within 3 years before the petition was filed.

Taxes resulting from a recapture, occasioned by a transfer during bankruptcy, of a tax credit or deduction taken during an earlier tax year (§507(a)(6)(G)) are included. A typical example occurs when there is a sale by the trustee of depreciable property during the case and depreciation deductions taken in prepetition years are subject to recapture under section 1250 of the Code [title 26].

Taxes owed by the debtor as a transferee of assets from another person who is liable for a tax, if the tax claim against the transferor would have received priority in a chapter 11 case commenced by the transferor within 1 year before the date of the petition filed by the transferee (§507(a)(6)(H)), are included.

Also included are certain tax payments required to have been made during the 1 year immediately before the petition was filed, where the debtor had previously entered into a deferred payment agreement (including an offer in compromise) to pay an agreed liability in periodic installments but had become delinquent in one or more installments before the petition was filed (§507(a)(6)(I)). This priority covers all types of deferred or part payment agreements. The priority covers only installments which first became due during the 1 year before the petition but which remained unpaid at the date of the petition. The priority does not come into play, however, if before the case began or during the case, the debtor and the taxing authority agree to a further extension of time to pay the delinquent amounts.

Certain tax-related liabilities which are not true taxes or which are not collected by regular assessment procedures (§507(a)(6)(J)) are included. One type of liability covered in this category is the liability under section 3505 of the Internal Revenue Code [title 26] of a lender who pays wages directly to employees of another employer or who supplies funds to an employer for the payment of wages. Another is the liability under section 6332 of the Internal Revenue Code [title 26], of a person who fails to turn over money or property of the taxpayer in response to a levy. Since the taxing authority must collect such a liability from the third party by suit rather than normal assessment procedures, an extra year is added to the normal 3-year priority periods. If a suit was commenced by the taxing authority within the four-year period and before the petition was filed, the priority is also preserved, provided that the suit had not terminated more than 1 year before the date of the filing of the petition.

Also included are certain unpaid customs duties which have not grown unreasonably "stale" (§507(a)(6)(K)). These include duties on imports entered for consumption with 3 years before the filing of the petition if the duties are still unliquidated on the petition date. If an import entry has been liquidated (in general, liquidation is in an administrative determination of the value and tariff rate of the item) or reliquidated, within two years of the filing of the petition the customs liability is given priority. If the Secretary of the Treasury certifies that customs duties were not liquidated because of an investigation into possible assessment of antidumping or countervailing duties, or because of fraud penalties, duties not liquidated for this reason during the five years before the importer filed under title 11 also will receive priority.

Subsection (a) of this section also provides specifically that interest on sixth priority tax claims accrued before the filing of the petition is also entitled to sixth priority.

Subsection (b) of this section provides that any fine or penalty which represents compensation for actual pecuniary loss of a governmental unit, and which involves a tax liability entitled to sixth priority, is to receive the same priority.

Subsection (b) also provides that a claim arising from an erroneous refund or credit of tax is to be given the same priority as the tax to which the refund or credit relates.

AMENDMENTS

2005—Subsec. (a)(1). Pub. L. 109–8, §212(9), added par. (1). Former par. (1) redesignated (2).

Subsec. (a)(2). Pub. L. 109–8, §212(2), (3), redesignated par. (1) as (2) and substituted "Second" for "First". Former par. (2) redesignated (3).

Subsec. (a)(3). Pub. L. 109–8, §212(2), (4), redesignated par. (2) as (3) and substituted "Third" for "Second". Former par. (3) redesignated (4).

Subsec. (a)(4). Pub. L. 109–8, §1401, which directed amendment of par. (4), "as amended by section 212", by substituting "$10,000" for "$4,000" and "180" for "90" in introductory provisions, effective Apr. 20, 2005, was executed to this par., which was par. (3), to reflect the probable intent of Congress, notwithstanding that the redesignation of this par. as (4) by Pub. L. 109–8, §212(2), was effective 180 days after Apr. 20, 2005. See Effective Date of 2005 Amendment notes below.

Pub. L. 109–8, §212(2), (5), redesignated par. (3) as (4) and substituted "Fourth" for "Third" in introductory provisions and a period for semicolon at end. Former par. (4) redesignated (5).

Subsec. (a)(5). Pub. L. 109–8, §212(2), (6), redesignated par. (4) as (5) and substituted "Fifth" for "Fourth" in introductory provisions. Former par. (5) redesignated (6).

Subsec. (a)(5)(B)(i). Pub. L. 109–8, §1401(2), which directed amendment of par. (5), "as amended by section 212", by substituting "$10,000" for "$4,000", effective

Apr. 20, 2005, was executed to this par., which was par. (4), to reflect the probable intent of Congress, notwithstanding that the redesignation of this par. as (5) by Pub. L. 109–8, §212(2), was effective 180 days after Apr. 20, 2005. See Effective Date of 2005 Amendment notes below.

Subsec. (a)(5)(B)(ii). Pub. L. 109–8, §1502(a)(1)(A)(i), substituted "paragraph (4)" for "paragraph (3)".

Subsec. (a)(6). Pub. L. 109–8, §212(2), (7), redesignated par. (5) as (6) and substituted "Sixth" for "Fifth" in introductory provisions. Former par. (6) redesignated (7).

Subsec. (a)(7). Pub. L. 109–8, §212(1), (2), (8), redesignated par. (6) as (7), substituted "Seventh" for "Sixth", and struck out former par. (7) which read as follows: "Seventh, allowed claims for debts to a spouse, former spouse, or child of the debtor, for alimony to, maintenance for, or support of such spouse or child, in connection with a separation agreement, divorce decree or other order of a court of record, determination made in accordance with State or territorial law by a governmental unit, or property settlement agreement, but not to the extent that such debt—

"(A) is assigned to another entity, voluntarily, by operation of law, or otherwise; or

"(B) includes a liability designated as alimony, maintenance, or support, unless such liability is actually in the nature of alimony, maintenance or support."

Subsec. (a)(8). Pub. L. 109–8, §705(2), inserted at end "An otherwise applicable time period specified in this paragraph shall be suspended for any period during which a governmental unit is prohibited under applicable nonbankruptcy law from collecting a tax as a result of a request by the debtor for a hearing and an appeal of any collection action taken or proposed against the debtor, plus 90 days; plus any time during which the stay of proceedings was in effect in a prior case under this title or during which collection was precluded by the existence of 1 or more confirmed plans under this title, plus 90 days."

Subsec. (a)(8)(A). Pub. L. 109–8, §705(1)(A), inserted "for a taxable year ending on or before the date of the filing of the petition" after "gross receipts" in introductory provisions.

Subsec. (a)(8)(A)(i). Pub. L. 109–8, §705(1)(B), struck out "for a taxable year ending on or before the date of the filing of the petition" before "for which a return".

Subsec. (a)(8)(A)(ii). Pub. L. 109–8, §705(1)(C), added cl. (ii) and struck out former cl. (ii) which read as follows: "assessed within 240 days, plus any time plus 30 days during which an offer in compromise with respect to such tax that was made within 240 days after such assessment was pending, before the date of the filing of the petition; or".

Subsec. (a)(8)(B). Pub. L. 109–8, §706, substituted "incurred" for "assessed".

Subsec. (a)(8)(D). Pub. L. 109–8, §1502(a)(1)(A)(ii), substituted "paragraph (4)" for "paragraph (3)".

Subsec. (a)(10). Pub. L. 109–8, §223, added par. (10).

Subsec. (b). Pub. L. 109–8, §1502(a)(1)(B), substituted "subsection (a)(2)" for "subsection (a)(1)".

Subsec. (d). Pub. L. 109–8, §1502(a)(1)(C), substituted "subsection (a)(1)" for "subsection (a)(3)".

1994—Subsec. (a)(3). Pub. L. 103–394, §207, amended par. (3) generally. Prior to amendment, par. (3) read as follows: "Third, allowed unsecured claims for wages, salaries, or commissions, including vacation, severance, and sick leave pay—

"(A) earned by an individual within 90 days before the date of the filing of the petition or the date of the cessation of the debtor's business, whichever occurs first, but only

"(B) to the extent of $2,000 for each such individual."

Subsec. (a)(4)(B)(i). Pub. L. 103–394, §108(c)(1), substituted "$4,000" for "$2,000".

Subsec. (a)(5). Pub. L. 103–394, §§108(c)(2), 501(b)(3), substituted "section 557(b)" for "section 557(b)(1)" after "grain, as defined in" and "section 557(b)" for "section 557(b)(2)" after "facility, as defined in" in subpar. (A) and "$4,000" for "$2,000" in concluding provisions.

Subsec. (a)(6). Pub. L. 103–394, §108(c)(3), substituted "$1,800" for "$900".

Subsec. (a)(7). Pub. L. 103–394, §304(c)(3), added par. (7). Former par. (7) redesignated (8).

Subsec. (a)(8). Pub. L. 103–394, §304(c)(2), redesignated par. (7) as (8) and substituted "Eighth" for "Seventh". Former par. (8) redesignated (9).

Subsec. (a)(9). Pub. L. 103–394, §§304(c)(1), 501(d)(11)(A), redesignated par. (8) as (9) and substituted "Ninth" for "Eighth" and "a Federal depository institutions regulatory agency (or predecessor to such agency)" for "the Federal Deposit Insurance Corporation, the Resolution Trust Corporation, the Director of the Office of Thrift Supervision, the Comptroller of the Currency, or the Board of Governors of the Federal Reserve System, or their predecessors or successors,".

Subsec. (d). Pub. L. 103–394, §501(d)(11)(B), substituted "(a)(6), (a)(7), (a)(8), or (a)(9)" for "or (a)(6)".

1990—Subsec. (a)(8). Pub. L. 101–647 added par. (8).

1984—Subsec. (a)(3). Pub. L. 98–353, §449(a)(1), inserted a comma after "severance".

Subsec. (a)(4). Pub. L. 98–353, §449(a)(2), substituted "an employee benefit plan" for "employee benefit plans" in provisions preceding subpar. (A).

Subsec. (a)(4)(B)(i). Pub. L. 98–353, §449(a)(3), inserted "each" after "covered by".

Subsec. (a)(5). Pub. L. 98–353, §350(3), added par. (5). Former par. (5) redesignated (6).

Subsec. (a)(6). Pub. L. 98–353, §350(1), redesignated former par. (5) as (6) and substituted "Sixth" for "Fifth". Former par. (6) redesignated (7).

Subsec. (a)(7). Pub. L. 98–353, §§350(2), 449(a)(4), redesignated former par. (6) as (7), substituted "Seventh" for "Sixth", and inserted "only" after "units,".

Subsec. (c). Pub. L. 98–353, §449(b), substituted "has the same priority" for "shall be treated the same".

Effective Date of 2005 Amendment

Pub. L. 109–8, title XIV, §1406, Apr. 20, 2005, 119 Stat. 215, provided that:

"(a) Effective Date.—Except as provided in subsection (b), this title [amending this section and sections 523, 548, 1104, and 1114 of this title and enacting provisions set out as a note under section 523 of this title] and the amendments made by this title shall take effect on the date of the enactment of this Act [Apr. 20, 2005].

"(b) Application of Amendments.—

"(1) In general.—[Ex]cept as provided in paragraph (2), the amendments made by this title shall apply only with respect to cases commenced under title 11 of the United States Code on or after the date of the enactment of this Act [Apr. 20, 2005].

"(2) Avoidance period.—The amendment made by section 1402(1) [amending section 548 of this title] shall apply only with respect to cases commenced under title 11 of the United States Code more than 1 year after the date of the enactment of this Act."

Amendment by sections 212, 223, 705, 706, and 1502(a)(1) of Pub. L. 109–8 effective 180 days after Apr. 20, 2005, and not applicable with respect to cases commenced under this title before such effective date, except as otherwise provided, see section 1501 of Pub. L. 109–8, set out as a note under section 101 of this title.

Effective Date of 1994 Amendment

Amendment by Pub. L. 103–394 effective Oct. 22, 1994, and not applicable with respect to cases commenced under this title before Oct. 22, 1994, see section 702 of Pub. L. 103–394, set out as a note under section 101 of this title.

Effective Date of 1984 Amendment

Amendment by Pub. L. 98–353 effective with respect to cases filed 90 days after July 10, 1984, see section 552(a) of Pub. L. 98–353, set out as a note under section 101 of this title.

Adjustment of Dollar Amounts

For adjustment of dollar amounts specified in subsec. (a)(4) to (7) of this section by the Judicial Conference of the United States, see note set out under section 104 of this title.

§ 508. Effect of distribution other than under this title

If a creditor of a partnership debtor receives, from a general partner that is not a debtor in a case under chapter 7 of this title, payment of, or a transfer of property on account of, a claim that is allowed under this title and that is not secured by a lien on property of such partner, such creditor may not receive any payment under this title on account of such claim until each of the other holders of claims on account of which such holders are entitled to share equally with such creditor under this title has received payment under this title equal in value to the consideration received by such creditor from such general partner.

(Pub. L. 95–598, Nov. 6, 1978, 92 Stat. 2585; Pub. L. 109–8, title VIII, § 802(d)(7), Apr. 20, 2005, 119 Stat. 146.)

HISTORICAL AND REVISION NOTES

LEGISLATIVE STATEMENTS

Section 508(b) of the House amendment is new and provides an identical rule with respect to a creditor of a partnership who receives payment from a partner, to that of a creditor of a debtor who receives a payment in a foreign proceeding involving the debtor.

SENATE REPORT NO. 95–989

This section prohibits a creditor from receiving any distribution in the bankruptcy case if he has received payment of a portion of his claim in a foreign proceeding, until the other creditors in the bankruptcy case in this country that are entitled to share equally with that creditor have received as much as he has in the foreign proceeding.

AMENDMENTS

2005—Pub. L. 109–8 designated subsec. (b) as entire section and struck out subsec. (a) which read as follows: "If a creditor receives, in a foreign proceeding, payment of, or a transfer of property on account of, a claim that is allowed under this title, such creditor may not receive any payment under this title on account of such claim until each of the other holders of claims on account of which such holders are entitled to share equally with such creditor under this title has received payment under this title equal in value to the consideration received by such creditor in such foreign proceeding."

EFFECTIVE DATE OF 2005 AMENDMENT

Amendment by Pub. L. 109–8 effective 180 days after Apr. 20, 2005, and not applicable with respect to cases commenced under this title before such effective date, except as otherwise provided, see section 1501 of Pub. L. 109–8, set out as a note under section 101 of this title.

§ 509. Claims of codebtors

(a) Except as provided in subsection (b) or (c) of this section, an entity that is liable with the debtor on, or that has secured, a claim of a creditor against the debtor, and that pays such claim, is subrogated to the rights of such creditor to the extent of such payment.

(b) Such entity is not subrogated to the rights of such creditor to the extent that—

(1) a claim of such entity for reimbursement or contribution on account of such payment of such creditor's claim is—

(A) allowed under section 502 of this title;

(B) disallowed other than under section 502(e) of this title; or

(C) subordinated under section 510 of this title; or

(2) as between the debtor and such entity, such entity received the consideration for the claim held by such creditor.

(c) The court shall subordinate to the claim of a creditor and for the benefit of such creditor an allowed claim, by way of subrogation under this section, or for reimbursement or contribution, of an entity that is liable with the debtor on, or that has secured, such creditor's claim, until such creditor's claim is paid in full, either through payments under this title or otherwise.

(Pub. L. 95–598, Nov. 6, 1978, 92 Stat. 2585; Pub. L. 98–353, title III, § 450, July 10, 1984, 98 Stat. 375.)

HISTORICAL AND REVISION NOTES

LEGISLATIVE STATEMENTS

Section 509 of the House amendment represents a substantial revision of provisions contained in H.R. 8200 as passed by the House and in the Senate amendment. Section 509(a) states a general rule that a surety or codebtor is subrogated to the rights of a creditor assured by the surety or co-debtor to the extent the surety or co-debtor pays such creditor. Section 509(b) states a general exception indicating that subrogation is not granted to the extent that a claim of a surety or codebtor for reimbursement or contribution is allowed under section 502 or disallowed other than under section 502(e). Additionally, section 509(b)(1)(C) provides that such claims for subrogation are subordinated to the extent that a claim of the surety or co-debtor for reimbursement or contribution is subordinated under section 510(a)(1) or 510(b). Section 509(b)(2) reiterates the well-known rule that prevents a debtor that is ultimately liable on the debt from recovering from a surety or a co-debtor. Although the language in section 509(b)(2) focuses in terms of receipt of consideration, legislative history appearing elsewhere indicates that an agreement to share liabilities should prevail over an agreement to share profits throughout title 11. This is particularly important in the context of co-debtors who are partners. Section 509(c) subordinates the claim of a surety or co-debtor to the claim of an assured creditor until the creditor's claim is paid in full.

SENATE REPORT NO. 95–989

Section 509 deals with codebtors generally, and is in addition to the disallowance provision in section 502(e). This section is based on the notion that the only rights available to a surety, guarantor, or comaker are contribution, reimbursement, and subrogation. The right that applies in a particular situation will depend on the agreement between the debtor and the codebtor, and on whether and how payment was made by the codebtor to the creditor. The claim of a surety or codebtor for contribution or reimbursement is discharged even if the claim is never filed, as is any claim for subrogation even if the surety or codebtor chooses to file a claim for contribution or reimbursement instead.

Subsection (a) subrogates the codebtor (whether as a codebtor, surety, or guarantor) to the rights of the creditor, to the extent of any payment made by the codebtor to the creditor. Whether the creditor's claim was filed under section 501(a) or 501(b) is irrelevant. The right of subrogation will exist even if the primary creditor's claim is allowed by virtue of being listed under proposed 11 U.S.C. 924 or 1111, and not by reason of a proof of claim.

Subsection (b) permits a subrogated codebtor to receive payments in the bankruptcy case only if the creditor has been paid in full, either through payments under the bankruptcy code or otherwise.

AMENDMENTS

1984—Subsec. (a). Pub. L. 98-353, §450(a), substituted "subsection (b) or" for "subsections (b) and", and inserted "against the debtor" after "a creditor".

Subsec. (b)(1). Pub. L. 98-353, §450(b), substituted "of such" for "of a" after "account".

Subsec. (c). Pub. L. 98-353, §450(c), substituted "this section" for "section 509 of this title".

EFFECTIVE DATE OF 1984 AMENDMENT

Amendment by Pub. L. 98-353 effective with respect to cases filed 90 days after July 10, 1984, see section 552(a) of Pub. L. 98-353, set out as a note under section 101 of this title.

§ 510. Subordination

(a) A subordination agreement is enforceable in a case under this title to the same extent that such agreement is enforceable under applicable nonbankruptcy law.

(b) For the purpose of distribution under this title, a claim arising from rescission of a purchase or sale of a security of the debtor or of an affiliate of the debtor, for damages arising from the purchase or sale of such a security, or for reimbursement or contribution allowed under section 502 on account of such a claim, shall be subordinated to all claims or interests that are senior to or equal the claim or interest represented by such security, except that if such security is common stock, such claim has the same priority as common stock.

(c) Notwithstanding subsections (a) and (b) of this section, after notice and a hearing, the court may—

(1) under principles of equitable subordination, subordinate for purposes of distribution all or part of an allowed claim to all or part of another allowed claim or all or part of an allowed interest to all or part of another allowed interest; or

(2) order that any lien securing such a subordinated claim be transferred to the estate.

(Pub. L. 95-598, Nov. 6, 1978, 92 Stat. 2586; Pub. L. 98-353, title III, §451, July 10, 1984, 98 Stat. 375.)

HISTORICAL AND REVISION NOTES

LEGISLATIVE STATEMENTS

Section 510(c)(1) of the House amendment represents a compromise between similar provisions in the House bill and Senate amendment. After notice and a hearing, the court may, under principles of equitable subordination, subordinate for purposes of distribution all or part of an allowed claim to all or part of another allowed claim or all or part of an allowed interest to all or part of another allowed interest. As a matter of equity, it is reasonable that a court subordinate claims to claims and interests to interests. It is intended that the term "principles of equitable subordination" follow existing case law and leave to the courts development of this principle. To date, under existing law, a claim is generally subordinated only if holder of such claim is guilty of inequitable conduct, or the claim itself is of a status susceptible to subordination, such as a penalty or a claim for damages arising from the purchase or sale of a security of the debtor. The fact that such a claim may be secured is of no consequence to the issue of subordination. However, it is inconceivable that the status of a claim as a secured claim could ever be grounds for justifying equitable subordination.

Subordination: Since the House amendment authorizes subordination of claims only under principles of equitable subordination, and thus incorporates principles of existing case law, a tax claim would rarely be subordinated under this provision of the bill.

Section 511 of the Senate amendment is deleted. Its substance is adopted in section 502(b)(9) of the House amendment which reflects an identical provision contained in H.R. 8200 as passed by the House.

SENATE REPORT NO. 95-989

Subsection (a) requires the court to enforce subordination agreements. A subordination agreement will not be enforced, however, in a reorganization case in which the class that is the beneficiary of the agreement has accepted, as specified in proposed 11 U.S.C. 1126, a plan that waives their rights under the agreement. Otherwise, the agreement would prevent just what chapter 11 contemplates: that seniors may give up rights to juniors in the interest of confirmation of a plan and rehabilitation of the debtor. The subsection also requires the court to subordinate in payment any claim for rescission of a purchase or sale of a security of the debtor or of an affiliate, or for damages arising from the purchase or sale of such a security, to all claims and interests that are senior to the claim or interest represented by the security. Thus, the later subordination varies with the claim or interest involved. If the security is a debt instrument, the damages or rescission claim will be granted the status of a general unsecured claim. If the security is an equity security, the damages or rescission claim is subordinated to all creditors and treated the same as the equity security itself.

Subsection (b) authorizes the bankruptcy court, in ordering distribution of assets, to subordinate all or any part of any claim to all or any part of another claim, regardless of the priority ranking of either claim. In addition, any lien securing such a subordinated claim may be transferred to the estate. The bill provides, however, that any subordination ordered under this provision must be based on principles of equitable subordination. These principles are defined by case law, and have generally indicated that a claim may normally be subordinated only if its holder is guilty of misconduct. As originally introduced, the bill provided specifically that a tax claim may not be subordinated on equitable grounds. The bill deletes this express exception, but the effect under the amendment should be much the same in most situations since, under the judicial doctrine of equitable subordination, a tax claim would rarely be subordinated.

AMENDMENTS

1984—Subsec. (b). Pub. L. 98-353 amended subsec. (b) generally. Prior to amendment, subsec. (b) read as follows: "Any claim for recission of a purchase or sale of a security of the debtor or of an affiliate or for damages arising from the purchase or sale of such a security shall be subordinated for purposes of distribution to all claims and interests that are senior or equal to the claim or interest represented by such security."

EFFECTIVE DATE OF 1984 AMENDMENT

Amendment by Pub. L. 98-353 effective with respect to cases filed 90 days after July 10, 1984, see section 552(a) of Pub. L. 98-353, set out as a note under section 101 of this title.

§ 511. Rate of interest on tax claims

(a) If any provision of this title requires the payment of interest on a tax claim or on an administrative expense tax, or the payment of interest to enable a creditor to receive the present value of the allowed amount of a tax claim, the rate of interest shall be the rate determined under applicable nonbankruptcy law.

(b) In the case of taxes paid under a confirmed plan under this title, the rate of interest shall be determined as of the calendar month in which the plan is confirmed.

(Added Pub. L. 109–8, title VII, §704(a), Apr. 20, 2005, 119 Stat. 125.)

EFFECTIVE DATE

Section effective 180 days after Apr. 20, 2005, and not applicable with respect to cases commenced under this title before such effective date, except as otherwise provided, see section 1501 of Pub. L. 109–8, set out as an Effective Date of 2005 Amendment note under section 101 of this title.

SUBCHAPTER II—DEBTOR'S DUTIES AND BENEFITS

§ 521. Debtor's duties

(a) The debtor shall—

(1) file—

(A) a list of creditors; and

(B) unless the court orders otherwise—

(i) a schedule of assets and liabilities;

(ii) a schedule of current income and current expenditures;

(iii) a statement of the debtor's financial affairs and, if section 342(b) applies, a certificate—

(I) of an attorney whose name is indicated on the petition as the attorney for the debtor, or a bankruptcy petition preparer signing the petition under section 110(b)(1), indicating that such attorney or the bankruptcy petition preparer delivered to the debtor the notice required by section 342(b); or

(II) if no attorney is so indicated, and no bankruptcy petition preparer signed the petition, of the debtor that such notice was received and read by the debtor;

(iv) copies of all payment advices or other evidence of payment received within 60 days before the date of the filing of the petition, by the debtor from any employer of the debtor;

(v) a statement of the amount of monthly net income, itemized to show how the amount is calculated; and

(vi) a statement disclosing any reasonably anticipated increase in income or expenditures over the 12-month period following the date of the filing of the petition;

(2) if an individual debtor's schedule of assets and liabilities includes debts which are secured by property of the estate—

(A) within thirty days after the date of the filing of a petition under chapter 7 of this title or on or before the date of the meeting of creditors, whichever is earlier, or within such additional time as the court, for cause, within such period fixes, the debtor shall file with the clerk a statement of his intention with respect to the retention or surrender of such property and, if applicable, specifying that such property is claimed as exempt, that the debtor intends to redeem such property, or that the debtor intends to reaffirm debts secured by such property;

(B) within 30 days after the first date set for the meeting of creditors under section 341(a), or within such additional time as the court, for cause, within such 30-day period fixes, the debtor shall perform his intention with respect to such property, as specified by subparagraph (A) of this paragraph; and

(C) nothing in subparagraphs (A) and (B) of this paragraph shall alter the debtor's or the trustee's rights with regard to such property under this title, except as provided in section 362(h);

(3) if a trustee is serving in the case or an auditor serving under section 586(f) of title 28, cooperate with the trustee as necessary to enable the trustee to perform the trustee's duties under this title;

(4) if a trustee is serving in the case or an auditor serving under section 586(f) of title 28, surrender to the trustee all property of the estate and any recorded information, including books, documents, records, and papers, relating to property of the estate, whether or not immunity is granted under section 344 of this title;

(5) appear at the hearing required under section 524(d) of this title;

(6) in a case under chapter 7 of this title in which the debtor is an individual, not retain possession of personal property as to which a creditor has an allowed claim for the purchase price secured in whole or in part by an interest in such personal property unless the debtor, not later than 45 days after the first meeting of creditors under section 341(a), either—

(A) enters into an agreement with the creditor pursuant to section 524(c) with respect to the claim secured by such property; or

(B) redeems such property from the security interest pursuant to section 722; and

(7) unless a trustee is serving in the case, continue to perform the obligations required of the administrator (as defined in section 3 of the Employee Retirement Income Security Act of 1974) of an employee benefit plan if at the time of the commencement of the case the debtor (or any entity designated by the debtor) served as such administrator.

If the debtor fails to so act within the 45-day period referred to in paragraph (6), the stay under section 362(a) is terminated with respect to the personal property of the estate or of the debtor which is affected, such property shall no longer be property of the estate, and the creditor may take whatever action as to such property as is permitted by applicable nonbankruptcy law, unless the court determines on the motion of the trustee filed before the expiration of such 45-day period, and after notice and a hearing, that such property is of consequential value or benefit to the estate, orders appropriate adequate protection of the creditor's interest, and orders the debtor to deliver any collateral in the debtor's possession to the trustee.

(b) In addition to the requirements under subsection (a), a debtor who is an individual shall file with the court—

(1) a certificate from the approved nonprofit budget and credit counseling agency that provided the debtor services under section 109(h) describing the services provided to the debtor; and

(2) a copy of the debt repayment plan, if any, developed under section 109(h) through the ap-

proved nonprofit budget and credit counseling agency referred to in paragraph (1).

(c) In addition to meeting the requirements under subsection (a), a debtor shall file with the court a record of any interest that a debtor has in an education individual retirement account (as defined in section 530(b)(1) of the Internal Revenue Code of 1986) or under a qualified State tuition program (as defined in section 529(b)(1) of such Code).

(d) If the debtor fails timely to take the action specified in subsection (a)(6) of this section, or in paragraphs (1) and (2) of section 362(h), with respect to property which a lessor or bailor owns and has leased, rented, or bailed to the debtor or as to which a creditor holds a security interest not otherwise voidable under section 522(f), 544, 545, 547, 548, or 549, nothing in this title shall prevent or limit the operation of a provision in the underlying lease or agreement that has the effect of placing the debtor in default under such lease or agreement by reason of the occurrence, pendency, or existence of a proceeding under this title or the insolvency of the debtor. Nothing in this subsection shall be deemed to justify limiting such a provision in any other circumstance.

(e)(1) If the debtor in a case under chapter 7 or 13 is an individual and if a creditor files with the court at any time a request to receive a copy of the petition, schedules, and statement of financial affairs filed by the debtor, then the court shall make such petition, such schedules, and such statement available to such creditor.

(2)(A) The debtor shall provide—

(i) not later than 7 days before the date first set for the first meeting of creditors, to the trustee a copy of the Federal income tax return required under applicable law (or at the election of the debtor, a transcript of such return) for the most recent tax year ending immediately before the commencement of the case and for which a Federal income tax return was filed; and

(ii) at the same time the debtor complies with clause (i), a copy of such return (or if elected under clause (i), such transcript) to any creditor that timely requests such copy.

(B) If the debtor fails to comply with clause (i) or (ii) of subparagraph (A), the court shall dismiss the case unless the debtor demonstrates that the failure to so comply is due to circumstances beyond the control of the debtor.

(C) If a creditor requests a copy of such tax return or such transcript and if the debtor fails to provide a copy of such tax return or such transcript to such creditor at the time the debtor provides such tax return or such transcript to the trustee, then the court shall dismiss the case unless the debtor demonstrates that the failure to provide a copy of such tax return or such transcript is due to circumstances beyond the control of the debtor.

(3) If a creditor in a case under chapter 13 files with the court at any time a request to receive a copy of the plan filed by the debtor, then the court shall make available to such creditor a copy of the plan—

(A) at a reasonable cost; and

(B) not later than 7 days after such request is filed.

(f) At the request of the court, the United States trustee, or any party in interest in a case under chapter 7, 11, or 13, a debtor who is an individual shall file with the court—

(1) at the same time filed with the taxing authority, a copy of each Federal income tax return required under applicable law (or at the election of the debtor, a transcript of such tax return) with respect to each tax year of the debtor ending while the case is pending under such chapter;

(2) at the same time filed with the taxing authority, each Federal income tax return required under applicable law (or at the election of the debtor, a transcript of such tax return) that had not been filed with such authority as of the date of the commencement of the case and that was subsequently filed for any tax year of the debtor ending in the 3-year period ending on the date of the commencement of the case;

(3) a copy of each amendment to any Federal income tax return or transcript filed with the court under paragraph (1) or (2); and

(4) in a case under chapter 13—

(A) on the date that is either 90 days after the end of such tax year or 1 year after the date of the commencement of the case, whichever is later, if a plan is not confirmed before such later date; and

(B) annually after the plan is confirmed and until the case is closed, not later than the date that is 45 days before the anniversary of the confirmation of the plan;

a statement, under penalty of perjury, of the income and expenditures of the debtor during the tax year of the debtor most recently concluded before such statement is filed under this paragraph, and of the monthly income of the debtor, that shows how income, expenditures, and monthly income are calculated.

(g)(1) A statement referred to in subsection (f)(4) shall disclose—

(A) the amount and sources of the income of the debtor;

(B) the identity of any person responsible with the debtor for the support of any dependent of the debtor; and

(C) the identity of any person who contributed, and the amount contributed, to the household in which the debtor resides.

(2) The tax returns, amendments, and statement of income and expenditures described in subsections (e)(2)(A) and (f) shall be available to the United States trustee (or the bankruptcy administrator, if any), the trustee, and any party in interest for inspection and copying, subject to the requirements of section 315(c) of the Bankruptcy Abuse Prevention and Consumer Protection Act of 2005.

(h) If requested by the United States trustee or by the trustee, the debtor shall provide—

(1) a document that establishes the identity of the debtor, including a driver's license, passport, or other document that contains a photograph of the debtor; or

(2) such other personal identifying information relating to the debtor that establishes the identity of the debtor.

(i)(1) Subject to paragraphs (2) and (4) and notwithstanding section 707(a), if an individual debtor in a voluntary case under chapter 7 or 13 fails to file all of the information required under subsection (a)(1) within 45 days after the date of the filing of the petition, the case shall be automatically dismissed effective on the 46th day after the date of the filing of the petition.

(2) Subject to paragraph (4) and with respect to a case described in paragraph (1), any party in interest may request the court to enter an order dismissing the case. If requested, the court shall enter an order of dismissal not later than 7 days after such request.

(3) Subject to paragraph (4) and upon request of the debtor made within 45 days after the date of the filing of the petition described in paragraph (1), the court may allow the debtor an additional period of not to exceed 45 days to file the information required under subsection (a)(1) if the court finds justification for extending the period for the filing.

(4) Notwithstanding any other provision of this subsection, on the motion of the trustee filed before the expiration of the applicable period of time specified in paragraph (1), (2), or (3), and after notice and a hearing, the court may decline to dismiss the case if the court finds that the debtor attempted in good faith to file all the information required by subsection (a)(1)(B)(iv) and that the best interests of creditors would be served by administration of the case.

(j)(1) Notwithstanding any other provision of this title, if the debtor fails to file a tax return that becomes due after the commencement of the case or to properly obtain an extension of the due date for filing such return, the taxing authority may request that the court enter an order converting or dismissing the case.

(2) If the debtor does not file the required return or obtain the extension referred to in paragraph (1) within 90 days after a request is filed by the taxing authority under that paragraph, the court shall convert or dismiss the case, whichever is in the best interests of creditors and the estate.

(Pub. L. 95–598, Nov. 6, 1978, 92 Stat. 2586; Pub. L. 98–353, title III, §§305, 452, July 10, 1984, 98 Stat. 352, 375; Pub. L. 99–554, title II, §283(h), Oct. 27, 1986, 100 Stat. 3117; Pub. L. 109–8, title I, §106(d), title II, §225(b), title III, §§304(1), 305(2), 315(b), 316, title IV, §446(a), title VI, §603(c), title VII, §720, Apr. 20, 2005, 119 Stat. 38, 66, 78, 80, 89, 92, 118, 123, 133; Pub. L. 111–16, §2(5), (6), May 7, 2009, 123 Stat. 1607.)

Historical and Revision Notes

Legislative Statements

Section 521 of the House amendment modifies a comparable provision contained in the House bill and Senate amendment. The Rules of Bankruptcy Procedure should provide where the list of creditors is to be filed. In addition, the debtor is required to attend the hearing on discharge under section 524(d).

Senate Report No. 95–989

This section lists three duties of the debtor in a bankruptcy case. The Rules of Bankruptcy Procedure will specify the means of carrying out these duties. The first duty is to file with the court a list of creditors and, unless the court orders otherwise, a schedule of assets and liabilities and a statement of his financial affairs. Second, the debtor is required to cooperate with the trustee as necessary to enable the trustee to perform the trustee's duties. Finally, the debtor must surrender to the trustee all property of the estate, and any recorded information, including books, documents, records, and papers, relating to property of the estate. This phrase "recorded information, including books, documents, records, and papers," has been used here and throughout the bill as a more general term, and includes such other forms of recorded information as data in computer storage or in other machine readable forms.

The list in this section is not exhaustive of the debtor's duties. Others are listed elsewhere in proposed title 11, such as in section 343, which requires the debtor to submit to examination, or in the Rules of Bankruptcy Procedure, as continued by §404(a) of S. 2266, such as the duty to attend any hearing on discharge, Rule 402(2).

References in Text

Section 3 of the Employee Retirement Income Security Act of 1974, referred to in subsec. (a)(7), is classified to section 1002 of Title 29, Labor.

Sections 530(b)(1) and 529(b)(1) of the Internal Revenue Code of 1986, referred to in subsec. (c), are classified to sections 530(b)(1) and 529(b)(1), respectively, of Title 26, Internal Revenue Code.

Section 315(c) of the Bankruptcy Abuse Prevention and Consumer Protection Act of 2005, referred to in subsec. (g)(2), is section 315(c) of Pub. L. 109–8, which is set out as a note under this section.

Amendments

2009—Subsec. (e)(3)(B). Pub. L. 111–16, §2(5), substituted "7 days" for "5 days".

Subsec. (i)(2). Pub. L. 111–16, §2(6), substituted "7 days" for "5 days".

2005—Pub. L. 109–8, §106(d)(1), designated existing provisions as subsec. (a).

Subsec. (a). Pub. L. 109–8, §304(1), added concluding provisions.

Subsec. (a)(1). Pub. L. 109–8, §315(b)(1), amended par. (1) generally. Prior to amendment, par. (1) read as follows: "file a list of creditors, and unless the court orders otherwise, a schedule of assets and liabilities, a schedule of current income and current expenditures, and a statement of the debtor's financial affairs;".

Subsec. (a)(2). Pub. L. 109–8, §305(2)(A), struck out "consumer" before "debts" in introductory provisions.

Subsec. (a)(2)(B). Pub. L. 109–8, §305(2)(B), substituted "30 days after the first date set for the meeting of creditors under section 341(a)" for "forty-five days after the filing of a notice of intent under this section" and "30-day" for "forty-five day".

Subsec. (a)(2)(C). Pub. L. 109–8, §305(2)(C), inserted ", except as provided in section 362(h)" before semicolon.

Subsec. (a)(3), (4). Pub. L. 109–8, §603(c), inserted "or an auditor serving under section 586(f) of title 28" after "serving in the case".

Subsec. (a)(6). Pub. L. 109–8, §304(1), added par. (6).

Subsec. (a)(7). Pub. L. 109–8, §446(a), added par. (7).

Subsec. (b). Pub. L. 109–8, §106(d)(2), added subsec. (b).

Subsec. (c). Pub. L. 109–8, §225(b), added subsec. (c).

Subsec. (d). Pub. L. 109–8, §305(2)(D), added subsec. (d).

Subsecs. (e) to (h). Pub. L. 109–8, §315(b)(2), added subsecs. (e) to (h).

Subsec. (i). Pub. L. 109–8, §316, added subsec. (i).

Subsec. (j). Pub. L. 109–8, §720, added subsec. (j).

1986—Par. (4). Pub. L. 99–554 inserted ", whether or not immunity is granted under section 344 of this title" after second reference to "estate".

1984—Par. (1). Pub. L. 98–353, §305(2), inserted "a schedule of current income and current expenditures," after "liabilities,".

Pars. (2) to (5). Pub. L. 98–353, §305(1), (3), added par. (2), redesignated former pars. (2) to (4) as (3) to (5), respectively.

Pub. L. 98–353, §452, which directed the insertion of ", whether or not immunity is granted under section 344 of this title" after second reference to "estate" in par. (3) as redesignated above, could not be executed because such reference appeared in par. (4) rather than in par. (3).

EFFECTIVE DATE OF 2009 AMENDMENT

Amendment by Pub. L. 111–16 effective Dec. 1, 2009, see section 7 of Pub. L. 111–16, set out as a note under section 109 of this title.

EFFECTIVE DATE OF 2005 AMENDMENT

Pub. L. 109–8, title VI, §603(e), Apr. 20, 2005, 119 Stat. 123, provided that: "The amendments made by this section [amending this section, section 727 of this title and section 586 of Title 28, Judiciary and Judicial Procedure, and enacting provisions set out as a note under section 586 of Title 28] shall take effect 18 months after the date of enactment of this Act [Apr. 20, 2005]."

Amendment by sections 106(d), 225(b), 304(1), 305(2), 315(b), 316, 446(a), and 720 of Pub. L. 109–8 effective 180 days after Apr. 20, 2005, and not applicable with respect to cases commenced under this title before such effective date, except as otherwise provided, see section 1501 of Pub. L. 109–8, set out as a note under section 101 of this title.

EFFECTIVE DATE OF 1986 AMENDMENT

Amendment by Pub. L. 99–554 effective 30 days after Oct. 27, 1986, see section 302(a) of Pub. L. 99–554, set out as a note under section 581 of Title 28, Judiciary and Judicial Procedure.

EFFECTIVE DATE OF 1984 AMENDMENT

Amendment by Pub. L. 98–353 effective with respect to cases filed 90 days after July 10, 1984, see section 552(a) of Pub. L. 98–353, set out as a note under section 101 of this title.

CONFIDENTIALITY OF TAX INFORMATION

Pub. L. 109–8, title III, §315(c), Apr. 20, 2005, 119 Stat. 91, provided that:

"(1) Not later than 180 days after the date of the enactment of this Act [Apr. 20, 2005], the Director of the Administrative Office of the United States Courts shall establish procedures for safeguarding the confidentiality of any tax information required to be provided under this section.

"(2) The procedures under paragraph (1) shall include restrictions on creditor access to tax information that is required to be provided under this section.

"(3) Not later than 540 days after the date of enactment of this Act, the Director of the Administrative Office of the United States Courts shall prepare and submit to the President pro tempore of the Senate and the Speaker of the House of Representatives a report that—

"(A) assesses the effectiveness of the procedures established under paragraph (1); and

"(B) if appropriate, includes proposed legislation to—

"(i) further protect the confidentiality of tax information; and

"(ii) provide penalties for the improper use by any person of the tax information required to be provided under this section."

PROVIDING REQUESTED TAX DOCUMENTS TO THE COURT

Pub. L. 109–8, title XII, §1228, Apr. 20, 2005, 119 Stat. 200, provided that:

"(a) CHAPTER 7 CASES.—The court shall not grant a discharge in the case of an individual who is a debtor in a case under chapter 7 of title 11, United States Code, unless requested tax documents have been provided to the court.

"(b) CHAPTER 11 AND CHAPTER 13 CASES.—The court shall not confirm a plan of reorganization in the case of an individual under chapter 11 or 13 of title 11, United States Code, unless requested tax documents have been filed with the court.

"(c) DOCUMENT RETENTION.—The court shall destroy documents submitted in support of a bankruptcy claim not sooner than 3 years after the date of the conclusion of a case filed by an individual under chapter 7, 11, or 13 of title 11, United States Code. In the event of a pending audit or enforcement action, the court may extend the time for destruction of such requested tax documents."

§522. Exemptions

(a) In this section—

(1) "dependent" includes spouse, whether or not actually dependent; and

(2) "value" means fair market value as of the date of the filing of the petition or, with respect to property that becomes property of the estate after such date, as of the date such property becomes property of the estate.

(b)(1) Notwithstanding section 541 of this title, an individual debtor may exempt from property of the estate the property listed in either paragraph (2) or, in the alternative, paragraph (3) of this subsection. In joint cases filed under section 302 of this title and individual cases filed under section 301 or 303 of this title by or against debtors who are husband and wife, and whose estates are ordered to be jointly administered under Rule 1015(b) of the Federal Rules of Bankruptcy Procedure, one debtor may not elect to exempt property listed in paragraph (2) and the other debtor elect to exempt property listed in paragraph (3) of this subsection. If the parties cannot agree on the alternative to be elected, they shall be deemed to elect paragraph (2), where such election is permitted under the law of the jurisdiction where the case is filed.

(2) Property listed in this paragraph is property that is specified under subsection (d), unless the State law that is applicable to the debtor under paragraph (3)(A) specifically does not so authorize.

(3) Property listed in this paragraph is—

(A) subject to subsections (*o*) and (p), any property that is exempt under Federal law, other than subsection (d) of this section, or State or local law that is applicable on the date of the filing of the petition at the place in which the debtor's domicile has been located for the 730 days immediately preceding the date of the filing of the petition or if the debtor's domicile has not been located at a single State for such 730-day period, the place in which the debtor's domicile was located for 180 days immediately preceding the 730-day period or for a longer portion of such 180-day period than in any other place;

(B) any interest in property in which the debtor had, immediately before the commencement of the case, an interest as a tenant by the entirety or joint tenant to the extent that such interest as a tenant by the entirety or joint tenant is exempt from process under applicable nonbankruptcy law; and

(C) retirement funds to the extent that those funds are in a fund or account that is exempt from taxation under section 401, 403, 408, 408A, 414, 457, or 501(a) of the Internal Revenue Code of 1986.

If the effect of the domiciliary requirement under subparagraph (A) is to render the debtor ineligible for any exemption, the debtor may elect to exempt property that is specified under subsection (d).

(4) For purposes of paragraph (3)(C) and subsection (d)(12), the following shall apply:

(A) If the retirement funds are in a retirement fund that has received a favorable determination under section 7805 of the Internal Revenue Code of 1986, and that determination is in effect as of the date of the filing of the petition in a case under this title, those funds shall be presumed to be exempt from the estate.

(B) If the retirement funds are in a retirement fund that has not received a favorable determination under such section 7805, those funds are exempt from the estate if the debtor demonstrates that—

(i) no prior determination to the contrary has been made by a court or the Internal Revenue Service; and

(ii)(I) the retirement fund is in substantial compliance with the applicable requirements of the Internal Revenue Code of 1986; or

(II) the retirement fund fails to be in substantial compliance with the applicable requirements of the Internal Revenue Code of 1986 and the debtor is not materially responsible for that failure.

(C) A direct transfer of retirement funds from 1 fund or account that is exempt from taxation under section 401, 403, 408, 408A, 414, 457, or 501(a) of the Internal Revenue Code of 1986, under section 401(a)(31) of the Internal Revenue Code of 1986, or otherwise, shall not cease to qualify for exemption under paragraph (3)(C) or subsection (d)(12) by reason of such direct transfer.

(D)(i) Any distribution that qualifies as an eligible rollover distribution within the meaning of section 402(c) of the Internal Revenue Code of 1986 or that is described in clause (ii) shall not cease to qualify for exemption under paragraph (3)(C) or subsection (d)(12) by reason of such distribution.

(ii) A distribution described in this clause is an amount that—

(I) has been distributed from a fund or account that is exempt from taxation under section 401, 403, 408, 408A, 414, 457, or 501(a) of the Internal Revenue Code of 1986; and

(II) to the extent allowed by law, is deposited in such a fund or account not later than 60 days after the distribution of such amount.

(c) Unless the case is dismissed, property exempted under this section is not liable during or after the case for any debt of the debtor that arose, or that is determined under section 502 of this title as if such debt had arisen, before the commencement of the case, except—

(1) a debt of a kind specified in paragraph (1) or (5) of section 523(a) (in which case, notwithstanding any provision of applicable nonbankruptcy law to the contrary, such property shall be liable for a debt of a kind specified in section 523(a)(5));

(2) a debt secured by a lien that is—

(A)(i) not avoided under subsection (f) or (g) of this section or under section 544, 545, 547, 548, 549, or 724(a) of this title; and

(ii) not void under section 506(d) of this title; or

(B) a tax lien, notice of which is properly filed;

(3) a debt of a kind specified in section 523(a)(4) or 523(a)(6) of this title owed by an institution-affiliated party of an insured depository institution to a Federal depository institutions regulatory agency acting in its capacity as conservator, receiver, or liquidating agent for such institution; or

(4) a debt in connection with fraud in the obtaining or providing of any scholarship, grant, loan, tuition, discount, award, or other financial assistance for purposes of financing an education at an institution of higher education (as that term is defined in section 101 of the Higher Education Act of 1965 (20 U.S.C. 1001)).

(d) The following property may be exempted under subsection (b)(2) of this section:

(1) The debtor's aggregate interest, not to exceed $15,000 in value, in real property or personal property that the debtor or a dependent of the debtor uses as a residence, in a cooperative that owns property that the debtor or a dependent of the debtor uses as a residence, or in a burial plot for the debtor or a dependent of the debtor.

(2) The debtor's interest, not to exceed $2,400 in value, in one motor vehicle.

(3) The debtor's interest, not to exceed $400 in value in any particular item or $8,000 in aggregate value, in household furnishings, household goods, wearing apparel, appliances, books, animals, crops, or musical instruments, that are held primarily for the personal, family, or household use of the debtor or a dependent of the debtor.

(4) The debtor's aggregate interest, not to exceed $1,000 in value, in jewelry held primarily for the personal, family, or household use of the debtor or a dependent of the debtor.

(5) The debtor's aggregate interest in any property, not to exceed in value $800 plus up to $7,500 of any unused amount of the exemption provided under paragraph (1) of this subsection.

(6) The debtor's aggregate interest, not to exceed $1,500 in value, in any implements, professional books, or tools, of the trade of the debtor or the trade of a dependent of the debtor.

(7) Any unmatured life insurance contract owned by the debtor, other than a credit life insurance contract.

(8) The debtor's aggregate interest, not to exceed in value $8,000 less any amount of property of the estate transferred in the manner specified in section 542(d) of this title, in any accrued dividend or interest under, or loan value of, any unmatured life insurance contract owned by the debtor under which the insured is the debtor or an individual of whom the debtor is a dependent.

(9) Professionally prescribed health aids for the debtor or a dependent of the debtor.

(10) The debtor's right to receive—

(A) a social security benefit, unemployment compensation, or a local public assistance benefit;

(B) a veterans' benefit;

(C) a disability, illness, or unemployment benefit;

(D) alimony, support, or separate maintenance, to the extent reasonably necessary for the support of the debtor and any dependent of the debtor;

(E) a payment under a stock bonus, pension, profitsharing, annuity, or similar plan or contract on account of illness, disability, death, age, or length of service, to the extent reasonably necessary for the support of the debtor and any dependent of the debtor, unless—

(i) such plan or contract was established by or under the auspices of an insider that employed the debtor at the time the debtor's rights under such plan or contract arose;

(ii) such payment is on account of age or length of service; and

(iii) such plan or contract does not qualify under section 401(a), 403(a), 403(b), or 408 of the Internal Revenue Code of 1986.

(11) The debtor's right to receive, or property that is traceable to—

(A) an award under a crime victim's reparation law;

(B) a payment on account of the wrongful death of an individual of whom the debtor was a dependent, to the extent reasonably necessary for the support of the debtor and any dependent of the debtor;

(C) a payment under a life insurance contract that insured the life of an individual of whom the debtor was a dependent on the date of such individual's death, to the extent reasonably necessary for the support of the debtor and any dependent of the debtor;

(D) a payment, not to exceed $15,000, on account of personal bodily injury, not including pain and suffering or compensation for actual pecuniary loss, of the debtor or an individual of whom the debtor is a dependent; or

(E) a payment in compensation of loss of future earnings of the debtor or an individual of whom the debtor is or was a dependent, to the extent reasonably necessary for the support of the debtor and any dependent of the debtor.

(12) Retirement funds to the extent that those funds are in a fund or account that is exempt from taxation under section 401, 403, 408, 408A, 414, 457, or 501(a) of the Internal Revenue Code of 1986.

(e) A waiver of an exemption executed in favor of a creditor that holds an unsecured claim against the debtor is unenforceable in a case under this title with respect to such claim against property that the debtor may exempt under subsection (b) of this section. A waiver by the debtor of a power under subsection (f) or (h) of this section to avoid a transfer, under subsection (g) or (i) of this section to exempt property, or under subsection (i) of this section to recover property or to preserve a transfer, is unenforceable in a case under this title.

(f)(1) Notwithstanding any waiver of exemptions but subject to paragraph (3), the debtor may avoid the fixing of a lien on an interest of the debtor in property to the extent that such lien impairs an exemption to which the debtor would have been entitled under subsection (b) of this section, if such lien is—

(A) a judicial lien, other than a judicial lien that secures a debt of a kind that is specified in section 523(a)(5); or

(B) a nonpossessory, nonpurchase-money security interest in any—

(i) household furnishings, household goods, wearing apparel, appliances, books, animals, crops, musical instruments, or jewelry that are held primarily for the personal, family, or household use of the debtor or a dependent of the debtor;

(ii) implements, professional books, or tools, of the trade of the debtor or the trade of a dependent of the debtor; or

(iii) professionally prescribed health aids for the debtor or a dependent of the debtor.

(2)(A) For the purposes of this subsection, a lien shall be considered to impair an exemption to the extent that the sum of—

(i) the lien;

(ii) all other liens on the property; and

(iii) the amount of the exemption that the debtor could claim if there were no liens on the property;

exceeds the value that the debtor's interest in the property would have in the absence of any liens.

(B) In the case of a property subject to more than 1 lien, a lien that has been avoided shall not be considered in making the calculation under subparagraph (A) with respect to other liens.

(C) This paragraph shall not apply with respect to a judgment arising out of a mortgage foreclosure.

(3) In a case in which State law that is applicable to the debtor—

(A) permits a person to voluntarily waive a right to claim exemptions under subsection (d) or prohibits a debtor from claiming exemptions under subsection (d); and

(B) either permits the debtor to claim exemptions under State law without limitation in amount, except to the extent that the debtor has permitted the fixing of a consensual lien on any property or prohibits avoidance of a consensual lien on property otherwise eligible to be claimed as exempt property;

the debtor may not avoid the fixing of a lien on an interest of the debtor or a dependent of the debtor in property if the lien is a nonpossessory, nonpurchase-money security interest in implements, professional books, or tools of the trade of the debtor or a dependent of the debtor or farm animals or crops of the debtor or a dependent of the debtor to the extent the value of such implements, professional books, tools of the trade, animals, and crops exceeds $5,000.

(4)(A) Subject to subparagraph (B), for purposes of paragraph (1)(B), the term "household goods" means—

(i) clothing;
(ii) furniture;
(iii) appliances;
(iv) 1 radio;
(v) 1 television;
(vi) 1 VCR;
(vii) linens;
(viii) china;
(ix) crockery;
(x) kitchenware;
(xi) educational materials and educational equipment primarily for the use of minor dependent children of the debtor;
(xii) medical equipment and supplies;
(xiii) furniture exclusively for the use of minor children, or elderly or disabled dependents of the debtor;
(xiv) personal effects (including the toys and hobby equipment of minor dependent children and wedding rings) of the debtor and the dependents of the debtor; and
(xv) 1 personal computer and related equipment.

(B) The term "household goods" does not include—
(i) works of art (unless by or of the debtor, or any relative of the debtor);
(ii) electronic entertainment equipment with a fair market value of more than $500 in the aggregate (except 1 television, 1 radio, and 1 VCR);
(iii) items acquired as antiques with a fair market value of more than $500 in the aggregate;
(iv) jewelry with a fair market value of more than $500 in the aggregate (except wedding rings); and
(v) a computer (except as otherwise provided for in this section), motor vehicle (including a tractor or lawn tractor), boat, or a motorized recreational device, conveyance, vehicle, watercraft, or aircraft.

(g) Notwithstanding sections 550 and 551 of this title, the debtor may exempt under subsection (b) of this section property that the trustee recovers under section 510(c)(2), 542, 543, 550, 551, or 553 of this title, to the extent that the debtor could have exempted such property under subsection (b) of this section if such property had not been transferred, if—
(1)(A) such transfer was not a voluntary transfer of such property by the debtor; and
(B) the debtor did not conceal such property; or
(2) the debtor could have avoided such transfer under subsection (f)(1)(B) of this section.

(h) The debtor may avoid a transfer of property of the debtor or recover a setoff to the extent that the debtor could have exempted such property under subsection (g)(1) of this section if the trustee had avoided such transfer, if—
(1) such transfer is avoidable by the trustee under section 544, 545, 547, 548, 549, or 724(a) of this title or recoverable by the trustee under section 553 of this title; and
(2) the trustee does not attempt to avoid such transfer.

(i)(1) If the debtor avoids a transfer or recovers a setoff under subsection (f) or (h) of this section, the debtor may recover in the manner prescribed by, and subject to the limitations of, section 550 of this title, the same as if the trustee had avoided such transfer, and may exempt any property so recovered under subsection (b) of this section.
(2) Notwithstanding section 551 of this title, a transfer avoided under section 544, 545, 547, 548, 549, or 724(a) of this title, under subsection (f) or (h) of this section, or property recovered under section 553 of this title, may be preserved for the benefit of the debtor to the extent that the debtor may exempt such property under subsection (g) of this section or paragraph (1) of this subsection.
(j) Notwithstanding subsections (g) and (i) of this section, the debtor may exempt a particular kind of property under subsections (g) and (i) of this section only to the extent that the debtor has exempted less property in value of such kind than that to which the debtor is entitled under subsection (b) of this section.
(k) Property that the debtor exempts under this section is not liable for payment of any administrative expense except—
(1) the aliquot share of the costs and expenses of avoiding a transfer of property that the debtor exempts under subsection (g) of this section, or of recovery of such property, that is attributable to the value of the portion of such property exempted in relation to the value of the property recovered; and
(2) any costs and expenses of avoiding a transfer under subsection (f) or (h) of this section, or of recovery of property under subsection (i)(1) of this section, that the debtor has not paid.

(*l*) The debtor shall file a list of property that the debtor claims as exempt under subsection (b) of this section. If the debtor does not file such a list, a dependent of the debtor may file such a list, or may claim property as exempt from property of the estate on behalf of the debtor. Unless a party in interest objects, the property claimed as exempt on such list is exempt.
(m) Subject to the limitation in subsection (b), this section shall apply separately with respect to each debtor in a joint case.
(n) For assets in individual retirement accounts described in section 408 or 408A of the Internal Revenue Code of 1986, other than a simplified employee pension under section 408(k) of such Code or a simple retirement account under section 408(p) of such Code, the aggregate value of such assets exempted under this section, without regard to amounts attributable to rollover contributions under section 402(c), 402(e)(6), 403(a)(4), 403(a)(5), and 403(b)(8) of the Internal Revenue Code of 1986, and earnings thereon, shall not exceed $1,000,000 in a case filed by a debtor who is an individual, except that such amount may be increased if the interests of justice so require.
(*o*) For purposes of subsection (b)(3)(A), and notwithstanding subsection (a), the value of an interest in—
(1) real or personal property that the debtor or a dependent of the debtor uses as a residence;

(2) a cooperative that owns property that the debtor or a dependent of the debtor uses as a residence;

(3) a burial plot for the debtor or a dependent of the debtor; or

(4) real or personal property that the debtor or a dependent of the debtor claims as a homestead;

shall be reduced to the extent that such value is attributable to any portion of any property that the debtor disposed of in the 10-year period ending on the date of the filing of the petition with the intent to hinder, delay, or defraud a creditor and that the debtor could not exempt, or that portion that the debtor could not exempt, under subsection (b), if on such date the debtor had held the property so disposed of.

(p)(1) Except as provided in paragraph (2) of this subsection and sections 544 and 548, as a result of electing under subsection (b)(3)(A) to exempt property under State or local law, a debtor may not exempt any amount of interest that was acquired by the debtor during the 1215-day period preceding the date of the filing of the petition that exceeds in the aggregate $125,000 in value in—

(A) real or personal property that the debtor or a dependent of the debtor uses as a residence;

(B) a cooperative that owns property that the debtor or a dependent of the debtor uses as a residence;

(C) a burial plot for the debtor or a dependent of the debtor; or

(D) real or personal property that the debtor or dependent of the debtor claims as a homestead.

(2)(A) The limitation under paragraph (1) shall not apply to an exemption claimed under subsection (b)(3)(A) by a family farmer for the principal residence of such farmer.

(B) For purposes of paragraph (1), any amount of such interest does not include any interest transferred from a debtor's previous principal residence (which was acquired prior to the beginning of such 1215-day period) into the debtor's current principal residence, if the debtor's previous and current residences are located in the same State.

(q)(1) As a result of electing under subsection (b)(3)(A) to exempt property under State or local law, a debtor may not exempt any amount of an interest in property described in subparagraphs (A), (B), (C), and (D) of subsection (p)(1) which exceeds in the aggregate $125,000 if—

(A) the court determines, after notice and a hearing, that the debtor has been convicted of a felony (as defined in section 3156 of title 18), which under the circumstances, demonstrates that the filing of the case was an abuse of the provisions of this title; or

(B) the debtor owes a debt arising from—

(i) any violation of the Federal securities laws (as defined in section 3(a)(47) of the Securities Exchange Act of 1934), any State securities laws, or any regulation or order issued under Federal securities laws or State securities laws;

(ii) fraud, deceit, or manipulation in a fiduciary capacity or in connection with the purchase or sale of any security registered under section 12 or 15(d) of the Securities Exchange Act of 1934 or under section 6 of the Securities Act of 1933;

(iii) any civil remedy under section 1964 of title 18; or

(iv) any criminal act, intentional tort, or willful or reckless misconduct that caused serious physical injury or death to another individual in the preceding 5 years.

(2) Paragraph (1) shall not apply to the extent the amount of an interest in property described in subparagraphs (A), (B), (C), and (D) of subsection (p)(1) is reasonably necessary for the support of the debtor and any dependent of the debtor.

(Pub. L. 95–598, Nov. 6, 1978, 92 Stat. 2586; Pub. L. 98–353, title III, §§306, 453, July 10, 1984, 98 Stat. 353, 375; Pub. L. 99–554, title II, §283(i), Oct. 27, 1986, 100 Stat. 3117; Pub. L. 101–647, title XXV, §2522(b), Nov. 29, 1990, 104 Stat. 4866; Pub. L. 103–394, title I, §108(d), title III, §§303, 304(d), 310, title V, §501(d)(12), Oct. 22, 1994, 108 Stat. 4112, 4132, 4133, 4137, 4145; Pub. L. 106–420, §4, Nov. 1, 2000, 114 Stat. 1868; Pub. L. 109–8, title II, §§216, 224(a), (e)(1), title III, §§307, 308, 313(a), 322(a), Apr. 20, 2005, 119 Stat. 55, 62, 65, 81, 87, 96.)

HISTORICAL AND REVISION NOTES

LEGISLATIVE STATEMENTS

Section 522 of the House amendment represents a compromise on the issue of exemptions between the position taken in the House bill, and that taken in the Senate amendment. Dollar amounts specified in section 522(d) of the House bill have been reduced from amounts as contained in H.R. 8200 as passed by the House. The States may, by passing a law, determine whether the Federal exemptions will apply as an alternative to State exemptions in bankruptcy cases.

Section 522(c)(1) tracks the House bill and provides that dischargeable tax claims may not be collected out of exempt property.

Section 522(f)(2) is derived from the Senate amendment restricting the debtor to avoidance of nonpossessory, nonpurchase money security interests.

Exemptions: Section 522(c)(1) of the House amendment adopts a provision contained in the House bill that dischargeable taxes cannot be collected from exempt assets. This changes present law, which allows collection of dischargeable taxes from exempt property, a rule followed in the Senate amendment. Nondischargeable taxes, however, will continue to the [be] collectable out of exempt property. It is anticipated that in the next session Congress will review the exemptions from levy currently contained in the Internal Revenue Code [title 26] with a view to increasing the exemptions to more realistic levels.

SENATE REPORT NO. 95–989

Subsection (a) of this section defines two terms: "dependent" includes the debtor's spouse, whether or not actually dependent; and "value" means fair market value as of the date of the filing of the petition.

Subsection (b) tracks current law. It permits a debtor the exemptions to which he is entitled under other Federal law and the law of the State of his domicile. Some of the items that may be exempted under Federal laws other than title 11 include:

Foreign Service Retirement and Disability payments, 22 U.S.C. 1104;[1]

Social security payments, 42 U.S.C. 407;

Injury or death compensation payments from war risk hazards, 42 U.S.C. 1717;

[1] Replaced by 22 U.S.C. 4060(c).

Wages of fishermen, seamen, and apprentices, 46 U.S.C. 601;[2]

Civil service retirement benefits, 5 U.S.C. 729, 2265;[3]

Longshoremen's and Harbor Workers' Compensation Act death and disability benefits, 33 U.S.C. 916;

Railroad Retirement Act annuities and pensions, 45 U.S.C. 228(L);[4]

Veterans benefits, 45 U.S.C. 352(E);[5]

Special pensions paid to winners of the Congressional Medal of Honor, 38 U.S.C. 3101;[6] and

Federal homestead lands on debts contracted before issuance of the patent, 43 U.S.C. 175.

He may also exempt an interest in property in which the debtor had an interest as a tenant by the entirety or joint tenant to the extent that interest would have been exempt from process under applicable nonbankruptcy law.

Under proposed section 541, all property of the debtor becomes property of the estate, but the debtor is permitted to exempt certain property from property of the estate under this section. Property may be exempted even if it is subject to a lien, but only the unencumbered portion of the property is to be counted in computing the "value" of the property for the purposes of exemption.

As under current law, the debtor will be permitted to convert nonexempt property into exempt property before filing a bankruptcy petition. The practice is not fraudulent as to creditors, and permits the debtor to make full use of the exemptions to which he is entitled under the law.

Subsection (c) insulates exempt property from prepetition claims other than tax claims (whether or not dischargeable), and other than alimony, maintenance, or support claims that are excepted from discharge. The bankruptcy discharge does not prevent enforcement of valid liens. The rule of *Long v. Bullard*, 117 U.S. 617 (1886), is accepted with respect to the enforcement of valid liens on nonexempt property as well as on exempt property. Cf. *Louisville Joint Stock Land Bank v. Radford*, 295 U.S. 555, 583 (1935).

Subsection (c)(3) permits the collection of dischargeable taxes from exempt assets. Only assets exempted from levy under Section 6334 of the Internal Revenue Code [title 26] or under applicable state or local tax law cannot be applied to satisfy these tax claims. This rule applies to prepetition tax claims against the debtor regardless of whether the claims do or do not receive priority and whether they are dischargeable or nondischargeable. Thus, even if a tax is dischargeable vis-a-vis the debtor's after-acquired assets, it may nevertheless be collectible from exempt property held by the estate. (Taxes incurred by the debtor's estate which are collectible as first priority administrative expenses are not collectible from the debtor's estate which are collectible as first priority administrative expenses are not collectible from the debtor's exempt assets.)

Subsection (d) protects the debtor's exemptions, either Federal or State, by making unenforceable in a bankruptcy case a waiver of exemptions or a waiver of the debtor's avoiding powers under the following subsections.

Subsection (e) protects the debtor's exemptions, his discharge, and thus his fresh start by permitting him to avoid certain liens on exempt property. The debtor may avoid a judicial lien on any property to the extent that the property could have been exempted in the absence of the lien, and may similarly avoid a nonpurchase-money security interest in certain household and personal goods. The avoiding power is independent of any waiver of exemptions.

Subsection (f) gives the debtor the ability to exempt property that the trustee recovers under one of the trustee's avoiding powers if the property was involuntarily transferred away from the debtor (such as by the fixing of a judicial lien) and if the debtor did not conceal the property. The debtor is also permitted to exempt property that the trustee recovers as the result of the avoiding of the fixing of certain security interests to the extent that the debtor could otherwise have exempted the property.

Subsection (g) provides that if the trustee does not exercise an avoiding power to recover a transfer of property that would be exempt, the debtor may exercise it and exempt the property, if the transfer was involuntary and the debtor did not conceal the property. If the debtor wishes to preserve his right to pursue any action under this provision, then he must intervene in any action brought by the trustee based on the same cause of action. It is not intended that the debtor be given an additional opportunity to avoid a transfer or that the transferee should have to defend the same action twice. Rather, the section is primarily designed to give the debtor the rights the trustee could have, but has not, pursued. The debtor is given no greater rights under this provision than the trustee, and thus, the debtor's avoiding powers under proposed sections 544, 545, 547, and 548, are subject to proposed 546, as are the trustee's powers.

These subsections are cumulative. The debtor is not required to choose which he will use to gain an exemption. Instead, he may use more than one in any particular instance, just as the trustee's avoiding powers are cumulative.

Subsection (h) permits recovery by the debtor of property transferred by an avoided transfer from either the initial or subsequent transferees. It also permits preserving a transfer for the benefit of the debtor. In either event, the debtor may exempt the property recovered or preserved.

Subsection (i) makes clear that the debtor may exempt property under the avoiding subsections (f) and (h) only to the extent he has exempted less property than allowed under subsection (b).

Subsection (j) makes clear that the liability of the debtor's exempt property is limited to the debtor's aliquot share of the costs and expenses recovery of property that the trustee recovers and the debtor later exempts, and any costs and expenses of avoiding a transfer by the debtor that the debtor has not already paid.

Subsection (k) requires the debtor to file a list of property that he claims as exempt from property of the estate. Absent an objection to the list, the property is exempted. A dependent of the debtor may file it and thus be protected if the debtor fails to file the list.

Subsection (*l*) provides the rule for a joint case.

HOUSE REPORT NO. 95–595

Subsection (a) of this section defines two terms: "dependent" includes the debtor's spouse, whether or not actually dependent; and "value" means fair market value as of the date of the filing of the petition.

Subsection (b), the operative subsection of this section, is a significant departure from present law. It permits an individual debtor in a bankruptcy case a choice between exemption systems. The debtor may choose the Federal exemptions prescribed in subsection (d), or he may choose the exemptions to which he is entitled under other Federal law and the law of the State of his domicile. If the debtor chooses the latter, some of the items that may be exempted under other Federal laws include:

—Foreign Service Retirement and Disability payments, 22 U.S.C. 1104;[7]

—Social security payments, 42 U.S.C. 407;

—Injury or death compensation payments from war risk hazards, 42 U.S.C. 1717;

—Wages of fishermen, seamen, and apprentices, 46 U.S.C. 601;[8]

---

[2] Replaced by 46 U.S.C. 11108, 11109.

[3] Replaced by 5 U.S.C. 8346.

[4] Replaced by 45 U.S.C. 231m.

[5] Railroad unemployment benefits are covered by 45 U.S.C. 352(e).

[6] Veterans benefits generally are covered by 38 U.S.C. 3101 [now 5301].

[7] Replaced by 22 U.S.C. 4060(c).

[8] Replaced by 46 U.S.C. 11108, 11109.

—Civil service retirement benefits, 5 U.S.C. 729, 2265;[9]
—Longshoremen's and Harbor Workers' Compensation Act death and disability benefits, 33 U.S.C. 916;
—Railroad Retirement Act annuities and pensions, 45 U.S.C. 228(*l*);[10]
—Veterans benefits, 45 U.S.C. 352(E);[11]
—Special pensions paid to winners of the Congressional Medal of Honor, 38 U.S.C. 3101;[12] and
—Federal homestead lands on debts contracted before issuance of the patent, 43 U.S.C. 175.

He may also exempt an interest in property in which the debtor had an interest as a tenant by the entirety or joint tenant to the extent that interest would have been exempt from process under applicable nonbankruptcy law. The Rules will provide for the situation where the debtor's choice of exemption, Federal or State, was improvident and should be changed, for example, where the court has ruled against the debtor with respect to a major exemption.

Under proposed 11 U.S.C. 541, all property of the debtor becomes property of the estate, but the debtor is permitted to exempt certain property from property of the estate under this section. Property may be exempted even if it is subject to a lien, but only the unencumbered portion of the property is to be counted in computing the "value" of the property for the purposes of exemption. Thus, for example, a residence worth $30,000 with a mortgage of $25,000 will be exemptable [sic] to the extent of $5,000. This follows current law. The remaining value of the property will be dealt with in the bankruptcy case as is any interest in property that is subject to a lien.

As under current law, the debtor will be permitted to convert nonexempt property into exempt property before filing a bankruptcy petition. See Hearings, pt. 3, at 1355–58. The practice is not fraudulent as to creditors and permits the debtor to make full use of the exemptions to which he is entitled under the law.

Subsection (c) insulates exempt property from prepetition claims, except tax and alimony, maintenance, or support claims that are excepted from discharge. The bankruptcy discharge will not prevent enforcement of valid liens. The rule of *Long v. Bullard*, 117 U.S. 617 (1886) [6 S.Ct. 917, 29 L.Ed. 1004], is accepted with respect to the enforcement of valid liens on nonexempt property as well as on exempt property. Cf. *Louisville Joint Stock Land Bank v. Radford*, 295 U.S. 555, 583 (1935) [55 S.Ct. 854].

Subsection (d) specifies the Federal exemptions to which the debtor is entitled. They are derived in large part from the Uniform Exemptions Act, promulgated by the Commissioners of Uniform State Laws in August, 1976. Eleven categories of property are exempted. First is a homestead to the extent of $10,000, which may be claimed in real or personal property that the debtor or a dependent of the debtor uses as a residence. Second, the debtor may exempt a motor vehicle to the extent of $1500. Third, the debtor may exempt household goods, furnishings, clothing, and similar household items, held primarily for the personal, family, or household use of the debtor or a dependent of the debtor. "Animals" includes all animals, such as pets, livestock, poultry, and fish, if they are held primarily for personal, family or household use. The limitation for third category items is $300 on any particular item. The debtor may also exempt up to $750 of personal jewelry.

Paragraph (5) permits the exemption of $500, plus any unused amount of the homestead exemption, in any property, in order not to discriminate against the nonhomeowner. Paragraph (6) grants the debtor up to $1000 in implements, professional books, or tools, of the trade of the debtor or a dependent. Paragraph (7) exempts a life insurance contract, other than a credit life insurance contract, owned by the debtor. This paragraph refers to the life insurance contract itself. It does not encompass any other rights under the contract, such as the right to borrow out the loan value. Because of this provision, the trustee may not surrender a life insurance contract, which remains property of the debtor if he chooses the Federal exemptions. Paragraph (8) permits the debtor to exempt up to $5000 in loan value in a life insurance policy owned by the debtor under which the debtor or an individual of whom the debtor is a dependent is the insured. The exemption provided by this paragraph and paragraph (7) will also include the debtor's rights in a group insurance certificate under which the insured is an individual of whom the debtor is a dependent (assuming the debtor has rights in the policy that could be exempted) or the debtor. A trustee is authorized to collect the entire loan value on every life insurance policy owned by the debtor as property of the estate. First, however, the debtor will choose which policy or policies under which the loan value will be exempted. The $5000 figure is reduced by the amount of any automatic premium loan authorized after the date of the filing of the petition under section 542(d). Paragraph (9) exempts professionally prescribed health aids.

Paragraph (10) exempts certain benefits that are akin to future earnings of the debtor. These include social security, unemployment compensation, or public assistance benefits, veteran's benefits, disability, illness, or unemployment benefits, alimony, support, or separate maintenance (but only to the extent reasonably necessary for the support of the debtor and any dependents of the debtor), and benefits under a certain stock bonus, pension, profitsharing, annuity or similar plan based on illness, disability, death, age or length of service. Paragraph (11) allows the debtor to exempt certain compensation for losses. These include crime victim's reparation benefits, wrongful death benefits (with a reasonably necessary for support limitation), life insurance proceeds (same limitation), compensation for bodily injury, not including pain and suffering ($10,000 limitation), and loss of future earnings payments (support limitation). This provision in subparagraph (D)(11) is designed to cover payments in compensation of actual bodily injury, such as the loss of a limb, and is not intended to include the attendant costs that accompany such a loss, such as medical payments, pain and suffering, or loss of earnings. Those items are handled separately by the bill.

Subsection (e) protects the debtor's exemptions, either Federal or State, by making unenforceable in a bankruptcy case a waiver of exemptions or a waiver of the debtor's avoiding powers under the following subsections.

Subsection (f) protects the debtor's exemptions, his discharge, and thus his fresh start by permitting him to avoid certain liens on exempt property. The debtor may avoid a judicial lien on any property to the extent that the property could have been exempted in the absence of the lien, and may similarly avoid a nonpurchase-money security interest in certain household and personal goods. The avoiding power is independent of any waiver of exemptions.

Subsection (g) gives the debtor the ability to exempt property that the trustee recovers under one of the trustee's avoiding powers if the property was involuntarily transferred away from the debtor (such as by the fixing of a judicial lien) and if the debtor did not conceal the property. The debtor is also permitted to exempt property that the trustee recovers as the result of the avoiding of the fixing of certain security interests to the extent that the debtor could otherwise have exempted the property.

If the trustee does not pursue an avoiding power to recover a transfer of property that would be exempt, the debtor may pursue it and exempt the property, if the transfer was involuntary and the debtor did not conceal the property. If the debtor wishes to preserve his right to pursue an action under this provision, then he must intervene in any action brought by the trustee

[9] Replaced by 5 U.S.C. 8346.

[10] Replaced by 45 U.S.C. 231m.

[11] Railroad unemployment benefits are covered by 45 U.S.C. 352(e).

[12] Veterans benefits generally are covered by 38 U.S.C. 3101 [now 5301].

based on the same cause of action. It is not intended that the debtor be given an additional opportunity to avoid a transfer or that the transferee have to defend the same action twice. Rather, the section is primarily designed to give the debtor the rights the trustee could have pursued if the trustee chooses not to pursue them. The debtor is given no greater rights under this provision than the trustee, and thus the debtor's avoiding powers under proposed 11 U.S.C. 544, 545, 547, and 548, are subject to proposed 11 U.S.C. 546, as are the trustee's powers.

These subsections are cumulative. The debtor is not required to choose which he will use to gain an exemption. Instead, he may use more than one in any particular instance, just as the trustee's avoiding powers are cumulative.

Subsection (i) permits recovery by the debtor of property transferred in an avoided transfer from either the initial or subsequent transferees. It also permits preserving a transfer for the benefit of the debtor. Under either case the debtor may exempt the property recovered or preserved.

Subsection (k) makes clear that the debtor's aliquot share of the costs and expenses [for] recovery of property that the trustee recovers and the debtor later exempts, and any costs and expenses of avoiding a transfer by the debtor that the debtor has not already paid.

Subsection (*l*) requires the debtor to file a list of property that he claims as exempt from property of the estate. Absent an objection to the list, the property is exempted. A dependent of the debtor may file it and thus be protected if the debtor fails to file the list.

Subsection (m) requires the clerk of the bankruptcy court to give notice of any exemptions claimed under subsection (*l*), in order that parties in interest may have an opportunity to object to the claim.

Subsection (n) provides the rule for a joint case: each debtor is entitled to the Federal exemptions provided under this section or to the State exemptions, whichever the debtor chooses.

References in Text

The Federal Rules of Bankruptcy Procedure, referred to in subsec. (b)(1), are set out in the Appendix to this title.

The Internal Revenue Code of 1986, referred to in subsecs. (b)(3)(C), (4), (d)(10)(E)(iii), (12), and (n), is classified generally to Title 26, Internal Revenue Code.

Sections 3(a)(47), 12, and 15(d) of the Securities Exchange Act of 1934, referred to in subsec. (q)(1)(B)(i), (ii), are classified to sections 78c(a)(47), 78*l*, and 78*o*(d), respectively, of Title 15, Commerce and Trade.

Section 6 of the Securities Exchange Act of 1933, referred to in subsec. (q)(1)(B)(ii), is classified to section 77f of Title 15, Commerce and Trade.

Amendments

2005—Subsec. (b). Pub. L. 109–8, §224(a)(1)(B)–(F), designated introductory provisions of subsec. (b) as par. (1), substituted "paragraph (3)" for "paragraph (2)" in two places and "paragraph (2)" for "paragraph (1)" wherever appearing, struck out "Such property is—" after "case is filed.", and struck out former par. (1) which read: "property that is specified under subsection (d) of this section, unless the State law that is applicable to the debtor under paragraph (2)(A) of this subsection specifically does not so authorize; or, in the alternative,".

Subsec. (b)(2). Pub. L. 109–8, §224(a)(1)(B), added par. (2). Former par. (2) redesignated (3).

Subsec. (b)(2)(C). Pub. L. 109–8, §224(a)(1)(A)(i)–(iii), added subpar. (C).

Subsec. (b)(3). Pub. L. 109–8, §307(2), inserted "If the effect of the domiciliary requirement under subparagraph (A) is to render the debtor ineligible for any exemption, the debtor may elect to exempt property that is specified under subsection (d)." at end.

Pub. L. 109–8, §224(a)(1)(A)(iv), redesignated par. (2) as (3) and inserted introductory provisions.

Subsec. (b)(3)(A). Pub. L. 109–8, §308(1), inserted "subject to subsections (*o*) and (p)," before "any property".

Pub. L. 109–8, §307(1), substituted "730 days" for "180 days" and "or if the debtor's domicile has not been located at a single State for such 730-day period, the place in which the debtor's domicile was located for 180 days immediately preceding the 730-day period or for a longer portion of such 180-day period than in any other place" for ", or for a longer portion of such 180-day period than in any other place".

Subsec. (b)(4). Pub. L. 109–8, §224(a)(1)(G), added par. (4).

Subsec. (c)(1). Pub. L. 109–8, §216(1), added par. (1) and struck out former par. (1) which read as follows: "a debt of a kind specified in section 523(a)(1) or 523(a)(5) of this title;".

Subsec. (d). Pub. L. 109–8, §224(a)(2)(A), substituted "subsection (b)(2)" for "subsection (b)(1)" in introductory provisions.

Subsec. (d)(12). Pub. L. 109–8, §224(a)(2)(B), added par. (12).

Subsec. (f)(1)(A). Pub. L. 109–8, §216(2), substituted "a debt of a kind that is specified in section 523(a)(5); or" for "a debt—

"(i) to a spouse, former spouse, or child of the debtor, for alimony to, maintenance for, or support of such spouse or child, in connection with a separation agreement, divorce decree or other order of a court of record, determination made in accordance with State or territorial law by a governmental unit, or property settlement agreement; and

"(ii) to the extent that such debt—

"(I) is not assigned to another entity, voluntarily, by operation of law, or otherwise; and

"(II) includes a liability designated as alimony, maintenance, or support, unless such liability is actually in the nature of alimony, maintenance or support.; or".

Subsec. (f)(4). Pub. L. 109–8, §313(a), added par. (4).

Subsec. (g)(2). Pub. L. 109–8, §216(3), substituted "subsection (f)(1)(B)" for "subsection (f)(2)".

Subsec. (n). Pub. L. 109–8, §224(e)(1), added subsec. (n).

Subsec. (*o*). Pub. L. 109–8, §308(2), added subsec. (*o*).

Subsecs. (p), (q). Pub. L. 109–8, §322(a), added subsecs. (p) and (q).

2000—Subsec. (c)(4). Pub. L. 106–420 added par. (4).

1994—Subsec. (b). Pub. L. 103–394, §501(d)(12)(A), substituted "Federal Rules of Bankruptcy Procedure" for "Bankruptcy Rules".

Subsec. (d)(1) to (6). Pub. L. 103–394, §108(d)(1)–(6), substituted "$15,000" for "$7,500" in par. (1), "$2,400" for "$1,200" in par. (2), "$400" and "$8,000" for "$200" and "$4,000", respectively, in par. (3), "$1,000" for "$500" in par. (4), "$800" and "$7,500" for "$400" and "$3,750", respectively, in par. (5), and "$1,500" for "$750" in par. (6).

Subsec. (d)(8). Pub. L. 103–394, §108(d)(7), substituted "$8,000" for "$4,000".

Subsec. (d)(10)(E)(iii). Pub. L. 103–394, §501(d)(12)(B), substituted "or 408" for "408, or 409" and "Internal Revenue Code of 1986" for "Internal Revenue Code of 1954 (26 U.S.C. 401(a), 403(a), 403(b), 408, or 409)".

Subsec. (d)(11)(D). Pub. L. 103–394, §108(d)(8), substituted "$15,000" for "$7,500".

Subsec. (f)(1). Pub. L. 103–394, §§303(3), 310(1), designated existing provisions as par. (1) and inserted "but subject to paragraph (3)" after "waiver of exemptions" in introductory provisions. Former par. (1) redesignated subpar. (A) of par. (1).

Subsec. (f)(1)(A). Pub. L. 103–394, §§303(2), 304(d), redesignated par. (1) as subpar. (A) of par. (1) and inserted ", other than a judicial lien that secures a debt—

"(i) to a spouse, former spouse, or child of the debtor, for alimony to, maintenance for, or support of such spouse or child, in connection with a separation agreement, divorce decree or other order of a court of record, determination made in accordance with State or territorial law by a governmental unit, or property settlement agreement; and

"(ii) to the extent that such debt—

"(I) is not assigned to another entity, voluntarily, by operation of law, or otherwise; and

"(II) includes a liability designated as alimony, maintenance, or support, unless such liability is actually in the nature of alimony, maintenance or support."

Subsec. (f)(1)(B). Pub. L. 103–394, §303(1), redesignated par. (2) as subpar. (B) of par. (1) and subpars. (A) to (C) of par. (2) as cls. (i) to (iii), respectively, of subpar. (B) of par. (1).

Subsec. (f)(2). Pub. L. 103–394, §303(4), added par. (2). Former par. (2) redesignated subpar. (B) of par. (1).

Subsec. (f)(3). Pub. L. 103–394, §310(2), added par. (3).

1990—Subsec. (c)(3). Pub. L. 101–647 added par. (3).

1986—Subsec. (h)(1). Pub. L. 99–554, §283(i)(1), substituted "553 of this title" for "553 of this tittle".

Subsec. (i)(2). Pub. L. 99–554, §283(i)(2), substituted "this" for "his" after "subsection (g) of".

1984—Subsec. (a)(2). Pub. L. 98–353, §453(a), inserted "or, with respect to property that becomes property of an estate after such date, as of the date such property becomes property of the estate".

Subsec. (b). Pub. L. 98–353, §306(a), inserted provision that in joint cases filed under section 302 of this title and individual cases filed under section 301 or 303 of this title by or against debtors who are husband and wife, and whose estates are ordered to be jointly administered under Rule 1015(b) of the Bankruptcy Rules, one debtor may not elect to exempt property listed in paragraph (1) and the other debtor elect to exempt property listed in paragraph (2) of this subsection, but that if the parties cannot agree on the alternative to be elected, they shall be deemed to elect paragraph (1), where such election is permitted under the law of the jurisdiction where the case is filed.

Subsec. (c). Pub. L. 98–353, §453(b), amended subsec. (c) generally. Prior to amendment, subsec. (c) read as follows: "Unless the case is dismissed, property exempted under this section is not liable during or after the case for any debt of the debtor that arose, or that is determined under section 502 of this title as if such claim had arisen before the commencement of the case, except—

"(1) a debt of a kind specified in section 523(a)(1) or section 523(a)(5) of this title; or

"(2) a lien that is—

"(A) not avoided under section 544, 545, 547, 548, 549, or 724(a) of this title;

"(B) not voided under section 506(d) of this title; or

"(C)(i) a tax lien, notice of which is properly filed; and

"(ii) avoided under section 545(2) of this title."

Subsec. (d)(3). Pub. L. 98–353, §306(b), inserted "or $4,000 in aggregate value".

Subsec. (d)(5). Pub. L. 98–353, §306(c), amended par. (5) generally. Prior to amendment, par. (5) read as follows: "The debtor's aggregate interest, not to exceed in value $400 plus any unused amount of the exemption provided under paragraph (1) of this subsection, in any property."

Subsec. (e). Pub. L. 98–353, §453(c), substituted "an exemption" for "exemptions".

Subsec. (m). Pub. L. 98–353, §306(d), substituted "Subject to the limitation in subsection (b), this section shall apply separately with respect to each debtor in a joint case" for "This section shall apply separately with respect to each debtor in a joint case".

EFFECTIVE DATE OF 2005 AMENDMENT

Amendment by Pub. L. 109–8 effective 180 days after Apr. 20, 2005, with amendments by sections 216, 224(a), (e)(1), 307, and 313(a) of Pub. L. 109–8 not applicable with respect to cases commenced under this title before such effective date, except as otherwise provided, and amendments by sections 308 and 322(a) of Pub. L. 109–8 applicable with respect to cases commenced under this title on or after Apr. 20, 2005, see section 1501 of Pub. L. 109–8, set out as a note under section 101 of this title.

EFFECTIVE DATE OF 1994 AMENDMENT

Amendment by Pub. L. 103–394 effective Oct. 22, 1994, and not applicable with respect to cases commenced under this title before Oct. 22, 1994, see section 702 of Pub. L. 103–394, set out as a note under section 101 of this title.

EFFECTIVE DATE OF 1986 AMENDMENT

Amendment by Pub. L. 99–554 effective 30 days after Oct. 27, 1986, see section 302(a) of Pub. L. 99–554, set out as a note under section 581 of Title 28, Judiciary and Judicial Procedure.

EFFECTIVE DATE OF 1984 AMENDMENT

Amendment by Pub. L. 98–353 effective with respect to cases filed 90 days after July 10, 1984, see section 552(a) of Pub. L. 98–353, set out as a note under section 101 of this title.

ADJUSTMENT OF DOLLAR AMOUNTS

For adjustment of dollar amounts specified in subsecs. (d)(1) to (6), (8), (11)(D), (f)(3), (4), (n), (p), and (q) of this section by the Judicial Conference of the United States, see note set out under section 104 of this title.

§ 523. Exceptions to discharge

(a) A discharge under section 727, 1141, 1228(a), 1228(b), or 1328(b) of this title does not discharge an individual debtor from any debt—

(1) for a tax or a customs duty—

(A) of the kind and for the periods specified in section 507(a)(3) or 507(a)(8) of this title, whether or not a claim for such tax was filed or allowed;

(B) with respect to which a return, or equivalent report or notice, if required—

(i) was not filed or given; or

(ii) was filed or given after the date on which such return, report, or notice was last due, under applicable law or under any extension, and after two years before the date of the filing of the petition; or

(C) with respect to which the debtor made a fraudulent return or willfully attempted in any manner to evade or defeat such tax;

(2) for money, property, services, or an extension, renewal, or refinancing of credit, to the extent obtained by—

(A) false pretenses, a false representation, or actual fraud, other than a statement respecting the debtor's or an insider's financial condition;

(B) use of a statement in writing—

(i) that is materially false;

(ii) respecting the debtor's or an insider's financial condition;

(iii) on which the creditor to whom the debtor is liable for such money, property, services, or credit reasonably relied; and

(iv) that the debtor caused to be made or published with intent to deceive; or

(C)(i) for purposes of subparagraph (A)—

(I) consumer debts owed to a single creditor and aggregating more than $500 for luxury goods or services incurred by an individual debtor on or within 90 days before the order for relief under this title are presumed to be nondischargeable; and

(II) cash advances aggregating more than $750 that are extensions of consumer credit under an open end credit plan obtained by an individual debtor on or within 70 days before the order for relief under this title, are presumed to be nondischargeable; and

(ii) for purposes of this subparagraph—

(I) the terms "consumer", "credit", and "open end credit plan" have the same meanings as in section 103 of the Truth in Lending Act; and

(II) the term "luxury goods or services" does not include goods or services reasonably necessary for the support or maintenance of the debtor or a dependent of the debtor.

(3) neither listed nor scheduled under section 521(1) of this title, with the name, if known to the debtor, of the creditor to whom such debt is owed, in time to permit—

(A) if such debt is not of a kind specified in paragraph (2), (4), or (6) of this subsection, timely filing of a proof of claim, unless such creditor had notice or actual knowledge of the case in time for such timely filing; or

(B) if such debt is of a kind specified in paragraph (2), (4), or (6) of this subsection, timely filing of a proof of claim and timely request for a determination of dischargeability of such debt under one of such paragraphs, unless such creditor had notice or actual knowledge of the case in time for such timely filing and request;

(4) for fraud or defalcation while acting in a fiduciary capacity, embezzlement, or larceny;

(5) for a domestic support obligation;

(6) for willful and malicious injury by the debtor to another entity or to the property of another entity;

(7) to the extent such debt is for a fine, penalty, or forfeiture payable to and for the benefit of a governmental unit, and is not compensation for actual pecuniary loss, other than a tax penalty—

(A) relating to a tax of a kind not specified in paragraph (1) of this subsection; or

(B) imposed with respect to a transaction or event that occurred before three years before the date of the filing of the petition;

(8) unless excepting such debt from discharge under this paragraph would impose an undue hardship on the debtor and the debtor's dependents, for—

(A)(i) an educational benefit overpayment or loan made, insured, or guaranteed by a governmental unit, or made under any program funded in whole or in part by a governmental unit or nonprofit institution; or

(ii) an obligation to repay funds received as an educational benefit, scholarship, or stipend; or

(B) any other educational loan that is a qualified education loan, as defined in section 221(d)(1) of the Internal Revenue Code of 1986, incurred by a debtor who is an individual;

(9) for death or personal injury caused by the debtor's operation of a motor vehicle, vessel, or aircraft if such operation was unlawful because the debtor was intoxicated from using alcohol, a drug, or another substance;

(10) that was or could have been listed or scheduled by the debtor in a prior case concerning the debtor under this title or under the Bankruptcy Act in which the debtor waived discharge, or was denied a discharge under section 727(a)(2), (3), (4), (5), (6), or (7) of this title, or under section 14c(1), (2), (3), (4), (6), or (7) of such Act;

(11) provided in any final judgment, unreviewable order, or consent order or decree entered in any court of the United States or of any State, issued by a Federal depository institutions regulatory agency, or contained in any settlement agreement entered into by the debtor, arising from any act of fraud or defalcation while acting in a fiduciary capacity committed with respect to any depository institution or insured credit union;

(12) for malicious or reckless failure to fulfill any commitment by the debtor to a Federal depository institutions regulatory agency to maintain the capital of an insured depository institution, except that this paragraph shall not extend any such commitment which would otherwise be terminated due to any act of such agency;

(13) for any payment of an order of restitution issued under title 18, United States Code;

(14) incurred to pay a tax to the United States that would be nondischargeable pursuant to paragraph (1);

(14A) incurred to pay a tax to a governmental unit, other than the United States, that would be nondischargeable under paragraph (1);

(14B) incurred to pay fines or penalties imposed under Federal election law;

(15) to a spouse, former spouse, or child of the debtor and not of the kind described in paragraph (5) that is incurred by the debtor in the course of a divorce or separation or in connection with a separation agreement, divorce decree or other order of a court of record, or a determination made in accordance with State or territorial law by a governmental unit;

(16) for a fee or assessment that becomes due and payable after the order for relief to a membership association with respect to the debtor's interest in a unit that has condominium ownership, in a share of a cooperative corporation, or a lot in a homeowners association, for as long as the debtor or the trustee has a legal, equitable, or possessory ownership interest in such unit, such corporation, or such lot, but nothing in this paragraph shall except from discharge the debt of a debtor for a membership association fee or assessment for a period arising before entry of the order for relief in a pending or subsequent bankruptcy case;

(17) for a fee imposed on a prisoner by any court for the filing of a case, motion, complaint, or appeal, or for other costs and expenses assessed with respect to such filing, regardless of an assertion of poverty by the debtor under subsection (b) or (f)(2) of section 1915 of title 28 (or a similar non-Federal law), or the debtor's status as a prisoner, as defined in section 1915(h) of title 28 (or a similar non-Federal law);

(18) owed to a pension, profit-sharing, stock bonus, or other plan established under section 401, 403, 408, 408A, 414, 457, or 501(c) of the Internal Revenue Code of 1986, under—

(A) a loan permitted under section 408(b)(1) of the Employee Retirement Income Security Act of 1974, or subject to section 72(p) of the Internal Revenue Code of 1986; or

(B) a loan from a thrift savings plan permitted under subchapter III of chapter 84 of title 5, that satisfies the requirements of section 8433(g) of such title;

but nothing in this paragraph may be construed to provide that any loan made under a governmental plan under section 414(d), or a contract or account under section 403(b), of the Internal Revenue Code of 1986 constitutes a claim or a debt under this title; or

(19) that—

(A) is for—

(i) the violation of any of the Federal securities laws (as that term is defined in section 3(a)(47) of the Securities Exchange Act of 1934), any of the State securities laws, or any regulation or order issued under such Federal or State securities laws; or

(ii) common law fraud, deceit, or manipulation in connection with the purchase or sale of any security; and

(B) results, before, on, or after the date on which the petition was filed, from—

(i) any judgment, order, consent order, or decree entered in any Federal or State judicial or administrative proceeding;

(ii) any settlement agreement entered into by the debtor; or

(iii) any court or administrative order for any damages, fine, penalty, citation, restitutionary payment, disgorgement payment, attorney fee, cost, or other payment owed by the debtor.

For purposes of this subsection, the term "return" means a return that satisfies the requirements of applicable nonbankruptcy law (including applicable filing requirements). Such term includes a return prepared pursuant to section 6020(a) of the Internal Revenue Code of 1986, or similar State or local law, or a written stipulation to a judgment or a final order entered by a nonbankruptcy tribunal, but does not include a return made pursuant to section 6020(b) of the Internal Revenue Code of 1986, or a similar State or local law.

(b) Notwithstanding subsection (a) of this section, a debt that was excepted from discharge under subsection (a)(1), (a)(3), or (a)(8) of this section, under section 17a(1), 17a(3), or 17a(5) of the Bankruptcy Act, under section 439A[1] of the Higher Education Act of 1965, or under section 733(g)[1] of the Public Health Service Act in a prior case concerning the debtor under this title, or under the Bankruptcy Act, is dischargeable in a case under this title unless, by the terms of subsection (a) of this section, such debt is not dischargeable in the case under this title.

(c)(1) Except as provided in subsection (a)(3)(B) of this section, the debtor shall be discharged from a debt of a kind specified in paragraph (2), (4), or (6) of subsection (a) of this section, unless, on request of the creditor to whom such debt is owed, and after notice and a hearing, the court determines such debt to be excepted from discharge under paragraph (2), (4), or (6), as the case may be, of subsection (a) of this section.

[1] See References in Text note below.

(2) Paragraph (1) shall not apply in the case of a Federal depository institutions regulatory agency seeking, in its capacity as conservator, receiver, or liquidating agent for an insured depository institution, to recover a debt described in subsection (a)(2), (a)(4), (a)(6), or (a)(11) owed to such institution by an institution-affiliated party unless the receiver, conservator, or liquidating agent was appointed in time to reasonably comply, or for a Federal depository institutions regulatory agency acting in its corporate capacity as a successor to such receiver, conservator, or liquidating agent to reasonably comply, with subsection (a)(3)(B) as a creditor of such institution-affiliated party with respect to such debt.

(d) If a creditor requests a determination of dischargeability of a consumer debt under subsection (a)(2) of this section, and such debt is discharged, the court shall grant judgment in favor of the debtor for the costs of, and a reasonable attorney's fee for, the proceeding if the court finds that the position of the creditor was not substantially justified, except that the court shall not award such costs and fees if special circumstances would make the award unjust.

(e) Any institution-affiliated party of an insured depository institution shall be considered to be acting in a fiduciary capacity with respect to the purposes of subsection (a)(4) or (11).

(Pub. L. 95–598, Nov. 6, 1978, 92 Stat. 2590; Pub. L. 96–56, §3, Aug. 14, 1979, 93 Stat. 387; Pub. L. 97–35, title XXIII, §2334(b), Aug. 13, 1981, 95 Stat. 863; Pub. L. 98–353, title III, §§307, 371, 454, July 10, 1984, 98 Stat. 353, 364, 375; Pub. L. 99–554, title II, §§257(n), 281, 283(j), Oct. 27, 1986, 100 Stat. 3115–3117; Pub. L. 101–581, §2(a), Nov. 15, 1990, 104 Stat. 2865; Pub. L. 101–647, title XXV, §2522(a), title XXXI, §3102(a), title XXXVI, §3621, Nov. 29, 1990, 104 Stat. 4865, 4916, 4964; Pub. L. 103–322, title XXXII, §320934, Sept. 13, 1994, 108 Stat. 2135; Pub. L. 103–394, title II, §221, title III, §§304(e), (h)(3), 306, 309, title V, §501(d)(13), Oct. 22, 1994, 108 Stat. 4129, 4133–4135, 4137, 4145; Pub. L. 104–134, title I, §101[(a)] [title VIII, §804(b)], Apr. 26, 1996, 110 Stat. 1321, 1321–74; renumbered title I, Pub. L. 104–140, §1(a), May 2, 1996, 110 Stat. 1327; Pub. L. 104–193, title III, §374(a), Aug. 22, 1996, 110 Stat. 2255; Pub. L. 105–244, title IX, §971(a), Oct. 7, 1998, 112 Stat. 1837; Pub. L. 107–204, title VIII, §803, July 30, 2002, 116 Stat. 801; Pub. L. 109–8, title II, §§215, 220, 224(c), title III, §§301, 310, 314(a), title IV, §412, title VII, §714, title XII, §§1209, 1235, title XIV, §1404(a), title XV, §1502(a)(2), Apr. 20, 2005, 119 Stat. 54, 59, 64, 75, 84, 88, 107, 128, 194, 204, 215, 216.)

Historical and Revision Notes

Legislative Statements

Section 523(a)(1) represents a compromise between the position taken in the House bill and the Senate amendment. Section 523(a)(2) likewise represents a compromise between the position taken in the House bill and the Senate amendment with respect to the false financial statement exception to discharge. In order to clarify that a "renewal of credit" includes a "refinancing of credit", explicit reference to a refinancing of credit is made in the preamble to section 523(a)(2). A renewal of credit or refinancing of credit that was obtained by a false financial statement within the terms of section 523(a)(2) is nondischargeable. However, each of the provisions of section 523(a)(2) must be proved. Thus, under section 523(a)(2)(A) a creditor must prove that the debt was obtained by false pretenses, a false representation, or actual fraud, other than a statement respecting the debtor's or an insider's financial condition. Subparagraph (A) is intended to codify current case law e.g., *Neal v. Clark*, 95 U.S. 704 (1887) [24 L. Ed. 586], which interprets "fraud" to mean actual or positive fraud rather than fraud implied in law. Subparagraph (A) is mutually exclusive from subparagraph (B). Subparagraph (B) pertains to the so-called false financial statement. In order for the debt to be nondischargeable, the creditor must prove that the debt was obtained by the use of a statement in writing (i) that is materially false; (ii) respecting the debtor's or an insider's financial condition; (iii) on which the creditor to whom the debtor is liable for obtaining money, property, services, or credit reasonably relied; (iv) that the debtor caused to be made or published with intent to deceive. Section 523(a)(2)(B)(iv) is not intended to change from present law since the statement that the debtor causes to be made or published with the intent to deceive automatically includes a statement that the debtor actually makes or publishes with an intent to deceive. Section 523(a)(2)(B) is explained in the House report. Under section 523(a)(2)(B)(i) a discharge is barred only as to that portion of a loan with respect to which a false financial statement is materially false.

In many cases, a creditor is required by state law to refinance existing credit on which there has been no default. If the creditor does not forfeit remedies or otherwise rely to his detriment on a false financial statement with respect to existing credit, then an extension, renewal, or refinancing of such credit is nondischargeable only to the extent of the new money advanced; on the other hand, if an existing loan is in default or the creditor otherwise reasonably relies to his detriment on a false financial statement with regard to an existing loan, then the entire debt is nondischargeable under section 523(a)(2)(B). This codifies the reasoning expressed by the second circuit in *In re Danns*, 558 F.2d 114 (2d Cir. 1977).

Section 523(a)(3) of the House amendment is derived from the Senate amendment. The provision is intended to overrule *Birkett v. Columbia Bank*, 195 U.S. 345 (1904) [25 S.Ct. 38, 49 L.Ed. 231, 12 Am.Bankr.Rep. 691].

Section 523(a)(4) of the House amendment represents a compromise between the House bill and the Senate amendment.

Section 523(a)(5) is a compromise between the House bill and the Senate amendment. The provision excepts from discharge a debt owed to a spouse, former spouse or child of the debtor, in connection with a separation agreement, divorce decree, or property settlement agreement, for alimony to, maintenance for, or support of such spouse or child but not to the extent that the debt is assigned to another entity. If the debtor has assumed an obligation of the debtor's spouse to a third party in connection with a separation agreement, property settlement agreement, or divorce proceeding, such debt is dischargeable to the extent that payment of the debt by the debtor is not actually in the nature of alimony, maintenance, or support of debtor's spouse, former spouse, or child.

Section 523(a)(6) adopts the position taken in the House bill and rejects the alternative suggested in the Senate amendment. The phrase "willful and malicious injury" covers a willful and malicious conversion.

Section 523(a)(7) of the House amendment adopts the position taken in the Senate amendment and rejects the position taken in the House bill. A penalty relating to a tax cannot be nondischargeable unless the tax itself is nondischargeable.

Section 523(a)(8) represents a compromise between the House bill and the Senate amendment regarding educational loans. This provision is broader than current law which is limited to federally insured loans. Only educational loans owing to a governmental unit or a nonprofit institution of higher education are made nondischargeable under this paragraph.

Section 523(b) is new. The section represents a modification of similar provisions contained in the House bill and the Senate amendment.

Section 523(c) of the House amendment adopts the position taken in the Senate amendment.

Section 523(d) represents a compromise between the position taken in the House bill and the Senate amendment on the issue of attorneys' fees in false financial statement complaints to determine dischargeability. The provision contained in the House bill permitting the court to award damages is eliminated. The court must grant the debtor judgment or a reasonable attorneys' fee unless the granting of judgment would be clearly inequitable.

Nondischargeable debts: The House amendment retains the basic categories of nondischargeable tax liabilities contained in both bills, but restricts the time limits on certain nondischargeable taxes. Under the amendment, nondischargeable taxes cover taxes entitled to priority under section 507(a)(6) of title 11 and, in the case of individual debtors under chapters 7, 11, or 13, tax liabilities with respect to which no required return had been filed or as to which a late return had been filed if the return became last due, including extensions, within 2 years before the date of the petition or became due after the petition or as to which the debtor made a fraudulent return, entry or invoice or fraudulently attempted to evade or defeat the tax.

In the case of individuals in liquidation under chapter 7 or in reorganization under chapter 11 of title 11, section 1141(d)(2) incorporates by reference the exceptions to discharge continued in section 523. Different rules concerning the discharge of taxes where a partnership or corporation reorganizes under chapter 11, apply under section 1141.

The House amendment also deletes the reduction rule contained in section 523(e) of the Senate amendment. Under that rule, the amount of an otherwise nondischargeable tax liability would be reduced by the amount which a governmental tax authority could have collected from the debtor's estate if it had filed a timely claim against the estate but which it did not collect because no such claim was filed. This provision is deleted in order not to effectively compel a tax authority to file claim against the estate in "no asset" cases, along with a dischargeability petition. In no-asset cases, therefore, if the tax authority is not potentially penalized by failing to file a claim, the debtor in such cases will have a better opportunity to choose the prepayment forum, bankruptcy court or the Tax Court, in which to litigate his personal liability for a nondischargeable tax.

The House amendment also adopts the Senate amendment provision limiting the nondischargeability of punitive tax penalties, that is, penalties other than those which represent collection of a principal amount of tax liability through the form of a "penalty." Under the House amendment, tax penalties which are basically punitive in nature are to be nondischargeable only if the penalty is computed by reference to a related tax liability which is nondischargeable or, if the amount of the penalty is not computed by reference to a tax liability, the transaction or event giving rise to the penalty occurred during the 3-year period ending on the date of the petition.

SENATE REPORT NO. 95–989

This section specifies which of the debtor's debts are not discharged in a bankruptcy case, and certain procedures for effectuating the section. The provision in Bankruptcy Act §17c [section 35(c) of former title 11] granting the bankruptcy courts jurisdiction to determine dischargeability is deleted as unnecessary, in view of the comprehensive grant of jurisdiction prescribed in proposed 28 U.S.C. 1334(b), which is adequate to cover the full jurisdiction that the bankruptcy courts have today over dischargeability and related issues under Bankruptcy Act §17c. The Rules of Bankruptcy Procedure will specify, as they do today, who may request determinations of dischargeability, subject, of course, to proposed 11 U.S.C. 523(c), and when such a request may be made. Proposed 11 U.S.C. 350, providing for reopening of cases, provides one possible procedure for a determination of dischargeability and related issues after a case is closed.

Subsection (a) lists nine kinds of debts excepted from discharge. Taxes that are excepted from discharge are set forth in paragraph (1). These include claims against the debtor which receive priority in the second, third and sixth categories (§507(a)(3)(B) and (c) and (6)). These categories include taxes for which the tax authority failed to file a claim against the estate or filed its claim late. Whether or not the taxing authority's claim is secured will also not affect the claim's nondischargeability if the tax liability in question is otherwise entitled to priority.

Also included in the nondischargeable debts are taxes for which the debtor had not filed a required return as of the petition date, or for which a return had been filed beyond its last permitted due date (§523(a)(1)(B)). For this purpose, the date of the tax year to which the return relates is immaterial. The late return rule applies, however, only to the late returns filed within three years before the petition was filed, and to late returns filed after the petition in title 11 was filed. For this purpose, the taxable year in question need not be one or more of the three years immediately preceding the filing of the petition.

Tax claims with respect to which the debtor filed a fraudulent return, entry or invoice, or fraudulently attempted to evade or defeat any tax (§523(a)(1)(C)) are included. The date of the taxable year with regard to which the fraud occurred is immaterial.

Also included are tax payments due under an agreement for deferred payment of taxes, which a debtor had entered into with the Internal Revenue Service (or State or local tax authority) before the filing of the petition and which relate to a prepetition tax liability (§523(a)(1)(D)) are also nondischargeable. This classification applies only to tax claims which would have received priority under section 507(a) if the taxpayer had filed a title 11 petition on the date on which the deferred payment agreement was entered into. This rule also applies only to installment payments which become due during and after the commencement of the title 11 case. Payments which had become due within one year before the filing of the petition receive sixth priority, and will be nondischargeable under the general rule of section 523(a)(1)(A).

The above categories of nondischargeability apply to customs duties as well as to taxes.

Paragraph (2) provides that as under Bankruptcy Act §17a(2) [section 35(a)(2) of former title 11], a debt for obtaining money, property, services, or a refinancing extension or renewal of credit by false pretenses, a false representation, or actual fraud, or by use of a statement in writing respecting the debtor's financial condition that is materially false, on which the creditor reasonably relied, and which the debtor made or published with intent to deceive, is excepted from discharge. This provision is modified only slightly from current section 17a(2). First, "actual fraud" is added as a ground for exception from discharge. Second, the creditor must not only have relied on a false statement in writing, but the reliance must have been reasonable. This codifies case law construing present section 17a(2). Third, the phrase "in any manner whatsoever" that appears in current law after "made or published" is deleted as unnecessary, the word "published" is used in the same sense that it is used in defamation cases.

Unscheduled debts are excepted from discharge under paragraph (3). The provision, derived from section 17a(3) [section 35(a)(3) of former title 11], follows current law, but clarifies some uncertainties generated by the case law construing 17a(3). The debt is excepted from discharge if it was not scheduled in time to permit timely action by the creditor to protect his rights, unless the creditor had notice or actual knowledge of the case.

Paragraph (4) excepts debts for fraud incurred by the debtor while acting in a fiduciary capacity or for defalcation, embezzlement, or misappropriation.

Paragraph (5) provides that debts for willful and malicious conversion or injury by the debtor to another entity or the property of another entity are nondischargeable. Under this paragraph "willful" means deliberate or intentional. To the extent that *Tinker v. Colwell*, 139 U.S. 473 (1902), held that a less strict standard is intended, and to the extent that other cases have relied on *Tinker* to apply a "reckless disregard" standard, they are overruled.

Paragraph (6) excepts from discharge debts to a spouse, former spouse, or child of the debtor for alimony to, maintenance for, or support of the spouse or child. This language, in combination with the repeal of section 456(b) of the Social Security Act (42 U.S.C. 656(b)) by section 326 of the bill, will apply to make nondischargeable only alimony, maintenance, or support owed directly to a spouse or dependent. What constitutes alimony, maintenance, or support, will be determined under the bankruptcy law, not State law. Thus, cases such as *In re Waller*, 494 F.2d 447 (6th Cir. 1974), are overruled, and the result in cases such as *Fife v. Fife*, 1 Utah 2d 281, 265 P.2d 642 (1952) is followed. The proviso, however, makes nondischargeable any debts resulting from an agreement by the debtor to hold the debtor's spouse harmless on joint debts, to the extent that the agreement is in payment of alimony, maintenance, or support of the spouse, as determined under bankruptcy law considerations as to whether a particular agreement to pay money to a spouse is actually alimony or a property settlement.

Paragraph (7) makes nondischargeable certain liabilities for penalties including tax penalties if the underlying tax with respect to which the penalty was imposed is also nondischargeable (sec. 523(a)(7)). These latter liabilities cover those which, but are penal in nature, as distinct from so-called "pecuniary loss" penalties which, in the case of taxes, involve basically the collection of a tax under the label of a "penalty." This provision differs from the bill as introduced, which did not link the nondischarge of a tax penalty with the treatment of the underlying tax. The amended provision reflects the existing position of the Internal Revenue Service as to tax penalties imposed by the Internal Revenue Code (Rev.Rul. 68-574, 1968-2 C.B. 595).

Paragraph (8) follows generally current law and excerpts from discharge student loans until such loans have been due and owing for five years. Such loans include direct student loans as well as insured and guaranteed loans. This provision is intended to be self-executing and the lender or institution is not required to file a complaint to determine the nondischargeability of any student loan.

Paragraph (9) excepts from discharge debts that the debtor owed before a previous bankruptcy case concerning the debtor in which the debtor was denied a discharge other than on the basis of the six-year bar.

Subsection (b) of this section permits discharge in a bankruptcy case of an unscheduled debt from a prior case. This provision is carried over from Bankruptcy Act §17b [section 35(b) of former title 11]. The result dictated by the subsection would probably not be different if the subsection were not included. It is included nevertheless for clarity.

Subsection (c) requires a creditor who is owed a debt that may be excepted from discharge under paragraph (2), (4), or (5), (false statements, defalcation or larceny misappropriation, or willful and malicious injury) to initiate proceedings in the bankruptcy court for an exception to discharge. If the creditor does not act, the debt is discharged. This provision does not change current law.

Subsection (d) is new. It provides protection to a consumer debtor that dealt honestly with a creditor who sought to have a debt excepted from discharge on the ground of falsity in the incurring of the debt. The debtor may be awarded costs and a reasonable attorney's fee for the proceeding to determine the dischargeability of a debt under subsection (a)(2), if the court finds that the proceeding was frivolous or not brought by its creditor in good faith.

The purpose of the provision is to discourage creditors from initiating proceedings to obtaining a false financial statement exception to discharge in the hope of obtaining a settlement from an honest debtor anxious to save attorney's fees. Such practices impair the debtor's fresh start and are contrary to the spirit of the bankruptcy laws.

HOUSE REPORT NO. 95–595

Subsection (a) lists eight kinds of debts excepted from discharge. Taxes that are entitled to priority are excepted from discharge under paragraph (1). In addition, taxes with respect to which the debtor made a fraudulent return or willfully attempted to evade or defeat, or with respect to which a return (if required) was not filed or was not filed after the due date and after one year before the bankruptcy case are excepted from discharge. If the taxing authority's claim has been disallowed, then it would be barred by the more modern rules of collateral estoppel from reasserting that claim against the debtor after the case was closed. See Plumb, The Tax Recommendations of the Commission on the Bankruptcy Laws: Tax Procedures, 88 Harv.L.Rev. 1360, 1388 (1975).

As under Bankruptcy Act §17a(2) [section 35(a)(2) of former title 11], debt for obtaining money, property, services, or an extension or renewal of credit by false pretenses, a false representation, or actual fraud, or by use of a statement in writing respecting the debtor's financial condition that is materially false, on which the creditor reasonably relied, and that the debtor made or published with intent to deceive, is excepted from discharge. This provision is modified only slightly from current section 17a(2). First, "actual fraud" is added as a grounds for exception from discharge. Second, the creditor must not only have relied on a false statement in writing, the reliance must have been reasonable. This codifies case law construing this provision. Third, the phrase "in any manner whatsoever" that appears in current law after "made or published" is deleted as unnecessary. The word "published" is used in the same sense that it is used in slander actions.

Unscheduled debts are excepted from discharge under paragraph (3). The provision, derived from section 17a(3) [section 35(a)(3) of former title 11], follows current law, but clarifies some uncertainties generated by the case law construing 17a(3). The debt is excepted from discharge if it was not scheduled in time to permit timely action by the creditor to protect his rights, unless the creditor had notice or actual knowledge of the case.

Paragraph (4) excepts debts for embezzlement or larceny. The deletion of willful and malicious conversion from §17a(2) of the Bankruptcy Act [section 35(a)(2) of former title 11] is not intended to effect a substantive change. The intent is to include in the category of nondischargeable debts a conversion under which the debtor willfully and maliciously intends to borrow property for a short period of time with no intent to inflict injury but on which injury is in fact inflicted.

Paragraph (5) excepts from discharge debts to a spouse, former spouse, or child of the debtor for alimony to, maintenance for, or support of, the spouse or child. This language, in combination with the repeal of section 456(b) of the Social Security Act (42 U.S.C. 656(b)) by section 327 of the bill, will apply to make nondischargeable only alimony, maintenance, or support owed directly to a spouse or dependent. See Hearings, pt. 2, at 942. What constitutes alimony, maintenance, or support, will be determined under the bankruptcy laws, not State law. Thus, cases such as *In re Waller*, 494 F.2d 447 (6th Cir. 1974); Hearings, pt. 3, at 1308–10, are overruled, and the result in cases such as *Fife v. Fife*, 1 Utah 2d 281, 265 P.2d 642 (1952) is followed. This provision will, however, make nondischargeable any debts resulting from an agreement by the debtor to hold the debtor's spouse harmless on joint debts, to the extent that the agreement is in payment of alimony, maintenance, or support of the spouse, as determined under bankruptcy law considerations that are similar to considerations of whether a particular agreement to pay money to a spouse is actually alimony or a property settlement. See Hearings, pt. 3, at 1287–1290.

Paragraph (6) excepts debts for willful and malicious injury by the debtor to another person or to the property of another person. Under this paragraph, "willful" means deliberate or intentional. To the extent that *Tinker v. Colwell*, 193 U.S. 473 (1902) [24 S.Ct. 505, 48 L.Ed. 754, 11 Am.Bankr.Rep. 568], held that a looser standard is intended, and to the extent that other cases have relied on *Tinker* to apply a "reckless disregard" standard, they are overruled.

Paragraph (7) excepts from discharge a debt for a fine, penalty, or forfeiture payable to and for the benefit of a governmental unit, that is not compensation for actual pecuniary loss.

Paragraph (8) [enacted as (9)] excepts from discharge debts that the debtor owed before a previous bankruptcy case concerning the debtor in which the debtor was denied a discharge other than on the basis of the six-year bar.

Subsection (d) is new. It provides protection to a consumer debtor that dealt honestly with a creditor who sought to have a debt excepted from discharge on grounds of falsity in the incurring of the debt. The debtor is entitled to costs of and a reasonable attorney's fee for the proceeding to determine the dischargeability of a debt under subsection (a)(2), if the creditor initiated the proceeding and the debt was determined to be dischargeable. The court is permitted to award any actual pecuniary loss that the debtor may have suffered as a result of the proceeding (such as loss of a day's pay). The purpose of the provision is to discourage creditors from initiating false financial statement exception to discharge actions in the hopes of obtaining a settlement from an honest debtor anxious to save attorney's fees. Such practices impair the debtor's fresh start.

REFERENCES IN TEXT

The Internal Revenue Code of 1986, referred to in subsec. (a), is classified generally to Title 26, Internal Revenue Code.

Section 103 of the Truth in Lending Act, referred to in subsec. (a)(2)(C)(ii)(I), is classified to section 1602 of Title 15, Commerce and Trade.

The Bankruptcy Act, referred to in subsecs. (a)(10) and (b), is act July 1, 1898, ch. 541, 30 Stat. 544, as amended, which was classified generally to former Title 11. Sections 14c and 17a of the Bankruptcy Act were classified to sections 32(c) and 35(a) of former Title 11.

Section 408(b)(1) of the Employee Retirement Income Security Act of 1974, referred to in subsec. (a)(18)(A), is classified to section 1108(b)(1) of Title 29, Labor.

Section 3(a)(47) of the Securities Exchange Act of 1934, referred to in subsec. (a)(19)(A)(i), is classified to section 78c(a)(47) of Title 15, Commerce and Trade.

Section 439A of the Higher Education Act of 1965, referred to in subsec. (b), was classified to section 1087–3 of Title 20, Education, and was repealed by Pub. L. 95–598, title III, §317, Nov. 6, 1978, 92 Stat. 2678.

Section 733(g) of the Public Health Service Act, referred to in subsec. (b), was repealed by Pub. L. 95–598, title III, §327, Nov. 6, 1978, 92 Stat. 2679. A subsec. (g), containing similar provisions, was added to section 733 by Pub. L. 97–35, title XXVII, §2730, Aug. 13, 1981, 95 Stat. 919. Section 733 was subsequently omitted in the general revision of subchapter V of chapter 6A of Title 42, The Public Health and Welfare, by Pub. L. 102–408, title I, §102, Oct. 13, 1992, 106 Stat. 1994. See section 292f(g) of Title 42.

AMENDMENTS

2005—Pub. L. 109–8, §1209(1), transferred par. (15) and inserted it after subsec. (a)(14A). See 1994 Amendments note below.

Pub. L. 109–8, §215(3), in par. (15), inserted "to a spouse, former spouse, or child of the debtor and" before "not of the kind" and "or" after "court of record," and substituted a semicolon for "unless—

"(A) the debtor does not have the ability to pay such debt from income or property of the debtor not reasonably necessary to be expended for the maintenance or support of the debtor or a dependent of the debtor and, if the debtor is engaged in a business, for the payment of expenditures necessary for the continuation, preservation, and operation of such business; or

"(B) discharging such debt would result in a benefit to the debtor that outweighs the detrimental consequences to a spouse, former spouse, or child of the debtor;".

Subsec. (a). Pub. L. 109–8, §714(2), inserted at end "For purposes of this subsection, the term 'return' means a return that satisfies the requirements of applicable nonbankruptcy law (including applicable filing requirements). Such term includes a return prepared pursuant to section 6020(a) of the Internal Revenue Code of 1986, or similar State or local law, or a written stipulation to a judgment or a final order entered by a nonbankruptcy tribunal, but does not include a return made pursuant to section 6020(b) of the Internal Revenue Code of 1986, or a similar State or local law."

Subsec. (a)(1)(A). Pub. L. 109–8, §1502(a)(2), substituted "507(a)(3)" for "507(a)(2)".

Subsec. (a)(1)(B). Pub. L. 109–8, §714(1)(A), inserted "or equivalent report or notice," after "a return," in introductory provisions.

Subsec. (a)(1)(B)(i). Pub. L. 109–8, §714(1)(B), inserted "or given" after "filed".

Subsec. (a)(1)(B)(ii). Pub. L. 109–8, §714(1)(C), inserted "or given" after "filed" and ", report, or notice" after "return".

Subsec. (a)(2)(C). Pub. L. 109–8, §310, amended subpar. (C) generally. Prior to amendment, subpar. (C) read as follows: "for purposes of subparagraph (A) of this paragraph, consumer debts owed to a single creditor and aggregating more than $1,000 for 'luxury goods or services' incurred by an individual debtor on or within 60 days before the order for relief under this title, or cash advances aggregating more than $1,000 that are extensions of consumer credit under an open end credit plan obtained by an individual debtor on or within 60 days before the order for relief under this title, are presumed to be nondischargeable; 'luxury goods or services' do not include goods or services reasonably acquired for the support or maintenance of the debtor or a dependent of the debtor; an extension of consumer credit under an open end credit plan is to be defined for purposes of this subparagraph as it is defined in the Consumer Credit Protection Act;".

Subsec. (a)(5). Pub. L. 109–8, §215(1)(A), added par. (5) and struck out former par. (5) which read as follows: "to a spouse, former spouse, or child of the debtor, for alimony to, maintenance for, or support of such spouse or child, in connection with a separation agreement, divorce decree or other order of a court of record, determination made in accordance with State or territorial law by a governmental unit, or property settlement agreement, but not to the extent that—

"(A) such debt is assigned to another entity, voluntarily, by operation of law, or otherwise (other than debts assigned pursuant to section 408(a)(3) of the Social Security Act, or any such debt which has been assigned to the Federal Government or to a State or any political subdivision of such State); or

"(B) such debt includes a liability designated as alimony, maintenance, or support, unless such liability is actually in the nature of alimony, maintenance, or support;".

Subsec. (a)(8). Pub. L. 109–8, §220, added par. (8) and struck out former par. (8) which read as follows: "for an educational benefit overpayment or loan made, insured or guaranteed by a governmental unit, or made under any program funded in whole or in part by a governmental unit or nonprofit institution, or for an obligation to repay funds received as an educational benefit, scholarship or stipend, unless excepting such debt from discharge under this paragraph will impose an undue hardship on the debtor and the debtor's dependents;".

Subsec. (a)(9). Pub. L. 109–8, §1209(2), substituted "motor vehicle, vessel, or aircraft" for "motor vehicle".

Subsec. (a)(14A). Pub. L. 109–8, §314(a), added par. (14A).

Subsec. (a)(14B). Pub. L. 109–8, §1235, added par. (14B).

Subsec. (a)(16). Pub. L. 109–8, §412, struck out "dwelling" after "debtor's interest in a" and "housing" after "share of a cooperative" and substituted "ownership," for "ownership or" and "or a lot in a homeowners association, for as long as the debtor or the trustee has a legal, equitable, or possessory ownership interest in such unit, such corporation, or such lot," for "but only if such fee or assessment is payable for a period during which—

"(A) the debtor physically occupied a dwelling unit in the condominium or cooperative project; or

"(B) the debtor rented the dwelling unit to a tenant and received payments from the tenant for such period,".

Subsec. (a)(17). Pub. L. 109–8, §301, substituted "on a prisoner by any court" for "by a court" and "subsection (b) or (f)(2) of section 1915" for "section 1915(b) or (f)" and inserted "(or a similar non-Federal law)" after "title 28" in two places.

Subsec. (a)(18). Pub. L. 109–8, §224(c), added par. (18).

Pub. L. 109–8, §215(1)(B), struck out par. (18) which read as follows: "owed under State law to a State or municipality that is—

"(A) in the nature of support, and

"(B) enforceable under part D of title IV of the Social Security Act (42 U.S.C. 601 et seq.); or".

Subsec. (a)(19)(B). Pub. L. 109–8, §1404(a), inserted ", before, on, or after the date on which the petition was filed," after "results" in introductory provisions.

Subsec. (c)(1). Pub. L. 109–8, §215(2), substituted "or (6)" for "(6), or (15)" in two places.

Subsec. (e). Pub. L. 109–8, §1209(3), substituted "an insured" for "a insured".

2002—Subsec. (a)(19). Pub. L. 107–204 added par. (19).

1998—Subsec. (a)(8). Pub. L. 105–244 substituted "stipend, unless" for "stipend, unless—" and struck out "(B)" before "excepting such debt" and subpar. (A) which read as follows: "such loan, benefit, scholarship, or stipend overpayment first became due more than 7 years (exclusive of any applicable suspension of the repayment period) before the date of the filing of the petition; or".

1996—Subsec. (a)(5)(A). Pub. L. 104–193, §374(a)(4), substituted "section 408(a)(3)" for "section 402(a)(26)".

Subsec. (a)(17). Pub. L. 104–134 added par. (17).

Subsec. (a)(18). Pub. L. 104–193, §374(a)(1)–(3), added par. (18).

1994—Par. (15). Pub. L. 103–394, §304(e)[(1)], amended this section by adding par. (15) at the end. See 2005 Amendment note above.

Subsec. (a). Pub. L. 103–394, §501(d)(13)(A)(i), substituted "1141," for "1141,," in introductory provisions.

Subsec. (a)(1)(A). Pub. L. 103–394, §304(h)(3), substituted "507(a)(8)" for "507(a)(7)".

Subsec. (a)(2)(C). Pub. L. 103–394, §§306, 501(d)(13)(A)(ii), substituted "$1,000 for" for "$500 for", "60" for "forty" after "incurred by an individual debtor on or within", and "60" for "twenty" after "obtained by an individual debtor on or within", and struck out "(15 U.S.C. 1601 et seq.)" after "Protection Act".

Subsec. (a)(11). Pub. L. 103–322, §320934(1), struck out "or" after semicolon at end.

Subsec. (a)(12). Pub. L. 103–322, §320934(2), which directed the substitution of "; or" for a period at end of par. (12), could not be executed because a period did not appear at end.

Subsec. (a)(13). Pub. L. 103–394, §221(1), substituted semicolon for period at end.

Pub. L. 103–322, §320934(3), added par. (13).

Subsec. (a)(14). Pub. L. 103–394, §221(2), added par. (14).

Subsec. (a)(16). Pub. L. 103–394, §309, added par. (16).

Subsec. (b). Pub. L. 103–394, §501(d)(13)(B), struck out "(20 U.S.C. 1087–3)" after "Act of 1965" and "(42 U.S.C. 294f)" after "Service Act".

Subsec. (c)(1). Pub. L. 103–394, §304(e)(2), substituted "(6), or (15)" for "or (6)" in two places.

Subsec. (e). Pub. L. 103–394, §501(d)(13)(C), substituted "insured depository institution" for "depository institution or insured credit union".

1990—Subsec. (a)(8). Pub. L. 101–647, §3621, substituted "for an educational benefit overpayment or loan made, insured or guaranteed by a governmental unit, or made under any program funded in whole or in part by a governmental unit or nonprofit institution, or for an obligation to repay funds received as an educational benefit, scholarship or stipend, unless" for "for an educational loan made, insured, or guaranteed by a governmental unit, or made under any program funded in whole or in part by a governmental unit or a nonprofit institution, unless" in introductory provisions and amended subpar. (A) generally. Prior to amendment, subpar. (A) read as follows: "such loan first became due before five years (exclusive of any applicable suspension of the repayment period) before the date of the filing of the petition; or".

Subsec. (a)(9). Pub. L. 101–581 and Pub. L. 101–647, §3102(a), identically amended par. (9) generally. Prior to amendment, par. (9) read as follows: "to any entity, to the extent that such debt arises from a judgment or consent decree entered in a court of record against the debtor wherein liability was incurred by such debtor as a result of the debtor's operation of a motor vehicle while legally intoxicated under the laws or regulations of any jurisdiction within the United States or its territories wherein such motor vehicle was operated and within which such liability was incurred; or".

Subsec. (a)(11), (12). Pub. L. 101–647, §2522(a)(1), added pars. (11) and (12).

Subsec. (c). Pub. L. 101–647, §2522(a)(3), designated existing provisions as par. (1) and added par. (2).

Subsec. (e). Pub. L. 101–647, §2522(a)(2), added subsec. (e).

1986—Subsec. (a). Pub. L. 99–554, §257(n), inserted reference to sections 1228(a) and 1228(b) of this title.

Subsec. (a)(1)(A). Pub. L. 99–554, §283(j)(1)(A), substituted "507(a)(7)" for "507(a)(6)".

Subsec. (a)(5). Pub. L. 99–554, §281, struck out the comma after "decree" and inserted ", determination made in accordance with State or territorial law by a governmental unit," after "record".

Subsec. (a)(9), (10). Pub. L. 99–554, §283(j)(1)(B), redesignated par. (9) relating to debts incurred by persons driving while intoxicated, added by Pub. L. 98–353, as (10).

Subsec. (b). Pub. L. 99–554, §283(j)(2), substituted "Service" for "Services".

1984—Subsec. (a)(2). Pub. L. 98–353, §454(a)(1), in provisions preceding subpar. (A), struck out "obtaining" after "for", and substituted "refinancing of credit, to the extent obtained" for "refinance of credit,".

Subsec. (a)(2)(A). Pub. L. 98–353, §307(a)(1), struck out "or" at end.

Subsec. (a)(2)(B). Pub. L. 98–353, §307(a)(2), inserted "or" at end.

Subsec. (a)(2)(B)(iii). Pub. L. 98–353, §454(a)(1)(A), struck out "obtaining" before "such".

Subsec. (a)(2)(C). Pub. L. 98–353, §307(a)(3), added subpar. (C).

Subsec. (a)(5). Pub. L. 98–353, §454(b)(1), inserted "or other order of a court of record" after "divorce decree," in provisions preceding subpar. (A).

Subsec. (a)(5)(A). Pub. L. 98–353, §454(b)(2), inserted ", or any such debt which has been assigned to the Federal Government or to a State or any political subdivision of such State".

Subsec. (a)(8). Pub. L. 98–353, §§371(1), 454(a)(2), struck out "of higher education" after "a nonprofit institution of" and struck out "or" at end.

Subsec. (a)(9). Pub. L. 98–353, §371(2), added the par. (9) relating to debts incurred by persons driving while intoxicated.

Subsec. (c). Pub. L. 98–353, §454(c), inserted "of a kind" after "debt".

Subsec. (d). Pub. L. 98–353, §307(b), substituted "the court shall grant judgment in favor of the debtor for the costs of, and a reasonable attorney's fee for, the proceeding if the court finds that the position of the creditor was not substantially justified, except that the court shall not award such costs and fees if special circumstances would make the award unjust" for "the court shall grant judgment against such creditor and in favor of the debtor for the costs of, and a reasonable attorney's fee for, the proceeding to determine dischargeability, unless such granting of judgment would be clearly inequitable".

1981—Subsec. (a)(5)(A). Pub. L. 97–35 substituted "law, or otherwise (other than debts assigned pursuant to section 402(a)(26) of the Social Security Act);" for "law, or otherwise;".

1979—Subsec. (a)(8). Pub. L. 96–56 substituted "for an educational loan made, insured, or guaranteed by a governmental unit, or made under any program funded in whole or in part by a governmental unit or a nonprofit institution of higher education" for "to a governmental unit, or a nonprofit institution of higher education, for an educational loan" in the provisions preceding subpar. (A) and inserted "(exclusive of any applicable suspension of the repayment period)" after "before five years" in subpar. (A).

Effective Date of 2005 Amendment

Pub. L. 109–8, title XIV, §1404(b), Apr. 20, 2005, 119 Stat. 215, provided that: "The amendment made by subsection (a) [amending this section] is effective beginning July 30, 2002."

Amendment by sections 215, 220, 224(c), 301, 310, 314(a), 412, 714, 1209, 1235, and 1502(a)(2) of Pub. L. 109–8 effective 180 days after Apr. 20, 2005, and not applicable with respect to cases commenced under this title before such effective date, except as otherwise provided, see section 1501 of Pub. L. 109–8, set out as a note under section 101 of this title.

Effective Date of 1998 Amendment

Pub. L. 105–244, title IX, §971(b), Oct. 7, 1998, 112 Stat. 1837, provided that: "The amendment made by subsection (a) [amending this section] shall apply only with respect to cases commenced under title 11, United States Code, after the date of enactment of this Act [Oct. 7, 1998]."

Effective Date of 1996 Amendment

Section 374(c) of Pub. L. 104–193 provided that: "The amendments made by this section [amending this section and section 656 of Title 42, The Public Health and Welfare] shall apply only with respect to cases commenced under title 11 of the United States Code after the date of the enactment of this Act [Aug. 22, 1996]."

For provisions relating to effective date of title III of Pub. L. 104–193, see section 395(a)–(c) of Pub. L. 104–193, set out as a note under section 654 of Title 42, The Public Health and Welfare.

Effective Date of 1994 Amendment

Amendment by Pub. L. 103–394 effective Oct. 22, 1994, and not applicable with respect to cases commenced under this title before Oct. 22, 1994, see section 702 of Pub. L. 103–394, set out as a note under section 101 of this title.

Effective Date of 1990 Amendments

Section 3104 of title XXXI of Pub. L. 101–647 provided that:

"(a) Effective Date.—This title and the amendments made by this title [amending this section and section 1328 of this title and enacting provisions set out as a note under section 101 of this title] shall take effect on the date of the enactment of this Act [Nov. 29, 1990].

"(b) Application of Amendments.—The amendments made by this title [amending this section and section 1328 of this title] shall not apply with respect to cases commenced under title 11 of the United States Code before the date of the enactment of this Act."

Amendment by section 3621 of Pub. L. 101–647 effective 180 days after Nov. 29, 1990, see section 3631 of Pub. L. 101–647, set out as an Effective Date note under section 3001 of Title 28, Judiciary and Judicial Procedure.

Section 4 of Pub. L. 101–581 provided that:

"(a) EFFECTIVE DATE.—This Act and the amendments made by this Act [amending this section and section 1328 of this title and enacting provisions set out as a note under section 101 of this title] shall take effect on the date of the enactment of this Act [Nov. 15, 1990].

"(b) APPLICATION OF AMENDMENTS.—The amendments made by this Act [amending this section and section 1328 of this title] shall not apply with respect to cases commenced under title 11 of the United States Code before the date of the enactment of this Act."

EFFECTIVE DATE OF 1986 AMENDMENT

Amendment by section 257 of Pub. L. 99–554 effective 30 days after Oct. 27, 1986, but not applicable to cases commenced under this title before that date, see section 302(a), (c)(1) of Pub. L. 99–554, set out as a note under section 581 of Title 28, Judiciary and Judicial Procedure.

Amendment by sections 281 and 283 of Pub. L. 99–554 effective 30 days after Oct. 27, 1986, see section 302(a) of Pub. L. 99–554.

EFFECTIVE DATE OF 1984 AMENDMENT

Amendment by Pub. L. 98–353 effective with respect to cases filed 90 days after July 10, 1984, see section 552(a) of Pub. L. 98–353, set out as a note under section 101 of this title.

EFFECTIVE DATE OF 1981 AMENDMENT

Amendment by Pub. L. 97–35 effective Aug. 13, 1981, see section 2334(c) of Pub. L. 97–35, set out as a note under section 656 of Title 42, The Public Health and Welfare.

ADJUSTMENT OF DOLLAR AMOUNTS

For adjustment of dollar amounts specified in subsec. (a)(2)(C)(i) of this section by the Judicial Conference of the United States, see note set out under section 104 of this title.

§ 524. Effect of discharge

(a) A discharge in a case under this title—

(1) voids any judgment at any time obtained, to the extent that such judgment is a determination of the personal liability of the debtor with respect to any debt discharged under section 727, 944, 1141, 1228, or 1328 of this title, whether or not discharge of such debt is waived;

(2) operates as an injunction against the commencement or continuation of an action, the employment of process, or an act, to collect, recover or offset any such debt as a personal liability of the debtor, whether or not discharge of such debt is waived; and

(3) operates as an injunction against the commencement or continuation of an action, the employment of process, or an act, to collect or recover from, or offset against, property of the debtor of the kind specified in section 541(a)(2) of this title that is acquired after the commencement of the case, on account of any allowable community claim, except a community claim that is excepted from discharge under section 523, 1228(a)(1), or 1328(a)(1), or that would be so excepted, determined in accordance with the provisions of sections 523(c) and 523(d) of this title, in a case concerning the debtor's spouse commenced on the date of the filing of the petition in the case concerning the debtor, whether or not discharge of the debt based on such community claim is waived.

(b) Subsection (a)(3) of this section does not apply if—

(1)(A) the debtor's spouse is a debtor in a case under this title, or a bankrupt or a debtor in a case under the Bankruptcy Act, commenced within six years of the date of the filing of the petition in the case concerning the debtor; and

(B) the court does not grant the debtor's spouse a discharge in such case concerning the debtor's spouse; or

(2)(A) the court would not grant the debtor's spouse a discharge in a case under chapter 7 of this title concerning such spouse commenced on the date of the filing of the petition in the case concerning the debtor; and

(B) a determination that the court would not so grant such discharge is made by the bankruptcy court within the time and in the manner provided for a determination under section 727 of this title of whether a debtor is granted a discharge.

(c) An agreement between a holder of a claim and the debtor, the consideration for which, in whole or in part, is based on a debt that is dischargeable in a case under this title is enforceable only to any extent enforceable under applicable nonbankruptcy law, whether or not discharge of such debt is waived, only if—

(1) such agreement was made before the granting of the discharge under section 727, 1141, 1228, or 1328 of this title;

(2) the debtor received the disclosures described in subsection (k) at or before the time at which the debtor signed the agreement;

(3) such agreement has been filed with the court and, if applicable, accompanied by a declaration or an affidavit of the attorney that represented the debtor during the course of negotiating an agreement under this subsection, which states that—

(A) such agreement represents a fully informed and voluntary agreement by the debtor;

(B) such agreement does not impose an undue hardship on the debtor or a dependent of the debtor; and

(C) the attorney fully advised the debtor of the legal effect and consequences of—

(i) an agreement of the kind specified in this subsection; and

(ii) any default under such an agreement;

(4) the debtor has not rescinded such agreement at any time prior to discharge or within sixty days after such agreement is filed with the court, whichever occurs later, by giving notice of rescission to the holder of such claim;

(5) the provisions of subsection (d) of this section have been complied with; and

(6)(A) in a case concerning an individual who was not represented by an attorney during the course of negotiating an agreement under this subsection, the court approves such agreement as—

(i) not imposing an undue hardship on the debtor or a dependent of the debtor; and

(ii) in the best interest of the debtor.

(B) Subparagraph (A) shall not apply to the extent that such debt is a consumer debt secured by real property.

(d) In a case concerning an individual, when the court has determined whether to grant or not to grant a discharge under section 727, 1141, 1228, or 1328 of this title, the court may hold a hearing at which the debtor shall appear in person. At any such hearing, the court shall inform the debtor that a discharge has been granted or the reason why a discharge has not been granted. If a discharge has been granted and if the debtor desires to make an agreement of the kind specified in subsection (c) of this section and was not represented by an attorney during the course of negotiating such agreement, then the court shall hold a hearing at which the debtor shall appear in person and at such hearing the court shall—

(1) inform the debtor—

(A) that such an agreement is not required under this title, under nonbankruptcy law, or under any agreement not made in accordance with the provisions of subsection (c) of this section; and

(B) of the legal effect and consequences of—

(i) an agreement of the kind specified in subsection (c) of this section; and

(ii) a default under such an agreement; and

(2) determine whether the agreement that the debtor desires to make complies with the requirements of subsection (c)(6) of this section, if the consideration for such agreement is based in whole or in part on a consumer debt that is not secured by real property of the debtor.

(e) Except as provided in subsection (a)(3) of this section, discharge of a debt of the debtor does not affect the liability of any other entity on, or the property of any other entity for, such debt.

(f) Nothing contained in subsection (c) or (d) of this section prevents a debtor from voluntarily repaying any debt.

(g)(1)(A) After notice and hearing, a court that enters an order confirming a plan of reorganization under chapter 11 may issue, in connection with such order, an injunction in accordance with this subsection to supplement the injunctive effect of a discharge under this section.

(B) An injunction may be issued under subparagraph (A) to enjoin entities from taking legal action for the purpose of directly or indirectly collecting, recovering, or receiving payment or recovery with respect to any claim or demand that, under a plan of reorganization, is to be paid in whole or in part by a trust described in paragraph (2)(B)(i), except such legal actions as are expressly allowed by the injunction, the confirmation order, or the plan of reorganization.

(2)(A) Subject to subsection (h), if the requirements of subparagraph (B) are met at the time an injunction described in paragraph (1) is entered, then after entry of such injunction, any proceeding that involves the validity, application, construction, or modification of such injunction, or of this subsection with respect to such injunction, may be commenced only in the district court in which such injunction was entered, and such court shall have exclusive jurisdiction over any such proceeding without regard to the amount in controversy.

(B) The requirements of this subparagraph are that—

(i) the injunction is to be implemented in connection with a trust that, pursuant to the plan of reorganization—

(I) is to assume the liabilities of a debtor which at the time of entry of the order for relief has been named as a defendant in personal injury, wrongful death, or property-damage actions seeking recovery for damages allegedly caused by the presence of, or exposure to, asbestos or asbestos-containing products;

(II) is to be funded in whole or in part by the securities of 1 or more debtors involved in such plan and by the obligation of such debtor or debtors to make future payments, including dividends;

(III) is to own, or by the exercise of rights granted under such plan would be entitled to own if specified contingencies occur, a majority of the voting shares of—

(aa) each such debtor;

(bb) the parent corporation of each such debtor; or

(cc) a subsidiary of each such debtor that is also a debtor; and

(IV) is to use its assets or income to pay claims and demands; and

(ii) subject to subsection (h), the court determines that—

(I) the debtor is likely to be subject to substantial future demands for payment arising out of the same or similar conduct or events that gave rise to the claims that are addressed by the injunction;

(II) the actual amounts, numbers, and timing of such future demands cannot be determined;

(III) pursuit of such demands outside the procedures prescribed by such plan is likely to threaten the plan's purpose to deal equitably with claims and future demands;

(IV) as part of the process of seeking confirmation of such plan—

(aa) the terms of the injunction proposed to be issued under paragraph (1)(A), including any provisions barring actions against third parties pursuant to paragraph (4)(A), are set out in such plan and in any disclosure statement supporting the plan; and

(bb) a separate class or classes of the claimants whose claims are to be addressed by a trust described in clause (i) is established and votes, by at least 75 percent of those voting, in favor of the plan; and

(V) subject to subsection (h), pursuant to court orders or otherwise, the trust will operate through mechanisms such as structured, periodic, or supplemental payments, pro rata distributions, matrices, or periodic review of estimates of the numbers and values of present claims and future demands, or other comparable mechanisms, that provide reasonable assurance that the trust will value, and be in a financial position to pay, present claims and future demands that involve similar claims in substantially the same manner.

(3)(A) If the requirements of paragraph (2)(B) are met and the order confirming the plan of reorganization was issued or affirmed by the district court that has jurisdiction over the reorganization case, then after the time for appeal of the order that issues or affirms the plan—

(i) the injunction shall be valid and enforceable and may not be revoked or modified by any court except through appeal in accordance with paragraph (6);

(ii) no entity that pursuant to such plan or thereafter becomes a direct or indirect transferee of, or successor to any assets of, a debtor or trust that is the subject of the injunction shall be liable with respect to any claim or demand made against such entity by reason of its becoming such a transferee or successor; and

(iii) no entity that pursuant to such plan or thereafter makes a loan to such a debtor or trust or to such a successor or transferee shall, by reason of making the loan, be liable with respect to any claim or demand made against such entity, nor shall any pledge of assets made in connection with such a loan be upset or impaired for that reason;

(B) Subparagraph (A) shall not be construed to—

(i) imply that an entity described in subparagraph (A)(ii) or (iii) would, if this paragraph were not applicable, necessarily be liable to any entity by reason of any of the acts described in subparagraph (A);

(ii) relieve any such entity of the duty to comply with, or of liability under, any Federal or State law regarding the making of a fraudulent conveyance in a transaction described in subparagraph (A)(ii) or (iii); or

(iii) relieve a debtor of the debtor's obligation to comply with the terms of the plan of reorganization, or affect the power of the court to exercise its authority under sections 1141 and 1142 to compel the debtor to do so.

(4)(A)(i) Subject to subparagraph (B), an injunction described in paragraph (1) shall be valid and enforceable against all entities that it addresses.

(ii) Notwithstanding the provisions of section 524(e), such an injunction may bar any action directed against a third party who is identifiable from the terms of such injunction (by name or as part of an identifiable group) and is alleged to be directly or indirectly liable for the conduct of, claims against, or demands on the debtor to the extent such alleged liability of such third party arises by reason of—

(I) the third party's ownership of a financial interest in the debtor, a past or present affiliate of the debtor, or a predecessor in interest of the debtor;

(II) the third party's involvement in the management of the debtor or a predecessor in interest of the debtor, or service as an officer, director or employee of the debtor or a related party;

(III) the third party's provision of insurance to the debtor or a related party; or

(IV) the third party's involvement in a transaction changing the corporate structure, or in a loan or other financial transaction affecting the financial condition, of the debtor or a related party, including but not limited to—

(aa) involvement in providing financing (debt or equity), or advice to an entity involved in such a transaction; or

(bb) acquiring or selling a financial interest in an entity as part of such a transaction.

(iii) As used in this subparagraph, the term "related party" means—

(I) a past or present affiliate of the debtor;

(II) a predecessor in interest of the debtor; or

(III) any entity that owned a financial interest in—

(aa) the debtor;

(bb) a past or present affiliate of the debtor; or

(cc) a predecessor in interest of the debtor.

(B) Subject to subsection (h), if, under a plan of reorganization, a kind of demand described in such plan is to be paid in whole or in part by a trust described in paragraph (2)(B)(i) in connection with which an injunction described in paragraph (1) is to be implemented, then such injunction shall be valid and enforceable with respect to a demand of such kind made, after such plan is confirmed, against the debtor or debtors involved, or against a third party described in subparagraph (A)(ii), if—

(i) as part of the proceedings leading to issuance of such injunction, the court appoints a legal representative for the purpose of protecting the rights of persons that might subsequently assert demands of such kind, and

(ii) the court determines, before entering the order confirming such plan, that identifying such debtor or debtors, or such third party (by name or as part of an identifiable group), in such injunction with respect to such demands for purposes of this subparagraph is fair and equitable with respect to the persons that might subsequently assert such demands, in light of the benefits provided, or to be provided, to such trust on behalf of such debtor or debtors or such third party.

(5) In this subsection, the term "demand" means a demand for payment, present or future, that—

(A) was not a claim during the proceedings leading to the confirmation of a plan of reorganization;

(B) arises out of the same or similar conduct or events that gave rise to the claims addressed by the injunction issued under paragraph (1); and

(C) pursuant to the plan, is to be paid by a trust described in paragraph (2)(B)(i).

(6) Paragraph (3)(A)(i) does not bar an action taken by or at the direction of an appellate court on appeal of an injunction issued under

paragraph (1) or of the order of confirmation that relates to the injunction.

(7) This subsection does not affect the operation of section 1144 or the power of the district court to refer a proceeding under section 157 of title 28 or any reference of a proceeding made prior to the date of the enactment of this subsection.

(h) APPLICATION TO EXISTING INJUNCTIONS.—For purposes of subsection (g)—

(1) subject to paragraph (2), if an injunction of the kind described in subsection (g)(1)(B) was issued before the date of the enactment of this Act, as part of a plan of reorganization confirmed by an order entered before such date, then the injunction shall be considered to meet the requirements of subsection (g)(2)(B) for purposes of subsection (g)(2)(A), and to satisfy subsection (g)(4)(A)(ii), if—

(A) the court determined at the time the plan was confirmed that the plan was fair and equitable in accordance with the requirements of section 1129(b);

(B) as part of the proceedings leading to issuance of such injunction and confirmation of such plan, the court had appointed a legal representative for the purpose of protecting the rights of persons that might subsequently assert demands described in subsection (g)(4)(B) with respect to such plan; and

(C) such legal representative did not object to confirmation of such plan or issuance of such injunction; and

(2) for purposes of paragraph (1), if a trust described in subsection (g)(2)(B)(i) is subject to a court order on the date of the enactment of this Act staying such trust from settling or paying further claims—

(A) the requirements of subsection (g)(2)(B)(ii)(V) shall not apply with respect to such trust until such stay is lifted or dissolved; and

(B) if such trust meets such requirements on the date such stay is lifted or dissolved, such trust shall be considered to have met such requirements continuously from the date of the enactment of this Act.

(i) The willful failure of a creditor to credit payments received under a plan confirmed under this title, unless the order confirming the plan is revoked, the plan is in default, or the creditor has not received payments required to be made under the plan in the manner required by the plan (including crediting the amounts required under the plan), shall constitute a violation of an injunction under subsection (a)(2) if the act of the creditor to collect and failure to credit payments in the manner required by the plan caused material injury to the debtor.

(j) Subsection (a)(2) does not operate as an injunction against an act by a creditor that is the holder of a secured claim, if—

(1) such creditor retains a security interest in real property that is the principal residence of the debtor;

(2) such act is in the ordinary course of business between the creditor and the debtor; and

(3) such act is limited to seeking or obtaining periodic payments associated with a valid security interest in lieu of pursuit of in rem relief to enforce the lien.

(k)(1) The disclosures required under subsection (c)(2) shall consist of the disclosure statement described in paragraph (3), completed as required in that paragraph, together with the agreement specified in subsection (c), statement, declaration, motion and order described, respectively, in paragraphs (4) through (8), and shall be the only disclosures required in connection with entering into such agreement.

(2) Disclosures made under paragraph (1) shall be made clearly and conspicuously and in writing. The terms "Amount Reaffirmed" and "Annual Percentage Rate" shall be disclosed more conspicuously than other terms, data or information provided in connection with this disclosure, except that the phrases "Before agreeing to reaffirm a debt, review these important disclosures" and "Summary of Reaffirmation Agreement" may be equally conspicuous. Disclosures may be made in a different order and may use terminology different from that set forth in paragraphs (2) through (8), except that the terms "Amount Reaffirmed" and "Annual Percentage Rate" must be used where indicated.

(3) The disclosure statement required under this paragraph shall consist of the following:

(A) The statement: "Part A: Before agreeing to reaffirm a debt, review these important disclosures:";

(B) Under the heading "Summary of Reaffirmation Agreement", the statement: "This Summary is made pursuant to the requirements of the Bankruptcy Code";

(C) The "Amount Reaffirmed", using that term, which shall be—

(i) the total amount of debt that the debtor agrees to reaffirm by entering into an agreement of the kind specified in subsection (c), and

(ii) the total of any fees and costs accrued as of the date of the disclosure statement, related to such total amount.

(D) In conjunction with the disclosure of the "Amount Reaffirmed", the statements—

(i) "The amount of debt you have agreed to reaffirm"; and

(ii) "Your credit agreement may obligate you to pay additional amounts which may come due after the date of this disclosure. Consult your credit agreement.".

(E) The "Annual Percentage Rate", using that term, which shall be disclosed as—

(i) if, at the time the petition is filed, the debt is an extension of credit under an open end credit plan, as the terms "credit" and "open end credit plan" are defined in section 103 of the Truth in Lending Act, then—

(I) the annual percentage rate determined under paragraphs (5) and (6) of section 127(b) of the Truth in Lending Act, as applicable, as disclosed to the debtor in the most recent periodic statement prior to entering into an agreement of the kind specified in subsection (c) or, if no such periodic statement has been given to the debtor during the prior 6 months, the annual percentage rate as it would have been so disclosed at the time the disclosure statement is given to the debtor, or to the extent this annual percentage rate is not readily available or not applicable, then

(II) the simple interest rate applicable to the amount reaffirmed as of the date the disclosure statement is given to the debtor, or if different simple interest rates apply to different balances, the simple interest rate applicable to each such balance, identifying the amount of each such balance included in the amount reaffirmed, or

(III) if the entity making the disclosure elects, to disclose the annual percentage rate under subclause (I) and the simple interest rate under subclause (II); or

(ii) if, at the time the petition is filed, the debt is an extension of credit other than under an open end credit plan, as the terms "credit" and "open end credit plan" are defined in section 103 of the Truth in Lending Act, then—

(I) the annual percentage rate under section 128(a)(4) of the Truth in Lending Act, as disclosed to the debtor in the most recent disclosure statement given to the debtor prior to the entering into an agreement of the kind specified in subsection (c) with respect to the debt, or, if no such disclosure statement was given to the debtor, the annual percentage rate as it would have been so disclosed at the time the disclosure statement is given to the debtor, or to the extent this annual percentage rate is not readily available or not applicable, then

(II) the simple interest rate applicable to the amount reaffirmed as of the date the disclosure statement is given to the debtor, or if different simple interest rates apply to different balances, the simple interest rate applicable to each such balance, identifying the amount of such balance included in the amount reaffirmed, or

(III) if the entity making the disclosure elects, to disclose the annual percentage rate under (I) and the simple interest rate under (II).

(F) If the underlying debt transaction was disclosed as a variable rate transaction on the most recent disclosure given under the Truth in Lending Act, by stating "The interest rate on your loan may be a variable interest rate which changes from time to time, so that the annual percentage rate disclosed here may be higher or lower.".

(G) If the debt is secured by a security interest which has not been waived in whole or in part or determined to be void by a final order of the court at the time of the disclosure, by disclosing that a security interest or lien in goods or property is asserted over some or all of the debts the debtor is reaffirming and listing the items and their original purchase price that are subject to the asserted security interest, or if not a purchase-money security interest then listing by items or types and the original amount of the loan.

(H) At the election of the creditor, a statement of the repayment schedule using 1 or a combination of the following—

(i) by making the statement: "Your first payment in the amount of $_____ is due on _____ but the future payment amount may be different. Consult your reaffirmation agreement or credit agreement, as applicable.", and stating the amount of the first payment and the due date of that payment in the places provided;

(ii) by making the statement: "Your payment schedule will be:", and describing the repayment schedule with the number, amount, and due dates or period of payments scheduled to repay the debts reaffirmed to the extent then known by the disclosing party; or

(iii) by describing the debtor's repayment obligations with reasonable specificity to the extent then known by the disclosing party.

(I) The following statement: "Note: When this disclosure refers to what a creditor 'may' do, it does not use the word 'may' to give the creditor specific permission. The word 'may' is used to tell you what might occur if the law permits the creditor to take the action. If you have questions about your reaffirming a debt or what the law requires, consult with the attorney who helped you negotiate this agreement reaffirming a debt. If you don't have an attorney helping you, the judge will explain the effect of your reaffirming a debt when the hearing on the reaffirmation agreement is held.".

(J)(i) The following additional statements:

"Reaffirming a debt is a serious financial decision. The law requires you to take certain steps to make sure the decision is in your best interest. If these steps are not completed, the reaffirmation agreement is not effective, even though you have signed it.

"1. Read the disclosures in this Part A carefully. Consider the decision to reaffirm carefully. Then, if you want to reaffirm, sign the reaffirmation agreement in Part B (or you may use a separate agreement you and your creditor agree on).

"2. Complete and sign Part D and be sure you can afford to make the payments you are agreeing to make and have received a copy of the disclosure statement and a completed and signed reaffirmation agreement.

"3. If you were represented by an attorney during the negotiation of your reaffirmation agreement, the attorney must have signed the certification in Part C.

"4. If you were not represented by an attorney during the negotiation of your reaffirmation agreement, you must have completed and signed Part E.

"5. The original of this disclosure must be filed with the court by you or your creditor. If a separate reaffirmation agreement (other than the one in Part B) has been signed, it must be attached.

"6. If you were represented by an attorney during the negotiation of your reaffirmation agreement, your reaffirmation agreement becomes effective upon filing with the court unless the reaffirmation is presumed to be an undue hardship as explained in Part D.

"7. If you were not represented by an attorney during the negotiation of your reaffirmation agreement, it will not be effective unless the court approves it. The court will notify you of the hearing on your reaffirmation agreement. You must attend this hearing in bankruptcy court where the judge will review your reaffirmation agreement. The bankruptcy court must approve your reaffirmation agreement as consistent with your best interests, except that no court approval is required if your reaffirmation agreement is for a consumer debt secured by a mortgage, deed of trust, security deed, or other lien on your real property, like your home.

"Your right to rescind (cancel) your reaffirmation agreement. You may rescind (cancel) your reaffirmation agreement at any time before the bankruptcy court enters a discharge order, or before the expiration of the 60-day period that begins on the date your reaffirmation agreement is filed with the court, whichever occurs later. To rescind (cancel) your reaffirmation agreement, you must notify the creditor that your reaffirmation agreement is rescinded (or canceled).

"What are your obligations if you reaffirm the debt? A reaffirmed debt remains your personal legal obligation. It is not discharged in your bankruptcy case. That means that if you default on your reaffirmed debt after your bankruptcy case is over, your creditor may be able to take your property or your wages. Otherwise, your obligations will be determined by the reaffirmation agreement which may have changed the terms of the original agreement. For example, if you are reaffirming an open end credit agreement, the creditor may be permitted by that agreement or applicable law to change the terms of that agreement in the future under certain conditions.

"Are you required to enter into a reaffirmation agreement by any law? No, you are not required to reaffirm a debt by any law. Only agree to reaffirm a debt if it is in your best interest. Be sure you can afford the payments you agree to make.

"What if your creditor has a security interest or lien? Your bankruptcy discharge does not eliminate any lien on your property. A 'lien' is often referred to as a security interest, deed of trust, mortgage or security deed. Even if you do not reaffirm and your personal liability on the debt is discharged, because of the lien your creditor may still have the right to take the security property if you do not pay the debt or default on it. If the lien is on an item of personal property that is exempt under your State's law or that the trustee has abandoned, you may be able to redeem the item rather than reaffirm the debt. To redeem, you make a single payment to the creditor equal to the current value of the security property, as agreed by the parties or determined by the court.".

(ii) In the case of a reaffirmation under subsection (m)(2), numbered paragraph 6 in the disclosures required by clause (i) of this subparagraph shall read as follows:

"6. If you were represented by an attorney during the negotiation of your reaffirmation agreement, your reaffirmation agreement becomes effective upon filing with the court.".

(4) The form of such agreement required under this paragraph shall consist of the following:

"Part B: Reaffirmation Agreement. I (we) agree to reaffirm the debts arising under the credit agreement described below.

"Brief description of credit agreement:

"Description of any changes to the credit agreement made as part of this reaffirmation agreement:

"Signature: Date:

"Borrower:

"Co-borrower, if also reaffirming these debts:

"Accepted by creditor:

"Date of creditor acceptance:".

(5) The declaration shall consist of the following:

(A) The following certification:

"Part C: Certification by Debtor's Attorney (If Any).

"I hereby certify that (1) this agreement represents a fully informed and voluntary agreement by the debtor; (2) this agreement does not impose an undue hardship on the debtor or any dependent of the debtor; and (3) I have fully advised the debtor of the legal effect and consequences of this agreement and any default under this agreement.

"Signature of Debtor's Attorney: Date:".

(B) If a presumption of undue hardship has been established with respect to such agreement, such certification shall state that in the opinion of the attorney, the debtor is able to make the payment.

(C) In the case of a reaffirmation agreement under subsection (m)(2), subparagraph (B) is not applicable.

(6)(A) The statement in support of such agreement, which the debtor shall sign and date prior to filing with the court, shall consist of the following:

"Part D: Debtor's Statement in Support of Reaffirmation Agreement.

"1. I believe this reaffirmation agreement will not impose an undue hardship on my dependents or me. I can afford to make the payments on the reaffirmed debt because my monthly income (take home pay plus any other income received) is $______, and my actual current monthly expenses including monthly payments on post-bankruptcy debt and other reaffirmation agreements total $______, leaving $______ to make the required payments on this reaffirmed debt. I understand that if my income less my monthly expenses does not leave enough to make the payments, this reaffirmation agreement is presumed to be an undue hardship on me and must be reviewed by the court. However, this presumption may be overcome if I explain to the satisfaction of the court how I can afford to make the payments here: ______.

"2. I received a copy of the Reaffirmation Disclosure Statement in Part A and a completed and signed reaffirmation agreement.".

(B) Where the debtor is represented by an attorney and is reaffirming a debt owed to a creditor defined in section 19(b)(1)(A)(iv) of the Federal Reserve Act, the statement of support of the reaffirmation agreement, which the debtor shall sign and date prior to filing with the court, shall consist of the following:

"I believe this reaffirmation agreement is in my financial interest. I can afford to make the payments on the reaffirmed debt. I received a copy of the Reaffirmation Disclosure Statement in Part A and a completed and signed reaffirmation agreement.".

(7) The motion that may be used if approval of such agreement by the court is required in order for it to be effective, shall be signed and dated by the movant and shall consist of the following:

"Part E: Motion for Court Approval (To be completed only if the debtor is not represented by an attorney.). I (we), the debtor(s), affirm the following to be true and correct:

"I am not represented by an attorney in connection with this reaffirmation agreement.

"I believe this reaffirmation agreement is in my best interest based on the income and expenses I have disclosed in my Statement in Support of this reaffirmation agreement, and because (provide any additional relevant reasons the court should consider):

"Therefore, I ask the court for an order approving this reaffirmation agreement.".

(8) The court order, which may be used to approve such agreement, shall consist of the following:

"Court Order: The court grants the debtor's motion and approves the reaffirmation agreement described above.".

(*l*) Notwithstanding any other provision of this title the following shall apply:

(1) A creditor may accept payments from a debtor before and after the filing of an agreement of the kind specified in subsection (c) with the court.

(2) A creditor may accept payments from a debtor under such agreement that the creditor believes in good faith to be effective.

(3) The requirements of subsections (c)(2) and (k) shall be satisfied if disclosures required under those subsections are given in good faith.

(m)(1) Until 60 days after an agreement of the kind specified in subsection (c) is filed with the court (or such additional period as the court, after notice and a hearing and for cause, orders before the expiration of such period), it shall be presumed that such agreement is an undue hardship on the debtor if the debtor's monthly income less the debtor's monthly expenses as shown on the debtor's completed and signed statement in support of such agreement required under subsection (k)(6)(A) is less than the scheduled payments on the reaffirmed debt. This presumption shall be reviewed by the court. The presumption may be rebutted in writing by the debtor if the statement includes an explanation that identifies additional sources of funds to make the payments as agreed upon under the terms of such agreement. If the presumption is not rebutted to the satisfaction of the court, the court may disapprove such agreement. No agreement shall be disapproved without notice and a hearing to the debtor and creditor, and such hearing shall be concluded before the entry of the debtor's discharge.

(2) This subsection does not apply to reaffirmation agreements where the creditor is a credit union, as defined in section 19(b)(1)(A)(iv) of the Federal Reserve Act.

(Pub. L. 95–598, Nov. 6, 1978, 92 Stat. 2592; Pub. L. 98–353, title III, §§308, 455, July 10, 1984, 98 Stat. 354, 376; Pub. L. 99–554, title II, §§257(*o*), 282, 283(k), Oct. 27, 1986, 100 Stat. 3115–3117; Pub. L. 103–394, title I, §§103, 111(a), title V, §501(d)(14), Oct. 22, 1994, 108 Stat. 4108, 4113, 4145; Pub. L. 109–8, title II, §§202, 203(a), title XII, §1210, Apr. 20, 2005, 119 Stat. 43, 194.)

Historical and Revision Notes

LEGISLATIVE STATEMENTS

Section 524(a) of the House amendment represents a compromise between the House bill and the Senate amendment. Section 524(b) of the House amendment is new, and represents standards clarifying the operation of section 524(a)(3) with respect to community property.

Sections 524(c) and (d) represent a compromise between the House bill and Senate amendment on the issue of reaffirmation of a debt discharged in bankruptcy. Every reaffirmation to be enforceable must be approved by the court, and any debtor may rescind a reaffirmation for 30 days from the time the reaffirmation becomes enforceable. If the debtor is an individual the court must advise the debtor of various effects of reaffirmation at a hearing. In addition, to any extent the debt is a consumer debt that is not secured by real property of the debtor reaffirmation is permitted only if the court approves the reaffirmation agreement, before granting a discharge under section 727, 1141, or 1328, as not imposing a hardship on the debtor or a dependent of the debtor and in the best interest of the debtor; alternatively, the court may approve an agreement entered into in good faith that is in settlement of litigation of a complaint to determine dischargeability or that is entered into in connection with redemption under section 722. The hearing on discharge under section 524(d) will be held whether or not the debtor desires to reaffirm any debts.

SENATE REPORT NO. 95–989

Subsection (a) specifies that a discharge in a bankruptcy case voids any judgment to the extent that it is a determination of the personal liability of the debtor with respect to a prepetition debt, and operates as an injunction against the commencement or continuation of an action, the employment of process, or any act, including telephone calls, letters, and personal contacts, to collect, recover, or offset any discharged debt as a personal liability of the debtor, or from property of the debtor, whether or not the debtor has waived discharge of the debt involved. The injunction is to give complete effect to the discharge and to eliminate any doubt concerning the effect of the discharge as a total prohibition on debt collection efforts. This paragraph has been expanded over a comparable provision in Bankruptcy Act §14f [section 32(f) of former title 11] to cover any act to collect, such as dunning by telephone or letter, or indirectly through friends, relatives, or employers, harassment, threats of repossession, and the like. The change is consonant with the new policy forbidding binding reaffirmation agreements under proposed 11 U.S.C. 524(b), and is intended to insure that once a debt is discharged, the debtor will not be pressured in any way to repay it. In effect, the discharge extinguishes the debt, and creditors may not attempt to avoid that. The language "whether or not discharge of such debt is waived" is intended to prevent waiver of discharge of a particular debt from defeating the purposes of this section. It is directed at waiver of discharge of a particular debt, not waiver of discharge in toto as permitted under section 727(a)(9).

Subsection (a) also codifies the split discharge for debtors in community property states. If community property was in the estate and community claims were discharged, the discharge is effective against community creditors of the nondebtor spouse as well as of the debtor spouse.

Subsection (b) gives further effect to the discharge. It prohibits reaffirmation agreements after the commencement of the case with respect to any dischargeable debt. The prohibition extends to agreements the consideration for which in whole or in part is based on a dischargeable debt, and it applies whether or not discharge of the debt involved in the agreement has been waived. Thus, the prohibition on reaffirmation agreements extends to debts that are based on discharged debts. Thus, "second generation" debts, which included all or a part of a discharged debt could not be included in any new agreement for new money. This subsection will not have any effect on reaffirmations of debts discharged under the Bankruptcy Act [former title 11]. It will only apply to discharges granted if commenced under the new title 11 bankruptcy code.

Subsection (c) grants an exception to the anti-reaffirmation provision. It permits reaffirmation in connection with the settlement of a proceeding to determine the dischargeability of the debt being reaffirmed, or in connection with a redemption agreement permitted under section 722. In either case, the reaffirmation agreement must be entered into in good faith and must be approved by the court.

Subsection (d) provides the discharge of the debtor does not affect co-debtors or guarantors.

REFERENCES IN TEXT

The Bankruptcy Act, referred to in subsec. (b)(1), is act July 1, 1898, ch. 541, 30 Stat. 544, as amended, which was classified generally to former Title 11.

The date of the enactment of this subsection, referred to in subsec. (g)(7), is the date of enactment of Pub. L. 103–394, which enacted subsec. (g) and was approved Oct. 22, 1994.

The date of the enactment of this Act, referred to in subsec. (h), probably means the date of enactment of Pub. L. 103–394, which enacted subsec. (h) and was approved Oct. 22, 1994.

The Truth in Lending Act, referred to in subsec. (k), is title I of Pub. L. 90–321, May 29, 1968, 82 Stat. 146, as amended, which is classified generally to subchapter I (§1601 et seq.) of chapter 41 of Title 15, Commerce and Trade. Sections 103, 127(b), and 128(a)(4) of the Act are classified to sections 1602, 1637(b), and 1638(a)(4), respectively, of Title 15. For complete classification of this Act to the Code, see Short Title note set out under section 1601 of Title 15 and Tables.

Section 19(b)(1)(A)(iv) of the Federal Reserve Act, referred to in subsecs. (k)(6)(B) and (m)(2), is classified to section 461(b)(1)(A)(iv) of Title 12, Banks and Banking.

AMENDMENTS

2005—Subsec. (a)(3). Pub. L. 109–8, §1210, substituted "section 523, 1228(a)(1), or 1328(a)(1), or that" for "section 523, 1228(a)(1), or 1328(a)(1) of this title, or that".

Subsec. (c)(2). Pub. L. 109–8, §203(a)(1), added par. (2) and struck out former par. (2) which read as follows:

"(2)(A) such agreement contains a clear and conspicuous statement which advises the debtor that the agreement may be rescinded at any time prior to discharge or within sixty days after such agreement is filed with the court, whichever occurs later, by giving notice of rescission to the holder of such claim; and

"(B) such agreement contains a clear and conspicuous statement which advises the debtor that such agreement is not required under this title, under nonbankruptcy law, or under any agreement not in accordance with the provisions of this subsection;".

Subsecs. (i), (j). Pub. L. 109–8, §202, added subsecs. (i) and (j).

Subsecs. (k) to (m). Pub. L. 109–8, §203(a)(2), added subsecs. (k) to (m).

1994—Subsec. (a)(3). Pub. L. 103–394, §501(d)(14)(A), substituted "1328(a)(1)" for "1328(c)(1)". See 1986 Amendment note below.

Subsec. (c)(2). Pub. L. 103–394, §103(a)(1), designated existing provisions as subpar. (A), inserted "and" at end, and added subpar. (B).

Subsec. (c)(3). Pub. L. 103–394, §103(a)(2), struck out "such agreement" after "which states that" in introductory provisions, struck out "and" at end of subpar. (A), inserted "such agreement" in subpars. (A) and (B), and added subpar. (C).

Subsec. (c)(4). Pub. L. 103–394, §501(d)(14)(B), substituted "rescission" for "recission".

Subsec. (d). Pub. L. 103–394, §103(b), inserted "and was not represented by an attorney during the course of negotiating such agreement" after "this section" in introductory provisions.

Subsec. (d)(1)(B)(ii). Pub. L. 103–394, §501(d)(14)(C), inserted "and" at end.

Subsecs. (g), (h). Pub. L. 103–394, §111(a), added subsecs. (g) and (h).

1986—Subsec. (a)(1). Pub. L. 99–554, §257(*o*)(1), inserted reference to section 1228 of this title.

Subsec. (a)(3). Pub. L. 99–554, §257(*o*)(2), which directed the substitution of ", 1228(a)(1), or 1328(a)(1)" for "or 1328(a)(1)" was executed by making the substitution for "or 1328(c)(1)" to reflect the probable intent of Congress. See 1994 Amendment note above.

Subsec. (c)(1). Pub. L. 99–554, §257(*o*)(1), inserted reference to section 1228 of this title.

Subsec. (d). Pub. L. 99–554, §257(*o*)(1), inserted reference to section 1228 of this title.

Pub. L. 99–554, §282, substituted "shall" for "may" before "hold" in first sentence, inserted "any" after "At" in second sentence, and inserted "the court shall hold a hearing at which the debtor shall appear in person and" after "then" in third sentence.

Subsec. (d)(2). Pub. L. 99–554, §283(k), substituted "section" for "subsection" after "subsection (c)(6) of this".

1984—Subsec. (a)(2). Pub. L. 98–353, §§308(a), 455, struck out "or from property of the debtor," before "whether or not discharge", and substituted "an act" for "any act".

Subsec. (a)(3). Pub. L. 98–353, §455, substituted "an act" for "any act".

Subsec. (c)(2). Pub. L. 98–353, §308(b)(1), (3), added par. (2). Former par. (2), which related to situations where the debtor had not rescinded the agreement within 30 days after the agreement became enforceable, was struck out.

Subsec. (c)(3), (4). Pub. L. 98–352, §308(b)(3), added pars. (3) and (4). Former pars. (3) and (4) redesignated (5) and (6), respectively.

Subsec. (c)(5). Pub. L. 98–353, §308(b)(2), redesignated former par. (3) as (5).

Subsec. (c)(6). Pub. L. 98–353, §308(b)(2), (4), redesignated former par. (4) as (6) and generally amended par. (6), as so redesignated, thereby striking out provisions relating to court approval of such agreements as are entered into in good faith and are in settlement of litigation under section 523 of this title or provide for redemption under section 722 of this title.

Subsec. (d)(2). Pub. L. 98–353, §308(c), substituted "subsection (c)(6)" for "subsection (c)(4)".

Subsec. (f). Pub. L. 98–353, §308(d), added subsec. (f).

EFFECTIVE DATE OF 2005 AMENDMENT

Amendment by Pub. L. 109–8 effective 180 days after Apr. 20, 2005, and not applicable with respect to cases commenced under this title before such effective date, except as otherwise provided, see section 1501 of Pub. L. 109–8, set out as a note under section 101 of this title.

EFFECTIVE DATE OF 1994 AMENDMENT

Amendment by Pub. L. 103–394 effective Oct. 22, 1994, and, except with respect to amendment by section 111(a) of Pub. L. 103–394, amendment by Pub. L. 103–394 not applicable with respect to cases commenced under this title before Oct. 22, 1994, see section 702 of Pub. L. 103–394, set out as a note under section 101 of this title.

EFFECTIVE DATE OF 1986 AMENDMENT

Amendment by section 257 of Pub. L. 99–554 effective 30 days after Oct. 27, 1986, but not applicable to cases commenced under this title before that date, see section 302(a), (c)(1) of Pub. L. 99–554, set out as a note under section 581 of Title 28, Judiciary and Judicial Procedure.

Amendment by sections 282 and 283 of Pub. L. 99–554 effective 30 days after Oct. 27, 1986, see section 302(a) of Pub. L. 99–554.

EFFECTIVE DATE OF 1984 AMENDMENT

Amendment by Pub. L. 98–353 effective with respect to cases filed 90 days after July 10, 1984, see section 552(a) of Pub. L. 98–353, set out as a note under section 101 of this title.

CONSTRUCTION

Section 111(b) of Pub. L. 103–394 provided that: "Nothing in subsection (a), or in the amendments made by subsection (a) [amending this section], shall be construed to modify, impair, or supersede any other authority the court has to issue injunctions in connection with an order confirming a plan of reorganization."

§ 525. Protection against discriminatory treatment

(a) Except as provided in the Perishable Agricultural Commodities Act, 1930, the Packers and Stockyards Act, 1921, and section 1 of the Act entitled "An Act making appropriations for the Department of Agriculture for the fiscal year ending June 30, 1944, and for other purposes," approved July 12, 1943, a governmental unit may not deny, revoke, suspend, or refuse to renew a license, permit, charter, franchise, or other similar grant to, condition such a grant to, discriminate with respect to such a grant against, deny employment to, terminate the employment of, or discriminate with respect to employment against, a person that is or has been a debtor under this title or a bankrupt or a debtor under the Bankruptcy Act, or another person with whom such bankrupt or debtor has been associated, solely because such bankrupt or debtor is or has been a debtor under this title or a bankrupt or debtor under the Bankruptcy Act, has been insolvent before the commencement of the case under this title, or during the case but before the debtor is granted or denied a discharge, or has not paid a debt that is dischargeable in the case under this title or that was discharged under the Bankruptcy Act.

(b) No private employer may terminate the employment of, or discriminate with respect to employment against, an individual who is or has been a debtor under this title, a debtor or bankrupt under the Bankruptcy Act, or an individual associated with such debtor or bankrupt, solely because such debtor or bankrupt—

(1) is or has been a debtor under this title or a debtor or bankrupt under the Bankruptcy Act;

(2) has been insolvent before the commencement of a case under this title or during the case but before the grant or denial of a discharge; or

(3) has not paid a debt that is dischargeable in a case under this title or that was discharged under the Bankruptcy Act.

(c)(1) A governmental unit that operates a student grant or loan program and a person engaged in a business that includes the making of loans guaranteed or insured under a student loan program may not deny a student grant, loan, loan guarantee, or loan insurance to a person that is or has been a debtor under this title or a bankrupt or debtor under the Bankruptcy Act, or another person with whom the debtor or bankrupt has been associated, because the debtor or bankrupt is or has been a debtor under this title or a bankrupt or debtor under the Bankruptcy Act, has been insolvent before the commencement of a case under this title or during the pendency of the case but before the debtor is granted or denied a discharge, or has not paid a debt that is dischargeable in the case under this title or that was discharged under the Bankruptcy Act.

(2) In this section, "student loan program" means any program operated under title IV of the Higher Education Act of 1965 or a similar program operated under State or local law.

(Pub. L. 95–598, Nov. 6, 1978, 92 Stat. 2593; Pub. L. 98–353, title III, §309, July 10, 1984, 98 Stat. 354; Pub. L. 103–394, title III, §313, title V, §501(d)(15), Oct. 22, 1994, 108 Stat. 4140, 4145; Pub. L. 109–8, title XII, §1211, Apr. 20, 2005, 119 Stat. 194.)

HISTORICAL AND REVISION NOTES

SENATE REPORT NO. 95–989

This section is additional debtor protection. It codifies the result of *Perez v. Campbell*, 402 U.S. 637 (1971), which held that a State would frustrate the Congressional policy of a fresh start for a debtor if it were permitted to refuse to renew a drivers license because a tort judgment resulting from an automobile accident had been unpaid as a result of a discharge in bankruptcy.

Notwithstanding any other laws, section 525 prohibits a governmental unit from denying, revoking, suspending, or refusing to renew a license, permit, charter, franchise, or other similar grant to, from conditioning such a grant to, from discrimination with respect to such a grant against, deny employment to, terminate the employment of, or discriminate with respect to employment against, a person that is or has been a debtor or that is or has been associated with a debtor. The prohibition extends only to discrimination or other action based solely on the basis of the bankruptcy, on the basis of insolvency before or during bankruptcy prior to a determination of discharge, or on the basis of nonpayment of a debt discharged in the bankruptcy case (the *Perez* situation). It does not prohibit consideration of other factors, such as future financial responsibility or ability, and does not prohibit imposition of requirements such as net capital rules, if applied nondiscriminatorily.

In addition, the section is not exhaustive. The enumeration of various forms of discrimination against former bankrupts is not intended to permit other forms of discrimination. The courts have been developing the *Perez* rule. This section permits further development to prohibit actions by governmental or quasi-governmental organizations that perform licensing functions, such as a State bar association or a medical society, or by other organizations that can seriously affect the debtors' livelihood or fresh start, such as exclusion from a union on the basis of discharge of a debt to the union's credit union.

The effect of the section, and of further interpretations of the *Perez* rule, is to strengthen the anti-reaffirmation policy found in section 524(b). Discrimination based solely on nonpayment could encourage reaffirmations, contrary to the expressed policy.

The section is not so broad as a comparable section proposed by the Bankruptcy Commission, S. 236, 94th Cong., 1st Sess. §4–508 (1975), which would have extended the prohibition to any discrimination, even by private parties. Nevertheless, it is not limiting either, as noted. The courts will continue to mark the contours of the anti-discrimination provision in pursuit of sound bankruptcy policy.

REFERENCES IN TEXT

The Perishable Agricultural Commodities Act, 1930, referred to in subsec. (a), is act June 10, 1930, ch. 436, 46 Stat. 531, as amended, which is classified generally to chapter 20A (§499a et seq.) of Title 7, Agriculture. For complete classification of this Act to the Code, see section 499a(a) of Title 7 and Tables.

The Packers and Stockyards Act, 1921, referred to in subsec. (a), is act Aug. 15, 1921, ch. 64, 42 Stat. 159, as amended, which is classified generally to chapter 9 (§181 et seq.) of Title 7. For complete classification of this Act to the Code, see section 181 of Title 7 and Tables.

Section 1 of the Act entitled "An Act making appropriations for the Department of Agriculture for the fiscal year ending June 30, 1944, and for other purposes," approved July 12, 1943, referred to in subsec. (a), is classified to section 204 of Title 7.

The Bankruptcy Act, referred to in text, is act July 1, 1898, ch. 541, 30 Stat. 544, as amended, which was classified generally to former Title 11.

The Higher Education Act of 1965, referred to in subsec. (c)(2), is Pub. L. 89-329, Nov. 8, 1965, 79 Stat. 1219, as amended. Title IV of the Act is classified generally to subchapter IV (§1070 et seq.) of chapter 28 of Title 20, Education, and part C (§2751 et seq.) of subchapter I of chapter 34 of Title 42, The Public Health and Welfare. For complete classification of this Act to the Code, see Short Title note set out under section 1001 of Title 20 and Tables.

AMENDMENTS

2005—Subsec. (c)(1). Pub. L. 109-8, §1211(1), inserted "student" before "grant, loan,".

Subsec. (c)(2). Pub. L. 109-8, §1211(2), substituted "any program operated under" for "the program operated under part B, D, or E of".

1994—Subsec. (a). Pub. L. 103-394, §501(d)(15), struck out "(7 U.S.C. 499a-499s)" after "Act, 1930", "(7 U.S.C. 181-229)" after "Act, 1921", and "(57 Stat. 422; 7 U.S.C. 204)" after "July 12, 1943".

Subsec. (c). Pub. L. 103-394, §313, added subsec. (c).

1984—Pub. L. 98-353 designated existing provisions as subsec. (a), inserted "the" before "Perishable", and added subsec. (b).

EFFECTIVE DATE OF 2005 AMENDMENT

Amendment by Pub. L. 109-8 effective 180 days after Apr. 20, 2005, and not applicable with respect to cases commenced under this title before such effective date, except as otherwise provided, see section 1501 of Pub. L. 109-8, set out as a note under section 101 of this title.

EFFECTIVE DATE OF 1994 AMENDMENT

Amendment by Pub. L. 103-394 effective Oct. 22, 1994, and not applicable with respect to cases commenced under this title before Oct. 22, 1994, see section 702 of Pub. L. 103-394, set out as a note under section 101 of this title.

EFFECTIVE DATE OF 1984 AMENDMENT

Amendment by Pub. L. 98-353 effective with respect to cases filed 90 days after July 10, 1984, see section 552(a) of Pub. L. 98-353, set out as a note under section 101 of this title.

§526. Restrictions on debt relief agencies

(a) A debt relief agency shall not—

(1) fail to perform any service that such agency informed an assisted person or prospective assisted person it would provide in connection with a case or proceeding under this title;

(2) make any statement, or counsel or advise any assisted person or prospective assisted person to make a statement in a document filed in a case or proceeding under this title, that is untrue and misleading, or that upon the exercise of reasonable care, should have been known by such agency to be untrue or misleading;

(3) misrepresent to any assisted person or prospective assisted person, directly or indirectly, affirmatively or by material omission, with respect to—

(A) the services that such agency will provide to such person; or

(B) the benefits and risks that may result if such person becomes a debtor in a case under this title; or

(4) advise an assisted person or prospective assisted person to incur more debt in contemplation of such person filing a case under this title or to pay an attorney or bankruptcy petition preparer fee or charge for services performed as part of preparing for or representing a debtor in a case under this title.

(b) Any waiver by any assisted person of any protection or right provided under this section shall not be enforceable against the debtor by any Federal or State court or any other person, but may be enforced against a debt relief agency.

(c)(1) Any contract for bankruptcy assistance between a debt relief agency and an assisted person that does not comply with the material requirements of this section, section 527, or section 528 shall be void and may not be enforced by any Federal or State court or by any other person, other than such assisted person.

(2) Any debt relief agency shall be liable to an assisted person in the amount of any fees or charges in connection with providing bankruptcy assistance to such person that such debt relief agency has received, for actual damages, and for reasonable attorneys' fees and costs if such agency is found, after notice and a hearing, to have—

(A) intentionally or negligently failed to comply with any provision of this section, section 527, or section 528 with respect to a case or proceeding under this title for such assisted person;

(B) provided bankruptcy assistance to an assisted person in a case or proceeding under this title that is dismissed or converted to a case under another chapter of this title because of such agency's intentional or negligent failure to file any required document including those specified in section 521; or

(C) intentionally or negligently disregarded the material requirements of this title or the Federal Rules of Bankruptcy Procedure applicable to such agency.

(3) In addition to such other remedies as are provided under State law, whenever the chief law enforcement officer of a State, or an official or agency designated by a State, has reason to believe that any person has violated or is violating this section, the State—

(A) may bring an action to enjoin such violation;

(B) may bring an action on behalf of its residents to recover the actual damages of assisted persons arising from such violation, including any liability under paragraph (2); and

(C) in the case of any successful action under subparagraph (A) or (B), shall be awarded the costs of the action and reasonable attorneys' fees as determined by the court.

(4) The district courts of the United States for districts located in the State shall have concurrent jurisdiction of any action under subparagraph (A) or (B) of paragraph (3).

(5) Notwithstanding any other provision of Federal law and in addition to any other remedy provided under Federal or State law, if the court, on its own motion or on the motion of the United States trustee or the debtor, finds that a person intentionally violated this section, or engaged in a clear and consistent pattern or practice of violating this section, the court may—

(A) enjoin the violation of such section; or

(B) impose an appropriate civil penalty against such person.

(d) No provision of this section, section 527, or section 528 shall—

(1) annul, alter, affect, or exempt any person subject to such sections from complying with any law of any State except to the extent that such law is inconsistent with those sections, and then only to the extent of the inconsistency; or

(2) be deemed to limit or curtail the authority or ability—

(A) of a State or subdivision or instrumentality thereof, to determine and enforce qualifications for the practice of law under the laws of that State; or

(B) of a Federal court to determine and enforce the qualifications for the practice of law before that court.

(Added Pub. L. 109–8, title II, §227(a), Apr. 20, 2005, 119 Stat. 67.)

REFERENCES IN TEXT

The Federal Rules of Bankruptcy Procedure, referred to in subsec. (c)(2)(C), are set out in the Appendix to this title.

EFFECTIVE DATE

Section effective 180 days after Apr. 20, 2005, and not applicable with respect to cases commenced under this title before such effective date, except as otherwise provided, see section 1501 of Pub. L. 109–8, set out as an Effective Date of 2005 Amendment note under section 101 of this title.

§ 527. Disclosures

(a) A debt relief agency providing bankruptcy assistance to an assisted person shall provide—

(1) the written notice required under section 342(b)(1); and

(2) to the extent not covered in the written notice described in paragraph (1), and not later than 3 business days after the first date on which a debt relief agency first offers to provide any bankruptcy assistance services to an assisted person, a clear and conspicuous written notice advising assisted persons that—

(A) all information that the assisted person is required to provide with a petition and thereafter during a case under this title is required to be complete, accurate, and truthful;

(B) all assets and all liabilities are required to be completely and accurately disclosed in the documents filed to commence the case, and the replacement value of each asset as defined in section 506 must be stated in those documents where requested after reasonable inquiry to establish such value;

(C) current monthly income, the amounts specified in section 707(b)(2), and, in a case under chapter 13 of this title, disposable income (determined in accordance with section 707(b)(2)), are required to be stated after reasonable inquiry; and

(D) information that an assisted person provides during their case may be audited pursuant to this title, and that failure to provide such information may result in dismissal of the case under this title or other sanction, including a criminal sanction.

(b) A debt relief agency providing bankruptcy assistance to an assisted person shall provide each assisted person at the same time as the notices required under subsection (a)(1) the following statement, to the extent applicable, or one substantially similar. The statement shall be clear and conspicuous and shall be in a single document separate from other documents or notices provided to the assisted person:

"IMPORTANT INFORMATION ABOUT BANKRUPTCY ASSISTANCE SERVICES FROM AN ATTORNEY OR BANKRUPTCY PETITION PREPARER.

"If you decide to seek bankruptcy relief, you can represent yourself, you can hire an attorney to represent you, or you can get help in some localities from a bankruptcy petition preparer who is not an attorney. THE LAW REQUIRES AN ATTORNEY OR BANKRUPTCY PETITION PREPARER TO GIVE YOU A WRITTEN CONTRACT SPECIFYING WHAT THE ATTORNEY OR BANKRUPTCY PETITION PREPARER WILL DO FOR YOU AND HOW MUCH IT WILL COST. Ask to see the contract before you hire anyone.

"The following information helps you understand what must be done in a routine bankruptcy case to help you evaluate how much service you need. Although bankruptcy can be complex, many cases are routine.

"Before filing a bankruptcy case, either you or your attorney should analyze your eligibility for different forms of debt relief available under the Bankruptcy Code and which form of relief is most likely to be beneficial for you. Be sure you understand the relief you can obtain and its limitations. To file a bankruptcy case, documents called a Petition, Schedules and Statement of Financial Affairs, as well as in some cases a Statement of Intention need to be prepared correctly and filed with the bankruptcy court. You will have to pay a filing fee to the bankruptcy court. Once your case starts, you will have to attend the required first meeting of creditors where you may be questioned by a court official called a 'trustee' and by creditors.

"If you choose to file a chapter 7 case, you may be asked by a creditor to reaffirm a debt. You may want help deciding whether to do so. A creditor is not permitted to coerce you into reaffirming your debts.

"If you choose to file a chapter 13 case in which you repay your creditors what you can afford over 3 to 5 years, you may also want help with preparing your chapter 13 plan and with the confirmation hearing on your plan which will be before a bankruptcy judge.

"If you select another type of relief under the Bankruptcy Code other than chapter 7 or chapter 13, you will want to find out what should be done from someone familiar with that type of relief.

"Your bankruptcy case may also involve litigation. You are generally permitted to represent yourself in litigation in bankruptcy court, but only attorneys, not bankruptcy petition preparers, can give you legal advice.".

(c) Except to the extent the debt relief agency provides the required information itself after reasonably diligent inquiry of the assisted person or others so as to obtain such information reasonably accurately for inclusion on the petition, schedules or statement of financial affairs, a debt relief agency providing bankruptcy assistance to an assisted person, to the extent permitted by nonbankruptcy law, shall provide each assisted person at the time required for the notice required under subsection (a)(1) reasonably sufficient information (which shall be provided in a clear and conspicuous writing) to the assisted person on how to provide all the information the assisted person is required to provide under this title pursuant to section 521, including—

(1) how to value assets at replacement value, determine current monthly income, the amounts specified in section 707(b)(2) and, in a chapter 13 case, how to determine disposable income in accordance with section 707(b)(2) and related calculations;

(2) how to complete the list of creditors, including how to determine what amount is owed and what address for the creditor should be shown; and

(3) how to determine what property is exempt and how to value exempt property at replacement value as defined in section 506.

(d) A debt relief agency shall maintain a copy of the notices required under subsection (a) of this section for 2 years after the date on which the notice is given the assisted person.

(Added Pub. L. 109-8, title II, §228(a), Apr. 20, 2005, 119 Stat. 69.)

EFFECTIVE DATE

Section effective 180 days after Apr. 20, 2005, and not applicable with respect to cases commenced under this title before such effective date, except as otherwise provided, see section 1501 of Pub. L. 109-8, set out as an Effective Date of 2005 Amendment note under section 101 of this title.

§ 528. Requirements for debt relief agencies

(a) A debt relief agency shall—

(1) not later than 5 business days after the first date on which such agency provides any bankruptcy assistance services to an assisted person, but prior to such assisted person's petition under this title being filed, execute a written contract with such assisted person that explains clearly and conspicuously—

(A) the services such agency will provide to such assisted person; and

(B) the fees or charges for such services, and the terms of payment;

(2) provide the assisted person with a copy of the fully executed and completed contract;

(3) clearly and conspicuously disclose in any advertisement of bankruptcy assistance services or of the benefits of bankruptcy directed to the general public (whether in general media, seminars or specific mailings, telephonic or electronic messages, or otherwise) that the services or benefits are with respect to bankruptcy relief under this title; and

(4) clearly and conspicuously use the following statement in such advertisement: "We are a debt relief agency. We help people file for bankruptcy relief under the Bankruptcy Code." or a substantially similar statement.

(b)(1) An advertisement of bankruptcy assistance services or of the benefits of bankruptcy directed to the general public includes—

(A) descriptions of bankruptcy assistance in connection with a chapter 13 plan whether or not chapter 13 is specifically mentioned in such advertisement; and

(B) statements such as "federally supervised repayment plan" or "Federal debt restructuring help" or other similar statements that could lead a reasonable consumer to believe that debt counseling was being offered when in fact the services were directed to providing bankruptcy assistance with a chapter 13 plan or other form of bankruptcy relief under this title.

(2) An advertisement, directed to the general public, indicating that the debt relief agency provides assistance with respect to credit defaults, mortgage foreclosures, eviction proceedings, excessive debt, debt collection pressure, or inability to pay any consumer debt shall—

(A) disclose clearly and conspicuously in such advertisement that the assistance may involve bankruptcy relief under this title; and

(B) include the following statement: "We are a debt relief agency. We help people file for bankruptcy relief under the Bankruptcy Code." or a substantially similar statement.

(Added Pub. L. 109-8, title II, §229(a), Apr. 20, 2005, 119 Stat. 71.)

EFFECTIVE DATE

Section effective 180 days after Apr. 20, 2005, and not applicable with respect to cases commenced under this title before such effective date, except as otherwise provided, see section 1501 of Pub. L. 109-8, set out as an Effective Date of 2005 Amendment note under section 101 of this title.

SUBCHAPTER III—THE ESTATE

§ 541. Property of the estate

(a) The commencement of a case under section 301, 302, or 303 of this title creates an estate. Such estate is comprised of all the following property, wherever located and by whomever held:

(1) Except as provided in subsections (b) and (c)(2) of this section, all legal or equitable interests of the debtor in property as of the commencement of the case.

(2) All interests of the debtor and the debtor's spouse in community property as of the commencement of the case that is—

(A) under the sole, equal, or joint management and control of the debtor; or

(B) liable for an allowable claim against the debtor, or for both an allowable claim against the debtor and an allowable claim against the debtor's spouse, to the extent that such interest is so liable.

(3) Any interest in property that the trustee recovers under section 329(b), 363(n), 543, 550, 553, or 723 of this title.

(4) Any interest in property preserved for the benefit of or ordered transferred to the estate under section 510(c) or 551 of this title.

(5) Any interest in property that would have been property of the estate if such interest had been an interest of the debtor on the date of the filing of the petition, and that the debtor acquires or becomes entitled to acquire within 180 days after such date—

(A) by bequest, devise, or inheritance;

(B) as a result of a property settlement agreement with the debtor's spouse, or of an interlocutory or final divorce decree; or

(C) as a beneficiary of a life insurance policy or of a death benefit plan.

(6) Proceeds, product, offspring, rents, or profits of or from property of the estate, except such as are earnings from services performed by an individual debtor after the commencement of the case.

(7) Any interest in property that the estate acquires after the commencement of the case.

(b) Property of the estate does not include—

(1) any power that the debtor may exercise solely for the benefit of an entity other than the debtor;

(2) any interest of the debtor as a lessee under a lease of nonresidential real property that has terminated at the expiration of the stated term of such lease before the commencement of the case under this title, and ceases to include any interest of the debtor as a lessee under a lease of nonresidential real property that has terminated at the expiration of the stated term of such lease during the case;

(3) any eligibility of the debtor to participate in programs authorized under the Higher Education Act of 1965 (20 U.S.C. 1001 et seq.; 42 U.S.C. 2751 et seq.), or any accreditation status or State licensure of the debtor as an educational institution;

(4) any interest of the debtor in liquid or gaseous hydrocarbons to the extent that—

(A)(i) the debtor has transferred or has agreed to transfer such interest pursuant to a farmout agreement or any written agreement directly related to a farmout agreement; and

(ii) but for the operation of this paragraph, the estate could include the interest referred to in clause (i) only by virtue of section 365 or 544(a)(3) of this title; or

(B)(i) the debtor has transferred such interest pursuant to a written conveyance of a production payment to an entity that does not participate in the operation of the property from which such production payment is transferred; and

(ii) but for the operation of this paragraph, the estate could include the interest referred to in clause (i) only by virtue of section 365 or 542 of this title;

(5) funds placed in an education individual retirement account (as defined in section 530(b)(1) of the Internal Revenue Code of 1986) not later than 365 days before the date of the filing of the petition in a case under this title, but—

(A) only if the designated beneficiary of such account was a child, stepchild, grandchild, or stepgrandchild of the debtor for the taxable year for which funds were placed in such account;

(B) only to the extent that such funds—

(i) are not pledged or promised to any entity in connection with any extension of credit; and

(ii) are not excess contributions (as described in section 4973(e) of the Internal Revenue Code of 1986); and

(C) in the case of funds placed in all such accounts having the same designated beneficiary not earlier than 720 days nor later than 365 days before such date, only so much of such funds as does not exceed $5,000;

(6) funds used to purchase a tuition credit or certificate or contributed to an account in accordance with section 529(b)(1)(A) of the Internal Revenue Code of 1986 under a qualified State tuition program (as defined in section 529(b)(1) of such Code) not later than 365 days before the date of the filing of the petition in a case under this title, but—

(A) only if the designated beneficiary of the amounts paid or contributed to such tuition program was a child, stepchild, grandchild, or stepgrandchild of the debtor for the taxable year for which funds were paid or contributed;

(B) with respect to the aggregate amount paid or contributed to such program having the same designated beneficiary, only so much of such amount as does not exceed the total contributions permitted under section 529(b)(7) of such Code with respect to such beneficiary, as adjusted beginning on the date of the filing of the petition in a case under this title by the annual increase or decrease (rounded to the nearest tenth of 1 percent) in the education expenditure category of the Consumer Price Index prepared by the Department of Labor; and

(C) in the case of funds paid or contributed to such program having the same designated beneficiary not earlier than 720 days nor later than 365 days before such date, only so much of such funds as does not exceed $5,000;

(7) any amount—

(A) withheld by an employer from the wages of employees for payment as contributions—

(i) to—

(I) an employee benefit plan that is subject to title I of the Employee Retirement Income Security Act of 1974 or under an employee benefit plan which is a governmental plan under section 414(d) of the Internal Revenue Code of 1986;

(II) a deferred compensation plan under section 457 of the Internal Revenue Code of 1986; or

(III) a tax-deferred annuity under section 403(b) of the Internal Revenue Code of 1986;

except that such amount under this subparagraph shall not constitute disposable income as defined in section 1325(b)(2); or

(ii) to a health insurance plan regulated by State law whether or not subject to such title; or

(B) received by an employer from employees for payment as contributions—

(i) to—

(I) an employee benefit plan that is subject to title I of the Employee Retirement Income Security Act of 1974 or under an employee benefit plan which is a governmental plan under section 414(d) of the Internal Revenue Code of 1986;

(II) a deferred compensation plan under section 457 of the Internal Revenue Code of 1986; or

(III) a tax-deferred annuity under section 403(b) of the Internal Revenue Code of 1986;

except that such amount under this subparagraph shall not constitute disposable income, as defined in section 1325(b)(2); or

(ii) to a health insurance plan regulated by State law whether or not subject to such title;

(8) subject to subchapter III of chapter 5, any interest of the debtor in property where the debtor pledged or sold tangible personal property (other than securities or written or printed evidences of indebtedness or title) as collateral for a loan or advance of money given by a person licensed under law to make such loans or advances, where—

(A) the tangible personal property is in the possession of the pledgee or transferee;

(B) the debtor has no obligation to repay the money, redeem the collateral, or buy back the property at a stipulated price; and

(C) neither the debtor nor the trustee have exercised any right to redeem provided under the contract or State law, in a timely manner as provided under State law and section 108(b); or

(9) any interest in cash or cash equivalents that constitute proceeds of a sale by the debtor of a money order that is made—

(A) on or after the date that is 14 days prior to the date on which the petition is filed; and

(B) under an agreement with a money order issuer that prohibits the commingling of such proceeds with property of the debtor (notwithstanding that, contrary to the agreement, the proceeds may have been commingled with property of the debtor),

unless the money order issuer had not taken action, prior to the filing of the petition, to require compliance with the prohibition.

Paragraph (4) shall not be construed to exclude from the estate any consideration the debtor retains, receives, or is entitled to receive for transferring an interest in liquid or gaseous hydrocarbons pursuant to a farmout agreement.

(c)(1) Except as provided in paragraph (2) of this subsection, an interest of the debtor in property becomes property of the estate under subsection (a)(1), (a)(2), or (a)(5) of this section notwithstanding any provision in an agreement, transfer instrument, or applicable nonbankruptcy law—

(A) that restricts or conditions transfer of such interest by the debtor; or

(B) that is conditioned on the insolvency or financial condition of the debtor, on the commencement of a case under this title, or on the appointment of or taking possession by a trustee in a case under this title or a custodian before such commencement, and that effects or gives an option to effect a forfeiture, modification, or termination of the debtor's interest in property.

(2) A restriction on the transfer of a beneficial interest of the debtor in a trust that is enforceable under applicable nonbankruptcy law is enforceable in a case under this title.

(d) Property in which the debtor holds, as of the commencement of the case, only legal title and not an equitable interest, such as a mortgage secured by real property, or an interest in such a mortgage, sold by the debtor but as to which the debtor retains legal title to service or supervise the servicing of such mortgage or interest, becomes property of the estate under subsection (a)(1) or (2) of this section only to the extent of the debtor's legal title to such property, but not to the extent of any equitable interest in such property that the debtor does not hold.

(e) In determining whether any of the relationships specified in paragraph (5)(A) or (6)(A) of subsection (b) exists, a legally adopted child of an individual (and a child who is a member of an individual's household, if placed with such individual by an authorized placement agency for legal adoption by such individual), or a foster child of an individual (if such child has as the child's principal place of abode the home of the debtor and is a member of the debtor's household) shall be treated as a child of such individual by blood.

(f) Notwithstanding any other provision of this title, property that is held by a debtor that is a corporation described in section 501(c)(3) of the Internal Revenue Code of 1986 and exempt from tax under section 501(a) of such Code may be transferred to an entity that is not such a corporation, but only under the same conditions as would apply if the debtor had not filed a case under this title.

(Pub. L. 95–598, Nov. 6, 1978, 92 Stat. 2594; Pub. L. 98–353, title III, §§363(a), 456, July 10, 1984, 98 Stat. 363, 376; Pub. L. 101–508, title III, §3007(a)(2), Nov. 5, 1990, 104 Stat. 1388–28; Pub. L. 102–486, title XXX, §3017(b), Oct. 24, 1992, 106 Stat. 3130; Pub. L. 103–394, title II, §§208(b), 223, Oct. 22, 1994, 108 Stat. 4124, 4129; Pub. L. 109–8, title II, §225(a), title III, §323, title XII, §§1212, 1221(c), 1230, Apr. 20, 2005, 119 Stat. 65, 97, 194, 196, 201.)

HISTORICAL AND REVISION NOTES

LEGISLATIVE STATEMENTS

Section 541(a)(7) is new. The provision clarifies that any interest in property that the estate acquires after the commencement of the case is property of the estate; for example, if the estate enters into a contract, after the commencement of the case, such a contract would be property of the estate. The addition of this provision by the House amendment merely clarifies that section 541(a) is an all-embracing definition which includes charges on property, such as liens held by the debtor on property of a third party, or beneficial rights and interests that the debtor may have in property of another. However, only the debtor's interest in such property becomes property of the estate. If the debtor holds bare legal title or holds property in trust for another, only those rights which the debtor would have otherwise had emanating from such interest pass to the estate under section 541. Neither this section nor section 545 will affect various statutory provisions that give a creditor a lien that is valid both inside and outside bankruptcy against a bona fide purchaser of property from the debtor, or that creates a trust fund for the benefit of creditors meeting similar criteria. See Packers and Stockyards Act §206, 7 U.S.C. 196 (1976).

Section 541(c)(2) follows the position taken in the House bill and rejects the position taken in the Senate amendment with respect to income limitations on a spend-thrift trust.

Section 541(d) of the House amendment is derived from section 541(e) of the Senate amendment and reiterates the general principle that where the debtor holds bare legal title without any equitable interest, that the estate acquires bare legal title without any equitable interest in the property. The purpose of section 541(d) as applied to the secondary mortgage market is identical to the purpose of section 541(e) of the Senate amendment and section 541(d) will accomplish the same result as would have been accomplished by section 541(e). Even if a mortgage seller retains for purposes of servicing legal title to mortgages or interests in mortgages sold in the secondary mortgage market, the trustee would be required by section 541(d) to turn over the mortgages or interests in mortgages to the purchaser of those mortgages.

The seller of mortgages in the secondary mortgage market will often retain the original mortgage notes and related documents and the seller will not endorse the notes to reflect the sale to the purchaser. Similarly, the purchaser will often not record the purchaser's ownership of the mortgages or interests in mortgages under State recording statutes. These facts are irrelevant and the seller's retention of the mortgage documents and the purchaser's decision not to record do not change the trustee's obligation to turn the mortgages or interests in mortgages over to the purchaser. The application of section 541(d) to secondary mortgage market transactions will not be affected by the terms of the servicing agreement between the mortgage servicer and the purchaser of the mortgages. Under section 541(d), the trustee is required to recognize the purchaser's title to the mortgages or interests in mortgages and to turn this property over to the purchaser. It makes no difference whether the servicer and the purchaser characterize their relationship as one of trust, agency, or independent contractor.

The purpose of section 541(d) as applied to the secondary mortgage market is therefore to make certain that secondary mortgage market sales as they are currently structured are not subject to challenge by bankruptcy trustees and that purchasers of mortgages will be able to obtain the mortgages or interests in mortgages which they have purchased from trustees without the trustees asserting that a sale of mortgages is a loan from the purchaser to the seller.

Thus, as section 541(a)(1) clearly states, the estate is comprised of all legal or equitable interests of the debtor in property as of the commencement of the case. To the extent such an interest is limited in the hands of the debtor, it is equally limited in the hands of the estate except to the extent that defenses which are personal against the debtor are not effective against the estate.

Property of the estate: The Senate amendment provided that property of the estate does not include amounts held by the debtor as trustee and any taxes withheld or collected from others before the commencement of the case. The House amendment removes these two provisions. As to property held by the debtor as a trustee, the House amendment provides that property of the estate will include whatever interest the debtor held in the property at the commencement of the case. Thus, where the debtor held only legal title to the property and the beneficial interest in that property belongs to another, such as exists in the case of property held in trust, the property of the estate includes the legal title, but not the beneficial interest in the property.

As to withheld taxes, the House amendment deletes the rule in the Senate bill as unnecessary since property of the estate does not include the beneficial interest in property held by the debtor as a trustee. Under the Internal Revenue Code of 1954 (section 7501) [26 U.S.C. 7501], the amounts of withheld taxes are held to be a special fund in trust for the United States. Where the Internal Revenue Service can demonstrate that the amounts of taxes withheld are still in the possession of the debtor at the commencement of the case, then if a trust is created, those amounts are not property of the estate. Compare *In re Shakesteers Coffee Shops*, 546 F.2d 821 (9th Cir. 1976) with *In re Glynn Wholesale Building Materials, Inc.* (S.D. Ga. 1978) and *In re Progress Tech Colleges, Inc.*, 42 Aftr 2d 78–5573 (S.D. Ohio 1977).

Where it is not possible for the Internal Revenue Service to demonstrate that the amounts of taxes withheld are still in the possession of the debtor at the commencement of the case, present law generally includes amounts of withheld taxes as property of the estate. See, e.g., *United States v. Randall*, 401 U.S. 513 (1973) [91 S. Ct. 991, 28 L.Ed.2d 273] and *In re Tamasha Town and Country Club*, 483 F.2d 1377 (9th Cir. 1973). Nonetheless, a serious problem exists where "trust fund taxes" withheld from others are held to be property of the estate where the withheld amounts are commingled with other assets of the debtor. The courts should permit the use of reasonable assumptions under which the Internal Revenue Service, and other tax authorities, can demonstrate that amounts of withheld taxes are still in the possession of the debtor at the commencement of the case. For example, where the debtor had commingled that amount of withheld taxes in his general checking account, it might be reasonable to assume that any remaining amounts in that account on the commencement of the case are the withheld taxes. In addition, Congress may consider future amendments to the Internal Revenue Code [title 26] making clear that amounts of withheld taxes are held by the debtor in a trust relationship and, consequently, that such amounts are not property of the estate.

SENATE REPORT NO. 95–989

This section defines property of the estate, and specifies what property becomes property of the estate. The commencement of a bankruptcy case creates an estate. Under paragraph (1) of subsection (a), the estate is comprised of all legal or equitable interest of the debtor in property, wherever located, as of the commencement of the case. The scope of this paragraph is broad. It includes all kinds of property, including tangible or intangible property, causes of action (see Bankruptcy Act §70a(6) [section 110(a)(6) of former title 11]), and all other forms of property currently specified in section 70a of the Bankruptcy Act §70a [section 110(a) of former title 11], as well as property recovered by the trustee under section 542 of proposed title 11, if the property recovered was merely out of the possession of the debtor, yet remained "property of the debtor." The debtor's interest in property also includes "title" to property, which is an interest, just as are a possessory interest, or lease-hold interest, for example. The result of *Segal v. Rochelle*, 382 U.S. 375 (1966), is followed, and the right to a refund is property of the estate.

Though this paragraph will include choses in action and claims by the debtor against others, it is not intended to expand the debtor's rights against others more than they exist at the commencement of the case. For example, if the debtor has a claim that is barred at the time of the commencement of the case by the statute of limitations, then the trustee would not be able to pursue that claim, because he too would be barred. He could take no greater rights than the debtor himself had. But see proposed 11 U.S.C. 108, which would permit the trustee a tolling of the statute of limitations if it had not run before the date of the filing of the petition.

Paragraph (1) has the effect of overruling *Lockwood v. Exchange Bank*, 190 U.S. 294 (1903), because it includes as property of the estate all property of the debtor, even that needed for a fresh start. After the property comes into the estate, then the debtor is permitted to exempt it under proposed 11 U.S.C. 522, and the court will have jurisdiction to determine what property may be exempted and what remains as property of the estate. The broad jurisdictional grant in proposed 28 U.S.C. 1334 would have the effect of overruling *Lockwood* independently of the change made by this provision.

Paragraph (1) also has the effect of overruling *Lines v. Frederick*, 400 U.S. 18 (1970).

Situations occasionally arise where property ostensibly belonging to the debtor will actually not be property of the debtor, but will be held in trust for another. For example, if the debtor has incurred medical bills that were covered by insurance, and the insurance company had sent the payment of the bills to the debtor before the debtor had paid the bill for which the payment was reimbursement, the payment would actually be held in a constructive trust for the person to whom the bill was owed. This section and proposed 11 U.S.C. 545 also will not affect various statutory provisions that give a creditor of the debtor a lien that is valid outside as well as inside bankruptcy, or that creates a trust fund for the benefit of a creditor of the debtor. See Packers and Stockyards Act §206, 7 U.S.C. 196.

Bankruptcy Act §8 [section 26 of former title 11] has been deleted as unnecessary. Once the estate is created, no interests in property of the estate remain in the debtor. Consequently, if the debtor dies during the case, only property exempted from property of the estate or acquired by the debtor after the commencement of the case and not included as property of the estate will be available to the representative of the debtor's probate estate. The bankruptcy proceeding will continue in rem with respect to property of the state, and the discharge will apply in personam to relieve the debtor, and thus his probate representative, of liability for dischargeable debts.

The estate also includes the interests of the debtor and the debtor's spouse in community property, subject to certain limitations; property that the trustee recovers under the avoiding powers; property that the debtor acquires by bequest, devise, inheritance, a property settlement agreement with the debtor's spouse, or as the beneficiary of a life insurance policy within 180 days after the petition; and proceeds, product, offspring, rents, and profits of or from property of the estate, except such as are earning from services performed by an individual debtor after the commencement of the case. Proceeds here is not used in a confining sense, as defined in the Uniform Commercial Code, but is intended to be a broad term to encompass all proceeds of property of the estate. The conversion in form of property of the estate does not change its character as property of the estate.

Subsection (b) excludes from property of the estate any power, such as a power of appointment, that the debtor may exercise solely for the benefit of an entity other than the debtor. This changes present law which excludes powers solely benefiting other persons but not other entities.

Subsection (c) invalidates restrictions on the transfer of property of the debtor, in order that all of the interests of the debtor in property will become property of the estate. The provisions invalidated are those that restrict or condition transfer of the debtor's interest, and those that are conditioned on the insolvency or financial condition of the debtor, on the commencement of a bankruptcy case, or on the appointment of a custodian of the debtor's property. Paragraph (2) of subsection (c), however, preserves restrictions on a transfer of a spendthrift trust that the restriction is enforceable nonbankruptcy law to the extent of the income reasonably necessary for the support of a debtor and his dependents.

Subsection (d) [enacted as (e)], derived from section 70c of the Bankruptcy Act [section 110(c) of former title 11], gives the estate the benefit of all defenses available to the debtor as against an entity other than the estate, including such defenses as statutes of limitations, statutes of frauds, usury, and other personal defenses, and makes waiver by the debtor after the commencement of the case ineffective to bind the estate.

Section 541(e) [enacted as (d)] confirms the current status under the Bankruptcy Act [former title 11] of bona fide secondary mortgage market transactions as the purchase and sale of assets. Mortgages or interests in mortgages sold in the secondary market should not be considered as part of the debtor's estate. To permit the efficient servicing of mortgages or interests in mortgages the seller often retains the original mortgage notes and related documents, and the purchaser records under State recording statutes the purchaser's ownership of the mortgages or interests in mortgages purchased. Section 541(e) makes clear that the seller's retention of the mortgage documents and the purchaser's decision not to record do not impair the asset sale character of secondary mortgage market transactions. The committee notes that in secondary mortgage market transactions the parties may characterize their relationship as one of trust, agency, or independent contractor. The characterization adopted by the parties should not affect the statutes in bankruptcy on bona fide secondary mortgage market purchases and sales.

REFERENCES IN TEXT

The Higher Education Act of 1965, referred to in subsec. (b)(3), is Pub. L. 89–329, Nov. 8, 1965, 79 Stat. 1219, as amended, which is classified principally to chapter 28 (§1001 et seq.) of Title 20, Education. For complete classification of this Act to the Code, see Short Title note set out under section 1001 of Title 20 and Tables.

The Internal Revenue Code of 1986, referred to in subsecs. (b)(5) to (7) and (f), is classified generally to Title 26, Internal Revenue Code.

The Employee Retirement Income Security Act of 1974, referred to in subsec. (b)(7)(A)(i)(I), (B)(i)(I), is Pub. L. 93–406, Sept. 2, 1974, 88 Stat. 829, as amended. Title I of the Act is classified generally to subchapter I (§1001 et seq.) of chapter 18 of Title 29, Labor. For complete classification of this Act to the Code, see Short Title note set out under section 1001 of Title 29 and Tables.

AMENDMENTS

2005—Subsec. (b)(4). Pub. L. 109–8, §225(a)(1)(A), struck out "or" at end.

Subsec. (b)(4)(B)(ii). Pub. L. 109–8, §1212, inserted "365 or" before "542".

Subsec. (b)(5), (6). Pub. L. 109–8, §225(a)(1)(C), added pars. (5) and (6). Former par. (5) redesignated (9).

Subsec. (b)(7). Pub. L. 109–8, §323, added par. (7).

Subsec. (b)(8). Pub. L. 109–8, §1230, added par. (8).

Subsec. (b)(9). Pub. L. 109–8, §225(a)(1)(B), redesignated par. (5) as (9).

Subsec. (e). Pub. L. 109–8, §225(a)(2), added subsec. (e).

Subsec. (f). Pub. L. 109–8, §1221(c), added subsec. (f).

1994—Subsec. (b)(4). Pub. L. 103–394, §208(b), designated existing provisions of subpar. (A) as cl. (i) of subpar. (A), redesignated subpar. (B) as cl. (ii) of subpar. (A), substituted "the interest referred to in clause (i)" for "such interest", substituted "; or" for period at end of cl. (ii), and added subpar. (B).

Pub. L. 103–394, §223(2), which directed the amendment of subsec. (b)(4) by striking out period at end and inserting "; or", was executed by inserting "or" after semicolon at end of subsec. (b)(4)(B)(ii), as added by Pub. L. 103–394, §208(b)(3), to reflect the probable intent of Congress.

Subsec. (b)(5). Pub. L. 103–394, §223, added par. (5).

1992—Subsec. (b). Pub. L. 102–486 added par. (4) and closing provisions.

1990—Subsec. (b)(3). Pub. L. 101–508 added par. (3).

1984—Subsec. (a). Pub. L. 98–353, §456(a)(1), (2), struck out "under" after "under" and inserted "and by whomever held" after "located".

Subsec. (a)(3). Pub. L. 98–353, §456(a)(3), inserted "329(b), 363(n),".

Subsec. (a)(5). Pub. L. 98–353, §456(a)(4), substituted "Any" for "An".

Subsec. (a)(6). Pub. L. 98–353, §456(a)(5), substituted "or profits" for "and profits".

Subsec. (b). Pub. L. 98–353, §363(a), amended subsec. (b) generally. Prior to amendment, subsec. (b) read as follows: "Property of the estate does not include any power that the debtor may only exercise solely for the benefit of an entity other than the debtor."

Subsec. (c)(1). Pub. L. 98–353, §456(b)(1), inserted "in an agreement, transfer, instrument, or applicable nonbankruptcy law".

Subsec. (c)(1)(B). Pub. L. 98–353, §456(b)(2), substituted "taking" for "the taking", and inserted "before such commencement" after "custodian".

Subsec. (d). Pub. L. 98–353, §456(c), inserted "(1) or (2)" after "(a)".

Subsec. (e). Pub. L. 98–353, §456(d), struck out subsec. (e) which read as follows: "The estate shall have the benefit of any defense available to the debtor as against an entity other than the estate, including statutes of limitation, statutes of frauds, usury, and other personal defenses. A waiver of any such defense by the debtor after the commencement of the case does not bind the estate."

EFFECTIVE DATE OF 2005 AMENDMENT

Amendment by section 1221(c) of Pub. L. 109–8 applicable to cases pending under this title on Apr. 20, 2005, or filed under this title on or after Apr. 20, 2005, with certain exceptions, see section 1221(d) of Pub. L. 109–8, set out as a note under section 363 of this title.

Amendment by sections 225(a), 323, 1212, and 1230 of Pub. L. 109–8 effective 180 days after Apr. 20, 2005, and not applicable with respect to cases commenced under this title before such effective date, except as otherwise provided, see section 1501 of Pub. L. 109–8, set out as a note under section 101 of this title.

EFFECTIVE DATE OF 1994 AMENDMENT

Amendment by Pub. L. 103–394 effective Oct. 22, 1994, and not applicable with respect to cases commenced under this title before Oct. 22, 1994, see section 702 of Pub. L. 103–394, set out as a note under section 101 of this title.

EFFECTIVE DATE OF 1992 AMENDMENT

Amendment by Pub. L. 102–486 effective Oct. 24, 1992, but not applicable with respect to cases commenced under this title before Oct. 24, 1992, see section 3017(c) of Pub. L. 102–486, set out as a note under section 101 of this title.

EFFECTIVE DATE OF 1984 AMENDMENT

Amendment by Pub. L. 98–353 effective with respect to cases filed 90 days after July 10, 1984, see section 552(a) of Pub. L. 98–353, set out as a note under section 101 of this title.

ADJUSTMENT OF DOLLAR AMOUNTS

For adjustment of dollar amounts specified in subsec. (b)(5)(C), (6)(C) of this section by the Judicial Conference of the United States, see note set out under section 104 of this title.

§ 542. Turnover of property to the estate

(a) Except as provided in subsection (c) or (d) of this section, an entity, other than a custodian, in possession, custody, or control, during the case, of property that the trustee may use, sell, or lease under section 363 of this title, or that the debtor may exempt under section 522 of this title, shall deliver to the trustee, and account for, such property or the value of such property, unless such property is of inconsequential value or benefit to the estate.

(b) Except as provided in subsection (c) or (d) of this section, an entity that owes a debt that is property of the estate and that is matured, payable on demand, or payable on order, shall pay such debt to, or on the order of, the trustee, except to the extent that such debt may be offset under section 553 of this title against a claim against the debtor.

(c) Except as provided in section 362(a)(7) of this title, an entity that has neither actual notice nor actual knowledge of the commencement of the case concerning the debtor may transfer property of the estate, or pay a debt owing to the debtor, in good faith and other than in the manner specified in subsection (d) of this section, to an entity other than the trustee, with the same effect as to the entity making such transfer or payment as if the case under this title concerning the debtor had not been commenced.

(d) A life insurance company may transfer property of the estate or property of the debtor to such company in good faith, with the same effect with respect to such company as if the case under this title concerning the debtor had not been commenced, if such transfer is to pay a premium or to carry out a nonforfeiture insurance option, and is required to be made automatically, under a life insurance contract with such company that was entered into before the date of the filing of the petition and that is property of the estate.

(e) Subject to any applicable privilege, after notice and a hearing, the court may order an attorney, accountant, or other person that holds recorded information, including books, documents, records, and papers, relating to the debtor's property or financial affairs, to turn over or disclose such recorded information to the trustee.

(Pub. L. 95–598, Nov. 6, 1978, 92 Stat. 2595; Pub. L. 98–353, title III, §457, July 10, 1984, 98 Stat. 376; Pub. L. 103–394, title V, §501(d)(16), Oct. 22, 1994, 108 Stat. 4146.)

HISTORICAL AND REVISION NOTES

LEGISLATIVE STATEMENTS

Section 542(a) of the House amendment modifies similar provisions contained in the House bill and the Senate amendment treating with turnover of property to the estate. The section makes clear that any entity, other than a custodian, is required to deliver property of the estate to the trustee or debtor in possession whenever such property is acquired by the entity during the case, if the trustee or debtor in possession may use, sell, or lease the property under section 363, or if the debtor may exempt the property under section 522, unless the property is of inconsequential value or benefit to the estate. This section is not intended to require an entity to deliver property to the trustee if such entity has obtained an order of the court authorizing the entity to retain possession, custody or control of the property.

The House amendment adopts section 542(c) of the House bill in preference to a similar provision contained in section 542(c) of the Senate amendment. Protection afforded by section 542(c) applies only to the transferor or payor and not to a transferee or payee receiving a transfer or payment, as the case may be. Such transferee or payee is treated under section 549 and section 550 of title 11.

The extent to which the attorney client privilege is valid against the trustee is unclear under current law and is left to be determined by the courts on a case by case basis.

SENATE REPORT NO. 95–989

Subsection (a) of this section requires anyone holding property of the estate on the date of the filing of the petition, or property that the trustee may use, sell, or lease under section 363, to deliver it to the trustee. The subsection also requires an accounting. The holder of property of the estate is excused from the turnover requirement of this subsection if the property held is of inconsequential value to the estate. However, this provision must be read in conjunction with the remainder of the subsection, so that if the property is of inconsequential monetary value, yet has a significant use value for the estate, the holder of the property would not be excused from turnover.

Subsection (b) requires an entity that owes money to the debtor as of the date of the petition, or that holds money payable on demand or payable on order, to pay the money to the order of the trustee. An exception is made to the extent that the entity has a valid right of setoff, as recognized by section 553.

Subsection (c) provides an exception to subsections (a) and (b). It protects an entity that has neither actual notice nor actual knowledge of the case and that transfers, in good faith, property that is deliverable or payable to the trustee to someone other than to the estate or on order of the estate. This subsection codifies the result of *Bank of Marin v. England*, 385 U.S. 99 (1966), but does not go so far as to permit bank setoff in violation of the automatic stay, proposed 11 U.S.C. 362(a)(7), even if the bank offsetting the debtor's balance has no knowledge of the case.

Subsection (d) protects life insurance companies that are required by contract to make automatic premium loans from property that might otherwise be property of the estate.

Subsection (e) requires an attorney, accountant, or other professional that holds recorded information relating to the debtor's property or financial affairs, to surrender it to the trustee. This duty is subject to any applicable claim of privilege, such as attorney-client privilege. It is a new provision that deprives accountants and attorneys of the leverage that they have today, under State law lien provisions, to receive payment in full ahead of other creditors when the information they hold is necessary to the administration of the estate.

AMENDMENTS

1994—Subsec. (e). Pub. L. 103–394 substituted "to" for "to to" after "financial affairs,".

1984—Subsec. (e). Pub. L. 98–353 inserted "to turn over or" before "disclose".

EFFECTIVE DATE OF 1994 AMENDMENT

Amendment by Pub. L. 103–394 effective Oct. 22, 1994, and not applicable with respect to cases commenced under this title before Oct. 22, 1994, see section 702 of Pub. L. 103–394, set out as a note under section 101 of this title.

EFFECTIVE DATE OF 1984 AMENDMENT

Amendment by Pub. L. 98–353 effective with respect to cases filed 90 days after July 10, 1984, see section 552(a) of Pub. L. 98–353, set out as a note under section 101 of this title.

§ 543. Turnover of property by a custodian

(a) A custodian with knowledge of the commencement of a case under this title concerning the debtor may not make any disbursement from, or take any action in the administration of, property of the debtor, proceeds, product, offspring, rents, or profits of such property, or property of the estate, in the possession, custody, or control of such custodian, except such action as is necessary to preserve such property.

(b) A custodian shall—

(1) deliver to the trustee any property of the debtor held by or transferred to such custodian, or proceeds, product, offspring, rents, or profits of such property, that is in such custodian's possession, custody, or control on the date that such custodian acquires knowledge of the commencement of the case; and

(2) file an accounting of any property of the debtor, or proceeds, product, offspring, rents, or profits of such property, that, at any time, came into the possession, custody, or control of such custodian.

(c) The court, after notice and a hearing, shall—

(1) protect all entities to which a custodian has become obligated with respect to such property or proceeds, product, offspring, rents, or profits of such property;

(2) provide for the payment of reasonable compensation for services rendered and costs and expenses incurred by such custodian; and

(3) surcharge such custodian, other than an assignee for the benefit of the debtor's creditors that was appointed or took possession more than 120 days before the date of the filing of the petition, for any improper or excessive disbursement, other than a disbursement that has been made in accordance with applicable law or that has been approved, after notice and a hearing, by a court of competent jurisdiction before the commencement of the case under this title.

(d) After notice and hearing, the bankruptcy court—

(1) may excuse compliance with subsection (a), (b), or (c) of this section if the interests of creditors and, if the debtor is not insolvent, of equity security holders would be better served by permitting a custodian to continue in possession, custody, or control of such property, and

(2) shall excuse compliance with subsections (a) and (b)(1) of this section if the custodian is an assignee for the benefit of the debtor's creditors that was appointed or took possession more than 120 days before the date of the filing of the petition, unless compliance with such subsections is necessary to prevent fraud or injustice.

(Pub. L. 95–598, Nov. 6, 1978, 92 Stat. 2595; Pub. L. 98–353, title III, § 458, July 10, 1984, 98 Stat. 376; Pub. L. 103–394, title V, § 501(d)(17), Oct. 22, 1994, 108 Stat. 4146.)

HISTORICAL AND REVISION NOTES

LEGISLATIVE STATEMENTS

Section 543(a) is a modification of similar provisions contained in the House bill and the Senate amendment. The provision clarifies that a custodian may always act as is necessary to preserve property of the debtor. Section 543(c)(3) excepts from surcharge a custodian that is an assignee for the benefit of creditors, who was appointed or took possession before 120 days before the date of the filing of the petition, whichever is later. The provision also prevents a custodian from being surcharged in connection with payments made in accordance with applicable law.

SENATE REPORT NO. 95–989

This section requires a custodian appointed before the bankruptcy case to deliver to the trustee and to account for property that has come into his possession, custody, or control as a custodian. "Property of the debtor" in section (a) includes property that was property of the debtor at the time the custodian took the property, but the title to which passed to the custodian. The section requires the court to protect any obligations incurred by the custodian, provide for the payment of reasonable compensation for services rendered and costs and expenses incurred by the custodian, and to surcharge the custodian for any improper or excessive disbursement, unless it has been approved by a court of competent jurisdiction. Subsection (d) reinforces the general abstention policy in section 305 by permitting the bankruptcy court to authorize the custodianship to proceed notwithstanding this section.

AMENDMENTS

1994—Subsec. (d)(1). Pub. L. 103–394 struck out comma after "section".

1984—Subsec. (a). Pub. L. 98–353, §458(a), inserted ", product, offspring, rents, or profits" after "proceeds".

Subsec. (b)(1). Pub. L. 98–353, §458(b)(1), inserted "held by or" after "debtor", and ", product, offspring, rents, or profits" after "proceeds".

Subsec. (b)(2). Pub. L. 98–353, §458(b)(2), inserted ", product, offspring, rents, or profits" after "proceeds".

Subsec. (c)(1). Pub. L. 98–353, §458(c)(1), inserted "or proceeds, product, offspring, rents, or profits of such property" after "property".

Subsec. (c)(3). Pub. L. 98–353, §458(c)(2), inserted "that has been" before "approved".

Subsec. (d). Pub. L. 98–353, §458(d), designated existing provisions as par. (1) and added par. (2).

EFFECTIVE DATE OF 1994 AMENDMENT

Amendment by Pub. L. 103–394 effective Oct. 22, 1994, and not applicable with respect to cases commenced under this title before Oct. 22, 1994, see section 702 of Pub. L. 103–394, set out as a note under section 101 of this title.

EFFECTIVE DATE OF 1984 AMENDMENT

Amendment by Pub. L. 98–353 effective with respect to cases filed 90 days after July 10, 1984, see section 552(a) of Pub. L. 98–353, set out as a note under section 101 of this title.

§544. Trustee as lien creditor and as successor to certain creditors and purchasers

(a) The trustee shall have, as of the commencement of the case, and without regard to any knowledge of the trustee or of any creditor, the rights and powers of, or may avoid any transfer of property of the debtor or any obligation incurred by the debtor that is voidable by—

(1) a creditor that extends credit to the debtor at the time of the commencement of the case, and that obtains, at such time and with respect to such credit, a judicial lien on all property on which a creditor on a simple contract could have obtained such a judicial lien, whether or not such a creditor exists;

(2) a creditor that extends credit to the debtor at the time of the commencement of the case, and obtains, at such time and with respect to such credit, an execution against the debtor that is returned unsatisfied at such time, whether or not such a creditor exists; or

(3) a bona fide purchaser of real property, other than fixtures, from the debtor, against whom applicable law permits such transfer to be perfected, that obtains the status of a bona fide purchaser and has perfected such transfer at the time of the commencement of the case, whether or not such a purchaser exists.

(b)(1) Except as provided in paragraph (2), the trustee may avoid any transfer of an interest of the debtor in property or any obligation incurred by the debtor that is voidable under applicable law by a creditor holding an unsecured claim that is allowable under section 502 of this title or that is not allowable only under section 502(e) of this title.

(2) Paragraph (1) shall not apply to a transfer of a charitable contribution (as that term is defined in section 548(d)(3)) that is not covered under section 548(a)(1)(B), by reason of section 548(a)(2). Any claim by any person to recover a transferred contribution described in the preceding sentence under Federal or State law in a Federal or State court shall be preempted by the commencement of the case.

(Pub. L. 95–598, Nov. 6, 1978, 92 Stat. 2596; Pub. L. 98–353, title III, §459, July 10, 1984, 98 Stat. 377; Pub. L. 105–183, §3(b), June 19, 1998, 112 Stat. 518.)

HISTORICAL AND REVISION NOTES

LEGISLATIVE STATEMENTS

Section 544(a)(3) modifies similar provisions contained in the House bill and Senate amendment so as not to require a creditor to perform the impossible in order to perfect his interest. Both the lien creditor test in section 544(a)(1), and the bona fide purchaser test in section 544(a)(3) should not require a transferee to perfect a transfer against an entity with respect to which applicable law does not permit perfection. The avoiding powers under section 544(a)(1), (2), and (3) are new. In particular, section 544(a)(1) overrules *Pacific Finance Corp. v. Edwards*, 309 F.2d 224 (9th Cir. 1962), and *In re Federals, Inc.*, 553 F.2d 509 (6th Cir. 1977), insofar as those cases held that the trustee did not have the status of a creditor who extended credit immediately prior to the commencement of the case.

The House amendment deletes section 544(c) of the House bill.

SENATE REPORT NO. 95–989

Subsection (a) is the "strong arm clause" of current law, now found in Bankruptcy Act §70c [section 110(c) of former title 11]. It gives the trustee the rights of a creditor on a simple contract with a judicial lien on the property of the debtor as of the date of the petition; of a creditor with a writ of execution against the property of the debtor unsatisfied as of the date of the petition; and a bona fide purchaser of the real property of the debtor as of the date of the petition. "Simple contract" as used here is derived from Bankruptcy Act §60a(4) [section 96(a)(4) of former title 11]. The third status, that of a bona fide purchaser of real property, is new.

Subsection (b) is derived from current section 70e [section 110(e) of former title 11]. It gives the trustee the rights of actual unsecured creditors under applicable law to void transfers. It follows *Moore v. Bay*, 284 U.S. 4 (1931), and overrules those cases that hold section 70e gives the trustee the rights of secured creditors.

AMENDMENTS

1998—Subsec. (b). Pub. L. 105–183 designated existing provisions as par. (1), substituted "Except as provided in paragraph (2), the trustee" for "The trustee", and added par. (2).

1984—Subsec. (a)(1). Pub. L. 98–353, §459(1), inserted "such" after "obtained".

Subsec. (a)(2). Pub. L. 98–353, §459(2), substituted "; or" for "; and".

Subsec. (a)(3). Pub. L. 98–353, §459(3), inserted ", other than fixtures," after "property", and "and has perfected such transfer" after "purchaser" the second place it appeared.

EFFECTIVE DATE OF 1998 AMENDMENT

Pub. L. 105–183, §5, June 19, 1998, 112 Stat. 518, provided that: "This Act [amending this section and sections 546, 548, 707, and 1325 of this title and enacting provisions set out as notes under this section and section 101 of this title] and the amendments made by this Act shall apply to any case brought under an applicable provision of title 11, United States Code, that is pending or commenced on or after the date of enactment of this Act [June 19, 1998]."

EFFECTIVE DATE OF 1984 AMENDMENT

Amendment by Pub. L. 98–353 effective with respect to cases filed 90 days after July 10, 1984, see section 552(a) of Pub. L. 98–353, set out as a note under section 101 of this title.

CONSTRUCTION OF 1998 AMENDMENT

Pub. L. 105–183, §6, June 19, 1998, 112 Stat. 519, provided that: "Nothing in the amendments made by this Act [amending this section and sections 546, 548, 707, and 1325 of this title] is intended to limit the applicability of the Religious Freedom Restoration Act of 1993 (42 U.S.C. 2002bb [2000bb] et seq.)."

§545. Statutory liens

The trustee may avoid the fixing of a statutory lien on property of the debtor to the extent that such lien—

(1) first becomes effective against the debtor—

(A) when a case under this title concerning the debtor is commenced;

(B) when an insolvency proceeding other than under this title concerning the debtor is commenced;

(C) when a custodian is appointed or authorized to take or takes possession;

(D) when the debtor becomes insolvent;

(E) when the debtor's financial condition fails to meet a specified standard; or

(F) at the time of an execution against property of the debtor levied at the instance of an entity other than the holder of such statutory lien;

(2) is not perfected or enforceable at the time of the commencement of the case against a bona fide purchaser that purchases such property at the time of the commencement of the case, whether or not such a purchaser exists, except in any case in which a purchaser is a purchaser described in section 6323 of the Internal Revenue Code of 1986, or in any other similar provision of State or local law;

(3) is for rent; or

(4) is a lien of distress for rent.

(Pub. L. 95–598, Nov. 6, 1978, 92 Stat. 2597; Pub. L. 98–353, title III, §460, July 10, 1984, 98 Stat. 377; Pub. L. 109–8, title VII, §711, Apr. 20, 2005, 119 Stat. 127.)

HISTORICAL AND REVISION NOTES

LEGISLATIVE STATEMENTS

Section 545 of the House amendment modifies similar provisions contained in the House bill and Senate amendment to make clear that a statutory lien may be avoided under section 545 only to the extent the lien violates the perfection standards of section 545. Thus a Federal tax lien is invalid under section 545(2) with respect to property specified in sections 6323(b) and (c) of the Internal Revenue Code of 1954 [title 26]. As a result of this modification, section 545(b) of the Senate amendment is deleted as unnecessary.

Statutory liens: The House amendment retains the provision of section 545(2) of the House bill giving the trustee in a bankruptcy case the same power which a bona fide purchaser has to take over certain kinds of personal property despite the existence of a tax lien covering that property. The amendment thus retains present law, and deletes section 545(b) of the Senate amendment which would have no longer allowed the trustee to step into the shoes of a bona fide purchaser for this purpose.

SENATE REPORT NO. 95–989

This section permits the trustee to avoid the fixing of certain statutory liens. It is derived from subsections 67b and 67c of present law [section 107(b) and (c) of former title 11]. Liens that first become effective on the bankruptcy or insolvency of the debtor are voidable by the trustee. Liens that are not perfected or enforceable on the date of the petition against a bona fide purchaser are voidable. If a transferee is able to perfect under section 546(a) and that perfection relates back to an earlier date, then in spite of the filing of the bankruptcy petition, the trustee would not be able to defeat the lien, because the lien would be perfected and enforceable against a bona fide purchaser that purchased the property on the date of the filing of the petition. Finally, a lien for rent or of distress for rent is voidable, whether the lien is a statutory lien or a common law lien of distress for rent. See proposed 11 U.S.C. 101(37); Bankruptcy Act §67(c)(1)(C). The trustee may avoid a lien under this section even if the lien has been enforced by sale before the commencement of the case. To that extent, Bankruptcy Act §67c(5) is not followed.

Subsection (b) limits the trustee's power to avoid tax liens under Federal, state, or local law. For example, under §6323 of the Internal Revenue Code [Title 26]. Once public notice of a tax lien has been filed, the Government is generally entitled to priority over subsequent lienholders. However, certain purchasers who acquire an interest in certain specific kinds of personal property will take free of an existing filed tax lien attaching to such property. Among the specific kinds of personal property which a purchaser can acquire free of an existing tax lien (unless the buyer knows of the existence of the lien) are stocks and securities, motor vehicles, inventory, and certain household goods. Under the present Bankruptcy Act (§67(c)(1)) [section 107(c)(1) of former title 11], the trustee may be viewed as a bona fide purchaser, so that he can take over any such designated items free of tax liens even if the tax authority has perfected its lien. However, the reasons for enabling a bona fide purchaser to take these kinds of assets free of an unfiled tax lien, that is, to encourage free movement of these assets in general commerce, do not apply to a trustee in a title 11 case, who is not in the same position as an ordinary bona fide purchaser as to such property. The bill accordingly adds a new subsection (b) to sec. 545 providing, in effect, that a trustee in bankruptcy does not have the right under this section to take otherwise specially treated items of personal property free of a tax lien filed before the filing of the petition.

REFERENCES IN TEXT

Section 6323 of the Internal Revenue Code of 1986, referred to in par. (2), is classified to section 6323 of Title 26, Internal Revenue Code.

AMENDMENTS

2005—Par. (2). Pub. L. 109–8 inserted before semicolon at end ", except in any case in which a purchaser is a purchaser described in section 6323 of the Internal Revenue Code of 1986, or in any other similar provision of State or local law".

1984—Par. (1)(A). Pub. L. 98–353, §460(1), struck out "is" after "is".

Par. (1)(C). Pub. L. 98–353, §460(2), substituted "appointed or authorized to take" for "apponted".

Par. (2). Pub. L. 98–353, §460(3), substituted "at the time of the commencement of the case" for "on the date of the filing of the petition" in two places.

EFFECTIVE DATE OF 2005 AMENDMENT

Amendment by Pub. L. 109–8 effective 180 days after Apr. 20, 2005, and not applicable with respect to cases commenced under this title before such effective date, except as otherwise provided, see section 1501 of Pub. L. 109–8, set out as a note under section 101 of this title.

EFFECTIVE DATE OF 1984 AMENDMENT

Amendment by Pub. L. 98–353 effective with respect to cases filed 90 days after July 10, 1984, see section 552(a) of Pub. L. 98–353, set out as a note under section 101 of this title.

§ 546. Limitations on avoiding powers

(a) An action or proceeding under section 544, 545, 547, 548, or 553 of this title may not be commenced after the earlier of—

(1) the later of—

(A) 2 years after the entry of the order for relief; or

(B) 1 year after the appointment or election of the first trustee under section 702, 1104, 1163, 1202, or 1302 of this title if such appointment or such election occurs before the expiration of the period specified in subparagraph (A); or

(2) the time the case is closed or dismissed.

(b)(1) The rights and powers of a trustee under sections 544, 545, and 549 of this title are subject to any generally applicable law that—

(A) permits perfection of an interest in property to be effective against an entity that acquires rights in such property before the date of perfection; or

(B) provides for the maintenance or continuation of perfection of an interest in property to be effective against an entity that acquires rights in such property before the date on which action is taken to effect such maintenance or continuation.

(2) If—

(A) a law described in paragraph (1) requires seizure of such property or commencement of an action to accomplish such perfection, or maintenance or continuation of perfection of an interest in property; and

(B) such property has not been seized or such an action has not been commenced before the date of the filing of the petition;

such interest in such property shall be perfected, or perfection of such interest shall be maintained or continued, by giving notice within the time fixed by such law for such seizure or such commencement.

(c)(1) Except as provided in subsection (d) of this section and in section 507(c), and subject to the prior rights of a holder of a security interest in such goods or the proceeds thereof, the rights and powers of the trustee under sections 544(a), 545, 547, and 549 are subject to the right of a seller of goods that has sold goods to the debtor, in the ordinary course of such seller's business, to reclaim such goods if the debtor has received such goods while insolvent, within 45 days before the date of the commencement of a case under this title, but such seller may not reclaim such goods unless such seller demands in writing reclamation of such goods—

(A) not later than 45 days after the date of receipt of such goods by the debtor; or

(B) not later than 20 days after the date of commencement of the case, if the 45-day period expires after the commencement of the case.

(2) If a seller of goods fails to provide notice in the manner described in paragraph (1), the seller still may assert the rights contained in section 503(b)(9).

(d) In the case of a seller who is a producer of grain sold to a grain storage facility, owned or operated by the debtor, in the ordinary course of such seller's business (as such terms are defined in section 557 of this title) or in the case of a United States fisherman who has caught fish sold to a fish processing facility owned or operated by the debtor in the ordinary course of such fisherman's business, the rights and powers of the trustee under sections 544(a), 545, 547, and 549 of this title are subject to any statutory or common law right of such producer or fisherman to reclaim such grain or fish if the debtor has received such grain or fish while insolvent, but—

(1) such producer or fisherman may not reclaim any grain or fish unless such producer or fisherman demands, in writing, reclamation of such grain or fish before ten days after receipt thereof by the debtor; and

(2) the court may deny reclamation to such a producer or fisherman with a right of reclamation that has made such a demand only if the court secures such claim by a lien.

(e) Notwithstanding sections 544, 545, 547, 548(a)(1)(B), and 548(b) of this title, the trustee may not avoid a transfer that is a margin payment, as defined in section 101, 741, or 761 of this title, or settlement payment, as defined in section 101 or 741 of this title, made by or to (or for the benefit of) a commodity broker, forward contract merchant, stockbroker, financial institution, financial participant, or securities clearing agency, or that is a transfer made by or to (or for the benefit of) a commodity broker, forward contract merchant, stockbroker, financial institution, financial participant, or securities clearing agency, in connection with a securities contract, as defined in section 741(7), commodity contract, as defined in section 761(4), or forward contract, that is made before the commencement of the case, except under section 548(a)(1)(A) of this title.

(f) Notwithstanding sections 544, 545, 547, 548(a)(1)(B), and 548(b) of this title, the trustee may not avoid a transfer made by or to (or for the benefit of) a repo participant or financial participant, in connection with a repurchase agreement and that is made before the commencement of the case, except under section 548(a)(1)(A) of this title.

(g) Notwithstanding sections 544, 545, 547, 548(a)(1)(B) and 548(b) of this title, the trustee may not avoid a transfer, made by or to (or for the benefit of) a swap participant or financial participant, under or in connection with any swap agreement and that is made before the commencement of the case, except under section 548(a)(1)(A) of this title.

(h) Notwithstanding the rights and powers of a trustee under sections 544(a), 545, 547, 549, and 553, if the court determines on a motion by the trustee made not later than 120 days after the date of the order for relief in a case under chapter 11 of this title and after notice and a hearing, that a return is in the best interests of the estate, the debtor, with the consent of a creditor and subject to the prior rights of holders of security interests in such goods or the proceeds of such goods, may return goods shipped to the debtor by the creditor before the commencement of the case, and the creditor may offset the purchase price of such goods against any claim of the creditor against the debtor that arose before the commencement of the case.

(i)(1) Notwithstanding paragraphs (2) and (3) of section 545, the trustee may not avoid a warehouseman's lien for storage, transportation, or other costs incidental to the storage and handling of goods.

(2) The prohibition under paragraph (1) shall be applied in a manner consistent with any State statute applicable to such lien that is similar to section 7–209 of the Uniform Commercial Code, as in effect on the date of enactment of the Bankruptcy Abuse Prevention and Consumer Protection Act of 2005, or any successor to such section 7–209.

(j) Notwithstanding sections 544, 545, 547, 548(a)(1)(B), and 548(b) the trustee may not avoid a transfer made by or to (or for the benefit of) a master netting agreement participant under or in connection with any master netting agreement or any individual contract covered thereby that is made before the commencement of the case, except under section 548(a)(1)(A) and except to the extent that the trustee could otherwise avoid such a transfer made under an individual contract covered by such master netting agreement.

(Pub. L. 95–598, Nov. 6, 1978, 92 Stat. 2597; Pub. L. 97–222, §4, July 27, 1982, 96 Stat. 236; Pub. L. 98–353, title III, §§351, 393, 461, July 10, 1984, 98 Stat. 358, 365, 377; Pub. L. 99–554, title II, §§257(d), 283(*l*), Oct. 27, 1986, 100 Stat. 3114, 3117; Pub. L. 101–311, title I, §103, title II, §203, June 25, 1990, 104 Stat. 268, 269; Pub. L. 103–394, title II, §§204(b), 209, 216, 222(a), title V, §501(b)(4), Oct. 22, 1994, 108 Stat. 4122, 4125, 4126, 4129, 4142; Pub. L. 105–183, §3(c), June 19, 1998, 112 Stat. 518; Pub. L. 109–8, title IV, §406, title IX, §907(e), (*o*)(2), (3), title XII, §1227(a), Apr. 20, 2005, 119 Stat. 105, 177, 182, 199; Pub. L. 109–390, §5(b), Dec. 12, 2006, 120 Stat. 2697.)

Historical and Revision Notes

legislative statements

Section 546(a) of the House amendment is derived from section 546(c) of the Senate amendment. Section 546(c) of the House amendment is derived from section 546(b) of the Senate amendment. It applies to receipt of goods on credit as well as by cash sales. The section clarifies that a demand for reclamation must be made in writing anytime before 10 days after receipt of the goods by the debtor. The section also permits the court to grant the reclaiming creditor a lien or an administrative expense in lieu of turning over the property.

senate report no. 95–989

The trustee's rights and powers under certain of the avoiding powers are limited by section 546. First, if an interest holder against whom the trustee would have rights still has, under applicable nonbankruptcy law, and as of the date of the petition, the opportunity to perfect his lien against an intervening interest holder, then he may perfect his interest against the trustee. If applicable law requires seizure for perfection, then perfection is by notice to the trustee instead. The rights granted to a creditor under this subsection prevail over the trustee only if the transferee has perfected the transfer in accordance with applicable law, and that perfection relates back to a date that is before the commencement of the case.

The phrase "generally applicable law" relates to those provisions of applicable law that apply both in bankruptcy cases and outside of bankruptcy cases. For example, many State laws, under the Uniform Commercial Code, permit perfection of a purchase-money security interest to relate back to defeat an earlier levy by another creditor if the former was perfected within ten days of delivery of the property. U.C.C. §9–301(2). Such perfection would then be able to defeat an intervening hypothetical judicial lien creditor on the date of the filing of the petition. The purpose of the subsection is to protect, in spite of the surprise intervention of a bankruptcy petition, those whom State law protects by allowing them to perfect their liens or interests as of an effective date that is earlier than the date of perfection. It is not designed to give the States an opportunity to enact disguised priorities in the form of liens that apply only in bankruptcy cases.

Subsection (b) [enacted as (c)] specifies that the trustee's rights and powers under the strong arm clause, the successor to creditors provision, the preference section, and the postpetition transaction section are all subject to any statutory or common-law right of a seller, in the ordinary course of business, of goods to the debtor to reclaim the goods if the debtor received the goods on credit while insolvent. The seller must demand reclamation within ten days after receipt of the goods by the debtor. As under nonbankruptcy law, the right is subject to any superior rights of secured creditors. The purpose of the provision is to recognize, in part, the validity of section 2–702 of the Uniform Commercial Code, which has generated much litigation, confusion, and divergent decisions in different circuits. The right is subject, however, to the power of the court to deny reclamation and protect the seller by granting him a priority as an administrative expense for his claim arising out of the sale of the goods.

Subsection (c) [enacted as (a)] adds a statute of limitations to the use by the trustee of the avoiding powers. The limitation is two years after his appointment, or the time the case is closed or dismissed, whichever occurs later.

References in Text

The date of enactment of the Bankruptcy Abuse Prevention and Consumer Protection Act of 2005, referred to in subsec. (i)(2), is the date of enactment of Pub. L. 109–8, which was approved Apr. 20 2005.

Amendments

2006—Subsec. (e). Pub. L. 109–390, §5(b)(1), inserted "(or for the benefit of)" before "a commodity broker" and "or that is a transfer made by or to (or for the benefit of) a commodity broker, forward contract merchant, stockbroker, financial institution, financial participant, or securities clearing agency, in connection with a securities contract, as defined in section 741(7), commodity contract, as defined in section 761(4), or forward contract," after "securities clearing agency,".

Subsec. (f). Pub. L. 109–390, §5(b)(2), struck out "that is a margin payment, as defined in section 741 or 761 of this title, or settlement payment, as defined in section 741 of this title," after "avoid a transfer" and inserted "(or for the benefit of)" before "a repo participant".

Subsec. (g). Pub. L. 109–390, §5(b)(3), inserted "(or for the benefit of)" before "a swap participant".

Subsec. (j). Pub. L. 109–390, §5(b)(4), inserted "(or for the benefit of)" before "a master netting agreement participant".

2005—Subsec. (c). Pub. L. 109–8, §1227(a), amended subsec. (c) generally. Prior to amendment, subsec. (c) consisted of pars. (1) and (2) relating to reclamation of goods sold to an insolvent debtor.

Subsec. (e). Pub. L. 109–8, §907(*o*)(3), inserted "financial participant," after "financial institution,".

Subsec. (f). Pub. L. 109–8, §907(*o*)(2), inserted "or financial participant" after "repo participant".

Subsec. (g). Pub. L. 109–8, §907(e)(1), struck out "under a swap agreement" after "avoid a transfer", substituted "under or in connection with any swap agreement" for "in connection with a swap agreement", and inserted "or financial participant" after "swap participant".

Pub. L. 109–8, §406(1), redesignated subsec. (g) relating to return of goods as (h).

Subsec. (h). Pub. L. 109–8, §406(2), inserted "and subject to the prior rights of holders of security interests in such goods or the proceeds of such goods" after "consent of a creditor".

Pub. L. 109–8, §406(1), redesignated subsec. (g) relating to return of goods as (h).

Subsec. (i). Pub. L. 109–8, §406(3), added subsec. (i).

Subsec. (j). Pub. L. 109–8, §907(e)(2), added subsec. (j).

1998—Subsecs. (e) to (g). Pub. L. 105–183 substituted "548(a)(1)(B)" for "548(a)(2)" and "548(a)(1)(A)" for "548(a)(1)".

1994—Subsec. (a)(1). Pub. L. 103–394, §216, amended par. (1) generally. Prior to amendment, par. (1) read as follows: "two years after the appointment of a trustee under section 702, 1104, 1163, 1302, or 1202 of this title; or".

Subsec. (b). Pub. L. 103–394, §204(b), amended subsec. (b) generally. Prior to amendment, subsec. (b) read as follows: "The rights and powers of a trustee under sections 544, 545, and 549 of this title are subject to any generally applicable law that permits perfection of an interest in property to be effective against an entity that acquires rights in such property before the date of such perfection. If such law requires seizure of such property or commencement of an action to accomplish such perfection, and such property has not been seized or such action has not been commenced before the date of the filing of the petition, such interest in such property shall be perfected by notice within the time fixed by such law for such seizure or commencement."

Subsec. (c)(1). Pub. L. 103–394, §209, amended par. (1) generally. Prior to amendment, par. (1) read as follows: "such a seller may not reclaim any such goods unless such seller demands in writing reclamation of such goods before ten days after receipt of such goods by the debtor; and".

Subsec. (e). Pub. L. 103–394, §501(b)(4)(A), substituted "section 101, 741, or 761" for "section 101(34), 741(5), or 761(15)" and "section 101 or 741" for "section 101(35) or 741(8)".

Subsec. (f). Pub. L. 103–394, §501(b)(4)(B), substituted "section 741 or 761" for "section 741(5) or 761(15)" and "section 741" for "section 741(8)".

Subsec. (g). Pub. L. 103–394, §222(a), added subsec. (g) relating to return of goods.

1990—Subsec. (e). Pub. L. 101–311, §203, inserted reference to sections 101(34) and 101(35) of this title.

Subsec. (g). Pub. L. 101–311, §103, added subsec. (g) relating to trustee's authority to avoid transfer involving swap agreement.

1986—Subsec. (a)(1). Pub. L. 99–554, §257(d), inserted reference to section 1202 of this title.

Subsec. (e). Pub. L. 99–554, §283(*l*), inserted a comma after "stockbroker".

1984—Subsec. (a)(1). Pub. L. 98–353, §461(a), substituted "; or" for "; and".

Subsec. (b). Pub. L. 98–353, §461(b), substituted "a trustee under sections 544, 545, and" for "the trustee under sections 544, 545, or".

Subsec. (c). Pub. L. 98–353, §§351(1), 461(c)(1)–(4), substituted "Except as provided in subsection (d) of this section, the" for "The", substituted "a trustee" for "the trustee", struck out "right" before "or common-law", inserted "of goods that has sold goods to the debtor" after "seller", and struck out "of goods to the debtor" after "business,".

Subsec. (c)(2). Pub. L. 98–353, §461(c)(5)(A), inserted "the" after "if" in provisions preceding subpar. (A).

Subsec. (c)(2)(A). Pub. L. 98–353, §461(c)(5)(B), substituted "a claim of a kind specified in section 503(b) of this title" for "an administrative expense".

Subsec. (d). Pub. L. 98–353, §351(3), added subsec. (d). Former subsec. (d) redesignated (e).

Subsec. (e). Pub. L. 98–353, §§351(2), 461(d), redesignated former subsec. (d) as (e) and inserted "financial institution" after "stockbroker".

Subsec. (f). Pub. L. 98–353, §393, added subsec. (f).

1982—Subsec. (d). Pub. L. 97–222 added subsec. (d).

EFFECTIVE DATE OF 2006 AMENDMENT

Amendment by Pub. L. 109–390 not applicable to any cases commenced under this title or to appointments made under any Federal or State law, before Dec. 12, 2006, see section 7 of Pub. L. 109–390, set out as a note under section 101 of this title.

EFFECTIVE DATE OF 2005 AMENDMENT

Amendment by Pub. L. 109–8 effective 180 days after Apr. 20, 2005, and not applicable with respect to cases commenced under this title before such effective date, except as otherwise provided, see section 1501 of Pub. L. 109–8, set out as a note under section 101 of this title.

EFFECTIVE DATE OF 1998 AMENDMENT

Amendment by Pub. L. 105–183 applicable to any case brought under an applicable provision of this title that is pending or commenced on or after June 19, 1998, see section 5 of Pub. L. 105–183, set out as a note under section 544 of this title.

EFFECTIVE DATE OF 1994 AMENDMENT

Amendment by Pub. L. 103–394 effective Oct. 22, 1994, and not applicable with respect to cases commenced under this title before Oct. 22, 1994, see section 702 of Pub. L. 103–394, set out as a note under section 101 of this title.

EFFECTIVE DATE OF 1986 AMENDMENT

Amendment by section 257 of Pub. L. 99–554 effective 30 days after Oct. 27, 1986, but not applicable to cases commenced under this title before that date, see section 302(a), (c)(1) of Pub. L. 99–554, set out as a note under section 581 of Title 28, Judiciary and Judicial Procedure.

Amendment by section 283 of Pub. L. 99–554 effective 30 days after Oct. 27, 1986, see section 302(a) of Pub. L. 99–554.

EFFECTIVE DATE OF 1984 AMENDMENT

Amendment by Pub. L. 98–353 effective with respect to cases filed 90 days after July 10, 1984, see section 552(a) of Pub. L. 98–353, set out as a note under section 101 of this title.

§547. Preferences

(a) In this section—

(1) "inventory" means personal property leased or furnished, held for sale or lease, or to be furnished under a contract for service, raw

materials, work in process, or materials used or consumed in a business, including farm products such as crops or livestock, held for sale or lease;

(2) "new value" means money or money's worth in goods, services, or new credit, or release by a transferee of property previously transferred to such transferee in a transaction that is neither void nor voidable by the debtor or the trustee under any applicable law, including proceeds of such property, but does not include an obligation substituted for an existing obligation;

(3) "receivable" means right to payment, whether or not such right has been earned by performance; and

(4) a debt for a tax is incurred on the day when such tax is last payable without penalty, including any extension.

(b) Except as provided in subsections (c) and (i) of this section, the trustee may avoid any transfer of an interest of the debtor in property—

(1) to or for the benefit of a creditor;

(2) for or on account of an antecedent debt owed by the debtor before such transfer was made;

(3) made while the debtor was insolvent;

(4) made—

(A) on or within 90 days before the date of the filing of the petition; or

(B) between ninety days and one year before the date of the filing of the petition, if such creditor at the time of such transfer was an insider; and

(5) that enables such creditor to receive more than such creditor would receive if—

(A) the case were a case under chapter 7 of this title;

(B) the transfer had not been made; and

(C) such creditor received payment of such debt to the extent provided by the provisions of this title.

(c) The trustee may not avoid under this section a transfer—

(1) to the extent that such transfer was—

(A) intended by the debtor and the creditor to or for whose benefit such transfer was made to be a contemporaneous exchange for new value given to the debtor; and

(B) in fact a substantially contemporaneous exchange;

(2) to the extent that such transfer was in payment of a debt incurred by the debtor in the ordinary course of business or financial affairs of the debtor and the transferee, and such transfer was—

(A) made in the ordinary course of business or financial affairs of the debtor and the transferee; or

(B) made according to ordinary business terms;

(3) that creates a security interest in property acquired by the debtor—

(A) to the extent such security interest secures new value that was—

(i) given at or after the signing of a security agreement that contains a description of such property as collateral;

(ii) given by or on behalf of the secured party under such agreement;

(iii) given to enable the debtor to acquire such property; and

(iv) in fact used by the debtor to acquire such property; and

(B) that is perfected on or before 30 days after the debtor receives possession of such property;

(4) to or for the benefit of a creditor, to the extent that, after such transfer, such creditor gave new value to or for the benefit of the debtor—

(A) not secured by an otherwise unavoidable security interest; and

(B) on account of which new value the debtor did not make an otherwise unavoidable transfer to or for the benefit of such creditor;

(5) that creates a perfected security interest in inventory or a receivable or the proceeds of either, except to the extent that the aggregate of all such transfers to the transferee caused a reduction, as of the date of the filing of the petition and to the prejudice of other creditors holding unsecured claims, of any amount by which the debt secured by such security interest exceeded the value of all security interests for such debt on the later of—

(A)(i) with respect to a transfer to which subsection (b)(4)(A) of this section applies, 90 days before the date of the filing of the petition; or

(ii) with respect to a transfer to which subsection (b)(4)(B) of this section applies, one year before the date of the filing of the petition; or

(B) the date on which new value was first given under the security agreement creating such security interest;

(6) that is the fixing of a statutory lien that is not avoidable under section 545 of this title;

(7) to the extent such transfer was a bona fide payment of a debt for a domestic support obligation;

(8) if, in a case filed by an individual debtor whose debts are primarily consumer debts, the aggregate value of all property that constitutes or is affected by such transfer is less than $600; or

(9) if, in a case filed by a debtor whose debts are not primarily consumer debts, the aggregate value of all property that constitutes or is affected by such transfer is less than $5,000.

(d) The trustee may avoid a transfer of an interest in property of the debtor transferred to or for the benefit of a surety to secure reimbursement of such a surety that furnished a bond or other obligation to dissolve a judicial lien that would have been avoidable by the trustee under subsection (b) of this section. The liability of such surety under such bond or obligation shall be discharged to the extent of the value of such property recovered by the trustee or the amount paid to the trustee.

(e)(1) For the purposes of this section—

(A) a transfer of real property other than fixtures, but including the interest of a seller or purchaser under a contract for the sale of real property, is perfected when a bona fide purchaser of such property from the debtor against whom applicable law permits such transfer to be perfected cannot acquire an interest that is superior to the interest of the transferee; and

(B) a transfer of a fixture or property other than real property is perfected when a creditor on a simple contract cannot acquire a judicial lien that is superior to the interest of the transferee.

(2) For the purposes of this section, except as provided in paragraph (3) of this subsection, a transfer is made—

(A) at the time such transfer takes effect between the transferor and the transferee, if such transfer is perfected at, or within 30 days after, such time, except as provided in subsection (c)(3)(B);

(B) at the time such transfer is perfected, if such transfer is perfected after such 30 days; or

(C) immediately before the date of the filing of the petition, if such transfer is not perfected at the later of—

(i) the commencement of the case; or

(ii) 30 days after such transfer takes effect between the transferor and the transferee.

(3) For the purposes of this section, a transfer is not made until the debtor has acquired rights in the property transferred.

(f) For the purposes of this section, the debtor is presumed to have been insolvent on and during the 90 days immediately preceding the date of the filing of the petition.

(g) For the purposes of this section, the trustee has the burden of proving the avoidability of a transfer under subsection (b) of this section, and the creditor or party in interest against whom recovery or avoidance is sought has the burden of proving the nonavoidability of a transfer under subsection (c) of this section.

(h) The trustee may not avoid a transfer if such transfer was made as a part of an alternative repayment schedule between the debtor and any creditor of the debtor created by an approved nonprofit budget and credit counseling agency.

(i) If the trustee avoids under subsection (b) a transfer made between 90 days and 1 year before the date of the filing of the petition, by the debtor to an entity that is not an insider for the benefit of a creditor that is an insider, such transfer shall be considered to be avoided under this section only with respect to the creditor that is an insider.

(Pub. L. 95–598, Nov. 6, 1978, 92 Stat. 2597; Pub. L. 98–353, title III, §§310, 462, July 10, 1984, 98 Stat. 355, 377; Pub. L. 99–554, title II, §283(m), Oct. 27, 1986, 100 Stat. 3117; Pub. L. 103–394, title II, §203, title III, §304(f), Oct. 22, 1994, 108 Stat. 4121, 4133; Pub. L. 109–8, title II, §§201(b), 217, title IV, §§403, 409, title XII, §§1213(a), 1222, Apr. 20, 2005, 119 Stat. 42, 55, 104, 106, 194, 196.)

HISTORICAL AND REVISION NOTES

LEGISLATIVE STATEMENTS

No limitation is provided for payments to commodity brokers as in section 766 of the Senate amendment other than the amendment to section 548 of title 11. Section 547(c)(2) protects most payments.

Section 547(b)(2) of the House amendment adopts a provision contained in the House bill and rejects an alternative contained in the Senate amendment relating to the avoidance of a preferential transfer that is payment of a tax claim owing to a governmental unit. As provided, section 106(c) of the House amendment overrules contrary language in the House report with the result that the Government is subject to avoidance of preferential transfers.

Contrary to language contained in the House report, payment of a debt by means of a check is equivalent to a cash payment, unless the check is dishonored. Payment is considered to be made when the check is delivered for purposes of sections 547(c)(1) and (2).

Section 547(c)(6) of the House bill is deleted and is treated in a different fashion in section 553 of the House amendment.

Section 547(c)(6) represents a modification of a similar provision contained in the House bill and Senate amendment. The exception relating to satisfaction of a statutory lien is deleted. The exception for a lien created under title 11 is deleted since such a lien is a statutory lien that will not be avoidable in a subsequent bankruptcy.

Section 547(e)(1)(B) is adopted from the House bill and Senate amendment without change. It is intended that the simple contract test used in this section will be applied as under section 544(a)(1) not to require a creditor to perfect against a creditor on a simple contract in the event applicable law makes such perfection impossible. For example, a purchaser from a debtor at an improperly noticed bulk sale may take subject to the rights of a creditor on a simple contract of the debtor for 1 year after the bulk sale. Since the purchaser cannot perfect against such a creditor on a simple contract, he should not be held responsible for failing to do the impossible. In the event the debtor goes into bankruptcy within a short time after the bulk sale, the trustee should not be able to use the avoiding powers under section 544(a)(1) or 547 merely because State law has made some transfers of personal property subject to the rights of a creditor on a simple contract to acquire a judicial lien with no opportunity to perfect against such a creditor.

Preferences: The House amendment deletes from the category of transfers on account of antecedent debts which may be avoided under the preference rules, section 547(b)(2), the exception in the Senate amendment for taxes owed to governmental authorities. However, for purposes of the "ordinary course" exception to the preference rules contained in section 547(c)(2), the House amendment specifies that the 45-day period referred to in section 547(c)(2)(B) is to begin running, in the case of taxes from the last due date, including extensions, of the return with respect to which the tax payment was made.

SENATE REPORT NO. 95–989

This section is a substantial modification of present law. It modernizes the preference provisions and brings them more into conformity with commercial practice and the Uniform Commercial Code.

Subsection (a) contains three definitions. Inventory, new value, and receivable are defined in their ordinary senses, but are defined to avoid any confusion or uncertainty surrounding the terms.

Subsection (b) is the operative provision of the section. It authorizes the trustee to avoid a transfer if five conditions are met. These are the five elements of a preference action. First, the transfer must be to or for the benefit of a creditor. Second, the transfer must be for or on account of an antecedent debt owed by the debtor before the transfer was made. Third, the transfer must have been made when the debtor was insolvent. Fourth, the transfer must have been made during the 90 days immediately preceding the commencement of the case. If the transfer was to an insider, the trustee may avoid the transfer if it was made during the period that begins one year before the filing of the petition and ends 90 days before the filing, if the insider to whom the transfer was made had reasonable cause to believe the debtor was insolvent at the time the transfer was made.

Finally, the transfer must enable the creditor to whom or for whose benefit it was made to receive a greater percentage of his claim than he would receive under the distributive provisions of the bankruptcy code. Specifically, the creditor must receive more than he would if the case were a liquidation case, if the transfer had not been made, and if the creditor received payment of the debt to the extent provided by the provisions of the code.

The phrasing of the final element changes the application of the greater percentage test from that employed under current law. Under this language, the court must focus on the relative distribution between classes as well as the amount that will be received by the members of the class of which the creditor is a member. The language also requires the court to focus on the allowability of the claim for which the preference was made. If the claim would have been entirely disallowed, for example, then the test of paragraph (5) will be met, because the creditor would have received nothing under the distributive provisions of the bankruptcy code.

The trustee may avoid a transfer of a lien under this section even if the lien has been enforced by sale before the commencement of the case.

Subsection (b)(2) of this section in effect exempts from the preference rules payments by the debtor of tax liabilities, regardless of their priority status.

Subsection (c) contains exceptions to the trustee's avoiding power. If a creditor can qualify under any one of the exceptions, then he is protected to that extent. If he can qualify under several, he is protected by each to the extent that he can qualify under each.

The first exception is for a transfer that was intended by all parties to be a contemporaneous exchange for new value, and was in fact substantially contemporaneous. Normally, a check is a credit transaction. However, for the purposes of this paragraph, a transfer involving a check is considered to be "intended to be contemporaneous", and if the check is presented for payment in the normal course of affairs, which the Uniform Commercial Code specifies as 30 days, U.C.C. §3-503(2)(a), that will amount to a transfer that is "in fact substantially contemporaneous."

The second exception protects transfers in the ordinary course of business (or of financial affairs, where a business is not involved) transfers. For the case of a consumer, the paragraph uses the phrase "financial affairs" to include such nonbusiness activities as payment of monthly utility bills. If the debt on account of which the transfer was made was incurred in the ordinary course of both the debtor and the transferee, if the transfer was made not later than 45 days after the debt was incurred, if the transfer itself was made in the ordinary course of both the debtor and the transferee, and if the transfer was made according to ordinary business terms, then the transfer is protected. The purpose of this exception is to leave undisturbed normal financial relations, because it does not detract from the general policy of the preference section to discourage unusual action by either the debtor or his creditors during the debtor's slide into bankruptcy.

The third exception is for enabling loans in connection with which the debtor acquires the property that the loan enabled him to purchase after the loan is actually made.

The fourth exception codifies the net result rule in section 60c of current law [section 96(c) of former title 11]. If the creditor and the debtor have more than one exchange during the 90-day period, the exchanges are netted out according to the formula in paragraph (4). Any new value that the creditor advances must be unsecured in order for it to qualify under this exception.

Paragraph (5) codifies the improvement in position test, and thereby overrules such cases as *DuBay v. Williams*, 417 F.2d 1277 (C.A.9, 1966), and *Grain Merchants of Indiana, Inc. v. Union Bank and Savings Co.*, 408 F.2d 209 (C.A.7, 1969). A creditor with a security interest in a floating mass, such as inventory or accounts receivable, is subject to preference attack to the extent he improves his position during the 90-day period before bankruptcy. The test is a two-point test, and requires determination of the secured creditor's position 90 days before the petition and on the date of the petition. If new value was first given after 90 days before the case, the date on which it was first given substitutes for the 90-day point.

Paragraph (6) excepts statutory liens validated under section 545 from preference attack. It also protects transfers in satisfaction of such liens, and the fixing of a lien under section 365(j), which protects a vendee whose contract to purchase real property from the debtor is rejected.

Subsection (d), derived from section 67a of the Bankruptcy Act [section 107(a) of former title 11], permits the trustee to avoid a transfer to reimburse a surety that posts a bond to dissolve a judicial lien that would have been avoidable under this section. The second sentence protects the surety from double liability.

Subsection (e) determines when a transfer is made for the purposes of the preference section. Paragraph (1) defines when a transfer is perfected. For real property, a transfer is perfected when it is valid against a bona fide purchaser. For personal property and fixtures, a transfer is perfected when it is valid against a creditor on a simple contract that obtains a judicial lien after the transfer is perfected. "Simple contract" as used here is derived from Bankruptcy Act §60a(4) [section 96(a)(4) of former title 11]. Paragraph (2) specifies that a transfer is made when it takes effect between the transferor and the transferee if it is perfected at or within 10 days after that time. Otherwise, it is made when the transfer is perfected. If it is not perfected before the commencement of the case, it is made immediately before the commencement of the case. Paragraph (3) specifies that a transfer is not made until the debtor has acquired rights in the property transferred. This provision, more than any other in the section, overrules *DuBay* and *Grain Merchants*, and in combination with subsection (b)(2), overrules *In re King-Porter Co.*, 446 F.2d 722 (5th Cir. 1971).

Subsection (e) is designed to reach the different results under the 1962 version of Article 9 of the U.C.C. and under the 1972 version because different actions are required under each version in order to make a security agreement effective between the parties.

Subsection (f) creates a presumption of insolvency for the 90 days preceding the bankruptcy case. The presumption is as defined in Rule 301 of the Federal Rules of Evidence, made applicable in bankruptcy cases by sections 224 and 225 of the bill. The presumption requires the party against whom the presumption exists to come forward with some evidence to rebut the presumption, but the burden of proof remains on the party in whose favor the presumption exists.

AMENDMENTS

2005—Subsec. (b). Pub. L. 109-8, §1213(a)(1), substituted "subsections (c) and (i)" for "subsection (c)" in introductory provisions.

Subsec. (c)(2). Pub. L. 109-8, §409(1), added par. (2) and struck out former par. (2) which read as follows: "to the extent that such transfer was—

"(A) in payment of a debt incurred by the debtor in the ordinary course of business or financial affairs of the debtor and the transferee;

"(B) made in the ordinary course of business or financial affairs of the debtor and the transferee; and

"(C) made according to ordinary business terms;".

Subsec. (c)(3)(B). Pub. L. 109-8, §1222, substituted "30 days" for "20 days".

Subsec. (c)(7). Pub. L. 109-8, §217, amended par. (7) generally. Prior to amendment, par. (7) read as follows: "to the extent such transfer was a bona fide payment of a debt to a spouse, former spouse, or child of the debtor, for alimony to, maintenance for, or support of such spouse or child, in connection with a separation agreement, divorce decree or other order of a court of record, determination made in accordance with State or territorial law by a governmental unit, or property settlement agreement, but not to the extent that such debt—

"(A) is assigned to another entity, voluntarily, by operation of law, or otherwise; or

"(B) includes a liability designated as alimony, maintenance, or support, unless such liability is actually in the nature of alimony, maintenance or support; or".

Subsec. (c)(9). Pub. L. 109–8, §409(2), (3), added par. (9).

Subsec. (e)(2). Pub. L. 109–8, §403, substituted "30" for "10" wherever appearing.

Subsec. (h). Pub. L. 109–8, §201(b), added subsec. (h).

Subsec. (i). Pub. L. 109–8, §1213(a)(2), added subsec. (i).

1994—Subsec. (c)(3)(B). Pub. L. 103–394, §203(1), substituted "20" for "10".

Subsec. (c)(7), (8). Pub. L. 103–394, §304(f), added par. (7) and redesignated former par. (7) as (8).

Subsec. (e)(2)(A). Pub. L. 103–394, §203(2), inserted before semicolon at end ", except as provided in subsection (c)(3)(B)".

1986—Subsec. (b)(4)(B). Pub. L. 99–554 inserted "and" after the semicolon.

1984—Subsec. (a)(2). Pub. L. 98–353, §462(a)(1), inserted "including proceeds of such property," after "law,".

Subsec. (a)(4). Pub. L. 98–353, §462(a)(2), struck out ", without penalty" after "any extension", and inserted "without penalty" after "payable".

Subsec. (b). Pub. L. 98–353, §462(b)(1), substituted "of an interest of the debtor in property" for "of property of the debtor" in provisions preceding par. (1).

Subsec. (b)(4)(B). Pub. L. 98–353, §462(b)(2), amended subpar. (B) generally. Prior to amendment, subpar. (B) read as follows: "between 90 days and one year before the date of the filing of the petition, if such creditor, at the time of such transfer—

"(i) was an insider; and

"(ii) had reasonable cause to believe the debtor was insolvent at the time of such transfer; and".

Subsec. (c)(2)(A). Pub. L. 98–353, §462(d)(1), inserted "by the debtor" after "incurred".

Subsec. (c)(2)(B) to (D). Pub. L. 98–353, §462(c), struck out subpar. (B) which read as follows: "made not later than 45 days after such debt was incurred;" and redesignated subpars. (C) and (D) as (B) and (C), respectively.

Subsec. (c)(3). Pub. L. 98–353, §462(d)(2), substituted "that creates" for "of".

Subsec. (c)(3)(B). Pub. L. 98–353, §462(d)(3), inserted "on or" after "perfected", and substituted "the debtor receives possession of such property" for "such security interest attaches".

Subsec. (c)(5). Pub. L. 98–353, §462(d)(4), substituted "that creates" for "of", and "all security interests" for "all security interest".

Subsec. (c)(5)(A)(ii). Pub. L. 98–353, §462(d)(5), substituted "or" for "and".

Subsec. (c)(7). Pub. L. 98–353, §310(3), added par. (7).

Subsec. (d). Pub. L. 98–353, §462(e), substituted "The" for "A" before "trustee may avoid", inserted "an interest in" after "transfer of", inserted "to or for the benefit of a surety" after "transferred", and inserted "such" after "reimbursement of".

Subsec. (e)(2)(C)(i). Pub. L. 98–353, §462(f), substituted "or" for "and".

Subsec. (g). Pub. L. 98–353, §462(g), added subsec. (g).

EFFECTIVE DATE OF 2005 AMENDMENT

Pub. L. 109–8, title XII, §1213(b), Apr. 20, 2005, 119 Stat. 195, provided that: "The amendments made by this section [amending this section] shall apply to any case that is pending or commenced on or after the date of enactment of this Act [Apr. 20, 2005]."

Amendment by Pub. L. 109–8 effective 180 days after Apr. 20, 2005, and not applicable with respect to cases commenced under this title before such effective date, except as otherwise provided, see section 1501 of Pub. L. 109–8, set out as a note under section 101 of this title.

EFFECTIVE DATE OF 1994 AMENDMENT

Amendment by Pub. L. 103–394 effective Oct. 22, 1994, and not applicable with respect to cases commenced under this title before Oct. 22, 1994, see section 702 of Pub. L. 103–394, set out as a note under section 101 of this title.

EFFECTIVE DATE OF 1986 AMENDMENT

Amendment by Pub. L. 99–554 effective 30 days after Oct. 27, 1986, see section 302(a) of Pub. L. 99–554, set out as a note under section 581 of Title 28, Judiciary and Judicial Procedure.

EFFECTIVE DATE OF 1984 AMENDMENT

Amendment by Pub. L. 98–353 effective with respect to cases filed 90 days after July 10, 1984, see section 552(a) of Pub. L. 98–353, set out as a note under section 101 of this title.

ADJUSTMENT OF DOLLAR AMOUNTS

For adjustment of dollar amounts specified in subsec. (c)(9) of this section by the Judicial Conference of the United States, see note set out under section 104 of this title.

§548. Fraudulent transfers and obligations

(a)(1) The trustee may avoid any transfer (including any transfer to or for the benefit of an insider under an employment contract) of an interest of the debtor in property, or any obligation (including any obligation to or for the benefit of an insider under an employment contract) incurred by the debtor, that was made or incurred on or within 2 years before the date of the filing of the petition, if the debtor voluntarily or involuntarily—

(A) made such transfer or incurred such obligation with actual intent to hinder, delay, or defraud any entity to which the debtor was or became, on or after the date that such transfer was made or such obligation was incurred, indebted; or

(B)(i) received less than a reasonably equivalent value in exchange for such transfer or obligation; and

(ii)(I) was insolvent on the date that such transfer was made or such obligation was incurred, or became insolvent as a result of such transfer or obligation;

(II) was engaged in business or a transaction, or was about to engage in business or a transaction, for which any property remaining with the debtor was an unreasonably small capital;

(III) intended to incur, or believed that the debtor would incur, debts that would be beyond the debtor's ability to pay as such debts matured; or

(IV) made such transfer to or for the benefit of an insider, or incurred such obligation to or for the benefit of an insider, under an employment contract and not in the ordinary course of business.

(2) A transfer of a charitable contribution to a qualified religious or charitable entity or organization shall not be considered to be a transfer covered under paragraph (1)(B) in any case in which—

(A) the amount of that contribution does not exceed 15 percent of the gross annual income of the debtor for the year in which the transfer of the contribution is made; or

(B) the contribution made by a debtor exceeded the percentage amount of gross annual income specified in subparagraph (A), if the transfer was consistent with the practices of the debtor in making charitable contributions.

(b) The trustee of a partnership debtor may avoid any transfer of an interest of the debtor in property, or any obligation incurred by the debtor, that was made or incurred on or within 2 years before the date of the filing of the petition, to a general partner in the debtor, if the debtor was insolvent on the date such transfer was made or such obligation was incurred, or became insolvent as a result of such transfer or obligation.

(c) Except to the extent that a transfer or obligation voidable under this section is voidable under section 544, 545, or 547 of this title, a transferee or obligee of such a transfer or obligation that takes for value and in good faith has a lien on or may retain any interest transferred or may enforce any obligation incurred, as the case may be, to the extent that such transferee or obligee gave value to the debtor in exchange for such transfer or obligation.

(d)(1) For the purposes of this section, a transfer is made when such transfer is so perfected that a bona fide purchaser from the debtor against whom applicable law permits such transfer to be perfected cannot acquire an interest in the property transferred that is superior to the interest in such property of the transferee, but if such transfer is not so perfected before the commencement of the case, such transfer is made immediately before the date of the filing of the petition.

(2) In this section—

(A) "value" means property, or satisfaction or securing of a present or antecedent debt of the debtor, but does not include an unperformed promise to furnish support to the debtor or to a relative of the debtor;

(B) a commodity broker, forward contract merchant, stockbroker, financial institution, financial participant, or securities clearing agency that receives a margin payment, as defined in section 101, 741, or 761 of this title, or settlement payment, as defined in section 101 or 741 of this title, takes for value to the extent of such payment;

(C) a repo participant or financial participant that receives a margin payment, as defined in section 741 or 761 of this title, or settlement payment, as defined in section 741 of this title, in connection with a repurchase agreement, takes for value to the extent of such payment;

(D) a swap participant or financial participant that receives a transfer in connection with a swap agreement takes for value to the extent of such transfer; and

(E) a master netting agreement participant that receives a transfer in connection with a master netting agreement or any individual contract covered thereby takes for value to the extent of such transfer, except that, with respect to a transfer under any individual contract covered thereby, to the extent that such master netting agreement participant otherwise did not take (or is otherwise not deemed to have taken) such transfer for value.

(3) In this section, the term "charitable contribution" means a charitable contribution, as that term is defined in section 170(c) of the Internal Revenue Code of 1986, if that contribution—

(A) is made by a natural person; and

(B) consists of—

(i) a financial instrument (as that term is defined in section 731(c)(2)(C) of the Internal Revenue Code of 1986); or

(ii) cash.

(4) In this section, the term "qualified religious or charitable entity or organization" means—

(A) an entity described in section 170(c)(1) of the Internal Revenue Code of 1986; or

(B) an entity or organization described in section 170(c)(2) of the Internal Revenue Code of 1986.

(e)(1) In addition to any transfer that the trustee may otherwise avoid, the trustee may avoid any transfer of an interest of the debtor in property that was made on or within 10 years before the date of the filing of the petition, if—

(A) such transfer was made to a self-settled trust or similar device;

(B) such transfer was by the debtor;

(C) the debtor is a beneficiary of such trust or similar device; and

(D) the debtor made such transfer with actual intent to hinder, delay, or defraud any entity to which the debtor was or became, on or after the date that such transfer was made, indebted.

(2) For the purposes of this subsection, a transfer includes a transfer made in anticipation of any money judgment, settlement, civil penalty, equitable order, or criminal fine incurred by, or which the debtor believed would be incurred by—

(A) any violation of the securities laws (as defined in section 3(a)(47) of the Securities Exchange Act of 1934 (15 U.S.C. 78c(a)(47))), any State securities laws, or any regulation or order issued under Federal securities laws or State securities laws; or

(B) fraud, deceit, or manipulation in a fiduciary capacity or in connection with the purchase or sale of any security registered under section 12 or 15(d) of the Securities Exchange Act of 1934 (15 U.S.C. 78*l* and 78*o*(d)) or under section 6 of the Securities Act of 1933 (15 U.S.C. 77f).

(Pub. L. 95–598, Nov. 6, 1978, 92 Stat. 2600; Pub. L. 97–222, §5, July 27, 1982, 96 Stat. 236; Pub. L. 98–353, title III, §§394, 463, July 10, 1984, 98 Stat. 365, 378; Pub. L. 99–554, title II, §283(n), Oct. 27, 1986, 100 Stat. 3117; Pub. L. 101–311, title I, §104, title II, §204, June 25, 1990, 104 Stat. 268, 269; Pub. L. 103–394, title V, §501(b)(5), Oct. 22, 1994, 108 Stat. 4142; Pub. L. 105–183, §§2, 3(a), June 19, 1998, 112 Stat. 517; Pub. L. 109–8, title IX, §907(f), (*o*)(4)–(6), title XIV, §1402, Apr. 20, 2005, 119 Stat. 177, 182, 214.)

HISTORICAL AND REVISION NOTES

LEGISLATIVE STATEMENTS

Section 548(d)(2) is modified to reflect general application of a provision contained in section 766 of the Senate amendment with respect to commodity brokers. In particular, section 548(d)(2)(B) of the House amendment makes clear that a commodity broker who receives a margin payment is considered to receive the margin payment in return for "value" for purposes of section 548.

SENATE REPORT NO. 95–989

This section is derived in large part from section 67d of the Bankruptcy Act [section 107(d) of former title 11]. It permits the trustee to avoid transfers by the debtor in fraud of his creditors. Its history dates from the statute of 13 Eliz. c. 5 (1570).

The trustee may avoid fraudulent transfers or obligations if made with actual intent to hinder, delay, or defraud a past or future creditor. Transfers made for less than a reasonably equivalent consideration are also vulnerable if the debtor was or thereby becomes insolvent, was engaged in business with an unreasonably small capital, or intended to incur debts that would be beyond his ability to repay.

The trustee of a partnership debtor may avoid any transfer of partnership property to a partner in the debtor if the debtor was or thereby became insolvent.

If a transferee's only liability to the trustee is under this section, and if he takes for value and in good faith, then subsection (c) grants him a lien on the property transferred, or other similar protection.

Subsection (d) specifies that for the purposes of fraudulent transfer section, a transfer is made when it is valid against a subsequent bona fide purchaser. If not made before the commencement of the case, it is considered made immediately before then. Subsection (d) also defines "value" to mean property, or the satisfaction or securing of a present or antecedent debt, but does not include an unperformed promise to furnish support to the debtor or a relative of the debtor.

REFERENCES IN TEXT

Sections 170(c) and 731(c)(2)(C) of the Internal Revenue Code of 1986, referred to in subsec. (d)(3), (4), are classified to sections 170(c) and 731(c)(2)(C), respectively, of Title 26, Internal Revenue Code.

AMENDMENTS

2005—Subsec. (a)(1). Pub. L. 109–8, §1402(2), in introductory provisions, inserted "(including any transfer to or for the benefit of an insider under an employment contract)" after "avoid any transfer" and "(including any obligation to or for the benefit of an insider under an employment contract)" after "or any obligation".

Pub. L. 109–8, §1402(1), substituted "2 years" for "one year" in introductory provisions

Subsec. (a)(1)(B)(ii)(IV). Pub. L. 109–8, §1402(3), added subcl. (IV).

Subsec. (b). Pub. L. 109–8, §1402(1), substituted "2 years" for "one year".

Subsec. (d)(2)(B). Pub. L. 109–8, §907(*o*)(4), inserted "financial participant," after "financial institution,".

Subsec. (d)(2)(C). Pub. L. 109–8, §907(*o*)(5), inserted "or financial participant" after "repo participant".

Subsec. (d)(2)(D). Pub. L. 109–8, §907(*o*)(6), inserted "or financial participant" after "swap participant".

Subsec. (d)(2)(E). Pub. L. 109–8, §907(f), added subpar. (E).

Subsec. (e). Pub. L. 109–8, §1402(4), added subsec. (e).

1998—Subsec. (a). Pub. L. 105–183, §3(a), designated existing provisions as par. (1), redesignated former pars. (1) and (2) as par. (1)(A) and (B), respectively, redesignated former par. (2)(A) and (B) as par. (1)(B)(i) and (ii), respectively, and redesignated former par. (2)(B)(i) to (iii) as par. (1)(B)(ii)(I) to (III), respectively, and added par. (2).

Subsec. (d)(3), (4). Pub. L. 105–183, §2, added pars. (3) and (4).

1994—Subsec. (d)(2)(B). Pub. L. 103–394, §501(b)(5)(A) substituted "section 101, 741, or 761" for "section 101(34), 741(5) or 761(15)" and "section 101 or 741" for "section 101(35) or 741(8)".

Subsec. (d)(2)(C). Pub. L. 103–394, §501(b)(5)(B), substituted "section 741 or 761" for "section 741(5) or 761(15)" and "section 741" for "section 741(8)".

1990—Subsec. (d)(2)(B). Pub. L. 101–311, §204, inserted reference to sections 101(34) and 101(35) of this title.

Subsec. (d)(2)(D). Pub. L. 101–311, §104, added subpar. (D).

1986—Subsec. (d)(2)(B). Pub. L. 99–554 substituted ", financial institution" for "financial institution,".

1984—Subsec. (a). Pub. L. 98–353, §463(a)(1), substituted "if the debtor voluntarily or involuntarily" for "if the debtor" in provisions preceding par. (1).

Subsec. (a)(1). Pub. L. 98–353, §463(a)(2), substituted "was made" for "occurred".

Subsec. (a)(2)(B)(ii). Pub. L. 98–353, §463(a)(3), inserted "or a transaction" after "engaged in business".

Subsec. (c). Pub. L. 98–353, §463(b), inserted "or may retain" after "lien on" and struck out ", may retain any lien transferred," before "or may enforce any obligation incurred".

Subsec. (d)(1). Pub. L. 98–353, §463(c)(1), substituted "is so" for "becomes so far", "applicable law permits such transfer to be" for "such transfer could have been", and "is made" for "occurs".

Subsec. (d)(2)(B). Pub. L. 98–353, §463(c)(2), inserted "financial institution," after "stockbroker".

Subsec. (d)(2)(C). Pub. L. 98–353, §394(2), added subpar. (C).

1982—Subsec. (d)(2)(B). Pub. L. 97–222 substituted "a commodity broker, forward contract merchant, stockbroker, or securities clearing agency that receives a margin payment, as defined in section 741(5) or 761(15) of this title, or settlement payment, as defined in section 741(8) of this title, takes for value to extent of such payment" for "a commodity broker or forward contract merchant that receives a margin payment, as defined in section 761(15) of this title, takes for value".

EFFECTIVE DATE OF 2005 AMENDMENT

Amendment by section 1402 of Pub. L. 109–8 effective Apr. 20, 2005, and applicable only with respect to cases commenced under this title on or after such date, with amendment by par. (1) of such section applicable only with respect to cases commenced under this title more than 1 year after Apr. 20, 2005, see section 1406 of Pub. L. 109–8, set out as a note under section 507 of this title.

Amendment by section 907 of Pub. L. 109–8 effective 180 days after Apr. 20, 2005, and not applicable with respect to cases commenced under this title before such effective date, except as otherwise provided, see section 1501 of Pub. L. 109–8, set out as a note under section 101 of this title.

EFFECTIVE DATE OF 1998 AMENDMENT

Amendment by Pub. L. 105–183 applicable to any case brought under an applicable provision of this title that is pending or commenced on or after June 19, 1998, see section 5 of Pub. L. 105–183, set out as a note under section 544 of this title.

EFFECTIVE DATE OF 1994 AMENDMENT

Amendment by Pub. L. 103–394 effective Oct. 22, 1994, and not applicable with respect to cases commenced under this title before Oct. 22, 1994, see section 702 of Pub. L. 103–394, set out as a note under section 101 of this title.

EFFECTIVE DATE OF 1986 AMENDMENT

Amendment by Pub. L. 99–554 effective 30 days after Oct. 27, 1986, see section 302(a) of Pub. L. 99–554, set out as a note under section 581 of Title 28, Judiciary and Judicial Procedure.

EFFECTIVE DATE OF 1984 AMENDMENT

Amendment by Pub. L. 98–353 effective with respect to cases filed 90 days after July 10, 1984, see section 552(a) of Pub. L. 98–353, set out as a note under section 101 of this title.

§549. Postpetition transactions

(a) Except as provided in subsection (b) or (c) of this section, the trustee may avoid a transfer of property of the estate—

(1) that occurs after the commencement of the case; and

(2)(A) that is authorized only under section 303(f) or 542(c) of this title; or

(B) that is not authorized under this title or by the court.

(b) In an involuntary case, the trustee may not avoid under subsection (a) of this section a transfer made after the commencement of such case but before the order for relief to the extent any value, including services, but not including satisfaction or securing of a debt that arose before the commencement of the case, is given after the commencement of the case in exchange for such transfer, notwithstanding any notice or knowledge of the case that the transferee has.

(c) The trustee may not avoid under subsection (a) of this section a transfer of an interest in real property to a good faith purchaser without knowledge of the commencement of the case and for present fair equivalent value unless a copy or notice of the petition was filed, where a transfer of an interest in such real property may be recorded to perfect such transfer, before such transfer is so perfected that a bona fide purchaser of such real property, against whom applicable law permits such transfer to be perfected, could not acquire an interest that is superior to such interest of such good faith purchaser. A good faith purchaser without knowledge of the commencement of the case and for less than present fair equivalent value has a lien on the property transferred to the extent of any present value given, unless a copy or notice of the petition was so filed before such transfer was so perfected.

(d) An action or proceeding under this section may not be commenced after the earlier of—

(1) two years after the date of the transfer sought to be avoided; or

(2) the time the case is closed or dismissed.

(Pub. L. 95–598, Nov. 6, 1978, 92 Stat. 2601; Pub. L. 98–353, title III, §464, July 10, 1984, 98 Stat. 379; Pub. L. 99–554, title II, §283(*o*), Oct. 27, 1986, 100 Stat. 3117; Pub. L. 103–394, title V, §501(d)(18), Oct. 22, 1994, 108 Stat. 4146; Pub. L. 109–8, title XII, §1214, Apr. 20, 2005, 119 Stat. 195.)

HISTORICAL AND REVISION NOTES

LEGISLATIVE STATEMENTS

Section 549 of the House amendment has been redrafted in order to incorporate sections 342(b) and (c) of the Senate amendment. Those sections have been consolidated and redrafted in section 549(c) of the House amendment. Section 549(d) of the House amendment adopts a provision contained in section 549(c) of the Senate amendment.

SENATE REPORT NO. 95–989

This section modifies section 70d of current law [section 110(d) of former title 11]. It permits the trustee to avoid transfers of property that occur after the commencement of the case. The transfer must either have been unauthorized, or authorized under a section that protects only the transferor. Subsection (b) protects "involuntary gap" transferees to the extent of any value (including services, but not including satisfaction of a debt that arose before the commencement of the case), given after commencement in exchange for the transfer. Notice or knowledge of the transferee is irrelevant in determining whether he is protected under this provision.

AMENDMENTS

2005—Subsec. (c). Pub. L. 109–8 inserted "an interest in" after "transfer of" in two places and substituted "purchaser of such real property" for "purchaser of such property" and "such interest" for "the interest".

1994—Subsec. (b). Pub. L. 103–394 inserted "the trustee may not avoid under subsection (a) of this section" after "involuntary case.".

1986—Subsec. (b). Pub. L. 99–554 substituted "made" for "that occurs", and "to the extent" for "is valid against the trustee to the extent of", and inserted "is" before "given".

1984—Subsec. (a). Pub. L. 98–353, §464(a)(1), (2), substituted "(b) or (c)" for "(b) and (c)" in provisions preceding par. (1) and inserted "only" between "authorized" and "under" in par. (2)(A). In the original of Pub. L. 98–353, subsec. (a)(2) of section 464 thereof ended with a period but was followed by pars. (3), (4), and (5). Such pars. (3), (4), and (5) purported to amend subsec. (a) of this section in ways not susceptible of execution. In a predecessor bill [S. 445], these pars. (3), (4), and (5) formed a part of a subsec. (b) of section 361 thereof which amended subsec. (b) of this section. Such subsec. (b) of section 361 of S. 445 was not carried into Pub. L. 98–353, §464.

Subsec. (c). Pub. L. 98–353, §464(c), amended subsec. (c) generally. Prior to amendment, subsec. (c) read as follows: "The trustee may not avoid under subsection (a) of this section a transfer, to a good faith purchaser without knowledge of the commencement of the case and for present fair equivalent value or to a purchaser at a judicial sale, of real property located other than in the county in which the case is commenced, unless a copy of the petition was filed in the office where conveyances of real property in such county are recorded before such transfer was so far perfected that a bona fide purchaser of such property against whom applicable law permits such transfer to be perfected cannot acquire an interest that is superior to the interest of such good faith or judicial sale purchaser. A good faith purchaser, without knowledge of the commencement of the case and for less than present fair equivalent value, of real property located other than in the county in which the case is commenced, under a transfer that the trustee may avoid under this section, has a lien on the property transferred to the extent of any present value given, unless a copy of the petition was so filed before such transfer was so perfected."

Subsec. (d)(1). Pub. L. 98–353, §464(d), substituted "or" for "and".

EFFECTIVE DATE OF 2005 AMENDMENT

Amendment by Pub. L. 109–8 effective 180 days after Apr. 20, 2005, and not applicable with respect to cases commenced under this title before such effective date, except as otherwise provided, see section 1501 of Pub. L. 109–8, set out as a note under section 101 of this title.

EFFECTIVE DATE OF 1994 AMENDMENT

Amendment by Pub. L. 103–394 effective Oct. 22, 1994, and not applicable with respect to cases commenced under this title before Oct. 22, 1994, see section 702 of Pub. L. 103–394, set out as a note under section 101 of this title.

EFFECTIVE DATE OF 1986 AMENDMENT

Amendment by Pub. L. 99–554 effective 30 days after Oct. 27, 1986, see section 302(a) of Pub. L. 99–554, set out as a note under section 581 of Title 28, Judiciary and Judicial Procedure.

EFFECTIVE DATE OF 1984 AMENDMENT

Amendment by Pub. L. 98–353 effective with respect to cases filed 90 days after July 10, 1984, see section 552(a) of Pub. L. 98–353, set out as a note under section 101 of this title.

§ 550. Liability of transferee of avoided transfer

(a) Except as otherwise provided in this section, to the extent that a transfer is avoided under section 544, 545, 547, 548, 549, 553(b), or

724(a) of this title, the trustee may recover, for the benefit of the estate, the property transferred, or, if the court so orders, the value of such property, from—

(1) the initial transferee of such transfer or the entity for whose benefit such transfer was made; or

(2) any immediate or mediate transferee of such initial transferee.

(b) The trustee may not recover under section (a)(2) of this section from—

(1) a transferee that takes for value, including satisfaction or securing of a present or antecedent debt, in good faith, and without knowledge of the voidability of the transfer avoided; or

(2) any immediate or mediate good faith transferee of such transferee.

(c) If a transfer made between 90 days and one year before the filing of the petition—

(1) is avoided under section 547(b) of this title; and

(2) was made for the benefit of a creditor that at the time of such transfer was an insider;

the trustee may not recover under subsection (a) from a transferee that is not an insider.

(d) The trustee is entitled to only a single satisfaction under subsection (a) of this section.

(e)(1) A good faith transferee from whom the trustee may recover under subsection (a) of this section has a lien on the property recovered to secure the lesser of—

(A) the cost, to such transferee, of any improvement made after the transfer, less the amount of any profit realized by or accruing to such transferee from such property; and

(B) any increase in the value of such property as a result of such improvement, of the property transferred.

(2) In this subsection, "improvement" includes—

(A) physical additions or changes to the property transferred;

(B) repairs to such property;

(C) payment of any tax on such property;

(D) payment of any debt secured by a lien on such property that is superior or equal to the rights of the trustee; and

(E) preservation of such property.

(f) An action or proceeding under this section may not be commenced after the earlier of—

(1) one year after the avoidance of the transfer on account of which recovery under this section is sought; or

(2) the time the case is closed or dismissed.

(Pub. L. 95–598, Nov. 6, 1978, 92 Stat. 2601; Pub. L. 98–353, title III, §465, July 10, 1984, 98 Stat. 379; Pub. L. 103–394, title II, §202, Oct. 22, 1994, 108 Stat. 4121.)

Historical and Revision Notes

legislative statements

Section 550(a)(1) of the House amendment has been modified in order to permit recovery from an entity for whose benefit an avoided transfer is made in addition to a recovery from the initial transferee of the transfer. Section 550(c) would still apply, and the trustee is entitled only to a single satisfaction. The liability of a transferee under section 550(a) applies only "to the extent that a transfer is avoided". This means that liability is not imposed on a transferee to the extent that a transferee is protected under a provision such as section 548(c) which grants a good faith transferee for value of a transfer that is avoided only as a fraudulent transfer, a lien on the property transferred to the extent of value given.

Section 550(b) of the House amendment is modified to indicate that value includes satisfaction or securing of a present antecedent debt. This means that the trustee may not recover under subsection (a)(2) from a subsequent transferee that takes for "value", provided the subsequent transferee also takes in good faith and without knowledge of the transfer avoided.

Section 550(e) of the House amendment is derived from section 550(e) of the Senate amendment.

senate report no. 95–989

Section 550 prescribes the liability of a transferee of an avoided transfer, and enunciates the separation between the concepts of avoiding a transfer and recovering from the transferee. Subsection (a) permits the trustee to recover from the initial transferee of an avoided transfer or from any immediate or mediate transferee of the initial transferee. The words "to the extent that" in the lead in to this subsection are designed to incorporate the protection of transferees found in proposed 11 U.S.C. 549(b) and 548(c). Subsection (b) limits the liability of an immediate or mediate transferee of the initial transferee if such secondary transferee takes for value, in good faith and without knowledge of the voidability of the transfer. An immediate or mediate good faith transferee of a protected secondary transferee is also shielded from liability. This subsection is limited to the trustee's right to recover from subsequent transferees under subsection (a)(2). It does not limit the trustee's rights against the initial transferee under subsection (a)(1). The phrase "good faith" in this paragraph is intended to prevent a transferee from whom the trustee could recover from transferring the recoverable property to an innocent transferee, and receiving a retransfer from him, that is, "washing" the transaction through an innocent third party. In order for the transferee to be excepted from liability under this paragraph, he himself must be a good faith transferee. Subsection (c) is a further limitation on recovery. It specifies that the trustee is entitled to only one satisfactory, under subsection (a), even if more than one transferee is liable.

Subsection (d) protects good faith transferees, either initial or subsequent, to the extent of the lesser of the cost of any improvement the transferee makes in the transferred property and the increase in value of the property as a result of the improvement. Paragraph (2) of the subsection defines improvement to include physical additions or changes to the property, repairs, payment of taxes on the property, payment of a debt secured by a lien on the property, discharge of a lien on the property, and preservation of the property.

Subsection (e) establishes a statute of limitations on avoidance by the Trustee. The limitation is one year after the avoidance of the transfer or the time the case is closed or dismissed, whichever is earlier.

Amendments

1994—Subsecs. (c) to (f). Pub. L. 103–394 added subsec. (c) and redesignated former subsecs. (c) to (e) as (d) to (f), respectively.

1984—Subsec. (a). Pub. L. 98–353, §465(a), substituted "549, 553(b), or 724(a) of this title" for "549, or 724(a) of this title".

Subsec. (d)(1)(A). Pub. L. 98–353, §465(b)(1), inserted "or accruing to" after "by".

Subsec. (d)(1)(B). Pub. L. 98–353, §465(b)(2), substituted "the value of such property" for "value".

Subsec. (d)(2)(D). Pub. L. 98–353, §465(b)(3), substituted "payment of any debt secured by a lien on such property that is superior or equal to the rights of the trustee; and" for "payment of any debt secured by a lien on such property."

Subsec. (d)(2)(E), (F). Pub. L. 98-353, §465(b)(3), (4), struck out subpar. (E) "discharge of any lien against such property that is superior or equal to the rights of the trustee; and" and redesignated subpar. (F) as (E).

Subsec. (e)(1). Pub. L. 98-353, §465(c), substituted "or" for "and".

EFFECTIVE DATE OF 1994 AMENDMENT

Amendment by Pub. L. 103-394 effective Oct. 22, 1994, and not applicable with respect to cases commenced under this title before Oct. 22, 1994, see section 702 of Pub. L. 103-394, set out as a note under section 101 of this title.

EFFECTIVE DATE OF 1984 AMENDMENT

Amendment by Pub. L. 98-353 effective with respect to cases filed 90 days after July 10, 1984, see section 552(a) of Pub. L. 98-353, set out as a note under section 101 of this title.

§ 551. Automatic preservation of avoided transfer

Any transfer avoided under section 522, 544, 545, 547, 548, 549, or 724(a) of this title, or any lien void under section 506(d) of this title, is preserved for the benefit of the estate but only with respect to property of the estate.

(Pub. L. 95-598, Nov. 6, 1978, 92 Stat. 2602.)

HISTORICAL AND REVISION NOTES

LEGISLATIVE STATEMENTS

Section 551 is adopted from the House bill and the alternative in the Senate amendment is rejected. The section is clarified to indicate that a transfer avoided or a lien that is void is preserved for the benefit of the estate, but only with respect to property of the estate. This prevents the trustee from asserting an avoided tax lien against after acquired property of the debtor.

SENATE REPORT NO. 95-989

This section is a change from present law. It specifies that any avoided transfer is automatically preserved for the benefit of the estate. Under current law, the court must determine whether or not the transfer should be preserved. The operation of the section is automatic, unlike current law, even though preservation may not benefit the estate in every instance. A preserved lien may be abandoned by the trustee under proposed 11 U.S.C. 554 if the preservation does not benefit the estate. The section as a whole prevents junior lienors from improving their position at the expense of the estate when a senior lien is avoided.

§ 552. Postpetition effect of security interest

(a) Except as provided in subsection (b) of this section, property acquired by the estate or by the debtor after the commencement of the case is not subject to any lien resulting from any security agreement entered into by the debtor before the commencement of the case.

(b)(1) Except as provided in sections 363, 506(c), 522, 544, 545, 547, and 548 of this title, if the debtor and an entity entered into a security agreement before the commencement of the case and if the security interest created by such security agreement extends to property of the debtor acquired before the commencement of the case and to proceeds, products, offspring, or profits of such property, then such security interest extends to such proceeds, products, offspring, or profits acquired by the estate after the commencement of the case to the extent provided by such security agreement and by applicable nonbankruptcy law, except to any extent that the court, after notice and a hearing and based on the equities of the case, orders otherwise.

(2) Except as provided in sections 363, 506(c), 522, 544, 545, 547, and 548 of this title, and notwithstanding section 546(b) of this title, if the debtor and an entity entered into a security agreement before the commencement of the case and if the security interest created by such security agreement extends to property of the debtor acquired before the commencement of the case and to amounts paid as rents of such property or the fees, charges, accounts, or other payments for the use or occupancy of rooms and other public facilities in hotels, motels, or other lodging properties, then such security interest extends to such rents and such fees, charges, accounts, or other payments acquired by the estate after the commencement of the case to the extent provided in such security agreement, except to any extent that the court, after notice and a hearing and based on the equities of the case, orders otherwise.

(Pub. L. 95-598, Nov. 6, 1978, 92 Stat. 2602; Pub. L. 98-353, title III, §466, July 10, 1984, 98 Stat. 380; Pub. L. 103-394, title II, §214(a), Oct. 22, 1994, 108 Stat. 4126; Pub. L. 109-8, title XII, §1204(2), Apr. 20, 2005, 119 Stat. 194.)

HISTORICAL AND REVISION NOTES

LEGISLATIVE STATEMENTS

Section 552(a) is derived from the House bill and the alternative provision in the Senate amendment is rejected. Section 552(b) represents a compromise between the House bill and the Senate amendment. Proceeds coverage, but not after acquired property clauses, are valid under title 11. The provision allows the court to consider the equities in each case. In the course of such consideration the court may evaluate any expenditures by the estate relating to proceeds and any related improvement in position of the secured party. Although this section grants a secured party a security interest in proceeds, product, offspring, rents, or profits, the section is explicitly subject to other sections of title 11. For example, the trustee or debtor in possession may use, sell, or lease proceeds, product, offspring, rents or profits under section 363.

SENATE REPORT NO. 95-989

Under the Uniform Commercial Code, article 9, creditors may take security interests in after-acquired property. Section 552 governs the effect of such a prepetition security interest in postpetition property. It applies to all security interests as defined in section 101(37) of the bankruptcy code, not only to U.C.C. security interests.

As a general rule, if a security agreement is entered into before the commencement of the case, then property that the estate acquires is not subject to the security interest created by a provision in the security agreement extending the security interest to after-acquired property. Subsection (b) provides an important exception consistent with the Uniform Commercial Code. If the security agreement extends to proceeds, product, offspring, rents, or profits of the property in question, then the proceeds would continue to be subject to the security interest pursuant to the terms of the security agreement and provisions of applicable law, except to the extent that where the estate acquires the proceeds at the expense of other creditors holding unsecured claims, the expenditure resulted in an improvement in the position of the secured party.

The exception covers the situation where raw materials, for example, are converted into inventory, or inventory into accounts, at some expense to the estate, thus depleting the fund available for general unsecured creditors, but is limited to the benefit inuring to the secured party thereby. Situations in which the estate incurs expense in simply protecting collateral are governed by 11 U.S.C. 506(c). In ordinary circumstances, the risk of loss in continued operations will remain with the estate.

HOUSE REPORT NO. 95–595

Under the Uniform Commercial Code, Article 9, creditors may take security interests in after-acquired property. This section governs the effect of such a prepetition security interest in postpetition property. It applies to all security interests as defined in section 101 of the bankruptcy code, not only to U.C.C. security interests.

As a general rule, if a security agreement is entered into before the case, then property that the estate acquires is not subject to the security interest created by the security agreement. Subsection (b) provides the only exception. If the security agreement extends to proceeds, product, offspring, rents, or profits of property that the debtor had before the commencement of the case, then the proceeds, etc., continue to be subject to the security interest, except to the extent that the estate acquired the proceeds to the prejudice of other creditors holding unsecured claims. "Extends to" as used here would include an automatically arising security interest in proceeds, as permitted under the 1972 version of the Uniform Commercial Code, as well as an interest in proceeds specifically designated, as required under the 1962 Code or similar statutes covering property not covered by the Code. "Prejudice" is not intended to be a broad term here, but is designed to cover the situation where the estate expends funds that result in an increase in the value of collateral. The exception is to cover the situation where raw materials, for example, are converted into inventory, or inventory into accounts, at some expense to the estate, thus depleting the fund available for general unsecured creditors. The term "proceeds" is not limited to the technical definition of that term in the U.C.C., but covers any property into which property subject to the security interest is converted.

AMENDMENTS

2005—Subsec. (b)(1). Pub. L. 109–8 substituted "products" for "product" in two places.

1994—Subsec. (b). Pub. L. 103–394 designated existing provisions as par. (1), struck out "rents," after "offspring," in two places, and added par. (2).

1984—Subsec. (b). Pub. L. 98–353 inserted "522," after "506(c),", substituted "an entity entered" for "a secured party enter", and substituted "except to any extent" for "except to the extent".

EFFECTIVE DATE OF 2005 AMENDMENT

Amendment by Pub. L. 109–8 effective 180 days after Apr. 20, 2005, and not applicable with respect to cases commenced under this title before such effective date, except as otherwise provided, see section 1501 of Pub. L. 109–8, set out as a note under section 101 of this title.

EFFECTIVE DATE OF 1994 AMENDMENT

Amendment by Pub. L. 103–394 effective Oct. 22, 1994, and not applicable with respect to cases commenced under this title before Oct. 22, 1994, see section 702 of Pub. L. 103–394, set out as a note under section 101 of this title.

EFFECTIVE DATE OF 1984 AMENDMENT

Amendment by Pub. L. 98–353 effective with respect to cases filed 90 days after July 10, 1984, see section 552(a) of Pub. L. 98–353, set out as a note under section 101 of this title.

§ 553. Setoff

(a) Except as otherwise provided in this section and in sections 362 and 363 of this title, this title does not affect any right of a creditor to offset a mutual debt owing by such creditor to the debtor that arose before the commencement of the case under this title against a claim of such creditor against the debtor that arose before the commencement of the case, except to the extent that—

(1) the claim of such creditor against the debtor is disallowed;

(2) such claim was transferred, by an entity other than the debtor, to such creditor—

(A) after the commencement of the case; or

(B)(i) after 90 days before the date of the filing of the petition; and

(ii) while the debtor was insolvent (except for a setoff of a kind described in section 362(b)(6), 362(b)(7), 362(b)(17), 362(b)(27), 555, 556, 559, 560, or 561); or

(3) the debt owed to the debtor by such creditor was incurred by such creditor—

(A) after 90 days before the date of the filing of the petition;

(B) while the debtor was insolvent; and

(C) for the purpose of obtaining a right of setoff against the debtor (except for a setoff of a kind described in section 362(b)(6), 362(b)(7), 362(b)(17), 362(b)(27), 555, 556, 559, 560, or 561).

(b)(1) Except with respect to a setoff of a kind described in section 362(b)(6), 362(b)(7), 362(b)(17), 362(b)(27), 555, 556, 559, 560, 561, 365(h), 546(h), or 365(i)(2) of this title, if a creditor offsets a mutual debt owing to the debtor against a claim against the debtor on or within 90 days before the date of the filing of the petition, then the trustee may recover from such creditor the amount so offset to the extent that any insufficiency on the date of such setoff is less than the insufficiency on the later of—

(A) 90 days before the date of the filing of the petition; and

(B) the first date during the 90 days immediately preceding the date of the filing of the petition on which there is an insufficiency.

(2) In this subsection, "insufficiency" means amount, if any, by which a claim against the debtor exceeds a mutual debt owing to the debtor by the holder of such claim.

(c) For the purposes of this section, the debtor is presumed to have been insolvent on and during the 90 days immediately preceding the date of the filing of the petition.

(Pub. L. 95–598, Nov. 6, 1978, 92 Stat. 2602; Pub. L. 98–353, title III, §§ 395, 467, July 10, 1984, 98 Stat. 365, 380; Pub. L. 101–311, title I, § 106, June 25, 1990, 104 Stat. 268; Pub. L. 103–394, title II, §§ 205(b), 222(b), title V, § 501(d)(19), Oct. 22, 1994, 108 Stat. 4123, 4129, 4146; Pub. L. 109–8, title IX, § 907(n), Apr. 20, 2005, 119 Stat. 181.)

HISTORICAL AND REVISION NOTES

LEGISLATIVE STATEMENTS

Section 553 of the House amendment is derived from a similar provision contained in the Senate amendment, but is modified to clarify application of a two-point test with respect to setoffs.

SENATE REPORT NO. 95–989

This section preserves, with some changes, the right of setoff in bankruptcy cases now found in section 68 of the Bankruptcy Act [section 108 of former title 11]. One exception to the right is the automatic stay, discussed in connection with proposed 11 U.S.C. 362. Another is the right of the trustee to use property under section 363 that is subject to a right of setoff.

The section states that the right of setoff is unaffected by the bankruptcy code except to the extent that the creditor's claim is disallowed, the creditor acquired (other than from the debtor) the claim during the 90 days preceding the case while the debtor was insolvent, the debt being offset was incurred for the purpose of obtaining a right of setoff, while the debtor was insolvent and during the 90-day prebankruptcy period, or the creditor improved his position in the 90-day period (similar to the improvement in position test found in the preference section 547(c)(5)). Only the last exception is an addition to current law.

As under section 547(f), the debtor is presumed to have been insolvent during the 90 days before the case.

AMENDMENTS

2005—Subsec. (a)(2)(B)(ii). Pub. L. 109–8, §907(n)(1), inserted "(except for a setoff of a kind described in section 362(b)(6), 362(b)(7), 362(b)(17), 362(b)(27), 555, 556, 559, 560, or 561)" before semicolon.

Subsec. (a)(3)(C). Pub. L. 109–8, §907(n)(2), inserted "(except for a setoff of a kind described in section 362(b)(6), 362(b)(7), 362(b)(17), 362(b)(27), 555, 556, 559, 560, or 561)" before period.

Subsec. (b)(1). Pub. L. 109–8, §907(n)(3), substituted "362(b)(17), 362(b)(27), 555, 556, 559, 560, 561," for "362(b)(14)," in introductory provisions.

1994—Subsec. (a)(1). Pub. L. 103–394, §501(d)(19)(A), struck out before semicolon at end "other than under section 502(b)(3) of this title".

Subsec. (b)(1). Pub. L. 103–394, §501(d)(19)(B), substituted "section 362(b)(14)," for "section 362(b)(14),,".

Pub. L. 103–394, §222(b), which directed the amendment of section 553(b)(1) by inserting "546(h)," after "365(h)," was executed by making the insertion in section 553(b)(1) of this title to reflect the probable intent of Congress.

Pub. L. 103–394, §205(b), substituted "365(h)" for "365(h)(2)".

1990—Subsec. (b)(1). Pub. L. 101–311 substituted "362(b)(7), 362(b)(14)," for "362(b)(7),".

1984—Subsec. (b)(1). Pub. L. 98–353 inserted ", 362(b)(7)," after "362(b)(6)", and substituted ", 365(h)(2), or 365(i)(2)" for "or 365(h)(1)".

EFFECTIVE DATE OF 2005 AMENDMENT

Amendment by Pub. L. 109–8 effective 180 days after Apr. 20, 2005, and not applicable with respect to cases commenced under this title before such effective date, except as otherwise provided, see section 1501 of Pub. L. 109–8, set out as a note under section 101 of this title.

EFFECTIVE DATE OF 1994 AMENDMENT

Amendment by Pub. L. 103–394 effective Oct. 22, 1994, and not applicable with respect to cases commenced under this title before Oct. 22, 1994, see section 702 of Pub. L. 103–394, set out as a note under section 101 of this title.

EFFECTIVE DATE OF 1984 AMENDMENT

Amendment by Pub. L. 98–353 effective with respect to cases filed 90 days after July 10, 1984, see section 552(a) of Pub. L. 98–353, set out as a note under section 101 of this title.

§554. Abandonment of property of the estate

(a) After notice and a hearing, the trustee may abandon any property of the estate that is burdensome to the estate or that is of inconsequential value and benefit to the estate.

(b) On request of a party in interest and after notice and a hearing, the court may order the trustee to abandon any property of the estate that is burdensome to the estate or that is of inconsequential value and benefit to the estate.

(c) Unless the court orders otherwise, any property scheduled under section 521(1) of this title not otherwise administered at the time of the closing of a case is abandoned to the debtor and administered for purposes of section 350 of this title.

(d) Unless the court orders otherwise, property of the estate that is not abandoned under this section and that is not administered in the case remains property of the estate.

(Pub. L. 95–598, Nov. 6, 1978, 92 Stat. 2603; Pub. L. 98–353, title III, §468, July 10, 1984, 98 Stat. 380; Pub. L. 99–554, title II, §283(p), Oct. 27, 1986, 100 Stat. 3118.)

HISTORICAL AND REVISION NOTES

LEGISLATIVE STATEMENTS

Section 554(b) is new and permits a party in interest to request the court to order the trustee to abandon property of the estate that is burdensome to the estate or that is of inconsequential value to the estate.

SENATE REPORT NO. 95–989

Under this section the court may authorize the trustee to abandon any property of the estate that is burdensome to the estate or that is of inconsequential value to the estate. Abandonment may be to any party with a possessory interest in the property abandoned. In order to aid administration of the case, subsection (b) deems the court to have authorized abandonment of any property that is scheduled under section 521(1) and that is not administered before the case is closed. That property is deemed abandoned to the debtor. Subsection (c) specifies that if property is neither abandoned nor administered it remains property of the estate.

AMENDMENTS

1986—Subsec. (c). Pub. L. 99–554 substituted "521(1)" for "521(a)(1)".

1984—Subsecs. (a), (b). Pub. L. 98–353, §468(a), inserted "and benefit" after "value".

Subsec. (c). Pub. L. 98–353, §468(b), amended subsec. (c) generally. Prior to amendment, subsec. (c) read as follows: "Unless the court orders otherwise, any property that is scheduled under section 521(1) of this title and that is not administered before a case is closed under section 350 of this title is deemed abandoned."

Subsec. (d). Pub. L. 98–353, §468(c), struck out "section (a) or (b) of" after "not abandoned under".

EFFECTIVE DATE OF 1986 AMENDMENT

Amendment by Pub. L. 99–554 effective 30 days after Oct. 27, 1986, see section 302(a) of Pub. L. 99–554, set out as a note under section 581 of Title 28, Judiciary and Judicial Procedure.

EFFECTIVE DATE OF 1984 AMENDMENT

Amendment by Pub. L. 98–353 effective with respect to cases filed 90 days after July 10, 1984, see section 552(a) of Pub. L. 98–353, set out as a note under section 101 of this title.

§555. Contractual right to liquidate, terminate, or accelerate a securities contract

The exercise of a contractual right of a stockbroker, financial institution, financial participant, or securities clearing agency to cause the liquidation, termination, or acceleration of a securities contract, as defined in section 741 of this title, because of a condition of the kind specified in section 365(e)(1) of this title shall not be stayed, avoided, or otherwise limited by operation of any provision of this title or by order of a court or administrative agency in any proceeding under this title unless such order is authorized under the provisions of the Securities Investor Protection Act of 1970 or any statute administered by the Securities and Exchange Commission. As used in this section, the term "contractual right" includes a right set forth in a rule or bylaw of a derivatives clearing organization (as defined in the Commodity Exchange Act), a multilateral clearing organization (as defined in the Federal Deposit Insurance Corporation Improvement Act of 1991), a national securities exchange, a national securities association, a securities clearing agency, a contract market designated under the Commodity Exchange Act, a derivatives transaction execution facility registered under the Commodity Exchange Act, or a board of trade (as defined in the Commodity Exchange Act), or in a resolution of the governing board thereof, and a right, whether or not in writing, arising under common law, under law merchant, or by reason of normal business practice.

(Added Pub. L. 97–222, §6(a), July 27, 1982, 96 Stat. 236; amended Pub. L. 98–353, title III, §469, July 10, 1984, 98 Stat. 380; Pub. L. 103–394, title V, §501(b)(6), (d)(20), Oct. 22, 1994, 108 Stat. 4143, 4146; Pub. L. 109–8, title IX, §907(g), (*o*)(7), Apr. 20, 2005, 119 Stat. 177, 182.)

REFERENCES IN TEXT

The Securities Investor Protection Act of 1970, referred to in text, is Pub. L. 91–598, Dec. 30, 1970, 84 Stat. 1636, as amended, which is classified generally to chapter 2B–1 (§78aaa et seq.) of Title 15, Commerce and Trade. For complete classification of this Act to the Code, see section 78aaa of Title 15 and Tables.

The Commodity Exchange Act, referred to in text, is act Sept. 21, 1922, ch. 369, 42 Stat. 998, as amended, which is classified generally to chapter 1 (§1 et seq.) of Title 7, Agriculture. For complete classification of this Act to the Code, see section 1 of Title 7 and Tables.

The Federal Deposit Insurance Corporation Improvement Act of 1991, referred to in text, is Pub. L. 102–242, Dec. 19, 1991, 105 Stat. 2236, as amended. For complete classification of this Act to the Code, see Short Title of 1991 Amendment note set out under section 1811 of Title 12, Banks and Banking, and Tables.

AMENDMENTS

2005—Pub. L. 109–8, §907(g)(1), substituted "Contractual right to liquidate, terminate, or accelerate a securities contract" for "Contractual right to liquidate a securities contract" in section catchline.

Pub. L. 109–8, §907(g)(2), (*o*)(7), in first sentence, inserted "financial participant," after "financial institution," and substituted "liquidation, termination, or acceleration" for "liquidation", and substituted second sentence for former second sentence which read as follows: "As used in this section, the term 'contractual right' includes a right set forth in a rule or bylaw of a national securities exchange, a national securities association, or a securities clearing agency."

1994—Pub. L. 103–394 substituted "section 741 of this title" for "section 741(7)" and struck out "(15 U.S.C. 78aaa et seq.)" after "Act of 1970".

1984—Pub. L. 98–353 inserted ", financial institution," after "stockbroker".

EFFECTIVE DATE OF 2005 AMENDMENT

Amendment by Pub. L. 109–8 effective 180 days after Apr. 20, 2005, and not applicable with respect to cases commenced under this title before such effective date, except as otherwise provided, see section 1501 of Pub. L. 109–8, set out as a note under section 101 of this title.

EFFECTIVE DATE OF 1994 AMENDMENT

Amendment by Pub. L. 103–394 effective Oct. 22, 1994, and not applicable with respect to cases commenced under this title before Oct. 22, 1994, see section 702 of Pub. L. 103–394, set out as a note under section 101 of this title.

EFFECTIVE DATE OF 1984 AMENDMENT

Amendment by Pub. L. 98–353 effective with respect to cases filed 90 days after July 10, 1984, see section 552(a) of Pub. L. 98–353, set out as a note under section 101 of this title.

§556. Contractual right to liquidate, terminate, or accelerate a commodities contract or forward contract

The contractual right of a commodity broker, financial participant, or forward contract merchant to cause the liquidation, termination, or acceleration of a commodity contract, as defined in section 761 of this title, or forward contract because of a condition of the kind specified in section 365(e)(1) of this title, and the right to a variation or maintenance margin payment received from a trustee with respect to open commodity contracts or forward contracts, shall not be stayed, avoided, or otherwise limited by operation of any provision of this title or by the order of a court in any proceeding under this title. As used in this section, the term "contractual right" includes a right set forth in a rule or bylaw of a derivatives clearing organization (as defined in the Commodity Exchange Act), a multilateral clearing organization (as defined in the Federal Deposit Insurance Corporation Improvement Act of 1991), a national securities exchange, a national securities association, a securities clearing agency, a contract market designated under the Commodity Exchange Act, a derivatives transaction execution facility registered under the Commodity Exchange Act, or a board of trade (as defined in the Commodity Exchange Act) or in a resolution of the governing board thereof and a right, whether or not evidenced in writing, arising under common law, under law merchant or by reason of normal business practice.

(Added Pub. L. 97–222, §6(a), July 27, 1982, 96 Stat. 236; amended Pub. L. 101–311, title II, §205, June 25, 1990, 104 Stat. 270; Pub. L. 103–394, title V, §501(b)(7), Oct. 22, 1994, 108 Stat. 4143; Pub. L. 109–8, title IX, §§907(h), (*o*)(8), Apr. 20, 2005, 119 Stat. 178, 182.)

REFERENCES IN TEXT

The Commodity Exchange Act, referred to in text, is act Sept. 21, 1922, ch. 369, 42 Stat. 998, as amended, which is classified generally to chapter 1 (§1 et seq.) of Title 7, Agriculture. For complete classification of this Act to the Code, see section 1 of Title 7 and Tables.

The Federal Deposit Insurance Corporation Improvement Act of 1991, referred to in text, is Pub. L. 102–242, Dec. 19, 1991, 105 Stat. 2236, as amended. For complete classification of this Act to the Code, see Short Title of 1991 Amendment note set out under section 1811 of Title 12, Banks and Banking, and Tables.

AMENDMENTS

2005—Pub. L. 109-8, §907(o)(8), inserted ", financial participant," after "commodity broker" in first sentence.

Pub. L. 109-8, §907(h), substituted "Contractual right to liquidate, terminate, or accelerate a commodities contract or forward contract" for "Contractual right to liquidate a commodities contract or forward contract" in section catchline, "liquidation, termination, or acceleration" for "liquidation" in first sentence, and "As used in this section, the term 'contractual right' includes a right set forth in a rule or bylaw of a derivatives clearing organization (as defined in the Commodity Exchange Act), a multilateral clearing organization (as defined in the Federal Deposit Insurance Corporation Improvement Act of 1991), a national securities exchange, a national securities association, a securities clearing agency, a contract market designated under the Commodity Exchange Act, a derivatives transaction execution facility registered under the Commodity Exchange Act, or a board of trade (as defined in the Commodity Exchange Act) or in a resolution of the governing board thereof and a right," for "As used in this section, the term 'contractual right' includes a right set forth in a rule or bylaw of a clearing organization or contract market or in a resolution of the governing board thereof and a right," in second sentence.

1994—Pub. L. 103-394 substituted "section 761 of this title" for "section 761(4)".

1990—Pub. L. 101-311 inserted before period at end "and a right, whether or not evidenced in writing, arising under common law, under law merchant or by reason of normal business practice".

EFFECTIVE DATE OF 2005 AMENDMENT

Amendment by Pub. L. 109-8 effective 180 days after Apr. 20, 2005, and not applicable with respect to cases commenced under this title before such effective date, except as otherwise provided, see section 1501 of Pub. L. 109-8, set out as a note under section 101 of this title.

EFFECTIVE DATE OF 1994 AMENDMENT

Amendment by Pub. L. 103-394 effective Oct. 22, 1994, and not applicable with respect to cases commenced under this title before Oct. 22, 1994, see section 702 of Pub. L. 103-394, set out as a note under section 101 of this title.

§557. Expedited determination of interests in, and abandonment or other disposition of grain assets

(a) This section applies only in a case concerning a debtor that owns or operates a grain storage facility and only with respect to grain and the proceeds of grain. This section does not affect the application of any other section of this title to property other than grain and proceeds of grain.

(b) In this section—

(1) "grain" means wheat, corn, flaxseed, grain sorghum, barley, oats, rye, soybeans, other dry edible beans, or rice;

(2) "grain storage facility" means a site or physical structure regularly used to store grain for producers, or to store grain acquired from producers for resale; and

(3) "producer" means an entity which engages in the growing of grain.

(c)(1) Notwithstanding sections 362, 363, 365, and 554 of this title, on the court's own motion the court may, and on the request of the trustee or an entity that claims an interest in grain or the proceeds of grain the court shall, expedite the procedures for the determination of interests in and the disposition of grain and the proceeds of grain, by shortening to the greatest extent feasible such time periods as are otherwise applicable for such procedures and by establishing, by order, a timetable having a duration of not to exceed 120 days for the completion of the applicable procedure specified in subsection (d) of this section. Such time periods and such timetable may be modified by the court, for cause, in accordance with subsection (f) of this section.

(2) The court shall determine the extent to which such time periods shall be shortened, based upon—

(A) any need of an entity claiming an interest in such grain or the proceeds of grain for a prompt determination of such interest;

(B) any need of such entity for a prompt disposition of such grain;

(C) the market for such grain;

(D) the conditions under which such grain is stored;

(E) the costs of continued storage or disposition of such grain;

(F) the orderly administration of the estate;

(G) the appropriate opportunity for an entity to assert an interest in such grain; and

(H) such other considerations as are relevant to the need to expedite such procedures in the case.

(d) The procedures that may be expedited under subsection (c) of this section include—

(1) the filing of and response to—

(A) a claim of ownership;

(B) a proof of claim;

(C) a request for abandonment;

(D) a request for relief from the stay of action against property under section 362(a) of this title;

(E) a request for determination of secured status;

(F) a request for determination of whether such grain or the proceeds of grain—

(i) is property of the estate;

(ii) must be turned over to the estate; or

(iii) may be used, sold, or leased; and

(G) any other request for determination of an interest in such grain or the proceeds of grain;

(2) the disposition of such grain or the proceeds of grain, before or after determination of interests in such grain or the proceeds of grain, by way of—

(A) sale of such grain;

(B) abandonment;

(C) distribution; or

(D) such other method as is equitable in the case;

(3) subject to sections 701, 702, 703, 1104, 1202, and 1302 of this title, the appointment of a trustee or examiner and the retention and compensation of any professional person required to assist with respect to matters relevant to the determination of interests in or disposition of such grain or the proceeds of grain; and

(4) the determination of any dispute concerning a matter specified in paragraph (1), (2), or (3) of this subsection.

(e)(1) Any governmental unit that has regulatory jurisdiction over the operation or liquidation of the debtor or the debtor's business shall be given notice of any request made or order entered under subsection (c) of this section.

(2) Any such governmental unit may raise, and may appear and be heard on, any issue relating to grain or the proceeds of grain in a case in which a request is made, or an order is entered, under subsection (c) of this section.

(3) The trustee shall consult with such governmental unit before taking any action relating to the disposition of grain in the possession, custody, or control of the debtor or the estate.

(f) The court may extend the period for final disposition of grain or the proceeds of grain under this section beyond 120 days if the court finds that—

(1) the interests of justice so require in light of the complexity of the case; and

(2) the interests of those claimants entitled to distribution of grain or the proceeds of grain will not be materially injured by such additional delay.

(g) Unless an order establishing an expedited procedure under subsection (c) of this section, or determining any interest in or approving any disposition of grain or the proceeds of grain, is stayed pending appeal—

(1) the reversal or modification of such order on appeal does not affect the validity of any procedure, determination, or disposition that occurs before such reversal or modification, whether or not any entity knew of the pendency of the appeal; and

(2) neither the court nor the trustee may delay, due to the appeal of such order, any proceeding in the case in which such order is issued.

(h)(1) The trustee may recover from grain and the proceeds of grain the reasonable and necessary costs and expenses allowable under section 503(b) of this title attributable to preserving or disposing of grain or the proceeds of grain, but may not recover from such grain or the proceeds of grain any other costs or expenses.

(2) Notwithstanding section 326(a) of this title, the dollar amounts of money specified in such section include the value, as of the date of disposition, of any grain that the trustee distributes in kind.

(i) In all cases where the quantity of a specific type of grain held by a debtor operating a grain storage facility exceeds ten thousand bushels, such grain shall be sold by the trustee and the assets thereof distributed in accordance with the provisions of this section.

(Added Pub. L. 98–353, title III, §352(a), July 10, 1984, 98 Stat. 359; amended Pub. L. 99–554, title II, §257(p), Oct. 27, 1986, 100 Stat. 3115.)

AMENDMENTS

1986—Subsec. (d)(3). Pub. L. 99–554 inserted reference to section 1202 of this title.

EFFECTIVE DATE OF 1986 AMENDMENT

Amendment by Pub. L. 99–554 effective 30 days after Oct. 27, 1986, but not applicable to cases commenced under this title before that date, see section 302(a), (c)(1) of Pub. L. 99–554, set out as a note under section 581 of Title 28, Judiciary and Judicial Procedure.

EFFECTIVE DATE

Section effective with respect to cases filed 90 days after July 10, 1984, see section 552(a) of Pub. L. 98–353, set out as an Effective Date of 1984 Amendment note under section 101 of this title.

§ 558. Defenses of the estate

The estate shall have the benefit of any defense available to the debtor as against any entity other than the estate, including statutes of limitation, statutes of frauds, usury, and other personal defenses. A waiver of any such defense by the debtor after the commencement of the case does not bind the estate.

(Added Pub. L. 98–353, title III, §470(a), July 10, 1984, 98 Stat. 380.)

EFFECTIVE DATE

Section effective with respect to cases filed 90 days after July 10, 1984, see section 552(a) of Pub. L. 98–353, set out as an Effective Date of 1984 Amendment note under section 101 of this title.

§ 559. Contractual right to liquidate, terminate, or accelerate a repurchase agreement

The exercise of a contractual right of a repo participant or financial participant to cause the liquidation, termination, or acceleration of a repurchase agreement because of a condition of the kind specified in section 365(e)(1) of this title shall not be stayed, avoided, or otherwise limited by operation of any provision of this title or by order of a court or administrative agency in any proceeding under this title, unless, where the debtor is a stockbroker or securities clearing agency, such order is authorized under the provisions of the Securities Investor Protection Act of 1970 or any statute administered by the Securities and Exchange Commission. In the event that a repo participant or financial participant liquidates one or more repurchase agreements with a debtor and under the terms of one or more such agreements has agreed to deliver assets subject to repurchase agreements to the debtor, any excess of the market prices received on liquidation of such assets (or if any such assets are not disposed of on the date of liquidation of such repurchase agreements, at the prices available at the time of liquidation of such repurchase agreements from a generally recognized source or the most recent closing bid quotation from such a source) over the sum of the stated repurchase prices and all expenses in connection with the liquidation of such repurchase agreements shall be deemed property of the estate, subject to the available rights of setoff. As used in this section, the term "contractual right" includes a right set forth in a rule or bylaw of a derivatives clearing organization (as defined in the Commodity Exchange Act), a multilateral clearing organization (as defined in the Federal Deposit Insurance Corporation Improvement Act of 1991), a national securities exchange, a national securities association, a securities clearing agency, a contract market designated under the Commodity Exchange Act, a derivatives transaction execution facility registered under the Commodity Exchange Act, or a board of trade (as defined in the Commodity Exchange Act) or in a resolution of the governing board thereof and a right, whether or not evidenced in writing, arising under common law, under law merchant or by reason of normal business practice.

(Added Pub. L. 98–353, title III, §396(a), July 10, 1984, 98 Stat. 366; amended Pub. L. 103–394, title V, §501(d)(21), Oct. 22, 1994, 108 Stat. 4146; Pub. L. 109–8, title IX, §907(i), (*o*)(9), Apr. 20, 2005, 119 Stat. 178, 182.)

REFERENCES IN TEXT

The Securities Investor Protection Act of 1970, referred to in text, is Pub. L. 91–598, Dec. 30, 1970, 84 Stat. 1636, as amended, which is classified generally to chapter 2B–1 (§78aaa et seq.) of Title 15, Commerce and Trade. For complete classification of this Act to the Code, see section 78aaa of Title 15 and Tables.

The Commodity Exchange Act, referred to in text, is act Sept. 21, 1922, ch. 369, 42 Stat. 998, as amended, which is classified generally to chapter 1 (§1 et seq.) of Title 7, Agriculture. For complete classification of this Act to the Code, see section 1 of Title 7 and Tables.

The Federal Deposit Insurance Corporation Improvement Act of 1991, referred to in text, is Pub. L. 102–242, Dec. 19, 1991, 105 Stat. 2236, as amended. For complete classification of this Act to the Code, see Short Title of 1991 Amendment note set out under section 1811 of Title 12, Banks and Banking, and Tables.

AMENDMENTS

2005—Pub. L. 109–8, §907(*o*)(9), inserted "or financial participant" after "repo participant" in two places.

Pub. L. 109–8, §907(i), substituted "Contractual right to liquidate, terminate, or accelerate a repurchase agreement" for "Contractual right to liquidate a repurchase agreement" in section catchline, "liquidation, termination, or acceleration" for "liquidation" in first sentence, and "As used in this section, the term 'contractual right' includes a right set forth in a rule or bylaw of a derivatives clearing organization (as defined in the Commodity Exchange Act), a multilateral clearing organization (as defined in the Federal Deposit Insurance Corporation Improvement Act of 1991), a national securities exchange, a national securities association, a securities clearing agency, a contract market designated under the Commodity Exchange Act, a derivatives transaction execution facility registered under the Commodity Exchange Act, or a board of trade (as defined in the Commodity Exchange Act) or in a resolution of the governing board thereof and a right," for "As used in this section, the term 'contractual right' includes a right set forth in a rule or bylaw, applicable to each party to the repurchase agreement, of a national securities exchange, a national securities association, or a securities clearing agency, and a right," in third sentence.

1994—Pub. L. 103–394 struck out "(15 U.S.C. 78aaa et seq.)" after "Act of 1970".

EFFECTIVE DATE OF 2005 AMENDMENT

Amendment by Pub. L. 109–8 effective 180 days after Apr. 20, 2005, and not applicable with respect to cases commenced under this title before such effective date, except as otherwise provided, see section 1501 of Pub. L. 109–8, set out as a note under section 101 of this title.

EFFECTIVE DATE OF 1994 AMENDMENT

Amendment by Pub. L. 103–394 effective Oct. 22, 1994, and not applicable with respect to cases commenced under this title before Oct. 22, 1994, see section 702 of Pub. L. 103–394, set out as a note under section 101 of this title.

EFFECTIVE DATE

Section effective with respect to cases filed 90 days after July 10, 1984, see section 552(a) of Pub. L. 98–353, set out as an Effective Date of 1984 Amendment note under section 101 of this title.

§560. Contractual right to liquidate, terminate, or accelerate a swap agreement

The exercise of any contractual right of any swap participant or financial participant to cause the liquidation, termination, or acceleration of one or more swap agreements because of a condition of the kind specified in section 365(e)(1) of this title or to offset or net out any termination values or payment amounts arising under or in connection with the termination, liquidation, or acceleration of one or more swap agreements shall not be stayed, avoided, or otherwise limited by operation of any provision of this title or by order of a court or administrative agency in any proceeding under this title. As used in this section, the term "contractual right" includes a right set forth in a rule or bylaw of a derivatives clearing organization (as defined in the Commodity Exchange Act), a multilateral clearing organization (as defined in the Federal Deposit Insurance Corporation Improvement Act of 1991), a national securities exchange, a national securities association, a securities clearing agency, a contract market designated under the Commodity Exchange Act, a derivatives transaction execution facility registered under the Commodity Exchange Act, or a board of trade (as defined in the Commodity Exchange Act) or in a resolution of the governing board thereof and a right, whether or not evidenced in writing, arising under common law, under law merchant, or by reason of normal business practice.

(Added Pub. L. 101–311, title I, §106(a), June 25, 1990, 104 Stat. 268; amended Pub. L. 109–8, title IX, §907(j), (*o*)(10), Apr. 20, 2005, 119 Stat. 178, 182.)

REFERENCES IN TEXT

The Commodity Exchange Act, referred to in text, is act Sept. 21, 1922, ch. 369, 42 Stat. 998, as amended, which is classified generally to chapter 1 (§1 et seq.) of Title 7, Agriculture. For complete classification of this Act to the Code, see section 1 of Title 7 and Tables.

The Federal Deposit Insurance Corporation Improvement Act of 1991, referred to in text, is Pub. L. 102–242, Dec. 19, 1991, 105 Stat. 2236, as amended. For complete classification of this Act to the Code, see Short Title of 1991 Amendment note set out under section 1811 of Title 12, Banks and Banking, and Tables.

AMENDMENTS

2005—Pub. L. 109–8, §907(*o*)(10), inserted "or financial participant" after "swap participant" in first sentence.

Pub. L. 109–8, §907(j)(1), in section catchline, substituted "Contractual right to liquidate, terminate, or accelerate a swap agreement" for "Contractual right to terminate a swap agreement", in first sentence, substituted "liquidation, termination, or acceleration of one or more swap agreements" for "termination of a swap agreement" and "in connection with the termination, liquidation, or acceleration of one or more swap agreements" for "in connection with any swap agreement", and in second sentence, substituted "As used in this section, the term 'contractual right' includes a right set forth in a rule or bylaw of a derivatives clearing organization (as defined in the Commodity Exchange Act), a multilateral clearing organization (as defined in the Federal Deposit Insurance Corporation Improvement Act of 1991), a national securities exchange, a national securities association, a securities clearing agency, a contract market designated under the Commodity Exchange Act, a derivatives transaction execution facility registered under the Commodity Exchange Act, or a board of trade (as defined in the Commodity Exchange Act) or in a resolution of the governing board thereof and a right," for "As used in this section, the term 'contractual right' includes a right.".

EFFECTIVE DATE OF 2005 AMENDMENT

Amendment by Pub. L. 109–8 effective 180 days after Apr. 20, 2005, and not applicable with respect to cases commenced under this title before such effective date, except as otherwise provided, see section 1501 of Pub. L. 109–8, set out as a note under section 101 of this title.

§ 561. Contractual right to terminate, liquidate, accelerate, or offset under a master netting agreement and across contracts; proceedings under chapter 15

(a) Subject to subsection (b), the exercise of any contractual right, because of a condition of the kind specified in section 365(e)(1), to cause the termination, liquidation, or acceleration of or to offset or net termination values, payment amounts, or other transfer obligations arising under or in connection with one or more (or the termination, liquidation, or acceleration of one or more)—

(1) securities contracts, as defined in section 741(7);

(2) commodity contracts, as defined in section 761(4);

(3) forward contracts;

(4) repurchase agreements;

(5) swap agreements; or

(6) master netting agreements,

shall not be stayed, avoided, or otherwise limited by operation of any provision of this title or by any order of a court or administrative agency in any proceeding under this title.

(b)(1) A party may exercise a contractual right described in subsection (a) to terminate, liquidate, or accelerate only to the extent that such party could exercise such a right under section 555, 556, 559, or 560 for each individual contract covered by the master netting agreement in issue.

(2) If a debtor is a commodity broker subject to subchapter IV of chapter 7—

(A) a party may not net or offset an obligation to the debtor arising under, or in connection with, a commodity contract traded on or subject to the rules of a contract market designated under the Commodity Exchange Act or a derivatives transaction execution facility registered under the Commodity Exchange Act against any claim arising under, or in connection with, other instruments, contracts, or agreements listed in subsection (a) except to the extent that the party has positive net equity in the commodity accounts at the debtor, as calculated under such subchapter; and

(B) another commodity broker may not net or offset an obligation to the debtor arising under, or in connection with, a commodity contract entered into or held on behalf of a customer of the debtor and traded on or subject to the rules of a contract market designated under the Commodity Exchange Act or a derivatives transaction execution facility registered under the Commodity Exchange Act against any claim arising under, or in connection with, other instruments, contracts, or agreements listed in subsection (a).

(3) No provision of subparagraph (A) or (B) of paragraph (2) shall prohibit the offset of claims and obligations that arise under—

(A) a cross-margining agreement or similar arrangement that has been approved by the Commodity Futures Trading Commission or submitted to the Commodity Futures Trading Commission under paragraph (1) or (2) of section 5c(c) of the Commodity Exchange Act and has not been abrogated or rendered ineffective by the Commodity Futures Trading Commission; or

(B) any other netting agreement between a clearing organization (as defined in section 761) and another entity that has been approved by the Commodity Futures Trading Commission.

(c) As used in this section, the term "contractual right" includes a right set forth in a rule or bylaw of a derivatives clearing organization (as defined in the Commodity Exchange Act), a multilateral clearing organization (as defined in the Federal Deposit Insurance Corporation Improvement Act of 1991), a national securities exchange, a national securities association, a securities clearing agency, a contract market designated under the Commodity Exchange Act, a derivatives transaction execution facility registered under the Commodity Exchange Act, or a board of trade (as defined in the Commodity Exchange Act) or in a resolution of the governing board thereof, and a right, whether or not evidenced in writing, arising under common law, under law merchant, or by reason of normal business practice.

(d) Any provisions of this title relating to securities contracts, commodity contracts, forward contracts, repurchase agreements, swap agreements, or master netting agreements shall apply in a case under chapter 15, so that enforcement of contractual provisions of such contracts and agreements in accordance with their terms will not be stayed or otherwise limited by operation of any provision of this title or by order of a court in any case under this title, and to limit avoidance powers to the same extent as in a proceeding under chapter 7 or 11 of this title (such enforcement not to be limited based on the presence or absence of assets of the debtor in the United States).

(Added Pub. L. 109–8, title IX, § 907(k)(1), Apr. 20, 2005, 119 Stat. 179.)

REFERENCES IN TEXT

The Commodity Exchange Act, referred to in subsecs. (b)(2) and (c), is act Sept. 21, 1922, ch. 369, 42 Stat. 998, as amended, which is classified generally to chapter 1 (§ 1 et seq.) of Title 7, Agriculture. Section 5c(c) of the Act is classified to section 7a–2(c) of Title 7. For complete classification of this Act to the Code, see section 1 of Title 7 and Tables.

The Federal Deposit Insurance Corporation Improvement Act of 1991, referred to in subsec. (c), is Pub. L. 102–242, Dec. 19, 1991, 105 Stat. 2236, as amended. For complete classification of this Act to the Code, see Short Title of 1991 Amendment note set out under section 1811 of Title 12, Banks and Banking, and Tables.

EFFECTIVE DATE

Section effective 180 days after Apr. 20, 2005, and not applicable with respect to cases commenced under this title before such effective date, except as otherwise provided, see section 1501 of Pub. L. 109–8, set out as an Effective Date of 2005 Amendment note under section 101 of this title.

§ 562. Timing of damage measurement in connection with swap agreements, securities contracts, forward contracts, commodity contracts, repurchase agreements, and master netting agreements

(a) If the trustee rejects a swap agreement, securities contract (as defined in section 741), forward contract, commodity contract (as defined in section 761), repurchase agreement, or master netting agreement pursuant to section 365(a), or if a forward contract merchant, stockbroker, financial institution, securities clearing agency, repo participant, financial participant, master netting agreement participant, or swap participant liquidates, terminates, or accelerates such contract or agreement, damages shall be measured as of the earlier of—

(1) the date of such rejection; or

(2) the date or dates of such liquidation, termination, or acceleration.

(b) If there are not any commercially reasonable determinants of value as of any date referred to in paragraph (1) or (2) of subsection (a), damages shall be measured as of the earliest subsequent date or dates on which there are commercially reasonable determinants of value.

(c) For the purposes of subsection (b), if damages are not measured as of the date or dates of rejection, liquidation, termination, or acceleration, and the forward contract merchant, stockbroker, financial institution, securities clearing agency, repo participant, financial participant, master netting agreement participant, or swap participant or the trustee objects to the timing of the measurement of damages—

(1) the trustee, in the case of an objection by a forward contract merchant, stockbroker, financial institution, securities clearing agency, repo participant, financial participant, master netting agreement participant, or swap participant; or

(2) the forward contract merchant, stockbroker, financial institution, securities clearing agency, repo participant, financial participant, master netting agreement participant, or swap participant, in the case of an objection by the trustee,

has the burden of proving that there were no commercially reasonable determinants of value as of such date or dates.

(Added Pub. L. 109–8, title IX, § 910(a)(1), Apr. 20, 2005, 119 Stat. 184.)

EFFECTIVE DATE

Section effective 180 days after Apr. 20, 2005, and not applicable with respect to cases commenced under this title before such effective date, except as otherwise provided, see section 1501 of Pub. L. 109–8, set out as an Effective Date of 2005 Amendment note under section 101 of this title.

CHAPTER 7—LIQUIDATION

SUBCHAPTER I—OFFICERS AND ADMINISTRATION

AMENDMENTS

2005—Pub. L. 109–8, title I, § 102(k), title VII, § 719(b)(2), title IX, § 907(p)(2), Apr. 20, 2005, 119 Stat. 35, 133, 182, added items 753 and 767, substituted "Dismissal of a case or conversion to a case under chapter 11 or 13" for "Dismissal" in item 707, and struck out item 728 "Special tax provisions".

2000—Pub. L. 106–554, § 1(a)(5) [title I, § 112(d)], Dec. 21, 2000, 114 Stat. 2763, 2763A–396, added subchapter V heading and items 781 to 784.

1984—Pub. L. 98–353, title III, § 471, July 10, 1984, 98 Stat. 380, substituted "Successor" for "Succesor" in item 703.

SUBCHAPTER I—OFFICERS AND ADMINISTRATION

§ 701. Interim trustee

(a)(1) Promptly after the order for relief under this chapter, the United States trustee shall appoint one disinterested person that is a member of the panel of private trustees established under section 586(a)(1) of title 28 or that is serving as trustee in the case immediately before the order for relief under this chapter to serve as interim trustee in the case.

(2) If none of the members of such panel is willing to serve as interim trustee in the case, then the United States trustee may serve as interim trustee in the case.

(b) The service of an interim trustee under this section terminates when a trustee elected or designated under section 702 of this title to serve as trustee in the case qualifies under section 322 of this title.

(c) An interim trustee serving under this section is a trustee in a case under this title.

(Pub. L. 95-598, Nov. 6, 1978, 92 Stat. 2604; Pub. L. 99-554, title II, §215, Oct. 27, 1986, 100 Stat. 3100.)

HISTORICAL AND REVISION NOTES

LEGISLATIVE STATEMENTS

The House amendment deletes section 701(d) of the Senate amendment. It is anticipated that the Rules of Bankruptcy Procedure will require the appointment of an interim trustee at the earliest practical moment in commodity broker bankruptcies, but no later than noon of the day after the date of the filing of the petition, due to the volatility of such cases.

SENATE REPORT NO. 95-989

This section requires the court to appoint an interim trustee. The appointment must be made from the panel of private trustees established and maintained by the Director of the Administrative Office under proposed 28 U.S.C. 604(e).

Subsection (a) requires the appointment of an interim trustee to be made promptly after the order for relief, unless a trustee is already serving in the case, such as before a conversion from a reorganization to a liquidation case.

Subsection (b) specifies that the appointment of an interim trustee expires when the permanent trustee is elected or designated under section 702.

Subsection (c) makes clear that an interim trustee is a trustee in a case under the bankruptcy code.

Subsection (d) provides that in a commodity broker case where speed is essential the interim trustee must be appointed by noon of the business day immediately following the order for relief.

AMENDMENTS

1986—Subsec. (a). Pub. L. 99-554 designated existing provisions as par. (1), substituted "the United States trustee shall appoint" for "the court shall appoint", "586(a)(1)" for "604(f)", "that is serving" for "that was serving", and added par. (2).

EFFECTIVE DATE OF 1986 AMENDMENT

Effective date and applicability of amendment by Pub. L. 99-554 dependent upon the judicial district involved, see section 302(d), (e) of Pub. L. 99-554, set out as a note under section 581 of Title 28, Judiciary and Judicial Procedure.

§ 702. Election of trustee

(a) A creditor may vote for a candidate for trustee only if such creditor—

(1) holds an allowable, undisputed, fixed, liquidated, unsecured claim of a kind entitled to distribution under section 726(a)(2), 726(a)(3), 726(a)(4), 752(a), 766(h), or 766(i) of this title;

(2) does not have an interest materially adverse, other than an equity interest that is not substantial in relation to such creditor's interest as a creditor, to the interest of creditors entitled to such distribution; and

(3) is not an insider.

(b) At the meeting of creditors held under section 341 of this title, creditors may elect one person to serve as trustee in the case if election of a trustee is requested by creditors that may vote under subsection (a) of this section, and that hold at least 20 percent in amount of the claims specified in subsection (a)(1) of this section that are held by creditors that may vote under subsection (a) of this section.

(c) A candidate for trustee is elected trustee if—

(1) creditors holding at least 20 percent in amount of the claims of a kind specified in subsection (a)(1) of this section that are held by creditors that may vote under subsection (a) of this section vote; and

(2) such candidate receives the votes of creditors holding a majority in amount of claims specified in subsection (a)(1) of this section that are held by creditors that vote for a trustee.

(d) If a trustee is not elected under this section, then the interim trustee shall serve as trustee in the case.

(Pub. L. 95-598, Nov. 6, 1978, 92 Stat. 2604; Pub. L. 97-222, §7, July 27, 1982, 96 Stat. 237; Pub. L. 98-353, title III, §472, July 10, 1984, 98 Stat. 380.)

HISTORICAL AND REVISION NOTES

LEGISLATIVE STATEMENTS

The House amendment adopts section 702(a)(2) of the Senate amendment. An insubstantial equity interest does not disqualify a creditor from voting for a candidate for trustee.

SENATE REPORT NO. 95-989

Subsection (a) of this section specifies which creditors may vote for a trustee. Only a creditor that holds an allowable, undisputed, fixed, liquidated, unsecured claim that is not entitled to priority, that does not have an interest materially adverse to the interest of general unsecured creditors, and that is not an insider may vote for a trustee. The phrase "materially adverse" is currently used in the Rules of Bankruptcy Procedure, rule 207(d). The application of the standard requires a balancing of various factors, such as the nature of the adversity. A creditor with a very small equity position would not be excluded from voting solely because he holds a small equity in the debtor. The Rules of Bankruptcy Procedure also currently provide for temporary allowance of claims, and will continue to do so for the purposes of determining who is eligible to vote under this provision.

Subsection (b) permits creditors at the meeting of creditors to elect one person to serve as trustee in the case. Creditors holding at least 20 percent in amount of the claims specified in the preceding paragraph must request election before creditors may elect a trustee. Subsection (c) specifies that a candidate for trustee is elected trustee if creditors holding at least 20 percent in amount of those claims actually vote, and if the candidate receives a majority in amount of votes actually cast.

Subsection (d) specifies that if a trustee is not elected, then the interim trustee becomes the permanent trustee and serves in the case permanently.

AMENDMENTS

1984—Subsec. (b). Pub. L. 98-353, §472(a), inserted "held" after "meeting of creditors".

Subsec. (c)(1). Pub. L. 98–353, §472(b)(1), inserted "of a kind" after "claims".

Subsec. (c)(2). Pub. L. 98–353, §472(b)(2), substituted "for a trustee" for "for trustee".

Subsec. (d). Pub. L. 98–353, §472(c), substituted "this section" for "subsection (c) of this section".

1982—Subsec. (a)(1). Pub. L. 97–222 substituted "726(a)(4), 752(a), 766(h), or 766(i)" for "or 726(a)(4)".

EFFECTIVE DATE OF 1984 AMENDMENT

Amendment by Pub. L. 98–353 effective with respect to cases filed 90 days after July 10, 1984, see section 552(a) of Pub. L. 98–353, set out as a note under section 101 of this title.

§ 703. Successor trustee

(a) If a trustee dies or resigns during a case, fails to qualify under section 322 of this title, or is removed under section 324 of this title, creditors may elect, in the manner specified in section 702 of this title, a person to fill the vacancy in the office of trustee.

(b) Pending election of a trustee under subsection (a) of this section, if necessary to preserve or prevent loss to the estate, the United States trustee may appoint an interim trustee in the manner specified in section 701(a).

(c) If creditors do not elect a successor trustee under subsection (a) of this section or if a trustee is needed in a case reopened under section 350 of this title, then the United States trustee—

(1) shall appoint one disinterested person that is a member of the panel of private trustees established under section 586(a)(1) of title 28 to serve as trustee in the case; or

(2) may, if none of the disinterested members of such panel is willing to serve as trustee, serve as trustee in the case.

(Pub. L. 95–598, Nov. 6, 1978, 92 Stat. 2605; Pub. L. 98–353, title III, §473, July 10, 1984, 98 Stat. 381; Pub. L. 99–554, title II, §216, Oct. 27, 1986, 100 Stat. 3100.)

HISTORICAL AND REVISION NOTES

SENATE REPORT NO. 95–989

If the office of trustee becomes vacant during the case, this section makes provision for the selection of a successor trustee. The office might become vacant through death, resignation, removal, failure to qualify under section 322 by posting bond, or the reopening of a case. If it does, creditors may elect a successor in the same manner as they may elect a trustee under the previous section. Pending the election of a successor, the court may appoint an interim trustee in the usual manner if necessary to preserve or prevent loss to the estate. If creditors do not elect a successor, or if a trustee is needed in a reopened case, then the court appoints a disinterested member of the panel of private trustees to serve.

AMENDMENTS

1986—Subsec. (b). Pub. L. 99–554 amended subsec. (b) generally, substituting "the United States trustee may appoint" for "the court may appoint" and "manner specified in section 701(a)" for "manner and subject to the provisions of section 701 of this title".

Subsec. (c). Pub. L. 99–554 amended subsec. (c) generally, substituting "this section or" for "this section, or", "then the United States trustee" for "then the court", designating part of existing provisions as par. (1), and, as so designated, substituting "586(a)(1)" for "604(f)", "in the case; or" for "in the case.", and adding par. (2).

1984—Subsec. (b). Pub. L. 98–353 substituted "and subject to the provisions of section 701 of this title" for "specified in section 701(a) of this title. Sections 701(b) and 701(c) of this title apply to such interim trustee".

EFFECTIVE DATE OF 1986 AMENDMENT

Effective date and applicability of amendment by Pub. L. 99–554 dependent upon the judicial district involved, see section 302(d), (e) of Pub. L. 99–554, set out as a note under section 581 of Title 28, Judiciary and Judicial Procedure.

EFFECTIVE DATE OF 1984 AMENDMENT

Amendment by Pub. L. 98–353 effective with respect to cases filed 90 days after July 10, 1984, see section 552(a) of Pub. L. 98–353, set out as a note under section 101 of this title.

§ 704. Duties of trustee

(a) The trustee shall—

(1) collect and reduce to money the property of the estate for which such trustee serves, and close such estate as expeditiously as is compatible with the best interests of parties in interest;

(2) be accountable for all property received;

(3) ensure that the debtor shall perform his intention as specified in section 521(2)(B) of this title;

(4) investigate the financial affairs of the debtor;

(5) if a purpose would be served, examine proofs of claims and object to the allowance of any claim that is improper;

(6) if advisable, oppose the discharge of the debtor;

(7) unless the court orders otherwise, furnish such information concerning the estate and the estate's administration as is requested by a party in interest;

(8) if the business of the debtor is authorized to be operated, file with the court, with the United States trustee, and with any governmental unit charged with responsibility for collection or determination of any tax arising out of such operation, periodic reports and summaries of the operation of such business, including a statement of receipts and disbursements, and such other information as the United States trustee or the court requires;

(9) make a final report and file a final account of the administration of the estate with the court and with the United States trustee;

(10) if with respect to the debtor there is a claim for a domestic support obligation, provide the applicable notice specified in subsection (c);

(11) if, at the time of the commencement of the case, the debtor (or any entity designated by the debtor) served as the administrator (as defined in section 3 of the Employee Retirement Income Security Act of 1974) of an employee benefit plan, continue to perform the obligations required of the administrator; and

(12) use all reasonable and best efforts to transfer patients from a health care business that is in the process of being closed to an appropriate health care business that—

(A) is in the vicinity of the health care business that is closing;

(B) provides the patient with services that are substantially similar to those provided by the health care business that is in the process of being closed; and

(C) maintains a reasonable quality of care.

(b)(1) With respect to a debtor who is an individual in a case under this chapter—

(A) the United States trustee (or the bankruptcy administrator, if any) shall review all materials filed by the debtor and, not later than 10 days after the date of the first meeting of creditors, file with the court a statement as to whether the debtor's case would be presumed to be an abuse under section 707(b); and

(B) not later than 7 days after receiving a statement under subparagraph (A), the court shall provide a copy of the statement to all creditors.

(2) The United States trustee (or bankruptcy administrator, if any) shall, not later than 30 days after the date of filing a statement under paragraph (1), either file a motion to dismiss or convert under section 707(b) or file a statement setting forth the reasons the United States trustee (or the bankruptcy administrator, if any) does not consider such a motion to be appropriate, if the United States trustee (or the bankruptcy administrator, if any) determines that the debtor's case should be presumed to be an abuse under section 707(b) and the product of the debtor's current monthly income, multiplied by 12 is not less than—

(A) in the case of a debtor in a household of 1 person, the median family income of the applicable State for 1 earner; or

(B) in the case of a debtor in a household of 2 or more individuals, the highest median family income of the applicable State for a family of the same number or fewer individuals.

(c)(1) In a case described in subsection (a)(10) to which subsection (a)(10) applies, the trustee shall—

(A)(i) provide written notice to the holder of the claim described in subsection (a)(10) of such claim and of the right of such holder to use the services of the State child support enforcement agency established under sections 464 and 466 of the Social Security Act for the State in which such holder resides, for assistance in collecting child support during and after the case under this title;

(ii) include in the notice provided under clause (i) the address and telephone number of such State child support enforcement agency; and

(iii) include in the notice provided under clause (i) an explanation of the rights of such holder to payment of such claim under this chapter;

(B)(i) provide written notice to such State child support enforcement agency of such claim; and

(ii) include in the notice provided under clause (i) the name, address, and telephone number of such holder; and

(C) at such time as the debtor is granted a discharge under section 727, provide written notice to such holder and to such State child support enforcement agency of—

(i) the granting of the discharge;

(ii) the last recent known address of the debtor;

(iii) the last recent known name and address of the debtor's employer; and

(iv) the name of each creditor that holds a claim that—

(I) is not discharged under paragraph (2), (4), or (14A) of section 523(a); or

(II) was reaffirmed by the debtor under section 524(c).

(2)(A) The holder of a claim described in subsection (a)(10) or the State child support enforcement agency of the State in which such holder resides may request from a creditor described in paragraph (1)(C)(iv) the last known address of the debtor.

(B) Notwithstanding any other provision of law, a creditor that makes a disclosure of a last known address of a debtor in connection with a request made under subparagraph (A) shall not be liable by reason of making such disclosure.

(Pub. L. 95–598, Nov. 6, 1978, 92 Stat. 2605; Pub. L. 98–353, title III, §§311(a), 474, July 10, 1984, 98 Stat. 355, 381; Pub. L. 99–554, title II, §217, Oct. 27, 1986, 100 Stat. 3100; Pub. L. 109–8, title I, §102(c), title II, §219(a), title IV, §446(b), title XI, §1105(a), Apr. 20, 2005, 119 Stat. 32, 55, 118, 192; Pub. L. 111–16, §2(7), May 7, 2009, 123 Stat. 1607.)

Historical and Revision Notes

Legislative Statements

Section 704(8) of the Senate amendment is deleted in the House amendment. Trustees should give constructive notice of the commencement of the case in the manner specified under section 549(c) of title 11.

Senate Report No. 95–989

The essential duties of the trustee are enumerated in this section. Others, or elaborations on these, may be prescribed by the Rules of Bankruptcy Procedure to the extent not inconsistent with those prescribed by this section. The duties are derived from section 47a of the Bankruptcy Act [section 75(a) of former title 11].

The trustee's principal duty is to collect and reduce to money the property of the estate for which he serves, and to close up the estate as expeditiously as is compatible with the best interests of parties in interest. He must be accountable for all property received, and must investigate the financial affairs of the debtor. If a purpose would be served (such as if there are assets that will be distributed), the trustee is required to examine proofs of claims and object to the allowance of any claim that is improper. If advisable, the trustee must oppose the discharge of the debtor, which is for the benefit of general unsecured creditors whom the trustee represents.

The trustee is responsible to furnish such information concerning the estate and its administration as is requested by a party in interest. If the business of the debtor is authorized to be operated, then the trustee is required to file with governmental units charged with the responsibility for collection or determination of any tax arising out of the operation of the business periodic reports and summaries of the operation, including a statement of receipts and disbursements, and such other information as the court requires. He is required to give constructive notice of the commencement of the case in the manner specified under section 342(b).

References in Text

Section 3 of the Employee Retirement Income Security Act of 1974, referred to in subsec. (a)(11), is classified to section 1002 of Title 29, Labor.

Sections 464 and 466 of the Social Security Act, referred to in subsec. (c)(1)(A)(i), are classified to sections 664 and 666, respectively, of Title 42, The Public Health and Welfare.

AMENDMENTS

2009—Subsec. (b)(1)(B). Pub. L. 111–16 substituted "7 days" for "5 days".

2005—Pub. L. 109–8, §102(c)(1), designated existing provisions as subsec. (a).

Subsec. (a)(10). Pub. L. 109–8, §219(a)(1), added par. (10).

Subsec. (a)(11). Pub. L. 109–8, §446(b), added par. (11).

Subsec. (a)(12). Pub. L. 109–8, §1105(a), added par. (12).

Subsec. (b). Pub. L. 109–8, §102(c)(2), added subsec. (b).

Subsec. (c). Pub. L. 109–8, §219(a)(2), added subsec. (c).

1986—Par. (8). Pub. L. 99–554, §217(1), inserted ", with the United States trustee," after "with the court" and "the United States trustee or" after "information as".

Par. (9). Pub. L. 99–554, §217(2), inserted "with the United States trustee" after "court".

1984—Par. (1). Pub. L. 98–353, §474, substituted "close such estate" for "close up such estate".

Pars. (3) to (9). Pub. L. 98–353, §311(a), added par. (3) and redesignated former pars. (3) to (8) as (4) to (9), respectively.

EFFECTIVE DATE OF 2009 AMENDMENT

Amendment by Pub. L. 111–16 effective Dec. 1, 2009, see section 7 of Pub. L. 111–16, set out as a note under section 109 of this title.

EFFECTIVE DATE OF 2005 AMENDMENT

Amendment by Pub. L. 109–8 effective 180 days after Apr. 20, 2005, and not applicable with respect to cases commenced under this title before such effective date, except as otherwise provided, see section 1501 of Pub. L. 109–8, set out as a note under section 101 of this title.

EFFECTIVE DATE OF 1986 AMENDMENT

Effective date and applicability of amendment by Pub. L. 99–554 dependent upon the judicial district involved, see section 302(d), (e) of Pub. L. 99–554, set out as a note under section 581 of Title 28, Judiciary and Judicial Procedure.

EFFECTIVE DATE OF 1984 AMENDMENT

Amendment by Pub. L. 98–353 effective with respect to cases filed 90 days after July 10, 1984, see section 552(a) of Pub. L. 98–353, set out as a note under section 101 of this title.

§ 705. Creditors' committee

(a) At the meeting under section 341(a) of this title, creditors that may vote for a trustee under section 702(a) of this title may elect a committee of not fewer than three, and not more than eleven, creditors, each of whom holds an allowable unsecured claim of a kind entitled to distribution under section 726(a)(2) of this title.

(b) A committee elected under subsection (a) of this section may consult with the trustee or the United States trustee in connection with the administration of the estate, make recommendations to the trustee or the United States trustee respecting the performance of the trustee's duties, and submit to the court or the United States trustee any question affecting the administration of the estate.

(Pub. L. 95–598, Nov. 6, 1978, 92 Stat. 2605; Pub. L. 99–554, title II, §218, Oct. 27, 1986, 100 Stat. 3100.)

HISTORICAL AND REVISION NOTES

LEGISLATIVE STATEMENTS

Section 705(a) of the House amendment adopts a provision contained in the Senate amendment that limits a committee of creditors to not more than 11; the House bill contained no maximum limitation.

SENATE REPORT NO. 95–989

This section is derived from section 44b of the Bankruptcy Act [section 72(b) of former title 11] without substantial change. It permits election by general unsecured creditors of a committee of not fewer than 3 members and not more than 11 members to consult with the trustee in connection with the administration of the estate, to make recommendations to the trustee respecting the performance of his duties, and to submit to the court any question affecting the administration of the estate. There is no provision for compensation or reimbursement of its counsel.

AMENDMENTS

1986—Subsec. (b). Pub. L. 99–554 inserted "or the United States trustee" in three places.

EFFECTIVE DATE OF 1986 AMENDMENT

Effective date and applicability of amendment by Pub. L. 99–554 dependent upon the judicial district involved, see section 302(d), (e) of Pub. L. 99–554, set out as a note under section 581 of Title 28, Judiciary and Judicial Procedure.

§ 706. Conversion

(a) The debtor may convert a case under this chapter to a case under chapter 11, 12, or 13 of this title at any time, if the case has not been converted under section 1112, 1208, or 1307 of this title. Any waiver of the right to convert a case under this subsection is unenforceable.

(b) On request of a party in interest and after notice and a hearing, the court may convert a case under this chapter to a case under chapter 11 of this title at any time.

(c) The court may not convert a case under this chapter to a case under chapter 12 or 13 of this title unless the debtor requests or consents to such conversion.

(d) Notwithstanding any other provision of this section, a case may not be converted to a case under another chapter of this title unless the debtor may be a debtor under such chapter.

(Pub. L. 95–598, Nov. 6, 1978, 92 Stat. 2606; Pub. L. 99–554, title II, §257(q), Oct. 27, 1986, 100 Stat. 3115; Pub. L. 103–394, title V, §501(d)(22), Oct. 22, 1994, 108 Stat. 4146; Pub. L. 109–8, title I, §101, Apr. 20, 2005, 119 Stat. 27.)

HISTORICAL AND REVISION NOTES

LEGISLATIVE STATEMENTS

Section 706(a) of the House amendment adopts a provision contained in the Senate amendment indicating that a waiver of the right to convert a case under section 706(a) is unenforceable. The explicit reference in title 11 forbidding the waiver of certain rights is not intended to imply that other rights, such as the right to file a voluntary bankruptcy case under section 301, may be waived.

Section 706 of the House amendment adopts a similar provision contained in H.R. 8200 as passed by the House. Competing proposals contained in section 706(c) and section 706(d) of the Senate amendment are rejected.

SENATE REPORT NO. 95–989

Subsection (a) of this section gives the debtor the one-time absolute right of conversion of a liquidation case to a reorganization or individual repayment plan case. If the case has already once been converted from chapter 11 or 13 to chapter 7, then the debtor does not have that right. The policy of the provision is that the debtor should always be given the opportunity to repay his debts, and a waiver of the right to convert a case is unenforceable.

Subsection (b) permits the court, on request of a party in interest and after notice and a hearing, to convert the case to chapter 11 at any time. The decision whether to convert is left in the sound discretion of the court, based on what will most inure to the benefit of all parties in interest.

Subsection (c) is part of the prohibition against involuntary chapter 13 cases, and prohibits the court from converting a case to chapter 13 without the debtor's consent.

Subsection (d) reinforces section 109 by prohibiting conversion to a chapter unless the debtor is eligible to be a debtor under that chapter.

AMENDMENTS

2005—Subsec. (c). Pub. L. 109–8 inserted "or consents to" after "requests".

1994—Subsec. (a). Pub. L. 103–394 substituted "1208, or 1307" for "1307, or 1208".

1986—Subsec. (a). Pub. L. 99–554, §257(q)(1), inserted references to chapter 12 and section 1208 of this title.

Subsec. (c). Pub. L. 99–554, §257(q)(2), inserted reference to chapter 12.

EFFECTIVE DATE OF 2005 AMENDMENT

Amendment by Pub. L. 109–8 effective 180 days after Apr. 20, 2005, and not applicable with respect to cases commenced under this title before such effective date, except as otherwise provided, see section 1501 of Pub. L. 109–8, set out as a note under section 101 of this title.

EFFECTIVE DATE OF 1994 AMENDMENT

Amendment by Pub. L. 103–394 effective Oct. 22, 1994, and not applicable with respect to cases commenced under this title before Oct. 22, 1994, see section 702 of Pub. L. 103–394, set out as a note under section 101 of this title.

EFFECTIVE DATE OF 1986 AMENDMENT

Amendment by Pub. L. 99–554 effective 30 days after Oct. 27, 1986, but not applicable to cases commenced under this title before that date, see section 302(a), (c)(1) of Pub. L. 99–554, set out as a note under section 581 of Title 28, Judiciary and Judicial Procedure.

§707. Dismissal of a case or conversion to a case under chapter 11 or 13

(a) The court may dismiss a case under this chapter only after notice and a hearing and only for cause, including—

(1) unreasonable delay by the debtor that is prejudicial to creditors;

(2) nonpayment of any fees or charges required under chapter 123 of title 28; and

(3) failure of the debtor in a voluntary case to file, within fifteen days or such additional time as the court may allow after the filing of the petition commencing such case, the information required by paragraph (1) of section 521, but only on a motion by the United States trustee.

(b)(1) After notice and a hearing, the court, on its own motion or on a motion by the United States trustee, trustee (or bankruptcy administrator, if any), or any party in interest, may dismiss a case filed by an individual debtor under this chapter whose debts are primarily consumer debts, or, with the debtor's consent, convert such a case to a case under chapter 11 or 13 of this title, if it finds that the granting of relief would be an abuse of the provisions of this chapter. In making a determination whether to dismiss a case under this section, the court may not take into consideration whether a debtor has made, or continues to make, charitable contributions (that meet the definition of "charitable contribution" under section 548(d)(3)) to any qualified religious or charitable entity or organization (as that term is defined in section 548(d)(4)).

(2)(A)(i) In considering under paragraph (1) whether the granting of relief would be an abuse of the provisions of this chapter, the court shall presume abuse exists if the debtor's current monthly income reduced by the amounts determined under clauses (ii), (iii), and (iv), and multiplied by 60 is not less than the lesser of—

(I) 25 percent of the debtor's nonpriority unsecured claims in the case, or $6,000, whichever is greater; or

(II) $10,000.

(ii)(I) The debtor's monthly expenses shall be the debtor's applicable monthly expense amounts specified under the National Standards and Local Standards, and the debtor's actual monthly expenses for the categories specified as Other Necessary Expenses issued by the Internal Revenue Service for the area in which the debtor resides, as in effect on the date of the order for relief, for the debtor, the dependents of the debtor, and the spouse of the debtor in a joint case, if the spouse is not otherwise a dependent. Such expenses shall include reasonably necessary health insurance, disability insurance, and health savings account expenses for the debtor, the spouse of the debtor, or the dependents of the debtor. Notwithstanding any other provision of this clause, the monthly expenses of the debtor shall not include any payments for debts. In addition, the debtor's monthly expenses shall include the debtor's reasonably necessary expenses incurred to maintain the safety of the debtor and the family of the debtor from family violence as identified under section 309 of the Family Violence Prevention and Services Act,[1] or other applicable Federal law. The expenses included in the debtor's monthly expenses described in the preceding sentence shall be kept confidential by the court. In addition, if it is demonstrated that it is reasonable and necessary, the debtor's monthly expenses may also include an additional allowance for food and clothing of up to 5 percent of the food and clothing categories as specified by the National Standards issued by the Internal Revenue Service.

(II) In addition, the debtor's monthly expenses may include, if applicable, the continuation of actual expenses paid by the debtor that are reasonable and necessary for care and support of an elderly, chronically ill, or disabled household member or member of the debtor's immediate family (including parents, grandparents, siblings, children, and grandchildren of the debtor, the dependents of the debtor, and the spouse of the debtor in a joint case who is not a dependent) and who is unable to pay for such reasonable and necessary expenses.

(III) In addition, for a debtor eligible for chapter 13, the debtor's monthly expenses may include the actual administrative expenses of administering a chapter 13 plan for the district in which the debtor resides, up to an amount of 10 percent of the projected plan payments, as determined under schedules issued by the Executive Office for United States Trustees.

[1] See References in Text note below.

(IV) In addition, the debtor's monthly expenses may include the actual expenses for each dependent child less than 18 years of age, not to exceed $1,500 per year per child, to attend a private or public elementary or secondary school if the debtor provides documentation of such expenses and a detailed explanation of why such expenses are reasonable and necessary, and why such expenses are not already accounted for in the National Standards, Local Standards, or Other Necessary Expenses referred to in subclause (I).

(V) In addition, the debtor's monthly expenses may include an allowance for housing and utilities, in excess of the allowance specified by the Local Standards for housing and utilities issued by the Internal Revenue Service, based on the actual expenses for home energy costs if the debtor provides documentation of such actual expenses and demonstrates that such actual expenses are reasonable and necessary.

(iii) The debtor's average monthly payments on account of secured debts shall be calculated as the sum of—

(I) the total of all amounts scheduled as contractually due to secured creditors in each month of the 60 months following the date of the petition; and

(II) any additional payments to secured creditors necessary for the debtor, in filing a plan under chapter 13 of this title, to maintain possession of the debtor's primary residence, motor vehicle, or other property necessary for the support of the debtor and the debtor's dependents, that serves as collateral for secured debts;

divided by 60.

(iv) The debtor's expenses for payment of all priority claims (including priority child support and alimony claims) shall be calculated as the total amount of debts entitled to priority, divided by 60.

(B)(i) In any proceeding brought under this subsection, the presumption of abuse may only be rebutted by demonstrating special circumstances, such as a serious medical condition or a call or order to active duty in the Armed Forces, to the extent such special circumstances that justify additional expenses or adjustments of current monthly income for which there is no reasonable alternative.

(ii) In order to establish special circumstances, the debtor shall be required to itemize each additional expense or adjustment of income and to provide—

(I) documentation for such expense or adjustment to income; and

(II) a detailed explanation of the special circumstances that make such expenses or adjustment to income necessary and reasonable.

(iii) The debtor shall attest under oath to the accuracy of any information provided to demonstrate that additional expenses or adjustments to income are required.

(iv) The presumption of abuse may only be rebutted if the additional expenses or adjustments to income referred to in clause (i) cause the product of the debtor's current monthly income reduced by the amounts determined under clauses (ii), (iii), and (iv) of subparagraph (A) when multiplied by 60 to be less than the lesser of—

(I) 25 percent of the debtor's nonpriority unsecured claims, or $6,000, whichever is greater; or

(II) $10,000.

(C) As part of the schedule of current income and expenditures required under section 521, the debtor shall include a statement of the debtor's current monthly income, and the calculations that determine whether a presumption arises under subparagraph (A)(i), that show how each such amount is calculated.

(D) Subparagraphs (A) through (C) shall not apply, and the court may not dismiss or convert a case based on any form of means testing—

(i) if the debtor is a disabled veteran (as defined in section 3741(1) of title 38), and the indebtedness occurred primarily during a period during which he or she was—

(I) on active duty (as defined in section 101(d)(1) of title 10); or

(II) performing a homeland defense activity (as defined in section 901(1) of title 32); or

(ii) with respect to the debtor, while the debtor is—

(I) on, and during the 540-day period beginning immediately after the debtor is released from, a period of active duty (as defined in section 101(d)(1) of title 10) of not less than 90 days; or

(II) performing, and during the 540-day period beginning immediately after the debtor is no longer performing, a homeland defense activity (as defined in section 901(1) of title 32) performed for a period of not less than 90 days;

if after September 11, 2001, the debtor while a member of a reserve component of the Armed Forces or a member of the National Guard, was called to such active duty or performed such homeland defense activity.

(3) In considering under paragraph (1) whether the granting of relief would be an abuse of the provisions of this chapter in a case in which the presumption in subparagraph (A)(i) of such paragraph does not arise or is rebutted, the court shall consider—

(A) whether the debtor filed the petition in bad faith; or

(B) the totality of the circumstances (including whether the debtor seeks to reject a personal services contract and the financial need for such rejection as sought by the debtor) of the debtor's financial situation demonstrates abuse.

(4)(A) The court, on its own initiative or on the motion of a party in interest, in accordance with the procedures described in rule 9011 of the Federal Rules of Bankruptcy Procedure, may order the attorney for the debtor to reimburse the trustee for all reasonable costs in prosecuting a motion filed under section 707(b), including reasonable attorneys' fees, if—

(i) a trustee files a motion for dismissal or conversion under this subsection; and

(ii) the court—

(I) grants such motion; and

(II) finds that the action of the attorney for the debtor in filing a case under this chapter violated rule 9011 of the Federal Rules of Bankruptcy Procedure.

(B) If the court finds that the attorney for the debtor violated rule 9011 of the Federal Rules of Bankruptcy Procedure, the court, on its own initiative or on the motion of a party in interest, in accordance with such procedures, may order—

(i) the assessment of an appropriate civil penalty against the attorney for the debtor; and

(ii) the payment of such civil penalty to the trustee, the United States trustee (or the bankruptcy administrator, if any).

(C) The signature of an attorney on a petition, pleading, or written motion shall constitute a certification that the attorney has—

(i) performed a reasonable investigation into the circumstances that gave rise to the petition, pleading, or written motion; and

(ii) determined that the petition, pleading, or written motion—

(I) is well grounded in fact; and

(II) is warranted by existing law or a good faith argument for the extension, modification, or reversal of existing law and does not constitute an abuse under paragraph (1).

(D) The signature of an attorney on the petition shall constitute a certification that the attorney has no knowledge after an inquiry that the information in the schedules filed with such petition is incorrect.

(5)(A) Except as provided in subparagraph (B) and subject to paragraph (6), the court, on its own initiative or on the motion of a party in interest, in accordance with the procedures described in rule 9011 of the Federal Rules of Bankruptcy Procedure, may award a debtor all reasonable costs (including reasonable attorneys' fees) in contesting a motion filed by a party in interest (other than a trustee or United States trustee (or bankruptcy administrator, if any)) under this subsection if—

(i) the court does not grant the motion; and

(ii) the court finds that—

(I) the position of the party that filed the motion violated rule 9011 of the Federal Rules of Bankruptcy Procedure; or

(II) the attorney (if any) who filed the motion did not comply with the requirements of clauses (i) and (ii) of paragraph (4)(C), and the motion was made solely for the purpose of coercing a debtor into waiving a right guaranteed to the debtor under this title.

(B) A small business that has a claim of an aggregate amount less than $1,000 shall not be subject to subparagraph (A)(ii)(I).

(C) For purposes of this paragraph—

(i) the term "small business" means an unincorporated business, partnership, corporation, association, or organization that—

(I) has fewer than 25 full-time employees as determined on the date on which the motion is filed; and

(II) is engaged in commercial or business activity; and

(ii) the number of employees of a wholly owned subsidiary of a corporation includes the employees of—

(I) a parent corporation; and

(II) any other subsidiary corporation of the parent corporation.

(6) Only the judge or United States trustee (or bankruptcy administrator, if any) may file a motion under section 707(b), if the current monthly income of the debtor, or in a joint case, the debtor and the debtor's spouse, as of the date of the order for relief, when multiplied by 12, is equal to or less than—

(A) in the case of a debtor in a household of 1 person, the median family income of the applicable State for 1 earner;

(B) in the case of a debtor in a household of 2, 3, or 4 individuals, the highest median family income of the applicable State for a family of the same number or fewer individuals; or

(C) in the case of a debtor in a household exceeding 4 individuals, the highest median family income of the applicable State for a family of 4 or fewer individuals, plus $525 per month for each individual in excess of 4.

(7)(A) No judge, United States trustee (or bankruptcy administrator, if any), trustee, or other party in interest may file a motion under paragraph (2) if the current monthly income of the debtor, including a veteran (as that term is defined in section 101 of title 38), and the debtor's spouse combined, as of the date of the order for relief when multiplied by 12, is equal to or less than—

(i) in the case of a debtor in a household of 1 person, the median family income of the applicable State for 1 earner;

(ii) in the case of a debtor in a household of 2, 3, or 4 individuals, the highest median family income of the applicable State for a family of the same number or fewer individuals; or

(iii) in the case of a debtor in a household exceeding 4 individuals, the highest median family income of the applicable State for a family of 4 or fewer individuals, plus $525 per month for each individual in excess of 4.

(B) In a case that is not a joint case, current monthly income of the debtor's spouse shall not be considered for purposes of subparagraph (A) if—

(i)(I) the debtor and the debtor's spouse are separated under applicable nonbankruptcy law; or

(II) the debtor and the debtor's spouse are living separate and apart, other than for the purpose of evading subparagraph (A); and

(ii) the debtor files a statement under penalty of perjury—

(I) specifying that the debtor meets the requirement of subclause (I) or (II) of clause (i); and

(II) disclosing the aggregate, or best estimate of the aggregate, amount of any cash or money payments received from the debtor's spouse attributed to the debtor's current monthly income.

(c)(1) In this subsection—

(A) the term "crime of violence" has the meaning given such term in section 16 of title 18; and

(B) the term "drug trafficking crime" has the meaning given such term in section 924(c)(2) of title 18.

(2) Except as provided in paragraph (3), after notice and a hearing, the court, on a motion by the victim of a crime of violence or a drug trafficking crime, may when it is in the best interest of the victim dismiss a voluntary case filed under this chapter by a debtor who is an individual if such individual was convicted of such crime.

(3) The court may not dismiss a case under paragraph (2) if the debtor establishes by a preponderance of the evidence that the filing of a case under this chapter is necessary to satisfy a claim for a domestic support obligation.

(Pub. L. 95–598, Nov. 6, 1978, 92 Stat. 2606; Pub. L. 98–353, title III, §§312, 475, July 10, 1984, 98 Stat. 355, 381; Pub. L. 99–554, title II, §219, Oct. 27, 1986, 100 Stat. 3100; Pub. L. 105–183, §4(b), June 19, 1998, 112 Stat. 518; Pub. L. 109–8, title I, §102(a), (f), Apr. 20, 2005, 119 Stat. 27, 33; Pub. L. 110–438, §2, Oct. 20, 2008, 122 Stat. 5000.)

HISTORICAL AND REVISION NOTES

LEGISLATIVE STATEMENTS

Section 707 of the House amendment indicates that the court may dismiss a case only after notice and a hearing.

SENATE REPORT NO. 95–989

This section authorizes the court to dismiss a liquidation case only for cause, such as unreasonable delay by the debtor that is prejudicial to creditors or nonpayment of any fees and charges required under chapter 123 [§1911 et seq.] of title 28. These causes are not exhaustive, but merely illustrative. The section does not contemplate, however, that the ability of the debtor to repay his debts in whole or in part constitutes adequate cause for dismissal. To permit dismissal on that ground would be to enact a non-uniform mandatory chapter 13, in lieu of the remedy of bankruptcy.

REFERENCES IN TEXT

Section 309 of the Family Violence Prevention and Services Act, referred to in subsec. (b)(2)(A)(ii)(I), was redesignated section 320 of the Act by Pub. L. 108–36, title IV, §415(5), June 25, 2003, 117 Stat. 830, and is classified to section 10421 of Title 42, The Public Health and Welfare.

The Federal Rules of Bankruptcy Procedure, referred to in subsec. (b)(4)(A), (B), (5)(A), are set out in the Appendix to this title.

AMENDMENTS

2008—Subsec. (b)(2)(D). Pub. L. 110–438 substituted "testing—" for "testing." in introductory provisions, inserted cl. (i) designation before "if the debtor", redesignated former cls. (i) and (ii) as subcls. (I) and (II), respectively, of cl. (i) and added cl. (ii).

2005—Pub. L. 109–8, §102(a)(1), substituted "Dismissal of a case or conversion to a case under chapter 11 or 13" for "Dismissal" in section catchline.

Subsec. (b). Pub. L. 109–8, §102(a)(2), designated existing provisions as par. (1), substituted "trustee (or bankruptcy administrator, if any), or" for "but not at the request or suggestion of" and "an abuse" for "a substantial abuse", inserted ", or, with the debtor's consent, convert such a case to a case under chapter 11 or 13 of this title," after "consumer debts", struck out "There shall be a presumption in favor of granting the relief requested by the debtor." before "In making", and added pars. (2) to (7).

Subsec. (c). Pub. L. 109–8, §102(f), added subsec. (c).

1998—Subsec. (b). Pub. L. 105–183 inserted at end "In making a determination whether to dismiss a case under this section, the court may not take into consideration whether a debtor has made, or continues to make, charitable contributions (that meet the definition of 'charitable contribution' under section 548(d)(3)) to any qualified religious or charitable entity or organization (as that term is defined in section 548(d)(4))."

1986—Subsec. (a)(3). Pub. L. 99–554, §219(a), added par. (3).

Subsec. (b). Pub. L. 99–554, §219(b), substituted "motion or on a motion by the United States trustee, but" for "motion and".

1984—Pub. L. 98–353 designated existing provisions as subsec. (a) and in pars. (1) and (2) substituted "or" for "and", and added subsec. (b).

EFFECTIVE DATE OF 2008 AMENDMENT

Pub. L. 110–438, §4, Oct. 20, 2008, 122 Stat. 5002, provided that:

"(a) EFFECTIVE DATE.—Except as provided in subsection (b), this Act [amending this section and enacting provisions set out as a note under section 101 of this title] and the amendments made by this Act shall take effect 60 days after the date of enactment of this Act [Oct. 20, 2008].

"(b) APPLICATION OF AMENDMENTS.—The amendments made by this Act [amending this section] shall apply only with respect to cases commenced under title 11 of the United States Code in the 3-year period beginning on the effective date of this Act."

EFFECTIVE DATE OF 2005 AMENDMENT

Amendment by Pub. L. 109–8 effective 180 days after Apr. 20, 2005, and not applicable with respect to cases commenced under this title before such effective date, except as otherwise provided, see section 1501 of Pub. L. 109–8, set out as a note under section 101 of this title.

EFFECTIVE DATE OF 1998 AMENDMENT

Amendment by Pub. L. 105–183 applicable to any case brought under an applicable provision of this title that is pending or commenced on or after June 19, 1998, see section 5 of Pub. L. 105–183, set out as a note under section 544 of this title.

EFFECTIVE DATE OF 1986 AMENDMENT

Effective date and applicability of amendment by Pub. L. 99–554 dependent upon the judicial district involved, see section 302(d), (e) of Pub. L. 99–554, set out as a note under section 581 of Title 28, Judiciary and Judicial Procedure.

EFFECTIVE DATE OF 1984 AMENDMENT

Amendment by Pub. L. 98–353 effective with respect to cases filed 90 days after July 10, 1984, see section 552(a) of Pub. L. 98–353, set out as a note under section 101 of this title.

SCHEDULES OF REASONABLE AND NECESSARY EXPENSES

Pub. L. 109–8, title I, §107, Apr. 20, 2005, 119 Stat. 42, provided that: "For purposes of section 707(b) of title 11, United States Code, as amended by this Act, the Director of the Executive Office for United States Trustees shall, not later than 180 days after the date of enactment of this Act [Apr. 20, 2005], issue schedules of reasonable and necessary administrative expenses of administering a chapter 13 plan for each judicial district of the United States."

ADJUSTMENT OF DOLLAR AMOUNTS

For adjustment of dollar amounts specified in subsec. (b)(2)(A)(i), (ii)(IV), (5)(B), (6)(C), (7)(A) of this section by the Judicial Conference of the United States, see note set out under section 104 of this title.

RULES PROMULGATED BY SUPREME COURT

United States Supreme Court to prescribe general rules implementing the practice and procedure to be followed under subsec. (b) of this section, with section 2075 of Title 28, Judiciary and Judicial Procedure, to apply with respect to such general rules, see section 320 of Pub. L. 98–353, set out as a note under section 2075 of Title 28.

SUBCHAPTER II—COLLECTION, LIQUIDATION, AND DISTRIBUTION OF THE ESTATE

§ 721. Authorization to operate business

The court may authorize the trustee to operate the business of the debtor for a limited period, if such operation is in the best interest of the estate and consistent with the orderly liquidation of the estate.

(Pub. L. 95–598, Nov. 6, 1978, 92 Stat. 2606.)

HISTORICAL AND REVISION NOTES

SENATE REPORT NO. 95–989

This section is derived from section 2a(5) of the Bankruptcy Act [section 11(a)(5) of former title 11]. It permits the court to authorize the operation of any business of the debtor for a limited period, if the operation is in the best interest of the estate and consistent with orderly liquidation of the estate. An example is the operation of a watch company to convert watch movements and cases into completed watches which will bring much higher prices than the component parts would have brought.

§ 722. Redemption

An individual debtor may, whether or not the debtor has waived the right to redeem under this section, redeem tangible personal property intended primarily for personal, family, or household use, from a lien securing a dischargeable consumer debt, if such property is exempted under section 522 of this title or has been abandoned under section 554 of this title, by paying the holder of such lien the amount of the allowed secured claim of such holder that is secured by such lien in full at the time of redemption.

(Pub. L. 95–598, Nov. 6, 1978, 92 Stat. 2606; Pub. L. 109–8, title III, § 304(2), Apr. 20, 2005, 119 Stat. 79.)

HISTORICAL AND REVISION NOTES

LEGISLATIVE STATEMENTS

Section 722 of the House amendment adopts the position taken in H.R. 8200 as passed by the House and rejects the alternative contained in section 722 of the Senate amendment.

SENATE REPORT NO. 95–989

This section is new and is broader than rights of redemption under the Uniform Commercial Code. It authorizes an individual debtor to redeem tangible personal property intended primarily for personal, family, or household use, from a lien securing a nonpurchase money dischargeable consumer debt. It applies only if the debtor's interest in the property is exempt or has been abandoned.

This right to redeem is a very substantial change from current law. To prevent abuses such as may occur when the debtor deliberately allows the property to depreciate in value, the debtor will be required to pay the fair market value of the goods or the amount of the claim if the claim is less. The right is personal to the debtor and not assignable.

HOUSE REPORT NO. 95–595

This section is new and is broader than rights of redemption under the Uniform Commercial Code. It authorizes an individual debtor to redeem tangible personal property intended primarily for personal, family, or household use, from a lien securing a dischargeable consumer debt. It applies only if the debtor's interest in the property is exempt or has been abandoned.

The right to redeem extends to the whole of the property, not just the debtor's exempt interest in it. Thus, for example, if a debtor owned a $2,000 car, subject to a $1,200 lien, the debtor could exempt his $800 interest in the car. The debtor is permitted a $1,500 exemption in a car, proposed 11 U.S.C. 522(d)(2). This section permits him to pay the holder of the lien $1,200 and redeem the entire car, not just the remaining $700 of his exemption. The redemption is accomplished by paying the holder of the lien the amount of the allowed claim secured by the lien. The provision amounts to a right of first refusal for the debtor in consumer goods that might otherwise be repossessed. The right of redemption under this section is not waivable.

AMENDMENTS

2005—Pub. L. 109–8 inserted "in full at the time of redemption" before period at end.

EFFECTIVE DATE OF 2005 AMENDMENT

Amendment by Pub. L. 109–8 effective 180 days after Apr. 20, 2005, and not applicable with respect to cases commenced under this title before such effective date, except as otherwise provided, see section 1501 of Pub. L. 109–8, set out as a note under section 101 of this title.

§ 723. Rights of partnership trustee against general partners

(a) If there is a deficiency of property of the estate to pay in full all claims which are allowed in a case under this chapter concerning a partnership and with respect to which a general partner of the partnership is personally liable, the trustee shall have a claim against such general partner to the extent that under applicable nonbankruptcy law such general partner is personally liable for such deficiency.

(b) To the extent practicable, the trustee shall first seek recovery of such deficiency from any general partner in such partnership that is not a debtor in a case under this title. Pending determination of such deficiency, the court may order any such partner to provide the estate with indemnity for, or assurance of payment of, any deficiency recoverable from such partner, or not to dispose of property.

(c) Notwithstanding section 728(c)[1] of this title, the trustee has a claim against the estate of each general partner in such partnership that is a debtor in a case under this title for the full amount of all claims of creditors allowed in the case concerning such partnership. Notwithstanding section 502 of this title, there shall not be allowed in such partner's case a claim against such partner on which both such partner and such partnership are liable, except to any extent that such claim is secured only by property of such partner and not by property of such partnership. The claim of the trustee under this subsection is entitled to distribution in such partner's case under section 726(a) of this title the same as any other claim of a kind specified in such section.

(d) If the aggregate that the trustee recovers from the estates of general partners under subsection (c) of this section is greater than any de-

[1] See References in Text note below.

ficiency not recovered under subsection (b) of this section, the court, after notice and a hearing, shall determine an equitable distribution of the surplus so recovered, and the trustee shall distribute such surplus to the estates of the general partners in such partnership according to such determination.

(Pub. L. 95-598, Nov. 6, 1978, 92 Stat. 2606; Pub. L. 98-353, title III, §476, July 10, 1984, 98 Stat. 381; Pub. L. 103-394, title II, §212, Oct. 22, 1994, 108 Stat. 4125.)

HISTORICAL AND REVISION NOTES

LEGISLATIVE STATEMENTS

Section 723(c) of the House amendment is a compromise between similar provisions contained in the House bill and Senate amendment. The section makes clear that the trustee of a partnership has a claim against each general partner for the full amount of all claims of creditors allowed in the case concerning the partnership. By restricting the trustee's rights to claims of "creditors," the trustee of the partnership will not have a claim against the general partners for administrative expenses or claims allowed in the case concerning the partnership. As under present law, sections of the Bankruptcy Act [former title 11] applying to codebtors and sureties apply to the relationship of a partner with respect to a partnership debtor. See sections 501(b), 502(e), 506(d)(2), 509, 524(d), and 1301 of title 11.

SENATE REPORT NO. 95-989

This section is a significant departure from present law. It repeals the jingle rule, which, for ease of administration, denied partnership creditors their rights against general partners by permitting general partners' individual creditors to share in their estates first to the exclusion of partnership creditors. The result under this section more closely tracks generally applicable partnership law, without a significant administrative burden.

Subsection (a) specifies that each general partner in a partnership debtor is liable to the partnership's trustee for any deficiency of partnership property to pay in full all administrative expenses and all claims against the partnership.

Subsection (b) requires the trustee to seek recovery of the deficiency from any general partner that is not a debtor in a bankruptcy case. The court is empowered to order that partner to indemnify the estate or not to dispose of property pending a determination of the deficiency. The language of the subsection is directed to cases under the bankruptcy code. However, if, during the early stages of the transition period, a partner in a partnership is proceeding under the Bankruptcy Act [former title 11] while the partnership is proceeding under the bankruptcy code, the trustee should not first seek recovery against the Bankruptcy Act partner. Rather, the Bankruptcy Act partner should be deemed for the purposes of this section and the rights of the trustee to be proceeding under title 11.

Subsection (c) requires the partnership trustee to seek recovery of the full amount of the deficiency from the estate of each general partner that is a debtor in a bankruptcy case. The trustee will share equally with the partners' individual creditors in the assets of the partners' estates. Claims of partnership creditors who may have filed against the partner will be disallowed to avoid double counting.

Subsection (d) provides for the case where the total recovery from all of the bankrupt general partners is greater than the deficiency of which the trustee sought recovery. This case would most likely occur for a partnership with a large number of general partners. If the situation arises, the court is required to determine an equitable redistribution of the surplus to the estate of the general partners. The determination will be based on factors such as the relative liability of each of the general partners under the partnership agreement and the relative rights of each of the general partners in the profits of the enterprise under the partnership agreement.

REFERENCES IN TEXT

Section 728(c) of this title, referred to in subsec. (c), was repealed by Pub. L. 109-8, title VII, §719(b)(1), Apr. 20, 2005, 119 Stat. 133.

AMENDMENTS

1994—Subsec. (a). Pub. L. 103-394 substituted "to the extent that under applicable nonbankruptcy law such general partner is personally liable for such deficiency" for "for the full amount of the deficiency".

1984—Subsec. (a). Pub. L. 98-353, §476, substituted provisions that the trustee shall have a claim for the full amount of the deficiency against a general partner who is personally liable with respect to claims concerning partnerships which are allowed in a case under this chapter, for provisions that each general partner in the partnership would be liable to the trustee for the full amount of such deficiency.

Subsec. (c). Pub. L. 98-353, §476(b), substituted "such partner's case" for "such case" in two places, "by property of such partnership" for "be property of such partnership", and "a kind specified in such section" for "the kind specified in such section".

EFFECTIVE DATE OF 1994 AMENDMENT

Amendment by Pub. L. 103-394 effective Oct. 22, 1994, and not applicable with respect to cases commenced under this title before Oct. 22, 1994, see section 702 of Pub. L. 103-394, set out as a note under section 101 of this title.

EFFECTIVE DATE OF 1984 AMENDMENT

Amendment by Pub. L. 98-353 effective with respect to cases filed 90 days after July 10, 1984, see section 552(a) of Pub. L. 98-353, set out as a note under section 101 of this title.

§ 724. Treatment of certain liens

(a) The trustee may avoid a lien that secures a claim of a kind specified in section 726(a)(4) of this title.

(b) Property in which the estate has an interest and that is subject to a lien that is not avoidable under this title (other than to the extent that there is a properly perfected unavoidable tax lien arising in connection with an ad valorem tax on real or personal property of the estate) and that secures an allowed claim for a tax, or proceeds of such property, shall be distributed—

(1) first, to any holder of an allowed claim secured by a lien on such property that is not avoidable under this title and that is senior to such tax lien;

(2) second, to any holder of a claim of a kind specified in section 507(a)(1) (except that such expenses, other than claims for wages, salaries, or commissions that arise after the date of the filing of the petition, shall be limited to expenses incurred under chapter 7 of this title and shall not include expenses incurred under chapter 11 of this title), 507(a)(2), 507(a)(3), 507(a)(4), 507(a)(5), 507(a)(6), or 507(a)(7) of this title, to the extent of the amount of such allowed tax claim that is secured by such tax lien;

(3) third, to the holder of such tax lien, to any extent that such holder's allowed tax

claim that is secured by such tax lien exceeds any amount distributed under paragraph (2) of this subsection;

(4) fourth, to any holder of an allowed claim secured by a lien on such property that is not avoidable under this title and that is junior to such tax lien;

(5) fifth, to the holder of such tax lien, to the extent that such holder's allowed claim secured by such tax lien is not paid under paragraph (3) of this subsection; and

(6) sixth, to the estate.

(c) If more than one holder of a claim is entitled to distribution under a particular paragraph of subsection (b) of this section, distribution to such holders under such paragraph shall be in the same order as distribution to such holders would have been other than under this section.

(d) A statutory lien the priority of which is determined in the same manner as the priority of a tax lien under section 6323 of the Internal Revenue Code of 1986 shall be treated under subsection (b) of this section the same as if such lien were a tax lien.

(e) Before subordinating a tax lien on real or personal property of the estate, the trustee shall—

(1) exhaust the unencumbered assets of the estate; and

(2) in a manner consistent with section 506(c), recover from property securing an allowed secured claim the reasonable, necessary costs and expenses of preserving or disposing of such property.

(f) Notwithstanding the exclusion of ad valorem tax liens under this section and subject to the requirements of subsection (e), the following may be paid from property of the estate which secures a tax lien, or the proceeds of such property:

(1) Claims for wages, salaries, and commissions that are entitled to priority under section 507(a)(4).

(2) Claims for contributions to an employee benefit plan entitled to priority under section 507(a)(5).

(Pub. L. 95-598, Nov. 6, 1978, 92 Stat. 2607; Pub. L. 98-353, title III, §477, July 10, 1984, 98 Stat. 381; Pub. L. 99-554, title II, §283(r), Oct. 27, 1986, 100 Stat. 3118; Pub. L. 103-394, title III, §304(h)(4), title V, §501(d)(23), Oct. 22, 1994, 108 Stat. 4134, 4146; Pub. L. 109-8, title VII, §701(a), Apr. 20, 2005, 119 Stat. 124.)

Historical and Revision Notes

LEGISLATIVE STATEMENTS

Section 724 of the House amendment adopts the provision taken in the House bill and rejects the provision taken in the Senate amendment. In effect, a tax claim secured by a lien is treated as a claim between the fifth and sixth priority in a case under chapter 7 rather than as a secured claim.

Treatment of certain liens: The House amendment modifies present law by requiring the subordination of tax liens on both real and personal property to the payment of claims having a priority. This means that assets are to be distributed from the debtor's estate to pay higher priority claims before the tax claims are paid, even though the tax claims are properly secured. Under present law and the Senate amendment only tax liens on personal property, but not on real property, are subordinated to the payment of claims having a priority above the priority for tax claims.

SENATE REPORT NO. 95-989

Subsection (a) of section 724 permits the trustee to avoid a lien that secures a fine, penalty, forfeiture, or multiple, punitive, or exemplary damages claim to the extent that the claim is not compensation for actual pecuniary loss. The subsection follows the policy found in section 57j of the Bankruptcy Act [section 93(j) of former title 11] of protecting unsecured creditors from the debtor's wrongdoing, but expands the protection afforded. The lien is made voidable rather than void in chapter 7, in order to permit the lien to be revived if the case is converted to chapter 11 under which penalty liens are not voidable. To make the lien void would be to permit the filing of a chapter 7, the voiding of the lien, and the conversion to a chapter 11, simply to avoid a penalty lien, which should be valid in a reorganization case.

Subsection (b) governs tax liens. This provision retains the rule of present bankruptcy law (§67(C)(3) of the Bankruptcy Act [section 107(c)(3) of former title 11]) that a tax lien on personal property, if not avoidable by the trustee, is subordinated in payment to unsecured claims having a higher priority than unsecured tax claims. Those other claims may be satisfied from the amount that would otherwise have been applied to the tax lien, and any excess of the amount of the lien is then applied to the tax. Any personal property (or sale proceeds) remaining is to be used to satisfy claims secured by liens which are junior to the tax lien. Any proceeds remaining are next applied to pay any unpaid balance of the tax lien.

Subsection (d) specifies that any statutory lien whose priority is determined in the same manner as a tax lien is to be treated as a tax lien under this section, even if the lien does not secure a claim for taxes. An example is the ERISA [29 U.S.C. 1001 et seq.] lien.

HOUSE REPORT NO. 95-595

Subsection (b) governs tax liens. It is derived from section 67c(3) of the Bankruptcy Act [section 107(c)(3) of former title 11], without substantial modification in result. It subordinates tax liens to administrative expense and wage claims, and solves certain circuity of liens problems that arise in connection with the subordination. The order of distribution of property subject to a tax lien is as follows: First, to holders of liens senior to the tax lien; second, to administrative expenses, wage claims, and consumer creditors that are granted priority, but only to the extent of the amount of the allowed tax claim secured by the lien. In other words, the priority claimants step into the shoes of the tax collector. Third, to the tax claimant, to the extent that priority claimants did not use up his entire claim. Fourth, to junior lien holders. Fifth, to the tax collector to the extent that he was not paid under paragraph (3). Finally, any remaining property goes to the estate. The result of these provisions are to leave senior and junior lienors and holders of unsecured claims undisturbed. If there are any liens that are equal in status to the tax lien, they share pari passu with the tax lien under the distribution provisions of this subsection.

References in Text

Section 6323 of the Internal Revenue Code of 1986, referred to in subsec. (d), is classified to section 6323 of Title 26, Internal Revenue Code.

Amendments

2005—Subsec. (b). Pub. L. 109-8, §701(a)(1), inserted "(other than to the extent that there is a properly perfected unavoidable tax lien arising in connection with an ad valorem tax on real or personal property of the estate)" after "under this title" in introductory provisions.

Subsec. (b)(2). Pub. L. 109-8, §701(a)(2), inserted "(except that such expenses, other than claims for wages, salaries, or commissions that arise after the date of the filing of the petition, shall be limited to expenses incurred under chapter 7 of this title and shall not include expenses incurred under chapter 11 of this title)" after "section 507(a)(1)".

Subsecs. (e), (f). Pub. L. 109–8, §701(a)(3), added subsecs. (e) and (f).

1994—Subsec. (b)(2). Pub. L. 103–394, §304(h)(4), substituted "507(a)(6), or 507(a)(7)" for "or 507(a)(6)".

Subsec. (d). Pub. L. 103–394, §501(d)(23), substituted "Internal Revenue Code of 1986" for "Internal Revenue Code of 1954 (26 U.S.C. 6323)".

1986—Subsec. (b)(2). Pub. L. 99–554 inserted reference to section 507(a)(6) of this title.

1984—Subsec. (b). Pub. L. 98–353, §477(a)(1), substituted "a tax" for "taxes" in provisions preceding par. (1).

Subsec. (b)(2). Pub. L. 98–353, §477(a)(2), substituted "any holder of a claim of a kind specified" for "claims specified", "section 507(a)(1)" for "sections 507(a)(1)", and "or 507(a)(5) of this title" for "and 507(a)(5) of this title".

Subsec. (b)(3). Pub. L. 98–353, §477(a)(3), substituted "allowed tax claim" for "allowed claim".

Subsec. (c). Pub. L. 98–353, §477(b), substituted "holder of a claim is entitled" for "creditor is entitled" and "holders" for "creditors" in two places.

Subsec. (d). Pub. L. 98–353, §477(c), substituted "the priority of which" for "whose priority" and "the same as if such lien were a tax lien" for "the same as a tax lien".

EFFECTIVE DATE OF 2005 AMENDMENT

Amendment by Pub. L. 109–8 effective 180 days after Apr. 20, 2005, and not applicable with respect to cases commenced under this title before such effective date, except as otherwise provided, see section 1501 of Pub. L. 109–8, set out as a note under section 101 of this title.

EFFECTIVE DATE OF 1994 AMENDMENT

Amendment by Pub. L. 103–394 effective Oct. 22, 1994, and not applicable with respect to cases commenced under this title before Oct. 22, 1994, see section 702 of Pub. L. 103–394, set out as a note under section 101 of this title.

EFFECTIVE DATE OF 1986 AMENDMENT

Amendment by Pub. L. 99–554 effective 30 days after Oct. 27, 1986, see section 302(a) of Pub. L. 99–554, set out as a note under section 581 of Title 28, Judiciary and Judicial Procedure.

EFFECTIVE DATE OF 1984 AMENDMENT

Amendment by Pub. L. 98–353 effective with respect to cases filed 90 days after July 10, 1984, see section 552(a) of Pub. L. 98–353, set out as a note under section 101 of this title.

§ 725. Disposition of certain property

After the commencement of a case under this chapter, but before final distribution of property of the estate under section 726 of this title, the trustee, after notice and a hearing, shall dispose of any property in which an entity other than the estate has an interest, such as a lien, and that has not been disposed of under another section of this title.

(Pub. L. 95–598, Nov. 6, 1978, 92 Stat. 2607; Pub. L. 98–353, title III, §478, July 10, 1984, 98 Stat. 381.)

HISTORICAL AND REVISION NOTES

LEGISLATIVE STATEMENTS

Section 725 of the House amendment adopts the substance contained in both the House bill and Senate amendment but transfers an administrative function to the trustee in accordance with the general thrust of this legislation to separate the administrative and the judicial functions where appropriate.

SENATE REPORT NO. 95–989

This section requires the court to determine the appropriate disposition of property in which the estate and an entity other than the estate have an interest. It would apply, for example, to property subject to a lien or property co-owned by the estate and another entity. The court must make the determination with respect to property that is not disposed of under another section of the bankruptcy code, such as by abandonment under section 554, by sale or distribution under 363, or by allowing foreclosure by a secured creditor by lifting the stay under section 362. The purpose of the section is to give the court appropriate authority to ensure that collateral or its proceeds is returned to the proper secured creditor, that consigned or bailed goods are returned to the consignor or bailor and so on. Current law is curiously silent on this point, though case law has grown to fill the void. The section is in lieu of a section that would direct a certain distribution to secured creditors. It gives the court greater flexibility to meet the circumstances, and it is broader, permitting disposition of property subject to a co-ownership interest.

AMENDMENTS

1984—Pub. L. 98–353 substituted "distribution of property of the estate" for "distribution".

EFFECTIVE DATE OF 1984 AMENDMENT

Amendment by Pub. L. 98–353 effective with respect to cases filed 90 days after July 10, 1984, see section 552(a) of Pub. L. 98–353, set out as a note under section 101 of this title.

§ 726. Distribution of property of the estate

(a) Except as provided in section 510 of this title, property of the estate shall be distributed—

(1) first, in payment of claims of the kind specified in, and in the order specified in, section 507 of this title, proof of which is timely filed under section 501 of this title or tardily filed on or before the earlier of—

(A) the date that is 10 days after the mailing to creditors of the summary of the trustee's final report; or

(B) the date on which the trustee commences final distribution under this section;

(2) second, in payment of any allowed unsecured claim, other than a claim of a kind specified in paragraph (1), (3), or (4) of this subsection, proof of which is—

(A) timely filed under section 501(a) of this title;

(B) timely filed under section 501(b) or 501(c) of this title; or

(C) tardily filed under section 501(a) of this title, if—

(i) the creditor that holds such claim did not have notice or actual knowledge of the case in time for timely filing of a proof of such claim under section 501(a) of this title; and

(ii) proof of such claim is filed in time to permit payment of such claim;

(3) third, in payment of any allowed unsecured claim proof of which is tardily filed under section 501(a) of this title, other than a claim of the kind specified in paragraph (2)(C) of this subsection;

(4) fourth, in payment of any allowed claim, whether secured or unsecured, for any fine, penalty, or forfeiture, or for multiple, exemplary, or punitive damages, arising before the earlier of the order for relief or the appointment of a trustee, to the extent that such fine, penalty, forfeiture, or damages are not compensation for actual pecuniary loss suffered by the holder of such claim;

(5) fifth, in payment of interest at the legal rate from the date of the filing of the petition, on any claim paid under paragraph (1), (2), (3), or (4) of this subsection; and

(6) sixth, to the debtor.

(b) Payment on claims of a kind specified in paragraph (1), (2), (3), (4), (5), (6), (7), or (8) of section 507(a) of this title, or in paragraph (2), (3), (4), or (5) of subsection (a) of this section, shall be made pro rata among claims of the kind specified in each such particular paragraph, except that in a case that has been converted to this chapter under section 1112, 1208, or 1307 of this title, a claim allowed under section 503(b) of this title incurred under this chapter after such conversion has priority over a claim allowed under section 503(b) of this title incurred under any other chapter of this title or under this chapter before such conversion and over any expenses of a custodian superseded under section 543 of this title.

(c) Notwithstanding subsections (a) and (b) of this section, if there is property of the kind specified in section 541(a)(2) of this title, or proceeds of such property, in the estate, such property or proceeds shall be segregated from other property of the estate, and such property or proceeds and other property of the estate shall be distributed as follows:

(1) Claims allowed under section 503 of this title shall be paid either from property of the kind specified in section 541(a)(2) of this title, or from other property of the estate, as the interest of justice requires.

(2) Allowed claims, other than claims allowed under section 503 of this title, shall be paid in the order specified in subsection (a) of this section, and, with respect to claims of a kind specified in a particular paragraph of section 507 of this title or subsection (a) of this section, in the following order and manner:

(A) First, community claims against the debtor or the debtor's spouse shall be paid from property of the kind specified in section 541(a)(2) of this title, except to the extent that such property is solely liable for debts of the debtor.

(B) Second, to the extent that community claims against the debtor are not paid under subparagraph (A) of this paragraph, such community claims shall be paid from property of the kind specified in section 541(a)(2) of this title that is solely liable for debts of the debtor.

(C) Third, to the extent that all claims against the debtor including community claims against the debtor are not paid under subparagraph (A) or (B) of this paragraph such claims shall be paid from property of the estate other than property of the kind specified in section 541(a)(2) of this title.

(D) Fourth, to the extent that community claims against the debtor or the debtor's spouse are not paid under subparagraph (A), (B), or (C) of this paragraph, such claims shall be paid from all remaining property of the estate.

(Pub. L. 95–598, Nov. 6, 1978, 92 Stat. 2608; Pub. L. 98–353, title III, §479, July 10, 1984, 98 Stat. 381; Pub. L. 99–554, title II, §§257(r), 283(s), Oct. 27, 1986, 100 Stat. 3115, 3118; Pub. L. 103–394, title II, §213(b), title III, §304(h)(5), title V, §501(d)(24), Oct. 22, 1994, 108 Stat. 4126, 4134, 4146; Pub. L. 109–8, title VII, §713, title XII, §1215, Apr. 20, 2005, 119 Stat. 128, 195.)

Historical and Revision Notes

legislative statements

Section 726(a)(4) adopts a provision contained in the Senate amendment subordinating prepetition penalties and penalties arising in the involuntary gap period to the extent the penalties are not compensation for actual pecuniary laws.

The House amendment deletes a provision following section 726(a)(6) of the Senate amendment providing that the term "claim" includes interest due owed before the date of the filing of the petition as unnecessary since a right to payment for interest due is a right to payment which is within the definition of "claim" in section 101(4) of the House amendment.

senate report no. 95–989

This section is the general distribution section for liquidation cases. It dictates the order in which distribution of property of the estate, which has usually been reduced to money by the trustee under the requirements of section 704(1).

First, property is distributed among priority claimants, as determined by section 507, and in the order prescribed by section 507. Second, distribution is to general unsecured creditors. This class excludes priority creditors and the two classes of subordinated creditors specified below. The provision is written to permit distribution to creditors that tardily file claims if their tardiness was due to lack of notice or knowledge of the case. Though it is in the interest of the estate to encourage timely filing, when tardy filing is not the result of a failure to act by the creditor, the normal subordination penalty should not apply. Third distribution is to general unsecured creditors who tardily file. Fourth distribution is to holders of fine, penalty, forfeiture, or multiple, punitive, or exemplary damage claims. More of these claims are disallowed entirely under present law. They are simply subordinated here.

Paragraph (4) provides that punitive penalties, including prepetition tax penalties, are subordinated to the payment of all other classes of claims, except claims for interest accruing during the case. In effect, these penalties are payable out of the estate's assets only if and to the extent that a surplus of assets would otherwise remain at the close of the case for distribution back to the debtor.

Paragraph (5) provides that postpetition interest on prepetition claims is also to be paid to the creditor in a subordinated position. Like prepetition penalties, such interest will be paid from the estate only if and to the extent that a surplus of assets would otherwise remain for return to the debtor at the close of the case.

This section also specifies that interest accrued on all claims (including priority and nonpriority tax claims) which accrued before the date of the filing of the title 11 petition is to be paid in the same order of distribution of the estate's assets as the principal amount of the related claims.

Any surplus is paid to the debtor under paragraph (6).

Subsection (b) follows current law. It specifies that claims within a particular class are to be paid pro rata. This provision will apply, of course, only when there are inadequate funds to pay the holders of claims of a particular class in full. The exception found in the section, which also follows current law, specifies that liquidation administrative expenses are to be paid ahead of reorganization administrative expenses if the case has been converted from a reorganization case to a liquidation case, or from an individual repayment plan case to a liquidation case.

Subsection (c) governs distributions in cases in which there is community property and other property of the estate. The section requires the two kinds of property to be segregated. The distribution is as follows: First, administrative expenses are to be paid, as the court determines on any reasonable equitable basis, from both kinds of property. The court will divide administrative expenses according to such factors as the amount of each kind of property in the estate, the cost of preservation and liquidation of each kind of property, and whether any particular administrative expenses are attributable to one kind of property or the other. Second, claims are to be paid as provided under subsection (a) (the normal liquidation case distribution rules) in the following order and manner: First, community claims against the debtor or the debtor's spouse are paid from community property, except such as is liable solely for the debts of the debtor.

Second, community claims against the debtor, to the extent not paid under the first provision, are paid from community property that is solely liable for the debts of the debtor. Third, community claims, to the extent they remain unpaid, and all other claims against the debtor, are paid from noncommunity property. Fourth, if any community claims against the debtor or the debtor's spouse remain unpaid, they are paid from whatever property remains in the estate. This would occur if community claims against the debtor's spouse are large in amount and most of the estate's property is property solely liable, under nonbankruptcy law, for debts of the debtor.

The marshalling rules in this section apply only to property of the estate. However, they will provide a guide to the courts in the interpretation of proposed 11 U.S.C. 725, relating to distribution of collateral, in cases in which there is community property. If a secured creditor has a lien on both community and noncommunity property, the marshalling rules here—by analogy would dictate that the creditor be satisfied first out of community property, and then out of separate property.

AMENDMENTS

2005—Subsec. (a)(1). Pub. L. 109–8, §713, substituted "on or before the earlier of—" and subpars. (A) and (B) for "before the date on which the trustee commences distribution under this section;".

Subsec. (b). Pub. L. 109–8, §1215, struck out "1009," before "1112".

1994—Subsec. (a)(1). Pub. L. 103–394, §213(b), inserted before semicolon at end ", proof of which is timely filed under section 501 of this title or tardily filed before the date on which the trustee commences distribution under this section".

Subsec. (b). Pub. L. 103–394, §§304(h)(5), 501(d)(24), substituted ", (7), or (8)" for "or (7)" and "chapter under section 1009, 1112," for "chapter under section 1112".

1986—Subsec. (b). Pub. L. 99–554, §283(s), inserted reference to par. (7) of section 507(a) of this title.

Pub. L. 99–554, §257(r), inserted reference to section 1208 of this title.

1984—Subsec. (b). Pub. L. 98–353, §479(a), substituted "each such particular paragraph" for "a particular paragraph", "a claim allowed under section 503(b) of this title" for "administrative expenses" in two places, and "has priority over" for "have priority over".

Subsec. (c)(1). Pub. L. 98–353, §479(b)(1), substituted "Claims allowed under section 503 of this title" for "Administrative expenses".

Subsec. (c)(2). Pub. L. 98–353, §479(b)(2), substituted "Allowed claims, other than claims allowed under section 503 of this title," for "Claims other than for administrative expenses".

EFFECTIVE DATE OF 2005 AMENDMENT

Amendment by Pub. L. 109–8 effective 180 days after Apr. 20, 2005, and not applicable with respect to cases commenced under this title before such effective date, except as otherwise provided, see section 1501 of Pub. L. 109–8, set out as a note under section 101 of this title.

EFFECTIVE DATE OF 1994 AMENDMENT

Amendment by Pub. L. 103–394 effective Oct. 22, 1994, and not applicable with respect to cases commenced under this title before Oct. 22, 1994, see section 702 of Pub. L. 103–394, set out as a note under section 101 of this title.

EFFECTIVE DATE OF 1986 AMENDMENT

Amendment by section 257 of Pub. L. 99–554 effective 30 days after Oct. 27, 1986, but not applicable to cases commenced under this title before that date, see section 302(a), (c)(1) of Pub. L. 99–554, set out as a note under section 581 of Title 28, Judiciary and Judicial Procedure.

Amendment by section 283 of Pub. L. 99–554 effective 30 days after Oct. 27, 1986, see section 302(a) of Pub. L. 99–554.

EFFECTIVE DATE OF 1984 AMENDMENT

Amendment by Pub. L. 98–353 effective with respect to cases filed 90 days after July 10, 1984, see section 552(a) of Pub. L. 98–353, set out as a note under section 101 of this title.

§ 727. Discharge

(a) The court shall grant the debtor a discharge, unless—

(1) the debtor is not an individual;

(2) the debtor, with intent to hinder, delay, or defraud a creditor or an officer of the estate charged with custody of property under this title, has transferred, removed, destroyed, mutilated, or concealed, or has permitted to be transferred, removed, destroyed, mutilated, or concealed—

(A) property of the debtor, within one year before the date of the filing of the petition; or

(B) property of the estate, after the date of the filing of the petition;

(3) the debtor has concealed, destroyed, mutilated, falsified, or failed to keep or preserve any recorded information, including books, documents, records, and papers, from which the debtor's financial condition or business transactions might be ascertained, unless such act or failure to act was justified under all of the circumstances of the case;

(4) the debtor knowingly and fraudulently, in or in connection with the case—

(A) made a false oath or account;

(B) presented or used a false claim;

(C) gave, offered, received, or attempted to obtain money, property, or advantage, or a promise of money, property, or advantage, for acting or forbearing to act; or

(D) withheld from an officer of the estate entitled to possession under this title, any recorded information, including books, documents, records, and papers, relating to the debtor's property or financial affairs;

(5) the debtor has failed to explain satisfactorily, before determination of denial of discharge under this paragraph, any loss of assets or deficiency of assets to meet the debtor's liabilities;

(6) the debtor has refused, in the case—

(A) to obey any lawful order of the court, other than an order to respond to a material question or to testify;

(B) on the ground of privilege against self-incrimination, to respond to a material question approved by the court or to testify, after the debtor has been granted immunity with respect to the matter concerning which such privilege was invoked; or

(C) on a ground other than the properly invoked privilege against self-incrimination, to respond to a material question approved by the court or to testify;

(7) the debtor has committed any act specified in paragraph (2), (3), (4), (5), or (6) of this subsection, on or within one year before the date of the filing of the petition, or during the case, in connection with another case, under this title or under the Bankruptcy Act, concerning an insider;

(8) the debtor has been granted a discharge under this section, under section 1141 of this title, or under section 14, 371, or 476 of the Bankruptcy Act, in a case commenced within 8 years before the date of the filing of the petition;

(9) the debtor has been granted a discharge under section 1228 or 1328 of this title, or under section 660 or 661 of the Bankruptcy Act, in a case commenced within six years before the date of the filing of the petition, unless payments under the plan in such case totaled at least—

(A) 100 percent of the allowed unsecured claims in such case; or

(B)(i) 70 percent of such claims; and

(ii) the plan was proposed by the debtor in good faith, and was the debtor's best effort;

(10) the court approves a written waiver of discharge executed by the debtor after the order for relief under this chapter;

(11) after filing the petition, the debtor failed to complete an instructional course concerning personal financial management described in section 111, except that this paragraph shall not apply with respect to a debtor who is a person described in section 109(h)(4) or who resides in a district for which the United States trustee (or the bankruptcy administrator, if any) determines that the approved instructional courses are not adequate to service the additional individuals who would otherwise be required to complete such instructional courses under this section (The United States trustee (or the bankruptcy administrator, if any) who makes a determination described in this paragraph shall review such determination not later than 1 year after the date of such determination, and not less frequently than annually thereafter.); or

(12) the court after notice and a hearing held not more than 10 days before the date of the entry of the order granting the discharge finds that there is reasonable cause to believe that—

(A) section 522(q)(1) may be applicable to the debtor; and

(B) there is pending any proceeding in which the debtor may be found guilty of a felony of the kind described in section 522(q)(1)(A) or liable for a debt of the kind described in section 522(q)(1)(B).

(b) Except as provided in section 523 of this title, a discharge under subsection (a) of this section discharges the debtor from all debts that arose before the date of the order for relief under this chapter, and any liability on a claim that is determined under section 502 of this title as if such claim had arisen before the commencement of the case, whether or not a proof of claim based on any such debt or liability is filed under section 501 of this title, and whether or not a claim based on any such debt or liability is allowed under section 502 of this title.

(c)(1) The trustee, a creditor, or the United States trustee may object to the granting of a discharge under subsection (a) of this section.

(2) On request of a party in interest, the court may order the trustee to examine the acts and conduct of the debtor to determine whether a ground exists for denial of discharge.

(d) On request of the trustee, a creditor, or the United States trustee, and after notice and a hearing, the court shall revoke a discharge granted under subsection (a) of this section if—

(1) such discharge was obtained through the fraud of the debtor, and the requesting party did not know of such fraud until after the granting of such discharge;

(2) the debtor acquired property that is property of the estate, or became entitled to acquire property that would be property of the estate, and knowingly and fraudulently failed to report the acquisition of or entitlement to such property, or to deliver or surrender such property to the trustee;

(3) the debtor committed an act specified in subsection (a)(6) of this section; or

(4) the debtor has failed to explain satisfactorily—

(A) a material misstatement in an audit referred to in section 586(f) of title 28; or

(B) a failure to make available for inspection all necessary accounts, papers, documents, financial records, files, and all other papers, things, or property belonging to the debtor that are requested for an audit referred to in section 586(f) of title 28.

(e) The trustee, a creditor, or the United States trustee may request a revocation of a discharge—

(1) under subsection (d)(1) of this section within one year after such discharge is granted; or

(2) under subsection (d)(2) or (d)(3) of this section before the later of—

(A) one year after the granting of such discharge; and

(B) the date the case is closed.

(Pub. L. 95–598, Nov. 6, 1978, 92 Stat. 2609; Pub. L. 98–353, title III, §480, July 10, 1984, 98 Stat. 382; Pub. L. 99–554, title II, §§220, 257(s), Oct. 27, 1986, 100 Stat. 3101, 3116; Pub. L. 109–8, title I, §106(b), title III, §§312(1), 330(a), title VI, §603(d), Apr. 20, 2005, 119 Stat. 38, 86, 101, 123.)

HISTORICAL AND REVISION NOTES

LEGISLATIVE STATEMENTS

Sections 727(a) (8) and (9) of the House amendment represent a compromise between provisions contained in section 727(a)(8) of the House bill and Senate amendment. Section 727(a)(8) of the House amendment adopts section 727(a)(8) of the House bill. However, section 727(a)(9) of the House amendment contains a compromise based on section 727(a)(8) of the Senate amendment with respect to the circumstances under which a plan by way of composition under Chapter XIII of the Bankruptcy Act [chapter 13 of former title 11] should be a bar to discharge in a subsequent proceeding under title 11. The paragraph provides that a discharge under section 660 or 661 of the Bankruptcy Act [section 1060 or 1061 of former title 11] or section 1328 of title 11 in a case commenced within 6 years before the date of the filing of the petition in a subsequent case, operates as a bar to discharge unless, first, payments under the plan totaled at least 100 percent of the allowed unsecured claims in the case; or second, payments under the plan totaled at least 70 percent of the allowed unsecured claims in the case and the plan was proposed by the debtor in good faith and was the debtor's best effort.

It is expected that the Rules of Bankruptcy Procedure will contain a provision permitting the debtor to request a determination of whether a plan is the debtor's "best effort" prior to confirmation of a plan in a case under chapter 13 of title 11. In determining whether a plan is the debtor's "best effort" the court will evaluate several factors. Different facts and circumstances in cases under chapter 13 operate to make any rule of thumb of limited usefulness. The court should balance the debtor's assets, including family income, health insurance, retirement benefits, and other wealth, a sum which is generally determinable, against the foreseeable necessary living expenses of the debtor and the debtor's dependents, which unfortunately is rarely quantifiable. In determining the expenses of the debtor and the debtor's dependents, the court should consider the stability of the debtor's employment, if any, the age of the debtor, the number of the debtor's dependents and their ages, the condition of equipment and tools necessary to the debtor's employment or to the operation of his business, and other foreseeable expenses that the debtor will be required to pay during the period of the plan, other than payments to be made to creditors under the plan.

Section 727(a)(10) of the House amendment clarifies a provision contained in section 727(a)(9) of the House bill and Senate amendment indicating that a discharge may be barred if the court approves a waiver of discharge executed in writing by the debtor after the order for relief under chapter 7.

Section 727(b) of the House amendment adopts a similar provision contained in the Senate amendment modifying the effect of discharge. The provision makes clear that the debtor is discharged from all debts that arose before the date of the order for relief under chapter 7 in addition to any debt which is determined under section 502 as if it were a prepetition claim. Thus, if a case is converted from chapter 11 or chapter 13 to a case under chapter 7, all debts prior to the time of conversion are discharged, in addition to debts determined after the date of conversion of a kind specified in section 502, that are to be determined as prepetition claims. This modification is particularly important with respect to an individual debtor who files a petition under chapter 11 or chapter 13 of title 11 if the case is converted to chapter 7. The logical result of the House amendment is to equate the result that obtains whether the case is converted from another chapter to chapter 7, or whether the other chapter proceeding is dismissed and a new case is commenced by filing a petition under chapter 7.

SENATE REPORT NO. 95–989

This section is the heart of the fresh start provisions of the bankruptcy law. Subsection (a) requires the court to grant a debtor a discharge unless one of nine conditions is met. The first condition is that the debtor is not an individual. This is a change from present law, under which corporations and partnerships may be discharged in liquidation cases, though they rarely are. The change in policy will avoid trafficking in corporate shells and in bankrupt partnerships. "Individual" includes a deceased individual, so that if the debtor dies during the bankruptcy case, he will nevertheless be released from his debts, and his estate will not be liable for them. Creditors will be entitled to only one satisfaction—from the bankruptcy estate and not from the probate estate.

The next three grounds for denial of discharge center on the debtor's wrongdoing in or in connection with the bankruptcy case. They are derived from Bankruptcy Act §14c [section 32(c) of former title 11]. If the debtor, with intent to hinder, delay, or defraud his creditors or an officer of the estate, has transferred, removed, destroyed, mutilated, or concealed, or has permitted any such action with respect to, property of the debtor within the year preceding the case, or property of the estate after the commencement of the case, then the debtor is denied discharge. The debtor is also denied discharge if he has concealed, destroyed, mutilated, falsified, or failed to keep or preserve any books and records from which his financial condition might be ascertained, unless the act or failure to act was justified under all the circumstances of the case. The fourth ground for denial of discharge is the commission of a bankruptcy crime, although the standard of proof is preponderance of the evidence rather than proof beyond a reasonable doubt. These crimes include the making of a false oath or account, the use or presentation of a false claim, the giving or receiving of money for acting or forbearing to act, and the withholding from an officer of the estate entitled to possession of books and records relating to the debtor's financial affairs.

The fifth ground for denial of discharge is the failure of the debtor to explain satisfactorily any loss of assets or deficiency of assets to meet the debtor's liabilities. The sixth ground concerns refusal to testify. It is a change from present law, under which the debtor may be denied discharge for legitimately exercising his right against self-incrimination. Under this provision, the debtor may be denied discharge if he refuses to obey any lawful order of the court, or if he refuses to testify after having been granted immunity or after improperly invoking the constitutional privilege against self-incrimination.

The seventh ground for denial of discharge is the commission of an act specified in grounds two through six during the year before the debtor's case in connection with another bankruptcy case concerning an insider.

The eighth ground for denial of discharge is derived from §14c(5) of the Bankruptcy Act [section 32(c)(5) of former title 11]. If the debtor has been granted a discharge in a case commenced within 6 years preceding the present bankruptcy case, he is denied discharge. This provision, which is no change from current law with respect to straight bankruptcy, is the 6-year bar to discharge. Discharge under chapter 11 will bar a discharge for 6 years. As under current law, confirmation of a composition wage earner plan under chapter 13 is a basis for invoking the 6-year bar.

The ninth ground is approval by the court of a waiver of discharge.

Subsection (b) specifies that the discharge granted under this section discharges the debtor from all debts that arose before the date of the order for relief. It is irrelevant whether or not a proof of claim was filed with respect to the debt, and whether or not the claim based on the debt was allowed.

Subsection (c) permits the trustee, or a creditor, to object to discharge. It also permits the court, on request of a party in interest, to order the trustee to examine the acts and conduct of the debtor to determine whether a ground for denial of discharge exists.

Subsection (d) requires the court to revoke a discharge already granted in certain circumstances. If the debtor obtained the discharge through fraud, if he acquired and concealed property of the estate, or if he refused to obey a court order or to testify, the discharge is to be revoked.

Subsection (e) permits the trustee or a creditor to request revocation of a discharge within 1 year after the discharge is granted, on the grounds of fraud, and within one year of discharge or the date of the closing of the case, whichever is later, on other grounds.

REFERENCES IN TEXT

The Bankruptcy Act, referred to in subsec. (a)(7), is act July 1, 1898, ch. 541, 30 Stat. 544, as amended, which was classified generally to former Title 11.

Sections 14, 371, and 476 of the Bankruptcy Act, referred to in subsec. (a)(8), are section 14 of act July 1, 1898, ch. 541, 30 Stat. 550, section 371 of act July 1, 1898, ch. 541, as added June 22, 1938, ch. 575, §1, 52 Stat. 912, and section 476 of act July 1, 1898, ch. 541, as added June 22, 1938, ch. 575, §1, 52 Stat. 924, which were classified to sections 32, 771, and 876 of former Title 11.

Sections 660 and 661 of the Bankruptcy Act, referred to in subsec. (a)(9), are sections 660 and 661 of act July 1, 1898, ch. 541, as added June 22, 1938, ch. 575, §1, 52 Stat. 935, 936, which were classified to sections 1060 and 1061 of former Title 11.

AMENDMENTS

2005—Subsec. (a)(8). Pub. L. 109-8, §312(1), substituted "8 years" for "six years".

Subsec. (a)(11). Pub. L. 109-8, §106(b), added par. (11).

Subsec. (a)(12). Pub. L. 109-8, §330(a), added par. (12).

Subsec. (d)(4). Pub. L. 109-8, §603(d), added par. (4).

1986—Subsec. (a)(9). Pub. L. 99-554, §257(s), inserted reference to section 1228 of this title.

Subsec. (c). Pub. L. 99-554, §220, amended subsec. (c) generally, substituting "The trustee, a creditor, or the United States trustee may object" for "The trustee or a creditor may object" in par. (1).

Subsec. (d). Pub. L. 99-554, §220, amended subsec. (d) generally, substituting ", a creditor, or the United States trustee," for "or a creditor," in provisions preceding par. (1) and "acquisition of or entitlement to such property" for "acquisition of, or entitlement to, such property" in par. (2).

Subsec. (e). Pub. L. 99-554, §220, amended subsec. (e) generally, substituting "The trustee, a creditor, or the United States trustee may" for "The trustee or a creditor may" in provisions preceding par. (1), "section within" for "section, within" and "discharge is granted" for "discharge was granted" in par. (1), "section before" for "section, before" in provisions of par. (2) preceding subpar. (A), and "discharge; and" for "discharge; or" in par. (2)(A).

1984—Subsec. (a)(6)(C). Pub. L. 98-353, §480(a)(1), substituted "properly" for "property".

Subsec. (a)(7). Pub. L. 98-353, §480(a)(2), inserted ", under this title or under the Bankruptcy Act," after "another case".

Subsec. (a)(8). Pub. L. 98-353, §480(a)(3), substituted "371," for "371".

Subsec. (c)(1). Pub. L. 98-353, §480(b), substituted "to the granting of a discharge" for "to discharge".

Subsec. (e)(2)(A). Pub. L. 98-353, §480(c), substituted "or" for "and".

EFFECTIVE DATE OF 2005 AMENDMENT

Amendment by section 603(d) of Pub. L. 109-8 effective 18 months after Apr. 20, 2005, see section 603(e) of Pub. L. 109-8, set out as a note under section 521 of this title.

Amendments by sections 106(b), 312(1), and 330(a) of Pub. L. 109-8 effective 180 days after Apr. 20, 2005, with amendments by sections 106(b) and 312(1) of Pub. L. 109-8 not applicable with respect to cases commenced under this title before such effective date, except as otherwise provided, and amendment by section 330(a) of Pub. L. 109-8 applicable with respect to cases commenced under this title on or after Apr. 20, 2005, see section 1501 of Pub. L. 109-8, set out as a note under section 101 of this title.

EFFECTIVE DATE OF 1986 AMENDMENT

Amendment by section 257 of Pub. L. 99-554 effective 30 days after Oct. 27, 1986, but not applicable to cases commenced under this title before that date, see section 302(a), (c)(1) of Pub. L. 99-554, set out as a note under section 581 of Title 28, Judiciary and Judicial Procedure.

Effective date and applicability of amendment by section 220 of Pub. L. 99-554 dependent upon the judicial district involved, see section 302(d), (e) of Pub. L. 99-554.

EFFECTIVE DATE OF 1984 AMENDMENT

Amendment by Pub. L. 98-353 effective with respect to cases filed 90 days after July 10, 1984, see section 552(a) of Pub. L. 98-353, set out as a note under section 101 of this title.

[§728. Repealed. Pub. L. 109-8, title VII, §719(b)(1), Apr. 20, 2005, 119 Stat. 133]

Section, Pub. L. 95-598, Nov. 6, 1978, 92 Stat. 2611; Pub. L. 98-353, title III, §481, July 10, 1984, 98 Stat. 382; Pub. L. 99-554, title II, §257(t), Oct. 27, 1986, 100 Stat. 3116, related to special tax provisions.

EFFECTIVE DATE OF REPEAL

Repeal effective 180 days after Apr. 20, 2005, and not applicable with respect to cases commenced under this title before such effective date, except as otherwise provided, see section 1501 of Pub. L. 109-8, set out as an Effective Date of 2005 Amendment note under section 101 of this title.

SUBCHAPTER III—STOCKBROKER LIQUIDATION

§741. Definitions for this subchapter

In this subchapter—

(1) "Commission" means Securities and Exchange Commission;

(2) "customer" includes—

(A) entity with whom a person deals as principal or agent and that has a claim against such person on account of a security received, acquired, or held by such person in the ordinary course of such person's business as a stockbroker, from or for the securities account or accounts of such entity—

(i) for safekeeping;

(ii) with a view to sale;

(iii) to cover a consummated sale;

(iv) pursuant to a purchase;

(v) as collateral under a security agreement; or

(vi) for the purpose of effecting registration of transfer; and

(B) entity that has a claim against a person arising out of—

(i) a sale or conversion of a security received, acquired, or held as specified in subparagraph (A) of this paragraph; or

(ii) a deposit of cash, a security, or other property with such person for the purpose of purchasing or selling a security;

(3) "customer name security" means security—

(A) held for the account of a customer on the date of the filing of the petition by or on behalf of the debtor;

(B) registered in such customer's name on such date or in the process of being so registered under instructions from the debtor; and

(C) not in a form transferable by delivery on such date;

(4) "customer property" means cash, security, or other property, and proceeds of such cash, security, or property, received, acquired, or held by or for the account of the debtor, from or for the securities account of a customer—

(A) including—

(i) property that was unlawfully converted from and that is the lawful property of the estate;

(ii) a security held as property of the debtor to the extent such security is necessary to meet a net equity claim of a customer based on a security of the same class and series of an issuer;

(iii) resources provided through the use or realization of a customer's debit cash balance or a debit item includible in the Formula for Determination of Reserve Requirement for Brokers and Dealers as promulgated by the Commission under the Securities Exchange Act of 1934; and

(iv) other property of the debtor that any applicable law, rule, or regulation requires to be set aside or held for the benefit of a customer, unless including such property as customer property would not significantly increase customer property; but

(B) not including—

(i) a customer name security delivered to or reclaimed by a customer under section 751 of this title; or

(ii) property to the extent that a customer does not have a claim against the debtor based on such property;

(5) "margin payment" means payment or deposit of cash, a security, or other property, that is commonly known to the securities trade as original margin, initial margin, maintenance margin, or variation margin, or as a mark-to-market payment, or that secures an obligation of a participant in a securities clearing agency;

(6) "net equity" means, with respect to all accounts of a customer that such customer has in the same capacity—

(A)(i) aggregate dollar balance that would remain in such accounts after the liquidation, by sale or purchase, at the time of the filing of the petition, of all securities positions in all such accounts, except any customer name securities of such customer; minus

(ii) any claim of the debtor against such customer in such capacity that would have been owing immediately after such liquidation; plus

(B) any payment by such customer to the trustee, within 60 days after notice under section 342 of this title, of any business related claim of the debtor against such customer in such capacity;

(7) "securities contract"—

(A) means—

(i) a contract for the purchase, sale, or loan of a security, a certificate of deposit, a mortgage loan, any interest in a mortgage loan, a group or index of securities, certificates of deposit, or mortgage loans or interests therein (including an interest therein or based on the value thereof), or option on any of the foregoing, including an option to purchase or sell any such security, certificate of deposit, mortgage loan, interest, group or index, or option, and including any repurchase or reverse repurchase transaction on any such security, certificate of deposit, mortgage loan, interest, group or index, or option (whether or not such repurchase or reverse repurchase transaction is a "repurchase agreement", as defined in section 101);

(ii) any option entered into on a national securities exchange relating to foreign currencies;

(iii) the guarantee (including by novation) by or to any securities clearing agency of a settlement of cash, securities, certificates of deposit, mortgage loans or interests therein, group or index of securities, or mortgage loans or interests therein (including any interest therein or based on the value thereof), or option on any of the foregoing, including an option to purchase or sell any such security, certificate of deposit, mortgage loan, interest, group or index, or option (whether or not such settlement is in connection with any agreement or transaction referred to in clauses (i) through (xi));

(iv) any margin loan;

(v) any extension of credit for the clearance or settlement of securities transactions;

(vi) any loan transaction coupled with a securities collar transaction, any prepaid forward securities transaction, or any total return swap transaction coupled with a securities sale transaction;

(vii) any other agreement or transaction that is similar to an agreement or transaction referred to in this subparagraph;

(viii) any combination of the agreements or transactions referred to in this subparagraph;

(ix) any option to enter into any agreement or transaction referred to in this subparagraph;

(x) a master agreement that provides for an agreement or transaction referred to in clause (i), (ii), (iii), (iv), (v), (vi), (vii), (viii), or (ix), together with all supplements to any such master agreement, without regard to whether the master agreement provides for an agreement or transaction that is not a securities contract under this subparagraph, except that such master agreement shall be considered to be a securities contract under this subparagraph only with respect to each agreement or transaction under such master agreement that is referred to in clause (i), (ii), (iii), (iv), (v), (vi), (vii), (viii), or (ix); or

(xi) any security agreement or arrangement or other credit enhancement related to any agreement or transaction referred to in this subparagraph, including any guarantee or reimbursement obligation by or to a stockbroker, securities clearing agency, financial institution, or financial participant in connection with any agreement or transaction referred to in this subparagraph, but not to exceed the damages in connection with any such agreement or transaction, measured in accordance with section 562; and

(B) does not include any purchase, sale, or repurchase obligation under a participation in a commercial mortgage loan;

(8) "settlement payment" means a preliminary settlement payment, a partial settlement payment, an interim settlement payment, a settlement payment on account, a final settlement payment, or any other similar payment commonly used in the securities trade; and

(9) "SIPC" means Securities Investor Protection Corporation.

(Pub. L. 95–598, Nov. 6, 1978, 92 Stat. 2611; Pub. L. 97–222, §8, July 27, 1982, 96 Stat. 237; Pub. L. 98–353, title III, §482, July 10, 1984, 98 Stat. 382; Pub. L. 103–394, title V, §501(d)(25), Oct. 22, 1994, 108 Stat. 4146; Pub. L. 109–8, title IX, §907(a)(2), Apr. 20, 2005, 119 Stat. 173; Pub. L. 109–390, §5(a)(3), Dec. 12, 2006, 120 Stat. 2697.)

HISTORICAL AND REVISION NOTES

LEGISLATIVE STATEMENTS

Section 741(6) of the House bill and Senate amendment is deleted by the House amendment since the defined term is used only in section 741(4)(A)(iii). A corresponding change is made in that section.

SENATE REPORT NO. 95–989

Section 741 sets forth definitions for subchapter III of chapter 7.

Paragraph (1) defines "Commission" to mean the Securities and Exchange Commission.

Paragraph (2) defines "customer" to include anybody that interacts with the debtor in a capacity that concerns securities transactions. The term embraces cash or margin customers of a broker or dealer in the broadest sense.

Paragraph (3) defines "customer name security" in a restrictive fashion to include only non-transferable securities that are registered, or in the process of being registered in a customer's own name. The securities must not be endorsed by the customer and the stockbroker must not be able to legally transfer the securities by delivery, by a power of attorney, or otherwise.

Paragraph (4) defines "customer property" to include all property of the debtor that has been segregated for customers or property that should have been segregated but was unlawfully converted. Clause (i) refers to customer property not properly segregated by the debtor or customer property converted and then recovered so as to become property of the estate. Unlawfully converted property that has been transferred to a third party is excluded until it is recovered as property of the estate by virtue of the avoiding powers. The concept excludes customer name securities that have been delivered to or reclaimed by a customer and any property properly belonging to the stockholder, such as money deposited by a customer to pay for securities that the stockholder has distributed to such customer.

Paragraph (5) [enacted as (6)] defines "net equity" to establish the extent to which a customer will be entitled to share in the single and separate fund. Accounts of a customer are aggregated and offset only to the extent the accounts are held by the customer in the same capacity. Thus, a personal account is separate from an account held as trustee. In a community property state an account held for the community is distinct from an account held as separate property.

The net equity is computed by liquidating all securities positions in the accounts and crediting the account with any amount due to the customer. Regardless of the actual dates, if any, of liquidation, the customer is only entitled to the liquidation value at the time of the filing of the petition. To avoid double counting, the liquidation value of customer name securities belonging to a customer is excluded from net equity. Thus, clause (ii) includes claims against a customer resulting from the liquidation of a security under clause (i). The value of a security on which trading has been suspended at the time of the filing of the petition will be estimated. Once the net liquidation value is computed, any amount that the customer owes to the stockbroker is subtracted including any amount that would be owing after the hypothetical liquidation, such as brokerage fees. Debts owed by the customer to the debtor, other than in a securities related transaction, will not reduce the net equity of the customer. Finally, net equity is increased by any payment by the customer to the debtor actually paid within 60 days after notice. The principal reason a customer would make such a payment is to reclaim customer name securities under §751.

Paragraph (6) defines "1934 Act" to mean the Securities Exchange Act of 1934 [15 U.S.C. 78a et seq.].

Paragraph (7) [enacted as (9)] defines "SIPC" to mean the Securities Investor Protection Corporation.

REFERENCES IN TEXT

The Securities Exchange Act of 1934, referred to in par. (4)(A)(iii), is act June 6, 1934, ch. 404, 48 Stat. 881, as amended, which is classified principally to chapter 2B (§78a et seq.) of Title 15, Commerce and Trade. For complete classification of this Act to the Code, see section 78a of Title 15 and Tables.

AMENDMENTS

2006—Par. (7)(A)(i). Pub. L. 109–390, §5(a)(3)(A), substituted "a mortgage loan," for "a mortgage loan or" and inserted "(whether or not such repurchase or reverse repurchase transaction is a 'repurchase agreement', as defined in section 101)" before semicolon at end.

Par. (7)(A)(iii). Pub. L. 109–390, §5(a)(3)(B), inserted "(including by novation)" after "the guarantee" and "(whether or not such settlement is in connection with any agreement or transaction referred to in clauses (i) through (xi))" before semicolon at end.

Par. (7)(A)(v) to (vii). Pub. L. 109–390, §5(a)(3)(D), (E), added cls. (v) and (vi) and redesignated former cl. (v) as (vii). Former cls. (vi) and (vii) redesignated (viii) and (ix), respectively.

Par. (7)(A)(viii). Pub. L. 109–390, §5(a)(3)(D), redesignated cl. (vi) as (viii). Former cl. (viii) redesignated (x).

Pub. L. 109–390, §5(a)(3)(C), substituted "(vii), (viii), or (ix)" for "or (vii)" in two places.

Par. (7)(A)(ix) to (xi). Pub. L. 109–390, §5(a)(3)(D), redesignated cls. (vii) to (ix) as (ix) to (xi), respectively.

2005—Par. (7). Pub. L. 109–8 added par. (7) and struck out former par. (7) which read as follows: "'securities contract' means contract for the purchase, sale, or loan of a security, including an option for the purchase or sale of a security, certificate of deposit, or group or index of securities (including any interest therein or based on the value thereof), or any option entered into on a national securities exchange relating to foreign currencies, or the guarantee of any settlement of cash or securities by or to a securities clearing agency;".

1994—Par. (4)(A)(iii). Pub. L. 103–394 struck out "(15 U.S.C. 78a et seq.)" after "Act of 1934".

1984—Par. (2)(A). Pub. L. 98–353, §482(1), substituted "with whom a person deals" for "with whom the debtor deals", "that has a claim" for "that holds a claim", "against such person" for "against the debtor", "held by such person" for "held by the debtor", and "such person's business as a stockbroker," for "business as a stockbroker".

Par. (2)(B). Pub. L. 98–353, §482(2)(A), (B), substituted "has a claim" for "holds a claim" and "against a person" for "against the debtor" in provisions preceding cl. (i).

Par. (2)(B)(ii). Pub. L. 98–353, §482(2)(C), substituted "such person" for "the debtor".

Par. (4)(A)(i). Pub. L. 98–353, §482(3), substituted "from and that is the lawful" for "and that is".

Par. (6)(A)(i). Pub. L. 98–353, §482(4), inserted a comma after "petition" and "any" after "except".

Par. (7). Pub. L. 98–353, §482(5), amended par. (7) generally, inserting provisions relating to options for the purchase or sale of certificates of deposit, or a group or index of securities (including any interest therein or based on the value thereof), or any option entered into on a national securities exchange relating to foreign currencies.

Par. (8). Pub. L. 98–353, §482(6), inserted "a final settlement payment,".

1982—Par. (4). Pub. L. 97–222, §8(1), struck out "at any time" after "security, or property," in provisions preceding subpar. (A), and inserted "of a customer" after "claim" in subpar. (A)(ii).

Par. (5). Pub. L. 97–222, §8(3), added par. (5). Former par. (5) redesignated (6).

Par. (6). Pub. L. 97–222, §8(2), (4), redesignated former par. (5) as (6), in provisions preceding subpar. (A), substituted "all accounts of a customer that such customer has" for "the aggregate of all of a customer's accounts that such customer holds", in subpar. (A)(2) inserted "in such capacity", and in subpar. (B) inserted "in such capacity". Former par. (6) redesignated (9).

Pars. (7), (8). Pub. L. 97–222, §8(5), added pars. (7) and (8).

Par. (9). Pub. L. 97–222, §8(2), (6), redesignated former par. (6) as (9) and substituted "Securities" for "Security".

EFFECTIVE DATE OF 2006 AMENDMENT

Amendment by Pub. L. 109–390 not applicable to any cases commenced under this title or to appointments made under any Federal or State law, before Dec. 12, 2006, see section 7 of Pub. L. 109–390, set out as a note under section 101 of this title.

EFFECTIVE DATE OF 2005 AMENDMENT

Amendment by Pub. L. 109–8 effective 180 days after Apr. 20, 2005, and not applicable with respect to cases commenced under this title before such effective date, except as otherwise provided, see section 1501 of Pub. L. 109–8, set out as a note under section 101 of this title.

EFFECTIVE DATE OF 1994 AMENDMENT

Amendment by Pub. L. 103–394 effective Oct. 22, 1994, and not applicable with respect to cases commenced under this title before Oct. 22, 1994, see section 702 of Pub. L. 103–394, set out as a note under section 101 of this title.

EFFECTIVE DATE OF 1984 AMENDMENT

Amendment by Pub. L. 98–353 effective with respect to cases filed 90 days after July 10, 1984, see section 552(a) of Pub. L. 98–353, set out as a note under section 101 of this title.

§742. Effect of section 362 of this title in this subchapter

Notwithstanding section 362 of this title, SIPC may file an application for a protective decree under the Securities Investor Protection Act of 1970. The filing of such application stays all proceedings in the case under this title unless and until such application is dismissed. If SIPC completes the liquidation of the debtor, then the court shall dismiss the case.

(Pub. L. 95–598, Nov. 6, 1978, 92 Stat. 2613; Pub. L. 97–222, §9, July 27, 1982, 96 Stat. 237; Pub. L. 103–394, title V, §501(d)(26), Oct. 22, 1994, 108 Stat. 4146.)

HISTORICAL AND REVISION NOTES

LEGISLATIVE STATEMENTS

Section 742 of the House amendment deletes a sentence contained in the Senate amendment requiring the trustee in an interstate stock-brokerage liquidation to comply with the provisions of subchapter IV of chapter 7 if the debtor is also a commodity broker. The House amendment expands the requirement to require the SIPC trustee to perform such duties, if the debtor is a commodity broker, under section 7(b) of the Securities Investor Protection Act [15 U.S.C. 78ggg(b)]. The requirement is deleted from section 742 since the trustee of an intrastate stockbroker will be bound by the provisions of subchapter IV of chapter 7 if the debtor is also a commodity broker by reason of section 103 of title 11.

SENATE REPORT NO. 95–989

Section 742 indicates that the automatic stay does not prevent SIPC from filing an application for a protective decree under SIPA. If SIPA does file such an application, then all bankruptcy proceedings are suspended until the SIPC action is completed. If SIPC completes liquidation of the stockbroker then the bankruptcy case is dismissed.

REFERENCES IN TEXT

The Securities Investor Protection Act of 1970, referred to in text, is Pub. L. 91–598, Dec. 30, 1970, 84 Stat. 1636, as amended, which is classified generally to chapter 2B–1 (§78aaa et seq.) of Title 15, Commerce and Trade. For complete classification of this Act to the Code, see section 78aaa of Title 15 and Tables.

AMENDMENTS

1994—Pub. L. 103–394 struck out "(15 U.S.C. 78aaa et seq.)" after "Act of 1970".

1982—Pub. L. 97–222 substituted "title" for "chapter" after "all proceedings in the case under this".

EFFECTIVE DATE OF 1994 AMENDMENT

Amendment by Pub. L. 103–394 effective Oct. 22, 1994, and not applicable with respect to cases commenced under this title before Oct. 22, 1994, see section 702 of Pub. L. 103–394, set out as a note under section 101 of this title.

§743. Notice

The clerk shall give the notice required by section 342 of this title to SIPC and to the Commission.

(Pub. L. 95–598, Nov. 6, 1978, 92 Stat. 2613; Pub. L. 99–554, title II, §283(t), Oct. 27, 1986, 100 Stat. 3118; Pub. L. 103–394, title V, §501(d)(27), Oct. 22, 1994, 108 Stat. 4146.)

HISTORICAL AND REVISION NOTES

SENATE REPORT NO. 95–989

Section 743 requires that notice of the order for relief be given to SIPC and to the SEC in every stockbroker case.

AMENDMENTS

1994—Pub. L. 103–394 substituted "342" for "342(a)".

1986—Pub. L. 99–554, which directed the amendment of this section by striking "(d)", rather than "(a)", could not be executed because "(d)" did not appear in text. See 1994 Amendment note above.

EFFECTIVE DATE OF 1994 AMENDMENT

Amendment by Pub. L. 103–394 effective Oct. 22, 1994, and not applicable with respect to cases commenced under this title before Oct. 22, 1994, see section 702 of Pub. L. 103–394, set out as a note under section 101 of this title.

EFFECTIVE DATE OF 1986 AMENDMENT

Amendment by Pub. L. 99–554 effective 30 days after Oct. 27, 1986, see section 302(a) of Pub. L. 99–554, set out as a note under section 581 of Title 28, Judiciary and Judicial Procedure.

§ 744. Executory contracts

Notwithstanding section 365(d)(1) of this title, the trustee shall assume or reject, under section 365 of this title, any executory contract of the debtor for the purchase or sale of a security in the ordinary course of the debtor's business, within a reasonable time after the date of the order for relief, but not to exceed 30 days. If the trustee does not assume such a contract within such time, such contract is rejected.

(Pub. L. 95–598, Nov. 6, 1978, 92 Stat. 2613; Pub. L. 97–222, § 10, July 27, 1982, 96 Stat. 238.)

HISTORICAL AND REVISION NOTES

SENATE REPORT NO. 95–989

Section 744 instructs the court to give the trustee a reasonable time, not to exceed 30 days, to assume or reject any executory contract of the stockbroker to buy or sell securities. Any contract not assumed within the time fixed by the court is considered to be rejected.

AMENDMENTS

1982—Pub. L. 97–222 inserted "but" after "relief,".

§ 745. Treatment of accounts

(a) Accounts held by the debtor for a particular customer in separate capacities shall be treated as accounts of separate customers.

(b) If a stockbroker or a bank holds a customer net equity claim against the debtor that arose out of a transaction for a customer of such stockbroker or bank, each such customer of such stockbroker or bank shall be treated as a separate customer of the debtor.

(c) Each trustee's account specified as such on the debtor's books, and supported by a trust deed filed with, and qualified as such by, the Internal Revenue Service, and under the Internal Revenue Code of 1986, shall be treated as a separate customer account for each beneficiary under such trustee account.

(Pub. L. 95–598, Nov. 6, 1978, 92 Stat. 2613; Pub. L. 97–222, § 11, July 27, 1982, 96 Stat. 238; Pub. L. 98–353, title III, § 483, July 10, 1984, 98 Stat. 383; Pub. L. 103–394, title V, § 501(d)(28), Oct. 22, 1994, 108 Stat. 4146.)

HISTORICAL AND REVISION NOTES

SENATE REPORT NO. 95–989

Section 745(a) indicates that each account held by a customer in a separate capacity is to be considered a separate account. This prevents the offset of accounts held in different capacities.

Subsection (b) indicates that a bank or another stockbroker that is a customer of a debtor is considered to hold its customers accounts in separate capacities. Thus a bank or other stockbroker is not treated as a mutual fund for purposes of bulk investment. This protects unrelated customers of a bank or other stockholder from having their accounts offset.

Subsection (c) effects the same result with respect to a trust so that each beneficiary is treated as the customer of the debtor rather than the trust itself. This eliminates any doubt whether a trustee holds a personal account in a separate capacity from his trustee's account.

REFERENCES IN TEXT

The Internal Revenue Code of 1986, referred to in subsec. (c), is classified generally to Title 26, Internal Revenue Code.

AMENDMENTS

1994—Subsec. (c). Pub. L. 103–394 substituted "Internal Revenue Code of 1986" for "Internal Revenue Code of 1954 (26 U.S.C. 1 et seq.)".

1984—Subsec. (a). Pub. L. 98–353 inserted "the debtor for" after "by".

1982—Subsec. (c). Pub. L. 97–222 substituted "Each" for "A".

EFFECTIVE DATE OF 1994 AMENDMENT

Amendment by Pub. L. 103–394 effective Oct. 22, 1994, and not applicable with respect to cases commenced under this title before Oct. 22, 1994, see section 702 of Pub. L. 103–394, set out as a note under section 101 of this title.

EFFECTIVE DATE OF 1984 AMENDMENT

Amendment by Pub. L. 98–353 effective with respect to cases filed 90 days after July 10, 1984, see section 552(a) of Pub. L. 98–353, set out as a note under section 101 of this title.

§ 746. Extent of customer claims

(a) If, after the date of the filing of the petition, an entity enters into a transaction with the debtor, in a manner that would have made such entity a customer had such transaction occurred before the date of the filing of the petition, and such transaction was entered into by such entity in good faith and before the qualification under section 322 of this title of a trustee, such entity shall be deemed a customer, and the date of such transaction shall be deemed to be the date of the filing of the petition for the purpose of determining such entity's net equity.

(b) An entity does not have a claim as a customer to the extent that such entity transferred to the debtor cash or a security that, by contract, agreement, understanding, or operation of law, is—

(1) part of the capital of the debtor; or

(2) subordinated to the claims of any or all creditors.

(Pub. L. 95–598, Nov. 6, 1978, 92 Stat. 2613; Pub. L. 97–222, § 12, July 27, 1982, 96 Stat. 238.)

HISTORICAL AND REVISION NOTES

SENATE REPORT NO. 95–989

Section 746(a) protects entities who deal in good faith with the debtor after the filing of the petition and before a trustee is appointed by deeming such entities to be customers. The principal application of this section will be in an involuntary case before the order for relief, because § 701(b) requires prompt appointment of an interim trustee after the order for relief.

Subsection (b) indicates that an entity who holds securities that are either part of the capital of the debtor or that are subordinated to the claims of any creditor of the debtor is not a customer with respect to those securities. This subsection will apply when the stockbroker has sold securities in itself to the customer or when the customer has otherwise placed such securities in an account with the stockbroker.

AMENDMENTS

1982—Pub. L. 97–222, § 12(c), substituted "claims" for "claim" in section catchline.

Subsec. (a). Pub. L. 97–222, § 12(a), substituted "enters into" for "effects, with respect to cash or a security,", struck out "with respect to such cash or security" wherever appearing, and substituted "the date of the filing of the petition" for "such date", and "entered into" for "effected".

Subsec. (b). Pub. L. 97–222, §12(b), substituted "transferred to the debtor" for "has a claim for" in provisions preceding par. (1), and struck out "is" in par. (2).

§747. Subordination of certain customer claims

Except as provided in section 510 of this title, unless all other customer net equity claims have been paid in full, the trustee may not pay in full or pay in part, directly or indirectly, any net equity claim of a customer that was, on the date the transaction giving rise to such claim occurred—

(1) an insider;

(2) a beneficial owner of at least five percent of any class of equity securities of the debtor, other than—

(A) nonconvertible stock having fixed preferential dividend and liquidation rights; or

(B) interests of limited partners in a limited partnership;

(3) a limited partner with a participation of at least five percent in the net assets or net profits of the debtor; or

(4) an entity that, directly or indirectly, through agreement or otherwise, exercised or had the power to exercise control over the management or policies of the debtor.

(Pub. L. 95–598, Nov. 6, 1978, 92 Stat. 2613; Pub. L. 97–222, §13, July 27, 1982, 96 Stat. 238.)

HISTORICAL AND REVISION NOTES

SENATE REPORT NO. 95–989

Section 747 subordinates to other customer claims, all claims of a customer who is an insider, a five percent owner of the debtor, or otherwise in control of the debtor.

AMENDMENTS

1982—Pub. L. 97–222 substituted "the transaction giving rise to such claim occurred" for "such claim arose" in provisions preceding par. (1).

§748. Reduction of securities to money

As soon as practicable after the date of the order for relief, the trustee shall reduce to money, consistent with good market practice, all securities held as property of the estate, except for customer name securities delivered or reclaimed under section 751 of this title.

(Pub. L. 95–598, Nov. 6, 1978, 92 Stat. 2614.)

HISTORICAL AND REVISION NOTES

SENATE REPORT NO. 95–989

Section 748 requires the trustee to liquidate all securities, except for customer name securities, of the estate in a manner consistent with good market practice. The trustee should refrain from flooding a thin market with a large percentage of shares in any one issue. If the trustee holds restricted securities or securities in which trading has been suspended, then the trustee must arrange to liquidate such securities in accordance with the securities laws. A private placement may be the only exemption available with the customer of the debtor the best prospect for such a placement. The subsection does not permit such a customer to bid in his net equity as part of the purchase price; a contrary result would permit a customer to receive a greater percentage on his net equity claim than other customers.

§749. Voidable transfers

(a) Except as otherwise provided in this section, any transfer of property that, but for such transfer, would have been customer property, may be avoided by the trustee, and such property shall be treated as customer property, if and to the extent that the trustee avoids such transfer under section 544, 545, 547, 548, or 549 of this title. For the purpose of such sections, the property so transferred shall be deemed to have been property of the debtor and, if such transfer was made to a customer or for a customer's benefit, such customer shall be deemed, for the purposes of this section, to have been a creditor.

(b) Notwithstanding sections 544, 545, 547, 548, and 549 of this title, the trustee may not avoid a transfer made before seven days after the order for relief if such transfer is approved by the Commission by rule or order, either before or after such transfer, and if such transfer is—

(1) a transfer of a securities contract entered into or carried by or through the debtor on behalf of a customer, and of any cash, security, or other property margining or securing such securities contract; or

(2) the liquidation of a securities contract entered into or carried by or through the debtor on behalf of a customer.

(Pub. L. 95–598, Nov. 6, 1978, 92 Stat. 2614; Pub. L. 97–222, §14, July 27, 1982, 96 Stat. 238; Pub. L. 111–16, §2(8), May 7, 2009, 123 Stat. 1607.)

HISTORICAL AND REVISION NOTES

SENATE REPORT NO. 95–989

Section 749 indicates that if the trustee avoids a transfer, property recovered is customer property to any extent it would have been customer property but for the transfer. The section clarifies that a customer who receives a transfer of property of the debtor is a creditor and that property in a customer's account is property of a creditor for purposes of the avoiding powers.

AMENDMENTS

2009—Subsec. (b). Pub. L. 111–16 substituted "seven days" for "five days" in introductory provisions.

1982—Pub. L. 97–222 substituted "(a) Except as otherwise provided in this section, any" for "Any", and "but" for "except", inserted "such property", substituted "or 549" for "549, or 724(a)", and added subsec. (b).

EFFECTIVE DATE OF 2009 AMENDMENT

Amendment by Pub. L. 111–16 effective Dec. 1, 2009, see section 7 of Pub. L. 111–16, set out as a note under section 109 of this title.

§750. Distribution of securities

The trustee may not distribute a security except under section 751 of this title.

(Pub. L. 95–598, Nov. 6, 1978, 92 Stat. 2614.)

HISTORICAL AND REVISION NOTES

SENATE REPORT NO. 95–989

Section 750 forbids the trustee from distributing a security other than a customer name security. The term "distribution" refers to a distribution to customers in satisfaction of net equity claims and is not intended to preclude the trustee from liquidating securities under proposed 11 U.S.C. 748.

§ 751. Customer name securities

The trustee shall deliver any customer name security to or on behalf of the customer entitled to such security, unless such customer has a negative net equity. With the approval of the trustee, a customer may reclaim a customer name security after payment to the trustee, within such period as the trustee allows, of any claim of the debtor against such customer to the extent that such customer will not have a negative net equity after such payment.

(Pub. L. 95–598, Nov. 6, 1978, 92 Stat. 2614.)

HISTORICAL AND REVISION NOTES

SENATE REPORT NO. 95–989

Section 751 requires the trustee to deliver a customer name security to the customer entitled to such security unless the customer has a negative net equity. The customer's net equity will be negative when the amount owed by the customer to the stockbroker exceeds the liquidation value of the non-customer name securities in the customer's account. If the customer is a net debtor of the stockbroker, then the trustee may permit the customer to repay debts to the stockbroker so that the customer will no longer be in debt to the stockbroker. If the customer refuses to pay such amount, then the court may order the customer to endorse the security in order that the trustee may liquidate such property.

§ 752. Customer property

(a) The trustee shall distribute customer property ratably to customers on the basis and to the extent of such customers' allowed net equity claims and in priority to all other claims, except claims of the kind specified in section 507(a)(2) of this title that are attributable to the administration of such customer property.

(b)(1) The trustee shall distribute customer property in excess of that distributed under subsection (a) of this section in accordance with section 726 of this title.

(2) Except as provided in section 510 of this title, if a customer is not paid the full amount of such customer's allowed net equity claim from customer property, the unpaid portion of such claim is a claim entitled to distribution under section 726 of this title.

(c) Any cash or security remaining after the liquidation of a security interest created under a security agreement made by the debtor, excluding property excluded under section 741(4)(B) of this title, shall be apportioned between the general estate and customer property in the same proportion as the general estate of the debtor and customer property were subject to such security interest.

(Pub. L. 95–598, Nov. 6, 1978, 92 Stat. 2614; Pub. L. 97–222, § 15, July 27, 1982, 96 Stat. 238; Pub. L. 98–353, title III, § 484, July 10, 1984, 98 Stat. 383; Pub. L. 109–8, title XV, § 1502(a)(3), Apr. 20, 2005, 119 Stat. 216.)

HISTORICAL AND REVISION NOTES

SENATE REPORT NO. 95–989

Section 752(a) requires the trustee to distribute customer property to customers based on the amount of their net equity claims. Customer property is to be distributed in priority to all claims except expenses of administration entitled to priority under § 507(1). It is anticipated that the court will apportion such administrative claims on an equitable basis between the general estate and the customer property of the debtor.

Subsection (b)(1) indicates that in the event customer property exceeds customers net equity claims and administrative expenses, the excess pours over into the general estate. This event would occur if the value of securities increased dramatically after the order for relief but before liquidation by the trustee. Subsection (b)(2) indicates that the unpaid portion of a customer's net equity claim is entitled to share in the general estate as an unsecured claim unless subordinated by the court under proposed 11 U.S.C. 501. A net equity claim of a customer that is subordinated under section 747 is entitled to share in distribution under section 726(a)(2) unless subordinated under section 510 independently of the subordination under section 747.

Subsection (c) provides for apportionment between customer property and the general estate of any equity of the debtor in property remaining after a secured creditor liquidates a security interest. This might occur if a stockbroker hypothecates securities of his own and of his customers if the value of the hypothecated securities exceeds the debt owed to the secured party. The apportionment is to be made according to the ratio of customer property and general property of the debtor that comprised the collateral. The subsection refers to cash and securities of customers to include any customer property unlawfully converted by the stockbroker in the course of such a transaction. The apportionment is made subject to section 741(4)(B) to insure that property in a customer's account that is owed to the stockbroker will not be considered customer property. This recognizes the right of the stockbroker to withdraw money that has been erroneously placed in a customer's account or that is otherwise owing to the stockbroker.

AMENDMENTS

2005—Subsec. (a). Pub. L. 109–8 substituted "507(a)(2)" for "507(a)(1)".

1984—Subsec. (a). Pub. L. 98–353, § 484(a), substituted "customers' allowed" for "customers allowed", "except claims of the kind" for "except claims", and "such customer property" for "customer property".

Subsec. (b)(2). Pub. L. 98–353, § 484(b), substituted "section 726" for "section 726(a)".

1982—Subsec. (c). Pub. L. 97–222 substituted "Any cash or security remaining after the liquidation of a security interest created under a security agreement made by the debtor, excluding property excluded under section 741(4)(B) of this title, shall be apportioned between the general estate and customer property in the same proportion as the general estate of the debtor and customer property were subject to such security interest" for "Subject to section 741(4)(B) of this title, any cash or security remaining after the liquidation of a security interest created under a security agreement made by the debtor shall be apportioned between the general estate and customer property in the proportion that the general property of the debtor and the cash or securities of customers were subject to such security interest".

EFFECTIVE DATE OF 2005 AMENDMENT

Amendment by Pub. L. 109–8 effective 180 days after Apr. 20, 2005, and not applicable with respect to cases commenced under this title before such effective date, except as otherwise provided, see section 1501 of Pub. L. 109–8, set out as a note under section 101 of this title.

EFFECTIVE DATE OF 1984 AMENDMENT

Amendment by Pub. L. 98–353 effective with respect to cases filed 90 days after July 10, 1984, see section 552(a) of Pub. L. 98–353, set out as a note under section 101 of this title.

§ 753. Stockbroker liquidation and forward contract merchants, commodity brokers, stockbrokers, financial institutions, financial participants, securities clearing agencies, swap participants, repo participants, and master netting agreement participants

Notwithstanding any other provision of this title, the exercise of rights by a forward contract merchant, commodity broker, stockbroker, financial institution, financial participant, securities clearing agency, swap participant, repo participant, or master netting agreement participant under this title shall not affect the priority of any unsecured claim it may have after the exercise of such rights.

(Added Pub. L. 109–8, title IX, § 907(m), Apr. 20, 2005, 119 Stat. 181.)

EFFECTIVE DATE

Section effective 180 days after Apr. 20, 2005, and not applicable with respect to cases commenced under this title before such effective date, except as otherwise provided, see section 1501 of Pub. L. 109–8, set out as an Effective Date of 2005 Amendment note under section 101 of this title.

SUBCHAPTER IV—COMMODITY BROKER LIQUIDATION

§ 761. Definitions for this subchapter

In this subchapter—

(1) "Act" means Commodity Exchange Act;

(2) "clearing organization" means a derivatives clearing organization registered under the Act;

(3) "Commission" means Commodity Futures Trading Commission;

(4) "commodity contract" means—

(A) with respect to a futures commission merchant, contract for the purchase or sale of a commodity for future delivery on, or subject to the rules of, a contract market or board of trade;

(B) with respect to a foreign futures commission merchant, foreign future;

(C) with respect to a leverage transaction merchant, leverage transaction;

(D) with respect to a clearing organization, contract for the purchase or sale of a commodity for future delivery on, or subject to the rules of, a contract market or board of trade that is cleared by such clearing organization, or commodity option traded on, or subject to the rules of, a contract market or board of trade that is cleared by such clearing organization;

(E) with respect to a commodity options dealer, commodity option;

(F) any other agreement or transaction that is similar to an agreement or transaction referred to in this paragraph;

(G) any combination of the agreements or transactions referred to in this paragraph;

(H) any option to enter into an agreement or transaction referred to in this paragraph;

(I) a master agreement that provides for an agreement or transaction referred to in subparagraph (A), (B), (C), (D), (E), (F), (G), or (H), together with all supplements to such master agreement, without regard to whether the master agreement provides for an agreement or transaction that is not a commodity contract under this paragraph, except that the master agreement shall be considered to be a commodity contract under this paragraph only with respect to each agreement or transaction under the master agreement that is referred to in subparagraph (A), (B), (C), (D), (E), (F), (G), or (H); or

(J) any security agreement or arrangement or other credit enhancement related to any agreement or transaction referred to in this paragraph, including any guarantee or reimbursement obligation by or to a commodity broker or financial participant in connection with any agreement or transaction referred to in this paragraph, but not to exceed the damages in connection with any such agreement or transaction, measured in accordance with section 562;

(5) "commodity option" means agreement or transaction subject to regulation under section 4c(b) of the Act;

(6) "commodity options dealer" means person that extends credit to, or that accepts cash, a security, or other property from, a customer of such person for the purchase or sale of an interest in a commodity option;

(7) "contract market" means a registered entity;

(8) "contract of sale", "commodity", "derivatives clearing organization", "future delivery", "board of trade", "registered entity", and "futures commission merchant" have the meanings assigned to those terms in the Act;

(9) "customer" means—

(A) with respect to a futures commission merchant—

(i) entity for or with whom such futures commission merchant deals and that holds a claim against such futures commission merchant on account of a commodity contract made, received, acquired, or held by or through such futures commission merchant in the ordinary course of such futures commission merchant's business as a futures commission merchant from or for the commodity futures account of such entity; or

(ii) entity that holds a claim against such futures commission merchant arising out of—

(I) the making, liquidation, or change in the value of a commodity contract of a kind specified in clause (i) of this subparagraph;

(II) a deposit or payment of cash, a security, or other property with such futures commission merchant for the purpose of making or margining such a commodity contract; or

(III) the making or taking of delivery on such a commodity contract;

(B) with respect to a foreign futures commission merchant—

(i) entity for or with whom such foreign futures commission merchant deals and that holds a claim against such foreign futures commission merchant on account of a commodity contract made, received, acquired, or held by or through such foreign futures commission merchant in the ordinary course of such foreign futures commission merchant's business as a foreign futures commission merchant from or for the foreign futures account of such entity; or

(ii) entity that holds a claim against such foreign futures commission merchant arising out of—

(I) the making, liquidation, or change in value of a commodity contract of a kind specified in clause (i) of this subparagraph;

(II) a deposit or payment of cash, a security, or other property with such foreign futures commission merchant for the purpose of making or margining such a commodity contract; or

(III) the making or taking of delivery on such a commodity contract;

(C) with respect to a leverage transaction merchant—

(i) entity for or with whom such leverage transaction merchant deals and that holds a claim against such leverage transaction merchant on account of a commodity contract engaged in by or with such leverage transaction merchant in the ordinary course of such leverage transaction merchant's business as a leverage transaction merchant from or for the leverage account of such entity; or

(ii) entity that holds a claim against such leverage transaction merchant arising out of—

(I) the making, liquidation, or change in value of a commodity contract of a kind specified in clause (i) of this subparagraph;

(II) a deposit or payment of cash, a security, or other property with such leverage transaction merchant for the purpose of entering into or margining such a commodity contract; or

(III) the making or taking of delivery on such a commodity contract;

(D) with respect to a clearing organization, clearing member of such clearing organization with whom such clearing organization deals and that holds a claim against such clearing organization on account of cash, a security, or other property received by such clearing organization to margin, guarantee, or secure a commodity contract in such clearing member's proprietary account or customers' account; or

(E) with respect to a commodity options dealer—

(i) entity for or with whom such commodity options dealer deals and that holds a claim on account of a commodity contract made, received, acquired, or held by or through such commodity options dealer in the ordinary course of such commodity options dealer's business as a commodity options dealer from or for the commodity options account of such entity; or

(ii) entity that holds a claim against such commodity options dealer arising out of—

(I) the making of, liquidation of, exercise of, or a change in value of, a commodity contract of a kind specified in clause (i) of this subparagraph; or

(II) a deposit or payment of cash, a security, or other property with such commodity options dealer for the purpose of making, exercising, or margining such a commodity contract;

(10) "customer property" means cash, a security, or other property, or proceeds of such cash, security, or property, received, acquired, or held by or for the account of the debtor, from or for the account of a customer—

(A) including—

(i) property received, acquired, or held to margin, guarantee, secure, purchase, or sell a commodity contract;

(ii) profits or contractual or other rights accruing to a customer as a result of a commodity contract;

(iii) an open commodity contract;

(iv) specifically identifiable customer property;

(v) warehouse receipt or other document held by the debtor evidencing ownership of or title to property to be delivered to fulfill a commodity contract from or for the account of a customer;

(vi) cash, a security, or other property received by the debtor as payment for a commodity to be delivered to fulfill a commodity contract from or for the account of a customer;

(vii) a security held as property of the debtor to the extent such security is necessary to meet a net equity claim based on a security of the same class and series of an issuer;

(viii) property that was unlawfully converted from and that is the lawful property of the estate; and

(ix) other property of the debtor that any applicable law, rule, or regulation requires to be set aside or held for the benefit of a customer, unless including such property as customer property would not significantly increase customer property; but

(B) not including property to the extent that a customer does not have a claim against the debtor based on such property;

(11) "foreign future" means contract for the purchase or sale of a commodity for future delivery on, or subject to the rules of, a board of trade outside the United States;

(12) "foreign futures commission merchant" means entity engaged in soliciting or accepting orders for the purchase or sale of a foreign future or that, in connection with such a solicitation or acceptance, accepts cash, a security, or other property, or extends credit to margin, guarantee, or secure any trade or contract that results from such a solicitation or acceptance;

(13) "leverage transaction" means agreement that is subject to regulation under section 19 of the Commodity Exchange Act, and that is commonly known to the commodities trade as a margin account, margin contract, leverage account, or leverage contract;

(14) "leverage transaction merchant" means person in the business of engaging in leverage transactions;

(15) "margin payment" means payment or deposit of cash, a security, or other property, that is commonly known to the commodities trade as original margin, initial margin, maintenance margin, or variation margin, including mark-to-market payments, settlement payments, variation payments, daily settlement payments, and final settlement payments made as adjustments to settlement prices;

(16) "member property" means customer property received, acquired, or held by or for the account of a debtor that is a clearing organization, from or for the proprietary account of a customer that is a clearing member of the debtor; and

(17) "net equity" means, subject to such rules and regulations as the Commission promulgates under the Act, with respect to the aggregate of all of a customer's accounts that such customer has in the same capacity—

(A) the balance remaining in such customer's accounts immediately after—

(i) all commodity contracts of such customer have been transferred, liquidated, or become identified for delivery; and

(ii) all obligations of such customer in such capacity to the debtor have been offset; plus

(B) the value, as of the date of return under section 766 of this title, of any specifically identifiable customer property actually returned to such customer before the date specified in subparagraph (A) of this paragraph; plus

(C) the value, as of the date of transfer, of—

(i) any commodity contract to which such customer is entitled that is transferred to another person under section 766 of this title; and

(ii) any cash, security, or other property of such customer transferred to such other person under section 766 of this title to margin or secure such transferred commodity contract.

(Pub. L. 95–598, Nov. 6, 1978, 92 Stat. 2615; Pub. L. 97–222, §16, July 27, 1982, 96 Stat. 238; Pub. L. 98–353, title III, §485, July 10, 1984, 98 Stat. 383; Pub. L. 103–394, title V, §501(d)(29), Oct. 22, 1994, 108 Stat. 4146; Pub. L. 106–554, §1(a)(5) [title I, §112(c)(6)], Dec. 21, 2000, 114 Stat. 2763, 2763A–395; Pub. L. 109–8, title IX, §907(a)(3), Apr. 20, 2005, 119 Stat. 174.)

Historical and Revision Notes

Legislative Statements

Subchapter IV of chapter 7 represents a compromise between similar chapters in the House bill and Senate amendment. Section 761(2) of the House amendment defines "clearing organization" to cover an organization that clears commodity contracts on a contract market or a board of trade; the expansion of the definition is intended to include clearing organizations that clear commodity options. Section 761(4) of the House amendment adopts the term "commodity contract" as used in section 761(5) of the Senate amendment but with the more precise substantive definitions contained in section 761(8) of the House bill. The definition is modified to insert "board of trade" to cover commodity options. Section 761(5) of the House amendment adopts the definition contained in section 761(6) of the Senate amendment in preference to the definition contained in section 761(4) of the House bill which erroneously included onions. Section 761(9) of the House amendment represents a compromise between similar provisions contained in section 761(10) of the Senate amendment and section 761(9) of the House bill. The compromise adopts the substance contained in the House bill and adopts the terminology of "commodity contract" in lieu of "contractual commitment" as suggested in the Senate amendment. Section 761(10) of the House amendment represents a compromise between similar sections in the House bill and Senate amendment regarding the definition of "customer property." The definition of "distribution share" contained in section 761(12) of the Senate amendment is deleted as unnecessary. Section 761(12) of the House amendment adopts a definition of "foreign futures commission merchant" similar to the definition contained in section 761(14) of the Senate amendment. The definition is modified to cover either an entity engaged in soliciting orders or the purchase or sale of a foreign future, or an entity that accepts cash, a security, or other property for credit in connection with such a solicitation or acceptance. Section 761(13) of the House amendment adopts a definition of "leverage transaction" identical to the definition contained in section 761(15) of the Senate amendment. Section 761(15) of the House amendment adopts the definition of "margin payment" contained in section 761(17) of the Senate amendment. Section 761(17) of the House amendment adopts a definition of "net equity" derived from section 761(15) of the House bill.

Senate Report No. 95–989

Paragraph (1) defines "Act" to mean the Commodity Exchange Act [7 U.S.C. 1 et seq.].

Paragraph (2) defines "clearing organization" to mean an organization that clears (i.e., matches purchases and sales) commodity futures contracts made on or subject to the rules of a contract market or commodity options transactions made on or subject to the rules of a commodity option exchange. Although commodity option trading on exchanges is currently prohibited, it is anticipated that CFTC may permit such trading in the future.

Paragraphs (3) and (4) define terms "Commission" and "commodity futures contract".

Paragraph (5) [enacted as (4)] defines "commodity contract" to mean a commodity futures contract (§761(4)), a commodity option (§761(6)), or a leverage contract (§761(15)).

Paragraph (b) [probably should be "(6)" which was enacted as (5)] defines "commodity option" by reference to section 4c(b) of the Commodity Exchange Act [7 U.S.C. 6c(b)].

Paragraphs (7), (8), and (9) [enacted as (6), (7), and (8)] define "commodity options dealer," "contract market," "contract of sale," "commodity," "future delivery," "board of trade," and "futures commission merchant."

Paragraph (10) [enacted as (9)] defines the term "customer" to mean with respect to a futures commission merchant or a foreign futures commission merchant, the entity for whom the debtor carries a commodity futures contract or foreign future, or with whom such a contract is carried (such as another commodity broker), or from whom the debtor has received, acquired, or holds cash, securities, or other property arising out of or connected with specified transactions involving commodity futures contracts or foreign futures. This section also defines "customer" in the context of leverage transaction merchants, clearing organizations, and commodity options dealers. Persons associated with a commodity broker, such as its employees, officers, or partners, may be customers under this definition.

The definition of "customer" serves to isolate that class of persons entitled to the protection subchapter

IV provides to customers. In addition, section 101(5) defines "commodity broker" to mean a futures commission merchant, foreign futures commission merchant, clearing organization, leverage transaction merchant, or commodity options dealer, with respect to which there is a customer. Accordingly, the definition of customer also serves to designate those entities which must utilize chapter 7 and are precluded from reorganizing under chapter 11.

Paragraph (11) [enacted as (10)] defines "customer property" to mean virtually all property or proceeds thereof, received, acquired, or held by or for the account of the debtor for a customer arising out of or in connection with a transaction involving a commodity contract.

Paragraph (12) defines "distribution share" to mean the amount to which a customer is entitled under section 765(a).

Paragraphs (13), (14), (15), and (16) [enacted as (11), (12), (13), and (14)] define "foreign future," "foreign futures commission merchant," "leverage transaction," and "leverage transaction merchant."

Paragraph (17) [enacted as (15)] defines "margin payment" to mean a payment or deposit commonly known to the commodities trade as original margin, initial margin, or variation margin.

Paragraph (18) [enacted as (16)] defines "member property."

Paragraph (19) [enacted as (17)] defines "net equity" to be the sum of (A) the value of all customer property remaining in a customer's account immediately after all commodity contracts of such customer have been transferred, liquidated, or become identified for delivery and all obligations of such customer to the debtor have been offset (such as margin payments, whether or not called, and brokerage commissions) plus (B) the value of specifically identifiable customer property previously returned to the customer by the trustee, plus (C) if the trustee has transferred any commodity contract to which the customer is entitled or any margin or security for such contract, the value of such contract and margin or security. Net equity, therefore, will be the total amount of customer property to which a customer is entitled as of the date of the filing of the bankruptcy petition, although valued at subsequent dates. The Commission is given authority to promulgate rules and regulations to further refine this definition.

HOUSE REPORT NO. 95–595

Paragraph (8) [enacted as (4)] is a dynamic definition of "contractual commitment". The definition will vary depending on the character of the debtor in each case. If the debtor is a futures commission merchant or a clearing organization, then subparagraphs (A) and (D) indicate that the definition means a contract of sale of a commodity for future delivery on a contract market. If the debtor is a foreign futures commission merchant, a leverage transaction merchant, or a commodity options dealer, then subparagraphs (B), (C), and (E) indicate that the definition means foreign future, leverage transaction, or commodity option, respectively.

Paragraph (9) defines "customer" in a similar style. It is anticipated that a debtor with multifaceted characteristics will have separate estates for each different kind of customer. Thus, a debtor that is a leverage transaction merchant and a commodity options dealer would have separate estates for the leverage transaction customers and for the options customers, and a general estate for other creditors. Customers for each kind of commodity broker, except the clearing organization, arise from either of two relationships. In subparagraphs (A), (B), (C), and (E), clause (i) treats with customers to the extent of contractual commitments with the debtor in either a broker or a dealer relationship. Clause (ii) treats with customers to the extent of proceeds from contractual commitments or deposits for the purpose of making contractual commitments. The customer of the clearing organization is a member with a proprietary or customers' account.

Paragraph (10) defines "customer property" to include all property in customer accounts and property that should have been in those accounts but was diverted through conversion or mistake. Clause (i) refers to customer property not properly segregated by the debtor or customer property converted and then recovered so as to become property of the estate. Clause (vii) is intended to exclude property that would cost more to recover from a third party than the value of the property itself. Subparagraph (B) excludes property in a customer's account that belongs to the commodity broker, such as a contract placed in the account by error, or cash due the broker for a margin payment that the broker has made.

Paragraph (15) [enacted as (17)] defines "net equity" to include the value of all contractual commitments at the time of liquidation or transfer less any obligations owed by the customer to the debtor, such as brokerage fees. In addition, the term includes the value of any specifically identifiable property as of the date of return to the customer and the value of any customer property transferred to another commodity broker as of the date of transfer. This definition places the risk of market fluctuations on the customer until commitments leave the estate.

REFERENCES IN TEXT

The Commodity Exchange Act, referred to in pars. (1), (2), (8), and (17), is act Sept. 21, 1922, ch. 369, 42 Stat. 998, as amended, which is classified generally to chapter 1 (§1 et seq.) of Title 7, Agriculture. Sections 4c(b) and 19 of the Act are classified to sections 6c(b) and 23, respectively, of Title 7. For complete classification of this Act to the Code, see section 1 of Title 7 and Tables.

AMENDMENTS

2005—Par. (4)(F) to (J). Pub. L. 109–8 added subpars. (F) to (J).

2000—Par. (2). Pub. L. 106–554, §1(a)(5) [title I, §112(c)(6)(A)], amended par. (2) generally. Prior to amendment, par. (2) read as follows: "'clearing organization' means organization that clears commodity contracts made on, or subject to the rules of, a contract market or board of trade;".

Par. (7). Pub. L. 106–554, §1(a)(5) [title I, §112(c)(6)(B)], amended par. (7) generally. Prior to amendment, par. (7) read as follows: "'contract market' means board of trade designated as a contract market by the Commission under the Act;".

Par. (8). Pub. L. 106–554, §1(a)(5) [title I, §112(c)(6)(C)], amended par. (8) generally. Prior to amendment, par. (8) read as follows: "'contract of sale', 'commodity', 'future delivery', 'board of trade', and 'futures commission merchant' have the meanings assigned to those terms in the Act;".

1994—Par. (1). Pub. L. 103–394, §501(d)(29)(A), struck out "(7 U.S.C. 1 et seq.)" after "Act".

Par. (5). Pub. L. 103–394, §501(d)(29)(B), struck out "(7 U.S.C. 6c(b))" after "Act".

Par. (13). Pub. L. 103–394, §501(d)(29)(C), struck out "(7 U.S.C. 23)" after "Act".

1984—Par. (10)(A)(viii). Pub. L. 98–353 substituted "from and that is the lawful property" for "and that is property".

1982—Par. (2). Pub. L. 97–222, §16(1), inserted "made" after "commodity contracts".

Par. (4). Pub. L. 97–222, §16(2), substituted "with respect to" for "if the debtor is" wherever appearing, and substituted "cleared by such clearing organization, or commodity option traded on, or subject to the rules of, a contract market or board of trade that is cleared by such clearing organization" for "cleared by the debtor" in subpar. (D).

Par. (9). Pub. L. 97–222, §16(3), substituted "with respect to" for "if the debtor is" wherever appearing, in subpar. (A) substituted "such futures commission merchant" for "the debtor" wherever appearing and "such futures commission merchant's" for "the debtor's", in subpar. (B) substituted "such foreign futures commission merchant" for "the debtor" wherever appearing and "such foreign futures commission merchant's" for "the debtor's", in subpar. (C) substituted "such leverage transaction merchant" for "the debtor" wherever appearing and "such leverage transaction merchant's" for "the debtor's", inserted "or" after the semicolon in cl. (i), and substituted "holds" for "hold" in cl. (ii), in subpar. (D) substituted "such clearing organization" for "the debtor" wherever appearing, and in subpar. (E) substituted "such commodity options dealer" for "the debtor" wherever appearing and "such commodity options dealer's" for "the debtor's".

Par. (10). Pub. L. 97–222, §16(4), struck out "at any time" after "security, or property," in provisions preceding subpar. (A).

Par. (12). Pub. L. 97–222, §16(5), inserted a comma after "property" and struck out the comma after "credit".

Par. (13). Pub. L. 97–222, §16(6), substituted "section 19 of the Commodity Exchange Act (7 U.S.C. 23)" for "section 217 of the Commodity Futures Trading Commission Act of 1974 (7 U.S.C. 15a)".

Par. (14). Pub. L. 97–222, §16(7), struck out "that is engaged" after "means person".

Par. (15). Pub. L. 97–222, §16(8), substituted "mark-to-market payments, settlement payments, variation payments, daily settlement payments, and final settlement payments made as adjustments to settlement prices" for "a daily variation settlement payment".

Par. (16). Pub. L. 97–222, §16(9), struck out "at any time" after "customer property".

Par. (17). Pub. L. 97–222, §16(10), in provisions preceding subpar. (A) substituted "has" for "holds", in subpar. (A) inserted "the" after "(A)" in provisions preceding cl. (i), and "in such capacity" after "customer" in cl. (ii).

EFFECTIVE DATE OF 2005 AMENDMENT

Amendment by Pub. L. 109–8 effective 180 days after Apr. 20, 2005, and not applicable with respect to cases commenced under this title before such effective date, except as otherwise provided, see section 1501 of Pub. L. 109–8, set out as a note under section 101 of this title.

EFFECTIVE DATE OF 1994 AMENDMENT

Amendment by Pub. L. 103–394 effective Oct. 22, 1994, and not applicable with respect to cases commenced under this title before Oct. 22, 1994, see section 702 of Pub. L. 103–394, set out as a note under section 101 of this title.

EFFECTIVE DATE OF 1984 AMENDMENT

Amendment by Pub. L. 98–353 effective with respect to cases filed 90 days after July 10, 1984, see section 552(a) of Pub. L. 98–353, set out as a note under section 101 of this title.

§762. Notice to the Commission and right to be heard

(a) The clerk shall give the notice required by section 342 of this title to the Commission.

(b) The Commission may raise and may appear and be heard on any issue in a case under this chapter.

(Pub. L. 95–598, Nov. 6, 1978, 92 Stat. 2618.)

HISTORICAL AND REVISION NOTES

SENATE REPORT NO. 95–989

Section 762 provides that the Commission shall be given such notice as is appropriate of an order for relief in a bankruptcy case and that the Commission may raise and may appear and may be heard on any issue in case involving a commodity broker liquidation.

§763. Treatment of accounts

(a) Accounts held by the debtor for a particular customer in separate capacities shall be treated as accounts of separate customers.

(b) A member of a clearing organization shall be deemed to hold such member's proprietary account in a separate capacity from such member's customers' account.

(c) The net equity in a customer's account may not be offset against the net equity in the account of any other customer.

(Pub. L. 95–598, Nov. 6, 1978, 92 Stat. 2618; Pub. L. 98–353, title III, §486, July 10, 1984, 98 Stat. 383.)

HISTORICAL AND REVISION NOTES

SENATE REPORT NO. 95–989

Section 763 provides for separate treatment of accounts held in separate capacities. A deficit in one account held for a customer may not be offset against the net equity in another account held by the same customer in a separate capacity or held by another customer.

AMENDMENTS

1984—Subsec. (a). Pub. L. 98–353 substituted "by the debtor for" for "by" and "treated as" for "deemed to be".

EFFECTIVE DATE OF 1984 AMENDMENT

Amendment by Pub. L. 98–353 effective with respect to cases filed 90 days after July 10, 1984, see section 552(a) of Pub. L. 98–353, set out as a note under section 101 of this title.

§764. Voidable transfers

(a) Except as otherwise provided in this section, any transfer by the debtor of property that, but for such transfer, would have been customer property, may be avoided by the trustee, and such property shall be treated as customer property, if and to the extent that the trustee avoids such transfer under section 544, 545, 547, 548, 549, or 724(a) of this title. For the purpose of such sections, the property so transferred shall be deemed to have been property of the debtor, and, if such transfer was made to a customer or for a customer's benefit, such customer shall be deemed, for the purposes of this section, to have been a creditor.

(b) Notwithstanding sections 544, 545, 547, 548, 549, and 724(a) of this title, the trustee may not avoid a transfer made before seven days after the order for relief, if such transfer is approved by the Commission by rule or order, either before or after such transfer, and if such transfer is—

(1) a transfer of a commodity contract entered into or carried by or through the debtor on behalf of a customer, and of any cash, securities, or other property margining or securing such commodity contract; or

(2) the liquidation of a commodity contract entered into or carried by or through the debtor on behalf of a customer.

(Pub. L. 95–598, Nov. 6, 1978, 92 Stat. 2618; Pub. L. 97–222, §17, July 27, 1982, 96 Stat. 240; Pub. L. 98–353, title III, §487, July 10, 1984, 98 Stat. 383; Pub. L. 111–16, §2(9), May 7, 2009, 123 Stat. 1607.)

HISTORICAL AND REVISION NOTES

LEGISLATIVE STATEMENTS

Section 764 of the House amendment is derived from the House bill.

SENATE REPORT NO. 95–989

Section 764 permits the trustee to void any transfer of property that, except for such transfer, would have been customer property, to the extent permitted under section 544, 545, 547, 548, 549, or 724(a).

HOUSE REPORT NO. 95–595

Section 764 indicates the extent to which the avoiding powers may be used by the trustee under subchapter IV of chapter 7. If property recovered would have been customer property if never transferred, then subsection (a) indicates that it will be so treated when recovered.

Subsection (b) prohibits avoiding any transaction that occurs before or within five days after the petition if the transaction is approved by the Commission and concerns an open contractual commitment. This enables the Commission to exercise its discretion to protect the integrity of the market by insuring that transactions cleared with other brokers will not be undone on a preference or a fraudulent transfer theory.

Subsection (c) insulates variation margin payments and other deposits from the avoiding powers except to the extent of actual fraud under section 548(a)(1). This facilitates prepetition transfers and protects the ordinary course of business in the market.

AMENDMENTS

2009—Subsec. (b). Pub. L. 111–16 substituted "seven days" for "five days" in introductory provisions.

1984—Subsec. (a). Pub. L. 98–353 substituted "any transfer by the debtor" for "any transfer".

1982—Subsec. (a). Pub. L. 97–222, §17(a), substituted "but" for "except", inserted "such property" after "trustee, and", and substituted "shall be" for "is" wherever appearing.

Subsec. (b). Pub. L. 97–222, §17(b), substituted "order for relief" for "date of the filing of the petition".

Subsec. (c). Pub. L. 97–222, §17(c), struck out subsec. (c) which provided that the trustee could not avoid a transfer that was a margin payment to or deposit with a commodity broker or forward contract merchant or was a settlement payment made by a clearing organization and that occurred before the commencement of the case.

EFFECTIVE DATE OF 2009 AMENDMENT

Amendment by Pub. L. 111–16 effective Dec. 1, 2009, see section 7 of Pub. L. 111–16, set out as a note under section 109 of this title.

EFFECTIVE DATE OF 1984 AMENDMENT

Amendment by Pub. L. 98–353 effective with respect to cases filed 90 days after July 10, 1984, see section 552(a) of Pub. L. 98–353, set out as a note under section 101 of this title.

§ 765. Customer instructions

(a) The notice required by section 342 of this title to customers shall instruct each customer—

(1) to file a proof of such customer's claim promptly, and to specify in such claim any specifically identifiable security, property, or commodity contract; and

(2) to instruct the trustee of such customer's desired disposition, including transfer under section 766 of this title or liquidation, of any commodity contract specifically identified to such customer.

(b) The trustee shall comply, to the extent practicable, with any instruction received from a customer regarding such customer's desired disposition of any commodity contract specifically identified to such customer. If the trustee has transferred, under section 766 of this title, such a commodity contract, the trustee shall transmit any such instruction to the commodity broker to whom such commodity contract was so transferred.

(Pub. L. 95–598, Nov. 6, 1978, 92 Stat. 2619; Pub. L. 97–222, §18, July 27, 1982, 96 Stat. 240; Pub. L. 98–353, title III, §488, July 10, 1984, 98 Stat. 383.)

HISTORICAL AND REVISION NOTES

For Historical and Revision Notes for this section, see Historical and Revision Notes set out under section 766 of this title.

AMENDMENTS

1984—Subsec. (a). Pub. L. 98–353 substituted "notice required by" for "notice under".

1982—Subsec. (b). Pub. L. 97–222 substituted "commodity contract" for "commitment".

EFFECTIVE DATE OF 1984 AMENDMENT

Amendment by Pub. L. 98–353 effective with respect to cases filed 90 days after July 10, 1984, see section 552(a) of Pub. L. 98–353, set out as a note under section 101 of this title.

§ 766. Treatment of customer property

(a) The trustee shall answer all margin calls with respect to a specifically identifiable commodity contract of a customer until such time as the trustee returns or transfers such commodity contract, but the trustee may not make a margin payment that has the effect of a distribution to such customer of more than that to which such customer is entitled under subsection (h) or (i) of this section.

(b) The trustee shall prevent any open commodity contract from remaining open after the last day of trading in such commodity contract, or into the first day on which notice of intent to deliver on such commodity contract may be tendered, whichever occurs first. With respect to any commodity contract that has remained open after the last day of trading in such commodity contract or with respect to which delivery must be made or accepted under the rules of the contract market on which such commodity contract was made, the trustee may operate the business of the debtor for the purpose of—

(1) accepting or making tender of notice of intent to deliver the physical commodity underlying such commodity contract;

(2) facilitating delivery of such commodity; or

(3) disposing of such commodity if a party to such commodity contract defaults.

(c) The trustee shall return promptly to a customer any specifically identifiable security, property, or commodity contract to which such customer is entitled, or shall transfer, on such customer's behalf, such security, property, or commodity contract to a commodity broker that is not a debtor under this title, subject to such rules or regulations as the Commission may prescribe, to the extent that the value of such security, property, or commodity contract does not exceed the amount to which such customer would be entitled under subsection (h) or (i) of this section if such security, property, or commodity contract were not returned or transferred under this subsection.

(d) If the value of a specifically identifiable security, property, or commodity contract exceeds the amount to which the customer of the debtor is entitled under subsection (h) or (i) of this section, then such customer to whom such security, property, or commodity contract is specifically identified may deposit cash with the trustee equal to the difference between the value of such security, property, or commodity contract and such amount, and the trustee then shall—

(1) return promptly such security, property, or commodity contract to such customer; or

(2) transfer, on such customer's behalf, such security, property, or commodity contract to a commodity broker that is not a debtor under this title, subject to such rules or regulations as the Commission may prescribe.

(e) Subject to subsection (b) of this section, the trustee shall liquidate any commodity contract that—

(1) is identified to a particular customer and with respect to which such customer has not timely instructed the trustee as to the desired disposition of such commodity contract;

(2) cannot be transferred under subsection (c) of this section; or

(3) cannot be identified to a particular customer.

(f) As soon as practicable after the commencement of the case, the trustee shall reduce to money, consistent with good market practice, all securities and other property, other than commodity contracts, held as property of the estate, except for specifically identifiable securities or property distributable under subsection (h) or (i) of this section.

(g) The trustee may not distribute a security or other property except under subsection (h) or (i) of this section.

(h) Except as provided in subsection (b) of this section, the trustee shall distribute customer property ratably to customers on the basis and to the extent of such customers' allowed net equity claims, and in priority to all other claims, except claims of a kind specified in section 507(a)(2) of this title that are attributable to the administration of customer property. Such distribution shall be in the form of—

(1) cash;

(2) the return or transfer, under subsection (c) or (d) of this section, of specifically identifiable customer securities, property, or commodity contracts; or

(3) payment of margin calls under subsection (a) of this section.

Notwithstanding any other provision of this subsection, a customer net equity claim based on a proprietary account, as defined by Commission rule, regulation, or order, may not be paid either in whole or in part, directly or indirectly, out of customer property unless all other customer net equity claims have been paid in full.

(i) If the debtor is a clearing organization, the trustee shall distribute—

(1) customer property, other than member property, ratably to customers on the basis and to the extent of such customers' allowed net equity claims based on such customers' accounts other than proprietary accounts, and in priority to all other claims, except claims of a kind specified in section 507(a)(2) of this title that are attributable to the administration of such customer property; and

(2) member property ratably to customers on the basis and to the extent of such customers' allowed net equity claims based on such customers' proprietary accounts, and in priority to all other claims, except claims of a kind specified in section 507(a)(2) of this title that are attributable to the administration of member property or customer property.

(j)(1) The trustee shall distribute customer property in excess of that distributed under subsection (h) or (i) of this section in accordance with section 726 of this title.

(2) Except as provided in section 510 of this title, if a customer is not paid the full amount of such customer's allowed net equity claim from customer property, the unpaid portion of such claim is a claim entitled to distribution under section 726 of this title.

(Pub. L. 95–598, Nov. 6, 1978, 92 Stat. 2619; Pub. L. 97–222, §19, July 27, 1982, 96 Stat. 240; Pub. L. 98–353, title III, §489, July 10, 1984, 98 Stat. 383; Pub. L. 109–8, title XV, §1502(a)(4), Apr. 20, 2005, 119 Stat. 216.)

Historical and Revision Notes

legislative statements

Sections 765 and 766 of the House amendment represent a consolidation and redraft of sections 765, 766, 767, and 768 of the House bill and sections 765, 766, 767, and 768 of the Senate amendment. In particular, section 765(a) of the House amendment is derived from section 765(a) of the House bill and section 767(a) of the Senate amendment. Under section 765(a) of the House amendment customers are notified of the opportunity to immediately file proofs of claim and to identify specifically identifiable securities, property, or commodity contracts. The customer is also afforded an opportunity to instruct the trustee regarding the customer's desires concerning disposition of the customer's commodity contracts. Section 767(b) [probably should be 765(b)] makes clear that the trustee must comply with instructions received to the extent practicable, but in the event the trustee has transferred commodity contracts to a commodity broker, such instructions shall be forwarded to the broker.

Section 766(a) of the House amendment is derived from section 768(c) of the House bill and section 767(f) of the Senate amendment. Section 766(b) of the House amendment is derived from section 765(d) of the House bill, and section 767(g) of the Senate amendment. Section 766(c) of the House amendment is derived from section 768(a) of the House bill and section 767(e) of the Senate amendment. Section 766(d) of the House amendment is derived from section 768(b) of the House bill and the second sentence of section 767(e) of the Senate amendment.

Section 766(e) of the House amendment is derived from section 765(c) of the House bill and sections 767(c) and (d) of the Senate amendment. The provision clarifies that the trustee may liquidate a commodity contract only if the commodity contract cannot be transferred to a commodity broker under section 766(c), cannot be identified to a particular customer, or has been identified with respect to a particular customer, but with respect to which the customer's instructions have not been received.

Section 766(f) of the House amendment is derived from section 766(b) of the House bill and section 767(h) of the Senate amendment. The term "all securities and other property" is not intended to include a commodity contract. Section 766(g) of the House amendment is derived from section 766(a) of the House bill. Section 766(h) of the House amendment is derived from section 767(a) of the House bill and section 765(a) of the Senate amendment. In order to induce private trustees to undertake the difficult and risky job of liquidating a commodity broker, the House amendment contains a provision insuring that a pro rata share of administrative claims will be paid. The provision represents a compromise between the position taken in the House bill, subordinating customer property to all expenses of administration, and the position taken in the Senate amendment requiring the distribution of customer property in advance of any expenses of administration. The position in the Senate amendment is rejected since customers, in any event, would have to pay a brokerage commission or fee in the ordinary course of business. The compromise provision requires customers to pay only those administrative expenses that are attributable to the administration of customer property.

Section 766(i) of the House amendment is derived from section 767(b) of the House bill and contains a similar compromise with respect to expenses of administration as the compromise detailed in connection with section 766(h) of the House amendment. Section 766(j) of the House amendment is derived from section 767(c) of the House bill. No counterpart is contained in the Senate amendment. The provision takes account of the rare case where the estate has customer property in excess of customer claims and administrative expenses attributable to those claims. The section also specifies that to the extent a customer is not paid in full out of customer property, that the unpaid claim will be treated the same as any other general unsecured creditor.

Section 768 of the Senate amendment was deleted from the House amendment as unwise. The provision in the Senate amendment would have permitted the trustee to distribute customer property based upon an estimate of value of the customer's account, with no provision for recapture of excessive disbursements. Moreover, the section would have exonerated the trustee from any liability for such an excessive disbursement. Furthermore, the section is unclear with respect to the customer's rights in the event the trustee makes a distribution less than the share to which the customer is entitled. The provision is deleted in the House amendment so that this difficult problem may be handled on a case-by-case basis by the courts as the facts and circumstances of each case require.

Section 769 of the Senate amendment is deleted in the House amendment as unnecessary. The provision was intended to codify *Board of Trade v. Johnson*, 264 U.S. 1 (1924) [Ill.1924, 44 S.Ct. 232]. *Board of Trade against Johnson* is codified in section 363(f) of the House amendment which indicates the only five circumstances in which property may be sold free and clear of an interest in such property of an entity other than the estate.

Section 770 of the Senate amendment is deleted in the House amendment as unnecessary. That section would have permitted commodity brokers to liquidate commodity contracts, notwithstanding any contrary order of the court. It would require an extraordinary circumstance, such as a threat to the national security, to enjoin a commodity broker from liquidating a commodity contract. However, in those circumstances, an injunction must prevail. Failure of the House amendment to incorporate section 770 of the Senate amendment does not imply that the automatic stay prevents liquidation of commodity contracts by commodity brokers. To the contrary, whenever by contract, or otherwise, a commodity broker is entitled to liquidate a position as a result of a condition specified in a contract, other than a condition or default of the kind specified in section 365(b)(2) of title 11, the commodity broker may engage in such liquidation. To this extent, the commodity broker's contract with his customer is treated no differently than any other contract under section 365 of title 11.

SENATE REPORT NO. 95–989

[Section 765] Subsection (a) of this section [enacted as section 766(h)] provides that with respect to liquidation of commodity brokers which are not clearing organizations, the trustee shall distribute customer property to customers on the basis and to the extent of such customers' allowed net equity claims, and in priority to all other claims. This section grants customers' claims first priority in the distribution of the estate. Subsection (b) [enacted as section 766(i)] grants the same priority to member property and other customer property in the liquidation of a clearing organization. A fundamental purpose of these provisions is to ensure that the property entrusted by customers to their brokers will not be subject to the risks of the broker's business and will be available for disbursement to customers if the broker becomes bankrupt.

As a result of section 765, a customer need not trace any funds in order to avoid treatment as a general creditor as was required by the Seventh Circuit in *In re Rosenbaum Grain Corporation*.

Section 766 lists certain transfers which are not voidable by the trustee of a commodity broker. Subsection (a) exempts transfers approved by the Commission by rule or order, either before or after the transfer. It is expected that the Commission will use this power sparingly and only when necessary to effectuate the remedial purposes of this legislation, bearing in mind that the immediate transfer of customer accounts from bankrupt commodity brokers to solvent commodity brokers is one of the primary goals of this subchapter. The committee considered and rejected a provision in subsection (b) that would have exempted payments made to a commodity broker. The Commission may not by rule exempt such transfers. The Commission's prompt attention to the promulgation of such rules and regulations is expected.

Subsection (b) [enacted as section 764(c)] provides for the nonavoidability of margin payments made by a commodity broker, other than a clearing organization. If such payments are made by or to a clearing organization, they are nonavoidable pursuant to subsection (c). All other margin payments made by a commodity broker, other than a clearing organization, are nonavoidable if they meet the conditions set forth in subsection (b). Subsections (b)(1) and (b)(2) parallel the requirements for avoidance of fraudulent transfers and obligations under section 548. Subsection (b)(3) adds a requirement that there be collusion between the transferee and transferor in order for such payments to be voidable. It would be unfair to permit recovery from an innocent commodity broker since such brokers are, for the most part, simply conduits for margin payments and do not retain margin for use in their operations. Subsection (b)(4) would permit recovery of a subsequent transferee only if it had actual knowledge at the time of that subsequent transfer of the scheme to defraud. Again it should be noted that if the transfer is a margin payment and the subsequent transferee is a clearing organization, the transfer is nonavoidable under section 766(c).

Subsection (c) [enacted as section 548(d)(2)] overrules *Seligson v. New York Produce Exchange*, and provides as a matter of law that margin payments made by or to a clearing organization are not voidable.

Section 767 sets forth the procedures to be followed by the trustee. It should be emphasized that many of the duties imposed on the trustee are required to be discharged by the trustee immediately upon his appointment. The earlier these duties are discharged the less potential market disruption can result.

The initial duty of the trustee is to endeavor to transfer to another commodity broker or brokers all identified customer accounts together with the customer property margining such accounts, to the extent the trustee deems appropriate. Although it is preferable for all such accounts to be transferred, exigencies may dictate a partial transfer. The requirement that the value of the accounts and property transferred not exceed the customer's distribution share may necessitate a slight delay until the trustee can submit to the court, for its disapproval, an estimate of each customer's distribution share pursuant to section 768.

Subsection (c) [enacted as section 766(e)] provides that contemporaneously with the estimate of the distribution share and the transfer of identified customer accounts and property, subsection (c) provides that the trustee should make arrangements for the liquidation of all commodity contracts maintained by the debtor that are not identifiable to specific customers. These contracts would, of course, include all such contracts held in the debtor's proprietory [sic] account.

At approximately the same time, the trustee should notify each customer of the debtor's bankruptcy and instruct each customer immediately to submit a claim including any claim to a specifically identifiable security or other property, and advise the trustee as to the desired disposition of commodity contracts carried by the debtor for the customer.

This requirement is placed upon the trustee to insure that producers who have hedged their production in the commodities market are allowed the opportunity to preserve their positions. The theory of the commodity market is that it exists for producers and buyers of commodities and not for the benefit of the speculators whose transactions now comprise the overwhelming majority of trades. Maintenance of positions by hedges may require them to put up additional margin payments in the hours and days following the commodity broker bankruptcy, which they may be unable or unwilling to do. In such cases, their positions will be quickly liquidated by the trustee, but they must have the opportunity to make those margin payments before they are summarily liquidated out of the market to the detriment of their growing crop. The failure of the customer to advise the trustee as to disposition of the customer's commodity contract will not delay a transfer of a contract pursuant to subsection (b) so long as the contract can otherwise be identified to the customer. Nor will the failure of the customer to submit a claim prevent the customer from recovering the net equity in that customer's account, absent a claim the customer cannot participate in the determination of the net equity in the account.

If the customer submits instructions pursuant to subsection (a) after the customer's commodity contracts are transferred to another commodity broker, the trustee must transmit the instruction to the transferee. If the customer's commodity contracts are not transferred before the customer's instructions are received, the trustee must attempt to comply with the instruction, subject to the provisions of section 767(d).

Under subsection (d) [enacted as section 766(e)], the trustee has discretion to liquidate any commodity contract carried by the debtor at any time. This discretion must be exercised with restraint in such cases, consistent with the purposes of this subchapter and good business practices. The committee intends that hedged accounts will be given special consideration before liquidation as discussed in connection with subsection (c).

Subsection (e) [enacted as section 766(c)] instructs the trustee as to the disposition of any security or other property, not disposed of pursuant to subsection (b) or (d), that is specifically identifiable to a customer and to which the customer is entitled. Such security or other property must be returned to the customer or promptly transferred to another commodity broker for the benefit of the customer. If the value of the security or other property retained or transferred, together with any other distribution made by the trustee to or on behalf of the customer, exceeds the customer's distribution share the customer must deposit cash with the trustee equal to that difference before the return or transfer of the security or other property.

Subsection (f) [enacted as section 766(a)] requires the trustee to answer margin calls on specifically identifiable customer commodity contracts, but only to the extent that the margin payment, together with any other distribution made by the trustee to or on behalf of the customer, does not exceed the customer's distribution share.

Subsection (g) [enacted as section 766(b)] requires the trustee to liquidate all commodity futures contracts prior to the close of trading in that contract, or the first day on which notice of intent to deliver on that contract may be tendered, whichever occurs first. If the customer desires that the contract be kept open for delivery, the contract should be transferred to another commodity broker pursuant to subsection (b).

If for some reason the trustee is unable to transfer a contract on which delivery must be made or accepted and is unable to close out such contract, the trustee is authorized to operate the business of the debtor for the purpose of accepting or making tender of notice of intent to deliver the physical commodity underlying the contract, facilitating delivery of the physical commodity or disposing of the physical commodity in the event of a default. Any property received, not previously held, by the trustee in connection with its operation of the business of the debtor for these purposes, is not by the terms of this subchapter specifically included in the definition of customer property.

Finally, subsection (h) [enacted as section 766(f)] requires the trustee to liquidate the debtor's estate as soon as practicable and consistent with good market practice, except for specifically identifiable securities or other property distributable under subsection (e).

Section 768 is an integral part of the commodity broker liquidation procedures outlined in section 767. Prompt action by the trustee to transfer or liquidate customer commodity contracts is necessary to protect customers, the debtor's estate, and the marketplace generally. However, transfers of customer accounts and property valued in excess of the customer's distribution share are prohibited. Since a determination of the customer's distribution share requires a determination of the customer's net equity and the total dollar value of customer property held by or for the account of the debtor, it is possible that the customer's distribution share will not be determined, and thus the customer's contracts and property will not be transferred, on a timely basis. To avoid this problem, and to expedite transfers of customer property, section 768 permits the trustee to make distributions to customers in accordance with a preliminary estimate of the debtor's customer property and each customer's distribution share.

It is acknowledged that the necessity for prompt action may not allow the trustee to assemble all relevant facts before such an estimate is made. However, the trustee is expected to develop as accurate an estimate as possible based on the available facts. Further, in order to permit expeditious action, section 768 does not require that notice be given to customers or other creditors before the court approves or disapproves the estimate. Nor does section 768 require that customer claims be received pursuant to section 767(a) before the trustee may act upon and in accordance with the estimate. If the estimate is inaccurate, the trustee is absolved of liability for a distribution which exceeds the customer's actual distribution share so long as the distribution did not exceed the customer's estimated distribution share. However, a trustee may have a claim back against a customer who received more than its actual distribution share.

HOUSE REPORT NO. 95-595

Section 765(a) indicates that a customer must file a proof of claim, including any claim to specifically identifiable property, within such time as the court fixes.

Subsection (c) [of section 765 (enacted as section 766(e))] sets forth the general rule requiring the trustee to liquidate contractual commitments that are either not specifically identifiable or with respect to which a customer has not instructed the trustee during the time fixed by the court. Subsection (d) [enacted as section 766(b)] indicates an exception to the time limits in the rule by requiring the trustee to liquidate any open contractual commitment before the last day of trading or the first day during which delivery may be demanded, whichever first occurs, if transfer cannot be effectuated.

Section 766(a) [enacted as section 766(g)] indicates that the trustee may distribute securities or other property only under section 768. This does not preclude a distribution of cash under section 767(a) or distribution of any excess customer property under section 767(c) to the general estate.

Subsection (b) [enacted as section 766(f)] indicates that the trustee shall liquidate all securities and other property that is not specifically identifiable property as soon as practicable after the commencement of the case and in accordance with good market practice. If securities are restricted or trading has been suspended, the trustee will have to make an exempt sale or file a registration statement. In the event of a private placement, a customer is not entitled to "bid in" his net equity claim. To do so would enable him to receive a greater percentage recovery than other customers.

Section 767(a) [enacted as section 766(h)] provides for the trustee to distribute customer property pro rata according to customers' net equity claims. The court will determine an equitable portion of customer property to pay administrative expenses. Paragraphs (2) and (3) indicate that the return of specifically identifiable property constitutes a distribution of net equity.

Subsection (b) [enacted as section 766(i)] indicates that if the debtor is a clearing organization, customer property is to be segregated into customers' accounts and proprietary accounts and distributed accordingly without offset. This protects a member's customers from having their claims offset against the member's proprietary account. Subsection (c)(1) [enacted as section 766(j)(1)] indicates that any excess customer property will pour over into the general estate. This unlikely event would occur only if customers fail to file proofs of claim. Subsection (c)(2) [enacted as section 766(j)(2)] indicates that to the extent customers are not paid in full, they are entitled to share in the general estate as unsecured creditors, unless subordinated by the court under proposed 11 U.S.C. 510.

Section 768(a) [enacted as section 766(c)] requires the trustee to return specifically identifiable property to the extent that such distribution will not exceed a customer's net equity claim. Thus, if the customer owes money to a commodity broker, this will be offset under section 761(15)(A)(ii). If the value of the specifically identifiable property exceeds the net equity claim, then the customer may deposit cash with the trustee to make up the difference after which the trustee may return or transfer the customer's property.

Subsection (c) [enacted as section 766(a)] permits the trustee to answer all margin calls, to the extent of the customer's net equity claim, with respect to any specifically identifiable open contractual commitment. It should be noted that any payment under subsections (a) or (c) will be considered a reduction of the net equity claim under section 767(a). Thus the customer's net equity claim is a dynamic amount that varies with distributions of specifically identifiable property or margin payments on such property. This approach differs from the priority given to specifically identifiable property under subchapter III of chapter 7 by limiting the priority effect to a right to receive specific property as part of, rather than in addition to, a ratable share of customer property. This policy is designed to protect the small customer who is unlikely to have property in specifically identifiable form as compared with the professional trader. The CFTC is authorized to make rules defining specifically identifiable property under section 302 of the bill, in title III.

AMENDMENTS

2005—Subsec. (h). Pub. L. 109–8, §1502(a)(4)(A), substituted "507(a)(2)" for "507(a)(1)" in introductory provisions.

Subsec. (i). Pub. L. 109–8, §1502(a)(4)(B), substituted "507(a)(2)" for "507(a)(1)" in pars. (1) and (2).

1984—Subsec. (j)(2). Pub. L. 98–353 substituted "section 726" for "section 726(a)".

1982—Subsec. (a). Pub. L. 97–222, §19(a), inserted "to such customer" after "distribution".

Subsec. (b). Pub. L. 97–222, §19(b), struck out "that is being actively traded as of the date of the filing of the petition" after "any open commodity contract" and inserted "the" after "rules of".

Subsec. (d). Pub. L. 97–222, §19(c), substituted "the amount to which the customer of the debtor is entitled under subsection (h) or (i) of this section, then such" for "such amount, then the" and "the trustee then shall" for "the trustee shall".

Subsec. (h). Pub. L. 97–222, §19(d), inserted provision that notwithstanding any other provision of this subsection, a customer net equity claim based on a proprietary account, as defined by Commission rule, regulation, or order, may not be paid either in whole or in part, directly or indirectly, out of customer property unless all other customer net equity claims have been paid in full.

EFFECTIVE DATE OF 2005 AMENDMENT

Amendment by Pub. L. 109–8 effective 180 days after Apr. 20, 2005, and not applicable with respect to cases commenced under this title before such effective date, except as otherwise provided, see section 1501 of Pub. L. 109–8, set out as a note under section 101 of this title.

EFFECTIVE DATE OF 1984 AMENDMENT

Amendment by Pub. L. 98–353 effective with respect to cases filed 90 days after July 10, 1984, see section 552(a) of Pub. L. 98–353, set out as a note under section 101 of this title.

§767. Commodity broker liquidation and forward contract merchants, commodity brokers, stockbrokers, financial institutions, financial participants, securities clearing agencies, swap participants, repo participants, and master netting agreement participants

Notwithstanding any other provision of this title, the exercise of rights by a forward contract merchant, commodity broker, stockbroker, financial institution, financial participant, securities clearing agency, swap participant, repo participant, or master netting agreement participant under this title shall not affect the priority of any unsecured claim it may have after the exercise of such rights.

(Added Pub. L. 109–8, title IX, §907(*l*), Apr. 20, 2005, 119 Stat. 181.)

EFFECTIVE DATE

Section effective 180 days after Apr. 20, 2005, and not applicable with respect to cases commenced under this title before such effective date, except as otherwise provided, see section 1501 of Pub. L. 109–8, set out as an Effective Date of 2005 Amendment note under section 101 of this title.

SUBCHAPTER V—CLEARING BANK LIQUIDATION

§781. Definitions

For purposes of this subchapter, the following definitions shall apply:

(1) BOARD.—The term "Board" means the Board of Governors of the Federal Reserve System.

(2) DEPOSITORY INSTITUTION.—The term "depository institution" has the same meaning as in section 3 of the Federal Deposit Insurance Act.

(3) CLEARING BANK.—The term "clearing bank" means an uninsured State member bank, or a corporation organized under section 25A of the Federal Reserve Act, which operates, or operates as, a multilateral clearing organization pursuant to section 409 of the Federal Deposit Insurance Corporation Improvement Act of 1991.

(Added Pub. L. 106–554, §1(a)(5) [title I, §112(c)(5)(B)], Dec. 21, 2000, 114 Stat. 2763, 2763A–394.)

REFERENCES IN TEXT

Section 3 of the Federal Deposit Insurance Act, referred to in par. (2), is classified to section 1813 of Title 12, Banks and Banking.

Section 25A of the Federal Reserve Act, referred to in par. (3), popularly known as the Edge Act, is classified to subchapter II (§611 et seq.) of chapter 6 of Title 12, Banks and Banking. For complete classification of this Act to the Code, see Short Title note set out under section 611 of Title 12 and Tables.

Section 409 of the Federal Deposit Insurance Corporation Improvement Act of 1991, referred to in par. (3), is classified to section 4422 of Title 12, Banks and Banking.

§ 782. Selection of trustee

(a) IN GENERAL.—

(1) APPOINTMENT.—Notwithstanding any other provision of this title, the conservator or receiver who files the petition shall be the trustee under this chapter, unless the Board designates an alternative trustee.

(2) SUCCESSOR.—The Board may designate a successor trustee if required.

(b) AUTHORITY OF TRUSTEE.—Whenever the Board appoints or designates a trustee, chapter 3 and sections 704 and 705 of this title shall apply to the Board in the same way and to the same extent that they apply to a United States trustee.

(Added Pub. L. 106–554, §1(a)(5) [title I, §112(c)(5)(B)], Dec. 21, 2000, 114 Stat. 2763, 2763A–394.)

§ 783. Additional powers of trustee

(a) DISTRIBUTION OF PROPERTY NOT OF THE ESTATE.—The trustee under this subchapter has power to distribute property not of the estate, including distributions to customers that are mandated by subchapters III and IV of this chapter.

(b) DISPOSITION OF INSTITUTION.—The trustee under this subchapter may, after notice and a hearing—

(1) sell the clearing bank to a depository institution or consortium of depository institutions (which consortium may agree on the allocation of the clearing bank among the consortium);

(2) merge the clearing bank with a depository institution;

(3) transfer contracts to the same extent as could a receiver for a depository institution under paragraphs (9) and (10) of section 11(e) of the Federal Deposit Insurance Act;

(4) transfer assets or liabilities to a depository institution; and

(5) transfer assets and liabilities to a bridge depository institution as provided in paragraphs (1), (3)(A), (5), and (6) of section 11(n) of the Federal Deposit Insurance Act, paragraphs (9) through (13) of such section, and subparagraphs (A) through (H) and subparagraph (K) of paragraph (4) of such section 11(n), except that—

(A) the bridge depository institution to which such assets or liabilities are transferred shall be treated as a clearing bank for the purpose of this subsection; and

(B) any references in any such provision of law to the Federal Deposit Insurance Corporation shall be construed to be references to the appointing agency and that references to deposit insurance shall be omitted.

(c) CERTAIN TRANSFERS INCLUDED.—Any reference in this section to transfers of liabilities includes a ratable transfer of liabilities within a priority class.

(Added Pub. L. 106–554, §1(a)(5) [title I, §112(c)(5)(B)], Dec. 21, 2000, 114 Stat. 2763, 2763A–395; amended Pub. L. 110–289, div. A, title VI, §1604(b)(3), July 30, 2008, 122 Stat. 2829.)

REFERENCES IN TEXT

Section 11 of the Federal Deposit Insurance Act, referred to in subsec. (b)(3), (5), is classified to section 1821 of Title 12, Banks and Banking.

AMENDMENTS

2008—Subsec. (b)(5). Pub. L. 110–289, which directed amendment of this section by substituting "bridge depository institution" for "bridge bank", was executed by making the substitution in introductory provisions and subpar. (A) of subsec. (b)(5), to reflect the probable intent of Congress.

§ 784. Right to be heard

The Board or a Federal reserve bank (in the case of a clearing bank that is a member of that bank) may raise and may appear and be heard on any issue in a case under this subchapter.

(Added Pub. L. 106–554, §1(a)(5) [title I, §112(c)(5)(B)], Dec. 21, 2000, 114 Stat. 2763, 2763A–395.)

CHAPTER 9—ADJUSTMENT OF DEBTS OF A MUNICIPALITY

SUBCHAPTER I—GENERAL PROVISIONS

AMENDMENTS

1988—Pub. L. 100–597, §11, Nov. 3, 1988, 102 Stat. 3030, added items 927 to 929 and redesignated former item 927 as 930.

SUBCHAPTER I—GENERAL PROVISIONS

§ 901. Applicability of other sections of this title

(a) Sections 301, 344, 347(b), 349, 350(b), 361, 362, 364(c), 364(d), 364(e), 364(f), 365, 366, 501, 502, 503, 504, 506, 507(a)(2), 509, 510, 524(a)(1), 524(a)(2), 544, 545, 546, 547, 548, 549(a), 549(c), 549(d), 550, 551, 552, 553, 555, 556, 557, 559, 560, 561, 562, 1102, 1103, 1109, 1111(b), 1122, 1123(a)(1), 1123(a)(2), 1123(a)(3), 1123(a)(4), 1123(a)(5), 1123(b), 1123(d), 1124, 1125, 1126(a), 1126(b), 1126(c), 1126(e), 1126(f), 1126(g), 1127(d), 1128, 1129(a)(2), 1129(a)(3), 1129(a)(6), 1129(a)(8), 1129(a)(10), 1129(b)(1), 1129(b)(2)(A), 1129(b)(2)(B), 1142(b), 1143, 1144, and 1145 of this title apply in a case under this chapter.

(b) A term used in a section of this title made applicable in a case under this chapter by subsection (a) of this section or section 103(e)[1] of this title has the meaning defined for such term for the purpose of such applicable section, unless such term is otherwise defined in section 902 of this title.

(c) A section made applicable in a case under this chapter by subsection (a) of this section that is operative if the business of the debtor is authorized to be operated is operative in a case under this chapter.

(Pub. L. 95–598, Nov. 6, 1978, 92 Stat. 2621; Pub. L. 98–353, title III, §§ 353, 490, July 10, 1984, 98 Stat. 361, 383; Pub. L. 100–597, § 3, Nov. 3, 1988, 102 Stat. 3028; Pub. L. 109–8, title V, § 502, title XII, § 1216, title XV, § 1502(a)(5), Apr. 20, 2005, 119 Stat. 118, 195, 216.)

HISTORICAL AND REVISION NOTES

LEGISLATIVE STATEMENTS

Chapter 9 of the House amendment represents a compromise between chapter 9 of the House bill and 9 of the Senate amendment. In most respects this chapter follows current law with respect to the adjustment of debts of a municipality. Stylistic changes and minor substantive revisions have been made in order to conform this chapter with other new chapters of the bankruptcy code. There are few major differences between the House bill and the Senate amendment on this issue. Section 901 indicates the applicability of other sections of title 11 in cases under chapter 9. Included are sections providing for creditors' committees under sections 1102 and 1103.

HOUSE REPORT NO. 95–595

Section 901 makes applicable appropriate provisions of other chapters of proposed title 11. The general rule set out in section 103(e) is that only the provisions of chapters 1 and 9 apply in a chapter 9 case. Section 901 is the exception, and specifies other provisions that do apply. They are as follows:

§ 301. Voluntary cases. Application of this section makes clear, as under current chapter IX [chapter 9 of former title 11], that a municipal case can be commenced only by the municipality itself. There are no involuntary chapter 9 cases.

§ 344. Self-incrimination; immunity. Application of this section is of no substantive effect for the administration of the case, but merely provides that the general rules in part V [§ 6001 et seq.] of title 18 govern immunity.

§ 347(b). Unclaimed property. This provision currently appears in section 96(d) of chapter IX [section 416(d) of former title 11].

§ 349. Effect of dismissal. This section governs the effect of a dismissal of a chapter 9 case. It provides in substance that rights that existed before the case that were disturbed by the commencement of the case are reinstated. This section does not concern grounds for dismissal, which are found in section 926.

§ 361. Adequate protection. Section 361 provides the general standard for the protection of secured creditors whose property is used in a case under title 11. Its importance lies in its application to sections 362 and 364.

§ 362. Automatic stay. The automatic stay provisions of the general portions of the title are incorporated into chapter 9. There is an automatic stay provided in current Bankruptcy Act § 85(e) [section 405(e) of former title 11]. The thrust of section 362 is the same as that of section 85(e), but, of course, its application in chapter 9 is modernized and drafted to conform with the stay generally applicable under the bankruptcy code. An additional part of the automatic stay applicable only to municipal cases is included in section 922.

§§ 364(c), 364(d), 364(e). Obtaining credit. This section governs the borrowing of money by a municipality in reorganization. It is narrower than a comparable provision in current law, section 82(b)(2) [section 402(b)(2) of former title 11]. The difference lies mainly in the removal under the bill of the authority of the court to supervise borrowing by the municipality in instances in which none of the special bankruptcy powers are involved. That is, if a municipality could borrow money outside of the bankruptcy court, then it should have the same authority in bankruptcy court, under the doctrine of *Ashton v. Cameron Water District No. 1*, 298 U.S. 513 (1936) [Tex.1936, 56 S.Ct. 892, 80 L.Ed. 1309, 31 Am.Bankr.Rep.N.S. 96, rehearing denied 57 S.Ct. 5, 299 U.S. 619, 81 L.Ed. 457] and *National League of Cities v. Usery*, 426 U.S. 833 (1976) [Dist.Col.1976, 96 S.Ct. 2465, 49 L.Ed.2d 245, on remand 429 F. Supp. 703]. Only when the municipality needs special authority, such as subordination of existing liens, or special priority for the borrowed funds, will the court become involved in the authorization.

§ 365. Executory contracts and unexpired leases. The applicability of section 365 incorporates the general power of a bankruptcy court to authorize the assumption or rejection of executory contracts or unexpired leases found in other chapters of the title. This section is comparable to section 82(b)(1) of current law [section 402(b)(1) of former title 11].

§ 366. Utility service. This section gives a municipality the same authority as any other debtor with respect to continuation of utility service during the proceeding, provided adequate assurance of future payment is provided. No comparable explicit provision is found in current law, although the case law seems to support the same result.

§ 501. Filing of proofs of claims. This section permits filing of proofs of claims in a chapter 9 case. Note, however, that section 924 permits listing of creditors' claims, as under chapter 11 and under section 85(b) of chapter IX [section 405(b) of former title 11].

§ 502. Allowance of claims. This section applies the general allowance rules to chapter 9 cases. This is no change from current law.

§ 503. Administrative expenses. Administrative expenses as defined in section 503 will be paid in a chapter 9 case, as provided under section 89(1) of current law [section 409(1) of former title 11].

§ 504. Sharing of compensation. There is no comparable provision in current law. However, this provision applies generally throughout the proposed law, and will not affect the progress of the case, only the interrelations between attorneys and other professionals that participate in the case.

§ 506. Determination of secured status. Section 506 specifies that claims secured by a lien should be separated, to the extent provided, into secured and unsecured claims. It applies generally. Current law follows this result, though there is no explicit provision.

§ 507(1). Priorities. Paragraph (1) of section 507 requires that administrative expenses be paid first. This rule will apply in chapter 9 cases. It is presently found in section 89(1) [section 409(1) of former title 11]. The two

[1] See References in Text note below.

other priorities presently found in section 89 have been deleted. The second for claims arising within 3 months before the case is commenced, is deleted from the statute, but may be within the court's equitable power to award, under the case of *Fosdick v. Schall*, 99 U.S. 235 (1878) [25 L.Ed. 339]. Leaving the provision to the courts permits greater flexibility, as under railroad cases, than an absolute three-month rule. The third priority under current law, for claims which are entitled to priority under the laws of the United States, is deleted because of the proposed amendment to section 3466 of the Revised Statutes [former 31 U.S.C. 191, see 31 U.S.C. 3713(a)] contained in section 321(a) of title III of the bill, which previously has given the United States an absolute first priority in chapter X [chapter 10 of former title 11] and section 77 [section 205 of former title 11] cases. Because the priority rules are regularized and brought together in the bankruptcy laws by this bill, the need for incorporation of priorities elsewhere specified is eliminated.

§509. Claims of codebtors. This section provides for the treatment of sureties, guarantors, and codebtors. The general rule of postponement found in the other chapters will apply in chapter 9. This section adopts current law.

§510. Subordination of claims. This section permits the court to subordinate, on equitable grounds, any claim, and requires enforcement of contractual subordination agreements, and subordination of securities rescission claims. The section recognizes the inherent equitable power of the court under current law, and the practice followed with respect to contractual provisions.

§547. Preferences. Incorporation of section 547 will permit the debtor to recover preferences. This power will be used primarily when those who gave the preferences have been replaced by new municipal officers or when creditors coerced preferential payments. Unlike Bankruptcy Act §85(h) [section 405(h) of former title 11], the section does not permit the appointment of a trustee for the purpose of pursuing preferences. Moreover, this bill does not incorporate the other avoiding powers of a trustee for chapter 9, found in current section 85(h).

§550. Liability of transfers. Incorporation of this section is made necessary by the incorporation of the preference section, and permits recovery by the debtor from a transferee of an avoided preference.

§551. Automatic preservation of avoided transfer. Application of section 551 requires preservation of any avoided preference for the benefit of the estate.

§552. Postpetition effect of security interest. This section will govern the applicability after the commencement of the case of security interests granted by the debtor before the commencement of the case.

§553. Setoff. Under current law, certain setoff is stayed. Application of this section preserves that result, though the setoffs that are permitted under section 553 are better defined than under present law. Application of this section is necessary to stay the setoff and to provide the offsetting creditor with the protection to which he is entitled under present law.

§1122. Classification of claims. This section is derived from current section 88(b) [section 408(b) of former title 11], and is substantially similar.

§1123(a)(1)–(4), (b). Contents of plan. The general provisions governing contents of a chapter 11 plan are made applicable here, with two exceptions relating to the rights of stockholders, which are not applicable in chapter 9 cases. This section expands current law by specifying the contents of a plan in some detail. Section 91 of current law [section 411 of former title 11] speaks only in general terms. The substance of the two sections is substantially the same, however.

§1124. Impairment of claims. The confirmation standards adopted in chapter 9 are the same as those of chapter 11. This changes current chapter IX [chapter 9 of former title 11], which requires compliance with the fair and equitable rule. The greater flexibility of proposed chapter 11 is carried over into chapter 9, for there appears to be no reason why the confirmation standards for the two chapters should be different, or why the elimination of the fair and equitable rule from corporate reorganizations should not be followed in municipal debt adjustments. The current chapter IX rule is based on the confirmation rules of current chapter X [chapter 10 of former title 11]. The change in the latter suggests a corresponding change in the former. Section 1124 is one part of the new confirmation standard. It defines impairment, for use in section 1129.

§1125. Postpetition disclosure and solicitation. The change in the confirmation standard necessitates a corresponding change in the disclosure requirements for solicitation of acceptances of a plan. Under current chapter IX [chapter 9 of former title 11] there is no disclosure requirement. Incorporation of section 1125 will insure that creditors receive adequate information before they are required to vote on a plan.

§1126(a), (b), (c), (e), (f), (g). Acceptance of plan. Section 1126 incorporates the current chapter IX [chapter 9 of former title 11] acceptance requirement: two-thirds in amount and a majority in number, Bankruptcy Act §92 [section 412 of former title 11]. Section 1125 permits exclusion of certain acceptances from the computation if the acceptances were obtained in bad faith or, unlike current law, if there is a conflict of interest motivating the acceptance.

§1127(d). Modification of plan. This section governs the change of a creditor's vote on the plan after a modification is proposed. It is derived from current section 92(e) [section 412(e) of former title 11].

§1128. Hearing on confirmation. This section requires a hearing on the confirmation of the plan, and permits parties in interest to object. It is the same as Bankruptcy Act §§93 and 94(a) [sections 413 and 414(a) of former title 11], though the provision, comparable to section 206 of current chapter X [section 606 of former title 11], permitting a labor organization to appear and be heard on the economic soundness of the plan, has been deleted as more appropriate for the Rules.

§1129(a)(2), (3), (8), (b)(1), (2). Confirmation of plan. This section provides the boiler-plate language that the plan be proposed in good faith and that it comply with the provisions of the chapter, and also provides the financial standard for confirmation, which replaces the fair and equitable rule. See §1124, supra.

§1142(b). Execution of plan. Derived from Bankruptcy Act §96(b) [section 416(b) of former title 11], this section permits the court to order execution and delivery of instruments in order to execute the plan.

§1143. Distribution. This section is the same in substance as section 96(d) [section 416(d) of former title 11], which requires presentment or delivery of securities within five years, and bars creditors that do not act within that time.

§1144. Revocation of order of confirmation. This section permits the court to revoke the order of confirmation and the discharge if the confirmation of the plan was procured by fraud. There is no comparable provision in current chapter IX [chapter 9 of former title 11].

REFERENCES IN TEXT

Section 103(e) of this title, referred to in subsec. (b), was redesignated section 103(f) and a new section 103(e) was added by Pub. L. 106–554, §1(a)(5) [title I, §112(c)(5)(A)], Dec. 21, 2000, 114 Stat. 2763, 2763A–394.

AMENDMENTS

2005—Subsec. (a). Pub. L. 109–8, §1502(a)(5), substituted "507(a)(2)" for "507(a)(1)".

Pub. L. 109–8, §1216, inserted "1123(d)," after "1123(b),".

Pub. L. 109–8, §502, inserted "555, 556," after "553," and "559, 560, 561, 562," after "557,".

1988—Subsec. (a). Pub. L. 100–597 inserted "1129(a)(6)," after "1129(a)(3),".

1984—Subsec. (a). Pub. L. 98–353 inserted "557," after "553," and substituted "1111(b)," for "1111(b)".

EFFECTIVE DATE OF 2005 AMENDMENT

Amendment by Pub. L. 109–8 effective 180 days after Apr. 20, 2005, and not applicable with respect to cases commenced under this title before such effective date, except as otherwise provided, see section 1501 of Pub. L. 109–8, set out as a note under section 101 of this title.

EFFECTIVE DATE OF 1988 AMENDMENT

Amendment by Pub. L. 100–597 effective Nov. 3, 1988, but not applicable to any case commenced under this title before that date, see section 12 of Pub. L. 100–597, set out as a note under section 101 of this title.

EFFECTIVE DATE OF 1984 AMENDMENT

Amendment by Pub. L. 98–353 effective with respect to cases filed 90 days after July 10, 1984, see section 552(a) of Pub. L. 98–353, set out as a note under section 101 of this title.

§ 902. Definitions for this chapter

In this chapter—

(1) "property of the estate", when used in a section that is made applicable in a case under this chapter by section 103(e)[1] or 901 of this title, means property of the debtor;

(2) "special revenues" means—

(A) receipts derived from the ownership, operation, or disposition of projects or systems of the debtor that are primarily used or intended to be used primarily to provide transportation, utility, or other services, including the proceeds of borrowings to finance the projects or systems;

(B) special excise taxes imposed on particular activities or transactions;

(C) incremental tax receipts from the benefited area in the case of tax-increment financing;

(D) other revenues or receipts derived from particular functions of the debtor, whether or not the debtor has other functions; or

(E) taxes specifically levied to finance one or more projects or systems, excluding receipts from general property, sales, or income taxes (other than tax-increment financing) levied to finance the general purposes of the debtor;

(3) "special tax payer" means record owner or holder of legal or equitable title to real property against which a special assessment or special tax has been levied the proceeds of which are the sole source of payment of an obligation issued by the debtor to defray the cost of an improvement relating to such real property;

(4) "special tax payer affected by the plan" means special tax payer with respect to whose real property the plan proposes to increase the proportion of special assessments or special taxes referred to in paragraph (2) of this section assessed against such real property; and

(5) "trustee", when used in a section that is made applicable in a case under this chapter by section 103(e)[1] or 901 of this title, means debtor, except as provided in section 926 of this title.

(Pub. L. 95–598, Nov. 6, 1978, 92 Stat. 2622; Pub. L. 98–353, title III, § 491, July 10, 1984, 98 Stat. 383; Pub. L. 100–597, § 4, Nov. 3, 1988, 102 Stat. 3028.)

HISTORICAL AND REVISION NOTES

LEGISLATIVE STATEMENTS

Section 902(2) of the Senate amendment is deleted since the bankruptcy court will have jurisdiction over all cases under chapter 9. The concept of a claim being materially and adversely affected reflected in section 902(1) of the Senate amendment has been deleted and replaced with the new concept of "impairment" set forth in section 1124 of the House amendment and incorporated by reference into chapter 9.

SENATE REPORT NO. 95–989

There are six definitions for use in chapter 9. Paragraph (1) defines what claims are included in a chapter 9 case and adopts the definition now found in section 81(1) [section 401(1) of former title 11]. All claims against the petitioner generally will be included, with one significant exception. Municipalities are authorized, under section 103(c) of the Internal Revenue Code of 1954, as amended [title 26], to issue tax-exempt industrial development revenue bonds to provide for the financing of certain projects for privately owned companies. The bonds are sold on the basis of the credit of the company on whose behalf they are issued, and the principal, interest, and premium, if any, are payable solely from payments made by the company to the trustee under the bond indenture and do not constitute claims on the tax revenues or other funds of the issuing municipalities. The municipality merely acts as the vehicle to enable the bonds to be issued on a tax-exempt basis. Claims that arise by virtue of these bonds are not among the claims defined by this paragraph and amounts owed by private companies to the holders of industrial development revenue bonds are not to be included among the assets of the municipality that would be affected by the plan. See Cong. Record, 94th Cong., 1st Sess. H.R. 12073 (statement by Mr. Don Edwards, floor manager of the bill in the House). Paragraph (2) defines the court which means the federal district court or federal district judge before which the case is pending. Paragraph (3) [enacted as (1)] specifies that when the term "property of the estate" is used in a section in another chapter made applicable in chapter 9 cases, the term means "property of the debtor". Paragraphs (4) and (5) [enacted as (2) and (3)] adopt the definition of "special taxpayer affected by the plan" that appears in current sections 81(10) and 81(11) of the Bankruptcy Act [section 401(10) and (11) of former title 11]. Paragraph (6) [enacted as (4)] provides that "trustee" means "debtor" when used in conjunction with chapter 9.

HOUSE REPORT NO. 95–595

There are only four definitions for use only in chapter 9. The first specifies that when the term "property of the estate" is used in a section in another chapter made applicable in chapter 9 cases, the term will mean "property of the debtor". Paragraphs (2) and (3) adopt the definition of "special taxpayer affected by the plan" that appears in current sections 81(10) and 81(11) [section 401(10) and (11) of former title 11]. Paragraph (4) provides for "trustee" the same treatment as provided for "property of the estate", specifying that it means "debtor" when used in conjunction with chapter 9.

REFERENCES IN TEXT

Section 103(e) of this title, referred to in pars. (1) and (5), was redesignated section 103(f) and a new section 103(e) was added by Pub. L. 106–554, § 1(a)(5) [title I, § 112(c)(5)(A)], Dec. 21, 2000, 114 Stat. 2763, 2763A–394.

AMENDMENTS

1988—Pars. (2) to (5). Pub. L. 100–597 added par. (2) and redesignated former pars. (2) to (4) as (3) to (5), respectively.

1984—Par. (2). Pub. L. 98–353 substituted "legal or equitable title to real property against which a special assessment or special tax has been levied" for "title, legal or equitable, to real property against which has been levied a special assessment or special tax".

EFFECTIVE DATE OF 1988 AMENDMENT

Amendment by Pub. L. 100–597 effective Nov. 3, 1988, but not applicable to any case commenced under this

[1] See References in Text note below.

title before that date, see section 12 of Pub. L. 100–597, set out as a note under section 101 of this title.

EFFECTIVE DATE OF 1984 AMENDMENT

Amendment by Pub. L. 98–353 effective with respect to cases filed 90 days after July 10, 1984, see section 552(a) of Pub. L. 98–353, set out as a note under section 101 of this title.

§ 903. Reservation of State power to control municipalities

This chapter does not limit or impair the power of a State to control, by legislation or otherwise, a municipality of or in such State in the exercise of the political or governmental powers of such municipality, including expenditures for such exercise, but—

(1) a State law prescribing a method of composition of indebtedness of such municipality may not bind any creditor that does not consent to such composition; and

(2) a judgment entered under such a law may not bind a creditor that does not consent to such composition.

(Pub. L. 95–598, Nov. 6, 1978, 92 Stat. 2622; Pub. L. 98–353, title III, § 492, July 10, 1984, 98 Stat. 383.)

HISTORICAL AND REVISION NOTES

LEGISLATIVE STATEMENTS

Section 903 of the House amendment represents a stylistic revision of section 903 of the Senate amendment. To the extent section 903 of the House bill would have changed present law, such section is rejected.

SENATE REPORT NO. 95–989

Section 903 is derived, with stylistic changes, from section 83 of current Chapter IX [section 403 of former title 11]. It sets forth the primary authority of a State, through its constitution, laws, and other powers, over its municipalities. The proviso in section 83, prohibiting State composition procedures for municipalities, is retained. Deletion of the provision would "permit all States to enact their own versions of Chapter IX [chapter 9 of former title 11]", Municipal Insolvency, 50 Am.Bankr.L.J. 55, 65, which would frustrate the constitutional mandate of uniform bankruptcy laws. Constitution of the United States, Art. I, Sec. 8.

This section provides that the municipality can consent to the court's orders in regard to use of its income or property. It is contemplated that such consent will be required by the court for the issuance of certificates of indebtedness under section 364(c). Such consent could extend to enforcement of the conditions attached to the certificates or the municipal services to be provided during the proceedings.

AMENDMENTS

1984—Par. (2). Pub. L. 98–353 struck out "to" before "that does not consent".

EFFECTIVE DATE OF 1984 AMENDMENT

Amendment by Pub. L. 98–353 effective with respect to cases filed 90 days after July 10, 1984, see section 552(a) of Pub. L. 98–353, set out as a note under section 101 of this title.

§ 904. Limitation on jurisdiction and powers of court

Notwithstanding any power of the court, unless the debtor consents or the plan so provides, the court may not, by any stay, order, or decree, in the case or otherwise, interfere with—

(1) any of the political or governmental powers of the debtor;

(2) any of the property or revenues of the debtor; or

(3) the debtor's use or enjoyment of any income-producing property.

(Pub. L. 95–598, Nov. 6, 1978, 92 Stat. 2622.)

HISTORICAL AND REVISION NOTES

SENATE REPORT NO. 95–989

This section adopts the policy of section 82(c) of current law [section 402(c) of former title 11]. The only change in this section from section 82(c) is to conform the section to the style and cross-references of S. 2266.

HOUSE REPORT NO. 95–595

This section adopts the policy of section 82(c) of current law [section 402(c) of former title 11]. The *Usery* case underlines the need for this limitation on the court's powers. The only change in this section from section 82(c) is to conform the section to the style and cross-references of H.R. 8200. This section makes clear that the court may not interfere with the choices a municipality makes as to what services and benefits it will provide to its inhabitants.

SUBCHAPTER II—ADMINISTRATION

AMENDMENTS

1984—Pub. L. 98–353, title III, § 493, July 10, 1984, 98 Stat. 383, substituted "SUBCHAPTER" for "SUBCHAPER".

§ 921. Petition and proceedings relating to petition

(a) Notwithstanding sections 109(d) and 301 of this title, a case under this chapter concerning an unincorporated tax or special assessment district that does not have such district's own officials is commenced by the filing under section 301 of this title of a petition under this chapter by such district's governing authority or the board or body having authority to levy taxes or assessments to meet the obligations of such district.

(b) The chief judge of the court of appeals for the circuit embracing the district in which the case is commenced shall designate the bankruptcy judge to conduct the case.

(c) After any objection to the petition, the court, after notice and a hearing, may dismiss the petition if the debtor did not file the petition in good faith or if the petition does not meet the requirements of this title.

(d) If the petition is not dismissed under subsection (c) of this section, the court shall order relief under this chapter notwithstanding section 301(b).

(e) The court may not, on account of an appeal from an order for relief, delay any proceeding under this chapter in the case in which the appeal is being taken; nor shall any court order a stay of such proceeding pending such appeal. The reversal on appeal of a finding of jurisdiction does not affect the validity of any debt incurred that is authorized by the court under section 364(c) or 364(d) of this title.

(Pub. L. 95–598, Nov. 6, 1978, 92 Stat. 2622; Pub. L. 98–353, title III, § 494, July 10, 1984, 98 Stat. 383; Pub. L. 109–8, title V, § 501(a), Apr. 20, 2005, 119 Stat. 118.)

HISTORICAL AND REVISION NOTES

LEGISLATIVE STATEMENTS

Section 905 of the Senate amendment is incorporated as section 921(b) of the House amendment with the difference that the chief judge of the circuit embracing the district in which the case is commenced designates a bankruptcy judge to conduct the case in lieu of a district judge as under present law. It is intended that a municipality may commence a case in any district in which the municipality is located, as under present law. Section 906 of the Senate amendment has been adopted in substance in section 109(c) of the House amendment.

SENATE REPORT NO. 95–989

Section 905 [enacted as section 921(b)] adopts the procedures for selection of the judge for the chapter 9 case as found in current section 82(d) [section 402(d) of former title 11]. It is expected that the large chapter 9 case might take up almost all the judicial time of the presiding judge and involve very complex legal questions. Selection should not be left to chance or the luck of the draw. This provision will insure that calendar demands and levels of experience can be considered in the selection of the judge in a chapter 9 case.

HOUSE REPORT NO. 95–595

Subsection (a) is derived from section 85(a) [section 405(a) of former title 11], second sentence, of current law. There is no substantive change in the law. The subsection permits a municipality that does not have its own officers to be moved into chapter 9 by the action of the body or board that has authority to levy taxes for the municipality.

Subsection (b) permits a party in interest to object to the filing of the petition not later than 15 days after notice. This provision tracks the third sentence of section 85(a) [section 405(a) of former title 11], except that the provision for publication in section 85(a) is left to the Rules (see Rule 9–14), and therefore the determinative date is left less definite.

Subsection (c) permits the court to dismiss a petition not filed in good faith or not filed in compliance with the requirements of the chapter. This provision is the fourth sentence of section 85(a) [section 405(a) of former title 11].

Subsection (d) directs the court to order relief on the petition if it does not dismiss the case under subsection (c).

Subsection (e) contains the fifth and sixth sentences of section 85(a) [section 405(a) of former title 11].

AMENDMENTS

2005—Subsec. (d). Pub. L. 109–8 inserted "notwithstanding section 301(b)" before period at end.

1984—Subsec. (a). Pub. L. 98–353, §494(c), substituted "109(d)" for "109(c)".

Subsec. (c). Pub. L. 98–353, §494(a), substituted "any" for "an", and "petition if the debtor did not file the petition in good faith" for "petition, if the debtor did not file the petition in good faith,".

Subsec. (d). Pub. L. 98–353, §494(b), (d), redesignated subsec. (e) as (d) and substituted "subsection (c)" for "subsection (d)". No former subsec. (d) had been enacted.

Subsecs. (e), (f). Pub. L. 98–353, §494(b), redesignated subsec. (f) as (e). Former subsec. (e) redesignated (d).

EFFECTIVE DATE OF 2005 AMENDMENT

Amendment by Pub. L. 109–8 effective 180 days after Apr. 20, 2005, and not applicable with respect to cases commenced under this title before such effective date, except as otherwise provided, see section 1501 of Pub. L. 109–8, set out as a note under section 101 of this title.

EFFECTIVE DATE OF 1984 AMENDMENT

Amendment by Pub. L. 98–353 effective with respect to cases filed 90 days after July 10, 1984, see section 552(a) of Pub. L. 98–353, set out as a note under section 101 of this title.

§922. Automatic stay of enforcement of claims against the debtor

(a) A petition filed under this chapter operates as a stay, in addition to the stay provided by section 362 of this title, applicable to all entities, of—

(1) the commencement or continuation, including the issuance or employment of process, of a judicial, administrative, or other action or proceeding against an officer or inhabitant of the debtor that seeks to enforce a claim against the debtor; and

(2) the enforcement of a lien on or arising out of taxes or assessments owed to the debtor.

(b) Subsections (c), (d), (e), (f), and (g) of section 362 of this title apply to a stay under subsection (a) of this section the same as such subsections apply to a stay under section 362(a) of this title.

(c) If the debtor provides, under section 362, 364, or 922 of this title, adequate protection of the interest of the holder of a claim secured by a lien on property of the debtor and if, notwithstanding such protection such creditor has a claim arising from the stay of action against such property under section 362 or 922 of this title or from the granting of a lien under section 364(d) of this title, then such claim shall be allowable as an administrative expense under section 503(b) of this title.

(d) Notwithstanding section 362 of this title and subsection (a) of this section, a petition filed under this chapter does not operate as a stay of application of pledged special revenues in a manner consistent with section 927 of this title to payment of indebtedness secured by such revenues.

(Pub. L. 95–598, Nov. 6, 1978, 92 Stat. 2623; Pub. L. 98–353, title III, §495, July 10, 1984, 98 Stat. 384; Pub. L. 100–597, §5, Nov. 3, 1988, 102 Stat. 3029.)

HISTORICAL AND REVISION NOTES

HOUSE REPORT NO. 95–595

The automatic stay provided under section 362 of title 11 is incomplete for a municipality, because there is the possibility of action by a creditor against an officer or inhabitant of the municipality to collect taxes due the municipality. Section 85(e)(1) of current chapter IX [section 405(e)(1) of former title 11] stays such actions. Section 922 carries over that protection into the proposed chapter 9. Subsection (b) applies the provisions for relief from the stay that apply generally in section 362 to the stay under section 922.

AMENDMENTS

1988—Subsecs. (c), (d). Pub. L. 100–597 added subsecs. (c) and (d).

1984—Subsec. (a)(1). Pub. L. 98–353 substituted "a judicial" for "judicial", and "action or proceeding" for "proceeding".

EFFECTIVE DATE OF 1988 AMENDMENT

Amendment by Pub. L. 100–597 effective Nov. 3, 1988, but not applicable to any case commenced under this title before that date, see section 12 of Pub. L. 100–597, set out as a note under section 101 of this title.

EFFECTIVE DATE OF 1984 AMENDMENT

Amendment by Pub. L. 98–353 effective with respect to cases filed 90 days after July 10, 1984, see section

552(a) of Pub. L. 98–353, set out as a note under section 101 of this title.

§ 923. Notice

There shall be given notice of the commencement of a case under this chapter, notice of an order for relief under this chapter, and notice of the dismissal of a case under this chapter. Such notice shall also be published at least once a week for three successive weeks in at least one newspaper of general circulation published within the district in which the case is commenced, and in such other newspaper having a general circulation among bond dealers and bondholders as the court designates.

(Pub. L. 95–598, Nov. 6, 1978, 92 Stat. 2623.)

HISTORICAL AND REVISION NOTES

LEGISLATIVE STATEMENTS

Section 923 of the House amendment represents a compromise with respect to the notice provisions contained in comparable provisions of the House bill and Senate amendment. As a general matter, title 11 leaves most procedural issues to be determined by the Rules of Bankruptcy Procedure. Section 923 of the House amendment contains certain important aspects of procedure that have been retained from present law. It is anticipated that the Rules of Bankruptcy Procedure will adopt rules similar to the present rules for chapter IX of the Bankruptcy Act [chapter 9 of former title 11].

HOUSE REPORT NO. 95–595

The notice provisions in section 923 are significantly more sparse than those provided under section 85(d) of chapter IX [section 405(d) of former title 11]. The exact contours of the notice to be given under chapter 9 are left to the Rules. Because the Rules deal with notice in a municipal case (Rule 9–14), and because section 405(d) of title IV of the bill continues those Rules in effect to the extent not inconsistent with the bill, the notice provisions of current law and Rules would continue to apply.

§ 924. List of creditors

The debtor shall file a list of creditors.

(Pub. L. 95–598, Nov. 6, 1978, 92 Stat. 2623.)

HISTORICAL AND REVISION NOTES

LEGISLATIVE STATEMENTS

Section 924 of the House amendment is derived from section 924 of the House bill with the location of the filing of the list of creditors to be determined by the rules of bankruptcy procedure. The detailed requirements of section 724 [probably should be "924"] of the Senate bill are anticipated to be incorporated in the rules of bankruptcy procedure.

SENATE REPORT NO. 95–989

This section adopts the provision presently contained in section 85(b) of Chapter IX [section 405(b) of former title 11]. A list of creditors, as complete and accurate as practicable, must be filed with the court.

HOUSE REPORT NO. 95–595

This section directs the debtor to file a list of creditors with the court. A comparable provision is presently contained in section 85(b) of chapter IX [section 405(b) of former title 11]. The Rules, in Rule 9–7, copy the provisions of section 85(b), with additional matter. As noted above, section 405(d) of title IV will continue those Rules in effect. Because the form, time of filing, and nature of the list, are procedural matters that may call for some flexibility, those details have been left to the Rules.

§ 925. Effect of list of claims

A proof of claim is deemed filed under section 501 of this title for any claim that appears in the list filed under section 924 of this title, except a claim that is listed as disputed, contingent, or unliquidated.

(Pub. L. 95–598, Nov. 6, 1978, 92 Stat. 2623.)

HISTORICAL AND REVISION NOTES

LEGISLATIVE STATEMENTS

Section 925 of the Senate amendment regarding venue and fees has been deleted.

SENATE REPORT NO. 95–989

Section 926 [enacted as section 925] follows the policy contained in section 88(a) of the present Act [section 408(a) of former title 11], though certain details are left to the Rules. The language of section 926 is the same as that of proposed 11 U.S.C. 1111, which applies in chapter 11 cases. The list of creditors filed under section 924 is given weight as prima facie evidence of the claims listed (except claims that are listed as disputed, contingent, or unliquidated), which are deemed filed under section 501, obviating the need for listed creditors to file proofs of claim.

§ 926. Avoiding powers

(a) If the debtor refuses to pursue a cause of action under section 544, 545, 547, 548, 549(a), or 550 of this title, then on request of a creditor, the court may appoint a trustee to pursue such cause of action.

(b) A transfer of property of the debtor to or for the benefit of any holder of a bond or note, on account of such bond or note, may not be avoided under section 547 of this title.

(Pub. L. 95–598, Nov. 6, 1978, 92 Stat. 2623; Pub. L. 100–597, § 6, Nov. 3, 1988, 102 Stat. 3029.)

HISTORICAL AND REVISION NOTES

LEGISLATIVE STATEMENTS

Section 926 of the House amendment is derived from section 928 of the Senate bill. The provision enables creditors to request the court to appoint a trustee to pursue avoiding powers if the debtor refuses to exercise those powers. Section 901 of the House amendment makes a corresponding change to incorporate avoiding powers included in the Senate amendment, but excluded from the House bill.

SENATE REPORT NO. 95–989

This section [928 (enacted as section 926)] adopts current section 85(h) [section 405(h) of former title 11] which provides for a trustee to be appointed for the purpose of pursuing an action under an avoiding power, if the debtor refuses to do so. This section is necessary because a municipality might, by reason of political pressure or desire for future good relations with a particular creditor or class of creditors, make payments to such creditors in the days preceding the petition to the detriment of all other creditors. No change in the elected officials of such a city would automatically occur upon filing of the petition, and it might be very awkward for those same officials to turn around and demand the return of the payments following the filing of the petition. Hence, the need for a trustee for such purpose.

The general avoiding powers are incorporated by reference in section 901 and are broader than under current law. Preference, fraudulent conveyances, and other kinds of transfers will thus be voidable.

Incorporated by reference also is the power to accept or reject executory contracts and leases (section 365).

Within the definition of executory contracts are collective bargaining agreements between the city and its employees. Such contracts may be rejected despite contrary State laws. Courts should readily allow the rejection of such contracts where they are burdensome, the rejection will aid in the municipality's reorganization and in consideration of the equities of each case. On the last point, "[e]quities in favor of the city in chapter 9 will be far more compelling than the equities in favor of the employer in chapter 11. Onerous employment obligations may prevent a city from balancing its budget for some time. The prospect of an unbalanced budget may preclude judicial confirmation of the plan. Unless a city can reject its labor contracts, lack of funds may force cutbacks in police, fire, sanitation, and welfare services, imposing hardships on many citizens. In addition, because cities in the past have often seemed immune to the constraint of "profitability" faced by private businesses, their wage contracts may be relatively more onerous than those in the private sector." Executory Contracts and Municipal Bankruptcy, 85 Yale L. J. 957, 965 (1976) (footnote omitted). Rejection of the contracts may require the municipalities to renegotiate such contracts by state collective bargaining laws. It is intended that the power to reject collective bargaining agreements will pre-empt state termination provisions, but not state collective bargaining laws. Thus, a city would not be required to maintain existing employment terms during the renegotiation period.

AMENDMENTS

1988—Pub. L. 100-597 designated existing provisions as subsec. (a) and added subsec. (b).

EFFECTIVE DATE OF 1988 AMENDMENT

Amendment by Pub. L. 100-597 effective Nov. 3, 1988, but not applicable to any case commenced under this title before that date, see section 12 of Pub. L. 100-597, set out as a note under section 101 of this title.

§ 927. Limitation on recourse

The holder of a claim payable solely from special revenues of the debtor under applicable nonbankruptcy law shall not be treated as having recourse against the debtor on account of such claim pursuant to section 1111(b) of this title.

(Added Pub. L. 100-597, § 7(2), Nov. 3, 1988, 102 Stat. 3029.)

PRIOR PROVISIONS

A prior section 927 was renumbered section 930 of this title.

EFFECTIVE DATE

Section effective Nov. 3, 1988, but not applicable to any case commenced under this title before that date, see section 12 of Pub. L. 100-597, set out as an Effective Date of 1988 Amendment note under section 101 of this title.

§ 928. Post petition effect of security interest

(a) Notwithstanding section 552(a) of this title and subject to subsection (b) of this section, special revenues acquired by the debtor after the commencement of the case shall remain subject to any lien resulting from any security agreement entered into by the debtor before the commencement of the case.

(b) Any such lien on special revenues, other than municipal betterment assessments, derived from a project or system shall be subject to the necessary operating expenses of such project or system, as the case may be.

(Added Pub. L. 100-597, § 8, Nov. 3, 1988, 102 Stat. 3029.)

EFFECTIVE DATE

Section effective Nov. 3, 1988, but not applicable to any case commenced under this title before that date, see section 12 of Pub. L. 100-597, set out as an Effective Date of 1988 Amendment note under section 101 of this title.

§ 929. Municipal leases

A lease to a municipality shall not be treated as an executory contract or unexpired lease for the purposes of section 365 or 502(b)(6) of this title solely by reason of its being subject to termination in the event the debtor fails to appropriate rent.

(Added Pub. L. 100-597, § 9, Nov. 3, 1988, 102 Stat. 3030.)

EFFECTIVE DATE

Section effective Nov. 3, 1988, but not applicable to any case commenced under this title before that date, see section 12 of Pub. L. 100-597, set out as an Effective Date of 1988 Amendment note under section 101 of this title.

§ 930. Dismissal

(a) After notice and a hearing, the court may dismiss a case under this chapter for cause, including—

(1) want of prosecution;

(2) unreasonable delay by the debtor that is prejudicial to creditors;

(3) failure to propose a plan within the time fixed under section 941 of this title;

(4) if a plan is not accepted within any time fixed by the court;

(5) denial of confirmation of a plan under section 943(b) of this title and denial of additional time for filing another plan or a modification of a plan; or

(6) if the court has retained jurisdiction after confirmation of a plan—

(A) material default by the debtor with respect to a term of such plan; or

(B) termination of such plan by reason of the occurrence of a condition specified in such plan.

(b) The court shall dismiss a case under this chapter if confirmation of a plan under this chapter is refused.

(Pub. L. 95-598, Nov. 6, 1978, 92 Stat. 2623, § 927; Pub. L. 98-353, title III, § 496, July 10, 1984, 98 Stat. 384; renumbered § 930, Pub. L. 100-597, § 7(1), Nov. 3, 1988, 102 Stat. 3029.)

HISTORICAL AND REVISION NOTES

LEGISLATIVE STATEMENTS

Section 927(b) of the House amendment is derived from section 927(b) of the Senate bill. The provision requires mandatory dismissal if confirmation of a plan is refused.

The House amendment deletes section 929 of the Senate amendment as unnecessary since the bankruptcy court has original exclusive jurisdiction of all cases under chapter 9.

The House amendment deletes section 930 of the Senate amendment and incorporates section 507(a)(1) by reference.

SENATE REPORT NO. 95-989

Section 927 conforms to section 98 of current law [section 418 of former title 11]. The Section permits dismissal by the court for unreasonable delay by the debtor, failure to propose a plan, failure of acceptance of a plan, or default by the debtor under a conformed plan. Mandatory dismissal is required if confirmation is refused.

HOUSE REPORT NO. 95–595

Section 926 [enacted as section 927] generally conforms to section 98(a) [section 418(a) of former title 11] of current law. Stylistic changes have been made to conform the language with that used in chapter 11, section 1112. The section permits dismissal by the court for unreasonable delay by the debtor that is prejudicial to creditors, failure to propose a plan, failure of confirmation of a plan, or material default by the debtor under a confirmed plan. The only significant change from current law lies in the second ground. Currently, section 98(a)(2) provides for dismissal if a proposed plan is not accepted, and section 98(b) *requires* dismissal if an accepted plan is not confirmed. In order to provide greater flexibility to the court, the debtor, and creditors, the bill allows the court to permit the debtor to propose another plan if the first plan is not confirmed. In that event the debtor need not, as under current law, commence the case all over again. This could provide savings in time and administrative expenses if a plan is denied confirmation.

AMENDMENTS

1984—Subsec. (b). Pub. L. 98–353 substituted "confirmation of a plan under this chapter" for "confirmation".

EFFECTIVE DATE OF 1984 AMENDMENT

Amendment by Pub. L. 98–353 effective with respect to cases filed 90 days after July 10, 1984, see section 552(a) of Pub. L. 98–353, set out as a note under section 101 of this title.

SUBCHAPTER III—THE PLAN

§ 941. Filing of plan

The debtor shall file a plan for the adjustment of the debtor's debts. If such a plan is not filed with the petition, the debtor shall file such a plan at such later time as the court fixes.

(Pub. L. 95–598, Nov. 6, 1978, 92 Stat. 2624.)

HISTORICAL AND REVISION NOTES

SENATE REPORT NO. 95–989

Section 941 gives the debtor the exclusive right to propose a plan, and directs that the debtor propose one either with the petition or within such time as the court directs. The section follows section 90(a) of current law [section 410(a) of former title 11].

§ 942. Modification of plan

The debtor may modify the plan at any time before confirmation, but may not modify the plan so that the plan as modified fails to meet the requirements of this chapter. After the debtor files a modification, the plan as modified becomes the plan.

(Pub. L. 95–598, Nov. 6, 1978, 92 Stat. 2624.)

HISTORICAL AND REVISION NOTES

LEGISLATIVE STATEMENTS

The House amendment deletes section 942 of the Senate amendment in favor of incorporating section 1125 by cross-reference. Similarly, the House amendment does not incorporate section 944 or 945 of the Senate amendment since incorporation of several sections in chapter 11 in section 901 is sufficient.

SENATE REPORT NO. 95–989

Section 942 permits the debtor to modify the plan at any time before confirmation, as does section 90(a) of current law [section 410(a) of former title 11].

§ 943. Confirmation

(a) A special tax payer may object to confirmation of a plan.

(b) The court shall confirm the plan if—

(1) the plan complies with the provisions of this title made applicable by sections 103(e)[1] and 901 of this title;

(2) the plan complies with the provisions of this chapter;

(3) all amounts to be paid by the debtor or by any person for services or expenses in the case or incident to the plan have been fully disclosed and are reasonable;

(4) the debtor is not prohibited by law from taking any action necessary to carry out the plan;

(5) except to the extent that the holder of a particular claim has agreed to a different treatment of such claim, the plan provides that on the effective date of the plan each holder of a claim of a kind specified in section 507(a)(2) of this title will receive on account of such claim cash equal to the allowed amount of such claim;

(6) any regulatory or electoral approval necessary under applicable nonbankruptcy law in order to carry out any provision of the plan has been obtained, or such provision is expressly conditioned on such approval; and

(7) the plan is in the best interests of creditors and is feasible.

(Pub. L. 95–598, Nov. 6, 1978, 92 Stat. 2624; Pub. L. 98–353, title III, § 497, July 10, 1984, 98 Stat. 384; Pub. L. 100–597, § 10, Nov. 3, 1988, 102 Stat. 3030; Pub. L. 109–8, title XV, § 1502(a)(6), Apr. 20, 2005, 119 Stat. 216.)

HISTORICAL AND REVISION NOTES

LEGISLATIVE STATEMENTS

Section 943(a) of the House amendment makes clear that a special taxpayer may object to confirmation of a plan. Section 943(b) of the House amendment is derived from section 943 of the House bill respecting confirmation of a plan under chapter 9. It must be emphasized that these standards of confirmation are in addition to standards in section 1129 that are made applicable to chapter 9 by section 901 of the House amendment. In particular, if the requirements of sections 1129(a)(8) are not complied with, then the proponent may request application of section 1129(b). The court will then be required to confirm the plan if it complies with the "fair and equitable" test and is in the best interests of creditors. The best interests of creditors test does not mean liquidation value as under chapter XI of the Bankruptcy Act [chapter 11 of former title 11]. In making such a determination, it is expected that the court will be guided by standards set forth in *Kelley v. Everglades Drainage District*, 319 U.S. 415 (1943) [Fla.1943, 63 S.Ct. 1141, 87 L.Ed. 1485, rehearing denied 63 S.Ct. 1444, 320 U.S. 214, 87 L.Ed. 1851, motion denied 64 S.Ct 783, 321 U.S. 754, 88 L.Ed. 1054] and *Fano v. Newport Heights Irrigation Dist.*, 114 F.2d 563 (9th Cir. 1940), as under present law, the bankruptcy court should make findings as detailed as possible to support a conclusion that this test has been met. However, it must be emphasized that un-

[1] See References in Text note below.

like current law, the fair and equitable test under section 1129(b) will not apply if section 1129(a)(8) has been satisfied in addition to the other confirmation standards specified in section 943 and incorporated by reference in section 901 of the House amendment. To the extent that *American United Mutual Life Insurance Co. v. City of Avon Park*, 311 U.S. 138 (1940) [Fla.1940, 61 S.Ct. 157, 85 L.Ed. 91, 136 A.L.R. 860, rehearing denied 61 S.Ct. 395, 311 U.S. 730, 85 L.Ed. 475] and other cases are to the contrary, such cases are overruled to that extent.

SENATE REPORT NO. 95–989

Section 946 [enacted as section 943] is adopted from current section 94 [section 414 of former title 11]. The test for confirmation is whether or not the plan is fair and equitable and feasible. The fair and equitable test tracts current chapter X [chapter 10 of former title 11] and is known as the strict priority rule. Creditors must be provided, under the plan, the going concern value of their claims. The going concern value contemplates a "comparison of revenues and expenditures taking into account the taxing power and the extent to which tax increases are both necessary and feasible" Municipal Insolvency, supra, at p. 64, and is intended to provide more of a return to creditors than the liquidation value if the city's assets could be liquidated like those of a private corporation.

HOUSE REPORT NO. 95–595

In addition to the confirmation requirements incorporated from section 1129 by section 901, this section specifies additional requirements. Paragraph (1) requires compliance with the provisions of the title made applicable in chapter 9 cases. This provision follows section 94(b)(2) [section 414(b)(2) of former title 11]. Paragraph (2) requires compliance with the provisions of chapter 9, as does section 94(b)(2). Paragraph (3) adopts section 94(b)(4), requiring disclosure and reasonableness of all payments to be made in connection with the plan or the case. Paragraph (4), copied from section 92(b)(6) [probably should be "94(b)(6)" which was section 414(b)(6) of former title 11], requires that the debtor not be prohibited by law from taking any action necessary to carry out the plan. Paragraph (5) departs from current law by requiring that administrative expenses be paid in full, but not necessarily in cash. Finally, paragraph (6) requires that the plan be in the best interest of creditors and feasible. The best interest test was deleted in section 94(b)(1) of current chapter IX from previous chapter IX [chapter 9 of former title 11] because it was redundant with the fair and equitable rule. However, this bill proposes a new confirmation standard generally for reorganization, one element of which is the best interest of creditors test; see section 1129(a)(7). In that section, the test is phrased in terms of liquidation of the debtor. Because that is not possible in a municipal case, the test here is phrased in its more traditional form, using the words of art "best interest of creditors." The best interest of creditors test here is in addition to the financial standards imposed on the plan by sections 1129(a)(8) and 1129(b), just as those provisions are in addition to the comparable best interest test in chapter 11. 11 U.S.C. 1129(a)(7). The feasibility requirement, added in the revision of chapter IX last year, is retained.

REFERENCES IN TEXT

Section 103(e) of this title, referred to in subsec. (b)(1), was redesignated section 103(f) and a new section 103(e) was added by Pub. L. 106–554, §1(a)(5) [title I, §112(c)(5)(A)], Dec. 21, 2000, 114 Stat. 2763, 2763A–394.

AMENDMENTS

2005—Subsec. (b)(5). Pub. L. 109–8 substituted "507(a)(2)" for "507(a)(1)".

1988—Subsec. (b)(6), (7). Pub. L. 100–597 added par. (6) and redesignated former par. (6) as (7).

1984—Subsec. (b)(4). Pub. L. 98–353, §497(1), struck out "to be taken" after "necessary".

Subsec. (b)(5). Pub. L. 98–353, §497(2), substituted provisions requiring the plan to provide payment of cash in an amount equal to the allowed amount of a claim except to the extent that the holder of a particular claim has agreed to different treatment of such claim, for provisions which required the plan to provide for payment of property of a value equal to the allowed amount of such claim except to the extent that the holder of a particular claim has waived such payment on such claim.

EFFECTIVE DATE OF 2005 AMENDMENT

Amendment by Pub. L. 109–8 effective 180 days after Apr. 20, 2005, and not applicable with respect to cases commenced under this title before such effective date, except as otherwise provided, see section 1501 of Pub. L. 109–8, set out as a note under section 101 of this title.

EFFECTIVE DATE OF 1988 AMENDMENT

Amendment by Pub. L. 100–597 effective Nov. 3, 1988, but not applicable to any case commenced under this title before that date, see section 12 of Pub. L. 100–597, set out as a note under section 101 of this title.

EFFECTIVE DATE OF 1984 AMENDMENT

Amendment by Pub. L. 98–353 effective with respect to cases filed 90 days after July 10, 1984, see section 552(a) of Pub. L. 98–353, set out as a note under section 101 of this title.

§ 944. Effect of confirmation

(a) The provisions of a confirmed plan bind the debtor and any creditor, whether or not—

(1) a proof of such creditor's claim is filed or deemed filed under section 501 of this title;

(2) such claim is allowed under section 502 of this title; or

(3) such creditor has accepted the plan.

(b) Except as provided in subsection (c) of this section, the debtor is discharged from all debts as of the time when—

(1) the plan is confirmed;

(2) the debtor deposits any consideration to be distributed under the plan with a disbursing agent appointed by the court; and

(3) the court has determined—

(A) that any security so deposited will constitute, after distribution, a valid legal obligation of the debtor; and

(B) that any provision made to pay or secure payment of such obligation is valid.

(c) The debtor is not discharged under subsection (b) of this section from any debt—

(1) excepted from discharge by the plan or order confirming the plan; or

(2) owed to an entity that, before confirmation of the plan, had neither notice nor actual knowledge of the case.

(Pub. L. 95–598, Nov. 6, 1978, 92 Stat. 2624.)

HISTORICAL AND REVISION NOTES

SENATE REPORT NO. 95–989

[Section 947] Subsection (a) [enacted as section 944(a)] makes the provisions of a confirmed plan binding on the debtor and creditors. It is derived from section 95(a) of chapter 9 [section 415(a) of former title 11].

Subsections (b) and (c) [enacted as section 944(b) and (c)] provide for the discharge of a municipality. The discharge is essentially the same as that granted under section 95(b) of the Bankruptcy Act [section 415(b) of former title 11].

§ 945. Continuing jurisdiction and closing of the case

(a) The court may retain jurisdiction over the case for such period of time as is necessary for the successful implementation of the plan.

(b) Except as provided in subsection (a) of this section, the court shall close the case when administration of the case has been completed.

(Pub. L. 95–598, Nov. 6, 1978, 92 Stat. 2625; Pub. L. 98–353, title III, § 498, July 10, 1984, 98 Stat. 384.)

HISTORICAL AND REVISION NOTES

SENATE REPORT NO. 95–989

Section 948 [enacted as section 945] permits the court to retain jurisdiction over the case to ensure successful execution of the plan. The provision is the same as that found in section 96(e) of Chapter 9 of the present Act [section 416(e) of former title 11].

AMENDMENTS

1984—Subsec. (a). Pub. L. 98–353 substituted "implementation" for "execution".

EFFECTIVE DATE OF 1984 AMENDMENT

Amendment by Pub. L. 98–353 effective with respect to cases filed 90 days after July 10, 1984, see section 552(a) of Pub. L. 98–353, set out as a note under section 101 of this title.

§ 946. Effect of exchange of securities before the date of the filing of the petition

The exchange of a new security under the plan for a claim covered by the plan, whether such exchange occurred before or after the date of the filing of the petition, does not limit or impair the effectiveness of the plan or of any provision of this chapter. The amount and number specified in section 1126(c) of this title include the amount and number of claims formerly held by a creditor that has participated in any such exchange.

(Pub. L. 95–598, Nov. 6, 1978, 92 Stat. 2625.)

HISTORICAL AND REVISION NOTES

LEGISLATIVE STATEMENTS

The House amendment deletes section 950 of the Senate amendment as unnecessary. The constitutionality of chapter 9 of the House amendment is beyond doubt.

SENATE REPORT NO. 95–989

[Section 949] This section [enacted as section 946], which follows section 97 of current law [section 417 of former title 11], permits an exchange of a security before the case is filed to constitute an acceptance of the plan if the exchange was under a proposal that later becomes the plan.

CHAPTER 11—REORGANIZATION

SUBCHAPTER I—OFFICERS AND ADMINISTRATION

HISTORICAL AND REVISION NOTES

LEGISLATIVE STATEMENTS

Chapter 11 of the House amendment is derived in large part from chapter 11 as contained in the House bill. Unlike chapter 11 of the Senate amendment, chapter 11 of the House amendment does not represent an extension of chapter X of current law [chapter 10 of former title 11] or any other chapter of the Bankruptcy Act [former title 11]. Rather chapter 11 of the House amendment takes a new approach consolidating subjects dealt with under chapters VIII, X, XI, and XII of the Bankruptcy Act [chapters 8, 10, 11, and 12 of former title 11]. The new consolidated chapter 11 contains no special procedure for companies with public debt or equity security holders. Instead, factors such as the standard to be applied to solicitation of acceptances of a plan of reorganization are left to be determined by the court on a case-by-case basis. In order to insure that adequate investigation of the debtor is conducted to determine fraud or wrongdoing on the part of present management, an examiner is required to be appointed in all cases in which the debtor's fixed, liquidated, and unsecured debts, other than debts for goods, services, or taxes, or owing to an insider, exceed $5 million. This should adequately represent the needs of public security holders in most cases. However, in addition, section 1109 of the House amendment enables both the Securities and Exchange Commission and any party in interest who is creditor, equity security holder, indenture trustee, or any committee representing creditors or equity security holders to raise and appear and be heard on any issue in a case under chapter 11. This will enable the bankruptcy court to evaluate all sides of a position and to determine the public interest. This approach is sharply contrasted to that under chapter X of present law in which the public interest is often determined only in terms of the interest of public security holders. The advisory role of the Securities and Exchange Commission will enable the court to balance the needs of public security holders against equally important public needs relating to the economy, such as employment and production, and other factors such as the public health and safety of the people or protection of the national interest. In this context, the new chapter 11 deletes archaic rules contained in certain chapters of present law such as the requirement of an approval hearing and the prohibition of prepetition solicitation. Such requirements were written in an age before the enactment of the Trust Indenture Act [15 U.S.C. 77aaa et seq.] and the development of securities laws had occurred. The benefits of these provisions have long been outlived but the detriment of the provisions served to frustrate and delay effective reorganization in those chapters of the Bankruptcy Act in which such provisions applied. Chapter 11 thus represents a much needed revision of reorganization laws. A brief discussion of the history of this important achievement is useful to an appreciation of the monumental reform embraced in chapter 11.

Under the existing Bankruptcy Act [former title 11] debtors seeking reorganization may choose among three reorganization chapters, chapter X, chapter XI, and chapter XII [chapters 10, 11, and 12 of former title 11]. Individuals and partnerships may file under chapter XI or, if they own property encumbered by mortgage liens, they may file under chapter XII. A corporation may file under either chapter X or chapter XI, but is ineligible to file under chapter XII. Chapter X was designed to facilitate the pervasive reorganization of corporations whose creditors include holders of publicly issued debt securities. Chapter XI, on the other hand, was designed to permit smaller enterprises to negotiate composition or extension plans with their unsecured creditors. The essential differences between chapters X and XI are as follows. Chapter X mandates that, first, an independent trustee be appointed and assume management control from the officers and directors of the debtor corporation; second, the Securities and Exchange Commission must be afforded an opportunity to participate both as an adviser to the court and as a representative of the interests of public security holders; third, the court must approve any proposed plan of reorganization, and prior to such approval, acceptances of creditors and shareholders may not be solicited; fourth, the court must apply the absolute priority rule; and fifth, the court has the power to affect, and grant the debtor a discharge in respect of, all types of claims, whether secured or unsecured and whether arising by reason of fraud or breach of contract.

The Senate amendment consolidates chapters X, XI, and XII [chapters 10, 11, and 12 of former title 11], but establishes a separate and distinct reorganization procedure for "public companies." The special provisions applicable to "public companies" are tantamount to the codification of chapter X of the existing Bankruptcy Act and thus result in the creation of a "two-track system." The narrow definition of the term "public company" would require many businesses which could have been rehabilitated under chapter XI to instead use the more cumbersome procedures of chapter X, whether needed or not.

The special provisions of the Senate amendment applicable to a "public company" are as follows:

(a) Section 1101(3) defines a "public company" as a debtor who, within 12 months prior to the filing of the petition, had outstanding $5 million or more in debt and had not less than 1000 security holders;

(b) Section 1104(a) requires the appointment of a disinterested trustee irrespective of whether creditors support such appointment and whether there is cause for such appointment;

(c) Section 1125(f) prohibits the solicitation of acceptances of a plan of reorganization prior to court approval of such plan even though the solicitation complies with all applicable securities laws;

(d) Section 1128(a) requires the court to conduct a hearing on any plan of reorganization proposed by the trustee or any other party;

(e) Section 1128(b) requires the court to refer any plans "worthy of consideration" to the Securities and Exchange Commission for their examination and report, prior to court approval of a plan; and

(f) Section 1128(c) and section 1130(a)(7) requires the court to approve a plan or plans which are "fair and equitable" and comply with the other provisions of chapter 11.

The record of the Senate hearings on S. 2266 and the House hearings on H.R. 8200 is replete with evidence of the failure of the reorganization provisions of the existing Bankruptcy Act [former title 11] to meet the needs of insolvent corporations in today's business environment. Chapter X [chapter 10 of former title 11] was designed to impose rigid and formalized procedures upon the reorganization of corporations and, although designed to protect public creditors, has often worked to the detriment of such creditors. As the House report has noted:

The negative results under chapter X [chapter 10 of former title 11] have resulted from the stilted procedures, under which management is always ousted and replaced by an independent trustee, the courts and the Securities and Exchange Commission examine the plan of reorganization in great detail, no matter how long that takes, and the court values the business, a time consuming and inherently uncertain procedure.

The House amendment deletes the "public company" exception, because it would codify the well recognized infirmities of chapter X [chapter 10 of former title 11], because it would extend the chapter X approach to a large number of new cases without regard to whether the rigid and formalized procedures of chapter X are needed, and because it is predicated upon the myth that provisions similar to those contained in chapter X are necessary for the protection of public investors. Bankruptcy practice in large reorganization cases has also changed substantially in the 40 years since the Chandler Act [June 22, 1938, ch. 575, 52 Stat. 883, amending former title 11] was enacted. This change is, in large part, attributable to the pervasive effect of the Federal securities laws and the extraordinary success of the Securities and Exchange Commission in sensitizing both management and members of the bar to the need for full disclosure and fair dealing in transactions involving publicly held securities.

It is important to note that Congress passed the Chandler Act [June 22, 1938, ch. 575, 52 Stat. 883, amending former title 11] prior to enactment of the Trust Indenture Act of 1939 [15 U.S.C. section 77aaa et seq.] and prior to the definition and enforcement of the disclosure requirements of the Securities Act of 1933 [15 U.S.C. 77a et seq.] and the Securities Exchange Act of 1934 [15 U.S.C. 78a et seq.]. The judgments made by the 75th Congress in enacting the Chandler Act are not equally applicable to the financial markets of 1978. First of all, most public debenture holders are neither weak nor unsophisticated investors. In most cases, a significant portion of the holders of publicly issued debentures are sophisticated institutions, acting for their own account or as trustees for investment funds, pension funds, or private trusts. In addition, debenture holders, sophisticated and unsophisticated alike, are represented by indenture trustees, qualified under section 77ggg of the Trust Indenture Act [probably should be "section 307" which is 15 U.S.C. 77ggg]. Given the high standard of care to which indenture trustees are bound, they are invariably active and sophisticated participants in efforts to rehabilitate corporate debtors in distress.

It is also important to note that in 1938 when the Chandler Act [June 22, 1938, ch. 575, 52 Stat. 883, amending former title 11] was enacted, public investors commonly held senior, not subordinated, debentures and corporations were very often privately owned. In this environment, the absolute priority rule protected debenture holders from an erosion of their position in favor of equity holders. Today, however, if there are public security holders in a case, they are likely to be holders of subordinated debentures and equity and thus the application of the absolute priority rule under chapter X [chapter 10 of former title 11] leads to the exclusion, rather than the protection, of the public.

The primary problem posed by chapter X [chapter 10 of former title 11] is delay. The modern corporation is a complex and multifaceted entity. Most corporations do not have a significant market share of the lines of business in which they compete. The success, and even the survival, of a corporation in contemporary markets depends on three elements: First, the ability to attract and hold skilled management; second, the ability to obtain credit; and third, the corporation's ability to project to the public an image of vitality. Over and over again, it is demonstrated that corporations which must avail themselves of the provisions of the Bankruptcy Act [former title 11] suffer appreciable deterioration if they are caught in a chapter X proceeding for any substantial period of time.

There are exceptions to this rule. For example, King Resources filed a chapter X [chapter 10 of former title 11] petition in the District of Colorado and it emerged from such proceeding as a solvent corporation. The debtor's new found solvency was not, however, so much attributable to a brilliant rehabilitation program conceived by a trustee, but rather to a substantial appreciation in the value of the debtor's oil and uranium properties during the pendency of the proceedings.

Likewise, Equity Funding is always cited as an example of a successful chapter X [chapter 10 of former title 11] case. But it should be noted that in Equity Funding there was no question about retaining existing management. Rather, Equity Funding involved fraud on a grand scale. Under the House amendment with the deletion of the mandatory appointment of a trustee in cases involving "public companies," a bankruptcy judge, in a case like Equity Funding, would presumably have little difficulty in concluding that a trustee should be appointed under section 1104(6).

While I will not undertake to list the chapter X [chapter 10 of former title 11] failures, it is important to note a number of cases involving corporations which would be "public companies" under the Senate amendment which have successfully skirted the shoals of chapter X and confirmed plans of arrangement in chapter XI [chapter 11 of former title 11]. Among these are Daylin, Inc. ("Daylin") and Colwell Mortgage Investors ("Colwell").

Daylin filed a chapter XI [chapter 11 of former title 11] petition on February 26, 1975, and confirmed its plan of arrangement on October 20, 1976. The success of its turnaround is best evidenced by the fact that it had consolidated net income of $6,473,000 for the first three quarters of the 1978 fiscal year.

Perhaps the best example of the contrast between chapter XI and chapter X [chapters 11 and 10 of former title 11] is the recent case of *In re Colwell Mortgage Investors*. Colwell negotiated a recapitalization plan with its institutional creditors, filed a proxy statement with the Securities and Exchange Commission, and solicited consents of its creditors and shareholders prior to filing its chapter XI petition. Thereafter, Colwell confirmed its plan of arrangement 41 days after filing its chapter XI petition. This result would have been impossible under the Senate amendment since Colwell would have been a "public company."

There are a number of other corporations with publicly held debt which have successfully reorganized under chapter XI [chapter 11 of former title 11]. Among these are National Mortgage Fund (NMF), which filed a chapter XI petition in the northern district of Ohio on June 30, 1976. Prior to commencement of the chapter XI proceeding, NMF filed a proxy statement with the Securities and Exchange Commission and solicited acceptances to a proposed plan of arrangement. The NMF plan was subsequently confirmed on December 14, 1976. The Securities and Exchange Commission did not file a motion under section 328 of the Bankruptcy Act [section 728 of former title 11] to transfer the case to chapter X [chapter 10 of former title 11] and a transfer motion which was filed by private parties was denied by the court.

While there are other examples of large publicly held companies which have successfully reorganized in chapter XI [chapter 11 of former title 11], including Esgrow, Inc. (C.D.Cal. 73-02510), Sherwood Diversified Services Inc. (S.D.N.Y. 73-B-213), and United Merchants and Manufacturers, Inc. (S.D.N.Y. 77-B-1513), the numerous successful chapter XI cases demonstrate two points: first, the complicated and time-consuming provisions of chapter X [chapter 10 of former title 11] are not always necessary for the successful reorganization of a company with publicly held debt, and second, the more flexible provisions in chapter XI permit a debtor to obtain relief under the Bankruptcy Act [former title 11] in significantly less time than is required to confirm a plan of reorganization under chapter X of the Bankruptcy Act.

One cannot overemphasize the advantages of speed and simplicity to both creditors and debtors. Chapter XI [chapter 11 of former title 11] allows a debtor to negotiate a plan outside of court and, having reached a settlement with a majority in number and amount of each class of creditors, permits the debtor to bind all unsecured creditors to the terms of the arrangement. From the perspective of creditors, early confirmation of a plan of arrangement: first, generally reduces administrative expenses which have priority over the claims of unsecured creditors; second, permits creditors to receive prompt distributions on their claims with respect to which interest does not accrue after the filing date; and third, increases the ultimate recovery on creditor claims by minimizing the adverse effect on the business which often accompanies efforts to operate an enterprise under the protection of the Bankruptcy Act [former title 11].

Although chapter XI [chapter 11 of former title 11] offers the corporate debtor flexibility and continuity of management, successful rehabilitation under chapter XI is often impossible for a number of reasons. First, chapter XI does not permit a debtor to "affect" secured creditors or shareholders, in the absence of their consent. Second, whereas a debtor corporation in chapter X [chapter 10 of former title 11], upon the consummation of the plan or reorganization, is discharged from all its debts and liabilities, a corporation in chapter XI may not be able to get a discharge in respect of certain kinds of claims including fraud claims, even in cases where the debtor is being operated under new management. The language of chapter 11 in the House amendment solves these problems and thus increases the utility and flexibility of the new chapter 11, as compared to chapter XI of the existing Bankruptcy Act [chapter 11 of former title 11].

Those who would urge the adoption of a two-track system have two major obstacles to meet. First, the practical experience of those involved in business rehabilitation cases, practitioners, debtors, and bankruptcy judges, has been that the more simple and expeditious procedures of chapter XI [chapter 11 of former title 11] are appropriate in the great majority of cases. While attempts have been made to convince the courts that a chapter X [chapter 10 of former title 11] proceeding is required in every case where public debt is present, the courts have categorically rejected such arguments. Second, chapter X has been far from a success. Of the 991 chapter X cases filed during the period of January 1, 1967, through December 31, 1977, only 664 have been terminated. Of those cases recorded as "terminated," only 140 resulted in consummated plans. This 21 percent success rate suggests one of the reasons for the unpopularity of chapter X.

In summary, it has been the experience of the great majority of those who have testified before the Senate and House subcommittees that a consolidated approach to business rehabilitation is warranted. Such approach is adopted in the House amendment.

Having discussed the general reasons why chapter 11 of the House amendment is sorely needed, a brief discussion of the differences between the House bill, Senate amendment, and the House amendment, is in order. Since chapter 11 of the House amendment rejects the concept of separate treatment for a public company, sections 1101(3), 1104(a), 1125(f), 1128, and 1130(a)(7) of the Senate amendment have been deleted.

AMENDMENTS

2005—Pub. L. 109–8, title III, §321(a)(2), title IV, §436(b), Apr. 20, 2005, 119 Stat. 95, 113, added items 1115 and 1116.

1988—Pub. L. 100–334, §2(c), June 16, 1988, 102 Stat. 613, added item 1114.

1984—Pub. L. 98–353, title III, §§514(b), 541(b), July 10, 1984, 98 Stat. 387, 391, added item 1113 and substituted "Implementation" for "Execution" in item 1142.

1983—Pub. L. 97–449, §5(a)(1), Jan. 12, 1983, 96 Stat. 2442, substituted "subtitle IV of title 49" for "Interstate Commerce Act" in item 1166.

SUBCHAPTER I—OFFICERS AND ADMINISTRATION

§1101. Definitions for this chapter

In this chapter—

(1) "debtor in possession" means debtor except when a person that has qualified under section 322 of this title is serving as trustee in the case;

(2) "substantial consummation" means—

(A) transfer of all or substantially all of the property proposed by the plan to be transferred;

(B) assumption by the debtor or by the successor to the debtor under the plan of the business or of the management of all or substantially all of the property dealt with by the plan; and

(C) commencement of distribution under the plan.

(Pub. L. 95–598, Nov. 6, 1978, 92 Stat. 2626.)

HISTORICAL AND REVISION NOTES

SENATE REPORT NO. 95–989

This section contains definitions of three terms that are used in chapter 11. Paragraph (1) defines debtor in possession to mean the debtor, except when a trustee who has qualified in serving in the case.

Paragraph (2), derived from section 229a of current law [section 629(a) of former title 11], defines substantial consummation. Substantial consummation of a plan occurs when transfer of all or substantially all of the property proposed by the plan to be transferred is actually transferred; when the debtor (or its successor) has assumed the business of the debtor or the management of all or substantially all of the property dealt with by the plan; and when distribution under the plan has commenced.

Paragraph (3) defines for purposes of Chapter 11 a public company to mean "a debtor who, within 12 months prior to the filing of a petition for relief under this chapter, had outstanding liabilities of $5 million or more, exclusive of liabilities for goods, services, or taxes and not less than 1,000 security holders." There are, as noted, special safeguards for public investors related to the reorganization of a public company, as so defined.

Both requirements must be met: liabilities, excluding tax obligations and trade liabilities, must be $5 million or more; and (2) the number of holders of securities, debt or equity, or both, must be not less than 1,000. The amount and number are to be determined as of any time within 12 months prior to the filing of the petition for reorganization.

§1102. Creditors' and equity security holders' committees

(a)(1) Except as provided in paragraph (3), as soon as practicable after the order for relief under chapter 11 of this title, the United States trustee shall appoint a committee of creditors holding unsecured claims and may appoint additional committees of creditors or of equity security holders as the United States trustee deems appropriate.

(2) On request of a party in interest, the court may order the appointment of additional committees of creditors or of equity security holders if necessary to assure adequate representation of creditors or of equity security holders. The United States trustee shall appoint any such committee.

(3) On request of a party in interest in a case in which the debtor is a small business debtor and for cause, the court may order that a committee of creditors not be appointed.

(4) On request of a party in interest and after notice and a hearing, the court may order the United States trustee to change the membership of a committee appointed under this subsection, if the court determines that the change is necessary to ensure adequate representation of creditors or equity security holders. The court may order the United States trustee to increase the number of members of a committee to include a creditor that is a small business concern (as described in section 3(a)(1) of the Small Business Act), if the court determines that the creditor holds claims (of the kind represented by the committee) the aggregate amount of which, in comparison to the annual gross revenue of that creditor, is disproportionately large.

(b)(1) A committee of creditors appointed under subsection (a) of this section shall ordinarily consist of the persons, willing to serve, that hold the seven largest claims against the debtor of the kinds represented on such committee, or of the members of a committee organized by creditors before the commencement of the case under this chapter, if such committee was fairly chosen and is representative of the different kinds of claims to be represented.

(2) A committee of equity security holders appointed under subsection (a)(2) of this section shall ordinarily consist of the persons, willing to serve, that hold the seven largest amounts of equity securities of the debtor of the kinds represented on such committee.

(3) A committee appointed under subsection (a) shall—

(A) provide access to information for creditors who—

(i) hold claims of the kind represented by that committee; and

(ii) are not appointed to the committee;

(B) solicit and receive comments from the creditors described in subparagraph (A); and

(C) be subject to a court order that compels any additional report or disclosure to be made to the creditors described in subparagraph (A).

(Pub. L. 95–598, Nov. 6, 1978, 92 Stat. 2626; Pub. L. 98–353, title III, §499, July 10, 1984, 98 Stat. 384;

Pub. L. 99–554, title II, §221, Oct. 27, 1986, 100 Stat. 3101; Pub. L. 103–394, title II, §217(b), Oct. 22, 1994, 108 Stat. 4127; Pub. L. 109–8, title IV, §§405, 432(b), Apr. 20, 2005, 119 Stat. 105, 110.)

HISTORICAL AND REVISION NOTES

LEGISLATIVE STATEMENTS

Section 1102(a) of the House amendment adopts a compromise between the House bill and Senate amendment requiring appointment of a committee of creditors holding unsecured claims by the court; the alternative of creditor committee election is rejected.

Section 1102(b) of the House amendment represents a compromise between the House bill and the Senate amendment by preventing the appointment of creditors who are unwilling to serve on a creditors committee.

SENATE REPORT NO. 95–989

This section provides for the election and appointment of committees. Subsection (c) provides that this section does not apply in case of a public company, as to which a trustee, appointed under section 1104(a) will have responsibility to administer the estate and to formulate a plan as provided in section 1106(a).

There is no need for the election or appointment of committees for which the appointment of a trustee is mandatory. In the case of a public company there are likely to be several committees, each representing a different class of security holders and seeking authority to retain accountants, lawyers, and other experts, who will expect to be paid. If in the case of a public company creditors or stockholders wish to organize committees, they may do so, as authorized under section 1109(a). Compensation and reimbursement will be allowed for contributions to the reorganization pursuant to section 503(b) (3) and (4).

HOUSE REPORT NO. 95–595

This section provides for the appointment of creditors' and equity security holders' committees, which will be the primary negotiating bodies for the formulation of the plan of reorganization. They will represent the various classes of creditors and equity security holders from which they are selected. They will also provide supervision of the debtor in possession and of the trustee, and will protect their constituents' interests.

Subsection (a) requires the court to appoint at least one committee. That committee is to be composed of creditors holding unsecured claims. The court is authorized to appoint such additional committees as are necessary to assure adequate representation of creditors and equity security holders. The provision will be relied upon in cases in which the debtor proposes to affect several classes of debt or equity holders under the plan, and in which they need representation.

Subsection (b) contains precatory language directing the court to appoint the persons holding the seven largest claims against the debtor of the kinds represented on a creditors' committee, or the members of a prepetition committee organized by creditors before the order for relief under chapter 11. The court may continue prepetition committee members only if the committee was fairly chosen and is representative of the different kinds of claims to be represented. The court is restricted to the appointment of persons in order to exclude governmental holders of claims or interests.

Paragraph (2) of subsection (b) requires similar treatment for equity security holders' committees. The seven largest holders are normally to be appointed, but the language is only precatory.

Subsection (c) authorizes the court, on request of a party in interest, to change the size or the membership of a creditors' or equity security holders' committee if the membership of the committee is not representative of the different kinds of claims or interests to be represented. This subsection is intended, along with the nonbinding nature of subsection (b), to afford the court latitude in appointing a committee that is manageable and representative in light of the circumstances of the case.

REFERENCES IN TEXT

Section 3(a)(1) of the Small Business Act, referred to in subsec. (a)(4), is classified to section 632(a)(1) of Title 15, Commerce and Trade.

AMENDMENTS

2005—Subsec. (a)(3). Pub. L. 109–8, §432(b), inserted "debtor" after "small business".

Subsec. (a)(4). Pub. L. 109–8, §405(a), added par. (4).

Subsec. (b)(3). Pub. L. 109–8, §405(b), added par. (3).

1994—Subsec. (a). Pub. L. 103–394 substituted "Except as provided in paragraph (3), as" for "As" in par. (1) and added par. (3).

1986—Subsec. (a). Pub. L. 99–554, §221(1), amended subsec. (a) generally, substituting "chapter 11 of this title, the United States trustee shall appoint a committee of creditors holding unsecured claims and may appoint additional committees of creditors or of equity security holders as the United States trustee deems appropriate" for "this chapter, the court shall appoint a committee of creditors holding unsecured claims" in par. (1) and "United States trustee" for "court" in par. (2).

Subsec. (c). Pub. L. 99–554, §221(2), struck out subsec. (c) which read as follows: "On request of a party in interest and after notice and a hearing, the court may change the membership or the size of a committee appointed under subsection (a) of this section if the membership of such committee is not representative of the different kinds of claims or interests to be represented."

1984—Subsec. (b)(1). Pub. L. 98–353 substituted "commencement of the case" for "order for relief".

EFFECTIVE DATE OF 2005 AMENDMENT

Amendment by Pub. L. 109–8 effective 180 days after Apr. 20, 2005, and not applicable with respect to cases commenced under this title before such effective date, except as otherwise provided, see section 1501 of Pub. L. 109–8, set out as a note under section 101 of this title.

EFFECTIVE DATE OF 1994 AMENDMENT

Amendment by Pub. L. 103–394 effective Oct. 22, 1994, and not applicable with respect to cases commenced under this title before Oct. 22, 1994, see section 702 of Pub. L. 103–394, set out as a note under section 101 of this title.

EFFECTIVE DATE OF 1986 AMENDMENT

Effective date and applicability of amendment by Pub. L. 99–554 dependent upon the judicial district involved, see section 302(d), (e) of Pub. L. 99–554, set out as a note under section 581 of Title 28, Judiciary and Judicial Procedure.

EFFECTIVE DATE OF 1984 AMENDMENT

Amendment by Pub. L. 98–353 effective with respect to cases filed 90 days after July 10, 1984, see section 552(a) of Pub. L. 98–353, set out as a note under section 101 of this title.

§1103. Powers and duties of committees

(a) At a scheduled meeting of a committee appointed under section 1102 of this title, at which a majority of the members of such committee are present, and with the court's approval, such committee may select and authorize the employment by such committee of one or more attorneys, accountants, or other agents, to represent or perform services for such committee.

(b) An attorney or accountant employed to represent a committee appointed under section

1102 of this title may not, while employed by such committee, represent any other entity having an adverse interest in connection with the case. Representation of one or more creditors of the same class as represented by the committee shall not per se constitute the representation of an adverse interest.

(c) A committee appointed under section 1102 of this title may—

(1) consult with the trustee or debtor in possession concerning the administration of the case;

(2) investigate the acts, conduct, assets, liabilities, and financial condition of the debtor, the operation of the debtor's business and the desirability of the continuance of such business, and any other matter relevant to the case or to the formulation of a plan;

(3) participate in the formulation of a plan, advise those represented by such committee of such committee's determinations as to any plan formulated, and collect and file with the court acceptances or rejections of a plan;

(4) request the appointment of a trustee or examiner under section 1104 of this title; and

(5) perform such other services as are in the interest of those represented.

(d) As soon as practicable after the appointment of a committee under section 1102 of this title, the trustee shall meet with such committee to transact such business as may be necessary and proper.

(Pub. L. 95-598, Nov. 6, 1978, 92 Stat. 2627; Pub. L. 98-353, title III, §§324, 500, July 10, 1984, 98 Stat. 358, 384.)

HISTORICAL AND REVISION NOTES

SENATE REPORT NO. 95-989

This section defines the powers and duties of a committee elected or appointed under section 1102.

Under subsection (a) the committee may, if authorized by the court, employ one or more attorneys, accountants, or other agents to represent or perform services for the committee. Normally one attorney should suffice; more than one may be authorized for good cause. The same considerations apply to the services of others, if the need for any at all is demonstrated.

Under subsections (c) and (d) the committee, like any party in interest, may confer with the trustee or debtor regarding the administration of the estate; may advise the court on the need for a trustee under section 1104(b). The committee may investigate matters specified in paragraph (2) of subsection (c), but only if authorized by the court and if no trustee or examiner is appointed.

HOUSE REPORT NO. 95-595

Subsection (a) of this section authorizes a committee appointed under section 1102 to select and authorize the employment of counsel, accountants, or other agents, to represent or perform services for the committee. The committee's selection and authorization is subject to the court's approval, and may only be done at a meeting of the committee at which a majority of its members are present. The subsection provides for the employment of more than one attorney. However, this will be the exception, and not the rule; cause must be shown to depart from the normal standard.

Subsection (b) requires a committee's counsel to cease representation of any other entity in connection with the case after he begins to represent the committee. This will prevent the potential of severe conflicts of interest.

Subsection (c) lists a committee's functions in a chapter 11 case. The committee may consult with the trustee or debtor in possession concerning the administration of the case, may investigate the acts, conduct, assets, liabilities and financial condition of the debtor, the operation of the debtor's business, and the desirability of the continuance of the business, and any other matter relevant to the case or to the formulation of a plan. The committee may participate in the formulation of a plan, advise those it represents of the committee's recommendation with respect to any plan formulated, and collect and file acceptances. These will be its most important functions. The committee may also determine the need for the appointment of a trustee, if one has not previously been appointed, and perform such other services as are in the interest of those represented.

Subsection (d) requires the trustee and each committee to meet as soon as practicable after their appointments to transact such business as may be necessary and proper.

AMENDMENTS

1984—Subsec. (b). Pub. L. 98-353, §§324, 500(a), substituted "An attorney or accountant" for "A person", substituted "entity having an adverse interest" for "entity", and inserted provision that representation of one or more creditors of the same class as represented by the committee shall not per se constitute the representation of an adverse interest.

Subsec. (c)(3). Pub. L. 98-353, §500(b)(1), substituted "determinations" for "recommendations", and "acceptances or rejections" for "acceptances".

Subsec. (c)(4). Pub. L. 98-353, §500(b)(2), struck out "if a trustee or examiner, as the case may be, has not previously been appointed under this chapter in the case" after "section 1104 of this title".

EFFECTIVE DATE OF 1984 AMENDMENT

Amendment by Pub. L. 98-353 effective with respect to cases filed 90 days after July 10, 1984, see section 552(a) of Pub. L. 98-353, set out as a note under section 101 of this title.

§ 1104. Appointment of trustee or examiner

(a) At any time after the commencement of the case but before confirmation of a plan, on request of a party in interest or the United States trustee, and after notice and a hearing, the court shall order the appointment of a trustee—

(1) for cause, including fraud, dishonesty, incompetence, or gross mismanagement of the affairs of the debtor by current management, either before or after the commencement of the case, or similar cause, but not including the number of holders of securities of the debtor or the amount of assets or liabilities of the debtor;

(2) if such appointment is in the interests of creditors, any equity security holders, and other interests of the estate, without regard to the number of holders of securities of the debtor or the amount of assets or liabilities of the debtor; or

(3) if grounds exist to convert or dismiss the case under section 1112, but the court determines that the appointment of a trustee or an examiner is in the best interests of creditors and the estate.

(b)(1) Except as provided in section 1163 of this title, on the request of a party in interest made not later than 30 days after the court orders the appointment of a trustee under subsection (a), the United States trustee shall convene a meeting of creditors for the purpose of electing one disinterested person to serve as trustee in the case. The election of a trustee shall be conducted in the manner provided in subsections (a), (b), and (c) of section 702 of this title.

(2)(A) If an eligible, disinterested trustee is elected at a meeting of creditors under paragraph (1), the United States trustee shall file a report certifying that election.

(B) Upon the filing of a report under subparagraph (A)—

(i) the trustee elected under paragraph (1) shall be considered to have been selected and appointed for purposes of this section; and

(ii) the service of any trustee appointed under subsection (d) shall terminate.

(C) The court shall resolve any dispute arising out of an election described in subparagraph (A).

(c) If the court does not order the appointment of a trustee under this section, then at any time before the confirmation of a plan, on request of a party in interest or the United States trustee, and after notice and a hearing, the court shall order the appointment of an examiner to conduct such an investigation of the debtor as is appropriate, including an investigation of any allegations of fraud, dishonesty, incompetence, misconduct, mismanagement, or irregularity in the management of the affairs of the debtor of or by current or former management of the debtor, if—

(1) such appointment is in the interests of creditors, any equity security holders, and other interests of the estate; or

(2) the debtor's fixed, liquidated, unsecured debts, other than debts for goods, services, or taxes, or owing to an insider, exceed $5,000,000.

(d) If the court orders the appointment of a trustee or an examiner, if a trustee or an examiner dies or resigns during the case or is removed under section 324 of this title, or if a trustee fails to qualify under section 322 of this title, then the United States trustee, after consultation with parties in interest, shall appoint, subject to the court's approval, one disinterested person other than the United States trustee to serve as trustee or examiner, as the case may be, in the case.

(e) The United States trustee shall move for the appointment of a trustee under subsection (a) if there are reasonable grounds to suspect that current members of the governing body of the debtor, the debtor's chief executive or chief financial officer, or members of the governing body who selected the debtor's chief executive or chief financial officer, participated in actual fraud, dishonesty, or criminal conduct in the management of the debtor or the debtor's public financial reporting.

(Pub. L. 95–598, Nov. 6, 1978, 92 Stat. 2627; Pub. L. 99–554, title II, §222, Oct. 27, 1986, 100 Stat. 3102; Pub. L. 103–394, title II, §211(a), title V, §501(d)(30), Oct. 22, 1994, 108 Stat. 4125, 4146; Pub. L. 109–8, title IV, §§416, 442(b), title XIV, §1405, Apr. 20, 2005, 119 Stat. 107, 116, 215.)

Historical and Revision Notes

Legislative Statements

Section 1104 of the House amendment represents a compromise between the House bill and the Senate amendment concerning the appointment of a trustee or examiner. The method of appointment rather than election, is derived from the House bill; the two alternative standards of appointment are derived with modifications from the Senate amendment, instead of the standard stated in the House bill. For example, if the current management of the debtor gambled away rental income before the filing of the petition, a trustee should be appointed after the petition, whether or not postpetition mismanagement can be shown. However, under no circumstances will cause include the number of security holders of the debtor or the amount of assets or liabilities of the debtor. The standard also applies to the appointment of an examiner in those circumstances in which mandatory appointment, as previously detailed, is not required.

Senate Report No. 95–989

Subsection (a) provides for the mandatory appointment of a disinterested trustee in the case of a public company, as defined in section 1101(3), within 10 days of the order for relief, or of a successor, in the event of a vacancy, as soon as practicable.

Section 156 of chapter X ([former] 11 U.S.C. 516 [556]) requires the appointment of a disinterested trustee if the debtor's liabilities are $250,000 or over. Section 1104(a) marks a substantial change. The appointment of a trustee is mandatory only for a public company, which under section 1101(3), has $5 million in liabilities, excluding tax and trade obligations, and 1,000 security holders. In view of past experience, cases involving public companies will under normal circumstances probably be relatively few in number but of vast importance in terms of public investor interest.

In case of a nonpublic company, the appointment or election of a trustee is discretionary if the interests of the estate and its security holders would be served thereby. A test based on probable costs and benefits of a trusteeship is not practical. The appointment may be made at any time prior to confirmation of the plan.

In case of a nonpublic company, if no trustee is appointed, the court may under subsection (c) appoint an examiner, if the appointment would serve the interests of the estate and security holders. The purpose of his appointment is specified in section 1106(b).

House Report No. 95–595

Subsection (a) of this section governs the appointment of trustees in reorganization cases. The court is permitted to order the appointment of one trustee at any time after the commencement of the case if a party in interest so requests. The court may order appointment only if the protection afforded by a trustee is needed and the costs and expenses of a trustee would not be disproportionately higher than the value of the protection afforded.

The protection afforded by a trustee would be needed, for example, in cases where the current management of the debtor has been fraudulent or dishonest, or has grossly mismanaged the company, or where the debtor's management has abandoned the business. A trustee would not necessarily be needed to investigate misconduct of former management of the debtor, because an examiner appointed under this section might well be able to serve that function adequately without displacing the current management. Generally, a trustee would not be needed in any case where the protection afforded by a trustee could equally be afforded by an examiner. Though the device of examiner appears in current chapter X [chapter 10 of former title 11], it is rarely used because of the nearly absolute presumption in favor of the appointment of a trustee. Its use here will give the courts, debtors, creditors, and equity security holders greater flexibility in handling the affairs of an insolvent debtor, permitting the court to tailor the remedy to the case.

The second test, relating to the costs and expenses of a trustee, is not intended to be a strict cost/benefit analysis. It is included to require the court to have due regard for any additional costs or expenses that the appointment of a trustee would impose on the estate.

Subsection (b) permits the court, at any time after the commencement of the case and on request of a party in interest, to order the appointment of an examiner, if the court has not ordered the appointment of a trustee. The examiner would be appointed to conduct such an investigation of the debtor as is appropriate under the particular circumstances of the case, including an investigation of any allegations of fraud, dishonesty, or gross mismanagement of the debtor of or by current or former management of the debtor. The standards for the appointment of an examiner are the same as those for the appointment of a trustee: the protection must be needed, and the costs and expenses must not be disproportionately high.

By virtue of proposed 11 U.S.C. 1109, an indenture trustee and the Securities and Exchange Commission will be parties in interest for the purpose of requesting the appointment of a trustee or examiner.

Subsection (c) directs that the United States trustee actually select and appoint the trustee or examiner ordered appointed under this section. The United States trustee is required to consult with various parties in interest before selecting and appointing a trustee. He is not bound to select one of the members of the panel of private trustees established under proposed 28 U.S.C. 586(a)(1) which exists only for the purpose of providing trustees for chapter 7 cases. Neither is he precluded from selecting a panel member if the member is qualified to serve as chapter 11 trustee. Appointment by the United States trustee will remove the court from the often criticized practice of appointing an officer that will appear in litigation before the court against an adverse party.

AMENDMENTS

2005—Subsec. (a)(3). Pub. L. 109–8, §442(b), added par. (3).

Subsec. (b). Pub. L. 109–8, §416, designated existing provisions as par. (1) and added par. (2).

Subsec. (e). Pub. L. 109–8, §1405, added subsec. (e).

1994—Subsec. (b). Pub. L. 103–394, §211(a)(2), added subsec. (b). Former subsec. (b) redesignated (c).

Subsec. (c). Pub. L. 103–394, §211(a)(1), redesignated subsec. (b) as (c). Former subsec. (c) redesignated (d).

Subsec. (d). Pub. L. 103–394, §§211(a)(1), 501(d)(30), redesignated subsec. (c) as (d) and inserted comma after "interest".

1986—Subsecs. (a), (b). Pub. L. 99–554, §222(1), (2), inserted "or the United States trustee" after "party in interest".

Subsec. (c). Pub. L. 99–554, §222(3), substituted "the United States trustee, after consultation with parties in interest shall appoint, subject to the court's approval, one disinterested person other than the United States trustee to serve" for "the court shall appoint one disinterested person to serve".

EFFECTIVE DATE OF 2005 AMENDMENT

Amendment by section 1405 of Pub. L. 109–8 effective Apr. 20, 2005, and applicable only with respect to cases commenced under this title on or after Apr. 20, 2005, see section 1406 of Pub. L. 109–8, set out as a note under section 507 of this title.

Amendment by sections 416 and 442(b) of Pub. L. 109–8 effective 180 days after Apr. 20, 2005, and not applicable with respect to cases commenced under this title before such effective date, except as otherwise provided, see section 1501 of Pub. L. 109–8, set out as a note under section 101 of this title.

EFFECTIVE DATE OF 1994 AMENDMENT

Amendment by Pub. L. 103–394 effective Oct. 22, 1994, and not applicable with respect to cases commenced under this title before Oct. 22, 1994, see section 702 of Pub. L. 103–394, set out as a note under section 101 of this title.

EFFECTIVE DATE OF 1986 AMENDMENT

Effective date and applicability of amendment by Pub. L. 99–554 dependent upon the judicial district involved, see section 302(d), (e) of Pub. L. 99–554, set out as a note under section 581 of Title 28, Judiciary and Judicial Procedure.

§ 1105. Termination of trustee's appointment

At any time before confirmation of a plan, on request of a party in interest or the United States trustee, and after notice and a hearing, the court may terminate the trustee's appointment and restore the debtor to possession and management of the property of the estate and of the operation of the debtor's business.

(Pub. L. 95–598, Nov. 6, 1978, 92 Stat. 2628; Pub. L. 98–353, title III, §501, July 10, 1984, 98 Stat. 384; Pub. L. 99–554, title II, §223, Oct. 27, 1986, 100 Stat. 3102.)

HISTORICAL AND REVISION NOTES

SENATE REPORT NO. 95–989

This section authorizes the court to terminate the trustee's appointment and to restore the debtor to possession and management of the property of the estate and to operation of the debtor's business. Section 1104(a) provides that this section does not apply in the case of a public company, for which the appointment of a trustee is mandatory.

HOUSE REPORT NO. 95–595

This section authorizes the court to terminate the trustee's appointment and to restore the debtor to possession and management of the property of the estate, and to operation of the debtor's business. This section would permit the court to reverse its decision to order the appointment of a trustee in light of new evidence.

AMENDMENTS

1986—Pub. L. 99–554 inserted "or the United States trustee" after "party in interest".

1984—Pub. L. 98–353 substituted "estate and of the" for "estate, and".

EFFECTIVE DATE OF 1986 AMENDMENT

Effective date and applicability of amendment by Pub. L. 99–554 dependent upon the judicial district involved, see section 302(d), (e) of Pub. L. 99–554, set out as a note under section 581 of Title 28, Judiciary and Judicial Procedure.

EFFECTIVE DATE OF 1984 AMENDMENT

Amendment by Pub. L. 98–353 effective with respect to cases filed 90 days after July 10, 1984, see section 552(a) of Pub. L. 98–353, set out as a note under section 101 of this title.

§ 1106. Duties of trustee and examiner

(a) A trustee shall—

(1) perform the duties of the trustee, as specified in paragraphs (2), (5), (7), (8), (9), (10), (11), and (12) of section 704;

(2) if the debtor has not done so, file the list, schedule, and statement required under section 521(1) of this title;

(3) except to the extent that the court orders otherwise, investigate the acts, conduct, assets, liabilities, and financial condition of the debtor, the operation of the debtor's business and the desirability of the continuance of such business, and any other matter relevant to the case or to the formulation of a plan;

(4) as soon as practicable—

(A) file a statement of any investigation conducted under paragraph (3) of this subsection, including any fact ascertained pertaining to fraud, dishonesty, incompetence, misconduct, mismanagement, or irregularity in the management of the affairs of the debtor, or to a cause of action available to the estate; and

(B) transmit a copy or a summary of any such statement to any creditors' committee or equity security holders' committee, to any indenture trustee, and to such other entity as the court designates;

(5) as soon as practicable, file a plan under section 1121 of this title, file a report of why the trustee will not file a plan, or recommend conversion of the case to a case under chapter 7, 12, or 13 of this title or dismissal of the case;

(6) for any year for which the debtor has not filed a tax return required by law, furnish, without personal liability, such information as may be required by the governmental unit with which such tax return was to be filed, in light of the condition of the debtor's books and records and the availability of such information;

(7) after confirmation of a plan, file such reports as are necessary or as the court orders; and

(8) if with respect to the debtor there is a claim for a domestic support obligation, provide the applicable notice specified in subsection (c).

(b) An examiner appointed under section 1104(d) of this title shall perform the duties specified in paragraphs (3) and (4) of subsection (a) of this section, and, except to the extent that the court orders otherwise, any other duties of the trustee that the court orders the debtor in possession not to perform.

(c)(1) In a case described in subsection (a)(8) to which subsection (a)(8) applies, the trustee shall—

(A)(i) provide written notice to the holder of the claim described in subsection (a)(8) of such claim and of the right of such holder to use the services of the State child support enforcement agency established under sections 464 and 466 of the Social Security Act for the State in which such holder resides, for assistance in collecting child support during and after the case under this title; and

(ii) include in the notice required by clause (i) the address and telephone number of such State child support enforcement agency;

(B)(i) provide written notice to such State child support enforcement agency of such claim; and

(ii) include in the notice required by clause (i) the name, address, and telephone number of such holder; and

(C) at such time as the debtor is granted a discharge under section 1141, provide written notice to such holder and to such State child support enforcement agency of—

(i) the granting of the discharge;

(ii) the last recent known address of the debtor;

(iii) the last recent known name and address of the debtor's employer; and

(iv) the name of each creditor that holds a claim that—

(I) is not discharged under paragraph (2), (4), or (14A) of section 523(a); or

(II) was reaffirmed by the debtor under section 524(c).

(2)(A) The holder of a claim described in subsection (a)(8) or the State child enforcement support agency of the State in which such holder resides may request from a creditor described in paragraph (1)(C)(iv) the last known address of the debtor.

(B) Notwithstanding any other provision of law, a creditor that makes a disclosure of a last known address of a debtor in connection with a request made under subparagraph (A) shall not be liable by reason of making such disclosure.

(Pub. L. 95–598, Nov. 6, 1978, 92 Stat. 2628; Pub. L. 98–353, title III, §§311(b)(1), 502, July 10, 1984, 98 Stat. 355, 384; Pub. L. 99–554, title II, §257(c), Oct. 27, 1986, 100 Stat. 3114; Pub. L. 103–394, title II, §211(b), Oct. 22, 1994, 108 Stat. 4125; Pub. L. 109–8, title II, §219(b), title IV, §446(c), title XI, §1105(b), Apr. 20, 2005, 119 Stat. 56, 118, 192.)

Historical and Revision Notes

Senate Report No. 95–989

Subsection (a) of this section prescribes the trustee's duties. He is required to perform the duties of a trustee in a liquidation case specified in section 704 (2), (4), (6), (7), (8), and (9). These include reporting and informational duties, and accountability for all property received. Paragraph (2) of this subsection requires the trustee to file with the court, if the debtor has not done so, the list of creditors, schedule of assets and liabilities, and statement of affairs required under section 521(1).

Paragraph (3) of S. 1106 requires the trustee to investigate the acts, conduct, assets, liabilities, and financial condition of the debtor, the operation of the debtor's business, and the desirability of the continuance of the business, and any other matter relevant to the case or to the formulation of a plan. Paragraph (4) requires the trustee to report the results of his investigation to the court and to creditors' committees, equity security holders' committees, indenture trustees and any other entity the court designates.

Paragraph (5) requires the trustee to file a plan or to report why a plan cannot be formulated, or to recommend conversion to liquidation or to an individual repayment plan case, or dismissal. It is anticipated that the trustee will consult with creditors and other parties in interest in the formulation of a plan, just as the debtor in possession would.

Paragraph (6) [enacted as (7)] requires final reports by the trustee, as the court orders.

Subsection (b) gives the trustee's investigative duties to an examiner, if one is appointed. The court is authorized to give the examiner additional duties as the circumstances warrant.

Paragraphs (3), (4), and (5) of subsection (a) are derived from sections 165 and 169 of chapter X [sections 565 and 569 of former title 11].

References in Text

Sections 464 and 466 of the Social Security Act, referred to in subsec. (c)(1)(A)(i), are classified to sections 664 and 666, respectively, of Title 42, The Public Health and Welfare.

Amendments

2005—Subsec. (a)(1). Pub. L. 109–8, §1105(b), substituted "(11), and (12)" for "and (11)".

Pub. L. 109–8, §446(c), amended par. (1) generally. Prior to amendment, par. (1) read as follows: "perform the duties of a trustee specified in sections 704(2), 704(5), 704(7), 704(8), and 704(9) of this title;".

Subsec. (a)(8). Pub. L. 109–8, §219(b)(1), added par. (8).

Subsec. (c). Pub. L. 109–8, §219(b)(2), added subsec. (c).

1994—Subsec. (b). Pub. L. 103–394 substituted "1104(d)" for "1104(c)".

1986—Subsec. (a)(5). Pub. L. 99–554 inserted reference to chapter 12.

1984—Subsec. (a)(1). Pub. L. 98–353, §311(b)(1), substituted "704(5), 704(7), 704(8), and 704(9)" for "704(4), 704(6), 704(7) and 704(8)".

Subsec. (b). Pub. L. 98–353, §502, inserted ", except to the extent that the court orders otherwise.".

EFFECTIVE DATE OF 2005 AMENDMENT

Amendment by Pub. L. 109–8 effective 180 days after Apr. 20, 2005, and not applicable with respect to cases commenced under this title before such effective date, except as otherwise provided, see section 1501 of Pub. L. 109–8, set out as a note under section 101 of this title.

EFFECTIVE DATE OF 1994 AMENDMENT

Amendment by Pub. L. 103–394 effective Oct. 22, 1994, and not applicable with respect to cases commenced under this title before Oct. 22, 1994, see section 702 of Pub. L. 103–394, set out as a note under section 101 of this title.

EFFECTIVE DATE OF 1986 AMENDMENT

Amendment by Pub. L. 99–554 effective 30 days after Oct. 27, 1986, but not applicable to cases commenced under this title before that date, see section 302(a), (c)(1) of Pub. L. 99–554, set out as a note under section 581 of Title 28, Judiciary and Judicial Procedure.

EFFECTIVE DATE OF 1984 AMENDMENT

Amendment by Pub. L. 98–353 effective with respect to cases filed 90 days after July 10, 1984, see section 552(a) of Pub. L. 98–353, set out as a note under section 101 of this title.

PAYMENT OF CERTAIN BENEFITS TO RETIRED FORMER EMPLOYEES

Pub. L. 99–500, §101(b) [title VI, §608], Oct. 18, 1986, 100 Stat. 1783–39, 1783–74, and Pub. L. 99–591, §101(b) [title VI, §608], Oct. 30, 1986, 100 Stat. 3341–39, 3341–74, as amended by Pub. L. 100–41, May 15, 1987, 101 Stat. 309; Pub. L. 100–99, Aug. 18, 1987, 101 Stat. 716; Pub. L. 100–334, §3(a), June 16, 1988, 102 Stat. 613, provided that:

"(a)(1) Subject to paragraphs (2), (3), (4), and (5), and notwithstanding title 11 of the United States Code, the trustee shall pay benefits to retired former employees under a plan, fund, or program maintained or established by the debtor prior to filing a petition (through the purchase of insurance or otherwise) for the purpose of providing medical, surgical, or hospital care benefits, or benefits in the event of sickness, accident, disability, or death.

"(2) The level of benefits required to be paid by this subsection may be modified prior to confirmation of a plan under section 1129 of such title if—

"(A) the trustee and an authorized representative of the former employees with respect to whom such benefits are payable agree to the modification of such benefit payments; or

"(B) the court finds that a modification proposed by the trustee meets the standards of section 1113(b)(1)(A) of such title and the balance of the equities clearly favors the modification.

If such benefits are covered by a collective bargaining agreement, the authorized representative shall be the labor organization that is signatory to such collective bargaining agreement unless there is a conflict of interest.

"(3) The trustee shall pay benefits in accordance with this subsection until—

"(A) the dismissal of the case involved; or

"(B) the effective date of a plan confirmed under section 1129 of such title which provides for the continued payment after confirmation of the plan of all such benefits at the level established under paragraph (2) of this subsection, at any time prior to the confirmation of the plan, for the duration of the period the debtor (as defined in such title) has obligated itself to provide such benefits.

"(4) No such benefits paid between the filing of a petition in a case covered by this section and the time a plan confirmed under section 1129 of such title with respect to such case becomes effective shall be deducted or offset from the amount allowed as claims for any benefits which remain unpaid, or from the amount to be paid under the plan with respect to such claims for unpaid benefits, whether such claims for unpaid benefits are based upon or arise from a right to future benefits or from any benefit not paid as a result of modifications allowed pursuant to this section.

"(5) No claim for benefits covered by this section shall be limited by section 502(b)(7) of such title.

"(b)(1) Notwithstanding any provision of title 11 of the United States Code, the trustee shall pay an allowable claim of any person for a benefit paid—

"(A) before the filing of the petition under title 11 of the United States Code; and

"(B) directly or indirectly to a retired former employee under a plan, fund, or program described in subsection (a)(1);

if, as determined by the court, such person is entitled to recover from such employee, or any provider of health care to such employee, directly or indirectly, the amount of such benefit for which such person receives no payment from the debtor.

"(2) For purposes of paragraph (1), the term 'provider of health care' means a person who—

"(A) is the direct provider of health care (including a physician, dentist, nurse, podiatrist, optometrist, physician assistant, or ancillary personnel employed under the supervision of a physician); or

"(B) administers a facility or institution (including a hospital, alcohol and drug abuse treatment facility, outpatient facility, or health maintenance organization) in which health care is provided.

"(c) This section is effective with respect to cases commenced under chapter 11, of title 11, United States Code, in which a plan for reorganization has not been confirmed by the court and in which any such benefit is still being paid on October 2, 1986, and in cases that become subject to chapter 11, title 11, United States Code, after October 2, 1986 and before the date of the enactment of the Retiree Benefits Bankruptcy Protection Act of 1988 [June 16, 1988].

"(d) This section shall not apply during any period in which a case is subject to chapter 7, title 11, United States Code."

Similar provisions were contained in Pub. L. 99–656, §2, Nov. 14, 1986, 100 Stat. 3668, as amended by Pub. L. 100–41, May 15, 1987, 101 Stat. 309; Pub. L. 100–99, Aug. 18, 1987, 101 Stat. 716, and were repealed by Pub. L. 100–334, §3(b), June 16, 1988, 102 Stat. 614.

§1107. Rights, powers, and duties of debtor in possession

(a) Subject to any limitations on a trustee serving in a case under this chapter, and to such limitations or conditions as the court prescribes, a debtor in possession shall have all the rights, other than the right to compensation under section 330 of this title, and powers, and shall perform all the functions and duties, except the duties specified in sections 1106(a)(2), (3), and (4) of this title, of a trustee serving in a case under this chapter.

(b) Notwithstanding section 327(a) of this title, a person is not disqualified for employment under section 327 of this title by a debtor in possession solely because of such person's employment by or representation of the debtor before the commencement of the case.

(Pub. L. 95–598, Nov. 6, 1978, 92 Stat. 2628; Pub. L. 98–353, title III, §503, July 10, 1984, 98 Stat. 384.)

HISTORICAL AND REVISION NOTES

LEGISLATIVE STATEMENTS

The House amendment adopts section 1107(b) of the Senate amendment which clarifies a point not covered by the House bill.

SENATE REPORT NO. 95–989

This section places a debtor in possession in the shoes of a trustee in every way. The debtor is given the rights and powers of a chapter 11 trustee. He is required to perform the functions and duties of a chapter 11 trustee (except the investigative duties). He is also subject to any limitations on a chapter 11 trustee, and to such other limitations and conditions as the court prescribes cf. *Wolf v. Weinstein*, 372 U.S. 633, 649–650 (1963).

AMENDMENTS

1984—Subsec. (a). Pub. L. 98–353 substituted "on a trustee serving in a case" for "on a trustee".

EFFECTIVE DATE OF 1984 AMENDMENT

Amendment by Pub. L. 98–353 effective with respect to cases filed 90 days after July 10, 1984, see section 552(a) of Pub. L. 98–353, set out as a note under section 101 of this title.

§ 1108. Authorization to operate business

Unless the court, on request of a party in interest and after notice and a hearing, orders otherwise, the trustee may operate the debtor's business.

(Pub. L. 95–598, Nov. 6, 1978, 92 Stat. 2629; Pub. L. 98–353, title III, § 504, July 10, 1984, 98 Stat. 384.)

HISTORICAL AND REVISION NOTES

LEGISLATIVE STATEMENTS

The House amendment adopts section 1108 of the House bill in preference to the style of an identical substantive provision contained in the Senate amendment. Throughout title 11 references to a "trustee" is read to include other parties under various sections of the bill. For example, section 1107 applies to give the debtor in possession all the rights and powers of a trustee in a case under chapter 11; this includes the power of the trustee to operate the debtor's business under section 1108.

SENATE REPORT NO. 95–989

This section permits the debtor's business to continue to be operated, unless the court orders otherwise. Thus, in a reorganization case, operation of the business will be the rule, and it will not be necessary to go to the court to obtain an order authorizing operation.

HOUSE REPORT NO. 95–595

This section does not presume that a trustee will be appointed to operate the business of the debtor. Rather, the power granted to trustee under this section is one of the powers that a debtor in possession acquires by virtue of proposed 11 U.S.C. 1107.

AMENDMENTS

1984—Pub. L. 98–353 inserted ", on request of a party in interest and after notice and a hearing,".

EFFECTIVE DATE OF 1984 AMENDMENT

Amendment by Pub. L. 98–353 effective with respect to cases filed 90 days after July 10, 1984, see section 552(a) of Pub. L. 98–353, set out as a note under section 101 of this title.

§ 1109. Right to be heard

(a) The Securities and Exchange Commission may raise and may appear and be heard on any issue in a case under this chapter, but the Securities and Exchange Commission may not appeal from any judgment, order, or decree entered in the case.

(b) A party in interest, including the debtor, the trustee, a creditors' committee, an equity security holders' committee, a creditor, an equity security holder, or any indenture trustee, may raise and may appear and be heard on any issue in a case under this chapter.

(Pub. L. 95–598, Nov. 6, 1978, 92 Stat. 2629.)

HISTORICAL AND REVISION NOTES

LEGISLATIVE STATEMENTS

Section 1109 of the House amendment represents a compromise between comparable provisions in the House bill and Senate amendment. As previously discussed the section gives the Securities and Exchange Commission the right to appear and be heard and to raise any issue in a case under chapter 11; however, the Securities and Exchange Commission is not a party in interest and the Commission may not appeal from any judgment, order, or decree entered in the case. Under section 1109(b) a party in interest, including the debtor, the trustee, creditors committee, equity securities holders committee, a creditor, an equity security holder, or an indentured trustee, may raise and may appear and be heard on any issue in a case under chapter 11. Section 1109(c) of the Senate amendment has been moved to subchapter IV pertaining to Railroad Reorganizations.

SENATE REPORT NO. 95–989

Subsection (a) provides, in unqualified terms, that any creditor, equity security holder, or an indenture trustee shall have the right to be heard as a party in interest under this chapter in person, by an attorney, or by a committee. It is derived from section 206 of chapter X ([former] 11 U.S.C. 606).

Subsection (b) provides that the Securities and Exchange Commission may appear by filing an appearance in a case of a public company and may appear in other cases if authorized or requested by the court. As a party in interest in either case, the Commission may raise and be heard on any issue. The Commission may not appeal from a judgment, order, or decree in a case, but may participate in any appeal by any other party in interest. This is the present law under section 208 of chapter X ([former] 11 U.S.C. 608).

HOUSE REPORT NO. 95–595

Section 1109 authorizes the Securities and Exchange Commission and any indenture trustee to intervene in the case at any time on any issue. They may raise an issue or may appear and be heard on an issue that is raised by someone else. The section, following current law, denies the right of appeal to the Securities and Exchange Commission. It does not, however, prevent the Commission from joining or participating in an appeal taken by a true party in interest. The Commission is merely prevented from initiating the appeal in any capacity.

§ 1110. Aircraft equipment and vessels

(a)(1) Except as provided in paragraph (2) and subject to subsection (b), the right of a secured party with a security interest in equipment described in paragraph (3), or of a lessor or conditional vendor of such equipment, to take possession of such equipment in compliance with a security agreement, lease, or conditional sale contract, and to enforce any of its other rights or remedies, under such security agreement, lease, or conditional sale contract, to sell, lease, or otherwise retain or dispose of such equipment, is not limited or otherwise affected by any other provision of this title or by any power of the court.

(2) The right to take possession and to enforce the other rights and remedies described in paragraph (1) shall be subject to section 362 if—

(A) before the date that is 60 days after the date of the order for relief under this chapter, the trustee, subject to the approval of the court, agrees to perform all obligations of the debtor under such security agreement, lease, or conditional sale contract; and

(B) any default, other than a default of a kind specified in section 365(b)(2), under such security agreement, lease, or conditional sale contract—

(i) that occurs before the date of the order is cured before the expiration of such 60-day period;

(ii) that occurs after the date of the order and before the expiration of such 60-day period is cured before the later of—

(I) the date that is 30 days after the date of the default; or

(II) the expiration of such 60-day period; and

(iii) that occurs on or after the expiration of such 60-day period is cured in compliance with the terms of such security agreement, lease, or conditional sale contract, if a cure is permitted under that agreement, lease, or contract.

(3) The equipment described in this paragraph—

(A) is—

(i) an aircraft, aircraft engine, propeller, appliance, or spare part (as defined in section 40102 of title 49) that is subject to a security interest granted by, leased to, or conditionally sold to a debtor that, at the time such transaction is entered into, holds an air carrier operating certificate issued pursuant to chapter 447 of title 49 for aircraft capable of carrying 10 or more individuals or 6,000 pounds or more of cargo; or

(ii) a vessel documented under chapter 121 of title 46 that is subject to a security interest granted by, leased to, or conditionally sold to a debtor that is a water carrier that, at the time such transaction is entered into, holds a certificate of public convenience and necessity or permit issued by the Department of Transportation; and

(B) includes all records and documents relating to such equipment that are required, under the terms of the security agreement, lease, or conditional sale contract, to be surrendered or returned by the debtor in connection with the surrender or return of such equipment.

(4) Paragraph (1) applies to a secured party, lessor, or conditional vendor acting in its own behalf or acting as trustee or otherwise in behalf of another party.

(b) The trustee and the secured party, lessor, or conditional vendor whose right to take possession is protected under subsection (a) may agree, subject to the approval of the court, to extend the 60-day period specified in subsection (a)(1).

(c)(1) In any case under this chapter, the trustee shall immediately surrender and return to a secured party, lessor, or conditional vendor, described in subsection (a)(1), equipment described in subsection (a)(3), if at any time after the date of the order for relief under this chapter such secured party, lessor, or conditional vendor is entitled pursuant to subsection (a)(1) to take possession of such equipment and makes a written demand for such possession to the trustee.

(2) At such time as the trustee is required under paragraph (1) to surrender and return equipment described in subsection (a)(3), any lease of such equipment, and any security agreement or conditional sale contract relating to such equipment, if such security agreement or conditional sale contract is an executory contract, shall be deemed rejected.

(d) With respect to equipment first placed in service on or before October 22, 1994, for purposes of this section—

(1) the term "lease" includes any written agreement with respect to which the lessor and the debtor, as lessee, have expressed in the agreement or in a substantially contemporaneous writing that the agreement is to be treated as a lease for Federal income tax purposes; and

(2) the term "security interest" means a purchase-money equipment security interest.

(Pub. L. 95–598, Nov. 6, 1978, 92 Stat. 2629; Pub. L. 103–272, §5(c), July 5, 1994, 108 Stat. 1373; Pub. L. 103–394, title II, §201(a), Oct. 22, 1994, 108 Stat. 4119; Pub. L. 106–181, title VII, §744(b), Apr. 5, 2000, 114 Stat. 177; Pub. L. 109–304, §17(b)(2), Oct. 6, 2006, 120 Stat. 1707.)

Historical and Revision Notes

Legislative Statements

Section 1110 of the House amendment adopts an identical provision contained in the House bill without modifications contained in the Senate amendment. This section protects a limited class of financiers of aircraft and vessels and is intended to be narrowly construed to prevent secured parties or lessors from gaining the protection of the section unless the interest of such lessor or secured party is explicitly enumerated therein. It should be emphasized that under section 1110(a) a debtor in possession or trustee is given 60 days after the order for relief in a case under chapter 11, to have an opportunity to comply with the provisions of section 1110(a).

During this time the automatic stay will apply and may not be lifted prior to the expiration of the 60-day period. Under section 1110(b), the debtor and secured party or lessor are given an opportunity to extend the 60-day period, but no right to reduce the period is intended. It should additionally be noted that under section 1110(a) the trustee or debtor in possession is not required to assume the executory contract or unexpired lease under section 1110; rather, if the trustee or debtor in possession complies with the requirements of section 1110(a), the trustee or debtor in possession is entitled to retain the aircraft or vessels subject to the normal requirements of section 365. The discussion regarding aircraft and vessels likewise applies with respect to railroad rolling stock in a railroad reorganization under section 1168.

Senate Report No. 95–989

This section, to a large degree, preserves the protection given lessors and conditional vendors of aircraft to a certificated air carrier or of vessels to a certificated water carrier under section 116(5) and 116(6) of present

Chapter X [section 516(5) and (6) of former title 11]. It is modified to conform with the consolidation of Chapters X and XI [chapters 10 and 11 of former title 11] and with the new chapter 11 generally. It is also modified to give the trustee in a reorganization case an opportunity to continue in possession of the equipment in question by curing defaults and by making the required lease or purchase payments. This removes the absolute veto power over a reorganization that lessors and conditional vendors have under present law, while entitling them to protection of their investment.

The section overrides the automatic stay or any power of the court to enjoin taking of possession of certain leased, conditionally sold, or liened equipment, unless, the trustee agrees to perform the debtor's obligations and cures all prior defaults (other than defaults under ipso facto or bankruptcy clauses) within 60 days after the order for relief. The trustee and the equipment financer are permitted to extend the 60-day period by agreement. During the first 60 days, the automatic stay will apply to prevent foreclosure unless the creditor gets relief from the stay.

The effect of this section will be the same if the debtor has granted the security interest to the financer or if the debtor is leasing equipment from a financer that has leveraged the lease and leased the equipment subject to a security interest of a third party.

AMENDMENTS

2006—Subsec. (a)(3)(A)(ii). Pub. L. 109–304 substituted "vessel documented under chapter 121 of title 46" for "documented vessel (as defined in section 30101(1) of title 46)".

2000—Pub. L. 106–181 amended section catchline and text generally, substituting present provisions consisting of subsecs. (a) to (d) for former subsecs. (a) to (c) which contained somewhat similar provisions.

1994—Pub. L. 103–394 amended section generally. Prior to amendment, section read as follows:

"(a) The right of a secured party with a purchase-money equipment security interest in, or of a lessor or conditional vendor of, whether as trustee or otherwise, aircraft, aircraft engines, propellers, appliances, or spare parts, as defined in section 40102(a) of title 49, or vessels of the United States, as defined in section 30101 of title 46, that are subject to a purchase-money equipment security interest granted by, leased to, or conditionally sold to, a debtor that is an air carrier operating under a certificate of convenience and necessity issued by the Secretary of Transportation, or a water carrier that holds a certificate of public convenience and necessity or permit issued by the Interstate Commerce Commission, as the case may be, to take possession of such equipment in compliance with the provisions of a purchase-money equipment security agreement, lease, or conditional sale contract, as the case may be, is not affected by section 362 or 363 of this title or by any power of the court to enjoin such taking of possession, unless—

"(1) before 60 days after the date of the order for relief under this chapter, the trustee, subject to the court's approval, agrees to perform all obligations of the debtor that become due on or after such date under such security agreement, lease, or conditional sale contract, as the case may be; and

"(2) any default, other than a default of a kind specified in section 365(b)(2) of this title, under such security agreement, lease, or conditional sale contract, as the case may be—

"(A) that occurred before such date is cured before the expiration of such 60-day period; and

"(B) that occurs after such date is cured before the later of—

"(i) 30 days after the date of such default; and

"(ii) the expiration of such 60-day period.

"(b) The trustee and the secured party, lessor, or conditional vendor, as the case may be, whose right to take possession is protected under subsection (a) of this section may agree, subject to the court's approval, to extend the 60-day period specified in subsection (a)(1) of this section."

Subsec. (a). Pub. L. 103–272 substituted "section 40102(a) of title 49" for "section 101 of the Federal Aviation Act of 1958 (49 U.S.C. 1301)", "section 30101 of title 46" for "subsection B(4) of the Ship Mortgage Act, 1920 (46 U.S.C. 911(4))", and "Secretary of Transportation" for "Civil Aeronautics Board".

EFFECTIVE DATE OF 2000 AMENDMENT

Amendment by Pub. L. 106–181 applicable only to fiscal years beginning after Sept. 30, 1999, see section 3 of Pub. L. 106–181, set out as a note under section 106 of Title 49, Transportation.

EFFECTIVE DATE OF 1994 AMENDMENT

Amendment by Pub. L. 103–394 effective Oct. 22, 1994, with this section, as amended by section 201 of Pub. L. 103–394, applicable with respect to any lease, as defined by subsec. (c) of this section, entered into in connection with a settlement of any proceeding in any case pending under this title on Oct. 22, 1994, see section 702 of Pub. L. 103–394, set out as a note under section 101 of this title.

ABOLITION OF INTERSTATE COMMERCE COMMISSION AND TRANSFER OF FUNCTIONS

Interstate Commerce Commission abolished and functions of Commission transferred, except as otherwise provided in Pub. L. 104–88, to Surface Transportation Board effective Jan. 1, 1996, by section 702 of Title 49, Transportation, and section 101 of Pub. L. 104–88, set out as a note under section 701 of Title 49. References to Interstate Commerce Commission deemed to refer to Surface Transportation Board, a member or employee of the Board, or Secretary of Transportation, as appropriate, see section 205 of Pub. L. 104–88, set out as a note under section 701 of Title 49.

AIRCRAFT EQUIPMENT SETTLEMENT LEASES

Pub. L. 103–7, Mar. 17, 1993, 107 Stat. 36, provided that:

"SECTION 1. SHORT TITLE.

"This Act may be cited as the 'Aircraft Equipment Settlement Leases Act of 1993'.

"SEC. 2. TREATMENT OF AIRCRAFT EQUIPMENT SETTLEMENT LEASES WITH THE PENSION BENEFIT GUARANTY CORPORATION.

"In the case of any settlement of liability under title IV of the Employee Retirement Income Security Act of 1974 [29 U.S.C. 1301 et seq.] entered into by the Pension Benefit Guaranty Corporation and one or more other parties, if—

"(1) such settlement was entered into before, on, or after the date of the enactment of this Act [Mar. 17, 1993],

"(2) at least one party to such settlement was a debtor under title 11 of the United States Code, and

"(3) an agreement that is entered into as part of such settlement provides that such agreement is to be treated as a lease,

then such agreement shall be treated as a lease for purposes of section 1110 of such title 11."

§ 1111. Claims and interests

(a) A proof of claim or interest is deemed filed under section 501 of this title for any claim or interest that appears in the schedules filed under section 521(1) or 1106(a)(2) of this title, except a claim or interest that is scheduled as disputed, contingent, or unliquidated.

(b)(1)(A) A claim secured by a lien on property of the estate shall be allowed or disallowed under section 502 of this title the same as if the holder of such claim had recourse against the debtor on account of such claim, whether or not such holder has such recourse, unless—

(i) the class of which such claim is a part elects, by at least two-thirds in amount and more than half in number of allowed claims of such class, application of paragraph (2) of this subsection; or

(ii) such holder does not have such recourse and such property is sold under section 363 of this title or is to be sold under the plan.

(B) A class of claims may not elect application of paragraph (2) of this subsection if—

(i) the interest on account of such claims of the holders of such claims in such property is of inconsequential value; or

(ii) the holder of a claim of such class has recourse against the debtor on account of such claim and such property is sold under section 363 of this title or is to be sold under the plan.

(2) If such an election is made, then notwithstanding section 506(a) of this title, such claim is a secured claim to the extent that such claim is allowed.

(Pub. L. 95–598, Nov. 6, 1978, 92 Stat. 2630.)

HISTORICAL AND REVISION NOTES

LEGISLATIVE STATEMENTS

A discussion of section 1111(b) of the House amendment is best considered in the context of confirmation and will therefore, be discussed in connection with section 1129.

SENATE REPORT NO. 95–989

This section dispenses with the need for every creditor and equity security holder to file a proof of claim or interest in a reorganization case. Usually the debtor's schedules are accurate enough that they will suffice to determine the claims or interests allowable in the case. Thus, the section specifies that any claim or interest included on the debtor's schedules is deemed filed under section 501. This does not apply to claims or interests that are scheduled as disputed, contingent, or unliquidated.

§ 1112. Conversion or dismissal

(a) The debtor may convert a case under this chapter to a case under chapter 7 of this title unless—

(1) the debtor is not a debtor in possession;

(2) the case originally was commenced as an involuntary case under this chapter; or

(3) the case was converted to a case under this chapter other than on the debtor's request.

(b)(1) Except as provided in paragraph (2) of this subsection, subsection (c) of this section, and section 1104(a)(3), on request of a party in interest, and after notice and a hearing, absent unusual circumstances specifically identified by the court that establish that the requested conversion or dismissal is not in the best interests of creditors and the estate, the court shall convert a case under this chapter to a case under chapter 7 or dismiss a case under this chapter, whichever is in the best interests of creditors and the estate, if the movant establishes cause.

(2) The relief provided in paragraph (1) shall not be granted absent unusual circumstances specifically identified by the court that establish that such relief is not in the best interests of creditors and the estate, if the debtor or another party in interest objects and establishes that—

(A) there is a reasonable likelihood that a plan will be confirmed within the timeframes established in sections 1121(e) and 1129(e) of this title, or if such sections do not apply, within a reasonable period of time; and

(B) the grounds for granting such relief include an act or omission of the debtor other than under paragraph (4)(A)—

(i) for which there exists a reasonable justification for the act or omission; and

(ii) that will be cured within a reasonable period of time fixed by the court.

(3) The court shall commence the hearing on a motion under this subsection not later than 30 days after filing of the motion, and shall decide the motion not later than 15 days after commencement of such hearing, unless the movant expressly consents to a continuance for a specific period of time or compelling circumstances prevent the court from meeting the time limits established by this paragraph.

(4) For purposes of this subsection, the term "cause" includes—

(A) substantial or continuing loss to or diminution of the estate and the absence of a reasonable likelihood of rehabilitation;

(B) gross mismanagement of the estate;

(C) failure to maintain appropriate insurance that poses a risk to the estate or to the public;

(D) unauthorized use of cash collateral substantially harmful to 1 or more creditors;

(E) failure to comply with an order of the court;

(F) unexcused failure to satisfy timely any filing or reporting requirement established by this title or by any rule applicable to a case under this chapter;

(G) failure to attend the meeting of creditors convened under section 341(a) or an examination ordered under rule 2004 of the Federal Rules of Bankruptcy Procedure without good cause shown by the debtor;

(H) failure timely to provide information or attend meetings reasonably requested by the United States trustee (or the bankruptcy administrator, if any);

(I) failure timely to pay taxes owed after the date of the order for relief or to file tax returns due after the date of the order for relief;

(J) failure to file a disclosure statement, or to file or confirm a plan, within the time fixed by this title or by order of the court;

(K) failure to pay any fees or charges required under chapter 123 of title 28;

(L) revocation of an order of confirmation under section 1144;

(M) inability to effectuate substantial consummation of a confirmed plan;

(N) material default by the debtor with respect to a confirmed plan;

(O) termination of a confirmed plan by reason of the occurrence of a condition specified in the plan; and

(P) failure of the debtor to pay any domestic support obligation that first becomes payable after the date of the filing of the petition.

(c) The court may not convert a case under this chapter to a case under chapter 7 of this title if the debtor is a farmer or a corporation that is not a moneyed, business, or commercial corporation, unless the debtor requests such conversion.

(d) The court may convert a case under this chapter to a case under chapter 12 or 13 of this title only if—

(1) the debtor requests such conversion;

(2) the debtor has not been discharged under section 1141(d) of this title; and

(3) if the debtor requests conversion to chapter 12 of this title, such conversion is equitable.

(e) Except as provided in subsections (c) and (f), the court, on request of the United States trustee, may convert a case under this chapter to a case under chapter 7 of this title or may dismiss a case under this chapter, whichever is in the best interest of creditors and the estate if the debtor in a voluntary case fails to file, within fifteen days after the filing of the petition commencing such case or such additional time as the court may allow, the information required by paragraph (1) of section 521, including a list containing the names and addresses of the holders of the twenty largest unsecured claims (or of all unsecured claims if there are fewer than twenty unsecured claims), and the approximate dollar amounts of each of such claims.

(f) Notwithstanding any other provision of this section, a case may not be converted to a case under another chapter of this title unless the debtor may be a debtor under such chapter.

(Pub. L. 95-598, Nov. 6, 1978, 92 Stat. 2630; Pub. L. 98-353, title III, §505, July 10, 1984, 98 Stat. 384; Pub. L. 99-554, title II, §§224, 256, Oct. 27, 1986, 100 Stat. 3102, 3114; Pub. L. 103-394, title II, §217(c), Oct. 22, 1994, 108 Stat. 4127; Pub. L. 109-8, title IV, §442(a), Apr. 20, 2005, 119 Stat. 115.)

Historical and Revision Notes

Legislative Statements

Section 1112 of the House amendment represents a compromise between the House bill and Senate amendment with respect to the factors constituting cause for conversion of a case to chapter 7 or dismissal. The House amendment combines two separate factors contained in section 1112(b)(1) and section 1112(b)(2) of the Senate amendment. Section 1112(b)(1) of the House amendment permits the court to convert a case to a case under chapter 7 or to dismiss the case if there is both a continuing loss to or diminution of the estate and the absence of a reasonable likelihood of rehabilitation; requiring both factors to be present simultaneously represents a compromise from the House bill which eliminated both factors from the list of causes enumerated.

Sections 1112(c) and 1112(d) of the House amendment is derived from the House bill which differs from the Senate amendment only as a matter of style.

Senate Report No. 95-989

This section brings together all of the conversion and dismissal rules for chapter 11 cases. Subsection (a) gives the debtor an absolute right to convert a voluntarily commenced chapter 11 case in which the debtor remains in possession to a liquidation case.

Subsection (b) gives wide discretion to the court to make an appropriate disposition of the case sua sponte or upon motion of a party in interest, or the court is permitted to convert a reorganization case to a liquidation case or to dismiss the case, whichever is in the best interest of creditors and the estate, but only for cause. Cause may include the continuing loss to or dimunition [sic] of the estate of an insolvent debtor, the absence of a reasonable likelihood of rehabilitation, the inability to effectuate a plan, unreasonable delay by the debtor that is prejudicial to creditors, failure to file a plan within the appropriate time limits, denial of confirmation and any opportunity to modify or propose a new plan, revocation of confirmation and denial of confirmation of a modified plan, inability to effectuate substantial consummation of a confirmed plan, material default by the debtor under the plan, and termination of the plan by reason of the occurrence of a condition specified in the plan. This list is not exhaustive. The court will be able to consider other factors as they arise, and to use its equitable powers to reach an appropriate result in individual cases. The power of the court to act sua sponte should be used sparingly and only in emergency situations.

Subsection (c) prohibits the court from converting a case concerning a farmer or an eleemosynary institution to a liquidation case unless the debtor consents.

Subsection (d) prohibits conversion of a reorganization case to a chapter 13 case unless the debtor requests conversion and his discharge has not been granted or has been revoked.

Subsection (e) reinforces section 109 by prohibiting conversion of a chapter 11 case to a case under another chapter proceedings under which the debtor is not permitted to proceed.

References in Text

The Federal Rules of Bankruptcy Procedure, referred to in subsec. (b)(4)(G), are set out in the Appendix to this title.

Amendments

2005—Subsec. (b). Pub. L. 109-8 added subsec. (b) and struck out former subsec. (b) which consisted of introductory provisions and pars. (1) to (10) relating to conversion of cases under this chapter to chapter 7 cases or dismissal for cause in the best interest of creditors and the estate.

1994—Subsec. (b). Pub. L. 103-394 inserted "or bankruptcy administrator" after "United States trustee".

1986—Subsec. (b). Pub. L. 99-554, §224(1)(A), inserted "or the United States trustee" after "party in interest".

Subsec. (b)(10). Pub. L. 99-554, §224(1)(B)-(D), added par. (10).

Subsec. (d). Pub. L. 99-554, §256, inserted reference to chapter 12 and added par. (3).

Subsecs. (e), (f). Pub. L. 99-554, §224(2), (3), added subsec. (e) and redesignated former subsec. (e) as (f).

1984—Subsec. (a)(2). Pub. L. 98-353, §505(a)(1), substituted "originally was commenced as an involuntary case" for "is an involuntary case originally commenced".

Subsec. (a)(3). Pub. L. 98-353, §505(a)(2), substituted "other than on" for "on other than".

Subsec. (b)(5). Pub. L. 98-353, §505(b)(1), inserted "a request made for" before "additional".

Subsec. (b)(8). Pub. L. 98-353, §505(b)(2), substituted "or" for "and".

Effective Date of 2005 Amendment

Amendment by Pub. L. 109-8 effective 180 days after Apr. 20, 2005, and not applicable with respect to cases commenced under this title before such effective date, except as otherwise provided, see section 1501 of Pub. L. 109-8, set out as a note under section 101 of this title.

Effective Date of 1994 Amendment

Amendment by Pub. L. 103-394 effective Oct. 22, 1994, and not applicable with respect to cases commenced under this title before Oct. 22, 1994, see section 702 of Pub. L. 103-394, set out as a note under section 101 of this title.

Effective Date of 1986 Amendment

Effective date and applicability of amendment by section 224 of Pub. L. 99-554 dependent upon the judicial district involved, see section 302(d), (e) of Pub. L. 99-554, set out as a note under section 581 of Title 28, Judiciary and Judicial Procedure.

Amendment by section 256 of Pub. L. 99–554 effective 30 days after Oct. 27, 1986, but not applicable to cases commenced under this title before that date, see section 302(a), (c)(1) of Pub. L. 99–554.

EFFECTIVE DATE OF 1984 AMENDMENT

Amendment by Pub. L. 98–353 effective with respect to cases filed 90 days after July 10, 1984, see section 552(a) of Pub. L. 98–353, set out as a note under section 101 of this title.

§ 1113. Rejection of collective bargaining agreements

(a) The debtor in possession, or the trustee if one has been appointed under the provisions of this chapter, other than a trustee in a case covered by subchapter IV of this chapter and by title I of the Railway Labor Act, may assume or reject a collective bargaining agreement only in accordance with the provisions of this section.

(b)(1) Subsequent to filing a petition and prior to filing an application seeking rejection of a collective bargaining agreement, the debtor in possession or trustee (hereinafter in this section "trustee" shall include a debtor in possession), shall—

(A) make a proposal to the authorized representative of the employees covered by such agreement, based on the most complete and reliable information available at the time of such proposal, which provides for those necessary modifications in the employees benefits and protections that are necessary to permit the reorganization of the debtor and assures that all creditors, the debtor and all of the affected parties are treated fairly and equitably; and

(B) provide, subject to subsection (d)(3), the representative of the employees with such relevant information as is necessary to evaluate the proposal.

(2) During the period beginning on the date of the making of a proposal provided for in paragraph (1) and ending on the date of the hearing provided for in subsection (d)(1), the trustee shall meet, at reasonable times, with the authorized representative to confer in good faith in attempting to reach mutually satisfactory modifications of such agreement.

(c) The court shall approve an application for rejection of a collective bargaining agreement only if the court finds that—

(1) the trustee has, prior to the hearing, made a proposal that fulfills the requirements of subsection (b)(1);

(2) the authorized representative of the employees has refused to accept such proposal without good cause; and

(3) the balance of the equities clearly favors rejection of such agreement.

(d)(1) Upon the filing of an application for rejection the court shall schedule a hearing to be held not later than fourteen days after the date of the filing of such application. All interested parties may appear and be heard at such hearing. Adequate notice shall be provided to such parties at least ten days before the date of such hearing. The court may extend the time for the commencement of such hearing for a period not exceeding seven days where the circumstances of the case, and the interests of justice require such extension, or for additional periods of time to which the trustee and representative agree.

(2) The court shall rule on such application for rejection within thirty days after the date of the commencement of the hearing. In the interests of justice, the court may extend such time for ruling for such additional period as the trustee and the employees' representative may agree to. If the court does not rule on such application within thirty days after the date of the commencement of the hearing, or within such additional time as the trustee and the employees' representative may agree to, the trustee may terminate or alter any provisions of the collective bargaining agreement pending the ruling of the court on such application.

(3) The court may enter such protective orders, consistent with the need of the authorized representative of the employee to evaluate the trustee's proposal and the application for rejection, as may be necessary to prevent disclosure of information provided to such representative where such disclosure could compromise the position of the debtor with respect to its competitors in the industry in which it is engaged.

(e) If during a period when the collective bargaining agreement continues in effect, and if essential to the continuation of the debtor's business, or in order to avoid irreparable damage to the estate, the court, after notice and a hearing, may authorize the trustee to implement interim changes in the terms, conditions, wages, benefits, or work rules provided by a collective bargaining agreement. Any hearing under this paragraph shall be scheduled in accordance with the needs of the trustee. The implementation of such interim changes shall not render the application for rejection moot.

(f) No provision of this title shall be construed to permit a trustee to unilaterally terminate or alter any provisions of a collective bargaining agreement prior to compliance with the provisions of this section.

(Added Pub. L. 98–353, title III, § 541(a), July 10, 1984, 98 Stat. 390.)

REFERENCES IN TEXT

The Railway Labor Act, referred to in subsec. (a), is act May 20, 1926, ch. 347, 44 Stat. 577, as amended. Title I of the Railway Labor Act is classified principally to subchapter I (§ 151 et seq.) of chapter 8 of Title 45, Railroads. For complete classification of this Act to the Code, see section 151 of Title 45 and Tables.

EFFECTIVE DATE

Section 541(c) of Pub. L. 98–353 provided that: "The amendments made by this section [enacting this section] shall become effective upon the date of enactment of this Act [July 10, 1984]; provided that this section shall not apply to cases filed under title 11 of the United States Code which were commenced prior to the date of enactment of this section."

§ 1114. Payment of insurance benefits to retired employees

(a) For purposes of this section, the term "retiree benefits" means payments to any entity or person for the purpose of providing or reimbursing payments for retired employees and their spouses and dependents, for medical, surgical, or hospital care benefits, or benefits in the event of sickness, accident, disability, or death under any plan, fund, or program (through the purchase of insurance or otherwise) maintained or established in whole or in part by the debtor prior to filing a petition commencing a case under this title.

(b)(1) For purposes of this section, the term "authorized representative" means the authorized representative designated pursuant to subsection (c) for persons receiving any retiree benefits covered by a collective bargaining agreement or subsection (d) in the case of persons receiving retiree benefits not covered by such an agreement.

(2) Committees of retired employees appointed by the court pursuant to this section shall have the same rights, powers, and duties as committees appointed under sections 1102 and 1103 of this title for the purpose of carrying out the purposes of sections 1114 and 1129(a)(13) and, as permitted by the court, shall have the power to enforce the rights of persons under this title as they relate to retiree benefits.

(c)(1) A labor organization shall be, for purposes of this section, the authorized representative of those persons receiving any retiree benefits covered by any collective bargaining agreement to which that labor organization is signatory, unless (A) such labor organization elects not to serve as the authorized representative of such persons, or (B) the court, upon a motion by any party in interest, after notice and hearing, determines that different representation of such persons is appropriate.

(2) In cases where the labor organization referred to in paragraph (1) elects not to serve as the authorized representative of those persons receiving any retiree benefits covered by any collective bargaining agreement to which that labor organization is signatory, or in cases where the court, pursuant to paragraph (1) finds different representation of such persons appropriate, the court, upon a motion by any party in interest, and after notice and a hearing, shall appoint a committee of retired employees if the debtor seeks to modify or not pay the retiree benefits or if the court otherwise determines that it is appropriate, from among such persons, to serve as the authorized representative of such persons under this section.

(d) The court, upon a motion by any party in interest, and after notice and a hearing, shall order the appointment of a committee of retired employees if the debtor seeks to modify or not pay the retiree benefits or if the court otherwise determines that it is appropriate, to serve as the authorized representative, under this section, of those persons receiving any retiree benefits not covered by a collective bargaining agreement. The United States trustee shall appoint any such committee.

(e)(1) Notwithstanding any other provision of this title, the debtor in possession, or the trustee if one has been appointed under the provisions of this chapter (hereinafter in this section "trustee" shall include a debtor in possession), shall timely pay and shall not modify any retiree benefits, except that—

(A) the court, on motion of the trustee or authorized representative, and after notice and a hearing, may order modification of such payments, pursuant to the provisions of subsections (g) and (h) of this section, or

(B) the trustee and the authorized representative of the recipients of those benefits may agree to modification of such payments,

after which such benefits as modified shall continue to be paid by the trustee.

(2) Any payment for retiree benefits required to be made before a plan confirmed under section 1129 of this title is effective has the status of an allowed administrative expense as provided in section 503 of this title.

(f)(1) Subsequent to filing a petition and prior to filing an application seeking modification of the retiree benefits, the trustee shall—

(A) make a proposal to the authorized representative of the retirees, based on the most complete and reliable information available at the time of such proposal, which provides for those necessary modifications in the retiree benefits that are necessary to permit the reorganization of the debtor and assures that all creditors, the debtor and all of the affected parties are treated fairly and equitably; and

(B) provide, subject to subsection (k)(3), the representative of the retirees with such relevant information as is necessary to evaluate the proposal.

(2) During the period beginning on the date of the making of a proposal provided for in paragraph (1), and ending on the date of the hearing provided for in subsection (k)(1), the trustee shall meet, at reasonable times, with the authorized representative to confer in good faith in attempting to reach mutually satisfactory modifications of such retiree benefits.

(g) The court shall enter an order providing for modification in the payment of retiree benefits if the court finds that—

(1) the trustee has, prior to the hearing, made a proposal that fulfills the requirements of subsection (f);

(2) the authorized representative of the retirees has refused to accept such proposal without good cause; and

(3) such modification is necessary to permit the reorganization of the debtor and assures that all creditors, the debtor, and all of the affected parties are treated fairly and equitably, and is clearly favored by the balance of the equities;

except that in no case shall the court enter an order providing for such modification which provides for a modification to a level lower than that proposed by the trustee in the proposal found by the court to have complied with the requirements of this subsection and subsection (f): *Provided, however*, That at any time after an order is entered providing for modification in the payment of retiree benefits, or at any time after an agreement modifying such benefits is made between the trustee and the authorized representative of the recipients of such benefits, the authorized representative may apply to the court for an order increasing those benefits which order shall be granted if the increase in retiree benefits sought is consistent with the standard set forth in paragraph (3): *Provided further*, That neither the trustee nor the authorized representative is precluded from making more than one motion for a modification order governed by this subsection.

(h)(1) Prior to a court issuing a final order under subsection (g) of this section, if essential to the continuation of the debtor's business, or in order to avoid irreparable damage to the estate, the court, after notice and a hearing, may authorize the trustee to implement interim modifications in retiree benefits.

(2) Any hearing under this subsection shall be scheduled in accordance with the needs of the trustee.

(3) The implementation of such interim changes does not render the motion for modification moot.

(i) No retiree benefits paid between the filing of the petition and the time a plan confirmed under section 1129 of this title becomes effective shall be deducted or offset from the amounts allowed as claims for any benefits which remain unpaid, or from the amounts to be paid under the plan with respect to such claims for unpaid benefits, whether such claims for unpaid benefits are based upon or arise from a right to future unpaid benefits or from any benefits not paid as a result of modifications allowed pursuant to this section.

(j) No claim for retiree benefits shall be limited by section 502(b)(7) of this title.

(k)(1) Upon the filing of an application for modifying retiree benefits, the court shall schedule a hearing to be held not later than fourteen days after the date of the filing of such application. All interested parties may appear and be heard at such hearing. Adequate notice shall be provided to such parties at least ten days before the date of such hearing. The court may extend the time for the commencement of such hearing for a period not exceeding seven days where the circumstances of the case, and the interests of justice require such extension, or for additional periods of time to which the trustee and the authorized representative agree.

(2) The court shall rule on such application for modification within ninety days after the date of the commencement of the hearing. In the interests of justice, the court may extend such time for ruling for such additional period as the trustee and the authorized representative may agree to. If the court does not rule on such application within ninety days after the date of the commencement of the hearing, or within such additional time as the trustee and the authorized representative may agree to, the trustee may implement the proposed modifications pending the ruling of the court on such application.

(3) The court may enter such protective orders, consistent with the need of the authorized representative of the retirees to evaluate the trustee's proposal and the application for modification, as may be necessary to prevent disclosure of information provided to such representative where such disclosure could compromise the position of the debtor with respect to its competitors in the industry in which it is engaged.

(*l*) If the debtor, during the 180-day period ending on the date of the filing of the petition—

(1) modified retiree benefits; and

(2) was insolvent on the date such benefits were modified;

the court, on motion of a party in interest, and after notice and a hearing, shall issue an order reinstating as of the date the modification was made, such benefits as in effect immediately before such date unless the court finds that the balance of the equities clearly favors such modification.

(m) This section shall not apply to any retiree, or the spouse or dependents of such retiree, if such retiree's gross income for the twelve months preceding the filing of the bankruptcy petition equals or exceeds $250,000, unless such retiree can demonstrate to the satisfaction of the court that he is unable to obtain health, medical, life, and disability coverage for himself, his spouse, and his dependents who would otherwise be covered by the employer's insurance plan, comparable to the coverage provided by the employer on the day before the filing of a petition under this title.

(Added Pub. L. 100–334, §2(a), June 16, 1988, 102 Stat. 610; amended Pub. L. 109–8, title IV, §447, title XIV, §1403, Apr. 20, 2005, 119 Stat. 118, 215.)

Amendments

2005—Subsec. (d). Pub. L. 109–8, §447, substituted "order the appointment of" for "appoint" and inserted "The United States trustee shall appoint any such committee." at end.

Subsecs. (*l*), (m). Pub. L. 109–8, §1403, added subsec. (*l*) and redesignated former subsec. (*l*) as (m).

Effective Date of 2005 Amendment

Amendment by section 1403 of Pub. L. 109–8 effective Apr. 20, 2005, and applicable only with respect to cases commenced under this title on or after Apr. 20, 2005, see section 1406 of Pub. L. 109–8, set out as a note under section 507 of this title.

Amendment by section 447 of Pub. L. 109–8 effective 180 days after Apr. 20, 2005, and not applicable with respect to cases commenced under this title before such effective date, except as otherwise provided, see section 1501 of Pub. L. 109–8, set out as a note under section 101 of this title.

Effective Date

Section 4 of Pub. L. 100–334 provided that:

"(a) General Effective Date.—Except as provided in subsection (b), this Act and the amendments made by this Act [enacting this section, amending section 1129 of this title, enacting provisions set out as a note under section 101 of this title, and amending and repealing provisions set out as notes under section 1106 of this title] shall take effect on the date of the enactment of this Act [June 16, 1988].

"(b) Application of Amendments.—The amendments made by section 2 [enacting this section and amending section 1129 of this title] shall not apply with respect to cases commenced under title 11 of the United States Code before the date of the enactment of this Act [June 16, 1988]."

Payment of Certain Benefits to Retired Former Employees

For payment of benefits by bankruptcy trustee to retired employees in enumerated circumstances with respect to cases commenced under this chapter in which a plan for reorganization had not been confirmed by the court and in which any such benefit was still being paid on October 2, 1986, and in cases that became subject to this chapter after October 2, 1986, and before June 16, 1988, see section 101(b) [title VI, §608] of Pub. L. 99–500, and Pub. L. 99–591, as amended, set out as a note under section 1106 of this title.

§1115. Property of the estate

(a) In a case in which the debtor is an individual, property of the estate includes, in addition to the property specified in section 541—

(1) all property of the kind specified in section 541 that the debtor acquires after the commencement of the case but before the case is closed, dismissed, or converted to a case under chapter 7, 12, or 13, whichever occurs first; and

(2) earnings from services performed by the debtor after the commencement of the case but before the case is closed, dismissed, or converted to a case under chapter 7, 12, or 13, whichever occurs first.

(b) Except as provided in section 1104 or a confirmed plan or order confirming a plan, the debtor shall remain in possession of all property of the estate.

(Added Pub. L. 109–8, title III, §321(a)(1), Apr. 20, 2005, 119 Stat. 94.)

EFFECTIVE DATE

Section effective 180 days after Apr. 20, 2005, and not applicable with respect to cases commenced under this title before such effective date, except as otherwise provided, see section 1501 of Pub. L. 109–8, set out as an Effective Date of 2005 Amendment note under section 101 of this title.

§ 1116. Duties of trustee or debtor in possession in small business cases

In a small business case, a trustee or the debtor in possession, in addition to the duties provided in this title and as otherwise required by law, shall—

(1) append to the voluntary petition or, in an involuntary case, file not later than 7 days after the date of the order for relief—

(A) its most recent balance sheet, statement of operations, cash-flow statement, and Federal income tax return; or

(B) a statement made under penalty of perjury that no balance sheet, statement of operations, or cash-flow statement has been prepared and no Federal tax return has been filed;

(2) attend, through its senior management personnel and counsel, meetings scheduled by the court or the United States trustee, including initial debtor interviews, scheduling conferences, and meetings of creditors convened under section 341 unless the court, after notice and a hearing, waives that requirement upon a finding of extraordinary and compelling circumstances;

(3) timely file all schedules and statements of financial affairs, unless the court, after notice and a hearing, grants an extension, which shall not extend such time period to a date later than 30 days after the date of the order for relief, absent extraordinary and compelling circumstances;

(4) file all postpetition financial and other reports required by the Federal Rules of Bankruptcy Procedure or by local rule of the district court;

(5) subject to section 363(c)(2), maintain insurance customary and appropriate to the industry;

(6)(A) timely file tax returns and other required government filings; and

(B) subject to section 363(c)(2), timely pay all taxes entitled to administrative expense priority except those being contested by appropriate proceedings being diligently prosecuted; and

(7) allow the United States trustee, or a designated representative of the United States trustee, to inspect the debtor's business premises, books, and records at reasonable times, after reasonable prior written notice, unless notice is waived by the debtor.

(Added Pub. L. 109–8, title IV, §436(a), Apr. 20, 2005, 119 Stat. 112.)

REFERENCES IN TEXT

The Federal Rules of Bankruptcy Procedure, referred to in par. (4), are set out in the Appendix to this title.

EFFECTIVE DATE

Section effective 180 days after Apr. 20, 2005, and not applicable with respect to cases commenced under this title before such effective date, except as otherwise provided, see section 1501 of Pub. L. 109–8, set out as an Effective Date of 2005 Amendment note under section 101 of this title.

SUBCHAPTER II—THE PLAN

§ 1121. Who may file a plan

(a) The debtor may file a plan with a petition commencing a voluntary case, or at any time in a voluntary case or an involuntary case.

(b) Except as otherwise provided in this section, only the debtor may file a plan until after 120 days after the date of the order for relief under this chapter.

(c) Any party in interest, including the debtor, the trustee, a creditors' committee, an equity security holders' committee, a creditor, an equity security holder, or any indenture trustee, may file a plan if and only if—

(1) a trustee has been appointed under this chapter;

(2) the debtor has not filed a plan before 120 days after the date of the order for relief under this chapter; or

(3) the debtor has not filed a plan that has been accepted, before 180 days after the date of the order for relief under this chapter, by each class of claims or interests that is impaired under the plan.

(d)(1) Subject to paragraph (2), on request of a party in interest made within the respective periods specified in subsections (b) and (c) of this section and after notice and a hearing, the court may for cause reduce or increase the 120-day period or the 180-day period referred to in this section.

(2)(A) The 120-day period specified in paragraph (1) may not be extended beyond a date that is 18 months after the date of the order for relief under this chapter.

(B) The 180-day period specified in paragraph (1) may not be extended beyond a date that is 20 months after the date of the order for relief under this chapter.

(e) In a small business case—

(1) only the debtor may file a plan until after 180 days after the date of the order for relief, unless that period is—

(A) extended as provided by this subsection, after notice and a hearing; or

(B) the court, for cause, orders otherwise;

(2) the plan and a disclosure statement (if any) shall be filed not later than 300 days after the date of the order for relief; and

(3) the time periods specified in paragraphs (1) and (2), and the time fixed in section 1129(e) within which the plan shall be confirmed, may be extended only if—

(A) the debtor, after providing notice to parties in interest (including the United States trustee), demonstrates by a preponderance of the evidence that it is more likely than not that the court will confirm a plan within a reasonable period of time;

(B) a new deadline is imposed at the time the extension is granted; and

(C) the order extending time is signed before the existing deadline has expired.

(Pub. L. 95–598, Nov. 6, 1978, 92 Stat. 2631; Pub. L. 98–353, title III, §506, July 10, 1984, 98 Stat. 385; Pub. L. 99–554, title II, §283(u), Oct. 27, 1986, 100 Stat. 3118; Pub. L. 103–394, title II, §217(d), Oct. 22, 1994, 108 Stat. 4127; Pub. L. 109–8, title IV, §§411, 437, Apr. 20, 2005, 119 Stat. 106, 113.)

HISTORICAL AND REVISION NOTES

LEGISLATIVE STATEMENTS

Section 1121 of the House amendment is derived from section 1121 of the House bill; section 1121(c)(1) will be satisfied automatically in a case under subchapter IV of title 11.

SENATE REPORT NO. 95–989

Subsection (a) permits the debtor to file a reorganization plan with a petition commencing a voluntary case or at any time during a voluntary or involuntary case.

Subsection (b) gives the debtor the exclusive right to file a plan during the first 120 days of the case. There are exceptions, however, enumerated in subsection (c). If a trustee has been appointed, if the debtor does not meet the 120-day deadline, or if the debtor fails to obtain the required consent within 180 days after the filing of the petition, any party in interest may propose a plan. This includes the debtor, the trustee, a creditors' committee, an equity security holders' committee, a creditor, an equity security holder, and an indenture trustee. The list is not exhaustive. In the case of a public company, a trustee is appointed within 10 days of the petition. In such a case, for all practical purposes, any party in interest may file a plan.

Subsection (d) permits the court, for cause, to increase or reduce the 120-day and 180-day periods specified. Since, the debtor has an exclusive privilege for 6 months during which others may not file a plan, the granted extension should be based on a showing of some promise of probable success. An extension should not be employed as a tactical device to put pressure on parties in interest to yield to a plan they consider unsatisfactory.

AMENDMENTS

2005—Subsec. (d). Pub. L. 109–8, §411, designated existing provisions as par. (1), substituted "Subject to paragraph (2), on" for "On", and added par. (2).

Subsec. (e). Pub. L. 109–8, §437, added subsec. (e) and struck out former subsec. (e) which read as follows: "In a case in which the debtor is a small business and elects to be considered a small business—

"(1) only the debtor may file a plan until after 100 days after the date of the order for relief under this chapter;

"(2) all plans shall be filed within 160 days after the date of the order for relief; and

"(3) on request of a party in interest made within the respective periods specified in paragraphs (1) and (2) and after notice and a hearing, the court may—

"(A) reduce the 100-day period or the 160-day period specified in paragraph (1) or (2) for cause; and

"(B) increase the 100-day period specified in paragraph (1) if the debtor shows that the need for an increase is caused by circumstances for which the debtor should not be held accountable."

1994—Subsec. (e). Pub. L. 103–394 added subsec. (e).

1986—Subsec. (d). Pub. L. 99–554 inserted reference to subsection (b) of this section.

1984—Subsec. (c)(3). Pub. L. 98–353, §506(a), substituted "of claims or interests that is" for "the claims or interests of which are".

Subsec. (d). Pub. L. 98–353, §506(b), inserted "made within the respective periods specified in subsection (c) of this section".

EFFECTIVE DATE OF 2005 AMENDMENT

Amendment by Pub. L. 109–8 effective 180 days after Apr. 20, 2005, and not applicable with respect to cases commenced under this title before such effective date, except as otherwise provided, see section 1501 of Pub. L. 109–8, set out as a note under section 101 of this title.

EFFECTIVE DATE OF 1994 AMENDMENT

Amendment by Pub. L. 103–394 effective Oct. 22, 1994, and not applicable with respect to cases commenced under this title before Oct. 22, 1994, see section 702 of Pub. L. 103–394, set out as a note under section 101 of this title.

EFFECTIVE DATE OF 1986 AMENDMENT

Amendment by Pub. L. 99–554 effective 30 days after Oct. 27, 1986, see section 302(a) of Pub. L. 99–554, set out as a note under section 581 of Title 28, Judiciary and Judicial Procedure.

EFFECTIVE DATE OF 1984 AMENDMENT

Amendment by Pub. L. 98–353 effective with respect to cases filed 90 days after July 10, 1984, see section 552(a) of Pub. L. 98–353, set out as a note under section 101 of this title.

§1122. Classification of claims or interests

(a) Except as provided in subsection (b) of this section, a plan may place a claim or an interest in a particular class only if such claim or interest is substantially similar to the other claims or interests of such class.

(b) A plan may designate a separate class of claims consisting only of every unsecured claim that is less than or reduced to an amount that the court approves as reasonable and necessary for administrative convenience.

(Pub. L. 95–598, Nov. 6, 1978, 92 Stat. 2631.)

HISTORICAL AND REVISION NOTES

SENATE REPORT NO. 95–989

This section codifies current case law surrounding the classification of claims and equity securities. It requires classification based on the nature of the claims or interests classified, and permits inclusion of claims or interests in a particular class only if the claim or interest being included is substantially similar to the other claims or interests of the class.

Subsection (b), also a codification of existing practice, contains an exception. The plan may designate a separate class of claims consisting only of every unsecured claim that is less than or reduced to an amount that the court approves as reasonable and necessary for administrative convenience.

§1123. Contents of plan

(a) Notwithstanding any otherwise applicable nonbankruptcy law, a plan shall—

(1) designate, subject to section 1122 of this title, classes of claims, other than claims of a kind specified in section 507(a)(2), 507(a)(3), or 507(a)(8) of this title, and classes of interests;

(2) specify any class of claims or interests that is not impaired under the plan;

(3) specify the treatment of any class of claims or interests that is impaired under the plan;

(4) provide the same treatment for each claim or interest of a particular class, unless the holder of a particular claim or interest agrees to a less favorable treatment of such particular claim or interest;

(5) provide adequate means for the plan's implementation, such as—

(A) retention by the debtor of all or any part of the property of the estate;

(B) transfer of all or any part of the property of the estate to one or more entities, whether organized before or after the confirmation of such plan;

(C) merger or consolidation of the debtor with one or more persons;

(D) sale of all or any part of the property of the estate, either subject to or free of any lien, or the distribution of all or any part of the property of the estate among those having an interest in such property of the estate;

(E) satisfaction or modification of any lien;

(F) cancellation or modification of any indenture or similar instrument;

(G) curing or waiving of any default;

(H) extension of a maturity date or a change in an interest rate or other term of outstanding securities;

(I) amendment of the debtor's charter; or

(J) issuance of securities of the debtor, or of any entity referred to in subparagraph (B) or (C) of this paragraph, for cash, for property, for existing securities, or in exchange for claims or interests, or for any other appropriate purpose;

(6) provide for the inclusion in the charter of the debtor, if the debtor is a corporation, or of any corporation referred to in paragraph (5)(B) or (5)(C) of this subsection, of a provision prohibiting the issuance of nonvoting equity securities, and providing, as to the several classes of securities possessing voting power, an appropriate distribution of such power among such classes, including, in the case of any class of equity securities having a preference over another class of equity securities with respect to dividends, adequate provisions for the election of directors representing such preferred class in the event of default in the payment of such dividends;

(7) contain only provisions that are consistent with the interests of creditors and equity security holders and with public policy with respect to the manner of selection of any officer, director, or trustee under the plan and any successor to such officer, director, or trustee; and

(8) in a case in which the debtor is an individual, provide for the payment to creditors under the plan of all or such portion of earnings from personal services performed by the debtor after the commencement of the case or other future income of the debtor as is necessary for the execution of the plan.

(b) Subject to subsection (a) of this section, a plan may—

(1) impair or leave unimpaired any class of claims, secured or unsecured, or of interests;

(2) subject to section 365 of this title, provide for the assumption, rejection, or assignment of any executory contract or unexpired lease of the debtor not previously rejected under such section;

(3) provide for—

(A) the settlement or adjustment of any claim or interest belonging to the debtor or to the estate; or

(B) the retention and enforcement by the debtor, by the trustee, or by a representative of the estate appointed for such purpose, of any such claim or interest;

(4) provide for the sale of all or substantially all of the property of the estate, and the distribution of the proceeds of such sale among holders of claims or interests;

(5) modify the rights of holders of secured claims, other than a claim secured only by a security interest in real property that is the debtor's principal residence, or of holders of unsecured claims, or leave unaffected the rights of holders of any class of claims; and

(6) include any other appropriate provision not inconsistent with the applicable provisions of this title.

(c) In a case concerning an individual, a plan proposed by an entity other than the debtor may not provide for the use, sale, or lease of property exempted under section 522 of this title, unless the debtor consents to such use, sale, or lease.

(d) Notwithstanding subsection (a) of this section and sections 506(b), 1129(a)(7), and 1129(b) of this title, if it is proposed in a plan to cure a default the amount necessary to cure the default shall be determined in accordance with the underlying agreement and applicable nonbankruptcy law.

(Pub. L. 95–598, Nov. 6, 1978, 92 Stat. 2631; Pub. L. 98–353, title III, §507, July 10, 1984, 98 Stat. 385; Pub. L. 103–394, title II, §206, title III, §§304(h)(6), 305(a), title V, §501(d)(31), Oct. 22, 1994, 108 Stat. 4123, 4134, 4146; Pub. L. 109–8, title III, §321(b), title XV, §1502(a)(7), Apr. 20, 2005, 119 Stat. 95, 216.)

HISTORICAL AND REVISION NOTES

LEGISLATIVE STATEMENTS

Section 1123 of the House amendment represents a compromise between similar provisions in the House bill and Senate amendment. The section has been clarified to clearly indicate that both secured and unsecured claims, or either of them, may be impaired in a case under title 11. In addition assumption or rejection of an executory contract under a plan must comply with section 365 of title 11. Moreover, section 1123(a)(1) has been substantively modified to permit classification of certain kinds of priority claims. This is important for purposes of confirmation under section 1129(a)(9).

Section 1123(a)(5) of the House amendment is derived from a similar provision in the House bill and Senate amendment but deletes the language pertaining to "fair upset price" as an unnecessary restriction. Section 1123 is also intended to indicate that a plan may provide for any action specified in section 1123 in the case of a corporation without a resolution of the board of directors. If the plan is confirmed, then any action proposed in the plan may be taken notwithstanding any otherwise applicable nonbankruptcy law in accordance with section 1142(a) of title 11.

SENATE REPORT NO. 95–989

Subsection (a) specifies what a plan of reorganization must contain. The plan must designate classes of claims and interests, and specify, by class, the claims or interests that are unimpaired under the plan. Priority claims are not required to be classified because they may not have arisen when the plan is filed. The plan must provide the same treatment for each claim or interest of a particular class, unless the holder of a particular claim or interest agrees to a different, but not better, treatment of his claim or interest.

Paragraph (3) applies to claims, not creditors. Thus, if a creditor is undersecured, and thus has a secured claim and an unsecured claim, this paragraph will be applied independently to each of his claims.

Paragraph (4) of subsection (a) is derived from section 216 of chapter X [section 616 of former title 11] with some modifications. It requires the plan to provide adequate means for the plans execution. These means may include retention by the debtor of all or any part of the property of the estate, transfer of all or any part of the property of the estate to one or more entities, whether organized pre- or postconfirmation, merger or consolidation of the debtor with one or more persons, sale and distribution of all or any part of the property of the estate, satisfaction or modification of any lien, cancellation or modification of any indenture or similar instrument, curing or waiving of any default, extension of maturity dates or change in interest rates of securities, amendment of the debtor's charter, and issuance of securities.

Subparagraph (C), as it applies in railroad cases, has the effect of overruling *St. Joe Paper Co. v. Atlantic Coast Line R. R.*, 347 U.S. 298 (1954). It will allow the trustee or creditors to propose a plan of merger with another railroad without the consent of the debtor, and the debtor will be bound under proposed 11 U.S.C. 1141(a). See Hearings, pt. 3, at 1616. "Similar instrument" referred to in subparagraph (F) might include a deposit with an agent for distribution, other than an indenture trustee, such as an agent under an agreement in a railroad conditional sale or lease financing agreement.

Paragraphs (5) and (6) and subsection (b) are derived substantially from Section 216 of Chapter X ([former] 11 U.S.C. 616). Paragraph (5) requires the plan to prohibit the issuance of nonvoting equity securities, and to provide for an appropriate distribution of voting power among the various classes of equity securities. Paragraph (6) requires that the plan contain only provisions that are consistent with the interests of creditors and equity security holders, and with public policy with respect to the selection of officers, directors, and trustees, and their successors.

Subsection (b) specifies the matters that the plan may propose. The plan may impair or leave unimpaired any claim or interest. The plan may provide for the assumption or rejection of executory contracts or unexpired leases not previously rejected under section 365. The plan may also provide for the treatment of claims by the debtor against other entities that are not settled before the confirmation of the plan. The plan may propose settlement or adjustment of any claim or equity security belonging to the estate, or may propose retention and enforcement of such claim or interest by the debtor or by an agent appointed for that purpose.

The plan may also propose the sale of all or substantially all of the property of the estate, and the distribution of the proceeds of the sale among creditors and equity security holders. This would be a liquidating plan. The subsection permits the plan to include any other appropriate provision not inconsistent with the applicable provisions of the bankruptcy code.

Subsection (c) protects an individual debtor's exempt property by prohibiting its use, sale, or lease under a plan proposed by someone other than the debtor, unless the debtor consents.

AMENDMENTS

2005—Subsec. (a)(1). Pub. L. 109–8, §1502(a)(7), substituted "507(a)(2), 507(a)(3)" for "507(a)(1), 507(a)(2)".

Subsec. (a)(8). Pub. L. 109–8, §321(b), added par. (8).

1994—Subsec. (a)(1). Pub. L. 103–394, §§304(h)(6), 501(d)(31), substituted "507(a)(8) of this title," for "507(a)(7) of this title".

Subsec. (b)(5), (6). Pub. L. 103–394, §206, added par. (5) and redesignated former par. (5) as (6).

Subsec. (d). Pub. L. 103–394, §305(a), added subsec. (d).

1984—Subsec. (a). Pub. L. 98–353, §507(a)(1), in provisions preceding par. (1) substituted "Notwithstanding any otherwise applicable nonbankruptcy law, a" for "A".

Subsec. (a)(1). Pub. L. 98–353, §507(a)(2), inserted a comma after "classes of claims" and substituted "507(a)(7) of this title," for "507(a)(6) of this title".

Subsec. (a)(3). Pub. L. 98–353, §507(a)(3), struck out "shall" before "specify the treatment".

Subsec. (a)(5). Pub. L. 98–353, §507(a)(4), substituted "implementation" for "execution".

Subsec. (a)(5)(G). Pub. L. 98–353, §507(a)(5), inserted "of" after "waiving".

Subsec. (b)(2). Pub. L. 98–353, §507(b), substituted "rejection, or assignment" for "or rejection", and "under such section" for "under section 365 of this title".

EFFECTIVE DATE OF 2005 AMENDMENT

Amendment by Pub. L. 109–8 effective 180 days after Apr. 20, 2005, and not applicable with respect to cases commenced under this title before such effective date, except as otherwise provided, see section 1501 of Pub. L. 109–8, set out as a note under section 101 of this title.

EFFECTIVE DATE OF 1994 AMENDMENT

Amendment by sections 206, 304(h)(6), and 501(d)(31) of Pub. L. 103–394 effective Oct. 22, 1994, and not applicable with respect to cases commenced under this title before Oct. 22, 1994, and amendment by section 305(a) of Pub. L. 103–394 effective Oct. 22, 1994, and applicable only to agreements entered into after Oct. 22, 1994, see section 702 of Pub. L. 103–394, set out as a note under section 101 of this title.

EFFECTIVE DATE OF 1984 AMENDMENT

Amendment by Pub. L. 98–353 effective with respect to cases filed 90 days after July 10, 1984, see section 552(a) of Pub. L. 98–353, set out as a note under section 101 of this title.

§ 1124. Impairment of claims or interests

Except as provided in section 1123(a)(4) of this title, a class of claims or interests is impaired under a plan unless, with respect to each claim or interest of such class, the plan—

(1) leaves unaltered the legal, equitable, and contractual rights to which such claim or interest entitles the holder of such claim or interest; or

(2) notwithstanding any contractual provision or applicable law that entitles the holder of such claim or interest to demand or receive accelerated payment of such claim or interest after the occurrence of a default—

(A) cures any such default that occurred before or after the commencement of the case under this title, other than a default of a kind specified in section 365(b)(2) of this title or of a kind that section 365(b)(2) expressly does not require to be cured;

(B) reinstates the maturity of such claim or interest as such maturity existed before such default;

(C) compensates the holder of such claim or interest for any damages incurred as a result of any reasonable reliance by such holder on such contractual provision or such applicable law;

(D) if such claim or such interest arises from any failure to perform a nonmonetary obligation, other than a default arising from failure to operate a nonresidential real property lease subject to section 365(b)(1)(A), compensates the holder of such claim or such interest (other than the debtor or an insider) for any actual pecuniary loss incurred by such holder as a result of such failure; and

(E) does not otherwise alter the legal, equitable, or contractual rights to which such claim or interest entitles the holder of such claim or interest.

(Pub. L. 95–598, Nov. 6, 1978, 92 Stat. 2633; Pub. L. 98–353, title III, §508, July 10, 1984, 98 Stat. 385; Pub. L. 103–394, title II, §213(d), Oct. 22, 1994, 108 Stat. 4126; Pub. L. 109–8, title III, §328(b), Apr. 20, 2005, 119 Stat. 100.)

Historical and Revision Notes

LEGISLATIVE STATEMENTS

Section 1124 of the House amendment is derived from a similar provision in the House bill and Senate amendment. The section defines the new concept of "impairment" of claims or interests; the concept differs significantly from the concept of "materially and adversely affected" under the Bankruptcy Act [former title 11]. Section 1124(3) of the House amendment provides that a holder of a claim or interest is not impaired, if the plan provides that the holder will receive the allowed amount of the holder's claim, or in the case of an interest with a fixed liquidation preference or redemption price, the greater of such price. This adopts the position contained in the House bill and rejects the contrary standard contained in the Senate amendment.

Section 1124(3) of the House amendment rejects a provision contained in section 1124(3)(B)(iii) of the House bill which would have considered a class of interest not to be impaired by virtue of the fact that the plan provided cash or property for the value of the holder's interest in the debtor.

The effect of the House amendment is to permit an interest not to be impaired only if the interest has a fixed liquidation preference or redemption price. Therefore, a class of interests such as common stock, must either accept a plan under section 1129(a)(8), or the plan must satisfy the requirements of section 1129(b)(2)(C) in order for a plan to be confirmed.

A compromise reflected in section 1124(2)(C) of the House amendment indicates that a class of claims is not impaired under the circumstances of section 1124(2) if damages are paid to rectify reasonable reliance engaged in by the holder of a claim or interest arising from the prepetition breach of a contractual provision, such as an ipso facto or bankruptcy clause, or law. Where the rights of third parties are concerned, such as in the case of lease premises which have been rerented to a third party, it is not intended that there will be adequate damages to compensate the third party.

SENATE REPORT NO. 95–989

The basic concept underlying this section is not new. It rests essentially on Section 107 of Chapter X ([former] 11 U.S.C. 507), which states that creditors or stockholders or any class thereof "shall be deemed to be 'affected' by a plan only if their or its interest shall be materially and adversely affected thereby."

This section is designated to indicate when contractual rights of creditors or interest holders are not materially affected. It specifies three ways in which the plan may leave a claim or interest unimpaired.

First, the plan may propose not to alter the legal, equitable, or contractual rights to which the claim or interest entitled its holder.

Second, a claim or interest is unimpaired by curing the effect of a default and reinstating the original terms of an obligation when maturity was brought on or accelerated by the default. The intervention of bankruptcy and the defaults represent a temporary crisis which the plan of reorganization is intended to clear away. The holder of a claim or interest who under the plan is restored to his original position, when others receive less or get nothing at all, is fortunate indeed and has no cause to complain. Curing of the default and the assumption of the debt in accordance with its terms is an important reorganization technique for dealing with a particular class of claims, especially secured claims.

Third, a claim or interest is unimpaired if the plan provides for their payment in cash. In the case of a debt liability, the cash payment is for the allowed amount of the claim, which does not include a redemption premium. If it is an equity security with a fixed liquidation preference, such as a preferred stock, the allowed amount is such liquidation preference, with no redemption premium. With respect to any other equity security, such as a common stock, cash payment must be equal to the "value of such holder's interest in the debtor."

Section 1124 does not include payment "in property" other than cash. Except for a rare case, claims or interests are not by their terms payable in property, but a plan may so provide and those affected thereby may accept or reject the proposed plan. They may not be forced to accept a plan declaring the holders' claims or interests to be "unimpaired."

HOUSE REPORT NO. 95–595

This section is new. It is designed to indicate when contractual rights of creditors or interest holders are not materially affected. The section specifies three ways in which the plan may leave a claim or interest unimpaired.

First, the plan may propose not to alter the legal, equitable, or contractual rights to which the claim or interest entitled its holder.

Second, the plan is permitted to reinstate a claim or interest and thus leave it unimpaired. Reinstatement consists of curing any default (other than a default under an ipso facto or bankruptcy clause) and reinstatement of the maturity of the claim or interest. Further, the plan may not otherwise alter any legal, equitable, or contractual right to which the claim or interest entitles its holder.

Third, the plan may leave a claim or interest unimpaired by paying its amount in full other than in securities of the debtor, an affiliate of the debtor participating in a joint plan, or a successor to the debtor. These securities are excluded because determination of their value would require a valuation of the business being reorganized. Use of them to pay a creditor or equity security holder without his consent may be done only under section 1129(b) and only after a valuation of the debtor. Under this paragraph, the plan must pay the allowed amount of the claim in full, in cash or other property, or, in the case of an equity security, must pay the greatest of any fixed liquidation preference to which the terms of the equity security entitle its holder, any fixed price at which the debtor, under the terms of the equity security may redeem such equity security, and the value, as of the effective date of the plan, of the holder's interest in the debtor. The value of the holder's interest need not be determined precisely by valuing the debtor's business if such value is clearly below redemption or liquidation preference values. If such value would require a full-scale valuation of the business, then such interest should be treated as impaired. But, if the debtor corporation is clearly insolvent, then the value of the common stock holder's interest in the debtor is zero, and offering them nothing under the plan of reorganization will not impair their rights.

"Value, as of the effective date of the plan," as used in paragraph (3) and in proposed 11 U.S.C. 1179(a)(7)(B), 1129(a)(9), 1129(b), 1172(2), 1325(a)(4), 1325(a)(5)(B), and 1328(b), indicates that the promised payment under the plan must be discounted to present value as of the effective date of the plan. The discounting should be based only on the unpaid balance of the amount due under the plan, until that amount, including interest, is paid in full.

AMENDMENTS

2005—Par. (2)(A). Pub. L. 109–8, §328(b)(1), inserted "or of a kind that section 365(b)(2) expressly does not require to be cured" before semicolon at end.

Par. (2)(D), (E). Pub. L. 109–8, §328(b)(2)–(4), added subpar. (D) and redesignated former subpar. (D) as (E).

1994—Par. (3). Pub. L. 103–394 struck out par. (3) which read as follows: "provides that, on the effective date of the plan, the holder of such claim or interest receives, on account of such claim or interest, cash equal to—

"(A) with respect to a claim, the allowed amount of such claim; or

"(B) with respect to an interest, if applicable, the greater of—

"(i) any fixed liquidation preference to which the terms of any security representing such interest entitle the holder of such interest; or

"(ii) any fixed price at which the debtor, under the terms of such security, may redeem such security from such holder."

1984—Par. (2)(A). Pub. L. 98–353, §508(1), amended subpar. (A) generally. Prior to amendment, subpar. (A) read as follows: "cures any such default, other than a default of a kind specified in section 365(b)(2) of this title, that occurred before or after the commencement of the case under this title;".

Par. (3)(B)(i). Pub. L. 98–353, §508(2), substituted "or" for "and".

EFFECTIVE DATE OF 2005 AMENDMENT

Amendment by Pub. L. 109–8 effective 180 days after Apr. 20, 2005, and not applicable with respect to cases commenced under this title before such effective date, except as otherwise provided, see section 1501 of Pub. L. 109–8, set out as a note under section 101 of this title.

EFFECTIVE DATE OF 1994 AMENDMENT

Amendment by Pub. L. 103–394 effective Oct. 22, 1994, and not applicable with respect to cases commenced under this title before Oct. 22, 1994, see section 702 of Pub. L. 103–394, set out as a note under section 101 of this title.

EFFECTIVE DATE OF 1984 AMENDMENT

Amendment by Pub. L. 98–353 effective with respect to cases filed 90 days after July 10, 1984, see section 552(a) of Pub. L. 98–353, set out as a note under section 101 of this title.

§1125. Postpetition disclosure and solicitation

(a) In this section—

(1) "adequate information" means information of a kind, and in sufficient detail, as far as is reasonably practicable in light of the nature and history of the debtor and the condition of the debtor's books and records, including a discussion of the potential material Federal tax consequences of the plan to the debtor, any successor to the debtor, and a hypothetical investor typical of the holders of claims or interests in the case, that would enable such a hypothetical investor of the relevant class to make an informed judgment about the plan, but adequate information need not include such information about any other possible or proposed plan and in determining whether a disclosure statement provides adequate information, the court shall consider the complexity of the case, the benefit of additional information to creditors and other parties in interest, and the cost of providing additional information; and

(2) "investor typical of holders of claims or interests of the relevant class" means investor having—

(A) a claim or interest of the relevant class;

(B) such a relationship with the debtor as the holders of other claims or interests of such class generally have; and

(C) such ability to obtain such information from sources other than the disclosure required by this section as holders of claims or interests in such class generally have.

(b) An acceptance or rejection of a plan may not be solicited after the commencement of the case under this title from a holder of a claim or interest with respect to such claim or interest, unless, at the time of or before such solicitation, there is transmitted to such holder the plan or a summary of the plan, and a written disclosure statement approved, after notice and a hearing, by the court as containing adequate information. The court may approve a disclosure statement without a valuation of the debtor or an appraisal of the debtor's assets.

(c) The same disclosure statement shall be transmitted to each holder of a claim or interest of a particular class, but there may be transmitted different disclosure statements, differing in amount, detail, or kind of information, as between classes.

(d) Whether a disclosure statement required under subsection (b) of this section contains adequate information is not governed by any otherwise applicable nonbankruptcy law, rule, or regulation, but an agency or official whose duty is to administer or enforce such a law, rule, or regulation may be heard on the issue of whether a disclosure statement contains adequate information. Such an agency or official may not appeal from, or otherwise seek review of, an order approving a disclosure statement.

(e) A person that solicits acceptance or rejection of a plan, in good faith and in compliance with the applicable provisions of this title, or that participates, in good faith and in compliance with the applicable provisions of this title, in the offer, issuance, sale, or purchase of a security, offered or sold under the plan, of the debtor, of an affiliate participating in a joint plan with the debtor, or of a newly organized successor to the debtor under the plan, is not liable, on account of such solicitation or participation, for violation of any applicable law, rule, or regulation governing solicitation of acceptance or rejection of a plan or the offer, issuance, sale, or purchase of securities.

(f) Notwithstanding subsection (b), in a small business case—

(1) the court may determine that the plan itself provides adequate information and that a separate disclosure statement is not necessary;

(2) the court may approve a disclosure statement submitted on standard forms approved

by the court or adopted under section 2075 of title 28; and

(3)(A) the court may conditionally approve a disclosure statement subject to final approval after notice and a hearing;

(B) acceptances and rejections of a plan may be solicited based on a conditionally approved disclosure statement if the debtor provides adequate information to each holder of a claim or interest that is solicited, but a conditionally approved disclosure statement shall be mailed not later than 25 days before the date of the hearing on confirmation of the plan; and

(C) the hearing on the disclosure statement may be combined with the hearing on confirmation of a plan.

(g) Notwithstanding subsection (b), an acceptance or rejection of the plan may be solicited from a holder of a claim or interest if such solicitation complies with applicable nonbankruptcy law and if such holder was solicited before the commencement of the case in a manner complying with applicable nonbankruptcy law.

(Pub. L. 95–598, Nov. 6, 1978, 92 Stat. 2633; Pub. L. 98–353, title III, §509, July 10, 1984, 98 Stat. 385; Pub. L. 103–394, title II, §217(e), Oct. 22, 1994, 108 Stat. 4127; Pub. L. 109–8, title IV, §§408, 431, title VII, §717, Apr. 20, 2005, 119 Stat. 106, 109, 131.)

HISTORICAL AND REVISION NOTES

LEGISLATIVE STATEMENTS

Section 1125 of the House amendment is derived from section 1125 of the House bill and Senate amendment except with respect to section 1125(f) of the Senate amendment. It will not be necessary for the court to consider the report of the examiner prior to approval of a disclosure statement. The investigation of the examiner is to proceed on an independent basis from the procedure of the reorganization under chapter 11. In order to ensure that the examiner's report will be expeditious and fair, the examiner is precluded from serving as a trustee in the case or from representing a trustee if a trustee is appointed, whether the case remains in chapter 11 or is converted to chapter 7 or 13.

SENATE REPORT NO. 95–989

This section extends disclosure requirements in connection with solicitations to all cases under chapter 11. Heretofore this subject was dealt with by the Bankruptcy Act [former title 11] mainly in the special contexts of railroad reorganizations and chapter X [chapter 10 of former title 11] cases.

Subsection (a) defines (1) the subject matter of disclosure as "adequate information" and relates the standard of adequacy to an (2) "investor typical of holders or claims or interests of the relevant class." "Investor" is used broadly here, for it will almost always include a trade creditor or other creditors who originally had no investment intent or interest. It refers to the investment-type decision by those called upon to accept a plan to modify their claims or interests, which typically will involve acceptance of new securities or of a cash payment in lieu thereof.

Both the kind and form of information are left essentially to the judicial discretion of the court, guided by the specification in subparagraph (a)(1) that it be of a kind and in sufficient detail that a reasonable and typical investor can make an informed judgment about the plan. The information required will necessarily be governed by the circumstances of the case.

Reporting and audit standards devised for solvent and continuing businesses do not necessarily fit a debtor in reorganization. Subsection (a)(1) expressly incorporates consideration of the nature and history of the debtor and the condition of its books and records into the determination of what is reasonably practicable to supply. These factors are particularly pertinent to historical data and to discontinued operations of no future relevance.

A plan is necessarily predicated on knowledge of the assets and liabilities being dealt with and on factually supported expectations as to the future course of the business sufficient to meet the feasibility standard in section 1130(a)(11) of this title. It may thus be necessary to provide estimates or judgments for that purpose. Yet it remains practicable to describe, in such detail as may be relevant and needed, the basis for the plan and the data on which supporters of the plan rely.

Subsection (b) establishes the jurisdiction of the court over this subject by prohibiting solicitation of acceptance or rejection of a plan after the commencement of the case, unless the person solicited receives, before or at the time of the solicitation, a written disclosure statement approved by the court, after notice and hearing, as containing adequate information. As under present law, determinations of value, by appraisal or otherwise, are not required if not needed to accomplish the purpose specified in subsection (a)(1).

Subsection (c) requires that the same disclosure statement be transmitted to each member of a class. It recognizes that the information needed for an informed judgment about the plan may differ among classes. A class whose rights under the plan center on a particular fund or asset would have no use for an extensive description of other matters that could not affect them.

Subsection (d) relieves the court of the need to follow any otherwise applicable Federal or state law in determining the adequacy of the information contained in the disclosure statement submitted for its approval. It authorizes an agency or official, Federal or state, charged with administering cognate laws so preempted to advise the court on the adequacy of proposed disclosure statement. But they are not authorized to appeal the court's decision.

Solicitations with respect to a plan do not involve just mere requests for opinions. Acceptance of the plan vitally affects creditors and shareholders, and most frequently the solicitation involves an offering of securities in exchange for claims or interests. The present bankruptcy statute [former title 11] has exempted such offerings under each of its chapters from the registration and disclosure requirements of the Securities Act of 1933 [15 U.S.C. 77a et seq.], an exemption also continued by section 1145(a)(2) of this title. The extension of the disclosure requirements to all chapter 11 cases justifies the coordinate extension of these exemptions. By the same token, no valid purpose is served not to exempt from the requirements of similar state laws in a matter under the exclusive jurisdiction of the Federal bankruptcy laws.

Subsection (e) exonerates any person who, in good faith and in compliance with this title, solicits or participates in the offer, issuance, sale or purchase, under the plan, of a security from any liability, on account of such solicitation or participation, for violation of any law, rule, or regulation governing the offer, issuance, sale, or purchase of securities. This exoneration is coordinate with the exemption from Federal or State registration or licensing requirements provided by section 1145 of this title.

In the nonpublic case, the court, when approving the disclosure statement, has before it the texts of the plan, a proposed disclosure document, and such other information the plan proponents and other interested parties may present at the hearing. In the final analysis the exoneration which subsection (e) grants must depend on the good faith of the plan proponents and of those who participate in the preparation of the disclosure statement and in the solicitation. Subsection (e) does not affect civil or criminal liability for defects and inadequacies that are beyond the limits of the exoneration that good faith provides.

Section 1125 applies to public companies as well, subject to the qualifications of subsection (f). In case of a public company no solicitations of acceptance is permitted unless authorized by the court upon or after approval of the plan pursuant to section 1128(c). In addition to the documents specified in subsection (b), subsection (f) requires transmission of the opinion and order of the court approving the plan and, if filed, the advisory report of the Securities and Exchange Commission or a summary thereof prepared by the Commission.

HOUSE REPORT NO. 95–595

This section is new. It is the heart of the consolidation of the various reorganization chapters found in current law. It requires disclosure before solicitation of acceptances of a plan or reorganization.

Subsection (a) contains two definitions. First, "adequate information" is defined to mean information of a kind, and insufficient detail, as far as is reasonably practical in light of the nature and history of the debtor and the condition of the debtor's books and records, that would enable a hypothetical reasonable investor typical of holders of claims or interests of the relevant class to make an informed judgment about the plan. Second, "investor typical of holders of claims or interests of the relevant class" is defined to mean an investor having a claim or interest of the relevant class, having such a relationship with the debtor as the holders of other claims or interests of the relevant class have, and having such ability to obtain information from sources other than the disclosure statement as holders of claims or interests of the relevant class have, and having such ability to obtain information from sources other than the disclosure statement as holders of claims or interests of the relevant class have. That is, the hypothetical investor against which the disclosure is measured must not be an insider if other members of the class are not insiders, and so on. In other words, the adequacy of disclosure is measured against the typical investor, not an extraordinary one.

The Supreme Court's rulemaking power will not extend to rulemaking that will prescribe what constitutes adequate information. That standard is a substantive standard. Precisely what constitutes adequate information in any particular instance will develop on a case-by-case basis. Courts will take a practical approach as to what is necessary under the circumstances of each case, such as the cost of preparation of the statements, the need for relative speed in solicitation and confirmation, and, of course, the need for investor protection. There will be a balancing of interests in each case. In reorganization cases, there is frequently great uncertainty. Therefore the need for flexibility is greatest.

Subsection (b) is the operative subsection. It prohibits solicitation of acceptances or rejections of a plan after the commencement of the case unless, at the time of the solicitation or before, there is transmitted to the solicitee the plan or a summary of the plan, and a written disclosure statement approved by the court as containing adequate information. The subsection permits approval of the statement without the necessity of a valuation of the debtor or an appraisal of the debtor's assets. However, in some cases, a valuation or appraisal will be necessary to develop adequate information. The court will be able to determine what is necessary in light of the facts and circumstances of each particular case.

Subsection (c) requires that the same disclosure statement go to all members of a particular class, but permits different disclosure to different classes.

Subsection (d) excepts the disclosure statements from the requirements of the securities laws (such as section 14 of the 1934 Act [15 U.S.C. 78n] and section 5 of the 1933 Act [15 U.S.C. 77e]), and from similar State securities laws (blue sky laws, for example). The subsection permits an agency or official whose duty is to administer or enforce such laws (such as the Securities and Exchange Commission or State Corporation Commissioners) to appear and be heard on the issue of whether a disclosure statement contains adequate information, but the agencies and officials are not granted the right of appeal from an adverse determination in any capacity. They may join in an appeal by a true party in interest, however.

Subsection (e) is a safe harbor provision, and is necessary to make the exemption provided by subsection (d) effective. Without it, a creditor that solicited an acceptance or rejection in reliance on the court's approval of a disclosure statement would be potentially liable under antifraud sections designed to enforce the very sections of the securities laws from which subsection (d) excuses compliance. The subsection protects only persons that solicit in good faith and in compliance with the applicable provisions of the reorganization chapter. It provides protection from legal liability as well as from equitable liability based on an injunctive action by the SEC or other agency or official.

AMENDMENTS

2005—Subsec. (a)(1). Pub. L. 109–8, §717, inserted "including a discussion of the potential material Federal tax consequences of the plan to the debtor, any successor to the debtor, and a hypothetical investor typical of the holders of claims or interests in the case," after "records," and substituted "such a hypothetical investor" for "a hypothetical reasonable investor typical of holders of claims or interests".

Pub. L. 109–8, §431(1), inserted before semicolon "and in determining whether a disclosure statement provides adequate information, the court shall consider the complexity of the case, the benefit of additional information to creditors and other parties in interest, and the cost of providing additional information".

Subsec. (f). Pub. L. 109–8, §431(2), added subsec. (f) and struck out former subsec. (f) which read as follows: "Notwithstanding subsection (b), in a case in which the debtor has elected under section 1121(e) to be considered a small business—

"(1) the court may conditionally approve a disclosure statement subject to final approval after notice and a hearing;

"(2) acceptances and rejections of a plan may be solicited based on a conditionally approved disclosure statement as long as the debtor provides adequate information to each holder of a claim or interest that is solicited, but a conditionally approved disclosure statement shall be mailed at least 10 days prior to the date of the hearing on confirmation of the plan; and

"(3) a hearing on the disclosure statement may be combined with a hearing on confirmation of a plan."

Subsec. (g). Pub. L. 109–8, §408, added subsec. (g).

1994—Subsec. (f). Pub. L. 103–394 added subsec. (f).

1984—Subsec. (a)(1). Pub. L. 98–353, §509(a)(1), inserted ", but adequate information need not include such information about any other possible or proposed plan".

Subsec. (a)(2)(B). Pub. L. 98–353, §509(a)(2), inserted "the" after "with".

Subsec. (a)(2)(C). Pub. L. 98–353, §509(a)(3), inserted "of" after "holders".

Subsec. (d). Pub. L. 98–353, §509(b), inserted "required under subsection (b) of this section" and ", or otherwise seek review of,".

Subsec. (e). Pub. L. 98–353, §509(c), inserted "acceptance or rejection of a plan" after "solicits", and "solicitation of acceptance or rejection of a plan or" after "governing".

EFFECTIVE DATE OF 2005 AMENDMENT

Amendment by Pub. L. 109–8 effective 180 days after Apr. 20, 2005, and not applicable with respect to cases commenced under this title before such effective date, except as otherwise provided, see section 1501 of Pub. L. 109–8, set out as a note under section 101 of this title.

EFFECTIVE DATE OF 1994 AMENDMENT

Amendment by Pub. L. 103–394 effective Oct. 22, 1994, and not applicable with respect to cases commenced under this title before Oct. 22, 1994, see section 702 of

Pub. L. 103–394, set out as a note under section 101 of this title.

EFFECTIVE DATE OF 1984 AMENDMENT

Amendment by Pub. L. 98–353 effective with respect to cases filed 90 days after July 10, 1984, see section 552(a) of Pub. L. 98–353, set out as a note under section 101 of this title.

§ 1126. Acceptance of plan

(a) The holder of a claim or interest allowed under section 502 of this title may accept or reject a plan. If the United States is a creditor or equity security holder, the Secretary of the Treasury may accept or reject the plan on behalf of the United States.

(b) For the purposes of subsections (c) and (d) of this section, a holder of a claim or interest that has accepted or rejected the plan before the commencement of the case under this title is deemed to have accepted or rejected such plan, as the case may be, if—

(1) the solicitation of such acceptance or rejection was in compliance with any applicable nonbankruptcy law, rule, or regulation governing the adequacy of disclosure in connection with such solicitation; or

(2) if there is not any such law, rule, or regulation, such acceptance or rejection was solicited after disclosure to such holder of adequate information, as defined in section 1125(a) of this title.

(c) A class of claims has accepted a plan if such plan has been accepted by creditors, other than any entity designated under subsection (e) of this section, that hold at least two-thirds in amount and more than one-half in number of the allowed claims of such class held by creditors, other than any entity designated under subsection (e) of this section, that have accepted or rejected such plan.

(d) A class of interests has accepted a plan if such plan has been accepted by holders of such interests, other than any entity designated under subsection (e) of this section, that hold at least two-thirds in amount of the allowed interests of such class held by holders of such interests, other than any entity designated under subsection (e) of this section, that have accepted or rejected such plan.

(e) On request of a party in interest, and after notice and a hearing, the court may designate any entity whose acceptance or rejection of such plan was not in good faith, or was not solicited or procured in good faith or in accordance with the provisions of this title.

(f) Notwithstanding any other provision of this section, a class that is not impaired under a plan, and each holder of a claim or interest of such class, are conclusively presumed to have accepted the plan, and solicitation of acceptances with respect to such class from the holders of claims or interests of such class is not required.

(g) Notwithstanding any other provision of this section, a class is deemed not to have accepted a plan if such plan provides that the claims or interests of such class do not entitle the holders of such claims or interests to receive or retain any property under the plan on account of such claims or interests.

(Pub. L. 95–598, Nov. 6, 1978, 92 Stat. 2634; Pub. L. 98–353, title III, § 510, July 10, 1984, 98 Stat. 386.)

HISTORICAL AND REVISION NOTES

LEGISLATIVE STATEMENTS

Section 1126 of the House amendment deletes section 1126(e) as contained in the House bill. Section 105 of the bill constitutes sufficient power in the court to designate exclusion of a creditor's claim on the basis of a conflict of interest. Section 1126(f) of the House amendment adopts a provision contained in section 1127(f) of the Senate bill indicating that a class that is not impaired under a plan is deemed to have accepted a plan and solicitation of acceptances from such class is not required.

SENATE REPORT NO. 95–989

Subsection (a) of this section permits the holder of a claim or interest allowed under section 502 to accept or reject a proposed plan of reorganization. The subsection also incorporates a provision now found in section 199 of chapter X [section 599 of former title 11] that authorizes the Secretary of the Treasury to accept or reject a plan on behalf of the United States when the United States is a creditor or equity security holder.

Subsection (b) governs acceptances and rejections of plans obtained before commencement of a reorganization for a nonpublic company. Paragraph (3) expressly states that subsection (b) does not apply to a public company.

Prepetition solicitation is a common practice under chapter XI [chapter 11 of former title 11] today, and chapter IX [chapter 9 of former title 11] current makes explicit provision for it. Section 1126(b) counts a prepetition acceptance or rejection toward the required amounts and number of acceptances only if the solicitation of the acceptance or rejection was in compliance with any applicable nonbankruptcy law, rule, or regulation governing the adequacy of disclosure in connection with such solicitation. If there is not any such applicable law, rule, or regulation, then the acceptance or rejection is counted only if it was solicited after disclosure of adequate information, to the holder, as defined in section 1125(a)(1). This permits the court to ensure that the requirements of section 1125 are not avoided by prepetition solicitation.

Subsection (c) specifies the required amount and number of acceptances for a class of creditors. A class of creditors has accepted a plan if at least two-thirds in amount and more than one-half in number of the allowed claims of the class that are voted are cast in favor of the plan. The amount and number are computed on the basis of claims actually voted for or against the plan, not as under chapter X [chapter 10 of former title 11] on the basis of the allowed claims in the class. Subsection (f) excludes from all these calculations claims not voted in good faith, and claims procured or solicited not in good faith or not in accordance with the provisions of this title.

Subsection (e) requires that the same disclosure statement be transmitted to each member of a class. It recognizes that the information needed for an informed judgment about the plan may differ among classes. A class whose rights under the plan center on a particular fund or asset would have no use for an extensive description of other matters that could not affect them.

Subsection (d) relieves the court of the need to follow any otherwise applicable Federal or state law in determining the adequacy of the information contained in the disclosure statement submitted for its approval. It authorizes an agency or official, Federal or state, charged with administering cognate laws so pre-empted to advise the court on the adequacy of proposed disclosure statement. But they are not authorized to appeal the court's decision.

Solicitations with respect to a plan do not involve just mere requests for opinions. Acceptance of the plan vitally affects creditors and shareholders, and most frequently the solicitation involves an offering of securities in exchange for claims or interests. The present Bankruptcy Act [former title 11] has exempted such offerings under each of its chapters from the registration and disclosure requirements of the Securities Act of 1933 [15 U.S.C. 77a et seq.], an exemption also continued by section 1145 of this title. The extension of the disclosure requirements to all chapter 11 cases is justified by the integration of the separate chapters into the single chapter 11. By the same token, no valid purpose is served by failing to provide exemption from the requirements of similar state laws in a matter under the exclusive jurisdiction of the Federal bankruptcy laws.

Under subsection (d), with respect to a class of equity securities, it is sufficient for acceptance of the plan if the amount of securities voting for the plan is at least two-thirds of the total actually voted.

Subsection (e) provides that no acceptances are required from any class whose claims or interests are unimpaired under the plan or in the order confirming the plan.

Subsection (g) provides that any class denied participation under the plan is conclusively deemed to have rejected the plan. There is obviously no need to submit a plan for a vote by a class that is to receive nothing. But under subsection (g) the excluded class is like a class that has not accepted, and is a dissenting class for purposes of confirmation under section 1130.

AMENDMENTS

1984—Subsec. (b)(2). Pub. L. 98–353, §510(a), substituted "1125(a)" for "1125(a)(1)".

Subsec. (d). Pub. L. 98–353, §510(b), inserted a comma after "such interests".

Subsec. (f). Pub. L. 98–353, §510(c), substituted ", and each holder of a claim or interest of such class, are conclusively presumed" for "is deemed", "solicitation" for "solicititation", and "interests" for "interest".

Subsec. (g). Pub. L. 98–353, §510(d), substituted "receive or retain any property" for "any payment or compensation".

EFFECTIVE DATE OF 1984 AMENDMENT

Amendment by Pub. L. 98–353 effective with respect to cases filed 90 days after July 10, 1984, see section 552(a) of Pub. L. 98–353, set out as a note under section 101 of this title.

§ 1127. Modification of plan

(a) The proponent of a plan may modify such plan at any time before confirmation, but may not modify such plan so that such plan as modified fails to meet the requirements of sections 1122 and 1123 of this title. After the proponent of a plan files a modification of such plan with the court, the plan as modified becomes the plan.

(b) The proponent of a plan or the reorganized debtor may modify such plan at any time after confirmation of such plan and before substantial consummation of such plan, but may not modify such plan so that such plan as modified fails to meet the requirements of sections 1122 and 1123 of this title. Such plan as modified under this subsection becomes the plan only if circumstances warrant such modification and the court, after notice and a hearing, confirms such plan as modified, under section 1129 of this title.

(c) The proponent of a modification shall comply with section 1125 of this title with respect to the plan as modified.

(d) Any holder of a claim or interest that has accepted or rejected a plan is deemed to have accepted or rejected, as the case may be, such plan as modified, unless, within the time fixed by the court, such holder changes such holder's previous acceptance or rejection.

(e) If the debtor is an individual, the plan may be modified at any time after confirmation of the plan but before the completion of payments under the plan, whether or not the plan has been substantially consummated, upon request of the debtor, the trustee, the United States trustee, or the holder of an allowed unsecured claim, to—

(1) increase or reduce the amount of payments on claims of a particular class provided for by the plan;

(2) extend or reduce the time period for such payments; or

(3) alter the amount of the distribution to a creditor whose claim is provided for by the plan to the extent necessary to take account of any payment of such claim made other than under the plan.

(f)(1) Sections 1121 through 1128 and the requirements of section 1129 apply to any modification under subsection (a).

(2) The plan, as modified, shall become the plan only after there has been disclosure under section 1125 as the court may direct, notice and a hearing, and such modification is approved.

(Pub. L. 95–598, Nov. 6, 1978, 92 Stat. 2635; Pub. L. 98–353, title III, §511, July 10, 1984, 98 Stat. 386; Pub. L. 109–8, title III, §321(e), Apr. 20, 2005, 119 Stat. 96.)

HISTORICAL AND REVISION NOTES

LEGISLATIVE STATEMENTS

Section 1127(a) of the House amendment adopts a provision contained in the House bill permitting only the proponent of a plan to modify the plan and rejecting the alternative of open modification contained in the Senate amendment.

SENATE REPORT NO. 95–989

Under subsection (a) the proponent may file a proposal to modify a plan prior to confirmation. In the case of a public company the modifying proposal may be filed prior to approval.

Subsection (b) provides that a party in interest eligible to file a plan may file instead of a plan a proposal to modify a plan filed by another. Under subsection (c) a party in interest objecting to some feature of a plan may submit a proposal to modify the plan to meet the objection.

After a plan has been confirmed, but before its substantial consummation, a plan may be modified by leave of court, which subsection (d) provides shall be granted for good cause. Subsection (e) provides that a proposal to modify a plan is subject to the disclosure requirements of section 1125 and as provided in subsection (f). It provides that a creditor or stockholder who voted for or against a plan is deemed to have accepted or rejected the modifying proposal. But if the modification materially and adversely affects any of their interests, they must be afforded an opportunity to change their vote in accordance with the disclosure and solicitation requirements of section 1125.

Under subsection (g) a plan, if modified prior to confirmation, shall be confirmed if it meets the requirements of section 1130.

HOUSE REPORT NO. 95–595

Subsection (a) permits the proponent of a plan to modify it at any time before confirmation, subject, of course, to the requirements of sections 1122 and 1123, governing classification and contents of a plan. After the proponent of a plan files a modification with the court, the plan as modified becomes the plan, and is to be treated the same as an original plan.

Subsection (b) permits modification of a plan after confirmation under certain circumstances. The modification must be proposed before substantial consummation of the plan. The requirements of sections 1122 and 1123 continue to apply. The plan as modified under this subsection becomes the plan only if the court confirms the plan as modified under section 1129 and the circumstances warrant the modification.

Subsection (c) requires the proponent of a modification to comply with the disclosure provisions of section 1125. Of course, if the modification were sufficiently minor, the court might determine that additional disclosure was not required under the circumstances.

Subsection (d) simplifies modification procedure by deeming any creditor or equity security holder that has already accepted or rejected the plan to have accepted or rejected the modification, unless, within the time fixed by the court, the creditor or equity security holder changes this previous acceptance or rejection.

AMENDMENTS

2005—Subsecs. (e), (f). Pub. L. 109–8 added subsecs. (e) and (f).

1984—Subsec. (a). Pub. L. 98–353, §511(a), inserted "of a plan" after "After the proponent", and "of such plan" after "modification".

Subsec. (b). Pub. L. 98–353, §511(b), substituted "circumstances warrant such modification and the court, after notice and a hearing, confirms such plan as modified, under section 1129 of this title" for "the court, after notice and a hearing, confirms such plan, as modified, under section 1129 of this title, and circumstances warrant such modification".

EFFECTIVE DATE OF 2005 AMENDMENT

Amendment by Pub. L. 109–8 effective 180 days after Apr. 20, 2005, and not applicable with respect to cases commenced under this title before such effective date, except as otherwise provided, see section 1501 of Pub. L. 109–8, set out as a note under section 101 of this title.

EFFECTIVE DATE OF 1984 AMENDMENT

Amendment by Pub. L. 98–353 effective with respect to cases filed 90 days after July 10, 1984, see section 552(a) of Pub. L. 98–353, set out as a note under section 101 of this title.

§1128. Confirmation hearing

(a) After notice, the court shall hold a hearing on confirmation of a plan.

(b) A party in interest may object to confirmation of a plan.

(Pub. L. 95–598, Nov. 6, 1978, 92 Stat. 2635.)

HISTORICAL AND REVISION NOTES

SENATE REPORT NO. 95–989

[Section 1129 (enacted as section 1128)] Subsection (a) requires that there be a hearing in every case on the confirmation of the plan. Notice is required.

Subsection (b) permits any party in interest to object to the confirmation of the plan. The Securities and Exchange Commission and indenture trustees, as parties in interest under section 1109, may object to confirmation of the plan.

§1129. Confirmation of plan

(a) The court shall confirm a plan only if all of the following requirements are met:

(1) The plan complies with the applicable provisions of this title.

(2) The proponent of the plan complies with the applicable provisions of this title.

(3) The plan has been proposed in good faith and not by any means forbidden by law.

(4) Any payment made or to be made by the proponent, by the debtor, or by a person issuing securities or acquiring property under the plan, for services or for costs and expenses in or in connection with the case, or in connection with the plan and incident to the case, has been approved by, or is subject to the approval of, the court as reasonable.

(5)(A)(i) The proponent of the plan has disclosed the identity and affiliations of any individual proposed to serve, after confirmation of the plan, as a director, officer, or voting trustee of the debtor, an affiliate of the debtor participating in a joint plan with the debtor, or a successor to the debtor under the plan; and

(ii) the appointment to, or continuance in, such office of such individual, is consistent with the interests of creditors and equity security holders and with public policy; and

(B) the proponent of the plan has disclosed the identity of any insider that will be employed or retained by the reorganized debtor, and the nature of any compensation for such insider.

(6) Any governmental regulatory commission with jurisdiction, after confirmation of the plan, over the rates of the debtor has approved any rate change provided for in the plan, or such rate change is expressly conditioned on such approval.

(7) With respect to each impaired class of claims or interests—

(A) each holder of a claim or interest of such class—

(i) has accepted the plan; or

(ii) will receive or retain under the plan on account of such claim or interest property of a value, as of the effective date of the plan, that is not less than the amount that such holder would so receive or retain if the debtor were liquidated under chapter 7 of this title on such date; or

(B) if section 1111(b)(2) of this title applies to the claims of such class, each holder of a claim of such class will receive or retain under the plan on account of such claim property of a value, as of the effective date of the plan, that is not less than the value of such holder's interest in the estate's interest in the property that secures such claims.

(8) With respect to each class of claims or interests—

(A) such class has accepted the plan; or

(B) such class is not impaired under the plan.

(9) Except to the extent that the holder of a particular claim has agreed to a different treatment of such claim, the plan provides that—

(A) with respect to a claim of a kind specified in section 507(a)(2) or 507(a)(3) of this title, on the effective date of the plan, the holder of such claim will receive on account of such claim cash equal to the allowed amount of such claim;

(B) with respect to a class of claims of a kind specified in section 507(a)(1), 507(a)(4), 507(a)(5), 507(a)(6), or 507(a)(7) of this title, each holder of a claim of such class will receive—

(i) if such class has accepted the plan, deferred cash payments of a value, as of the effective date of the plan, equal to the allowed amount of such claim; or

(ii) if such class has not accepted the plan, cash on the effective date of the plan equal to the allowed amount of such claim;

(C) with respect to a claim of a kind specified in section 507(a)(8) of this title, the holder of such claim will receive on account of such claim regular installment payments in cash—

(i) of a total value, as of the effective date of the plan, equal to the allowed amount of such claim;

(ii) over a period ending not later than 5 years after the date of the order for relief under section 301, 302, or 303; and

(iii) in a manner not less favorable than the most favored nonpriority unsecured claim provided for by the plan (other than cash payments made to a class of creditors under section 1122(b)); and

(D) with respect to a secured claim which would otherwise meet the description of an unsecured claim of a governmental unit under section 507(a)(8), but for the secured status of that claim, the holder of that claim will receive on account of that claim, cash payments, in the same manner and over the same period, as prescribed in subparagraph (C).

(10) If a class of claims is impaired under the plan, at least one class of claims that is impaired under the plan has accepted the plan, determined without including any acceptance of the plan by any insider.

(11) Confirmation of the plan is not likely to be followed by the liquidation, or the need for further financial reorganization, of the debtor or any successor to the debtor under the plan, unless such liquidation or reorganization is proposed in the plan.

(12) All fees payable under section 1930 of title 28, as determined by the court at the hearing on confirmation of the plan, have been paid or the plan provides for the payment of all such fees on the effective date of the plan.

(13) The plan provides for the continuation after its effective date of payment of all retiree benefits, as that term is defined in section 1114 of this title, at the level established pursuant to subsection (e)(1)(B) or (g) of section 1114 of this title, at any time prior to confirmation of the plan, for the duration of the period the debtor has obligated itself to provide such benefits.

(14) If the debtor is required by a judicial or administrative order, or by statute, to pay a domestic support obligation, the debtor has paid all amounts payable under such order or such statute for such obligation that first become payable after the date of the filing of the petition.

(15) In a case in which the debtor is an individual and in which the holder of an allowed unsecured claim objects to the confirmation of the plan—

(A) the value, as of the effective date of the plan, of the property to be distributed under the plan on account of such claim is not less than the amount of such claim; or

(B) the value of the property to be distributed under the plan is not less than the projected disposable income of the debtor (as defined in section 1325(b)(2)) to be received during the 5-year period beginning on the date that the first payment is due under the plan, or during the period for which the plan provides payments, whichever is longer.

(16) All transfers of property of the plan shall be made in accordance with any applicable provisions of nonbankruptcy law that govern the transfer of property by a corporation or trust that is not a moneyed, business, or commercial corporation or trust.

(b)(1) Notwithstanding section 510(a) of this title, if all of the applicable requirements of subsection (a) of this section other than paragraph (8) are met with respect to a plan, the court, on request of the proponent of the plan, shall confirm the plan notwithstanding the requirements of such paragraph if the plan does not discriminate unfairly, and is fair and equitable, with respect to each class of claims or interests that is impaired under, and has not accepted, the plan.

(2) For the purpose of this subsection, the condition that a plan be fair and equitable with respect to a class includes the following requirements:

(A) With respect to a class of secured claims, the plan provides—

(i)(I) that the holders of such claims retain the liens securing such claims, whether the property subject to such liens is retained by the debtor or transferred to another entity, to the extent of the allowed amount of such claims; and

(II) that each holder of a claim of such class receive on account of such claim deferred cash payments totaling at least the allowed amount of such claim, of a value, as of the effective date of the plan, of at least the value of such holder's interest in the estate's interest in such property;

(ii) for the sale, subject to section 363(k) of this title, of any property that is subject to the liens securing such claims, free and clear of such liens, with such liens to attach to the proceeds of such sale, and the treatment of such liens on proceeds under clause (i) or (iii) of this subparagraph; or

(iii) for the realization by such holders of the indubitable equivalent of such claims.

(B) With respect to a class of unsecured claims—

(i) the plan provides that each holder of a claim of such class receive or retain on account of such claim property of a value, as of the effective date of the plan, equal to the allowed amount of such claim; or

(ii) the holder of any claim or interest that is junior to the claims of such class will not receive or retain under the plan on account of such junior claim or interest any property, except that in a case in which the debtor is an individual, the debtor may retain property included in the estate under section 1115, subject to the requirements of subsection (a)(14) of this section.

(C) With respect to a class of interests—

(i) the plan provides that each holder of an interest of such class receive or retain on account of such interest property of a value, as of the effective date of the plan, equal to the greatest of the allowed amount of any fixed liquidation preference to which such holder is entitled, any fixed redemption price to which such holder is entitled, or the value of such interest; or

(ii) the holder of any interest that is junior to the interests of such class will not receive or retain under the plan on account of such junior interest any property.

(c) Notwithstanding subsections (a) and (b) of this section and except as provided in section 1127(b) of this title, the court may confirm only one plan, unless the order of confirmation in the case has been revoked under section 1144 of this title. If the requirements of subsections (a) and (b) of this section are met with respect to more than one plan, the court shall consider the preferences of creditors and equity security holders in determining which plan to confirm.

(d) Notwithstanding any other provision of this section, on request of a party in interest that is a governmental unit, the court may not confirm a plan if the principal purpose of the plan is the avoidance of taxes or the avoidance of the application of section 5 of the Securities Act of 1933. In any hearing under this subsection, the governmental unit has the burden of proof on the issue of avoidance.

(e) In a small business case, the court shall confirm a plan that complies with the applicable provisions of this title and that is filed in accordance with section 1121(e) not later than 45 days after the plan is filed unless the time for confirmation is extended in accordance with section 1121(e)(3).

(Pub. L. 95–598, Nov. 6, 1978, 92 Stat. 2635; Pub. L. 98–353, title III, §512, July 10, 1984, 98 Stat. 386; Pub. L. 99–554, title II, §§225, 283(v), Oct. 27, 1986, 100 Stat. 3102, 3118; Pub. L. 100–334, §2(b), June 16, 1988, 102 Stat. 613; Pub. L. 103–394, title III, §304(h)(7), title V, §501(d)(32), Oct. 22, 1994, 108 Stat. 4134, 4146; Pub. L. 109–8, title II, §213(1), title III, §321(c), title IV, §438, title VII, §710, title XII, §1221(b), title XV, §1502(a)(8), Apr. 20, 2005, 119 Stat. 52, 95, 113, 127, 196, 216.)

HISTORICAL AND REVISION NOTES

LEGISLATIVE STATEMENTS

Section 1129 of the House amendment relates to confirmation of a plan in a case under chapter 11. Section 1129(a)(3) of the House amendment adopts the position taken in the Senate amendment and section 1129(a)(5) takes the position adopted in the House bill. Section 1129(a)(7) adopts the position taken in the House bill in order to insure that the dissenting members of an accepting class will receive at least what they would otherwise receive under the best interest of creditors test; it also requires that even the members of a class that has rejected the plan be protected by the best interest of creditors test for those rare cramdown cases where a class of creditors would receive more on liquidation than under reorganization of the debtor. Section 1129(a)(7)(C) is discussed in connection with section 1129(b) and section 1111(b). Section 1129(a)(8) of the House amendment adopts the provision taken in the House bill which permits confirmation of a plan as to a particular class without resort to the fair and equitable test if the class has accepted a plan or is unimpaired under the plan.

Section 1129(a)(9) represents a compromise between a similar provision contained in the House bill and the Senate amendment. Under subparagraph (A) claims entitled to priority under section 507(a)(1) or (2) are entitled to receive cash on the effective date of the plan equal to the amount of the claim. Under subparagraph (B) claims entitled to priority under section 507(a)(3), (4), or (5), are entitled to receive deferred cash payments of a present value as of the effective date of the plan equal to the amount of the claims if the class has accepted the plan or cash payments on the effective date of the plan otherwise. Tax claims entitled to priority under section 507(a)(6) of different governmental units may not be contained in one class although all claims of one such unit may be combined and such unit may be required to take deferred cash payments over a period not to exceed 6 years after the date of assessment of the tax with the present value equal to the amount of the claim.

Section 1129(a)(10) is derived from section 1130(a)(12) of the Senate amendment.

Section 1129(b) is new. Together with section 1111(b) and section 1129(a)(7)(C), this section provides when a plan may be confirmed, notwithstanding the failure of an impaired class to accept the plan under section 1129(a)(8). Before discussing section 1129(b) an understanding of section 1111(b) is necessary. Section 1111(b)(1), the general rule that a secured claim is to be treated as a recourse claim in chapter 11 whether or not the claim is nonrecourse by agreement or applicable law. This preferred status for a nonrecourse loan terminates if the property securing the loan is sold under section 363 or is to be sold under the plan.

The preferred status also terminates if the class of which the secured claim is a part elects application of section 1111(b)(2). Section 1111(b)(2) provides that an allowed claim is a secured claim to the full extent the claim is allowed rather than to the extent of the collateral as under section 506(a). A class may elect application of paragraph (2) only if the security is not of inconsequential value and, if the creditor is a recourse creditor, the collateral is not sold under section 363 or to be sold under the plan. Sale of property under section 363 or under the plan is excluded from treatment under section 1111(b) because of the secured party's right to bid in the full amount of his allowed claim at any sale of collateral under section 363(k) of the House amendment.

As previously noted, section 1129(b) sets forth a standard by which a plan may be confirmed notwithstanding the failure of an impaired class to accept the plan.

Paragraph (1) makes clear that this alternative confirmation standard, referred to as "cram down," will be called into play only on the request of the proponent of the plan. Under this cramdown test, the court must confirm the plan if the plan does not discriminate unfairly, and is "fair and equitable," with respect to each class of claims or interests that is impaired under, and has not accepted, the plan. The requirement of the House bill that a plan not "discriminate unfairly" with respect to a class is included for clarity; the language in the House report interpreting that requirement, in the context of subordinated debentures, applies equally under the requirements of section 1129(b)(1) of the House amendment.

Although many of the factors interpreting "fair and equitable" are specified in paragraph (2), others, which were explicated in the description of section 1129(b) in the House report, were omitted from the House amendment to avoid statutory complexity and because they would undoubtedly be found by a court to be fundamental to "fair and equitable" treatment of a dissenting class. For example, a dissenting class should be assured that no senior class receives more than 100 percent of the amount of its claims. While that requirement was explicitly included in the House bill, the deletion is intended to be one of style and not one of substance.

Paragraph (2) provides guidelines for a court to determine whether a plan is fair and equitable with respect to a dissenting class. It must be emphasized that the fair and equitable requirement applies only with respect to dissenting classes. Therefore, unlike the fair and equitable rule contained in chapter X [chapter 10 of former title 11] and section 77 of the Bankruptcy Act [section 205 of former title 11] under section 1129(b)(2), senior accepting classes are permitted to give up value to junior classes as long as no dissenting intervening class receives less than the amount of its claims in full. If there is no dissenting intervening class and the only dissent is from a class junior to the class to which value have been given up, then the plan may still be fair and equitable with respect to the dissenting class, as long as no class senior to the dissenting class has received more than 100 percent of the amount of its claims.

Paragraph (2) contains three subparagraphs, each of which applies to a particular kind of class of claims or interests that is impaired and has not accepted the plan. Subparagraph (A) applies when a class of secured claims is impaired and has not accepted the plan. The provision applies whether or not section 1111(b) applies. The plan may be crammed down notwithstanding the dissent of a secured class only if the plan complies with clause (i), (ii), or (iii).

Clause (i) permits cramdown if the dissenting class of secured claims will retain its lien on the property whether the property is retained by the debtor or transferred. It should be noted that the lien secures the allowed secured claim held by such holder. The meaning of "allowed secured claim" will vary depending on whether section 1111(b)(2) applies to such class.

If section 1111(b)(2) applies then the "electing" class is entitled to have the entire allowed amount of the debt related to such property secured by a lien even if the value of the collateral is less than the amount of the debt. In addition, the plan must provide for the holder to receive, on account of the allowed secured claims, payments, either present or deferred, of a principal face amount equal to the amount of the debt and of a present value equal to the value of the collateral.

For example, if a creditor loaned $15,000,000 to a debtor secured by real property worth $18,000,000 and the value of the real property had dropped to $12,000,000 by the date when the debtor commenced a proceeding under chapter 11, the plan could be confirmed notwithstanding the dissent of the creditor as long as the lien remains on the collateral to secure a $15,000,000 debt, the face amount of present or extended payments to be made to the creditor under the plan is at least $15,000,000, and the present value of the present or deferred payments is not less than $12,000,000. The House report accompanying the House bill described what is meant by "present value".

Clause (ii) is self explanatory. Clause (iii) requires the court to confirm the plan notwithstanding the dissent of the electing secured class if the plan provides for the realization by the secured class of the indubitable equivalents of the secured claims. The standard of "indubitable equivalents" is taken from *In re Murel Holding Corp.*, 75 F.2d 941 (2d Cir. 1935) (Learned Hand, Jr.).

Abandonment of the collateral to the creditor would clearly satisfy indubitable equivalence, as would a lien on similar collateral. However, present cash payments less than the secured claim would not satisfy the standard because the creditor is deprived of an opportunity to gain from a future increase in value of the collateral. Unsecured notes as to the secured claim or equity securities of the debtor would not be the indubitable equivalent. With respect to an oversecured creditor, the secured claim will never exceed the allowed claim.

Although the same language applies, a different result pertains with respect to a class of secured claims to which section 1111(b)(2) does not apply. This will apply to all claims secured by a right of setoff. The court must confirm the plan notwithstanding the dissent of such a class of secured claims if any of three alternative requirements is met. Under clause (i) the plan may be confirmed if the class retains a right of setoff or a lien securing the allowed secured claims of the class and the holders will receive payments of a present value equal to the allowed amount of their secured claims. Contrary to electing classes of secured creditors who retain a lien under subparagraph (A)(i)(I) to the extent of the entire claims secured by such lien, nonelecting creditors retain a lien on collateral only to the extent of their allowed secured claims and not to the extent of any deficiency, and such secured creditors must receive present or deferred payments with a present value equal to the allowed secured claim, which in turn is only the equivalent of the value of the collateral under section 506(a).

Any deficiency claim of a nonelecting class of secured claims is treated as an unsecured claim and is not provided for under subparagraph (A). The plan may be confirmed under clause (ii) if the plan proposes to sell the property free and clear of the secured party's lien as long as the lien will attach to the proceeds and will receive treatment under clause (i) or (iii). Clause (iii) permits confirmation if the plan provides for the realization by the dissenting nonelecting class of secured claims of the indubitable equivalent of the secured claims of such class.

Contrary to an "electing" class to which section 1111(b)(2) applies, the nonelecting class need not be protected with respect to any future appreciation in value of the collateral since the secured claim of such a class is never undersecured by reason of section 506(a). Thus the lien secures only the value of interest of such creditor in the collateral. To the extent deferred payments exceed that amount, they represent interest. In the event of a subsequent default, the portion of the face amount of deferred payments representing unaccrued interest will not be secured by the lien.

Subparagraph (B) applies to a dissenting class of unsecured claims. The court must confirm the plan notwithstanding the dissent of a class of impaired unsecured claims if the plan provides for such claims to receive property with a present value equal to the allowed amount of the claims. Unsecured claims may receive any kind of "property," which is used in its broadest sense, as long as the present value of the property given to the holders of unsecured claims is equal to the allowed amount of the claims. Some kinds of property, such as securities, may require difficult valuations by the court; in such circumstances the court need only determine that there is a reasonable likelihood that the property given the dissenting class of impaired unsecured claims equals the present value of such allowed claims.

Alternatively, under clause (ii), the court must confirm the plan if the plan provides that holders of any claims or interests junior to the interests of the dissenting class of impaired unsecured claims will not receive any property under the plan on account of such junior claims or interests. As long as senior creditors have not been paid more than in full, and classes of equal claims are being treated so that the dissenting class of impaired unsecured claims is not being discriminated against unfairly, the plan may be confirmed if the impaired class of unsecured claims receives less than 100 cents on the dollar (or nothing at all) as long as no class junior to the dissenting class receives anything at all. Such an impaired dissenting class may not prevent confirmation of a plan by objection merely because a senior class has elected to give up value to a junior class that is higher in priority than the impaired dissenting class of unsecured claims as long as the above safeguards are met.

Subparagraph (C) applies to a dissenting class of impaired interests. Such interests may include the interests of general or limited partners in a partnership, the interests of a sole proprietor in a proprietorship, or the interest of common or preferred stockholders in a corporation. If the holders of such interests are entitled to a fixed liquidation preference or fixed redemption price on account of such interests then the plan may be confirmed notwithstanding the dissent of such class of interests as long as it provides the holders property of a present value equal to the greatest of the fixed redemption price, or the value of such interests. In the event there is no fixed liquidation preference or redemption price, then the plan may be confirmed as long as it provides the holders of such interests property of a present value equal to the value of such interests. If the interests are "under water" then they will be valueless and the plan may be confirmed notwithstanding the dissent of that class of interests even if the plan provides that the holders of such interests will not receive any property on account of such interests.

Alternatively, under clause (ii), the court must confirm the plan notwithstanding the dissent of a class of interests if the plan provides that holders of any interests junior to the dissenting class of interests will not receive or retain any property on account of such junior interests. Clearly, if there are no junior interests junior to the class of dissenting interests, then the condition of clause (ii) is satisfied. The safeguards that no claim or interest receive more than 100 percent of the allowed amount of such claim or interest and that no class be discriminated against unfairly will insure that the plan is fair and equitable with respect to the dissenting class of interests.

Except to the extent of the treatment of secured claims under subparagraph (A) of this statement, the House report remains an accurate description of confirmation of section 1129(b). Contrary to the example contained in the Senate report, a senior class will not be able to give up value to a junior class over the dissent of an intervening class unless the intervening class receives the full amount, as opposed to value, of its claims or interests.

One last point deserves explanation with respect to the admittedly complex subject of confirmation. Section 1129(a)(7)(C) in effect exempts secured creditors making an election under section 1111(b)(2) from application of the best interest of creditors test. In the absence of an election the amount such creditors receive in a plan of liquidation would be the value of their collateral plus any amount recovered on the deficiency in the case of a recourse loan. However, under section 1111(b)(2), the creditors are given an allowed secured claim to the full extent the claim is allowed and have no unsecured deficiency. Since section 1129(b)(2)(A) makes clear that an electing class need receive payments of a present value only equal to the value of the collateral, it is conceivable that under such a "cram down" the electing creditors would receive nothing with respect to their deficiency. The advantage to the electing creditors is that they have a lien securing the full amount of the allowed claim so that if the value of the collateral increases after the case is closed, the deferred payments will be secured claims. Thus it is both reasonable and necessary to exempt such electing class from application of section 1129(a)(7) as a logical consequence of permitting election under section 1111(b)(2).

Section 1131 of the Senate amendment is deleted as unnecessary in light of the protection given a secured creditor under section 1129(b) of the House amendment.

Payment of taxes in reorganizations: Under the provisions of section 1141 as revised by the House amendment, an individual in reorganization under chapter 11 will not be discharged from any debt, including prepetition tax liabilities, which are nondischargeable under section 523. Thus, an individual debtor whose plan of reorganization is confirmed under chapter 11 will remain liable for prepetition priority taxes, as defined in section 507, and for tax liabilities which receive no priority but are nondischargeable under section 523, including no return, late return, and fraud liabilities.

In the case of a partnership or a corporation in reorganization under chapter 11 of title 11, section 1141(d)(1) of the House amendment adopts a provision limiting the taxes that must be provided for in a plan before a plan can be confirmed to taxes which receive priority under section 507. In addition, the House amendment makes dischargeable, in effect, tax liabilities attributable to no return, late return, or fraud situations. The amendment thus does not adopt a shareholder continuity test such as was contained in section 1141(d)(2)(A)(iii) of the Senate amendment. However, the House amendment amends section 1106, relating to duties of the trustee, to require the trustee to furnish, on request of a tax authority and without personal liability, information available to the trustee concerning potential prepetition tax liabilities for unfiled returns of the debtor. Depending on the condition of the debtor's books and records, this information may include schedules and files available to the business. The House amendment also does not prohibit a tax authority from disallowing any tax benefit claimed after the reorganization if the item originated in a deduction, credit, or other item improperly reported before the reorganization occurred. It may also be appropriate for the Congress to consider in the future imposing civil or criminal liability on corporate officers for preparing a false or fraudulent tax return. The House amendment also contemplates that the Internal Revenue Service will monitor the relief from liabilities under this provision and advise the Congress if, and to the extent, any significant tax abuse may be resulting from the provision.

Medium of payment of taxes: Federal, State, and local taxes incurred during the administration period of the estate, and during the "gap" period in an involuntary case, are to be paid solely in cash. Taxes relating to third priority wages are to be paid, under the general rules, in cash on the effective date of the plan, if the class has not accepted the plan, in an amount equal to the allowed amount of the claim. If the class has accepted the plan, the taxes must be paid in cash but the payments must be made at the time the wages are paid which may be paid in deferred periodic installments having a value, on the effective date of the plan, equal to the allowed amount of the tax claims. Prepetition taxes entitled to sixth priority under section 507(a)(6) also must be paid in cash, but the plan may also permit the debtor whether a corporation, partnership, or an individual, to pay the allowed taxes in installments over a period not to exceed 6 years following the date on which the tax authority assesses the tax liability, provided the value of the deferred payments representing principal and interest, as of the effective date of the plan, equals the allowed amount of the tax claim.

The House amendment also modifies the provisions of both bills dealing with the time when tax liabilities of a debtor in reorganization may be assessed by the tax authority. The House amendment follows the Senate amendment in deleting the limitation in present law under which a priority tax assessed after a reorganization plan is confirmed must be assessed within 1 year after the date of the filing of the petition. The House amendment specifies broadly that after the bankruptcy court determines the liability of the estate for a prepetition tax or for an administration period tax, the governmental unit may thereafter assess the tax against the estate, debtor, or successor to the debtor. The party to be assessed will, of course, depend on whether the case is under chapter 7, 11, or 13, whether the debtor is an individual, partnership, or a corporation, and whether the court is determining an individual debtor's personal liability for a nondischargeable tax. Assessment of the tax may only be made, however, within the limits of otherwise applicable law, such as the statute of limitations under the tax law.

Tax avoidance purpose: The House bill provided that no reorganization plan may be approved if the principal purpose of the plan is the avoidance of taxes. The Senate amendment modified the rule so that the bankruptcy court need make a determination of tax avoidance purpose only if it is asked to do so by the appropriate tax authority. Under the Senate amendment, if the tax authority does not request the bankruptcy court to rule on the purpose of the plan, the tax authority would not be barred from later asserting a tax avoidance motive with respect to allowance of a deduction or other tax benefit claimed after the reorganization. The House amendment adopts the substance of the Senate amendment, but does not provide a basis by which a tax authority may collaterally attack confirmation of a plan of reorganization other than under section 1144.

SENATE REPORT NO. 95–989

[Section 1130 (enacted as section 1129)] Subsection (a) enumerates the requirement governing confirmation of a plan. The court is required to confirm a plan if and only if all of the requirements are met.

Paragraph (1) requires that the plan comply with the applicable provisions of chapter 11, such as sections 1122 and 1123, governing classification and contents of plan.

Paragraph (2) requires that the proponent of the plan comply with the applicable provisions of chapter 11, such as section 1125 regarding disclosure.

Paragraph (3) requires that the plan have been proposed in good faith, and not by any means forbidden by law.

Paragraph (4) is derived from section 221 of chapter X [section 621 of former title 11]. It requires that any payment made or promised by the proponent, the debtor, or person issuing securities or acquiring property under the plan, for services or for costs and expenses in, or in connection with the case, or in connection with the plan and incident to the case, be disclosed to the court. In addition, any payment made before confirmation must have been reasonable, and any payment to be fixed after confirmation must be subject to the approval of the court as reasonable.

Paragraph (5) is also derived from section 221 of chapter X [section 621 of former title 11]. It requires the plan to disclose the identity and affiliations of any individual proposed to serve, after confirmation, as a director, officer, or voting trustee of the reorganized debtor. The appointment to or continuance in one of these offices by the individual must be consistent with the interests of creditors and equity security holders and with public policy. The plan must also disclose the identity of any insider that will be employed or retained by the reorganized debtor, and the nature of any compensation to be paid to the insider.

Paragraph (6) permits confirmation only if any regulatory commission that will have jurisdiction over the debtor after confirmation of the plan has approved any rate change provided for in the plan. As an alternative, the rate change may be conditioned on such approval.

Paragraph (7) provides that in the case of a public company the court shall confirm the plan if it finds the plan to be fair and equitable and the plan either (1) has been accepted by classes of claims or interests as provided in section 1126, or (2), if not so accepted, satisfies the requirements of subsection (b) of this section.

Paragraphs (8) and (9) apply only in nonpublic cases. Paragraph (8) does not apply the fair and equitable standards in two situations. The first occurs if there is unanimous consent of all affected holders of claims and interests. It is also sufficient for purposes of confirmation if each holder of a claim or interest receives or retains consideration of a value, as of the effective date of the plan, that is not less than each would have or receive if the debtor were liquidated under chapter 7 of this title. This standard adapts the test of "best interest of creditors" as interpreted by the courts under chapter XI [chapter 11 of former title 11]. It is given broader application in chapter 11 of this title since a plan under chapter 11 may affect not only unsecured claims but secured claims and stock as well.

Under paragraph (9)(A), if a class of claims or interests has not accepted the plan, the court will confirm the plan if, for the dissenting class and any class of equal rank, the negotiated plan provides in value no less than under a plan that is fair and equitable. Such review and determination are not required for any other classes that accepted the plan.

Paragraph (9)(A) would permit a senior creditor to adjust his participation for the benefit of stockholders. In such a case, junior creditors, who have not been satisfied in full, may not object if, absent the "give-up", they are receiving all that a fair and equitable plan would give them. To illustrate, suppose the estate is valued at $1.5 million and claims and stock are:

	Claims and stock (millions)	*Equity (millions)*
(1) Senior debt	$1.2	$1.2
(2) Junior debt	.5	.3
(3) Stock	([1])	--
Total	1.7	1.5

[1] No value.

Under the plan, the senior creditor gives up $100,000 in value for the benefit of stockholders as follows:

	Millions
(1) Senior debt	$1.1
(2) Junior debt	.3
(3) Stock	.1
Total	1.5

If the junior creditors dissent, the court may nevertheless confirm the plan since under the fair and equitable standard they had an equity of only $300,000 and the allocation to equity security holders did not affect them.

Paragraph (9)(A) provides a special alternative with respect to secured claims. A plan may be confirmed against a dissenting class of secured claims if the plan or order of confirmation provides for the realization of their security (1) by the retention of the property subject to such security; (2) by a sale of the property and transfer of the claim to the proceeds of sale if the secured creditors were permitted to bid at the sale and set off against the purchase price up to the allowed amount of their claims; or (3) by such other method that will assure them the realization of the indubitable equivalent of the allowed amount of their secured claims. The indubitable equivalent language is intended to follow the strict approach taken by Judge Learned Hand in *In Re Murel Holding Corp.* 75. F.2d 941 (2nd Cir. 1935).

Paragraph (9)(B) provides that, if a class of claims or interests is excluded from participation under the plan, the court may nevertheless confirm the plan if it determines that no class on a parity with or junior to such participates under the plan. In the previous illustration, no confirmation would be permitted if the negotiated plan would grant a participation to stockholders but nothing for junior creditors. As noted elsewhere, by reason of section 1126(g), an excluded class is a dissenting class under section 1130.

Paragraph (10) states that, to be confirmed, the plan must provide that each holder of a claim under section 507 will receive property, as therein noted, of a value equal to the allowed amount of the claim. There are two exceptions: (A) The holder thereof may agree to a different settlement in part or in whole; (B) where a debtor's business is reorganized under chapter 11, this provision requires that taxes entitled to priority (including administrative claims or taxes) must be paid in cash not later than 120 days after the plan is confirmed, unless the Secretary of the Treasury agrees to other terms or kinds of payment. The bill, as introduced, required full payment in cash within 60 days after the plan is confirmed.

Paragraph (11) requires a determination regarding feasibility of the plan. It is a slight elaboration of the law that has developed in the application of the word "feasible" in Chapter X of the present Act [chapter 10 of former title 11].

Paragraph (12) requires that at least one class must accept the plan, but any claims or interests held by insiders are not to be included for purposes of determining the number and amount of acceptances.

Subsection (b) provides that if, in the case of a public company, the plan meets the requirements of subsection (a) (except paragraphs (8) and (9) which do not apply to such a company), the court is to confirm the plan if the plan or the order of confirmation provides adequate protection for the realization of the value of the claims or interests of each class not accepting the plan. The intent is to incorporate inclusively, as a guide to the meaning of subsection (a) the provisions of section 216(7) ([former] 11 U.S.C. 616(7)) with respect to claims and section 216(8) ([former] 11 U.S.C. 616(8)) with respect to equity security interests.

Under subsection (c) the court may confirm only one plan, unless the order of confirmation has been revoked under section 1144. If the requirements for confirmation are met with respect to more than one plan, the court shall consider the preferences of creditors and stockholders in deciding which plan to confirm.

Subsection (d) provides that the bankruptcy court may not confirm a plan of reorganization if its principal purpose is the avoidance of taxes or the avoidance of section 5 of the Securities Act of 1933 (15 U.S.C. 77e). This rules modifies a similar provision of present law (section 269 of the Bankruptcy Act [section 669 of former title 11]).

HOUSE REPORT NO. 95–595

Paragraph (7) [of subsec. (a)] incorporates the former "best interest of creditors" test found in chapter 11, but spells out precisely what is intended. With respect to each class, the holders of the claims or interests of that class must receive or retain under the plan on account of those claims or interest property of a value, as of the effective date of the plan, that is not less than the amount that they would so receive or retain if the debtor were liquidated under chapter 7 on the effective date of the plan.

In order to determine the hypothetical distribution in a liquidation, the court will have to consider the various subordination provisions of proposed 11 U.S.C. 510, 726(a)(3), 726(a)(4), and the postponement provisions of proposed 11 U.S.C. 724. Also applicable in appropriate cases will be the rules governing partnership distributions under proposed 11 U.S.C. 723, and distributions of community property under proposed 11 U.S.C. 726(c). Under subparagraph (A), a particular holder is permitted to accept less than liquidation value, but his acceptance does not bind the class.

Property under subparagraph (B) may include securities of the debtor. Thus, the provision will apply in cases in which the plan is confirmed under proposed 11 U.S.C. 1129(b).

Paragraph (8) is central to the confirmation standards. It requires that each class either have accepted the plan or be unimpaired.

Paragraph (9) augments the requirements of paragraph (8) by requiring payment of each priority claim in full. It permits payments over time and payment other than in cash, but payment in securities is not intended to be permitted without consent of the priority claimant even if the class has consented. It also permits a particular claimant to accept less than full payment.

Subsection (b) permits the court to confirm a plan notwithstanding failure of compliance with paragraph (8) of subsection (a). The plan must comply with all other paragraphs of subsection (a), including paragraph (9). This subsection contains the so-called cramdown. It requires simply that the plan meet certain standards of fairness to dissenting creditors or equity security holders. The general principle of the subsection permits confirmation notwithstanding nonacceptance by an impaired class if that class and all below it in priority are treated according to the absolute priority rule. The dissenting class must be paid in full before any junior class may share under the plan. If it is paid in full, then junior classes may share. Treatment of classes of secured creditors is slightly different because they do not fall in the priority ladder, but the principle is the same.

Specifically, the court may confirm a plan over the objection of a class of secured claims if the members of that class are unimpaired or if they are to receive under the plan property of a value equal to the allowed amount of their secured claims, as determined under proposed 11 U.S.C. 506(a). The property is to be valued as of the effective date of the plan, thus recognizing the time-value of money. As used throughout this subsection, "property" includes both tangible and intangible property, such as a security of the debtor or a successor to the debtor under a reorganization plan.

The court may confirm over the dissent of a class of unsecured claims, including priority claims, only if the members of the class are unimpaired, if they will receive under the plan property of a value equal to the allowed amount of their unsecured claims, or if no class junior will share under the plan. That is, if the class is impaired, then they must be paid in full or, if paid less than in full, then no class junior may receive anything under the plan. This codifies the absolute priority rule from the dissenting class on down.

With respect to classes of equity, the court may confirm over a dissent if the members of the class are unimpaired, if they receive their liquidation preference or redemption rights, if any, or if no class junior shares under the plan. This, too, is a codification of the absolute priority rule with respect to equity. If a partnership agreement subordinates limited partners to general partners to any degree, then the general principles of paragraph (3) of this subsection would apply to prevent the general partners from being squeezed out.

One requirement applies generally to all classes before the court may confirm under this subsection. No class may be paid more than in full.

The partial codification of the absolute priority rule here is not intended to deprive senior creditor of compensation for being required to take securities in the reorganized debtor that are of an equal priority with the securities offered to a junior class. Under current law, seniors are entitled to compensation for their loss of priority, and the increased risk put upon them by being required to give up their priority will be reflected in a lower value of the securities given to them than the value of comparable securities given to juniors that have not lost a priority position.

Finally, the proponent must request use of this subsection. The court may not confirm notwithstanding nonacceptance unless the proponent requests and the court may then confirm only if subsection (b) is complied with. The court may not rewrite the plan.

A more detailed explanation follows:

The test to be applied by the court is set forth in the various paragraphs of section 1129(b). The elements of the test are new[,] departing from both the absolute priority rule and the best interests of creditors tests found under the Bankruptcy Act [former title 11]. The court is not permitted to alter the terms of the plan. It must merely decide whether the plan complies with the requirements of section 1129(b). If so, the plan is confirmed, if not the plan is denied confirmation.

The procedure followed is simple. The court examines each class of claims or interests designated under section 1123(a)(1) to see if the requirements of section 1129(b) are met. If the class is a class of secured claims, then paragraph (1) contains two tests that must be complied with in order for confirmation to occur. First, under subparagraph (A), the court must be able to find that the consideration given under the plan on account of the secured claim does not exceed the allowed amount of the claim. This condition is not prescribed as a matter of law under section 1129(a), because if the secured claim is compensated in securities of the debtor, a valuation of the business would be necessary to determine the value of the consideration. While section 1129(a) does not contemplate a valuation of the debtor's business, such a valuation will almost always be required under section 1129(b) in order to determine the value of the consideration to be distributed under the plan. Once the valuation is performed, it becomes a simple matter to impose the criterion that no claim will be paid more than in full.

Application of the test under subparagraph (A) also requires a valuation of the consideration "as of the effective date of the plan". This contemplates a present value analysis that will discount value to be received in the future; of course, if the interest rate paid is equivalent to the discount rate used, the present value and face future value will be identical. On the other hand, if no interest is proposed to be paid, the present value will be less than the face future value. For example, consider an allowed secured claim of $1,000 in a class by itself. One plan could propose to pay $1,000 on account of this claim as of the effective date of the plan. Another plan could propose to give a note with a $1,000 face amount due five years after the effective date of the plan on account of this claim. A third plan could propose to give a note in a face amount of $1,000 due five years from the effective date of the plan plus six percent annual interest commencing on the effective date of the plan on account of this claim. The first plan clearly meets the requirements of subparagraph (A) because the amount received on account of the second claim has an equivalent present value as of the effective date of the plan equal to the allowed amount of such claim.

The second plan also meets the requirements of subparagraph (A) because the present value of the five years note as of the effective date of the plan will never exceed the allowed amount of the secured claim; the higher the discount rate, the less present value the note will have. Whether the third plan complies with subparagraph (A) depends on whether the discount rate is less than six percent. Normally, the interest rate used in the plan will be prima facie evidence of the discount rate because the interest rate will reflect an arms length determination of the risk of the security involved and feasibility considerations will tend to understate interest payments. If the court found the discount rate to be greater than or equal to the interest rate used in the plan, then subparagraph (A) would be complied with because the value of the note as of the effective date of the plan would not exceed the allowed amount of the second claim. If, however, the court found the discount rate to be less than the interest rate proposed under the plan, then the present value of the note would exceed $1,000 and the plan would fail of confirmation. On the other hand, it is important to recognize that the future principal amount of a note in excess of the allowed amount of a secured claim may have a present value less than such allowed amount, if the interest rate under the plan is correspondingly less than the discount rate.

Even if the requirements of subparagraph (A) are complied with, the class of secured claims must satisfy one of the three clauses in paragraph (B) in order to pass muster. It is sufficient for confirmation if the class has accepted the plan, or if the claims of the class are unimpaired, or if each holder of a secured claim in the class will receive property of a value as of the effective date of the plan equal to the allowed amount of such claim (unless he has agreed to accept less). It is important to note that under section 506(a), the allowed amount of the secured claim will not include any extent to which the amount of such claim exceeds the value of the property securing such claim. Thus, instead of focusing on secured creditors or unsecured creditors, the statute focuses on secured claims and unsecured claims.

After the court has applied paragraph (1) to each class of secured claims, it then applies paragraph (2) to each class of unsecured claims. Again two separate components must be tested. Subparagraph (A) is identical with the test under section 1129(b)(1)(A) insofar as the holder of an unsecured claim is not permitted to receive property of a value as of the effective date of the plan on account of such claim that is greater than the allowed amount of such claim. In addition, subparagraph (B) requires compliance with one of four conditions. The conditions in clauses (i)-(iii) mirror the conditions of acceptance unimpairment, or full value found in connection with secured claims in section 1129(b)(1)(B).

The condition contained in section 1129(b)(2)(B)(iv) provides another basis for confirming the plan with respect to a class of unsecured claims. It will be of greatest use when an impaired class that has not accepted the plan is to receive less than full value under the plan. The plan may be confirmed under clause (iv) in those circumstances if the class is not unfairly discriminated against with respect to equal classes and if junior classes will receive nothing under the plan. The second criterion is the easier to understand. It is designed to prevent a senior class from giving up consideration to a junior class unless every intermediate class consents, is paid in full, or is unimpaired. This gives intermediate creditors a great deal of leverage in negotiating with senior or secured creditors who wish to have a plan that gives value to equity. One aspect of this test that is not obvious is that whether one class is senior, equal, or junior to another class is relative and not absolute. Thus from the perspective of trade creditors holding unsecured claims, claims of senior and subordinated debentures may be entitled to share on an equal basis with the trade claims. However, from the perspective of the senior unsecured debt, the subordinated debentures are junior.

This point illustrates the lack of precision in the first criterion which demands that a class not be unfairly discriminated against with respect to equal classes. From the perspective of unsecured trade claims, there is no unfair discrimination as long as the total consideration given all other classes of equal rank does not exceed the amount that would result from an exact aliquot distribution. Thus if trade creditors, senior debt, and subordinate debt are each owed $100 and the plan proposes to pay the trade debt $15, the senior debt $30, and the junior debt $0, the plan would not unfairly discriminate against the trade debt nor would any other allocation of consideration under the plan between the senior and junior debt be unfair as to the trade debt as long as the aggregate consideration is less than $30. The senior debt could take $25 and give up $5 to the junior debt and the trade debt would have no cause to complain because as far as it is concerned the junior debt is an equal class.

However, in this latter case the senior debt would have been unfairly discriminated against because the trade debt was being unfairly over-compensated; of course the plan would also fail unless the senior debt was unimpaired, received full value, or accepted the plan, because from its perspective a junior class received property under the plan. Application of the test from the perspective of senior debt is best illustrated by the plan that proposes to pay trade debt $15, senior debt $25, and junior debt $0. Here the senior debt is being unfairly discriminated against with respect to the equal trade debt even though the trade debt receives less than the senior debt. The discrimination arises from the fact that the senior debt is entitled to the rights of the junior debt which in this example entitle the senior debt to share on a 2:1 basis with the trade debt.

Finally, it is necessary to interpret the first criterion from the perspective of subordinated debt. The junior debt is subrogated to the rights of senior debt once the senior debt is paid in full. Thus, while the plan that pays trade debt $15, senior debt $25, and junior debt $0 is not unfairly discriminatory against the junior debt, a plan that proposes to pay trade debt $55, senior debt $100, and junior debt $1, would be unfairly discriminatory. In order to avoid discriminatory treatment against the junior debt, at least $10 would have to be received by such debt under those facts.

The criterion of unfair discrimination is not derived from the fair and equitable rule or from the best interests of creditors test. Rather it preserves just treatment of a dissenting class from the class's own perspective.

If each class of secured claims satisfies the requirements of section 1129(b)(1) and each class of unsecured claims satisfies the requirements of section 1129(b)(2), then the court must still see if each class of interests satisfies section 1129(b)(3) before the plan may be confirmed. Again, two separate criteria must be met. Under subparagraph (A) if the interest entitles the holder thereof to a fixed liquidation preference or if such interest may be redeemed at a fixed price, then the holder of such interest must not receive under the plan on account of such interest property of a value as of the effective date of the plan greater than the greater of these two values of the interest. Preferred stock would be an example of an interest likely to have liquidation preference or redemption price.

If an interest such as most common stock or the interest of a general partnership has neither a fixed liquidation preference nor a fixed redemption price, then the criterion in subparagraph (A) is automatically fulfilled. In addition subparagraph (B) contains five clauses that impose alternative conditions of which at least one must be satisfied in order to warrant confirmation. The first two clauses contain requirements of acceptance or unimpairment similar to the first two clauses in paragraphs (1)(B) and (2)(B). Clause (iii) is similar to the unimpairment test contained in section 1124(3)(B), except that it will apply to cover the issuance securities of the debtor of a value as of the effective date of the plan equal to the greater of any fixed liquidation preference or redemption price. The fourth clause allows confirmation if junior interests are not compensated under the plan and the fifth clause allows confirmation if there are no junior interests. These clauses recognized that as long as senior classes receive no more than full payment, the objection of a junior class will not defeat confirmation unless a class junior to it is receiving value under the plan and the objecting class is impaired. While a determination of impairment may be made under section 1124(3)(B)(iii) without a precise valuation of the business when common stock is clearly under water, once section 1129(b) is used, a more detailed valuation is a necessary byproduct. Thus, if no property is given to a holder of an interest under the plan, the interest should be clearly worthless in order to find unimpairment under section 1124(3)(B)(iii) and section 1129(a)(8); otherwise, since a class of interests receiving no property is deemed to object under section 1126(g), the more precise valuation of section 1129(b) should be used.

If all of the requirements of section 1129(b) are complied with, then the court may confirm the plan subject to other limitations such as those found in section 1129(a) and (d).

Subsection (c) of section 1129 governs confirmation when more than one plan meets the requirements of the section. The court must consider the preferences of creditors and equity security holders in determining which plan to confirm.

Subsection (d) requires the court to deny confirmation if the principal purpose of the plan is the avoidance of taxes (through use of sections 346 and 1146, and applicable provisions of State law or the Internal Revenue Code [title 26] governing bankruptcy reorganizations) or the avoidance of section 5 of the Securities Act of 1933 [15 U.S.C. 77e] (through use of section 1145).

References in Text

Section 5 of the Securities Act of 1933, referred to in subsec. (d), is classified to section 77e of Title 15, Commerce and Trade.

Amendments

2005—Subsec. (a)(9)(A). Pub. L. 109–8, §1502(a)(8)(A), substituted "507(a)(2) or 507(a)(3)" for "507(a)(1) or 507(a)(2)".

Subsec. (a)(9)(B). Pub. L. 109–8, §1502(a)(8)(B), substituted "507(a)(1)" for "507(a)(3)".

Subsec. (a)(9)(C). Pub. L. 109–8, §710(2), substituted "regular installment payments in cash—" and cls. (i) to (iii) for "deferred cash payments, over a period not exceeding six years after the date of assessment of such claim, of a value, as of the effective date of the plan, equal to the allowed amount of such claim."

Subsec. (a)(9)(D). Pub. L. 109–8, §710(1), (3), added subpar. (D).

Subsec. (a)(14). Pub. L. 109–8, §213(1), added par. (14).

Subsec. (a)(15). Pub. L. 109–8, §321(c)(1), added par. (15).

Subsec. (a)(16). Pub. L. 109–8, §1221(b), added par. (16).

Subsec. (b)(2)(B)(ii). Pub. L. 109–8, §321(c)(2), inserted before period at end ", except that in a case in which the debtor is an individual, the debtor may retain property included in the estate under section 1115, subject to the requirements of subsection (a)(14) of this section".

Subsec. (e). Pub. L. 109–8, §438, added subsec. (e).

1994—Subsec. (a)(4). Pub. L. 103–394, §501(d)(32)(A)(i), substituted period for semicolon at end.

Subsec. (a)(9)(B). Pub. L. 103–394, §304(h)(7)(i), substituted ", 507(a)(6), or 507(a)(7)" for "or 507(a)(6)".

Subsec. (a)(9)(C). Pub. L. 103–394, §304(h)(7)(ii), substituted "507(a)(8)" for "507(a)(7)".

Subsec. (a)(12). Pub. L. 103–394, §501(d)(32)(A)(ii), inserted "of title 28" after "section 1930".

Subsec. (d). Pub. L. 103–394, §501(d)(32)(B), struck out "(15 U.S.C. 77e)" after "Act of 1933".

1988—Subsec. (a)(13). Pub. L. 100–334 added par. (13).

1986—Subsec. (a)(7). Pub. L. 99–554, §283(v)(1), struck out "of" after "to".

Subsec. (a)(9)(B). Pub. L. 99–554, §283(v)(2), inserted reference to section 507(a)(6).

Subsec. (a)(9)(C). Pub. L. 99–554, §283(v)(3), substituted "507(a)(7)" for "507(a)(6)".

Subsec. (a)(12). Pub. L. 99–554, §225, added par. (12).

1984—Subsec. (a)(1), (2). Pub. L. 98–353, §512(a)(1), (2), substituted "title" for "chapter".

Subsec. (a)(4). Pub. L. 98–353, §512(a)(3), amended par. (4) generally. Prior to amendment, par. (4) read as follows: "(A) Any payment made or promised by the proponent, by the debtor, or by a person issuing securities or acquiring property under the plan, for services or for costs and expenses in, or in connection with, the case, or in connection with the plan and incident to the case, has been disclosed to the court; and (B)(i) any such payment made before confirmation of the plan is reasonable; or (ii) if such payment is to be fixed after confirmation of the plan, such payment is subject to the approval of the court as reasonable."

Subsec. (a)(5)(A)(ii). Pub. L. 98–353, §512(a)(4), substituted "; and" for the period at the end.

Subsec. (a)(5)(B). Pub. L. 98–353, §512(a)(5), substituted "the" for "The".

Subsec. (a)(6). Pub. L. 98–353, §512(a)(6), inserted "governmental" after "Any".

Subsec. (a)(7). Pub. L. 98–353, §512(a)(7)(A), substituted "of each impaired class of claims or interests" for "each class".

Subsec. (a)(7)(B). Pub. L. 98–353, §512(a)(7)(B), substituted "holder's" for "creditor's".

Subsec. (a)(8). Pub. L. 98–353, §512(a)(8), inserted "of claims or interests" after "each class".

Subsec. (a)(10). Pub. L. 98–353, §512(a)(9), substituted "If a class of claims is impaired under the plan, at least one class of claims that is impaired under the plan has accepted the plan, determined without including any acceptance of the plan by any insider" for "At least one class of claims has accepted the plan, determined without including any acceptance of the plan by any insider holding a claim of such class".

Subsec. (b)(2)(A)(i)(I), (ii). Pub. L. 98–353, §512(b)(1), substituted "liens" for "lien" wherever appearing.

Subsec. (b)(2)(B)(ii). Pub. L. 98–353, §512(b)(2), inserted "under the plan" after "retain".

Subsec. (b)(2)(C)(i). Pub. L. 98–353, §512(b)(3), substituted "interest" for "claim", and "or the value" for "and the value".

Subsec. (d). Pub. L. 98–353, §512(c), inserted "the application of" and provisions requiring that in any hearing under this subsection, the governmental unit has the burden of proof on the issue of avoidance.

Effective Date of 2005 Amendment

Amendment by section 1221(b) of Pub. L. 109–8 applicable to cases pending under this title on Apr. 20, 2005, or filed under this title on or after Apr. 20, 2005, with certain exceptions, see section 1221(d) of Pub. L. 109–8, set out as a note under section 363 of this title.

Amendment by sections 213(1), 321(c), 438, 710, and 1502(a)(8) of Pub. L. 109–8 effective 180 days after Apr.

20, 2005, and not applicable with respect to cases commenced under this title before such effective date, except as otherwise provided, see section 1501 of Pub. L. 109-8, set out as a note under section 101 of this title.

EFFECTIVE DATE OF 1994 AMENDMENT

Amendment by Pub. L. 103-394 effective Oct. 22, 1994, and not applicable with respect to cases commenced under this title before Oct. 22, 1994, see section 702 of Pub. L. 103-394, set out as a note under section 101 of this title.

EFFECTIVE DATE OF 1988 AMENDMENT

Amendment by Pub. L. 100-334 effective June 16, 1988, but not applicable to cases commenced under this title before that date, see section 4 of Pub. L. 100-334, set out as an Effective Date note under section 1114 of this title.

EFFECTIVE DATE OF 1986 AMENDMENT

Effective date and applicability of amendment by section 225 of Pub. L. 99-554 dependent upon the judicial district involved, see section 302(d), (e) of Pub. L. 99-554, set out as a note under section 581 of Title 28, Judiciary and Judicial Procedure.

Amendment by section 283 of Pub. L. 99-554 effective 30 days after Oct. 27, 1986, see section 302(a) of Pub. L. 99-554.

EFFECTIVE DATE OF 1984 AMENDMENT

Amendment by Pub. L. 98-353 effective with respect to cases filed 90 days after July 10, 1984, see section 552(a) of Pub. L. 98-353, set out as a note under section 101 of this title.

SUBCHAPTER III—POSTCONFIRMATION MATTERS

§ 1141. Effect of confirmation

(a) Except as provided in subsections (d)(2) and (d)(3) of this section, the provisions of a confirmed plan bind the debtor, any entity issuing securities under the plan, any entity acquiring property under the plan, and any creditor, equity security holder, or general partner in the debtor, whether or not the claim or interest of such creditor, equity security holder, or general partner is impaired under the plan and whether or not such creditor, equity security holder, or general partner has accepted the plan.

(b) Except as otherwise provided in the plan or the order confirming the plan, the confirmation of a plan vests all of the property of the estate in the debtor.

(c) Except as provided in subsections (d)(2) and (d)(3) of this section and except as otherwise provided in the plan or in the order confirming the plan, after confirmation of a plan, the property dealt with by the plan is free and clear of all claims and interests of creditors, equity security holders, and of general partners in the debtor.

(d)(1) Except as otherwise provided in this subsection, in the plan, or in the order confirming the plan, the confirmation of a plan—

(A) discharges the debtor from any debt that arose before the date of such confirmation, and any debt of a kind specified in section 502(g), 502(h), or 502(i) of this title, whether or not—

(i) a proof of the claim based on such debt is filed or deemed filed under section 501 of this title;

(ii) such claim is allowed under section 502 of this title; or

(iii) the holder of such claim has accepted the plan; and

(B) terminates all rights and interests of equity security holders and general partners provided for by the plan.

(2) A discharge under this chapter does not discharge a debtor who is an individual from any debt excepted from discharge under section 523 of this title.

(3) The confirmation of a plan does not discharge a debtor if—

(A) the plan provides for the liquidation of all or substantially all of the property of the estate;

(B) the debtor does not engage in business after consummation of the plan; and

(C) the debtor would be denied a discharge under section 727(a) of this title if the case were a case under chapter 7 of this title.

(4) The court may approve a written waiver of discharge executed by the debtor after the order for relief under this chapter.

(5) In a case in which the debtor is an individual—

(A) unless after notice and a hearing the court orders otherwise for cause, confirmation of the plan does not discharge any debt provided for in the plan until the court grants a discharge on completion of all payments under the plan;

(B) at any time after the confirmation of the plan, and after notice and a hearing, the court may grant a discharge to the debtor who has not completed payments under the plan if—

(i) the value, as of the effective date of the plan, of property actually distributed under the plan on account of each allowed unsecured claim is not less than the amount that would have been paid on such claim if the estate of the debtor had been liquidated under chapter 7 on such date; and

(ii) modification of the plan under section 1127 is not practicable; and

(C) unless after notice and a hearing held not more than 10 days before the date of the entry of the order granting the discharge, the court finds that there is no reasonable cause to believe that—

(i) section 522(q)(1) may be applicable to the debtor; and

(ii) there is pending any proceeding in which the debtor may be found guilty of a felony of the kind described in section 522(q)(1)(A) or liable for a debt of the kind described in section 522(q)(1)(B).

(6) Notwithstanding paragraph (1), the confirmation of a plan does not discharge a debtor that is a corporation from any debt—

(A) of a kind specified in paragraph (2)(A) or (2)(B) of section 523(a) that is owed to a domestic governmental unit, or owed to a person as the result of an action filed under subchapter III of chapter 37 of title 31 or any similar State statute; or

(B) for a tax or customs duty with respect to which the debtor—

(i) made a fraudulent return; or

(ii) willfully attempted in any manner to evade or to defeat such tax or such customs duty.

(Pub. L. 95–598, Nov. 6, 1978, 92 Stat. 2638; Pub. L. 98–353, title III, §513, July 10, 1984, 98 Stat. 387; Pub. L. 109–8, title III, §§321(d), 330(b), title VII, §708, Apr. 20, 2005, 119 Stat. 95, 101, 126.)

HISTORICAL AND REVISION NOTES

LEGISLATIVE STATEMENTS

Section 1141(d) of the House amendment is derived from a comparable provision contained in the Senate amendment. However, section 1141(d)(2) of the House amendment is derived from the House bill as preferable to the Senate amendment. It is necessary for a corporation or partnership undergoing reorganization to be able to present its creditors with a fixed list of liabilities upon which the creditors or third parties can make intelligent decisions. Retaining an exception for discharge with respect to nondischargeable taxes would leave an undesirable uncertainty surrounding reorganizations that is unacceptable. Section 1141(d)(3) is derived from the Senate amendment. Section 1141(d)(4) is likewise derived from the Senate amendment.

SENATE REPORT NO. 95–989

Subsection (a) of this section makes the provisions of a confirmed plan binding on the debtor, any entity issuing securities under the plan, any entity acquiring property under the plan, and any creditor, equity security holder, or general partner in the debtor, whether or not the claim or interest of the creditor, equity security holder, or partner is impaired under the plan and whether or not he has accepted the plan. There are two exceptions, enumerated in paragraph (2) and (3) of subsection (d).

Unless the plan or the order confirming the plan provides otherwise, the confirmation of a plan vests all of the property of the estate in the debtor and releases it from all claims and interests of creditors, equity security holders and general partners.

Subsection (d) contains the discharge for a reorganized debtor. Paragraph (1) specifies that the confirmation of a plan discharges the debtor from any debt that arose before the date of the order for relief unless the plan or the order confirming the plan provides otherwise. The discharge is effective against those claims whether or not proof of the claim is filed (or deemed filed), and whether or not the claim is allowed. The discharge also terminates all rights and interests of equity security holders and general partners provided for by the plan. The paragraph permits the plan or the order confirming the plan to provide otherwise, and excepts certain debts from the discharge as provided in paragraphs (2) and (3).

Paragraph (2) of subsection (d) makes clear what taxes remain nondischargeable in the case of a corporate debtor emerging from a reorganization under chapter 11. Nondischargeable taxes in such a reorganization are the priority taxes (under section 507) and tax payments which come due during and after the proceeding under a deferred or part-payment agreement which the debtor had entered into with the tax authority before the bankruptcy proceedings began. On the other hand, a corporation which is taken over by its creditors through a plan of reorganization will not continue to be liable for nonpriority taxes arising from the corporation's prepetition fraud, failure to file a return, or failure to file a timely return, since the creditors who take over the reorganized company should not bear the burden of acts for which the creditors were not at fault.

Paragraph (3) specifies that the debtor is not discharged by the confirmation of a plan if the plan is a liquidating plan and if the debtor would be denied discharge in a liquidation case under section 727. Specifically, if all or substantially all of the distribution under the plan is of all or substantially all of the property of the estate or the proceeds of it, if the business, if any, of the debtor does not continue, and if the debtor would be denied a discharge under section 727 (such as if the debtor were not an individual or if he had committed an act that would lead to a denial of discharge), the chapter 11 discharge is not granted.

Paragraph (4) authorizes the court to approve a waiver of discharge by the debtor.

HOUSE REPORT NO. 95–595

Paragraph (2) [of subsec. (d)] makes applicable to an individual debtor the general exceptions to discharge that are enumerated in section 523(a) of the bankruptcy code.

AMENDMENTS

2005—Subsec. (d)(2). Pub. L. 109–8, §321(d)(1), substituted "A discharge under this chapter does not discharge a debtor who is an individual" for "The confirmation of a plan does not discharge an individual debtor".

Subsec. (d)(5). Pub. L. 109–8, §321(d)(2), added par. (5).

Subsec. (d)(5)(C). Pub. L. 109–8, §330(b), added subpar. (C).

Subsec. (d)(6). Pub. L. 109–8, §708, added par. (6).

1984—Subsec. (a). Pub. L. 98–353, §513(a), substituted "any creditor, equity security holder, or general partner in" for "any creditor or equity security holder of, or general partner in,".

Subsec. (c). Pub. L. 98–353, §513(b), amended subsec. (c) generally. Prior to amendment, subsec. (c) read as follows: "After confirmation of a plan, the property dealt with by the plan is free and clear of all claims and interests of creditors, of equity security holders, and of general partners in the debtor, except as otherwise provided in the plan or in the order confirming the plan."

EFFECTIVE DATE OF 2005 AMENDMENT

Amendments by Pub. L. 109–8 effective 180 days after Apr. 20, 2005, with amendments by sections 321(d) and 708 of Pub. L. 109–8 not applicable with respect to cases commenced under this title before such effective date, except as otherwise provided, and amendment by section 330(b) of Pub. L. 109–8 applicable with respect to cases commenced under this title on or after Apr. 20, 2005, see section 1501 of Pub. L. 109–8, set out as a note under section 101 of this title.

EFFECTIVE DATE OF 1984 AMENDMENT

Amendment by Pub. L. 98–353 effective with respect to cases filed 90 days after July 10, 1984, see section 552(a) of Pub. L. 98–353, set out as a note under section 101 of this title.

§ 1142. Implementation of plan

(a) Notwithstanding any otherwise applicable nonbankruptcy law, rule, or regulation relating to financial condition, the debtor and any entity organized or to be organized for the purpose of carrying out the plan shall carry out the plan and shall comply with any orders of the court.

(b) The court may direct the debtor and any other necessary party to execute or deliver or to join in the execution or delivery of any instrument required to effect a transfer of property dealt with by a confirmed plan, and to perform any other act, including the satisfaction of any lien, that is necessary for the consummation of the plan.

(Pub. L. 95–598, Nov. 6, 1978, 92 Stat. 2639; Pub. L. 98–353, title III, §514(a), (c), (d), July 10, 1984, 98 Stat. 387.)

AMENDMENTS

1984—Pub. L. 98–353, §514(a), substituted "Implementation" for "Execution" in section catchline.

Subsec. (a). Pub. L. 98–353, §514(c), struck out the comma after "shall carry out the plan".

Subsec. (b). Pub. L. 98-353, §514(d), inserted "a" after "by".

EFFECTIVE DATE OF 1984 AMENDMENT

Amendment by Pub. L. 98-353 effective with respect to cases filed 90 days after July 10, 1984, see section 552(a) of Pub. L. 98-353, set out as a note under section 101 of this title.

§ 1143. Distribution

If a plan requires presentment or surrender of a security or the performance of any other act as a condition to participation in distribution under the plan, such action shall be taken not later than five years after the date of the entry of the order of confirmation. Any entity that has not within such time presented or surrendered such entity's security or taken any such other action that the plan requires may not participate in distribution under the plan.

(Pub. L. 95-598, Nov. 6, 1978, 92 Stat. 2639.)

HISTORICAL AND REVISION NOTES

SENATE REPORT NO. 95-989

Section 1143 fixes a 5-year limitation on presentment or surrender of securities or the performance of any other act that is a condition to participation in distribution under the plan. The 5 years runs from the date of the entry of the order of confirmation. Any entity that does not take the appropriate action with the 5-year period is barred from participation in the distribution under the plan.

§ 1144. Revocation of an order of confirmation

On request of a party in interest at any time before 180 days after the date of the entry of the order of confirmation, and after notice and a hearing, the court may revoke such order if and only if such order was procured by fraud. An order under this section revoking an order of confirmation shall—

(1) contain such provisions as are necessary to protect any entity acquiring rights in good faith reliance on the order of confirmation; and

(2) revoke the discharge of the debtor.

(Pub. L. 95-598, Nov. 6, 1978, 92 Stat. 2639; Pub. L. 98-353, title III, §515, July 10, 1984, 98 Stat. 387.)

HISTORICAL AND REVISION NOTES

SENATE REPORT NO. 95-989

If an order of confirmation was procured by fraud, then the court may revoke the order on request of a party in interest if the request is made before 180 days after the date of the entry of the order of confirmation. The order revoking the order of confirmation must revoke the discharge of the debtor, and contain such provisions as are necessary to protect any entity acquiring rights in good faith reliance on the order of confirmation.

AMENDMENTS

1984—Pub. L. 98-353 inserted "if and only" after "revoke such order".

EFFECTIVE DATE OF 1984 AMENDMENT

Amendment by Pub. L. 98-353 effective with respect to cases filed 90 days after July 10, 1984, see section 552(a) of Pub. L. 98-353, set out as a note under section 101 of this title.

§ 1145. Exemption from securities laws

(a) Except with respect to an entity that is an underwriter as defined in subsection (b) of this section, section 5 of the Securities Act of 1933 and any State or local law requiring registration for offer or sale of a security or registration or licensing of an issuer of, underwriter of, or broker or dealer in, a security do not apply to—

(1) the offer or sale under a plan of a security of the debtor, of an affiliate participating in a joint plan with the debtor, or of a successor to the debtor under the plan—

(A) in exchange for a claim against, an interest in, or a claim for an administrative expense in the case concerning, the debtor or such affiliate; or

(B) principally in such exchange and partly for cash or property;

(2) the offer of a security through any warrant, option, right to subscribe, or conversion privilege that was sold in the manner specified in paragraph (1) of this subsection, or the sale of a security upon the exercise of such a warrant, option, right, or privilege;

(3) the offer or sale, other than under a plan, of a security of an issuer other than the debtor or an affiliate, if—

(A) such security was owned by the debtor on the date of the filing of the petition;

(B) the issuer of such security is—

(i) required to file reports under section 13 or 15(d) of the Securities Exchange Act of 1934; and

(ii) in compliance with the disclosure and reporting provision of such applicable section; and

(C) such offer or sale is of securities that do not exceed—

(i) during the two-year period immediately following the date of the filing of the petition, four percent of the securities of such class outstanding on such date; and

(ii) during any 180-day period following such two-year period, one percent of the securities outstanding at the beginning of such 180-day period; or

(4) a transaction by a stockbroker in a security that is executed after a transaction of a kind specified in paragraph (1) or (2) of this subsection in such security and before the expiration of 40 days after the first date on which such security was bona fide offered to the public by the issuer or by or through an underwriter, if such stockbroker provides, at the time of or before such transaction by such stockbroker, a disclosure statement approved under section 1125 of this title, and, if the court orders, information supplementing such disclosure statement.

(b)(1) Except as provided in paragraph (2) of this subsection and except with respect to ordinary trading transactions of an entity that is not an issuer, an entity is an underwriter under section 2(11) of the Securities Act of 1933,[1] if such entity—

(A) purchases a claim against, interest in, or claim for an administrative expense in the case concerning, the debtor, if such purchase is with a view to distribution of any security received or to be received in exchange for such a claim or interest;

[1] See References in Text note below.

(B) offers to sell securities offered or sold under the plan for the holders of such securities;

(C) offers to buy securities offered or sold under the plan from the holders of such securities, if such offer to buy is—

(i) with a view to distribution of such securities; and

(ii) under an agreement made in connection with the plan, with the consummation of the plan, or with the offer or sale of securities under the plan; or

(D) is an issuer, as used in such section 2(11), with respect to such securities.

(2) An entity is not an underwriter under section 2(11) of the Securities Act of 1933 [1] or under paragraph (1) of this subsection with respect to an agreement that provides only for—

(A)(i) the matching or combining of fractional interests in securities offered or sold under the plan into whole interests; or

(ii) the purchase or sale of such fractional interests from or to entities receiving such fractional interests under the plan; or

(B) the purchase or sale for such entities of such fractional or whole interests as are necessary to adjust for any remaining fractional interests after such matching.

(3) An entity other than an entity of the kind specified in paragraph (1) of this subsection is not an underwriter under section 2(11) of the Securities Act of 1933 [1] with respect to any securities offered or sold to such entity in the manner specified in subsection (a)(1) of this section.

(c) An offer or sale of securities of the kind and in the manner specified under subsection (a)(1) of this section is deemed to be a public offering.

(d) The Trust Indenture Act of 1939 does not apply to a note issued under the plan that matures not later than one year after the effective date of the plan.

(Pub. L. 95–598, Nov. 6, 1978, 92 Stat. 2639; Pub. L. 98–353, title III, §516, July 10, 1984, 98 Stat. 387; Pub. L. 103–394, title V, §501(d)(33), Oct. 22, 1994, 108 Stat. 4146.)

HISTORICAL AND REVISION NOTES

LEGISLATIVE STATEMENTS

Section 1145 of the House amendment deletes a provision contained in section 1145(a)(1) of the House bill in favor of a more adequate provision contained in section 364(f) of the House amendment. In addition, section 1145(d) has been added to indicate that the Trust Indenture Act [15 U.S.C. 77aaa et seq.] does not apply to a commercial note issued under a plan, if the note matures not later than 1 year after the effective date of the plan. Some commercial notes receive such an exemption under 304(a)(4) of the Trust Indenture Act of 1939 (15 U.S.C. §77ddd(a)(4)) and others may receive protection by incorporation by reference into the Trust Indenture Act of securities exempt under section 3a(3), (7), (9), or (10) of the Securities Act of 1933 [15 U.S.C. 77c(a)(3), (7), (9), (10)].

In light of the amendments made to the Securities Act of 1933 [15 U.S.C. 77a et seq.] in title III of the House amendment to H.R. 8200, a specific exemption from the Trust Indenture Act [15 U.S.C. 77aaa et seq.] is required in order to create certainty regarding plans of reorganization. Section 1145(d) is not intended to imply that commercial notes issued under a plan that matures more than 1 year after the effective date of the plan are automatically covered by the Trust Indenture Act of 1939 since such notes may fall within another exemption thereto.

One other point with respect to Section 1145 deserves comment. Section 1145(a)(3) grants a debtor in possession or trustee in chapter 11 an extremely narrow portfolio security exemption from section 5 of the Securities Act of 1933 [15 U.S.C. 77e] or any comparable State law. The provision was considered by Congress and adopted after much study. The exemption is reasonable and is more restrictive than comparable provisions under the Securities Act [15 U.S.C. 77a et seq.] relating to the estates of decedents. Subsequent to passage of H.R. 8200 by the House of Representatives, the Securities and Exchange Commission promulgated Rule 148 to treat with this problem under existing law. Members of Congress received opinions from attorneys indicating dissatisfaction with the Commission's rule although the rule has been amended, the ultimate limitation of 1 percent promulgated by the Commission is wholly unacceptable.

The Commission rule would permit a trustee or debtor in possession to distribute securities at the rate of 1 percent every 6 months. Section 1145(a)(3) permits the trustee to distribute 4 percent of the securities during the 2-year period immediately following the date of the filing of the petition. In addition, the security must be of a reporting company under section 13 of the Securities and Exchange Act of 1934 [15 U.S.C. 78m], and must be in compliance with all applicable requirements for the continuing of trading in the security on the date that the trustee offers or sells the security.

With these safeguards the trustee or debtor in possession should be able to distribute 4 percent of the securities of a class at any time during the 2-year period immediately following the date of the filing of the petition in the interests of expediting bankruptcy administration. The same rationale that applies in expeditiously terminating decedents' estates applies no less to an estate under title 11.

SENATE REPORT NO. 95–989

This section, derived from similar provisions found in sections 264, 393, and 518 of the Bankruptcy Act [sections 664, 793, and 918 of former title 11], provides a limited exemption from the securities laws for securities issued under a plan of reorganization and for certain other securities. Subsection (a) exempts from the requirements of section 5 of the Securities Act of 1933 [15 U.S.C. 77e] and from any State or local law requiring registration or licensing of an issuer of, underwriter of, or broker or dealer in, a security, the offer or sale of certain securities.

Paragraph (1) of subsection (a) exempts the offer or sale under section 364 of any security that is not an equity security or convertible into an equity security. This paragraph is designed to facilitate the issuance of certificates of indebtedness, and should be read in light of the amendment made in section 306 of title III to section 3(a)(7) of the 1933 act [15 U.S.C. 77c(a)(7)].

Paragraph (2) of subsection (a) exempts the offer or sale of any security of the debtor, a successor to the debtor, or an affiliate in a joint plan, distributed under a plan if such security is exchanged in principal part for securities of the debtor or for allowed claims or administrative expenses. This exemption is carried over from present law, except as to administrative claims, but is limited to prevent distribution of securities to other than claim holders or equity security holders of the debtor or the estate.

Paragraph (3) of subsection (a) exempts the offer or sale of any security that arises from the exercise of a subscription right or from the exercise of a conversion privilege when such subscription right or conversion privilege was issued under a plan. This exemption is necessary in order to enhance the marketability of subscription rights or conversion privileges, including warrants, offered or sold under a plan. This is present law.

Paragraph (4) of subsection (a) exempts sales of portfolio securities, excluding securities of the debtor or its affiliate, owned by the debtor on the date of the filing of the petition. The purpose of this exemption is to allow the debtor or trustee to sell or distribute, without allowing manipulation schemes, restricted portfolio securities held or acquired by the debtor. Subparagraph (B) of section 1145(a)(4) limits the exemption to securities of a company that is required to file reports under section 13 of the Securities Act [15 U.S.C. 78m] and that is in compliance with all requirements for the continuance of trading those securities. This limitation effectively prevents selling into the market "cats and dogs" of a nonreporting company. Subparagraph (C) places a limitation on the amount of restricted securities that may be distributed. During the case, the trustee may sell up to 4 percent of each class of restricted securities at any time during the first 2 years and 1 percent during any 180-day period thereafter. This relaxation of the resale rules for debtors in holding restricted securities is similar to but less extensive than the relaxation in SEC Rule 144(c)(3)(v) for the estates of deceased holders of securities.

Paragraph (5) contains an exemption for brokers and dealers (stockbrokers, as defined in title 11) akin to the exemption provided by section 4(3)(A) of the Securities Act of 1933 [15 U.S.C. 77d(3)(A)]. Instead of being required to supply a prospectus, however, the stockbroker is required to supply the approved disclosure statement, and if the court orders, information supplementing the disclosure statement. Under present law, the stockholder is not required to supply anything.

Subsection (b) is new. The subsection should be read in light of the amendment in section 306 of title III to the 1933 act [15 U.S.C. 77c(a)(7), (9), (10)]. It specifies the standards under which a creditor, equity security holder, or other entity acquiring securities under the plan may resell them. The Securities Act places limitations on sales by underwriters. This subsection defines who is an underwriter, and thus restricted, and who is free to resell. Paragraph (1) enumerates real underwriters that participate in a classical underwriting. A person is an underwriter if he purchases a claim against, interest in, or claim for an administrative expense in the case concerning, the debtor, with a view to distribution or interest. This provision covers the purchase of a certificate of indebtedness issued under proposed 11 U.S.C. 364 and purchased from the debtor, if the purchase of the certificate was with a view to distribution.

A person is also an underwriter if he offers to sell securities offered or sold under the plan for the holders of such securities, or offers to buy securities offered or sold under the plan from the holders of such securities, if the offer to buy is with a view to distribution of the securities and under an agreement made in connection with the plan, with the consummation of the plan or with the offer or sale of securities under the plan. Finally, a person is an underwriter if he is an issuer, as used in section 2(11) of the Securities Act of 1933 [15 U.S.C. 77b(11)].

Paragraph (2) of subsection (b) exempts from the definition of underwriter any entity to the extent that any agreement that would bring the entity under the definition in paragraph (1) provides only for the matching combination of fractional interests in the covered securities or the purchase or sale of fractional interests. This paragraph and paragraph (1) are modeled after former rule 133 of the Securities and Exchange Commission.

Paragraph (3) specifies that if an entity is not an underwriter under the provisions of paragraph (1), as limited by paragraph (2), then the entity is not an underwriter for the purposes of the Securities Act of 1933 [15 U.S.C. 77a et seq.] with respect to the covered securities, that is, those offered or sold in an exempt transaction specified in subsection (a)(2). This makes clear that the current definition of underwriter in section 2(11) of the Securities Act of 1933 [15 U.S.C. 77b(11)] does not apply to such a creditor. The definition in that section technically applies to any person that purchases securities with "a view to distribution." If literally applied, it would prevent any creditor in a bankruptcy case from selling securities received without filing a registration statement or finding another exemption.

Subsection (b) is a first run transaction exemption and does not exempt a creditor that, for example, some years later becomes an underwriter by reacquiring securities originally issued under a plan.

Subsection (c) makes an offer or sale of securities under the plan in an exempt transaction (as specified in subsection (a)(2)) a public offering, in order to prevent characterization of the distribution as a "private placement" which would result in restrictions, under rule 144 of the SEC, on the resale of the securities.

REFERENCES IN TEXT

Section 5 of the Securities Act of 1933, referred to in subsec. (a), is classified to section 77e of Title 15, Commerce and Trade.

Sections 13 and 15(d) of the Securities Exchange Act of 1934, referred to in subsec. (a)(3)(B)(i), are classified to sections 78m and 78*o*(d), respectively, of Title 15, Commerce and Trade.

Section 2(11) of the Securities Act of 1933, referred to in subsec. (b), was redesignated section 2(a)(11) of the Act by Pub. L. 104–290, title I, §106(a)(1), Oct. 11, 1996, 110 Stat. 3424, and is classified to section 77b(a)(11) of Title 15, Commerce and Trade.

The Trust Indenture Act of 1939, referred to in subsec. (d), is title III of act May 27, 1933, ch. 38, as added Aug. 3, 1939, ch. 411, 53 Stat. 1149, as amended, which is classified generally to subchapter III (§77aaa et seq.) of chapter 2A of Title 15, Commerce and Trade. For complete classification of this Act to the Code, see section 77aaa of Title 15 and Tables.

AMENDMENTS

1994—Subsec. (a). Pub. L. 103–394, §501(d)(33)(A), in introductory provisions struck out "(15 U.S.C. 77e)" after "Act of 1933" and substituted "do not apply" for "does not apply" and in par. (3)(B)(i) struck out "(15 U.S.C. 78m or 78*o*(d))" after "Act of 1934".

Subsec. (b)(1). Pub. L. 103–394, §501(d)(33)(B), struck out "(15 U.S.C. 77b(11))" after "Act of 1933".

Subsec. (d). Pub. L. 103–394, §501(d)(33)(C), struck out "(15 U.S.C. 77aaa et seq.)" after "Act of 1939".

1984—Subsec. (a)(3)(B)(i). Pub. L. 98–353, §516(a)(1), inserted "or 15(d)" after "13", and "or 78*o*(d)" after "78m".

Subsec. (a)(3)(B)(ii). Pub. L. 98–353, §516(a)(2), amended cl. (ii) generally. Prior to amendment, cl. (ii) read as follows: "in compliance with all applicable requirements for the continuance of trading in such security on the date of such offer or sale; and".

Subsec. (a)(4). Pub. L. 98–353, §516(a)(3), substituted "stockbroker" for "stockholder" in two places.

Subsec. (b)(1). Pub. L. 98–353, §516(b)(1), inserted "and except with respect to ordinary trading transactions of an entity that is not an issuer".

Subsec. (b)(1)(C). Pub. L. 98–353, §516(b)(2), substituted "from" for "for".

Subsec. (b)(2)(A)(i). Pub. L. 98–353, §516(b)(3), substituted "or combining" for "combination".

Subsec. (b)(2)(A)(ii). Pub. L. 98–353, §516(b)(4), substituted "from or to" for "among".

Subsec. (d). Pub. L. 98–353, §516(c), struck out "commercial" before "note".

EFFECTIVE DATE OF 1994 AMENDMENT

Amendment by Pub. L. 103–394 effective Oct. 22, 1994, and not applicable with respect to cases commenced under this title before Oct. 22, 1994, see section 702 of Pub. L. 103–394, set out as a note under section 101 of this title.

EFFECTIVE DATE OF 1984 AMENDMENT

Amendment by Pub. L. 98–353 effective with respect to cases filed 90 days after July 10, 1984, see section 552(a) of Pub. L. 98–353, set out as a note under section 101 of this title.

§ 1146. Special tax provisions

(a) The issuance, transfer, or exchange of a security, or the making or delivery of an instrument of transfer under a plan confirmed under section 1129 of this title, may not be taxed under any law imposing a stamp tax or similar tax.

(b) The court may authorize the proponent of a plan to request a determination, limited to questions of law, by a State or local governmental unit charged with responsibility for collection or determination of a tax on or measured by income, of the tax effects, under section 346 of this title and under the law imposing such tax, of the plan. In the event of an actual controversy, the court may declare such effects after the earlier of—

(1) the date on which such governmental unit responds to the request under this subsection; or

(2) 270 days after such request.

(Pub. L. 95–598, Nov. 6, 1978, 92 Stat. 2641; Pub. L. 98–353, title III, § 517, July 10, 1984, 98 Stat. 388; Pub. L. 109–8, title VII, § 719(b)(3), Apr. 20, 2005, 119 Stat. 133.)

HISTORICAL AND REVISION NOTES

LEGISLATIVE STATEMENTS

Section 1146 of the House amendment represents a compromise between the House bill and Senate amendment.

Special tax provisions: reorganization: The House bill provided rules on the effect of bankruptcy on the taxable year of the debtor and on tax return filing requirements for State and local taxes only. The House bill also exempted from State or local stamp taxes the issuance, transfer, or exchange of a security, or the making or delivery of an instrument of transfer under a plan. The House bill also authorized the bankruptcy court to declare the tax effects of a reorganization plan after the proponent of the plan had requested a ruling from State or local tax authority and either had received an unfavorable ruling or the tax authority had not issued a ruling within 270 days.

The Senate amendment deleted the rules concerning the taxable years of the debtor and tax return filing requirements since the Federal rules were to be considered in the next Congress. It broadened the rule exempting transfers of securities to include Federal stamp or similar taxes, if any. In addition, the Senate amendment deleted the provision which permitted the bankruptcy court to determine the tax effects of a plan.

The House amendment retains the State and local rules in the House bill with one modification. Under the House amendment, the power of the bankruptcy court to declare the tax effects of the plan is limited to issues of law and not to questions of fact such as the allowance of specific deductions. Thus, the bankruptcy court could declare whether the reorganization qualified for taxfree status under State or local tax rules, but it could not declare the dollar amount of any tax attributes that survive the reorganization.

SENATE REPORT NO. 95–989

Section 1146 provides special tax rules applicable to Title 11 reorganizations. Subsection (a) provides that the taxable period of an individual debtor terminates on the date of the order for relief, unless the case has been converted into a reorganization from a liquidation proceeding.

Subsection (b) requires the trustee of the estate of an individual debtor in a reorganization to file a tax return for each taxable period while the case is pending after the order for relief. For corporations in chapter 11, the trustee is required to file the tax returns due while the case is pending (sec. 346(c)(2)).

Subsection (c) exempts from Federal, State, or local stamp taxes the issuance, transfer, or exchange of a security, or the making or delivery of an instrument of transfer under a plan. This subsection is derived from section 267 of the present Bankruptcy Act [section 667 of former title 11].

Subsection (d) permits the court to authorize the proponent of a reorganization plan to request from the Internal Revenue Service (or State or local tax authority) an advance ruling on the tax effects of the proposed plan. If a ruling is not obtained within 270 days after the request was made, or if a ruling is obtained but the proponent of the plan disagrees with the ruling, the bankruptcy court may resolve the dispute and determine the tax effects of the proposed plan.

Subsection (e) provides that prepetition taxes which are nondischargeable in a reorganization, and all taxes arising during the administration period of the case, may be assessed and collected from the debtor or the debtor's successor in a reorganization (see sec. 505(c) of the bill).

HOUSE REPORT NO. 95–595

Section 1146 of title 11 specifies five subsections which embody special tax provisions that apply in a case under chapter 11 of title 11. Subsection (a) indicates that the tax year of an individual debtor terminates on the date of the order for relief under chapter 11. Termination of the taxable year of the debtor commences the tax period of the estate. If the case was converted from chapter 7 of title 11 then the estate is created as a separate taxable entity dating from the order for relief under chapter 7. If multiple conversion of the case occurs, then the estate is treated as a separate taxable entity on the date of the order for relief under the first chapter under which the estate is a separate taxable entity.

Subsection (d) permits the court to authorize the proponent of a plan to request a taxing authority to declare the tax effects of such plan. In the event of an actual controversy, the court may declare the tax effects of the plan of reorganization at any time after the earlier of action by such taxing authority or 270 days after the request. Such a declaration, unless appealed, becomes a final judgment and binds any tax authority that was requested by the proponent to determine the tax effects of the plan.

AMENDMENTS

2005—Pub. L. 109–8 redesignated subsecs. (c) and (d) as (a) and (b), respectively, and struck out former subsecs. (a) and (b) which read as follows:

"(a) For the purposes of any State or local law imposing a tax on or measured by income, the taxable period of a debtor that is an individual shall terminate on the date of the order for relief under this chapter, unless the case was converted under section 706 of this title.

"(b) The trustee shall make a State or local tax return of income for the estate of an individual debtor in a case under this chapter for each taxable period after the order for relief under this chapter during which the case is pending."

1984—Subsec. (c). Pub. L. 98–353, § 517(a), struck out "State or local" before "law imposing a stamp tax".

Subsec. (d)(1). Pub. L. 98–353, § 517(b), substituted "or" for "and".

EFFECTIVE DATE OF 2005 AMENDMENT

Amendment by Pub. L. 109–8 effective 180 days after Apr. 20, 2005, and not applicable with respect to cases commenced under this title before such effective date, except as otherwise provided, see section 1501 of Pub. L. 109–8, set out as a note under section 101 of this title.

EFFECTIVE DATE OF 1984 AMENDMENT

Amendment by Pub. L. 98–353 effective with respect to cases filed 90 days after July 10, 1984, see section

552(a) of Pub. L. 98–353, set out as a note under section 101 of this title.

SUBCHAPTER IV—RAILROAD REORGANIZATION

§ 1161. Inapplicability of other sections

Sections 341, 343, 1102(a)(1), 1104, 1105, 1107, 1129(a)(7), and 1129(c) of this title do not apply in a case concerning a railroad.

(Pub. L. 95–598, Nov. 6, 1978, 92 Stat. 2641.)

HISTORICAL AND REVISION NOTES

SENATE REPORT NO. 95–989

This section makes inapplicable sections of the bill which are either inappropriate in railroad reorganizations, or relate to matters which are otherwise dealt with in subchapter IV.

§ 1162. Definition

In this subchapter, "Board" means the "Surface Transportation Board".

(Added Pub. L. 104–88, title III, § 302(1), Dec. 29, 1995, 109 Stat. 943.)

PRIOR PROVISIONS

A prior section 1162, Pub. L. 95–598, Nov. 6, 1978, 92 Stat. 2641, defined "Commission", prior to repeal by Pub. L. 104–88, title III, § 302(1), Dec. 29, 1995, 109 Stat. 943.

EFFECTIVE DATE

Section effective Jan. 1, 1996, see section 2 of Pub. L. 104–88, set out as a note under section 701 of Title 49, Transportation.

§ 1163. Appointment of trustee

As soon as practicable after the order for relief the Secretary of Transportation shall submit a list of five disinterested persons that are qualified and willing to serve as trustees in the case. The United States trustee shall appoint one of such persons to serve as trustee in the case.

(Pub. L. 95–598, Nov. 6, 1978, 92 Stat. 2641; Pub. L. 99–554, title II, § 226, Oct. 27, 1986, 100 Stat. 3102.)

HISTORICAL AND REVISION NOTES

LEGISLATIVE STATEMENTS

Section 1163 of the House amendment represents a compromise between the House bill and Senate amendment with respect to the appointment of a trustee in a railroad reorganization. As soon as practicable after the order for relief, the Secretary of Transportation is required to submit a list of five disinterested persons who are qualified to serve as trustee and the court will than appoint one trustee from the list to serve as trustee in the case.

The House amendment deletes section 1163 of the Senate amendment in order to cover intrastate railroads in a case under subchapter IV of chapter 11. The bill does not confer jurisdiction on the Interstate Commerce Commission with respect to intrastate railroads.

SENATE REPORT NO. 95–989

[Section 1166 (enacted as section 1163)] Requires the court to appoint a trustee in every case. Since the trustee may employ whatever help he needs, multiple trusteeships are unnecessary and add to the cost of administration. The present requirement of section 77(c)(1) [section 205(c)(1) of former title 11] that the trustee be approved by the Interstate Commerce Commission is unnecessary, since the trustee will be selected either from the panel established under section 606(f) of title 28, or someone certified by the Director of the Administrative Office of the United States Courts as qualified to become a member of that panel.

HOUSE REPORT NO. 95–595

[Section 1162] This section [enacted as section 1163] requires the appointment of an independent trustee in a railroad reorganization case. The court may appoint one or more disinterested persons to serve as trustee in the case.

AMENDMENTS

1986—Pub. L. 99–554 amended section generally, substituting "relief the Secretary" for "relief, the Secretary" and "The United States trustee shall appoint" for "The court shall appoint".

EFFECTIVE DATE OF 1986 AMENDMENT

Effective date and applicability of amendment by Pub. L. 99–554 dependent upon the judicial district involved, see section 302(d), (e) of Pub. L. 99–554, set out as a note under section 581 of Title 28, Judiciary and Judicial Procedure.

§ 1164. Right to be heard

The Board, the Department of Transportation, and any State or local commission having regulatory jurisdiction over the debtor may raise and may appear and be heard on any issue in a case under this chapter, but may not appeal from any judgment, order, or decree entered in the case.

(Pub. L. 95–598, Nov. 6, 1978, 92 Stat. 2641; Pub. L. 104–88, title III, § 302(2), Dec. 29, 1995, 109 Stat. 943.)

HISTORICAL AND REVISION NOTES

LEGISLATIVE STATEMENTS

Section 1164 of the Senate amendment is deleted as a matter to be left to the Rules of Bankruptcy Procedure. It is anticipated that the rules will require a petition in a railroad reorganization to be filed with the Interstate Commerce Commission and the Secretary of Transportation in a case concerning an interstate railroad.

Section 1164 of the House amendment is derived from section 1163 of the House bill. The section makes clear that the Interstate Commerce Commission, the Department of Transportation, and any State or local commission having regulatory jurisdiction over the debtor may raise and appear and be heard on any issue in a case under subchapter IV of chapter 11, but may not appeal from any judgment, order, or decree in the case. As under section 1109 of title 11, such intervening parties are not parties in interest.

HOUSE REPORT NO. 95–595

[Section 1163] This section [enacted as section 1164] gives the same right to raise, and appear and be heard on, any issue in a railroad reorganization case to the Interstate Commerce Commission, the Department of Transportation, and any State or local commission having regulatory jurisdiction over the debtor as is given to the SEC and indenture trustees under section 1109 in ordinary reorganization cases. The right of appeal is denied the ICC, the Department of Transportation, and State and local regulatory agencies, the same as it is denied the SEC.

AMENDMENTS

1995—Pub. L. 104–88 substituted "Board" for "Commission".

EFFECTIVE DATE OF 1995 AMENDMENT

Amendment by Pub. L. 104–88 effective Jan. 1, 1996, see section 2 of Pub. L. 104–88, set out as an Effective Date note under section 701 of Title 49, Transportation.

§ 1165. Protection of the public interest

In applying sections 1166, 1167, 1169, 1170, 1171, 1172, 1173, and 1174 of this title, the court and the trustee shall consider the public interest in addition to the interests of the debtor, creditors, and equity security holders.

(Pub. L. 95–598, Nov. 6, 1978, 92 Stat. 2641.)

HISTORICAL AND REVISION NOTES

LEGISLATIVE STATEMENTS

Section 1165 of the House amendment represents a modification of sections 1165 and 1167 of the Senate amendment requiring the court and the trustee to consider the broad, general public interest in addition to the interests of the debtor, creditors, and equity security holders in applying specific sections of the subchapter.

SENATE REPORT NO. 95–989

Section 1165 requires the court, in consideration of the relief to be granted upon the filing of an involuntary petition, to take into account the "public interest" in the preservation of the debtor's rail service. This is an important factor in railroad reorganization, which distinguishes them from other business reorganizations. Hence, this section modifies the provisions in sections 303 and 305 that govern generally when the business of a debtor may continue to operate, when relief under the Act sought should be granted, and when the petition should be dismissed.

Section 1167 [enacted as section 1165] imposes on the trustee the obligations, in addition to his other duties and responsibilities, to take into account the "public interest" in the preservation of the debtor's rail service.

§ 1166. Effect of subtitle IV of title 49 and of Federal, State, or local regulations

Except with respect to abandonment under section 1170 of this title, or merger, modification of the financial structure of the debtor, or issuance or sale of securities under a plan, the trustee and the debtor are subject to the provisions of subtitle IV of title 49 that are applicable to railroads, and the trustee is subject to orders of any Federal, State, or local regulatory body to the same extent as the debtor would be if a petition commencing the case under this chapter had not been filed, but—

(1) any such order that would require the expenditure, or the incurring of an obligation for the expenditure, of money from the estate is not effective unless approved by the court; and

(2) the provisions of this chapter are subject to section 601(b) of the Regional Rail Reorganization Act of 1973.

(Pub. L. 95–598, Nov. 6, 1978, 92 Stat. 2642; Pub. L. 97–449, § 5(a)(2), Jan. 12, 1983, 96 Stat. 2442; Pub. L. 98–353, title III, § 518, July 10, 1984, 98 Stat. 388; Pub. L. 103–394, title V, § 501(d)(34), Oct. 22, 1994, 108 Stat. 4146.)

HISTORICAL AND REVISION NOTES

LEGISLATIVE STATEMENTS

Section 1166 of the House amendment is derived from sections 1164 and 1165 of the House bill. An alternative proposal contained in section 1168(1) of the Senate bill is rejected as violative of the principle of equal treatment of all creditors under title 11.

SENATE REPORT NO. 95–989

Section 1168 [enacted as section 1166] makes the trustee subject to the Interstate Commerce Act [49 U.S.C. 10101 et seq.] and to lawful orders of the Interstate Commerce Commission, the U.S. Department of Transportation, and State and regulatory bodies. The approval of the court is required, however, if the order requires the expenditure of money or the incurring of an expenditure other than the payment of certain interline accounts. The limitation of "lawful orders" of State commissions to those involving "safety, location of tracks, and terminal facilities," which is contained in present section 77(c)(2) [section 205(c)(2) of former title 11], is eliminated.

Subsection (1) further provides that the debtor must pay in cash all amounts owed other carriers for current balances owed for interline freight, passenger and per diem, including incentive per diem, for periods both prior and subsequent to the filing of the petition, without the necessity of court approval.

Subsection (2) makes the provisions of the chapter subject to section 601(b) of the Regional Rail Reorganization Act [45 U.S.C. 791(b)], which excludes the Interstate Commerce Commission from any participation in the reorganization of certain northeast railroads that have transferred their rail properties to Consolidated Rail Corporation (Conrail).

HOUSE REPORT NO. 95–595

Section 1164 [enacted as section 1166] makes the debtor railroad subject to the provisions of the Interstate Commerce Act [49 U.S.C. 10101 et seq.] that are applicable to railroads, and the trustee subject to the orders of the Interstate Commerce Commission to the same extent as the debtor would have been if the case had not been commenced. There are several exceptions. The section does not apply with respect to abandonment of rail lines, which is provided for under section 1169, or with respect to merger under a plan, modification of the financial structure of the debtor by reason of the plan, or the issuance or sale of securities under a plan. Further, the orders of the ICC are not effective if the order would require the expenditure or the incurring of an obligation for the expenditure of money from the estate, unless approved by the court, and the provisions of this chapter are subject to section 601(b) of the Regional Rail Reorganization Act of 1973 [45 U.S.C. 791(b)].

[Section 1165 (enacted as section 1166)] The same rules apply with respect to Federal, State, or local regulations. The trustee is subject to the orders of a Federal, State, or local regulatory body to the same extent as the debtor would be if the case had not been commenced. However, any order that would require the expenditure, or the incurring of an obligation for the expenditure, of money is not effective under [until] approved by the court.

REFERENCES IN TEXT

Section 601(b) of the Regional Rail Reorganization Act of 1973, referred to in par. (2), is classified to section 791(b) of Title 45, Railroads.

AMENDMENTS

1994—Par. (2). Pub. L. 103–394 struck out "(45 U.S.C. 791(b))" after "Act of 1973".

1984—Pub. L. 98–353 directed substitution of "subtitle IV of title 49" for "the Interstate Commerce Act (49 U.S.C. 1 et seq.)", which substitution had previously been made by Pub. L. 97–449.

1983—Pub. L. 97–449 substituted "subtitle IV of title 49" for "Interstate Commerce Act" in section catchline, and "subtitle IV of title 49" for "the Interstate Commerce Act (49 U.S.C. 1 et seq.)" in text.

EFFECTIVE DATE OF 1994 AMENDMENT

Amendment by Pub. L. 103–394 effective Oct. 22, 1994, and not applicable with respect to cases commenced under this title before Oct. 22, 1994, see section 702 of Pub. L. 103–394, set out as a note under section 101 of this title.

§ 1167. Collective bargaining agreements

Notwithstanding section 365 of this title, neither the court nor the trustee may change the wages or working conditions of employees of the debtor established by a collective bargaining agreement that is subject to the Railway Labor Act except in accordance with section 6 of such Act.

(Pub. L. 95–598, Nov. 6, 1978, 92 Stat. 2642; Pub. L. 103–394, title V, §501(d)(35), Oct. 22, 1994, 108 Stat. 4146.)

HISTORICAL AND REVISION NOTES

SENATE REPORT NO. 95–989

Section 1176 [enacted as section 1167] is derived from present section 77(n) [section 205(n) of former title 11]. It provides that notwithstanding the general section governing the rejection of executory contracts (section 365), neither the court nor the trustee may change the wages or working conditions of employees of the debtor established by a collective bargaining agreement that is subject to the Railway Labor Act [45 U.S.C. 151 et seq.], except in accordance with section 6 of that Act [45 U.S.C. 156]. As reported by the subcommittee this section provided that wages and salaries of rail employees could not be affected by the trustee, but that work rules could be rejected by the trustee. The reorganization court was given the authority to review the trustee's decisions and to settle any disputes arising from the rejection. This provision was withdrawn by the full committee, and hearings will be conducted next year by the Human Resources Committee in the area of rail labor contracts and the trustee's ability to reject them in a bankruptcy situation.

HOUSE REPORT NO. 95–595

Section 1167 is derived from present section 77(n) [section 205(n) of former title 11]. It provides that notwithstanding the general section governing the rejection of executory contracts (section 365), neither the court nor the trustee may change the wages or working conditions of employees of the debtor established by a collective bargaining agreement that is subject to the Railway Labor Act [45 U.S.C. 151 et seq.], except in accordance with section 6 of that Act [45 U.S.C. 156]. The subject of railway labor is too delicate and has too long a history for this code to upset established relationships. The balance has been struck over the years. This provision continues that balance unchanged.

REFERENCES IN TEXT

The Railway Labor Act, referred to in text, is act May 20, 1926, ch. 347, 44 Stat. 577, as amended, which is classified principally to chapter 8 (§151 et seq.) of Title 45, Railroads. Section 6 of the Act is classified to section 156 of Title 45. For complete classification of this Act to the Code, see section 151 of Title 45 and Tables.

AMENDMENTS

1994—Pub. L. 103–394 struck out "(45 U.S.C. 151 et seq.)" after "Railway Labor Act" and "(45 U.S.C. 156)" after "such Act".

EFFECTIVE DATE OF 1994 AMENDMENT

Amendment by Pub. L. 103–394 effective Oct. 22, 1994, and not applicable with respect to cases commenced under this title before Oct. 22, 1994, see section 702 of Pub. L. 103–394, set out as a note under section 101 of this title.

§1168. Rolling stock equipment

(a)(1) The right of a secured party with a security interest in or of a lessor or conditional vendor of equipment described in paragraph (2) to take possession of such equipment in compliance with an equipment security agreement, lease, or conditional sale contract, and to enforce any of its other rights or remedies under such security agreement, lease, or conditional sale contract, to sell, lease, or otherwise retain or dispose of such equipment, is not limited or otherwise affected by any other provision of this title or by any power of the court, except that right to take possession and enforce those other rights and remedies shall be subject to section 362, if—

(A) before the date that is 60 days after the date of commencement of a case under this chapter, the trustee, subject to the court's approval, agrees to perform all obligations of the debtor under such security agreement, lease, or conditional sale contract; and

(B) any default, other than a default of a kind described in section 365(b)(2), under such security agreement, lease, or conditional sale contract—

(i) that occurs before the date of commencement of the case and is an event of default therewith is cured before the expiration of such 60-day period;

(ii) that occurs or becomes an event of default after the date of commencement of the case and before the expiration of such 60-day period is cured before the later of—

(I) the date that is 30 days after the date of the default or event of the default; or

(II) the expiration of such 60-day period; and

(iii) that occurs on or after the expiration of such 60-day period is cured in accordance with the terms of such security agreement, lease, or conditional sale contract, if cure is permitted under that agreement, lease, or conditional sale contract.

(2) The equipment described in this paragraph—

(A) is rolling stock equipment or accessories used on rolling stock equipment, including superstructures or racks, that is subject to a security interest granted by, leased to, or conditionally sold to a debtor; and

(B) includes all records and documents relating to such equipment that are required, under the terms of the security agreement, lease, or conditional sale contract, that is to be surrendered or returned by the debtor in connection with the surrender or return of such equipment.

(3) Paragraph (1) applies to a secured party, lessor, or conditional vendor acting in its own behalf or acting as trustee or otherwise in behalf of another party.

(b) The trustee and the secured party, lessor, or conditional vendor whose right to take possession is protected under subsection (a) may agree, subject to the court's approval, to extend the 60-day period specified in subsection (a)(1).

(c)(1) In any case under this chapter, the trustee shall immediately surrender and return to a secured party, lessor, or conditional vendor, described in subsection (a)(1), equipment described in subsection (a)(2), if at any time after the date of commencement of the case under this chapter such secured party, lessor, or conditional vendor is entitled pursuant to subsection (a)(1) to take possession of such equipment and makes a written demand for such possession of the trustee.

(2) At such time as the trustee is required under paragraph (1) to surrender and return

equipment described in subsection (a)(2), any lease of such equipment, and any security agreement or conditional sale contract relating to such equipment, if such security agreement or conditional sale contract is an executory contract, shall be deemed rejected.

(d) With respect to equipment first placed in service on or prior to October 22, 1994, for purposes of this section—

(1) the term "lease" includes any written agreement with respect to which the lessor and the debtor, as lessee, have expressed in the agreement or in a substantially contemporaneous writing that the agreement is to be treated as a lease for Federal income tax purposes; and

(2) the term "security interest" means a purchase-money equipment security interest.

(e) With respect to equipment first placed in service after October 22, 1994, for purposes of this section, the term "rolling stock equipment" includes rolling stock equipment that is substantially rebuilt and accessories used on such equipment.

(Pub. L. 95–598, Nov. 6, 1978, 92 Stat. 2642; Pub. L. 98–353, title III, §519, July 10, 1984, 98 Stat. 388; Pub. L. 103–394, title II, §201(b), Oct. 22, 1994, 108 Stat. 4120; Pub. L. 106–181, title VII, §744(a), Apr. 5, 2000, 114 Stat. 175.)

HISTORICAL AND REVISION NOTES

LEGISLATIVE STATEMENTS

Section 1168 of the House amendment incorporates a provision contained in section 1166 of the House bill instead of the provision contained in section 1175 of the Senate amendment for the reasons stated in connection with the discussion of section 1110 of the House amendment.

SENATE REPORT NO. 95–989

Section 1175 [enacted as section 1168] continues the protection accorded in present section 77(j) [section 205(j) of former title 11] to the rights of holders of purchase-money equipment security, and of lessors or conditional vendors of railroad rolling stock, but accords to the trustee a limited period within which to assume the debtor's obligation and to cure any defaults. The rights of such lenders are not affected by the automatic stay and related provisions of sections 362 and 363, or by any power of the court, unless (1) within 60 days after the commencement of the case (or such longer period as may be agreed to by the secured party, lessor or conditional vendor) the trustees, with the approval of the court, agrees to perform all of the debtor's obligations under the security agreement, lease or conditional sale contract, and (2) all defaults are cured within the 60-day period. Defaults described in section 365(b)(2)—defaults which are breaches of provisions relating to the insolvency or financial condition of the debtor, or the commencement of a case under this title, or the appointment of a trustee—are for obvious reasons, excepted.

HOUSE REPORT NO. 95–595

[Section 1166] This section [enacted as section 1168], derived with changes from the last sentence of present section 77(j) [section 205(j) of former title 11], protects the interests of rolling stock equipment financers, while providing the trustee with some opportunity to cure defaults, agree to make payments, and retain and use the equipment. The provision is parallel to section 1110, concerning aircraft equipment and vessels.

AMENDMENTS

2000—Pub. L. 106–181 amended section catchline and text generally, substituting present provisions consisting of subsecs. (a) to (e) for former subsecs. (a) to (d) which contained somewhat similar provisions.

1994—Pub. L. 103–394 amended section generally. Prior to amendment, section read as follows:

"(a) The right of a secured party with a purchase-money equipment security interest in, or of a lessor or conditional vendor of, whether as trustee or otherwise, rolling stock equipment or accessories used on such equipment, including superstructures and racks, that are subject to a purchase-money equipment security interest granted by, leased to, or conditionally sold to, the debtor to take possession of such equipment in compliance with the provisions of a purchase-money equipment security agreement, lease, or conditional sale contract, as the case may be, is not affected by section 362 or 363 of this title or by any power of the court to enjoin such taking of possession, unless—

"(1) before 60 days after the date of the commencement of a case under this chapter, the trustee, subject to the court's approval, agrees to perform all obligations of the debtor under such security agreement, lease, or conditional sale contract, as the case may be; and

"(2) any default, other than a default of a kind specified in section 365(b)(2) of this title, under such security agreement, lease, or conditional sale contract, as the case may be—

"(A) that occurred before such date and is an event of default therewith is cured before the expiration of such 60-day period; and

"(B) that occurs or becomes an event of default after such date is cured before the later of—

"(i) 30 days after the date of such default or event of default; and

"(ii) the expiration of such 60-day period.

"(b) The trustee and the secured party, lessor, or conditional vendor, as the case may be, whose right to take possession is protected under subsection (a) of this section, may agree, subject to the court's approval, to extend the 60-day period specified in subsection (a)(1) of this section."

1984—Subsec. (b). Pub. L. 98–353 inserted a comma after "approval".

EFFECTIVE DATE OF 2000 AMENDMENT

Amendment by Pub. L. 106–181 applicable only to fiscal years beginning after Sept. 30, 1999, see section 3 of Pub. L. 106–181, set out as a note under section 106 of Title 49, Transportation.

EFFECTIVE DATE OF 1994 AMENDMENT

Amendment by Pub. L. 103–394 effective Oct. 22, 1994, and not applicable with respect to cases commenced under this title before Oct. 22, 1994, see section 702 of Pub. L. 103–394, set out as a note under section 101 of this title.

EFFECTIVE DATE OF 1984 AMENDMENT

Amendment by Pub. L. 98–353 effective with respect to cases filed 90 days after July 10, 1984, see section 552(a) of Pub. L. 98–353, set out as a note under section 101 of this title.

§1169. Effect of rejection of lease of railroad line

(a) Except as provided in subsection (b) of this section, if a lease of a line of railroad under which the debtor is the lessee is rejected under section 365 of this title, and if the trustee, within such time as the court fixes, and with the court's approval, elects not to operate the leased line, the lessor under such lease, after such approval, shall operate the line.

(b) If operation of such line by such lessor is impracticable or contrary to the public interest, the court, on request of such lessor, and after notice and a hearing, shall order the trustee to continue operation of such line for the account of such lessor until abandonment is ordered under section 1170 of this title, or until such operation is otherwise lawfully terminated, whichever occurs first.

(c) During any such operation, such lessor is deemed a carrier subject to the provisions of subtitle IV of title 49 that are applicable to railroads.

(Pub. L. 95–598, Nov. 6, 1978, 92 Stat. 2643; Pub. L. 97–449, §5(a)(3), Jan. 12, 1983, 96 Stat. 2442; Pub. L. 98–353, title III, §520, July 10, 1984, 98 Stat. 388.)

HISTORICAL AND REVISION NOTES

LEGISLATIVE STATEMENTS

Section 1169 of the Senate amendment is deleted from the House amendment as unnecessary since 28 U.S.C. 1407 treating with the judicial panel on multi-district litigation will apply by its terms to cases under title 11.

SENATE REPORT NO. 95–989

Section 1177 [enacted as section 1169] continues, essentially without change, the provisions relating to the rejection by the trustee of a lease of a line of railroad now contained in section 77(c)(6) [section 205(c)(6) of former title 11]. Subsection (a) requires the lessor of a line of railroad to operate it if the lease is rejected by the trustee and the trustee, with the approval of the court, elects not to operate the leased line. Subsection (b), however, further provides that if operation by the lessor is impractical or contrary to the public interest, the court shall require the trustee to operate the line for the account of the lessor until the operation is lawfully terminated. Subsection (c) provides that during such operation, the lessor is a carrier subject to the Interstate Commerce Act [49 U.S.C. 10101 et seq.].

HOUSE REPORT NO. 95–595

[Section 1168] This section [enacted as section 1169] governs the effect of the rejection by the trustee of an unexpired lease of railroad line under which the debtor is the lessee. If the trustee rejects such a lease, and if the trustee, within such time as the court allows, and with the approval of the court, elects not to operate the leased line, then the lessor under the lease must operate the line.

Subsection (b) excuses the lessor from the requirement to operate the line under certain circumstances. If operation of the line by the lessor is impracticable or contrary to the public interest, the court, on request of the lessor, must order the trustee to continue operation of the line for the account of the lessor until abandonment is ordered under section 1169, governing abandonments generally, or until the operation is otherwise lawfully terminated, such as by an order of the ICC.

Subsection (c) deems the lessor a carrier subject to the provisions of the Interstate Commerce Act [49 U.S.C. 10101 et seq.] during the operation of the line before abandonment.

AMENDMENTS

1984—Subsec. (c). Pub. L. 98–353 directed substitution of "subtitle IV of title 49" for "the Interstate Commerce Act (49 U.S.C. 1 et seq.)", which substitution had previously been made by Pub. L. 97–449.

1983—Subsec. (c). Pub. L. 97–449 substituted "subtitle IV of title 49" for "the Interstate Commerce Act (49 U.S.C. §1 et seq.)".

§ 1170. Abandonment of railroad line

(a) The court, after notice and a hearing, may authorize the abandonment of all or a portion of a railroad line if such abandonment is—

(1)(A) in the best interest of the estate; or

(B) essential to the formulation of a plan; and

(2) consistent with the public interest.

(b) If, except for the pendency of the case under this chapter, such abandonment would require approval by the Board under a law of the United States, the trustee shall initiate an appropriate application for such abandonment with the Board. The court may fix a time within which the Board shall report to the court on such application.

(c) After the court receives the report of the Board, or the expiration of the time fixed under subsection (b) of this section, whichever occurs first, the court may authorize such abandonment, after notice to the Board, the Secretary of Transportation, the trustee, any party in interest that has requested notice, any affected shipper or community, and any other entity prescribed by the court, and a hearing.

(d)(1) Enforcement of an order authorizing such abandonment shall be stayed until the time for taking an appeal has expired, or, if an appeal is timely taken, until such order has become final.

(2) If an order authorizing such abandonment is appealed, the court, on request of a party in interest, may authorize suspension of service on a line or a portion of a line pending the determination of such appeal, after notice to the Board, the Secretary of Transportation, the trustee, any party in interest that has requested notice, any affected shipper or community, and any other entity prescribed by the court, and a hearing. An appellant may not obtain a stay of the enforcement of an order authorizing such suspension by the giving of a supersedeas bond or otherwise, during the pendency of such appeal.

(e)(1) In authorizing any abandonment of a railroad line under this section, the court shall require the rail carrier to provide a fair arrangement at least as protective of the interests of employees as that established under section 11326(a) of title 49.

(2) Nothing in this subsection shall be deemed to affect the priorities or timing of payment of employee protection which might have existed in the absence of this subsection.

(Pub. L. 95–598, Nov. 6, 1978, 92 Stat. 2643; Pub. L. 96–448, title II, §227(a), Oct. 14, 1980, 94 Stat. 1931; Pub. L. 98–353, title III, §521, July 10, 1984, 98 Stat. 388; Pub. L. 104–88, title III, §302(2), Dec. 29, 1995, 109 Stat. 943; Pub. L. 109–8, title XII, §1217, Apr. 20, 2005, 119 Stat. 195.)

HISTORICAL AND REVISION NOTES

SENATE REPORT NO. 95–989

Subsection (a) of section 1178 [enacted as section 1170] permits the court to authorize the abandonment of a railroad line if the abandonment is consistent with the public interest and either in the best interest of the estate or essential to the formulation of a plan. This avoids the normal abandonment requirements of generally applicable railroad regulatory law.

Subsection (b) permits some participation by the Interstate Commerce Commission in the abandonment process. The Commission's role, however, is only advisory. The Commission will represent the public interest, while the trustee and various creditors and equity security holders will represent the interests of those who have invested money in the enterprise. The court will balance the various interests and make an appropriate decision. The subsection specifies that if, except for the pendency of the railroad reorganization case, the proposed abandonment would require Commission approval, then the trustee, with the approval of the court, must initiate an application for the abandonment with the Commission. The court may then fix a time within which the Commission must report to the court on the application.

Subsection (c) permits the court to act after it has received the report of the Commission or the time fixed under subsection (b) has expired, whichever occurs first. The court may then authorize the abandonment after notice and a hearing. The notice must go to the Commission, the Secretary of Transportation, the trustee, and party in interest that has requested notice, any affected shipper or community, and any other entity that the court specifies.

Subsection (d) stays the enforcement of an abandonment until the time for taking an appeal has expired, or if an appeal has been taken, until the order has become final. However, the court may, and after notice and a hearing, on request of a party in interest authorize termination of service on the line or a portion of the line pending the determination of the appeal. The notice required is the same as that required under subsection (c). If the court authorizes termination of service pending determination of the appeal, an appellant may not obtain a stay of the enforcement of the order authorizing termination, either by the giving of a supersedeas bond or otherwise, during the pendency of the appeal.

AMENDMENTS

2005—Subsec. (e)(1). Pub. L. 109–8 substituted "section 11326(a)" for "section 11347".

1995—Subsecs. (b), (c), (d)(2). Pub. L. 104–88 substituted "Board" for "Commission" wherever appearing.

1984—Subsec. (a). Pub. L. 98–353, §521(a), inserted "of all or a portion" after "the abandonment".

Subsec. (c). Pub. L. 98–353, §521(b), inserted a comma after "abandonment".

Subsec. (d)(2). Pub. L. 98–353, §521(c), substituted "such abandonment" for "the abandonment of a rail-road line", and "suspension" for "termination" in two places.

1980—Subsec. (e). Pub. L. 96–448 added subsec. (e).

EFFECTIVE DATE OF 2005 AMENDMENT

Amendment by Pub. L. 109–8 effective 180 days after Apr. 20, 2005, and not applicable with respect to cases commenced under this title before such effective date, except as otherwise provided, see section 1501 of Pub. L. 109–8, set out as a note under section 101 of this title.

EFFECTIVE DATE OF 1995 AMENDMENT

Amendment by Pub. L. 104–88 effective Jan. 1, 1996, see section 2 of Pub. L. 104–88, set out as an Effective Date note under section 701 of Title 49, Transportation.

EFFECTIVE DATE OF 1984 AMENDMENT

Amendment by Pub. L. 98–353 effective with respect to cases filed 90 days after July 10, 1984, see section 552(a) of Pub. L. 98–353, set out as a note under section 101 of this title.

EFFECTIVE DATE OF 1980 AMENDMENT

Section 710 of Pub. L. 96–448 provided that:

"(a) Except as provided in subsections (b), (c), and (d) of this section, the provisions of this Act and the amendments made by this Act [see Tables for classification] shall take effect on October 1, 1980.

"(b) Section 206 of this Act [enacting former section 10712 of Title 49, Transportation] shall take effect on January 1, 1981.

"(c) Section 218(b) of this Act [amending former section 10705 of Title 49] shall take effect on October 1, 1983.

"(d) Section 701 of this Act [enacting section 1018 of Title 45, Railroads, and amending sections 231f, 825, 906, 913, 914, 1002, 1005, 1007, and 1008 of Title 45] shall take effect on the date of enactment of this Act [Oct. 14, 1980]."

§ 1171. Priority claims

(a) There shall be paid as an administrative expense any claim of an individual or of the personal representative of a deceased individual against the debtor or the estate, for personal injury to or death of such individual arising out of the operation of the debtor or the estate, whether such claim arose before or after the commencement of the case.

(b) Any unsecured claim against the debtor that would have been entitled to priority if a receiver in equity of the property of the debtor had been appointed by a Federal court on the date of the order for relief under this title shall be entitled to the same priority in the case under this chapter.

(Pub. L. 95–598, Nov. 6, 1978, 92 Stat. 2643; Pub. L. 98–353, title III, §522, July 10, 1984, 98 Stat. 388.)

HISTORICAL AND REVISION NOTES

LEGISLATIVE STATEMENTS

Section 1171 of the House amendment is derived from section 1170 of the House bill in lieu of section 1173(a)(9) of the Senate amendment.

HOUSE REPORT NO. 95–595

[Section 1170] This section [enacted as section 1171] is derived from current law. Subsection (a) grants an administrative expense priority to the claim of any individual (or of the personal representative of a deceased individual) against the debtor or the estate for personal injury to or death of the individual arising out of the operation of the debtor railroad or the estate, whether the claim arose before or after commencement of the case. The priority under current law, found in section 77(n) [section 205(n) of former title 11], applies only to employees of the debtor. This subsection expands the protection provided.

Subsection (b) follows present section 77(b) of the Bankruptcy Act [section 205(b) of former title 11] by giving priority to any unsecured claims that would be entitled to priority if a receiver in equity of the property of the debtor had been appointed by a Federal court on the date of the order for relief under the bankruptcy laws. As under current law, the courts will determine the precise contours of the priority recognized by this subsection in each case.

AMENDMENTS

1984—Subsec. (b). Pub. L. 98–353 substituted "the same" for "such".

EFFECTIVE DATE OF 1984 AMENDMENT

Amendment by Pub. L. 98–353 effective with respect to cases filed 90 days after July 10, 1984, see section 552(a) of Pub. L. 98–353, set out as a note under section 101 of this title.

§ 1172. Contents of plan

(a) In addition to the provisions required or permitted under section 1123 of this title, a plan—

(1) shall specify the extent to and the means by which the debtor's rail service is proposed to be continued, and the extent to which any of the debtor's rail service is proposed to be terminated; and

(2) may include a provision for—

(A) the transfer of any or all of the operating railroad lines of the debtor to another operating railroad; or

(B) abandonment of any railroad line in accordance with section 1170 of this title.

(b) If, except for the pendency of the case under this chapter, transfer of, or operation of or over, any of the debtor's rail lines by an entity other than the debtor or a successor to the debtor under the plan would require approval by the Board under a law of the United States, then a plan may not propose such a transfer or such operation unless the proponent of the plan initiates an appropriate application for such a transfer or such operation with the Board and, within such time as the court may fix, not exceeding 180 days, the Board, with or without a hearing, as the Board may determine, and with or without modification or condition, approves such application, or does not act on such application. Any action or order of the Board approving, modifying, conditioning, or disapproving such application is subject to review by the court only under sections 706(2)(A), 706(2)(B), 706(2)(C), and 706(2)(D) of title 5.

(c)(1) In approving an application under subsection (b) of this section, the Board shall require the rail carrier to provide a fair arrangement at least as protective of the interests of employees as that established under section 11326(a) of title 49.

(2) Nothing in this subsection shall be deemed to affect the priorities or timing of payment of employee protection which might have existed in the absence of this subsection.

(Pub. L. 95-598, Nov. 6, 1978, 92 Stat. 2644; Pub. L. 96-448, title II, §227(b), Oct. 14, 1980, 94 Stat. 1931; Pub. L. 104-88, title III, §302(2), Dec. 29, 1995, 109 Stat. 943; Pub. L. 109-8, title XII, §1218, Apr. 20, 2005, 119 Stat. 195.)

HISTORICAL AND REVISION NOTES

LEGISLATIVE STATEMENTS

Section 1172 of the House amendment is derived from section 1171 of the House bill in preference to section 1170 of the Senate amendment with the exception that section 1170(4) of the Senate amendment is incorporated into section 1172(a)(1) of the House amendment.

Section 1172(b) of the House amendment is derived from section 1171(c) of the Senate amendment. The section gives the Interstate Commerce Commission the exclusive power to approve or disapprove the transfer of, or operation of or over, any of the debtor's rail lines over which the Commission has jurisdiction, subject to review under the Administrative Procedures Act [5 U.S.C. 551 et seq. and 701 et seq.]. The section does not apply to a transfer of railroad lines to a successor of the debtor under a plan of reorganization by merger or otherwise.

The House amendment deletes section 1171(a) of the Senate amendment as a matter to be determined by the Rules of Bankruptcy Procedure. It is anticipated that the rules will specify the period of time, such as 18 months, within which a trustee must file with the court a proposed plan of reorganization for the debtor or a report why a plan cannot be formulated. Incorporation by reference of section 1121 in section 1161 of title 11 means that a party in interest will also have a right to file a plan of reorganization. This differs from the position taken in the Senate amendment which would have permitted the Interstate Commerce Commission to file a plan of reorganization.

SENATE REPORT NO. 95-989

Section 1170 adds to the general provisions required or permitted in reorganization plans by section 1123. Subsection (1) requires that a reorganization plan under the railroad subchapter specify the means by which the value of the claims of creditors and the interests of equity holders which are materially and adversely affected by the plan are to be realized. Subsection (2) permits a plan to include provisions for the issuance of warrants. Subsection (3) requires that the plan provide for fixed charges by probable earnings for their payment. Subsection (4) requires that the plan specify the means by which, and the extent to which, the debtor's rail service is to be continued, and shall identify any rail service to be terminated. Subsection (5) permits other appropriate provisions not inconsistent with the chapter. With the exception of subsection (4), the requirements are comparable to those of present section 77(b) [section 205(b) of former title 11]; subsection (4) emphasizes the public interest in the preservation of rail transportation.

Section 1171 imposes on the court, rather than the Interstate Commerce Commission, as in present section 77 [section 205 of former title 11], the responsibility for the plan of reorganization. The Commission is empowered to make final decisions subject only to review by the court under the standards of the Administrative Procedure Act [5 U.S.C. 551 et seq. and 701 et seq.] as to any part of the plan which deals with transportation matters, such as the grant of operating rights of or over, or transfer of, the debtor's rail lines to other carriers.

Subsection (a) requires the trustee to file a plan of reorganization within 18 months after the petition is filed, and permits the court, for good cause shown, to extend such time limit. Subsection (b) permits a plan to be proposed by any interested person, and permits the trustee to revise his plan at any time before it is approved by the court.

Subsections (c), (d) and (e) require the court, when a plan is submitted by the trustee or, if the court deems it worthy of consideration, a plan submitted is proposed by any other person proposes the transfer of, or operation of or over, any of the debtor's lines by other carriers to refer to such provisions of the plan to the Interstate Commerce Commission. The Commission, within 240 days, and after a hearing if the Commission so determines, is to report to the court the effects of such provisions of the plan in the light of national transportation policy and sections 5(3)(f)(A), (B), and (D), (F)-(I) of the Interstate Commerce Act [49 U.S.C. 11350(b)(1), (2), (4), (6)-(9)]. The report of the Commission is conclusive in all further hearings on the plan by the court, subject only to review pursuant to 5 U.S.C. 706(2)(A)-(D).

HOUSE REPORT NO. 95-595

[Section 1171 (enacted as section 1172)] A plan in a railroad reorganization case may include provisions in addition to those required and permitted under an ordinary reorganization plan. It may provide for the transfer of any or all of the operating railroad lines of the debtor to another operating railroad.

Paragraph (1) contemplates a liquidating plan for the debtor's rail lines, much as occurred in the Penn Central case by transfer of operating lines to ConRail. Such a liquidating plan is not per se contrary to the public interest, and the court will have to determine on a case-by-case basis, with the guidance of the Interstate Commerce Commission and of other parties in interest, whether the particular plan proposed is in the public interest, as required under proposed 11 U.S.C. 1172(3).

The plan may also provide for abandonment in accordance with section 1169, governing abandonment generally. Neither of these provisions in a plan, transfer or abandonment of lines, requires ICC approval. Confirmation of the plan by the court authorizes the debtor to comply with the plan in accordance with section 1142(a) notwithstanding any bankruptcy law to the contrary.

AMENDMENTS

2005—Subsec. (c)(1). Pub. L. 109-8 substituted "section 11326(a)" for "section 11347".

1995—Subsecs. (b), (c)(1). Pub. L. 104-88 substituted "Board" for "Commission" wherever appearing.

1980—Subsec. (c). Pub. L. 96-448 added subsec. (c).

EFFECTIVE DATE OF 2005 AMENDMENT

Amendment by Pub. L. 109-8 effective 180 days after Apr. 20, 2005, and not applicable with respect to cases commenced under this title before such effective date, except as otherwise provided, see section 1501 of Pub. L. 109-8, set out as a note under section 101 of this title.

EFFECTIVE DATE OF 1995 AMENDMENT

Amendment by Pub. L. 104-88 effective Jan. 1, 1996, see section 2 of Pub. L. 104-88, set out as an Effective Date note under section 701 of Title 49, Transportation.

EFFECTIVE DATE OF 1980 AMENDMENT

Amendment by Pub. L. 96-448 effective Oct. 1, 1980, see section 710(a) of Pub. L. 96-448, set out as a note under section 1170 of this title.

NONAPPLICATION OF SUBSEC. (c)

For provision that subsec. (c) of this section does not apply to Amtrak and its employees, see section 142(d) of Pub. L. 105-134, set out in an Employee Protection Reforms note under section 24706 of Title 49, Transportation.

§ 1173. Confirmation of plan

(a) The court shall confirm a plan if—

(1) the applicable requirements of section 1129 of this title have been met;

(2) each creditor or equity security holder will receive or retain under the plan property of a value, as of the effective date of the plan, that is not less than the value of property that each such creditor or equity security holder would so receive or retain if all of the operating railroad lines of the debtor were sold, and the proceeds of such sale, and the other property of the estate, were distributed under chapter 7 of this title on such date;

(3) in light of the debtor's past earnings and the probable prospective earnings of the reorganized debtor, there will be adequate coverage by such prospective earnings of any fixed charges, such as interest on debt, amortization of funded debt, and rent for leased railroads, provided for by the plan; and

(4) the plan is consistent with the public interest.

(b) If the requirements of subsection (a) of this section are met with respect to more than one plan, the court shall confirm the plan that is most likely to maintain adequate rail service in the public interest.

(Pub. L. 95-598, Nov. 6, 1978, 92 Stat. 2644; Pub. L. 98-353, title III, § 523, July 10, 1984, 98 Stat. 388.)

HISTORICAL AND REVISION NOTES

LEGISLATIVE STATEMENTS

Section 1173 of the House amendment concerns confirmation of a plan of railroad reorganization and is derived from section 1172 of the House bill as modified. In particular, section 1173(a)(3) of the House amendment is derived from section 1170(3) of the Senate amendment. Section 1173(b) is derived from section 1173(a)(8) of the Senate amendment.

SENATE REPORT NO. 95-989

Section 1173 adapts the provisions dealing with reorganization plans generally contained in section 1130 to the particular requirements of railroad reorganization plans, as set out in present section 77(e) [section 205(e) of former title 11]. Subsection (a) specifies the findings which the court must make before approving a plan: (1) The plan complies with the applicable provisions of the chapter; (2) the proponent of the plan complies with the applicable provisions of the chapter; (3) the plan has been proposed in good faith; (4) any payments for services or for costs or expenses in connection with the case or the plan are disclosed to the court and are reasonable, or, if to be paid later, are subject to the approval of the court as reasonable; (5) the proponent of the plan has disclosed the identity and affiliations of the individuals who will serve as directors, officers, or voting trustees, such appointments or continuations in office are consistent with the interests of creditors, equity security holders, and the proponent the public, and has disclosed the identity and compensation of any insider who will be employed or retained under the plan; (6) that rate changes proposed in the plan have been approved by the appropriate regulatory commission, or that the plan is contingent on such approval; (7) that confirmation of the plan is not likely to be followed by further reorganization or liquidation, unless it is contemplated by the plan; (8) that the plan, if there is more than one, is the one most likely to maintain adequate rail service and (9) that the plan provides the priority traditionally accorded by section 77(b) [section 205(b) of former title 11] to claims by rail creditors for necessary services rendered during the 6 months preceding the filing of the petition in bankruptcy.

Subsection (b) continues the present power of the court in section 77(e) [section 205(e) of former title 11] to confirm a plan over the objections of creditors or equity security holders who are materially and adversely affected. The subsection also confirms the authority of the court to approve a transfer of all or part of a debtor's property or its merger over the objections of equity security holders if it finds (1) that the "public interest" in continued rail transportation outweighs any adverse effect on creditors and equity security holders, and (2) that the plan is fair and equitable, affords due recognition to the rights of each class, and does not discriminate unfairly against any class.

Subsection (c) permits modification of a plan confirmed by a final order only for fraud.

HOUSE REPORT NO. 95-595

[Section 1172] This section [enacted as section 1173] requires the court to confirm a plan if the applicable requirements of section 1129 (relating to confirmation of reorganization plans generally) are met, if the best interest test is met, and if the plan is compatible with the public interest.

The test in this paragraph is similar to the test prescribed for ordinary corporate reorganizations. However, since a railroad cannot liquidate its assets and sell them for scrap to satisfy its creditors, the test focuses on the value of the railroad as a going concern. That is, the test is based on what the assets, sold as operating rail lines, would bring.

The public interest requirement, found in current law, will now be decided by the court, with the ICC representing the public interest before the court, rather than in the first instance by the ICC. Liquidation of the debtor is not, per se, contrary to the public interest.

AMENDMENTS

1984—Subsec. (a)(4). Pub. L. 98-353 substituted "consistent" for "compatible".

EFFECTIVE DATE OF 1984 AMENDMENT

Amendment by Pub. L. 98-353 effective with respect to cases filed 90 days after July 10, 1984, see section

552(a) of Pub. L. 98–353, set out as a note under section 101 of this title.

§ 1174. Liquidation

On request of a party in interest and after notice and a hearing, the court may, or, if a plan has not been confirmed under section 1173 of this title before five years after the date of the order for relief, the court shall, order the trustee to cease the debtor's operation and to collect and reduce to money all of the property of the estate in the same manner as if the case were a case under chapter 7 of this title.

(Pub. L. 95–598, Nov. 6, 1978, 92 Stat. 2644.)

HISTORICAL AND REVISION NOTES

LEGISLATIVE STATEMENTS

Section 1174 of the House amendment represents a compromise between the House bill and Senate amendment on the issue of liquidation of a railroad. The provision permits a party in interest at any time to request liquidation. In addition, if a plan has not been confirmed under section 1173 of the House amendment before 5 years after the date of order for relief, the court must order the trustee to cease the debtor's operation and to collect and reduce to money all of the property of the estate in the same manner as if the case were a case under chapter 7 of title 11. The approach differs from the conversion to chapter 7 under section 1174 of the Senate bill in order to make special provisions contained in subchapter IV of chapter 11 applicable to liquidation. However, maintaining liquidation in the context of chapter 11 is not intended to delay liquidation of the railroad to a different extent than if the case were converted to chapter 7.

Although the House amendment does not adopt provisions contained in sections 1170(1), (2), (3), or (5), of the Senate amendment such provisions are contained explicitly or implicitly in section 1123 of the House amendment.

SENATE REPORT NO. 95–989

Section 1174 permits the court to convert the case to a liquidation under chapter 7 if the court finds that the debtor cannot be reorganized, or if various time limits specified in the subchapter are not met. Section 77 [section 205 of former title 11] does not authorize a liquidation of a railroad under the Bankruptcy Act [former title 11]. If the railroad is not reorganizable, the only action open to the court is to dismiss the petition, which would in all likelihood be followed by a State court receivership, with all of its attendant disadvantages. If reorganization is impossible, the debtor should be liquidated under the Bankruptcy Act.

CHAPTER 12—ADJUSTMENT OF DEBTS OF A FAMILY FARMER OR FISHERMAN WITH REGULAR ANNUAL INCOME

SUBCHAPTER I—OFFICERS, ADMINISTRATION, AND THE ESTATE

CODIFICATION

Chapter repealed effective Oct. 1, 1998, by Pub. L. 99–554, title III, §302(f), Oct. 27, 1986, 100 Stat. 3124, as amended by Pub. L. 103–65, §1, Aug. 6, 1993, 107 Stat. 311. Chapter, as in effect on Sept. 30, 1998, reenacted for the period beginning on Oct. 1, 1998, and ending on Apr. 1, 1999, by Pub. L. 105–277, div. C, title I, §149(a), Oct. 21, 1998, 112 Stat. 2681–610. Chapter reenacted for successive periods running from Mar. 31, 1999, to July 1, 2005, by Pub. L. 105–277, div. C, title I, §149(a), Oct. 21, 1998, 112 Stat. 2681–610, as successively amended by Pub. L. 106–5, Mar. 30, 1999, 113 Stat. 9; Pub. L. 106–70, Oct. 9, 1999, 113 Stat. 1031; Pub. L. 107–8, May 11, 2001, 115 Stat. 10; Pub. L. 107–17, June 26, 2001, 115 Stat. 151; Pub. L. 107–170, May 7, 2002, 116 Stat. 133; Pub. L. 107–171, title X, §10814, May 13, 2002, 116 Stat. 532; Pub. L. 107–377, §2, Dec. 19, 2002, 116 Stat. 3115; Pub. L. 108–73, §2, Aug. 15, 2003, 117 Stat. 891; Pub. L. 108–369, §2, Oct. 25, 2004, 118 Stat. 1749. Chapter, as in effect on June 30, 2005, permanently reenacted effective July 1, 2005, by Pub. L. 109–8, title X, §1001(a), Apr. 20, 2005, 119 Stat. 185. See Repeal, Reenactment, and Termination of Chapter notes and Effective Date notes set out under section 1201 of this title.

AMENDMENTS

2005—Pub. L. 109–8, title X, §1007(c)(1), Apr. 20, 2005, 119 Stat. 188, inserted "OR FISHERMAN" after "FAMILY FARMER" in chapter heading.

SUBCHAPTER I—OFFICERS, ADMINISTRATION, AND THE ESTATE

§ 1201. Stay of action against codebtor

(a) Except as provided in subsections (b) and (c) of this section, after the order for relief under this chapter, a creditor may not act, or commence or continue any civil action, to collect all or any part of a consumer debt of the debtor from any individual that is liable on such debt with the debtor, or that secured such debt, unless—

(1) such individual became liable on or secured such debt in the ordinary course of such individual's business; or

(2) the case is closed, dismissed, or converted to a case under chapter 7 of this title.

(b) A creditor may present a negotiable instrument, and may give notice of dishonor of such an instrument.

(c) On request of a party in interest and after notice and a hearing, the court shall grant relief from the stay provided by subsection (a) of this section with respect to a creditor, to the extent that—

(1) as between the debtor and the individual protected under subsection (a) of this section, such individual received the consideration for the claim held by such creditor;

(2) the plan filed by the debtor proposes not to pay such claim; or

(3) such creditor's interest would be irreparably harmed by continuation of such stay.

(d) Twenty days after the filing of a request under subsection (c)(2) of this section for relief from the stay provided by subsection (a) of this section, such stay is terminated with respect to the party in interest making such request, unless the debtor or any individual that is liable on such debt with the debtor files and serves upon such party in interest a written objection to the taking of the proposed action.

(Added and amended Pub. L. 99–554, title II, §255, title III, §302(f), Oct. 27, 1986, 100 Stat. 3105, 3124; Pub. L. 103–65, §1, Aug. 6, 1993, 107 Stat. 311; Pub. L. 105–277, div. C, title I, §149(a), Oct. 21, 1998, 112 Stat. 2681–610; Pub. L. 106–5, §1(1), (2), Mar. 30, 1999, 113 Stat. 9; Pub. L. 106–70, §1, Oct. 9, 1999, 113 Stat. 1031; Pub. L. 107–8, §1, May 11, 2001, 115 Stat. 10; Pub. L. 107–17, §1, June 26, 2001, 115 Stat. 151; Pub. L. 107–170, §1, May 7, 2002, 116 Stat. 133; Pub. L. 107–171, title X, §10814(a), May 13, 2002, 116 Stat. 532; Pub. L. 107–377, §2(a), Dec. 19, 2002, 116 Stat. 3115; Pub. L. 108–73, §2(a), Aug. 15, 2003, 117 Stat. 891; Pub. L. 108–369, §2(a), Oct. 25, 2004, 118 Stat. 1749; Pub. L. 109–8, title X, §1001(a)(1), (c), Apr. 20, 2005, 119 Stat. 185, 186.)

CODIFICATION

For repeal of section effective Oct. 1, 1998, and subsequent reenactment of section, see note set out preceding this section.

EFFECTIVE DATE OF 2004 AMENDMENT

Pub. L. 108–369, §2(b), Oct. 25, 2004, 118 Stat. 1749, provided that: "The amendments made by subsection (a) [amending this section and sections 1202 to 1208 and 1221 to 1231 of this title and amending provisions set out as a note under this section] are deemed to have taken effect on January 1, 2004."

EFFECTIVE DATE OF 2003 AMENDMENT

Pub. L. 108–73, §2(b), Aug. 15, 2003, 117 Stat. 891, provided that: "The amendments made by subsection (a) [amending this section and sections 1202 to 1208 and 1221 to 1231 of this title and amending provisions set out as a note under this section] take effect on July 1, 2003."

EFFECTIVE DATE OF 2002 AMENDMENTS

Pub. L. 107–377, §2(b), Dec. 19, 2002, 116 Stat. 3115, provided that: "The amendments made by subsection (a) [amending this section and sections 1202 to 1208 and 1221 to 1231 of this title and amending provisions set out as a note under this section] shall take effect on January 1, 2003."

Pub. L. 107–171, title X, §10814(b), May 13, 2002, 116 Stat. 532, provided that: "The amendments made by subsection (a) [amending this section and sections 1202 to 1208 and 1221 to 1231 of this title and amending provisions set out as a note under this section] shall take effect on June 1, 2002."

Pub. L. 107–170, §2, May 7, 2002, 116 Stat. 133, provided that: "The amendments made by section 1 [amending this section and sections 1202 to 1208 and 1221 to 1231 of this title and amending provisions set out as a note under this section] shall take effect on October 1, 2001."

EFFECTIVE DATE OF 2001 AMENDMENTS

Pub. L. 107–17, §2, June 26, 2001, 115 Stat. 151, provided that: "The amendments made by section 1 [amending this section and sections 1202 to 1208 and 1221 to 1231 of this title and amending provisions set out as a note under this section] shall take effect on June 1, 2001."

Pub. L. 107–8, §2, May 11, 2001, 115 Stat. 10, provided that: "The amendments made by section 1 [amending this section and sections 1202 to 1208 and 1221 to 1231 of this title and amending provisions set out as a note under this section] shall take effect on July 1, 2000."

EFFECTIVE DATE OF 1999 AMENDMENTS

Pub. L. 106–70, §2, Oct. 9, 1999, 113 Stat. 1031, provided that: "The amendments made by section 1 [amending this section and sections 1202 to 1208 and 1221 to 1231 of this title and amending provisions set out as a note under this section] shall take effect on October 1, 1999."

Pub. L. 106–5, §2, Mar. 30, 1999, 113 Stat. 9, provided that: "The amendments made by section 1 [amending this section and sections 1202 to 1208 and 1221 to 1231 of this title and amending provisions set out as a note under this section] shall take effect on April 1, 1999."

EFFECTIVE DATE

Chapter effective 30 days after Oct. 27, 1986, but not applicable to cases commenced under this title before that date, see section 302(a), (c)(1) of Pub. L. 99–554, set out as a note under section 581 of Title 28, Judiciary and Judicial Procedure.

REPEAL, REENACTMENT, AND TERMINATION OF CHAPTER

Pub. L. 109–8, title X, §1001(a), (b), Apr. 20, 2005, 119 Stat. 185, 186, provided that:

"(a) REENACTMENT.—

"(1) IN GENERAL.—Chapter 12 of title 11, United States Code, as reenacted by section 149 of division C of the Omnibus Consolidated and Emergency Supplemental Appropriations Act, 1999 (Public Law 105–277) [set out as a note below], and as in effect on June 30, 2005, is hereby reenacted.

"(2) EFFECTIVE DATE OF REENACTMENT.—Paragraph (1) shall take effect on July 1, 2005.

"(b) AMENDMENTS—Chapter 12 of title 11, United States Code, as reenacted by subsection (a), is amended by this Act [see Tables for classification]."

Pub. L. 105–277, div. C, title I, §149, Oct. 21, 1998, 112 Stat. 2681–610, as amended by Pub. L. 106–5, §1, Mar. 30, 1999, 113 Stat. 9; Pub. L. 106–70, §1, Oct. 9, 1999, 113 Stat. 1031; Pub. L. 107–8, §1, May 11, 2001, 115 Stat. 10; Pub. L. 107–17, §1, June 26, 2001, 115 Stat. 151; Pub. L. 107–170, §1, May 7, 2002, 116 Stat. 133; Pub. L. 107–171, title X, §10814(a), May 13, 2002, 116 Stat. 532; Pub. L. 107–377, §2(a), Dec. 19, 2002, 116 Stat. 3115; Pub. L. 108–73, §2(a), Aug. 15, 2003, 117 Stat. 891; Pub. L. 108–369, §2(a), Oct. 25, 2004, 118 Stat. 1749, provided that:

"(a) Chapter 12 of title 11 of the United States Code, as in effect on December 31, 2003, is hereby reenacted for the period beginning on January 1, 2004, and ending on July 1, 2005.

"(b) All cases commenced or pending under chapter 12 of title 11, United States Code, as reenacted under subsection (a), and all matters and proceedings in or relating to such cases, shall be conducted and determined under such chapter as if such chapter were continued in effect after July 1, 2005. The substantive rights of parties in connection with such cases, matters, and proceedings shall continue to be governed under the laws applicable to such cases, matters, and proceedings as if such chapter were continued in effect after July 1, 2005."

Chapter was repealed Oct. 1, 1998, except that cases commenced or pending under this chapter, and all matters and proceedings in or relating to such cases, were to be conducted and determined as if this chapter had not been repealed, and substantive rights of parties in connection with such cases, matters, and proceedings were to continue to be governed under the laws applicable to such cases, matters, and proceedings as if this chapter had not been repealed, see section 302(f) of Pub. L. 99–554, as amended, formerly set out in an Effective Date of 1986 Amendment note under section 581 of Title 28, Judiciary and Judicial Procedure.

§ 1202. Trustee

(a) If the United States trustee has appointed an individual under section 586(b) of title 28 to serve as standing trustee in cases under this chapter and if such individual qualifies as a trustee under section 322 of this title, then such individual shall serve as trustee in any case filed under this chapter. Otherwise, the United States trustee shall appoint one disinterested person to serve as trustee in the case or the United States trustee may serve as trustee in the case if necessary.

(b) The trustee shall—

(1) perform the duties specified in sections 704(2), 704(3), 704(5), 704(6), 704(7), and 704(9) of this title;

(2) perform the duties specified in section 1106(a)(3) and 1106(a)(4) of this title if the court, for cause and on request of a party in interest, the trustee, or the United States trustee, so orders;

(3) appear and be heard at any hearing that concerns—

(A) the value of property subject to a lien;

(B) confirmation of a plan;

(C) modification of the plan after confirmation; or

(D) the sale of property of the estate;

(4) ensure that the debtor commences making timely payments required by a confirmed plan;

(5) if the debtor ceases to be a debtor in possession, perform the duties specified in sections 704(8), 1106(a)(1), 1106(a)(2), 1106(a)(6), 1106(a)(7), and 1203; and

(6) if with respect to the debtor there is a claim for a domestic support obligation, provide the applicable notice specified in subsection (c).

(c)(1) In a case described in subsection (b)(6) to which subsection (b)(6) applies, the trustee shall—

(A)(i) provide written notice to the holder of the claim described in subsection (b)(6) of such claim and of the right of such holder to use the services of the State child support enforcement agency established under sections 464 and 466 of the Social Security Act for the State in which such holder resides, for assistance in collecting child support during and after the case under this title; and

(ii) include in the notice provided under clause (i) the address and telephone number of such State child support enforcement agency;

(B)(i) provide written notice to such State child support enforcement agency of such claim; and

(ii) include in the notice provided under clause (i) the name, address, and telephone number of such holder; and

(C) at such time as the debtor is granted a discharge under section 1228, provide written notice to such holder and to such State child support enforcement agency of—

(i) the granting of the discharge;

(ii) the last recent known address of the debtor;

(iii) the last recent known name and address of the debtor's employer; and

(iv) the name of each creditor that holds a claim that—

(I) is not discharged under paragraph (2), (4), or (14A) of section 523(a); or

(II) was reaffirmed by the debtor under section 524(c).

(2)(A) The holder of a claim described in subsection (b)(6) or the State child support enforcement agency of the State in which such holder resides may request from a creditor described in paragraph (1)(C)(iv) the last known address of the debtor.

(B) Notwithstanding any other provision of law, a creditor that makes a disclosure of a last known address of a debtor in connection with a request made under subparagraph (A) shall not be liable by reason of making that disclosure.

(Added and amended Pub. L. 99–554, title II, §§227, 255, title III, §302(f), Oct. 27, 1986, 100 Stat. 3103, 3106, 3124; Pub. L. 103–65, §1, Aug. 6, 1993, 107 Stat. 311; Pub. L. 105–277, div. C, title I, §149(a), Oct. 21, 1998, 112 Stat. 2681–610; Pub. L. 106–5, §1(1), (2), Mar. 30, 1999, 113 Stat. 9; Pub. L. 106–70, §1, Oct. 9, 1999, 113 Stat. 1031; Pub. L. 107–8, §1, May 11, 2001, 115 Stat. 10; Pub. L. 107–17, §1, June 26, 2001, 115 Stat. 151; Pub. L. 107–170, §1, May 7, 2002, 116 Stat. 133; Pub. L. 107–171, title X, §10814(a), May 13, 2002, 116 Stat. 532; Pub. L. 107–377, §2(a), Dec. 19, 2002, 116 Stat. 3115; Pub. L. 108–73, §2(a), Aug. 15, 2003, 117 Stat. 891; Pub. L. 108–369, §2(a), Oct. 25, 2004, 118 Stat. 1749; Pub. L. 109–8, title II, §219(c), title X, §1001(a)(1), (c), Apr. 20, 2005, 119 Stat. 57, 185, 186.)

REFERENCES IN TEXT

Sections 464 and 466 of the Social Security Act, referred to in subsec. (c)(1)(A)(i), are classified to sections 664 and 666, respectively, of Title 42, The Public Health and Welfare.

CODIFICATION

For repeal of section effective Oct. 1, 1998, and subsequent reenactment of section, see note set out preceding section 1201 of this title.

AMENDMENTS

2005—Subsec. (b)(6). Pub. L. 109–8, §219(c)(1), added par. (6).

Subsec. (c). Pub. L. 109–8, §219(c)(2), added subsec. (c).

1986—Subsecs. (c), (d). Pub. L. 99–554, §227, struck out subsecs. (c) and (d) which read as follows:

"(c) If the number of cases under this chapter commenced in a particular judicial district so warrants, the court may appoint one or more individuals to serve as standing trustee for such district in cases under this chapter.

"(d)(1) A court that has appointed an individual under subsection (a) of this section to serve as standing trustee in cases under this chapter shall set for such individual—

"(A) a maximum annual compensation not to exceed the lowest annual rate of basic pay in effect for grade GS–16 of the General Schedule prescribed under section 5332 of title 5; and

"(B) a percentage fee not to exceed the sum of—

"(i) not to exceed ten percent of the payments made under the plan of such debtor, with respect to payments in an aggregate amount not to exceed $450,000; and

"(ii) three percent of payments made under the plan of such debtor, with respect to payments made after the aggregate amount of payments made under the plan exceeds $450,000;

based on such maximum annual compensation and the actual, necessary expenses incurred by such individual as standing trustee.

"(2) Such individual shall collect such percentage fee from all payments under plans in the cases under this chapter for which such individual serves as standing trustee. Such individual shall pay annually to the Treasury—

"(A) any amount by which the actual compensation received by such individual exceeds five percent of all such payments made under plans in cases under this chapter for which such individual serves as standing trustee; and

"(B) any amount by which the percentage fee fixed under paragraph (1)(B) of this subsection for all such cases exceeds—

"(i) such individual's actual compensation for such cases, as adjusted under subparagraph (A) of this paragraph; plus

"(ii) the actual, necessary expenses incurred by such individual as standing trustee in such cases."

See section 586(b) and (e) of Title 28, Judiciary and Judicial Procedure.

EFFECTIVE DATE OF 2005 AMENDMENT

Amendment by section 219(c) of Pub. L. 109–8 effective 180 days after Apr. 20, 2005, and not applicable with respect to cases commenced under this title before such effective date, except as otherwise provided, see section 1501 of Pub. L. 109–8, set out as a note under section 101 of this title.

EFFECTIVE DATE

Section effective 30 days after Oct. 27, 1986, and before the amendment by section 227 of Pub. L. 99–554, see section 302(c)(2) of Pub. L. 99–554, set out as an Effective Date of 1986 Amendment note under section 581 of Title 28, Judiciary and Judicial Procedure.

Effective date and applicability of amendment by section 227 of Pub. L. 99–554 dependent upon the judicial district involved, see section 302(d), (e) of Pub. L. 99–554.

REFERENCES IN SUBSECTION (a) TEMPORARILY DEEMED TO BE REFERENCES TO OTHER PROVISIONS

Until the amendments made by subtitle A (§§201 to 231) of title II of Pub. L. 99–554 become effective in a district and apply to a case, in subsec. (a) of this section—

(1) the first two references to the United States trustee are deemed to be references to the court, and

(2) any reference to section 586(b) of Title 28, Judiciary and Judicial Procedure, is deemed to be a reference to subsec. (c) of this section,

see section 302(c)(3)(B), (d), (e) of Pub. L. 99–554, set out as an Effective Date note under section 581 of Title 28.

§ 1203. Rights and powers of debtor

Subject to such limitations as the court may prescribe, a debtor in possession shall have all the rights, other than the right to compensation under section 330, and powers, and shall perform all the functions and duties, except the duties specified in paragraphs (3) and (4) of section 1106(a), of a trustee serving in a case under chapter 11, including operating the debtor's farm or commercial fishing operation.

(Added and amended Pub. L. 99–554, title II, §255, title III, §302(f), Oct. 27, 1986, 100 Stat. 3107, 3124; Pub. L. 103–65, §1, Aug. 6, 1993, 107 Stat. 311; Pub. L. 105–277, div. C, title I, §149(a), Oct. 21, 1998, 112 Stat. 2681–610; Pub. L. 106–5, §1(1), (2), Mar. 30, 1999, 113 Stat. 9; Pub. L. 106–70, §1, Oct. 9, 1999, 113 Stat. 1031; Pub. L. 107–8, §1, May 11, 2001, 115 Stat. 10; Pub. L. 107–17, §1, June 26, 2001, 115 Stat. 151; Pub. L. 107–170, §1, May 7, 2002, 116 Stat. 133; Pub. L. 107–171, title X, §10814(a), May 13, 2002, 116 Stat. 532; Pub. L. 107–377, §2(a), Dec. 19, 2002, 116 Stat. 3115; Pub. L. 108–73, §2(a), Aug. 15, 2003, 117 Stat. 891; Pub. L. 108–369, §2(a), Oct. 25, 2004, 118 Stat. 1749; Pub. L. 109–8, title X, §§1001(a)(1), (c), 1007(c)(2), Apr. 20, 2005, 119 Stat. 185, 186, 188.)

CODIFICATION

For repeal of section effective Oct. 1, 1998, and subsequent reenactment of section, see note set out preceding section 1201 of this title.

AMENDMENTS

2005—Pub. L. 109–8, §1007(c)(2), inserted "or commercial fishing operation" after "farm".

EFFECTIVE DATE OF 2005 AMENDMENT

Amendment by section 1007(c)(2) of Pub. L. 109–8 effective 180 days after Apr. 20, 2005, and not applicable with respect to cases commenced under this title before such effective date, except as otherwise provided, see section 1501 of Pub. L. 109–8, set out as a note under section 101 of this title.

§ 1204. Removal of debtor as debtor in possession

(a) On request of a party in interest, and after notice and a hearing, the court shall order that the debtor shall not be a debtor in possession for cause, including fraud, dishonesty, incompetence, or gross mismanagement of the affairs of the debtor, either before or after the commencement of the case.

(b) On request of a party in interest, and after notice and a hearing, the court may reinstate the debtor in possession.

(Added and amended Pub. L. 99–554, title II, §255, title III, §302(f), Oct. 27, 1986, 100 Stat. 3107, 3124; Pub. L. 103–65, §1, Aug. 6, 1993, 107 Stat. 311; Pub. L. 105–277, div. C, title I, §149(a), Oct. 21, 1998, 112 Stat. 2681–610; Pub. L. 106–5, §1(1), (2), Mar. 30, 1999, 113 Stat. 9; Pub. L. 106–70, §1, Oct. 9, 1999, 113 Stat. 1031; Pub. L. 107–8, §1, May 11, 2001, 115 Stat. 10; Pub. L. 107–17, §1, June 26, 2001, 115 Stat. 151; Pub. L. 107–170, §1, May 7, 2002, 116 Stat. 133; Pub. L. 107–171, title X, §10814(a), May 13, 2002, 116 Stat. 532; Pub. L. 107–377, §2(a), Dec. 19, 2002, 116 Stat. 3115; Pub. L. 108–73, §2(a), Aug. 15, 2003, 117 Stat. 891; Pub. L. 108–369, §2(a), Oct. 25, 2004, 118 Stat. 1749; Pub. L. 109–8, title X, §1001(a)(1), (c), Apr. 20, 2005, 119 Stat. 185, 186.)

CODIFICATION

For repeal of section effective Oct. 1, 1998, and subsequent reenactment of section, see note set out preceding section 1201 of this title.

§ 1205. Adequate protection

(a) Section 361 does not apply in a case under this chapter.

(b) In a case under this chapter, when adequate protection is required under section 362, 363, or 364 of this title of an interest of an entity in property, such adequate protection may be provided by—

(1) requiring the trustee to make a cash payment or periodic cash payments to such entity, to the extent that the stay under section 362 of this title, use, sale, or lease under section 363 of this title, or any grant of a lien under section 364 of this title results in a decrease in the value of property securing a claim or of an entity's ownership interest in property;

(2) providing to such entity an additional or replacement lien to the extent that such stay, use, sale, lease, or grant results in a decrease in the value of property securing a claim or of an entity's ownership interest in property;

(3) paying to such entity for the use of farmland the reasonable rent customary in the community where the property is located, based upon the rental value, net income, and earning capacity of the property; or

(4) granting such other relief, other than entitling such entity to compensation allowable under section 503(b)(1) of this title as an administrative expense, as will adequately protect the value of property securing a claim or of such entity's ownership interest in property.

(Added and amended Pub. L. 99–554, title II, §255, title III, §302(f), Oct. 27, 1986, 100 Stat. 3107, 3124; Pub. L. 103–65, §1, Aug. 6, 1993, 107 Stat. 311; Pub. L. 105–277, div. C, title I, §149(a), Oct. 21, 1998, 112 Stat. 2681–610; Pub. L. 106–5, §1(1), (2), Mar. 30, 1999, 113 Stat. 9; Pub. L. 106–70, §1, Oct. 9, 1999, 113 Stat. 1031; Pub. L. 107–8, §1, May 11, 2001, 115 Stat. 10; Pub. L. 107–17, §1, June 26, 2001, 115 Stat. 151; Pub. L. 107–170, §1, May 7, 2002, 116 Stat. 133; Pub. L. 107–171, title X, §10814(a), May 13, 2002, 116 Stat. 532; Pub. L. 107–377, §2(a), Dec. 19, 2002, 116 Stat. 3115; Pub. L. 108–73, §2(a), Aug. 15, 2003, 117 Stat. 891; Pub. L. 108–369, §2(a), Oct. 25, 2004, 118 Stat. 1749; Pub. L. 109–8, title X, §1001(a)(1), (c), Apr. 20, 2005, 119 Stat. 185, 186.)

CODIFICATION

For repeal of section effective Oct. 1, 1998, and subsequent reenactment of section, see note set out preceding section 1201 of this title.

§1206. Sales free of interests

After notice and a hearing, in addition to the authorization contained in section 363(f), the trustee in a case under this chapter may sell property under section 363(b) and (c) free and clear of any interest in such property of an entity other than the estate if the property is farmland, farm equipment, or property used to carry out a commercial fishing operation (including a commercial fishing vessel), except that the proceeds of such sale shall be subject to such interest.

(Added and amended Pub. L. 99–554, title II, §255, title III, §302(f), Oct. 27, 1986, 100 Stat. 3108, 3124; Pub. L. 103–65, §1, Aug. 6, 1993, 107 Stat. 311; Pub. L. 105–277, div. C, title I, §149(a), Oct. 21, 1998, 112 Stat. 2681–610; Pub. L. 106–5, §1(1), (2), Mar. 30, 1999, 113 Stat. 9; Pub. L. 106–70, §1, Oct. 9, 1999, 113 Stat. 1031; Pub. L. 107–8, §1, May 11, 2001, 115 Stat. 10; Pub. L. 107–17, §1, June 26, 2001, 115 Stat. 151; Pub. L. 107–170, §1, May 7, 2002, 116 Stat. 133; Pub. L. 107–171, title X, §10814(a), May 13, 2002, 116 Stat. 532; Pub. L. 107–377, §2(a), Dec. 19, 2002, 116 Stat. 3115; Pub. L. 108–73, §2(a), Aug. 15, 2003, 117 Stat. 891; Pub. L. 108–369, §2(a), Oct. 25, 2004, 118 Stat. 1749; Pub. L. 109–8, title X, §§1001(a)(1), (c), 1007(c)(3), Apr. 20, 2005, 119 Stat. 185, 186, 188.)

CODIFICATION

For repeal of section effective Oct. 1, 1998, and subsequent reenactment of section, see note set out preceding section 1201 of this title.

AMENDMENTS

2005—Pub. L. 109–8, §1007(c)(3), substituted "if the property is farmland, farm equipment, or property used to carry out a commercial fishing operation (including a commercial fishing vessel)" for "if the property is farmland or farm equipment".

EFFECTIVE DATE OF 2005 AMENDMENT

Amendment by section 1007(c)(3) of Pub. L. 109–8 effective 180 days after Apr. 20, 2005, and not applicable with respect to cases commenced under this title before such effective date, except as otherwise provided, see section 1501 of Pub. L. 109–8, set out as a note under section 101 of this title.

§1207. Property of the estate

(a) Property of the estate includes, in addition to the property specified in section 541 of this title—

(1) all property of the kind specified in such section that the debtor acquires after the commencement of the case but before the case is closed, dismissed, or converted to a case under chapter 7 of this title, whichever occurs first; and

(2) earnings from services performed by the debtor after the commencement of the case but before the case is closed, dismissed, or converted to a case under chapter 7 of this title, whichever occurs first.

(b) Except as provided in section 1204, a confirmed plan, or an order confirming a plan, the debtor shall remain in possession of all property of the estate.

(Added and amended Pub. L. 99–554, title II, §255, title III, §302(f), Oct. 27, 1986, 100 Stat. 3108, 3124; Pub. L. 103–65, §1, Aug. 6, 1993, 107 Stat. 311; Pub. L. 105–277, div. C, title I, §149(a), Oct. 21, 1998, 112 Stat. 2681–610; Pub. L. 106–5, §1(1), (2), Mar. 30, 1999, 113 Stat. 9; Pub. L. 106–70, §1, Oct. 9, 1999, 113 Stat. 1031; Pub. L. 107–8, §1, May 11, 2001, 115 Stat. 10; Pub. L. 107–17, §1, June 26, 2001, 115 Stat. 151; Pub. L. 107–170, §1, May 7, 2002, 116 Stat. 133; Pub. L. 107–171, title X, §10814(a), May 13, 2002, 116 Stat. 532; Pub. L. 107–377, §2(a), Dec. 19, 2002, 116 Stat. 3115; Pub. L. 108–73, §2(a), Aug. 15, 2003, 117 Stat. 891; Pub. L. 108–369, §2(a), Oct. 25, 2004, 118 Stat. 1749; Pub. L. 109–8, title X, §1001(a)(1), (c), Apr. 20, 2005, 119 Stat. 185, 186.)

CODIFICATION

For repeal of section effective Oct. 1, 1998, and subsequent reenactment of section, see note set out preceding section 1201 of this title.

§1208. Conversion or dismissal

(a) The debtor may convert a case under this chapter to a case under chapter 7 of this title at any time. Any waiver of the right to convert under this subsection is unenforceable.

(b) On request of the debtor at any time, if the case has not been converted under section 706 or 1112 of this title, the court shall dismiss a case under this chapter. Any waiver of the right to dismiss under this subsection is unenforceable.

(c) On request of a party in interest, and after notice and a hearing, the court may dismiss a case under this chapter for cause, including—

(1) unreasonable delay, or gross mismanagement, by the debtor that is prejudicial to creditors;

(2) nonpayment of any fees and charges required under chapter 123 of title 28;

(3) failure to file a plan timely under section 1221 of this title;

(4) failure to commence making timely payments required by a confirmed plan;

(5) denial of confirmation of a plan under section 1225 of this title and denial of a request made for additional time for filing another plan or a modification of a plan;

(6) material default by the debtor with respect to a term of a confirmed plan;

(7) revocation of the order of confirmation under section 1230 of this title, and denial of confirmation of a modified plan under section 1229 of this title;

(8) termination of a confirmed plan by reason of the occurrence of a condition specified in the plan;

(9) continuing loss to or diminution of the estate and absence of a reasonable likelihood of rehabilitation; and

(10) failure of the debtor to pay any domestic support obligation that first becomes payable after the date of the filing of the petition.

(d) On request of a party in interest, and after notice and a hearing, the court may dismiss a case under this chapter or convert a case under this chapter to a case under chapter 7 of this title upon a showing that the debtor has committed fraud in connection with the case.

(e) Notwithstanding any other provision of this section, a case may not be converted to a case under another chapter of this title unless the debtor may be a debtor under such chapter.

(Added and amended Pub. L. 99–554, title II, §255, title III, §302(f), Oct. 27, 1986, 100 Stat. 3108, 3124; Pub. L. 103–65, §1, Aug. 6, 1993, 107 Stat. 311; Pub. L. 105–277, div. C, title I, §149(a), Oct. 21, 1998, 112 Stat. 2681–610; Pub. L. 106–5, §1(1), (2), Mar. 30, 1999, 113 Stat. 9; Pub. L. 106–70, §1, Oct. 9, 1999, 113 Stat. 1031; Pub. L. 107–8, §1, May 11, 2001, 115 Stat. 10; Pub. L. 107–17, §1, June 26, 2001, 115 Stat. 151; Pub. L. 107–170, §1, May 7, 2002, 116 Stat. 133; Pub. L. 107–171, title X, §10814(a), May 13, 2002, 116 Stat. 532; Pub. L. 107–377, §2(a), Dec. 19, 2002, 116 Stat. 3115; Pub. L. 108–73, §2(a), Aug. 15, 2003, 117 Stat. 891; Pub. L. 108–369, §2(a), Oct. 25, 2004, 118 Stat. 1749; Pub. L. 109–8, title II, §213(2), title X, §1001(a)(1), (c), Apr. 20, 2005, 119 Stat. 52, 185, 186.)

CODIFICATION

For repeal of section effective Oct. 1, 1998, and subsequent reenactment of section, see note set out preceding section 1201 of this title.

AMENDMENTS

2005—Subsec. (c)(10). Pub. L. 109–8, §213(2), added par. (10).

EFFECTIVE DATE OF 2005 AMENDMENT

Amendment by section 213(2) of Pub. L. 109–8 effective 180 days after Apr. 20, 2005, and not applicable with respect to cases commenced under this title before such effective date, except as otherwise provided, see section 1501 of Pub. L. 109–8, set out as a note under section 101 of this title.

SUBCHAPTER II—THE PLAN

§1221. Filing of plan

The debtor shall file a plan not later than 90 days after the order for relief under this chapter, except that the court may extend such period if the need for an extension is attributable to circumstances for which the debtor should not justly be held accountable.

(Added and amended Pub. L. 99–554, title II, §255, title III, §302(f), Oct. 27, 1986, 100 Stat. 3109, 3124; Pub. L. 103–65, §§1, 2, Aug. 6, 1993, 107 Stat. 311; Pub. L. 105–277, div. C, title I, §149(a), Oct. 21, 1998, 112 Stat. 2681–610; Pub. L. 106–5, §1(1), (2), Mar. 30, 1999, 113 Stat. 9; Pub. L. 106–70, §1, Oct. 9, 1999, 113 Stat. 1031; Pub. L. 107–8, §1, May 11, 2001, 115 Stat. 10; Pub. L. 107–17, §1, June 26, 2001, 115 Stat. 151; Pub. L. 107–170, §1, May 7, 2002, 116 Stat. 133; Pub. L. 107–171, title X, §10814(a), May 13, 2002, 116 Stat. 532; Pub. L. 107–377, §2(a), Dec. 19, 2002, 116 Stat. 3115; Pub. L. 108–73, §2(a), Aug. 15, 2003, 117 Stat. 891; Pub. L. 108–369, §2(a), Oct. 25, 2004, 118 Stat. 1749; Pub. L. 109–8, title X, §1001(a)(1), (c), Apr. 20, 2005, 119 Stat. 185, 186.)

CODIFICATION

For repeal of section effective Oct. 1, 1998, and subsequent reenactment of section, see note set out preceding section 1201 of this title.

AMENDMENTS

1993—Pub. L. 103–65 substituted "the need for an extension is attributable to circumstances for which the debtor should not justly be held accountable" for "an extension is substantially justified".

EFFECTIVE DATE OF 1993 AMENDMENT

Section 3 of Pub. L. 103–65 provided that:

"(a) EFFECTIVE DATE.—Except as provided in subsection (b), this Act [amending this section and provisions set out as a note under section 581 of Title 28, Judiciary and Judicial Procedure] and the amendments made by this Act shall take effect on the date of the enactment of this Act [Aug. 6, 1993].

"(b) APPLICATION OF AMENDMENT MADE BY SECTION 2.—The amendment made by section 2 [amending this section] shall not apply with respect to cases commenced under title 11 of the United States Code before the date of the enactment of this Act."

§1222. Contents of plan

(a) The plan shall—

(1) provide for the submission of all or such portion of future earnings or other future income of the debtor to the supervision and control of the trustee as is necessary for the execution of the plan;

(2) provide for the full payment, in deferred cash payments, of all claims entitled to priority under section 507, unless—

(A) the claim is a claim owed to a governmental unit that arises as a result of the sale, transfer, exchange, or other disposition of any farm asset used in the debtor's farming operation, in which case the claim shall be treated as an unsecured claim that is not entitled to priority under section 507, but the debt shall be treated in such manner only if the debtor receives a discharge; or

(B) the holder of a particular claim agrees to a different treatment of that claim;

(3) if the plan classifies claims and interests, provide the same treatment for each claim or interest within a particular class unless the holder of a particular claim or interest agrees to less favorable treatment; and

(4) notwithstanding any other provision of this section, a plan may provide for less than full payment of all amounts owed for a claim entitled to priority under section 507(a)(1)(B) only if the plan provides that all of the debtor's projected disposable income for a 5-year period beginning on the date that the first payment is due under the plan will be applied to make payments under the plan.

(b) Subject to subsections (a) and (c) of this section, the plan may—

(1) designate a class or classes of unsecured claims, as provided in section 1122 of this title, but may not discriminate unfairly against any class so designated; however, such plan may treat claims for a consumer debt of the debtor if an individual is liable on such consumer debt with the debtor differently than other unsecured claims;

(2) modify the rights of holders of secured claims, or of holders of unsecured claims, or leave unaffected the rights of holders of any class of claims;

(3) provide for the curing or waiving of any default;

(4) provide for payments on any unsecured claim to be made concurrently with payments on any secured claim or any other unsecured claim;

(5) provide for the curing of any default within a reasonable time and maintenance of payments while the case is pending on any unsecured claim or secured claim on which the last payment is due after the date on which the final payment under the plan is due;

(6) subject to section 365 of this title, provide for the assumption, rejection, or assignment of any executory contract or unexpired lease of the debtor not previously rejected under such section;

(7) provide for the payment of all or part of a claim against the debtor from property of the estate or property of the debtor;

(8) provide for the sale of all or any part of the property of the estate or the distribution of all or any part of the property of the estate among those having an interest in such property;

(9) provide for payment of allowed secured claims consistent with section 1225(a)(5) of this title, over a period exceeding the period permitted under section 1222(c);

(10) provide for the vesting of property of the estate, on confirmation of the plan or at a later time, in the debtor or in any other entity;

(11) provide for the payment of interest accruing after the date of the filing of the petition on unsecured claims that are nondischargeable under section 1228(a), except that such interest may be paid only to the extent that the debtor has disposable income available to pay such interest after making provision for full payment of all allowed claims; and

(12) include any other appropriate provision not inconsistent with this title.

(c) Except as provided in subsections (b)(5) and (b)(9), the plan may not provide for payments over a period that is longer than three years unless the court for cause approves a longer period, but the court may not approve a period that is longer than five years.

(d) Notwithstanding subsection (b)(2) of this section and sections 506(b) and 1225(a)(5) of this title, if it is proposed in a plan to cure a default, the amount necessary to cure the default, shall be determined in accordance with the underlying agreement and applicable nonbankruptcy law.

(Added and amended Pub. L. 99–554, title II, §255, title III, §302(f), Oct. 27, 1986, 100 Stat. 3109, 3124; Pub. L. 103–65, §1, Aug. 6, 1993, 107 Stat. 311; Pub. L. 103–394, title III, §305(b), Oct. 22, 1994, 108 Stat. 4134; Pub. L. 105–277, div. C, title I, §149(a), Oct. 21, 1998, 112 Stat. 2681–610; Pub. L. 106–5, §1(1), (2), Mar. 30, 1999, 113 Stat. 9; Pub. L. 106–70, §1, Oct. 9, 1999, 113 Stat. 1031; Pub. L. 107–8, §1, May 11, 2001, 115 Stat. 10; Pub. L. 107–17, §1, June 26, 2001, 115 Stat. 151; Pub. L. 107–170, §1, May 7, 2002, 116 Stat. 133; Pub. L. 107–171, title X, §10814(a), May 13, 2002, 116 Stat. 532; Pub. L. 107–377, §2(a), Dec. 19, 2002, 116 Stat. 3115; Pub. L. 108–73, §2(a), Aug. 15, 2003, 117 Stat. 891; Pub. L. 108–369, §2(a), Oct. 25, 2004, 118 Stat. 1749; Pub. L. 109–8, title II, §213(3), (4), title X, §§1001(a)(1), (c), 1003(a), Apr. 20, 2005, 119 Stat. 52, 185, 186.)

CODIFICATION

For repeal of section effective Oct. 1, 1998, and subsequent reenactment of section, see note set out preceding section 1201 of this title.

AMENDMENTS

2005—Subsec. (a)(2). Pub. L. 109–8, §1003(a), amended par. (2) generally. Prior to amendment, par. (2) read as follows: "provide for the full payment, in deferred cash payments, of all claims entitled to priority under section 507 of this title, unless the holder of a particular claim agrees to a different treatment of such claim;".

Subsec. (a)(4). Pub. L. 109–8, §213(3), added par. (4).

Subsec. (b)(11), (12). Pub. L. 109–8, §213(4), added par. (11) and redesignated former par. (11) as (12).

1994—Subsec. (d). Pub. L. 103–394 added subsec. (d).

EFFECTIVE DATE OF 2005 AMENDMENT

Pub. L. 109–8, title X, §1003(c), Apr. 20, 2005, 119 Stat. 186, provided that: "This section [amending this section and section 1231 of this title] and the amendments made by this section shall take effect on the date of the enactment of this Act [Apr. 20, 2005] and shall not apply with respect to cases commenced under title 11 of the United States Code before such date."

Amendment by section 213(3), (4) of Pub. L. 109–8 effective 180 days after Apr. 20, 2005, and not applicable with respect to cases commenced under this title before such effective date, except as otherwise provided, see section 1501 of Pub. L. 109–8, set out as a note under section 101 of this title.

EFFECTIVE DATE OF 1994 AMENDMENT

Amendment by Pub. L. 103–394 effective Oct. 22, 1994, and applicable only to agreements entered into after Oct. 22, 1994, see section 702 of Pub. L. 103–394, set out as a note under section 101 of this title.

§1223. Modification of plan before confirmation

(a) The debtor may modify the plan at any time before confirmation, but may not modify the plan so that the plan as modified fails to meet the requirements of section 1222 of this title.

(b) After the debtor files a modification under this section, the plan as modified becomes the plan.

(c) Any holder of a secured claim that has accepted or rejected the plan is deemed to have accepted or rejected, as the case may be, the plan as modified, unless the modification provides for a change in the rights of such holder from what such rights were under the plan before modification, and such holder changes such holder's previous acceptance or rejection.

(Added and amended Pub. L. 99–554, title II, §255, title III, §302(f), Oct. 27, 1986, 100 Stat. 3110, 3124;

Pub. L. 103–65, §1, Aug. 6, 1993, 107 Stat. 311; Pub. L. 105–277, div. C, title I, §149(a), Oct. 21, 1998, 112 Stat. 2681–610; Pub. L. 106–5, §1(1), (2), Mar. 30, 1999, 113 Stat. 9; Pub. L. 106–70, §1, Oct. 9, 1999, 113 Stat. 1031; Pub. L. 107–8, §1, May 11, 2001, 115 Stat. 10; Pub. L. 107–17, §1, June 26, 2001, 115 Stat. 151; Pub. L. 107–170, §1, May 7, 2002, 116 Stat. 133; Pub. L. 107–171, title X, §10814(a), May 13, 2002, 116 Stat. 532; Pub. L. 107–377, §2(a), Dec. 19, 2002, 116 Stat. 3115; Pub. L. 108–73, §2(a), Aug. 15, 2003, 117 Stat. 891; Pub. L. 108–369, §2(a), Oct. 25, 2004, 118 Stat. 1749; Pub. L. 109–8, title X, §1001(a)(1), (c), Apr. 20, 2005, 119 Stat. 185, 186.)

CODIFICATION

For repeal of section effective Oct. 1, 1998, and subsequent reenactment of section, see note set out preceding section 1201 of this title.

§1224. Confirmation hearing

After expedited notice, the court shall hold a hearing on confirmation of the plan. A party in interest, the trustee, or the United States trustee may object to the confirmation of the plan. Except for cause, the hearing shall be concluded not later than 45 days after the filing of the plan.

(Added and amended Pub. L. 99–554, title II, §255, title III, §302(f), Oct. 27, 1986, 100 Stat. 3110, 3124; Pub. L. 103–65, §1, Aug. 6, 1993, 107 Stat. 311; Pub. L. 105–277, div. C, title I, §149(a), Oct. 21, 1998, 112 Stat. 2681–610; Pub. L. 106–5, §1(1), (2), Mar. 30, 1999, 113 Stat. 9; Pub. L. 106–70, §1, Oct. 9, 1999, 113 Stat. 1031; Pub. L. 107–8, §1, May 11, 2001, 115 Stat. 10; Pub. L. 107–17, §1, June 26, 2001, 115 Stat. 151; Pub. L. 107–170, §1, May 7, 2002, 116 Stat. 133; Pub. L. 107–171, title X, §10814(a), May 13, 2002, 116 Stat. 532; Pub. L. 107–377, §2(a), Dec. 19, 2002, 116 Stat. 3115; Pub. L. 108–73, §2(a), Aug. 15, 2003, 117 Stat. 891; Pub. L. 108–369, §2(a), Oct. 25, 2004, 118 Stat. 1749; Pub. L. 109–8, title X, §1001(a)(1), (c), Apr. 20, 2005, 119 Stat. 185, 186.)

CODIFICATION

For repeal of section effective Oct. 1, 1998, and subsequent reenactment of section, see note set out preceding section 1201 of this title.

§1225. Confirmation of plan

(a) Except as provided in subsection (b), the court shall confirm a plan if—

(1) the plan complies with the provisions of this chapter and with the other applicable provisions of this title;

(2) any fee, charge, or amount required under chapter 123 of title 28, or by the plan, to be paid before confirmation, has been paid;

(3) the plan has been proposed in good faith and not by any means forbidden by law;

(4) the value, as of the effective date of the plan, of property to be distributed under the plan on account of each allowed unsecured claim is not less than the amount that would be paid on such claim if the estate of the debtor were liquidated under chapter 7 of this title on such date;

(5) with respect to each allowed secured claim provided for by the plan—

(A) the holder of such claim has accepted the plan;

(B)(i) the plan provides that the holder of such claim retain the lien securing such claim; and

(ii) the value, as of the effective date of the plan, of property to be distributed by the trustee or the debtor under the plan on account of such claim is not less than the allowed amount of such claim; or

(C) the debtor surrenders the property securing such claim to such holder;

(6) the debtor will be able to make all payments under the plan and to comply with the plan; and

(7) the debtor has paid all amounts that are required to be paid under a domestic support obligation and that first become payable after the date of the filing of the petition if the debtor is required by a judicial or administrative order, or by statute, to pay such domestic support obligation.

(b)(1) If the trustee or the holder of an allowed unsecured claim objects to the confirmation of the plan, then the court may not approve the plan unless, as of the effective date of the plan—

(A) the value of the property to be distributed under the plan on account of such claim is not less than the amount of such claim;

(B) the plan provides that all of the debtor's projected disposable income to be received in the three-year period, or such longer period as the court may approve under section 1222(c), beginning on the date that the first payment is due under the plan will be applied to make payments under the plan; or

(C) the value of the property to be distributed under the plan in the 3-year period, or such longer period as the court may approve under section 1222(c), beginning on the date that the first distribution is due under the plan is not less than the debtor's projected disposable income for such period.

(2) For purposes of this subsection, "disposable income" means income which is received by the debtor and which is not reasonably necessary to be expended—

(A) for the maintenance or support of the debtor or a dependent of the debtor or for a domestic support obligation that first becomes payable after the date of the filing of the petition; or

(B) for the payment of expenditures necessary for the continuation, preservation, and operation of the debtor's business.

(c) After confirmation of a plan, the court may order any entity from whom the debtor receives income to pay all or any part of such income to the trustee.

(Added and amended Pub. L. 99–554, title II, §255, title III, §302(f), Oct. 27, 1986, 100 Stat. 3110, 3124; Pub. L. 103–65, §1, Aug. 6, 1993, 107 Stat. 311; Pub. L. 105–277, div. C, title I, §149(a), Oct. 21, 1998, 112 Stat. 2681–610; Pub. L. 106–5, §1(1), (2), Mar. 30, 1999, 113 Stat. 9; Pub. L. 106–70, §1, Oct. 9, 1999, 113 Stat. 1031; Pub. L. 107–8, §1, May 11, 2001, 115 Stat. 10; Pub. L. 107–17, §1, June 26, 2001, 115 Stat. 151; Pub. L. 107–170, §1, May 7, 2002, 116 Stat. 133; Pub. L. 107–171, title X, §10814(a), May 13, 2002, 116 Stat. 532; Pub. L. 107–377, §2(a), Dec. 19, 2002, 116 Stat. 3115; Pub. L. 108–73, §2(a), Aug. 15, 2003, 117 Stat. 891; Pub. L. 108–369, §2(a), Oct. 25, 2004, 118 Stat. 1749; Pub. L. 109–8, title II, §§213(5), 218, title X, §§1001(a)(1), (c), 1006(a), Apr. 20, 2005, 119 Stat. 52, 55, 185–187.)

CODIFICATION

For repeal of section effective Oct. 1, 1998, and subsequent reenactment of section, see note set out preceding section 1201 of this title.

AMENDMENTS

2005—Subsec. (a)(7). Pub. L. 109–8, §213(5), added par. (7).

Subsec. (b)(1)(C). Pub. L. 109–8, §1006(a), added subpar. (C).

Subsec. (b)(2)(A). Pub. L. 109–8, §218, inserted "or for a domestic support obligation that first becomes payable after the date of the filing of the petition" after "dependent of the debtor".

EFFECTIVE DATE OF 2005 AMENDMENT

Amendment by sections 213(5), 218, and 1006(a) of Pub. L. 109–8 effective 180 days after Apr. 20, 2005, and not applicable with respect to cases commenced under this title before such effective date, except as otherwise provided, see section 1501 of Pub. L. 109–8, set out as a note under section 101 of this title.

§1226. Payments

(a) Payments and funds received by the trustee shall be retained by the trustee until confirmation or denial of confirmation of a plan. If a plan is confirmed, the trustee shall distribute any such payment in accordance with the plan. If a plan is not confirmed, the trustee shall return any such payments to the debtor, after deducting—

(1) any unpaid claim allowed under section 503(b) of this title; and

(2) if a standing trustee is serving in the case, the percentage fee fixed for such standing trustee.

(b) Before or at the time of each payment to creditors under the plan, there shall be paid—

(1) any unpaid claim of the kind specified in section 507(a)(2) of this title; and

(2) if a standing trustee appointed under section 1202(c)[1] of this title is serving in the case, the percentage fee fixed for such standing trustee under section 1202(d)[1] of this title.

(c) Except as otherwise provided in the plan or in the order confirming the plan, the trustee shall make payments to creditors under the plan.

(Added and amended Pub. L. 99–554, title II, §255, title III, §302(f), Oct. 27, 1986, 100 Stat. 3111, 3124; Pub. L. 103–65, §1, Aug. 6, 1993, 107 Stat. 311; Pub. L. 103–394, title V, §501(d)(36), Oct. 22, 1994, 108 Stat. 4147; Pub. L. 105–277, div. C, title I, §149(a), Oct. 21, 1998, 112 Stat. 2681–610; Pub. L. 106–5, §1(1), (2), Mar. 30, 1999, 113 Stat. 9; Pub. L. 106–70, §1, Oct. 9, 1999, 113 Stat. 1031; Pub. L. 107–8, §1, May 11, 2001, 115 Stat. 10; Pub. L. 107–17, §1, June 26, 2001, 115 Stat. 151; Pub. L. 107–170, §1, May 7, 2002, 116 Stat. 133; Pub. L. 107–171, title X, §10814(a), May 13, 2002, 116 Stat. 532; Pub. L. 107–377, §2(a), Dec. 19, 2002, 116 Stat. 3115; Pub. L. 108–73, §2(a), Aug. 15, 2003, 117 Stat. 891; Pub. L. 108–369, §2(a), Oct. 25, 2004, 118 Stat. 1749; Pub. L. 109–8, title X, §1001(a)(1), (c), title XV, §1502(a)(9), Apr. 20, 2005, 119 Stat. 185, 186, 217.)

REFERENCES IN TEXT

Section 1202(c) and (d) of this title, referred to in subsec. (b)(2), was repealed by section 227 of Pub. L. 99–554, and provisions relating to appointment of and fixing percentage fees for standing trustees are contained in section 586(b) and (e) of Title 28, Judiciary and Judicial Procedure, as amended by section 113(b), (c) of Pub. L. 99–554.

CODIFICATION

For repeal of section effective Oct. 1, 1998, and subsequent reenactment of section, see note set out preceding section 1201 of this title.

AMENDMENTS

2005—Subsec. (b)(1). Pub. L. 109–8, §1502(a)(9), substituted "507(a)(2)" for "507(a)(1)".

1994—Subsec. (b)(2). Pub. L. 103–394 substituted "1202(c)" for "1202(d)" and "1202(d)" for "1202(e)".

EFFECTIVE DATE OF 2005 AMENDMENT

Amendment by section 1502(a)(9) of Pub. L. 109–8 effective 180 days after Apr. 20, 2005, and not applicable with respect to cases commenced under this title before such effective date, except as otherwise provided, see section 1501 of Pub. L. 109–8, set out as a note under section 101 of this title.

EFFECTIVE DATE OF 1994 AMENDMENT

Amendment by Pub. L. 103–394 effective Oct. 22, 1994, and not applicable with respect to cases commenced under this title before Oct. 22, 1994, see section 702 of Pub. L. 103–394, set out as a note under section 101 of this title.

§1227. Effect of confirmation

(a) Except as provided in section 1228(a) of this title, the provisions of a confirmed plan bind the debtor, each creditor, each equity security holder, and each general partner in the debtor, whether or not the claim of such creditor, such equity security holder, or such general partner in the debtor is provided for by the plan, and whether or not such creditor, such equity security holder, or such general partner in the debtor has objected to, has accepted, or has rejected the plan.

(b) Except as otherwise provided in the plan or the order confirming the plan, the confirmation of a plan vests all of the property of the estate in the debtor.

(c) Except as provided in section 1228(a) of this title and except as otherwise provided in the plan or in the order confirming the plan, the property vesting in the debtor under subsection (b) of this section is free and clear of any claim or interest of any creditor provided for by the plan.

(Added and amended Pub. L. 99–554, title II, §255, title III, §302(f), Oct. 27, 1986, 100 Stat. 3112, 3124; Pub. L. 103–65, §1, Aug. 6, 1993, 107 Stat. 311; Pub. L. 105–277, div. C, title I, §149(a), Oct. 21, 1998, 112 Stat. 2681–610; Pub. L. 106–5, §1(1), (2), Mar. 30, 1999, 113 Stat. 9; Pub. L. 106–70, §1, Oct. 9, 1999, 113 Stat. 1031; Pub. L. 107–8, §1, May 11, 2001, 115 Stat. 10; Pub. L. 107–17, §1, June 26, 2001, 115 Stat. 151; Pub. L. 107–170, §1, May 7, 2002, 116 Stat. 133; Pub. L. 107–171, title X, §10814(a), May 13, 2002, 116 Stat. 532; Pub. L. 107–377, §2(a), Dec. 19, 2002, 116 Stat. 3115; Pub. L. 108–73, §2(a), Aug. 15, 2003, 117 Stat. 891; Pub. L. 108–369, §2(a), Oct. 25, 2004, 118 Stat. 1749; Pub. L. 109–8, title X, §1001(a)(1), (c), Apr. 20, 2005, 119 Stat. 185, 186.)

CODIFICATION

For repeal of section effective Oct. 1, 1998, and subsequent reenactment of section, see note set out preceding section 1201 of this title.

[1] See References in Text note below.

§ 1228. Discharge

(a) Subject to subsection (d), as soon as practicable after completion by the debtor of all payments under the plan, and in the case of a debtor who is required by a judicial or administrative order, or by statute, to pay a domestic support obligation, after such debtor certifies that all amounts payable under such order or such statute that are due on or before the date of the certification (including amounts due before the petition was filed, but only to the extent provided for by the plan) have been paid, other than payments to holders of allowed claims provided for under section 1222(b)(5) or 1222(b)(9) of this title, unless the court approves a written waiver of discharge executed by the debtor after the order for relief under this chapter, the court shall grant the debtor a discharge of all debts provided for by the plan allowed under section 503 of this title or disallowed under section 502 of this title, except any debt—

(1) provided for under section 1222(b)(5) or 1222(b)(9) of this title; or

(2) of the kind specified in section 523(a) of this title.

(b) Subject to subsection (d), at any time after the confirmation of the plan and after notice and a hearing, the court may grant a discharge to a debtor that has not completed payments under the plan only if—

(1) the debtor's failure to complete such payments is due to circumstances for which the debtor should not justly be held accountable;

(2) the value, as of the effective date of the plan, of property actually distributed under the plan on account of each allowed unsecured claim is not less than the amount that would have been paid on such claim if the estate of the debtor had been liquidated under chapter 7 of this title on such date; and

(3) modification of the plan under section 1229 of this title is not practicable.

(c) A discharge granted under subsection (b) of this section discharges the debtor from all unsecured debts provided for by the plan or disallowed under section 502 of this title, except any debt—

(1) provided for under section 1222(b)(5) or 1222(b)(9) of this title; or

(2) of a kind specified in section 523(a) of this title.

(d) On request of a party in interest before one year after a discharge under this section is granted, and after notice and a hearing, the court may revoke such discharge only if—

(1) such discharge was obtained by the debtor through fraud; and

(2) the requesting party did not know of such fraud until after such discharge was granted.

(e) After the debtor is granted a discharge, the court shall terminate the services of any trustee serving in the case.

(f) The court may not grant a discharge under this chapter unless the court after notice and a hearing held not more than 10 days before the date of the entry of the order granting the discharge finds that there is no reasonable cause to believe that—

(1) section 522(q)(1) may be applicable to the debtor; and

(2) there is pending any proceeding in which the debtor may be found guilty of a felony of the kind described in section 522(q)(1)(A) or liable for a debt of the kind described in section 522(q)(1)(B).

(Added and amended Pub. L. 99–554, title II, § 255, title III, § 302(f), Oct. 27, 1986, 100 Stat. 3112, 3124; Pub. L. 103–65, § 1, Aug. 6, 1993, 107 Stat. 311; Pub. L. 105–277, div. C, title I, § 149(a), Oct. 21, 1998, 112 Stat. 2681–610; Pub. L. 106–5, § 1(1), (2), Mar. 30, 1999, 113 Stat. 9; Pub. L. 106–70, § 1, Oct. 9, 1999, 113 Stat. 1031; Pub. L. 106–518, title II, § 208, Nov. 13, 2000, 114 Stat. 2415; Pub. L. 107–8, § 1, May 11, 2001, 115 Stat. 10; Pub. L. 107–17, § 1, June 26, 2001, 115 Stat. 151; Pub. L. 107–170, § 1, May 7, 2002, 116 Stat. 133; Pub. L. 107–171, title X, § 10814(a), May 13, 2002, 116 Stat. 532; Pub. L. 107–377, § 2(a), Dec. 19, 2002, 116 Stat. 3115; Pub. L. 108–73, § 2(a), Aug. 15, 2003, 117 Stat. 891; Pub. L. 108–369, § 2(a), Oct. 25, 2004, 118 Stat. 1749; Pub. L. 109–8, title II, § 213(6), title III, § 330(c), title X, § 1001(a)(1), (c), Apr. 20, 2005, 119 Stat. 53, 101, 185, 186.)

CODIFICATION

For repeal of section effective Oct. 1, 1998, and subsequent reenactment of section, see note set out preceding section 1201 of this title.

AMENDMENTS

2005—Subsec. (a). Pub. L. 109–8, § 330(c)(1), substituted "Subject to subsection (d), as" for "As" in introductory provisions.

Pub. L. 109–8, § 213(6), inserted ", and in the case of a debtor who is required by a judicial or administrative order, or by statute, to pay a domestic support obligation, after such debtor certifies that all amounts payable under such order or such statute that are due on or before the date of the certification (including amounts due before the petition was filed, but only to the extent provided for by the plan) have been paid" after "completion by the debtor of all payments under the plan" in introductory provisions.

Subsec. (b). Pub. L. 109–8, § 330(c)(2), substituted "Subject to subsection (d), at" for "At" in introductory provisions.

Subsec. (f). Pub. L. 109–8, § 330(c)(3), added subsec. (f).

2000—Subsecs. (a), (c)(1). Pub. L. 106–518 substituted "1222(b)(9)" for "1222(b)(10)" wherever appearing.

EFFECTIVE DATE OF 2005 AMENDMENT

Amendments by sections 213(6) and 330(c) of Pub. L. 109–8 effective 180 days after Apr. 20, 2005, with amendment by section 213(6) of Pub. L. 109–8 not applicable with respect to cases commenced under this title before such effective date, except as otherwise provided, and amendment by section 330(c) of Pub. L. 109–8 applicable with respect to cases commenced under this title on or after Apr. 20, 2005, see section 1501 of Pub. L. 109–8, set out as a note under section 101 of this title.

§ 1229. Modification of plan after confirmation

(a) At any time after confirmation of the plan but before the completion of payments under such plan, the plan may be modified, on request of the debtor, the trustee, or the holder of an allowed unsecured claim, to—

(1) increase or reduce the amount of payments on claims of a particular class provided for by the plan;

(2) extend or reduce the time for such payments; or

(3) alter the amount of the distribution to a creditor whose claim is provided for by the plan to the extent necessary to take account

of any payment of such claim other than under the plan.

(b)(1) Sections 1222(a), 1222(b), and 1223(c) of this title and the requirements of section 1225(a) of this title apply to any modification under subsection (a) of this section.

(2) The plan as modified becomes the plan unless, after notice and a hearing, such modification is disapproved.

(c) A plan modified under this section may not provide for payments over a period that expires after three years after the time that the first payment under the original confirmed plan was due, unless the court, for cause, approves a longer period, but the court may not approve a period that expires after five years after such time.

(d) A plan may not be modified under this section—

(1) to increase the amount of any payment due before the plan as modified becomes the plan;

(2) by anyone except the debtor, based on an increase in the debtor's disposable income, to increase the amount of payments to unsecured creditors required for a particular month so that the aggregate of such payments exceeds the debtor's disposable income for such month; or

(3) in the last year of the plan by anyone except the debtor, to require payments that would leave the debtor with insufficient funds to carry on the farming operation after the plan is completed.

(Added and amended Pub. L. 99–554, title II, §255, title III, §302(f), Oct. 27, 1986, 100 Stat. 3113, 3124; Pub. L. 103–65, §1, Aug. 6, 1993, 107 Stat. 311; Pub. L. 105–277, div. C, title I, §149(a), Oct. 21, 1998, 112 Stat. 2681–610; Pub. L. 106–5, §1(1), (2), Mar. 30, 1999, 113 Stat. 9; Pub. L. 106–70, §1, Oct. 9, 1999, 113 Stat. 1031; Pub. L. 107–8, §1, May 11, 2001, 115 Stat. 10; Pub. L. 107–17, §1, June 26, 2001, 115 Stat. 151; Pub. L. 107–170, §1, May 7, 2002, 116 Stat. 133; Pub. L. 107–171, title X, §10814(a), May 13, 2002, 116 Stat. 532; Pub. L. 107–377, §2(a), Dec. 19, 2002, 116 Stat. 3115; Pub. L. 108–73, §2(a), Aug. 15, 2003, 117 Stat. 891; Pub. L. 108–369, §2(a), Oct. 25, 2004, 118 Stat. 1749; Pub. L. 109–8, title X, §§1001(a)(1), (c), 1006(b), Apr. 20, 2005, 119 Stat. 185–187.)

CODIFICATION

For repeal of section effective Oct. 1, 1998, and subsequent reenactment of section, see note set out preceding section 1201 of this title.

AMENDMENTS

2005—Subsec. (d). Pub. L. 109–8, §1006(b), added subsec. (d).

EFFECTIVE DATE OF 2005 AMENDMENT

Amendment by section 1006(b) of Pub. L. 109–8 effective 180 days after Apr. 20, 2005, and not applicable with respect to cases commenced under this title before such effective date, except as otherwise provided, see section 1501 of Pub. L. 109–8, set out as a note under section 101 of this title.

§1230. Revocation of an order of confirmation

(a) On request of a party in interest at any time within 180 days after the date of the entry of an order of confirmation under section 1225 of this title, and after notice and a hearing, the court may revoke such order if such order was procured by fraud.

(b) If the court revokes an order of confirmation under subsection (a) of this section, the court shall dispose of the case under section 1207 of this title, unless, within the time fixed by the court, the debtor proposes and the court confirms a modification of the plan under section 1229 of this title.

(Added and amended Pub. L. 99–554, title II, §255, title III, §302(f), Oct. 27, 1986, 100 Stat. 3113, 3124; Pub. L. 103–65, §1, Aug. 6, 1993, 107 Stat. 311; Pub. L. 105–277, div. C, title I, §149(a), Oct. 21, 1998, 112 Stat. 2681–610; Pub. L. 106–5, §1(1), (2), Mar. 30, 1999, 113 Stat. 9; Pub. L. 106–70, §1, Oct. 9, 1999, 113 Stat. 1031; Pub. L. 107–8, §1, May 11, 2001, 115 Stat. 10; Pub. L. 107–17, §1, June 26, 2001, 115 Stat. 151; Pub. L. 107–170, §1, May 7, 2002, 116 Stat. 133; Pub. L. 107–171, title X, §10814(a), May 13, 2002, 116 Stat. 532; Pub. L. 107–377, §2(a), Dec. 19, 2002, 116 Stat. 3115; Pub. L. 108–73, §2(a), Aug. 15, 2003, 117 Stat. 891; Pub. L. 108–369, §2(a), Oct. 25, 2004, 118 Stat. 1749; Pub. L. 109–8, title X, §1001(a)(1), (c), Apr. 20, 2005, 119 Stat. 185, 186.)

CODIFICATION

For repeal of section effective Oct. 1, 1998, and subsequent reenactment of section, see note set out preceding section 1201 of this title.

§1231. Special tax provisions

(a) The issuance, transfer, or exchange of a security, or the making or delivery of an instrument of transfer under a plan confirmed under section 1225 of this title, may not be taxed under any law imposing a stamp tax or similar tax.

(b) The court may authorize the proponent of a plan to request a determination, limited to questions of law, by any governmental unit charged with responsibility for collection or determination of a tax on or measured by income, of the tax effects, under section 346 of this title and under the law imposing such tax, of the plan. In the event of an actual controversy, the court may declare such effects after the earlier of—

(1) the date on which such governmental unit responds to the request under this subsection; or

(2) 270 days after such request.

(Added and amended Pub. L. 99–554, title II, §255, title III, §302(f), Oct. 27, 1986, 100 Stat. 3113, 3124; Pub. L. 103–65, §1, Aug. 6, 1993, 107 Stat. 311; Pub. L. 105–277, div. C, title I, §149(a), Oct. 21, 1998, 112 Stat. 2681–610; Pub. L. 106–5, §1(1), (2), Mar. 30, 1999, 113 Stat. 9; Pub. L. 106–70, §1, Oct. 9, 1999, 113 Stat. 1031; Pub. L. 107–8, §1, May 11, 2001, 115 Stat. 10; Pub. L. 107–17, §1, June 26, 2001, 115 Stat. 151; Pub. L. 107–170, §1, May 7, 2002, 116 Stat. 133; Pub. L. 107–171, title X, §10814(a), May 13, 2002, 116 Stat. 532; Pub. L. 107–377, §2(a), Dec. 19, 2002, 116 Stat. 3115; Pub. L. 108–73, §2(a), Aug. 15, 2003, 117 Stat. 891; Pub. L. 108–369, §2(a), Oct. 25, 2004, 118 Stat. 1749; Pub. L. 109–8, title VII, §719(b)(4), title X, §§1001(a)(1), (c), 1003(b), Apr. 20, 2005, 119 Stat. 133, 185, 186.)

CODIFICATION

For repeal of section effective Oct. 1, 1998, and subsequent reenactment of section, see note set out preceding section 1201 of this title.

AMENDMENTS

2005—Subsec. (a). Pub. L. 109–8, §719(b)(4), redesignated subsec. (c) as (a) and struck out former subsec. (a) which read as follows: "For the purpose of any State or local law imposing a tax on or measured by income, the taxable period of a debtor that is an individual shall terminate on the date of the order for relief under this chapter, unless the case was converted under section 706 of this title."

Subsec. (b). Pub. L. 109–8, §1003(b), substituted "any governmental unit" for "a State or local governmental unit".

Pub. L. 109–8, §719(b)(4), redesignated subsec. (d) as (b) and struck out former subsec. (b) which read as follows: "The trustee shall make a State or local tax return of income for the estate of an individual debtor in a case under this chapter for each taxable period after the order for relief under this chapter during which the case is pending."

Subsecs. (c), (d). Pub. L. 109–8, §719(b)(4)(B), redesignated subsecs. (c) and (d) as (a) and (b), respectively.

EFFECTIVE DATE OF 2005 AMENDMENT

Amendment by section 1003(b) of Pub. L. 109–8 effective Apr. 20, 2005, and not applicable with respect to cases commenced under this title before Apr. 20, 2005, see section 1003(c) of Pub. L. 109–8, set out as a note under section 1222 of this title.

Amendment by section 719(b)(4) of Pub. L. 109–8 effective 180 days after Apr. 20, 2005, and not applicable with respect to cases commenced under this title before such effective date, except as otherwise provided, see section 1501 of Pub. L. 109–8, set out as a note under section 101 of this title.

CHAPTER 13—ADJUSTMENT OF DEBTS OF AN INDIVIDUAL WITH REGULAR INCOME

SUBCHAPTER I—OFFICERS, ADMINISTRATION, AND THE ESTATE

AMENDMENTS

2005—Pub. L. 109–8, title VII, §716(b)(2), Apr. 20, 2005, 119 Stat. 130, added item 1308.

SUBCHAPTER I—OFFICERS, ADMINISTRATION, AND THE ESTATE

§1301. Stay of action against codebtor

(a) Except as provided in subsections (b) and (c) of this section, after the order for relief under this chapter, a creditor may not act, or commence or continue any civil action, to collect all or any part of a consumer debt of the debtor from any individual that is liable on such debt with the debtor, or that secured such debt, unless—

(1) such individual became liable on or secured such debt in the ordinary course of such individual's business; or

(2) the case is closed, dismissed, or converted to a case under chapter 7 or 11 of this title.

(b) A creditor may present a negotiable instrument, and may give notice of dishonor of such an instrument.

(c) On request of a party in interest and after notice and a hearing, the court shall grant relief from the stay provided by subsection (a) of this section with respect to a creditor, to the extent that—

(1) as between the debtor and the individual protected under subsection (a) of this section, such individual received the consideration for the claim held by such creditor;

(2) the plan filed by the debtor proposes not to pay such claim; or

(3) such creditor's interest would be irreparably harmed by continuation of such stay.

(d) Twenty days after the filing of a request under subsection (c)(2) of this section for relief from the stay provided by subsection (a) of this section, such stay is terminated with respect to the party in interest making such request, unless the debtor or any individual that is liable on such debt with the debtor files and serves upon such party in interest a written objection to the taking of the proposed action.

(Pub. L. 95–598, Nov. 6, 1978, 92 Stat. 2645; Pub. L. 98–353, title III, §§313, 524, July 10, 1984, 98 Stat. 355, 388.)

HISTORICAL AND REVISION NOTES

LEGISLATIVE STATEMENTS

Section 1301 of the House amendment is identical with the provision contained in section 1301 of the House bill and adopted by the Senate amendment. Section 1301(c)(1) indicates that a basis for lifting the stay is that the debtor did not receive consideration for the claim by the creditor, or in other words, the debtor is really the "codebtor." As with other sections in title 11, the standard of receiving consideration is a general rule, but where two co-debtors have agreed to share liabilities in a different manner than profits it is the individual who does not ultimately bear the liability that is protected by the stay under section 1301.

SENATE REPORT NO. 95–989

Subsection (a) automatically stays the holder of a claim based on a consumer debt of the chapter 13 debtor from acting or proceeding in any way, except as authorized pursuant to subsections (b) and (c), against an individual or the property of an individual liable with the chapter 13 debtor, unless such codebtor became liable in the ordinary course of his business, or unless the case is closed, dismissed, or converted to another chapter.

Under the terms of the agreement with the codebtor who is not in bankruptcy, the creditor has a right to collect all payments to the extent they are not made by the debtor at the time they are due. To the extent to which a chapter 13 plan does not propose to pay a creditor his claims, the creditor may obtain relief from the court from the automatic stay and collect such claims from the codebtor. Conversely, a codebtor obtains the benefit of any payments made to the creditor under the plan. If a debtor defaults on scheduled payments under the plan, then the codebtor would be liable for the remaining deficiency; otherwise, payments not made under the plan may never be made by the codebtor. The obligation of the codebtor to make the creditor whole at the time payments are due remains.

The automatic stay under this section pertains only to the collection of a consumer debt, defined by section 101(7) of this title to mean a debt incurred by an individual primarily for a personal, family, or household purpose. Therefore, not all debts owed by a chapter 13 debtor will be subject to the stay of the codebtor, particularly those business debts incurred by an individual with regular income, as defined by section 101(24) of this title, engaged in business, that is permitted by virtue of section 109(b) and section 1304 to obtain chapter 13 relief.

Subsection (b) excepts the giving of notice of dishonor of a negotiable instrument from the reach of the codebtor stay.

Under subsection (c), if the codebtor has property out of which the creditor's claim can be satisfied, the court can grant relief from the stay absent the transfer of a security interest in that property by the codebtor to the creditor. Correspondingly, if there is reasonable cause to believe that property is about to be disposed of by the codebtor which could be used to satisfy his obligation to the creditor, the court should lift the stay to allow the creditor to perfect his rights against such property. Likewise, if property is subject to rapid depreciation or decrease in value the stay should be lifted to allow the creditor to protect his rights to reach such property. Otherwise, the creditor's interest would be irreparably harmed by such stay. Property which could be used to satisfy the claim could be disposed of or encumbered and placed beyond the reach of the creditor. The creditor should be allowed to protect his rights to reach property which could satisfy his claim and prevent its erosion in value, disposal, or encumbrance.

HOUSE REPORT NO. 95–595

This section is new. It is designed to protect a debtor operating under a chapter 13 individual repayment plan case by insulating him from indirect pressures from his creditors exerted through friends or relatives that may have cosigned an obligation of the debtor. The protection is limited, however, to ensure that the creditor involved does not lose the benefit of the bargain he made for a cosigner. He is entitled to full compensation, including any interest, fees, and costs provided for by the agreement under which the debtor obtained his loan. The creditor is simply required to share with other creditors to the extent that the debtor will repay him under the chapter 13 plan. The creditor is delayed, but his substantive rights are not affected.

Subsection (a) is the operative subsection. It stays action by a creditor after an order for relief under chapter 13. The creditor may not act, or commence or continue any civil action, to collect all or any part of a consumer debt of the debtor from any individual that is liable on such debt with the debtor, or that has secured the debt, unless the individual became liable or secured the debt in the ordinary course of his business, or the case is closed, dismissed, or converted to chapter 7 or 11.

Subsection (b) permits the creditor, notwithstanding the stay, to present a negotiable instrument and to give notice of dishonor of the instrument, in order to preserve his substantive rights against the codebtor as required by applicable nonbankruptcy law.

Subsection (c) requires the court to grant relief from the stay in certain circumstances. The court must grant relief to the extent that the debtor does not propose to pay, under the plan, the amount owed to the creditor. The court must also grant relief to the extent that the debtor was really the codebtor in the transaction, that is, to the extent that the nondebtor party actually received the consideration for the claim held by the creditor. Finally, the court must grant relief to the extent that the creditor's interest would be irreparably harmed by the stay, for example, where the codebtor filed bankruptcy himself, or threatened to leave the locale, or lost his job.

AMENDMENTS

1984—Subsec. (c)(3). Pub. L. 98–353, §524, inserted "continuation of" after "by".

Subsec. (d). Pub. L. 98–353, §313, added subsec. (d).

EFFECTIVE DATE OF 1984 AMENDMENT

Amendment by Pub. L. 98–353 effective with respect to cases filed 90 days after July 10, 1984, see section 552(a) of Pub. L. 98–353, set out as a note under section 101 of this title.

§ 1302. Trustee

(a) If the United States trustee appoints an individual under section 586(b) of title 28 to serve as standing trustee in cases under this chapter and if such individual qualifies under section 322 of this title, then such individual shall serve as trustee in the case. Otherwise, the United States trustee shall appoint one disinterested person to serve as trustee in the case or the United States trustee may serve as a trustee in the case.

(b) The trustee shall—

(1) perform the duties specified in sections 704(2), 704(3), 704(4), 704(5), 704(6), 704(7), and 704(9) of this title;

(2) appear and be heard at any hearing that concerns—

(A) the value of property subject to a lien;

(B) confirmation of a plan; or

(C) modification of the plan after confirmation;

(3) dispose of, under regulations issued by the Director of the Administrative Office of the United States Courts, moneys received or to be received in a case under chapter XIII of the Bankruptcy Act;

(4) advise, other than on legal matters, and assist the debtor in performance under the plan;

(5) ensure that the debtor commences making timely payments under section 1326 of this title; and

(6) if with respect to the debtor there is a claim for a domestic support obligation, provide the applicable notice specified in subsection (d).

(c) If the debtor is engaged in business, then in addition to the duties specified in subsection (b) of this section, the trustee shall perform the duties specified in sections 1106(a)(3) and 1106(a)(4) of this title.

(d)(1) In a case described in subsection (b)(6) to which subsection (b)(6) applies, the trustee shall—

(A)(i) provide written notice to the holder of the claim described in subsection (b)(6) of such claim and of the right of such holder to use the services of the State child support enforcement agency established under sections 464 and 466 of the Social Security Act for the State in which such holder resides, for assistance in collecting child support during and after the case under this title; and

(ii) include in the notice provided under clause (i) the address and telephone number of such State child support enforcement agency;

(B)(i) provide written notice to such State child support enforcement agency of such claim; and

(ii) include in the notice provided under clause (i) the name, address, and telephone number of such holder; and

(C) at such time as the debtor is granted a discharge under section 1328, provide written notice to such holder and to such State child support enforcement agency of—

(i) the granting of the discharge;

(ii) the last recent known address of the debtor;

(iii) the last recent known name and address of the debtor's employer; and

(iv) the name of each creditor that holds a claim that—

(I) is not discharged under paragraph (2) or (4) of section 523(a); or

(II) was reaffirmed by the debtor under section 524(c).

(2)(A) The holder of a claim described in subsection (b)(6) or the State child support enforcement agency of the State in which such holder resides may request from a creditor described in paragraph (1)(C)(iv) the last known address of the debtor.

(B) Notwithstanding any other provision of law, a creditor that makes a disclosure of a last known address of a debtor in connection with a request made under subparagraph (A) shall not be liable by reason of making that disclosure.

(Pub. L. 95–598, Nov. 6, 1978, 92 Stat. 2645; Pub. L. 98–353, title III, §§314, 525, July 10, 1984, 98 Stat. 356, 388; Pub. L. 99–554, title II, §§228, 283(w), Oct. 27, 1986, 100 Stat. 3103, 3118; Pub. L. 103–394, title V, §501(d)(37), Oct. 22, 1994, 108 Stat. 4147; Pub. L. 109–8, title II, §219(d), Apr. 20, 2005, 119 Stat. 58.)

Historical and Revision Notes

LEGISLATIVE STATEMENTS

Section 1302 of the House amendment adopts a provision contained in the Senate amendment instead of the position taken in the House bill. Sections 1302(d) and (e) are modeled on the standing trustee system contained in the House bill with the court assuming supervisory functions in districts not under the pilot program.

SENATE REPORT NO. 95–989

The principal administrator in a chapter 13 case is the chapter 13 trustee. Experience under chapter XIII of the Bankruptcy Act [chapter 13 of former title 11] has shown that the more efficient and effective wage earner programs have been conducted by standing chapter XIII trustees who exercise a broad range of responsibilities in both the design and the effectuation of debtor plans.

Subsection (a) provides administrative flexibility by permitting the bankruptcy judge to appoint an individual from the panel of trustees established pursuant to 28 U.S.C. §604(f) and qualified under section 322 of title 11, either to serve as a standing trustee in all chapter 13 cases filed in the district or a portion thereof, or to serve in a single case.

Subsection (b)(1) makes it clear that the chapter 13 trustee is no mere disbursing agent of the monies paid to him by the debtor under the plan [section 1322(a)(1)], by imposing upon him certain relevant duties of a liquidation trustee prescribed by section 704 of this title.

Subsection (b)(2) requires the chapter 13 trustee to appear before and be heard by the bankruptcy court whenever the value of property secured by a lien or the confirmation or modification of a plan after confirmation as provided by sections 1323–1325 is considered by the court.

Subsection (b)(3) requires the chapter 13 trustee to advise and counsel the debtor while under chapter 13, except on matters more appropriately left to the attorney for the debtor. The chapter 13 trustee must also assist the debtor in performance under the plan by attempting to tailor the requirements of the plan to the changing needs and circumstances of the debtor during the extension period.

Subsection (c) imposes on the trustee in a chapter 13 case filed by a debtor engaged in business the investigative and reporting duties normally required of a chapter 11 debtor or trustee as prescribed by section 1106(a)(3) and (4).

HOUSE REPORT NO. 95–595

Subsection (d) gives the trustee an additional duty if the debtor is engaged in business, as defined in section 1304. The trustee must perform the duties specified in sections 1106(a)(3) and 1106(a)(4), relating to investigation of the debtor.

References in Text

Chapter XIII of the Bankruptcy Act, referred to in subsec. (b)(3), is chapter XIII of act July 1, 1898, ch. 541, as added June 22, 1938, ch. 575, §1, 52 Stat. 930, which was classified to chapter 13 (§1001 et seq.) of former Title 11.

Sections 464 and 466 of the Social Security Act, referred to in subsec. (d)(1)(A)(i), are classified to sections 664 and 666, respectively, of Title 42, The Public Health and Welfare.

Amendments

2005—Subsec. (b)(6). Pub. L. 109–8, §219(d)(1), added par. (6).

Subsec. (d). Pub. L. 109–8, §219(d)(2), added subsec. (d).

1994—Subsec. (b)(3). Pub. L. 103–394 struck out "and" at end.

1986—Subsec. (a). Pub. L. 99–554, §228(1), amended subsec. (a) generally. Prior to amendment, subsec. (a) read as follows: "If the court has appointed an individual under subsection (d) of this section to serve as standing trustee in cases under this chapter and if such individual qualifies under section 322 of this title, then such individual shall serve as trustee in the case. Otherwise, the court shall appoint a person to serve as trustee in the case."

Subsec. (d). Pub. L. 99–554, §228(2), struck out subsec. (d) which read as follows: "If the number of cases under this chapter commenced in a particular judicial district so warrant, the court may appoint one or more individuals to serve as standing trustee for such district in cases under this chapter."

Subsec. (e). Pub. L. 99–554, §283(w), which directed the amendment of par. (1) by substituting "set for such individual" for "fix" could not be executed in view of the repeal of subsec. (e) by section 228(2) of Pub. L. 99–554. See 1984 Amendment note below.

Pub. L. 99–554, §228(2), struck out subsec. (e) which read as follows:

"(1) A court that has appointed an individual under subsection (d) of this section to serve as standing trustee in cases under this chapter shall set for such individual—

"(A) a maximum annual compensation, not to exceed the lowest annual rate of basic pay in effect for grade GS–16 of the General Schedule prescribed under section 5332 of title 5; and

"(B) a percentage fee, not to exceed ten percent, based on such maximum annual compensation and the actual, necessary expenses incurred by such individual as standing trustee.

"(2) Such individual shall collect such percentage fee from all payments under plans in the cases under this chapter for which such individual serves as standing trustee. Such individual shall pay annually to the Treasury—

"(A) any amount by which the actual compensation received by such individual exceeds five percent of all such payments made under plans in cases under this chapter for which such individual serves as standing trustee; and

"(B) any amount by which the percentage fee fixed under paragraph (1)(B) of this subsection for all such cases exceeds—

"(i) such individual's actual compensation for such cases, as adjusted under subparagraph (A) of this paragraph; plus

"(ii) the actual, necessary expenses incurred by such individual as standing trustee in such cases."

1984—Subsec. (b)(1). Pub. L. 98-353, §314(1), substituted "704(7), and 704(9) of this title" for "and 704(8) of this title".

Subsec. (b)(2). Pub. L. 98-353, §314(2), struck out "and" at the end.

Subsec. (b)(3) to (5). Pub. L. 98-353, §525(a), added par. (3) and redesignated former pars. (3) and (4) as (4) and (5), respectively.

Pub. L. 98-353, §314(3), (4), substituted "; and" for the period at end of par. (3) and added par. (4).

Subsec. (e)(1). Pub. L. 98-353, §525(b)(1), which directed the amendment of par. (4) by substituting "set for such individual" for "fix" was executed to par. (1) as the probable intent of Congress.

Subsec. (e)(1)(A). Pub. L. 98-353, §525(b)(2), struck out "for such individual" after "a maximum annual compensation".

Subsec. (e)(2)(A). Pub. L. 98-353, §525(b)(3), substituted "received by" for "of", and "of all such payments made" for "upon all payments".

EFFECTIVE DATE OF 2005 AMENDMENT

Amendment by Pub. L. 109-8 effective 180 days after Apr. 20, 2005, and not applicable with respect to cases commenced under this title before such effective date, except as otherwise provided, see section 1501 of Pub. L. 109-8, set out as a note under section 101 of this title.

EFFECTIVE DATE OF 1994 AMENDMENT

Amendment by Pub. L. 103-394 effective Oct. 22, 1994, and not applicable with respect to cases commenced under this title before Oct. 22, 1994, see section 702 of Pub. L. 103-394, set out as a note under section 101 of this title.

EFFECTIVE DATE OF 1986 AMENDMENT

Effective date and applicability of amendment by section 228 of Pub. L. 99-554 dependent upon the judicial district involved, see section 302(d), (e) of Pub. L. 99-554, set out as a note under section 581 of Title 28, Judiciary and Judicial Procedure.

Amendment by section 283 of Pub. L. 99-554 effective 30 days after Oct. 27, 1986, see section 302(a) of Pub. L. 99-554.

EFFECTIVE DATE OF 1984 AMENDMENT

Amendment by Pub. L. 98-353 effective with respect to cases filed 90 days after July 10, 1984, see section 552(a) of Pub. L. 98-353, set out as a note under section 101 of this title.

§1303. Rights and powers of debtor

Subject to any limitations on a trustee under this chapter, the debtor shall have, exclusive of the trustee, the rights and powers of a trustee under sections 363(b), 363(d), 363(e), 363(f), and 363(*l*), of this title.

(Pub. L. 95-598, Nov. 6, 1978, 92 Stat. 2646.)

HISTORICAL AND REVISION NOTES

LEGISLATIVE STATEMENTS

Section 1303 of the House amendment specifies rights and powers that the debtor has exclusive of the trustees. The section does not imply that the debtor does not also possess other powers concurrently with the trustee. For example, although section 1323 is not specified in section 1303, certainly it is intended that the debtor has the power to sue and be sued.

SENATE REPORT NO. 95-989

A chapter 13 debtor is vested with the identical rights and powers, and is subject to the same limitations in regard to their exercise, as those given a liquidation trustee by virtue of section 363(b), (d), (e), (f), and (h) of title 11, relating to the sale, use or lease of property.

§1304. Debtor engaged in business

(a) A debtor that is self-employed and incurs trade credit in the production of income from such employment is engaged in business.

(b) Unless the court orders otherwise, a debtor engaged in business may operate the business of the debtor and, subject to any limitations on a trustee under sections 363(c) and 364 of this title and to such limitations or conditions as the court prescribes, shall have, exclusive of the trustee, the rights and powers of the trustee under such sections.

(c) A debtor engaged in business shall perform the duties of the trustee specified in section 704(8) of this title.

(Pub. L. 95-598, Nov. 6, 1978, 92 Stat. 2646; Pub. L. 98-353, title III, §§311(b)(2), 526, July 10, 1984, 98 Stat. 355, 389.)

HISTORICAL AND REVISION NOTES

LEGISLATIVE STATEMENTS

Section 1304(b) of the House amendment adopts the approach taken in the comparable section of the Senate amendment as preferable to the position taken in the House bill.

SENATE REPORT NO. 95-989

Increased access to the simpler, speedier, and less expensive debtor relief provisions of chapter 13 is accomplished by permitting debtors engaged in business to proceed under chapter 13, provided their income is sufficiently stable and regular to permit compliance with a chapter 13 plan [section 101(24)] and that the debtor (or the debtor and spouse) do not owe liquidated, noncontingent unsecured debts of $50,000, or liquidated, noncontingent secured debts of $200,000 (§109(d)).

Section 1304(a) states that a self-employed individual who incurs trade credit in the production of income is a debtor engaged in business.

Subsection (b) empowers a chapter 13 debtor engaged in business to operate his business, subject to the rights, powers and limitations that pertain to a trustee under sections 363(c) and 364 of title 11, and subject to such further limitations and conditions as the court may prescribe.

Subsection (c) requires a chapter 13 debtor engaged in business to file with the court certain financial statements relating to the operation of the business.

AMENDMENTS

1984—Subsec. (b). Pub. L. 98-353, §526, struck out the comma after "of the debtor".

Subsec. (c). Pub. L. 98-353, §311(b)(2), substituted "section 704(8)" for "section 704(7)".

EFFECTIVE DATE OF 1984 AMENDMENT

Amendment by Pub. L. 98-353 effective with respect to cases filed 90 days after July 10, 1984, see section 552(a) of Pub. L. 98-353, set out as a note under section 101 of this title.

§ 1305. Filing and allowance of postpetition claims

(a) A proof of claim may be filed by any entity that holds a claim against the debtor—

(1) for taxes that become payable to a governmental unit while the case is pending; or

(2) that is a consumer debt, that arises after the date of the order for relief under this chapter, and that is for property or services necessary for the debtor's performance under the plan.

(b) Except as provided in subsection (c) of this section, a claim filed under subsection (a) of this section shall be allowed or disallowed under section 502 of this title, but shall be determined as of the date such claim arises, and shall be allowed under section 502(a), 502(b), or 502(c) of this title, or disallowed under section 502(d) or 502(e) of this title, the same as if such claim had arisen before the date of the filing of the petition.

(c) A claim filed under subsection (a)(2) of this section shall be disallowed if the holder of such claim knew or should have known that prior approval by the trustee of the debtor's incurring the obligation was practicable and was not obtained.

(Pub. L. 95–598, Nov. 6, 1978, 92 Stat. 2647.)

Historical and Revision Notes

legislative statements

Section 1305(a)(2) of the House amendment modifies similar provisions contained in the House and Senate bills by restricting application of the paragraph to a consumer debt. Debts of the debtor that are not consumer debts should not be subjected to section 1305(c) or section 1328(d) of the House amendment.

Section 1305(b) of the House amendment represents a technical modification of similar provisions contained in the House bill and Senate amendment.

The House amendment deletes section 1305(d) of the Senate amendment as unnecessary. Section 502(b)(1) is sufficient to disallow any claim to the extent the claim represents the usurious interest or any other charge forbidden by applicable law. It is anticipated that the Rules of Bankruptcy Procedure may require a creditor filing a proof of claim in a case under chapter 13 to include an affirmative statement as contemplated by section 1305(d) of the Senate amendment.

senate report no. 95–989

Section 1305, exclusively applicable in chapter 13 cases, supplements the provisions of sections 501–511 of title 11, dealing with the filing and allowance of claims. Sections 501–511 apply in chapter 13 cases by virtue of section 103(a) of this title. Section 1305(a) provides for the filing of a proof of claim for taxes and other obligations incurred after the filing of the chapter 13 case. Subsection (b) prescribes that section 502 of title 11 governs the allowance of section 1305(a) claims, except that its standards shall be applied as of the date of allowance of the claim, rather than the date of filing of the petition. Subsection (c) requires the disallowance of a postpetition claim for property or services necessary for the debtor's performance under the plan, if the holder of the claim knew or should have known that prior approval by the trustee of the debtor's incurring of the obligation was practicable and was not obtained.

house report no. 95–595

Subsection (a) permits the filing of a proof of a claim against the debtor that is for taxes that become payable to a governmental unit while the case is pending, or that arises after the date of the filing of the petition for property or services that are necessary for the debtor's performance under the plan, such as auto repairs in order that the debtor will be able to get to work, or medical bills. The effect of the latter provision, in paragraph (2), is to treat postpetition credit extended to a chapter 13 debtor the same as a prepetition claim for purposes of allowance, distribution, and so on.

§ 1306. Property of the estate

(a) Property of the estate includes, in addition to the property specified in section 541 of this title—

(1) all property of the kind specified in such section that the debtor acquires after the commencement of the case but before the case is closed, dismissed, or converted to a case under chapter 7, 11, or 12 of this title, whichever occurs first; and

(2) earnings from services performed by the debtor after the commencement of the case but before the case is closed, dismissed, or converted to a case under chapter 7, 11, or 12 of this title, whichever occurs first.

(b) Except as provided in a confirmed plan or order confirming a plan, the debtor shall remain in possession of all property of the estate.

(Pub. L. 95–598, Nov. 6, 1978, 92 Stat. 2647; Pub. L. 99–554, title II, § 257(u), Oct. 27, 1986, 100 Stat. 3116.)

Historical and Revision Notes

legislative statements

Section 1306(a)(2) adopts a provision contained in the Senate amendment in preference to a similar provision contained in the House bill.

senate report no. 95–989

Section 541 is expressly made applicable to chapter 13 cases by section 103(a). Section 1306 broadens the definition of property of the estate for chapter 13 purposes to include all property acquired and all earnings from services performed by the debtor after the commencement of the case.

Subsection (b) nullifies the effect of section 521(3), otherwise applicable, by providing that a chapter 13 debtor need not surrender possession of property of the estate, unless required by the plan or order of confirmation.

Amendments

1986—Subsec. (a). Pub. L. 99–554 inserted reference to chapter 12 in pars. (1) and (2).

Effective Date of 1986 Amendment

Amendment by Pub. L. 99–554 effective 30 days after Oct. 27, 1986, but not applicable to cases commenced under this title before that date, see section 302(a), (c)(1) of Pub. L. 99–554, set out as a note under section 581 of Title 28, Judiciary and Judicial Procedure.

§ 1307. Conversion or dismissal

(a) The debtor may convert a case under this chapter to a case under chapter 7 of this title at any time. Any waiver of the right to convert under this subsection is unenforceable.

(b) On request of the debtor at any time, if the case has not been converted under section 706, 1112, or 1208 of this title, the court shall dismiss a case under this chapter. Any waiver of the right to dismiss under this subsection is unenforceable.

(c) Except as provided in subsection (e)[1] of this section, on request of a party in interest or the United States trustee and after notice and a hearing, the court may convert a case under this chapter to a case under chapter 7 of this title, or may dismiss a case under this chapter, whichever is in the best interests of creditors and the estate, for cause, including—

(1) unreasonable delay by the debtor that is prejudicial to creditors;

(2) nonpayment of any fees and charges required under chapter 123 of title 28;

(3) failure to file a plan timely under section 1321 of this title;

(4) failure to commence making timely payments under section 1326 of this title;

(5) denial of confirmation of a plan under section 1325 of this title and denial of a request made for additional time for filing another plan or a modification of a plan;

(6) material default by the debtor with respect to a term of a confirmed plan;

(7) revocation of the order of confirmation under section 1330 of this title, and denial of confirmation of a modified plan under section 1329 of this title;

(8) termination of a confirmed plan by reason of the occurrence of a condition specified in the plan other than completion of payments under the plan;

(9) only on request of the United States trustee, failure of the debtor to file, within fifteen days, or such additional time as the court may allow, after the filing of the petition commencing such case, the information required by paragraph (1) of section 521;

(10) only on request of the United States trustee, failure to timely file the information required by paragraph (2) of section 521; or

(11) failure of the debtor to pay any domestic support obligation that first becomes payable after the date of the filing of the petition.

(d) Except as provided in subsection (e) of this section, at any time before the confirmation of a plan under section 1325 of this title, on request of a party in interest or the United States trustee and after notice and a hearing, the court may convert a case under this chapter to a case under chapter 11 or 12 of this title.

(e) Upon the failure of the debtor to file a tax return under section 1308, on request of a party in interest or the United States trustee and after notice and a hearing, the court shall dismiss a case or convert a case under this chapter to a case under chapter 7 of this title, whichever is in the best interest of the creditors and the estate.

(f) The court may not convert a case under this chapter to a case under chapter 7, 11, or 12 of this title if the debtor is a farmer, unless the debtor requests such conversion.

(g) Notwithstanding any other provision of this section, a case may not be converted to a case under another chapter of this title unless the debtor may be a debtor under such chapter.

(Pub. L. 95–598, Nov. 6, 1978, 92 Stat. 2647; Pub. L. 98–353, title III, §§315, 527, July 10, 1984, 98 Stat. 356, 389; Pub. L. 99–554, title II, §§229, 257(v), Oct. 27, 1986, 100 Stat. 3103, 3116; Pub. L. 109–8, title II, §213(7), title VII, §716(c), Apr. 20, 2005, 119 Stat. 53, 130.)

[1] See References in Text note below.

Historical and Revision Notes

Legislative Statements

Section 1307(a) is derived from the Senate amendment in preference to a comparable provision contained in the House bill.

Senate Report No. 95–989

Subsections (a) and (b) confirm, without qualification, the rights of a chapter 13 debtor to convert the case to a liquidating bankruptcy case under chapter 7 of title 11, at any time, or to have the chapter 13 case dismissed. Waiver of any such right is unenforceable. Subsection (c) specifies various conditions for the exercise of the power of the court to convert a chapter 13 case to one under chapter 7 or to dismiss the case. Subsection (d) deals with the conversion of a chapter 13 case to one under chapter 11. Subsection (e) prohibits conversion of the chapter 13 case filed by a farmer to chapter 7 or 11 except at the request of the debtor. No case is to be converted from chapter 13 to any other chapter, unless the debtor is an eligible debtor under the new chapter.

House Report No. 95–595

Subsection (f) reinforces section 109 by prohibiting conversion to a chapter under which the debtor is not eligible to proceed.

References in Text

Subsection (e) of this section, referred to in subsec. (c), was redesignated as subsec. (f) of this section, and a new subsec. (e) was added, by Pub. L. 109–8, title VII, §716(c), Apr. 20, 2005, 119 Stat. 130.

Amendments

2005—Subsec. (c)(11). Pub. L. 109–8, §213(7), added par. (11).

Subsecs. (e) to (g). Pub. L. 109–8, §716(c), added subsec. (e) and redesignated former subsecs. (e) and (f) as (f) and (g), respectively.

1986—Subsec. (b). Pub. L. 99–554, §257(v)(1), inserted reference to section 1208 of this title.

Subsec. (c). Pub. L. 99–554, §229(1)(A), inserted "or the United States trustee" after "party in interest" in provisions preceding par. (1).

Subsec. (c)(9), (10). Pub. L. 99–554, §229(1)(B)–(D), added pars. (9) and (10).

Subsec. (d). Pub. L. 99–554, §257(v)(2), inserted reference to chapter 12.

Pub. L. 99–554, §229(2), inserted "or the United States trustee" after "party in interest".

Subsec. (e). Pub. L. 99–554, §257(v)(3), inserted reference to chapter 12.

1984—Subsec. (b). Pub. L. 98–353, §527(a), inserted a comma after "time".

Subsec. (c)(4). Pub. L. 98–353, §315(2), added par. (4). Former par. (4) redesignated (5).

Subsec. (c)(5). Pub. L. 98–353, §§315(1), 527(b)(1), redesignated former par. (4) as (5) and inserted "a request made for" before "additional". Former par. (5) redesignated (6).

Subsec. (c)(6). Pub. L. 98–353, §315(1), redesignated former par. (5) as (6). Former par. (6) redesignated (7).

Subsec. (c)(7). Pub. L. 98–353, §§315(1), 527(b)(2), redesignated former par. (6) as (7) and substituted "or" for "and". Former par. (7) redesignated (8).

Subsec. (c)(8). Pub. L. 98–353, §§315(1), 527(b)(3), redesignated former par. (7) as (8) and inserted "other than completion of payments under the plan" after "in the plan".

Effective Date of 2005 Amendment

Amendment by Pub. L. 109–8 effective 180 days after Apr. 20, 2005, and not applicable with respect to cases commenced under this title before such effective date, except as otherwise provided, see section 1501 of Pub. L. 109–8, set out as a note under section 101 of this title.

EFFECTIVE DATE OF 1986 AMENDMENT

Effective date and applicability of amendment by section 229 of Pub. L. 99–554 dependent upon the judicial district involved, see section 302(d), (e) of Pub. L. 99–554, set out as a note under section 581 of Title 28, Judiciary and Judicial Procedure.

Amendment by section 257 of Pub. L. 99–554 effective 30 days after Oct. 27, 1986, but not applicable to cases commenced under this title before that date, see section 302(a), (c)(1) of Pub. L. 99–554.

EFFECTIVE DATE OF 1984 AMENDMENT

Amendment by Pub. L. 98–353 effective with respect to cases filed 90 days after July 10, 1984, see section 552(a) of Pub. L. 98–353, set out as a note under section 101 of this title.

§ 1308. Filing of prepetition tax returns

(a) Not later than the day before the date on which the meeting of the creditors is first scheduled to be held under section 341(a), if the debtor was required to file a tax return under applicable nonbankruptcy law, the debtor shall file with appropriate tax authorities all tax returns for all taxable periods ending during the 4-year period ending on the date of the filing of the petition.

(b)(1) Subject to paragraph (2), if the tax returns required by subsection (a) have not been filed by the date on which the meeting of creditors is first scheduled to be held under section 341(a), the trustee may hold open that meeting for a reasonable period of time to allow the debtor an additional period of time to file any unfiled returns, but such additional period of time shall not extend beyond—

(A) for any return that is past due as of the date of the filing of the petition, the date that is 120 days after the date of that meeting; or

(B) for any return that is not past due as of the date of the filing of the petition, the later of—

(i) the date that is 120 days after the date of that meeting; or

(ii) the date on which the return is due under the last automatic extension of time for filing that return to which the debtor is entitled, and for which request is timely made, in accordance with applicable nonbankruptcy law.

(2) After notice and a hearing, and order entered before the tolling of any applicable filing period determined under this subsection, if the debtor demonstrates by a preponderance of the evidence that the failure to file a return as required under this subsection is attributable to circumstances beyond the control of the debtor, the court may extend the filing period established by the trustee under this subsection for—

(A) a period of not more than 30 days for returns described in paragraph (1); and

(B) a period not to extend after the applicable extended due date for a return described in paragraph (2).[1]

(c) For purposes of this section, the term "return" includes a return prepared pursuant to subsection (a) or (b) of section 6020 of the Internal Revenue Code of 1986, or a similar State or local law, or a written stipulation to a judgment or a final order entered by a nonbankruptcy tribunal.

(Added Pub. L. 109–8, title VII, § 716(b)(1), Apr. 20, 2005, 119 Stat. 129.)

[1] So in original.

REFERENCES IN TEXT

Section 6020 of the Internal Revenue Code of 1986, referred to in subsec. (c), is classified to section 6020 of Title 26, Internal Revenue Code.

EFFECTIVE DATE

Section effective 180 days after Apr. 20, 2005, and not applicable with respect to cases commenced under this title before such effective date, except as otherwise provided, see section 1501 of Pub. L. 109–8, set out as an Effective Date of 2005 Amendment note under section 101 of this title.

SUBCHAPTER II—THE PLAN

§ 1321. Filing of plan

The debtor shall file a plan.

(Pub. L. 95–598, Nov. 6, 1978, 92 Stat. 2648.)

HISTORICAL AND REVISION NOTES

SENATE REPORT NO. 95–989

Chapter 13 contemplates the filing of a plan only by the debtor.

§ 1322. Contents of plan

(a) The plan shall—

(1) provide for the submission of all or such portion of future earnings or other future income of the debtor to the supervision and control of the trustee as is necessary for the execution of the plan;

(2) provide for the full payment, in deferred cash payments, of all claims entitled to priority under section 507 of this title, unless the holder of a particular claim agrees to a different treatment of such claim;

(3) if the plan classifies claims, provide the same treatment for each claim within a particular class; and

(4) notwithstanding any other provision of this section, a plan may provide for less than full payment of all amounts owed for a claim entitled to priority under section 507(a)(1)(B) only if the plan provides that all of the debtor's projected disposable income for a 5-year period beginning on the date that the first payment is due under the plan will be applied to make payments under the plan.

(b) Subject to subsections (a) and (c) of this section, the plan may—

(1) designate a class or classes of unsecured claims, as provided in section 1122 of this title, but may not discriminate unfairly against any class so designated; however, such plan may treat claims for a consumer debt of the debtor if an individual is liable on such consumer debt with the debtor differently than other unsecured claims;

(2) modify the rights of holders of secured claims, other than a claim secured only by a security interest in real property that is the debtor's principal residence, or of holders of

unsecured claims, or leave unaffected the rights of holders of any class of claims;

(3) provide for the curing or waiving of any default;

(4) provide for payments on any unsecured claim to be made concurrently with payments on any secured claim or any other unsecured claim;

(5) notwithstanding paragraph (2) of this subsection, provide for the curing of any default within a reasonable time and maintenance of payments while the case is pending on any unsecured claim or secured claim on which the last payment is due after the date on which the final payment under the plan is due;

(6) provide for the payment of all or any part of any claim allowed under section 1305 of this title;

(7) subject to section 365 of this title, provide for the assumption, rejection, or assignment of any executory contract or unexpired lease of the debtor not previously rejected under such section;

(8) provide for the payment of all or part of a claim against the debtor from property of the estate or property of the debtor;

(9) provide for the vesting of property of the estate, on confirmation of the plan or at a later time, in the debtor or in any other entity;

(10) provide for the payment of interest accruing after the date of the filing of the petition on unsecured claims that are nondischargeable under section 1328(a), except that such interest may be paid only to the extent that the debtor has disposable income available to pay such interest after making provision for full payment of all allowed claims; and

(11) include any other appropriate provision not inconsistent with this title.

(c) Notwithstanding subsection (b)(2) and applicable nonbankruptcy law—

(1) a default with respect to, or that gave rise to, a lien on the debtor's principal residence may be cured under paragraph (3) or (5) of subsection (b) until such residence is sold at a foreclosure sale that is conducted in accordance with applicable nonbankruptcy law; and

(2) in a case in which the last payment on the original payment schedule for a claim secured only by a security interest in real property that is the debtor's principal residence is due before the date on which the final payment under the plan is due, the plan may provide for the payment of the claim as modified pursuant to section 1325(a)(5) of this title.

(d)(1) If the current monthly income of the debtor and the debtor's spouse combined, when multiplied by 12, is not less than—

(A) in the case of a debtor in a household of 1 person, the median family income of the applicable State for 1 earner;

(B) in the case of a debtor in a household of 2, 3, or 4 individuals, the highest median family income of the applicable State for a family of the same number or fewer individuals; or

(C) in the case of a debtor in a household exceeding 4 individuals, the highest median family income of the applicable State for a family of 4 or fewer individuals, plus $525 per month for each individual in excess of 4,

the plan may not provide for payments over a period that is longer than 5 years.

(2) If the current monthly income of the debtor and the debtor's spouse combined, when multiplied by 12, is less than—

(A) in the case of a debtor in a household of 1 person, the median family income of the applicable State for 1 earner;

(B) in the case of a debtor in a household of 2, 3, or 4 individuals, the highest median family income of the applicable State for a family of the same number or fewer individuals; or

(C) in the case of a debtor in a household exceeding 4 individuals, the highest median family income of the applicable State for a family of 4 or fewer individuals, plus $525 per month for each individual in excess of 4,

the plan may not provide for payments over a period that is longer than 3 years, unless the court, for cause, approves a longer period, but the court may not approve a period that is longer than 5 years.

(e) Notwithstanding subsection (b)(2) of this section and sections 506(b) and 1325(a)(5) of this title, if it is proposed in a plan to cure a default, the amount necessary to cure the default, shall be determined in accordance with the underlying agreement and applicable nonbankruptcy law.

(f) A plan may not materially alter the terms of a loan described in section 362(b)(19) and any amounts required to repay such loan shall not constitute "disposable income" under section 1325.

(Pub. L. 95–598, Nov. 6, 1978, 92 Stat. 2648; Pub. L. 98–353, title III, §§316, 520, July 10, 1984, 98 Stat. 356, 389; Pub. L. 103–394, title III, §§301, 305(c), Oct. 22, 1994, 108 Stat. 4131, 4134; Pub. L. 109–8, title II, §§213(8), (9), 224(d), title III, §318(1), Apr. 20, 2005, 119 Stat. 53, 65, 93.)

HISTORICAL AND REVISION NOTES

LEGISLATIVE STATEMENTS

Section 1322(b)(2) of the House amendment represents a compromise agreement between similar provisions in the House bill and Senate amendment. Under the House amendment, the plan may modify the rights of holders of secured claims other than a claim secured by a security interest in real property that is the debtor's principal residence. It is intended that a claim secured by the debtor's principal residence may be treated with under section 1322(b)(5) of the House amendment.

Section 1322(c) adopts a 5-year period derived from the House bill in preference to a 4-year period contained in the Senate amendment. A conforming change is made in section 1329(c) adopting the provision in the House bill in preference to a comparable provision in the Senate amendment.

Tax payments in wage earner plans: The House bill provided that a wage earner plan had to provide that all priority claims would be paid in full. The Senate amendment contained a special rule in section 1325(c) requiring that Federal tax claims must be paid in cash, but that such tax claims can be paid in deferred cash installments under the general rules applicable to the payment of debts in a wage earner plan, unless the Internal Revenue Service negotiates with the debtor for some different medium or time for payment of the tax liability.

The House bill adopts the substance of the Senate amendment rule under section 1322(a)(2) of the House amendment. A wage earner plan must provide for full payment in deferred cash payments, of all priority claims, unless the holder of a particular claim agrees with a different treatment of such claim.

SENATE REPORT NO. 95–989

Chapter 13 is designed to serve as a flexible vehicle for the repayment of part or all of the allowed claims of the debtor. Section 1322 emphasizes that purpose by fixing a minimum of mandatory plan provisions.

Subsection (a) requires that the plan submit whatever portion of the future income of the debtor is necessary to implement the plan to the control of the trustee, mandates payment in full of all section 507 priority claims, and requires identical treatment for all claims of a particular class.

Subsection (b) permits a chapter 13 plan to (1) divide unsecured claims not entitled to priority under section 507 into classes in the manner authorized for chapter 11 claims; (2) modify the rights of holders of secured and unsecured claims, except claims wholly secured by real estate mortgages; (3) cure or waive any default; (4) propose payments on unsecured claims concurrently with payments on any secured claim or any other class of unsecured claims; (5) provide for curing any default on any secured or unsecured claim on which the final payment is due after the proposed final payment under the plan; (6) provide for payment of any allowed postpetition claim; (7) assume or reject any previously unrejected executory contract or unexpired lease of the debtor; (8) propose the payment of all or any part of any claim from property of the estate or of the debtor; (9) provide for the vesting of property of the estate; and (10) include any other provision not inconsistent with other provisions of title 11.

Subsection (c) limits the payment period under the plan to 3 years, except that a 4-year payment period may be permitted by the court.

AMENDMENTS

2005—Subsec. (a)(4). Pub. L. 109–8, §213(8), added par. (4).

Subsec. (b)(10), (11). Pub. L. 109–8, §213(9), added par. (10) and redesignated former par. (10) as (11).

Subsec. (d). Pub. L. 109–8, §318(1), amended subsec. (d) generally. Prior to amendment, subsec. (d) read as follows: "The plan may not provide for payments over a period that is longer than three years, unless the court, for cause, approves a longer period, but the court may not approve a period that is longer than five years."

Subsec. (f). Pub. L. 109–8, §224(d), added subsec. (f).

1994—Subsecs. (c), (d). Pub. L. 103–394, §301, added subsec. (c) and redesignated former subsec. (c) as (d).

Subsec. (e). Pub. L. 103–394, §305(c), added subsec. (e).

1984—Subsec. (a)(2). Pub. L. 98–353, §528(a), inserted a comma after "payments".

Subsec. (b)(1). Pub. L. 98–353, §316, inserted "; however, such plan may treat claims for a consumer debt of the debtor if an individual is liable on such consumer debt with the debtor differently than other unsecured claims".

Subsec. (b)(2). Pub. L. 98–353, §528(b)(1), inserted ", or leave unaffected the rights of the holders of any class of claims".

Subsec. (b)(4). Pub. L. 98–353, §528(b)(2), inserted "other" after "claim or any".

Subsec. (b)(7). Pub. L. 98–353, §528(b)(3), inserted "subject to section 365 of this title," before "provide", substituted ", rejection, or assignment" for "or rejection", and substituted "under such section" for "under section 365 of this title".

Subsec. (b)(8). Pub. L. 98–353, §528(b)(4), struck out "any" before "part of a claim".

EFFECTIVE DATE OF 2005 AMENDMENT

Amendment by Pub. L. 109–8 effective 180 days after Apr. 20, 2005, and not applicable with respect to cases commenced under this title before such effective date, except as otherwise provided, see section 1501 of Pub. L. 109–8, set out as a note under section 101 of this title.

EFFECTIVE DATE OF 1994 AMENDMENT

Amendment by section 301 of Pub. L. 103–394 effective Oct. 22, 1994, and not applicable with respect to cases commenced under this title before Oct. 22, 1994, and amendment by section 305(c) of Pub. L. 103–394 effective Oct. 22, 1994, and applicable only to agreements entered into after Oct. 22, 1994, see section 702 of Pub. L. 103–394, set out as a note under section 101 of this title.

EFFECTIVE DATE OF 1984 AMENDMENT

Amendment by Pub. L. 98–353 effective with respect to cases filed 90 days after July 10, 1984, see section 552(a) of Pub. L. 98–353, set out as a note under section 101 of this title.

ADJUSTMENT OF DOLLAR AMOUNTS

For adjustment of dollar amounts specified in subsec. (d) of this section by the Judicial Conference of the United States, see note set out under section 104 of this title.

§1323. Modification of plan before confirmation

(a) The debtor may modify the plan at any time before confirmation, but may not modify the plan so that the plan as modified fails to meet the requirements of section 1322 of this title.

(b) After the debtor files a modification under this section, the plan as modified becomes the plan.

(c) Any holder of a secured claim that has accepted or rejected the plan is deemed to have accepted or rejected, as the case may be, the plan as modified, unless the modification provides for a change in the rights of such holder from what such rights were under the plan before modification, and such holder changes such holder's previous acceptance or rejection.

(Pub. L. 95–598, Nov. 6, 1978, 92 Stat. 2649.)

HISTORICAL AND REVISION NOTES

SENATE REPORT NO. 95–989

The debtor is permitted to modify the plan before confirmation without court approval so long as the modified plan, which becomes the plan on filing, complies with the requirements of section 1322.

The original acceptance or rejection of a plan by the holder of a secured claim remains binding unless the modified plan changes the rights of the holder and the holder withdraws or alters its earlier acceptance or rejection.

§1324. Confirmation hearing

(a) Except as provided in subsection (b) and after notice, the court shall hold a hearing on confirmation of the plan. A party in interest may object to confirmation of the plan.

(b) The hearing on confirmation of the plan may be held not earlier than 20 days and not later than 45 days after the date of the meeting of creditors under section 341(a), unless the court determines that it would be in the best interests of the creditors and the estate to hold such hearing at an earlier date and there is no objection to such earlier date.

(Pub. L. 95–598, Nov. 6, 1978, 92 Stat. 2649; Pub. L. 98–353, title III, §529, July 10, 1984, 98 Stat. 389; Pub. L. 99–554, title II, §283(x), Oct. 27, 1986, 100

Stat. 3118; Pub. L. 109–8, title III, §317, Apr. 20, 2005, 119 Stat. 92.)

HISTORICAL AND REVISION NOTES

SENATE REPORT NO. 95–989

Any party in interest may object to the confirmation of a plan, as distinguished from merely rejecting a plan. An objection to confirmation is predicated on failure of the plan or the procedures employed prior to confirmation to conform with the requirements of chapter 13. The bankruptcy judge is required to provide notice and an opportunity for hearing any such objection to confirmation.

AMENDMENTS

2005—Pub. L. 109–8 designated existing provisions as subsec. (a), substituted "Except as provided in subsection (b) and after" for "After", and added subsec. (b).

1986—Pub. L. 99–554 struck out "the" after "object to".

1984—Pub. L. 98–353 struck out "the" before "confirmation of the plan".

EFFECTIVE DATE OF 2005 AMENDMENT

Amendment by Pub. L. 109–8 effective 180 days after Apr. 20, 2005, and not applicable with respect to cases commenced under this title before such effective date, except as otherwise provided, see section 1501 of Pub. L. 109–8, set out as a note under section 101 of this title.

EFFECTIVE DATE OF 1986 AMENDMENT

Amendment by Pub. L. 99–554 effective 30 days after Oct. 27, 1986, see section 302(a) of Pub. L. 99–554, set out as a note under section 581 of Title 28, Judiciary and Judicial Procedure.

EFFECTIVE DATE OF 1984 AMENDMENT

Amendment by Pub. L. 98–353 effective with respect to cases filed 90 days after July 10, 1984, see section 552(a) of Pub. L. 98–353, set out as a note under section 101 of this title.

§ 1325. Confirmation of plan

(a) Except as provided in subsection (b), the court shall confirm a plan if—

(1) The plan complies with the provisions of this chapter and with the other applicable provisions of this title;

(2) any fee, charge, or amount required under chapter 123 of title 28, or by the plan, to be paid before confirmation, has been paid;

(3) the plan has been proposed in good faith and not by any means forbidden by law;

(4) the value, as of the effective date of the plan, of property to be distributed under the plan on account of each allowed unsecured claim is not less than the amount that would be paid on such claim if the estate of the debtor were liquidated under chapter 7 of this title on such date;

(5) with respect to each allowed secured claim provided for by the plan—

(A) the holder of such claim has accepted the plan;

(B)(i) the plan provides that—

(I) the holder of such claim retain the lien securing such claim until the earlier of—

(aa) the payment of the underlying debt determined under nonbankruptcy law; or

(bb) discharge under section 1328; and

(II) if the case under this chapter is dismissed or converted without completion of the plan, such lien shall also be retained by such holder to the extent recognized by applicable nonbankruptcy law;

(ii) the value, as of the effective date of the plan, of property to be distributed under the plan on account of such claim is not less than the allowed amount of such claim; and

(iii) if—

(I) property to be distributed pursuant to this subsection is in the form of periodic payments, such payments shall be in equal monthly amounts; and

(II) the holder of the claim is secured by personal property, the amount of such payments shall not be less than an amount sufficient to provide to the holder of such claim adequate protection during the period of the plan; or

(C) the debtor surrenders the property securing such claim to such holder;

(6) the debtor will be able to make all payments under the plan and to comply with the plan;

(7) the action of the debtor in filing the petition was in good faith;

(8) the debtor has paid all amounts that are required to be paid under a domestic support obligation and that first become payable after the date of the filing of the petition if the debtor is required by a judicial or administrative order, or by statute, to pay such domestic support obligation; and

(9) the debtor has filed all applicable Federal, State, and local tax returns as required by section 1308.

For purposes of paragraph (5), section 506 shall not apply to a claim described in that paragraph if the creditor has a purchase money security interest securing the debt that is the subject of the claim, the debt was incurred within the 910-day preceding the date of the filing of the petition, and the collateral for that debt consists of a motor vehicle (as defined in section 30102 of title 49) acquired for the personal use of the debtor, or if collateral for that debt consists of any other thing of value, if the debt was incurred during the 1-year period preceding that filing.

(b)(1) If the trustee or the holder of an allowed unsecured claim objects to the confirmation of the plan, then the court may not approve the plan unless, as of the effective date of the plan—

(A) the value of the property to be distributed under the plan on account of such claim is not less than the amount of such claim; or

(B) the plan provides that all of the debtor's projected disposable income to be received in the applicable commitment period beginning on the date that the first payment is due under the plan will be applied to make payments to unsecured creditors under the plan.

(2) For purposes of this subsection, the term "disposable income" means current monthly income received by the debtor (other than child support payments, foster care payments, or disability payments for a dependent child made in accordance with applicable nonbankruptcy law

to the extent reasonably necessary to be expended for such child) less amounts reasonably necessary to be expended—

(A)(i) for the maintenance or support of the debtor or a dependent of the debtor, or for a domestic support obligation, that first becomes payable after the date the petition is filed; and

(ii) for charitable contributions (that meet the definition of "charitable contribution" under section 548(d)(3)[1] to a qualified religious or charitable entity or organization (as defined in section 548(d)(4)) in an amount not to exceed 15 percent of gross income of the debtor for the year in which the contributions are made; and

(B) if the debtor is engaged in business, for the payment of expenditures necessary for the continuation, preservation, and operation of such business.

(3) Amounts reasonably necessary to be expended under paragraph (2), other than subparagraph (A)(ii) of paragraph (2), shall be determined in accordance with subparagraphs (A) and (B) of section 707(b)(2), if the debtor has current monthly income, when multiplied by 12, greater than—

(A) in the case of a debtor in a household of 1 person, the median family income of the applicable State for 1 earner;

(B) in the case of a debtor in a household of 2, 3, or 4 individuals, the highest median family income of the applicable State for a family of the same number or fewer individuals; or

(C) in the case of a debtor in a household exceeding 4 individuals, the highest median family income of the applicable State for a family of 4 or fewer individuals, plus $525 per month for each individual in excess of 4.

(4) For purposes of this subsection, the "applicable commitment period"—

(A) subject to subparagraph (B), shall be—

(i) 3 years; or

(ii) not less than 5 years, if the current monthly income of the debtor and the debtor's spouse combined, when multiplied by 12, is not less than—

(I) in the case of a debtor in a household of 1 person, the median family income of the applicable State for 1 earner;

(II) in the case of a debtor in a household of 2, 3, or 4 individuals, the highest median family income of the applicable State for a family of the same number or fewer individuals; or

(III) in the case of a debtor in a household exceeding 4 individuals, the highest median family income of the applicable State for a family of 4 or fewer individuals, plus $525 per month for each individual in excess of 4; and

(B) may be less than 3 or 5 years, whichever is applicable under subparagraph (A), but only if the plan provides for payment in full of all allowed unsecured claims over a shorter period.

(c) After confirmation of a plan, the court may order any entity from whom the debtor receives income to pay all or any part of such income to the trustee.

(Pub. L. 95–598, Nov. 6, 1978, 92 Stat. 2649; Pub. L. 98–353, title III, §§317, 530, July 10, 1984, 98 Stat. 356, 389; Pub. L. 99–554, title II, §283(y), Oct. 27, 1986, 100 Stat. 3118; Pub. L. 105–183, §4(a), June 19, 1998, 112 Stat. 518; Pub. L. 109–8, title I, §102(g), (h), title II, §213(10), title III, §§306(a), (b), 309(c)(1), 318(2), (3), title VII, §716(a), Apr. 20, 2005, 119 Stat. 33, 53, 80, 83, 93, 129; Pub. L. 109–439, §2, Dec. 20, 2006, 120 Stat. 3285.)

HISTORICAL AND REVISION NOTES

LEGISLATIVE STATEMENTS

Section 1325(a)(5)(B) of the House amendment modifies the House bill and Senate amendment to significantly protect secured creditors in chapter 13. Unless the secured creditor accepts the plan, the plan must provide that the secured creditor retain the lien securing the creditor's allowed secured claim in addition to receiving value, as of the effective date of the plan of property to be distributed under the plan on account of the claim not less than the allowed amount of the claim. To this extent, a secured creditor in a case under chapter 13 is treated identically with a recourse creditor under section 1111(b)(1) of the House amendment except that the secured creditor in a case under chapter 13 may receive any property of a value as of the effective date of the plan equal to the allowed amount of the creditor's secured claim rather than being restricted to receiving deferred cash payments. Of course, the secured creditors' lien only secures the value of the collateral and to the extent property is distributed of a present value equal to the allowed amount of the creditor's secured claim the creditor's lien will have been satisfied in full. Thus the lien created under section 1325(a)(5)(B)(i) is effective only to secure deferred payments to the extent of the amount of the allowed secured claim. To the extent the deferred payments exceed the value of the allowed amount of the secured claim and the debtor subsequently defaults, the lien will not secure unaccrued interest represented in such deferred payments.

SENATE REPORT NO. 95–989

The bankruptcy court must confirm a plan if (1) the plan satisfies the provisions of chapter 13 and other applicable provisions of title 11; (2) it is proposed in good faith; (3) it is in the best interests of creditors, and defined by subsection (a)(4) of Section 1325; (4) it has been accepted by the holder of each allowed secured claim provided for the plan or where the holder of any such secured claim is to receive value under the plan not less than the amount of the allowed secured claim, or where the debtor surrenders to the holder the collateral securing any such allowed secured claim; (5) the plan is feasible; and (6) the requisite fees and charges have been paid.

Subsection (b) authorizes the court to order an entity, as defined by Section 101(15), to pay any income of the debtor to the trustee. Any governmental unit is an entity subject to such an order.

AMENDMENTS

2006—Subsec. (b)(3). Pub. L. 109–439 inserted ", other than subparagraph (A)(ii) of paragraph (2)," after "under paragraph (2)" in introductory provisions.

2005—Subsec. (a). Pub. L. 109–8, §306(b), inserted concluding provisions at end "For purposes of paragraph (5), section 506 shall not apply to a claim described in that paragraph if the creditor has a purchase money security interest securing the debt that is the subject of the claim, the debt was incurred within the 910-day preceding the date of the filing of the petition, and the collateral for that debt consists of a motor vehicle (as defined in section 30102 of title 49) acquired for the per-

[1] So in original. Probably should be followed by a second closing parenthesis.

sonal use of the debtor, or if collateral for that debt consists of any other thing of value, if the debt was incurred during the 1-year period preceding that filing."

Subsec. (a)(5)(B)(i). Pub. L. 109-8, §306(a), amended cl. (i) generally. Prior to amendment, cl. (i) read as follows: "the plan provides that the holder of such claim retain the lien securing such claim; and".

Subsec. (a)(5)(B)(iii). Pub. L. 109-8, §309(c)(1), added cl. (iii).

Subsec. (a)(7). Pub. L. 109-8, §102(g), added par. (7).

Subsec. (a)(8). Pub. L. 109-8, §213(10), added par. (8).

Subsec. (a)(9). Pub. L. 109-8, §716(a), added par. (9).

Subsec. (b)(1)(B). Pub. L. 109-8, §318(2), substituted "applicable commitment period" for "three-year period".

Pub. L. 109-8, §102(h)(1), inserted "to unsecured creditors" after "to make payments".

Subsec. (b)(2), (3). Pub. L. 109-8, §102(h)(2), added pars. (2) and (3) and struck out former par. (2) which read as follows: "For purposes of this subsection, 'disposable income' means income which is received by the debtor and which is not reasonably necessary to be expended—

"(A) for the maintenance or support of the debtor or a dependent of the debtor, including charitable contributions (that meet the definition of 'charitable contribution' under section 548(d)(3)) to a qualified religious or charitable entity or organization (as that term is defined in section 548(d)(4)) in an amount not to exceed 15 percent of the gross income of the debtor for the year in which the contributions are made; and

"(B) if the debtor is engaged in business, for the payment of expenditures necessary for the continuation, preservation, and operation of such business."

Subsec. (b)(4). Pub. L. 109-8, §318(3), added par. (4).

1998—Subsec. (b)(2)(A). Pub. L. 105-183 inserted before semicolon ", including charitable contributions (that meet the definition of 'charitable contribution' under section 548(d)(3)) to a qualified religious or charitable entity or organization (as that term is defined in section 548(d)(4)) in an amount not to exceed 15 percent of the gross income of the debtor for the year in which the contributions are made".

1986—Subsec. (b)(2)(A). Pub. L. 99-554 substituted "; and" for "; or".

1984—Subsec. (a). Pub. L. 98-353, §317(1), substituted "Except as provided in subsection (b), the" for "The".

Subsec. (a)(1). Pub. L. 98-353, §530, inserted "the" before "other".

Subsecs. (b), (c). Pub. L. 98-353, §317(2), (3), added subsec. (b) and redesignated former subsec. (b) as (c).

EFFECTIVE DATE OF 2005 AMENDMENT

Amendment by Pub. L. 109-8 effective 180 days after Apr. 20, 2005, and not applicable with respect to cases commenced under this title before such effective date, except as otherwise provided, see section 1501 of Pub. L. 109-8, set out as a note under section 101 of this title.

EFFECTIVE DATE OF 1998 AMENDMENT

Amendment by Pub. L. 105-183 applicable to any case brought under an applicable provision of this title that is pending or commenced on or after June 19, 1998, see section 5 of Pub. L. 105-183, set out as a note under section 544 of this title.

EFFECTIVE DATE OF 1986 AMENDMENT

Amendment by Pub. L. 99-554 effective 30 days after Oct. 27, 1986, see section 302(a) of Pub. L. 99-554, set out as a note under section 581 of Title 28, Judiciary and Judicial Procedure.

EFFECTIVE DATE OF 1984 AMENDMENT

Amendment by Pub. L. 98-353 effective with respect to cases filed 90 days after July 10, 1984, see section 552(a) of Pub. L. 98-353, set out as a note under section 101 of this title.

ADJUSTMENT OF DOLLAR AMOUNTS

For adjustment of dollar amounts specified in subsec. (b) of this section by the Judicial Conference of the United States, see note set out under section 104 of this title.

§1326. Payments

(a)(1) Unless the court orders otherwise, the debtor shall commence making payments not later than 30 days after the date of the filing of the plan or the order for relief, whichever is earlier, in the amount—

(A) proposed by the plan to the trustee;

(B) scheduled in a lease of personal property directly to the lessor for that portion of the obligation that becomes due after the order for relief, reducing the payments under subparagraph (A) by the amount so paid and providing the trustee with evidence of such payment, including the amount and date of payment; and

(C) that provides adequate protection directly to a creditor holding an allowed claim secured by personal property to the extent the claim is attributable to the purchase of such property by the debtor for that portion of the obligation that becomes due after the order for relief, reducing the payments under subparagraph (A) by the amount so paid and providing the trustee with evidence of such payment, including the amount and date of payment.

(2) A payment made under paragraph (1)(A) shall be retained by the trustee until confirmation or denial of confirmation. If a plan is confirmed, the trustee shall distribute any such payment in accordance with the plan as soon as is practicable. If a plan is not confirmed, the trustee shall return any such payments not previously paid and not yet due and owing to creditors pursuant to paragraph (3) to the debtor, after deducting any unpaid claim allowed under section 503(b).

(3) Subject to section 363, the court may, upon notice and a hearing, modify, increase, or reduce the payments required under this subsection pending confirmation of a plan.

(4) Not later than 60 days after the date of filing of a case under this chapter, a debtor retaining possession of personal property subject to a lease or securing a claim attributable in whole or in part to the purchase price of such property shall provide the lessor or secured creditor reasonable evidence of the maintenance of any required insurance coverage with respect to the use or ownership of such property and continue to do so for so long as the debtor retains possession of such property.

(b) Before or at the time of each payment to creditors under the plan, there shall be paid—

(1) any unpaid claim of the kind specified in section 507(a)(2) of this title;

(2) if a standing trustee appointed under section 586(b) of title 28 is serving in the case, the percentage fee fixed for such standing trustee under section 586(e)(1)(B) of title 28; and

(3) if a chapter 7 trustee has been allowed compensation due to the conversion or dismissal of the debtor's prior case pursuant to section 707(b), and some portion of that compensation remains unpaid in a case converted to this chapter or in the case dismissed under section 707(b) and refiled under this chapter,

the amount of any such unpaid compensation, which shall be paid monthly—

(A) by prorating such amount over the remaining duration of the plan; and

(B) by monthly payments not to exceed the greater of—

(i) $25; or

(ii) the amount payable to unsecured nonpriority creditors, as provided by the plan, multiplied by 5 percent, and the result divided by the number of months in the plan.

(c) Except as otherwise provided in the plan or in the order confirming the plan, the trustee shall make payments to creditors under the plan.

(d) Notwithstanding any other provision of this title—

(1) compensation referred to in subsection (b)(3) is payable and may be collected by the trustee under that paragraph, even if such amount has been discharged in a prior case under this title; and

(2) such compensation is payable in a case under this chapter only to the extent permitted by subsection (b)(3).

(Pub. L. 95–598, Nov. 6, 1978, 92 Stat. 2650; Pub. L. 98–353, title III, §§318(a), 531, July 10, 1984, 98 Stat. 357, 389; Pub. L. 99–554, title II, §§230, 283(z), Oct. 27, 1986, 100 Stat. 3103, 3118; Pub. L. 103–394, title III, §307, Oct. 22, 1994, 108 Stat. 4135; Pub. L. 109–8, title III, §309(c)(2), title XII, §1224, title XV, §1502(a)(10), Apr. 20, 2005, 119 Stat. 83, 199, 217.)

HISTORICAL AND REVISION NOTES

LEGISLATIVE STATEMENTS

Section 1326(a)(2) of the House amendment adopts a comparable provision contained in the House bill providing for standing trustees.

SENATE REPORT NO. 95–989

Section 1326 supplements the priorities provisions of section 507. Subsection (a) requires accrued costs of administration and filing fees, as well as fees due the chapter 13 trustee, to be disbursed before payments to creditors under the plan. Subsection (b) makes it clear that the chapter 13 trustee is normally to make distribution to creditors of the payments made under the plan by the debtor.

HOUSE REPORT NO. 95–595

Subsection (a) requires that before or at the time of each payment any outstanding administrative expenses [and] any percentage fee due for a private standing chapter 13 trustee be paid in full.

AMENDMENTS

2005—Subsec. (a). Pub. L. 109–8, §309(c)(2), amended subsec. (a) generally. Prior to amendment subsec. (a) read as follows:

"(a)(1) Unless the court orders otherwise, the debtor shall commence making the payments proposed by a plan within 30 days after the plan is filed.

"(2) A payment made under this subsection shall be retained by the trustee until confirmation or denial of confirmation of a plan. If a plan is confirmed, the trustee shall distribute any such payment in accordance with the plan as soon as practicable. If a plan is not confirmed, the trustee shall return any such payment to the debtor, after deducting any unpaid claim allowed under section 503(b) of this title."

Subsec. (b)(1). Pub. L. 109–8, §1502(a)(10), substituted "507(a)(2)" for "507(a)(1)".

Subsec. (b)(3). Pub. L. 109–8, §1224(1), added par. (3).

Subsec. (d). Pub. L. 109–8, §1224(2), added subsec. (d).

1994—Subsec. (a)(2). Pub. L. 103–394 inserted "as soon as practicable" before period at end of second sentence.

1986—Subsec. (a)(2). Pub. L. 99–554, §283(z), substituted "payment" for "payments" in last sentence.

Subsec. (b). Pub. L. 99–554, §230, amended subsec. (b) generally, substituting "586(b) of title 28" for "1302(d) of this title" and "586(e)(1)(B) of title 28" for "1302(e) of this title" in par. (2).

1984—Subsec. (a). Pub. L. 98–353, §318(a)(2), added subsec. (a). Former subsec. (a) redesignated (b).

Subsec. (b). Pub. L. 98–353, §318(a)(1), redesignated subsec. (a) as (b). Former subsec. (b) redesignated (c).

Subsec. (b)(2). Pub. L. 98–353, §531, inserted "of this title" after "1302(d)".

Subsec. (c). Pub. L. 98–353, §318(a)(1), redesignated former subsec. (b) as (c).

EFFECTIVE DATE OF 2005 AMENDMENT

Amendment by Pub. L. 109–8 effective 180 days after Apr. 20, 2005, and not applicable with respect to cases commenced under this title before such effective date, except as otherwise provided, see section 1501 of Pub. L. 109–8, set out as a note under section 101 of this title.

EFFECTIVE DATE OF 1994 AMENDMENT

Amendment by Pub. L. 103–394 effective Oct. 22, 1994, and not applicable with respect to cases commenced under this title before Oct. 22, 1994, see section 702 of Pub. L. 103–394, set out as a note under section 101 of this title.

EFFECTIVE DATE OF 1986 AMENDMENT

Effective date and applicability of amendment by section 230 of Pub. L. 99–554 dependent upon the judicial district involved, see section 302(d), (e) of Pub. L. 99–554, set out as a note under section 581 of Title 28, Judiciary and Judicial Procedure.

Amendment by section 283 of Pub. L. 99–554 effective 30 days after Oct. 27, 1986, see section 302(a) of Pub. L. 99–554.

EFFECTIVE DATE OF 1984 AMENDMENT

Amendment by Pub. L. 98–353 effective with respect to cases filed 90 days after July 10, 1984, see section 552(a) of Pub. L. 98–353, set out as a note under section 101 of this title.

ADJUSTMENT OF DOLLAR AMOUNTS

For adjustment of dollar amounts specified in subsec. (b)(3) of this section by the Judicial Conference of the United States, see note set out under section 104 of this title.

§ 1327. Effect of confirmation

(a) The provisions of a confirmed plan bind the debtor and each creditor, whether or not the claim of such creditor is provided for by the plan, and whether or not such creditor has objected to, has accepted, or has rejected the plan.

(b) Except as otherwise provided in the plan or the order confirming the plan, the confirmation of a plan vests all of the property of the estate in the debtor.

(c) Except as otherwise provided in the plan or in the order confirming the plan, the property vesting in the debtor under subsection (b) of this section is free and clear of any claim or interest of any creditor provided for by the plan.

(Pub. L. 95–598, Nov. 6, 1978, 92 Stat. 2650.)

HISTORICAL AND REVISION NOTES

SENATE REPORT NO. 95–989

Subsection (a) binds the debtor and each creditor to the provisions of a confirmed plan, whether or not the claim of the creditor is provided for by the plan and whether or not the creditor has accepted, rejected, or objected to the plan. Unless the plan itself or the order confirming the plan otherwise provides, confirmation is deemed to vest all property of the estate in the debtor, free and clear of any claim or interest of any creditor provided for by the plan.

§ 1328. Discharge

(a) Subject to subsection (d), as soon as practicable after completion by the debtor of all payments under the plan, and in the case of a debtor who is required by a judicial or administrative order, or by statute, to pay a domestic support obligation, after such debtor certifies that all amounts payable under such order or such statute that are due on or before the date of the certification (including amounts due before the petition was filed, but only to the extent provided for by the plan) have been paid, unless the court approves a written waiver of discharge executed by the debtor after the order for relief under this chapter, the court shall grant the debtor a discharge of all debts provided for by the plan or disallowed under section 502 of this title, except any debt—

(1) provided for under section 1322(b)(5);

(2) of the kind specified in section 507(a)(8)(C) or in paragraph (1)(B), (1)(C), (2), (3), (4), (5), (8), or (9) of section 523(a);

(3) for restitution, or a criminal fine, included in a sentence on the debtor's conviction of a crime; or

(4) for restitution, or damages, awarded in a civil action against the debtor as a result of willful or malicious injury by the debtor that caused personal injury to an individual or the death of an individual.

(b) Subject to subsection (d), at any time after the confirmation of the plan and after notice and a hearing, the court may grant a discharge to a debtor that has not completed payments under the plan only if—

(1) the debtor's failure to complete such payments is due to circumstances for which the debtor should not justly be held accountable;

(2) the value, as of the effective date of the plan, of property actually distributed under the plan on account of each allowed unsecured claim is not less than the amount that would have been paid on such claim if the estate of the debtor had been liquidated under chapter 7 of this title on such date; and

(3) modification of the plan under section 1329 of this title is not practicable.

(c) A discharge granted under subsection (b) of this section discharges the debtor from all unsecured debts provided for by the plan or disallowed under section 502 of this title, except any debt—

(1) provided for under section 1322(b)(5) of this title; or

(2) of a kind specified in section 523(a) of this title.

(d) Notwithstanding any other provision of this section, a discharge granted under this section does not discharge the debtor from any debt based on an allowed claim filed under section 1305(a)(2) of this title if prior approval by the trustee of the debtor's incurring such debt was practicable and was not obtained.

(e) On request of a party in interest before one year after a discharge under this section is granted, and after notice and a hearing, the court may revoke such discharge only if—

(1) such discharge was obtained by the debtor through fraud; and

(2) the requesting party did not know of such fraud until after such discharge was granted.

(f) Notwithstanding subsections (a) and (b), the court shall not grant a discharge of all debts provided for in the plan or disallowed under section 502, if the debtor has received a discharge—

(1) in a case filed under chapter 7, 11, or 12 of this title during the 4-year period preceding the date of the order for relief under this chapter, or

(2) in a case filed under chapter 13 of this title during the 2-year period preceding the date of such order.

(g)(1) The court shall not grant a discharge under this section to a debtor unless after filing a petition the debtor has completed an instructional course concerning personal financial management described in section 111.

(2) Paragraph (1) shall not apply with respect to a debtor who is a person described in section 109(h)(4) or who resides in a district for which the United States trustee (or the bankruptcy administrator, if any) determines that the approved instructional courses are not adequate to service the additional individuals who would otherwise be required to complete such instructional course by reason of the requirements of paragraph (1).

(3) The United States trustee (or the bankruptcy administrator, if any) who makes a determination described in paragraph (2) shall review such determination not later than 1 year after the date of such determination, and not less frequently than annually thereafter.

(h) The court may not grant a discharge under this chapter unless the court after notice and a hearing held not more than 10 days before the date of the entry of the order granting the discharge finds that there is no reasonable cause to believe that—

(1) section 522(q)(1) may be applicable to the debtor; and

(2) there is pending any proceeding in which the debtor may be found guilty of a felony of the kind described in section 522(q)(1)(A) or liable for a debt of the kind described in section 522(q)(1)(B).

(Pub. L. 95–598, Nov. 6, 1978, 92 Stat. 2650; Pub. L. 98–353, title III, § 532, July 10, 1984, 98 Stat. 389; Pub. L. 101–508, title III, § 3007(b)(1), Nov. 5, 1990, 104 Stat. 1388–28; Pub. L. 101–581, §§ 2(b), 3, Nov. 15, 1990, 104 Stat. 2865; Pub. L. 101–647, title XXXI, §§ 3102(b), 3103, Nov. 29, 1990, 104 Stat. 4916; Pub. L. 103–394, title III, § 302, title V, § 501(d)(38), Oct. 22, 1994, 108 Stat. 4132, 4147; Pub. L. 109–8, title I, § 106(c), title II, § 213(11), title III, §§ 312(2), 314(b), 330(d), title VII, § 707, Apr. 20, 2005, 119 Stat. 38, 53, 87, 88, 102, 126.)

Historical and Revision Notes

legislative statements

Section 1328(a) adopts a provision contained in the Senate amendment permitting the court to approve a waiver of discharge by the debtor. It is anticipated that such a waiver must be in writing executed after the order for relief in a case under chapter 13.

SENATE REPORT NO. 95–989

The court is to enter a discharge, unless waived, as soon as practicable after completion of payments under the plan. The debtor is to be discharged of all debts provided for by the plan or disallowed under section 502, except a debt provided for under the plan the last payment on which was not due until after the completion of the plan, or a debt incurred for willful and malicious conversion of or injury to the property or person of another.

Subsection (b) is the successor to Bankruptcy Act Section 661 [section 1061 of former title 11]. This subsection permits the bankruptcy judge to grant the debtor a discharge at any time after confirmation of a plan, if the court determines, after notice and hearing, that the failure to complete payments under the plan is due to circumstances for which the debtor should not justly be held accountable, the distributions made to each creditor under the plan equal in value the amount that would have been paid to the creditor had the estate been liquidated under chapter 7 of title 11 at the date of the hearing under this subsection, and that modification of the plan is impracticable. The discharge granted under subsection (b) relieves the debtor from all unsecured debts provided for by the plan or disallowed under section 502, except nondischargeable debts described in section 523(a) of title 11 or debts of the type covered by section 1322(b)(5).

Subsection (d) excepts from any chapter 13 discharge a debt based on an allowed section 1305(a)(2) postpetition claim, if prior trustee approval of the incurring of the debt was practicable but was not obtained.

A chapter 13 discharge obtained through fraud and before the moving party gained knowledge of the fraud may be revoked by the court under subsection (e), after notice and hearing, at the request of any party in interest made within 1 year after the discharge was granted.

AMENDMENTS

2005—Subsec. (a). Pub. L. 109–8, §330(d)(1), substituted "Subject to subsection (d), as" for "As" in introductory provisions.

Pub. L. 109–8, §314(b), added pars. (1) to (4) and struck out former pars. (1) to (3) which read as follows:

"(1) provided for under section 1322(b)(5) of this title;

"(2) of the kind specified in paragraph (5), (8), or (9) of section 523(a) of this title; or

"(3) for restitution, or a criminal fine, included in a sentence on the debtor's conviction of a crime."

Pub. L. 109–8, §213(11), inserted ", and in the case of a debtor who is required by a judicial or administrative order, or by statute, to pay a domestic support obligation, after such debtor certifies that all amounts payable under such order or such statute that are due on or before the date of the certification (including amounts due before the petition was filed, but only to the extent provided for by the plan) have been paid" after "completion by the debtor of all payments under the plan" in introductory provisions.

Subsec. (a)(2). Pub. L. 109–8, §707, substituted "section 507(a)(8)(C) or in paragraph (1)(B), (1)(C)," for "paragraph".

Subsec. (b). Pub. L. 109–8, §330(d)(2), substituted "Subject to subsection (d), at" for "At" in introductory provisions.

Subsec. (f). Pub. L. 109–8, §312(2), added subsec. (f).

Subsec. (g). Pub. L. 109–8, §106(c), added subsec. (g).

Subsec. (h). Pub. L. 109–8, §330(d)(3), added subsec. (h).

1994—Subsec. (a)(2). Pub. L. 103–394, §501(d)(38)(A), substituted "(5), (8), or (9)" for "(5) or (8)".

Subsec. (a)(3). Pub. L. 103–394, §501(d)(38)(B), struck out last par. (3). See 1990 Amendment note below.

Pub. L. 103–394, §302, inserted ", or a criminal fine," after "restitution".

1990—Subsec. (a)(1). Pub. L. 101–581, §3(1), and Pub. L. 101–647, §3103(1), made identical amendments striking "or" at end.

Subsec. (a)(2). Pub. L. 101–581, §3(2), and Pub. L. 101–647, §3103(2), made identical amendments substituting "; or" for period at end.

Pub. L. 101–581, §2(b), and Pub. L. 101–647, §3102(b), which directed identical insertions of "or 523(a)(9)" after "523(a)(5)", could not be executed because of prior amendment by Pub. L. 101–508. See below.

Pub. L. 101–508 substituted "paragraph (5) or (8) of section 523(a)" for "section 523(a)(5)".

Subsec. (a)(3). Pub. L. 101–581, §3(3), and Pub. L. 101–647, §3103(3), made identical amendments adding par. (3).

1984—Subsec. (e)(1). Pub. L. 98–353, §532(1), inserted "by the debtor" after "obtained".

Subsec. (e)(2). Pub. L. 98–353, §532(2), substituted "the requesting party did not know of such fraud until" for "knowledge of such fraud came to the requesting party".

EFFECTIVE DATE OF 2005 AMENDMENT

Amendments by Pub. L. 109–8 effective 180 days after Apr. 20, 2005, with amendments by sections 106(c), 213(11), 312(2), 314(b), and 707 of Pub. L. 109–8 not applicable with respect to cases commenced under this title before such effective date, except as otherwise provided, and amendment by section 330(d) of Pub. L. 109–8 applicable with respect to cases commenced under this title on or after Apr. 20, 2005, see section 1501 of Pub. L. 109–8, set out as a note under section 101 of this title.

EFFECTIVE DATE OF 1994 AMENDMENT

Amendment by Pub. L. 103–394 effective Oct. 22, 1994, and not applicable with respect to cases commenced under this title before Oct. 22, 1994, see section 702 of Pub. L. 103–394, set out as a note under section 101 of this title.

EFFECTIVE DATE OF 1990 AMENDMENTS

Amendment by Pub. L. 101–647 effective Nov. 29, 1990, but not applicable with respect to cases commenced under this title before Nov. 29, 1990, see section 3104 of Pub. L. 101–647, set out as a note under section 523 of this title.

Amendment by Pub. L. 101–581 effective Nov. 15, 1990, but not applicable with respect to cases commenced under this title before Nov. 15, 1990, see section 4 of Pub. L. 101–581, set out as a note under section 523 of this title.

Section 3007(b)(2) of Pub. L. 101–508 provided that: "The amendment made by paragraph (1) [amending this section] shall not apply to any case under the provisions of title 11, United States Code, commenced before the date of the enactment of this Act [Nov. 5, 1990]."

EFFECTIVE DATE OF 1984 AMENDMENT

Amendment by Pub. L. 98–353 effective with respect to cases filed 90 days after July 10, 1984, see section 552(a) of Pub. L. 98–353, set out as a note under section 101 of this title.

§ 1329. Modification of plan after confirmation

(a) At any time after confirmation of the plan but before the completion of payments under such plan, the plan may be modified, upon request of the debtor, the trustee, or the holder of an allowed unsecured claim, to—

(1) increase or reduce the amount of payments on claims of a particular class provided for by the plan;

(2) extend or reduce the time for such payments;

(3) alter the amount of the distribution to a creditor whose claim is provided for by the plan to the extent necessary to take account of any payment of such claim other than under the plan; or

(4) reduce amounts to be paid under the plan by the actual amount expended by the debtor to purchase health insurance for the debtor (and for any dependent of the debtor if such dependent does not otherwise have health insurance coverage) if the debtor documents the cost of such insurance and demonstrates that—

(A) such expenses are reasonable and necessary;

(B)(i) if the debtor previously paid for health insurance, the amount is not materially larger than the cost the debtor previously paid or the cost necessary to maintain the lapsed policy; or

(ii) if the debtor did not have health insurance, the amount is not materially larger than the reasonable cost that would be incurred by a debtor who purchases health insurance, who has similar income, expenses, age, and health status, and who lives in the same geographical location with the same number of dependents who do not otherwise have health insurance coverage; and

(C) the amount is not otherwise allowed for purposes of determining disposable income under section 1325(b) of this title;

and upon request of any party in interest, files proof that a health insurance policy was purchased.

(b)(1) Sections 1322(a), 1322(b), and 1323(c) of this title and the requirements of section 1325(a) of this title apply to any modification under subsection (a) of this section.

(2) The plan as modified becomes the plan unless, after notice and a hearing, such modification is disapproved.

(c) A plan modified under this section may not provide for payments over a period that expires after the applicable commitment period under section 1325(b)(1)(B) after the time that the first payment under the original confirmed plan was due, unless the court, for cause, approves a longer period, but the court may not approve a period that expires after five years after such time.

(Pub. L. 95–598, Nov. 6, 1978, 92 Stat. 2651; Pub. L. 98–353, title III, §§319, 533, July 10, 1984, 98 Stat. 357, 389; Pub. L. 109–8, title I, §102(i), title III, §318(4), Apr. 20, 2005, 119 Stat. 34, 94.)

HISTORICAL AND REVISION NOTES

SENATE REPORT NO. 95–989

At any time prior to the completion of payments under a confirmed plan, the plan may be modified, after notice and hearing, to change the amount of payments to creditors or a particular class of creditors and to extend or reduce the payment period. A modified plan may not contain any provision which could not be included in an original plan as prescribed by section 1322. A modified plan may not call for payments to be made beyond four years as measured from the date of the commencement of payments under the original plan.

AMENDMENTS

2005—Subsec. (a)(4). Pub. L. 109–8, §102(i), added par. (4).

Subsec. (c). Pub. L. 109–8, §318(4), substituted "the applicable commitment period under section 1325(b)(1)(B)" for "three years".

1984—Subsec. (a). Pub. L. 98–353, §§319, 533(1), (2), inserted "of the plan" after "confirmation", substituted "such plan" for "a plan", and inserted provisions respecting requests by the debtor, the trustee, or the holder of an allowed unsecured claim for modification.

Subsec. (a)(3). Pub. L. 98–353, §533(3), substituted "plan to" for "plan, to".

EFFECTIVE DATE OF 2005 AMENDMENT

Amendment by Pub. L. 109–8 effective 180 days after Apr. 20, 2005, and not applicable with respect to cases commenced under this title before such effective date, except as otherwise provided, see section 1501 of Pub. L. 109–8, set out as a note under section 101 of this title.

EFFECTIVE DATE OF 1984 AMENDMENT

Amendment by Pub. L. 98–353 effective with respect to cases filed 90 days after July 10, 1984, see section 552(a) of Pub. L. 98–353, set out as a note under section 101 of this title.

§1330. Revocation of an order of confirmation

(a) On request of a party in interest at any time within 180 days after the date of the entry of an order of confirmation under section 1325 of this title, and after notice and a hearing, the court may revoke such order if such order was procured by fraud.

(b) If the court revokes an order of confirmation under subsection (a) of this section, the court shall dispose of the case under section 1307 of this title, unless, within the time fixed by the court, the debtor proposes and the court confirms a modification of the plan under section 1329 of this title.

(Pub. L. 95–598, Nov. 6, 1978, 92 Stat. 2651.)

HISTORICAL AND REVISION NOTES

LEGISLATIVE STATEMENTS

Section 1331 of the House bill and Senate amendment is deleted in the House amendment.

Special tax provision: Section 1331 of title 11 of the House bill and the comparable provisions in sections 1322 and 1327(d) of the Senate amendment, pertaining to assessment and collection of taxes in wage earner plans, are deleted, and the governing rule is placed in section 505(c) of the House amendment. The provisions of both bills allowing assessment and collection of taxes after confirmation of the wage-earner plan are modified to allow assessment and collection after the court fixes the fact and amount of a tax liability, including administrative period taxes, regardless of whether this occurs before or after confirmation of the plan. The provision of the House bill limiting the collection of taxes to those assessed before one year after the filing of the petition is eliminated, thereby leaving the period of limitations on assessment of these nondischargeable tax liabilities the usual period provided by the Internal Revenue Code [Title 26].

SENATE REPORT NO. 95–989

The court may revoke an order of confirmation procured by fraud, after notice and hearing, on application of a party in interest filed within 180 days after the entry of the order. Thereafter, unless a modified plan is confirmed, the court is to convert or dismiss the chapter 13 case as provided in section 1307.

CHAPTER 15—ANCILLARY AND OTHER CROSS-BORDER CASES

PRIOR PROVISIONS

A prior chapter 15, consisting of sections 1501 to 151326, related to a pilot program for a United States trustee system, prior to repeal by Pub. L. 99–554, title II, §231, Oct. 27, 1986, 100 Stat. 3103.

§1501. Purpose and scope of application

(a) The purpose of this chapter is to incorporate the Model Law on Cross-Border Insolvency so as to provide effective mechanisms for dealing with cases of cross-border insolvency with the objectives of—

(1) cooperation between—

(A) courts of the United States, United States trustees, trustees, examiners, debtors, and debtors in possession; and

(B) the courts and other competent authorities of foreign countries involved in cross-border insolvency cases;

(2) greater legal certainty for trade and investment;

(3) fair and efficient administration of cross-border insolvencies that protects the interests of all creditors, and other interested entities, including the debtor;

(4) protection and maximization of the value of the debtor's assets; and

(5) facilitation of the rescue of financially troubled businesses, thereby protecting investment and preserving employment.

(b) This chapter applies where—

(1) assistance is sought in the United States by a foreign court or a foreign representative in connection with a foreign proceeding;

(2) assistance is sought in a foreign country in connection with a case under this title;

(3) a foreign proceeding and a case under this title with respect to the same debtor are pending concurrently; or

(4) creditors or other interested persons in a foreign country have an interest in requesting the commencement of, or participating in, a case or proceeding under this title.

(c) This chapter does not apply to—

(1) a proceeding concerning an entity, other than a foreign insurance company, identified by exclusion in section 109(b);

(2) an individual, or to an individual and such individual's spouse, who have debts within the limits specified in section 109(e) and who are citizens of the United States or aliens lawfully admitted for permanent residence in the United States; or

(3) an entity subject to a proceeding under the Securities Investor Protection Act of 1970, a stockbroker subject to subchapter III of chapter 7 of this title, or a commodity broker subject to subchapter IV of chapter 7 of this title.

(d) The court may not grant relief under this chapter with respect to any deposit, escrow, trust fund, or other security required or permitted under any applicable State insurance law or regulation for the benefit of claim holders in the United States.

(Added Pub. L. 109–8, title VIII, §801(a), Apr. 20, 2005, 119 Stat. 135.)

REFERENCES IN TEXT

The Securities Investor Protection Act of 1970, referred to in subsec. (c)(3), is Pub. L. 91–598, Dec. 30, 1970, 84 Stat. 1636, as amended, which is classified generally to chapter 2B–1 (§78aaa et seq.) of Title 15, Commerce and Trade. For complete classification of this Act to the Code, see section 78aaa of Title 15 and Tables.

PRIOR PROVISIONS

A prior section 1501, Pub. L. 95–598, Nov. 6, 1978, 92 Stat. 2652, related to applicability of chapter which provided a pilot program for a United States trustee system, prior to repeal by Pub. L. 99–554, title II, §231, Oct. 27, 1986, 100 Stat. 3103.

EFFECTIVE DATE

Chapter effective 180 days after Apr. 20, 2005, and not applicable with respect to cases commenced under this title before such effective date, except as otherwise provided, see section 1501 of Pub. L. 109–8, set out as an Effective Date of 2005 Amendment note under section 101 of this title.

SUBCHAPTER I—GENERAL PROVISIONS

§ 1502. Definitions

For the purposes of this chapter, the term—

(1) "debtor" means an entity that is the subject of a foreign proceeding;

(2) "establishment" means any place of operations where the debtor carries out a nontransitory economic activity;

(3) "foreign court" means a judicial or other authority competent to control or supervise a foreign proceeding;

(4) "foreign main proceeding" means a foreign proceeding pending in the country where the debtor has the center of its main interests;

(5) "foreign nonmain proceeding" means a foreign proceeding, other than a foreign main proceeding, pending in a country where the debtor has an establishment;

(6) "trustee" includes a trustee, a debtor in possession in a case under any chapter of this title, or a debtor under chapter 9 of this title;

(7) "recognition" means the entry of an order granting recognition of a foreign main proceeding or foreign nonmain proceeding under this chapter; and

(8) "within the territorial jurisdiction of the United States", when used with reference to property of a debtor, refers to tangible property located within the territory of the United States and intangible property deemed under applicable nonbankruptcy law to be located within that territory, including any property subject to attachment or garnishment that may properly be seized or garnished by an action in a Federal or State court in the United States.

(Added Pub. L. 109–8, title VIII, § 801(a), Apr. 20, 2005, 119 Stat. 135.)

§ 1503. International obligations of the United States

To the extent that this chapter conflicts with an obligation of the United States arising out of any treaty or other form of agreement to which it is a party with one or more other countries, the requirements of the treaty or agreement prevail.

(Added Pub. L. 109–8, title VIII, § 801(a), Apr. 20, 2005, 119 Stat. 136.)

§ 1504. Commencement of ancillary case

A case under this chapter is commenced by the filing of a petition for recognition of a foreign proceeding under section 1515.

(Added Pub. L. 109–8, title VIII, § 801(a), Apr. 20, 2005, 119 Stat. 136.)

§ 1505. Authorization to act in a foreign country

A trustee or another entity (including an examiner) may be authorized by the court to act in a foreign country on behalf of an estate created under section 541. An entity authorized to act under this section may act in any way permitted by the applicable foreign law.

(Added Pub. L. 109–8, title VIII, § 801(a), Apr. 20, 2005, 119 Stat. 136.)

§ 1506. Public policy exception

Nothing in this chapter prevents the court from refusing to take an action governed by this chapter if the action would be manifestly contrary to the public policy of the United States.

(Added Pub. L. 109–8, title VIII, § 801(a), Apr. 20, 2005, 119 Stat. 136.)

§ 1507. Additional assistance

(a) Subject to the specific limitations stated elsewhere in this chapter the court, if recognition is granted, may provide additional assistance to a foreign representative under this title or under other laws of the United States.

(b) In determining whether to provide additional assistance under this title or under other laws of the United States, the court shall consider whether such additional assistance, consistent with the principles of comity, will reasonably assure—

(1) just treatment of all holders of claims against or interests in the debtor's property;

(2) protection of claim holders in the United States against prejudice and inconvenience in the processing of claims in such foreign proceeding;

(3) prevention of preferential or fraudulent dispositions of property of the debtor;

(4) distribution of proceeds of the debtor's property substantially in accordance with the order prescribed by this title; and

(5) if appropriate, the provision of an opportunity for a fresh start for the individual that such foreign proceeding concerns.

(Added Pub. L. 109–8, title VIII, § 801(a), Apr. 20, 2005, 119 Stat. 136.)

§ 1508. Interpretation

In interpreting this chapter, the court shall consider its international origin, and the need to promote an application of this chapter that is consistent with the application of similar statutes adopted by foreign jurisdictions.

(Added Pub. L. 109–8, title VIII, § 801(a), Apr. 20, 2005, 119 Stat. 137.)

SUBCHAPTER II—ACCESS OF FOREIGN REPRESENTATIVES AND CREDITORS TO THE COURT

§ 1509. Right of direct access

(a) A foreign representative may commence a case under section 1504 by filing directly with the court a petition for recognition of a foreign proceeding under section 1515.

(b) If the court grants recognition under section 1517, and subject to any limitations that the court may impose consistent with the policy of this chapter—

(1) the foreign representative has the capacity to sue and be sued in a court in the United States;

(2) the foreign representative may apply directly to a court in the United States for appropriate relief in that court; and

(3) a court in the United States shall grant comity or cooperation to the foreign representative.

(c) A request for comity or cooperation by a foreign representative in a court in the United States other than the court which granted recognition shall be accompanied by a certified copy of an order granting recognition under section 1517.

(d) If the court denies recognition under this chapter, the court may issue any appropriate order necessary to prevent the foreign representative from obtaining comity or cooperation from courts in the United States.

(e) Whether or not the court grants recognition, and subject to sections 306 and 1510, a foreign representative is subject to applicable nonbankruptcy law.

(f) Notwithstanding any other provision of this section, the failure of a foreign representative to commence a case or to obtain recognition under this chapter does not affect any right the foreign representative may have to sue in a court in the United States to collect or recover a claim which is the property of the debtor.

(Added Pub. L. 109–8, title VIII, §801(a), Apr. 20, 2005, 119 Stat. 137.)

§ 1510. Limited jurisdiction

The sole fact that a foreign representative files a petition under section 1515 does not subject the foreign representative to the jurisdiction of any court in the United States for any other purpose.

(Added Pub. L. 109–8, title VIII, §801(a), Apr. 20, 2005, 119 Stat. 138.)

§ 1511. Commencement of case under section 301 or 303

(a) Upon recognition, a foreign representative may commence—

(1) an involuntary case under section 303; or

(2) a voluntary case under section 301 or 302, if the foreign proceeding is a foreign main proceeding.

(b) The petition commencing a case under subsection (a) must be accompanied by a certified copy of an order granting recognition. The court where the petition for recognition has been filed must be advised of the foreign representative's intent to commence a case under subsection (a) prior to such commencement.

(Added Pub. L. 109–8, title VIII, §801(a), Apr. 20, 2005, 119 Stat. 138.)

§ 1512. Participation of a foreign representative in a case under this title

Upon recognition of a foreign proceeding, the foreign representative in the recognized proceeding is entitled to participate as a party in interest in a case regarding the debtor under this title.

(Added Pub. L. 109–8, title VIII, §801(a), Apr. 20, 2005, 119 Stat. 138.)

§ 1513. Access of foreign creditors to a case under this title

(a) Foreign creditors have the same rights regarding the commencement of, and participation in, a case under this title as domestic creditors.

(b)(1) Subsection (a) does not change or codify present law as to the priority of claims under section 507 or 726, except that the claim of a foreign creditor under those sections shall not be given a lower priority than that of general unsecured claims without priority solely because the holder of such claim is a foreign creditor.

(2)(A) Subsection (a) and paragraph (1) do not change or codify present law as to the allowability of foreign revenue claims or other foreign public law claims in a proceeding under this title.

(B) Allowance and priority as to a foreign tax claim or other foreign public law claim shall be governed by any applicable tax treaty of the United States, under the conditions and circumstances specified therein.

(Added Pub. L. 109–8, title VIII, §801(a), Apr. 20, 2005, 119 Stat. 138.)

§ 1514. Notification to foreign creditors concerning a case under this title

(a) Whenever in a case under this title notice is to be given to creditors generally or to any class or category of creditors, such notice shall also be given to the known creditors generally, or to creditors in the notified class or category, that do not have addresses in the United States. The court may order that appropriate steps be taken with a view to notifying any creditor whose address is not yet known.

(b) Such notification to creditors with foreign addresses described in subsection (a) shall be given individually, unless the court considers that, under the circumstances, some other form of notification would be more appropriate. No letter or other formality is required.

(c) When a notification of commencement of a case is to be given to foreign creditors, such notification shall—

(1) indicate the time period for filing proofs of claim and specify the place for filing such proofs of claim;

(2) indicate whether secured creditors need to file proofs of claim; and

(3) contain any other information required to be included in such notification to creditors under this title and the orders of the court.

(d) Any rule of procedure or order of the court as to notice or the filing of a proof of claim shall provide such additional time to creditors with foreign addresses as is reasonable under the circumstances.

(Added Pub. L. 109–8, title VIII, §801(a), Apr. 20, 2005, 119 Stat. 138.)

SUBCHAPTER III—RECOGNITION OF A FOREIGN PROCEEDING AND RELIEF

§ 1515. Application for recognition

(a) A foreign representative applies to the court for recognition of a foreign proceeding in which the foreign representative has been appointed by filing a petition for recognition.

(b) A petition for recognition shall be accompanied by—

(1) a certified copy of the decision commencing such foreign proceeding and appointing the foreign representative;

(2) a certificate from the foreign court affirming the existence of such foreign proceeding and of the appointment of the foreign representative; or

(3) in the absence of evidence referred to in paragraphs (1) and (2), any other evidence acceptable to the court of the existence of such foreign proceeding and of the appointment of the foreign representative.

(c) A petition for recognition shall also be accompanied by a statement identifying all foreign proceedings with respect to the debtor that are known to the foreign representative.

(d) The documents referred to in paragraphs (1) and (2) of subsection (b) shall be translated into English. The court may require a translation into English of additional documents.

(Added Pub. L. 109–8, title VIII, §801(a), Apr. 20, 2005, 119 Stat. 139.)

§ 1516. Presumptions concerning recognition

(a) If the decision or certificate referred to in section 1515(b) indicates that the foreign proceeding is a foreign proceeding and that the person or body is a foreign representative, the court is entitled to so presume.

(b) The court is entitled to presume that documents submitted in support of the petition for recognition are authentic, whether or not they have been legalized.

(c) In the absence of evidence to the contrary, the debtor's registered office, or habitual residence in the case of an individual, is presumed to be the center of the debtor's main interests.

(Added Pub. L. 109–8, title VIII, §801(a), Apr. 20, 2005, 119 Stat. 139.)

§ 1517. Order granting recognition

(a) Subject to section 1506, after notice and a hearing, an order recognizing a foreign proceeding shall be entered if—

(1) such foreign proceeding for which recognition is sought is a foreign main proceeding or foreign nonmain proceeding within the meaning of section 1502;

(2) the foreign representative applying for recognition is a person or body; and

(3) the petition meets the requirements of section 1515.

(b) Such foreign proceeding shall be recognized—

(1) as a foreign main proceeding if it is pending in the country where the debtor has the center of its main interests; or

(2) as a foreign nonmain proceeding if the debtor has an establishment within the meaning of section 1502 in the foreign country where the proceeding is pending.

(c) A petition for recognition of a foreign proceeding shall be decided upon at the earliest possible time. Entry of an order recognizing a foreign proceeding constitutes recognition under this chapter.

(d) The provisions of this subchapter do not prevent modification or termination of recognition if it is shown that the grounds for granting it were fully or partially lacking or have ceased to exist, but in considering such action the court shall give due weight to possible prejudice to parties that have relied upon the order granting recognition. A case under this chapter may be closed in the manner prescribed under section 350.

(Added Pub. L. 109–8, title VIII, §801(a), Apr. 20, 2005, 119 Stat. 139.)

§ 1518. Subsequent information

From the time of filing the petition for recognition of a foreign proceeding, the foreign representative shall file with the court promptly a notice of change of status concerning—

(1) any substantial change in the status of such foreign proceeding or the status of the foreign representative's appointment; and

(2) any other foreign proceeding regarding the debtor that becomes known to the foreign representative.

(Added Pub. L. 109–8, title VIII, §801(a), Apr. 20, 2005, 119 Stat. 140.)

§ 1519. Relief that may be granted upon filing petition for recognition

(a) From the time of filing a petition for recognition until the court rules on the petition, the court may, at the request of the foreign representative, where relief is urgently needed to protect the assets of the debtor or the interests of the creditors, grant relief of a provisional nature, including—

(1) staying execution against the debtor's assets;

(2) entrusting the administration or realization of all or part of the debtor's assets located in the United States to the foreign representative or another person authorized by the court, including an examiner, in order to protect and preserve the value of assets that, by their nature or because of other circumstances, are perishable, susceptible to devaluation or otherwise in jeopardy; and

(3) any relief referred to in paragraph (3), (4), or (7) of section 1521(a).

(b) Unless extended under section 1521(a)(6), the relief granted under this section terminates when the petition for recognition is granted.

(c) It is a ground for denial of relief under this section that such relief would interfere with the administration of a foreign main proceeding.

(d) The court may not enjoin a police or regulatory act of a governmental unit, including a criminal action or proceeding, under this section.

(e) The standards, procedures, and limitations applicable to an injunction shall apply to relief under this section.

(f) The exercise of rights not subject to the stay arising under section 362(a) pursuant to paragraph (6), (7), (17), or (27) of section 362(b) or pursuant to section 362(n) shall not be stayed by any order of a court or administrative agency in any proceeding under this chapter.

(Added Pub. L. 109–8, title VIII, §801(a), Apr. 20, 2005, 119 Stat. 140.)

§ 1520. Effects of recognition of a foreign main proceeding

(a) Upon recognition of a foreign proceeding that is a foreign main proceeding—

(1) sections 361 and 362 apply with respect to the debtor and the property of the debtor that is within the territorial jurisdiction of the United States;

(2) sections 363, 549, and 552 apply to a transfer of an interest of the debtor in property that is within the territorial jurisdiction of the United States to the same extent that the sections would apply to property of an estate;

(3) unless the court orders otherwise, the foreign representative may operate the debtor's business and may exercise the rights and powers of a trustee under and to the extent provided by sections 363 and 552; and

(4) section 552 applies to property of the debtor that is within the territorial jurisdiction of the United States.

(b) Subsection (a) does not affect the right to commence an individual action or proceeding in a foreign country to the extent necessary to preserve a claim against the debtor.

(c) Subsection (a) does not affect the right of a foreign representative or an entity to file a petition commencing a case under this title or the right of any party to file claims or take other proper actions in such a case.

(Added Pub. L. 109–8, title VIII, §801(a), Apr. 20, 2005, 119 Stat. 141.)

§1521. Relief that may be granted upon recognition

(a) Upon recognition of a foreign proceeding, whether main or nonmain, where necessary to effectuate the purpose of this chapter and to protect the assets of the debtor or the interests of the creditors, the court may, at the request of the foreign representative, grant any appropriate relief, including—

(1) staying the commencement or continuation of an individual action or proceeding concerning the debtor's assets, rights, obligations or liabilities to the extent they have not been stayed under section 1520(a);

(2) staying execution against the debtor's assets to the extent it has not been stayed under section 1520(a);

(3) suspending the right to transfer, encumber or otherwise dispose of any assets of the debtor to the extent this right has not been suspended under section 1520(a);

(4) providing for the examination of witnesses, the taking of evidence or the delivery of information concerning the debtor's assets, affairs, rights, obligations or liabilities;

(5) entrusting the administration or realization of all or part of the debtor's assets within the territorial jurisdiction of the United States to the foreign representative or another person, including an examiner, authorized by the court;

(6) extending relief granted under section 1519(a); and

(7) granting any additional relief that may be available to a trustee, except for relief available under sections 522, 544, 545, 547, 548, 550, and 724(a).

(b) Upon recognition of a foreign proceeding, whether main or nonmain, the court may, at the request of the foreign representative, entrust the distribution of all or part of the debtor's assets located in the United States to the foreign representative or another person, including an examiner, authorized by the court, provided that the court is satisfied that the interests of creditors in the United States are sufficiently protected.

(c) In granting relief under this section to a representative of a foreign nonmain proceeding, the court must be satisfied that the relief relates to assets that, under the law of the United States, should be administered in the foreign nonmain proceeding or concerns information required in that proceeding.

(d) The court may not enjoin a police or regulatory act of a governmental unit, including a criminal action or proceeding, under this section.

(e) The standards, procedures, and limitations applicable to an injunction shall apply to relief under paragraphs (1), (2), (3), and (6) of subsection (a).

(f) The exercise of rights not subject to the stay arising under section 362(a) pursuant to paragraph (6), (7), (17), or (27) of section 362(b) or pursuant to section 362(n) shall not be stayed by any order of a court or administrative agency in any proceeding under this chapter.

(Added Pub. L. 109–8, title VIII, §801(a), Apr. 20, 2005, 119 Stat. 141.)

§1522. Protection of creditors and other interested persons

(a) The court may grant relief under section 1519 or 1521, or may modify or terminate relief under subsection (c), only if the interests of the creditors and other interested entities, including the debtor, are sufficiently protected.

(b) The court may subject relief granted under section 1519 or 1521, or the operation of the debtor's business under section 1520(a)(3), to conditions it considers appropriate, including the giving of security or the filing of a bond.

(c) The court may, at the request of the foreign representative or an entity affected by relief granted under section 1519 or 1521, or at its own motion, modify or terminate such relief.

(d) Section 1104(d) shall apply to the appointment of an examiner under this chapter. Any examiner shall comply with the qualification requirements imposed on a trustee by section 322.

(Added Pub. L. 109–8, title VIII, §801(a), Apr. 20, 2005, 119 Stat. 142.)

§1523. Actions to avoid acts detrimental to creditors

(a) Upon recognition of a foreign proceeding, the foreign representative has standing in a case concerning the debtor pending under another chapter of this title to initiate actions under sections 522, 544, 545, 547, 548, 550, 553, and 724(a).

(b) When a foreign proceeding is a foreign nonmain proceeding, the court must be satisfied that an action under subsection (a) relates to assets that, under United States law, should be administered in the foreign nonmain proceeding.

(Added Pub. L. 109–8, title VIII, §801(a), Apr. 20, 2005, 119 Stat. 142.)

§ 1524. Intervention by a foreign representative

Upon recognition of a foreign proceeding, the foreign representative may intervene in any proceedings in a State or Federal court in the United States in which the debtor is a party.

(Added Pub. L. 109–8, title VIII, § 801(a), Apr. 20, 2005, 119 Stat. 142.)

SUBCHAPTER IV—COOPERATION WITH FOREIGN COURTS AND FOREIGN REPRESENTATIVES

§ 1525. Cooperation and direct communication between the court and foreign courts or foreign representatives

(a) Consistent with section 1501, the court shall cooperate to the maximum extent possible with a foreign court or a foreign representative, either directly or through the trustee.

(b) The court is entitled to communicate directly with, or to request information or assistance directly from, a foreign court or a foreign representative, subject to the rights of a party in interest to notice and participation.

(Added Pub. L. 109–8, title VIII, § 801(a), Apr. 20, 2005, 119 Stat. 143.)

§ 1526. Cooperation and direct communication between the trustee and foreign courts or foreign representatives

(a) Consistent with section 1501, the trustee or other person, including an examiner, authorized by the court, shall, subject to the supervision of the court, cooperate to the maximum extent possible with a foreign court or a foreign representative.

(b) The trustee or other person, including an examiner, authorized by the court is entitled, subject to the supervision of the court, to communicate directly with a foreign court or a foreign representative.

(Added Pub. L. 109–8, title VIII, § 801(a), Apr. 20, 2005, 119 Stat. 143.)

§ 1527. Forms of cooperation

Cooperation referred to in sections 1525 and 1526 may be implemented by any appropriate means, including—

(1) appointment of a person or body, including an examiner, to act at the direction of the court;

(2) communication of information by any means considered appropriate by the court;

(3) coordination of the administration and supervision of the debtor's assets and affairs;

(4) approval or implementation of agreements concerning the coordination of proceedings; and

(5) coordination of concurrent proceedings regarding the same debtor.

(Added Pub. L. 109–8, title VIII, § 801(a), Apr. 20, 2005, 119 Stat. 143.)

SUBCHAPTER V—CONCURRENT PROCEEDINGS

§ 1528. Commencement of a case under this title after recognition of a foreign main proceeding

After recognition of a foreign main proceeding, a case under another chapter of this title may be commenced only if the debtor has assets in the United States. The effects of such case shall be restricted to the assets of the debtor that are within the territorial jurisdiction of the United States and, to the extent necessary to implement cooperation and coordination under sections 1525, 1526, and 1527, to other assets of the debtor that are within the jurisdiction of the court under sections 541(a) of this title, and 1334(e) of title 28, to the extent that such other assets are not subject to the jurisdiction and control of a foreign proceeding that has been recognized under this chapter.

(Added Pub. L. 109–8, title VIII, § 801(a), Apr. 20, 2005, 119 Stat. 143.)

§ 1529. Coordination of a case under this title and a foreign proceeding

If a foreign proceeding and a case under another chapter of this title are pending concurrently regarding the same debtor, the court shall seek cooperation and coordination under sections 1525, 1526, and 1527, and the following shall apply:

(1) If the case in the United States pending at the time the petition for recognition of such foreign proceeding is filed—

(A) any relief granted under section 1519 or 1521 must be consistent with the relief granted in the case in the United States; and

(B) section 1520 does not apply even if such foreign proceeding is recognized as a foreign main proceeding.

(2) If a case in the United States under this title commences after recognition, or after the date of the filing of the petition for recognition, of such foreign proceeding—

(A) any relief in effect under section 1519 or 1521 shall be reviewed by the court and shall be modified or terminated if inconsistent with the case in the United States; and

(B) if such foreign proceeding is a foreign main proceeding, the stay and suspension referred to in section 1520(a) shall be modified or terminated if inconsistent with the relief granted in the case in the United States.

(3) In granting, extending, or modifying relief granted to a representative of a foreign nonmain proceeding, the court must be satisfied that the relief relates to assets that, under the laws of the United States, should be administered in the foreign nonmain proceeding or concerns information required in that proceeding.

(4) In achieving cooperation and coordination under sections 1528 and 1529, the court may grant any of the relief authorized under section 305.

(Added Pub. L. 109–8, title VIII, § 801(a), Apr. 20, 2005, 119 Stat. 144.)

§ 1530. Coordination of more than 1 foreign proceeding

In matters referred to in section 1501, with respect to more than 1 foreign proceeding regarding the debtor, the court shall seek cooperation and coordination under sections 1525, 1526, and 1527, and the following shall apply:

(1) Any relief granted under section 1519 or 1521 to a representative of a foreign nonmain proceeding after recognition of a foreign main proceeding must be consistent with the foreign main proceeding.

(2) If a foreign main proceeding is recognized after recognition, or after the filing of a petition for recognition, of a foreign nonmain proceeding, any relief in effect under section 1519 or 1521 shall be reviewed by the court and shall be modified or terminated if inconsistent with the foreign main proceeding.

(3) If, after recognition of a foreign nonmain proceeding, another foreign nonmain proceeding is recognized, the court shall grant, modify, or terminate relief for the purpose of facilitating coordination of the proceedings.

(Added Pub. L. 109-8, title VIII, § 801(a), Apr. 20, 2005, 119 Stat. 144.)

§ 1531. Presumption of insolvency based on recognition of a foreign main proceeding

In the absence of evidence to the contrary, recognition of a foreign main proceeding is, for the purpose of commencing a proceeding under section 303, proof that the debtor is generally not paying its debts as such debts become due.

(Added Pub. L. 109-8, title VIII, § 801(a), Apr. 20, 2005, 119 Stat. 144.)

§ 1532. Rule of payment in concurrent proceedings

Without prejudice to secured claims or rights in rem, a creditor who has received payment with respect to its claim in a foreign proceeding pursuant to a law relating to insolvency may not receive a payment for the same claim in a case under any other chapter of this title regarding the debtor, so long as the payment to other creditors of the same class is proportionately less than the payment the creditor has already received.

(Added Pub. L. 109-8, title VIII, § 801(a), Apr. 20, 2005, 119 Stat. 145.)

PRIOR PROVISIONS

Sections 15101 to 151326 of prior chapter 15 were repealed by Pub. L. 99-554, title II, § 231, Oct. 27, 1986, 100 Stat. 3103.

Section 15101, Pub. L. 95-598, Nov. 6, 1978, 92 Stat. 2652, related to definitions.

Section 15102, Pub. L. 95-598, Nov. 6, 1978, 92 Stat. 2652, related to a rule of construction.

Section 15103, Pub. L. 95-598, Nov. 6, 1978, 92 Stat. 2652; Pub. L. 98-353, title III, §§ 311(b)(3), 318(b), July 10, 1984, 98 Stat. 355, 357, related to applicability of subchapters and sections.

Section 15303, Pub. L. 95-598, Nov. 6, 1978, 92 Stat. 2653, related to involuntary cases.

Section 15321, Pub. L. 95-598, Nov. 6, 1978, 92 Stat. 2653, related to eligibility to serve as trustee.

Section 15322, Pub. L. 95-598, Nov. 6, 1978, 92 Stat. 2653, related to qualification of trustee.

Section 15324, Pub. L. 95-598, Nov. 6, 1978, 92 Stat. 2653, related to removal of trustee or examiner.

Section 15326, Pub. L. 95-598, Nov. 6, 1978, 92 Stat. 2653, related to limitation on compensation of trustee.

Section 15330, Pub. L. 95-598, Nov. 6, 1978, 92 Stat. 2653, related to compensation of officers.

Section 15343, Pub. L. 95-598, Nov. 6, 1978, 92 Stat. 2653, related to examination of debtor.

Section 15345, Pub. L. 95-598, Nov. 6, 1978, 92 Stat. 2654; Pub. L. 97-258, § 3(c), Sept. 13, 1982, 96 Stat. 1064, related to money of estates.

Section 15701, Pub. L. 95-598, Nov. 6, 1978, 92 Stat. 2654, related to interim trustee.

Section 15703, Pub. L. 95-598, Nov. 6, 1978, 92 Stat. 2654, related to successor trustee.

Section 15704, Pub. L. 95-598, Nov. 6, 1978, 92 Stat. 2655, related to duties of trustee.

Section 15727, Pub. L. 95-598, Nov. 6, 1978, 92 Stat. 2655, related to discharge.

Section 151102, Pub. L. 95-598, Nov. 6, 1978, 92 Stat. 2655, related to creditors' and equity security holders' committees.

Section 151104, Pub. L. 95-598, Nov. 6, 1978, 92 Stat. 2655, related to appointment of trustee or examiner.

Section 151105, Pub. L. 95-598, Nov. 6, 1978, 92 Stat. 2656, related to termination of trustee's appointment.

Section 151163, Pub. L. 95-598, Nov. 6, 1978, 92 Stat. 2656, related to appointment of trustee.

Section 151302, Pub. L. 95-598, Nov. 6, 1978, 92 Stat. 2656; Pub. L. 98-353, title III, §§ 311(b)(4), 534, July 10, 1984, 98 Stat. 355, 390, related to trustees.

Section 151326, Pub. L. 95-598, Nov. 6, 1978, 92 Stat. 2657, related to payments.

Effective date and applicability of repeal by Pub. L. 99-554 dependent upon the judicial district involved, see section 302(d), (e) of Pub. L. 99-554, set out as an Effective Date note under section 581 of Title 28, Judiciary and Judicial Procedure.

Pub. L. 95-598, title IV, § 408(c), Nov. 6, 1978, 92 Stat. 2687, as amended by Pub. L. 98-166, title II, § 200, Nov. 28, 1983, 97 Stat. 1081; Pub. L. 98-353, title III, § 323, July 10, 1984, 98 Stat. 358; Pub. L. 99-429, Sept. 30, 1986, 100 Stat. 985; Pub. L. 99-500, § 101(b) [title II, § 200], Oct. 18, 1986, 100 Stat. 1783-39, 1783-45, and Pub. L. 99-591, § 101(b) [title II, § 200], Oct. 30, 1986, 100 Stat. 3341-39, 3341-45; Pub. L. 99-554, title III, § 307(a), Oct. 27, 1986, 100 Stat. 3125, provided for the repeal of prior chapter 15 at a prospective date, prior to repeal by Pub. L. 99-554, title III, § 307(b), Oct. 27, 1986, 100 Stat. 3125.

TITLE 11—APPENDIX

FEDERAL RULES OF BANKRUPTCY PROCEDURE AND OFFICIAL BANKRUPTCY FORMS

(Effective August 1, 1983, as amended to February 1, 2010)

HISTORICAL NOTE

The Federal Rules of Bankruptcy Procedure were adopted by order of the Supreme Court on Apr. 25, 1983, transmitted to Congress by the Chief Justice on the same day, and became effective Aug. 1, 1983.

The Rules have been amended Aug. 30, 1983, Pub. L. 98-91, §2(a), 97 Stat. 607, eff. Aug. 1, 1983; July 10, 1984, Pub. L. 98-353, title III, §321, 98 Stat. 357; Apr. 29, 1985, eff. Aug. 1, 1985; Mar. 30, 1987, eff. Aug. 1, 1987; Apr. 25, 1989, eff. Aug. 1, 1989; Apr. 30, 1991, eff. Aug. 1, 1991; Apr. 22, 1993, eff. Aug. 1, 1993; Apr. 29, 1994, eff. Aug. 1, 1994; Oct. 22, 1994, Pub. L. 103-394, title I, §114, 108 Stat. 4118; Apr. 27, 1995, eff. Dec. 1, 1995; Apr. 23, 1996, eff. Dec. 1, 1996; Apr. 11, 1997, eff. Dec. 1, 1997; Apr. 26, 1999, eff. Dec. 1, 1999; Apr. 17, 2000, eff. Dec. 1, 2000; Apr. 23, 2001, eff. Dec. 1, 2001; Apr. 29, 2002, eff. Dec. 1, 2002; Mar. 27, 2003, eff. Dec. 1, 2003; Apr. 26, 2004, eff. Dec. 1, 2004; Apr. 25, 2005, eff. Dec. 1, 2005; Apr. 12, 2006, eff. Dec. 1, 2006; Apr. 30, 2007, eff. Dec. 1, 2007; Apr. 23, 2008, eff. Dec. 1, 2008; Mar. 26, 2009, eff. Dec. 1, 2009.

BANKRUPTCY RULES

BANKRUPTCY RULES

EFFECTIVE DATE; APPLICATION; SUPERSEDURE OF PRIOR RULES; TRANSMISSION TO CONGRESS

Sections 2 to 4 of the Order of the Supreme Court, dated Apr. 25, 1983, provided:

"2. That the aforementioned Bankruptcy Rules shall take effect on August 1, 1983, and shall be applicable to proceedings then pending, except to the extent that in the opinion of the court their application in a pending proceeding would not be feasible or would work injustice, in which event the former procedure applies.

"3. That the Bankruptcy Rules, heretofore prescribed by this Court, be, and they hereby are, superseded by the new rules, effective August 1, 1983.

"4. That the Chief Justice be, and he hereby is, authorized to transmit these new Bankruptcy Rules to the Congress in accordance with the provisions of Section 2075 of Title 28, United States Code."

Rule 1001. Scope of Rules and Forms; Short Title

The Bankruptcy Rules and Forms govern procedure in cases under title 11 of the United States Code. The rules shall be cited as the Federal Rules of Bankruptcy Procedure and the forms as the Official Bankruptcy Forms. These rules shall be construed to secure the just, speedy, and inexpensive determination of every case and proceeding.

(As amended Mar. 30, 1987, eff. Aug. 1, 1987; Apr. 30, 1991, eff. Aug. 1, 1991.)

NOTES OF ADVISORY COMMITTEE ON RULES—1983

Section 247 of Public Law 95–598, 92 Stat. 2549 amended 28 U.S.C. §2075 by omitting the last sentence. The effect of the amendment is to require that procedural rules promulgated pursuant to 28 U.S.C. §2075 be consistent with the bankruptcy statute, both titles 11 and 28 U.S.C. Thus, although Rule 1001 sets forth the scope of the bankruptcy rules and forms, any procedural matters contained in title 11 or 28 U.S.C. with respect to cases filed under 11 U.S.C. would control. See 1 Collier, *Bankruptcy* ¶3.04 [2][c] (15th ed. 1980).

28 U.S.C. §151 establishes a United States Bankruptcy Court in each district as an adjunct to the district court. This provision does not, however, become effective until April 1, 1984. Public Law 95–598, §402(b). From October 1, 1979 through March 31, 1984, the courts of bankruptcy as defined in §1(10) of the Bankruptcy Act, and created in §2a of that Act continue to be the courts of bankruptcy. Public Law 95–598, §404(a). From their effective date these rules and forms are to be applicable in cases filed under chapters 7, 9, 11 and 13 of title 11 regardless of whether the court is established by the Bankruptcy Act or by 28 U.S.C. §151. Rule 9001 contains a broad and general definition of "bankruptcy court," "court" and "United States Bankruptcy Court" for this purpose.

"Bankruptcy Code" or "Code" as used in these rules means title 11 of the United States Code, the codification of the bankruptcy law. Public Law 95–598, §101. See Rule 9001.

"Bankruptcy Act" as used in the notes to these rules means the Bankruptcy Act of 1898 as amended which was repealed by §401(a) of Public Law 95–598.

These rules apply to all cases filed under the Code except as otherwise specifically stated.

The final sentence of the rule is derived from former Bankruptcy Rule 903. The objective of "expeditious and economical administration" of cases under the Code has frequently been recognized by the courts to be "a chief purpose of the bankruptcy laws." See *Katchen v. Landy*, 382 U.S. 323, 328 (1966); *Bailey v. Glover*, 88 U.S. (21 Wall.) 342, 346–47 (1874); *Ex parte Christy*, 44 U.S. (3 How.) 292, 312–14, 320–22 (1845). The rule also incorporates the wholesome mandate of the last sentence of Rule 1 of the Federal Rules of Civil Procedure. 2 Moore, *Federal Practice* ¶1.13 (2d ed. 1980); 4 Wright & Miller, *Federal Practice and Procedure-Civil* §1029 (1969).

NOTES OF ADVISORY COMMITTEE ON RULES—1987 AMENDMENT

Title I of the Bankruptcy Amendments and Federal Judgeship Act of 1984, Pub. L. No. 98–353, 98 Stat. 333 (hereinafter the 1984 amendments), created a new bankruptcy judicial system in which the role of the district court was substantially increased. 28 U.S.C. §1334 confers on the United States district courts original and exclusive jurisdiction over all cases under title 11 of the United States Code and original but not exclusive jurisdiction over civil proceedings arising under title 11 and civil proceedings arising in or related to a case under title 11.

Pursuant to 28 U.S.C. §157(a) the district court may but need not refer cases and proceedings within the district court's jurisdiction to the bankruptcy judges for the district. Judgments or orders of the bankruptcy judges entered pursuant to 28 U.S.C. §157(b)(1) and (c)(2) are subject to appellate review by the district courts or bankruptcy appellate panels under 28 U.S.C. §158(a).

Rule 81(a)(1) F.R.Civ.P. provides that the civil rules do not apply to proceedings in bankruptcy, except as they may be made applicable by rules promulgated by the Supreme Court, *e.g.*, Part VII of these rules. This amended Bankruptcy Rule 1001 makes the Bankruptcy Rules applicable to cases and proceedings under title 11, whether before the district judges or the bankruptcy judges of the district.

NOTES OF ADVISORY COMMITTEE ON RULES—1991 AMENDMENT

The citation to these rules is amended to conform to the citation form of the Federal Rules of Civil Procedure, Federal Rules of Appellate Procedure, and Federal Rules of Criminal Procedure.

PART I—COMMENCEMENT OF CASE; PROCEEDINGS RELATING TO PETITION AND ORDER FOR RELIEF

Rule 1002. Commencement of Case

(a) PETITION. A petition commencing a case under the Code shall be filed with the clerk.

(b) TRANSMISSION TO UNITED STATES TRUSTEE. The clerk shall forthwith transmit to the United States trustee a copy of the petition filed pursuant to subdivision (a) of this rule.

(As amended Mar. 30, 1987, eff. Aug. 1, 1987; Apr. 30, 1991, eff. Aug. 1, 1991.)

NOTES OF ADVISORY COMMITTEE ON RULES—1983

Under §§301–303 of the Code, a voluntary or involuntary case is commenced by filing a petition with the bankruptcy court. The voluntary petition may request relief under chapter 7, 9, 11, or 13 whereas an involuntary petition may be filed only under chapter 7 or 11. Section 109 of the Code specifies the types of debtors for whom the different forms of relief are available and §303(a) indicates the persons against whom involuntary petitions may be filed.

The rule in subdivision (a) is in harmony with the Code in that it requires the filing to be with the bankruptcy court.

The number of copies of the petition to be filed is specified in this rule but a local rule may require additional copies. This rule provides for filing sufficient copies for the court's files and for the trustee in a chapter 7 or 13 case.

Official Form No. 1 may be used to seek relief voluntarily under any of the chapters. Only the original need be signed and verified, but the copies must be conformed to the original. See Rules 1008 and 9011(c). As provided in §362(a) of the Code, the filing of a petition acts as a stay of certain acts and proceedings against the debtor, property of the debtor, and property of the estate.

NOTES OF ADVISORY COMMITTEE ON RULES—1987 AMENDMENT

Rules 1002(a), governing a voluntary petition, 1003(a), governing an involuntary petition, and 1003(e), governing a petition in a case ancillary to a foreign proceeding, are combined into this Rule 1002. If a bankruptcy clerk has been appointed for the district, the petition is filed with the bankruptcy clerk. Otherwise, the petition is filed with the clerk of the district court.

The elimination of the reference to the Official Forms of the petition is not intended to change the practice. Rule 9009 provides that the Official Forms "shall be observed and used" in cases and proceedings under the Code.

Subdivision (b) which provided for the distribution of copies of the petition to agencies of the United States has been deleted. Some of these agencies no longer wish to receive copies of the petition, while others not included in subdivision (b) have now requested copies. The Director of the Administrative Office will determine on an ongoing basis which government agencies will be provided a copy of the petition.

The number of copies of a petition that must be filed is a matter for local rule.

NOTES OF ADVISORY COMMITTEE ON RULES—1991 AMENDMENT

Subdivision (b) is derived from Rule X-1002(a). The duties of the United States trustee pursuant to the Code and 28 U.S.C. §586(a) require that the United States trustee be apprised of the commencement of every case under chapters 7, 11, 12 and 13 and this is most easily accomplished by providing that office with a copy of the petition. Although 28 U.S.C. §586(a) does not give the United States trustee an administrative role in chapter 9 cases, §1102 of the Code requires the United States trustee to appoint committees and that section is applicable in chapter 9 cases pursuant to §901(a). It is therefore appropriate that the United States trustee receive a copy of every chapter 9 petition.

Notwithstanding subdivision (b), pursuant to Rule 5005(b)(3), the clerk is not required to transmit a copy of the petition to the United States trustee if the United States trustee requests that it not be transmitted. Many rules require the clerk to transmit a certain document to the United States trustee, but Rule 5005(b)(3) relieves the clerk of that duty under this or any other rule if the United States trustee requests that such document not be transmitted.

Rule 1003. Involuntary Petition

(a) TRANSFEROR OR TRANSFEREE OF CLAIM. A transferor or transferee of a claim shall annex to the original and each copy of the petition a copy of all documents evidencing the transfer, whether transferred unconditionally, for security, or otherwise, and a signed statement that the claim was not transferred for the purpose of commencing the case and setting forth the consideration for and terms of the transfer. An entity that has transferred or acquired a claim for the purpose of commencing a case for liquidation under chapter 7 or for reorganization under chapter 11 shall not be a qualified petitioner.

(b) JOINDER OF PETITIONERS AFTER FILING. If the answer to an involuntary petition filed by fewer than three creditors avers the existence of 12 or more creditors, the debtor shall file with the answer a list of all creditors with their addresses, a brief statement of the nature of their claims, and the amounts thereof. If it appears that there are 12 or more creditors as provided in §303(b) of the Code, the court shall afford a reasonable opportunity for other creditors to join in the petition before a hearing is held thereon.

(As amended Mar. 30, 1987, eff. Aug. 1, 1987.)

NOTES OF ADVISORY COMMITTEE ON RULES—1983

Subdivision (a). Official Form No. 11 (Involuntary Case: Creditors' Petition), is prescribed for use by petitioning creditors to have a debtor's assets liquidated under chapter 7 of the Code or the business reorganized under chapter 11. It contains the required allegations as specified in §303(b) of the Code. Official Form 12 is prescribed for use by fewer than all the general partners to obtain relief for the partnership as governed by §303(b)(3) of the Code and Rule 1004(b).

Although the number of copies to be filed is specified in Rule 1002, a local rule may require additional copies.

Only the original need be signed and verified, but the copies must be conformed to the original. See Rules 1008 and 9011(c). The petition must be filed with the bankruptcy court. This provision implements §303(b) which provides that an involuntary case is commenced by filing the petition with the court.

As provided in §362 of the Code, the filing of the petition acts as a stay of certain acts and proceedings against the debtor, the debtor's property and property of the estate.

Subdivision (c) retains the explicitness of former Bankruptcy Rule 104(d) that a transfer of a claim for the purpose of commencing a case under the Code is a ground for disqualification of a party to the transfer as a petitioner.

Section 303(b) "is not intended to overrule Bankruptcy Rule 104(d), which places certain restrictions on the transfer of claims for the purpose of commencing an involuntary case." House Report No. 95–595, 95th Cong., 1st Sess. (1977) 322; Senate Report No. 95–989, 95th Cong., 2d Sess. (1978) 33.

The subdivision requires disclosure of any transfer of the petitioner's claim as well as a transfer to the petitioner and applies to transfers for security as well as unconditional transfers. *Cf. In re 69th & Crandon Bldg. Corp.*, 97 F.2d 392, 395 (7th Cir.), cert. denied, 305 U.S. 629 (1938), recognizing the right of a creditor to sign a bankruptcy petition notwithstanding a prior assignment of his claim for the purpose of security. This rule does not, however, qualify the requirement of §303(b)(1) that a petitioning creditor must have a claim not contingent as to liability.

Subdivision (d). Section 303(c) of the Code permits a creditor to join in the petition at any time before the case is dismissed or relief is ordered. While this rule does not require the court to give all creditors notice of the petition, the list of creditors filed by the debtor affords a petitioner the information needed to enable him to give notice for the purpose of obtaining the co-petitioners required to make the petition sufficient. After a reasonable opportunity has been afforded other creditors to join in an involuntary petition, the hearing on the petition should be held without further delay.

Subdivision (e). This subdivision implements §304. A petition for relief under §304 may only be filed by a foreign representative who is defined in §101(20) generally as a representative of an estate in a foreign proceeding. The term "foreign proceeding" is defined in §101(19).

Section 304(b) permits a petition filed thereunder to be contested by a party in interest. Subdivision (e)(2) therefore requires that the summons and petition be served on any person against whom the relief permitted by §304(b) is sought as well as on any other party the court may direct.

The rules applicable to the procedure when an involuntary petition is filed are made applicable generally when a case ancillary to a foreign proceeding is commenced. These rules include Rule 1010 with respect to issuance and service of a summons, Rule 1011 concerning responsive pleadings and motions, and Rule 1018 which makes various rules in Part VII applicable in proceedings on contested petitions.

The venue for a case ancillary to a foreign proceeding is provided in 28 U.S.C. §1474.

NOTES OF ADVISORY COMMITTEE ON RULES—1987 AMENDMENT

The subject matter of subdivisions (a), (b), and (e) has been incorporated in Rules 1002, 1010, 1011, and 1018.

Rule 1004. Involuntary Petition Against a Partnership

After filing of an involuntary petition under §303(b)(3) of the Code, (1) the petitioning partners or other petitioners shall promptly send to or serve on each general partner who is not a petitioner a copy of the petition; and (2) the clerk shall promptly issue a summons for service on each general partner who is not a petitioner. Rule 1010 applies to the form and service of the summons.

(As amended Apr. 29, 2002, eff. Dec. 1, 2002.)

NOTES OF ADVISORY COMMITTEE ON RULES—1983

This rule is adapted from former Bankruptcy Rule 105 and complements §§301 and 303(b)(3) of the Code.

Subdivision (a) specifies that while all general partners must consent to the filing of a voluntary petition, it is not necessary that they all execute the petition. It may be executed and filed on behalf of the partnership by fewer than all.

Subdivision (b) implements §303(b)(3) of the Code which provides that an involuntary petition may be filed by fewer than all the general partners or, when all the general partners are debtors, by a general partner, trustee of the partner or creditors of the partnership. Rule 1010, which governs service of a petition and summons in an involuntary case, specifies the time and mode of service on the partnership. When a petition is filed against a partnership under §303(b)(3), this rule requires an additional service on the nonfiling general partners. It is the purpose of this subdivision to protect the interests of the nonpetitioning partners and the partnership.

COMMITTEE NOTES ON RULES—2002 AMENDMENT

Section 303(b)(3)(A) of the Code provides that fewer than all of the general partners in a partnership may commence an involuntary case against the partnership. There is no counterpart provision in the Code setting out the manner in which a partnership commences a voluntary case. The Supreme Court has held in the corporate context that applicable nonbankruptcy law determines whether authority exists for a particular debtor to commence a bankruptcy case. *See Price v. Gurney*, 324 U.S. 100 (1945). The lower courts have followed this rule in the partnership context as well. *See, e.g., Jolly v. Pittore*, 170 B.R. 793 (S.D.N.Y. 1994); *Union Planters National Bank v. Hunters Horn Associates*, 158 B.R. 729 (Bankr. M.D. Tenn. 1993); *In re Channel 64 Joint Venture*, 61 B.R. 255 (Bankr. S.D. Oh. 1986). Rule 1004(a) could be construed as requiring the consent of all of the general partners to the filing of a voluntary petition, even if fewer than all of the general partners would have the authority under applicable nonbankruptcy law to commence a bankruptcy case for the partnership. Since this is a matter of substantive law beyond the scope of these rules, Rule 1004(a) is deleted as is the designation of subdivision (b).

The rule is retitled to reflect that it applies only to involuntary petitions filed against partnerships.

Changes Made After Publication and Comments. No changes since publication.

Rule 1004.1. Petition for an Infant or Incompetent Person

If an infant or incompetent person has a representative, including a general guardian, committee, conservator, or similar fiduciary, the representative may file a voluntary petition on behalf of the infant or incompetent person. An infant or incompetent person who does not have a duly appointed representative may file a voluntary petition by next friend or guardian ad litem. The court shall appoint a guardian ad litem for an infant or incompetent person who is a debtor and is not otherwise represented or shall make any other order to protect the infant or incompetent debtor.

(Added Apr. 29, 2002, eff. Dec. 1, 2002.)

COMMITTEE NOTES ON RULES—2002

This rule is derived from Rule 17(c) F.R. Civ. P. It does not address the commencement of a case filed on behalf of a missing person. *See, e.g., In re King*, 234 B.R. 515 (Bankr. D.N.M. 1999)

Changes Made After Publication and Comments. No changes were made.

Rule 1005. Caption of Petition

The caption of a petition commencing a case under the Code shall contain the name of the court, the title of the case, and the docket number. The title of the case shall include the following information about the debtor: name, employer identification number, last four digits of the social-security number or individual debtor's taxpayer-identification number, any other federal taxpayer-identification number, and all other names used within eight years before filing the petition. If the petition is not filed by the debtor, it shall include all names used by the debtor which are known to the petitioners.

(As amended Mar. 30, 1987, eff. Aug. 1, 1987; Mar. 27, 2003, eff. Dec. 1, 2003; Apr. 23, 2008, eff. Dec. 1, 2008.)

NOTES OF ADVISORY COMMITTEE ON RULES—1983

The title of the case should include all names used by the debtor, such as trade names, former married names and maiden name. See also Official Form No. 1 and the Advisory Committee Note to that Form. Additional names of the debtor are also required to appear in the caption of each notice to creditors. See Rule 2002(m).

COMMITTEE NOTES ON RULES—2003 AMENDMENT

The rule is amended to implement the Judicial Conference policy to limit the disclosure of a party's social security number and similar identifiers. Under the rule, as amended, only the last four digits of the debtor's social security number need be disclosed. Publication of the employer identification number does not present the same identity theft or privacy protection issues. Therefore, the caption must include the full employer identification number.

Debtors must submit with the petition a statement setting out their social security numbers. This enables the clerk to include the full social security number on the notice of the section 341 meeting of creditors, but the statement itself is not submitted in the case or maintained in the case file.

Changes Made After Publication and Comments. The rule was changed only slightly after publication. The rule was changed to make clear that only the debtor's social security number is truncated to the final four digits, but other numerical identifiers must be set out in full. The rule also was amended to include a requirement that a debtor list other federal taxpayer identification numbers that may be in use.

COMMITTEE NOTES ON RULES—2008 AMENDMENT

The rule is amended to require the disclosure of all names used by the debtor in the past eight years. Section 727(a)(8) was amended in 2005 to extend the time between chapter 7 discharges from six to eight years, and the rule is amended to implement that change. The rule also is amended to require the disclosure of the last four digits of an individual debtor's taxpayer-identification number. This truncation of the number applies only to individual debtors. This is consistent with the requirements of Rule 9037.

Changes Made After Publication. No changes were made after publication.

Rule 1006. Filing Fee

(a) GENERAL REQUIREMENT. Every petition shall be accompanied by the filing fee except as provided in subdivisions (b) and (c) of this rule. For the purpose of this rule, "filing fee" means the filing fee prescribed by 28 U.S.C. §1930(a)(1)-(a)(5) and any other fee prescribed by the Judicial Conference of the United States under 28 U.S.C. §1930(b) that is payable to the clerk upon the commencement of a case under the Code.

(b) PAYMENT OF FILING FEE IN INSTALLMENTS.

(1) *Application to Pay Filing Fee in Installments.* A voluntary petition by an individual shall be accepted for filing if accompanied by the debtor's signed application, prepared as prescribed by the appropriate Official Form, stating that the debtor is unable to pay the filing fee except in installments.

(2) *Action on Application.* Prior to the meeting of creditors, the court may order the filing fee paid to the clerk or grant leave to pay in installments and fix the number, amount and dates of payment. The number of installments shall not exceed four, and the final installment shall be payable not later than 120 days after filing the petition. For cause shown, the court may extend the time of any installment, provided the last installment is paid not later than 180 days after filing the petition.

(3) *Postponement of Attorney's Fees.* All installments of the filing fee must be paid in full before the debtor or chapter 13 trustee may make further payments to an attorney or any other person who renders services to the debtor in connection with the case.

(c) WAIVER OF FILING FEE. A voluntary chapter 7 petition filed by an individual shall be accepted for filing if accompanied by the debtor's application requesting a waiver under 28 U.S.C. §1930(f), prepared as prescribed by the appropriate Official Form.

(As amended Mar. 30, 1987, eff. Aug. 1, 1987; Apr. 23, 1996, eff. Dec. 1, 1996; Apr. 23, 2008, eff. Dec. 1, 2008.)

NOTES OF ADVISORY COMMITTEE ON RULES—1983

28 U.S.C. §1930 specifies the filing fees for petitions under chapters 7, 9, 11 and 13 of the Code. It also permits the payment in installments by individual debtors.

Subdivision (b) is adapted from former Bankruptcy Rule 107. The administrative cost of installments in excess of four is disproportionate to the benefits conferred. Prolonging the period beyond 180 days after the commencement of the case causes undesirable delays in administration. Paragraph (2) accordingly continues the imposition of a maximum of four on the number of installments and retains the maximum period of installment payments allowable on an original application at 120 days. Only in extraordinary cases should it be necessary to give an applicant an extension beyond the four months. The requirement of paragraph (3) that filing fees be paid in full before the debtor may pay an attorney for services in connection with the case codifies the rule declared in *In re Latham*, 271 Fed. 538 (N.D.N.Y. 1921), and *In re Darr*, 232 Fed. 415 (N.D. Cal. 1916).

NOTES OF ADVISORY COMMITTEE ON RULES—1987 AMENDMENT

Subdivision (b)(3) is expanded to prohibit payments by the debtor or the chapter 13 trustee not only to attorneys but to any person who renders services to the debtor in connection with the case.

NOTES OF ADVISORY COMMITTEE ON RULES—1996 AMENDMENT

The Judicial Conference prescribes miscellaneous fees pursuant to 28 U.S.C. §1930(b). In 1992, a $30 miscellaneous administrative fee was prescribed for all chapter 7 and chapter 13 cases. The Judicial Conference fee schedule was amended in 1993 to provide that an individual debtor may pay this fee in installments.

Subdivision (a) of this rule is amended to clarify that every petition must be accompanied by any fee prescribed under 28 U.S.C. §1930(b) that is required to be paid when a petition is filed, as well as the filing fee prescribed by 28 U.S.C. §1930(a). By defining "filing fee" to include Judicial Conference fees, the procedures set forth in subdivision (b) for paying the filing fee in installments will also apply with respect to any Judicial Conference fee required to be paid at the commencement of the case.

GAP Report on Rule 1006. No changes since publication, except for a stylistic change in subdivision (a).

COMMITTEE NOTES ON RULES—2008 AMENDMENT

Subdivision (a) is amended to include a reference to new subdivision (c), which deals with fee waivers under 28 U.S.C. §1930(f), which was added in 2005.

Subdivision (b)(1) is amended to delete the sentence requiring a disclosure that the debtor has not paid an attorney or other person in connection with the case. Inability to pay the filing fee in installments is one of the requirements for a fee waiver under the 2005 revisions to 28 U.S.C. §1930(f). If the attorney payment prohibition were retained, payment of an attorney's fee would render many debtors ineligible for installment payments and thus enhance their eligibility for the fee waiver. The deletion of this prohibition from the rule, which was not statutorily required, ensures that debtors who have the financial ability to pay the fee in installments will do so rather than request a waiver.

Subdivision (b)(3) is amended in conformance with the changes to subdivision (b)(1) to reflect the 2005 amendments. The change is meant to clarify that subdivision (b)(3) refers to payments made after the debtor has filed the bankruptcy case and after the debtor has received permission to pay the fee in installments. Otherwise, the subdivision may conflict with the intent and effect of the amendments to subdivision (b)(1).

Changes Made After Publication. No changes were made after publication.

Rule 1007. Lists, Schedules, Statements, and Other Documents; Time Limits

(a) CORPORATE OWNERSHIP STATEMENT, LIST OF CREDITORS AND EQUITY SECURITY HOLDERS, AND OTHER LISTS.

(1) *Voluntary Case.* In a voluntary case, the debtor shall file with the petition a list containing the name and address of each entity included or to be included on Schedules D, E, F, G, and H as prescribed by the Official Forms. If the debtor is a corporation, other than a governmental unit, the debtor shall file with the petition a corporate ownership statement containing the information described in Rule 7007.1. The debtor shall file a supplemental statement promptly upon any change in circumstances that renders the corporate ownership statement inaccurate.

(2) *Involuntary Case.* In an involuntary case, the debtor shall file within 14 days after entry of the order for relief, a list containing the name and address of each entity included or to be included on Schedules D, E, F, G, and H as prescribed by the Official Forms.

(3) *Equity Security Holders.* In a chapter 11 reorganization case, unless the court orders otherwise, the debtor shall file within 14 days after entry of the order for relief a list of the debtor's equity security holders of each class showing the number and kind of interests registered in the name of each holder, and the last known address or place of business of each holder.

(4) *Chapter 15 Case.* In addition to the documents required under §1515 of the Code, a foreign representative filing a petition for recognition under chapter 15 shall file with the petition: (A) a corporate ownership statement containing the information described in Rule 7007.1; and (B) unless the court orders otherwise, a list containing the names and addresses of all persons or bodies authorized to administer foreign proceedings of the debtor, all parties to litigation pending in the United States in which the debtor is a party at the time of the filing of the petition, and all entities against whom provisional relief is being sought under §1519 of the Code.

(5) *Extension of Time.* Any extension of time for the filing of the lists required by this subdivision may be granted only on motion for cause shown and on notice to the United States trustee and to any trustee, committee elected under §705 or appointed under §1102 of the Code, or other party as the court may direct.

(b) SCHEDULES, STATEMENTS, AND OTHER DOCUMENTS REQUIRED.

(1) Except in a chapter 9 municipality case, the debtor, unless the court orders otherwise, shall file the following schedules, statements, and other documents, prepared as prescribed by the appropriate Official Forms, if any:

(A) schedules of assets and liabilities;

(B) a schedule of current income and expenditures;

(C) a schedule of executory contracts and unexpired leases;

(D) a statement of financial affairs;

(E) copies of all payment advices or other evidence of payment, if any, received by the debtor from an employer within 60 days before the filing of the petition, with redaction of all but the last four digits of the debtor's social-security number or individual taxpayer-identification number; and

(F) a record of any interest that the debtor has in an account or program of the type specified in §521(c) of the Code.

(2) An individual debtor in a chapter 7 case shall file a statement of intention as required by §521(a) of the Code, prepared as prescribed by the appropriate Official Form. A copy of the statement of intention shall be served on the trustee and the creditors named in the statement on or before the filing of the statement.

(3) Unless the United States trustee has determined that the credit counseling requirement of §109(h) does not apply in the district, an individual debtor must file a statement of compliance with the credit counseling requirement, prepared as prescribed by the appropriate Official Form which must include one of the following:

(A) an attached certificate and debt repayment plan, if any, required by §521(b);

(B) a statement that the debtor has received the credit counseling briefing required by §109(h)(1) but does not have the certificate required by §521(b);

(C) a certification under §109(h)(3); or

(D) a request for a determination by the court under §109(h)(4).

(4) Unless §707(b)(2)(D) applies, an individual debtor in a chapter 7 case shall file a statement of current monthly income prepared as prescribed by the appropriate Official Form, and, if the current monthly income exceeds the median family income for the applicable state and household size, the information, including calculations, required by §707(b), prepared as prescribed by the appropriate Official Form.

(5) An individual debtor in a chapter 11 case shall file a statement of current monthly in-

come, prepared as prescribed by the appropriate Official Form.

(6) A debtor in a chapter 13 case shall file a statement of current monthly income, prepared as prescribed by the appropriate Official Form, and, if the current monthly income exceeds the median family income for the applicable state and household size, a calculation of disposable income made in accordance with §1325(b)(3), prepared as prescribed by the appropriate Official Form.

(7) An individual debtor in a chapter 7 or chapter 13 case shall file a statement of completion of a course concerning personal financial management, prepared as prescribed by the appropriate Official Form. An individual debtor shall file the statement in a chapter 11 case in which §1141(d)(3) applies.

(8) If an individual debtor in a chapter 11, 12, or 13 case has claimed an exemption under §522(b)(3)(A) in property of the kind described in §522(p)(1) with a value in excess of the amount set out in §522(q)(1), the debtor shall file a statement as to whether there is any proceeding pending in which the debtor may be found guilty of a felony of a kind described in §522(q)(1)(A) or found liable for a debt of the kind described in §522(q)(1)(B).

(c) TIME LIMITS. In a voluntary case, the schedules, statements, and other documents required by subdivision (b)(1), (4), (5), and (6) shall be filed with the petition or within 14 days thereafter, except as otherwise provided in subdivisions (d), (e), (f), and (h) of this rule. In an involuntary case, the list in subdivision (a)(2), and the schedules, statements, and other documents required by subdivision (b)(1) shall be filed by the debtor within 14 days of the entry of the order for relief. In a voluntary case, the documents required by paragraphs (A), (C), and (D) of subdivision (b)(3) shall be filed with the petition. Unless the court orders otherwise, a debtor who has filed a statement under subdivision (b)(3)(B), shall file the documents required by subdivision (b)(3)(A) within 14 days of the order for relief. In a chapter 7 case, the debtor shall file the statement required by subdivision (b)(7) within 45 days after the first date set for the meeting of creditors under §341 of the Code, and in a chapter 11 or 13 case no later than the date when the last payment was made by the debtor as required by the plan or the filing of a motion for a discharge under §1141(d)(5)(B) or §1328(b) of the Code. The court may, at any time and in its discretion, enlarge the time to file the statement required by subdivision (b)(7). The debtor shall file the statement required by subdivision (b)(8) no earlier than the date of the last payment made under the plan or the date of the filing of a motion for a discharge under §§1141(d)(5)(B),[1] 1228(b), or 1328(b) of the Code. Lists, schedules, statements, and other documents filed prior to the conversion of a case to another chapter shall be deemed filed in the converted case unless the court directs otherwise. Except as provided in §1116(3), any extension of time to file schedules, statements, and other documents required under this rule may be granted only on motion for cause shown and on notice to the United States trustee, any committee elected under §705 or appointed under §1102 of the Code, trustee, examiner, or other party as the court may direct. Notice of an extension shall be given to the United States trustee and to any committee, trustee, or other party as the court may direct.

(d) LIST OF 20 LARGEST CREDITORS IN CHAPTER 9 MUNICIPALITY CASE OR CHAPTER 11 REORGANIZATION CASE. In addition to the list required by subdivision (a) of this rule, a debtor in a chapter 9 municipality case or a debtor in a voluntary chapter 11 reorganization case shall file with the petition a list containing the name, address and claim of the creditors that hold the 20 largest unsecured claims, excluding insiders, as prescribed by the appropriate Official Form. In an involuntary chapter 11 reorganization case, such list shall be filed by the debtor within 2 days after entry of the order for relief under §303(h) of the Code.

(e) LIST IN CHAPTER 9 MUNICIPALITY CASES. The list required by subdivision (a) of this rule shall be filed by the debtor in a chapter 9 municipality case within such time as the court shall fix. If a proposed plan requires a revision of assessments so that the proportion of special assessments or special taxes to be assessed against some real property will be different from the proportion in effect at the date the petition is filed, the debtor shall also file a list showing the name and address of each known holder of title, legal or equitable, to real property adversely affected. On motion for cause shown, the court may modify the requirements of this subdivision and subdivision (a) of this rule.

(f) STATEMENT OF SOCIAL SECURITY NUMBER. An individual debtor shall submit a verified statement that sets out the debtor's social security number, or states that the debtor does not have a social security number. In a voluntary case, the debtor shall submit the statement with the petition. In an involuntary case, the debtor shall submit the statement within 14 days after the entry of the order for relief.

(g) PARTNERSHIP AND PARTNERS. The general partners of a debtor partnership shall prepare and file the list required under subdivision (a), schedules of the assets and liabilities, schedule of current income and expenditures, schedule of executory contracts and unexpired leases, and statement of financial affairs of the partnership. The court may order any general partner to file a statement of personal assets and liabilities within such time as the court may fix.

(h) INTERESTS ACQUIRED OR ARISING AFTER PETITION. If, as provided by §541(a)(5) of the Code, the debtor acquires or becomes entitled to acquire any interest in property, the debtor shall within 14 days after the information comes to the debtor's knowledge or within such further time the court may allow, file a supplemental schedule in the chapter 7 liquidation case, chapter 11 reorganization case, chapter 12 family farmer's debt adjustment case, or chapter 13 individual debt adjustment case. If any of the property required to be reported under this subdivision is claimed by the debtor as exempt, the debtor shall claim the exemptions in the supplemental schedule. The duty to file a supple-

[1] So in original. Probably should be only one section symbol.

mental schedule in accordance with this subdivision continues notwithstanding the closing of the case, except that the schedule need not be filed in a chapter 11, chapter 12, or chapter 13 case with respect to property acquired after entry of the order confirming a chapter 11 plan or discharging the debtor in a chapter 12 or chapter 13 case.

(i) DISCLOSURE OF LIST OF SECURITY HOLDERS. After notice and hearing and for cause shown, the court may direct an entity other than the debtor or trustee to disclose any list of security holders of the debtor in its possession or under its control, indicating the name, address and security held by any of them. The entity possessing this list may be required either to produce the list or a true copy thereof, or permit inspection or copying, or otherwise disclose the information contained on the list.

(j) IMPOUNDING OF LISTS. On motion of a party in interest and for cause shown the court may direct the impounding of the lists filed under this rule, and may refuse to permit inspection by any entity. The court may permit inspection or use of the lists, however, by any party in interest on terms prescribed by the court.

(k) PREPARATION OF LIST, SCHEDULES, OR STATEMENTS ON DEFAULT OF DEBTOR. If a list, schedule, or statement, other than a statement of intention, is not prepared and filed as required by this rule, the court may order the trustee, a petitioning creditor, committee, or other party to prepare and file any of these papers within a time fixed by the court. The court may approve reimbursement of the cost incurred in complying with such an order as an administrative expense.

(*l*) TRANSMISSION TO UNITED STATES TRUSTEE. The clerk shall forthwith transmit to the United States trustee a copy of every list, schedule, and statement filed pursuant to subdivision (a)(1), (a)(2), (b), (d), or (h) of this rule.

(m) INFANTS AND INCOMPETENT PERSONS. If the debtor knows that a person on the list of creditors or schedules is an infant or incompetent person, the debtor also shall include the name, address, and legal relationship of any person upon whom process would be served in an adversary proceeding against the infant or incompetent person in accordance with Rule 7004(b)(2).

(As amended Mar. 30, 1987, eff. Aug. 1, 1987; Apr. 30, 1991, eff. Aug. 1, 1991; Apr. 23, 1996, eff. Dec. 1, 1996; Apr. 23, 2001, eff. Dec. 1, 2001; Mar. 27, 2003, eff. Dec. 1, 2003; Apr. 25, 2005, eff. Dec. 1, 2005; Apr. 23, 2008, eff. Dec. 1, 2008; Mar. 26, 2009, eff. Dec. 1, 2009.)

NOTES OF ADVISORY COMMITTEE ON RULES—1983

This rule is an adaptation of former Rules 108, 8-106, 10-108 and 11-11. As specified in the rule, it is applicable in all types of cases filed under the Code.

Subdivision (a) requires at least a list of creditors with their names and addresses to be filed with the petition. This list is needed for notice of the meeting of creditors (Rule 2002) and notice of the order for relief (§342 of the Code). The list will also serve to meet the requirements of §521(1) of the Code. Subdivision (a) recognizes that it may be impossible to file the schedules required by §521(1) and subdivision (b) of the rule at the time the petition is filed but in order for the case to proceed expeditiously and efficiently it is necessary that the clerk have the names and addresses of creditors. It should be noted that subdivision (d) of the rule requires a special list of the 20 largest unsecured creditors in chapter 9 and 11 cases. That list is for the purpose of selecting a committee of unsecured creditors.

Subdivision (b) is derived from former Rule 11-11 and conforms with §521. This subdivision indicates the forms to be used. The court may dispense with the filing of schedules and the statement of affairs pursuant to §521.

Subdivisions (c) and (f) specify the time periods for filing the papers required by the rule as well as the number of copies. The provisions dealing with an involuntary case are derived from former Bankruptcy Rule 108. Under the Code, a chapter 11 case may be commenced by an involuntary petition (§303(a)), whereas under the Act, a Chapter XI case could have been commenced only by a voluntary petition. A motion for an extension of time to file the schedules and statements is required to be made on notice to parties, as the court may direct, including a creditors' committee if one has been appointed under §1102 of the Code and a trustee or examiner if one has been appointed pursuant to §1104 of the Code. Although written notice is preferable, it is not required by the rule; in proper circumstances the notice may be by telephone or otherwise.

Subdivision (d) is new and requires that a list of the 20 largest unsecured creditors, excluding insiders as defined in §101(25) of the Code, be filed with the petition. The court, pursuant to §1102 of the Code, is required to appoint a committee of unsecured creditors as soon as practicable after the order for relief. That committee generally is to consist of the seven largest unsecured creditors who are willing to serve. The list should, as indicated on Official Form No. 9, specify the nature and amount of the claim. It is important for the court to be aware of the different types of claims existing in the case and this form should supply such information.

Subdivision (e) applies only in chapter 9 municipality cases. It gives greater discretion to the court to determine the time for filing a list of creditors and any other matter related to the list. A list of creditors must at some point be filed since one is required by §924 of the Code. When the plan affects special assessments, the definitions in §902(2) and (3) for "special tax payer" and "special tax payer affected by the plan" become relevant.

Subdivision (g) is derived from former Rules 108(c) and 11-11. Nondebtor general partners are liable to the partnership's trustee for any deficiency in the partnership's estate to pay creditors in full as provided by §723 of the Code. Subdivision (g) authorizes the court to require a partner to file a statement of personal assets and liabilities to provide the trustee with the relevant information.

Subdivision (h) is derived from former Bankruptcy Rule 108(e) for chapter 7, 11 and 13 purposes. It implements the provisions in and language of §541(a)(5) of the Code.

Subdivisions (i) and (j) are adapted from §§165 and 166 of the Act and former Rule 10-108(b) and (c) without change in substance. The term "party in interest" is not defined in the Code or the rules, but reference may be made to §1109(b) of the Code. In the context of this subdivision, the term would include the debtor, the trustee, any indenture trustee, creditor, equity security holder or committee appointed pursuant to §1102 of the Code.

Subdivision (k) is derived from former Rules 108(d) and 10-108(a).

NOTES OF ADVISORY COMMITTEE ON RULES—1987 AMENDMENT

Subdivisions (b), (c), and (g) are amended to provide for the filing of a schedule of current income and current expenditures and the individual debtor's statement of intention. These documents are required by the 1984 amendments to §521 of the Code. Official Form No. 6A is prescribed for use by an individual debtor for filing a schedule of current income and current expenditures in a chapter 7 or chapter 11 case. Although a partnership or corporation is also required by §521(1) to file a schedule of current income and current expenditures, no Official Form is prescribed therefor.

The time for filing the statement of intention is governed by §521(2)(A). A copy of the statement of intention must be served on the trustee and the creditors named in the statement within the same time. The provisions of subdivision (c) governing the time for filing when a chapter 11 or chapter 13 case is converted to a chapter 7 case have been omitted from subdivision (c) as amended. Filing after conversion is now governed exclusively by Rule 1019.

Subdivision (f) has been abrogated. The number of copies of the documents required by this rule will be determined by local rule.

Subdivision (h) is amended to include a direct reference to §541(a)(5).

Subdivision (k) provides that the court may not order an entity other than the debtor to prepare and file the statement of intention.

NOTES OF ADVISORY COMMITTEE ON RULES—1991 AMENDMENT

References to Official Form numbers and to the Chapter 13 Statement are deleted and subdivision (b) is amended in anticipation of future revision and renumbering of the Official Forms. The debtor in a chapter 12 or chapter 13 case shall file the list, schedules and statements required in subdivisions (a)(1), (b)(1), and (h). It is expected that the information currently provided in the Chapter 13 Statement will be included in the schedules and statements as revised not later than the effective date of these rule amendments.

Subdivisions (a)(4) and (c) are amended to provide the United States trustee with notice of any motion to extend the time for the filing of any lists, schedules, or statements. Such notice enables the United States trustee to take appropriate steps to avoid undue delay in the administration of the case. See 28 U.S.C. §586(a)(3)(G). Subdivisions (a)(4) and (c) are amended further to provide notice to committees elected under §705 or appointed pursuant to §1102 of the Code. Committees of retired employees appointed pursuant to §1114 are not included.

The additions of references to unexpired leases in subdivisions (b)(1) and (g) indicate that the schedule requires the inclusion of unexpired leases as well as other executory contracts.

The words "with the court" in subdivisions (b)(1), (e), and (g) are deleted as unnecessary. See Rules 5005(a) and 9001(3).

Subdivision (l), which is derived from Rule X-1002(a), provides the United States trustee with the information required to perform certain administrative duties such as the appointment of a committee of unsecured creditors. In a chapter 7 case, the United States trustee should be aware of the debtor's intention with respect to collateral that secures a consumer debt so that the United States trustee may monitor the progress of the case. Pursuant to §307 of the Code, the United States trustee has standing to raise, appear and be heard on issues and the lists, schedules and statements contain information that, when provided to the United States trustee, enable that office to participate effectively in the case. The United States trustee has standing to move to dismiss a chapter 7 or 13 case for failure to file timely the list, schedules or statement required by §521(1) of the Code. See §§707(a)(3) and 1307(c)(9). It is therefore necessary for the United States trustee to receive notice of any extension of time to file such documents. Upon request, the United States trustee also may receive from the trustee or debtor in possession a list of equity security holders.

NOTES OF ADVISORY COMMITTEE ON RULES—1996 AMENDMENT

Subdivision (c) is amended to provide that schedules and statements filed prior to the conversion of a case to another chapter shall be deemed filed in the converted case, whether or not the case was a chapter 7 case prior to conversion. This amendment is in recognition of the 1991 amendments to the Official Forms that abrogated the Chapter 13 Statement and made the same forms for schedules and statements applicable in all cases.

This subdivision also contains a technical correction. The phrase "superseded case" creates the erroneous impression that conversion of a case results in a new case that is distinct from the original case. The effect of conversion of a case is governed by §348 of the Code.

GAP Report on Rule 1007(c). No changes since publication, except for stylistic changes.

COMMITTEE NOTES ON RULES—2001 AMENDMENT

Subdivision (m) is added to enable the person required to mail notices under Rule 2002 to mail them to the appropriate guardian or other representative when the debtor knows that a creditor or other person listed is an infant or incompetent person.

The proper mailing address of the representative is determined in accordance with Rule 7004(b)(2), which requires mailing to the person's dwelling house or usual place of abode or at the place where the person regularly conducts a business or profession.

Changes Made After Publication and Comments. No changes were made.

COMMITTEE NOTES ON RULES—2003 AMENDMENT

[*Subdivision (a).*] This rule is amended to require the debtor to file a corporate ownership statement setting out the information described in Rule 7007.1. Requiring debtors to file the statement provides the court with an opportunity to make judicial disqualification determinations at the outset of the case. This could reduce problems later in the case by preventing the initial assignment of the case to a judge who holds a financial interest in a parent company of the debtor or some other entity that holds a significant ownership interest in the debtor. Moreover, by including the disclosure statement filing requirement at the commencement of the case, the debtor does not have to make the same disclosure filing each time it is involved in an adversary proceeding throughout the case. The debtor also must file supplemental statements as changes in ownership might arise.

Changes Made After Publication and Comments. No changes since publication.

[*Subdivisions (c) and (f).*] The rule is amended to add a requirement that a debtor submit a statement setting out the debtor's social security number. The addition is necessary because of the corresponding amendment to Rule 1005 which now provides that the caption of the petition includes only the final four digits of the debtor's social security number. The debtor submits the statement, but it is not filed, nor is it included in the case file. The statement provides the information necessary to include on the service copy of the notice required under Rule 2002(a)(1). It will also provide the information to facilitate the ability of creditors to search the court record by a search of a social security number already in the creditor's possession.

Changes Made After Publication and Comments. The rule amendment is made in response to the extensive commentary that urged the Advisory Committee to continue the obligation contained in current Rule 1005 that a debtor must include his or her social security number on the caption of the bankruptcy petition. Rule 1005 is amended to limit that disclosure to the final four digits of the social security number, and Rule 1007 is amended to reinstate the obligation in a manner that will provide more protection of the debtor's privacy while continuing access to the information to those persons with legitimate need for that data. The debtor must disclose the information, but the method of disclosure is by a verified statement that is submitted to the clerk. The statement is not filed in the case and does not become a part of the court record. Therefore, it enables the clerk to deliver that information to the creditors and the trustee in the case, but it does not become a part of the court record governed by § 107 of the Bankruptcy Code and is not available to the public.

COMMITTEE NOTES ON RULES—2005 AMENDMENT

Notice to creditors and other parties in interest is essential to the operation of the bankruptcy system. Sending notice requires a convenient listing of the names and addresses of the entities to whom notice must be sent, and virtually all of the bankruptcy courts have adopted a local rule requiring the submission of a list of these entities with the petition and in a particular format. These lists are commonly called the "mailing matrix."

Given the universal adoption of these local rules, the need for such lists in all cases is apparent. Consequently, the rule is amended to require the debtor to submit such a list at the commencement of the case. This list may be amended when necessary. *See* Rule 1009(a).

The content of the list is described by reference to Schedules D through H of the Official Forms rather than by reference to creditors or persons holding claims. The cross reference to the Schedules as the source of the names for inclusion in the list ensures that persons such as codebtors or nondebtor parties to executory contracts and unexpired leases will receive appropriate notices in the case.

While this rule renders unnecessary, in part, local rules on the subject, this rule does not direct any particular format or form for the list to take. Local rules still may govern those particulars of the list.

Subdivision (c) is amended to reflect that subdivision (a)(1) no longer requires the debtor to file a schedule of liabilities with the petition in lieu of a list of creditors. The filing of the list is mandatory, and subdivision (b) of the rule requires the filing of schedules. Thus, subdivision (c) no longer needs to account for the possibility that the debtor can delay filing a schedule of liabilities when the petition is accompanied by a list of creditors. Subdivision (c) simply addresses the situation in which the debtor does not file schedules or statements with the petition, and the procedure for seeking an extension of time for filing.

Other changes are stylistic.

Changes Made After Publication and Comment. No changes since publication.

COMMITTEE NOTES ON RULES—2008 AMENDMENT

The title of this rule is expanded to refer to "documents" in conformity with the 2005 amendments to §521 and related provisions of the Bankruptcy Code that include a wider range of documentary requirements.

Subdivision (a) is amended to require that any foreign representative filing a petition for recognition to commence a case under chapter 15, which was added to the Code in 2005, file a list of entities with whom the debtor is engaged in litigation in the United States. The foreign representative filing the petition for recognition must also list any entities against whom provisional relief is being sought as well as all persons or bodies authorized to administer foreign proceedings of the debtor. This should ensure that entities most interested in the case, or their representatives, will receive notice of the petition under Rule 2002(q).

Subdivision (a)(4) is amended to require the foreign representative who files a petition for recognition under chapter 15 to file the documents described in §1515 of the Code as well as a corporate ownership statement. The subdivision is also amended to identify the foreign representative in language that more closely follows the text of the Code. Former subdivision (a)(4) is renumbered as subdivision (a)(5) and stylistic changes were made to the subdivision.

Subdivision (b)(1) addresses schedules, statements, and other documents that the debtor must file unless the court orders otherwise and other than in a case under chapter 9. This subdivision is amended to include documentary requirements added by the 2005 amendments to § 521 that apply to the same group of debtors and have the same time limits as the existing requirements of (b)(1). Consistent with the E-Government Act of 2002, Pub. L. No. 107-347, the payment advices should be redacted before they are filed.

Subdivision (b)(2) is amended to conform to the renumbering of the subsections of § 521.

Subdivisions (b)(3) through (b)(8) are new and implement the 2005 amendments to the Code. Subdivision (b)(3) provides for the filing of a document relating to the credit counseling requirement provided by the 2005 amendments to § 109 in the context of an Official Form that warns the debtor of the consequences of failing to comply with the credit counseling requirement.

Subdivision (b)(4) addresses the filing of information about current monthly income, as defined in § 101, for certain chapter 7 debtors and, if required, additional calculations of expenses required by the 2005 amendments to § 707(b).

Subdivision (b)(5) addresses the filing of information about current monthly income, as defined in § 101, for individual chapter 11 debtors. The 2005 amendments to § 1129(a)(15) condition plan confirmation for individual debtors on the commitment of disposable income, as defined in § 1325(b)(2), which is based on current monthly income.

Subdivision (b)(6) addresses the filing of information about current monthly income, as defined in § 101, for chapter 13 debtors and, if required, additional calculations of expenses. These changes are necessary because the 2005 amendments to § 1325 require that the determination of disposable income begin with current monthly income.

Subdivision (b)(7) reflects the 2005 amendments to §§ 727 and 1328 of the Code that condition the receipt of a discharge on the completion of a personal financial management course, with certain exceptions. Certain individual chapter 11 debtors may also be required to complete a personal financial management course under § 727(a)(11) as incorporated by § 1141(d)(3)(C). To evidence compliance with that requirement, the subdivision requires the debtor to file the appropriate Official Form certifying that the debtor has completed the personal financial management course.

Subdivision (b)(8) requires an individual debtor in a case under chapter 11, 12, or 13 to file a statement that there are no reasonable grounds to believe that the restrictions on a homestead exemption as set out in § 522(q) of the Code are applicable. Sections 1141(d)(5)(C), 1228(f), and 1328(h) each provide that the court shall not enter a discharge order unless it finds that there is no reasonable cause to believe that § 522(q) applies. Requiring the debtor to submit a statement to that effect in cases under chapters 11, 12, and 13 in which an exemption is claimed in excess of the amount allowed under § 522(q)(1) provides the court with a basis to conclude, in the absence of any contrary information, that § 522(q) does not apply. Creditors receive notice under Rule 2002(f)(11) of the time to request postponement of the entry of the discharge to permit an opportunity to challenge the debtor's assertions in the Rule 1007(b)(8) statement in appropriate cases.

Subdivision (c) is amended to include time limits for the filing requirements added to subdivision (b) due to the 2005 amendments to the Code, and to make conforming amendments. Separate time limits are provided for the documentation of credit counseling and for the statement of the completion of the financial management course. While most documents relating to credit counseling must be filed with the voluntary petition, the credit counseling certificate and debt repayment plan can be filed within 15 days of the filing of a voluntary petition if the debtor files a statement under subdivision (b)(3)(B) with the petition. Sections 727(a)(11), 1141(d)(3), and 1328(g) of the Code require individual debtors to complete a personal financial management course prior to the entry of a discharge. The amendment allows the court to enlarge the deadline for the debtor to file the statement of completion. Because no party is harmed by the enlargement, no specific restriction is placed on the court's discretion to enlarge the deadline, even after its expiration.

Subdivision (c) of the rule is also amended to recognize the limitation on the extension of time to file schedules and statements when the debtor is a small business debtor. Section 1116(3), added to the Code in 2005, establishes a specific standard for courts to apply in the event that the debtor in possession or the trustee seeks an extension for filing these forms for a period beyond 30 days after the order for relief.

Changes Made After Publication. Subdivision (a)(4) was amended to insert the requirement that the foreign representative who files the chapter 15 petition must file the corporate ownership statement. Subdivision (b)(4) was amended to provide that all individual debtors rather than just those whose debts are primarily consumer debts must file the statement of current monthly income. Subdivisions (b)(7) and (c) were amended to make the obligation to file a statement of the completion of a personal financial management course applicable to certain individual chapter 11 debtors as well as to individual debtors in chapters 7 and 13. Subdivision (c) is also amended to provide the court with broad discretion to enlarge the time to file the statement of completion of a personal financial management course. The Committee Note was amended to explain these changes.

COMMITTEE NOTES ON RULES—2009 AMENDMENT

The rule is amended to implement changes in connection with the amendment to Rule 9006(a) and the manner by which time is computed under the rules. Each deadline in the rule of fewer than 30 days is amended to substitute a deadline that is a multiple of seven days. Throughout the rules, deadlines are amended in the following manner:

- 5-day periods become 7-day periods
- 10-day periods become 14-day periods
- 15-day periods become 14-day periods
- 20-day periods become 21-day periods
- 25-day periods become 28-day periods

Rule 1008. Verification of Petitions and Accompanying Papers

All petitions, lists, schedules, statements and amendments thereto shall be verified or contain an unsworn declaration as provided in 28 U.S.C. §1746.

(As amended Apr. 30, 1991, eff. Aug. 1, 1991.)

NOTES OF ADVISORY COMMITTEE ON RULES—1983

This rule retains the requirement under the Bankruptcy Act and rules that petitions and accompanying papers must be verified. Only the original need be signed and verified, but the copies must be conformed to the original. See Rule 9011(c).

The verification may be replaced by an unsworn declaration as provided in 28 U.S.C. §1746. See also, Official Form No. 1 and Advisory Committee Note.

NOTES OF ADVISORY COMMITTEE ON RULES—1991 AMENDMENT

The amendments to this rule are stylistic.

Rule 1009. Amendments of Voluntary Petitions, Lists, Schedules and Statements

(a) GENERAL RIGHT TO AMEND. A voluntary petition, list, schedule, or statement may be amended by the debtor as a matter of course at any time before the case is closed. The debtor shall give notice of the amendment to the trustee and to any entity affected thereby. On motion of a party in interest, after notice and a hearing, the court may order any voluntary petition, list, schedule, or statement to be amended and the clerk shall give notice of the amendment to entities designated by the court.

(b) STATEMENT OF INTENTION. The statement of intention may be amended by the debtor at any time before the expiration of the period provided in §521(a) of the Code. The debtor shall give notice of the amendment to the trustee and to any entity affected thereby.

(c) STATEMENT OF SOCIAL SECURITY NUMBER. If a debtor becomes aware that the statement of social security number submitted under Rule 1007(f) is incorrect, the debtor shall promptly submit an amended verified statement setting forth the correct social security number. The debtor shall give notice of the amendment to all of the entities required to be included on the list filed under Rule 1007(a)(1) or (a)(2).

(d) TRANSMISSION TO UNITED STATES TRUSTEE. The clerk shall promptly transmit to the United States trustee a copy of every amendment filed or submitted under subdivision (a), (b), or (c) of this rule.

(As amended Mar. 30, 1987, eff. Aug. 1, 1987; Apr. 30, 1991, eff. Aug. 1, 1991; Apr. 12, 2006, eff. Dec. 1, 2006; Apr. 23, 2008, eff. Dec. 1, 2008.)

NOTES OF ADVISORY COMMITTEE ON RULES—1983

This rule continues the permissive approach adopted by former Bankruptcy Rule 110 to amendments of voluntary petitions and accompanying papers. Notice of any amendment is required to be given to the trustee. This is particularly important with respect to any amendment of the schedule of property affecting the debtor's claim of exemptions. Notice of any amendment of the schedule of liabilities is to be given to any creditor whose claim is changed or newly listed.

The rule does not continue the provision permitting the court to order an amendment on its own initiative. Absent a request in some form by a party in interest, the court should not be involved in administrative matters affecting the estate.

If a list or schedule is amended to include an additional creditor, the effect on the dischargeability of the creditor's claim is governed by the provisions of §523(a)(3) of the Code.

NOTES OF ADVISORY COMMITTEE ON RULES—1987 AMENDMENT

Subdivision (a) is amended to require notice and a hearing in the event a party in interest other than the debtor seeks to amend. The number of copies of the amendment will be determined by local rule of court.

Subdivision (b) is added to treat amendments of the statement of intention separately from other amendments. The intention of the individual debtor must be performed within 45 days of the filing of the statement, unless the court extends the period. Subdivision (b) limits the time for amendment to the time for performance under §521(2)(B) of the Code or any extension granted by the court.

NOTES OF ADVISORY COMMITTEE ON RULES—1991 AMENDMENT

The amendments to subdivision (a) are stylistic.

Subdivision (c) is derived from Rule X-1002(a) and is designed to provide the United States trustee with current information to enable that office to participate effectively in the case.

COMMITTEE NOTES ON RULES—2006 AMENDMENT

Subdivision (c). Rule 2002(a)(1) provides that the notice of the §341 meeting of creditors include the debtor's social security number. It provides creditors with the full number while limiting publication of the social security number otherwise to the final four digits of the number to protect the debtor's identity from others who do not have the same need for that information. If, however, the social security number that the debtor submitted under Rule 1007(f) is incorrect, then the only notice to the entities contained on the list filed under Rule 1007(a)(1) or (a)(2) would be incorrect. This amendment adds a new subdivision (c) that directs the debtor to submit a verified amended statement of social security number and to give notice of the new statement to all entities in the case who received the notice containing the erroneous social security number.

Subdivision (d). Former subdivision (c) becomes subdivision (d) and is amended to include new subdivision (c) amendments in the list of documents that the clerk must transmit to the United States trustee.

Other amendments are stylistic.

Changes Made After Publication. No changes since publication.

COMMITTEE NOTES ON RULES—2008 AMENDMENT

Subdivision (b) is amended to conform to the 2005 amendments to § 521 of the Code.

Changes Made After Publication. No changes were made after publication.

Rule 1010. Service of Involuntary Petition and Summons; Petition For Recognition of a Foreign Nonmain Proceeding

(a) SERVICE OF INVOLUNTARY PETITION AND SUMMONS; SERVICE OF PETITION FOR RECOGNITION OF FOREIGN NONMAIN PROCEEDING. On the filing of an involuntary petition or a petition for recognition of a foreign nonmain proceeding, the clerk shall forthwith issue a summons for service. When an involuntary petition is filed, service shall be made on the debtor. When a petition for recognition of a foreign nonmain proceeding is filed, service shall be made on the debtor, any entity against whom provisional relief is sought under § 1519 of the Code, and on any other party as the court may direct. The summons shall be served with a copy of the petition in the manner provided for service of a summons and complaint by Rule 7004(a) or (b). If service cannot be so made, the court may order that the summons and petition be served by mailing copies to the party's last known address, and by at least one publication in a manner and form directed by the court. The summons and petition may be served on the party anywhere. Rule 7004(e) and Rule 4(*l*) F.R.Civ.P. apply when service is made or attempted under this rule.

(b) CORPORATE OWNERSHIP STATEMENT. Each petitioner that is a corporation shall file with the involuntary petition a corporate ownership statement containing the information described in Rule 7007.1.

(As amended Mar. 30, 1987, eff. Aug. 1, 1987; Apr. 30, 1991, eff. Aug. 1, 1991; Apr. 22, 1993, eff. Aug. 1, 1993; Apr. 11, 1997, eff. Dec. 1, 1997; Apr. 23, 2008, eff. Dec. 1, 2008.)

NOTES OF ADVISORY COMMITTEE ON RULES—1983

This rule provides the procedure for service of the involuntary petition and summons. It does not deal with service of a summons and complaint instituting an adversary proceeding pursuant to Part VII.

While this rule is similar to former Bankruptcy Rule 111, it substitutes the clerk of the bankruptcy court for the clerk of the district court as the person who is to issue the summons.

The modes of service prescribed by the rule are personal or by mail, when service can be effected in one of these ways in the United States. Such service is to be made in the manner prescribed in adversary proceedings by Rule 7004(a) and (b). If service must be made in a foreign country, the mode of service is one of that set forth in Rule 4(i) F.R.Civ.P.

When the methods set out in Rule 7004(a) and (b) cannot be utilized, service by publication coupled with mailing to the last known address is authorized. *Cf.* Rule 7004(c). The court determines the form and manner of publication as provided in Rule 9007. The publication need not set out the petition or the order directing service by publication. In order to apprise the debtor fairly, however, the publication should include all the information required to be in the summons by Official Form No. 13 and a notice indicating how service is being effected and how a copy of the petition may be obtained.

There are no territorial limits on the service authorized by this rule, which continues the practice under the former rules and Act. There must, however, be a basis for jurisdiction pursuant to § 109(a) of the Code for the court to order relief. Venue provisions are set forth in 28 U.S.C. § 1472.

Subdivision (f) of Rule 7004 and subdivisions (g) and (h) of Rule 4 F.R.Civ.P. govern time and proof of service and amendment of process or of proof of service.

Rule 1004 provides for transmission to nonpetitioning partners of a petition filed against the partnership by fewer than all the general partners.

NOTES OF ADVISORY COMMITTEE ON RULES—1987 AMENDMENT

The rule has been broadened to include service of a petition commencing a case ancillary to a foreign proceeding, previously included in Rule 1003(e)(2).

NOTES OF ADVISORY COMMITTEE ON RULES—1991 AMENDMENT

Reference to the Official Form number is deleted in anticipation of future revision and renumbering of the Official Forms.

Rule 4(g) and (h) F.R.Civ.P. made applicable by this rule refers to Rule 4(g) and (h) F.R.Civ.P. in effect on January 1, 1990, notwithstanding any subsequent amendment thereto. See Rule 7004(g).

NOTES OF ADVISORY COMMITTEE ON RULES—1993 AMENDMENT

This rule is amended to delete the reference to the Official Form. The Official Form for the summons was abrogated in 1991. Other amendments are stylistic and make no substantive change.

NOTES OF ADVISORY COMMITTEE ON RULES—1997 AMENDMENT

The amendments to this rule are technical, are promulgated solely to conform to changes in subdivision designations in Rule 4, F.R.Civ.P., and in Rule 7004, and are not intended to effectuate any material change in substance.

In 1996, the letter designation of subdivision (f) of Rule 7004 (Summons; Time Limit for Service) was changed to subdivision (e). In 1993, the provisions of Rule 4, F.R.Civ.P., relating to proof of service contained in Rule 4(g) (Return) and Rule 4(h) (Amendments), were placed in the new subdivision (*l*) of Rule 4 (Proof of Service). The technical amendments to Rule 1010 are designed solely to conform to these new subdivision designations.

The 1996 amendments to Rule 7004 and the 1993 amendments to Rule 4, F.R.Civ.P., have not affected the availability of service by first class mail in accordance with Rule 7004(b) for the service of a summons and petition in an involuntary case commenced under § 303 or an ancillary case commenced under § 304 of the Code.

GAP Report on Rule 1010. These amendments, which are technical and conforming, were not published for comment.

COMMITTEE NOTES ON RULES—2008 AMENDMENT

This rule is amended to implement the 2005 amendments to the Code, which repealed §304 and replaced it with chapter 15 governing ancillary and other cross-border cases. Under chapter 15, a foreign representative commences a case by filing a petition for recognition of a pending foreign nonmain proceeding. The amendment requires service of the summons and petition on the debtor and any entity against whom the representative is seeking provisional relief. Until the court enters a recognition order under §1517, no stay is in effect unless the court enters some form of provisional relief under §1519. Thus, only those entities against whom specific provisional relief is sought need to be served. The court may, however, direct that service be made on additional entities as appropriate.

This rule does not apply to a petition for recognition of a foreign main proceeding.

The rule is also amended by renumbering the prior rule as subdivision (a) and adding a new subdivision (b) requiring any corporate creditor that files or joins an involuntary petition to file a corporate ownership statement.

Changes Made After Publication. No changes were made after publication.

REFERENCES IN TEXT

The Federal Rules of Civil Procedure, referred to in subd. (a), are set out in the Appendix to Title 28, Judiciary and Judicial Procedure.

Rule 1011. Responsive Pleading or Motion in Involuntary and Cross-Border Cases

(a) WHO MAY CONTEST PETITION. The debtor named in an involuntary petition, or a party in interest to a petition for recognition of a foreign proceeding, may contest the petition. In the case of a petition against a partnership under Rule 1004, a nonpetitioning general partner, or a person who is alleged to be a general partner but denies the allegation, may contest the petition.

(b) DEFENSES AND OBJECTIONS; WHEN PRESENTED. Defenses and objections to the petition shall be presented in the manner prescribed by Rule 12 F.R.Civ.P. and shall be filed and served within 21 days after service of the summons, except that if service is made by publication on a party or partner not residing or found within the state in which the court sits, the court shall prescribe the time for filing and serving the response.

(c) EFFECT OF MOTION. Service of a motion under Rule 12(b) F.R.Civ.P. shall extend the time for filing and serving a responsive pleading as permitted by Rule 12(a) F.R.Civ.P.

(d) CLAIMS AGAINST PETITIONERS. A claim against a petitioning creditor may not be asserted in the answer except for the purpose of defeating the petition.

(e) OTHER PLEADINGS. No other pleadings shall be permitted, except that the court may order a reply to an answer and prescribe the time for filing and service.

(f) CORPORATE OWNERSHIP STATEMENT. If the entity responding to the involuntary petition or the petition for recognition of a foreign proceeding is a corporation, the entity shall file with its first appearance, pleading, motion, response, or other request addressed to the court a corporate ownership statement containing the information described in Rule 7007.1.

(As amended Mar. 30, 1987, eff. Aug. 1, 1987; Apr. 26, 2004, eff. Dec. 1, 2004; Apr. 23, 2008, eff. Dec. 1, 2008; Mar. 26, 2009, eff. Dec. 1, 2009.)

NOTES OF ADVISORY COMMITTEE ON RULES—1983

This rule is derived from former Bankruptcy Rule 112. A petition filed by fewer than all the general partners under Rule 1004(b) to have an order for relief entered with respect to the partnership is referred to as a petition against the partnership because of the adversary character of the proceeding it commences. *Cf.* §303(b)(3) of the Code; 2 Collier *Bankruptcy* ¶303.05[5][a] (15th ed. 1981); 2 *id.* ¶¶18.33[2], 18.46 (14th ed. 1966). One who denies an allegation of membership in the firm is nevertheless recognized as a party entitled to contest a petition filed against a partnership under subdivision (b) of Rule 1004 in view of the possible consequences to him of an order for relief against the entity alleged to include him as a member. See §723 of the Code; *Francis v. McNeal*, 228 U.S. 695 (1913); *Manson v. Williams*, 213 U.S. 453 (1909); *Carter v. Whisler*, 275 Fed. 743, 746–747 (8th Cir. 1921). The rule preserves the features of the former Act and Rule 112 and the Code permitting no response by creditors to an involuntary petition or petition against a partnership under Rule 1004(b).

Subdivision (b): Rule 12 F.R.Civ.P. has been looked to by the courts as prescribing the mode of making a defense or objection to a petition in bankruptcy. See *Fada of New York, Inc. v. Organization Service Co., Inc.*, 125 F.2d 120, (2d Cir. 1942); *In the Matter of McDougald*, 17 F.R.D. 2, 5 (W.D. Ark. 1955); *In the Matter of Miller*, 6 Fed. Rules Serv. 12f.26, Case No. 1 (N.D. Ohio 1942); *Tatum v. Acadian Production Corp. of La.*, 35 F. Supp. 40, 50 (E.D. La. 1940); 2 Collier, *supra* ¶303.07 (15th ed. 1981); 2 *id.* at 134–40 (14th ed. 1966). As pointed out in the Note accompanying former Bankruptcy Rule 915 an objection that a debtor is neither entitled to the benefits of the Code nor amenable to an involuntary petition goes to jurisdiction of the subject matter and may be made at any time consistent with Rule 12(h)(3) F.R.Civ.P. Nothing in this rule recognizes standing in a creditor or any other person not authorized to contest a petition to raise an objection that a person eligible to file a voluntary petition cannot be the subject of an order for relief on an involuntary petition. See Seligson & King, *Jurisdiction and Venue in Bankruptcy*, 36 Ref.J. 36, 38–40 (1962).

As Collier has pointed out with respect to the Bankruptcy Act, "the mechanics of the provisions in §18a and b relating to time for appearance and pleading are unnecessarily confusing. . . . It would seem, though, to be more straightforward to provide, as does Federal Rule 12(a), that the time to respond runs from the date of service rather than the date of issuance of process." 2 Collier, *supra* at 119. The time normally allowed for the service and filing of an answer or motion under Rule 1011 runs from the date of the issuance of the summons. Compare Rule 7012. Service of the summons and petition will ordinarily be made by mail under Rule 1010 and must be made within 10 days of the issuance of the summons under Rule 7004(e), which governs the time of service. When service is made by publication, the court should fix the time for service and filing of the response in the light of all the circumstances so as to afford a fair opportunity to the debtor to enter a defense or objection without unduly delaying the hearing on the petition. *Cf.* Rule 12(a) F.R.Civ.P.

Subdivision (c): Under subdivision (c), the timely service of a motion permitted by Rule 12(b), (e), (f), or (h) F.R.Civ.P. alters the time within which an answer must be filed. If the court denies a motion or postpones its disposition until trial on the merits, the answer must be served within 10 days after notice of the court's action. If the court grants a motion for a more definite statement, the answer may be served any time within 10 days after the service of the more definite statement.

Many of the rules governing adversary proceedings apply to proceedings on a contested petition unless the court otherwise directs as provided in Rule 1018. The specific provisions of this Rule 1011 or 7005, however, govern the filing of an answer or motion responsive to a petition. The rules of Part VII are adaptations of the corresponding Federal Rules of Civil Procedure, and the effect of Rule 1018 is thus to make the provisions of Civil Rules 5, 8, 9, 15, and 56, *inter alia*, generally applicable to the making of defenses and objections to the petition. Rule 1018 follows prior law and practice in this respect. See 2 Collier, *Bankruptcy* ¶¶18.39–18.41 (14th ed. 1966).

Subdivision (d). This subdivision adopts the position taken in many cases that an affirmative judgment against a petitioning creditor cannot be sought by a counterclaim filed in an answer to an involuntary petition. See, *e.g.*, *Georgia Jewelers, Inc. v. Bulova Watch Co.*, 302 F.2d 362, 369–70 (5th Cir. 1962); *Associated Electronic Supply Co. of Omaha v. C.B.S. Electronic Sales Corp.*, 288 F.2d 683, 684–85 (8th Cir. 1961). The subdivision follows *Harris v. Capehart-Farnsworth Corp.*, 225 F.2d 268 (8th Cir. 1955), in permitting the debtor to challenge the standing of a petitioner by filing a counterclaim against him. It does not foreclose the court from rejecting a counterclaim that cannot be determined without unduly delaying the decision upon the petition. See *In the Matter of Bichel Optical Laboratories, Inc.*, 299 F. Supp. 545 (D. Minn. 1969).

Subdivision (e). This subdivision makes it clear that no reply needs to be made to an answer, including one asserting a counterclaim, unless the court orders otherwise.

NOTES OF ADVISORY COMMITTEE ON RULES—1987 AMENDMENT

The rule has been broadened to make applicable in ancillary cases the provisions concerning responsive pleadings to involuntary petitions.

COMMITTEE NOTES ON RULES—2004 AMENDMENT

The amendment to Rule 1004 that became effective on December 1, 2002, deleted former subdivision (a) of that rule leaving only the provisions relating to involuntary petitions against partnerships. The rule no longer includes subdivisions. Therefore, this technical amendment changes the reference to Rule 1004(b) to Rule 1004.

COMMITTEE NOTES ON RULES—2008 AMENDMENT

The rule is amended to reflect the 2005 amendments to the Code, which repealed §304 and added chapter 15. Section 304 covered cases ancillary to foreign proceedings, while chapter 15 governs ancillary and other cross-border cases and introduces the concept of a petition for recognition of a foreign proceeding.

The rule is also amended in tandem with the amendment to Rule 1010 to require the parties responding to an involuntary petition and a petition for recognition of a foreign proceeding to file corporate ownership statements to assist the court in determining whether recusal is necessary.

COMMITTEE NOTES ON RULES—2009 AMENDMENT

The rule is amended to implement changes in connection with the amendment to Rule 9006(a) and the manner by which time is computed under the rules. The deadline in the rule is amended to substitute a deadline that is a multiple of seven days. Throughout the rules, deadlines are amended in the following manner:

- 5-day periods become 7-day periods
- 10-day periods become 14-day periods
- 15-day periods become 14-day periods
- 20-day periods become 21-day periods
- 25-day periods become 28-day periods

Changes Made After Publication. No changes were made after publication.

REFERENCES IN TEXT

The Federal Rules of Civil Procedure, referred to in subds. (b) and (c), are set out in the Appendix to Title 28, Judiciary and Judicial Procedure.

[Rule 1012. Examination of Debtor, Including Discovery, on Issue of Nonpayment of Debts in Involuntary Cases.] (Abrogated Mar. 30, 1987, eff. Aug. 1, 1987)

NOTES OF ADVISORY COMMITTEE ON RULES—1987

This rule is abrogated. The discovery rules apply whenever an involuntary petition is contested. Rule 1018.

Rule 1013. Hearing and Disposition of a Petition in an Involuntary Case

(a) CONTESTED PETITION. The court shall determine the issues of a contested petition at the earliest practicable time and forthwith enter an order for relief, dismiss the petition, or enter any other appropriate order.

(b) DEFAULT. If no pleading or other defense to a petition is filed within the time provided by Rule 1011, the court, on the next day, or as soon thereafter as practicable, shall enter an order for the relief requested in the petition.

[(c) ORDER FOR RELIEF] (Abrogated Apr. 22, 1993, eff. Aug. 1, 1993)

(As amended Apr. 30, 1991, eff. Aug. 1, 1991; Apr. 22, 1993, eff. Aug. 1, 1993.)

NOTES OF ADVISORY COMMITTEE ON RULES—1983

This rule is adapted from former Bankruptcy Rule 115(a) and (c) and applies in chapter 7 and 11 cases. The right to trial by jury under §19a of the Bankruptcy Act has been abrogated and the availability of a trial by jury is within the discretion of the bankruptcy judge pursuant to 28 U.S.C. §1480(b). Rule 9015 governs the demand for a jury trial.

Subdivision (b) of Rule 1013 is derived from former Bankruptcy Rule 115(c) and §18(e) of the Bankruptcy Act. If an order for relief is not entered on default, dismissal will ordinarily be appropriate but the court may postpone definitive action. See also Rule 9024 with respect to setting aside an order for relief on default for cause.

Subdivision (e) of former Bankruptcy Rule 115 has not been carried over because its provisions are covered by §303(i) of the Code.

NOTES OF ADVISORY COMMITTEE ON RULES—1991 AMENDMENT

Reference to the Official Form number is deleted in anticipation of future revision and renumbering of the Official Forms.

NOTES OF ADVISORY COMMITTEE ON RULES—1993 AMENDMENT

Subdivision (c) is abrogated because the official form for the order for relief was abrogated in 1991. Other amendments are stylistic and make no substantive change.

Rule 1014. Dismissal and Change of Venue

(a) DISMISSAL AND TRANSFER OF CASES.

(1) *Cases Filed in Proper District*. If a petition is filed in the proper district, the court, on the timely motion of a party in interest or on its own motion, and after hearing on notice to the petitioners, the United States trustee, and other entities as directed by the court, may transfer the case to any other district if the court determines that the transfer is in the interest of justice or for the convenience of the parties.

(2) *Cases Filed in Improper District*. If a petition is filed in an improper district, the court,

on the timely motion of a party in interest or on its own motion, and after hearing on notice to the petitioners, the United States trustee, and other entities as directed by the court, may dismiss the case or transfer it to any other district if the court determines that transfer is in the interest of justice or for the convenience of the parties.

(b) PROCEDURE WHEN PETITIONS INVOLVING THE SAME DEBTOR OR RELATED DEBTORS ARE FILED IN DIFFERENT COURTS. If petitions commencing cases under the Code are filed in different districts by or against (1) the same debtor, or (2) a partnership and one or more of its general partners, or (3) two or more general partners, or (4) a debtor and an affiliate, on motion filed in the district in which the petition filed first is pending and after hearing on notice to the petitioners, the United States trustee, and other entities as directed by the court, the court may determine, in the interest of justice or for the convenience of the parties, the district or districts in which the case or cases should proceed. Except as otherwise ordered by the court in the district in which the petition filed first is pending, the proceedings on the other petitions shall be stayed by the courts in which they have been filed until the determination is made.

(As amended Mar. 30, 1987, eff. Aug. 1, 1987; Apr. 30, 1991, eff. Aug. 1, 1991; Apr. 30, 2007, eff. Dec. 1, 2007.)

NOTES OF ADVISORY COMMITTEE ON RULES—1983

This rule is derived from former Bankruptcy Rule 116 which contained venue as well as transfer provisions. Public Law 95-598, however, placed the venue provisions in 28 U.S.C. §1472, and no purpose is served by repeating them in this rule. Transfer of cases is provided in 28 U.S.C. §1475 but this rule adds the procedure for obtaining transfer. Pursuant to 28 U.S.C. §1472, proper venue for cases filed under the Code is either the district of domicile, residence, principal place of business, or location of principal assets for 180 days or the longer portion thereof immediately preceding the petition. 28 U.S.C. §1475 permits the court to transfer a case in the interest of justice and for the convenience of the parties. If the venue is improper, the court may retain or transfer the case in the interest of justice and for the convenience of the parties pursuant to 28 U.S.C. §1477.

Subdivision (a) of the rule is derived from former Bankruptcy Rule 116(b). It implements 28 U.S.C. §§1475 and 1477 and clarifies the procedure to be followed in requesting and effecting transfer of a case. Subdivision (a) protects the parties against being subjected to a transfer except on a timely motion of a party in interest. If the transfer would result in fragmentation or duplication of administration, increase expense, or delay closing the estate, such a factor would bear on the timeliness of the motion as well as on the propriety of the transfer under the standards prescribed in subdivision (a). Subdivision (a) of the rule requires the interest of justice and the convenience of the parties to be the grounds of any transfer of a case or of the retention of a case filed in an improper district as does 28 U.S.C. §1477. *Cf.* 28 U.S.C. §1404(a) (district court may transfer any civil action "[f]or the convenience of parties and witnesses, in the interest of justice"). It also expressly requires a hearing on notice to the petitioner or petitioners before the transfer of any case may be ordered. Under this rule, a motion by a party in interest is necessary. There is no provision for the court to act on its own initiative.

Subdivision (b) is derived from former Bankruptcy Rule 116(c). It authorizes the court in which the first petition is filed under the Code by or against a debtor to entertain a motion seeking a determination whether the case so commenced should continue or be transferred and consolidated or administered jointly with another case commenced by or against the same or related person in another court under a different chapter of the Code. Subdivision (b) is correlated with 28 U.S.C. §1472 which authorizes petitioners to file cases involving a partnership and partners or affiliated debtors.

The reference in subdivision (b) to petitions filed "by" a partner or "by" any other of the persons mentioned is to be understood as referring to voluntary petitions. It is not the purpose of this subdivision to permit more than one case to be filed in the same court because a creditor signing an involuntary petition happens to be a partner, a partnership, or an affiliate of a debtor.

Transfers of adversary proceedings in cases under title 11 are governed by Rule 7087 and 28 U.S.C. §1475.

NOTES OF ADVISORY COMMITTEE ON RULES—1987 AMENDMENT

Both paragraphs 1 and 2 of subdivision (a) are amended to conform to the standard for transfer in 28 U.S.C. §1412. Formerly, 28 U.S.C. §1477 authorized a court either to transfer or retain a case which had been commenced in a district where venue was improper. However, 28 U.S.C. §1412, which supersedes 28 U.S.C. §1477, authorizes only the transfer of a case. The rule is amended to delete the reference to retention of a case commenced in the improper district. Dismissal of a case commenced in the improper district as authorized by 28 U.S.C. §1406 has been added to the rule. If a timely motion to dismiss for improper venue is not filed, the right to object to venue is waived.

The last sentence of the rule has been deleted as unnecessary.

NOTES OF ADVISORY COMMITTEE ON RULES—1991 AMENDMENT

Subdivision (b) is amended to provide that a motion for transfer of venue under this subdivision shall be filed in the district in which the first petition is pending. If the case commenced by the first petition has been transferred to another district prior to the filing of a motion to transfer a related case under this subdivision, the motion must be filed in the district to which the first petition had been transferred.

The other amendments to this rule are consistent with the responsibilities of the United States trustee in the supervision and administration of cases pursuant to 28 U.S.C. §586(a)(3). The United States trustee may appear and be heard on issues relating to the transfer of the case or dismissal due to improper venue. See §307 of the Code.

COMMITTEE NOTES ON RULES—2007 AMENDMENT

Courts have generally held that they have the authority to dismiss or transfer cases on their own motion. The amendment recognizes this authority and also provides that dismissal or transfer of the case may take place only after notice and a hearing.

Other amendments are stylistic.

Changes Made After Publication. No changes since publication.

Rule 1015. Consolidation or Joint Administration of Cases Pending in Same Court

(a) CASES INVOLVING SAME DEBTOR. If two or more petitions are pending in the same court by or against the same debtor, the court may order consolidation of the cases.

(b) CASES INVOLVING TWO OR MORE RELATED DEBTORS. If a joint petition or two or more petitions are pending in the same court by or against (1) a husband and wife, or (2) a partnership and one or more of its general partners, or (3) two or more general partners, or (4) a debtor and an affiliate, the court may order a joint administration of the estates. Prior to entering an order the court shall give consideration to protecting creditors of different estates against potential conflicts of interest. An order directing joint administration of individual cases of a husband and wife shall, if one spouse has elected the exemptions under §522(b)(2) of the Code and the other has elected the exemptions under §522(b)(3), fix a reasonable time within which either may amend the election so that both shall have elected the same exemptions. The order shall notify the debtors that unless they elect the same exemptions within the time fixed by the court, they will be deemed to have elected the exemptions provided by §522(b)(2).

(c) EXPEDITING AND PROTECTIVE ORDERS. When an order for consolidation or joint administration of a joint case or two or more cases is entered pursuant to this rule, while protecting the rights of the parties under the Code, the court may enter orders as may tend to avoid unnecessary costs and delay.

(As amended Mar. 30, 1987, eff. Aug. 1, 1987; Apr. 23, 2008; eff. Dec. 1, 2008.)

NOTES OF ADVISORY COMMITTEE ON RULES—1983

Subdivision (a) of this rule is derived from former Bankruptcy Rule 117(a). It applies to cases when the same debtor is named in both voluntary and involuntary petitions, when husband and wife have filed a joint petition pursuant to §302 of the Code, and when two or more involuntary petitions are filed against the same debtor. It also applies when cases are pending in the same court by virtue of a transfer of one or more petitions from another court. Subdivision (c) allows the court discretion regarding the order of trial of issues raised by two or more involuntary petitions against the same debtor.

Subdivision (b) recognizes the propriety of joint administration of estates in certain kinds of cases. The election or appointment of one trustee for two or more jointly administered estates is authorized by Rule 2009. The authority of the court to order joint administration under subdivision (b) extends equally to the situation when the petitions are filed under different sections, *e.g.*, when one petition is voluntary and the other involuntary, and when all of the petitions are filed under the same section of the Code.

Consolidation of cases implies a unitary administration of the estate and will ordinarily be indicated under the circumstances to which subdivision (a) applies. This rule does not deal with the consolidation of cases involving two or more separate debtors. Consolidation of the estates of separate debtors may sometimes be appropriate, as when the affairs of an individual and a corporation owned or controlled by that individual are so intermingled that the court cannot separate their assets and liabilities. Consolidation, as distinguished from joint administration, is neither authorized nor prohibited by this rule since the propriety of consolidation depends on substantive considerations and affects the substantive rights of the creditors of the different estates. For illustrations of the substantive consolidation of separate estates, see *Sampsell v. Imperial Paper & Color Corp.*, 313 U.S. 215 (1941). See also *Chemical Bank N.Y. Trust Co. v. Kheel*, 369 F.2d 845 (2d Cir. 1966); Seligson & Mandell, *Multi-Debtor Petition—Consolidation of Debtors and Due Process of Law*, 73 Com.L.J. 341 (1968); Kennedy, *Insolvency and the Corporate Veil in the United States* in *Proceedings of the 8th International Symposium on Comparative Law* 232, 248–55 (1971).

Joint administration as distinguished from consolidation may include combining the estates by using a single docket for the matters occurring in the administration, including the listing of filed claims, the combining of notices to creditors of the different estates, and the joint handling of other purely administrative matters that may aid in expediting the cases and rendering the process less costly.

Subdivision (c) is an adaptation of the provisions of Rule 42(a) F.R.Civ.P. for the purposes of administration of estates under this rule. The rule does not deal with filing fees when an order for the consolidation of cases or joint administration of estates is made.

A joint petition of husband and wife, requiring the payment of a single filing fee, is permitted by §302 of the Code. Consolidation of such a case, however, rests in the discretion of the court; see §302(b) of the Code.

NOTES OF ADVISORY COMMITTEE ON RULES—1987 AMENDMENT

The amendment to subdivision (b) implements the provisions of §522(b) of the Code, as enacted by the 1984 amendments.

COMMITTEE NOTES ON RULES—2008 AMENDMENT

The rule is amended to conform to the change in the numbering of §522(b) of the Code that was made as a part of the 2005 amendments. Former subsections (b)(1) and (b)(2) of §522 were renumbered as subsections (b)(2) and (b)(3), respectively. The rule is amended to make the parallel change.

Changes Made After Publication. No changes were made after publication.

Rule 1016. Death or Incompetency of Debtor

Death or incompetency of the debtor shall not abate a liquidation case under chapter 7 of the Code. In such event the estate shall be administered and the case concluded in the same manner, so far as possible, as though the death or incompetency had not occurred. If a reorganization, family farmer's debt adjustment, or individual's debt adjustment case is pending under chapter 11, chapter 12, or chapter 13, the case may be dismissed; or if further administration is possible and in the best interest of the parties, the case may proceed and be concluded in the same manner, so far as possible, as though the death or incompetency had not occurred.

(As amended Apr. 30, 1991, eff. Aug. 1, 1991.)

NOTES OF ADVISORY COMMITTEE ON RULES—1983

This rule is derived from former Rules 118 and 11-16. In a chapter 11 reorganization case or chapter 13 individual's debt adjustment case, the likelihood is that the case will be dismissed.

NOTES OF ADVISORY COMMITTEE ON RULES—1991 AMENDMENT

This rule is amended to conform to 25 F.R.Civ.P. and to include chapter 12 cases.

Rule 1017. Dismissal or Conversion of Case; Suspension

(a) VOLUNTARY DISMISSAL; DISMISSAL FOR WANT OF PROSECUTION OR OTHER CAUSE. Except as provided in §§707(a)(3), 707(b), 1208(b), and 1307(b) of the Code, and in Rule 1017(b), (c), and (e), a case shall not be dismissed on motion of the petitioner, for want of prosecution or other cause, or by consent of the parties, before a hearing on notice as provided in Rule 2002. For the purpose of the notice, the debtor shall file a list of creditors with their addresses within the time fixed by the court unless the list was previously filed. If the debtor fails to file the list, the court may order the debtor or another entity to prepare and file it.

(b) DISMISSAL FOR FAILURE TO PAY FILING FEE.

(1) If any installment of the filing fee has not been paid, the court may, after a hearing on notice to the debtor and the trustee, dismiss the case.

(2) If the case is dismissed or closed without full payment of the filing fee, the installments collected shall be distributed in the same manner and proportions as if the filing fee had been paid in full.

(c) DISMISSAL OF VOLUNTARY CHAPTER 7 OR CHAPTER 13 CASE FOR FAILURE TO TIMELY FILE LIST OF CREDITORS, SCHEDULES, AND STATEMENT OF FINANCIAL AFFAIRS. The court may dismiss a voluntary chapter 7 or chapter 13 case under §707(a)(3) or §1307(c)(9) after a hearing on notice served by the United States trustee on the debtor, the trustee, and any other entities as the court directs.

(d) SUSPENSION. The court shall not dismiss a case or suspend proceedings under §305 before a hearing on notice as provided in Rule 2002(a).

(e) DISMISSAL OF AN INDIVIDUAL DEBTOR'S CHAPTER 7 CASE, OR CONVERSION TO A CASE UNDER CHAPTER 11 OR 13, FOR ABUSE. The court may dismiss or, with the debtor's consent, convert an individual debtor's case for abuse under §707(b) only on motion and after a hearing on notice to the debtor, the trustee, the United States trustee, and any other entity as the court directs.

(1) Except as otherwise provided in §704(b)(2), a motion to dismiss a case for abuse under §707(b) or (c) may be filed only within 60 days after the first date set for the meeting of creditors under §341(a), unless, on request filed before the time has expired, the court for cause extends the time for filing the motion to dismiss. The party filing the motion shall set forth in the motion all matters to be considered at the hearing. In addition, a motion to dismiss under §707(b)(1) and (3) shall state with particularity the circumstances alleged to constitute abuse.

(2) If the hearing is set on the court's own motion, notice of the hearing shall be served on the debtor no later than 60 days after the first date set for the meeting of creditors under §341(a). The notice shall set forth all matters to be considered by the court at the hearing.

(f) PROCEDURE FOR DISMISSAL, CONVERSION, OR SUSPENSION.

(1) Rule 9014 governs a proceeding to dismiss or suspend a case, or to convert a case to another chapter, except under §§706(a), 1112(a), 1208(a) or (b), or 1307(a) or (b).

(2) Conversion or dismissal under §§706(a), 1112(a), 1208(b), or 1307(b) shall be on motion filed and served as required by Rule 9013.

(3) A chapter 12 or chapter 13 case shall be converted without court order when the debtor files a notice of conversion under §§1208(a) or 1307(a). The filing date of the notice becomes the date of the conversion order for the purposes of applying §348(c) and Rule 1019. The clerk shall promptly transmit a copy of the notice to the United States trustee.

(As amended Mar. 30, 1987, eff. Aug. 1, 1987; Apr. 30, 1991, eff. Aug. 1, 1991; Apr. 22, 1993, eff. Aug. 1, 1993; Apr. 26, 1999, eff. Dec. 1, 1999; Apr. 17, 2000, eff. Dec. 1, 2000; Apr. 23, 2008, eff. Dec. 1, 2008.)

NOTES OF ADVISORY COMMITTEE ON RULES—1983

Subdivision (a) of this rule is derived from former Bankruptcy Rule 120(a). While the rule applies to voluntary and involuntary cases, the "consent of the parties" referred to is that of petitioning creditors and the debtor in an involuntary case. The last sentence recognizes that the court should not be confined to petitioning creditors in its choice of parties on whom to call for assistance in preparing the list of creditors when the debtor fails to do so. This subdivision implements §§303(j), 707, 1112 and 1307 of the Code by specifying the manner of and persons to whom notice shall be given and requiring the court to hold a hearing on the issue of dismissal.

Subdivision (b) is derived from former Bankruptcy Rule 120(b). A dismissal under this subdivision can occur only when the petition has been permitted to be filed pursuant to Rule 1006(b). The provision for notice in paragraph (3) is correlated with the provision in Rule 4006 when there is a waiver, denial, or revocation of a discharge. As pointed out in the Note accompanying Rule 4008, the purpose of notifying creditors of a debtor that no discharge has been granted is to correct their assumption to the contrary so that they can take appropriate steps to protect their claims.

Subdivision (c) is new and specifies the notice required for a hearing on dismissal or suspension pursuant to §305 of the Code. The suspension to which this subdivision refers is that of the case; it does not concern abstention of the court in hearing an adversary proceeding pursuant to 28 U.S.C. §1478(b).

Subdivision (d). Any proceeding, whether by a debtor or other party, to dismiss or convert a case under §§706, 707, 1112, or 1307 is commenced by a motion pursuant to Rule 9014.

NOTES OF ADVISORY COMMITTEE ON RULES—1987 AMENDMENT

Subdivision (d) is amended to provide that dismissal or conversion pursuant to §§706(a), 707(b), 1112(a), and 1307(b) is not automatically a contested matter under Rule 9014. Conversion or dismissal under these sections is initiated by the filing and serving of a motion as required by Rule 9013. No hearing is required on these motions unless the court directs.

Conversion of a chapter 13 case to a chapter 7 case as authorized by §1307(a) is accomplished by the filing of a notice of conversion. The notice of conversion procedure is modeled on the voluntary dismissal provision of Rule 41(a)(1) F.R.Civ.P. Conversion occurs on the filing of the notice. No court order is required.

Subdivision (e) is new and provides the procedure to be followed when a court on its own motion has made a preliminary determination that an individual debtor's chapter 7 case may be dismissed pursuant to §707(b) of the Code, which was added by the 1984 amendments. A debtor's failure to attend the hearing is not a ground for dismissal pursuant to §707(b).

NOTES OF ADVISORY COMMITTEE ON RULES—1991 AMENDMENT

Subdivision (a) is amended to clarify that all entities required to receive notice under Rule 2002, including but not limited to creditors, are entitled to the 20 day notice of the hearing to dismiss the case. The United States trustee receives the notice pursuant to Rule 2002(k).

The word "petition" is changed to "case" in subdivisions (a), (b), and (c) to conform to §§707, 930, 1112, 1208, and 1307.

Subdivision (d) is amended to conform to §348(c) of the Code which refers to the "conversion order."

Subdivisions (a) and (d) are amended to provide procedures for dismissal or conversion of a chapter 12 case. Procedures for dismissal or conversion under §1208(a) and (b) are the same as the procedures for dismissal or conversion of a chapter 13 case under §1307(a) and (b).

Subdivision (e) is amended to conform to the 1986 amendment to §707(b) of the Code which permits the United States trustee to make a motion to dismiss a case for substantial abuse. The time limit for such a motion is added by this subdivision. In general, the facts that are the basis for a motion to dismiss under §707(b) exist at the time the case is commenced and usually can be discovered early in the case by reviewing the debtor's schedules and examining the debtor at the meeting of creditors. Since dismissal for substantial abuse has the effect of denying the debtor a discharge in the chapter 7 case based on matters which may be discovered early, a motion to dismiss under §707(b) is analogous to an objection to discharge pursuant to Rule 4004 and, therefore, should be required to be made within a specified time period. If matters relating to substantial abuse are not discovered within the time period specified in subdivision (e) because of the debtor's false testimony, refusal to obey a court order, fraudulent schedules or other fraud, and the debtor receives a discharge, the debtor's conduct may constitute the basis for revocation of the discharge under §727(d) and (e) of the Code.

NOTES OF ADVISORY COMMITTEE ON RULES—1993 AMENDMENT

Subdivision (d) is amended to clarify that the date of the filing of a notice of conversion in a chapter 12 or chapter 13 case is treated as the date of the conversion order for the purpose of applying Rule 1019. Other amendments are stylistic and make no substantive change.

COMMITTEE NOTES ON RULES—1999 AMENDMENT

Subdivision (b)(3), which provides that notice of dismissal for failure to pay the filing fee shall be sent to all creditors within 30 days after the dismissal, is deleted as unnecessary. Rule 2002(f) provides for notice to creditors of the dismissal of a case.

Rule 2002(a) and this rule currently require notice to all creditors of a hearing on dismissal of a voluntary chapter 7 case for the debtor's failure to file a list of creditors, schedules, and statement of financial affairs within the time provided in §707(a)(3) of the Code. A new subdivision (c) is added to provide that the United States trustee, who is the only entity with standing to file a motion to dismiss under §707(a)(3) or §1307(c)(9), is required to serve the motion on only the debtor, the trustee, and any other entities as the court directs. This amendment, and the amendment to Rule 2002, will have the effect of avoiding the expense of sending notices of the motion to all creditors in a chapter 7 case.

New subdivision (f) is the same as current subdivision (d), except that it provides that a motion to suspend all proceedings in a case or to dismiss a case for substantial abuse of chapter 7 under §707(b) is governed by Rule 9014.

Other amendments to this rule are stylistic or for clarification.

GAP Report on Rule 1017. No changes since publication, except for stylistic changes in Rule 1017(e) and (f).

COMMITTEE NOTES ON RULES—2000 AMENDMENT

This rule is amended to permit the court to grant a timely request filed by the United States trustee for an extension of time to file a motion to dismiss a chapter 7 case under §707(b), whether the court rules on the request before or after the expiration of the 60-day period.

Reporter's Note on Text of Rule 1017(e). The above text of Rule 1017(e) is not based on the text of the rule in effect on this date. The above text embodies amendments that have been promulgated by the Supreme Court in April 1999 and, unless Congress acts with respect to the amendments, will become effective on December 1, 1999.

GAP Report on Rule 1017(e). No changes since publication.

COMMITTEE NOTES ON RULES—2008 AMENDMENT

Subdivision (e) is amended to implement the 2005 amendments to §707 of the Code. These statutory amendments permit conversion of a chapter 7 case to a case under chapter 11 or 13, change the basis for dismissal or conversion from "substantial abuse" to "abuse," authorize parties other than the United States trustee to bring motions under §707(b) under certain circumstances, and add §707(c) to create an explicit ground for dismissal based on the request of a victim of a crime of violence or drug trafficking. The conforming amendments to subdivision (e) preserve the time limits already in place for §707(b) motions, except to the extent that §704(b)(2) sets the deadline for the United States trustee to act. In contrast to the grounds for a motion to dismiss under §707(b)(2), which are quite specific, the grounds under §707(b)(1) and (3) are very general. Therefore, to enable the debtor to respond, subdivision (e) requires that motions to dismiss under §707(b)(1) and (3) state with particularity the circumstances alleged to constitute abuse.

Changes Made After Publication. No changes were made after publication.

Rule 1018. Contested Involuntary Petitions; Contested Petitions Commencing Ancillary Cases; Proceedings to Vacate Order for Relief; Applicability of Rules in Part VII Governing Adversary Proceedings

The following rules in Part VII apply to all proceedings relating to a contested involuntary petition, to proceedings relating to a contested petition commencing a case ancillary to a foreign proceeding, and to all proceedings to vacate an order for relief: Rules 7005, 7008–7010, 7015, 7016, 7024–7026, 7028–7037, 7052, 7054, 7056, and 7062, except as otherwise provided in Part I of these rules and unless the court otherwise directs. The court may direct that other rules in Part VII shall also apply. For the purposes of this rule a reference in the Part VII rules to adversary proceedings shall be read as a reference to proceedings relating to a contested involuntary petition, or contested ancillary petition, or proceedings to vacate an order for relief. Reference in the Federal Rules of Civil Procedure to the complaint shall be read as a reference to the petition.

(As amended Mar. 30, 1987, eff. Aug. 1, 1987.)

NOTES OF ADVISORY COMMITTEE ON RULES—1983

The rules in Part VII to which this rule refers are adaptations of the Federal Rules of Civil Procedure for the purpose of governing the procedure in adversary proceedings in cases under the Code. See the Note accompanying Rule 7001 *infra*. Because of the special need for dispatch and expedition in the determination of the issues in an involuntary petition, see *Acme Harvester Co. v. Beekman Lumber Co.*, 222 U.S. 300, 309 (1911), the objective of some of the Federal Rules of Civil Procedure and their adaptations in Part VII to facilitate the settlement of multiple controversies involving many persons in a single lawsuit is not compatible with the exigencies of bankruptcy administration. See *United States F. & G. Co. v. Bray*, 225 U.S. 205, 218 (1912). For that reason Rules 7013, 7014 and 7018–7023 will rarely be appropriate in a proceeding on a contested petition.

Certain terms used in the Federal Rules of Civil Procedure have altered meanings when they are made applicable in cases under the Code by these rules. See Rule 9002 *infra*. This Rule 1018 requires that the terms "adversary proceedings" when used in the rules in Part VII and "complaint" when used in the Federal Rules of Civil Procedure be given altered meanings when they are made applicable to proceedings relating to a contested petition or proceedings to vacate any order for relief. A motion to vacate an order for relief, whether or not made on a petition that was or could have been contested, is governed by the rules in Part VII referred to in this Rule 1018.

NOTES OF ADVISORY COMMITTEE ON RULES—1987 AMENDMENT

Rule 1018 is amended to include within its terms a petition commencing an ancillary case when it is contested. This provision was formerly included in Rule 1003(e)(4).

Although this rule does not contain an explicit authorization for the entry of an order for relief when a debtor refuses to cooperate in discovery relating to a contested involuntary petition, the court has ample power under Rule 37(b) F.R.Civ.P., as incorporated by Rule 7037, to enter an order for relief under appropriate circumstances. Rule 37(b) authorizes the court to enter judgment by default or an order that "facts shall be taken as established."

Rule 1019. Conversion of a Chapter 11 Reorganization Case, Chapter 12 Family Farmer's Debt Adjustment Case, or Chapter 13 Individual's Debt Adjustment Case to a Chapter 7 Liquidation Case

When a chapter 11, chapter 12, or chapter 13 case has been converted or reconverted to a chapter 7 case:

(1) *Filing of Lists, Inventories, Schedules, Statements.*

(A) Lists, inventories, schedules, and statements of financial affairs theretofore filed shall be deemed to be filed in the chapter 7 case, unless the court directs otherwise. If they have not been previously filed, the debtor shall comply with Rule 1007 as if an order for relief had been entered on an involuntary petition on the date of the entry of the order directing that the case continue under chapter 7.

(B) If a statement of intention is required, it shall be filed within 30 days after entry of the order of conversion or before the first date set for the meeting of creditors, whichever is earlier. The court may grant an extension of time for cause only on written motion filed, or oral request made during a hearing, before the time has expired. Notice of an extension shall be given to the United States trustee and to any committee, trustee, or other party as the court may direct.

(2) *New Filing Periods.* A new time period for filing a motion under §707(b) or (c), a claim, a complaint objecting to discharge, or a complaint to obtain a determination of dischargeability of any debt shall commence under Rules 1017, 3002, 4004, or 4007, but a new time period shall not commence if a chapter 7 case had been converted to a chapter 11, 12, or 13 case and thereafter reconverted to a chapter 7 case and the time for filing a motion under §707(b) or (c), a claim, a complaint objecting to discharge, or a complaint to obtain a determination of the dischargeability of any debt, or any extension thereof, expired in the original chapter 7 case.

(3) *Claims Filed Before Conversion.* All claims actually filed by a creditor before conversion of the case are deemed filed in the chapter 7 case.

(4) *Turnover of Records and Property.* After qualification of, or assumption of duties by the chapter 7 trustee, any debtor in possession or trustee previously acting in the chapter 11, 12, or 13 case shall, forthwith, unless otherwise ordered, turn over to the chapter 7 trustee all records and property of the estate in the possession or control of the debtor in possession or trustee.

(5) *Filing Final Report and Schedule of Postpetition Debts.*

(A) *Conversion of Chapter 11 or Chapter 12 Case.* Unless the court directs otherwise, if a chapter 11 or chapter 12 case is converted to chapter 7, the debtor in possession or, if the debtor is not a debtor in possession, the trustee serving at the time of conversion, shall:

(i) not later than 14 days after conversion of the case, file a schedule of unpaid debts incurred after the filing of the petition and before conversion of the case, including the name and address of each holder of a claim; and

(ii) not later than 30 days after conversion of the case, file and transmit to the United States trustee a final report and account;

(B) *Conversion of Chapter 13 Case.* Unless the court directs otherwise, if a chapter 13 case is converted to chapter 7,

(i) the debtor, not later than 14 days after conversion of the case, shall file a schedule of unpaid debts incurred after the filing of the petition and before conversion of the case, including the name and address of each holder of a claim; and

(ii) the trustee, not later than 30 days after conversion of the case, shall file and transmit to the United States trustee a final report and account;

(C) *Conversion After Confirmation of a Plan.* Unless the court orders otherwise, if a chapter 11, chapter 12, or chapter 13 case is converted to chapter 7 after confirmation of a plan, the debtor shall file:

(i) a schedule of property not listed in the final report and account acquired after the filing of the petition but before conversion, except if the case is converted from chapter 13 to chapter 7 and §348(f)(2) does not apply;

(ii) a schedule of unpaid debts not listed in the final report and account incurred after confirmation but before the conversion; and

(iii) a schedule of executory contracts and unexpired leases entered into or assumed after the filing of the petition but before conversion.

(D) *Transmission to United States Trustee.* The clerk shall forthwith transmit to the United States trustee a copy of every schedule filed pursuant to Rule 1019(5).

(6) *Postpetition Claims; Preconversion Administrative Expenses; Notice.* A request for payment of an administrative expense incurred before conversion of the case is timely filed under §503(a) of the Code if it is filed before conversion or a time fixed by the court. If the request is filed by a governmental unit, it is timely if it is filed before conversion or within

the later of a time fixed by the court or 180 days after the date of the conversion. A claim of a kind specified in §348(d) may be filed in accordance with Rules 3001(a)–(d) and 3002. Upon the filing of the schedule of unpaid debts incurred after commencement of the case and before conversion, the clerk, or some other person as the court may direct, shall give notice to those entities listed on the schedule of the time for filing a request for payment of an administrative expense and, unless a notice of insufficient assets to pay a dividend is mailed in accordance with Rule 2002(e), the time for filing a claim of a kind specified in §348(d).

(As amended Mar. 30, 1987, eff. Aug. 1, 1987; Apr. 30, 1991, eff. Aug. 1, 1991; Apr. 23, 1996, eff. Dec. 1, 1996; Apr. 11, 1997, eff. Dec. 1, 1997; Apr. 26, 1999, eff. Dec. 1, 1999; Apr. 23, 2008, eff. Dec. 1, 2008; Mar. 26, 2009, eff. Dec. 1, 2009.)

NOTES OF ADVISORY COMMITTEE ON RULES—1983

This rule is derived from former Bankruptcy Rule 122 and implements §348 of the Code. The rule applies to proceedings in a chapter 7 case following supersession of a case commenced under chapter 11 or 13, whether the latter was initiated by an original petition or was converted from a pending chapter 7 or another chapter case. The rule is not intended to invalidate any action taken in the superseded case before its conversion to chapter 7.

Paragraph (1): If requirements applicable in the superseded case respecting the filing of schedules of debts and property, or lists of creditors and inventory, and of statements of financial affairs have been complied with before the order directing conversion to liquidation, these documents will ordinarily provide all the information about the debts, property, financial affairs, and contracts of the debtor needed for the administration of the estate. If the information submitted in the superseded case is inadequate for the purposes of administration, however, the court may direct the preparation of further informational material and the manner and time of its submission pursuant to paragraph (1). If no schedules, lists, inventories, or statements were filed in the superseded case, this paragraph imposes the duty on the debtor to file schedules and a statement of affairs pursuant to Rule 1007 as if an involuntary petition had been filed on the date when the court directed the conversion of the case to a liquidation case.

Paragraphs (2) and (3). Paragraph (2) requires notice to be given to all creditors of the order of conversion. The notice is to be included in the notice of the meeting of creditors and Official Form No. 16 may be adapted for use. A meeting of creditors may have been held in the superseded case as required by §341(a) of the Code but that would not dispense with the need to hold one in the ensuing liquidation case. Section 701(a) of the Code permits the court to appoint the trustee acting in the chapter 11 or 13 case as interim trustee in the chapter 7 case. Section 702(a) of the Code allows creditors to elect a trustee but only at the meeting of creditors held under §341. The right to elect a trustee is not lost because the chapter 7 case follows a chapter 11 or 13 case. Thus a meeting of creditors is necessary. The date fixed for the meeting of creditors will control at least the time for filing claims pursuant to Rule 3002(c). That time will remain applicable in the ensuing chapter 7 case except as paragraph (3) provides, if that time had expired in an earlier chapter 7 case which was converted to the chapter 11 or 13 case, it is not revived in the subsequent chapter 7 case. The same is true if the time for filing a complaint objecting to discharge or to determine nondischargeability of a debt had expired. Paragraph (3), however, recognizes that such time may be extended by the court under Rule 4004 or 4007 on motion made within the original prescribed time.

Paragraph (4) renders it unnecessary to file anew claims that had been filed in the chapter 11 or 13 case before conversion to chapter 7.

Paragraph (5) contemplates that typically, after the court orders conversion of a chapter case to liquidation, a trustee under chapter 7 will forthwith take charge of the property of the estate and proceed expeditiously to liquidate it. The court may appoint the interim trustee in the chapter 7 case pursuant to §701(a) of the Code. If creditors do not elect a trustee under §702, the interim trustee becomes the trustee.

Paragraph (6) requires the trustee or debtor in possession acting in the chapter 11 or 13 case to file a final report and schedule of debts incurred in that case. This schedule will provide the information necessary for giving the notice required by paragraph (7) of the rule.

Paragraph (7) requires that claims that arose in the chapter 11 or 13 case be filed within 60 days after entry of the order converting the case to one under chapter 7. Claims not scheduled pursuant to paragraph (6) of the rule or arising from the rejection of an executory contract entered into during the chapter case may be filed within a time fixed by the court. Pursuant to §348(c) of the Code, the conversion order is treated as the order for relief to fix the time for the trustee to assume or reject executory contracts under §365(d).

Paragraph (8) permits the extension of the time for filing claims when claims are not timely filed but only with respect to any surplus that may remain in the estate. See also §726(a)(2)(C) and (3) of the Code.

NOTES OF ADVISORY COMMITTEE ON RULES—1987 AMENDMENT

Paragraph (1) is amended to provide for the filing of a statement of intention in a case converted to chapter 7. Paragraph (1)(B) is added to provide for the filing of the statement of intention when a case is converted to chapter 7. The time for filing the statement of intention and for an extension of that time is governed by §521(2)(A) of the Code. An extension of time for other required filings is governed by Rule 1007(c), which paragraph (1)(A) incorporates by reference. Because of the amendment to Rule 1007(c), the filing of new lists, schedules, and statements is now governed exclusively by Rule 1019(1).

Paragraph (3) of the rule is expanded to include the effect of conversion of a chapter 11 or 13 case to a chapter 7 case. On conversion of a case from chapter 11 or 13 to a chapter 7 case, parties have a new period within which to file claims or complaints relating to the granting of the discharge or the dischargeability of a debt. This amendment is consistent with the holding and reasoning of the court in *F & M Marquette Nat'l Bank v. Richards*, 780 F.2d 24 (8th Cir. 1985).

Paragraph (4) is amended to deal directly with the status of claims which are properly listed on the schedules filed in a chapter 11 case and deemed filed pursuant to §1111(a) of the Code. Section 1111(a) is only applicable to the chapter 11 case. On conversion of the chapter 11 case to a chapter 7 case, paragraph (4) governs the status of claims filed in the chapter 11 case. The Third Circuit properly construed paragraph (4) as applicable to claims deemed filed in the superseded chapter 11 case. *In re Crouthamel Potato Chip Co.*, 786 F.2d 141 (3d Cir. 1986).

The amendment to paragraph (4) changes that result by providing that only claims that are actually filed in the chapter 11 case are treated as filed in the superseding chapter 7 case. When chapter 11 cases are converted to chapter 7 cases, difficulties in obtaining and verifying the debtors' records are common. It is unfair to the chapter 7 trustee and creditors to require that they be bound by schedules which may not be subject to verification.

Paragraph (6) is amended to place the obligation on the chapter 13 debtor to file a schedule of unpaid debts incurred during the superseded chapter 13 case.

NOTES OF ADVISORY COMMITTEE ON RULES—1991 AMENDMENT

This rule is amended to include conversion of a case from chapter 12 to chapter 7 and to implement the United States trustee system.

The amendments to paragraph (1)(A) are stylistic. Reference to the statement of executory contracts is deleted to conform to the amendment to Rule 1007(b)(1) which changes the statement to a schedule of executory contracts and unexpired leases.

Paragraph (1)(B) is amended to enable the United States trustee to monitor the progress of the case and to take appropriate action to enforce the debtor's obligation to perform the statement of intention in a timely manner.

Paragraph (2) is deleted because notice of conversion of the case is required by Rules 1017(d), 2002(f)(2), and 9022. The United States trustee, who supervises trustees pursuant to 28 U.S.C. §586(a), may give notice of the conversion to the trustee in the superseded case.

Paragraph (6), renumbered as paragraph (5), is amended to reduce to 15 days the time for filing a schedule of postpetition debts and requires inclusion of the name and address of each creditor in connection with the postpetition debt. These changes will enable the clerk to send postpetition creditors a timely notice of the meeting of creditors held pursuant to §341(a) of the Code. The amendments to this paragraph also provide the United States trustee with the final report and account of the superseded case, and with a copy of every schedule filed after conversion of the case. Conversion to chapter 7 terminates the service of the trustee in the superseded case pursuant to §348(e) of the Code. Sections 704(a)(9), 1106(a)(1), 1107(a), 1202(b)(1), 1203 and 1302(b)(1) of the Code require the trustee or debtor in possession to file a final report and account with the court and the United States trustee. The words "with the court" are deleted as unnecessary. See Rules 5005(a) and 9001(3).

Paragraph (7), renumbered as paragraph (6), is amended to conform the time for filing postpetition claims to the time for filing prepetition claims pursuant to paragraph (3) (renumbered as paragraph (2)) of this rule and Rule 3002(c). This paragraph is also amended to eliminate the need for a court order to provide notice of the time for filing claims. It is anticipated that this notice will be given together with the notice of the meeting of creditors. It is amended further to avoid the need to fix a time for filing claims arising under §365(d) if it is a no asset case upon conversion. If assets become available for distribution, the court may fix a time for filing such claims pursuant to Rule 3002(c)(4).

The additions of references to unexpired leases in paragraph (1)(A) and in paragraphs (6) and (7) (renumbered as paragraphs (5) and (6)) are technical amendments to clarify that unexpired leases are included as well as other executory contracts.

NOTES OF ADVISORY COMMITTEE ON RULES—1996 AMENDMENT

Subdivision (7) is abrogated to conform to the abrogation of Rule 3002(c)(6).

GAP Report on Rule 1019. No changes were made to the text of the rule. The Committee Note was changed to conform to the proposed changes to Rule 3002 (see GAP Report on Rule 3002 below).

NOTES OF ADVISORY COMMITTEE ON RULES—1997 AMENDMENT

The amendments to subdivisions (3) and (5) are technical corrections and stylistic changes. The phrase "superseded case" is deleted because it creates the erroneous impression that conversion of a case results in a new case that is distinct from the original case. Similarly, the phrase "original petition" is deleted because it erroneously implies that there is a second petition with respect to a converted case. See §348 of the Code.

GAP Report on Rule 1019. No changes to the published draft.

COMMITTEE NOTES ON RULES—1999 AMENDMENT

Paragraph (1)(B) is amended to clarify that a motion for an extension of time to file a statement of intention must be made by written motion filed before the time expires, or by oral request made at a hearing before the time expires.

Subdivision (6) is amended to provide that a holder of an administrative expense claim incurred after the commencement of the case, but before conversion to chapter 7, is required to file a request for payment under §503(a) within a time fixed by the court, rather than a proof of claim under §501 and Rules 3001(a)–(d) and 3002. The 180-day period applicable to governmental units is intended to conform to §502(b)(9) of the Code and Rule 3002(c)(1). It is unnecessary for the court to fix a time for filing requests for payment if it appears that there are not sufficient assets to pay preconversion administrative expenses. If a time for filing a request for payment of an administrative expense is fixed by the court, it may be enlarged as provided in Rule 9006(b). If an administrative expense claimant fails to timely file the request, it may be tardily filed under §503(a) if permitted by the court for cause.

The final sentence of Rule 1019(6) is deleted because it is unnecessary in view of the other amendments to this paragraph. If a party has entered into a postpetition contract or lease with the trustee or debtor that constitutes an administrative expense, a timely request for payment must be filed in accordance with this paragraph and §503(b) of the Code. The time for filing a proof of claim in connection with the rejection of any other executory contract or unexpired lease is governed by Rule 3002(c)(4).

The phrase "including the United States, any state, or any subdivision thereof" is deleted as unnecessary. Other amendments to this rule are stylistic.

GAP Report on Rule 1019. The proposed amendments to Rule 1019(6) were changed to delete the deadline for filing requests for payment of preconversion administrative expenses that would be applicable in all cases, and to provide instead that the court may fix such a deadline. The committee note was revised to clarify that it is not necessary for the court to fix a deadline where there are insufficient assets to pay preconversion administrative expenses.

COMMITTEE NOTES ON RULES—2008 AMENDMENT

Subdivision (2) is amended to include a new filing period for motions under §707(b) and (c) of the Code when a case is converted to chapter 7. The establishment of a deadline for filing such motions is not intended to express a position as to whether such motions are permitted under the Code.

Changes Made After Publication. The Committee Note was amended by adding the second sentence to the Note stating explicitly that the rule was not intended to take a position on whether motions to dismiss a case under §707(b) and (c) are proper in a case that is converted from another chapter.

COMMITTEE NOTES ON RULES—2009 AMENDMENT

The rule is amended to implement changes in connection with the amendment to Rule 9006(a) and the manner by which time is computed under the rules. The deadlines in the rule are amended to substitute a deadline that is a multiple of seven days. Throughout the rules, deadlines are amended in the following manner:

- 5-day periods become 7-day periods
- 10-day periods become 14-day periods
- 15-day periods become 14-day periods
- 20-day periods become 21-day periods
- 25-day periods become 28-day periods

Rule 1020. Small Business Chapter 11 Reorganization Case

(a) SMALL BUSINESS DEBTOR DESIGNATION. In a voluntary chapter 11 case, the debtor shall state in the petition whether the debtor is a small business debtor. In an involuntary chapter 11 case, the debtor shall file within 14 days after entry of the order for relief a statement as to whether the debtor is a small business debtor. Except as provided in subdivision (c), the status of the case as a small business case shall be in accordance with the debtor's statement under this subdivision, unless and until the court enters an order finding that the debtor's statement is incorrect.

(b) OBJECTING TO DESIGNATION. Except as provided in subdivision (c), the United States trustee or a party in interest may file an objection to the debtor's statement under subdivision (a) no later than 30 days after the conclusion of the meeting of creditors held under § 341(a) of the Code, or within 30 days after any amendment to the statement, whichever is later.

(c) APPOINTMENT OF COMMITTEE OF UNSECURED CREDITORS. If a committee of unsecured creditors has been appointed under § 1102(a)(1), the case shall proceed as a small business case only if, and from the time when, the court enters an order determining that the committee has not been sufficiently active and representative to provide effective oversight of the debtor and that the debtor satisfies all the other requirements for being a small business. A request for a determination under this subdivision may be filed by the United States trustee or a party in interest only within a reasonable time after the failure of the committee to be sufficiently active and representative. The debtor may file a request for a determination at any time as to whether the committee has been sufficiently active and representative.

(d) PROCEDURE FOR OBJECTION OR DETERMINATION. Any objection or request for a determination under this rule shall be governed by Rule 9014 and served on: the debtor; the debtor's attorney; the United States trustee; the trustee; any committee appointed under § 1102 or its authorized agent, or, if no committee of unsecured creditors has been appointed under § 1102, the creditors included on the list filed under Rule 1007(d); and any other entity as the court directs.

(Added Apr. 11, 1997, eff. Dec. 1, 1997; amended Apr. 23, 2008, eff. Dec. 1, 2008; Mar. 26, 2009, eff. Dec. 1, 2009.)

NOTES OF ADVISORY COMMITTEE ON RULES—1997

This rule is designed to implement §§ 1121(e) and 1125(f) that were added to the Code by the Bankruptcy Reform Act of 1994.

GAP Report on Rule 1020. The phrase "or by a later date as the court, for cause, may fix" at the end of the published draft was deleted. The general provisions on reducing or extending time periods under Rule 9006 will be applicable.

COMMITTEE NOTES ON RULES—2008 AMENDMENT

Under the Code, as amended in 2005, there are no longer any provisions permitting or requiring a small business debtor to elect to be treated as a small business. Therefore, the election provisions in the rule are eliminated.

The 2005 amendments to the Code include several provisions relating to small business cases under chapter 11. Section 101 includes definitions of "small business debtor" and "small business case." The purpose of the new language in this rule is to provide a procedure for informing the parties, the United States trustee, and the court of whether the debtor is a small business debtor, and to provide procedures for resolving disputes regarding the proper characterization of the debtor. Because it is important to resolve such disputes early in the case, a time limit for objecting to the debtor's self-designation is imposed. Rule 9006(b)(1), which governs enlargement of time, is applicable to the time limits set forth in this rule.

An important factor in determining whether the debtor is a small business debtor is whether the United States trustee has appointed a committee of unsecured creditors under § 1102, and whether such a committee is sufficiently active and representative. Subdivision (c), relating to the appointment and activity of a committee of unsecured creditors, is designed to be consistent with the Code's definition of "small business debtor."

Changes Made After Publication. No changes were made after publication.

COMMITTEE NOTES ON RULES—2009 AMENDMENT

The rule is amended to implement changes in connection with the amendment to Rule 9006(a) and the manner by which time is computed under the rules. The deadline in the rule is amended to substitute a deadline that is a multiple of seven days. Throughout the rules, deadlines are amended in the following manner:

- 5-day periods become 7-day periods
- 10-day periods become 14-day periods
- 15-day periods become 14-day periods
- 20-day periods become 21-day periods
- 25-day periods become 28-day periods

Rule 1021. Health Care Business Case

(a) HEALTH CARE BUSINESS DESIGNATION. Unless the court orders otherwise, if a petition in a case under chapter 7, chapter 9, or chapter 11 states that the debtor is a health care business, the case shall proceed as a case in which the debtor is a health care business.

(b) MOTION. The United States trustee or a party in interest may file a motion to determine whether the debtor is a health care business. The motion shall be transmitted to the United States trustee and served on: the debtor; the trustee; any committee elected under § 705 or appointed under § 1102 of the Code or its authorized agent, or, if the case is a chapter 9 municipality case or a chapter 11 reorganization case and no committee of unsecured creditors has been appointed under § 1102, the creditors included on the list filed under Rule 1007(d); and any other entity as the court directs. The motion shall be governed by Rule 9014.

(Added Apr. 23, 2008, eff. Dec. 1, 2008.)

COMMITTEE NOTES ON RULES—2008

Section 101(27A) of the Code, added by the 2005 amendments, defines a health care business. This rule provides procedures for designating the debtor as a health care business. The debtor in a voluntary case, or petitioning creditors in an involuntary case, make that designation by checking the appropriate box on the petition. The rule also provides procedures for resolving disputes regarding the status of the debtor as a health care business.

Changes Made After Publication. No changes were made after publication.

PART II—OFFICERS AND ADMINISTRATION; NOTICES; MEETINGS; EXAMINATIONS; ELECTIONS; ATTORNEYS AND ACCOUNTANTS

Rule 2001. Appointment of Interim Trustee Before Order for Relief in a Chapter 7 Liquidation Case

(a) APPOINTMENT. At any time following the commencement of an involuntary liquidation case and before an order for relief, the court on written motion of a party in interest may order the appointment of an interim trustee under §303(g) of the Code. The motion shall set forth the necessity for the appointment and may be granted only after hearing on notice to the debtor, the petitioning creditors, the United States trustee, and other parties in interest as the court may designate.

(b) BOND OF MOVANT. An interim trustee may not be appointed under this rule unless the movant furnishes a bond in an amount approved by the court, conditioned to indemnify the debtor for costs, attorney's fee, expenses, and damages allowable under §303(i) of the Code.

(c) ORDER OF APPOINTMENT. The order directing the appointment of an interim trustee shall state the reason the appointment is necessary and shall specify the trustee's duties.

(d) TURNOVER AND REPORT. Following qualification of the trustee selected under §702 of the Code, the interim trustee, unless otherwise ordered, shall (1) forthwith deliver to the trustee all the records and property of the estate in possession or subject to control of the interim trustee and, (2) within 30 days thereafter file a final report and account.

(As amended Mar. 30, 1987, eff. Aug. 1, 1987; Apr. 30, 1991, eff. Aug. 1, 1991.)

NOTES OF ADVISORY COMMITTEE ON RULES—1983

This rule is adapted from former Bankruptcy Rule 201. See also former Chapter X Rule 10–201. In conformity with title 11 of the United States Code, this rule substitutes "interim trustee" for "receiver." Subdivision (a) and (e) of Rule 201 are not included because the provisions contained therein are found in detail in §303(g) of the Code, or they are inconsistent with §701 of the Code. Similarly, the provisions in Rule 201(d) relating to a debtor's counterbond are not included because of their presence in §303(g).

Subdivision (a) makes it clear that the court may not on its own motion order the appointment of an interim trustee before an order for relief is entered. Appointment may be ordered only on motion of a party in interest.

Subdivision (b) requires those seeking the appointment of an interim trustee to furnish a bond. The bond may be the same one required of petitioning creditors under §303(e) of the Code to indemnify the debtor for damages allowed by the court under §303(i).

Subdivision (c) requires that the order specify which duties enumerated in §303(g) shall be performed by the interim trustee. Reference should be made to Rule 2015 for additional duties required of an interim trustee including keeping records and filing periodic reports with the court.

Subdivision (d) requires turnover of records and property to the trustee selected under §702 of the Code, after qualification. That trustee may be the interim trustee who becomes the trustee because of the failure of creditors to elect one under §702(d) or the trustee elected by creditors under §702(b), (c).

NOTES OF ADVISORY COMMITTEE ON RULES—1991 AMENDMENT

This rule is amended to conform to §303(g) of the Code which provides that the United States trustee appoints the interim trustee. See Rule X-1003. This rule does not apply to the exercise by the court of the power to act sua sponte pursuant to §105(a) of the Code.

Rule 2002. Notices to Creditors, Equity Security Holders, Administrators in Foreign Proceedings, Persons Against Whom Provisional Relief is Sought in Ancillary and Other Cross-Border Cases, United States, and United States Trustee

(a) TWENTY-ONE-DAY NOTICES TO PARTIES IN INTEREST. Except as provided in subdivisions (h), (i), (*l*), (p), and (q) of this rule, the clerk, or some other person as the court may direct, shall give the debtor, the trustee, all creditors and indenture trustees at least 21 days' notice by mail of:

(1) the meeting of creditors under §341 or §1104(b) of the Code, which notice, unless the court orders otherwise, shall include the debtor's employer identification number, social security number, and any other federal taxpayer identification number;

(2) a proposed use, sale, or lease of property of the estate other than in the ordinary course of business, unless the court for cause shown shortens the time or directs another method of giving notice;

(3) the hearing on approval of a compromise or settlement of a controversy other than approval of an agreement pursuant to Rule 4001(d), unless the court for cause shown directs that notice not be sent;

(4) in a chapter 7 liquidation, a chapter 11 reorganization case, or a chapter 12 family farmer debt adjustment case, the hearing on the dismissal of the case or the conversion of the case to another chapter, unless the hearing is under §707(a)(3) or §707(b) or is on dismissal of the case for failure to pay the filing fee;

(5) the time fixed to accept or reject a proposed modification of a plan;

(6) a hearing on any entity's request for compensation or reimbursement of expenses if the request exceeds $1,000;

(7) the time fixed for filing proofs of claims pursuant to Rule 3003(c); and

(8) the time fixed for filing objections and the hearing to consider confirmation of a chapter 12 plan.

(b) TWENTY-EIGHT-DAY NOTICES TO PARTIES IN INTEREST. Except as provided in subdivision (*l*) of this rule, the clerk, or some other person as the court may direct, shall give the debtor, the trustee, all creditors and indenture trustees not less than 28 days' notice by mail of the time fixed (1) for filing objections and the hearing to consider approval of a disclosure statement or, under §1125(f), to make a final determination whether the plan provides adequate information so that a separate disclosure statement is not necessary; and (2) for filing objections and the hearing to consider confirmation of a chapter 9, chapter 11, or chapter 13 plan.

(c) CONTENT OF NOTICE.

(1) *Proposed Use, Sale, or Lease of Property.* Subject to Rule 6004, the notice of a proposed use, sale, or lease of property required by sub-

division (a)(2) of this rule shall include the time and place of any public sale, the terms and conditions of any private sale and the time fixed for filing objections. The notice of a proposed use, sale, or lease of property, including real estate, is sufficient if it generally describes the property. The notice of a proposed sale or lease of personally identifiable information under §363(b)(1) of the Code shall state whether the sale is consistent with any policy prohibiting the transfer of the information.

(2) *Notice of Hearing on Compensation*. The notice of a hearing on an application for compensation or reimbursement of expenses required by subdivision (a)(6) of this rule shall identify the applicant and the amounts requested.

(3) *Notice of Hearing on Confirmation When Plan Provides for an Injunction*. If a plan provides for an injunction against conduct not otherwise enjoined under the Code, the notice required under Rule 2002(b)(2) shall:

(A) include in conspicuous language (bold, italic, or underlined text) a statement that the plan proposes an injunction;

(B) describe briefly the nature of the injunction; and

(C) identify the entities that would be subject to the injunction.

(d) NOTICE TO EQUITY SECURITY HOLDERS. In a chapter 11 reorganization case, unless otherwise ordered by the court, the clerk, or some other person as the court may direct, shall in the manner and form directed by the court give notice to all equity security holders of (1) the order for relief; (2) any meeting of equity security holders held pursuant to §341 of the Code; (3) the hearing on the proposed sale of all or substantially all of the debtor's assets; (4) the hearing on the dismissal or conversion of a case to another chapter; (5) the time fixed for filing objections to and the hearing to consider approval of a disclosure statement; (6) the time fixed for filing objections to and the hearing to consider confirmation of a plan; and (7) the time fixed to accept or reject a proposed modification of a plan.

(e) NOTICE OF NO DIVIDEND. In a chapter 7 liquidation case, if it appears from the schedules that there are no assets from which a dividend can be paid, the notice of the meeting of creditors may include a statement to that effect; that it is unnecessary to file claims; and that if sufficient assets become available for the payment of a dividend, further notice will be given for the filing of claims.

(f) OTHER NOTICES. Except as provided in subdivision (*l*) of this rule, the clerk, or some other person as the court may direct, shall give the debtor, all creditors, and indenture trustees notice by mail of:

(1) the order for relief;

(2) the dismissal or the conversion of the case to another chapter, or the suspension of proceedings under §305;

(3) the time allowed for filing claims pursuant to Rule 3002;

(4) the time fixed for filing a complaint objecting to the debtor's discharge pursuant to §727 of the Code as provided in Rule 4004;

(5) the time fixed for filing a complaint to determine the dischargeability of a debt pursuant to §523 of the Code as provided in Rule 4007;

(6) the waiver, denial, or revocation of a discharge as provided in Rule 4006;

(7) entry of an order confirming a chapter 9, 11, or 12 plan;

(8) a summary of the trustee's final report in a chapter 7 case if the net proceeds realized exceed $1,500;

(9) a notice under Rule 5008 regarding the presumption of abuse;

(10) a statement under §704(b)(1) as to whether the debtor's case would be presumed to be an abuse under §707(b); and

(11) the time to request a delay in the entry of the discharge under §§1141(d)(5)(C), 1228(f), and 1328(h). Notice of the time fixed for accepting or rejecting a plan pursuant to Rule 3017(c) shall be given in accordance with Rule 3017(d).

(g) ADDRESSING NOTICES.

(1) Notices required to be mailed under Rule 2002 to a creditor, indenture trustee, or equity security holder shall be addressed as such entity or an authorized agent has directed in its last request filed in the particular case. For the purposes of this subdivision—

(A) a proof of claim filed by a creditor or indenture trustee that designates a mailing address constitutes a filed request to mail notices to that address, unless a notice of no dividend has been given under Rule 2002(e) and a later notice of possible dividend under Rule 3002(c)(5) has not been given; and

(B) a proof of interest filed by an equity security holder that designates a mailing address constitutes a filed request to mail notices to that address.

(2) Except as provided in §342(f) of the Code, if a creditor or indenture trustee has not filed a request designating a mailing address under Rule 2002(g)(1) or Rule 5003(e), the notices shall be mailed to the address shown on the list of creditors or schedule of liabilities, whichever is filed later. If an equity security holder has not filed a request designating a mailing address under Rule 2002(g)(1) or Rule 5003(e), the notices shall be mailed to the address shown on the list of equity security holders.

(3) If a list or schedule filed under Rule 1007 includes the name and address of a legal representative of an infant or incompetent person, and a person other than that representative files a request or proof of claim designating a name and mailing address that differs from the name and address of the representative included in the list or schedule, unless the court orders otherwise, notices under Rule 2002 shall be mailed to the representative included in the list or schedules and to the name and address designated in the request or proof of claim.

(4) Notwithstanding Rule 2002(g)(1)–(3), an entity and a notice provider may agree that when the notice provider is directed by the court to give a notice, the notice provider shall give the notice to the entity in the manner agreed to and at the address or addresses

the entity supplies to the notice provider. That address is conclusively presumed to be a proper address for the notice. The notice provider's failure to use the supplied address does not invalidate any notice that is otherwise effective under applicable law.

(5) A creditor may treat a notice as not having been brought to the creditor's attention under §342(g)(1) only if, prior to issuance of the notice, the creditor has filed a statement that designates the name and address of the person or organizational subdivision of the creditor responsible for receiving notices under the Code, and that describes the procedures established by the creditor to cause such notices to be delivered to the designated person or subdivision.

(h) NOTICES TO CREDITORS WHOSE CLAIMS ARE FILED. In a chapter 7 case, after 90 days following the first date set for the meeting of creditors under §341 of the Code, the court may direct that all notices required by subdivision (a) of this rule be mailed only to the debtor, the trustee, all indenture trustees, creditors that hold claims for which proofs of claim have been filed, and creditors, if any, that are still permitted to file claims by reason of an extension granted pursuant to Rule 3002(c)(1) or (c)(2). In a case where notice of insufficient assets to pay a dividend has been given to creditors pursuant to subdivision (e) of this rule, after 90 days following the mailing of a notice of the time for filing claims pursuant to Rule 3002(c)(5), the court may direct that notices be mailed only to the entities specified in the preceding sentence.

(i) NOTICES TO COMMITTEES. Copies of all notices required to be mailed pursuant to this rule shall be mailed to the committees elected under §705 or appointed under §1102 of the Code or to their authorized agents. Notwithstanding the foregoing subdivisions, the court may order that notices required by subdivision (a)(2), (3) and (6) of this rule be transmitted to the United States trustee and be mailed only to the committees elected under §705 or appointed under §1102 of the Code or to their authorized agents and to the creditors and equity security holders who serve on the trustee or debtor in possession and file a request that all notices be mailed to them. A committee appointed under §1114 shall receive copies of all notices required by subdivisions (a)(1), (a)(5), (b), (f)(2), and (f)(7), and such other notices as the court may direct.

(j) NOTICES TO THE UNITED STATES. Copies of notices required to be mailed to all creditors under this rule shall be mailed (1) in a chapter 11 reorganization case, to the Securities and Exchange Commission at any place the Commission designates, if the Commission has filed either a notice of appearance in the case or a written request to receive notices; (2) in a commodity broker case, to the Commodity Futures Trading Commission at Washington, D.C.; (3) in a chapter 11 case, to the Internal Revenue Service at its address set out in the register maintained under Rule 5003(e) for the district in which the case is pending; (4) if the papers in the case disclose a debt to the United States other than for taxes, to the United States attorney for the district in which the case is pending and to the department, agency, or instrumentality of the United States through which the debtor became indebted; or (5) if the filed papers disclose a stock interest of the United States, to the Secretary of the Treasury at Washington, D.C.

(k) NOTICES TO UNITED STATES TRUSTEE. Unless the case is a chapter 9 municipality case or unless the United States trustee requests otherwise, the clerk, or some other person as the court may direct, shall transmit to the United States trustee notice of the matters described in subdivisions (a)(2), (a)(3), (a)(4), (a)(8), (b), (f)(1), (f)(2), (f)(4), (f)(6), (f)(7), (f)(8), and (q) of this rule and notice of hearings on all applications for compensation or reimbursement of expenses. Notices to the United States trustee shall be transmitted within the time prescribed in subdivision (a) or (b) of this rule. The United States trustee shall also receive notice of any other matter if such notice is requested by the United States trustee or ordered by the court. Nothing in these rules requires the clerk or any other person to transmit to the United States trustee any notice, schedule, report, application or other document in a case under the Securities Investor Protection Act, 15 U.S.C. §78aaa *et. seq.*

(*l*) NOTICE BY PUBLICATION. The court may order notice by publication if it finds that notice by mail is impracticable or that it is desirable to supplement the notice.

(m) ORDERS DESIGNATING MATTER OF NOTICES. The court may from time to time enter orders designating the matters in respect to which, the entity to whom, and the form and manner in which notices shall be sent except as otherwise provided by these rules.

(n) CAPTION. The caption of every notice given under this rule shall comply with Rule 1005. The caption of every notice required to be given by the debtor to a creditor shall include the information required to be in the notice by §342(c) of the Code.

(*o*) NOTICE OF ORDER FOR RELIEF IN CONSUMER CASE. In a voluntary case commenced by an individual debtor whose debts are primarily consumer debts, the clerk or some other person as the court may direct shall give the trustee and all creditors notice by mail of the order for relief within 21 days from the date thereof.

(p) NOTICE TO A CREDITOR WITH A FOREIGN ADDRESS.

(1) If, at the request of the United States trustee or a party in interest, or on its own initiative, the court finds that a notice mailed within the time prescribed by these rules would not be sufficient to give a creditor with a foreign address to which notices under these rules are mailed reasonable notice under the circumstances, the court may order that the notice be supplemented with notice by other means or that the time prescribed for the notice by mail be enlarged.

(2) Unless the court for cause orders otherwise, a creditor with a foreign address to which notices under this rule are mailed shall be given at least 30 days' notice of the time fixed for filing a proof of claim under Rule 3002(c) or Rule 3003(c).

(3) Unless the court for cause orders otherwise, the mailing address of a creditor with a foreign address shall be determined under Rule 2002(g).

(q) NOTICE OF PETITION FOR RECOGNITION OF FOREIGN PROCEEDING AND OF COURT'S INTENTION TO COMMUNICATE WITH FOREIGN COURTS AND FOREIGN REPRESENTATIVES.

(1) *Notice of Petition for Recognition.* The clerk, or some other person as the court may direct, shall forthwith give the debtor, all persons or bodies authorized to administer foreign proceedings of the debtor, all entities against whom provisional relief is being sought under §1519 of the Code, all parties to litigation pending in the United States in which the debtor is a party at the time of the filing of the petition, and such other entities as the court may direct, at least 21 days' notice by mail of the hearing on the petition for recognition of a foreign proceeding. The notice shall state whether the petition seeks recognition as a foreign main proceeding or foreign nonmain proceeding.

(2) *Notice of Court's Intention to Communicate with Foreign Courts and Foreign Representatives.* The clerk, or some other person as the court may direct, shall give the debtor, all persons or bodies authorized to administer foreign proceedings of the debtor, all entities against whom provisional relief is being sought under §1519 of the Code, all parties to litigation pending in the United States in which the debtor is a party at the time of the filing of the petition, and such other entities as the court may direct, notice by mail of the court's intention to communicate with a foreign court or foreign representative.

(As amended Pub. L. 98–91, §2(a), Aug. 30, 1983, 97 Stat. 607; Pub. L. 98–353, title III, §321, July 10, 1984, 98 Stat. 357; Mar. 30, 1987, eff. Aug. 1, 1987; Apr. 30, 1991, eff. Aug. 1, 1991; Apr. 22, 1993, eff. Aug. 1, 1993; Apr. 23, 1996, eff. Dec. 1, 1996; Apr. 11, 1997, eff. Dec. 1, 1997; Apr. 26, 1999, eff. Dec. 1, 1999; Apr. 17, 2000, eff. Dec. 1, 2000; Apr. 23, 2001, eff. Dec. 1, 2001; Mar. 27, 2003, eff. Dec. 1, 2003; Apr. 26, 2004, eff. Dec. 1, 2004; Apr. 25, 2005, eff. Dec. 1, 2005; Apr. 23, 2008, eff. Dec. 1, 2008; Mar. 26, 2009, eff. Dec. 1, 2009.)

NOTES OF ADVISORY COMMITTEE ON RULES—1983

Some of the notices required by this rule may be given either by the clerk or as the court may otherwise direct. For example, the court may order the trustee or debtor in possession to transmit one or more of the notices required by this rule, such as, notice of a proposed sale of property. See §363(b) of the Code. When publication of notices is required or desirable, reference should be made to Rule 9008.

Notice of the order for relief is required to be given by §342 of the Code and by subdivision (f)(1) of this rule. That notice may be combined with the notice of the meeting of creditors as indicated in Official Form No. 16, the notice and order of the meeting of creditors.

Subdivision (a) sets forth the requirement that 20 days notice be given of the significant events in a case under the Bankruptcy Code. The former Act and Rules provided a ten day notice in bankruptcy and Chapter XI cases, and a 20 day notice in a Chapter X case. This rule generally makes uniform the 20 day notice provision except that subdivision (b) contains a 25 day period for certain events in a chapter 9, 11, or 13 case. Generally, Rule 9006 permits reduction of time periods. Since notice by mail is complete on mailing, the requirement of subdivision (a) is satisfied if the notices are deposited in the mail at least 20 days before the event. See Rule 9006(e). The exceptions referred to in the introductory phrase include the modifications in the notice procedure permitted by subdivision (h) as to non-filing creditors, subdivision (i) as to cases where a committee is functioning, and subdivision (k) where compliance with subdivision (a) is impracticable.

The notice of a proposed sale affords creditors an opportunity to object to the sale and raise a dispute for the court's attention. Section 363(b) of the Code permits the trustee or debtor in possession to sell property, other than in the ordinary course of business, only after notice and hearing. If no objection is raised after notice, §102(1) provides that there need not be an actual hearing. Thus, absent objection, there would be no court involvement with respect to a trustee's sale. Once an objection is raised, only the court may pass on it.

Prior to the Code the court could shorten the notice period for a proposed sale of property or dispense with notice. This subdivision (a), permits the 20 day period to be shortened in appropriate circumstances but the rule does not contain a provision allowing the court to dispense with notice. The rule is thus consistent with the Code, §§363(b) and 102(1)(A) of the Code. See 28 U.S.C. §2075. It may be necessary, in certain circumstances, however, to use a method of notice other than mail. Subdivision (a)(2) vests the court with discretion, on cause shown, to order a different method. Reference should also be made to Rule 6004 which allows a different type of notice of proposed sales when the property is of little value.

Notice of the hearing on an application for compensation or reimbursement of expenses totalling $100 or less need not be given. In chapter 13 cases relatively small amounts are sometimes allowed for post-confirmation services and it would not serve a useful purpose to require advance notice.

Subdivision (b) is similar to subdivision (a) but lengthens the notice time to 25 days with respect to those events particularly significant in chapter 9, 11 and 13 cases. The additional time may be necessary to formulate objections to a disclosure statement or confirmation of a plan and preparation for the hearing on approval of the disclosure statement or confirmation. The disclosure statement and hearing thereon is only applicable in chapter 9 cases (§901(a) of the Code), and chapter 11 cases (§1125 of the Code).

Subdivision (c) specifies certain matters that should be included in the notice of a proposed sale of property and notice of the hearing on an application for allowances. Rule 6004 fixes the time within which parties in interest may file objections to a proposed sale of property.

Subdivision (d) relates exclusively to the notices given to equity security holders in chapter 11 cases. Under chapter 11, a plan may impair the interests of the debtor's shareholders or a plan may be a relatively simple restructuring of unsecured debt. In some cases, it is necessary that equity interest holders receive various notices and in other cases there is no purpose to be served. This subdivision indicates that the court is not mandated to order notices but rather that the matter should be treated with some flexibility. The court may decide whether notice is to be given and how it is to be given. Under §341(b) of the Code, a meeting of equity security holders is not required in each case, only when it is ordered by the court. Thus subdivision (d)(2) requires notice only when the court orders a meeting.

In addition to the notices specified in this subdivision, there may be other events or matters arising in a case as to which equity security holders should receive notice. These are situations left to determination by the court.

Subdivision (e), authorizing a notice of the apparent insufficiency of assets for the payment of any dividend, is correlated with Rule 3002(c)(5), which provides for the issuance of an additional notice to creditors if the possibility of a payment later materializes.

Subdivision (f) provides for the transmission of other notices to which no time period applies. Clause (1) requires notice of the order for relief; this complements the mandate of §342 of the Code requiring such notice as is appropriate of the order for relief. This notice may be combined with the notice of the meeting of creditors to avoid the necessity of more than one mailing. See Official Form No. 16, notice of meeting of creditors.

Subdivision (g) recognizes that an agent authorized to receive notices for a creditor may, without a court order, designate where notices to the creditor he represents should be addressed. Agent includes an officer of a corporation, an attorney at law, or an attorney in fact if the requisite authority has been given him. It should be noted that Official Forms Nos. 17 and 18 do not include an authorization of the holder of a power of attorney to receive notices for the creditor. Neither these forms nor this rule carries any implication that such an authorization may not be given in a power of attorney or that a request for notices to be addressed to both the creditor or his duly authorized agent may not be filed.

Subdivision (h). After the time for filing claims has expired in a chapter 7 case, creditors who have not filed their claims in accordance with Rule 3002(c) are not entitled to share in the estate except as they may come within the special provisions of §726 of the Code or Rule 3002(c)(6). The elimination of notice to creditors who have no recognized stake in the estate may permit economies in time and expense. Reduction of the list of creditors to receive notices under this subdivision is discretionary. This subdivision does not apply to the notice of the meeting of creditors.

Subdivision (i) contains a list of matters of which notice may be given a creditors' committee or to its authorized agent in lieu of notice to the creditors. Such notice may serve every practical purpose of a notice to all the creditors and save delay and expense. *In re Schulte-United, Inc.*, 59 F.2d 553, 561 (8th Cir. 1932).

Subdivision (j). The premise for the requirement that the district director of internal revenue receive copies of notices that all creditors receive in a chapter 11 case is that every debtor is potentially a tax debtor of the United States. Notice to the district director alerts him to the possibility that a tax debtor's estate is about to be liquidated or reorganized and that the debtor may be discharged. When other indebtedness to the United States is indicated, the United States attorney is notified as the person in the best position to protect the interests of the government. In addition, the provision requires notice by mail to the head of any department, agency, or instrumentality of the United States through whose action the debtor became indebted to the United States. This rule is not intended to preclude a local rule from requiring a state or local tax authority to receive some or all of the notices to creditors under these rules.

Subdivision (k) specifies two kinds of situations in which notice by publication may be appropriate: (1) when notice by mail is impracticable; and (2) when notice by mail alone is less than adequate. Notice by mail may be impracticable when, for example, the debtor has disappeared or his records have been destroyed and the names and addresses of his creditors are unavailable, or when the number of creditors with nominal claims is very large and the estate to be distributed may be insufficient to defray the costs of issuing the notices. Supplementing notice by mail is also indicated when the debtor's records are incomplete or inaccurate and it is reasonable to believe that publication may reach some of the creditors who would otherwise be missed. Rule 9008 applies when the court directs notice by publication under this rule. Neither clause (2) of subdivision (a) nor subdivision (k) of this rule is concerned with the publication of advertisement to the general public of a sale of property of the estate at public auction under Rule 6004(b). See 3 Collier, *Bankruptcy* 522–23 (14th ed. 1971); 4B *id.* 1165–67 (1967); 2 *id.* ¶363.03 (15th ed. 1981).

Subdivision (m). Inclusion in notices to creditors of information as to other names used by the debtor as required by Rule 1005 will assist them in the preparation of their proofs of claim and in deciding whether to file a complaint objecting to the debtor's discharge. Additional names may be listed by the debtor on his statement of affairs when he did not file the petition. The mailing of notices should not be postponed to await a delayed filing of the statement of financial affairs.

NOTES OF ADVISORY COMMITTEE ON RULES—1987 AMENDMENT

Subdivision (a) is amended to provide that notice of a hearing on an application for compensation must be given only when the amount requested is in excess of $500.

Subdivision (d). A new notice requirement is added as clause (3). When a proposed sale is of all or substantially all of the debtor's assets, it is appropriate that equity security holders be given notice of the proposed sale. The clauses of subdivision (d) are renumbered to accommodate this addition.

Subdivision (f). Clause (7) is eliminated. Mailing of a copy of the discharge order is governed by Rule 4004(g).

Subdivision (g) is amended to relieve the clerk of the duty to mail notices to the address shown in a proof of claim when a notice of no dividend has been given pursuant to Rule 2002. This amendment avoids the necessity of the clerk searching proofs of claim which are filed in no dividend cases to ascertain whether a different address is shown.

Subdivision (n) was enacted by §321 of the 1984 amendments.

NOTES OF ADVISORY COMMITTEE ON RULES—1991 AMENDMENT

Subdivision (a)(3) is amended to exclude compromise or settlement agreements concerning adequate protection or which modify or terminate the automatic stay, provide for use of cash collateral, or create a senior or equal lien on collateral to obtain credit. Notice requirements relating to approval of such agreements are governed by Rule 4001(d).

Subdivision (a)(5) is amended to include a hearing on dismissal or conversion of a chapter 12 case. This subdivision does not apply when a hearing is not required. It is also amended to avoid the necessity of giving notice to all creditors of a hearing on the dismissal of a consumer debtor's case based on substantial abuse of chapter 7. Such hearings on dismissal under §707(b) of the Code are governed by Rule 1017(e).

Subdivision (a)(9) is added to provide for notice of the time fixed for filing objections and the hearing to consider confirmation of a plan in a chapter 12 case. Section 1224 of the Code requires "expedited notice" of the confirmation hearing in a chapter 12 case and requires that the hearing be concluded not later than 45 days after the filing of the plan unless the time is extended for cause. This amendment establishes 20 days as the notice period. The court may shorten this time on its own motion or on motion of a party in interest. The notice includes both the date of the hearing and the date for filing objections, and must be accompanied by a copy of the plan or a summary of the plan in accordance with Rule 3015(d).

Subdivision (b) is amended to delete as unnecessary the references to subdivisions (h) and (i).

Subdivision (d) does not require notice to equity security holders in a chapter 12 case. The procedural burden of requiring such notice is outweighed by the likelihood that all equity security holders of a family farmer will be informed of the progress of the case without formal notice. Subdivision (d) is amended to recognize that the United States trustee may convene a meeting of equity security holders pursuant to §341(b).

Subdivision (f)(2) is amended and subdivision (f)(4) is deleted to require notice of any conversion of the case, whether the conversion is by court order or is effectuated by the debtor filing a notice of conversion pursuant to §§1208(a) or 1307(a). Subdivision (f)(8), renumbered (f)(7), is amended to include entry of an order confirming a chapter 12 plan. Subdivision (f)(9) is amended to increase the amount to $1,500.

Subdivisions (g) and (j) are amended to delete the words "with the court" and subdivision (i) is amended to delete the words "with the clerk" because these phrases are unnecessary. See Rules 5005(a) and 9001(3).

Subdivision (i) is amended to require that the United States trustee receive notices required by subdivision (a)(2), (3) and (7) of this rule notwithstanding a court order limiting such notice to committees and to creditors and equity security holders who request such notices. Subdivision (i) is amended further to include committees elected pursuant to §705 of the Code and to provide that committees of retired employees appointed in chapter 11 cases receive certain notices.

Subdivision (k) is derived from Rule X-1008. The administrative functions of the United States trustee pursuant to 28 U.S.C. §586(a) and standing to be heard on issues under §307 and other sections of the Code require that the United States trustee be informed of developments and issues in every case except chapter 9 cases. The rule omits those notices described in subdivision (a)(1) because a meeting of creditors is convened only by the United States trustee, and those notices described in subdivision (a)(4) (date fixed for filing claims against a surplus), subdivision (a)(6) (time fixed to accept or reject proposed modification of a plan), subdivision (a)(8) (time fixed for filing proofs of claims in chapter 11 cases), subdivision (f)(3) (time fixed for filing claims in chapter 7, 12, and 13 cases), and subdivision (f)(5) (time fixed for filing complaint to determine dischargeability of debt) because these notices do not relate to matters that generally involve the United States trustee. Nonetheless, the omission of these notices does not prevent the United States trustee from receiving such notices upon request. The United States trustee also receives notice of hearings on applications for compensation or reimbursement without regard to the $500 limitation contained in subdivision (a)(7) of this rule. This rule is intended to be flexible in that it permits the United States trustee in a particular judicial district to request notices in certain categories, and to request not to receive notices in other categories, when the practice in that district makes that desirable.

NOTES OF ADVISORY COMMITTEE ON RULES—1993 AMENDMENT

Subdivision (j) is amended to avoid the necessity of sending an additional notice to the Washington, D.C. address of the Securities and Exchange Commission if the Commission prefers to have notices sent only to a local office. This change also clarifies that notices required to be mailed pursuant to this rule must be sent to the Securities and Exchange Commission only if it has filed a notice of appearance or has filed a written request. Other amendments are stylistic and make no substantive change.

NOTES OF ADVISORY COMMITTEE ON RULES—1996 AMENDMENT

Paragraph (a)(4) is abrogated to conform to the abrogation of Rule 3002(c)(6). The remaining paragraphs of subdivision (a) are renumbered, and references to these paragraphs contained in other subdivisions of this rule are amended accordingly.

Paragraph (f)(8) is amended so that a summary of the trustee's final account, which is prepared after distribution of property, does not have to be mailed to the debtor, all creditors, and indenture trustees in a chapter 7 case. Parties are sufficiently protected by receiving a summary of the trustee's final report that informs parties of the proposed distribution of property.

Subdivision (h) is amended (1) to provide that an order under this subdivision may not be issued if a notice of no dividend is given pursuant to Rule 2002(e) and the time for filing claims has not expired as provided in Rule 3002(c)(5); (2) to clarify that notices required to be mailed by subdivision (a) to parties other than creditors must be mailed to those entities despite an order issued pursuant to subdivision (h); (3) to provide that if the court, pursuant to Rule 3002(c)(1) or 3002(c)(2), has granted an extension of time to file a proof of claim, the creditor for whom the extension has been granted must continue to receive notices despite an order issued pursuant to subdivision (h); and (4) to delete references to subdivision (a)(4) and Rule 3002(c)(6), which have been abrogated.

Other amendments to this rule are stylistic.

GAP Report on Rule 2002. No changes since publication, except for stylistic changes and the correction of a typographical error in the committee note.

NOTES OF ADVISORY COMMITTEE ON RULES—1997 AMENDMENT

Paragraph (a)(1) is amended to include notice of a meeting of creditors convened under §1104(b) of the Code for the purpose of electing a trustee in a chapter 11 case. The court for cause shown may order the 20-day period reduced pursuant to Rule 9006(c)(1).

Subdivision (n) is amended to conform to the 1994 amendment to §342 of the Code. As provided in §342(c), the failure of a notice given by the debtor to a creditor to contain the information required by §342(c) does not invalidate the legal effect of the notice.

GAP Report on Rule 2002. No changes to the published draft.

COMMITTEE NOTES ON RULES—1999 AMENDMENT

Paragraph (a)(4) is amended to conform to the amendments to Rule 1017. If the United States trustee files a motion to dismiss a case for the debtor's failure to file the list of creditors, schedules, or the statement of financial affairs within the time specified in §707(a)(3), the amendments to this rule and to Rule 1017 eliminate the requirement that all creditors receive notice of the hearing.

Paragraph (a)(4) is amended further to conform to Rule 1017(b), which requires that notice of the hearing on dismissal of a case for failure to pay the filing fee be served on only the debtor and the trustee.

Paragraph (f)(2) is amended to provide for notice of the suspension of proceedings under §305.

GAP Report on Rule 2002. No changes since publication.

COMMITTEE NOTES ON RULES—2000 AMENDMENT

Paragraph (a)(6) is amended to increase the dollar amount from $500 to $1,000. The amount was last amended in 1987, when it was changed from $100 to $500. The amendment also clarifies that the notice is required only if a particular entity is requesting more than $1,000 as compensation or reimbursement of expenses. If several professionals are requesting compensation or reimbursement, and only one hearing will be held on all applications, notice under paragraph (a)(6) is required only with respect to the entities that have requested more than $1,000. If each applicant requests $1,000 or less, notice under paragraph (a)(6) is not required even though the aggregate amount of all applications to be considered at the hearing is more than $1,000.

If a particular entity had filed prior applications or had received compensation or reimbursement of expenses at an earlier time in the case, the amounts previously requested or awarded are not considered when determining whether the present application exceeds $1,000 for the purpose of applying this rule.

GAP Report on Rule 2002(a). No changes since publication.

COMMITTEE NOTES ON RULES—2001 AMENDMENT

Subdivision (c)(3) is added to assure that parties given notice of a hearing to consider confirmation of a plan under subdivision (b) are given adequate notice of an injunction provided for in the plan if it would enjoin conduct that is not otherwise enjoined by operation of the Code. The validity and effect of any injunction provided for in a plan are substantive law matters that are beyond the scope of these rules.

The notice requirement of subdivision (c)(3) is not applicable to an injunction contained in a plan if it is substantially the same as an injunction provided under the Code. For example, if a plan contains an injunction against acts to collect a discharged debt from the debtor, Rule 2002(c)(3) would not apply because that conduct would be enjoined under §524(a)(2) upon the debtor's discharge. But if a plan provides that creditors will be enjoined from asserting claims against persons who are not debtors in the case, the notice of the confirmation hearing must include the information required under Rule 2002(c)(3) because that conduct would not be enjoined by operation of the Code. *See* §524(e).

The requirement that the notice identify the entities that would be subject to the injunction requires only reasonable identification under the circumstances. If the entities that would be subject to the injunction cannot be identified by name, the notice may describe them by class or category if reasonable under the circumstances. For example, it may be sufficient for the notice to identify the entities as "all creditors of the debtor" and for the notice to be published in a manner that satisfies due process requirements.

Subdivision (g) has been revised to clarify that where a creditor or indenture trustee files both a proof of claim which includes a mailing address and a separate request designating a mailing address, the last paper filed determines the proper address. The amendments also clarify that a request designating a mailing address is effective only with respect to a particular case.

Under Rule 2002(g), a duly filed proof of claim is considered a request designating a mailing address if a notice of no dividend has been given under Rule 2002(e), but has been superseded by a subsequent notice of possible dividend under Rule 3002(c)(5). A duly filed proof of interest is considered a request designating a mailing address of an equity security holder.

Rule 2002(g)(3) is added to assure that notices to an infant or incompetent person under this rule are mailed to the appropriate guardian or other legal representative. Under Rule 1007(m), if the debtor knows that a creditor is an infant or incompetent person, the debtor is required to include in the list and schedule of creditors the name and address of the person upon whom process would be served in an adversary proceeding in accordance with Rule 7004(b)(2). If the infant or incompetent person, or another person, files a request or proof of claim designating a different name and mailing address, the notices would have to be mailed to both names and addresses until the court resolved the issue as to the proper mailing address.

The other amendments to Rule 2002(g) are stylistic.

Changes Made After Publication and Comments. In Rule 2002(c)(3), the word "highlighted" was replaced with "underlined" because highlighted documents are difficult to scan electronically for inclusion in the clerks' files. The Committee Note was revised to put in a more prominent position the statement that the validity and effect of any injunction provided for in a plan are substantive matters beyond the scope of the rules.

In Rule 2002(g), no changes were made.

COMMITTEE NOTES ON RULES—2003 AMENDMENT

Subdivision (a)(1) of the rule is amended to direct the clerk or other person giving notice of the §341 or §1104(b) meeting of creditors to include the debtor's full social security number on the notice. Official Form 9, the form of the notice of the meeting of creditors that will become a part of the court's file in the case, will include only the last four digits of the debtor's social security number. This rule, however, directs the clerk to include the full social security number on the notice that is served on the creditors and other identified parties, unless the court orders otherwise in a particular case. This will enable creditors and other parties in interest who are in possession of the debtor's social security number to verify the debtor's identity and proceed accordingly. The filed Official Form 9, however, will not include the debtor's full social security number. This will prevent the full social security number from becoming a part of the court's file in the case, and the number will not be included in the court's electronic records. Creditors who already have the debtor's social security number will be able to verify the existence of a case under the debtor's social security number, but any person searching the electronic case files without the number will not be able to acquire the debtor's social security number.

Changes Made After Publication and Comments. The rule amendment was made in response to concerns of both private creditors and taxing authorities that truncating the social security number of a debtor to the last four digits would unduly hamper their ability to identify the debtor and govern their actions accordingly. Therefore, the Advisory Committee amended Rule 2002 to require the clerk to include the debtor's full social security number on the notice informing creditors of the §341 meeting and other significant deadlines in the case. This is essentially a continuation of the practice under the current rules, and the amendment is necessary because of the amendment to Rule 1005 that restricts publication of the social security number on the caption of the petition to the final four digits of the number.

COMMITTEE NOTES ON RULES—2004 AMENDMENT

The rule is amended to reflect that the structure of the Internal Revenue Service no longer includes a District Director. Thus, rather than sending notice to the District Director, the rule now requires that the notices be sent to the location designated by the Service and set out in the register of addresses maintained by the clerk under Rule 5003(e). The other change is stylistic.

COMMITTEE NOTES ON RULES—2005 AMENDMENT

A new paragraph (g)(4) is inserted in the rule. The new paragraph authorizes an entity and a notice provider to agree that the notice provider will give notices to the entity at the address or addresses set out in their agreement. Rule 9001(9) sets out the definition of a notice provider.

The business of many entities is national in scope, and technology currently exists to direct the transmission of notice (both electronically and in paper form) to those entities in an accurate and much more efficient manner than by sending individual notices to the same creditor by separate mailings. The rule authorizes an entity and a notice provider to determine the manner of the service as well as to set the address or addresses to which the notices must be sent. For example, they could agree that all notices sent by the notice provider to the entity must be sent to a single, nationwide electronic or postal address. They could also establish local or regional addresses to which notices would be sent in matters pending in specific districts. Since the entity and notice provider also can agree on the date of the commencement of service under the agreement, there is no need to set a date in the rule after which notices would have to be sent to the address or addresses that the entity establishes. Furthermore, since the entity supplies the address to the notice provider, use of that address is conclusively presumed to be proper. Nonetheless, if that address is not used, the notice still may be effective if the notice is otherwise effective under applicable law. This is the same treatment given under Rule 5003(e) to notices sent to governmental units at addresses other than those set out in that register of addresses.

The remaining subdivisions of Rule 2002(g) continue to govern the addressing of a notice that is not sent pursuant to an agreement described in Rule 2002(g)(4).

Changes Made After Publication and Comment. No changes since publication.

COMMITTEE NOTES ON RULES—2008 AMENDMENT

Subdivision (b) is amended to provide for 25 days' notice of the time for the court to make a final determination whether the plan in a small business case can serve as a disclosure statement. Conditional approval of a disclosure statement in a small business case is governed by Rule 3017.1 and does not require 25 days' notice. The court may consider this matter in a hearing combined with the confirmation hearing in a small business case.

Because of the requirements of Rule 6004(g), subdivision (c)(1) is amended to require that a trustee leasing or selling personally identifiable information under §363(b)(1)(A) or (B) of the Code, as amended in 2005, include in the notice of the lease or sale transaction a statement as to whether the lease or sale is consistent with a policy prohibiting the transfer of the information.

Subdivisions (f)(9) and (10) are new. They reflect the 2005 amendments to §§342(d) and 704(b) of the Code. Section 342(d) requires the clerk to give notice to creditors shortly after the commencement of the case as to whether a presumption of abuse exists. Subdivision (f)(9) adds this notice to the list of notices that the clerk must give. Subdivision (f)(10) implements the amendment to §704(b), which requires the court to provide a copy to all creditors of a statement by the United States trustee or bankruptcy administrator as to whether the debtor's case would be presumed to be an abuse under §707(b) not later than five days after receiving it.

Subdivision (f)(11) is also added to provide notice to creditors of the debtor's filing of a statement in a chapter 11, 12, or 13 case that there is no reasonable cause to believe that §522(q) applies in the case. This allows a creditor who disputes that assertion to request a delay of the entry of the discharge in the case.

Subdivision (g)(2) of the rule is amended because the 2005 amendments to §342(f) of the Code permit creditors in chapter 7 and 13 individual debtor cases to file a notice with any bankruptcy court of the address to which the creditor wishes all notices to be sent. The amendment to Rule 2002(g)(2) therefore only limits application of the subdivision when a creditor files a notice under §342(f).

New subdivision (g)(5) implements §342(g)(1) which was added to the Code in 2005. Section 342(g)(1) allows a creditor to treat a notice as not having been brought to the creditor's attention, and so potentially ineffective, until it is received by a person or organizational subdivision that the creditor has designated to receive notices under the Bankruptcy Code. Under that section, the creditor must have established reasonable procedures for such notices to be delivered to the designated person or subdivision. The rule provides that, in order to challenge a notice under §342(g)(1), a creditor must have filed the name and address of the designated notice recipient, as well as a description of the procedures for directing notices to that recipient, prior to the time that the challenged notice was issued. The filing required by the rule may be made as part of a creditor's filing under §342(f), which allows a creditor to file a notice of the address to be used by all bankruptcy courts or by particular bankruptcy courts to provide notice to the creditor in cases under chapters 7 and 13. Filing the name and address of the designated notice recipient and the procedures for directing notices to that recipient will reduce uncertainty as to the proper party for receiving notice and limit factual disputes as to whether a notice recipient has been designated and as to the nature of procedures adopted to direct notices to the recipient.

Subdivision (k) is amended to add notices given under subdivision (q) to the list of notices which must be served on the United States trustee.

Section 1514(d) of the Code, added by the 2005 amendments, requires that such additional time as is reasonable under the circumstances be given to creditors with foreign addresses with respect to notices and the filing of a proof of claim. Thus, subdivision (p)(1) is added to this rule to give the court flexibility to direct that notice by other means shall supplement notice by mail, or to enlarge the notice period, for creditors with foreign addresses. If cause exists, such as likely delays in the delivery of mailed notices in particular locations, the court may order that notice also be given by email, facsimile, or private courier. Alternatively, the court may enlarge the notice period for a creditor with a foreign address. It is expected that in most situations involving foreign creditors, fairness will not require any additional notice or extension of the notice period. This rule recognizes that the court has discretion to establish procedures to determine, on its own initiative, whether relief under subdivision (p) is appropriate, but that the court is not required to establish such procedures and may decide to act only on request of a party in interest.

Subdivision (p)(2) is added to the rule to grant creditors with a foreign address to which notices are mailed at least 30 days' notice of the time within which to file proofs of claims if notice is mailed to the foreign address, unless the court orders otherwise. If cause exists, such as likely delays in the delivery of notices in particular locations, the court may extend the notice period for creditors with foreign addresses. The court may also shorten the additional notice time if circumstances so warrant. For example, if the court in a chapter 11 case determines that supplementing the notice to a foreign creditor with notice by electronic means, such as email or facsimile, would give the creditor reasonable notice, the court may order that the creditor be given only 20 days' notice in accordance with Rule 2002(a)(7).

Subdivision (p)(3) is added to provide that the court may, for cause, override a creditor's designation of a foreign address under Rule 2002(g). For example, if a party in interest believes that a creditor has wrongfully designated a foreign address to obtain additional time when it has a significant presence in the United States, the party can ask the court to order that notices to that creditor be sent to an address other than the one designated by the foreign creditor.

Subdivision (q) is added to require that notice of the hearing on the petition for recognition of a foreign proceeding be given to the debtor, all administrators in foreign proceedings of the debtor, entities against whom provisional relief is sought, and entities with whom the debtor is engaged in litigation at the time of the commencement of the case. There is no need at this stage of the proceedings to provide notice to all creditors. If the foreign representative should take action to commence a case under another chapter of the Code, the rules governing those proceedings will operate to provide that notice is given to all creditors.

The rule also requires notice of the court's intention to communicate with a foreign court or foreign representative.

Changes Made After Publication. Subdivision (g)(2) was amended to provide that the designated address of a governmental unit under Rule 5003(e) establishes an exception to the rule that a creditor's address is to be taken from the debtor's schedules. The fifth and sixth paragraphs of the Committee Note were amended to explain that change.

Subdivision (p)(3) was added to the rule to provide that the court may override a creditor's designation of a foreign mailing address under Rule 2002(g). This will permit a party in interest to seek court relief if a creditor has improperly designated a foreign address.

Subdivision (q)(1) and (2) were amended by adopting language from §101(24) to identify foreign representatives as "all persons or bodies authorized to administer foreign proceedings of the debtor" rather than as "all administrators in foreign proceedings of the debtor." References to Rule 5012 in subdivision (q)(2) and in the Committee Note were deleted.

Committee Notes on Rules—2009 Amendment

The rule is amended to implement changes in connection with the amendment to Rule 9006(a) and the manner by which time is computed under the rules. The deadlines in the rule are amended to substitute a deadline that is a multiple of seven days. Throughout the rules, deadlines are amended in the following manner:

- 5-day periods become 7-day periods
- 10-day periods become 14-day periods
- 15-day periods become 14-day periods
- 20-day periods become 21-day periods
- 25-day periods become 28-day periods

REFERENCES IN TEXT

The Securities Investor Protection Act, referred to in subd. (k), probably means the Securities Investor Protection Act of 1970, Pub. L. 91–598, Dec. 30, 1970, 84 Stat. 1636, as amended, which is classified generally to chapter 2B–1 (§78aaa et seq.) of Title 15, Commerce and Trade. For complete classification of this Act to the Code, see section 78aaa of Title 15 and Tables.

AMENDMENT BY PUBLIC LAW

1984—Subd. (n). Pub. L. 98–353 added subd. (n).

1983—Subd. (f). Pub. L. 98–91 inserted ", or some other person as the Court may direct," after "clerk".

EFFECTIVE DATE OF 1984 AMENDMENT

Amendment by Pub. L. 98–353 effective with respect to cases filed 90 days after July 10, 1984, see section 552(a) of Pub. L. 98–353, set out as a note under section 101 of this title.

EFFECTIVE DATE OF 1983 AMENDMENT

Section 1 of Pub. L. 98–91 provided: "That rule 2002(f) of the Bankruptcy Rules, as proposed by the United States Supreme Court in the order of April 25, 1983, of the Court, shall take effect on August 1, 1983, except as otherwise provided in section 2 [amending subd. (f) of this rule and enacting a provision set out as a note below]."

Section 2(b) of Pub. L. 98–91 provided that: "The amendment made by subsection (a) [amending subd. (f) of this rule] shall take effect on August 1, 1983."

Rule 2003. Meeting of Creditors or Equity Security Holders

(a) DATE AND PLACE. Except as otherwise provided in §341(e) of the Code, in a chapter 7 liquidation or a chapter 11 reorganization case, the United States trustee shall call a meeting of creditors to be held no fewer than 21 and no more than 40 days after the order for relief. In a chapter 12 family farmer debt adjustment case, the United States trustee shall call a meeting of creditors to be held no fewer than 21 and no more than 35 days after the order for relief. In a chapter 13 individual's debt adjustment case, the United States trustee shall call a meeting of creditors to be held no fewer than 21 and no more than 50 days after the order for relief. If there is an appeal from or a motion to vacate the order for relief, or if there is a motion to dismiss the case, the United States trustee may set a later date for the meeting. The meeting may be held at a regular place for holding court or at any other place designated by the United States trustee within the district convenient for the parties in interest. If the United States trustee designates a place for the meeting which is not regularly staffed by the United States trustee or an assistant who may preside at the meeting, the meeting may be held not more than 60 days after the order for relief.

(b) ORDER OF MEETING.

(1) *Meeting of Creditors.* The United States trustee shall preside at the meeting of creditors. The business of the meeting shall include the examination of the debtor under oath and, in a chapter 7 liquidation case, may include the election of a creditors' committee and, if the case is not under subchapter V of chapter 7, the election of a trustee. The presiding officer shall have the authority to administer oaths.

(2) *Meeting of Equity Security Holders.* If the United States trustee convenes a meeting of equity security holders pursuant to §341(b) of the Code, the United States trustee shall fix a date for the meeting and shall preside.

(3) *Right To Vote.* In a chapter 7 liquidation case, a creditor is entitled to vote at a meeting if, at or before the meeting, the creditor has filed a proof of claim or a writing setting forth facts evidencing a right to vote pursuant to §702(a) of the Code unless objection is made to the claim or the proof of claim is insufficient on its face. A creditor of a partnership may file a proof of claim or writing evidencing a right to vote for the trustee for the estate of the general partner notwithstanding that a trustee for the estate of the partnership has previously qualified. In the event of an objection to the amount or allowability of a claim for the purpose of voting, unless the court orders otherwise, the United States trustee shall tabulate the votes for each alternative presented by the dispute and, if resolution of such dispute is necessary to determine the result of the election, the tabulations for each alternative shall be reported to the court.

(c) RECORD OF MEETING. Any examination under oath at the meeting of creditors held pursuant to §341(a) of the Code shall be recorded verbatim by the United States trustee using electronic sound recording equipment or other means of recording, and such record shall be preserved by the United States trustee and available for public access until two years after the conclusion of the meeting of creditors. Upon request of any entity, the United States trustee shall certify and provide a copy or transcript of such recording at the entity's expense.

(d) REPORT OF ELECTION AND RESOLUTION OF DISPUTES IN A CHAPTER 7 CASE.

(1) *Report of Undisputed Election.* In a chapter 7 case, if the election of a trustee or a member of a creditors' committee is not disputed, the United States trustee shall promptly file a report of the election, including the name and address of the person or entity elected and a statement that the election is undisputed.

(2) *Disputed Election.* If the election is disputed, the United States trustee shall promptly file a report stating that the election is disputed, informing the court of the nature of the dispute, and listing the name and address of any candidate elected under any alternative presented by the dispute. No later than the date on which the report is filed, the United States trustee shall mail a copy of the report to any party in interest that has made a request to receive a copy of the report. Pending disposition by the court of a disputed election for trustee, the interim trustee shall continue in office. Unless a motion for the resolution of the dispute is filed no later than 14 days after the United States trustee files a report of a disputed election for trustee, the interim trustee shall serve as trustee in the case.

(e) ADJOURNMENT. The meeting may be adjourned from time to time by announcement at the meeting of the adjourned date and time without further written notice.

(f) SPECIAL MEETINGS. The United States trustee may call a special meeting of creditors on request of a party in interest or on the United States trustee's own initiative.

(g) FINAL MEETING. If the United States trustee calls a final meeting of creditors in a case in which the net proceeds realized exceed $1,500, the clerk shall mail a summary of the trustee's final account to the creditors with a notice of the meeting, together with a statement of the amount of the claims allowed. The trustee shall attend the final meeting and shall, if requested, report on the administration of the estate.

(As amended Mar. 30, 1987, eff. Aug. 1, 1987; Apr. 30, 1991, eff. Aug. 1, 1991; Apr. 22, 1993, eff. Aug. 1, 1993; Apr. 26, 1999, eff. Dec. 1, 1999; Mar. 27, 2003, eff. Dec. 1, 2003; Apr. 23, 2008, eff. Dec. 1, 2008; Mar. 26, 2009, eff. Dec. 1, 2009.)

NOTES OF ADVISORY COMMITTEE ON RULES—1983

Section 341(a) of the Code requires a meeting of creditors in a chapter 7, 11 or 13 case, and §341(b) permits the court to order a meeting of equity security holders. A major change from prior law, however, prohibits the judge from attending or presiding over the meeting. Section 341(c).

This rule does not apply either in a case for the reorganization of a railroad or for the adjustment of debts of a municipality. Sections 1161 and 901 render §§341 and 343 inapplicable in these types of cases. Section 341 sets the requirement for a meeting of creditors and §343 provides for the examination of the debtor.

Subdivision (a). The meeting is to be held between 20 and 40 days after the date of the order for relief. In a voluntary case, the date of the order for relief is the date of the filing of the petition (§301 of the Code); in an involuntary case, it is the date of an actual order (§303(i) of the Code).

Subdivision (b) provides flexibility as to who will preside at the meeting of creditors. The court may designate a person to serve as presiding officer, such as the interim trustee appointed under §701 of the Code. If the court does not designate anyone, the clerk will preside. In either case, creditors may elect a person of their own choosing. In any event, the clerk may remain to record the proceedings and take appearances. Use of the clerk is not contrary to the legislative policy of §341(c). The judge remains insulated from any information coming forth at the meeting and any information obtained by the clerk must not be relayed to the judge.

Although the clerk may preside at the meeting, the clerk is not performing any kind of judicial role, nor should the clerk give any semblance of performing such a role. It would be pretentious for the clerk to ascend the bench, don a robe or be addressed as "your honor". The clerk should not appear to parties or others as any type of judicial officer.

In a chapter 11 case, if a committee of unsecured creditors has been appointed pursuant to §1102(a)(1) of the Code and a chairman has been selected, the chairman will preside or a person, such as the attorney for the committee, may be designated to preside by the chairman.

Since the judge must fix the bond of the trustee but cannot be present at the meeting, the rule allows the creditors to recommend the amount of the bond. They should be able to obtain relevant information concerning the extent of assets of the debtor at the meeting.

Paragraph (1) authorizes the presiding officer to administer oaths. This is important because the debtor's examination must be under oath.

Paragraph (3) of subdivision (b) has application only in a chapter 7 case. That is the only type of case under the Code that permits election of a trustee or committee. In all other cases, no vote is taken at the meeting of creditors. If it is necessary for the court to make a determination with respect to a claim, the meeting may be adjourned until the objection or dispute is resolved.

The second sentence recognizes that partnership creditors may vote for a trustee of a partner's estate along with the separate creditors of the partner. Although §723(c) gives the trustee of a partnership a claim against a partner's estate for the full amount of partnership creditors' claims allowed, the purpose and function of this provision are to simplify distribution and prevent double proof, not to disfranchise partnership creditors in electing a trustee of an estate against which they hold allowable claims.

Subdivision (c) requires minutes and a record of the meeting to be maintained by the presiding officer. A verbatim record must be made of the debtor's examination but the rule is flexible as to the means used to record the examination.

Subdivision (d) recognizes that the court must be informed immediately about the election or nonelection of a trustee in a chapter 7 case. Pursuant to Rule 2008, the clerk officially informs the trustee of his election or appointment and how he is to qualify. The presiding person has no authority to resolve a disputed election.

For purposes of expediency, the results of the election should be obtained for each alternative presented by the dispute and immediately reported to the court. Thus, when an interested party presents the dispute to the court, its prompt resolution by the court will determine the dispute and a new or adjourned meeting to conduct the election may be avoided. The clerk is not an interested party.

A creditors' committee may be elected only in a chapter 7 case. In chapter 11 cases, a creditors' committee is appointed pursuant to §1102.

While a final meeting is not required, Rule 2002(f)(10) provides for the trustee's final account to be sent to creditors.

NOTES OF ADVISORY COMMITTEE ON RULES—1987 AMENDMENT

Subdivision (a). Many courts schedule meetings of creditors at various locations in the district. Because the clerk must schedule meetings at those locations, an additional 20 days for scheduling the meetings is provided under the amended rule.

NOTES OF ADVISORY COMMITTEE ON RULES—1991 AMENDMENT

The amendment to subdivision (a) relating to the calling of the meeting of creditors in a chapter 12 case is consistent with the expedited procedures of chapter 12. Subdivision (a) is also amended to clarify that the United States trustee does not call a meeting of creditors in a chapter 9 case. Pursuant to §901(a) of the Code, §341 is inapplicable in chapter 9 cases. The other amendments to subdivisions (a), (b)(1), and (b)(2) and the additions of subdivisions (f) and (g) are derived from Rule X-1006 and conform to the 1986 amendments to §341 of the Code. The second sentence of subdivision (b)(3) is amended because Rule 2009(e) is abrogated. Although the United States trustee fixes the date for the meeting, the clerk of the bankruptcy court transmits the notice of the meeting unless the court orders otherwise, as prescribed in Rule 2002(a)(1).

Pursuant to §702 and §705 of the Code, creditors may elect a trustee and a committee in a chapter 7 case. Subdivision (b) of this rule provides that the United States trustee shall preside over any election that is held under those sections. The deletion of the last sentence of subdivision (b)(1) does not preclude creditors from recommending to the United States trustee the amount of the trustee's bond when a trustee is elected. Trustees and committees are not elected in chapter 11, 12, and 13 cases.

If an election is disputed, the United States trustee shall not resolve the dispute. For purposes of expediency, the United States trustee shall tabulate the results of the election for each alternative presented by the dispute. However, if the court finds that such tabulation is not feasible under the circumstances, the United States trustee need not tabulate the votes. If such tabulation is feasible and if the disputed vote or votes would affect the result of the election, the tabulations of votes for each alternative presented by the dispute shall be reported to the court. If a motion is made for resolution of the dispute in accordance with subdivision (d) of this rule, the court will determine the issue and another meeting to conduct the election may not be necessary.

Subdivisions (f) and (g) are derived from Rule X-1006(d) and (e), except that the amount is increased to $1,500 to conform to the amendment to Rule 2002(f).

NOTES OF ADVISORY COMMITTEE ON RULES—1993 AMENDMENT

Subdivision (a) is amended to extend by ten days the time for holding the meeting of creditors in a chapter 13 case. This extension will provide more flexibility for scheduling the meeting of creditors. Other amendments are stylistic and make no substantive change.

COMMITTEE NOTES ON RULES—1999 AMENDMENT

Subdivision (d) is amended to require the United States trustee to mail a copy of a report of a disputed election to any party in interest that has requested a copy of it. Also, if the election is for a trustee, the rule as amended will give a party in interest ten days from the filing of the report, rather than from the date of the meeting of creditors, to file a motion to resolve the dispute.

The substitution of "United States trustee" for "presiding officer" is stylistic. Section 341(a) of the Code provides that the United States trustee shall preside at the meeting of creditors. Other amendments are designed to conform to the style of Rule 2007.1(b)(3) regarding the election of a trustee in a chapter 11 case.

GAP Report on Rule 2003. No changes since publication.

COMMITTEE NOTES ON RULES—2003 AMENDMENT

The rule is amended to reflect the enactment of subchapter V of chapter 7 of the Code governing multilateral clearing organization liquidations. Section 782 of the Code provides that the designation of a trustee or alternative trustee for the case is made by the Federal Reserve Board. Therefore, the meeting of creditors in those cases cannot include the election of a trustee.

Changes Made After Publication and Comments. No changes since publication.

COMMITTEE NOTES ON RULES—2008 AMENDMENT

If the debtor has solicited acceptances to a plan before commencement of the case, §341(e), which was added to the Code by the 2005 amendments, authorizes the court, on request of a party in interest and after notice and a hearing, to order that a meeting of creditors not be convened. The rule is amended to recognize that a meeting of creditors might not be held in those cases.

Changes Made After Publication. No changes were made after publication.

COMMITTEE NOTES ON RULES—2009 AMENDMENT

The rule is amended to implement changes in connection with the amendment to Rule 9006(a) and the manner by which time is computed under the rules. The deadlines in the rule are amended to substitute a deadline that is a multiple of seven days. Throughout the rules, deadlines are amended in the following manner:

- 5-day periods become 7-day periods
- 10-day periods become 14-day periods
- 15-day periods become 14-day periods
- 20-day periods become 21-day periods
- 25-day periods become 28-day periods

Rule 2004. Examination

(a) EXAMINATION ON MOTION. On motion of any party in interest, the court may order the examination of any entity.

(b) SCOPE OF EXAMINATION. The examination of an entity under this rule or of the debtor under §343 of the Code may relate only to the acts, conduct, or property or to the liabilities and financial condition of the debtor, or to any matter which may affect the administration of the debtor's estate, or to the debtor's right to a discharge. In a family farmer's debt adjustment case under chapter 12, an individual's debt adjustment case under chapter 13, or a reorganization case under chapter 11 of the Code, other than for the reorganization of a railroad, the examination may also relate to the operation of any business and the desirability of its continuance, the source of any money or property acquired or to be acquired by the debtor for purposes of consummating a plan and the consideration given or offered therefor, and any other matter relevant to the case or to the formulation of a plan.

(c) COMPELLING ATTENDANCE AND PRODUCTION OF DOCUMENTS. The attendance of an entity for examination and for the production of documents, whether the examination is to be conducted within or without the district in which the case is pending, may be compelled as provided in Rule 9016 for the attendance of a witness at a hearing or trial. As an officer of the court, an attorney may issue and sign a subpoena on behalf of the court for the district in which the examination is to be held if the attorney is admitted to practice in that court or in the court in which the case is pending.

(d) TIME AND PLACE OF EXAMINATION OF DEBTOR. The court may for cause shown and on terms as it may impose order the debtor to be examined under this rule at any time or place it designates, whether within or without the district wherein the case is pending.

(e) MILEAGE. An entity other than a debtor shall not be required to attend as a witness unless lawful mileage and witness fee for one day's attendance shall be first tendered. If the debtor resides more than 100 miles from the place of examination when required to appear for an examination under this rule, the mileage allowed by law to a witness shall be tendered for any distance more than 100 miles from the debtor's residence at the date of the filing of the first petition commencing a case under the Code or the residence at the time the debtor is required to appear for the examination, whichever is the lesser.

(As amended Mar. 30, 1987, eff. Aug. 1, 1987; Apr. 30, 1991, eff. Aug. 1, 1991; Apr. 29, 2002, eff. Dec. 1, 2002.)

NOTES OF ADVISORY COMMITTEE ON RULES—1983

Subdivision (a) of this rule is derived from former Bankruptcy Rule 205(a). See generally 2 Collier, *Bankruptcy* ¶¶343.02, 343.08, 343.13 (15th ed. 1981). It specifies the manner of moving for an examination. The motion may be heard *ex parte* or it may be heard on notice.

Subdivision (b) is derived from former Bankruptcy Rules 205(d) and 11-26.

Subdivision (c) specifies the mode of compelling attendance of a witness or party for an examination and for the production of evidence under this rule. The subdivision is substantially declaratory of the practice that had developed under §21a of the Act. See 2 Collier, *supra* ¶343.11.

This subdivision will be applicable for the most part to the examination of a person other than the debtor. The debtor is required to appear at the meeting of creditors for examination. The word "person" includes the debtor and this subdivision may be used if necessary to obtain the debtor's attendance for examination.

Subdivision (d) is derived from former Bankruptcy Rule 205(f) and is not a limitation on subdivision (c). Any person, including the debtor, served with a subpoena within the range of a subpoena must attend for examination pursuant to subdivision (c). Subdivision (d) applies only to the debtor and a subpoena need not be issued. There are no territorial limits on the service of an order on the debtor. See, *e.g.*, *In re Totem Lodge & Country Club, Inc.*, 134 F. Supp. 158 (S.D.N.Y. 1955).

Subdivision (e) is derived from former Bankruptcy Rule 205(g). The lawful mileage and fee for attendance at a United States court as a witness are prescribed by 28 U.S.C. §1821.

Definition of debtor. The word "debtor" as used in this rule includes the persons specified in the definition in Rule 9001(5).

Spousal privilege. The limitation on the spousal privilege formerly contained in §21a of the Act is not carried over in the Code. For privileges generally, see Rule 501 of the Federal Rules of Evidence made applicable in cases under the Code by Rule 1101 thereof.

NOTES OF ADVISORY COMMITTEE ON RULES—1991 AMENDMENT

This rule is amended to allow the examination in a chapter 12 case to cover the same matters that may be covered in an examination in a chapter 11 or 13 case.

COMMITTEE NOTES ON RULES—2002 AMENDMENT

Subdivision (c) is amended to clarify that an examination ordered under Rule 2004(a) may be held outside the district in which the case is pending if the subpoena is issued by the court for the district in which the examination is to be held and is served in the manner provided in Rule 45 F. R. Civ. P., made applicable by Rule 9016.

The subdivision is amended further to clarify that, in addition to the procedures for the issuance of a subpoena set forth in Rule 45 F. R. Civ. P., an attorney may issue and sign a subpoena on behalf of the court for the district in which a Rule 2004 examination is to be held if the attorney is authorized to practice, even if admitted pro hac vice, either in the court in which the case is pending or in the court for the district in which the examination is to be held. This provision supplements the procedures for the issuance of a subpoena set forth in Rule 45(a)(3)(A) and (B) F. R. Civ. P. and is consistent with one of the purposes of the 1991 amendments to Rule 45, to ease the burdens of interdistrict law practice.

Changes Made After Publication and Comments. The typographical error was corrected, but no other changes were made.

Rule 2005. Apprehension and Removal of Debtor to Compel Attendance for Examination

(a) ORDER TO COMPEL ATTENDANCE FOR EXAMINATION. On motion of any party in interest supported by an affidavit alleging (1) that the examination of the debtor is necessary for the proper administration of the estate and that there is reasonable cause to believe that the debtor is about to leave or has left the debtor's residence or principal place of business to avoid examination, or (2) that the debtor has evaded service of a subpoena or of an order to attend for examination, or (3) that the debtor has willfully disobeyed a subpoena or order to attend for examination, duly served, the court may issue to the marshal, or some other officer authorized by law, an order directing the officer to bring the debtor before the court without unnecessary delay. If, after hearing, the court finds the allegations to be true, the court shall thereupon cause the debtor to be examined forthwith. If necessary, the court shall fix conditions for further examination and for the debtor's obedience to all orders made in reference thereto.

(b) REMOVAL. Whenever any order to bring the debtor before the court is issued under this rule and the debtor is found in a district other than that of the court issuing the order, the debtor may be taken into custody under the order and removed in accordance with the following rules:

(1) If the debtor is taken into custody under the order at a place less than 100 miles from the place of issue of the order, the debtor shall be brought forthwith before the court that issued the order.

(2) If the debtor is taken into custody under the order at a place 100 miles or more from the place of issue of the order, the debtor shall be brought without unnecessary delay before the nearest available United States magistrate judge, bankruptcy judge, or district judge. If, after hearing, the magistrate judge, bankruptcy judge, or district judge finds that an order has issued under this rule and that the person in custody is the debtor, or if the person in custody waives a hearing, the magistrate judge, bankruptcy judge, or district judge shall order removal, and the person in custody shall be released on conditions ensuring prompt appearance before the court that issued the order to compel the attendance.

(c) CONDITIONS OF RELEASE. In determining what conditions will reasonably assure attendance or obedience under subdivision (a) of this rule or appearance under subdivision (b) of this rule, the court shall be governed by the provisions and policies of title 18, U.S.C., §3146(a) and (b).

(As amended Mar. 30, 1987, eff. Aug. 1, 1987; Apr. 22, 1993, eff. Aug. 1, 1993.)

NOTES OF ADVISORY COMMITTEE ON RULES—1983

This rule is derived from former Bankruptcy Rule 206. The rule requires the debtor to be examined as soon as possible if allegations of the movant for compulsory examination under this rule are found to be true after a hearing. Subdivision (b) includes in paragraphs (1) and (2) provisions adapted from subdivisions (a) and (b) of Rule 40 of the Federal Rules of Criminal Procedure, which governs the handling of a person arrested in one district on a warrant issued in another. Subdivision (c) incorporates by reference the features of subdivisions (a) and (b) of 18 U.S.C. §3146, which prescribe standards, procedures and factors to be considered in determining conditions of release of accused persons in noncapital cases prior to trial. The word "debtor" as used in this rule includes the persons named in Rule 9001(5).

The affidavit required to be submitted in support of the motion may be subscribed by the unsworn declaration provided for in 28 U.S.C. §1746.

NOTES OF ADVISORY COMMITTEE ON RULES—1993 AMENDMENT

Subdivision (b)(2) is amended to conform to §321 of the Judicial Improvements Act of 1990, Pub. L. No. 101-650.

which changed the title of "United States magistrate" to "United States magistrate judge." Other amendments are stylistic and make no substantive change.

Rule 2006. Solicitation and Voting of Proxies in Chapter 7 Liquidation Cases

(a) APPLICABILITY. This rule applies only in a liquidation case pending under chapter 7 of the Code.

(b) DEFINITIONS.

(1) *Proxy*. A proxy is a written power of attorney authorizing any entity to vote the claim or otherwise act as the owner's attorney in fact in connection with the administration of the estate.

(2) *Solicitation of Proxy*. The solicitation of a proxy is any communication, other than one from an attorney to a regular client who owns a claim or from an attorney to the owner of a claim who has requested the attorney to represent the owner, by which a creditor is asked, directly or indirectly, to give a proxy after or in contemplation of the filing of a petition by or against the debtor.

(c) AUTHORIZED SOLICITATION.

(1) A proxy may be solicited only by (A) a creditor owning an allowable unsecured claim against the estate on the date of the filing of the petition; (B) a committee elected pursuant to §705 of the Code; (C) a committee of creditors selected by a majority in number and amount of claims of creditors (i) whose claims are not contingent or unliquidated, (ii) who are not disqualified from voting under §702(a). of the Code and (iii) who were present or represented at a meeting of which all creditors having claims of over $500 or the 100 creditors having the largest claims had at least seven days' notice in writing and of which meeting written minutes were kept and are available reporting the names of the creditors present or represented and voting and the amounts of their claims; or (D) a bona fide trade or credit association, but such association may solicit only creditors who were its members or subscribers in good standing and had allowable unsecured claims on the date of the filing of the petition.

(2) A proxy may be solicited only in writing.

(d) SOLICITATION NOT AUTHORIZED. This rule does not permit solicitation (1) in any interest other than that of general creditors; (2) by or on behalf of any custodian; (3) by the interim trustee or by or on behalf of any entity not qualified to vote under §702(a) of the Code; (4) by or on behalf of an attorney at law; or (5) by or on behalf of a transferee of a claim for collection only.

(e) DATA REQUIRED FROM HOLDERS OF MULTIPLE PROXIES. At any time before the voting commences at any meeting of creditors pursuant to §341(a) of the Code, or at any other time as the court may direct, a holder of two or more proxies shall file and transmit to the United States trustee a verified list of the proxies to be voted and a verified statement of the pertinent facts and circumstances in connection with the execution and delivery of each proxy, including:

(1) a copy of the solicitation;

(2) identification of the solicitor, the forwarder, if the forwarder is neither the solicitor nor the owner of the claim, and the proxyholder, including their connections with the debtor and with each other. If the solicitor, forwarder, or proxyholder is an association, there shall also be included a statement that the creditors whose claims have been solicited and the creditors whose claims are to be voted were members or subscribers in good standing and had allowable unsecured claims on the date of the filing of the petition. If the solicitor, forwarder, or proxyholder is a committee of creditors, the statement shall also set forth the date and place the committee was organized, that the committee was organized in accordance with clause (B) or (C) of paragraph (c)(1) of this rule, the members of the committee, the amounts of their claims, when the claims were acquired, the amounts paid therefor, and the extent to which the claims of the committee members are secured or entitled to priority;

(3) a statement that no consideration has been paid or promised by the proxyholder for the proxy;

(4) a statement as to whether there is any agreement and, if so, the particulars thereof, between the proxyholder and any other entity for the payment of any consideration in connection with voting the proxy, or for the sharing of compensation with any entity, other than a member or regular associate of the proxyholder's law firm, which may be allowed the trustee or any entity for services rendered in the case, or for the employment of any person as attorney, accountant, appraiser, auctioneer, or other employee for the estate;

(5) if the proxy was solicited by an entity other than the proxyholder, or forwarded to the holder by an entity who is neither a solicitor of the proxy nor the owner of the claim, a statement signed and verified by the solicitor or forwarder that no consideration has been paid or promised for the proxy, and whether there is any agreement, and, if so, the particulars thereof, between the solicitor or forwarder and any other entity for the payment of any consideration in connection with voting the proxy, or for sharing compensation with any entity other than a member or regular associate of the solicitor's or forwarder's law firm which may be allowed the trustee or any entity for services rendered in the case, or for the employment of any person as attorney, accountant, appraiser, auctioneer, or other employee for the estate;

(6) if the solicitor, forwarder, or proxyholder is a committee, a statement signed and verified by each member as to the amount and source of any consideration paid or to be paid to such member in connection with the case other than by way of dividend on the member's claim.

(f) ENFORCEMENT OF RESTRICTIONS ON SOLICITATION. On motion of any party in interest or on its own initiative, the court may determine whether there has been a failure to comply with the provisions of this rule or any other impropriety in connection with the solicitation or voting of a proxy. After notice and a hearing the court may reject any proxy for cause, vacate any order entered in consequence of the voting of any proxy which should have been rejected, or take any other appropriate action.

(As amended Mar. 30, 1987, eff. Aug. 1, 1987; Apr. 30, 1991, eff. Aug. 1, 1991; Mar. 26, 2009, eff. Dec. 1, 2009.)

NOTES OF ADVISORY COMMITTEE ON RULES—1983

This rule is a comprehensive regulation of solicitation and voting of proxies in liquidation cases. It is derived from former Bankruptcy Rule 208. The rule applies only in chapter 7 cases because no voting occurs, other than on a plan, in a chapter 11 case. Former Bankruptcy Rule 208 did not apply to solicitations of acceptances of plans.

Creditor control was a basic feature of the Act and is continued, in part, by the Code. Creditor democracy is perverted and the congressional objective frustrated, however, if control of administration falls into the hands of persons whose principal interest is not in what the estate can be made to yield to the unsecured creditors but in what it can yield to those involved in its administration or in other ulterior objectives.

Subdivision (b). The definition of proxy in the first paragraph of subdivision (b) is derived from former Bankruptcy Rule 208.

Subdivision (c). The purpose of the rule is to protect creditors against loss of control of administration of their debtors' estates to holders of proxies having interests that differ from those of the creditors. The rule does not prohibit solicitation but restricts it to those who were creditors at the commencement of the case or their freely and fairly selected representatives. The special role occupied by credit and trade associations is recognized in the last clause of subdivision (c)(1). On the assumption that members or subscribers may have affiliated with an association in part for the purpose of obtaining its services as a representative in liquidation proceedings, an established association is authorized to solicit its own members, or its regular customers or clients, who were creditors on the date of the filing of the petition. Although the association may not solicit nonmembers or nonsubscribers for proxies, it may sponsor a meeting of creditors at which a committee entitled to solicit proxies may be selected in accordance with clause (C) of subdivision (c)(1).

Under certain circumstances, the relationship of a creditor, creditors' committee, or association to the estate or the case may be such as to warrant rejection of any proxy solicited by such a person or group. Thus a person who is forbidden by the Code to vote his own claim should be equally disabled to solicit proxies from creditors. Solicitation by or on behalf of the debtor has been uniformly condemned, *e.g., In re White*, 15 F.2d 371 (9th Cir. 1926), as has solicitation on behalf of a preferred creditor, *Matter of Law*, 13 Am.B.R. 650 (S.D. Ill. 1905). The prohibition on solicitation by a receiver or his attorney made explicit by General Order 39 has been collaterally supported by rulings rejecting proxies solicited by a receiver in equity, *In re Western States Bldg.-Loan Ass'n*, 54 F.2d 415 (S.D. Cal. 1931), and by an assignee for the benefit of creditors, *Lines v. Falstaff Brewing Co.*, 233 F.2d 927 (9th Cir. 1956).

Subdivision (d) prohibits solicitation by any person or group having a relationship described in the preceding paragraph. It also makes no exception for attorneys or transferees of claims for collection. The rule does not undertake to regulate communications between an attorney and his regular client or between an attorney and a creditor who has asked the attorney to represent him in a proceeding under the Code, but any other communication by an attorney or any other person or group requesting a proxy from the owner of a claim constitutes a regulated solicitation. Solicitation by an attorney of a proxy from a creditor who was not a client prior to the solicitation is objectionable not only as unethical conduct as recognized by such cases as *In the Matter of Darland Company*, 184 F. Supp. 760 (S.D. Iowa 1960) but also and more importantly because the practice carries a substantial risk that administration will fall into the hands of those whose interest is in obtaining fees from the estate rather than securing dividends for creditors. The same risk attaches to solicitation by the holder of a claim for collection only.

Subdivision (e). The regulation of solicitation and voting of proxies is achieved by the rule principally through the imposition of requirements of disclosure on the holders of two or more proxies. The disclosures must be made to the clerk before the meeting at which the proxies are to be voted to afford the clerk or a party in interest an opportunity to examine the circumstances accompanying the acquisition of the proxies in advance of any exercise of the proxies. In the light of the examination the clerk or a party in interest should bring to the attention of the judge any question that arises and the judge may permit the proxies that comply with the rule to be voted and reject those that do not unless the holders can effect or establish compliance in such manner as the court shall prescribe. The holders of single proxies are excused from the disclosure requirements because of the insubstantiality of the risk that such proxies have been solicited, or will be voted, in an interest other than that of general creditors.

Every holder of two or more proxies must include in the submission a verified statement that no consideration has been paid or promised for the proxy, either by the proxyholder or the solicitor or any forwarder of the proxy. Any payment or promise of consideration for a proxy would be conclusive evidence of a purpose to acquire control of the administration of an estate for an ulterior purpose. The holder of multiple proxies must also include in the submission a verified statement as to whether there is any agreement by the holder, the solicitor, or any forwarder of the proxy for the employment of any person in the administration of an estate or for the sharing of any compensation allowed in connection with the administration of the estate. The provisions requiring these statements implement the policy of the Code expressed in §504 as well as the policy of this rule to deter the acquisition of proxies for the purpose of obtaining a share in the outlays for administration. Finally the facts as to any consideration moving or promised to any member of a committee which functions as a solicitor, forwarder, or proxyholder must be disclosed by the proxyholder. Such information would be of significance to the court in evaluating the purpose of the committee in obtaining, transmitting, or voting proxies.

Subdivision (f) has counterparts in the local rules referred to in the Advisory Committee's Note to former Bankruptcy Rule 208. Courts have been accorded a wide range of discretion in the handling of disputes involving proxies. Thus the referee was allowed to reject proxies and to proceed forthwith to hold a scheduled election at the same meeting. *E.g., In re Portage Wholesale Co.*, 183 F.2d 959 (7th Cir. 1950); *In re McGill*, 106 Fed. 57 (6th Cir. 1901); *In re Deena Woolen Mills, Inc.*, 114 F. Supp. 260, 273 (D. Me. 1953); *In re Finlay*, 3 Am.B.R. 738 (S.D.N.Y. 1900). The bankruptcy judge may postpone an election to permit a determination of issues presented by a dispute as to proxies and to afford those creditors whose proxies are rejected an opportunity to give new proxies or to attend an adjourned meeting to vote their own claims. *Cf. In the Matter of Lenrick Sales, Inc.*, 369 F.2d 439, 442–43 (3d Cir.), cert. denied, 389 U.S. 822 (1967); *In the Matter of Construction Supply Corp.* 221 F. Supp. 124, 128 (E.D. Va. 1963). This rule is not intended to restrict the scope of the court's discretion in the handling of disputes as to proxies.

NOTES OF ADVISORY COMMITTEE ON RULES—1991 AMENDMENT

This rule is amended to give the United States trustee information in connection with proxies so that the United States trustee may perform responsibilities as presiding officer at the §341 meeting of creditors. See Rule 2003.

The words "with the clerk" are deleted as unnecessary. See Rules 5005(a) and 9001(3).

COMMITTEE NOTES ON RULES—2009 AMENDMENT

The rule is amended to implement changes in connection with the amendment to Rule 9006(a) and the manner by which time is computed under the rules. The deadline in the rule is amended to substitute a deadline that is a multiple of seven days. Throughout the rules, deadlines are amended in the following manner:

- 5-day periods become 7-day periods
- 10-day periods become 14-day periods
- 15-day periods become 14-day periods
- 20-day periods become 21-day periods
- 25-day periods become 28-day periods

Rule 2007. Review of Appointment of Creditors' Committee Organized Before Commencement of the Case

(a) MOTION TO REVIEW APPOINTMENT. If a committee appointed by the United States trustee pursuant to § 1102(a) of the Code consists of the members of a committee organized by creditors before the commencement of a chapter 9 or chapter 11 case, on motion of a party in interest and after a hearing on notice to the United States trustee and other entities as the court may direct, the court may determine whether the appointment of the committee satisfies the requirements of § 1102(b)(1) of the Code.

(b) SELECTION OF MEMBERS OF COMMITTEE. The court may find that a committee organized by unsecured creditors before the commencement of a chapter 9 or chapter 11 case was fairly chosen if:

(1) it was selected by a majority in number and amount of claims of unsecured creditors who may vote under § 702(a) of the Code and were present in person or represented at a meeting of which all creditors having unsecured claims of over $1,000 or the 100 unsecured creditors having the largest claims had at least seven days' notice in writing, and of which meeting written minutes reporting the names of the creditors present or represented and voting and the amounts of their claims were kept and are available for inspection;

(2) all proxies voted at the meeting for the elected committee were solicited pursuant to Rule 2006 and the lists and statements required by subdivision (e) thereof have been transmitted to the United States trustee; and

(3) the organization of the committee was in all other respects fair and proper.

(c) FAILURE TO COMPLY WITH REQUIREMENTS FOR APPOINTMENT. After a hearing on notice pursuant to subdivision (a) of this rule, the court shall direct the United States trustee to vacate the appointment of the committee and may order other appropriate action if the court finds that such appointment failed to satisfy the requirements of § 1102(b)(1) of the Code.

(As amended Mar. 30, 1987, eff. Aug. 1, 1987; Apr. 30, 1991, eff. Aug. 1, 1991; Mar. 26, 2009, eff. Dec. 1, 2009.)

NOTES OF ADVISORY COMMITTEE ON RULES—1983

Section 1102(b)(1) of the Code permits the court to appoint as the unsecured creditors' committee, the committee that was selected by creditors before the order for relief. This provision recognizes the propriety of continuing a "prepetition" committee in an official capacity. Such a committee, however, must be found to have been fairly chosen and representative of the different kinds of claims to be represented.

Subdivision (a) does not necessarily require a hearing but does require a party in interest to bring to the court's attention the fact that a prepetition committee had been organized and should be appointed. An application would suffice for this purpose. Party in interest would include the committee, any member of the committee, or any of its agents acting for the committee. Whether or not notice of the application should be given to any other party is left to the discretion of the court.

Subdivision (b) implements § 1102(b)(1). The Code provision allows the court to appoint, as the official § 1102(a) committee, a "prepetition" committee if its members were fairly chosen and the committee is representative of the different kinds of claims. This subdivision of the rule indicates some of the factors the court may consider in determining whether the requirements of § 1102(b)(1) have been satisfied. In effect, the subdivision provides various factors which are similar to those set forth in Rule 2006 with respect to the solicitation and voting of proxies in a chapter 7 liquidation case.

NOTES OF ADVISORY COMMITTEE ON RULES—1987 AMENDMENT

The rule is amended to conform to the 1984 amendments to § 1102(b)(1) of the Code.

NOTES OF ADVISORY COMMITTEE ON RULES—1991 AMENDMENT

This rule is amended to conform to the 1986 amendments to § 1102(a). The United States trustee appoints committees pursuant to § 1102 in chapter 11 cases. Section 1102 is applicable in chapter 9 cases pursuant to § 901(a).

Although § 1102(b)(1) of the Code permits the United States trustee to appoint a prepetition committee as the statutory committee if its members were fairly chosen and it is representative of the different kinds of claims to be represented, the amendment to this rule provides a procedure for judicial review of the appointment. The factors that may be considered by the court in determining whether the committee was fairly chosen are not new. A finding that a prepetition committee has not been fairly chosen does not prohibit the appointment of some or all of its members to the creditors' committee. Although this rule deals only with judicial review of the appointment of prepetition committees, it does not preclude judicial review under Rule 2020 regarding the appointment of other committees.

COMMITTEE NOTES ON RULES—2009 AMENDMENT

The rule is amended to implement changes in connection with the amendment to Rule 9006(a) and the manner by which time is computed under the rules. The deadline in the rule is amended to substitute a deadline that is a multiple of seven days. Throughout the rules, deadlines are amended in the following manner:

- 5-day periods become 7-day periods
- 10-day periods become 14-day periods
- 15-day periods become 14-day periods
- 20-day periods become 21-day periods
- 25-day periods become 28-day periods

Rule 2007.1. Appointment of Trustee or Examiner in a Chapter 11 Reorganization Case

(a) ORDER TO APPOINT TRUSTEE OR EXAMINER. In a chapter 11 reorganization case, a motion for an order to appoint a trustee or an examiner under § 1104(a) or § 1104(c) of the Code shall be made in accordance with Rule 9014.

(b) ELECTION OF TRUSTEE.

(1) *Request for an Election.* A request to convene a meeting of creditors for the purpose of electing a trustee in a chapter 11 reorganization case shall be filed and transmitted to the United States trustee in accordance with Rule 5005 within the time prescribed by § 1104(b) of

the Code. Pending court approval of the person elected, any person appointed by the United States trustee under § 1104(d) and approved in accordance with subdivision (c) of this rule shall serve as trustee.

(2) *Manner of Election and Notice.* An election of a trustee under § 1104(b) of the Code shall be conducted in the manner provided in Rules 2003(b)(3) and 2006. Notice of the meeting of creditors convened under § 1104(b) shall be given as provided in Rule 2002. The United States trustee shall preside at the meeting. A proxy for the purpose of voting in the election may be solicited only by a committee of creditors appointed under § 1102 of the Code or by any other party entitled to solicit a proxy pursuant to Rule 2006.

(3) *Report of Election and Resolution of Disputes.*

(A) *Report of Undisputed Election.* If no dispute arises out of the election, the United States trustee shall promptly file a report certifying the election, including the name and address of the person elected and a statement that the election is undisputed. The report shall be accompanied by a verified statement of the person elected setting forth that person's connections with the debtor, creditors, any other party in interest, their respective attorneys and accountants, the United States trustee, or any person employed in the office of the United States trustee.

(B) *Dispute Arising Out of an Election.* If a dispute arises out of an election, the United States trustee shall promptly file a report stating that the election is disputed, informing the court of the nature of the dispute, and listing the name and address of any candidate elected under any alternative presented by the dispute. The report shall be accompanied by a verified statement by each candidate elected under each alternative presented by the dispute, setting forth the person's connections with the debtor, creditors, any other party in interest, their respective attorneys and accountants, the United States trustee, or any person employed in the office of the United States trustee. Not later than the date on which the report of the disputed election is filed, the United States trustee shall mail a copy of the report and each verified statement to any party in interest that has made a request to convene a meeting under § 1104(b) or to receive a copy of the report, and to any committee appointed under § 1102 of the Code.

(c) APPROVAL OF APPOINTMENT. An order approving the appointment of a trustee or an examiner under § 1104(d) of the Code shall be made on application of the United States trustee. The application shall state the name of the person appointed and, to the best of the applicant's knowledge, all the person's connections with the debtor, creditors, any other parties in interest, their respective attorneys and accountants, the United States trustee, or persons employed in the office of the United States trustee. The application shall state the names of the parties in interest with whom the United States trustee consulted regarding the appointment. The application shall be accompanied by a verified statement of the person appointed setting forth the person's connections with the debtor, creditors, any other party in interest, their respective attorneys and accountants, the United States trustee, or any person employed in the office of the United States trustee.

(Added Apr. 30, 1991, eff. Aug. 1, 1991; amended Apr. 11, 1997, eff. Dec. 1, 1997; Apr. 23, 2008, eff. Dec. 1, 2008.)

NOTES OF ADVISORY COMMITTEE ON RULES—1991

This rule is added to implement the 1986 amendments to § 1104 of the Code regarding the appointment of a trustee or examiner in a chapter 11 case. A motion for an order to appoint a trustee or examiner is a contested matter. Although the court decides whether the appointment is warranted under the particular facts of the case, it is the United States trustee who makes the appointment pursuant to § 1104(c) of the Code. The appointment is subject to approval of the court, however, which may be obtained by application of the United States trustee. Section 1104(c) of the Code requires that the appointment be made after consultation with parties in interest and that the person appointed be disinterested.

The requirement that connections with the United States trustee or persons employed in the United States trustee's office be revealed is not intended to enlarge the definition of "disinterested person" in § 101(13) of the Code, to supersede executive regulations or other laws relating to appointments by United States trustees, or to otherwise restrict the United States trustee's discretion in making appointments. This information is required, however, in the interest of full disclosure and confidence in the appointment process and to give the court all information that may be relevant to the exercise of judicial discretion in approving the appointment of a trustee or examiner in a chapter 11 case.

NOTES OF ADVISORY COMMITTEE ON RULES—1997 AMENDMENT

This rule is amended to implement the 1994 amendments to § 1104 of the Code regarding the election of a trustee in a chapter 11 case.

Eligibility for voting in an election for a chapter 11 trustee is determined in accordance with Rule 2003(b)(3). Creditors whose claims are deemed filed under § 1111(a) are treated for voting purposes as creditors who have filed proofs of claim.

Proxies for the purpose of voting in the election may be solicited only by a creditors' committee appointed under § 1102 or by any other party entitled to solicit proxies pursuant to Rule 2006. Therefore, a trustee or examiner who has served in the case, or a committee of equity security holders appointed under § 1102, may not solicit proxies.

The procedures for reporting disputes to the court derive from similar provisions in Rule 2003(d) applicable to chapter 7 cases. An election may be disputed by a party in interest or by the United States trustee. For example, if the United States trustee believes that the person elected is ineligible to serve as trustee because the person is not "disinterested," the United States trustee should file a report disputing the election.

The word "only" is deleted from subdivision (b), redesignated as subdivision (c), to avoid any negative inference with respect to the availability of procedures for obtaining review of the United States trustee's acts or failure to act pursuant to Rule 2020.

GAP Report on Rule 2017.1. The published draft of proposed new subdivision (b)(3) of Rule 2017.1 [2007.1], and the Committee Note, was substantially revised to implement Mr. Patchan's recommendations (described above), to clarify how a disputed election will be reported, and to make stylistic improvements.

COMMITTEE NOTES ON RULES—2008 AMENDMENT

Under §1104(b)(2) of the Code, as amended in 2005, if an eligible, disinterested person is elected to serve as trustee in a chapter 11 case, the United States trustee is directed to file a report certifying the election. The person elected does not have to be appointed to the position. Rather, the filing of the report certifying the election itself constitutes the appointment. The section further provides that in the event of a dispute in the election of a trustee, the court must resolve the matter. The rule is amended to be consistent with §1104(b)(2).

When the United States trustee files a report certifying the election of a trustee, the person elected must provide a verified statement, similar to the statement required of professional persons under Rule 2014, disclosing connections with parties in interest and certain other persons connected with the case. Although court approval of the person elected is not required, the disclosure of the person's connections will enable parties in interest to determine whether the person is disinterested.

Changes Made After Publication. No changes were made after publication.

Rule 2007.2. Appointment of Patient Care Ombudsman in a Health Care Business Case

(a) ORDER TO APPOINT PATIENT CARE OMBUDSMAN. In a chapter 7, chapter 9, or chapter 11 case in which the debtor is a health care business, the court shall order the appointment of a patient care ombudsman under §333 of the Code, unless the court, on motion of the United States trustee or a party in interest filed no later than 21 days after the commencement of the case or within another time fixed by the court, finds that the appointment of a patient care ombudsman is not necessary under the specific circumstances of the case for the protection of patients.

(b) MOTION FOR ORDER TO APPOINT OMBUDSMAN. If the court has found that the appointment of an ombudsman is not necessary, or has terminated the appointment, the court, on motion of the United States trustee or a party in interest, may order the appointment at a later time if it finds that the appointment has become necessary to protect patients.

(c) NOTICE OF APPOINTMENT. If a patient care ombudsman is appointed under §333, the United States trustee shall promptly file a notice of the appointment, including the name and address of the person appointed. Unless the person appointed is a State Long-Term Care Ombudsman, the notice shall be accompanied by a verified statement of the person appointed setting forth the person's connections with the debtor, creditors, patients, any other party in interest, their respective attorneys and accountants, the United States trustee, and any person employed in the office of the United States trustee.

(d) TERMINATION OF APPOINTMENT. On motion of the United States trustee or a party in interest, the court may terminate the appointment of a patient care ombudsman if the court finds that the appointment is not necessary to protect patients.

(e) MOTION. A motion under this rule shall be governed by Rule 9014. The motion shall be transmitted to the United States trustee and served on: the debtor; the trustee; any committee elected under §705 or appointed under §1102 of the Code or its authorized agent, or, if the case is a chapter 9 municipality case or a chapter 11 reorganization case and no committee of unsecured creditors has been appointed under §1102, on the creditors included on the list filed under Rule 1007(d); and such other entities as the court may direct.

(Added Apr. 23, 2008, eff. Dec. 1, 2008; amended Mar. 26, 2009, eff. Dec. 1, 2009.)

COMMITTEE NOTES ON RULES—2008

Section 333 of the Code, added by the 2005 amendments, requires the court to order the appointment of a health care ombudsman within the first 30 days of a health care business case, unless the court finds that the appointment is not necessary for the protection of patients. The rule recognizes this requirement and provides a procedure by which a party may obtain a court order finding that the appointment of a patient care ombudsman is unnecessary. In the absence of a timely motion under subdivision (a) of this rule, the court will enter an order directing the United States trustee to appoint the ombudsman.

Subdivision (b) recognizes that, despite a previous order finding that a patient care ombudsman is not necessary, circumstances of the case may change or newly discovered evidence may demonstrate the necessity of an ombudsman to protect the interests of patients. In that event, a party may move the court for an order directing the appointment of an ombudsman.

When the appointment of a patient care ombudsman is ordered, the United States trustee is required to appoint a disinterested person to serve in that capacity. Court approval of the appointment is not required, but subdivision (c) requires the person appointed, if not a State Long-Term Care Ombudsman, to file a verified statement similar to the statement filed by professional persons under Rule 2014 so that parties in interest will have information relevant to disinterestedness. If a party believes that the person appointed is not disinterested, it may file a motion asking the court to find that the person is not eligible to serve.

Subdivision (d) permits parties in interest to move for the termination of the appointment of a patient care ombudsman. If the movant can show that there no longer is any need for the ombudsman, the court may order the termination of the appointment.

Changes Made After Publication. No changes were made after publication.

COMMITTEE NOTES ON RULES—2009 AMENDMENT

The rule is amended to implement changes in connection with the amendment to Rule 9006(a) and the manner by which time is computed under the rules. The deadline in the rule is amended to substitute a deadline that is a multiple of seven days. Throughout the rules, deadlines are amended in the following manner:

- 5-day periods become 7-day periods
- 10-day periods become 14-day periods
- 15-day periods become 14-day periods
- 20-day periods become 21-day periods
- 25-day periods become 28-day periods

Rule 2008. Notice to Trustee of Selection

The United States trustee shall immediately notify the person selected as trustee how to qualify and, if applicable, the amount of the trustee's bond. A trustee that has filed a blanket bond pursuant to Rule 2010 and has been selected as trustee in a chapter 7, chapter 12, or chapter 13 case that does not notify the court and the United States trustee in writing of rejection of the office within seven days after receipt of notice of selection shall be deemed to have accepted the office. Any other person selected as trustee shall notify the court and the United States trustee in writing of acceptance of the office within seven days after receipt of notice of selection or shall be deemed to have rejected the office.

(As amended Mar. 30, 1987, eff. Aug. 1, 1987; Apr. 30, 1991, eff. Aug. 1, 1991; Mar. 26, 2009, eff. Dec. 1, 2009.)

NOTES OF ADVISORY COMMITTEE ON RULES—1983

This rule is adapted from former Bankruptcy Rule 209(c). The remainder of that rule is inapplicable because its provisions are covered by §§701–703, 321 of the Code.

If the person selected as trustee accepts the office, he must qualify within five days after his selection, as required by §322(a) of the Code.

In districts having a standing trustee for chapter 13 cases, a blanket acceptance of the appointment would be sufficient for compliance by the standing trustee with this rule.

NOTES OF ADVISORY COMMITTEE ON RULES—1987 AMENDMENT

The rule is amended to eliminate the need for a standing chapter 13 trustee or member of the panel of chapter 7 trustees to accept or reject an appointment.

NOTES OF ADVISORY COMMITTEE ON RULES—1991 AMENDMENT

The amendments to this rule relating to the United States trustee are derived from Rule X–1004(a) and conform to the 1986 amendments to the Code and 28 U.S.C. §586 which provide that the United States trustee appoints and supervises trustees, and in a chapter 7 case presides over any election of a trustee. This rule applies when a trustee is either appointed or elected. This rule is also amended to provide for chapter 12 cases.

COMMITTEE NOTES ON RULES—2009 AMENDMENT

The rule is amended to implement changes in connection with the amendment to Rule 9006(a) and the manner by which time is computed under the rules. The deadline in the rule is amended to substitute a deadline that is a multiple of seven days. Throughout the rules, deadlines are amended in the following manner:

- 5-day periods become 7-day periods
- 10-day periods become 14-day periods
- 15-day periods become 14-day periods
- 20-day periods become 21-day periods
- 25-day periods become 28-day periods

Rule 2009. Trustees for Estates When Joint Administration Ordered

(a) ELECTION OF SINGLE TRUSTEE FOR ESTATES BEING JOINTLY ADMINISTERED. If the court orders a joint administration of two or more estates under Rule 1015(b), creditors may elect a single trustee for the estates being jointly administered, unless the case is under subchapter V of chapter 7 of the Code.

(b) RIGHT OF CREDITORS TO ELECT SEPARATE TRUSTEE. Notwithstanding entry of an order for joint administration under Rule 1015(b), the creditors of any debtor may elect a separate trustee for the estate of the debtor as provided in §702 of the Code, unless the case is under subchapter V of chapter 7.

(c) APPOINTMENT OF TRUSTEES FOR ESTATES BEING JOINTLY ADMINISTERED.

(1) *Chapter 7 Liquidation Cases*. Except in a case governed by subchapter V of chapter 7, the United States trustee may appoint one or more interim trustees for estates being jointly administered in chapter 7 cases.

(2) *Chapter 11 Reorganization Cases*. If the appointment of a trustee is ordered, the United States trustee may appoint one or more trustees for estates being jointly administered in chapter 11 cases.

(3) *Chapter 12 Family Farmer's Debt Adjustment Cases*. The United States trustee may appoint one or more trustees for estates being jointly administered in chapter 12 cases.

(4) *Chapter 13 Individual's Debt Adjustment Cases*. The United States trustee may appoint one or more trustees for estates being jointly administered in chapter 13 cases.

(d) POTENTIAL CONFLICTS OF INTEREST. On a showing that creditors or equity security holders of the different estates will be prejudiced by conflicts of interest of a common trustee who has been elected or appointed, the court shall order the selection of separate trustees for estates being jointly administered.

(e) SEPARATE ACCOUNTS. The trustee or trustees of estates being jointly administered shall keep separate accounts of the property and distribution of each estate.

(As amended Mar. 30, 1987, eff. Aug. 1, 1987; Apr. 30, 1991, eff. Aug. 1, 1991; Mar. 27, 2003, eff. Dec. 1, 2003.)

NOTES OF ADVISORY COMMITTEE ON RULES—1983

This rule is applicable in chapter 7 cases and, in part, in chapter 11 and 13 cases. The provisions in subdivisions (a) and (b) concerning creditor election of a trustee apply only in a chapter 7 case because it is only pursuant to §702 of the Code that creditors may elect a trustee. Subdivision (c) of the rule applies in chapter 11 and 13 as well as chapter 7 cases; pursuant to §1104 of the Code, the court may order the appointment of a trustee on application of a party in interest and, pursuant to §1163 of the Code, the court must appoint a trustee in a railroad reorganization case. Subdivision (c) should not be taken as an indication that more than one trustee may be appointed for a single debtor. Section 1104(c) permits only one trustee for each estate. In a chapter 13 case, if there is no standing trustee, the court is to appoint a person to serve as trustee pursuant to §1302 of the Code. There is no provision for a trustee in a chapter 9 case, except for a very limited purpose; see §926 of the Code.

This rule recognizes that economical and expeditious administration of two or more estates may be facilitated not only by the selection of a single trustee for a partnership and its partners, but by such selection whenever estates are being jointly administered pursuant to Rule 1015. See *In the Matter of International Oil Co.*, 427 F.2d 186, 187 (2d Cir. 1970). The rule is derived from former §5c of the Act and former Bankruptcy Rule 210. The premise of §5c of the Act was that notwithstanding the potentiality of conflict between the interests of the creditors of the partners and those of the creditors of the partnership, the conflict is not sufficiently serious or frequent in most cases to warrant the selection of separate trustees for the firm and the several partners. Even before the proviso was added to §5c of the Act in 1938 to permit the creditors of a general partner to elect their separate trustee for his estate, it was held that the court had discretion to permit such an election or to make a separate appointment when a conflict of interest was recognized. *In re Wood*, 248 Fed. 246, 249–50 (6th Cir.), cert. denied, 247 U.S. 512 (1918); 4 Collier, *Bankruptcy* ¶723.04 (15th ed. 1980). The rule retains in subdivision (e) the features of the practice respecting the selection of a trustee that was developed under §5 of the Act. Subdivisions (a) and (c) permit the court to authorize election of a single trustee or to make a single appointment when joint administration of estates of other kinds of debtors is ordered, but subdivision (d) requires the court to make a preliminary evaluation of the risks of conflict of interest. If after the election or appointment of a common trustee a conflict of interest materializes, the court must take appropriate action to deal with it.

Subdivision (f) is derived from §5e of the Act and former Bankruptcy Rule 210(f) and requires that the common trustee keep a separate account for each estate in all cases that are jointly administered.

NOTES OF ADVISORY COMMITTEE ON RULES—1991 AMENDMENT

One or more trustees may be appointed for estates being jointly administered in chapter 12 cases.

The amendments to this rule are derived from Rule X–1005 and are necessary because the United States trustee, rather than the court, has responsibility for appointing trustees pursuant to §§701, 1104, 1202, and 1302 of the Code.

If separate trustees are ordered for chapter 7 estates pursuant to subdivision (d), separate and successor trustees should be chosen as prescribed in §703 of the Code. If the occasion for another election arises, the United States trustee should call a meeting of creditors for this purpose. An order to select separate trustees does not disqualify an appointed or elected trustee from serving for one of the estates.

Subdivision (e) is abrogated because the exercise of discretion by the United States trustee, who is in the Executive Branch, is not subject to advance restriction by rule of court. United States v. Cox, 342 F.2d 167 (5th Cir. 1965), *cert. denied*, 365 U.S. 863 (1965); United States v. Frumento, 409 F.Supp. 136, 141 (E.D.Pa.), *aff'd*, 563 F.2d 1083 (3d Cir. 1977), *cert. denied*, 434 U.S. 1072 (1977); see, Smith v. United States, 375 F.2d 243 (5th Cir. 1967); House Report No. 95–595, 95th Cong., 1st Sess. 110 (1977). However, a trustee appointed by the United States trustee may be removed by the court for cause. See §324 of the Code. Subdivision (d) of this rule, as amended, is consistent with §324. Subdivision (f) is redesignated as subdivision (e).

COMMITTEE NOTES ON RULES—2003 AMENDMENT

The rule is amended to reflect the enactment of subchapter V of chapter 7 of the Code governing multilateral clearing organization liquidations. Section 782 of the Code provides that the designation of a trustee or alternative trustee for the case is made by the Federal Reserve Board. Therefore, neither the United States trustee nor the creditors can appoint or elect a trustee in these cases.

Other amendments are stylistic.

Changes Made After Publication and Comments. No changes since publication.

Rule 2010. Qualification by Trustee; Proceeding on Bond

(a) BLANKET BOND. The United States trustee may authorize a blanket bond in favor of the United States conditioned on the faithful performance of official duties by the trustee or trustees to cover (1) a person who qualifies as trustee in a number of cases, and (2) a number of trustees each of whom qualifies in a different case.

(b) PROCEEDING ON BOND. A proceeding on the trustee's bond may be brought by any party in interest in the name of the United States for the use of the entity injured by the breach of the condition.

(As amended Mar. 30, 1987, eff. Aug. 1, 1987; Apr. 30, 1991, eff. Aug. 1, 1991.)

NOTES OF ADVISORY COMMITTEE ON RULES—1983

Subdivisions (a) and (b). Subdivision (a) gives authority for approval by the court of a single bond to cover (1) a person who qualifies as trustee in a number of cases, and (2) a number of trustees each of whom qualifies in a different case. The cases need not be related in any way. Substantial economies can be effected if a single bond covering a number of different cases can be issued and approved at one time. When a blanket bond is filed, the trustee qualifies under subdivision (b) of the rule by filing an acceptance of the office.

Subdivision (c) prescribes the evidentiary effect of a certified copy of an order approving the trustee's bond given by a trustee under this rule or, when a blanket bond has been authorized, of a certified copy of acceptance. This rule supplements the Federal Rules of Evidence, which apply in bankruptcy cases. See Rule 1101 of the Federal Rules of Evidence. The order of approval should conform to Official Form No. 25. See, however, §549(c) of the Code which provides only for the filing of the petition in the real estate records to serve as constructive notice of the pendency of the case. See also Rule 2011 which prescribes the evidentiary effect of a certificate that the debtor is a debtor in possession.

Subdivision (d) is derived from former Bankruptcy Rule 212(f). Reference should be made to §322(a) and (d) of the Code which requires the bond to be filed with the bankruptcy court and places a two year limitation for the commencement of a proceeding on the bond. A bond filed under this rule should conform to Official Form No. 25. A proceeding on the bond of a trustee is governed by the rules in Part VII. See the Note accompanying Rule 7001. See also Rule 9025.

NOTES OF ADVISORY COMMITTEE ON RULES—1987 AMENDMENT

Subdivision (b) is deleted because of the amendment to Rule 2008.

NOTES OF ADVISORY COMMITTEE ON RULES—1991 AMENDMENT

This rule is amended to conform to the 1986 amendment of §322 of the Code. The United States trustee determines the amount and sufficiency of the trustee's bond. The amendment to subdivision (a) is derived from Rule X–1004(b).

Subdivision (b) is abrogated because an order approving a bond is no longer necessary in view of the 1986 amendments to §322 of the Code. Subdivision (c) is redesignated as subdivision (b).

Rule 2011. Evidence of Debtor in Possession or Qualification of Trustee

(a) Whenever evidence is required that a debtor is a debtor in possession or that a trustee has qualified, the clerk may so certify and the certificate shall constitute conclusive evidence of that fact.

(b) If a person elected or appointed as trustee does not qualify within the time prescribed by §322(a) of the Code, the clerk shall so notify the court and the United States trustee.

(As amended Apr. 30, 1991, eff. Aug. 1, 1991.)

NOTES OF ADVISORY COMMITTEE ON RULES—1983

This rule prescribes the evidentiary effect of a certificate issued by the clerk that the debtor is a debtor in possession. See Official Form No. 26. Only chapter 11 of the Code provides for a debtor in possession. See §1107(a) of the Code. If, however, a trustee is appointed in the chapter 11 case, there will not be a debtor in possession. See §§1101(1), 1105 of the Code.

NOTES OF ADVISORY COMMITTEE ON RULES—1991 AMENDMENT

This rule is amended to provide a procedure for proving that a trustee has qualified in accordance with §322 of the Code. *Subdivision (b)* is added so that the court and the United States trustee will be informed if the person selected as trustee pursuant to §§701, 702, 1104,

1202, 1302, or 1163 fails to qualify within the time prescribed in § 322(a).

Rule 2012. Substitution of Trustee or Successor Trustee; Accounting

(a) TRUSTEE. If a trustee is appointed in a chapter 11 case or the debtor is removed as debtor in possession in a chapter 12 case, the trustee is substituted automatically for the debtor in possession as a party in any pending action, proceeding, or matter.

(b) SUCCESSOR TRUSTEE. When a trustee dies, resigns, is removed, or otherwise ceases to hold office during the pendency of a case under the Code (1) the successor is automatically substituted as a party in any pending action, proceeding, or matter; and (2) the successor trustee shall prepare, file, and transmit to the United States trustee an accounting of the prior administration of the estate.

(As amended Mar. 30, 1987, eff. Aug. 1, 1987; Apr. 30, 1991, eff. Aug. 1, 1991.)

NOTES OF ADVISORY COMMITTEE ON RULES—1983

Paragraph (1) of this rule implements §325 of the Code. It provides that a pending action or proceeding continues without abatement and that the trustee's successor is automatically substituted as a party whether it be another trustee or the debtor returned to possession, as such party.

Paragraph (2) places it within the responsibility of a successor trustee to file an accounting of the prior administration of the estate. If an accounting is impossible to obtain from the prior trustee because of death or lack of cooperation, prior reports submitted in the earlier administration may be updated.

NOTES OF ADVISORY COMMITTEE ON RULES—1987 AMENDMENT

Subdivision (a) is new. The subdivision provides for the substitution of a trustee appointed in a chapter 11 case for the debtor in possession in any pending litigation.

The original provisions of the rule are now in subdivision (b).

NOTES OF ADVISORY COMMITTEE ON RULES—1991 AMENDMENT

Subdivision (a) is amended to include any chapter 12 case in which the debtor is removed as debtor in possession pursuant to § 1204(a) of the Code.

Subdivision (b) is amended to require that the accounting of the prior administration which must be filed with the court is also transmitted to the United States trustee who is responsible for supervising the administration of cases and trustees. See 28 U.S.C. § 586(a)(3). Because a court order is not required for the appointment of a successor trustee, requiring the court to fix a time for filing the accounting is inefficient and unnecessary. The United States trustee has supervisory powers over trustees and may require the successor trustee to file the accounting within a certain time period. If the successor trustee fails to file the accounting within a reasonable time, the United States trustee or a party in interest may take appropriate steps including a request for an appropriate court order. See 28 U.S.C. § 586(a)(3)(G). The words "with the court" are deleted in subdivision (b)(2) as unnecessary. See Rules 5005(a) and 9001(3).

Rule 2013. Public Record of Compensation Awarded to Trustees, Examiners, and Professionals

(a) RECORD TO BE KEPT. The clerk shall maintain a public record listing fees awarded by the court (1) to trustees and attorneys, accountants, appraisers, auctioneers and other professionals employed by trustees, and (2) to examiners. The record shall include the name and docket number of the case, the name of the individual or firm receiving the fee and the amount of the fee awarded. The record shall be maintained chronologically and shall be kept current and open to examination by the public without charge. "Trustees," as used in this rule, does not include debtors in possession.

(b) SUMMARY OF RECORD. At the close of each annual period, the clerk shall prepare a summary of the public record by individual or firm name, to reflect total fees awarded during the preceding year. The summary shall be open to examination by the public without charge. The clerk shall transmit a copy of the summary to the United States trustee.

(As amended Mar. 30, 1987, eff. Aug. 1, 1987; Apr. 30, 1991, eff. Aug. 1, 1991.)

NOTES OF ADVISORY COMMITTEE ON RULES—1983

This rule is adapted from former Rule 213. The first sentence of that rule is omitted because of the provisions in 28 U.S.C. §§ 586 and 604(f) creating panels of private trustees.

The rule is not applicable to standing trustees serving in chapter 13 cases. See § 1302 of the Code.

A basic purpose of the rule is to prevent what Congress has defined as "cronyism." Appointment or employment, whether in a chapter 7 or 11 case, should not center among a small select group of individuals unless the circumstances are such that it would be warranted. The public record of appointments to be kept by the clerk will provide a means for monitoring the appointment process.

Subdivision (b) provides a convenient source for public review of fees paid from debtors' estates in the bankruptcy courts. Thus, public recognition of appointments, fairly distributed and based on professional qualifications and expertise, will be promoted and notions of improper favor dispelled. This rule is in keeping with the findings of the Congressional subcommittees as set forth in the House Report of the Committee on the Judiciary, No. 95–595, 95th Cong., 1st Sess. 89–99 (1977). These findings included the observations that there were frequent appointments of the same person, contacts developed between the bankruptcy bar and the courts, and an unusually close relationship between the bar and the judges developed over the years. A major purpose of the new statute is to dilute these practices and instill greater public confidence in the system. Rule 2013 implements that laudatory purpose.

NOTES OF ADVISORY COMMITTEE ON RULES—1987 AMENDMENT

In subdivisions (b) and (c) the word awarded is substituted for the word paid. While clerks do not know if fees are paid, they can determine what fees are awarded by the court.

NOTES OF ADVISORY COMMITTEE ON RULES—1991 AMENDMENT

Subdivision (a) is deleted. The matter contained in this subdivision is more properly left for regulation by the United States trustee. When appointing trustees and examiners and when monitoring applications for employment of auctioneers, appraisers and other professionals, the United States trustee should be sensitive to disproportionate or excessive fees received by any person.

Subdivision (b), redesignated as subdivision (a), is amended to reflect the fact that the United States trustee appoints examiners subject to court approval.

Subdivision (c), redesignated as subdivision (b), is amended to furnish the United States trustee with a copy of the annual summary which may assist that office in the performance of its responsibilities under 28 U.S.C. §586 and the Code.

The rule is not applicable to standing trustees serving in chapter 12 cases. See §1202 of the Code.

Rule 2014. Employment of Professional Persons

(a) APPLICATION FOR AND ORDER OF EMPLOYMENT. An order approving the employment of attorneys, accountants, appraisers, auctioneers, agents, or other professionals pursuant to §327, §1103, or §1114 of the Code shall be made only on application of the trustee or committee. The application shall be filed and, unless the case is a chapter 9 municipality case, a copy of the application shall be transmitted by the applicant to the United States trustee. The application shall state the specific facts showing the necessity for the employment, the name of the person to be employed, the reasons for the selection, the professional services to be rendered, any proposed arrangement for compensation, and, to the best of the applicant's knowledge, all of the person's connections with the debtor, creditors, any other party in interest, their respective attorneys and accountants, the United States trustee, or any person employed in the office of the United States trustee. The application shall be accompanied by a verified statement of the person to be employed setting forth the person's connections with the debtor, creditors, any other party in interest, their respective attorneys and accountants, the United States trustee, or any person employed in the office of the United States trustee.

(b) SERVICES RENDERED BY MEMBER OR ASSOCIATE OF FIRM OF ATTORNEYS OR ACCOUNTANTS. If, under the Code and this rule, a law partnership or corporation is employed as an attorney, or an accounting partnership or corporation is employed as an accountant, or if a named attorney or accountant is employed, any partner, member, or regular associate of the partnership, corporation, or individual may act as attorney or accountant so employed, without further order of the court.

(As amended Mar. 30, 1987, eff. Aug. 1, 1987; Apr. 30, 1991, eff. Aug. 1, 1991.)

NOTES OF ADVISORY COMMITTEE ON RULES—1983

Subdivision (a) is adapted from the second sentence of former Bankruptcy Rule 215(a). The remainder of that rule is covered by §327 of the Code.

Subdivision (b) is derived from former Bankruptcy Rule 215(f). The compensation provisions are set forth in §504 of the Code.

NOTES OF ADVISORY COMMITTEE ON RULES—1991 AMENDMENT

This rule is amended to include retention of professionals by committees of retired employees pursuant to §1114 of the Code.

The United States trustee monitors applications filed under §327 of the Code and may file with the court comments with respect to the approval of such applications. See 28 U.S.C. §586(a)(3)(H). The United States trustee also monitors creditors' committees in accordance with 28 U.S.C. §586(a)(3)(E). The addition of the second sentence of subdivision (a) is designed to enable the United States trustee to perform these duties.

Subdivision (a) is also amended to require disclosure of the professional's connections with the United States trustee or persons employed in the United States trustee's office. This requirement is not intended to prohibit the employment of such persons in all cases or to enlarge the definition of "disinterested person" in §101(13) of the Code. However, the court may consider a connection with the United States trustee's office as a factor when exercising its discretion. Also, this information should be revealed in the interest of full disclosure and confidence in the bankruptcy system, especially since the United States trustee monitors and may be heard on applications for compensation and reimbursement of professionals employed under this rule.

The United States trustee appoints committees pursuant to §1102 of the Code which is applicable in chapter 9 cases under §901. In the interest of full disclosure and confidence in the bankruptcy system, a connection between the United States trustee and a professional employed by the committee should be revealed in every case, including a chapter 9 case. However, since the United States trustee does not have any role in the employment of professionals in chapter 9 cases, it is not necessary in such cases to transmit to the United States trustee a copy of the application under subdivision (a) of this rule. See 28 U.S.C. §586(a)(3)(H).

Rule 2015. Duty to Keep Records, Make Reports, and Give Notice of Case or Change of Status

(a) TRUSTEE OR DEBTOR IN POSSESSION. A trustee or debtor in possession shall:

(1) in a chapter 7 liquidation case and, if the court directs, in a chapter 11 reorganization case file and transmit to the United States trustee a complete inventory of the property of the debtor within 30 days after qualifying as a trustee or debtor in possession, unless such an inventory has already been filed;

(2) keep a record of receipts and the disposition of money and property received;

(3) file the reports and summaries required by §704(8) of the Code which shall include a statement, if payments are made to employees, of the amounts of deductions for all taxes required to be withheld or paid for and in behalf of employees and the place where these amounts are deposited;

(4) as soon as possible after the commencement of the case, give notice of the case to every entity known to be holding money or property subject to withdrawal or order of the debtor, including every bank, savings or building and loan association, public utility company, and landlord with whom the debtor has a deposit, and to every insurance company which has issued a policy having a cash surrender value payable to the debtor, except that notice need not be given to any entity who has knowledge or has previously been notified of the case;

(5) in a chapter 11 reorganization case, on or before the last day of the month after each calendar quarter during which there is a duty to pay fees under 28 U.S.C. §1930(a)(6), file and transmit to the United States trustee a statement of any disbursements made during that quarter and of any fees payable under 28 U.S.C. §1930(a)(6) for that quarter; and

(6) in a chapter 11 small business case, unless the court, for cause, sets another reporting interval, file and transmit to the United States trustee for each calendar month after the order for relief, on the appropriate Official Form, the report required by §308. If the order for relief is within the first 15 days of a cal-

endar month, a report shall be filed for the portion of the month that follows the order for relief. If the order for relief is after the 15th day of a calendar month, the period for the remainder of the month shall be included in the report for the next calendar month. Each report shall be filed no later than 21 days after the last day of the calendar month following the month covered by the report. The obligation to file reports under this subparagraph terminates on the effective date of the plan, or conversion or dismissal of the case.

(b) CHAPTER 12 TRUSTEE AND DEBTOR IN POSSESSION. In a chapter 12 family farmer's debt adjustment case, the debtor in possession shall perform the duties prescribed in clauses (2)–(4) of subdivision (a) of this rule and, if the court directs, shall file and transmit to the United States trustee a complete inventory of the property of the debtor within the time fixed by the court. If the debtor is removed as debtor in possession, the trustee shall perform the duties of the debtor in possession prescribed in this paragraph.

(c) CHAPTER 13 TRUSTEE AND DEBTOR.

(1) *Business Cases.* In a chapter 13 individual's debt adjustment case, when the debtor is engaged in business, the debtor shall perform the duties prescribed by clauses (2)–(4) of subdivision (a) of this rule and, if the court directs, shall file and transmit to the United States trustee a complete inventory of the property of the debtor within the time fixed by the court.

(2) *Nonbusiness Cases.* In a chapter 13 individual's debt adjustment case, when the debtor is not engaged in business, the trustee shall perform the duties prescribed by clause (2) of subdivision (a) of this rule.

(d) FOREIGN REPRESENTATIVE. In a case in which the court has granted recognition of a foreign proceeding under chapter 15, the foreign representative shall file any notice required under §1518 of the Code within 14 days after the date when the representative becomes aware of the subsequent information.

(e) TRANSMISSION OF REPORTS. In a chapter 11 case the court may direct that copies or summaries of annual reports and copies or summaries of other reports shall be mailed to the creditors, equity security holders, and indenture trustees. The court may also direct the publication of summaries of any such reports. A copy of every report or summary mailed or published pursuant to this subdivision shall be transmitted to the United States trustee.

(As amended Mar. 30, 1987, eff. Aug. 1, 1987; Apr. 30, 1991, eff. Aug. 1, 1991; Apr. 23, 1996, eff. Dec. 1, 1996; Apr. 29, 2002, eff. Dec. 1, 2002; Apr. 23, 2008, eff. Dec. 1, 2008; Mar. 26, 2009, eff. Dec. 1, 2009.)

NOTES OF ADVISORY COMMITTEE ON RULES—1983

This rule combines the provisions found in former Rules 218, 10–208, 11–30 and 13–208 of the Rules of Bankruptcy Procedure. It specifies various duties which are in addition to those required by §§704, 1106, 1302 and 1304 of the Code.

In *subdivision (a)* the times permitted to be fixed by the court in clause (3) for the filing of reports and summaries may be fixed by local rule or order.

Subdivision (b). This subdivision prescribes duties on either the debtor or trustee in chapter 13 cases, depending on whether or not the debtor is engaged in business (§1304 of the Code). The duty of giving notice prescribed by subdivision (a)(4) is not included in a nonbusiness case because of its impracticability.

Subdivision (c) is derived from former Chapter X Rule 10–208(c) which, in turn, was derived from §190 of the Act. The equity security holders to whom the reports should be sent are those of record at the time of transmittal of such reports.

NOTES OF ADVISORY COMMITTEE ON RULES—1987 AMENDMENT

Subdivision (a) is amended to add as a duty of the trustee or debtor in possession the filing of a notice of or a copy of the petition. The filing of such notice or a copy of the petition is essential to the protection of the estate from unauthorized post-petition conveyances of real property. Section 549(c) of the Code protects the title of a good faith purchaser for fair equivalent value unless the notice or copy of the petition is filed.

NOTES OF ADVISORY COMMITTEE ON RULES—1991 AMENDMENT

This rule is amended to provide the United States trustee with information needed to perform supervisory responsibilities in accordance with 28 U.S.C. §586(a)(3) and to exercise the right to raise, appear and be heard on issues pursuant to §307 of the Code.

Subdivision (a)(3) is amended to conform to the 1986 amendments to §704(8) of the Code and the United States trustee system. It may not be necessary for the court to fix a time to file reports if the United States trustee requests that they be filed within a specified time and there is no dispute regarding such time.

Subdivision (a)(5) is deleted because the filing of a notice of or copy of the petition to protect real property against unauthorized postpetition transfers in a particular case is within the discretion of the trustee.

The new subdivision (a)(5) was added to enable the United States trustee, parties in interest, and the court to determine the appropriate quarterly fee required by 28 U.S.C. §1930(a)(6). The requirements of subdivision (a)(5) should be satisfied whenever possible by including this information in other reports filed by the trustee or debtor in possession. Nonpayment of the fee may result in dismissal or conversion of the case pursuant to §1112(b) of the Code.

Rule X–1007(b), which provides that the trustee or debtor in possession shall cooperate with the United States trustee by furnishing information that the United States trustee reasonably requires, is deleted as unnecessary. The deletion of Rule X–1007(b) should not be construed as a limitation of the powers of the United States trustee or of the duty of the trustee or debtor in possession to cooperate with the United States trustee in the performance of the statutory responsibilities of that office.

Subdivision (a)(6) is abrogated as unnecessary. See §1106(a)(7) of the Code.

Subdivision (a)(7) is abrogated. The closing of a chapter 11 case is governed by Rule 3022.

New *subdivision (b)*, which prescribes the duties of the debtor in possession and trustee in a chapter 12 case, does not prohibit additional reporting requirements pursuant to local rule or court order.

NOTES OF ADVISORY COMMITTEE ON RULES—1996 AMENDMENT

Subdivision (a)(1) provides that the trustee in a chapter 7 case and, if the court directs, the trustee or debtor in possession in a chapter 11 case, is required to file and transmit to the United States trustee a complete inventory of the debtor's property within 30 days after qualifying as trustee or debtor in possession, unless such an inventory has already been filed. Subdivisions (b) and (c) are amended to clarify that a debtor in possession and trustee in a chapter 12 case, and a debtor in a chapter 13 case where the debtor is engaged in business, are not required to file and transmit to the United States trustee a complete inventory of the property of the debtor unless the court so directs. If the court so directs, the court also fixes the time limit for filing and transmitting the inventory.

GAP Report on Rule 2015. No changes since publication, except for a stylistic change in the first sentence of the committee note.

COMMITTEE NOTES ON RULES—2002 AMENDMENT

Subdivision (a)(5) is amended to provide that the duty to file quarterly disbursement reports continues only so long as there is an obligation to make quarterly payments to the United States trustee under 28 U.S.C. §1930(a)(6).

Other amendments are stylistic.

Changes Made After Publication and Comments. No changes were made.

COMMITTEE NOTES ON RULES—2008 AMENDMENT

Subparagraph (a)(6) implements §308 of the Code, added by the 2005 amendments. That section requires small business chapter 11 debtors to file periodic financial and operating reports, and the rule sets the time for filing those reports and requires the use of an Official Form for the report. The obligation to file reports under this rule does not relieve the trustee or debtor of any other obligations to provide information or documents to the United States trustee.

The rule also is amended to fix the time for the filing of notices under §1518, added to the Code in 2005. Former subdivision (d) is renumbered as subdivision (e).

Other changes are stylistic.

Changes Made After Publication. No changes were made after publication.

COMMITTEE NOTES ON RULES—2009 AMENDMENT

The rule is amended to implement changes in connection with the amendment to Rule 9006(a) and the manner by which time is computed under the rules. The deadlines in the rule are amended to substitute a deadline that is a multiple of seven days. Throughout the rules, deadlines are amended in the following manner:

- 5-day periods become 7-day periods
- 10-day periods become 14-day periods
- 15-day periods become 14-day periods
- 20-day periods become 21-day periods
- 25-day periods become 28-day periods

Rule 2015.1. Patient Care Ombudsman

(a) REPORTS. A patient care ombudsman, at least 14 days before making a report under §333(b)(2) of the Code, shall give notice that the report will be made to the court, unless the court orders otherwise. The notice shall be transmitted to the United States trustee, posted conspicuously at the health care facility that is the subject of the report, and served on: the debtor; the trustee; all patients; and any committee elected under §705 or appointed under §1102 of the Code or its authorized agent, or, if the case is a chapter 9 municipality case or a chapter 11 reorganization case and no committee of unsecured creditors has been appointed under §1102, on the creditors included on the list filed under Rule 1007(d); and such other entities as the court may direct. The notice shall state the date and time when the report will be made, the manner in which the report will be made, and, if the report is in writing, the name, address, telephone number, email address, and website, if any, of the person from whom a copy of the report may be obtained at the debtor's expense.

(b) AUTHORIZATION TO REVIEW CONFIDENTIAL PATIENT RECORDS. A motion by a patient care ombudsman under §333(c) to review confidential patient records shall be governed by Rule 9014, served on the patient and any family member or other contact person whose name and address have been given to the trustee or the debtor for the purpose of providing information regarding the patient's health care, and transmitted to the United States trustee subject to applicable nonbankruptcy law relating to patient privacy. Unless the court orders otherwise, a hearing on the motion may not be commenced earlier than 14 days after service of the motion.

(Added Apr. 23, 2008, eff. Dec. 1, 2008; amended Mar. 26, 2009, eff. Dec. 1, 2009.)

COMMITTEE NOTES ON RULES—2008

This rule is new and implements §333 of the Code, added by the 2005 amendments. Subdivision (a) is designed to give parties in interest, including patients or their representatives, sufficient notice so that they will be able to review written reports or attend hearings at which reports are made. The rule permits a notice to relate to a single report or to periodic reports to be given during the case. For example, the ombudsman may give notice that reports will be made at specified intervals or dates during the case.

Subdivision (a) of the rule also requires that the notice be posted conspicuously at the health care facility in a place where it will be seen by patients and their families or others visiting the patients. This may require posting in common areas and patient rooms within the facility. Because health care facilities and the patients they serve can vary greatly, the locations of the posted notice should be tailored to the specific facility that is the subject of the report.

Subdivision (b) requires the ombudsman to notify the patient and the United States trustee that the ombudsman is seeking access to confidential patient records so that they will be able to appear and be heard on the matter. This procedure should assist the court in reaching its decision both as to access to the records and appropriate restrictions on that access to ensure continued confidentiality. Notices given under this rule are subject to the provisions of applicable federal and state law that relate to the protection of patients' privacy, such as the Health Insurance Portability and Accountability Act of 1996, Pub. L. No. 104–191 (HIPAA).

Changes Made After Publication. Two stylistic changes were made to the rule. The reference to the court's authority to order otherwise was moved from the beginning to the end of the first sentence of subdivision (a). On line 19, the word "patient" was substituted for "health" to be consistent with the Code.

COMMITTEE NOTES ON RULES—2009 AMENDMENT

The rule is amended to implement changes in connection with the amendment to Rule 9006(a) and the manner by which time is computed under the rules. The deadlines in the rule are amended to substitute a deadline that is a multiple of seven days. Throughout the rules, deadlines are amended in the following manner:

- 5-day periods become 7-day periods
- 10-day periods become 14-day periods
- 15-day periods become 14-day periods
- 20-day periods become 21-day periods
- 25-day periods become 28-day periods

Rule 2015.2. Transfer of Patient in Health Care Business Case

Unless the court orders otherwise, if the debtor is a health care business, the trustee may not transfer a patient to another health care business under §704(a)(12) of the Code unless the trustee gives at least 14 days' notice of the transfer to the patient care ombudsman, if any, the patient, and any family member or other contact person whose name and address has been given to the trustee or the debtor for the purpose of providing information regarding the patient's health care. The notice is subject to applicable nonbankruptcy law relating to patient privacy.

(Added Apr. 23, 2008, eff. Dec. 1, 2008; amended Mar. 26, 2009, eff. Dec. 1, 2009.)

COMMITTEE NOTES ON RULES—2008

This rule is new. Section 704(a)(12), added to the Code by the 2005 amendments, authorizes the trustee to relocate patients when a health care business debtor's facility is in the process of being closed. The Code permits the trustee to take this action without the need for any court order, but the notice required by this rule will enable a patient care ombudsman appointed under §333, or a patient who contends that the trustee's actions violate §704(a)(12), to have those issues resolved before the patient is transferred.

This rule also permits the court to enter an order dispensing with or altering the notice requirement in proper circumstances. For example, a facility could be closed immediately, or very quickly, such that 10 days' notice would not be possible in some instances. In that event, the court may shorten the time required for notice.

Notices given under this rule are subject to the provisions of applicable federal and state law that relate to the protection of patients' privacy, such as the Health Insurance Portability and Accountability Act of 1996, Pub. L. No. 104–191 (HIPAA).

Changes Made After Publication. No changes were made after publication.

COMMITTEE NOTES ON RULES—2009 AMENDMENT

The rule is amended to implement changes in connection with the amendment to Rule 9006(a) and the manner by which time is computed under the rules. The deadline in the rule is amended to substitute a deadline that is a multiple of seven days. Throughout the rules, deadlines are amended in the following manner:

- 5-day periods become 7-day periods
- 10-day periods become 14-day periods
- 15-day periods become 14-day periods
- 20-day periods become 21-day periods
- 25-day periods become 28-day periods

Rule 2015.3. Reports of Financial Information on Entities in Which a Chapter 11 Estate Holds a Controlling or Substantial Interest

(a) REPORTING REQUIREMENT. In a chapter 11 case, the trustee or debtor in possession shall file periodic financial reports of the value, operations, and profitability of each entity that is not a publicly traded corporation or a debtor in a case under title 11, and in which the estate holds a substantial or controlling interest. The reports shall be prepared as prescribed by the appropriate Official Form, and shall be based upon the most recent information reasonably available to the trustee or debtor in possession.

(b) TIME FOR FILING; SERVICE. The first report required by this rule shall be filed no later than seven days before the first date set for the meeting of creditors under §341 of the Code. Subsequent reports shall be filed no less frequently than every six months thereafter, until the effective date of a plan or the case is dismissed or converted. Copies of the report shall be served on the United States trustee, any committee appointed under §1102 of the Code, and any other party in interest that has filed a request therefor.

(c) PRESUMPTION OF SUBSTANTIAL OR CONTROLLING INTEREST; JUDICIAL DETERMINATION. For purposes of this rule, an entity of which the estate controls or owns at least a 20 percent interest, shall be presumed to be an entity in which the estate has a substantial or controlling interest. An entity in which the estate controls or owns less than a 20 percent interest shall be presumed not to be an entity in which the estate has a substantial or controlling interest. Upon motion, the entity, any holder of an interest therein, the United States trustee, or any other party in interest may seek to rebut either presumption, and the court shall, after notice and a hearing, determine whether the estate's interest in the entity is substantial or controlling.

(d) MODIFICATION OF REPORTING REQUIREMENT. The court may, after notice and a hearing, vary the reporting requirement established by subdivision (a) of this rule for cause, including that the trustee or debtor in possession is not able, after a good faith effort, to comply with those reporting requirements, or that the information required by subdivision (a) is publicly available.

(e) NOTICE AND PROTECTIVE ORDERS. No later than 14 days before filing the first report required by this rule, the trustee or debtor in possession shall send notice to the entity in which the estate has a substantial or controlling interest, and to all holders—known to the trustee or debtor in possession—of an interest in that entity, that the trustee or debtor in possession expects to file and serve financial information relating to the entity in accordance with this rule. The entity in which the estate has a substantial or controlling interest, or a person holding an interest in that entity, may request protection of the information under §107 of the Code.

(f) EFFECT OF REQUEST. Unless the court orders otherwise, the pendency of a request under subdivisions (c), (d), or (e) of this rule shall not alter or stay the requirements of subdivision (a).

(Added Apr. 23, 2008, eff. Dec. 1, 2008; amended Mar. 26, 2009, eff. Dec. 1, 2009.)

COMMITTEE NOTES ON RULES—2008

This rule implements §419 of the Bankruptcy Abuse Prevention and Consumer Protection Act of 2005 ("BAPCPA"). Reports are to be made on the appropriate Official Form. While §419 of BAPCPA places the obligation to report upon the "debtor," this rule extends the obligation to include cases in which a trustee has been appointed. The court can order that the reports not be filed in appropriate circumstances, such as when the information that would be included in these reports is already available to interested parties.

Changes After Publication. In subdivision (e), the 20 day period was changed to 14 days. This better reconciles the timing of the notice and the scheduling of the §341 meeting of creditors, and it is also consistent with the upcoming time computation amendments.

COMMITTEE NOTES ON RULES—2009 AMENDMENT

The rule is amended to implement changes in connection with the amendment to Rule 9006(a) and the manner by which time is computed under the rules. The deadline in the rule is amended to substitute a deadline that is a multiple of seven days. Throughout the rules, deadlines are amended in the following manner:

- 5-day periods become 7-day periods
- 10-day periods become 14-day periods

- 15-day periods become 14-day periods
- 20-day periods become 21-day periods
- 25-day periods become 28-day periods

Rule 2016. Compensation for Services Rendered and Reimbursement of Expenses

(a) APPLICATION FOR COMPENSATION OR REIMBURSEMENT. An entity seeking interim or final compensation for services, or reimbursement of necessary expenses, from the estate shall file an application setting forth a detailed statement of (1) the services rendered, time expended and expenses incurred, and (2) the amounts requested. An application for compensation shall include a statement as to what payments have theretofore been made or promised to the applicant for services rendered or to be rendered in any capacity whatsoever in connection with the case, the source of the compensation so paid or promised, whether any compensation previously received has been shared and whether an agreement or understanding exists between the applicant and any other entity for the sharing of compensation received or to be received for services rendered in or in connection with the case, and the particulars of any sharing of compensation or agreement or understanding therefor, except that details of any agreement by the applicant for the sharing of compensation as a member or regular associate of a firm of lawyers or accountants shall not be required. The requirements of this subdivision shall apply to an application for compensation for services rendered by an attorney or accountant even though the application is filed by a creditor or other entity. Unless the case is a chapter 9 municipality case, the applicant shall transmit to the United States trustee a copy of the application.

(b) DISCLOSURE OF COMPENSATION PAID OR PROMISED TO ATTORNEY FOR DEBTOR. Every attorney for a debtor, whether or not the attorney applies for compensation, shall file and transmit to the United States trustee within 14 days after the order for relief, or at another time as the court may direct, the statement required by §329 of the Code including whether the attorney has shared or agreed to share the compensation with any other entity. The statement shall include the particulars of any such sharing or agreement to share by the attorney, but the details of any agreement for the sharing of the compensation with a member or regular associate of the attorney's law firm shall not be required. A supplemental statement shall be filed and transmitted to the United States trustee within 14 days after any payment or agreement not previously disclosed.

(c) DISCLOSURE OF COMPENSATION PAID OR PROMISED TO BANKRUPTCY PETITION PREPARER. Before a petition is filed, every bankruptcy petition preparer for a debtor shall deliver to the debtor, the declaration under penalty of perjury required by §110(h)(2). The declaration shall disclose any fee, and the source of any fee, received from or on behalf of the debtor within 12 months of the filing of the case and all unpaid fees charged to the debtor. The declaration shall also describe the services performed and documents prepared or caused to be prepared by the bankruptcy petition preparer. The declaration shall be filed with the petition. The petition preparer shall file a supplemental statement within 14 days after any payment or agreement not previously disclosed.

(As amended Mar. 30, 1987, eff. Aug. 1, 1987; Apr. 30, 1991, eff. Aug. 1, 1991; Mar. 27, 2003, eff. Dec. 1, 2003; Mar. 26, 2009, eff. Dec. 1, 2009.)

NOTES OF ADVISORY COMMITTEE ON RULES—1983

This rule is derived from former Rule 219. Many of the former rule's requirements are, however, set forth in the Code. Section 329 requires disclosure by an attorney of transactions with the debtor. §330 sets forth the bases for allowing compensation, and §504 prohibits sharing of compensation. This rule implements those various provisions.

Subdivision (a) includes within its provisions a committee, member thereof, agent, attorney or accountant for the committee when compensation or reimbursement of expenses is sought from the estate.

Regular associate of a law firm is defined in Rule 9001(9) to include any attorney regularly employed by, associated with, or counsel to that law firm. Firm is defined in Rule 9001(6) to include a partnership or professional corporation.

NOTES OF ADVISORY COMMITTEE ON RULES—1987 AMENDMENT

Subdivision (a) is amended to change "person" to "entity". There are occasions in which a governmental unit may be entitled to file an application under this rule. The requirement that the application contain a "detailed statement of services rendered, time expended and expenses incurred" gives to the court authority to ensure that the application is both comprehensive and detailed. No amendments are made to delineate further the requirements of the application because the amount of detail to be furnished is a function of the nature of the services rendered and the complexity of the case.

Subdivision (b) is amended to require that the attorney for the debtor file the §329 statement before the meeting of creditors. This will assist the parties in conducting the examination of the debtor. In addition the amended rule requires the attorney to supplement the §329 statement if an undisclosed payment is made to the attorney or a new or amended agreement is entered into by the debtor and the attorney.

NOTES OF ADVISORY COMMITTEE ON RULES—1991 AMENDMENT

Subdivision (a) is amended to enable the United States trustee to perform the duty to monitor applications for compensation and reimbursement filed under §330 of the Code. See 28 U.S.C. §586(a)(3)(A).

Subdivision (b) is amended to give the United States trustee the information needed to determine whether to request appropriate relief based on excessive fees under §329(b) of the Code. See Rule 2017.

The words "with the court" are deleted in subdivisions (a) and (b) as unnecessary. See Rules 5005(a) and 9001(3).

COMMITTEE NOTES ON RULES—2003 AMENDMENT

This rule is amended by adding subdivision (c) to implement §110(h)(1) of the Code.

Changes Made After Publication and Comments. No changes since publication.

COMMITTEE NOTES ON RULES—2009 AMENDMENT

The rule is amended to implement changes in connection with the amendment to Rule 9006(a) and the manner by which time is computed under the rules. The deadline in the rule is amended to substitute a deadline that is a multiple of seven days. Throughout the rules, deadlines are amended in the following manner:

- 5-day periods become 7-day periods
- 10-day periods become 14-day periods

- 15-day periods become 14-day periods
- 20-day periods become 21-day periods
- 25-day periods become 28-day periods

Subdivision (c) is amended to reflect the 2005 amendment to §110(h)(1) of the Bankruptcy Code which now requires that the declaration be filed with the petition. The statute previously required that the petition preparer file the declaration within 10 days after the filing of the petition. The amendment to the rule also corrects the cross reference to §110(h)(1), which was redesignated as subparagraph (h)(2) of §110 by the 2005 amendment to the Code.

Other changes are stylistic.

Rule 2017. Examination of Debtor's Transactions with Debtor's Attorney

(a) PAYMENT OR TRANSFER TO ATTORNEY BEFORE ORDER FOR RELIEF. On motion by any party in interest or on the court's own initiative, the court after notice and a hearing may determine whether any payment of money or any transfer of property by the debtor, made directly or indirectly and in contemplation of the filing of a petition under the Code by or against the debtor or before entry of the order for relief in an involuntary case, to an attorney for services rendered or to be rendered is excessive.

(b) PAYMENT OR TRANSFER TO ATTORNEY AFTER ORDER FOR RELIEF. On motion by the debtor, the United States trustee, or on the court's own initiative, the court after notice and a hearing may determine whether any payment of money or any transfer of property, or any agreement therefor, by the debtor to an attorney after entry of an order for relief in a case under the Code is excessive, whether the payment or transfer is made or is to be made directly or indirectly, if the payment, transfer, or agreement therefor is for services in any way related to the case.

(As amended Mar. 30, 1987, eff. Aug. 1, 1987; Apr. 30, 1991, eff. Aug. 1, 1991.)

NOTES OF ADVISORY COMMITTEE ON RULES—1983

This rule is derived from §60d of the Act and former Bankruptcy Rule 220 and implements §329 of the Code. Information required to be disclosed by the attorney for a debtor by §329 of the Code and by the debtor in his Statement of Financial Affairs (Item 15 of Form No. 7, Item 20 of Form No. 8) will assist the court in determining whether to proceed under this rule. Section 60d was enacted in recognition of "the temptation of a failing debtor to deal too liberally with his property in employing counsel to protect him in view of financial reverses and probable failure." *In re Wood & Henderson*, 210 U.S. 246, 253 (1908). This rule, like §60d of the Act and §329 of the Code, is premised on the need for and appropriateness of judicial scrutiny of arrangements between a debtor and his attorney to protect the creditors of the estate and the debtor against overreaching by an officer of the court who is in a peculiarly advantageous position to impose on both the creditors and his client. 2 Collier, *Bankruptcy* ¶329.02 (15th ed. 1980); MacLachlan, *Bankruptcy* 318 (1956). Rule 9014 applies to any contested matter arising under this rule.

This rule is not to be construed to permit post-petition payments or transfers which may be avoided under other provisions of the Code.

NOTES OF ADVISORY COMMITTEE ON RULES—1991 AMENDMENT

This rule is amended to include within subdivision (a) a payment or transfer of property by the debtor to an attorney after the filing of an involuntary petition but before the order for relief. Any party in interest should be able to make a motion for a determination of whether such payment or transfer is excessive because the funds or property transferred may be property of the estate.

The United States trustee supervises and monitors the administration of bankruptcy cases other than chapter 9 cases and pursuant to §307 of the Code may raise, appear and be heard on issues relating to fees paid to the debtor's attorney. It is consistent with that role to expect the United States trustee to review statements filed under Rule 2016(b) and to file motions relating to excessive fees pursuant to §329 of the Code.

Rule 2018. Intervention; Right to Be Heard

(a) PERMISSIVE INTERVENTION. In a case under the Code, after hearing on such notice as the court directs and for cause shown, the court may permit any interested entity to intervene generally or with respect to any specified matter.

(b) INTERVENTION BY ATTORNEY GENERAL OF A STATE. In a chapter 7, 11, 12, or 13 case, the Attorney General of a State may appear and be heard on behalf of consumer creditors if the court determines the appearance is in the public interest, but the Attorney General may not appeal from any judgment, order, or decree in the case.

(c) CHAPTER 9 MUNICIPALITY CASE. The Secretary of the Treasury of the United States may, or if requested by the court shall, intervene in a chapter 9 case. Representatives of the state in which the debtor is located may intervene in a chapter 9 case with respect to matters specified by the court.

(d) LABOR UNIONS. In a chapter 9, 11, or 12 case, a labor union or employees' association, representative of employees of the debtor, shall have the right to be heard on the economic soundness of a plan affecting the interests of the employees. A labor union or employees' association which exercises its right to be heard under this subdivision shall not be entitled to appeal any judgment, order, or decree relating to the plan, unless otherwise permitted by law.

(e) SERVICE ON ENTITIES COVERED BY THIS RULE. The court may enter orders governing the service of notice and papers on entities permitted to intervene or be heard pursuant to this rule.

(As amended Mar. 30, 1987, eff. Aug. 1, 1987; Apr. 30, 1991, eff. Aug. 1, 1991.)

NOTES OF ADVISORY COMMITTEE ON RULES—1983

This rule is derived from former Rules 8-210, 9-15 and 10-210 and it implements §§1109 and 1164 of the Code.

Pursuant to §1109 of the Code, parties in interest have a right to be heard and the Securities and Exchange Commission may raise and be heard on any issue but it may not take an appeal. That section is applicable in chapter 9 cases (§901 of the Code) and in chapter 11 cases, including cases under subchapter IV thereof for the reorganization of a railroad.

In a railroad reorganization case under subchapter IV of chapter 11, §1164 also gives the right to be heard to the Interstate Commerce Commission, the Department of Transportation and any state or local regulatory commission with jurisdiction over the debtor, but these entities may not appeal.

This rule does not apply in adversary proceedings. For intervention in adversary proceedings, see Rule 7024. The rules do not provide any right of compensation to or reimbursement of expenses for intervenors or others covered by this rule. Section 503(b)(3)(D) and (4) is not applicable to the entities covered by this rule.

Subdivision (a) is derived from former Chapter VIII Rule 8–210 and former Chapter X Rule 10–210. It permits intervention of an entity (see §101(14), (21) of the Code) not otherwise entitled to do so under the Code or this rule. Such a party seeking to intervene must show cause therefor.

Subdivision (b) specifically grants the appropriate state's Attorney General the right to appear and be heard on behalf of consumer creditors when it is in the public interest. See House Rep. No. 95–595, 95th Cong., 1st Sess. (1977) 189. While "consumer creditor" is not defined in the Code or elsewhere, it would include the type of individual entitled to priority under §507(a)(5) of the Code, that is, an individual who has deposited money for the purchase, lease or rental of property or the purchase of services for the personal, family, or household use of the individual. It would also include individuals who purchased or leased property for such purposes in connection with which there may exist claims for breach of warranty.

This subdivision does not grant the Attorney General the status of party in interest. In other contexts, the Attorney General will, of course, be a party in interest as for example, in representing a state in connection with a tax claim.

Subdivision (c) recognizes the possible interests of the Secretary of the Treasury or of the state of the debtor's locale when a municipality is the debtor. It is derived from former Chapter IX Rule 9–15 and §85(d) of the Act.

Subdivision (d) is derived from former Chapter X Rule 10–210 which, in turn, was derived from §206 of the Act. Section 206 has no counterpart in the Code.

Subdivision (e) is derived from former Chapter VIII Rule 8–210(d). It gives the court flexibility in directing the type of future notices to be given intervenors.

NOTES OF ADVISORY COMMITTEE ON RULES—1987 AMENDMENT

Subdivision (d) is amended to make it clear that the prohibition against appeals by labor unions is limited only to their participation in connection with the hearings on the plan as provided in subdivision (d). If a labor union would otherwise have the right to file an appeal or to be a party to an appeal, this rule does not preclude the labor union from exercising that right.

NOTES OF ADVISORY COMMITTEE ON RULES—1991 AMENDMENT

Subdivisions (b) and (d) are amended to include chapter 12.

Rule 2019. Representation of Creditors and Equity Security Holders in Chapter 9 Municipality and Chapter 11 Reorganization Cases

(a) DATA REQUIRED. In a chapter 9 municipality or chapter 11 reorganization case, except with respect to a committee appointed pursuant to §1102 or 1114 of the Code, every entity or committee representing more than one creditor or equity security holder and, unless otherwise directed by the court, every indenture trustee, shall file a verified statement setting forth (1) the name and address of the creditor or equity security holder; (2) the nature and amount of the claim or interest and the time of acquisition thereof unless it is alleged to have been acquired more than one year prior to the filing of the petition; (3) a recital of the pertinent facts and circumstances in connection with the employment of the entity or indenture trustee, and, in the case of a committee, the name or names of the entity or entities at whose instance, directly or indirectly, the employment was arranged or the committee was organized or agreed to act; and (4) with reference to the time of the employment of the entity, the organization or formation of the committee, or the appearance in the case of any indenture trustee, the amounts of claims or interests owned by the entity, the members of the committee or the indenture trustee, the times when acquired, the amounts paid therefor, and any sales or other disposition thereof. The statement shall include a copy of the instrument, if any, whereby the entity, committee, or indenture trustee is empowered to act on behalf of creditors or equity security holders. A supplemental statement shall be filed promptly, setting forth any material changes in the facts contained in the statement filed pursuant to this subdivision.

(b) FAILURE TO COMPLY; EFFECT. On motion of any party in interest or on its own initiative, the court may (1) determine whether there has been a failure to comply with the provisions of subdivision (a) of this rule or with any other applicable law regulating the activities and personnel of any entity, committee, or indenture trustee or any other impropriety in connection with any solicitation and, if it so determines, the court may refuse to permit that entity, committee, or indenture trustee to be heard further or to intervene in the case; (2) examine any representation provision of a deposit agreement, proxy, trust mortgage, trust indenture, or deed of trust, or committee or other authorization, and any claim or interest acquired by any entity or committee in contemplation or in the course of a case under the Code and grant appropriate relief; and (3) hold invalid any authority, acceptance, rejection, or objection given, procured, or received by an entity or committee who has not complied with this rule or with §1125(b) of the Code.

(As amended Mar. 30, 1987, eff. Aug. 1, 1987; Apr. 30, 1991, eff. Aug. 1, 1991.)

NOTES OF ADVISORY COMMITTEE ON RULES—1983

This rule is a comprehensive regulation of representation in chapter 9 municipality and in chapter 11 reorganization cases. It is derived from §§209–213 of the Act and former Chapter X Rule 10–211.

Subdivision (b) is derived from §§212, 213 of the Act. As used in clause (2), "other authorization" would include a power or warrant of attorney which are specifically mentioned in §212 of the Act. This rule deals with representation provisions in mortgages, trust deeds, etc. to protect the beneficiaries from unfair practices and the like. It does not deal with the validation or invalidation of security interests generally. If immediate compliance is not possible, the court may permit a representative to be heard on a specific matter, but there is no implicit waiver of compliance on a permanent basis.

NOTES OF ADVISORY COMMITTEE ON RULES—1991 AMENDMENT

Subdivision (a) is amended to exclude from the requirements of this rule committees of retired employees appointed pursuant to §1114 of the Code. The words "with the clerk" are deleted as unnecessary. See Rules 5005(a) and 9001(3).

Rule 2020. Review of Acts by United States Trustee

A proceeding to contest any act or failure to act by the United States trustee is governed by Rule 9014.

(Added Apr. 30, 1991, eff. Aug. 1, 1991.)

NOTES OF ADVISORY COMMITTEE ON RULES—1991

The United States trustee performs administrative functions, such as the convening of the meeting of creditors and the appointment of trustees and committees. Most of the acts of the United States trustee are not controversial and will go unchallenged. However, the United States trustee is not a judicial officer and does not resolve disputes regarding the propriety of its own actions. This rule, which is new, provides a procedure for judicial review of the United States trustee's acts or failure to act in connection with the administration of the case. For example, if the United States trustee schedules a §341 meeting to be held 90 days after the petition is filed, and a party in interest wishes to challenge the propriety of that act in view of §341(a) of the Code and Rule 2003 which requires that the meeting be held not more than 40 days after the order for relief, this rule permits the party to do so by motion.

This rule provides for review of acts already committed by the United States trustee, but does not provide for advisory opinions in advance of the act. This rule is not intended to limit the discretion of the United States trustee, provided that the United States trustee's act is authorized by, and in compliance with, the Code, title 28, these rules, and other applicable law.

PART III—CLAIMS AND DISTRIBUTION TO CREDITORS AND EQUITY INTEREST HOLDERS; PLANS

Rule 3001. Proof of Claim

(a) FORM AND CONTENT. A proof of claim is a written statement setting forth a creditor's claim. A proof of claim shall conform substantially to the appropriate Official Form.

(b) WHO MAY EXECUTE. A proof of claim shall be executed by the creditor or the creditor's authorized agent except as provided in Rules 3004 and 3005.

(c) CLAIM BASED ON A WRITING. When a claim, or an interest in property of the debtor securing the claim, is based on a writing, the original or a duplicate shall be filed with the proof of claim. If the writing has been lost or destroyed, a statement of the circumstances of the loss or destruction shall be filed with the claim.

(d) EVIDENCE OF PERFECTION OF SECURITY INTEREST. If a security interest in property of the debtor is claimed, the proof of claim shall be accompanied by evidence that the security interest has been perfected.

(e) TRANSFERRED CLAIM.

(1) *Transfer of Claim Other Than for Security Before Proof Filed.* If a claim has been transferred other than for security before proof of the claim has been filed, the proof of claim may be filed only by the transferee or an indenture trustee.

(2) *Transfer of Claim Other than for Security after Proof Filed.* If a claim other than one based on a publicly traded note, bond, or debenture has been transferred other than for security after the proof of claim has been filed, evidence of the transfer shall be filed by the transferee. The clerk shall immediately notify the alleged transferor by mail of the filing of the evidence of transfer and that objection thereto, if any, must be filed within 21 days of the mailing of the notice or within any additional time allowed by the court. If the alleged transferor files a timely objection and the court finds, after notice and a hearing, that the claim has been transferred other than for security, it shall enter an order substituting the transferee for the transferor. If a timely objection is not filed by the alleged transferor, the transferee shall be substituted for the transferor.

(3) *Transfer of Claim for Security Before Proof Filed.* If a claim other than one based on a publicly traded note, bond, or debenture has been transferred for security before proof of the claim has been filed, the transferor or transferee or both may file a proof of claim for the full amount. The proof shall be supported by a statement setting forth the terms of the transfer. If either the transferor or the transferee files a proof of claim, the clerk shall immediately notify the other by mail of the right to join in the filed claim. If both transferor and transferee file proofs of the same claim, the proofs shall be consolidated. If the transferor or transferee does not file an agreement regarding its relative rights respecting voting of the claim, payment of dividends thereon, or participation in the administration of the estate, on motion by a party in interest and after notice and a hearing, the court shall enter such orders respecting these matters as may be appropriate.

(4) *Transfer of Claim for Security after Proof Filed.* If a claim other than one based on a publicly traded note, bond, or debenture has been transferred for security after the proof of claim has been filed, evidence of the terms of the transfer shall be filed by the transferee. The clerk shall immediately notify the alleged transferor by mail of the filing of the evidence of transfer and that objection thereto, if any, must be filed within 21 days of the mailing of the notice or within any additional time allowed by the court. If a timely objection is filed by the alleged transferor, the court, after notice and a hearing, shall determine whether the claim has been transferred for security. If the transferor or transferee does not file an agreement regarding its relative rights respecting voting of the claim, payment of dividends thereon, or participation in the administration of the estate, on motion by a party in interest and after notice and a hearing, the court shall enter such orders respecting these matters as may be appropriate.

(5) *Service of Objection or Motion; Notice of Hearing.* A copy of an objection filed pursuant to paragraph (2) or (4) or a motion filed pursuant to paragraph (3) or (4) of this subdivision together with a notice of a hearing shall be mailed or otherwise delivered to the transferor or transferee, whichever is appropriate, at least 30 days prior to the hearing.

(f) EVIDENTIARY EFFECT. A proof of claim executed and filed in accordance with these rules shall constitute prima facie evidence of the validity and amount of the claim.

(g)[1] To the extent not inconsistent with the United States Warehouse Act or applicable State law, a warehouse receipt, scale ticket, or similar document of the type routinely issued as evidence of title by a grain storage facility, as defined in section 557 of title 11, shall constitute

[1] So in original. Subsec. (g) enacted without a catchline.

prima facie evidence of the validity and amount of a claim of ownership of a quantity of grain.

(As amended Pub. L. 98–353, title III, §354, July 10, 1984, 98 Stat. 361; Apr. 30, 1991, eff. Aug. 1, 1991; Mar. 26, 2009, eff. Dec. 1, 2009.)

NOTES OF ADVISORY COMMITTEE ON RULES—1983

This rule is adapted from former Bankruptcy Rules 301 and 302. The Federal Rules of Evidence, made applicable to cases under the Code by Rule 1101, do not prescribe the evidentiary effect to be accorded particular documents. Subdivision (f) of this rule supplements the Federal Rules of Evidence as they apply to cases under the Code.

Subdivision (c). This subdivision is similar to former Bankruptcy Rule 302(c) and continues the requirement for the filing of any written security agreement and provides that the filing of a duplicate of a writing underlying a claim authenticates the claim with the same effect as the filing of the original writing. *Cf.* Rules 1001(4) and 1003 of F.R. of Evid. Subdivision (d) together with the requirement in the first sentence of subdivision (c) for the filing of any written security agreement, is designed to facilitate the determination whether the claim is secured and properly perfected so as to be valid against the trustee.

Subdivision (d). "Satisfactory evidence" of perfection, which is to accompany the proof of claim, would include a duplicate of an instrument filed or recorded, a duplicate of a certificate of title when a security interest is perfected by notation on such a certificate, a statement that pledged property has been in possession of the secured party since a specified date, or a statement of the reasons why no action was necessary for perfection. The secured creditor may not be required to file a proof of claim under this rule if he is not seeking allowance of a claim for a deficiency. But see §506(d) of the Code.

Subdivision (e). The rule recognizes the differences between an unconditional transfer of a claim and a transfer for the purpose of security and prescribes a procedure for dealing with the rights of the transferor and transferee when the transfer is for security. The rule clarifies the procedure to be followed when a transfer precedes or follows the filing of the petition. The interests of sound administration are served by requiring the post-petition transferee to file with the proof of claim a statement of the transferor acknowledging the transfer and the consideration for the transfer. Such a disclosure will assist the court in dealing with evils that may arise out of post-bankruptcy traffic in claims against an estate. *Monroe v. Scofield*, 135 F.2d 725 (10th Cir. 1943); *In re Philadelphia & Western Ry.*, 64 F. Supp. 738 (E.D. Pa. 1946); *cf. In re Latham Lithographic Corp.*, 107 F.2d 749 (2d Cir. 1939). Both paragraphs (1) and (3) of this subdivision, which deal with a transfer before the filing of a proof of claim, recognize that the transferee may be unable to obtain the required statement from the transferor, but in that event a sound reason for such inability must accompany the proof of claim filed by the transferee.

Paragraphs (3) and (4) clarify the status of a claim transferred for the purpose of security. An assignee for security has been recognized as a rightful claimant in bankruptcy. *Feder v. John Engelhorn & Sons*, 202 F.2d 411 (2d Cir. 1953). An assignor's right to file a claim notwithstanding the assignment was sustained in *In re R & L Engineering Co.*, 182 F. Supp. 317 (S.D. Cal. 1960). Facilitation of the filing of proofs by both claimants as holders of interests in a single claim is consonant with equitable treatment of the parties and sound administration. See *In re Latham Lithographic Corp.*, 107 F.2d 749 (2d Cir. 1939).

Paragraphs (2) and (4) of subdivision (e) deal with the transfer of a claim after proof has been filed. Evidence of the terms of the transfer required to be disclosed to the court will facilitate the court's determination of the appropriate order to be entered because of the transfer.

Paragraph (5) describes the procedure to be followed when an objection is made by the transferor to the transferee's filed evidence of transfer.

NOTES OF ADVISORY COMMITTEE ON RULES—1987

Subdivision (g) was added by §354 of the 1984 amendments.

NOTES OF ADVISORY COMMITTEE ON RULES—1991 AMENDMENT

Subdivision (a) is amended in anticipation of future revision and renumbering of the Official Forms.

Subdivision (e) is amended to limit the court's role to the adjudication of disputes regarding transfers of claims. If a claim has been transferred prior to the filing of a proof of claim, there is no need to state the consideration for the transfer or to submit other evidence of the transfer. If a claim has been transferred other than for security after a proof of claim has been filed, the transferee is substituted for the transferor in the absence of a timely objection by the alleged transferor. In that event, the clerk should note the transfer without the need for court approval. If a timely objection is filed, the court's role is to determine whether a transfer has been made that is enforceable under nonbankruptcy law. This rule is not intended either to encourage or discourage postpetition transfers of claims or to affect any remedies otherwise available under nonbankruptcy law to a transferor or transferee such as for misrepresentation in connection with the transfer of a claim. "After notice and a hearing" as used in subdivision (e) shall be construed in accordance with paragraph (5).

The words "with the clerk" in subdivision (e)(2) and (e)(4) are deleted as unnecessary. See Rules 5005(a) and 9001(3).

COMMITTEE NOTES ON RULES—2009 AMENDMENT

The rule is amended to implement changes in connection with the amendment to Rule 9006(a) and the manner by which time is computed under the rules. The deadlines in the rule are amended to substitute a deadline that is a multiple of seven days. Throughout the rules, deadlines are amended in the following manner:

- 5-day periods become 7-day periods
- 10-day periods become 14-day periods
- 15-day periods become 14-day periods
- 20-day periods become 21-day periods
- 25-day periods become 28-day periods

REFERENCES IN TEXT

The United States Warehouse Act, referred to in subd. (g), is Part C of act Aug. 11, 1916, ch. 313, 39 Stat. 486, as amended, which is classified generally to chapter 10 (§241 et seq.) of Title 7, Agriculture. For complete classification of this Act to the Code, see Short Title note set out under section 241 of Title 7 and Tables.

AMENDMENT BY PUBLIC LAW

1984—Subd. (g). Pub. L. 98–353 added subd. (g).

EFFECTIVE DATE OF 1984 AMENDMENT

Amendment by Pub. L. 98–353 effective with respect to cases filed 90 days after July 10, 1984, see section 552(a) of Pub. L. 98–353, set out as a note under section 101 of this title.

Rule 3002. Filing Proof of Claim or Interest

(a) NECESSITY FOR FILING. An unsecured creditor or an equity security holder must file a proof of claim or interest for the claim or interest to be allowed, except as provided in Rules 1019(3), 3003, 3004, and 3005.

(b) PLACE OF FILING. A proof of claim or interest shall be filed in accordance with Rule 5005.

(c) TIME FOR FILING. In a chapter 7 liquidation, chapter 12 family farmer's debt adjustment, or chapter 13 individual's debt adjustment case, a proof of claim is timely filed if it is filed not later than 90 days after the first date set for the meeting of creditors called under §341(a) of the Code, except as follows:

(1) A proof of claim filed by a governmental unit, other than for a claim resulting from a tax return filed under §1308, is timely filed if it is filed not later than 180 days after the date of the order for relief. A proof of claim filed by a governmental unit for a claim resulting from a tax return filed under §1308 is timely filed if it is filed no later than 180 days after the date of the order for relief or 60 days after the date of the filing of the tax return. The court may, for cause, enlarge the time for a governmental unit to file a proof of claim only upon motion of the governmental unit made before expiration of the period for filing a timely proof of claim.

(2) In the interest of justice and if it will not unduly delay the administration of the case, the court may extend the time for filing a proof of claim by an infant or incompetent person or the representative of either.

(3) An unsecured claim which arises in favor of an entity or becomes allowable as a result of a judgment may be filed within 30 days after the judgment becomes final if the judgment is for the recovery of money or property from that entity or denies or avoids the entity's interest in property. If the judgment imposes a liability which is not satisfied, or a duty which is not performed within such period or such further time as the court may permit, the claim shall not be allowed.

(4) A claim arising from the rejection of an executory contract or unexpired lease of the debtor may be filed within such time as the court may direct.

(5) If notice of insufficient assets to pay a dividend was given to creditors under Rule 2002(e), and subsequently the trustee notifies the court that payment of a dividend appears possible, the clerk shall give at least 90 days' notice by mail to creditors of that fact and of the date by which proofs of claim must be filed.

(6) If notice of the time to file a proof of claim has been mailed to a creditor at a foreign address, on motion filed by the creditor before or after the expiration of the time, the court may extend the time by not more than 60 days if the court finds that the notice was insufficient under the circumstances to give the creditor a reasonable time to file a proof of claim.

(As amended Mar. 30, 1987, eff. Aug. 1, 1987; Apr. 30, 1991, eff. Aug. 1, 1991; Apr. 23, 1996, eff. Dec. 1, 1996; Apr. 23, 2008, eff. Dec. 1, 2008.)

NOTES OF ADVISORY COMMITTEE ON RULES—1983

Subdivision (a) of this rule is substantially a restatement of the general requirement that claims be proved and filed. The exceptions refer to Rule 3003 providing for the filing of claims in chapter 9 and 11 cases, and to Rules 3004 and 3005 authorizing claims to be filed by the debtor or trustee and the filing of a claim by a contingent creditor of the debtor.

A secured claim need not be filed or allowed under §502 or §506(d) unless a party in interest has requested a determination and allowance or disallowance under §502.

Subdivision (c) is adapted from former Bankruptcy Rule 302(e) but changes the time limits on the filing of claims in chapter 7 and 13 cases from six months to 90 days after the first date set for the meeting of creditors. The special rule for early filing by a secured creditor in a chapter 13 case, in former Rule 13-302(e)(1) is not continued.

Although the claim of a secured creditor may have arisen before the petition, a judgment avoiding the security interest may not have been entered until after the time for filing claims has expired. Under Rule 3002(c)(3) the creditor who did not file a secured claim may nevertheless file an unsecured claim within the time prescribed. A judgment does not become final for the purpose of starting the 30 day period provided for by paragraph (3) until the time for appeal has expired or, if an appeal is taken, until the appeal has been disposed of. *In re Tapp*, 61 F. Supp. 594 (W.D. Ky. 1945).

Paragraph (1) is derived from former Bankruptcy Rule 302(e). The governmental unit may move for an extension of the 90 day period. Pursuant to §501(c) of the Code, if the government does not file its claim within the proper time period, the debtor or trustee may file on its behalf. An extension is not needed by the debtor or trustee because the right to file does not arise until the government's time has expired.

Paragraph (4) is derived from former chapter rules. (See, *e.g.*, Rule 11-33(a)(2)(B). In light of the reduced time it is necessary that a party with a claim arising from the rejection of an executory contract have sufficient time to file that claim. This clause allows the court to fix an appropriate time.

Paragraph (5) of subdivision (c) is correlated with the provision in Rule 2002(e) authorizing notification to creditors of estates from which no dividends are anticipated. The clause permits creditors who have refrained from filing claims after receiving notification to be given an opportunity to file when subsequent developments indicate the possibility of a dividend. The notice required by this clause must be given in the manner provided in Rule 2002. The information relating to the discovery of assets will usually be obtained by the clerk from the trustee's interim reports or special notification by the trustee.

Provision is made in Rule 2002(a) and (h) for notifying all creditors of the fixing of a time for filing claims against a surplus under paragraph (6). This paragraph does not deal with the distribution of the surplus. Reference must also be made to §726(a)(2)(C) and (3) which permits distribution on late filed claims.

Paragraph (6) is only operative in a chapter 7 case. In chapter 13 cases, the plan itself provides the distribution to creditors which is not necessarily dependent on the size of the estate.

NOTES OF ADVISORY COMMITTEE ON RULES—1987 AMENDMENT

Subdivision (a) is amended by adding a reference to Rule 1019(4). Rule 1019(4) provides that claims actually filed by a creditor in a chapter 11 or 13 case shall be treated as filed in a superseding chapter 7 case. Claims deemed filed in a chapter 11 case pursuant to §1111(a) of the Code are not considered as filed in a superseding chapter 7 case. The creditor must file a claim in the superseding chapter 7 case.

NOTES OF ADVISORY COMMITTEE ON RULES—1991 AMENDMENT

Subdivision (a) is amended to conform to the renumbering of subdivisions of Rule 1019. Subdivision (c) is amended to include chapter 12 cases. Subdivision (c)(4) is amended to clarify that it includes a claim arising from the rejection of an unexpired lease.

NOTES OF ADVISORY COMMITTEE ON RULES—1996 AMENDMENT

The amendments are designed to conform to §§502(b)(9) and 726(a) of the Code as amended by the Bankruptcy Reform Act of 1994.

The Reform Act amended §726(a)(1) and added §502(b)(9) to the Code to govern the effects of a tardily filed claim. Under §502(b)(9), a tardily filed claim must be disallowed if an objection to the proof of claim is filed, except to the extent that a holder of a tardily filed claim is entitled to distribution under §726(a)(1), (2), or (3).

The phrase "in accordance with this rule" is deleted from Rule 3002(a) to clarify that the effect of filing a proof of claim after the expiration of the time prescribed in Rule 3002(c) is governed by §502(b)(9) of the Code, rather than by this rule.

Section 502(b)(9) of the Code provides that a claim of a governmental unit shall be timely filed if it is filed "before 180 days after the date of the order for relief" or such later time as the Bankruptcy Rules provide. To avoid any confusion as to whether a governmental unit's proof of claim is timely filed under §502(b)(9) if it is filed on the 180th day after the order for relief, paragraph (1) of subdivision (c) provides that a governmental unit's claim is timely if it is filed not later than 180 days after the order for relief.

References to "the United States, a state, or subdivision thereof" in paragraph (1) of subdivision (c) are changed to "governmental unit" to avoid different treatment among foreign and domestic governments.

GAP Report on Rule 3002. After publication of the proposed amendments, the Bankruptcy Reform Act of 1994 amended sections 726 and 502(b) of the Code to clarify the rights of creditors who tardily file a proof of claim. In view of the Reform Act, proposed new subdivision (d) of Rule 3002 has been deleted from the proposed amendments because it is no longer necessary. In addition, subdivisions (a) and (c) have been changed after publication to clarify that the effect of tardily filing a proof of claim is governed by §502(b)(9) of the Code, rather than by this rule.

The amendments to §502(b) also provide that a governmental unit's proof of claim is timely filed if it is filed before 180 days after the order for relief. Proposed amendments to Rule 3002(c)(1) were added to the published amendments to conform to this statutory change and to avoid any confusion as to whether a claim by a governmental unit is timely if it is filed on the 180th day.

The committee note has been re-written to explain the rule changes designed to conform to the Reform Act.

COMMITTEE NOTES ON RULES—2008 AMENDMENT

Subdivision (c)(1) is amended to reflect the addition of §1308 to the Bankruptcy Code in 2005. This provision requires that chapter 13 debtors file tax returns during the pendency of the case, and imposes bankruptcy-related consequences if debtors fail to do so. Subdivision (c)(1) provides additional time for governmental units to file a proof of claim for tax obligations with respect to tax returns filed during the pendency of a chapter 13 case. The amendment also allows the governmental unit to move for additional time to file a proof of claim prior to expiration of the applicable filing period.

Subdivision (c)(5) of the rule is amended to set a new period for providing notice to creditors that they may file a proof of claim in a case in which they were previously informed that there was no need to file a claim. Under Rule 2002(e), if it appears that there will be no distribution to creditors, the creditors are notified of this fact and are informed that if assets are later discovered and a distribution is likely that a new notice will be given to the creditors. This second notice is prescribed by Rule 3002(c)(5). The rule is amended to direct the clerk to give at least 90 days' notice of the time within which creditors may file a proof of claim. Setting the deadline in this manner allows the notices being sent to creditors to be more accurate regarding the deadline than was possible under the prior rule. The rule previously began the 90 day notice period from the time of the mailing of the notice, a date that could vary and generally would not even be known to the creditor. Under the amended rule, the notice will identify a specific bar date for filing proofs of claim thereby being more helpful to the creditors.

Subdivision (c)(6) is added to give the court discretion to extend the time for filing a proof of claim for a creditor who received notice of the time to file the claim at a foreign address, if the court finds that the notice was not sufficient, under the particular circumstances, to give the foreign creditor a reasonable time to file a proof of claim. This amendment is designed to comply with §1514(d), added to the Code by the 2005 amendments, and requires that the rules and orders of the court provide such additional time as is reasonable under the circumstances for foreign creditors to file claims in cases under all chapters of the Code.

Other changes are stylistic.

Changes Made After Publication. Subdivision (c)(1) was amended to allow governmental units to move for an enlargement of the time to file a proof of claim. The Committee Note was amended to describe this addition to the rule.

Rule 3003. Filing Proof of Claim or Equity Security Interest in Chapter 9 Municipality or Chapter 11 Reorganization Cases

(a) APPLICABILITY OF RULE. This rule applies in chapter 9 and 11 cases.

(b) SCHEDULE OF LIABILITIES AND LIST OF EQUITY SECURITY HOLDERS.

(1) *Schedule of Liabilities.* The schedule of liabilities filed pursuant to §521(l) of the Code shall constitute prima facie evidence of the validity and amount of the claims of creditors, unless they are scheduled as disputed, contingent, or unliquidated. It shall not be necessary for a creditor or equity security holder to file a proof of claim or interest except as provided in subdivision (c)(2) of this rule.

(2) *List of Equity Security Holders.* The list of equity security holders filed pursuant to Rule 1007(a)(3) shall constitute prima facie evidence of the validity and amount of the equity security interests and it shall not be necessary for the holders of such interests to file a proof of interest.

(c) FILING PROOF OF CLAIM.

(1) *Who May File.* Any creditor or indenture trustee may file a proof of claim within the time prescribed by subdivision (c)(3) of this rule.

(2) *Who Must File.* Any creditor or equity security holder whose claim or interest is not scheduled or scheduled as disputed, contingent, or unliquidated shall file a proof of claim or interest within the time prescribed by subdivision (c)(3) of this rule; any creditor who fails to do so shall not be treated as a creditor with respect to such claim for the purposes of voting and distribution.

(3) *Time for Filing.* The court shall fix and for cause shown may extend the time within which proofs of claim or interest may be filed. Notwithstanding the expiration of such time, a proof of claim may be filed to the extent and under the conditions stated in Rule 3002(c)(2), (c)(3), (c)(4), and (c)(6).

(4) *Effect of Filing Claim or Interest.* A proof of claim or interest executed and filed in accordance with this subdivision shall supersede any scheduling of that claim or interest pursuant to §521(a)(1) of the Code.

(5) *Filing by Indenture Trustee.* An indenture trustee may file a claim on behalf of all known

or unknown holders of securities issued pursuant to the trust instrument under which it is trustee.

(d) PROOF OF RIGHT TO RECORD STATUS. For the purposes of Rules 3017, 3018 and 3021 and for receiving notices, an entity who is not the record holder of a security may file a statement setting forth facts which entitle that entity to be treated as the record holder. An objection to the statement may be filed by any party in interest.

(As amended Mar. 30, 1987, eff. Aug. 1, 1987; Apr. 30, 1991, eff. Aug. 1, 1991; Apr. 23, 2008, eff. Dec. 1, 2008.)

NOTES OF ADVISORY COMMITTEE ON RULES—1983

Subdivision (a). This rule applies only in chapter 9 and chapter 11 cases. It is adapted from former Chapter X Rule 10–401 and provides an exception to the requirement for filing proofs of claim and interest as expressed in §§925 and 1111(a) of the Code.

Subdivision (b). This general statement implements §§925 and 1111(a) of the Code.

Subdivision (c). This subdivision permits, in paragraph (1), the filing of a proof of claim but does not make it mandatory. Paragraph (2) requires, as does the Code, filing when a claim is scheduled as disputed, contingent, or unliquidated as to amount. It is the creditor's responsibility to determine if the claim is accurately listed. Notice of the provision of this rule is provided for in Official Form No. 16, the order for the meeting of creditors. In an appropriate case the court may order creditors whose claims are scheduled as disputed, contingent, or unliquidated be notified of that fact but the procedure is left to the discretion of the court.

Subdivision (d) is derived from former Chapter X Rule 10–401(f).

Except with respect to the need and time for filing claims, the other aspects concerning claims covered by Rules 3001 and 3002 are applicable in chapter 9 and 11 cases.

Holders of equity security interests need not file proofs of interest. Voting and distribution participation is dependent on ownership as disclosed by the appropriate records of a transfer agent or the corporate or other business records at the time prescribed in Rules 3017 and 3021.

NOTES OF ADVISORY COMMITTEE ON RULES—1991 AMENDMENT

Paragraph (3) of subdivision (c) is amended to permit the late filing of claims by infants or incompetent persons under the same circumstances that permit late filings in cases under chapter 7, 12, or 13. The amendment also provides sufficient time in which to file a claim that arises from a postpetition judgment against the claimant for the recovery of money or property or the avoidance of a lien. It also provides for purposes of clarification that upon rejection of an executory contract or unexpired lease, the court shall set a time for filing a claim arising therefrom despite prior expiration of the time set for filing proofs of claim.

The caption of paragraph (4) of subdivision (c) is amended to indicate that it applies to a proof of claim.

COMMITTEE NOTES ON RULES—2008 AMENDMENT

Subdivision (c)(3) is amended to implement §1514(d) of the Code, which was added by the 2005 amendments. It makes the new Rule 3002(c)(6) applicable in chapter 9 and chapter 11 cases. This change was necessary so that creditors with foreign addresses be provided such additional time as is reasonable under the circumstances to file proofs of claims.

Changes Made After Publication. No changes were made after publication.

Rule 3004. Filing of Claims by Debtor or Trustee

If a creditor does not timely file a proof of claim under Rule 3002(c) or 3003(c), the debtor or trustee may file a proof of the claim within 30 days after the expiration of the time for filing claims prescribed by Rule 3002(c) or 3003(c), whichever is applicable. The clerk shall forthwith give notice of the filing to the creditor, the debtor and the trustee.

(As amended Mar. 30, 1987, eff. Aug. 1, 1987; Apr. 25, 2005, eff. Dec. 1, 2005.)

NOTES OF ADVISORY COMMITTEE ON RULES—1983

This rule is adapted from former Bankruptcy Rule 303 but conforms with the changes made by §501(c) of the Code. Rule 303 permitted only the filing of tax and wage claims by the debtor. Section 501(c) of the Code, however, permits the filing by the debtor or trustee on behalf of any creditor.

It is the policy of the Code that debtors' estates should be administered for the benefit of creditors without regard to the dischargeability of their claims. After their estates have been closed, however, discharged debtors may find themselves saddled with liabilities, particularly for taxes, which remain unpaid because of the failure of creditors holding nondischargeable claims to file proofs of claim and receive distributions thereon. The result is that the debtor is deprived of an important benefit of the Code without any fault or omission on the debtor's part and without any objective of the Code being served thereby.

Section 501(c) of the Code authorizes a debtor or trustee to file a proof of claim for any holder of a claim. Although all claims may not be nondischargeable, it may be difficult to determine, in particular, whether tax claims survive discharge. See Plumb, *Federal Tax Liens and Priorities in Bankruptcy*, 43 Ref. J. 37, 43–44 (1969); 1 Collier, *Bankruptcy* ¶17.14 (14th ed. 1967); 3 *id.* ¶523.06 (15th ed. 1979). To eliminate the necessity of the resolution of this troublesome issue, the option accorded the debtor by the Code does not depend on the nondischargeability of the claim. No serious administrative problems and no unfairness to creditors seemed to develop from adoption of Rule 303, the forerunner to §501(c). The authority to file is conditioned on the creditor's failure to file the proof of claim on or before the first date set for the meeting of creditors, which is the date a claim must ordinarily be filed in order to be voted in a chapter 7 case. Notice to the creditor is provided to enable him to file a proof of claim pursuant to Rule 3002, which proof, when filed, would supersede the proof filed by the debtor or trustee. Notice to the trustee would serve to alert the trustee to the special character of the proof and the possible need for supplementary evidence of the validity and amount of the claim. If the trustee does not qualify until after a proof of claim is filed by the debtor pursuant to this rule, he should be notified as soon as practicable thereafter.

To the extent the claim is allowed and dividends paid thereon, it will be reduced or perhaps paid in full. If the claim is also filed pursuant to Rule 3005, only one distribution thereon may be made. As expressly required by Rule 3005 and by the purpose of this rule such distribution must diminish the claim.

NOTES OF ADVISORY COMMITTEE ON RULES—1987 AMENDMENT

Under the rule as amended, the debtor or trustee in a chapter 7 or 13 case has 120 days from the first date set for the meeting of creditors to file a claim for the creditor. During the first 90 days of that period the creditor in a chapter 7 or 13 case may file a claim as provided by Rule 3002(c). If the creditor fails to file a claim, the debtor or trustee shall have an additional 30 days thereafter to file the claim. A proof of claim filed by a creditor supersedes a claim filed by the debtor or trustee only if it is timely filed within the 90 days allowed under Rule 3002(c).

COMMITTEE NOTES ON RULES—2005 AMENDMENT

The rule is amended to conform to §501(c) of the Code. Under that provision, the debtor or trustee may file proof of a claim if the creditor fails to do so in a timely fashion. The rule previously authorized the debtor and the trustee to file a claim as early as the day after the first date set for the meeting of creditors under §341(a). Under the amended rule, the debtor and trustee must wait until the creditor's opportunity to file a claim has expired. Providing the debtor and the trustee with the opportunity to file a claim ensures that the claim will participate in any distribution in the case. This is particularly important for claims that are nondischargeable.

Since the debtor and trustee cannot file a proof of claim until after the creditor's time to file has expired, the rule no longer permits the creditor to file a proof of claim that will supersede the claim filed by the debtor or trustee. The rule leaves to the courts the issue of whether to permit subsequent amendment of such proof of claim.

Other changes are stylistic.

Changes Made After Publication and Comment. No changes were made after publication. The Advisory Committee concluded that Mr. Van Allsburg's suggestion goes beyond the scope of the published proposal. Consequently, the Committee declined to adopt the suggestion but may consider it in greater detail at a future meeting.

Rule 3005. Filing of Claim, Acceptance, or Rejection by Guarantor, Surety, Indorser, or Other Codebtor

(a) FILING OF CLAIM. If a creditor does not timely file a proof of claim under Rule 3002(c) or 3003(c), any entity that is or may be liable with the debtor to that creditor, or who has secured that creditor, may file a proof of the claim within 30 days after the expiration of the time for filing claims prescribed by Rule 3002(c) or Rule 3003(c) whichever is applicable. No distribution shall be made on the claim except on satisfactory proof that the original debt will be diminished by the amount of distribution.

(b) FILING OF ACCEPTANCE OR REJECTION; SUBSTITUTION OF CREDITOR. An entity which has filed a claim pursuant to the first sentence of subdivision (a) of this rule may file an acceptance or rejection of a plan in the name of the creditor, if known, or if unknown, in the entity's own name but if the creditor files a proof of claim within the time permitted by Rule 3003(c) or files a notice prior to confirmation of a plan of the creditor's intention to act in the creditor's own behalf, the creditor shall be substituted for the obligor with respect to that claim.

(As amended Mar. 30, 1987, eff. Aug. 1, 1987; Apr. 30, 1991, eff. Aug. 1, 1991; Apr. 25, 2005, eff. Dec. 1, 2005.)

NOTES OF ADVISORY COMMITTEE ON RULES—1983

This rule is adapted from former Rules 304 and 10–402. Together with §501(b) of the Code, the rule makes clear that anyone who may be liable on a debt of the debtor, including a surety, guarantor, indorser, or other codebtor, is authorized to file in the name of the creditor of the debtor.

Subdivision (a). Rule 3002(c) provides the time period for filing proofs of claim in chapter 7 and 13 cases; Rule 3003(c) provides the time, when necessary, for filing claims in a chapter 9 or 11 case.

Subdivision (b). This subdivision applies in chapter 9 and 11 cases as distinguished from chapter 7 cases. It permits voting for or against a plan by an obligor who files a claim in place of the creditor.

NOTES OF ADVISORY COMMITTEE ON RULES—1991 AMENDMENT

The words "with the court" in subdivision (b) are deleted as unnecessary. See Rules 5005(a) and 9001(3).

COMMITTEE NOTES ON RULES—2005 AMENDMENT

The rule is amended to delete the last sentence of subdivision (a). The sentence is unnecessary because if a creditor has filed a timely claim under Rule 3002 or 3003(c), the codebtor cannot file a proof of such claim. The codebtor, consistent with §501(b) of the Code, may file a proof of such claim only after the creditor's time to file has expired. Therefore, the rule no longer permits the creditor to file a superseding claim. The rule leaves to the courts the issue of whether to permit subsequent amendment of the proof of claim.

The amendment conforms the rule to §501(b) by deleting language providing that the codebtor files proof of the claim in the name of the creditor.

Other amendments are stylistic.

Changes Made After Publication and Comment:

(a) The reference on line 2 of Rule 3005 to "Rule 3002 or 3003(c)" was changed to read "Rule 3002(c) or 3003(c)" to make it parallel to the language in Rule 3004.

(b) The phrase "file a proof of the claim" from line 7 of the proposed rule was moved up to line 4 of the proposed amendment immediately after the word "may". This makes the structure of Rules 3004 and 3005 more consistent.

Rule 3006. Withdrawal of Claim; Effect on Acceptance or Rejection of Plan

A creditor may withdraw a claim as of right by filing a notice of withdrawal, except as provided in this rule. If after a creditor has filed a proof of claim an objection is filed thereto or a complaint is filed against that creditor in an adversary proceeding, or the creditor has accepted or rejected the plan or otherwise has participated significantly in the case, the creditor may not withdraw the claim except on order of the court after a hearing on notice to the trustee or debtor in possession, and any creditors' committee elected pursuant to §705(a) or appointed pursuant to §1102 of the Code. The order of the court shall contain such terms and conditions as the court deems proper. Unless the court orders otherwise, an authorized withdrawal of a claim shall constitute withdrawal of any related acceptance or rejection of a plan.

(As amended Apr. 30, 1991, eff. Aug. 1, 1991.)

NOTES OF ADVISORY COMMITTEE ON RULES—1983

This rule is derived from former Rules 305 and 10–404.

Since 1938 it has generally been held that Rule 41 F.R.Civ.P. governs the withdrawal of a proof of claim. *In re Empire Coal Sales Corp.*, 45 F. Supp. 974, 976 (S.D.N.Y.), aff'd sub nom. *Kleid v. Ruthbell Coal Co.*, 131 F.2d 372, 373 (2d Cir. 1942); *Kelso v. MacLaren*, 122 F.2d 867, 870 (8th Cir. 1941); *In re Hills*, 35 F. Supp. 532, 533 (W.D. Wash. 1940). Accordingly, the cited cases held that after an objection has been filed a proof of claim may be withdrawn only subject to approval by the court. This constitutes a restriction of the right of withdrawal as recognized by some though by no means all of the cases antedating the promulgation of the Federal Rules of Civil Procedure. See 3 Collier *Bankruptcy*, ¶57.12 (14th ed. 1961); Note, 20 Bost. U. L. Rev. 121 (1940).

The filing of a claim does not commence an adversary proceeding but the filing of an objection to the claim initiates a contest that must be disposed of by the court. This rule recognizes the applicability of the considerations underlying Rule 41(a) F.R.Civ.P. to the withdrawal of a claim after it has been put in issue by an objection. Rule 41(a)(2) F.R.Civ.P. requires leave of court to obtain dismissal over the objection of a defendant who has pleaded a counterclaim prior to the service of the plaintiff's motion to dismiss. Although the applicability of this provision to the withdrawal of a claim was assumed in *Conway v. Union Bank of Switzerland*, 204 F.2d 603, 608 (2d Cir. 1953). *Kleid v. Ruthbell Coal Co., supra, Kelso v. MacLaren, supra*, and *In re Hills, supra*, this rule vests discretion in the court to grant, deny, or condition the request of a creditor to withdraw, without regard to whether the trustee has filed a merely defensive objection or a complaint seeking an affirmative recovery of money or property from the creditor.

A number of pre-1938 cases sustained denial of a creditor's request to withdraw proof of claim on the ground of estoppel or election of remedies. 2 Remington, *Bankruptcy* 186 (Henderson ed. 1956); *cf.* 3 Collier, *supra* ¶57.12, at 201 (1964). Voting a claim for a trustee was an important factor in the denial of a request to withdraw in *Standard Varnish Works v. Haydock*, 143 Fed. 318, 319–20 (6th Cir. 1906), and *In re Cann*, 47 F.2d 661, 662 (W.D. Pa. 1931). And it has frequently been recognized that a creditor should not be allowed to withdraw a claim after accepting a dividend. *In re Friedmann*, 1 Am. B. R. 510, 512 (Ref., S.D.N.Y. 1899); 3 Collier 205 (1964); *cf. In re O'Gara Coal Co.*, 12 F.2d 426, 429 (7th Cir.), cert. denied, 271 U.S. 683 (1926). It was held in *Industrial Credit Co. v. Hazen*, 222 F.2d 225 (8th Cir. 1955), however, that although a claimant had participated in the first meeting of creditors and in the examination of witnesses, the creditor was entitled under Rule 41(a)(1) F.R.Civ.P. to withdraw the claim as of right by filing a notice of withdrawal before the trustee filed an objection under §57g of the Act. While this rule incorporates the post-1938 case law referred to in the first paragraph of this note, it rejects the inference drawn in the *Hazen* case that Rule 41(a) F.R.Civ.P. supersedes the pre-1938 case law that vests discretion in the court to deny or restrict withdrawal of a claim by a creditor on the ground of estoppel or election of remedies. While purely formal or technical participation in a case by a creditor who has filed a claim should not deprive the creditor of the right to withdraw the claim, a creditor who has accepted a dividend or who has voted in the election of a trustee or otherwise participated actively in proceedings in a case should be permitted to withdraw only with the approval of the court on terms it deems appropriate after notice to the trustee. 3 Collier 205–06 (1964).

NOTES OF ADVISORY COMMITTEE ON RULES—1991 AMENDMENT

This amendment is stylistic. Notice of the hearing need not be given to committees of equity security holders appointed pursuant to §1102 or committees of retired employees appointed pursuant to §1114 of the Code.

Rule 3007. Objections to Claims

(a) OBJECTIONS TO CLAIMS. An objection to the allowance of a claim shall be in writing and filed. A copy of the objection with notice of the hearing thereon shall be mailed or otherwise delivered to the claimant, the debtor or debtor in possession, and the trustee at least 30 days prior to the hearing.

(b) DEMAND FOR RELIEF REQUIRING AN ADVERSARY PROCEEDING. A party in interest shall not include a demand for relief of a kind specified in Rule 7001 in an objection to the allowance of a claim, but may include the objection in an adversary proceeding.

(c) LIMITATION ON JOINDER OF CLAIMS OBJECTIONS. Unless otherwise ordered by the court or permitted by subdivision (d), objections to more than one claim shall not be joined in a single objection.

(d) OMNIBUS OBJECTION. Subject to subdivision (e), objections to more than one claim may be joined in an omnibus objection if all the claims were filed by the same entity, or the objections are based solely on the grounds that the claims should be disallowed, in whole or in part, because:

(1) they duplicate other claims;

(2) they have been filed in the wrong case;

(3) they have been amended by subsequently filed proofs of claim;

(4) they were not timely filed;

(5) they have been satisfied or released during the case in accordance with the Code, applicable rules, or a court order;

(6) they were presented in a form that does not comply with applicable rules, and the objection states that the objector is unable to determine the validity of the claim because of the noncompliance;

(7) they are interests, rather than claims; or

(8) they assert priority in an amount that exceeds the maximum amount under §507 of the Code.

(e) REQUIREMENTS FOR OMNIBUS OBJECTION. An omnibus objection shall:

(1) state in a conspicuous place that claimants receiving the objection should locate their names and claims in the objection;

(2) list claimants alphabetically, provide a cross-reference to claim numbers, and, if appropriate, list claimants by category of claims;

(3) state the grounds of the objection to each claim and provide a cross-reference to the pages in the omnibus objection pertinent to the stated grounds;

(4) state in the title the identity of the objector and the grounds for the objections;

(5) be numbered consecutively with other omnibus objections filed by the same objector; and

(6) contain objections to no more than 100 claims.

(f) FINALITY OF OBJECTION. The finality of any order regarding a claim objection included in an omnibus objection shall be determined as though the claim had been subject to an individual objection.

(As amended Apr. 30, 1991, eff. Aug. 1, 1991; Apr. 30, 2007, eff. Dec. 1, 2007.)

NOTES OF ADVISORY COMMITTEE ON RULES—1983

This rule is derived from §47a(8) of the Act and former Bankruptcy Rule 306. It prescribes the manner in which an objection to a claim shall be made and notice of the hearing thereon given to the claimant. The requirement of a writing does not apply to an objection to the allowance of a claim for the purpose of voting for a trustee or creditors' committee in a chapter 7 case. See Rule 2003.

The contested matter initiated by an objection to a claim is governed by rule 9014, unless a counterclaim by the trustee is joined with the objection to the claim. The filing of a counterclaim ordinarily commences an adversary proceeding subject to the rules in Part VII.

While the debtor's other creditors may make objections to the allowance of a claim, the demands of orderly and expeditious administration have led to a recognition that the right to object is generally exercised by the trustee. Pursuant to §502(a) of the Code, however, any party in interest may object to a claim. But under §704 the trustee, if any purpose would be served thereby, has the duty to examine proofs of claim and object to improper claims.

By virtue of the automatic allowance of a claim not objected to, a dividend may be paid on a claim which may thereafter be disallowed on objection made pursuant to this rule. The amount of the dividend paid before the disallowance in such event would be recoverable by the trustee in an adversary proceeding.

NOTES OF ADVISORY COMMITTEE ON RULES—1991 AMENDMENT

The words "with the court" are deleted as unnecessary. See Rules 5005(a) and 9001(3).

COMMITTEE NOTES ON RULES—2007 AMENDMENT

The rule is amended in a number of ways. First, the amendment prohibits a party in interest from including in a claim objection a request for relief that requires an adversary proceeding. A party in interest may, however, include an objection to the allowance of a claim in an adversary proceeding. Unlike a contested matter, an adversary proceeding requires the service of a summons and complaint, which puts the defendant on notice of the potential for an affirmative recovery. Permitting the plaintiff in the adversary proceeding to include an objection to a claim would not unfairly surprise the defendant as might be the case if the action were brought as a contested matter that included an action to obtain relief of a kind specified in Rule 7001.

The rule as amended does not require that a party include an objection to the allowance of a claim in an adversary proceeding. If a claim objection is filed separately from a related adversary proceeding, the court may consolidate the objection with the adversary proceeding under Rule 7042.

The rule also is amended to authorize the filing of a pleading that joins objections to more than one claim. Such filings present a significant opportunity for the efficient administration of large cases, but the rule includes restrictions on the use of these omnibus objections to ensure the protection of the due process rights of the claimants.

Unless the court orders otherwise, objections to more than one claim may be joined in a single pleading only if all of the claims were filed by the same entity, or if the objections are based solely on the grounds set out in subdivision (d) of the rule. Objections of the type listed in subdivision (d) often can be resolved without material factual or legal disputes. Objections to multiple claims permitted under the rule must comply with the procedural requirements set forth in subdivision (e). Among those requirements is the requirement in subdivision (e)(5) that these omnibus objections be consecutively numbered. Since these objections may not join more than 100 objections in any one omnibus objection, there may be a need for several omnibus objections to be filed in a particular case. Consecutive numbering of each omnibus objection and the identification of the objector in the title of the objection is essential to keep track of the objections on the court's docket. For example, the objections could be titled Debtor in Possession's First Omnibus Objection to Claims, Debtor in Possession's Second Omnibus Objection to Claims, Creditors' Committee's First Omnibus Objection to Claims, and so on. Titling the objections in this manner should avoid confusion and aid in tracking the objections on the docket.

Subdivision (f) provides that an order resolving an objection to any particular claim is treated, for purposes of finality, as if the claim had been the subject of an individual objection. A party seeking to appeal any such order is neither required, nor permitted, to await the court's resolution of all other joined objections. The rule permits the joinder of objections for convenience, and that convenience should not impede timely review of a court's decision with respect to each claim. Whether the court's action as to a particular objection is final, and the consequences of that finality, are not addressed by this amendment. Moreover, use of an omnibus objection generally does not preclude the objecting party from raising a subsequent objection to the claim on other grounds. See Restatement (Second) of Judgments §26(1)(d) (1982) (generally applicable rule barring multiple actions based on same transaction or series of transactions is overridden when a statutory scheme permits splitting of claims).

Changes Made After Publication. There were several changes made to the rule after its publication. The Advisory Committee declined to follow Mr. Sabino's suggestion, concluding that the rule as proposed includes sufficient flexibility, and that expanding the flexibility might lead to excessive deviation from the appropriate format for omnibus claims objections. The Advisory Committee also declined to follow Mr. Horsley's suggestion because the deadline for filing a proof of claim varies based on the nature of the creditor (governmental units have different deadlines from other creditors) as well as on the chapter under which the case is pending. The Advisory Committee rejected Judge Grant's suggestion that a party proposing an omnibus claims objection be required to demonstrate some special cause to allow the joinder of the objections. The Advisory Committee concluded that the rule includes sufficient protections for claimants such that omnibus objections should be allowed without the need for a special showing by the claims objector that joinder is proper.

The Advisory Committee did accept several of Judge Grant's suggestions, and the rule was amended by deleting the grounds for objection to claims based on the filing of a superceding proof of claim under proposed subdivision (d)(3) and the transfer of claims under proposed subdivision (d)(4). Subdivision (d)(3) now permits objections to claims that have been amended by a subsequently filed proof of claim and the paragraphs within subdivision (d) have been renumbered to reflect the deletion. The Committee Note also no longer includes any reliance on §502(j) for the statement indicating that a subsequent claim objection can be filed to a claim that was previously included in an omnibus claim objection.

Rule 3008. Reconsideration of Claims

A party in interest may move for reconsideration of an order allowing or disallowing a claim against the estate. The court after a hearing on notice shall enter an appropriate order.

NOTES OF ADVISORY COMMITTEE ON RULES—1983

Section 502(j) of the Code deals only with the reconsideration of allowed claims as did former §57k of the Act and General Order 21(b). It had sometimes been held that a referee had no jurisdiction to reconsider a disallowed claim, or the amount or priority of an allowed claim, at the instance of the claimant. See, *e.g.*, *In re Gouse*, 7 F. Supp. 106 (M.D. Pa. 1934); *In re Tomlinson & Dye, Inc.*, 3 F. Supp. 800 (N.D. Okla. 1933). This view disregarded §2a(2) of the Act and the "ancient and elementary power" of a referee as a court to reconsider orders. *In re Pottasch Brow. Co., Inc.*, 79 F.2d 613, 616 (2d Cir. 1935); *Castaner v. Mora*, 234 F.2d 710 (1st Cir. 1956). This rule recognizes, as did former Bankruptcy Rule 307, the power of the court to reconsider an order of disallowance on appropriate motion.

Reconsideration of a claim that has been previously allowed or disallowed after objection is discretionary with the court. The right to seek reconsideration of an allowed claim, like the right to object to its allowance, is generally exercised by the trustee if one has qualified and is performing the duties of that office with reasonable diligence and fidelity. A request for reconsideration of a disallowance would, on the other hand, ordinarily come from the claimant.

A proof of claim executed and filed in accordance with the rules in this Part III is prima facie evidence of the validity and the amount of the claim notwithstanding a motion for reconsideration of an order of allowance. Failure to respond does not constitute an admission, though it may be deemed a consent to a reconsideration. *In re Goble Boat Co.*, 190 Fed. 92 (N.D.N.Y. 1911). The court may decline to reconsider an order of allowance or disallowance without notice to any adverse party and without affording any hearing to the movant. If a motion to reconsider is granted, notice and hearing must be afforded to parties in interest before the previous action in the claim taken in respect to the claim may be vacated or modified. After reconsideration, the court may allow or disallow the claim, increase or decrease the amount of a prior allowance, accord the claim a priority different from that originally assigned it, or enter any other appropriate order.

The rule expands § 502(j) which provides for reconsideration of an allowance only before the case is closed. Authorities have disagreed as to whether reconsideration may be had after a case has been reopened. Compare 3 Collier *Bankruptcy* ¶57.23[4] (14th ed. 1964), see generally 3 *id.* ¶502.10 (15th ed. 1979), with 2 Remington, *Bankruptcy* 498 (Henderson ed. 1956). If a case is reopened as provided in § 350(b) of the Code, reconsideration of the allowance or disallowance of a claim may be sought and granted in accordance with this rule.

Rule 3009. Declaration and Payment of Dividends in a Chapter 7 Liquidation Case

In a chapter 7 case, dividends to creditors shall be paid as promptly as practicable. Dividend checks shall be made payable to and mailed to each creditor whose claim has been allowed, unless a power of attorney authorizing another entity to receive dividends has been executed and filed in accordance with Rule 9010. In that event, dividend checks shall be made payable to the creditor and to the other entity and shall be mailed to the other entity.

(As amended Mar. 30, 1987, eff. Aug. 1, 1987; Apr. 22, 1993, eff. Aug. 1, 1993.)

NOTES OF ADVISORY COMMITTEE ON RULES—1983

This rule is derived from former Rules 308 and 11-35(a). The preparation of records showing dividends declared and to whom payable is subject to prescription by the Director of the Administrative Office pursuant to Rule 5003(e). The rule governs distributions to creditors having priority as well as to general unsecured creditors. Notwithstanding the detailed statutory provisions regulating the declaration of dividends, a necessarily wide discretion over this matter has been recognized to reside in the court. See 3A Collier, *Bankruptcy* ¶65.03 (14th ed. 1975); 1 *Proceedings of Seminar for Newly Appointed Referees in Bankruptcy* 173 (1964). Although the rule leaves to the discretion of the court the amount and the times of dividend payments, it recognizes the creditors' right to as prompt payment as practicable.

The second and third sentences of the rule make explicit the method of payment of dividends and afford protection of the interests of the creditor and the holder of a power of attorney authorized to receive payment.

The rule does not permit variance at local option. This represents a marked change from former Bankruptcy Rule 308.

NOTES OF ADVISORY COMMITTEE ON RULES—1993 AMENDMENT

This rule is amended to delete the requirement that the court approve the amounts and times of distributions in chapter 7 cases. This change recognizes the role of the United States trustee in supervising trustees. Other amendments are stylistic and make no substantive change.

Rule 3010. Small Dividends and Payments in Chapter 7 Liquidation, Chapter 12 Family Farmer's Debt Adjustment, and Chapter 13 Individual's Debt Adjustment Cases

(a) CHAPTER 7 CASES. In a chapter 7 case no dividend in an amount less than $5 shall be distributed by the trustee to any creditor unless authorized by local rule or order of the court. Any dividend not distributed to a creditor shall be treated in the same manner as unclaimed funds as provided in § 347 of the Code.

(b) CHAPTER 12 AND CHAPTER 13 CASES. In a chapter 12 or chapter 13 case no payment in an amount less than $15 shall be distributed by the trustee to any creditor unless authorized by local rule or order of the court. Funds not distributed because of this subdivision shall accumulate and shall be paid whenever the accumulation aggregates $15. Any funds remaining shall be distributed with the final payment.

(As amended Mar. 30, 1987, eff. Aug. 1, 1987; Apr. 30, 1991, eff. Aug. 1, 1991.)

NOTES OF ADVISORY COMMITTEE ON RULES—1983

This rule permits a court to eliminate the disproportionate expense and inconvenience incurred by the issuance of a dividend check of less than $5 (or $15 in a chapter 13 case). Creditors are more irritated than pleased to receive such small dividends, but the money is held subject to their specific request as are unclaimed dividends under § 347(a) of the Code. When the trustee deposits undistributed dividends pursuant to a direction in accordance with this rule the trustee should file with the clerk a list of the names and addresses, so far as known, of the persons entitled to the money so deposited and the respective amounts payable to them pursuant to Rule 3011. In a chapter 13 case, the small dividend will accumulate and will be payable at the latest, with the final dividend. Local rule or order may change the practice permitted in this rule and, in that connection, the order may be incorporated in the order confirming a chapter 13 plan.

NOTES OF ADVISORY COMMITTEE ON RULES—1991 AMENDMENT

Subdivision (b) is amended to include chapter 12 cases.

Rule 3011. Unclaimed Funds in Chapter 7 Liquidation, Chapter 12 Family Farmer's Debt Adjustment, and Chapter 13 Individual's Debt Adjustment Cases

The trustee shall file a list of all known names and addresses of the entities and the amounts which they are entitled to be paid from remaining property of the estate that is paid into court pursuant to § 347(a) of the Code.

(As amended Mar. 30, 1987, eff. Aug. 1, 1987; Apr. 30, 1991, eff. Aug. 1, 1991.)

NOTES OF ADVISORY COMMITTEE ON RULES—1983

This rule is derived from former Bankruptcy Rule 310. The operative provisions of that rule, however, are contained in § 347(a) of the Code, requiring the trustee to stop payment of checks remaining unpaid 90 days after distribution. The rule adds the requirement of filing a list of the names and addresses of the persons entitled to these dividends. This rule applies in a chapter 7 or 13 case but not in a chapter 9 or 11 case. The latter cases are governed by § 347(b) of the Code which provides for unclaimed distributions to be returned to the debtor or other entity acquiring the assets of the debtor.

NOTES OF ADVISORY COMMITTEE ON RULES—1991 AMENDMENT

The title of this rule is amended to include chapter 12 cases. The words "with the clerk" are deleted as unnecessary. See Rules 5005(a) and 9001(3).

Rule 3012. Valuation of Security

The court may determine the value of a claim secured by a lien on property in which the estate has an interest on motion of any party in interest and after a hearing on notice to the holder of the secured claim and any other entity as the court may direct.

(As amended Mar. 30, 1987, eff. Aug. 1, 1987.)

NOTES OF ADVISORY COMMITTEE ON RULES—1983

Pursuant to §506(a) of the Code, secured claims are to be valued and allowed as secured to the extent of the value of the collateral and unsecured, to the extent it is enforceable, for the excess over such value. The valuation of secured claims may become important in different contexts *e.g.*, to determine the issue of adequate protection under §361, impairment under §1124, or treatment of the claim in a plan pursuant to §1129(b) of the Code. This rule permits the issue to be raised on motion by a party in interest. The secured creditor is entitled to notice of the hearing on the motion and the court may direct that others in the case also receive such notice.

An adversary proceeding is commenced when the validity, priority, or extent of a lien is at issue as prescribed by Rule 7001. That proceeding is relevant to the basis of the lien itself while valuation under Rule 3012 would be for the purposes indicated above.

Rule 3013. Classification of Claims and Interests

For the purposes of the plan and its acceptance, the court may, on motion after hearing on notice as the court may direct, determine classes of creditors and equity security holders pursuant to §§1122, 1222(b)(1), and 1322(b)(1) of the Code.

(As amended Apr. 30, 1991, eff. Aug. 1, 1991.)

NOTES OF ADVISORY COMMITTEE ON RULES—1983

Sections 1122 and 1322(b)(1) set the standards for classifying claims and interests but provide that such classification is accomplished in the plan. This rule does not change the standards; rather it recognizes that it may be desirable or necessary to establish proper classification before a plan can be formulated. It provides for a court hearing on such notice as the court may direct.

NOTES OF ADVISORY COMMITTEE ON RULES—1991 AMENDMENT

This rule is amended to include chapter 12 cases.

Rule 3014. Election Under §1111(b) by Secured Creditor in Chapter 9 Municipality or Chapter 11 Reorganization Case

An election of application of §1111(b)(2) of the Code by a class of secured creditors in a chapter 9 or 11 case may be made at any time prior to the conclusion of the hearing on the disclosure statement or within such later time as the court may fix. If the disclosure statement is conditionally approved pursuant to Rule 3017.1, and a final hearing on the disclosure statement is not held, the election of application of §1111(b)(2) may be made not later than the date fixed pursuant to Rule 3017.1(a)(2) or another date the court may fix. The election shall be in writing and signed unless made at the hearing on the disclosure statement. The election, if made by the majorities required by §1111(b)(1)(A)(i), shall be binding on all members of the class with respect to the plan.

(As amended Apr. 11, 1997, eff. Dec. 1, 1997.)

NOTES OF ADVISORY COMMITTEE ON RULES—1983

Pursuant to §1111(b)(1) of the Code, a nonrecourse secured loan is converted, automatically, into a recourse loan thereby entitling the creditor to an unsecured deficiency claim if the value of the collateral is less than the debt. The class, however, may retain the loan as a nonrecourse loan by electing application of §1111(b)(2) by the majorities stated in §1111(b)(1)(A)(i). That section does not specify any time periods for making the election.

Rule 3014 provides that if no agreement is negotiated, the election of §1111(b)(2) of the Code may be made at any time prior to conclusion of the hearing on the disclosure statement. Once the hearing has been concluded, it would be too late for a secured creditor class to demand different treatment unless the court has fixed a later time. This would be the case if, for example, a public class of secured creditors should have an approved disclosure statement prior to electing under §1111(b).

Generally it is important that the proponent of a plan ascertain the position of the secured creditor class before a plan is proposed. The secured creditor class must know the prospects of its treatment under the plan before it can intelligently determine its rights under §1111(b). The rule recognizes that there may be negotiations between the proponent of the plan and the secured creditor leading to a representation of desired treatment under §1111(b). If that treatment is approved by the requisite majorities of the class and culminates in a written, signed statement filed with the court, that statement becomes binding and the class may not thereafter demand different treatment under §1111(b) with respect to that plan. The proponent of the plan is thus enabled to seek approval of the disclosure statement and transmit the plan for voting in anticipation of confirmation. Only if that plan is not confirmed may the class of secured creditors thereafter change its prior election.

While this rule and the Code refer to a class of secured creditors it should be noted that ordinarily each secured creditor is in a separate and distinct class. In that event, the secured creditor has the sole power to determine application of §1111(b) with respect to that claim.

NOTES OF ADVISORY COMMITTEE ON RULES—1997 AMENDMENT

This amendment provides a deadline for electing application of §1111(b)(2) in a small business case in which a conditionally approved disclosure statement is finally approved without a hearing.

GAP Report on Rule 3014. No changes to the published draft.

Rule 3015. Filing, Objection to Confirmation, and Modification of a Plan in a Chapter 12 Family Farmer's Debt Adjustment or a Chapter 13 Individual's Debt Adjustment Case

(a) CHAPTER 12 PLAN. The debtor may file a chapter 12 plan with the petition. If a plan is not filed with the petition, it shall be filed within the time prescribed by §1221 of the Code.

(b) CHAPTER 13 PLAN. The debtor may file a chapter 13 plan with the petition. If a plan is not filed with the petition, it shall be filed within 14 days thereafter, and such time may not be further extended except for cause shown and on notice as the court may direct. If a case is converted to chapter 13, a plan shall be filed within 14 days thereafter, and such time may not be further extended except for cause shown and on notice as the court may direct.

(c) DATING. Every proposed plan and any modification thereof shall be dated.

(d) NOTICE AND COPIES. The plan or a summary of the plan shall be included with each notice of the hearing on confirmation mailed pursuant to Rule 2002. If required by the court, the debtor shall furnish a sufficient number of copies to enable the clerk to include a copy of the plan with the notice of the hearing.

(e) TRANSMISSION TO UNITED STATES TRUSTEE. The clerk shall forthwith transmit to the United States trustee a copy of the plan and any modification thereof filed pursuant to subdivision (a) or (b) of this rule.

(f) OBJECTION TO CONFIRMATION; DETERMINATION OF GOOD FAITH IN THE ABSENCE OF AN OBJECTION. An objection to confirmation of a plan shall be filed and served on the debtor, the trustee, and any other entity designated by the court, and shall be transmitted to the United States trustee, before confirmation of the plan. An objection to confirmation is governed by Rule 9014. If no objection is timely filed, the court may determine that the plan has been proposed in good faith and not by any means forbidden by law without receiving evidence on such issues.

(g) MODIFICATION OF PLAN AFTER CONFIRMATION. A request to modify a plan pursuant to §1229 or §1329 of the Code shall identify the proponent and shall be filed together with the proposed modification. The clerk, or some other person as the court may direct, shall give the debtor, the trustee, and all creditors not less than 21 days' notice by mail of the time fixed for filing objections and, if an objection is filed, the hearing to consider the proposed modification, unless the court orders otherwise with respect to creditors who are not affected by the proposed modification. A copy of the notice shall be transmitted to the United States trustee. A copy of the proposed modification, or a summary thereof, shall be included with the notice. If required by the court, the proponent shall furnish a sufficient number of copies of the proposed modification, or a summary thereof, to enable the clerk to include a copy with each notice. Any objection to the proposed modification shall be filed and served on the debtor, the trustee, and any other entity designated by the court, and shall be transmitted to the United States trustee. An objection to a proposed modification is governed by Rule 9014.

(As amended Apr. 30, 1991, eff. Aug. 1, 1991; Apr. 22, 1993, eff. Aug. 1, 1993; Mar. 26, 2009, eff. Dec. 1, 2009.)

NOTES OF ADVISORY COMMITTEE ON RULES—1983

Section 1321 provides only that the "debtor shall file a plan." No time periods are specified, nor is any other detail provided. The rule requires a chapter 13 plan to be filed either with the petition or within 15 days thereafter. The court may, for cause, extend the time. The rule permits a summary of the plan to be transmitted with the notice of the hearing on confirmation. The court may, however, require the plan itself to be transmitted and the debtor to supply enough copies for this purpose. In the former rules under Chapter XIII the plan would accompany the notice of the first meeting of creditors. It is more important for the plan or a summary of its terms to be sent with the notice of the confirmation hearing. At that hearing objections to the plan will be heard by the court.

NOTES OF ADVISORY COMMITTEE ON RULES—1991 AMENDMENT

This rule is amended to include chapter 12 plans. Section 1221 of the Code requires the debtor to file a chapter 12 plan not later than 90 days after the order for relief, except that the court may extend the period if an extension is "substantially justified."

Subdivision (e) enables the United States trustee to monitor chapter 12 and chapter 13 plans pursuant to 28 U.S.C. §586(a)(3)(C).

NOTES OF ADVISORY COMMITTEE ON RULES—1993 AMENDMENT

Subdivision (b) is amended to provide a time limit for filing a plan after a case has been converted to chapter 13. The substitution of "may" for "shall" is stylistic and makes no substantive change.

Subdivision (d) is amended to clarify that the plan or a summary of the plan must be included with each notice of the confirmation hearing in a chapter 12 case pursuant to Rule 2002(a).

Subdivision (f) is added to expand the scope of the rule to govern objections to confirmation in chapter 12 and chapter 13 cases. The subdivision also is amended to include a provision that permits the court, in the absence of an objection, to determine that the plan has been proposed in good faith and not by any means forbidden by law without the need to receive evidence on these issues. These matters are now governed by Rule 3020.

Subdivision (g) is added to provide a procedure for post-confirmation modification of chapter 12 and chapter 13 plans. These procedures are designed to be similar to the procedures for confirmation of plans. However, if no objection is filed with respect to a proposed modification of a plan after confirmation, the court is not required to hold a hearing. See §1229(b)(2) and §1329(b)(2) which provide that the plan as modified becomes the plan unless, after notice and a hearing, such modification is disapproved. See §102(1). The notice of the time fixed for filing objections to the proposed modification should set a date for a hearing to be held in the event that an objection is filed.

Amendments to the title of this rule are stylistic and make no substantive change.

COMMITTEE NOTES ON RULES—2009 AMENDMENT

The rule is amended to implement changes in connection with the amendment to Rule 9006(a) and the manner by which time is computed under the rules. The deadlines in the rule are amended to substitute a deadline that is a multiple of seven days. Throughout the rules, deadlines are amended in the following manner:

- 5-day periods become 7-day periods
- 10-day periods become 14-day periods
- 15-day periods become 14-day periods
- 20-day periods become 21-day periods
- 25-day periods become 28-day periods

Rule 3016. Filing of Plan and Disclosure Statement in a Chapter 9 Municipality or Chapter 11 Reorganization Case

(a) IDENTIFICATION OF PLAN. Every proposed plan and any modification thereof shall be dated and, in a chapter 11 case, identified with the name of the entity or entities submitting or filing it.

(b) DISCLOSURE STATEMENT. In a chapter 9 or 11 case, a disclosure statement under §1125 of the Code or evidence showing compliance with § 1126(b) shall be filed with the plan or within a time fixed by the court, unless the plan is intended to provide adequate information under § 1125(f)(1). If the plan is intended to provide adequate information under § 1125(f)(1), it shall be so designated and Rule 3017.1 shall apply as if the plan is a disclosure statement.

(c) INJUNCTION UNDER A PLAN. If a plan provides for an injunction against conduct not otherwise enjoined under the Code, the plan and disclosure statement shall describe in specific and conspicuous language (bold, italic, or underlined text) all acts to be enjoined and identify the entities that would be subject to the injunction.

(d) STANDARD FORM SMALL BUSINESS DISCLOSURE STATEMENT AND PLAN. In a small business case, the court may approve a disclosure statement and may confirm a plan that conform substantially to the appropriate Official Forms or other standard forms approved by the court.

(As amended Mar. 30, 1987, eff. Aug. 1, 1987; Apr. 30, 1991, eff. Aug. 1, 1991; Apr. 23, 1996, eff. Dec. 1, 1996; Apr. 23, 2001, eff. Dec. 1, 2001; Apr. 23, 2008, eff. Dec. 1, 2008.)

NOTES OF ADVISORY COMMITTEE ON RULES—1983

This rule implements the Code provisions concerning the filing of plans in chapters 9 and 11.

Chapter 9 Cases. Section 941 provides that the debtor may file a plan with the petition or thereafter but within a time fixed by the court. A rule, therefore, is unnecessary to specify the time for filing chapter 9 plans.

Chapter 11 Nonrailroad Cases. Section 1121 contains detailed provisions with respect to who may file a chapter 11 plan and, in part, the time period. Section 1121(a) permits a debtor to file a plan with the petition or at any time during the case. Section 1121(b) and (c) grants exclusive periods of 120 days and 180 days for the debtor to file and obtain acceptance of a plan. Failure to take advantage of these periods or the appointment of a trustee would permit other parties in interest to file a plan. These statutory provisions are not repeated in the rules.

Chapter 11 Railroad Cases. Pursuant to subchapter IV of chapter 11, § 1121 of the Code is applicable in railroad cases; see §§ 1161, 103(g). A trustee, however, is to be appointed in every case; thus, pursuant to § 1121(c), any party in interest may file a plan. See discussion of subdivision (a) of this rule, *infra*.

Subdivision (a). Section 1121(c), while permitting parties in interest a limited right to file plans, does not provide any time limitation. This subdivision sets as the deadline, the conclusion of the hearing on the disclosure statement. The court may, however, grant additional time. It is derived from former Chapter X Rule 10–301(c)(2) which used, as the cut-off time, the conclusion of the hearing on approval of a plan. As indicated, *supra*, § 1121(a) permits a debtor to file a plan at any time during the chapter 11 case. Under § 1121(c), parties other than a debtor may file a plan only after a trustee is appointed or the debtor's exclusive time expires.

Subdivision (b) requires plans to be properly identified.

Subdivision (c). This provision is new. In chapter 9 and 11 cases (including railroad reorganization cases) postpetition solicitation of votes on a plan requires transmittal of a disclosure statement, the contents of which have been approved by the court. See § 1125 of the Code. A prepetition solicitation must either have been in conformity with applicable nonbankruptcy law or, if none, the disclosure must have been of adequate information as set forth in § 1125 of the Code. See § 1126(b). Subdivision (c) of this rule provides the time for filing the disclosure statement or evidence of compliance with § 1126(b) which ordinarily will be with the plan but the court may allow a later time or the court may, pursuant to the last sentence, fix a time certain. Rule 3017 deals with the hearing on the disclosure statement. The disclosure statement, pursuant to § 1125 is to contain adequate information. "Adequate information" is defined in § 1125(a) as information that would permit a reasonable creditor or equity security holder to make an informed judgment on the plan.

NOTES OF ADVISORY COMMITTEE ON RULES—1991 AMENDMENT

Subdivision (a) is amended to enlarge the time for filing competing plans. A party in interest may not file a plan without leave of court only if an order approving a disclosure statement relating to another plan has been entered and a decision on confirmation of the plan has not been entered. This subdivision does not fix a deadline beyond which a debtor may not file a plan.

NOTES OF ADVISORY COMMITTEE ON RULES—1996 AMENDMENT

Section 1121(c) gives a party in interest the right to file a chapter 11 plan after expiration of the period when only the debtor may file a plan. Under § 1121(d), the exclusive period in which only the debtor may file a plan may be extended, but only if a party in interest so requests and the court, after notice and a hearing, finds cause for an extension. Subdivision (a) is abrogated because it could have the effect of extending the debtor's exclusive period for filing a plan without satisfying the requirements of § 1121(d). The abrogation of subdivision (a) does not affect the court's discretion with respect to the scheduling of hearings on the approval of disclosure statements when more than one plan has been filed.

The amendment to subdivision (c), redesignated as subdivision (b), is stylistic.

GAP Report on Rule 3016. No changes since publication, except for a stylistic change.

COMMITTEE NOTES ON RULES—2001 AMENDMENT

Subdivision (c) is added to assure that entities whose conduct would be enjoined under a plan, rather than by operation of the Code, are given adequate notice of the proposed injunction. The validity and effect of any injunction are substantive law matters that are beyond the scope of these rules.

Specific and conspicuous language is not necessary if the injunction contained in the plan is substantially the same as an injunction provided under the Code. For example, if a plan contains an injunction against acts to collect a discharged debt from the debtor, Rule 3016(c) would not apply because that conduct would be enjoined nonetheless under § 524(a)(2). But if a plan provides that creditors will be permanently enjoined from asserting claims against persons who are not debtors in the case, the plan and disclosure statement must highlight the injunctive language and comply with the requirements of Rule 3016(c). *See* § 524(e).

The requirement in this rule that the plan and disclosure statement identify the entities that would be subject to the injunction requires reasonable identification under the circumstances. If the entities that would be subject to the injunction cannot be identified by name, the plan and disclosure statement may describe them by class or category. For example, it may be sufficient to identify the subjects of the injunction as "all creditors of the debtor."

Changes Made After Publication and Comments. The word "highlighted" in the parenthesis was replaced with "underlined" because highlighted documents are difficult to scan electronically for inclusion in the clerks' files. The Committee Note was revised to put in a more prominent position the statement that the validity and effect of any injunction provided for in a plan are substantive matters beyond the scope of the rules. Other stylistic changes were made to the Committee Note.

COMMITTEE NOTES ON RULES—2008 AMENDMENT

Subdivision (b) is amended to recognize that, in 2005, §1125(f)(1) was added to the Code to provide that the plan proponent in a small business case need not file a disclosure statement if the plan itself includes adequate information and the court finds that a separate disclosure statement is unnecessary. If the plan is intended to provide adequate information in a small business case, it may be conditionally approved as a disclosure statement under Rule 3017.1 and is subject to all other rules applicable to disclosure statements in small business cases.

Subdivision (d) is added to the rule to implement §433 of the Bankruptcy Abuse Prevention and Consumer Protection Act of 2005 which requires the promulgation of Official Forms for plans and disclosure statements in small business cases. Section 1125(f)(2) of the Code provides that the court may approve a disclosure statement submitted on the appropriate Official Form or on a standard form approved by the court. The rule takes no position on whether a court may require a local standard form disclosure statement or plan of reorganization in lieu of the Official Forms.

Other amendments are stylistic.

Changes Made After Publication. No changes were made after publication.

Rule 3017. Court Consideration of Disclosure Statement in a Chapter 9 Municipality or Chapter 11 Reorganization Case

(a) HEARING ON DISCLOSURE STATEMENT AND OBJECTIONS. Except as provided in Rule 3017.1, after a disclosure statement is filed in accordance with Rule 3016(b), the court shall hold a hearing on at least 28 days' notice to the debtor, creditors, equity security holders and other parties in interest as provided in Rule 2002 to consider the disclosure statement and any objections or modifications thereto. The plan and the disclosure statement shall be mailed with the notice of the hearing only to the debtor, any trustee or committee appointed under the Code, the Securities and Exchange Commission and any party in interest who requests in writing a copy of the statement or plan. Objections to the disclosure statement shall be filed and served on the debtor, the trustee, any committee appointed under the Code, and any other entity designated by the court, at any time before the disclosure statement is approved or by an earlier date as the court may fix. In a chapter 11 reorganization case, every notice, plan, disclosure statement, and objection required to be served or mailed pursuant to this subdivision shall be transmitted to the United States trustee within the time provided in this subdivision.

(b) DETERMINATION ON DISCLOSURE STATEMENT. Following the hearing the court shall determine whether the disclosure statement should be approved.

(c) DATES FIXED FOR VOTING ON PLAN AND CONFIRMATION. On or before approval of the disclosure statement, the court shall fix a time within which the holders of claims and interests may accept or reject the plan and may fix a date for the hearing on confirmation.

(d) TRANSMISSION AND NOTICE TO UNITED STATES TRUSTEE, CREDITORS, AND EQUITY SECURITY HOLDERS. Upon approval of a disclosure statement,—[1] except to the extent that the court orders otherwise with respect to one or more unimpaired classes of creditors or equity security holders—the debtor in possession, trustee, proponent of the plan, or clerk as the court orders shall mail to all creditors and equity security holders, and in a chapter 11 reorganization case shall transmit to the United States trustee,

(1) the plan or a court-approved summary of the plan;

(2) the disclosure statement approved by the court;

(3) notice of the time within which acceptances and rejections of the plan may be filed; and

(4) any other information as the court may direct, including any court opinion approving the disclosure statement or a court-approved summary of the opinion.

In addition, notice of the time fixed for filing objections and the hearing on confirmation shall be mailed to all creditors and equity security holders in accordance with Rule 2002(b), and a form of ballot conforming to the appropriate Official Form shall be mailed to creditors and equity security holders entitled to vote on the plan. If the court opinion is not transmitted or only a summary of the plan is transmitted, the court opinion or the plan shall be provided on request of a party in interest at the plan proponent's expense. If the court orders that the disclosure statement and the plan or a summary of the plan shall not be mailed to any unimpaired class, notice that the class is designated in the plan as unimpaired and notice of the name and address of the person from whom the plan or summary of the plan and disclosure statement may be obtained upon request and at the plan proponent's expense, shall be mailed to members of the unimpaired class together with the notice of the time fixed for filing objections to and the hearing on confirmation. For the purposes of this subdivision, creditors and equity security holders shall include holders of stock, bonds, debentures, notes, and other securities of record on the date the order approving the disclosure statement is entered or another date fixed by the court, for cause, after notice and a hearing.

(e) TRANSMISSION TO BENEFICIAL HOLDERS OF SECURITIES. At the hearing held pursuant to subdivision (a) of this rule, the court shall consider the procedures for transmitting the documents and information required by subdivision (d) of this rule to beneficial holders of stock, bonds, debentures, notes, and other securities, determine the adequacy of the procedures, and enter any orders the court deems appropriate.

(f) NOTICE AND TRANSMISSION OF DOCUMENTS TO ENTITIES SUBJECT TO AN INJUNCTION UNDER A PLAN. If a plan provides for an injunction against conduct not otherwise enjoined under the Code and an entity that would be subject to the injunction is not a creditor or equity security holder, at the hearing held under Rule 3017(a), the court shall consider procedures for providing the entity with:

(1) at least 28 days' notice of the time fixed for filing objections and the hearing on confirmation of the plan containing the information described in Rule 2002(c)(3); and

(2) to the extent feasible, a copy of the plan and disclosure statement.

[1] So in original. The comma probably should not appear.

(As amended Mar. 30, 1987, eff. Aug. 1, 1987; Apr. 30, 1991, eff. Aug. 1, 1991; Apr. 11, 1997, eff. Dec. 1, 1997; Apr. 23, 2001, eff. Dec. 1, 2001; Mar. 26, 2009, eff. Dec. 1, 2009.)

NOTES OF ADVISORY COMMITTEE ON RULES—1983

This rule is adapted from former Rule 10-303 which dealt with the approval of a Chapter X plan by the court. There is no requirement for plan approval in a chapter 9 or 11 case under the Code but there is the requirement that a disclosure statement containing adequate financial information be approved by the court after notice and a hearing before votes on a plan are solicited. Section 1125(b) of the Code is made applicable in chapter 9 cases by §901(a). It is also applicable in railroad reorganization cases under subchapter IV of chapter 11; see §1161 of the Code.

Subdivision (a) of this rule provides for the hearing on the disclosure statement. Thus, a hearing would be required in all cases; whether it may be ex parte would depend on the circumstances of the case, but a mere absence of objections would not eliminate the need for a hearing; see §102(1) of the Code.

No provision similar to former Rule 10-303(f) is included. That subdivision together with former Rule 10-304 prohibited solicitation of votes until after entry of an order approving the plan. Section 1125(b) of the Code explicitly provides that votes on a plan may not be solicited until a disclosure statement approved by the court is transmitted. Pursuant to the change in rulemaking power, a comparable provision in this rule is unnecessary. 28 U.S.C. §2075.

Copies of the disclosure statement and plan need not be mailed with the notice of the hearing or otherwise transmitted prior to the hearing except with respect to the parties explicitly set forth in the subdivision.

It should be noted that, by construction, the singular includes the plural. Therefore, the phrase "plan or plans" or "disclosure statement or statements" has not been used although the possibility of multiple plans and statements is recognized.

Subdivision (d) permits the court to require a party other than the clerk of the bankruptcy court to bear the responsibility for transmitting the notices and documents specified in the rule when votes on the plan are solicited. Ordinarily the person responsible for such mailing will be the proponent of the plan. In rare cases the clerk may be directed to mail these documents, particularly when the trustee would have the responsibility but there is insufficient money in the estate to enable the trustee to perform this task.

NOTES OF ADVISORY COMMITTEE ON RULES—1987 AMENDMENT

Subdivision (d). Section 1125(c) of the Code requires that the entire approved disclosure statement be provided in connection with voting on a plan. The court is authorized by §1125(c) to approve different disclosure statements for different classes. Although the rule does not permit the mailing of a summary of the disclosure statement in place of the approved disclosure statement, the court may approve a summary of the disclosure statement to be mailed with the complete disclosure statement to those voting on the plan.

NOTES OF ADVISORY COMMITTEE ON RULES—1991 AMENDMENT

This rule is amended to enable the United States trustee to monitor and comment with regard to chapter 11 disclosure statements and plans. The United States trustee does not perform these functions in a chapter 9 municipal debt adjustment case. See 28 U.S.C. §586(a)(3)(B).

Subdivision (d) is amended to give the court the discretion to direct that one or more unimpaired classes shall not receive disclosure statements, plans, or summaries of plans. Members of unimpaired classes are not entitled to vote on the plan. Although disclosure statements enable members of unimpaired classes to make informed judgments as to whether to object to confirmation because of lack of feasibility or other grounds, in an unusual case the court may direct that disclosure statements shall not be sent to such classes if to do so would not be feasible considering the size of the unimpaired classes and the expense of printing and mailing. In any event, all creditors are entitled to notice of the time fixed for filing objections and notice of the hearing to consider confirmation of the plan pursuant to Rule 2002(b) and the requirement of such notice may not be excused with respect to unimpaired classes. The amendment to subdivision (d) also ensures that the members of unimpaired classes who do not receive such documents will have sufficient information so that they may request these documents in advance of the hearing on confirmation. The amendment to subdivision (d) is not intended to give the court the discretion to dispense with the mailing of the plan and disclosure statement to governmental units holding claims entitled to priority under §507(a)(7) because they may not be classified. See §1123(a)(1).

The words "with the court" in subdivision (a) are deleted as unnecessary. See Rules 5005(a) and 9001(3). Reference to the Official Form number in subdivision (d) is deleted in anticipation of future revision and renumbering of the Official Forms.

Subdivision (e) is designed to ensure that appropriate measures are taken for the plan, disclosure statement, ballot and other materials which are required to be transmitted to creditors and equity security holders under this rule to reach the beneficial holders of securities held in nominee name. Such measures may include orders directing the trustee or debtor in possession to reimburse the nominees out of the funds of the estate for the expenses incurred by them in distributing materials to beneficial holders. In most cases, the plan proponent will not know the identities of the beneficial holders and therefore it will be necessary to rely on the nominal holders of the securities to distribute the plan materials to the beneficial owners.

NOTES OF ADVISORY COMMITTEE ON RULES—1997 AMENDMENT

Subdivision (a) is amended to provide that it does not apply to the extent provided in new Rule 3017.1, which applies in small business cases.

Subdivision (d) is amended to provide flexibility in fixing the record date for the purpose of determining the holders of securities who are entitled to receive documents pursuant to this subdivision. For example, if there may be a delay between the oral announcement of the judge's order approving the disclosure statement and entry of the order on the court docket, the court may fix the date on which the judge orally approves the disclosure statement as the record date so that the parties may expedite preparation of the lists necessary to facilitate the distribution of the plan, disclosure statement, ballots, and other related documents.

The court may set a record date pursuant to subdivision (d) only after notice and a hearing as provided in §102(1) of the Code. Notice of a request for an order fixing the record date may be included in the notice of the hearing to consider approval of the disclosure statement mailed pursuant to Rule 2002(b).

If the court fixes a record date pursuant to subdivision (d) with respect to the holders of securities, and the holders are impaired by the plan, the judge also should order that the same record date applies for the purpose of determining eligibility for voting pursuant to Rule 3018(a).

Other amendments to this rule are stylistic.

GAP Report on Rule 3017. No changes to the published draft.

COMMITTEE NOTES ON RULES—2001 AMENDMENT

Subdivision (f) is added to assure that entities whose conduct would be enjoined under a plan, rather than by operation of the Code, and who will not receive the documents listed in subdivision (d) because they are neither creditors nor equity security holders, are provided with adequate notice of the proposed injunction. It does not address any substantive law issues relating to the validity or effect of any injunction provided under a plan, or any due process or other constitutional issues relating to notice. These issues are beyond the scope of these rules and are left for judicial determination.

This rule recognizes the need for adequate notice to subjects of an injunction, but that reasonable flexibility under the circumstances may be required. If a known and identifiable entity would be subject to the injunction, and the notice, plan, and disclosure statement could be mailed to that entity, the court should require that they be mailed at the same time that the plan, disclosure statement and related documents are mailed to creditors under Rule 3017(d). If mailing notices and other documents is not feasible because the entities subject to the injunction are described in the plan and disclosure statement by class or category and they cannot be identified individually by name and address, the court may require that notice under Rule 3017(f)(1) be published.

Changes Made After Publication and Comments. No changes were made in the text of the proposed amendments since publication. The Committee Note was revised to put in a more prominent position the statement that the rule does not address related substantive law issues which are beyond the scope of the rules.

COMMITTEE NOTES ON RULES—2009 AMENDMENT

The rule is amended to implement changes in connection with the amendment to Rule 9006(a) and the manner by which time is computed under the rules. The deadlines in the rule are amended to substitute a deadline that is a multiple of seven days. Throughout the rules, deadlines are amended in the following manner:

- 5-day periods become 7-day periods
- 10-day periods become 14-day periods
- 15-day periods become 14-day periods
- 20-day periods become 21-day periods
- 25-day periods become 28-day periods

Rule 3017.1. Court Consideration of Disclosure Statement in a Small Business Case

(a) CONDITIONAL APPROVAL OF DISCLOSURE STATEMENT. In a small business case, the court may, on application of the plan proponent or on its own initiative, conditionally approve a disclosure statement filed in accordance with Rule 3016. On or before conditional approval of the disclosure statement, the court shall:

(1) fix a time within which the holders of claims and interests may accept or reject the plan;

(2) fix a time for filing objections to the disclosure statement;

(3) fix a date for the hearing on final approval of the disclosure statement to be held if a timely objection is filed; and

(4) fix a date for the hearing on confirmation.

(b) APPLICATION OF RULE 3017. Rule 3017(a), (b), (c), and (e) do not apply to a conditionally approved disclosure statement. Rule 3017(d) applies to a conditionally approved disclosure statement, except that conditional approval is considered approval of the disclosure statement for the purpose of applying Rule 3017(d).

(c) FINAL APPROVAL.

(1) *Notice.* Notice of the time fixed for filing objections and the hearing to consider final approval of the disclosure statement shall be given in accordance with Rule 2002 and may be combined with notice of the hearing on confirmation of the plan.

(2) *Objections.* Objections to the disclosure statement shall be filed, transmitted to the United States trustee, and served on the debtor, the trustee, any committee appointed under the Code and any other entity designated by the court at any time before final approval of the disclosure statement or by an earlier date as the court may fix.

(3) *Hearing.* If a timely objection to the disclosure statement is filed, the court shall hold a hearing to consider final approval before or combined with the hearing on confirmation of the plan.

(Added Apr. 11, 1997, eff. Dec. 1, 1997; amended Apr. 23, 2008, eff. Dec. 1, 2008.)

NOTES OF ADVISORY COMMITTEE ON RULES—1997

This rule is added to implement §1125(f) that was added to the Code by the Bankruptcy Reform Act of 1994.

The procedures for electing to be considered a small business are set forth in Rule 1020. If the debtor is a small business and has elected to be considered a small business, §1125(f) permits the court to conditionally approve a disclosure statement subject to final approval after notice and a hearing. If a disclosure statement is conditionally approved, and no timely objection to the disclosure statement is filed, it is not necessary for the court to hold a hearing on final approval.

GAP Report on Rule 3017.1. No change to the published draft.

COMMITTEE NOTES ON RULES—2008 AMENDMENT

Section 101 of the Code, as amended in 2005, defines a "small business case" and "small business debtor," and eliminates any need to elect that status. Therefore, the reference in the rule to an election is deleted.

As provided in the amendment to Rule 3016(b), a plan intended to provide adequate information in a small business case under §1125(f)(1) may be conditionally approved and is otherwise treated as a disclosure statement under this rule.

Changes Made After Publication. No changes were made after publication.

Rule 3018. Acceptance or Rejection of Plan in a Chapter 9 Municipality or a Chapter 11 Reorganization Case

(a) ENTITIES ENTITLED TO ACCEPT OR REJECT PLAN; TIME FOR ACCEPTANCE OR REJECTION. A plan may be accepted or rejected in accordance with §1126 of the Code within the time fixed by the court pursuant to Rule 3017. Subject to subdivision (b) of this rule, an equity security holder or creditor whose claim is based on a security of record shall not be entitled to accept or reject a plan unless the equity security holder or creditor is the holder of record of the security on the date the order approving the disclosure statement is entered or on another date fixed by the court, for cause, after notice and a hearing. For cause shown, the court after notice and hearing may permit a creditor or equity security holder to change or withdraw an acceptance or rejection. Notwithstanding objection to a claim or interest, the court after notice and hearing may temporarily allow the claim or interest in an amount which the court deems proper for the purpose of accepting or rejecting a plan.

(b) ACCEPTANCES OR REJECTIONS OBTAINED BEFORE PETITION. An equity security holder or creditor whose claim is based on a security of record who accepted or rejected the plan before the commencement of the case shall not be deemed to have accepted or rejected the plan pursuant to §1126(b) of the Code unless the equity security holder or creditor was the holder of record of the security on the date specified in the solicitation of such acceptance or rejection for the purposes of such solicitation. A holder of a claim or interest who has accepted or rejected a plan before the commencement of the case under the Code shall not be deemed to have accepted or rejected the plan if the court finds after notice and hearing that the plan was not transmitted to substantially all creditors and equity security holders of the same class, that an unreasonably short time was prescribed for such creditors and equity security holders to accept or reject the plan, or that the solicitation was not in compliance with §1126(b) of the Code.

(c) FORM OF ACCEPTANCE OR REJECTION. An acceptance or rejection shall be in writing, identify the plan or plans accepted or rejected, be signed by the creditor or equity security holder or an authorized agent, and conform to the appropriate Official Form. If more than one plan is transmitted pursuant to Rule 3017, an acceptance or rejection may be filed by each creditor or equity security holder for any number of plans transmitted and if acceptances are filed for more than one plan, the creditor or equity security holder may indicate a preference or preferences among the plans so accepted.

(d) ACCEPTANCE OR REJECTION BY PARTIALLY SECURED CREDITOR. A creditor whose claim has been allowed in part as a secured claim and in part as an unsecured claim shall be entitled to accept or reject a plan in both capacities.

(As amended Mar. 30, 1987, eff. Aug. 1, 1987; Apr. 30, 1991, eff. Aug. 1, 1991; Apr. 22, 1993, eff. Aug. 1, 1993; Apr. 11, 1997, eff. Dec. 1, 1997.)

NOTES OF ADVISORY COMMITTEE ON RULES—1983

This rule applies in chapter 9, 11 and 13 cases under the Code. The references in the rule to equity security holders will not, however, be relevant in chapter 9 or 13 cases. The rule will be of little utility in a chapter 13 case because only secured creditors may be requested to vote on a plan; unsecured creditors are not entitled to vote; see §1325(a)(4), (5) of the Code.

Subdivision (a) is derived from former Rule 10–305(a). It substitutes, in a reorganization case, entry of the order approving the disclosure statement for the order approving a plan in conformity with the differences between Chapter X and chapter 11. In keeping with the underlying theory it continues to recognize that the lapse of time between the filing of the petition and entry of such order will normally be significant and, during that interim, bonds and equity interests can change ownership.

Subdivision (b) recognizes the former Chapter XI practice permitting a plan and acceptances to be filed with the petition, as does §1126(b) of the Code. However, because a plan under chapter 11 may affect shareholder interests, there should be reference to a record date of ownership. In this instance the appropriate record date is that used in the prepetition solicitation materials because it is those acceptances or rejections which are being submitted to the court.

While §1126(c), (d), and (e) prohibits use of an acceptance or rejection not procured in good faith, the added provision in subdivision (b) of the rule is somewhat more detailed. It would prohibit use of prepetition acceptances or rejections when some but not all impaired creditors or equity security holders are solicited or when they are not given a reasonable opportunity to submit their acceptances or rejections. This provision together with §1126(e) gives the court the power to nullify abusive solicitation procedures.

Subdivision (c). It is possible that multiple plans may be before the court for confirmation. Pursuant to §1129(c) of the Code, the court may confirm only one plan but is required to consider the preferences expressed by those accepting the plans in determining which one to confirm.

Subdivisions (d) and (e) of former Rule 10–305 are not continued since comparable provisions are contained in the statute; see §1126(c), (d), (e).

It should be noted that while the singular "plan" is used throughout, by construction the plural is included; see §102(7).

NOTES OF ADVISORY COMMITTEE ON RULES—1991 AMENDMENT

Subdivisions (a) and (b) are amended to delete provisions that duplicate §1126 of the Code. An entity who is not a record holder of a security, but who claims that it is entitled to be treated as a record holder, may file a statement pursuant to Rule 3003(d).

Subdivision (a) is amended further to allow the court to permit a creditor or equity security holder to change or withdraw an acceptance or rejection for cause shown whether or not the time fixed for voting has expired.

Subdivision (b) is also amended to give effect to a prepetition acceptance or rejection if solicitation requirements were satisfied with respect to substantially all members of the same class, instead of requiring proper solicitation with respect to substantially all members of all classes.

Subdivision (c) is amended to delete the Official Form number in anticipation of future revision and renumbering of the Official Forms.

NOTES OF ADVISORY COMMITTEE ON RULES—1993 AMENDMENT

The title of this rule is amended to indicate that it applies only in a chapter 9 or a chapter 11 case. The amendment of the word "Plans" to "Plan" is stylistic.

NOTES OF ADVISORY COMMITTEE ON RULES—1997 AMENDMENT

Subdivision (a) is amended to provide flexibility in fixing the record date for the purpose of determining the holders of securities who are entitled to vote on the plan. For example, if there may be a delay between the oral announcement of the judge's decision approving the disclosure statement and entry of the order on the court docket, the court may fix the date on which the judge orally approves the disclosure statement as the record date for voting purposes so that the parties may expedite preparation of the lists necessary to facilitate the distribution of the plan, disclosure statement, ballots, and other related documents in connection with the solicitation of votes.

The court may set a record date pursuant to subdivision (a) only after notice and a hearing as provided in §102(1) of the Code. Notice of a request for an order fixing the record date may be included in the notice of the hearing to consider approval of the disclosure statement mailed pursuant to Rule 2002(b).

If the court fixes the record date for voting purposes, the judge also should order that the same record date shall apply for the purpose of distributing the documents required to be distributed pursuant to Rule 3017(d).

GAP Report on Rule 3018. No changes to the published draft.

Rule 3019. Modification of Accepted Plan in a Chapter 9 Municipality or a Chapter 11 Reorganization Case

(a) MODIFICATION OF PLAN BEFORE CONFIRMATION. In a chapter 9 or chapter 11 case, after a plan has been accepted and before its confirmation, the proponent may file a modification of the plan. If the court finds after hearing on notice to the trustee, any committee appointed under the Code, and any other entity designated by the court that the proposed modification does not adversely change the treatment of the claim of any creditor or the interest of any equity security holder who has not accepted in writing the modification, it shall be deemed accepted by all creditors and equity security holders who have previously accepted the plan.

(b) MODIFICATION OF PLAN AFTER CONFIRMATION IN INDIVIDUAL DEBTOR CASE. If the debtor is an individual, a request to modify the plan under § 1127(e) of the Code is governed by Rule 9014. The request shall identify the proponent and shall be filed together with the proposed modification. The clerk, or some other person as the court may direct, shall give the debtor, the trustee, and all creditors not less than 21 days' notice by mail of the time fixed to file objections and, if an objection is filed, the hearing to consider the proposed modification, unless the court orders otherwise with respect to creditors who are not affected by the proposed modification. A copy of the notice shall be transmitted to the United States trustee, together with a copy of the proposed modification. Any objection to the proposed modification shall be filed and served on the debtor, the proponent of the modification, the trustee, and any other entity designated by the court, and shall be transmitted to the United States trustee.

(As amended Mar. 30, 1987, eff. Aug. 1, 1987; Apr. 22, 1993, eff. Aug. 1, 1993; Apr. 23, 2008, eff. Dec. 1, 2008; Mar. 26, 2009, eff. Dec. 1, 2009.)

NOTES OF ADVISORY COMMITTEE ON RULES—1983

This rule implements §§ 942, 1127 and 1323 of the Code. For example, § 1127 provides for modification before and after confirmation but does not deal with the minor modifications that do not adversely change any rights. The rule makes clear that a modification may be made, after acceptance of the plan without submission to creditors and equity security holders if their interests are not affected. To come within this rule, the modification should be one that does not change the rights of a creditor or equity security holder as fixed in the plan before modification.

NOTES OF ADVISORY COMMITTEE ON RULES—1993 AMENDMENT

This rule is amended to limit its application to chapter 9 and chapter 11 cases. Modification of plans after confirmation in chapter 12 and chapter 13 cases is governed by Rule 3015. The addition of the comma in the second sentence is stylistic and makes no substantive change.

COMMITTEE NOTES ON RULES—2008 AMENDMENT

The 2005 amendments to § 1127 of the Code provide for modification of a confirmed plan in an individual debtor chapter 11 case. Therefore, the rule is amended to establish the procedure for filing and objecting to a proposed modification of a confirmed plan.

Changes Made After Publication. The last sentence of the published rule provided that an objection to modification of a plan is governed by Rule 9014. The sentence is deleted and the reference to Rule 9014 is moved to the first sentence of subdivision (b) of the rule. The Committee Note was revised to make the reference to the 2005 amendments to the Bankruptcy Code consistent with their identification in other Committee Notes.

COMMITTEE NOTES ON RULES—2009 AMENDMENT

The rule is amended to implement changes in connection with the amendment to Rule 9006(a) and the manner by which time is computed under the rules. The deadline in the rule is amended to substitute a deadline that is a multiple of seven days. Throughout the rules, deadlines are amended in the following manner:

- 5-day periods become 7-day periods
- 10-day periods become 14-day periods
- 15-day periods become 14-day periods
- 20-day periods become 21-day periods
- 25-day periods become 28-day periods

Rule 3020. Deposit; Confirmation of Plan in a Chapter 9 Municipality or Chapter 11 Reorganization Case

(a) DEPOSIT. In a chapter 11 case, prior to entry of the order confirming the plan, the court may order the deposit with the trustee or debtor in possession of the consideration required by the plan to be distributed on confirmation. Any money deposited shall be kept in a special account established for the exclusive purpose of making the distribution.

(b) OBJECTION TO AND HEARING ON CONFIRMATION IN A CHAPTER 9 OR CHAPTER 11 CASE.

(1) *Objection.* An objection to confirmation of the plan shall be filed and served on the debtor, the trustee, the proponent of the plan, any committee appointed under the Code, and any other entity designated by the court, within a time fixed by the court. Unless the case is a chapter 9 municipality case, a copy of every objection to confirmation shall be transmitted by the objecting party to the United States trustee within the time fixed for filing objections. An objection to confirmation is governed by Rule 9014.

(2) *Hearing.* The court shall rule on confirmation of the plan after notice and hearing as provided in Rule 2002. If no objection is timely filed, the court may determine that the plan has been proposed in good faith and not by any means forbidden by law without receiving evidence on such issues.

(c) ORDER OF CONFIRMATION.

(1) The order of confirmation shall conform to the appropriate Official Form. If the plan provides for an injunction against conduct not otherwise enjoined under the Code, the order of confirmation shall (1) describe in reasonable detail all acts enjoined; (2) be specific in its terms regarding the injunction; and (3) identify the entities subject to the injunction.

(2) Notice of entry of the order of confirmation shall be mailed promptly to the debtor, the trustee, creditors, equity security holders, other parties in interest, and, if known, to any identified entity subject to an injunction provided for in the plan against conduct not otherwise enjoined under the Code.

(3) Except in a chapter 9 municipality case, notice of entry of the order of confirmation shall be transmitted to the United States trustee as provided in Rule 2002(k).

(d) RETAINED POWER. Notwithstanding the entry of the order of confirmation, the court may issue any other order necessary to administer the estate.

(e) STAY OF CONFIRMATION ORDER. An order confirming a plan is stayed until the expiration of 14 days after the entry of the order, unless the court orders otherwise.

(As amended Mar. 30, 1987, eff. Aug. 1, 1987; Apr. 30, 1991, eff. Aug. 1, 1991; Apr. 22, 1993, eff. Aug. 1, 1993; Apr. 26, 1999, eff. Dec. 1, 1999; Apr. 23, 2001, eff. Dec. 1, 2001; Mar. 26, 2009, eff. Dec. 1, 2009.)

NOTES OF ADVISORY COMMITTEE ON RULES—1983

This rule is adapted from former Rules 10–307, 11–38, and 13–213. It applies to cases filed under chapters 9, 11 and 13. Certain subdivisions of the earlier rules have not been included, such as, a subdivision revesting title in the debtor because §541 of the Code does not transfer title out of the debtor as did §70a of the Bankruptcy Act; see also §§1141(b), 1327(b). Subdivision (b) of former Rule 13–213 is not included because its provisions are contained in the statute; see §§1322, 1325(b), 105.

Subdivision (a) gives discretion to the court to require in chapter 11 cases the deposit of any consideration to be distributed on confirmation. If money is to be distributed, it is to be deposited in a special account to assure that it will not be used for any other purpose. The Code is silent in chapter 11 with respect to the need to make a deposit or the person with whom any deposit is to be made. Consequently, there is no statutory authority for any person to act in a capacity similar to the disbursing agent under former Chapter XI practice. This rule provides that only the debtor in possession or trustee should be appointed as the recipient of the deposit. Any consideration other than money, *e.g.*, notes or stock may be given directly to the debtor in possession or trustee and need not be left in any kind of special account. In chapter 9 cases, §944(b) provides for deposit with a disbursing agent appointed by the court of any consideration to be distributed under the plan.

Subdivision (d) clarifies the authority of the court to conclude matters pending before it prior to confirmation and to continue to administer the estate as necessary, *e.g.*, resolving objections to claims.

NOTES OF ADVISORY COMMITTEE ON RULES—1991 AMENDMENT

The United States trustee monitors chapter 11, chapter 12, and chapter 13 plans and has standing to be heard regarding confirmation of a plan. See 28 U.S.C. §586(a)(3). The amendments to subdivisions (b)(1) and (c) of this rule facilitate that role of the United States trustee. Subdivision (b)(1) is also amended to require service on the proponent of the plan of objections to confirmation. The words "with the court" in subdivision (b)(1) are deleted as unnecessary. See Rules 5005(a) and 9001(3).

In a chapter 12 case, the court is required to conduct and conclude the hearing on confirmation of the plan within the time prescribed in §1224 of the Code.

Subdivision (c) is also amended to require that the confirmation order be mailed to the trustee. Reference to the Official Form number is deleted in anticipation of future revision and renumbering of the Official Forms.

NOTES OF ADVISORY COMMITTEE ON RULES—1993 AMENDMENT

This rule is amended to limit its application to chapter 9 and chapter 11 cases. The procedures relating to confirmation of plans in chapter 12 and chapter 13 cases are provided in Rule 3015. Other amendments are stylistic and make no substantive change.

COMMITTEE NOTES ON RULES—1999 AMENDMENT

Subdivision (e) is added to provide sufficient time for a party to request a stay pending appeal of an order confirming a plan under chapter 9 or chapter 11 of the Code before the plan is implemented and an appeal becomes moot. Unless the court orders otherwise, any transfer of assets, issuance of securities, and cash distributions provided for in the plan may not be made before the expiration of the 10-day period. The stay of the confirmation order under subdivision (e) does not affect the time for filing a notice of appeal from the confirmation order in accordance with Rule 8002.

The court may, in its discretion, order that Rule 3020(e) is not applicable so that the plan may be implemented and distributions may be made immediately. Alternatively, the court may order that the stay under Rule 3020(e) is for a fixed period less than 10 days.

GAP Report on Rule 3020. No changes since publication.

COMMITTEE NOTES ON RULES—2001 AMENDMENT

Subdivision (c) is amended to provide notice to an entity subject to an injunction provided for in a plan against conduct not otherwise enjoined by operation of the Code. This requirement is not applicable to an injunction contained in a plan if it is substantially the same as an injunction provided under the Code. The validity and effect of any injunction provided for in a plan are substantive law matters that are beyond the scope of these rules.

The requirement that the order of confirmation identify the entities subject to the injunction requires only reasonable identification under the circumstances. If the entities that would be subject to the injunction cannot be identified by name, the order may describe them by class or category if reasonable under the circumstances. For example, it may be sufficient to identify the entities as "all creditors of the debtor."

Changes Made After Publication and Comments. No changes were made in the text of the proposed amendments. The Committee Note was revised to put in a more prominent position the statement that the validity and effect of injunctions provided for in plans is beyond the scope of the rules.

COMMITTEE NOTES ON RULES—2009 AMENDMENT

The rule is amended to implement changes in connection with the amendment to Rule 9006(a) and the manner by which time is computed under the rules. The deadline in the rule is amended to substitute a deadline that is a multiple of seven days. Throughout the rules, deadlines are amended in the following manner:

- 5-day periods become 7-day periods
- 10-day periods become 14-day periods
- 15-day periods become 14-day periods
- 20-day periods become 21-day periods
- 25-day periods become 28-day periods

Rule 3021. Distribution Under Plan

Except as provided in Rule 3020(e), after a plan is confirmed, distribution shall be made to creditors whose claims have been allowed, to interest holders whose interests have not been disallowed, and to indenture trustees who have filed claims under Rule 3003(c)(5) that have been allowed. For purposes of this rule, creditors include holders of bonds, debentures, notes, and other debt securities, and interest holders include the holders of stock and other equity securities, of record at the time of commencement of distribution, unless a different time is fixed by the plan or the order confirming the plan.

(As amended Apr. 11, 1997, eff. Dec. 1, 1997; Apr. 26, 1999, eff. Dec. 1, 1999.)

NOTES OF ADVISORY COMMITTEE ON RULES—1983

This rule is derived from former Chapter X Rule 10–405(a). Subdivision (b) of that rule is covered by §1143 of the Code.

NOTES OF ADVISORY COMMITTEE ON RULES—1997 AMENDMENT

This rule is amended to provide flexibility in fixing the record date for the purpose of making distributions to holders of securities of record. In a large case, it may be impractical for the debtor to determine the holders of record with respect to publicly held securities and also to make distributions to those holders at the same time. Under this amendment, the plan or the order confirming the plan may fix a record date for distributions that is earlier than the date on which distributions commence.

This rule also is amended to treat holders of bonds, debentures, notes, and other debt securities the same as any other creditors by providing that they shall receive a distribution only if their claims have been allowed. Finally, the amendments clarify that distributions are to be made to all interest holders—not only those that are within the definition of "equity security holders" under §101 of the Code—whose interests have not been disallowed.

GAP Report on Rule 3021. No changes to the published draft.

COMMITTEE NOTES ON RULES—1999 AMENDMENT

This amendment is to conform to the amendments to Rule 3020 regarding the ten-day stay of an order confirming a plan in a chapter 9 or chapter 11 case. The other amendments are stylistic.

GAP Report on Rule 3021. No changes since publication.

Rule 3022. Final Decree in Chapter 11 Reorganization Case

After an estate is fully administered in a chapter 11 reorganization case, the court, on its own motion or on motion of a party in interest, shall enter a final decree closing the case.

(As amended Mar. 30, 1987, eff. Aug. 1, 1987; Apr. 30, 1991, eff. Aug. 1, 1991.)

NOTES OF ADVISORY COMMITTEE ON RULES—1983

Section 350 of the Code requires the court to close the case after the estate is fully administered and the trustee has been discharged. Section 1143 places a five year limitation on the surrender of securities when required for participation under a plan but this provision should not delay entry of the final decree.

NOTES OF ADVISORY COMMITTEE ON RULES—1991 AMENDMENT

Entry of a final decree closing a chapter 11 case should not be delayed solely because the payments required by the plan have not been completed. Factors that the court should consider in determining whether the estate has been fully administered include (1) whether the order confirming the plan has become final, (2) whether deposits required by the plan have been distributed, (3) whether the property proposed by the plan to be transferred has been transferred, (4) whether the debtor or the successor of the debtor under the plan has assumed the business or the management of the property dealt with by the plan, (5) whether payments under the plan have commenced, and (6) whether all motions, contested matters, and adversary proceedings have been finally resolved.

The court should not keep the case open only because of the possibility that the court's jurisdiction may be invoked in the future. A final decree closing the case after the estate is fully administered does not deprive the court of jurisdiction to enforce or interpret its own orders and does not prevent the court from reopening the case for cause pursuant to §350(b) of the Code. For example, on motion of a party in interest, the court may reopen the case to revoke an order of confirmation procured by fraud under §1144 of the Code. If the plan or confirmation order provides that the case shall remain open until a certain date or event because of the likelihood that the court's jurisdiction may be required for specific purposes prior thereto, the case should remain open until that date or event.

PART IV—THE DEBTOR: DUTIES AND BENEFITS

Rule 4001. Relief from Automatic Stay; Prohibiting or Conditioning the Use, Sale, or Lease of Property; Use of Cash Collateral; Obtaining Credit; Agreements

(a) RELIEF FROM STAY; PROHIBITING OR CONDITIONING THE USE, SALE, OR LEASE OF PROPERTY.

(1) *Motion.* A motion for relief from an automatic stay provided by the Code or a motion to prohibit or condition the use, sale, or lease of property pursuant to §363(e) shall be made in accordance with Rule 9014 and shall be served on any committee elected pursuant to §705 or appointed pursuant to §1102 of the Code or its authorized agent, or, if the case is a chapter 9 municipality case or a chapter 11 reorganization case and no committee of unsecured creditors has been appointed pursuant to §1102, on the creditors included on the list filed pursuant to Rule 1007(d), and on such other entities as the court may direct.

(2) *Ex Parte Relief.* Relief from a stay under §362(a) or a request to prohibit or condition the use, sale, or lease of property pursuant to §363(e) may be granted without prior notice only if (A) it clearly appears from specific facts shown by affidavit or by a verified motion that immediate and irreparable injury, loss, or damage will result to the movant before the adverse party or the attorney for the adverse party can be heard in opposition, and (B) the movant's attorney certifies to the court in writing the efforts, if any, which have been made to give notice and the reasons why notice should not be required. The party obtaining relief under this subdivision and §362(f) or §363(e) shall immediately give oral notice thereof to the trustee or debtor in possession and to the debtor and forthwith mail or otherwise transmit to such adverse party or parties a copy of the order granting relief. On two days notice to the party who obtained relief from the stay without notice or on shorter notice to that party as the court may prescribe, the adverse party may appear and move reinstatement of the stay or reconsideration of the order prohibiting or conditioning the use, sale, or lease of property. In that event, the court shall proceed expeditiously to hear and determine the motion.

(3) *Stay of Order.* An order granting a motion for relief from an automatic stay made in accordance with Rule 4001(a)(1) is stayed until the expiration of 14 days after the entry of the order, unless the court orders otherwise.

(b) USE OF CASH COLLATERAL.

(1) *Motion; Service.*

(A) *Motion.* A motion for authority to use cash collateral shall be made in accordance with Rule 9014 and shall be accompanied by a proposed form of order.

(B) *Contents.* The motion shall consist of or (if the motion is more than five pages in length) begin with a concise statement of the relief requested, not to exceed five pages, that lists or summarizes, and sets out the location within the relevant documents of, all material provisions, including:

(i) the name of each entity with an interest in the cash collateral;

(ii) the purposes for the use of the cash collateral;

(iii) the material terms, including duration, of the use of the cash collateral; and

(iv) any liens, cash payments, or other adequate protection that will be provided to each entity with an interest in the cash collateral or, if no additional adequate protection is proposed, an explanation of why each entity's interest is adequately protected.

(C) *Service.* The motion shall be served on: (1) any entity with an interest in the cash collateral; (2) any committee elected under §705 or appointed under §1102 of the Code, or its authorized agent, or, if the case is a chapter 9 municipality case or a chapter 11 reorganization case and no committee of unsecured creditors has been appointed under §1102, the creditors included on the list filed under Rule 1007(d); and (3) any other entity that the court directs.

(2) *Hearing.* The court may commence a final hearing on a motion for authorization to use cash collateral no earlier than 14 days after service of the motion. If the motion so requests, the court may conduct a preliminary hearing before such 14-day period expires, but the court may authorize the use of only that amount of cash collateral as is necessary to avoid immediate and irreparable harm to the estate pending a final hearing.

(3) *Notice.* Notice of hearing pursuant to this subdivision shall be given to the parties on whom service of the motion is required by paragraph (1) of this subdivision and to such other entities as the court may direct.

(c) OBTAINING CREDIT.

(1) *Motion; Service.*

(A) *Motion.* A motion for authority to obtain credit shall be made in accordance with Rule 9014 and shall be accompanied by a copy of the credit agreement and a proposed form of order.

(B) *Contents.* The motion shall consist of or (if the motion is more than five pages in length) begin with a concise statement of the relief requested, not to exceed five pages, that lists or summarizes, and sets out the location within the relevant documents of, all material provisions of the proposed credit agreement and form of order, including interest rate, maturity, events of default, liens, borrowing limits, and borrowing conditions. If the proposed credit agreement or form of order includes any of the provisions listed below, the concise statement shall also: briefly list or summarize each one; identify its specific location in the proposed agreement and form of order; and identify any such provision that is proposed to remain in effect if interim approval is granted, but final relief is denied, as provided under Rule 4001(c)(2). In addition, the motion shall describe the nature and extent of each provision listed below:

(i) a grant of priority or a lien on property of the estate under §364(c) or (d);

(ii) the providing of adequate protection or priority for a claim that arose before the commencement of the case, including the granting of a lien on property of the estate to secure the claim, or the use of property of the estate or credit obtained under §364 to make cash payments on account of the claim;

(iii) a determination of the validity, enforceability, priority, or amount of a claim that arose before the commencement of the case, or of any lien securing the claim;

(iv) a waiver or modification of Code provisions or applicable rules relating to the automatic stay;

(v) a waiver or modification of any entity's authority or right to file a plan, seek an extension of time in which the debtor has the exclusive right to file a plan, request the use of cash collateral under §363(c), or request authority to obtain credit under §364;

(vi) the establishment of deadlines for filing a plan of reorganization, for approval of a disclosure statement, for a hearing on confirmation, or for entry of a confirmation order;

(vii) a waiver or modification of the applicability of nonbankruptcy law relating to the perfection of a lien on property of the estate, or on the foreclosure or other enforcement of the lien;

(viii) a release, waiver, or limitation on any claim or other cause of action belonging to the estate or the trustee, including any modification of the statute of limitations or other deadline to commence an action;

(ix) the indemnification of any entity;

(x) a release, waiver, or limitation of any right under §506(c); or

(xi) the granting of a lien on any claim or cause of action arising under §§544,[1] 545, 547, 548, 549, 553(b), 723(a), or 724(a).

(C) *Service.* The motion shall be served on: (1) any committee elected under §705 or appointed under §1102 of the Code, or its authorized agent, or, if the case is a chapter 9 municipality case or a chapter 11 reorganization case and no committee of unsecured creditors has been appointed under §1102, on the creditors included on the list filed under Rule 1007(d); and (2) on any other entity that the court directs.

(2) *Hearing.* The court may commence a final hearing on a motion for authority to obtain credit no earlier than 14 days after service of the motion. If the motion so requests, the court may conduct a hearing before such 14-day period expires, but the court may authorize the obtaining of credit only to the extent necessary to avoid immediate and irreparable harm to the estate pending a final hearing.

(3) *Notice.* Notice of hearing pursuant to this subdivision shall be given to the parties on whom service of the motion is required by paragraph (1) of this subdivision and to such other entities as the court may direct.

[1] So in original. Probably should be only one section symbol.

(d) AGREEMENT RELATING TO RELIEF FROM THE AUTOMATIC STAY, PROHIBITING OR CONDITIONING THE USE, SALE, OR LEASE OF PROPERTY, PROVIDING ADEQUATE PROTECTION, USE OF CASH COLLATERAL, AND OBTAINING CREDIT.

(1) *Motion; Service.*

(A) *Motion.* A motion for approval of any of the following shall be accompanied by a copy of the agreement and a proposed form of order:

(i) an agreement to provide adequate protection;

(ii) an agreement to prohibit or condition the use, sale, or lease of property;

(iii) an agreement to modify or terminate the stay provided for in §362;

(iv) an agreement to use cash collateral; or

(v) an agreement between the debtor and an entity that has a lien or interest in property of the estate pursuant to which the entity consents to the creation of a lien senior or equal to the entity's lien or interest in such property.

(B) *Contents.* The motion shall consist of or (if the motion is more than five pages in length) begin with a concise statement of the relief requested, not to exceed five pages, that lists or summarizes, and sets out the location within the relevant documents of, all material provisions of the agreement. In addition, the concise statement shall briefly list or summarize, and identify the specific location of, each provision in the proposed form of order, agreement, or other document of the type listed in subdivision (c)(1)(B). The motion shall also describe the nature and extent of each such provision.

(C) *Service.* The motion shall be served on: (1) any committee elected under §705 or appointed under §1102 of the Code, or its authorized agent, or, if the case is a chapter 9 municipality case or a chapter 11 reorganization case and no committee of unsecured creditors has been appointed under §1102, on the creditors included on the list filed under Rule 1007(d); and (2) on any other entity the court directs.

(2) *Objection.* Notice of the motion and the time within which objections may be filed and served on the debtor in possession or trustee shall be mailed to the parties on whom service is required by paragraph (1) of this subdivision and to such other entities as the court may direct. Unless the court fixes a different time, objections may be filed within 15 days of the mailing of notice.

(3) *Disposition; Hearing.* If no objection is filed, the court may enter an order approving or disapproving the agreement without conducting a hearing. If an objection is filed or if the court determines a hearing is appropriate, the court shall hold a hearing on no less than five days' notice to the objector, the movant, the parties on whom service is required by paragraph (1) of this subdivision and such other entities as the court may direct.

(4) *Agreement in Settlement of Motion.* The court may direct that the procedures prescribed in paragraphs (1), (2), and (3) of this subdivision shall not apply and the agreement may be approved without further notice if the court determines that a motion made pursuant to subdivisions (a), (b), or (c) of this rule was sufficient to afford reasonable notice of the material provisions of the agreement and opportunity for a hearing.

(As amended Mar. 30, 1987, eff. Aug. 1, 1987; Apr. 30, 1991, eff. Aug. 1, 1991; Apr. 26, 1999, eff. Dec. 1, 1999; Apr. 30, 2007; eff. Dec. 1, 2007; Mar. 26, 2009, eff. Dec. 1, 2009.)

NOTES OF ADVISORY COMMITTEE ON RULES—1983

This rule implements §362 of the Code which set forth provisions regarding the automatic stay that arises on the filing of a petition. That section and this rule are applicable in chapters 7, 9, 11 and 13 cases. It also implements §363(c)(2) concerning use of cash collateral.

Subdivision (a) transforms with respect to the automatic stay what was an adversary proceeding under the former rules to motion practice. The Code provides automatic stays in several sections, *e.g.*, §§362(a), 1301(a), and in §362(d) provides some grounds for relief from the stay. This rule specifies that the pleading seeking relief is by means of a motion. Thus the time period in Rule 7012 to answer a complaint would not be applicable and shorter periods may be fixed. Section 362(e) requires the preliminary hearing to be concluded within 30 days of it inception, rendering ordinary complaint and answer practice inappropriate.

This subdivision also makes clear that a motion under Rule 9014 is the proper procedure for a debtor to seek court permission to use cash collateral. See §363(c)(2). Pursuant to Rule 5005, the motion should be filed in the court in which the case in pending. The court or local rule may specify the persons to be served with the motion for relief from the stay; see Rule 9013.

Subdivision (b) of the rule fills a procedural void left by §362. Pursuant to §362(e), the automatic stay is terminated 30 days after a motion for relief is made unless the court continues the stay as a result of a final hearing or, pending final hearing, after a preliminary hearing. If a preliminary hearing is held, §362(e) requires the final hearing to be commenced within 30 days after the preliminary hearing. Although the expressed legislative intent is to require expeditious resolution of a secured party's motion for relief, §362 is silent as to the time within which the final hearing must be concluded. Subdivision (b) imposes a 30 day deadline on the court to resolve the dispute.

At the final hearing, the stay is to be terminated, modified, annulled, or conditioned for cause, which includes, *inter alia*, lack of adequate protection; §362(d). The burden of proving adequate protection is on the party opposing relief from the stay; §362(g)(2). Adequate protection is exemplified in §361.

Subdivision (c) implements §362(f) which permits ex parte relief from the stay when there will be irreparable damage. This subdivision sets forth the procedure to be followed when relief is sought under §362(f). It is derived from former Bankruptcy Rule 601(d).

NOTES OF ADVISORY COMMITTEE ON RULES—1987 AMENDMENT

The scope of this rule is expanded and the former subdivisions (a), (b) and (c) are now combined in subdivision (a). The new subdivision (a)(2) is amended to conform to the 1984 amendments to §362(e) of the Code.

Subdivision (b) deals explicitly with the procedures which follow after a motion to use cash collateral is made and served. Filing shall be pursuant to Rule 5005. Service of the motion may be made by any method authorized by Rule 7004 and, if service is by mail, service is complete on mailing. Rule 9006(e). Under subdivision (b)(2), the court may commence a final hearing on the motion within 15 days of service. Rule 9006(f) does not extend this 15 day period when service of the motion is by mail because the party served is not required to act within the 15 day period. In addition to service of the motion, notice of the hearing must be given. Rule 9007 authorizes the court to direct the form and manner of giving notice that is appropriate to the circumstances.

Section 363(c)(3) authorizes the court to conduct a preliminary hearing and to authorize the use of cash collateral "if there is a reasonable likelihood that the trustee will prevail at a final hearing." Subdivision (b)(2) of the rule permits a preliminary hearing to be held earlier than 15 days after service. Any order authorizing the use of cash collateral shall be limited to the amount necessary to protect the estate until a final hearing is held.

The objective of subdivision (b) is to accommodate both the immediate need of the debtor and the interest of the secured creditor in the cash collateral. The time for holding the final hearing may be enlarged beyond the 15 days prescribed when required by the circumstances.

The motion for authority to use cash collateral shall include (1) the amount of cash collateral sought to be used; (2) the name and address of each entity having an interest in the cash collateral; (3) the name and address of the entity in control or having possession of the cash collateral; (4) the facts demonstrating the need to use the cash collateral; and (5) the nature of the protection to be provided those having an interest in the cash collateral. If a preliminary hearing is requested, the motion shall also include the amount of cash collateral sought to be used pending final hearing and the protection to be provided.

Notice of the preliminary and final hearings may be combined. This rule does not limit the authority of the court under §363(c)(2)(B) and §102(1).

Subdivision (c) is new. The service, hearing, and notice requirements are similar to those imposed by subdivision (b). The motion to obtain credit shall include the amount and type of the credit to be extended, the name and address of the lender, the terms of the agreement, the need to obtain the credit, and the efforts made to obtain credit from other sources. If the motion is to obtain credit pursuant to §364(c) or (d), the motion shall describe the collateral, if any, and the protection for any existing interest in the collateral which may be affected by the proposed agreement.

Subdivision (d) is new. In the event the 15 day period for filing objections to the approval of an agreement of the parties described in this subdivision is too long, the parties either may move for a reduction of the period under Rule 9006(c)(1) or proceed under subdivision (b) or (c), if applicable. Rule 9006(c)(1) requires that cause be shown for the reduction of the period in which to object. In applying this criterion the court may consider the option of proceeding under subdivision (b) or (c) and grant a preliminary hearing and relief pending final hearing.

NOTES OF ADVISORY COMMITTEE ON RULES—1991 AMENDMENT

Subdivision (a) is expanded to include a request to prohibit or condition the use, sale, or lease of property as is necessary to provide adequate protection of a property interest pursuant to §363(e) of the Code.

Notice of the motion for relief from the automatic stay or to prohibit or condition the use, sale, or lease of property must be served on the entities entitled to receive notice of a motion to approve an agreement pursuant to subdivision (d). If the movant and the adverse party agree to settle the motion and the terms of the agreement do not materially differ from the terms set forth in the movant's motion papers, the court may approve the agreement without further notice pursuant to subdivision (d)(4).

Subdivision (a)(2) is deleted as unnecessary because of §362(e) of the Code.

Subdivisions (b)(1), (c)(1), and (d)(1) are amended to require service on committees that are elected in chapter 7 cases. Service on committees of retired employees appointed under §1114 of the Code is not required. These subdivisions are amended further to clarify that, in the absence of a creditors' committee, service on the creditors included on the list filed pursuant to Rule 1007(d) is required only in chapter 9 and chapter 11 cases. The other amendments to subdivision (d)(1) are for consistency of style and are not substantive.

Subdivision (d)(4) is added to avoid the necessity of further notice and delay for the approval of an agreement in settlement of a motion for relief from an automatic stay, to prohibit or condition the use, sale, or lease of property, for use of cash collateral, or for authority to obtain credit if the entities entitled to notice have already received sufficient notice of the scope of the proposed agreement in the motion papers and have had an opportunity to be heard. For example, if a trustee makes a motion to use cash collateral and proposes in the original motion papers to provide adequate protection of the interest of the secured party by granting a lien on certain equipment, and the secured creditor subsequently agrees to terms that are within the scope of those proposed in the motion, the court may enter an order approving the agreement without further notice if the entities that received the original motion papers have had a reasonable opportunity to object to the granting of the motion to use cash collateral.

If the motion papers served under subdivision (a), (b), or (c) do not afford notice sufficient to inform the recipients of the material provisions of the proposed agreement and opportunity for a hearing, approval of the settlement agreement may not be obtained unless the procedural requirements of subdivision (d)(1), (d)(2), and (d)(3) are satisfied. If the 15 day period for filing objections to the approval of the settlement agreement is too long under the particular circumstances of the case, the court may shorten the time for cause under Rule 9006(c)(1).

COMMITTEE NOTES ON RULES—1999 AMENDMENT

Paragraph (a)(3) is added to provide sufficient time for a party to request a stay pending appeal of an order granting relief from an automatic stay before the order is enforced or implemented. The stay under paragraph (a)(3) is not applicable to orders granted ex parte in accordance with Rule 4001(a)(2).

The stay of the order does not affect the time for filing a notice of appeal in accordance with Rule 8002. While the enforcement and implementation of an order granting relief from the automatic stay is temporarily stayed under paragraph (a)(3), the automatic stay continues to protect the debtor, and the moving party may not foreclose on collateral or take any other steps that would violate the automatic stay.

The court may, in its discretion, order that Rule 4001(a)(3) is not applicable so that the prevailing party may immediately enforce and implement the order granting relief from the automatic stay. Alternatively, the court may order that the stay under Rule 4001(a)(3) is for a fixed period less than 10 days.

GAP Report on Rule 4001. No changes since publication.

COMMITTEE NOTES ON RULES—2007 AMENDMENT

The rule is amended to require that parties seeking authority to use cash collateral, to obtain credit, and to obtain approval of agreements to provide adequate protection, modify or terminate the stay, or to grant a senior or equal lien on property, submit with those requests a proposed order granting the relief, and that they provide more extensive notice to interested parties of a number of specified terms. The motion must either not exceed five pages in length, or, if it is longer, begin with a concise statement of five pages or less, that summarizes or lists the material provisions and which will assist the court and interested parties in understanding the nature of the relief requested. The concise statement must also set out the location within the documents of the summarized or listed provisions. The parties to agreements and lending offers frequently have concise summaries of their transactions that contain a list of the material provisions of the agreements, even if the agreements themselves are very lengthy. A similar summary should allow the court and interested parties to understand the relief requested.

In addition to the concise statement, the rule requires that motions under subdivisions (c) and (d) state whether the movant is seeking approval of any of the provisions listed in subdivision (c)(1)(B), and where those provisions are located in the documents. The rule is intended to enhance the ability of the court and interested parties to find and evaluate those provisions.

The rule also provides that any motion for authority to obtain credit must identify any provision listed in subdivision (c)(1)(B)(i)–(xi) that is proposed to remain effective if the court grants the motion on an interim basis under Rule 4001(c)(2), but later denies final relief.

Other amendments are stylistic.

Changes Made After Publication.

1. The introductory language in subdivisions (b)(1)(B), (c)(1)(B), and (d)(1)(B) was revised to clarify that the motions filed under the rule can be either no more than five pages long or begin with a concise statement of that length. This permits the continued use of forms that have been effective in smaller cases. Subdivision (c)(1)(B) also is amended to require that the motion identify any provisionally approved term that would remain in effect even if the court denies the permanent relief requested.

2. A new subparagraph (c)(1)(B)(vi) was inserted into the rule and the remaining subparagraphs were renumbered accordingly. The new subparagraph requires that the motion identify any provisions setting deadlines for filing and confirming reorganization plans and disclosure statements.

3. Subdivisions (c)(1)(C) and (d)(1)(C) of the proposed rule were deleted as unnecessary. The court has whatever authority Rule 9024 provides, and making an explicit reference to that rule in these subdivisions brings unnecessary attention to Rule 9024 and could create a different standard of review under that rule than would apply in other instances. The Advisory Committee did not intend either consequence, so the subdivisions were deleted.

4. Subdivision (d)(1)(A) was restyled to form a vertical list of the motions subject to that provision.

COMMITTEE NOTES ON RULES—2009 AMENDMENT

The rule is amended to implement changes in connection with the amendment to Rule 9006(a) and the manner by which time is computed under the rules. The deadlines in the rule are amended to substitute a deadline that is a multiple of seven days. Throughout the rules, deadlines are amended in the following manner:

- 5-day periods become 7-day periods
- 10-day periods become 14-day periods
- 15-day periods become 14-day periods
- 20-day periods become 21-day periods
- 25-day periods become 28-day periods

Rule 4002. Duties of Debtor

(a) IN GENERAL. In addition to performing other duties prescribed by the Code and rules, the debtor shall:

(1) attend and submit to an examination at the times ordered by the court;

(2) attend the hearing on a complaint objecting to discharge and testify, if called as a witness;

(3) inform the trustee immediately in writing as to the location of real property in which the debtor has an interest and the name and address of every person holding money or property subject to the debtor's withdrawal or order if a schedule of property has not yet been filed pursuant to Rule 1007;

(4) cooperate with the trustee in the preparation of an inventory, the examination of proofs of claim, and the administration of the estate; and

(5) file a statement of any change of the debtor's address.

(b) INDIVIDUAL DEBTOR'S DUTY TO PROVIDE DOCUMENTATION.

(1) *Personal Identification.* Every individual debtor shall bring to the meeting of creditors under § 341:

(A) a picture identification issued by a governmental unit, or other personal identifying information that establishes the debtor's identity; and

(B) evidence of social-security number(s), or a written statement that such documentation does not exist.

(2) *Financial Information.* Every individual debtor shall bring to the meeting of creditors under § 341, and make available to the trustee, the following documents or copies of them, or provide a written statement that the documentation does not exist or is not in the debtor's possession:

(A) evidence of current income such as the most recent payment advice;

(B) unless the trustee or the United States trustee instructs otherwise, statements for each of the debtor's depository and investment accounts, including checking, savings, and money market accounts, mutual funds and brokerage accounts for the time period that includes the date of the filing of the petition; and

(C) documentation of monthly expenses claimed by the debtor if required by § 707(b)(2)(A) or (B).

(3) *Tax Return.* At least 7 days before the first date set for the meeting of creditors under § 341, the debtor shall provide to the trustee a copy of the debtor's federal income tax return for the most recent tax year ending immediately before the commencement of the case and for which a return was filed, including any attachments, or a transcript of the tax return, or provide a written statement that the documentation does not exist.

(4) *Tax Returns Provided to Creditors.* If a creditor, at least 14 days before the first date set for the meeting of creditors under § 341, requests a copy of the debtor's tax return that is to be provided to the trustee under subdivision (b)(3), the debtor, at least 7 days before the first date set for the meeting of creditors under § 341, shall provide to the requesting creditor a copy of the return, including any attachments, or a transcript of the tax return, or provide a written statement that the documentation does not exist.

(5) *Confidentiality of Tax Information.* The debtor's obligation to provide tax returns under Rule 4002(b)(3) and (b)(4) is subject to procedures for safeguarding the confidentiality of tax information established by the Director of the Administrative Office of the United States Courts.

(As amended Mar. 30, 1987, eff. Aug. 1, 1987; Apr. 23, 2008, eff. Dec. 1 2008; Mar. 26, 2009, eff. Dec. 1, 2009.)

NOTES OF ADVISORY COMMITTEE ON RULES—1983

This rule should be read together with §§343 and 521 of the Code and Rule 1007, all of which impose duties on the debtor. Clause (3) of this rule implements the provisions of Rule 2015(a).

NOTES OF ADVISORY COMMITTEE ON RULES—1987 AMENDMENT

New clause (5) of the rule imposes on the debtor the duty to advise the clerk of any change of the debtor's address.

COMMITTEE NOTES ON RULES—2008 AMENDMENT

This rule is amended to implement §521(a)(1)(B)(iv) and (e)(2), added to the Code by the 2005 amendments. These Code amendments expressly require the debtor to file with the court, or provide to the trustee, specific documents. The amendments to the rule implement these obligations and establish a time frame for creditors to make requests for a copy of the debtor's Federal income tax return. The rule also requires the debtor to provide documentation in support of claimed expenses under §707(b)(2)(A) and (B).

Subdivision (b) of the rule is also amended to require the debtor to cooperate with the trustee by providing materials and documents necessary to assist the trustee in the performance of the trustee's duties. Nothing in the rule, however, is intended to limit or restrict the debtor's duties under §521, or to limit the access of the Attorney General to any information provided by the debtor in the case. Subdivision (b)(2) does not require that the debtor create documents or obtain documents from third parties; rather, the debtor's obligation is to bring to the meeting of creditors under §341 the documents which the debtor possesses. Under subdivision (b)(2)(B), the trustee or the United States trustee can instruct debtors that they need not provide the documents described in that subdivision. Under subdivisions (b)(3) and (b)(4), the debtor must obtain and provide copies of tax returns or tax transcripts to the appropriate person, unless no such documents exist. Any written statement that the debtor provides indicating either that documents do not exist or are not in the debtor's possession must be verified or contain an unsworn declaration as required under Rule 1008.

Because the amendment implements the debtor's duty to cooperate with the trustee, the materials provided to the trustee would not be made available to any other party in interest at the §341 meeting of creditors other than the Attorney General. Some of the documents may contain otherwise private information that should not be disseminated. For example, pay stubs and financial account statements might include the social-security numbers of the debtor and the debtor's spouse and dependents, as well as the names of the debtor's children. The debtor should redact all but the last four digits of all social-security numbers and the names of any minors when they appear in these documents. This type of information would not usually be needed by creditors and others who may be attending the meeting. If a creditor perceives a need to review specific documents or other evidence, the creditor may proceed under Rule 2004.

Tax information produced under this rule is subject to procedures for safeguarding confidentiality established by the Director of the Administrative Office of the United States Courts.

Changes Made After Publication. The second paragraph of the Committee Note was amended to clarify that the debtor's duty to provide copies of tax returns or tax transcripts are governed by a different standard than the debtor's duty to provide other financial information.

COMMITTEE NOTES ON RULES—2009 AMENDMENT

The rule is amended to implement changes in connection with the amendment to Rule 9006(a) and the manner by which time is computed under the rules. The deadline in the rule is amended to substitute a deadline that is a multiple of seven days. Throughout the rules, deadlines are amended in the following manner:

- 5-day periods become 7-day periods
- 10-day periods become 14-day periods
- 15-day periods become 14-day periods
- 20-day periods become 21-day periods
- 25-day periods become 28-day periods

Rule 4003. Exemptions

(a) CLAIM OF EXEMPTIONS. A debtor shall list the property claimed as exempt under §522 of the Code on the schedule of assets required to be filed by Rule 1007. If the debtor fails to claim exemptions or file the schedule within the time specified in Rule 1007, a dependent of the debtor may file the list within 30 days thereafter.

(b) OBJECTING TO A CLAIM OF EXEMPTIONS.

(1) Except as provided in paragraphs (2) and (3), a party in interest may file an objection to the list of property claimed as exempt within 30 days after the meeting of creditors held under §341(a) is concluded or within 30 days after any amendment to the list or supplemental schedules is filed, whichever is later. The court may, for cause, extend the time for filing objections if, before the time to object expires, a party in interest files a request for an extension.

(2) The trustee may file an objection to a claim of exemption at any time prior to one year after the closing of the case if the debtor fraudulently asserted the claim of exemption. The trustee shall deliver or mail the objection to the debtor and the debtor's attorney, and to any person filing the list of exempt property and that person's attorney.

(3) An objection to a claim of exemption based on §522(q) shall be filed before the closing of the case. If an exemption is first claimed after a case is reopened, an objection shall be filed before the reopened case is closed.

(4) A copy of any objection shall be delivered or mailed to the trustee, the debtor and the debtor's attorney, and the person filing the list and that person's attorney.

(c) BURDEN OF PROOF. In any hearing under this rule, the objecting party has the burden of proving that the exemptions are not properly claimed. After hearing on notice, the court shall determine the issues presented by the objections.

(d) AVOIDANCE BY DEBTOR OF TRANSFERS OF EXEMPT PROPERTY. A proceeding by the debtor to avoid a lien or other transfer of property exempt under §522(f) of the Code shall be by motion in accordance with Rule 9014. Notwithstanding the provisions of subdivision (b), a creditor may object to a motion filed under §522(f) by challenging the validity of the exemption asserted to be impaired by the lien.

(As amended Mar. 30, 1987, eff. Aug. 1, 1987; Apr. 30, 1991, eff. Aug. 1, 1991; Apr. 17, 2000, eff. Dec. 1, 2000; Apr. 23, 2008, eff. Dec. 1, 2008.)

NOTES OF ADVISORY COMMITTEE ON RULES—1983

This rule is derived from §522(1) of the Code and, in part, former Bankruptcy Rule 403. The Code changes the thrust of that rule by making it the burden of the debtor to list his exemptions and the burden of parties in interest to raise objections in the absence of which "the property claimed as exempt on such list is exempt;" § 522(1).

Subdivision (a). While § 522(1) refers to a list of property claimed as exempt, the rule incorporates such a list as part of Official Form No. 6, the schedule of the debtor's assets, rather than requiring a separate list and filing. Rule 1007, to which subdivision (a) refers, requires that schedule to be filed within 15 days after the order for relief, unless the court extends the time.

Section 522(1) also provides that a dependent of the debtor may file the list if the debtor fails to do so. Subdivision (a) of the rule allows such filing from the expiration of the debtor's time until 30 days thereafter. Dependent is defined in § 522(a)(1).

Subdivision (d) provides that a proceeding by the debtor, permitted by § 522(f) of the Code, is a contested matter rather than the more formal adversary proceeding. Proceedings within the scope of this subdivision are distinguished from proceedings brought by the trustee to avoid transfers. The latter are classified as adversary proceedings by Rule 7001.

NOTES OF ADVISORY COMMITTEE ON RULES—1991 AMENDMENT

Subdivision (b) is amended to facilitate the filing of objections to exemptions claimed on a supplemental schedule filed under Rule 1007(h).

COMMITTEE NOTES ON RULES—2000 AMENDMENT

This rule is amended to permit the court to grant a timely request for an extension of time to file objections to the list of claimed exemptions, whether the court rules on the request before or after the expiration of the 30-day period. The purpose of this amendment is to avoid the harshness of the present rule which has been construed to deprive a bankruptcy court of jurisdiction to grant a timely request for an extension if it has failed to rule on the request within the 30-day period. See *In re Laurain*, 113 F.3d 595 (6th Cir. 1997), *Matter of Stoulig*, 45 F.3d 957 (5th Cir. 1995), *In re Brayshaw*, 912 F.2d 1255 (10th Cir. 1990). The amendments clarify that the extension may be granted only for cause. The amendments also conform the rule to § 522(*l*) of the Code by recognizing that any party in interest may file an objection or request for an extension of time under this rule. Other amendments are stylistic.

GAP Report on Rule 4003(b). The words "trustee or creditor" were replaced by "party in interest" to conform to § 522(*l*) of the Bankruptcy Code which permits any party in interest to object to claimed exemptions. Style revisions also were made to the published draft.

COMMITTEE NOTES ON RULES—2008 AMENDMENT

Subdivision (b) is rewritten to include four paragraphs.

Subdivision (b)(2) is added to the rule to permit the trustee to object to an exemption at any time up to one year after the closing of the case if the debtor fraudulently claimed the exemption. Extending the deadline for trustees to object to an exemption when the exemption claim has been fraudulently made will permit the court to review and, in proper circumstances, deny improperly claimed exemptions, thereby protecting the legitimate interests of creditors and the bankruptcy estate. However, similar to the deadline set in § 727(e) of the Code for revoking a discharge which was fraudulently obtained, an objection to an exemption that was fraudulently claimed must be filed within one year after the closing of the case. Subdivision (b)(2) extends the objection deadline only for trustees.

Subdivision (b)(3) is added to the rule to reflect the addition of subsection (q) to § 522 of the Code by the 2005 Act. Section 522(q) imposes a $136,875 limit on a state homestead exemption if the debtor has been convicted of a felony or owes a debt arising from certain causes of action. Other revised provisions of the Code, such as § 727(a)(12) and § 1328(h), suggest that the court may consider issues relating to § 522(q) late in the case, and the 30-day period for objections would not be appropriate for this provision.

Subdivision (d) is amended to clarify that a creditor with a lien on property that the debtor is attempting to avoid on the grounds that the lien impairs an exemption may raise in defense to the lien avoidance action any objection to the debtor's claimed exemption. The right to object is limited to an objection to the exemption of the property subject to the lien and for purposes of the lien avoidance action only. The creditor may not object to other exemption claims made by the debtor. Those objections, if any, are governed by Rule 4003(b).

Other changes are stylistic.

Changes Made After Publication. The deadline for filing objections to exemptions under subdivision (b)(1) was returned to 30 days after the conclusion of the § 341 meeting of creditors rather than the 60 day period proposed in the published rule. The second paragraph of the Committee Note which discussed this change was therefore deleted. Subdivisions (b)(2) and (b)(3) were amended to add the debtor and the debtor's attorney to the list of persons to whom objections to exemptions must be delivered.

Rule 4004. Grant or Denial of Discharge

(a) TIME FOR FILING COMPLAINT OBJECTING TO DISCHARGE; NOTICE OF TIME FIXED. In a chapter 7 liquidation case a complaint objecting to the debtor's discharge under § 727(a) of the Code shall be filed no later than 60 days after the first date set for the meeting of creditors under § 341(a). In a chapter 11 reorganization case, the complaint shall be filed no later than the first date set for the hearing on confirmation. At least 28 days' notice of the time so fixed shall be given to the United States trustee and all creditors as provided in Rule 2002(f) and (k) and to the trustee and the trustee's attorney.

(b) EXTENSION OF TIME. On motion of any party in interest, after hearing on notice, the court may for cause extend the time to file a complaint objecting to discharge. The motion shall be filed before the time has expired.

(c) GRANT OF DISCHARGE.

(1) In a chapter 7 case, on expiration of the time fixed for filing a complaint objecting to discharge and the time fixed for filing a motion to dismiss the case under Rule 1017(e), the court shall forthwith grant the discharge unless:

(A) the debtor is not an individual;

(B) a complaint objecting to the discharge has been filed;

(C) the debtor has filed a waiver under § 727(a)(10);

(D) a motion to dismiss the case under § 707 is pending;

(E) a motion to extend the time for filing a complaint objecting to the discharge is pending;

(F) a motion to extend the time for filing a motion to dismiss the case under Rule 1017(e)(1) is pending;

(G) the debtor has not paid in full the filing fee prescribed by 28 U.S.C. § 1930(a) and any other fee prescribed by the Judicial Conference of the United States under 28 U.S.C. § 1930(b) that is payable to the clerk upon the commencement of a case under the Code, unless the court has waived the fees under 28 U.S.C. § 1930(f);

(H) the debtor has not filed with the court a statement of completion of a course concerning personal financial management as required by Rule 1007(b)(7);

(I) a motion to delay or postpone discharge under §727(a)(12) is pending;

(J) a motion to enlarge the time to file a reaffirmation agreement under Rule 4008(a) is pending;

(K) a presumption has arisen under §524(m) that a reaffirmation agreement is an undue hardship; or

(L) a motion is pending to delay discharge, because the debtor has not filed with the court all tax documents required to be filed under §521(f).

(2) Notwithstanding Rule 4004(c)(1), on motion of the debtor, the court may defer the entry of an order granting a discharge for 30 days and, on motion within that period, the court may defer entry of the order to a date certain.

(3) If the debtor is required to file a statement under Rule 1007(b)(8), the court shall not grant a discharge earlier than 30 days after the statement is filed.

(d) APPLICABILITY OF RULES IN PART VII. A proceeding commenced by a complaint objecting to discharge is governed by Part VII of these rules.

(e) ORDER OF DISCHARGE. An order of discharge shall conform to the appropriate Official Form.

(f) REGISTRATION IN OTHER DISTRICTS. An order of discharge that has become final may be registered in any other district by filing a certified copy of the order in the office of the clerk of that district. When so registered the order of discharge shall have the same effect as an order of the court of the district where registered.

(g) NOTICE OF DISCHARGE. The clerk shall promptly mail a copy of the final order of discharge to those specified in subdivision (a) of this rule.

(As amended Mar. 30, 1987, eff. Aug. 1, 1987; Apr. 30, 1991, eff. Aug. 1, 1991; Apr. 23, 1996, eff. Dec. 1, 1996; Apr. 26, 1999, eff. Dec. 1, 1999; Apr. 17, 2000, eff. Dec. 1, 2000; Apr. 29, 2002, eff. Dec. 1, 2002; Apr. 23, 2008, eff. Dec. 1, 2008; Mar. 26, 2009, eff. Dec. 1, 2009.)

NOTES OF ADVISORY COMMITTEE ON RULES—1983

This rule is adapted from former Bankruptcy Rule 404.

Subdivisions (a) and (b) of this rule prescribe the procedure for determining whether a discharge will be granted pursuant to §727 of the Code. The time fixed by subdivision (a) may be enlarged as provided in subdivision (b).

The notice referred to in subdivision (a) is required to be given by mail and addressed to creditors as provided in Rule 2002.

An extension granted on a motion pursuant to subdivision (b) of the rule would ordinarily benefit only the movant, but its scope and effect would depend on the terms of the extension.

Subdivision (c). If a complaint objecting to discharge is filed, the court's grant or denial of the discharge will be entered at the conclusion of the proceeding as a judgment in accordance with Rule 9021. The inclusion of the clause in subdivision (c) qualifying the duty of the court to grant a discharge when a waiver has been filed is in accord with the construction of the Code. 4 Collier, *Bankruptcy* ¶727.12 (15th ed. 1979).

The last sentence of subdivision (c) takes cognizance of §524(c) of the Code which authorizes a debtor to enter into enforceable reaffirmation agreements only prior to entry of the order of discharge. Immediate entry of that order after expiration of the time fixed for filing complaints objecting to discharge may render it more difficult for a debtor to settle pending litigation to determine the dischargeability of a debt and execute a reaffirmation agreement as part of a settlement.

Subdivision (d). An objection to discharge is required to be made by a complaint, which initiates an adversary proceeding as provided in Rule 7003. Pursuant to Rule 5005, the complaint should be filed in the court in which the case is pending.

Subdivision (e). Official Form No. 27 to which subdivision (e) refers, includes notice of the effects of a discharge specified in §524(a) of the Code.

Subdivision (f). Registration may facilitate the enforcement of the order of discharge in a district other than that in which it was entered. See 2 Moore's *Federal Practice* ¶1.04[2] (2d ed. 1967). Because of the nationwide service of process authorized by Rule 7004, however, registration of the order of discharge is not necessary under these rules to enable a discharged debtor to obtain relief against a creditor proceeding anywhere in the United States in disregard of the injunctive provisions of the order of discharge.

Subdivision (g). Notice of discharge should be mailed promptly after the order becomes final so that creditors may be informed of entry of the order and of its injunctive provisions. Rule 2002 specifies the manner of the notice and persons to whom the notice is to be given.

NOTES OF ADVISORY COMMITTEE ON RULES—1991 AMENDMENT

This rule is amended to conform to §727(c) which gives the United States trustee the right to object to discharge. This amendment is derived from Rule X-1008(a)(1) and is consistent with Rule 2002. The amendment to subdivision (c) is to prevent a timely motion to dismiss a chapter 7 case for substantial abuse from becoming moot merely because a discharge order has been entered. Reference to the Official Form number in subdivision (e) is deleted in anticipation of future revision and renumbering of the Official Forms.

NOTES OF ADVISORY COMMITTEE ON RULES—1996 AMENDMENT

Subsection (c) is amended to delay entry of the order of discharge if a motion pursuant to Rule 4004(b) to extend the time for filing a complaint objecting to discharge is pending. Also, this subdivision is amended to delay entry of the discharge order if the debtor has not paid in full the filing fee and the administrative fee required to be paid upon the commencement of the case. If the debtor is authorized to pay the fees in installments in accordance with Rule 1006, the discharge order will not be entered until the final installment has been paid.

The other amendments to this rule are stylistic.

GAP Report on Rule 4004. No changes have been made since publication, except for stylistic changes.

COMMITTEE NOTES ON RULES—1999 AMENDMENT

Subdivision (a) is amended to clarify that, in a chapter 7 case, the deadline for filing a complaint objecting to discharge under §727(a) is 60 days after the first date set for the meeting of creditors, whether or not the meeting is held on that date. The time for filing the complaint is not affected by any delay in the commencement or conclusion of the meeting of creditors. This amendment does not affect the right of any party in interest to file a motion for an extension of time to file a complaint objecting to discharge in accordance with Rule 4004(b).

The substitution of the word "filed" for "made" in subdivision (b) is intended to avoid confusion regarding the time when a motion is "made" for the purpose of applying these rules. *See, e.g., In re Coggin,* 30 F.3d 1443 (11th Cir. 1994). As amended, this rule requires that a motion for an extension of time for filing a complaint objecting to discharge be *filed* before the time has expired.

Other amendments to this rule are stylistic.

GAP Report on Rule 4004. No changes since publication.

COMMITTEE NOTES ON RULES—2000 AMENDMENT

Subdivision (c) is amended so that a discharge will not be granted while a motion requesting an extension of time to file a motion to dismiss the case under §707(b) is pending. Other amendments are stylistic.

GAP Report on Rule 4004(c). No changes since publication except for style revisions.

COMMITTEE NOTES ON RULES—2002 AMENDMENT

Subdivision (c)(1)(D) is amended to provide that the filing of a motion to dismiss under §707 of the Bankruptcy Code postpones the entry of the discharge. Under the present version of the rule, only motions to dismiss brought under §707(b) cause the postponement of the discharge. This amendment would change the result in cases such as *In re Tanenbaum*, 210 B.R. 182 (Bankr. D. Colo. 1997).

Changes Made After Publication and Comments. No changes were made.

COMMITTEE NOTES ON RULES—2008 AMENDMENT

Subdivision (c)(1)(G) is amended to reflect the fee waiver provision in 28 U.S.C. §1930, added by the 2005 amendments.

Subdivision (c)(1)(H) is new. It reflects the 2005 addition to the Code of §§727(a)(11) and 1328(g), which require that individual debtors complete a course in personal financial management as a condition to the entry of a discharge. Including this requirement in the rule helps prevent the inadvertent entry of a discharge when the debtor has not complied with this requirement. If a debtor fails to file the required statement regarding a personal financial management course, the clerk will close the bankruptcy case without the entry of a discharge.

Subdivision (c)(1)(I) is new. It reflects the 2005 addition to the Code of §727(a)(12). This provision is linked to §522(q). Section 522(q) limits the availability of the homestead exemption for individuals who have been convicted of a felony or who owe a debt arising from certain causes of action within a particular time frame. The existence of reasonable cause to believe that §522(q) may be applicable to the debtor constitutes grounds for withholding the discharge.

Subdivision (c)(1)(J) is new. It accommodates the deadline for filing a reaffirmation agreement established by Rule 4008(a).

Subdivision (c)(1)(K) is new. It reflects the 2005 revisions to §524 of the Code that alter the requirements for approval of reaffirmation agreements. Section 524(m) sets forth circumstances under which a reaffirmation agreement is presumed to be an undue hardship. This triggers an obligation to review the presumption and may require notice and a hearing. Subdivision (c)(1)(J) has been added to prevent the discharge from being entered until the court approves or disapproves the reaffirmation agreement in accordance with §524(m).

Subdivision (c)(1)(L) is new. It implements §1228(a) of Public Law Number 109–8, an uncodified provision of the Bankruptcy Abuse Prevention and Consumer Protection Act of 2005, which prohibits entry of a discharge unless required tax documents have been provided to the court.

Subdivision (c)(3) is new. It postpones the entry of the discharge of an individual debtor in a case under chapter 11, 12, or 13 if there is a question as to the applicability of §522(q) of the Code. The postponement provides an opportunity for a creditor to file a motion to limit the debtor's exemption under that provision.

Other changes are stylistic.

Changes Made After Publication. No changes were made after publication.

COMMITTEE NOTES ON RULES—2009 AMENDMENT

The rule is amended to implement changes in connection with the amendment to Rule 9006(a) and the manner by which time is computed under the rules. The deadline in the rule is amended to substitute a deadline that is a multiple of seven days. Throughout the rules, deadlines are amended in the following manner:

- 5-day periods become 7-day periods
- 10-day periods become 14-day periods
- 15-day periods become 14-day periods
- 20-day periods become 21-day periods
- 25-day periods become 28-day periods

Rule 4005. Burden of Proof in Objecting to Discharge

At the trial on a complaint objecting to a discharge, the plaintiff has the burden of proving the objection.

(As amended Mar. 30, 1987, eff. Aug. 1, 1987.)

NOTES OF ADVISORY COMMITTEE ON RULES—1983

This rule does not address the burden of going forward with the evidence. Subject to the allocation by the rule of the initial burden of producing evidence and the ultimate burden of persuasion, the rule leaves to the courts the formulation of rules governing the shift of the burden of going forward with the evidence in the light of considerations such as the difficulty of proving the nonexistence of a fact and of establishing a fact as to which the evidence is likely to be more accessible to the debtor than to the objector. *See, e.g., In re Haggerty*, 165 F.2d 977, 979–80 (2d Cir. 1948); *Federal Provision Co. v. Ershowsky*, 94 F.2d 574, 575 (2d Cir. 1938); *In re Riceputo*, 41 F. Supp. 926, 927–28 (E.D.N.Y. 1941).

Rule 4006. Notice of No Discharge

If an order is entered: denying a discharge; revoking a discharge; approving a waiver of discharge; or, in the case of an individual debtor, closing the case without the entry of a discharge, the clerk shall promptly notify all parties in interest in the manner provided by Rule 2002.

(As amended Mar. 30, 1987, eff. Aug. 1, 1987; Apr. 23, 2008, eff. Dec. 1, 2008.)

NOTES OF ADVISORY COMMITTEE ON RULES—1983

The suspension by §108(c) of the Code of the statute of limitations affecting any debt of a debtor terminates within 30 days after the debtor is denied a discharge or otherwise loses his right to a discharge. If, however, a debtor's failure to receive a discharge does not come to the attention of his creditors until after the statutes of limitations have run, the debtor obtains substantially the same benefits from his bankruptcy as a debtor who is discharged.

This rule requires the clerk to notify creditors if a debtor fails to obtain a discharge because a waiver of discharge was filed under §727(a)(10) or as a result of an order denying or revoking the discharge under §727(a) or (d).

COMMITTEE NOTES ON RULES—2008 AMENDMENT

This amendment was necessary because the 2005 amendments to the Code require that individual debtors in a chapter 7 or 13 case complete a course in personal financial management as a condition to the entry of a discharge. If the debtor fails to complete the course, the case may be closed and no discharge will be entered. Reopening the case is governed by §350 and Rule 5010. The rule is amended to provide notice to parties in interest, including the debtor, that no discharge was entered.

Changes Made After Publication. No changes were made after publication.

Rule 4007. Determination of Dischargeability of a Debt

(a) PERSONS ENTITLED TO FILE COMPLAINT. A debtor or any creditor may file a complaint to obtain a determination of the dischargeability of any debt.

(b) TIME FOR COMMENCING PROCEEDING OTHER THAN UNDER §523(c) OF THE CODE. A complaint other than under §523(c) may be filed at any time. A case may be reopened without payment of an additional filing fee for the purpose of filing a complaint to obtain a determination under this rule.

(c) TIME FOR FILING COMPLAINT UNDER §523(c) IN A CHAPTER 7 LIQUIDATION, CHAPTER 11 REORGANIZATION, CHAPTER 12 FAMILY FARMER'S DEBT ADJUSTMENT CASE, OR CHAPTER 13 INDIVIDUAL'S DEBT ADJUSTMENT CASE; NOTICE OF TIME FIXED. Except as otherwise provided in subdivision (d), a complaint to determine the dischargeability of a debt under §523(c) shall be filed no later than 60 days after the first date set for the meeting of creditors under §341(a). The court shall give all creditors no less than 30 days' notice of the time so fixed in the manner provided in Rule 2002. On motion of a party in interest, after hearing on notice, the court may for cause extend the time fixed under this subdivision. The motion shall be filed before the time has expired.

(d) TIME FOR FILING COMPLAINT UNDER §523(a)(6) IN A CHAPTER 13 INDIVIDUAL'S DEBT ADJUSTMENT CASE; NOTICE OF TIME FIXED. On motion by a debtor for a discharge under §1328(b), the court shall enter an order fixing the time to file a complaint to determine the dischargeability of any debt under §523(a)(6) and shall give no less than 30 days' notice of the time fixed to all creditors in the manner provided in Rule 2002. On motion of any party in interest, after hearing on notice, the court may for cause extend the time fixed under this subdivision. The motion shall be filed before the time has expired.

(e) APPLICABILITY OF RULES IN PART VII. A proceeding commenced by a complaint filed under this rule is governed by Part VII of these rules.

(As amended Mar. 30, 1987, eff. Aug. 1, 1987; Apr. 30, 1991, eff. Aug. 1, 1991; Apr. 26, 1999, eff. Dec. 1, 1999; Apr. 23, 2008, eff. Dec. 1, 2008.)

NOTES OF ADVISORY COMMITTEE ON RULES—1983

This rule prescribes the procedure to be followed when a party requests the court to determine dischargeability of a debt pursuant to §523 of the Code.

Although a complaint that comes within §523(c) must ordinarily be filed before determining whether the debtor will be discharged, the court need not determine the issues presented by the complaint filed under this rule until the question of discharge has been determined under Rule 4004. A complaint filed under this rule initiates an adversary proceeding as provided in Rule 7003.

Subdivision (b) does not contain a time limit for filing a complaint to determine the dischargeability of a type of debt listed as nondischargeable under §523(a)(1), (3), (5), (7), (8), or (9). Jurisdiction over this issue on these debts is held concurrently by the bankruptcy court and any appropriate nonbankruptcy forum.

Subdivision (c) differs from subdivision (b) by imposing a deadline for filing complaints to determine the issue of dischargeability of debts set out in §523(a)(2), (4) or (6) of the Code. The bankruptcy court has exclusive jurisdiction to determine dischargeability of these debts. If a complaint is not timely filed, the debt is discharged. See §523(c).

Subdivision (e). The complaint required by this subdivision should be filed in the court in which the case is pending pursuant to Rule 5005.

NOTES OF ADVISORY COMMITTEE ON RULES—1991 AMENDMENT

Subdivision (a) is amended to delete the words "with the court" as unnecessary. See Rules 5005(a) and 9001(3).

Subdivision (c) is amended to apply in chapter 12 cases the same time period that applies in chapter 7 and 11 cases for filing a complaint under §523(c) of the Code to determine dischargeability of certain debts. Under §1228(a) of the Code, a chapter 12 discharge does not discharge the debts specified in §523(a) of the Code.

COMMITTEE NOTES ON RULES—1999 AMENDMENT

Subdivision (c) is amended to clarify that the deadline for filing a complaint to determine the dischargeability of a debt under §523(c) of the Code is 60 days after the first date set for the meeting of creditors, whether or not the meeting is held on that date. The time for filing the complaint is not affected by any delay in the commencement or conclusion of the meeting of creditors. This amendment does not affect the right of any party in interest to file a motion for an extension of time to file a complaint to determine the dischargeability of a debt in accordance with this rule.

The substitution of the word "filed" for "made" in the final sentences of subdivisions (c) and (d) is intended to avoid confusion regarding the time when a motion is "made" for the purpose of applying these rules. *See, e.g., In re Coggin*, 30 F.3d 1443 (11th Cir. 1994). As amended, these subdivisions require that a motion for an extension of time be *filed* before the time has expired.

The other amendments to this rule are stylistic.

GAP Report on Rule 4007. No changes since publication, except for stylistic changes in the heading of Rule 4007(d).

COMMITTEE NOTES ON RULES—2008 AMENDMENT

Subdivision (c) is amended because of the 2005 amendments to §1328(a) of the Code. This revision expands the exceptions to discharge upon completion of a chapter 13 plan. Subdivision (c) extends to chapter 13 the same time limits applicable to other chapters of the Code with respect to the two exceptions to discharge that have been added to §1328(a) and that are within §523(c).

The amendment to subdivision (d) reflects the 2005 amendments to §1328(a) that expands the exceptions to discharge upon completion of a chapter 13 plan, including two out of three of the provisions that fall within §523(c). However, the 2005 revisions to §1328(a) do not include a reference to §523(a)(6), which is the third provision to which §523(c) refers. Thus, subdivision (d) is now limited to that provision.

Changes Made After Publication. No changes were made after publication.

Rule 4008. Filing of Reaffirmation Agreement; Statement in Support of Reaffirmation Agreement

(a) FILING OF REAFFIRMATION AGREEMENT. A reaffirmation agreement shall be filed no later than 60 days after the first date set for the meeting of creditors under §341(a) of the Code. The reaffirmation agreement shall be accompanied by a cover sheet, prepared as prescribed by the appropriate Official Form. The court may, at any time and in its discretion, enlarge the time to file a reaffirmation agreement.

(b) STATEMENT IN SUPPORT OF REAFFIRMATION AGREEMENT. The debtor's statement required under §524(k)(6)(A) of the Code shall be accompanied by a statement of the total income and expenses stated on schedules I and J. If there is a difference between the total income and expenses stated on those schedules and the statement required under §524(k)(6)(A), the statement required by this subdivision shall include an explanation of the difference.

(As amended Apr. 30, 1991, eff. Aug. 1, 1991; Apr. 23, 2008, eff. Dec. 1, 2008; Mar. 26, 2009, eff. Dec. 1, 2009.)

NOTES OF ADVISORY COMMITTEE ON RULES—1983

Section 524(d) of the Code requires the court to hold a hearing to inform an individual debtor concerning the granting or denial of discharge and the law applicable to reaffirmation agreements.

The notice of the §524(d) hearing may be combined with the notice of the meeting of creditors or entered as a separate order.

The expression "not more than" contained in the first sentence of the rule is for the explicit purpose of requiring the hearing to occur within that time period and cannot be extended.

NOTES OF ADVISORY COMMITTEE ON RULES—1991 AMENDMENT

This rule is changed to conform to §524(d) of the Code as amended in 1986. A hearing under §524(d) is not mandatory unless the debtor desires to enter into a reaffirmation agreement.

COMMITTEE NOTES ON RULES—2008 AMENDMENT

This rule is amended to establish a deadline for filing reaffirmation agreements. The Code sets out a number of prerequisites to the enforceability of reaffirmation agreements. Among those requirements, §524(k)(6)(A) provides that each reaffirmation agreement must be accompanied by a statement indicating the debtor's ability to make the payments called for by the agreement. In the event that this statement reflects an insufficient income to allow payment of the reaffirmed debt, §524(m) provides that a presumption of undue hardship arises, allowing the court to disapprove the reaffirmation agreement, but only after a hearing conducted prior to the entry of discharge. Rule 4004(c)(1)(K) accommodates this provision by delaying the entry of discharge where a presumption of undue hardship arises. However, in order for that rule to be effective, the reaffirmation agreement itself must be filed before the entry of discharge. Under Rule 4004(c)(1) discharge is to be entered promptly after the expiration of the time for filing a complaint objecting to discharge, which, under Rule 4004(a), is 60 days after the first date set for the meeting of creditors under §341(a). Accordingly, that date is set as the deadline for filing a reaffirmation agreement.

Any party may file the agreement with the court. Thus, whichever party has a greater incentive to enforce the agreement usually will file it. In the event that the parties are unable to file a reaffirmation agreement in a timely fashion, the rule grants the court broad discretion to permit a late filing. A corresponding change to Rule 4004(c)(1)(J) accommodates such an extension by providing for a delay in the entry of discharge during the pendency of a motion to extend the time for filing a reaffirmation agreement.

Rule 4008 is also amended by deleting provisions regarding the timing of any reaffirmation and discharge hearing. As noted above, §524(m) itself requires that hearings on undue hardship be conducted prior to the entry of discharge. In other respects, including hearings to approve reaffirmation agreements of unrepresented debtors under §524(c)(6), the rule leaves discretion to the court to set the hearing at a time appropriate for the particular circumstances presented in the case and consistent with the scheduling needs of the parties.

Changes Made After Publication. The only change was stylistic. The phrase "of the Code" was added to subdivision (b).

COMMITTEE NOTES ON RULES—2009 AMENDMENT

Subdivision (a) of the rule is amended to require that the entity filing the reaffirmation agreement with the court also include Official Form 27, the Reaffirmation Agreement Cover Sheet. The form includes information necessary for the court to determine whether the proposed reaffirmation agreement is presumed to be an undue hardship for the debtor under §524(m) of the Code.

Changes Made After Publication. No changes since publication.

PART V—COURTS AND CLERKS

Rule 5001. Courts and Clerks' Offices

(a) COURTS ALWAYS OPEN. The courts shall be deemed always open for the purpose of filing any pleading or other proper paper, issuing and returning process, and filing, making, or entering motions, orders and rules.

(b) TRIALS AND HEARINGS; ORDERS IN CHAMBERS. All trials and hearings shall be conducted in open court and so far as convenient in a regular court room. Except as otherwise provided in 28 U.S.C. §152(c), all other acts or proceedings may be done or conducted by a judge in chambers and at any place either within or without the district; but no hearing, other than one ex parte, shall be conducted outside the district without the consent of all parties affected thereby.

(c) CLERK'S OFFICE. The clerk's office with the clerk or a deputy in attendance shall be open during business hours on all days except Saturdays, Sundays and the legal holidays listed in Rule 9006(a).

(As amended Mar. 30, 1987, eff. Aug. 1, 1987; Apr. 30, 1991, eff. Aug. 1, 1991; Apr. 23, 2008, eff. Dec. 1, 2008.)

NOTES OF ADVISORY COMMITTEE ON RULES—1983

This rule is adapted from subdivisions (a), (b) and (c) of Rule 77 F.R.Civ.P.

NOTES OF ADVISORY COMMITTEE ON RULES—1987 AMENDMENT

Rule 9001, as amended, defines court to mean the bankruptcy judge or district judge before whom a case or proceeding is pending. Clerk means the bankruptcy clerk, if one has been appointed for the district; if a bankruptcy clerk has not been appointed, clerk means clerk of the district court.

NOTES OF ADVISORY COMMITTEE ON RULES—1991 AMENDMENT

Subdivision (c) is amended to refer to Rule 9006(a) for a list of legal holidays. Reference to F.R.Civ.P. is not necessary for this purpose.

COMMITTEE NOTES ON RULES—2008 AMENDMENT

The rule is amended to permit bankruptcy judges to hold hearings outside of the district in which the case is pending to the extent that the circumstances lead to the authorization of the court to take such action under the 2005 amendment to 28 U.S.C. §152(c). Under that provision, bankruptcy judges may hold court outside of their districts in emergency situations and when the business of the court otherwise so requires. This amendment to the rule is intended to implement the legislation.

Changes Made After Publication. No changes were made after publication.

Rule 5002. Restrictions on Approval of Appointments

(a) APPROVAL OF APPOINTMENT OF RELATIVES PROHIBITED. The appointment of an individual as a trustee or examiner pursuant to § 1104 of the Code shall not be approved by the court if the individual is a relative of the bankruptcy judge approving the appointment or the United States trustee in the region in which the case is pending. The employment of an individual as an attorney, accountant, appraiser, auctioneer, or other professional person pursuant to §§ 327, 1103, or 1114 shall not be approved by the court if the individual is a relative of the bankruptcy judge approving the employment. The employment of an individual as attorney, accountant, appraiser, auctioneer, or other professional person pursuant to §§ 327, 1103, or 1114 may be approved by the court if the individual is a relative of the United States trustee in the region in which the case is pending, unless the court finds that the relationship with the United States trustee renders the employment improper under the circumstances of the case. Whenever under this subdivision an individual may not be approved for appointment or employment, the individual's firm, partnership, corporation, or any other form of business association or relationship, and all members, associates and professional employees thereof also may not be approved for appointment or employment.

(b) JUDICIAL DETERMINATION THAT APPROVAL OF APPOINTMENT OR EMPLOYMENT IS IMPROPER. A bankruptcy judge may not approve the appointment of a person as a trustee or examiner pursuant to § 1104 of the Code or approve the employment of a person as an attorney, accountant, appraiser, auctioneer, or other professional person pursuant to §§ 327, 1103, or 1114 of the Code if that person is or has been so connected with such judge or the United States trustee as to render the appointment or employment improper.

(As amended Apr. 29, 1985, eff. Aug. 1, 1985; Apr. 30, 1991, eff. Aug. 1, 1991.)

NOTES OF ADVISORY COMMITTEE ON RULES—1983

This rule is adapted from former Bankruptcy Rule 505(a). The scope of the prohibition on appointment or employment is expanded to include an examiner appointed under § 1104 of the Code and attorneys and other professional persons whose employment must be approved by the court under § 327 or § 1103.

The rule supplements two statutory provisions. Under 18 U.S.C. § 1910, it is a criminal offense for a judge to appoint a relative as a trustee and, under 28 U.S.C. § 458, a person may not be "appointed to or employed in any office or duty in any court" if he is a relative of any judge of that court. The rule prohibits the appointment or employment of a relative of a bankruptcy judge in a case pending before that bankruptcy judge or before other bankruptcy judges sitting within the district.

A relative is defined in § 101(34) of the Code to be an "individual related by affinity or consanguinity within the third degree as determined by the common law, or individual in a step or adoptive relationship within such third degree." Persons within the third degree under the common law system are as follows: first degree—parents, brothers and sisters, and children; second degree—grandparents, uncles and aunts, first cousins, nephews and nieces, and grandchildren; third degree—great grandparents, great uncles and aunts, first cousins once removed, second cousins, grand nephews and nieces, great grandchildren. Rule 9001 incorporates the definitions of § 101 of the Code.

In order for the policy of this rule to be meaningfully implemented, it is necessary to extend the prohibition against appointment or employment to the firm or other business association of the ineligible person and to those affiliated with the firm or business association. "Firm" is defined in Rule 9001 to include a professional partnership or corporation of attorneys or accountants. All other types of business and professional associations and relationships are covered by this rule.

NOTES OF ADVISORY COMMITTEE ON RULES—1985 AMENDMENT

The amended rule is divided into two subdivisions. Subdivision (a) applies to relatives of bankruptcy judges and subdivision (b) applies to persons who are or have been connected with bankruptcy judges. Subdivision (a) permits no judicial discretion; subdivision (b) allows judicial discretion. In both subdivisions of the amended rule "bankruptcy judge" has been substituted for "judge". The amended rule makes clear that it only applies to relatives of, or persons connected with, the bankruptcy judge. See *In re Hilltop Sand and Gravel, Inc.*, 35 B.R. 412 (N.D. Ohio 1983).

Subdivision (a). The original rule prohibited all bankruptcy judges in a district from appointing or approving the employment of (i) a relative of any bankruptcy judge serving in the district, (ii) the firm or business association of any ineligible relative and (iii) any member or professional employee of the firm or business association of an ineligible relative. In addition, the definition of relative, the third degree relationship under the common law, is quite broad. The restriction on the employment opportunities of relatives of bankruptcy judges was magnified by the fact that many law and accounting firms have practices and offices spanning the nation.

Relatives are not eligible for appointment or employment when the bankruptcy judge to whom they are related makes the appointment or approves the employment. Canon 3(b)(4) of the Code of Judicial Conduct, which provides that the judge "shall exercise his power of appointment only on the basis of merit, avoiding nepotism and favoritism," should guide a bankruptcy judge when a relative of a judge of the same bankruptcy court is considered for appointment or employment.

Subdivision (b), derived from clause (2) of the original rule, makes a person ineligible for appointment or employment if the person is so connected with a bankruptcy judge making the appointment or approving the employment as to render the appointment or approval of employment improper. The caption and text of the subdivision emphasize that application of the connection test is committed to the sound discretion of the bankruptcy judge who is to make the appointment or approve the employment. All relevant circumstances are to be taken into account by the court. The most important of those circumstances include: the nature and duration of the connection with the bankruptcy judge; whether the connection still exists, and, if not, when it was terminated; and the type of appointment or employment. These and other considerations must be carefully evaluated by the bankruptcy judge.

The policy underlying subdivision (b) is essentially the same as the policy embodied in the Code of Judicial Conduct. Canon 2 of the Code of Judicial Conduct instructs a judge to avoid impropriety and the appearance of impropriety, and Canon 3(b)(4) provides that the judge "should exercise his power of appointment only on the basis of merit, avoiding nepotism and favoritism." Subdivision (b) alerts the potential appointee or employee and party seeking approval of employment to consider the possible relevance or impact of subdivision (b) and indicates to them that appropriate disclosure must be made to the bankruptcy court before accepting appointment or employment. The information required may be made a part of the application for approval of employment. See Rule 2014(a).

Subdivision (b) departs from the former rule in an important respect: a firm or business association is not prohibited from appointment or employment merely because an individual member or employee of the firm or business association is ineligible under subdivision (b).

The emphasis given to the bankruptcy court's judicial discretion in applying subdivision (b) and the absence of a *per se* extension of ineligibility to the firm or business association or any ineligible individual complement the amendments to subdivision (a). The change is intended to moderate the prior limitation on the employment opportunities of attorneys, accountants and other professional persons who are or who have been connected in some way with the bankruptcy judge. For example, in all but the most unusual situations service as a law clerk to a bankruptcy judge is not the type of connection which alone precludes appointment or employment. Even if a bankruptcy judge determines that it is improper to appoint or approve the employment of a former law clerk in the period immediately after completion of the former law clerk's service with the judge, the firm which employs the former law clerk will, absent other circumstances, be eligible for employment. In each instance all the facts must be considered by the bankruptcy judge.

Subdivision (b) applies to persons connected with a bankruptcy judge. "Person" is defined in §101 of the Bankruptcy Code to include an "individual, partnership and corporation". A partnership or corporation may be appointed or employed to serve in a bankruptcy case. If a bankruptcy judge is connected in some way with a partnership or corporation, it is necessary for the court to determine whether the appointment or employment of that partnership or corporation is proper.

The amended rule does not regulate professional relationships which do not require approval of a bankruptcy judge. Disqualification of the bankruptcy judge pursuant to 28 U.S.C. §455 may, however, be appropriate. Under Rule 5004(a), a bankruptcy judge may find that disqualification from only some aspect of the case, rather than the entire case, is necessary. A situation may also arise in which the disqualifying circumstance only comes to light after services have been performed. Rule 5004(b) provides that if compensation from the estate is sought for these services, the bankruptcy judge is disqualified from awarding compensation.

NOTES OF ADVISORY COMMITTEE ON RULES—1991 AMENDMENT

The 1986 amendments to the Code provide that the United States trustee shall appoint trustees in chapter 7, chapter 12, and chapter 13 cases without the necessity of court approval. This rule is not intended to apply to the appointment of trustees in those cases because it would be inappropriate for a court rule to restrict in advance the exercise of discretion by the executive branch. See Committee Note to Rule 2009.

In chapter 11 cases, a trustee or examiner is appointed by the United States trustee after consultation with parties in interest and subject to court approval. Subdivision (a), as amended, prohibits the approval of the appointment of an individual as a trustee or examiner if the person is a relative of the United States trustee making the appointment or the bankruptcy judge approving the appointment.

The United States trustee neither appoints nor approves the employment of professional persons employed pursuant to §§327, 1103, or 1114 of the Code. Therefore, subdivision (a) is not a prohibition against judicial approval of employment of a professional person who is a relative of the United States trustee. However, the United States trustee monitors applications for compensation and reimbursement of expenses and may raise, appear and be heard on issues in the case. Employment of relatives of the United States trustee may be approved unless the court finds, after considering the relationship and the particular circumstances of the case, that the relationship would cause the employment to be improper. As used in this rule, "improper" includes the appearance of impropriety.

United States trustee is defined to include a designee or assistant United States trustee. See Rule 9001. Therefore, subdivision (a) is applicable if the person appointed as trustee or examiner or the professional to be employed is a relative of a designee of the United States trustee or any assistant United States trustee in the region in which the case is pending.

This rule is not exclusive of other laws or rules regulating ethical conduct. See, e.g., 28 CFR §45.735–5.

Rule 5003. Records Kept By the Clerk

(a) BANKRUPTCY DOCKETS. The clerk shall keep a docket in each case under the Code and shall enter thereon each judgment, order, and activity in that case as prescribed by the Director of the Administrative Office of the United States Courts. The entry of a judgment or order in a docket shall show the date the entry is made.

(b) CLAIMS REGISTER. The clerk shall keep in a claims register a list of claims filed in a case when it appears that there will be a distribution to unsecured creditors.

(c) JUDGMENTS AND ORDERS. The clerk shall keep, in the form and manner as the Director of the Administrative Office of the United States Courts may prescribe, a correct copy of every final judgment or order affecting title to or lien on real property or for the recovery of money or property, and any other order which the court may direct to be kept. On request of the prevailing party, a correct copy of every judgment or order affecting title to or lien upon real or personal property or for the recovery of money or property shall be kept and indexed with the civil judgments of the district court.

(d) INDEX OF CASES; CERTIFICATE OF SEARCH. The clerk shall keep indices of all cases and adversary proceedings as prescribed by the Director of the Administrative Office of the United States Courts. On request, the clerk shall make a search of any index and papers in the clerk's custody and certify whether a case or proceeding has been filed in or transferred to the court or if a discharge has been entered in its records.

(e) REGISTER OF MAILING ADDRESSES OF FEDERAL AND STATE GOVERNMENTAL UNITS AND CERTAIN TAXING AUTHORITIES. The United States or the state or territory in which the court is located may file a statement designating its mailing address. The United States, state, territory, or local governmental unit responsible for collecting taxes within the district in which the case is pending may also file a statement designating an address for service of requests under §505(b) of the Code, and the designation shall describe where further information concerning additional requirements for filing such requests may be found. The clerk shall keep, in the form and manner as the Director of the Administrative Office of the United States Courts may prescribe, a register that includes the mailing addresses designated under the first sentence of this subdivision, and a separate register of the addresses designated for the service of requests under §505(b) of the Code. The clerk is not required to include in any single register more than one mailing address for each department, agency, or instrumentality of the United States or the state or territory. If more than one address for a department, agency, or instrumentality is included in the register, the clerk shall also include information that would enable a user of the register to determine the circumstances when each address is applicable, and mailing notice to only one applicable address is sufficient to provide effective notice. The clerk shall update the register annually, effective January 2 of each year. The mailing address in the register is conclusively presumed to be a proper address for the governmental unit, but the failure to use that mailing address does not invalidate any notice that is otherwise effective under applicable law.

(f) OTHER BOOKS AND RECORDS OF THE CLERK. The clerk shall keep any other books and records required by the Director of the Administrative Office of the United States Courts.

(As amended Mar. 30, 1987, eff. Aug. 1, 1987; Apr. 17, 2000, eff. Dec. 1, 2000; Apr. 23, 2008, eff. Dec. 1, 2008.)

NOTES OF ADVISORY COMMITTEE ON RULES—1983

This rule consolidates former Bankruptcy Rules 504 and 507. The record-keeping duties of the referee under former Bankruptcy Rule 504 are transferred to the clerk. Subdivisions (a), (c), (d) and (e) are similar to subdivisions (a)–(d) of Rule 79 F.R.Civ.P.

Subdivision (b) requires that filed claims be listed on a claims register only when there may be a distribution to unsecured creditors. Compilation of the list for no asset or nominal asset cases would serve no purpose.

Rule 2013 requires the clerk to maintain a public record of fees paid from the estate and an annual summary thereof.

Former Bankruptcy Rules 507(d) and 508, which made materials in the clerk's office and files available to the public, are not necessary because §107 of the Code guarantees public access to files and dockets of cases under the Code.

NOTES OF ADVISORY COMMITTEE ON RULES—1987 AMENDMENT

Subdivision (a) has been made more specific.

Subdivision (c) is amended to require that on the request of the prevailing party the clerk of the district court shall keep and index bankruptcy judgments and orders affecting title to or lien upon real or personal property or for the recovery of money or property with the civil judgments of the district court. This requirement is derived from former Rule 9021(b). The Director of the Administrative Office will provide guidance to the bankruptcy and district court clerks regarding appropriate paperwork and retention procedures.

COMMITTEE NOTES ON RULES—2000 AMENDMENT

Subdivision (e) is added to provide a source where debtors, their attorneys, and other parties may go to determine whether the United States or the state or territory in which the court is located has filed a statement designating a mailing address for notice purposes. By using the address in the register—which must be available to the public—the sender is assured that the mailing address is proper. But the use of an address that differs from the address included in the register does not invalidate the notice if it is otherwise effective under applicable law.

The register may include a separate mailing address for each department, agency, or instrumentality of the United States or the state or territory. This rule does not require that addresses of municipalities or other local governmental units be included in the register, but the clerk may include them.

Although it is important for the register to be kept current, debtors, their attorneys, and other parties should be able to rely on mailing addresses listed in the register without the need to continuously inquire as to new or amended addresses. Therefore, the clerk must update the register, but only once each year.

To avoid unnecessary cost and burden on the clerk and to keep the register a reasonable length, the clerk is not required to include more than one mailing address for a particular agency, department, or instrumentality of the United States or the state or territory. But if more than one address is included, the clerk is required to include information so that a person using the register could determine when each address should be used. In any event, the inclusion of more than one address for a particular department, agency, or instrumentality does not impose on a person sending a notice the duty to send it to more than one address.

GAP Report on Rule 5003. No changes since publication.

COMMITTEE NOTES ON RULES—2008 AMENDMENT

The rule is amended to implement §505(b)(1) of the Code added by the 2005 amendments, which allows a taxing authority to designate an address to use for the service of requests under that subsection. Under the amendment, the clerk is directed to maintain a separate register for mailing addresses of governmental units solely for the service of requests under §505(b). This register is in addition to the register of addresses of governmental units already maintained by the clerk. The clerk is required to keep only one address for a governmental unit in each register.

Changes Made After Publication. Subdivision (e) was amended to clarify that the clerk must maintain a separate mailing address register that contains the addresses to which notices pertaining to actions under §505 of the Code are to be sent.

Rule 5004. Disqualification

(a) DISQUALIFICATION OF JUDGE. A bankruptcy judge shall be governed by 28 U.S.C. §455, and disqualified from presiding over the proceeding or contested matter in which the disqualifying circumstances[1] arises or, if appropriate, shall be disqualified from presiding over the case.

(b) DISQUALIFICATION OF JUDGE FROM ALLOWING COMPENSATION. A bankruptcy judge shall be disqualified from allowing compensation to a person who is a relative of the bankruptcy judge or with whom the judge is so connected as to render it improper for the judge to authorize such compensation.

(As amended Apr. 29, 1985, eff. Aug. 1, 1985; Mar. 30, 1987, eff. Aug. 1, 1987.)

NOTES OF ADVISORY COMMITTEE ON RULES—1983

Subdivision (a). Disqualification of a bankruptcy judge is governed by 28 U.S.C. §455. That section provides that the judge "shall disqualify himself in any proceeding in which his impartiality might reasonably be questioned" or under certain other circumstances. In a case under the Code it is possible that the disqualifying circumstance will be isolated to an adversary proceeding or contested matter. The rule makes it clear that when the disqualifying circumstance is limited in that way the judge need only disqualify himself from presiding over that adversary proceeding or contested matter.

It is possible, however, that even if the disqualifying circumstance arises in connection with an adversary proceeding, the effect will be so pervasive that disqualification from presiding over the case is appropriate. This distinction is consistent with the definition of "proceeding" in 28 U.S.C. §455(d)(1).

[1] So in original. Probably should be "circumstance".

Subdivision (b) precludes a bankruptcy judge from allowing compensation from the estate to a relative or other person closely associated with the judge. The subdivision applies where the judge has not appointed or approved the employment of the person requesting compensation. Perhaps the most frequent application of the subdivision will be in the allowance of administrative expenses under §503(b)(3)–(5) of the Code. For example, if an attorney or accountant is retained by an indenture trustee who thereafter makes a substantial contribution in a chapter 11 case, the attorney or accountant may seek compensation under §503(b)(4). If the attorney or accountant is a relative of or associated with the bankruptcy judge, the judge may not allow compensation to the attorney or accountant. Section 101(34) defines relative and Rule 9001 incorporates the definitions of the Code. See the Advisory Committee's Note to Rule 5002.

NOTES OF ADVISORY COMMITTEE ON RULES—1985 AMENDMENT

Subdivision (a) was affected by the Bankruptcy Amendments and Federal Judgeship Act of 1984, P.L. 98–353, 98 Stat. 333. The 1978 Bankruptcy Reform Act, P.L. 95–598, included bankruptcy judges in the definition of United States judges in 28 U.S.C. §451 and they were therefore subject to the provisions of 28 U.S.C. §455. This was to become effective on April 1, 1984. P.L. 95–598, §404(b). Section 113 of P.L. 98–353, however, appears to have rendered the amendment to 28 U.S.C. §451 ineffective. Subdivision (a) of the rule retains the substance and intent of the earlier draft by making bankruptcy judges subject to 28 U.S.C. §455.

The word "associated" in subdivision (b) has been changed to "connected" in order to conform with Rule 5002(b).

NOTES OF ADVISORY COMMITTEE ON RULES—1987 AMENDMENT

The rule is amended to be gender neutral. The bankruptcy judge before whom the matter is pending determines whether disqualification is required.

Rule 5005. Filing and Transmittal of Papers

(a) FILING.

(1) *Place of Filing.* The lists, schedules, statements, proofs of claim or interest, complaints, motions, applications, objections and other papers required to be filed by these rules, except as provided in 28 U.S.C. §1409, shall be filed with the clerk in the district where the case under the Code is pending. The judge of that court may permit the papers to be filed with the judge, in which event the filing date shall be noted thereon, and they shall be forthwith transmitted to the clerk. The clerk shall not refuse to accept for filing any petition or other paper presented for the purpose of filing solely because it is not presented in proper form as required by these rules or any local rules or practices.

(2) *Filing by Electronic Means.* A court may by local rule permit or require documents to be filed, signed, or verified by electronic means that are consistent with technical standards, if any, that the Judicial Conference of the United States establishes. A local rule may require filing by electronic means only if reasonable exceptions are allowed. A document filed by electronic means in compliance with a local rule constitutes a written paper for the purpose of applying these rules, the Federal Rules of Civil Procedure made applicable by these rules, and §107 of the Code.

(b) TRANSMITTAL TO THE UNITED STATES TRUSTEE.

(1) The complaints, motions, applications, objections and other papers required to be transmitted to the United States trustee by these rules shall be mailed or delivered to an office of the United States trustee, or to another place designated by the United States trustee, in the district where the case under the Code is pending.

(2) The entity, other than the clerk, transmitting a paper to the United States trustee shall promptly file as proof of such transmittal a verified statement identifying the paper and stating the date on which it was transmitted to the United States trustee.

(3) Nothing in these rules shall require the clerk to transmit any paper to the United States trustee if the United States trustee requests in writing that the paper not be transmitted.

(c) ERROR IN FILING OR TRANSMITTAL. A paper intended to be filed with the clerk but erroneously delivered to the United States trustee, the trustee, the attorney for the trustee, a bankruptcy judge, a district judge, the clerk of the bankruptcy appellate panel, or the clerk of the district court shall, after the date of its receipt has been noted thereon, be transmitted forthwith to the clerk of the bankruptcy court. A paper intended to be transmitted to the United States trustee but erroneously delivered to the clerk, the trustee, the attorney for the trustee, a bankruptcy judge, a district judge, the clerk of the bankruptcy appellate panel, or the clerk of the district court shall, after the date of its receipt has been noted thereon, be transmitted forthwith to the United States trustee. In the interest of justice, the court may order that a paper erroneously delivered shall be deemed filed with the clerk or transmitted to the United States trustee as of the date of its original delivery.

(As amended Mar. 30, 1987, eff. Aug. 1, 1987; Apr. 30, 1991, eff. Aug. 1, 1991; Apr. 22, 1993, eff. Aug. 1, 1993; Apr. 23, 1996, eff. Dec. 1, 1996; Apr. 12, 2006, eff. Dec. 1, 2006.)

NOTES OF ADVISORY COMMITTEE ON RULES—1983

Subdivision (a) is an adaptation of Rule 5(e) F.R.Civ.P. Sections 301–304 of the Code and Rules 1002 and 1003 require that cases under the Code be commenced by filing a petition "with the bankruptcy court." Other sections of the Code and other rules refer to or contemplate filing but there is no specific reference to filing with the bankruptcy court. For example, §501 of the Code requires filing of proofs of claim and Rule 3016(c) requires the filing of a disclosure statement. This subdivision applies to all situations in which filing is required. Except when filing in another district is authorized by 28 U.S.C. §1473, all papers, including complaints commencing adversary proceedings, must be filed in the court where the case under the Code is pending.

Subdivision (b) is the same as former Bankruptcy Rule 509(c).

NOTES OF ADVISORY COMMITTEE ON RULES—1987 AMENDMENT

Subdivision (a) is amended to conform with the 1984 amendments.

NOTES OF ADVISORY COMMITTEE ON RULES—1991 AMENDMENT

Subdivision (b)(1) is flexible in that it permits the United States trustee to designate a place or places for receiving papers within the district in which the case is pending. Transmittal of papers to the United States trustee may be accomplished by mail or delivery, including delivery by courier, and the technical requirements for service of process are not applicable. Although papers relating to a proceeding commenced in another district pursuant to 28 U.S.C. §1409 must be filed with the clerk in that district, the papers required to be transmitted to the United States trustee must be mailed or delivered to the United States trustee in the district in which the case under the Code is pending. The United States trustee in the district in which the case is pending monitors the progress of the case and should be informed of all developments in the case wherever the developments take place.

Subdivision (b)(2) requires that proof of transmittal to the United States trustee be filed with the clerk. If papers are served on the United States trustee by mail or otherwise, the filing of proof of service would satisfy the requirements of this subdivision. This requirement enables the court to assure that papers are actually transmitted to the United States trustee in compliance with the rules. When the rules require that a paper be transmitted to the United States trustee and proof of transmittal has not been filed with the clerk, the court should not schedule a hearing or should take other appropriate action to assure that the paper is transmitted to the United States trustee. The filing of the verified statement with the clerk also enables other parties in interest to determine whether a paper has been transmitted to the United States trustee.

Subdivision (b)(3) is designed to relieve the clerk of any obligation under these rules to transmit any paper to the United States trustee if the United States trustee does not wish to receive it.

Subdivision (c) is amended to include the erroneous delivery of papers intended to be transmitted to the United States trustee.

NOTES OF ADVISORY COMMITTEE ON RULES—1993 AMENDMENT

Subdivision (a) is amended to conform to the 1991 amendment to Rule 5(e) F.R.Civ.P. It is not a suitable role for the office of the clerk to refuse to accept for filing papers not conforming to requirements of form imposed by these rules or by local rules or practices. The enforcement of these rules and local rules is a role for a judge. This amendment does not require the clerk to accept for filing papers sent to the clerk's office by facsimile transmission.

NOTES OF ADVISORY COMMITTEE ON RULES—1996 AMENDMENT

The rule is amended to permit, but not require, courts to adopt local rules that allow filing, signing, or verifying of documents by electronic means. However, such local rules must be consistent with technical standards, if any, promulgated by the Judicial Conference of the United States.

An important benefit to be derived by permitting filing by electronic means is that the extensive volume of paper received and maintained as records in the clerk's office will be reduced substantially. With the receipt of electronic data transmissions by computer, the clerk may maintain records electronically without the need to reproduce them in tangible paper form.

Judicial Conference standards governing the technological aspects of electronic filing will result in uniformity among judicial districts to accommodate an increasingly national bar. By delegating to the Judicial Conference the establishment and future amendment of national standards for electronic filing, the Supreme Court and Congress will be relieved of the burden of reviewing and promulgating detailed rules dealing with complex technological standards. Another reason for leaving to the Judicial Conference the formulation of technological standards for electronic filing is that advances in computer technology occur often, and changes in the technological standards may have to be implemented more frequently than would be feasible by rule amendment under the Rules Enabling Act process.

It is anticipated that standards established by the Judicial Conference will govern technical specifications for electronic data transmission, such as requirements relating to the formatting of data, speed of transmission, means to transmit copies of supporting documentation, and security of communication procedures. In addition, before procedures for electronic filing are implemented, standards must be established to assure the proper maintenance and integrity of the record and to provide appropriate access and retrieval mechanisms. These matters will be governed by local rules until system-wide standards are adopted by the Judicial Conference.

Rule 9009 requires that the Official Forms shall be observed and used "with alterations as may be appropriate." Compliance with local rules and any Judicial Conference standards with respect to the formatting or presentation of electronically transmitted data, to the extent that they do not conform to the Official Forms, would be an appropriate alteration within the meaning of Rule 9009.

These rules require that certain documents be in writing. For example, Rule 3001 states that a proof of claim is a "written statement." Similarly, Rule 3007 provides that an objection to a claim "shall be in writing." Pursuant to the new subdivision (a)(2), any requirement under these rules that a paper be written may be satisfied by filing the document by electronic means, notwithstanding the fact that the clerk neither receives nor prints a paper reproduction of the electronic data.

Section 107(a) of the Code provides that a "paper" filed in a case is a public record open to examination by an entity at reasonable times without charge, except as provided in §107(b). The amendment to subdivision (a)(2) provides that an electronically filed document is to be treated as such a public record.

Although under subdivision (a)(2) electronically filed documents may be treated as written papers or as signed or verified writings, it is important to emphasize that such treatment is only for the purpose of applying these rules. In addition, local rules and Judicial Conference standards regarding verification must satisfy the requirements of 28 U.S.C. §1746.

GAP Report on Rule 5005. No changes since publication.

COMMITTEE NOTES ON RULES—2006 AMENDMENT

Subdivision (a). Amended Rule 5005(a)(2) acknowledges that many courts have required electronic filing by means of a standing order, procedures manual, or local rule. These local practices reflect the advantages that courts and most litigants realize from electronic filings. Courts requiring electronic filing must make reasonable exceptions for persons for whom electronic filing of documents constitutes an unreasonable denial of access to the courts. Experience with the rule will facilitate convergence on uniform exceptions in an amended Rule 5005(a)(2).

Subdivision (c). The rule is amended to include the clerk of the bankruptcy appellate panel among the list of persons required to transmit to the proper person erroneously filed or transmitted papers. The amendment is necessary because the bankruptcy appellate panels were not in existence at the time of the original promulgation of the rule. The amendment also inserts the district judge on the list of persons required to transmit papers intended for the United States trustee but erroneously sent to another person. The district judge is included in the list of persons who must transmit papers to the clerk of the bankruptcy court in the first part of the rule, and there is no reason to exclude the district judge from the list of persons who must transmit erroneously filed papers to the United States trustee.

Changes Made After Publication. The published version of the Rule did not include the sentence set out on lines 7–10 above [sic]. The Advisory Committee concluded, based on the written comments received and additonal Advisory Committee consideration, that the text of the rule should include a statement regarding the need for courts to protect access to the courts for those whose status might not allow for electronic participation in cases. The published version had relegated this notion to the Committee Note, but further deliberations led to the conclusion that this matter is too important to leave to the Committee Note and instead should be included in the text of the rule.

REFERENCES IN TEXT

The Federal Rules of Civil Procedure, referred to in subd. (a)(2), are set out in the Appendix to Title 28, Judiciary and Judicial Procedure.

Rule 5006. Certification of Copies of Papers

The clerk shall issue a certified copy of the record of any proceeding in a case under the Code or of any paper filed with the clerk on payment of any prescribed fee.

(As amended Apr. 30, 1991, eff. Aug. 1, 1991.)

NOTES OF ADVISORY COMMITTEE ON RULES—1983

Fees for certification and copying are fixed by the Judicial Conference under 28 U.S.C. §1930(b).

Rule 1101 F. R. Evid. makes the Federal Rules of Evidence applicable to cases under the Code. Rule 1005 F. R. Evid. allows the contents of an official record or of a paper filed with the court to be proved by a duly certified copy. A copy certified and issued in accordance with Rule 5006 is accorded authenticity by Rule 902(4) F. R. Evid.

Rule 5007. Record of Proceedings and Transcripts

(a) FILING OF RECORD OR TRANSCRIPT. The reporter or operator of a recording device shall certify the original notes of testimony, tape recording, or other original record of the proceeding and promptly file them with the clerk. The person preparing any transcript shall promptly file a certified copy.

(b) TRANSCRIPT FEES. The fees for copies of transcripts shall be charged at rates prescribed by the Judicial Conference of the United States. No fee may be charged for the certified copy filed with the clerk.

(c) ADMISSIBILITY OF RECORD IN EVIDENCE. A certified sound recording or a transcript of a proceeding shall be admissible as prima facie evidence to establish the record.

(As amended Mar. 30, 1987, eff. Aug. 1, 1987; Apr. 30, 1991, eff. Aug. 1, 1991.)

NOTES OF ADVISORY COMMITTEE ON RULES—1983

This rule supplements 28 U.S.C. §773. A record of proceedings before the bankruptcy judge is to be made whenever practicable. By whatever means the record is made, subdivision (a) requires that the preparer of the record certify and file the original notes, tape recording, or other form of sound recording of the proceedings. Similarly, if a transcript is requested, the preparer is to file a certified copy with the clerk.

Subdivision (b) is derived from 28 U.S.C. §753(f).

Subdivision (c) is derived from former Bankruptcy Rule 511(c). This subdivision extends to a sound recording the same evidentiary status as a transcript under 28 U.S.C. §773(b).

NOTES OF ADVISORY COMMITTEE ON RULES—1991 AMENDMENT

The words "with the clerk" in the final sentence of subdivision (a) are deleted as unnecessary. See Rules 5005(a) and 9001(3).

Rule 5008. Notice Regarding Presumption of Abuse in Chapter 7 Cases of Individual Debtors

If a presumption of abuse has arisen under §707(b) in a chapter 7 case of an individual with primarily consumer debts, the clerk shall within 10 days after the date of the filing of the petition notify creditors of the presumption of abuse in accordance with Rule 2002. If the debtor has not filed a statement indicating whether a presumption of abuse has arisen, the clerk shall within 10 days after the date of the filing of the petition notify creditors that the debtor has not filed the statement and that further notice will be given if a later filed statement indicates that a presumption of abuse has arisen. If a debtor later files a statement indicating that a presumption of abuse has arisen, the clerk shall notify creditors of the presumption of abuse as promptly as practicable.

(Added Apr. 23, 2008, eff. Dec. 1, 2008.)

NOTES OF ADVISORY COMMITTEE ON RULES—1991

This rule [Rule 5008. Funds of the Estate; abrogated Apr. 30, 1991, eff. Aug. 1, 1991] is abrogated in view of the amendments to §345(b) of the Code and the role of the United States trustee in approving bonds and supervising trustees.

COMMITTEE NOTES ON RULES—2008

This rule is new. The 2005 amendments to §342 of the Code require that clerks give written notice to all creditors not later than 10 days after the date of the filing of the petition that a presumption of abuse has arisen under §707(b). A statement filed by the debtor will be the source of the clerk's information about the presumption of abuse. This rule enables the clerk to meet its obligation to send the notice within the statutory time period set forth in §342. In the event that the court receives the debtor's statement after the clerk has sent the first notice, and the debtor's statement indicates a presumption of abuse, the rule requires that the clerk send a second notice.

Changes Made After Publication. No changes were made after publication.

Rule 5009. Closing Chapter 7 Liquidation, Chapter 12 Family Farmer's Debt Adjustment, and Chapter 13 Individual's Debt Adjustment Cases

If in a chapter 7, chapter 12, or chapter 13 case the trustee has filed a final report and final account and has certified that the estate has been fully administered, and if within 30 days no objection has been filed by the United States trustee or a party in interest, there shall be a presumption that the estate has been fully administered.

(As amended Apr. 30, 1991, eff. Aug. 1, 1991.)

NOTES OF ADVISORY COMMITTEE ON RULES—1983

This rule is the same as §350(a) of the Code. An estate may be closed even though the period allowed by Rule 3002(c) for filing claims has not expired. The closing of a case may be expedited when a notice of no dividends is given under Rule 2002(e). Dismissal of a case for want of prosecution or failure to pay filing fees is governed by Rule 1017.

NOTES OF ADVISORY COMMITTEE ON RULES—1991 AMENDMENT

The final report and account of the trustee is required to be filed with the court and the United States trustee under §§704(9), 1202(b)(1), and 1302(b)(1) of the Code. This amendment facilitates the United States trustee's performance of statutory duties to supervise trustees and administer cases under chapters 7, 12, and 13 pursuant to 28 U.S.C. §586. In the absence of a timely objection by the United States trustee or a party in interest, the court may discharge the trustee and close the case pursuant to §350(a) without the need to review the final report and account or to determine the merits of the trustee's certification that the estate has been fully administered.

Rule 3022 governs the closing of chapter 11 cases.

Rule 5010. Reopening Cases

A case may be reopened on motion of the debtor or other party in interest pursuant to §350(b) of the Code. In a chapter 7, 12, or 13 case a trustee shall not be appointed by the United States trustee unless the court determines that a trustee is necessary to protect the interests of creditors and the debtor or to insure efficient administration of the case.

(As amended Mar. 30, 1987, eff. Aug. 1, 1987; Apr. 30, 1991, eff. Aug. 1, 1991.)

NOTES OF ADVISORY COMMITTEE ON RULES—1983

Section 350(b) of the Code provides: "A case may be reopened in the court in which such case was closed to administer assets, to accord relief to the debtor, or for other cause."

Rule 9024, which incorporates Rule 60 F.R.Civ.P., exempts motions to reopen cases under the Code from the one year limitation of Rule 60(b).

Although a case has been closed the court may sometimes act without reopening the case. Under Rule 9024, clerical errors in judgments, orders, or other parts of the record or errors therein caused by oversight or omission may be corrected. A judgment determined to be non-dischargeable pursuant to Rule 4007 may be enforced after a case is closed by a writ of execution obtained pursuant to Rule 7069.

NOTES OF ADVISORY COMMITTEE ON RULES—1987 AMENDMENT

In order to avoid unnecessary cost and delay, the rule is amended to permit reopening of a case without the appointment of a trustee when the services of a trustee are not needed.

NOTES OF ADVISORY COMMITTEE ON RULES—1991 AMENDMENT

This rule is amended to conform to the 1986 amendments to the Code that give the United States trustee the duty to appoint trustees in chapter 7, 12 and 13 cases. See §§701, 702(d), 1202(a), and 1302(a) of the Code. In most reopened cases, a trustee is not needed because there are no assets to be administered. Therefore, in the interest of judicial economy, this rule is amended so that a motion will not be necessary unless the United States trustee or a party in interest seeks the appointment of a trustee in the reopened case.

Rule 5011. Withdrawal and Abstention from Hearing a Proceeding

(a) WITHDRAWAL. A motion for withdrawal of a case or proceeding shall be heard by a district judge.

(b) ABSTENTION FROM HEARING A PROCEEDING. A motion for abstention pursuant to 28 U.S.C. §1334(c) shall be governed by Rule 9014 and shall be served on the parties to the proceeding.

(c) EFFECT OF FILING OF MOTION FOR WITHDRAWAL OR ABSTENTION. The filing of a motion for withdrawal of a case or proceeding or for abstention pursuant to 28 U.S.C. §1334(c) shall not stay the administration of the case or any proceeding therein before the bankruptcy judge except that the bankruptcy judge may stay, on such terms and conditions as are proper, proceedings pending disposition of the motion. A motion for a stay ordinarily shall be presented first to the bankruptcy judge. A motion for a stay or relief from a stay filed in the district court shall state why it has not been presented to or obtained from the bankruptcy judge. Relief granted by the district judge shall be on such terms and conditions as the judge deems proper.

(Added Mar. 30, 1987, eff. Aug. 1, 1987; amended Apr. 30, 1991, eff. Aug. 1, 1991.)

NOTES OF ADVISORY COMMITTEE ON RULES—1987

Motions for withdrawal pursuant to 28 U.S.C. §157(d) or abstention pursuant to 28 U.S.C. §1334(c), like all other motions, are to be filed with the clerk as required by Rule 5005(a). If a bankruptcy clerk has been appointed for the district, all motions are filed with the bankruptcy clerk. The method for forwarding withdrawal motions to the district court will be established by administrative procedures.

Subdivision (a). Section 157(d) permits the district court to order withdrawal on its own motion or the motion of a party. Subdivision (a) of this rule makes it clear that the bankruptcy judge will not conduct hearings on a withdrawal motion. The withdrawal decision is committed exclusively to the district court.

Subdivision (b). A decision to abstain under 28 U.S.C. §1334(c) is not appealable. The district court is vested originally with jurisdiction and the decision to relinquish that jurisdiction must ultimately be a matter for the district court. The bankruptcy judge ordinarily will be in the best position to evaluate the grounds asserted for abstention. This subdivision (b) provides that the initial hearing on the motion is before the bankruptcy judge. The procedure for review of the report and recommendation are governed by Rule 9033.

This rule does not apply to motions under §305 of the Code for abstention from hearing a case. Judicial decisions will determine the scope of the bankruptcy judge's authority under §305.

Subdivision (c). Unless the court so orders, proceedings are not stayed when motions are filed for withdrawal or for abstention from hearing a proceeding. Because of the district court's authority over cases and proceedings, the subdivision authorizes the district court to order a stay or modify a stay ordered by the bankruptcy judge.

NOTES OF ADVISORY COMMITTEE ON RULES—1991 AMENDMENT

Subdivision (b) is amended to delete the restriction that limits the role of the bankruptcy court to the filing of a report and recommendation for disposition of a motion for abstention under 28 U.S.C. §1334(c)(2). This amendment is consistent with §309(b) of the Judicial Improvements Act of 1990 which amended §1334(c)(2) so that it allows an appeal to the district court of a bankruptcy court's order determining an abstention motion. This subdivision is also amended to clarify that the motion is a contested matter governed by Rule 9014 and that it must be served on all parties to the proceeding which is the subject of the motion.

PART VI—COLLECTION AND LIQUIDATION OF THE ESTATE

Rule 6001. Burden of Proof As to Validity of Postpetition Transfer

Any entity asserting the validity of a transfer under §549 of the Code shall have the burden of proof.

NOTES OF ADVISORY COMMITTEE ON RULES—1983

This rule is derived from former Bankruptcy Rule 603. The Act contained, in §70d, a provision placing the burden of proof on the same person as did Rule 603. The Code does not contain any directive with respect to the burden of proof. This omission, in all probability, resulted from the intention to leave matters affecting evidence to these rules. See H. Rep. No. 95–595, 95th Cong. 1st Sess. (1977) 293.

Rule 6002. Accounting by Prior Custodian of Property of the Estate

(a) ACCOUNTING REQUIRED. Any custodian required by the Code to deliver property in the custodian's possession or control to the trustee shall promptly file and transmit to the United States trustee a report and account with respect to the property of the estate and the administration thereof.

(b) EXAMINATION OF ADMINISTRATION. On the filing and transmittal of the report and account required by subdivision (a) of this rule and after an examination has been made into the superseded administration, after notice and a hearing, the court shall determine the propriety of the administration, including the reasonableness of all disbursements.

(As amended Mar. 30, 1987, eff. Aug. 1, 1987; Apr. 30, 1991, eff. Aug. 1, 1991; Apr. 22, 1993, eff. Aug. 1, 1993.)

NOTES OF ADVISORY COMMITTEE ON RULES—1983

"Custodian" is defined in §101(10) of the Code. The definition includes a trustee or receiver appointed in proceedings not under the Code, as well as an assignee for the benefit of creditors.

This rule prescribes the procedure to be followed by a custodian who under §543 of the Code is required to deliver property to the trustee and to account for its disposition. The examination under subdivision (b) may be initiated (1) on the motion of the custodian required to account under subdivision (a) for an approval of his account and discharge thereon, (2) on the motion of, or the filing of an objection to the custodian's account by, the trustee or any other party in interest, or (3) on the court's own initiative. Rule 9014 applies to any contested matter arising under this rule.

Section 543(d) is similar to an abstention provision. It grants the bankruptcy court discretion to permit the custodian to remain in possession and control of the property. In that event, the custodian is excused from complying with §543(a)–(c) and thus would not be required to turn over the property to the trustee. When there is no duty to turn over to the trustee, Rule 6002 would not be applicable.

NOTES OF ADVISORY COMMITTEE ON RULES—1991 AMENDMENT

This rule is amended to enable the United States trustee to review, object to, or to otherwise be heard regarding the custodian's report and accounting. See §§307 and 543 of the Code.

NOTES OF ADVISORY COMMITTEE ON RULES—1993 AMENDMENT

Subdivision (b) is amended to conform to the language of §102(1) of the Code.

Rule 6003. Interim and Final Relief Immediately Following the Commencement of the Case—Applications for Employment; Motions for Use, Sale, or Lease of Property; and Motions for Assumption or Assignment of Executory Contracts

Except to the extent that relief is necessary to avoid immediate and irreparable harm, the court shall not, within 21 days after the filing of the petition, grant relief regarding the following:

(a) an application under Rule 2014;

(b) a motion to use, sell, lease, or otherwise incur an obligation regarding property of the estate, including a motion to pay all or part of a claim that arose before the filing of the petition, but not a motion under Rule 4001; and

(c) a motion to assume or assign an executory contract or unexpired lease in accordance with §365.

(Added Apr. 30, 2007; eff. Dec. 1, 2007; amended Mar. 26, 2009, eff. Dec. 1, 2009.)

NOTES OF ADVISORY COMMITTEE ON RULES—1991

This rule [Former Rule 6003—Disbursement of Money of the Estate (Abrogated Apr. 30, 1991, eff. Aug. 1, 1991)] is abrogated in view of the role of the United States trustee in supervising trustees. Use of estate funds by a trustee or debtor in possession is governed by §363 of the Code.

COMMITTEE NOTES ON RULES—2007

There can be a flurry of activity during the first days of a bankruptcy case. This activity frequently takes place prior to the formation of a creditors' committee, and it also can include substantial amounts of materials for the court and parties in interest to review and evaluate. This rule is intended to alleviate some of the time pressures present at the start of a case so that full and close consideration can be given to matters that may have a fundamental impact on the case.

The rule provides that the court cannot grant relief on applications for the employment of professional persons, motions for the use, sale, or lease of property of the estate other than such a motion under Rule 4001, and motions to assume or assign executory contracts and unexpired leases for the first 20 days of the case, unless granting relief is necessary to avoid immediate and irreparable harm. This standard is taken from Rule 4001(b)(2) and (c)(2), and decisions under those provisions should provide guidance for the application of this provision.

This rule does not govern motions and applications made more than 20 days after the filing of the petition.

Changes After Publication. Subdivision (c) was amended by deleting the reference to the rejection of executory contracts or unexpired leases. The rule, as revised, now limits only the assumption or assignment of executory contracts or unexpired leases in that subdivision.

COMMITTEE NOTES ON RULES—2009 AMENDMENT

The rule is amended to implement changes in connection with the amendment to Rule 9006(a) and the manner by which time is computed under the rules. The deadline in the rule is amended to substitute a deadline that is a multiple of seven days. Throughout the rules, deadlines are amended in the following manner:

- 5-day periods become 7-day periods
- 10-day periods become 14-day periods
- 15-day periods become 14-day periods
- 20-day periods become 21-day periods
- 25-day periods become 28-day periods

Rule 6004. Use, Sale, or Lease of Property

(a) NOTICE OF PROPOSED USE, SALE, OR LEASE OF PROPERTY. Notice of a proposed use, sale, or lease of property, other than cash collateral, not in the ordinary course of business shall be given pursuant to Rule 2002(a)(2), (c)(1), (i), and (k) and, if applicable, in accordance with §363(b)(2) of the Code.

(b) OBJECTION TO PROPOSAL. Except as provided in subdivisions (c) and (d) of this rule, an objection to a proposed use, sale, or lease of property shall be filed and served not less than seven days before the date set for the proposed action or within the time fixed by the court. An objection to the proposed use, sale, or lease of property is governed by Rule 9014.

(c) SALE FREE AND CLEAR OF LIENS AND OTHER INTERESTS. A motion for authority to sell property free and clear of liens or other interests shall be made in accordance with Rule 9014 and shall be served on the parties who have liens or other interests in the property to be sold. The notice required by subdivision (a) of this rule shall include the date of the hearing on the motion and the time within which objections may be filed and served on the debtor in possession or trustee.

(d) SALE OF PROPERTY UNDER $2,500. Notwithstanding subdivision (a) of this rule, when all of the nonexempt property of the estate has an aggregate gross value less than $2,500, it shall be sufficient to give a general notice of intent to sell such property other than in the ordinary course of business to all creditors, indenture trustees, committees appointed or elected pursuant to the Code, the United States trustee and other persons as the court may direct. An objection to any such sale may be filed and served by a party in interest within 14 days of the mailing of the notice, or within the time fixed by the court. An objection is governed by Rule 9014.

(e) HEARING. If a timely objection is made pursuant to subdivision (b) or (d) of this rule, the date of the hearing thereon may be set in the notice given pursuant to subdivision (a) of this rule.

(f) CONDUCT OF SALE NOT IN THE ORDINARY COURSE OF BUSINESS.

(1) *Public or Private Sale.* All sales not in the ordinary course of business may be by private sale or by public auction. Unless it is impracticable, an itemized statement of the property sold, the name of each purchaser, and the price received for each item or lot or for the property as a whole if sold in bulk shall be filed on completion of a sale. If the property is sold by an auctioneer, the auctioneer shall file the statement, transmit a copy thereof to the United States trustee, and furnish a copy to the trustee, debtor in possession, or chapter 13 debtor. If the property is not sold by an auctioneer, the trustee, debtor in possession, or chapter 13 debtor shall file the statement and transmit a copy thereof to the United States trustee.

(2) *Execution of Instruments.* After a sale in accordance with this rule the debtor, the trustee, or debtor in possession, as the case may be, shall execute any instrument necessary or ordered by the court to effectuate the transfer to the purchaser.

(g) SALE OF PERSONALLY IDENTIFIABLE INFORMATION.

(1) *Motion.* A motion for authority to sell or lease personally identifiable information under §363(b)(1)(B) shall include a request for an order directing the United States trustee to appoint a consumer privacy ombudsman under §332. Rule 9014 governs the motion which shall be served on: any committee elected under §705 or appointed under §1102 of the Code, or if the case is a chapter 11 reorganization case and no committee of unsecured creditors has been appointed under §1102, on the creditors included on the list of creditors filed under Rule 1007(d); and on such other entities as the court may direct. The motion shall be transmitted to the United States trustee.

(2) *Appointment.* If a consumer privacy ombudsman is appointed under §332, no later than seven days before the hearing on the motion under §363(b)(1)(B), the United States trustee shall file a notice of the appointment, including the name and address of the person appointed. The United States trustee's notice shall be accompanied by a verified statement of the person appointed setting forth the person's connections with the debtor, creditors, any other party in interest, their respective attorneys and accountants, the United States trustee, or any person employed in the office of the United States trustee.

(h) STAY OF ORDER AUTHORIZING USE, SALE, OR LEASE OF PROPERTY. An order authorizing the use, sale, or lease of property other than cash collateral is stayed until the expiration of 14 days after entry of the order, unless the court orders otherwise.

(As amended Mar. 30, 1987, eff. Aug. 1, 1987; Apr. 30, 1991, eff. Aug. 1, 1991; Apr. 26, 1999, eff. Dec. 1, 1999; Apr. 23, 2008, eff. Dec. 1, 2008; Mar. 26, 2009, eff. Dec. 1, 2009.)

NOTES OF ADVISORY COMMITTEE ON RULES—1983

Subdivisions (a) and (b). Pursuant to §363(b) of the Code, a trustee or debtor in possession may use, sell, or lease property other than in the ordinary course of business only after notice and hearing. Rule 2002(a), (c) and (i) specifies the time when notice of sale is to be given, the contents of the notice and the persons to whom notice is to be given of sales of property. Subdivision (a) makes those provisions applicable as well to notices for proposed use and lease of property.

The Code does not provide the time within which parties may file objections to a proposed sale. Subdivision (b) of the rule requires the objection to be in writing and filed not less than five days before the proposed action is to take place. The objection should also be served within that time on the person who is proposing to take the action which would be either the trustee or debtor in possession. This time period is subject to change by the court. In some instances there is a need to conduct a sale in a short period of time and the court is given discretion to tailor the requirements to the circumstances.

Subdivision (c). In some situations a notice of sale for different pieces of property to all persons specified in Rule 2002(a) may be uneconomic and inefficient. This is particularly true in some chapter 7 liquidation cases when there is property of relatively little value which must be sold by the trustee. Subdivision (c) allows a general notice of intent to sell when the aggregate value of the estate's property is less than $2,500. The gross value is the value of the property without regard to the amount of any debt secured by a lien on the property. It is not necessary to give a detailed notice specifying the time and place of a particular sale. Thus, the requirements of Rule 2002(c) need not be met. If this method of providing notice of sales is used, the subdivision specifies that parties in interest may serve and file objections to the proposed sale of any property within the class and the time for service and filing is fixed at not later than 15 days after mailing the notice. The court may fix a different time. Subdivision (c) would have little utility in chapter 11 cases. Pursuant to Rule 2002(i), the court can limit notices of sale to the creditors' committee appointed under §1102 of the Code and the same burdens present in a small chapter 7 case would not exist.

Subdivision (d). If a timely objection is filed, a hearing is required with respect to the use, sale, or lease of property. Subdivision (d) renders the filing of an objection tantamount to requesting a hearing so as to require a hearing pursuant to §§363(b) and 102(1)(B)(i).

Subdivision (e) is derived in part from former Bankruptcy Rule 606(b) but does not carry forward the requirement of that rule that court approval be obtained for sales of property. Pursuant to §363(b) court approval is not required unless timely objection is made to the proposed sale. The itemized statement or information required by the subdivision is not necessary when it would be impracticable to prepare it or set forth the information. For example, a liquidation sale of retail goods although not in the ordinary course of business may be on a daily ongoing basis and only summaries may be available.

The duty imposed by paragraph (2) does not affect the power of the bankruptcy court to order third persons to execute instruments transferring property purchased at a sale under this subdivision. See, *e.g., In re Rosenberg*, 138 F.2d 409 (7th Cir. 1943).

NOTES OF ADVISORY COMMITTEE ON RULES—1987 AMENDMENT

Subdivision (a) is amended to conform to the 1984 amendments to §363(b)(2) of the Code.

Subdivision (b) is amended to provide that an objection to a proposed use, sale, or lease of property creates a contested matter governed by Rule 9014. A similar amendment is made to subdivision (d), which was formerly subdivision (c).

Subdivision (c) is new. Section 363(f) provides that sales free and clear of liens or other interests are only permitted if one of the five statutory requirements is satisfied. Rule 9013 requires that a motion state with particularity the grounds relied upon by the movant. A motion for approval of a sale free and clear of liens or other interests is subject to Rule 9014, service must be made on the parties holding liens or other interests in the property, and notice of the hearing on the motion and the time for filing objections must be included in the notice given under subdivision (a).

NOTES OF ADVISORY COMMITTEE ON RULES—1991 AMENDMENT

This rule is amended to provide notice to the United States trustee of a proposed use, sale or lease of property not in the ordinary course of business. See Rule 2002(k). Subdivision (f)(1) is amended to enable the United States trustee to monitor the progress of the case in accordance with 28 U.S.C. §586(a)(3)(G).

The words "with the clerk" in subdivision (f)(1) are deleted as unnecessary. See Rules 5005(a) and 9001(3).

COMMITTEE NOTES ON RULES—1999 AMENDMENT

Subdivision (g) is added to provide sufficient time for a party to request a stay pending appeal of an order authorizing the use, sale, or lease of property under §363(b) of the Code before the order is implemented. It does not affect the time for filing a notice of appeal in accordance with Rule 8002.

Rule 6004(g) does not apply to orders regarding the use of cash collateral and does not affect the trustee's right to use, sell, or lease property without a court order to the extent permitted under §363 of the Code.

The court may, in its discretion, order that Rule 6004(g) is not applicable so that the property may be used, sold, or leased immediately in accordance with the order entered by the court. Alternatively, the court may order that the stay under Rule 6004(g) is for a fixed period less than 10 days.

GAP Report on Rule 6004. No changes since publication.

COMMITTEE NOTES ON RULES—2008 AMENDMENT

The rule is amended by inserting a new subdivision (g) to implement §§332 and 363(b)(1)(B) of the Code, added by the 2005 amendments. This rule governs the proposed transfer of personally identifiable information in a manner inconsistent with any policy covering the transfer of the information. Rule 2002(c)(1) requires the seller to state in the notice of the sale or lease whether the transfer is consistent with and policy governing the transfer of the information.

Under §332 of the Code, the consumer privacy ombudsman must be appointed at least five days prior to the hearing on a sale or lease of personally identifiable information. In an appropriate case, the consumer privacy ombudsman may seek a continuance of the hearing on the proposed sale to perform the tasks required of the ombudsman by §332 of the Code.

Former subdivision (g) is redesignated as subdivision (h).

Changes Made After Publication. The Committee Note was amended to highlight the connection between this rule and Rule 2002 with regard to the obligation to provide notice of proposed transactions. It was also amended to recognize the ability of the consumer privacy ombudsman to seek a continuance of a hearing on the proposed sale of personally identifiable information.

COMMITTEE NOTES ON RULES—2009 AMENDMENT

The rule is amended to implement changes in connection with the amendment to Rule 9006(a) and the manner by which time is computed under the rules. The deadlines in the rule are amended to substitute a deadline that is a multiple of seven days. Throughout the rules, deadlines are amended in the following manner:

- 5-day periods become 7-day periods
- 10-day periods become 14-day periods
- 15-day periods become 14-day periods
- 20-day periods become 21-day periods
- 25-day periods become 28-day periods

Rule 6005. Appraisers and Auctioneers

The order of the court approving the employment of an appraiser or auctioneer shall fix the amount or rate of compensation. No officer or employee of the Judicial Branch of the United States or the United States Department of Justice shall be eligible to act as appraiser or auctioneer. No residence or licensing requirement shall disqualify an appraiser or auctioneer from employment.

(As amended Apr. 30, 1991, eff. Aug. 1, 1991.)

NOTES OF ADVISORY COMMITTEE ON RULES—1983

This rule is derived from former Bankruptcy Rule 606(c) and implements §327 of the Code. Pursuant to §327, the trustee or debtor in possession may employ one or more appraisers or auctioneers, subject to court approval. This rule requires the court order approving such employment to fix the amount or rate of compensation. The second sentence of the former rule is retained to continue to safeguard against imputations of favoritism which detract from public confidence in bankruptcy administration. The final sentence is to guard against imposition of parochial requirements not warranted by any consideration having to do with sound bankruptcy administration.

Reference should also be made to Rule 2013(a) regarding the limitation on employment of appraisers and auctioneers, and Rule 2014(a) regarding the application for appointment of an appraiser or auctioneer.

Rule 6006. Assumption, Rejection or Assignment of an Executory Contract or Unexpired Lease

(a) PROCEEDING TO ASSUME, REJECT, OR ASSIGN. A proceeding to assume, reject, or assign an executory contract or unexpired lease, other than as part of a plan, is governed by Rule 9014.

(b) PROCEEDING TO REQUIRE TRUSTEE TO ACT. A proceeding by a party to an executory contract or unexpired lease in a chapter 9 municipality case, chapter 11 reorganization case, chapter 12 family farmer's debt adjustment case, or chapter 13 individual's debt adjustment case, to require the trustee, debtor in possession, or debtor to determine whether to assume or reject the contract or lease is governed by Rule 9014.

(c) NOTICE. Notice of a motion made pursuant to subdivision (a) or (b) of this rule shall be given to the other party to the contract or lease, to other parties in interest as the court may direct, and, except in a chapter 9 municipality case, to the United States trustee.

(d) STAY OF ORDER AUTHORIZING ASSIGNMENT. An order authorizing the trustee to assign an executory contract or unexpired lease under § 365(f) is stayed until the expiration of 14 days after the entry of the order, unless the court orders otherwise.

(e) LIMITATIONS. The trustee shall not seek authority to assume or assign multiple executory contracts or unexpired leases in one motion unless: (1) all executory contracts or unexpired leases to be assumed or assigned are between the same parties or are to be assigned to the same assignee; (2) the trustee seeks to assume, but not assign to more than one assignee, unexpired leases of real property; or (3) the court otherwise authorizes the motion to be filed. Subject to subdivision (f), the trustee may join requests for authority to reject multiple executory contracts or unexpired leases in one motion.

(f) OMNIBUS MOTIONS. A motion to reject or, if permitted under subdivision (e), a motion to assume or assign multiple executory contracts or unexpired leases that are not between the same parties shall:

(1) state in a conspicuous place that parties receiving the omnibus motion should locate their names and their contracts or leases listed in the motion;

(2) list parties alphabetically and identify the corresponding contract or lease;

(3) specify the terms, including the curing of defaults, for each requested assumption or assignment;

(4) specify the terms, including the identity of each assignee and the adequate assurance of future performance by each assignee, for each requested assignment;

(5) be numbered consecutively with other omnibus motions to assume, assign, or reject executory contracts or unexpired leases; and

(6) be limited to no more than 100 executory contracts or unexpired leases.

(g) FINALITY OF DETERMINATION. The finality of any order respecting an executory contract or unexpired lease included in an omnibus motion shall be determined as though such contract or lease had been the subject of a separate motion.

(As amended Mar. 30, 1987, eff. Aug. 1, 1987; Apr. 30, 1991, eff. Aug. 1, 1991; Apr. 22, 1993, eff. Aug. 1, 1993; Apr. 26, 1999, eff. Dec. 1, 1999; Apr. 30 2007; eff. Dec. 1, 2007; Mar. 26, 2009, eff. Dec. 1, 2009.)

NOTES OF ADVISORY COMMITTEE ON RULES—1983

Section 365(a) of the Code requires court approval for the assumption or rejection of an executory contract by the trustee or debtor in possession. The trustee or debtor in possession may also assign an executory contract, § 365(f)(1), but must first assume the contract, § 365(f)(2). Rule 6006 provides a procedure for obtaining court approval. It does not apply to the automatic rejection of contracts which are not assumed in chapter 7 liquidation cases within 60 days after the order for relief, or to the assumption or rejection of contracts in a plan pursuant to § 1123(b)(2) or § 1322(b)(7).

Subdivision (a) by referring to Rule 9014 requires a motion to be brought for the assumption, rejection, or assignment of an executory contract. Normally, the motion will be brought by the trustee, debtor in possession or debtor in a chapter 9 or chapter 13 case. The authorization to assume a contract and to assign it may be sought in a single motion and determined by a single order.

Subdivision (b) makes applicable the same motion procedure when the other party to the contract seeks to require the chapter officer to take some action. Section 365(d)(2) recognizes that this procedure is available to these contractual parties. This provision of the Code and subdivision of the rule apply only in chapter 9, 11 and 13 cases. A motion is not necessary in chapter 7 cases because in those cases a contract is deemed rejected if the trustee does not timely assume it.

Subdivision (c) provides for the court to set a hearing on a motion made under subdivision (a) or (b). The other party to the contract should be given appropriate notice of the hearing and the court may order that other parties in interest, such as a creditors' committee, also be given notice.

NOTES OF ADVISORY COMMITTEE ON RULES—1987 AMENDMENT

Subdivisions (a) and (b) are amended to conform to the 1984 amendment to § 365 of the Code, which governs assumption or rejection of time share interests.

Section 1113, governing collective bargaining agreements, was added to the Code in 1984. It sets out requirements that must be met before a collective bargaining agreement may be rejected. The application to reject a collective bargaining agreement referred to in § 1113 shall be made by motion. The motion to reject creates a contested matter under Rule 9014, and service is made pursuant to Rule 7004 on the representative of the employees. The time periods set forth in § 1113(d) govern the scheduling of the hearing and disposition of a motion to reject the agreement.

NOTES OF ADVISORY COMMITTEE ON RULES—1991 AMENDMENT

References to time share interests are deleted as unnecessary. Time share interests are within the scope of this rule to the extent that they are governed by § 365 of the Code.

Subdivision (b) is amended to include chapter 12 cases.

Subdivision (c) is amended to enable the United States trustee to appear and be heard on the issues relating to the assumption or rejection of executory contracts and unexpired leases. See §§ 307, 365, and 1113 of the Code.

NOTES OF ADVISORY COMMITTEE ON RULES—1993 AMENDMENT

This rule is amended to delete the requirement for an actual hearing when no request for a hearing is made. See Rule 9014.

COMMITTEE NOTES ON RULES—1999 AMENDMENT

Subdivision (d) is added to provide sufficient time for a party to request a stay pending appeal of an order authorizing the assignment of an executory contract or unexpired lease under § 365(f) of the Code before the assignment is consummated. The stay under subdivision (d) does not affect the time for filing a notice of appeal in accordance with Rule 8002.

The court may, in its discretion, order that Rule 6006(d) is not applicable so that the executory contract or unexpired lease may be assigned immediately in accordance with the order entered by the court. Alternatively, the court may order that the stay under Rule 6006(d) is for a fixed period less than 10 days.

GAP Report on Rule 6006. No changes since publication.

COMMITTEE NOTES ON RULES—2007 AMENDMENT

The rule is amended to authorize the use of omnibus motions to reject multiple executory contracts and unexpired leases. In some cases there may be numerous executory contracts and unexpired leases, and this rule permits the combining of up to one hundred of these contracts and leases in a single motion to initiate the contested matter.

The rule also is amended to authorize the use of a single motion to assume or assign executory contracts and unexpired leases (i) when such contracts and leases are with a single nondebtor party, (ii) when such contracts and leases are being assigned to the same assignee, (iii) when the trustee proposes to assume, but not assign to more than one assignee, real property leases, or (iv) the court authorizes the filing of a joint motion to assume or to assume and assign executory contracts and unexpired leases under other circumstances that are not specifically recognized in the rule.

An omnibus motion to assume, assign, or reject multiple executory contracts and unexpired leases must comply with the procedural requirements set forth in subdivision (f) of the rule, unless the court orders otherwise. These requirements are intended to ensure that the nondebtor parties to the contracts and leases receive effective notice of the motion. Among those requirements is the requirement in subdivision (f)(5) that these motions be consecutively numbered (*e.g.*, Debtor in Possession's First Omnibus Motion for Authority to Assume Executory Contracts and Unexpired Leases, Debtor in Possession's Second Omnibus Motion for Authority to Assume Executory Contracts and Unexpired Leases, etc.). There may be a need for several of these motions in a particular case. Numbering the motions consecutively is essential to keep track of these motions on the court's docket and should avoid confusion that might otherwise result from similar or identically-titled motions.

Subdivision (g) of the rule provides that the finality of any order respecting an executory contract or unexpired lease included in an omnibus motion shall be determined as though such contract or lease had been the subject of a separate motion. A party seeking to appeal any such order is neither required, nor permitted, to await the court's resolution of all other contracts or leases included in the omnibus motion to obtain appellate review of the order. The rule permits the listing of multiple contracts or leases for convenience, and that convenience should not impede timely review of the court's decision with respect to each contract or lease.

Changes After Publication. Subdivision (e) of the proposed rule was amended as suggested by the NBC to insert a third category of requests that the trustee may make under an omnibus motion. The list of categories was numbered, and the new category is set out in (e)(2).

COMMITTEE NOTES ON RULES—2009 AMENDMENT

The rule is amended to implement changes in connection with the amendment to Rule 9006(a) and the manner by which time is computed under the rules. The deadline in the rule is amended to substitute a deadline that is a multiple of seven days. Throughout the rules, deadlines are amended in the following manner:

- 5-day periods become 7-day periods
- 10-day periods become 14-day periods
- 15-day periods become 14-day periods
- 20-day periods become 21-day periods
- 25-day periods become 28-day periods

Rule 6007. Abandonment or Disposition of Property

(a) NOTICE OF PROPOSED ABANDONMENT OR DISPOSITION; OBJECTIONS; HEARING. Unless otherwise directed by the court, the trustee or debtor in possession shall give notice of a proposed abandonment or disposition of property to the United States trustee, all creditors, indenture trustees, and committees elected pursuant to §705 or appointed pursuant to §1102 of the Code. A party in interest may file and serve an objection within 14 days of the mailing of the notice, or within the time fixed by the court. If a timely objection is made, the court shall set a hearing on notice to the United States trustee and to other entities as the court may direct.

(b) MOTION BY PARTY IN INTEREST. A party in interest may file and serve a motion requiring the trustee or debtor in possession to abandon property of the estate.

[(c) HEARING] (Abrogated Apr. 22, 1993, eff. Aug. 1, 1993)

(As amended Mar. 30, 1987, eff. Aug. 1, 1987; Apr. 30, 1991, eff. Aug. 1, 1991; Apr. 22, 1993, eff. Aug. 1, 1993; Mar. 26, 2009, eff. Dec. 1, 2009.)

NOTES OF ADVISORY COMMITTEE ON RULES—1983

Sections 554 and 725 of the Code permit and require abandonment and disposition of property of the estate. Pursuant to §554, the trustee may abandon property but only after notice and hearing. This section is applicable in chapter 7, 11 and 13 cases. Section 725 requires the trustee to dispose of property in which someone other than the estate has an interest, prior to final distribution. It applies only in chapter 7 cases. Notice and hearing are also required conditions. Section 102(1) provides that "notice and hearing" is construed to mean appropriate notice and an opportunity for a hearing. Neither §554 nor §725 specify to whom the notices are to be sent. This rule does not apply to §554(c). Pursuant to that subsection, property is deemed abandoned if it is not administered. A hearing is not required by the statute.

Subdivision (a) requires the notices to be sent to all creditors, indenture trustees, and committees elected under §705 or appointed under §1102 of the Code. This may appear burdensome, expensive and inefficient but the subdivision is in keeping with the Code's requirement for notice and the Code's intent to remove the bankruptcy judge from undisputed matters. The burden, expense and inefficiency can be alleviated in large measure by incorporating the notice into or together with the notice of the meeting of creditors so that separate notices would not be required.

Subdivision (b) implements §554(b) which specifies that a party in interest may request an order that the trustee abandon property. The rule specifies that the request be by motion and, pursuant to the Code, lists the parties who should receive notice.

Subdivision (c) requires a hearing when an objection under subdivision (a) is filed or a motion under subdivision (b) is made. Filing of an objection is sufficient to require a hearing; a separate or joined request for a hearing is unnecessary since the objection itself is tantamount to such a request.

NOTES OF ADVISORY COMMITTEE ON RULES—1991 AMENDMENT

This rule is amended to conform to the 1986 amendments to 28 U.S.C. §586(a) and to the Code. The United States trustee monitors the progress of the case and has standing to raise, appear and be heard on the issues relating to the abandonment or other disposition of property. See §§307 and 554 of the Code. Committees of retired employees appointed under §1114 are not entitled to notice under subdivision (a) of this rule.

NOTES OF ADVISORY COMMITTEE ON RULES—1993 AMENDMENT

This rule is amended to clarify that when a motion is made pursuant to subdivision (b), a hearing is not required if a hearing is not requested or if there is no opposition to the motion. See Rule 9014. Other amendments are stylistic and make no substantive change.

COMMITTEE NOTES ON RULES—2009 AMENDMENT

The rule is amended to implement changes in connection with the amendment to Rule 9006(a) and the manner by which time is computed under the rules. The deadline in the rule is amended to substitute a deadline that is a multiple of seven days. Throughout the rules, deadlines are amended in the following manner:

- 5-day periods become 7-day periods
- 10-day periods become 14-day periods
- 15-day periods become 14-day periods
- 20-day periods become 21-day periods
- 25-day periods become 28-day periods

Rule 6008. Redemption of Property from Lien or Sale

On motion by the debtor, trustee, or debtor in possession and after hearing on notice as the court may direct, the court may authorize the redemption of property from a lien or from a sale to enforce a lien in accordance with applicable law.

NOTES OF ADVISORY COMMITTEE ON RULES—1983

This rule is derived from former Bankruptcy Rule 609. No provision in the Code addresses the trustee's right of redemption. Ordinarily the secured creditor should be given notice of the trustee's motion so that any objection may be raised to the proposed redemption.

The rule applies also to a debtor exercising a right of redemption pursuant to §722. A proceeding under that section is governed by Rule 9014.

Rule 6009. Prosecution and Defense of Proceedings by Trustee or Debtor in Possession

With or without court approval, the trustee or debtor in possession may prosecute or may enter an appearance and defend any pending action or proceeding by or against the debtor, or commence and prosecute any action or proceeding in behalf of the estate before any tribunal.

NOTES OF ADVISORY COMMITTEE ON RULES—1983

This rule is derived from former Bankruptcy Rule 610.

Rule 6010. Proceeding to Avoid Indemnifying Lien or Transfer to Surety

If a lien voidable under §547 of the Code has been dissolved by the furnishing of a bond or other obligation and the surety thereon has been indemnified by the transfer of, or the creation of a lien upon, nonexempt property of the debtor, the surety shall be joined as a defendant in any proceeding to avoid the indemnifying transfer or lien. Such proceeding is governed by the rules in Part VII.

(As amended Apr. 30, 1991, eff. Aug. 1, 1991.)

NOTES OF ADVISORY COMMITTEE ON RULES—1983

This rule is derived from former Bankruptcy Rule 612.

NOTES OF ADVISORY COMMITTEE ON RULES—1991 AMENDMENT

This rule is amended to conform to §550(a) of the Code which provides that the trustee may recover the property transferred in a voidable transfer. The value of the property may be recovered in lieu of the property itself only if the court so orders.

Rule 6011. Disposal of Patient Records in Health Care Business Case

(a) NOTICE BY PUBLICATION UNDER §351(1)(A). A notice regarding the claiming or disposing of patient records under §351(1)(A) shall not identify any patient by name or other identifying information, but shall:

(1) identify with particularity the health care facility whose patient records the trustee proposes to destroy;

(2) state the name, address, telephone number, email address, and website, if any, of a person from whom information about the patient records may be obtained;

(3) state how to claim the patient records; and

(4) state the date by which patient records must be claimed, and that if they are not so claimed the records will be destroyed.

(b) NOTICE BY MAIL UNDER §351(1)(B). Subject to applicable nonbankruptcy law relating to patient privacy, a notice regarding the claiming or disposing of patient records under §351(1)(B) shall, in addition to including the information in subdivision (a), direct that a patient's family member or other representative who receives the notice inform the patient of the notice. Any notice under this subdivision shall be mailed to the patient and any family member or other contact person whose name and address have been given to the trustee or the debtor for the purpose of providing information regarding the patient's health care, to the Attorney General of the State where the health care facility is located, and to any insurance company known to have provided health care insurance to the patient.

(c) PROOF OF COMPLIANCE WITH NOTICE REQUIREMENT. Unless the court orders the trustee to file proof of compliance with §351(1)(B) under seal, the trustee shall not file, but shall maintain, the proof of compliance for a reasonable time.

(d) REPORT OF DESTRUCTION OF RECORDS. The trustee shall file, no later than 30 days after the destruction of patient records under §351(3), a report certifying that the unclaimed records have been destroyed and explaining the method used to effect the destruction. The report shall not identify any patient by name or other identifying information.

(Added Apr. 23, 2008, eff. Dec. 1, 2008.)

COMMITTEE NOTES ON RULES—2008

This rule is new. It implements §351(1), which was added to the Code by the 2005 amendments. That provision requires the trustee to notify patients that their patient records will be destroyed if they remain unclaimed for one year after the publication of a notice in an appropriate newspaper. The Code provision also requires that individualized notice be sent to each patient and to the patient's family member or other contact person.

The variety of health care businesses and the range of current and former patients present the need for flexibility in the creation and publication of the notices that will be given. Nevertheless, there are some matters that must be included in any notice being given to patients, their family members, and contact persons to ensure that sufficient information is provided to these persons regarding the trustee's intent to dispose of patient records. Subdivision (a) of this rule lists the minimum requirements for notices given under §351(1)(A), and subdivision (b) governs the form of notices under §351(1)(B). Notices given under this rule are subject to provisions under applicable federal and state law that relate to the protection of patients' privacy, such as the Health Insurance Portability and Accountability Act of 1996, Pub. L. No. 104-191 (HIPAA).

Subdivision (c) directs the trustee to maintain proof of compliance with §351(1)(B), but because the proof of compliance may contain patient names that should or must remain confidential, it prohibits filing the proof of compliance unless the court orders the trustee to file it under seal.

Subdivision (d) requires the trustee to file a report with the court regarding the destruction of patient records. This certification is intended to ensure that the trustee properly completed the destruction process. However, because the report will be filed with the court and ordinarily will be available to the public under §107, the names, addresses, and other identifying information of patients are not to be included in the report to protect patient privacy.

Changes Made After Publication. Subdivision (b)(2) was amended to add the Attorney General of the State where a health care facility is located to the list of entities entitled to notice of the disposal of patient records.

PART VII—ADVERSARY PROCEEDINGS

Rule 7001. Scope of Rules of Part VII

An adversary proceeding is governed by the rules of this Part VII. The following are adversary proceedings:

(1) a proceeding to recover money or property, other than a proceeding to compel the debtor to deliver property to the trustee, or a proceeding under §554(b) or §725 of the Code, Rule 2017, or Rule 6002;

(2) a proceeding to determine the validity, priority, or extent of a lien or other interest in property, other than a proceeding under Rule 4003(d);

(3) a proceeding to obtain approval under §363(h) for the sale of both the interest of the estate and of a co-owner in property;

(4) a proceeding to object to or revoke a discharge;

(5) a proceeding to revoke an order of confirmation of a chapter 11, chapter 12, or chapter 13 plan;

(6) a proceeding to determine the dischargeability of a debt;

(7) a proceeding to obtain an injunction or other equitable relief, except when a chapter 9, chapter 11, chapter 12, or chapter 13 plan provides for the relief;

(8) a proceeding to subordinate any allowed claim or interest, except when a chapter 9, chapter 11, chapter 12, or chapter 13 plan provides for subordination;

(9) a proceeding to obtain a declaratory judgment relating to any of the foregoing; or

(10) a proceeding to determine a claim or cause of action removed under 28 U.S.C. §1452.

(As amended Mar. 30, 1987, eff. Aug. 1, 1987; Apr. 30, 1991, eff. Aug. 1, 1991; Apr. 26, 1999, eff. Dec. 1, 1999.)

NOTES OF ADVISORY COMMITTEE ON RULES—1983

The rules in Part VII govern the procedural aspects of litigation involving the matters referred to in this Rule 7001. Under Rule 9014 some of the Part VII rules also apply to contested matters.

These Part VII rules are based on the premise that to the extent possible practice before the bankruptcy courts and the district courts should be the same. These rules either incorporate or are adaptations of most of the Federal Rules of Civil Procedure. Although the Part VII rules of the former Bankruptcy Rules also relied heavily on the F.R.Civ.P., the former Part VII rules departed from the civil practice in two significant ways: a trial or pretrial conference had to be scheduled as soon as the adversary proceeding was filed and pleadings had to be filed within periods shorter than those established by the F.R.Civ.P. These departures from the civil practice have been eliminated.

The content and numbering of these Part VII rules correlates to the content and numbering of the F.R.Civ.P. Most, but not all, of the F.R.Civ.P. have a comparable Part VII rule. When there is no Part VII rule with a number corresponding to a particular F.R.Civ.P., Parts V and IX of these rules must be consulted to determine if one of the rules in those parts deals with the subject. The list below indicates the F.R.Civ.P., or subdivision thereof, covered by a rule in either Part V or Part IX.

F.R.Civ.P.	Rule in Part V or IX
6	9006
7(b)	9013
10(a)	9004(b)
11	9011
38,39	9015(a)-(e)
47-51	9015(f)
43,44,44.1	9017
45	9016
58	9021
59	9023
60	9024
61	9005
63	9028
77(a),(b),(c)	5001
77(d)	9022(d)
79(a)-(d)	5003
81(c)	9027
83	9029
92	9030

Proceedings to which the rules in Part VII apply directly include those brought to avoid transfers by the debtor under §§544, 545, 547, 548 and 549 of the Code; subject to important exceptions, proceedings to recover money or property; proceedings on bonds under Rules 5008(d) and 9025; proceedings under Rule 4004 to determine whether a discharge in a chapter 7 or 11 case should be denied because of an objection grounded on §727 and proceedings in a chapter 7 or 13 case to revoke a discharge as provided in §§727(d) or 1328(e); and proceedings initiated pursuant to §523(c) of the Code to determine the dischargeability of a particular debt. Those proceedings were classified as adversary proceedings under former Bankruptcy Rule 701.

Also included as adversary proceedings are proceedings to revoke an order of confirmation of a plan in a chapter 11 or 13 case as provided in §§1144 and 1330, to subordinate under §510(c), other than as part of a plan, an allowed claim or interest, and to sell under §363(h) both the interest of the estate and a co-owner in property.

Declaratory judgments with respect to the subject matter of the various adversary proceedings are also adversary proceedings.

Any claim or cause of action removed to a bankruptcy court pursuant to 28 U.S.C. §1478 is also an adversary proceeding.

Unlike former Bankruptcy Rule 701, requests for relief from an automatic stay do not commence an adversary proceeding. Section 362(e) of the Code and Rule 4001 establish an expedited schedule for judicial disposition of requests for relief from the automatic stay. The formalities of the adversary proceeding process and the time for serving pleadings are not well suited to the expedited schedule. The motion practice prescribed in Rule 4001 is best suited to such requests because the court has the flexibility to fix hearing dates and other deadlines appropriate to the particular situation.

Clause (1) contains important exceptions. A person with an interest in property in the possession of the trustee or debtor in possession may seek to recover or reclaim that property under §554(b) or §725 of the Code. Since many attempts to recover or reclaim property under these two sections do not generate disputes, application of the formalities of the Part VII Rules is not appropriate. Also excluded from adversary proceedings is litigation arising from an examination under Rule 2017 of a debtor's payments of money or transfers of property to an attorney representing the debtor in a case under the Code or an examination of a superseded administration under Rule 6002.

Exemptions and objections thereto are governed by Rule 4003. Filing of proofs of claim and the allowances thereof are governed by Rules 3001–3005, and objections to claims are governed by Rule 3007. When an objection to a claim is joined with a demand for relief of the kind specified in this Rule 7001, the matter becomes an adversary proceeding. See Rule 3007.

NOTES OF ADVISORY COMMITTEE ON RULES—1987 AMENDMENT

Another exception is added to clause (1). A trustee may proceed by motion to recover property from the debtor.

NOTES OF ADVISORY COMMITTEE ON RULES—1991 AMENDMENT

Clauses (5) and (8) are amended to include chapter 12 plans.

COMMITTEE NOTES ON RULES—1999 AMENDMENT

This rule is amended to recognize that an adversary proceeding is not necessary to obtain injunctive or other equitable relief that is provided for in a plan under circumstances in which substantive law permits the relief. Other amendments are stylistic.

GAP Report on Rule 7001. No changes since publication, except for stylistic changes.

Rule 7002. References to Federal Rules of Civil Procedure

Whenever a Federal Rule of Civil Procedure applicable to adversary proceedings makes reference to another Federal Rule of Civil Procedure, the reference shall be read as a reference to the Federal Rule of Civil Procedure as modified in this Part VII.

NOTES OF ADVISORY COMMITTEE ON RULES—1983

Rules 5, 12, 13, 14, 25, 27, 30, 41 and 52 F.R.Civ.P. are made applicable to adversary proceedings by Part VII. Each of those rules contains a cross reference to another Federal Rule; however, the Part VII rule which incorporates the cross-referenced Federal Rule modifies the Federal Rule in some way. Under this Rule 7002 the cross reference is to the Federal Rule as modified by Part VII. For example, Rule 5 F.R.Civ.P., which is made applicable to adversary proceedings by Rule 7005, contains a reference to Rule 4 F.R.Civ.P. Under this Rule 7002, the cross reference is to Rule 4 F.R.Civ.P. as modified by Rule 7004.

Rules 7, 10, 12, 13, 14, 19, 22, 23.2, 24–37, 41, 45, 49, 50, 52, 55, 59, 60, 62 F.R.Civ.P. are made applicable to adversary proceedings by Part VII or generally to cases under the Code by Part IX. Each of those Federal Rules contains a cross reference to another Federal Rule which is not modified by the Part VII or Part IX rule which makes the cross-referenced Federal Rule applicable. Since the cross-referenced rule is not modified by a Part VII rule this Rule 7002 does not apply.

REFERENCES IN TEXT

The Federal Rules of Civil Procedure, referred to in text, are set out in the Appendix to Title 28, Judiciary and Judicial Procedure.

Rule 7003. Commencement of Adversary Proceeding

Rule 3 F.R.Civ.P. applies in adversary proceedings.

NOTES OF ADVISORY COMMITTEE ON RULES—1983

Rule 5005(a) requires that a complaint commencing an adversary proceeding be filed with the court in which the case under the Code is pending unless 28 U.S.C. §1473 authorizes the filing of the complaint in another district.

REFERENCES IN TEXT

The Federal Rules of Civil Procedure, referred to in text, are set out in the Appendix to Title 28, Judiciary and Judicial Procedure.

Rule 7004. Process; Service of Summons, Complaint

(a) SUMMONS; SERVICE; PROOF OF SERVICE.

(1) Except as provided in Rule 7004(a)(2), Rule 4(a), (b), (c)(1), (d)(1), (e)–(j), (*l*), and (m) F.R.Civ.P. applies in adversary proceedings. Personal service under Rule 4(e)–(j) F.R.Civ.P. may be made by any person at least 18 years of age who is not a party, and the summons may be delivered by the clerk to any such person.

(2) The clerk may sign, seal, and issue a summons electronically by putting an "s/" before the clerk's name and including the court's seal on the summons.

(b) SERVICE BY FIRST CLASS MAIL. Except as provided in subdivision (h), in addition to the methods of service authorized by Rule 4(e)–(j) F.R.Civ.P., service may be made within the United States by first class mail postage prepaid as follows:

(1) Upon an individual other than an infant or incompetent, by mailing a copy of the summons and complaint to the individual's dwelling house or usual place of abode or to the place where the individual regularly conducts a business or profession.

(2) Upon an infant or an incompetent person, by mailing a copy of the summons and complaint to the person upon whom process is prescribed to be served by the law of the state in which service is made when an action is brought against such a defendant in the courts of general jurisdiction of that state. The summons and complaint in that case shall be addressed to the person required to be served at that person's dwelling house or usual place of abode or at the place where the person regularly conducts a business or profession.

(3) Upon a domestic or foreign corporation or upon a partnership or other unincorporated association, by mailing a copy of the summons and complaint to the attention of an officer, a managing or general agent, or to any other agent authorized by appointment or by law to receive service of process and, if the agent is one authorized by statute to receive service and the statute so requires, by also mailing a copy to the defendant.

(4) Upon the United States, by mailing a copy of the summons and complaint addressed to the civil process clerk at the office of the United States attorney for the district in which the action is brought and by mailing a

copy of the summons and complaint to the Attorney General of the United States at Washington, District of Columbia, and in any action attacking the validity of an order of an officer or an agency of the United States not made a party, by also mailing a copy of the summons and complaint to that officer or agency. The court shall allow a reasonable time for service pursuant to this subdivision for the purpose of curing the failure to mail a copy of the summons and complaint to multiple officers, agencies, or corporations of the United States if the plaintiff has mailed a copy of the summons and complaint either to the civil process clerk at the office of the United States attorney or to the Attorney General of the United States.

(5) Upon any officer or agency of the United States, by mailing a copy of the summons and complaint to the United States as prescribed in paragraph (4) of this subdivision and also to the officer or agency. If the agency is a corporation, the mailing shall be as prescribed in paragraph (3) of this subdivision of this rule. The court shall allow a reasonable time for service pursuant to this subdivision for the purpose of curing the failure to mail a copy of the summons and complaint to multiple officers, agencies, or corporations of the United States if the plaintiff has mailed a copy of the summons and complaint either to the civil process clerk at the office of the United States attorney or to the Attorney General of the United States. If the United States trustee is the trustee in the case and service is made upon the United States trustee solely as trustee, service may be made as prescribed in paragraph (10) of this subdivision of this rule.

(6) Upon a state or municipal corporation or other governmental organization thereof subject to suit, by mailing a copy of the summons and complaint to the person or office upon whom process is prescribed to be served by the law of the state in which service is made when an action is brought against such a defendant in the courts of general jurisdiction of that state, or in the absence of the designation of any such person or office by state law, then to the chief executive officer thereof.

(7) Upon a defendant of any class referred to in paragraph (1) or (3) of this subdivision of this rule, it is also sufficient if a copy of the summons and complaint is mailed to the entity upon whom service is prescribed to be served by any statute of the United States or by the law of the state in which service is made when an action is brought against such a defendant in the court of general jurisdiction of that state.

(8) Upon any defendant, it is also sufficient if a copy of the summons and complaint is mailed to an agent of such defendant authorized by appointment or by law to receive service of process, at the agent's dwelling house or usual place of abode or at the place where the agent regularly carries on a business or profession and, if the authorization so requires, by mailing also a copy of the summons and complaint to the defendant as provided in this subdivision.

(9) Upon the debtor, after a petition has been filed by or served upon the debtor and until the case is dismissed or closed, by mailing a copy of the summons and complaint to the debtor at the address shown in the petition or to such other address as the debtor may designate in a filed writing.

(10) Upon the United States trustee, when the United States trustee is the trustee in the case and service is made upon the United States trustee solely as trustee, by mailing a copy of the summons and complaint to an office of the United States trustee or another place designated by the United States trustee in the district where the case under the Code is pending.

(c) SERVICE BY PUBLICATION. If a party to an adversary proceeding to determine or protect rights in property in the custody of the court cannot be served as provided in Rule 4(e)–(j) F.R.Civ.P. or subdivision (b) of this rule, the court may order the summons and complaint to be served by mailing copies thereof by first class mail, postage prepaid, to the party's last known address, and by at least one publication in such manner and form as the court may direct.

(d) NATIONWIDE SERVICE OF PROCESS. The summons and complaint and all other process except a subpoena may be served anywhere in the United States.

(e) SUMMONS: TIME LIMIT FOR SERVICE WITHIN THE UNITED STATES. Service made under Rule 4(e), (g), (h)(1), (i), or (j)(2) F.R.Civ.P. shall be by delivery of the summons and complaint within 14 days after the summons is issued. If service is by any authorized form of mail, the summons and complaint shall be deposited in the mail within 14 days after the summons is issued. If a summons is not timely delivered or mailed, another summons shall be issued and served. This subdivision does not apply to service in a foreign country.

(f) PERSONAL JURISDICTION. If the exercise of jurisdiction is consistent with the Constitution and laws of the United States, serving a summons or filing a waiver of service in accordance with this rule or the subdivisions of Rule 4 F.R.Civ.P. made applicable by these rules is effective to establish personal jurisdiction over the person of any defendant with respect to a case under the Code or a civil proceeding arising under the Code, or arising in or related to a case under the Code.

(g) SERVICE ON DEBTOR'S ATTORNEY. If the debtor is represented by an attorney, whenever service is made upon the debtor under this Rule, service shall also be made upon the debtor's attorney by any means authorized under Rule 5(b) F.R.Civ.P.

(h) SERVICE OF PROCESS ON AN INSURED DEPOSITORY INSTITUTION. Service on an insured depository institution (as defined in section 3 of the Federal Deposit Insurance Act) in a contested matter or adversary proceeding shall be made by certified mail addressed to an officer of the institution unless—

(1) the institution has appeared by its attorney, in which case the attorney shall be served by first class mail;

(2) the court orders otherwise after service upon the institution by certified mail of notice of an application to permit service on the institution by first class mail sent to an offi-

cer of the institution designated by the institution; or

(3) the institution has waived in writing its entitlement to service by certified mail by designating an officer to receive service.

(As amended Mar. 30, 1987, eff. Aug. 1, 1987; Apr. 30, 1991, eff. Aug. 1, 1991; Pub. L. 103–394, title I, §114, Oct. 22, 1994, 108 Stat. 4118; Apr. 23, 1996, eff. Dec. 1, 1996; Apr. 26, 1999, eff. Dec. 1, 1999; Apr. 25, 2005, eff. Dec. 1, 2005; Apr. 12, 2006, eff. Dec. 1, 2006; Mar. 26, 2009, eff. Dec. 1, 2009.)

NOTES OF ADVISORY COMMITTEE ON RULES—1983

Subdivision (a) of the rule, by incorporation of Rule 4(a), (b), (d), (e) and (g)–(i) F.R.Civ.P., governs the mechanics of issuance of a summons and its form, the manner of service on parties and their representatives, and service in foreign countries.

Subdivision (b), which is the same as former Rule 704(c), authorizes service of process by first class mail postage prepaid. This rule retains the modes of service contained in former Bankruptcy Rule 704. The former practice, in effect since 1976, has proven satisfactory.

Subdivision (c) is derived from former Bankruptcy Rule 704(d)(2).

Subdivision (d). Nationwide service of process is authorized by subdivision (d).

Subdivision (e) authorizes service by delivery on individuals and corporations in foreign countries if the party to be served is the debtor or any person required to perform the duties of the debtor and certain other persons, the adversary proceeding involves property in the custody of the bankruptcy court, or if federal or state law authorizes such service in a foreign country.

Subdivision (f). The requirement of former Bankruptcy Rule 704 that the summons be served within 10 days is carried over into these rules by subdivision (f).

NOTES OF ADVISORY COMMITTEE ON RULES—1987 AMENDMENT

Subdivision (a) is amended to make Rule 4(j) F.R.Civ.P. applicable to service of the summons. If service is not completed within 120 days of the filing of the complaint, the complaint may be dismissed.

Technical amendments are made to subdivisions (a), (b), (e), and (f) to conform to recent amendments to Rule 4 F.R.Civ.P.

NOTES OF ADVISORY COMMITTEE ON RULES—1991 AMENDMENT

The United States trustee may serve as trustee in a case pursuant to 28 U.S.C. §586(a)(2) and §§701(a)(2), 1202(a), and 1302(a) of the Code. This rule is amended to avoid the necessity of mailing copies of a summons and complaint or other pleadings to the Attorney General and to the United States attorney when service on the United States trustee is required only because the United States trustee is acting as a case trustee. For example, a proceeding commenced by a creditor to dismiss a case for unreasonable delay under §707(a) is governed by Rule 9014 which requires service on the trustee pursuant to the requirements of Rule 7004 for the service of a summons and complaint. The Attorney General and the United States attorney would have no interest in receiving a copy of the motion to dismiss. Mailing to the office of the United States trustee when acting as the case trustee is sufficient in such cases.

The words "with the court" in subdivision (b)(9) are deleted as unnecessary. See Rules 5005(a) and 9001(3).

The new paragraph (10) of subdivision (b) does not affect requirements for service of process on the United States trustee when sued or otherwise a party to a litigation unrelated to its capacity as a trustee. If a proceeding is commenced against the United States trustee which is unrelated to the United States trustee's role as trustee, the requirements of paragraph (5) of subdivision (b) of this rule would apply.

Subdivision (g) is added in anticipation of substantial amendment to, and restructuring of subdivisions of, Rule 4 F.R.Civ.P. Any amendment to Rule 4 will not affect service in bankruptcy cases and proceedings until further amendment to the Bankruptcy Rules. On January 1, 1990, Rule 4 F.R.Civ.P. read as follows:

RULE 4 F.R.CIV.P.

PROCESS

(a) SUMMONS: ISSUANCE. Upon the filing of the complaint the clerk shall forthwith issue a summons and deliver the summons to the plaintiff or the plaintiff's attorney, who shall be responsible for prompt service of the summons and a copy of the complaint. Upon request of the plaintiff separate or additional summons shall issue against any defendants.

(b) SAME: FORM. The summons shall be signed by the clerk, be under the seal of the court, contain the name of the court and the names of the parties, be directed to the defendant, state the name and address of the plaintiff's attorney, if any, otherwise the plaintiff's address, and the time within which these rules require the defendant to appear and defend, and shall notify the defendant that in case of the defendant's failure to do so judgment by default will be rendered against the defendant for the relief demanded in the complaint. When, under Rule 4(e), service is made pursuant to a statute or rule of court of a state, the summons, or notice, or order in lieu of summons shall correspond as nearly as may be to that required by the statute or rule.

(c) SERVICE.

(1) [Not applicable.]

(2)(A) [Not applicable.]

(B) [Not applicable.]

(C) A summons and complaint may be served upon a defendant of any class referred to in paragraph (1) or (3) of subdivision (d) of this rule—

(i) pursuant to the law of the State in which the district court is held for the service of summons or other like process upon such defendant in an action brought in the courts of general jurisdiction of that State, or

(ii) [Not applicable.]

(D) [Not applicable.]

(E) [Not applicable.]

(3) [Not applicable.]

(d) SUMMONS AND COMPLAINT: PERSON TO BE SERVED. The summons and complaint shall be served together. The plaintiff shall furnish the person making service with such copies as are necessary. Service shall be made as follows:

(1) Upon an individual other than an infant or an incompetent person, by delivering a copy of the summons and of the complaint to the individual personally or by leaving copies thereof at the individual's dwelling house or usual place of abode with some person of suitable age and discretion then residing therein or by delivering a copy of the summons and of the complaint to an agent authorized by appointment or by law to receive service of process.

(2) Upon an infant or an incompetent person, by serving the summons and complaint in the manner prescribed by the law of the state in which the service is made for the service of summons or other like process upon any such defendant in an action brought in the courts of general jurisdiction of that state.

(3) Upon a domestic or foreign corporation or upon a partnership or other unincorporated association which is subject to suit under a common name, by delivering a copy of the summons and of the complaint to an officer, a managing or general agent, or to any other agent authorized by appointment or by law to receive service of process and, if the agent is one authorized by statute to receive service and the statute so requires, by also mailing a copy to the defendant.

(4) Upon the United States, by delivering a copy of the summons and of the complaint to the United States attorney for the district in which the action is

brought or to an assistant United States attorney or clerical employee designated by the United States attorney in a writing filed with the clerk of the court and by sending a copy of the summons and of the complaint by registered or certified mail to the Attorney General of the United States at Washington, District of Columbia, and in any action attacking the validity of an order of an officer or agency of the United States not made a party, by also sending a copy of the summons and of the complaint by registered or certified mail to such officer or agency.

(5) Upon an officer or agency of the United States, by serving the United States and by sending a copy of the summons and of the complaint by registered or certified mail to such officer or agency. If the agency is a corporation the copy shall be delivered as provided in paragraph (3) of this subdivision of this rule.

(6) Upon a state or municipal corporation or other governmental organization thereof subject to suit, by delivering a copy of the summons and of the complaint to the chief executive officer thereof or by serving the summons and complaint in the manner prescribed by the law of that state for the service of summons or other like process upon any such defendant.

(e) SUMMONS: SERVICE UPON PARTY NOT INHABITANT OF OR FOUND WITHIN STATE. Whenever a statute of the United States or an order of court thereunder provides for service of a summons, or of a notice, or of an order in lieu of summons upon a party not an inhabitant of or found within the state in which the district court is held, service may be made under the circumstances and in the manner prescribed by the statute or order, or, if there is no provision therein prescribing the manner of service, in a manner stated in this rule. Whenever a statute or rule of court of the state in which the district court is held provides (1) for service of a summons, or of a notice, or of an order in lieu of summons upon a party not an inhabitant of or found within the state, or (2) for service upon or notice to such a party to appear and respond or defend in an action by reason of the attachment or garnishment or similar seizure of the party's property located within the state, service may in either case be made under the circumstances and in the manner prescribed in the statute or rule.

(f) [Not applicable.]

(g) RETURN. The person serving the process shall make proof of service thereof to the court promptly and in any event within the time during which the person served must respond to the process. If service is made by a person other than a United States marshal or deputy United States marshal, such person shall make affidavit thereof. If service is made under subdivision (c)(2)(C)(ii) of this rule, return shall be made by the sender's filing with the court the acknowledgment received pursuant to such subdivision. Failure to make proof of service does not affect the validity of the service.

(h) AMENDMENT. At any time in its discretion and upon such terms as it deems just, the court may allow any process or proof of service thereof to be amended, unless it clearly appears that material prejudice would result to the substantial rights of the party against whom the process issued.

(i) ALTERNATIVE PROVISIONS FOR SERVICE IN A FOREIGN COUNTRY.

(1) *Manner.* When the federal or state law referred to in subdivision (e) of this rule authorizes service upon a party not an inhabitant of or found within the state in which the district court is held, and service is to be effected upon the party in a foreign country, it is also sufficient if service of the summons and complaint is made: (A) in the manner prescribed by the law of the foreign country for service in that country in an action in any of its courts of general jurisdiction; or (B) as directed by the foreign authority in response to a letter rogatory, when service in either case is reasonably calculated to give actual notice; or (C) upon an individual, by delivery to the individual personally, and upon a corporation or partnership or association, by delivery to an officer, a managing or general agent; or (D) by any form of mail, requiring a signed receipt, to be addressed and dispatched by the clerk of the court to the party to be served; or (E) as directed by order of the court. Service under (C) or (E) above may be made by any person who is not a party and is not less than 18 years of age or who is designated by order of the district court or by the foreign court. On request, the clerk shall deliver the summons to the plaintiff for transmission to the person or the foreign court or officer who will make the service.

(2) *Return.* Proof of service may be made as prescribed by subdivision (g) of this rule, or by the law of the foreign country, or by order of the court. When service is made pursuant to subparagraph (1)(D) of this subdivision, proof of service shall include a receipt signed by the addressee or other evidence of delivery to the addressee satisfactory to the court.

(j) SUMMONS: TIME LIMIT FOR SERVICE. If a service of the summons and complaint is not made upon a defendant within 120 days after the filing of the complaint and the party on whose behalf such service was required cannot show good cause why such service was not made within that period, the action shall be dismissed as to that defendant without prejudice upon the court's own initiative with notice to such party or upon motion. This subdivision shall not apply to service in a foreign country pursuant to subdivision (i) of this rule.

NOTES OF ADVISORY COMMITTEE ON RULES—1996 AMENDMENT

The purpose of these amendments is to conform the rule to the 1993 revisions of Rule 4 F.R.Civ.P. and to make stylistic improvements. Rule 7004, as amended, continues to provide for service by first class mail as an alternative to the methods of personal service provided in Rule 4 F.R.Civ.P., except as provided in the new subdivision (h).

Rule 4(d)(2) F.R.Civ.P. provides a procedure by which the plaintiff may request by first class mail that the defendant waive service of the summons. This procedure is not applicable in adversary proceedings because it is not necessary in view of the availability of service by mail pursuant to Rule 7004(b). However, if a written waiver of service of a summons is made in an adversary proceeding, Rule 4(d)(1) F.R.Civ.P. applies so that the defendant does not thereby waive any objection to the venue or the jurisdiction of the court over the person of the defendant.

Subdivisions (b)(4) and (b)(5) are amended to conform to the 1993 amendments to Rule 4(i)(3) F.R.Civ.P., which protect the plaintiff from the hazard of losing a substantive right because of failure to comply with the requirements of multiple service when the United States or an officer, agency, or corporation of the United States is a defendant. These subdivisions also are amended to require that the summons and complaint be addressed to the civil process clerk at the office of the United States attorney.

Subdivision (e), which has governed service in a foreign country, is abrogated and Rule 4(f) and (h)(2) F.R.Civ.P., as substantially revised in 1993, are made applicable in adversary proceedings.

The new subdivision (f) is consistent with the 1993 amendments to F.R.Civ.P. 4(k)(2). It clarifies that service or filing a waiver of service in accordance with this rule or the applicable subdivisions of F.R.Civ.P. 4 is sufficient to establish personal jurisdiction over the defendant. See the committee note to the 1993 amendments to Rule 4 F.R.Civ.P.

Subdivision (g) is abrogated. This subdivision was promulgated in 1991 so that anticipated revisions to Rule 4 F.R.Civ.P. would not affect service of process in adversary proceedings until further amendment to Rule 7004.

Subdivision (h) and the first phrase of subdivision (b) were added by § 114 of the Bankruptcy Reform Act of 1994, Pub. L. No. 103-394, 108 Stat. 4106.

GAP Report on Rule 7004. After publication of the proposed amendments, Rule 7004(b) was amended and Rule

7004(h) was added by the Bankruptcy Reform Act of 1994 to provide for service by certified mail on an insured depository institution. The above draft includes those statutory amendments (without underlining new language or striking former language). No other changes have been made since publication, except for stylistic changes.

COMMITTEE NOTES ON RULES—1999 AMENDMENT

Subdivision (e) is amended so that the ten-day time limit for service of a summons does not apply if the summons is served in a foreign country.

GAP Report on Rule 7004. No changes since publication.

COMMITTEE NOTES ON RULES—2005 AMENDMENT

This amendment specifically authorizes the clerk to issue a summons electronically. In some bankruptcy cases the trustee or debtor in possession may commence hundreds of adversary proceedings simultaneously, and permitting the electronic signing and sealing of the summonses for those proceedings increases the efficiency of the clerk's office without any negative impact on any party. The rule only authorizes electronic issuance of the summons. It does not address the service requirements for the summons. Those requirements are set out elsewhere in Rule 7004, and nothing in Rule 7004(a)(2) should be construed as authorizing electronic service of a summons.

Changes Made After Publication and Comment. No changes were made after publication.

COMMITTEE NOTES ON RULES—2006 AMENDMENT

Under current Rule 7004, an entity may serve a summons and complaint upon the debtor by personal service or by mail. If the entity chooses to serve the debtor by mail, it must also serve a copy of the summons and complaint on the debtor's attorney by mail. If the entity effects personal service on the debtor, there is no requirement that the debtor's attorney also be served.

Subdivision (b)(9). The rule is amended to delete the reference in subdivision (b)(9) to the debtor's address as set forth in the statement of financial affairs. In 1991, the Official Form of the statement of financial affairs was revised and no longer includes a question regarding the debtor's current residence. Since that time, Official Form 1, the petition, has required the debtor to list both the debtor's residence and mailing address. Therefore, the subdivision is amended to delete the statement of financial affairs as a document that might contain an address at which the debtor can be served.

Subdivision (g). The rule is amended to require service on the debtor's attorney whenever the debtor is served with a summons and complaint. The amendment makes this change by deleting that portion of Rule 7004(b)(9) that requires service on the debtor's attorney when the debtor is served by mail, and relocates the obligation to serve the debtor's attorney into new subdivision (g). Service on the debtor's attorney is not limited to mail service, but may be accomplished by any means permitted under Rule 5(b) F.R.Civ.P.

Changes Made After Publication. The Committee Note was amended to add the final [second] paragraph of the Note. The new paragraph describes the reason for the deletion of the reference in the rule to the statement of affairs as a source for the debtor's address. This was a secondary reason for amending the rule, and even in the absence of public comment on the proposed amendment, the Advisory Committee believes that the additional explanation in the Committee Note is appropriate.

COMMITTEE NOTES ON RULES—2009 AMENDMENT

The rule is amended to implement changes in connection with the amendment to Rule 9006(a) and the manner by which time is computed under the rules. The deadlines in the rule are amended to substitute a deadline that is a multiple of seven days. Throughout the rules, deadlines are amended in the following manner:

- 5-day periods become 7-day periods
- 10-day periods become 14-day periods
- 15-day periods become 14-day periods
- 20-day periods become 21-day periods
- 25-day periods become 28-day periods

REFERENCES IN TEXT

The Federal Rules of Civil Procedure, referred to in text, are set out in the Appendix to Title 28, Judiciary and Judicial Procedure.

Section 3 of the Federal Deposit Insurance Act, referred to in subd. (h), is classified to section 1813 of Title 12, Banks and Banking.

AMENDMENT BY PUBLIC LAW

1994—Subd. (b). Pub. L. 103–394, §114(1), substituted "Except as provided in subdivision (h), in addition" for "In addition".

Subd. (h). Pub. L. 103–394, §114(2), added subd. (h).

EFFECTIVE DATE OF 1994 AMENDMENT

Amendment by Pub. L. 103–394 effective Oct. 22, 1994, and not applicable with respect to cases commenced under this title before Oct. 22, 1994, see section 702 of Pub. L. 103–394, set out as a note under section 101 of this title.

Rule 7005. Service and Filing of Pleadings and Other Papers

Rule 5 F.R.Civ.P. applies in adversary proceedings.

NOTES OF ADVISORY COMMITTEE ON RULES—1983

Rule 5 F.R.Civ.P. refers to Rule 4 F.R.Civ.P. Pursuant to Rule 7002 this reference is to Rule 4 F.R.Civ.P. as incorporated and modified by Rule 7004.

REFERENCES IN TEXT

The Federal Rules of Civil Procedure, referred to in text, are set out in the Appendix to Title 28, Judiciary and Judicial Procedure.

Rule 7007. Pleadings Allowed

Rule 7 F.R.Civ.P. applies in adversary proceedings.

REFERENCES IN TEXT

The Federal Rules of Civil Procedure, referred to in text, are set out in the Appendix to Title 28, Judiciary and Judicial Procedure.

Rule 7007.1. Corporate Ownership Statement

(a) REQUIRED DISCLOSURE. Any corporation that is a party to an adversary proceeding, other than the debtor or a governmental unit, shall file two copies of a statement that identifies any corporation, other than a governmental unit, that directly or indirectly owns 10% or more of any class of the corporation's equity interests, or states that there are no entities to report under this subdivision.

(b) TIME FOR FILING. A party shall file the statement required under Rule 7007.1(a) with its first appearance, pleading, motion, response, or other request addressed to the court. A party shall file a supplemental statement promptly upon any change in circumstances that this rule requires the party to identify or disclose.

(Added Mar. 27, 2003, eff. Dec. 1, 2003; amended Apr. 30, 2007; eff. Dec. 1, 2007.)

COMMITTEE NOTES ON RULES—2003

This rule is derived from Rule 26.1 of the Federal Rules of Appellate Procedure. The information that parties shall supply will support properly informed disqualification decisions in situations that call for automatic disqualification under Canon 3C(1)(c) of the Code of Conduct for United States Judges. This rule does not cover all of the circumstances that may call for disqualification under the subjective financial interest standard of Canon 3C, and does not deal at all with other circumstances that may call for disqualification. Nevertheless, the required disclosures are calculated to reach the majority of circumstances that are likely to call for disqualification under Canon 3C(1)(c).

The rule directs nongovernmental corporate parties to list those corporations that hold significant ownership interests in them. This includes listing membership interests in limited liability companies and similar entities that fall under the definition of a corporation in Bankruptcy Code §101.

Under subdivision (b), parties must file the statement with the first document that they file in any adversary proceeding. The rule also requires parties and other persons to file supplemental statements promptly whenever changed circumstances require disclosure of new or additional information.

The rule does not prohibit the adoption of local rules requiring disclosures beyond those called for in Rule 7007.1.

Changes Made After Publication and Comments. No changes since publication.

COMMITTEE NOTES ON RULES—2007 AMENDMENT

The rule is amended to clarify that a party must file a corporate ownership statement with its initial paper filed with the court in an adversary proceeding. The party's initial filing may be a document that is not a "pleading" as defined in Rule 7 F. R. Civ. P., which is made applicable in adversary proceedings by Rule 7007. The amendment also brings Rule 7007.1 more closely in line with Rule 7.1 F. R. Civ. P.

Changes After Publication. No changes were made after publication.

Rule 7008. General Rules of Pleading

(a) APPLICABILITY OF RULE 8 F.R.CIV.P. Rule 8 F.R.Civ.P. applies in adversary proceedings. The allegation of jurisdiction required by Rule 8(a) shall also contain a reference to the name, number, and chapter of the case under the Code to which the adversary proceeding relates and to the district and division where the case under the Code is pending. In an adversary proceeding before a bankruptcy judge, the complaint, counterclaim, cross-claim, or third-party complaint shall contain a statement that the proceeding is core or non-core and, if non-core, that the pleader does or does not consent to entry of final orders or judgment by the bankruptcy judge.

(b) ATTORNEY'S FEES. A request for an award of attorney's fees shall be pleaded as a claim in a complaint, cross-claim, third-party complaint, answer, or reply as may be appropriate.

(As amended Mar. 30, 1987, eff. Aug. 1, 1987.)

NOTES OF ADVISORY COMMITTEE ON RULES—1987 AMENDMENT

Proceedings before a bankruptcy judge are either core or non-core. 28 U.S.C. §157. A bankruptcy judge may enter a final order or judgment in a core proceeding. In a non-core proceeding, absent consent of the parties, the bankruptcy judge may not enter a final order or judgment but may only submit proposed findings of fact and conclusions of law to the district judge who will enter the final order or judgment. 28 U.S.C. §157(c)(1). The amendment to subdivision (a) of this rule requires an allegation as to whether a proceeding is core or non-core. A party who alleges that the proceeding is non-core shall state whether the party does or does not consent to the entry of a final order or judgment by the bankruptcy judge. Failure to include the statement of consent does not constitute consent. Only express consent in the pleadings or otherwise is effective to authorize entry of a final order or judgment by the bankruptcy judge in a non-core proceeding. Amendments to Rule 7012 require that the defendant admit or deny the allegation as to whether the proceeding is core or non-core.

REFERENCES IN TEXT

The Federal Rules of Civil Procedure, referred to in subd. (a), are set out in the Appendix to Title 28, Judiciary and Judicial Procedure.

Rule 7009. Pleading Special Matters

Rule 9 F.R.Civ.P. applies in adversary proceedings.

REFERENCES IN TEXT

The Federal Rules of Civil Procedure, referred to in text, are set out in the Appendix to Title 28, Judiciary and Judicial Procedure.

Rule 7010. Form of Pleadings

Rule 10 F.R.Civ.P. applies in adversary proceedings, except that the caption of each pleading in such a proceeding shall conform substantially to the appropriate Official Form.

(As amended Apr. 30, 1991, eff. Aug. 1, 1991.)

NOTES OF ADVISORY COMMITTEE ON RULES—1991 AMENDMENT

Reference to the Official Form number is deleted in anticipation of future revision and renumbering of the Official Forms.

REFERENCES IN TEXT

The Federal Rules of Civil Procedure, referred to in text, are set out in the Appendix to Title 28, Judiciary and Judicial Procedure.

Rule 7012. Defenses and Objections—When and How Presented—By Pleading or Motion—Motion for Judgment on the Pleadings

(a) WHEN PRESENTED. If a complaint is duly served, the defendant shall serve an answer within 30 days after the issuance of the summons, except when a different time is prescribed by the court. The court shall prescribe the time for service of the answer when service of a complaint is made by publication or upon a party in a foreign country. A party served with a pleading stating a cross-claim shall serve an answer thereto within 21 days after service. The plaintiff shall serve a reply to a counterclaim in the answer within 21 days after service of the answer or, if a reply is ordered by the court, within 21 days after service of the order, unless the order otherwise directs. The United States or an officer or agency thereof shall serve an answer to a complaint within 35 days after the issuance of the summons, and shall serve an answer to a cross-claim, or a reply to a counterclaim, within 35 days after service upon the United States attorney of the pleading in which the claim is asserted. The service of a motion permitted under this rule alters these periods of time as follows, unless a different time is fixed by order of the court: (1) if the court denies the motion or postpones its disposition until the trial on the merits, the responsive pleading shall be served within 14 days after notice of the court's action; (2) if the court grants a motion for a more definite statement, the responsive pleading shall be served within 14 days after the service of a more definite statement.

(b) APPLICABILITY OF RULE 12(b)–(i) F.R.CIV.P. Rule 12(b)–(i) F.R.Civ.P. applies in adversary proceedings. A responsive pleading shall admit or deny an allegation that the proceeding is core or non-core. If the response is that the proceeding is non-core, it shall include a statement that the party does or does not consent to entry of final orders or judgment by the bankruptcy judge. In non-core proceedings final orders and judgments shall not be entered on the bankruptcy judge's order except with the express consent of the parties.

(As amended Mar. 30, 1987, eff. Aug. 1, 1987; Apr. 23, 2008, eff. Dec. 1, 2008; Mar. 26, 2009, eff. Dec. 1, 2009.)

NOTES OF ADVISORY COMMITTEE ON RULES—1983

Subdivision (a) continues the practice of former Bankruptcy Rule 712(a) by requiring that the answer to a complaint be filed within 30 days after the issuance of the summons. Under Rule 7004(f), the summons must be served within 10 days of issuance. The other pleading periods in adversary proceedings are the same as those in civil actions before the district courts, except that the United States is allowed 35 rather than 60 days to respond.

Rule 12(b)(7) and (h)(2) F.R.Civ.P. refers to Rule 19 F.R.Civ.P. Pursuant to Rule 7002 these references are to Rule 19 F.R.Civ.P. as incorporated and modified by Rule 7019.

NOTES OF ADVISORY COMMITTEE ON RULES—1987 AMENDMENT

The amendment to subdivision (b) requires a response to the allegation that the proceeding is core or non-core. A final order of judgment may not be entered in a non-core proceeding heard by a bankruptcy judge unless all parties expressly consent. 28 U.S.C. §157(c).

COMMITTEE NOTES ON RULES—2008 AMENDMENT

The rule is amended to conform to the changes made to the Federal Rules of Civil Procedure through the restyling of those rules effective on December 1, 2007.

COMMITTEE NOTES ON RULES—2009 AMENDMENT

The rule is amended to implement changes in connection with the amendment to Rule 9006(a) and the manner by which time is computed under the rules. The deadlines in the rule are amended to substitute a deadline that is a multiple of seven days. Throughout the rules, deadlines are amended in the following manner:

- 5-day periods become 7-day periods
- 10-day periods become 14-day periods
- 15-day periods become 14-day periods
- 20-day periods become 21-day periods
- 25-day periods become 28-day periods

REFERENCES IN TEXT

The Federal Rules of Civil Procedure, referred to in subd. (b), are set out in the Appendix to Title 28, Judiciary and Judicial Procedure.

Rule 7013. Counterclaim and Cross-Claim

Rule 13 F.R.Civ.P. applies in adversary proceedings, except that a party sued by a trustee or debtor in possession need not state as a counterclaim any claim that the party has against the debtor, the debtor's property, or the estate, unless the claim arose after the entry of an order for relief. A trustee or debtor in possession who fails to plead a counterclaim through oversight, inadvertence, or excusable neglect, or when justice so requires, may by leave of court amend the pleading, or commence a new adversary proceeding or separate action.

(As amended Mar. 30, 1987, eff. Aug. 1, 1987.)

NOTES OF ADVISORY COMMITTEE ON RULES—1983

Rule 13(h) F.R.Civ.P. refers to Rule 19 F.R.Civ.P. Pursuant to Rule 7002 this reference is to Rule 19 F.R.Civ.P. as incorporated and modified by Rule 7019.

REFERENCES IN TEXT

The Federal Rules of Civil Procedure, referred to in text, are set out in the Appendix to Title 28, Judiciary and Judicial Procedure.

Rule 7014. Third-Party Practice

Rule 14 F.R.Civ.P. applies in adversary proceedings.

NOTES OF ADVISORY COMMITTEE ON RULES—1983

This rule does not purport to deal with questions of jurisdiction. The scope of the jurisdictional grant under 28 U.S.C. §1471 and whether the doctrines of pendent or ancillary jurisdiction are applicable to adversary proceedings will be determined by the courts.

Rule 14 F.R.Civ.P. refers to Rules 12 and 13 F.R.Civ.P. Pursuant to Rule 7002 those references are to Rules 12 and 13 as incorporated and modified by Rules 7012 and 7013.

REFERENCES IN TEXT

The Federal Rules of Civil Procedure, referred to in text, are set out in the Appendix to Title 28, Judiciary and Judicial Procedure.

Rule 7015. Amended and Supplemental Pleadings

Rule 15 F.R.Civ.P. applies in adversary proceedings.

REFERENCES IN TEXT

The Federal Rules of Civil Procedure, referred to in text, are set out in the Appendix to Title 28, Judiciary and Judicial Procedure.

Rule 7016. Pre-Trial Procedure; Formulating Issues

Rule 16 F.R.Civ.P. applies in adversary proceedings.

REFERENCES IN TEXT

The Federal Rules of Civil Procedure, referred to in text, are set out in the Appendix to Title 28, Judiciary and Judicial Procedure.

Rule 7017. Parties Plaintiff and Defendant; Capacity

Rule 17 F.R.Civ.P. applies in adversary proceedings, except as provided in Rule 2010(b).

(As amended Apr. 30, 1991, eff. Aug. 1, 1991.)

NOTES OF ADVISORY COMMITTEE ON RULES—1983

Rules 2010(d) and 5008(d), which implement §§322 and 345 of the Code, authorize a party in interest to prosecute a claim on the bond of a trustee or depository in the name of the United States.

NOTES OF ADVISORY COMMITTEE ON RULES—1991 AMENDMENT

Reference to Rule 5008(d) is deleted because of the abrogation of Rule 5008.

REFERENCES IN TEXT

The Federal Rules of Civil Procedure, referred to in text, are set out in the Appendix to Title 28, Judiciary and Judicial Procedure.

Rule 7018. Joinder of Claims and Remedies

Rule 18 F.R.Civ.P. applies in adversary proceedings.

REFERENCES IN TEXT

The Federal Rules of Civil Procedure, referred to in text, are set out in the Appendix to Title 28, Judiciary and Judicial Procedure.

Rule 7019. Joinder of Persons Needed for Just Determination

Rule 19 F.R.Civ.P. applies in adversary proceedings, except that (1) if an entity joined as a party raises the defense that the court lacks jurisdiction over the subject matter and the defense is sustained, the court shall dismiss such entity from the adversary proceedings and (2) if an entity joined as a party properly and timely raises the defense of improper venue, the court shall determine, as provided in 28 U.S.C. §1412, whether that part of the proceeding involving the joined party shall be transferred to another district, or whether the entire adversary proceeding shall be transferred to another district.

(As amended Mar. 30, 1987, eff. Aug. 1, 1987.)

NOTES OF ADVISORY COMMITTEE ON RULES—1983

This rule addresses a situation different from that encountered by the district court when its jurisdiction is based on diversity of citizenship under 28 U.S.C. §1332. Joining of a party whose citizenship is the same as that of an adversary destroys the district court's jurisdiction over the entire civil action but under 28 U.S.C. §1471 the attempted joinder of such a person would not affect the bankruptcy court's jurisdiction over the original adversary proceeding.

NOTES OF ADVISORY COMMITTEE ON RULES—1987 AMENDMENT

The rule is amended to delete the reference to retention of the adversary proceeding if venue is improper. See 28 U.S.C. §1412.

REFERENCES IN TEXT

The Federal Rules of Civil Procedure, referred to in text, are set out in the Appendix to Title 28, Judiciary and Judicial Procedure.

Rule 7020. Permissive Joinder of Parties

Rule 20 F.R.Civ.P. applies in adversary proceedings.

REFERENCES IN TEXT

The Federal Rules of Civil Procedure, referred to in text, are set out in the Appendix to Title 28, Judiciary and Judicial Procedure.

Rule 7021. Misjoinder and Non-Joinder of Parties

Rule 21 F.R.Civ.P. applies in adversary proceedings.

REFERENCES IN TEXT

The Federal Rules of Civil Procedure, referred to in text, are set out in the Appendix to Title 28, Judiciary and Judicial Procedure.

Rule 7022. Interpleader

Rule 22(a) F.R.Civ.P. applies in adversary proceedings. This rule supplements—and does not limit—the joinder of parties allowed by Rule 7020.

(As amended Apr. 23, 2008, eff. Dec. 1, 2008.)

COMMITTEE NOTES ON RULES—2008 AMENDMENT

The rule is amended to conform to the changes made to the Federal Rules of Civil Procedure through the restyling of those rules effective on December 1, 2007.

REFERENCES IN TEXT

The Federal Rules of Civil Procedure, referred to in text, are set out in the Appendix to Title 28, Judiciary and Judicial Procedure.

Rule 7023. Class Proceedings

Rule 23 F.R.Civ.P. applies in adversary proceedings.

REFERENCES IN TEXT

The Federal Rules of Civil Procedure, referred to in text, are set out in the Appendix to Title 28, Judiciary and Judicial Procedure.

Rule 7023.1. Derivative Actions

Rule 23.1 F.R.Civ.P. applies in adversary proceedings.

(As amended Apr. 23, 2008, eff. Dec. 1, 2008.)

COMMITTEE NOTES ON RULES—2008 AMENDMENT

The rule is amended to conform to the changes made to the Federal Rules of Civil Procedure through the restyling of those rules effective on December 1, 2007.

REFERENCES IN TEXT

The Federal Rules of Civil Procedure, referred to in text, are set out in the Appendix to Title 28, Judiciary and Judicial Procedure.

Rule 7023.2. Adversary Proceedings Relating to Unincorporated Associations

Rule 23.2 F.R.Civ.P. applies in adversary proceedings.

REFERENCES IN TEXT

The Federal Rules of Civil Procedure, referred to in text, are set out in the Appendix to Title 28, Judiciary and Judicial Procedure.

Rule 7024. Intervention

Rule 24 F.R.Civ.P. applies in adversary proceedings.

NOTES OF ADVISORY COMMITTEE ON RULES—1983

A person may seek to intervene in the case under the Code or in an adversary proceeding relating to the case under the Code. Intervention in a case under the Code is governed by Rule 2018 and intervention in an adversary proceeding is governed by this rule. Intervention in a case and intervention in an adversary proceeding must be sought separately.

REFERENCES IN TEXT

The Federal Rules of Civil Procedure, referred to in text, are set out in the Appendix to Title 28, Judiciary and Judicial Procedure.

Rule 7025. Substitution of Parties

Subject to the provisions of Rule 2012, Rule 25 F.R.Civ.P. applies in adversary proceedings.

NOTES OF ADVISORY COMMITTEE ON RULES—1983

Rule 25 F.R.Civ.P. refers to Rule 4 F.R.Civ.P. Pursuant to Rule 7002 that reference is to Rule 4 as incorporated and modified by Rule 7004.

REFERENCES IN TEXT

The Federal Rules of Civil Procedure, referred to in text, are set out in the Appendix to Title 28, Judiciary and Judicial Procedure.

Rule 7026. General Provisions Governing Discovery

Rule 26 F.R.Civ.P. applies in adversary proceedings.

REFERENCES IN TEXT

The Federal Rules of Civil Procedure, referred to in text, are set out in the Appendix to Title 28, Judiciary and Judicial Procedure.

Rule 7027. Depositions Before Adversary Proceedings or Pending Appeal

Rule 27 F.R.Civ.P. applies to adversary proceedings.

NOTES OF ADVISORY COMMITTEE ON RULES—1983

Rule 27(a)(2) F.R.Civ.P. refers to Rule 4 F.R.Civ.P. Pursuant to Rule 7002 the reference is to Rule 4 F.R.Civ.P. as incorporated and modified by Rule 7004.

REFERENCES IN TEXT

The Federal Rules of Civil Procedure, referred to in text, are set out in the Appendix to Title 28, Judiciary and Judicial Procedure.

Rule 7028. Persons Before Whom Depositions May Be Taken

Rule 28 F.R.Civ.P. applies in adversary proceedings.

REFERENCES IN TEXT

The Federal Rules of Civil Procedure, referred to in text, are set out in the Appendix to Title 28, Judiciary and Judicial Procedure.

Rule 7029. Stipulations Regarding Discovery Procedure

Rule 29 F.R.Civ.P. applies in adversary proceedings.

REFERENCES IN TEXT

The Federal Rules of Civil Procedure, referred to in text, are set out in the Appendix to Title 28, Judiciary and Judicial Procedure.

Rule 7030. Depositions Upon Oral Examination

Rule 30 F.R.Civ.P. applies in adversary proceedings.

NOTES OF ADVISORY COMMITTEE ON RULES—1983

Rule 30 F.R.Civ.P. refers to Rule 4 F.R.Civ.P. Pursuant to Rule 7002 that reference is a reference to Rule 4 F.R.Civ.P. as incorporated and modified by Rule 7004.

REFERENCES IN TEXT

The Federal Rules of Civil Procedure, referred to in text, are set out in the Appendix to Title 28, Judiciary and Judicial Procedure.

Rule 7031. Deposition Upon Written Questions

Rule 31 F.R.Civ.P. applies in adversary proceedings.

REFERENCES IN TEXT

The Federal Rules of Civil Procedure, referred to in text, are set out in the Appendix to Title 28, Judiciary and Judicial Procedure.

Rule 7032. Use of Depositions in Adversary Proceedings

Rule 32 F.R.Civ.P. applies in adversary proceedings.

REFERENCES IN TEXT

The Federal Rules of Civil Procedure, referred to in text, are set out in the Appendix to Title 28, Judiciary and Judicial Procedure.

Rule 7033. Interrogatories to Parties

Rule 33 F.R.Civ.P. applies in adversary proceedings.

REFERENCES IN TEXT

The Federal Rules of Civil Procedure, referred to in text, are set out in the Appendix to Title 28, Judiciary and Judicial Procedure.

Rule 7034. Production of Documents and Things and Entry Upon Land for Inspection and Other Purposes

Rule 34 F.R.Civ.P. applies in adversary proceedings.

REFERENCES IN TEXT

The Federal Rules of Civil Procedure, referred to in text, are set out in the Appendix to Title 28, Judiciary and Judicial Procedure.

Rule 7035. Physical and Mental Examination of Persons

Rule 35 F.R.Civ.P. applies in adversary proceedings.

REFERENCES IN TEXT

The Federal Rules of Civil Procedure, referred to in text, are set out in the Appendix to Title 28, Judiciary and Judicial Procedure.

Rule 7036. Requests for Admission

Rule 36 F.R.Civ.P. applies in adversary proceedings.

REFERENCES IN TEXT

The Federal Rules of Civil Procedure, referred to in text, are set out in the Appendix to Title 28, Judiciary and Judicial Procedure.

Rule 7037. Failure to Make Discovery: Sanctions

Rule 37 F.R.Civ.P. applies in adversary proceedings.

REFERENCES IN TEXT

The Federal Rules of Civil Procedure, referred to in text, are set out in the Appendix to Title 28, Judiciary and Judicial Procedure.

Rule 7040. Assignment of Cases for Trial

Rule 40 F.R.Civ.P. applies in adversary proceedings.

REFERENCES IN TEXT

The Federal Rules of Civil Procedure, referred to in text, are set out in the Appendix to Title 28, Judiciary and Judicial Procedure.

Rule 7041. Dismissal of Adversary Proceedings

Rule 41 F.R.Civ.P. applies in adversary proceedings, except that a complaint objecting to the debtor's discharge shall not be dismissed at the plaintiff's instance without notice to the trustee, the United States trustee, and such other persons as the court may direct, and only on order of the court containing terms and conditions which the court deems proper.

(As amended Apr. 30, 1991, eff. Aug. 1, 1991.)

NOTES OF ADVISORY COMMITTEE ON RULES—1983

Dismissal of a complaint objecting to a discharge raises special concerns because the plaintiff may have been induced to dismiss by an advantage given or promised by the debtor or someone acting in his interest. Some courts by local rule or order have required the debtor and his attorney or the plaintiff to file an affidavit that nothing has been promised to the plaintiff in consideration of the withdrawal of the objection. By specifically authorizing the court to impose conditions in the order of dismissal this rule permits the continuation of this salutary practice.

Rule 41 F.R.Civ.P. refers to Rule 19 F.R.Civ.P. Pursuant to Rule 7002 that reference is to Rule 19 F.R.Civ.P. as incorporated and modified by Rule 7019.

NOTES OF ADVISORY COMMITTEE ON RULES—1991 AMENDMENT

The United States trustee has standing to object to the debtor's discharge pursuant to §727(c) and may have refrained from commencing an adversary proceeding objecting to discharge within the time limits provided in Rule 4004 only because another party commenced such a proceeding. The United States trustee may oppose dismissal of the original proceeding.

The rule is also amended to clarify that the court may direct that other persons receive notice of a plaintiff's motion to dismiss a complaint objecting to discharge.

REFERENCES IN TEXT

The Federal Rules of Civil Procedure, referred to in text, are set out in the Appendix to Title 28, Judiciary and Judicial Procedure.

Rule 7042. Consolidation of Adversary Proceedings; Separate Trials

Rule 42 F.R.Civ.P. applies in adversary proceedings.

REFERENCES IN TEXT

The Federal Rules of Civil Procedure, referred to in text, are set out in the Appendix to Title 28, Judiciary and Judicial Procedure.

Rule 7052. Findings by the Court

Rule 52 F.R.Civ.P. applies in adversary proceedings, except that any motion under subdivision (b) of that rule for amended or additional findings shall be filed no later than 14 days after entry of judgment. In these proceedings, the reference in Rule 52 F.R.Civ.P. to the entry of judgment under Rule 58 F.R.Civ.P. shall be read as a reference to the entry of a judgment or order under Rule 5003(a).

(As amended Mar. 26, 2009, eff. Dec. 1, 2009.)

NOTES OF ADVISORY COMMITTEE ON RULES—1983

Rule 52(a) F.R.Civ.P. refers to Rule 12 F.R.Civ.P. Pursuant to Rule 7002 this reference is to Rule 12 F.R.Civ.P. as incorporated and modified by Rule 7012.

COMMITTEE NOTES ON RULES—2009 AMENDMENT

The rule is amended by limiting the time for filing post judgment motions for amended or additional findings. In 2009, Rule 52 F. R. Civ. P. was amended to extend the deadline for filing those post judgment motions to no later than 28 days after entry of the judgment. That deadline corresponds to the 30-day deadline for filing a notice of appeal in a civil case under Rule 4(a)(1)(A) F. R. App. P. In a bankruptcy case, the deadline for filing a notice of appeal is 14 days. Therefore, the 28-day deadline for filing a motion for amended or additional findings would effectively override the notice of appeal deadline under Rule 8002(a) but for this amendment.

The rule is amended to clarify that the reference in Rule 52 F. R. Civ. P. to Rule 58 F. R. Civ. P. and its provisions is construed as a reference to the entry of a judgment or order under Rule 5003(a).

Changes Made After Publication. No changes since publication.

REFERENCES IN TEXT

The Federal Rules of Civil Procedure, referred to in text, are set out in the Appendix to Title 28, Judiciary and Judicial Procedure.

Rule 7054. Judgments; Costs

(a) JUDGMENTS. Rule 54(a)–(c) F.R.Civ.P. applies in adversary proceedings.

(b) COSTS. The court may allow costs to the prevailing party except when a statute of the United States or these rules otherwise provides. Costs against the United States, its officers and agencies shall be imposed only to the extent permitted by law. Costs may be taxed by the clerk on one day's notice; on motion served within five days thereafter, the action of the clerk may be reviewed by the court.

REFERENCES IN TEXT

The Federal Rules of Civil Procedure, referred to in subd. (a), are set out in the Appendix to Title 28, Judiciary and Judicial Procedure.

Rule 7055. Default

Rule 55 F.R.Civ.P. applies in adversary proceedings.

REFERENCES IN TEXT

The Federal Rules of Civil Procedure, referred to in text, are set out in the Appendix to Title 28, Judiciary and Judicial Procedure.

Rule 7056. Summary Judgment

Rule 56 F.R.Civ.P. applies in adversary proceedings.

REFERENCES IN TEXT

The Federal Rules of Civil Procedure, referred to in text, are set out in the Appendix to Title 28, Judiciary and Judicial Procedure.

Rule 7058. Entering Judgment in Adversary Proceeding

Rule 58 F.R.Civ.P. applies in adversary proceedings. In these proceedings, the reference in Rule 58 F.R.Civ.P. to the civil docket shall be read as a reference to the docket maintained by the clerk under Rule 5003(a).

(Added Mar. 26, 2009, eff. Dec. 1, 2009.)

COMMITTEE NOTES ON RULES—2009

This rule makes Rule 58 F.R.Civ.P. applicable in adversary proceedings and is added in connection with the amendments to Rule 9021.

Changes Made After Publication. No changes since publication.

REFERENCES IN TEXT

The Federal Rules of Civil Procedure, referred to in text, are set out in the Appendix to Title 28, Judiciary and Judicial Procedure.

Rule 7062. Stay of Proceedings to Enforce a Judgment

Rule 62 F.R.Civ.P. applies in adversary proceedings.

(As amended Apr. 30, 1991, eff. Aug. 1, 1991; Apr. 26, 1999, eff. Dec. 1, 1999.)

NOTES OF ADVISORY COMMITTEE ON RULES—1983

The additional exceptions set forth in this rule make applicable to those matters the consequences contained in Rule 62(c) and (d) with respect to orders in actions for injunctions.

NOTES OF ADVISORY COMMITTEE ON RULES—1991 AMENDMENT

This rule is amended to include as additional exceptions to Rule 62(a) an order granting relief from the automatic stay of actions against codebtors provided by §1201 of the Code, the sale or lease of property of the estate under §363, and the assumption or assignment of an executory contract under §365.

COMMITTEE NOTES ON RULES—1999 AMENDMENT

The additional exceptions to Rule 62(a) consist of orders that are issued in contested matters. These exceptions are deleted from this rule because of the amendment to Rule 9014 that renders this rule inapplicable in contested matters unless the court orders otherwise. *See also* the amendments to Rules 3020, 3021, 4001, 6004, and 6006 that delay the implementation of certain types of orders for a period of ten days unless the court otherwise directs.

GAP Report on Rule 7062. No changes since publication.

REFERENCES IN TEXT

The Federal Rules of Civil Procedure, referred to in text, are set out in the Appendix to Title 28, Judiciary and Judicial Procedure.

Rule 7064. Seizure of Person or Property

Rule 62 F.R.Civ.P. applies in adversary proceedings.

REFERENCES IN TEXT

The Federal Rules of Civil Procedure, referred to in text, are set out in the Appendix to Title 28, Judiciary and Judicial Procedure.

Rule 7065. Injunctions

Rule 65 F.R.Civ.P. applies in adversary proceedings, except that a temporary restraining order or preliminary injunction may be issued on application of a debtor, trustee, or debtor in possession without compliance with Rule 65(c).

REFERENCES IN TEXT

The Federal Rules of Civil Procedure, referred to in text, are set out in the Appendix to Title 28, Judiciary and Judicial Procedure.

Rule 7067. Deposit in Court

Rule 67 F.R.Civ.P. applies in adversary proceedings.

REFERENCES IN TEXT

The Federal Rules of Civil Procedure, referred to in text, are set out in the Appendix to Title 28, Judiciary and Judicial Procedure.

Rule 7068. Offer of Judgment

Rule 68 F.R.Civ.P. applies in adversary proceedings.

REFERENCES IN TEXT

The Federal Rules of Civil Procedure, referred to in text, are set out in the Appendix to Title 28, Judiciary and Judicial Procedure.

Rule 7069. Execution

Rule 69 F.R.Civ.P. applies in adversary proceedings.

REFERENCES IN TEXT

The Federal Rules of Civil Procedure, referred to in text, are set out in the Appendix to Title 28, Judiciary and Judicial Procedure.

Rule 7070. Judgment for Specific Acts; Vesting Title

Rule 70 F.R.Civ.P. applies in adversary proceedings and the court may enter a judgment divesting the title of any party and vesting title in others whenever the real or personal property involved is within the jurisdiction of the court.

(As amended Mar. 30, 1987, eff. Aug. 1, 1987.)

NOTES OF ADVISORY COMMITTEE ON RULES—1987 AMENDMENT

The reference to court is used in the amendment because the district court may preside over an adversary proceeding.

REFERENCES IN TEXT

The Federal Rules of Civil Procedure, referred to in text, are set out in the Appendix to Title 28, Judiciary and Judicial Procedure.

Rule 7071. Process in Behalf of and Against Persons Not Parties

Rule 71 F.R.Civ.P. applies in adversary proceedings.

REFERENCES IN TEXT

The Federal Rules of Civil Procedure, referred to in text, are set out in the Appendix to Title 28, Judiciary and Judicial Procedure.

Rule 7087. Transfer of Adversary Proceeding

On motion and after a hearing, the court may transfer an adversary proceeding or any part thereof to another district pursuant to 28 U.S.C. §1412, except as provided in Rule 7019(2).

(As amended Mar. 30, 1987, eff. Aug. 1, 1987.)

NOTES OF ADVISORY COMMITTEE ON RULES—1987 AMENDMENT

The reference to the venue section of title 28 is amended to conform to the 1984 amendments to title 28.

PART VIII—APPEALS TO DISTRICT COURT OR BANKRUPTCY APPELLATE PANEL

Rule 8001. Manner of Taking Appeal; Voluntary Dismissal; Certification to Court of Appeals

(a) APPEAL AS OF RIGHT; HOW TAKEN. An appeal from a judgment, order, or decree of a bankruptcy judge to a district court or bankruptcy appellate panel as permitted by 28 U.S.C. §158(a)(1) or (a)(2) shall be taken by filing a notice of appeal with the clerk within the time allowed by Rule 8002. An appellant's failure to take any step other than timely filing a notice of appeal does not affect the validity of the appeal, but is ground only for such action as the district court or bankruptcy appellate panel deems appropriate, which may include dismissal of the appeal. The notice of appeal shall (1) conform substantially to the appropriate Official Form, (2) contain the names of all parties to the judgment, order, or decree appealed from and the names, addresses, and telephone numbers of their respective attorneys, and (3) be accompanied by the prescribed fee. Each appellant shall file a sufficient number of copies of the notice of appeal to enable the clerk to comply promptly with Rule 8004.

(b) APPEAL BY LEAVE; HOW TAKEN. An appeal from an interlocutory judgment, order, or decree of a bankruptcy judge as permitted by 28 U.S.C. §158(a)(3) shall be taken by filing a notice of appeal, as prescribed in subdivision (a) of this rule, accompanied by a motion for leave to appeal prepared in accordance with Rule 8003 and with proof of service in accordance with Rule 8008.

(c) VOLUNTARY DISMISSAL.

(1) *Before Docketing.* If an appeal has not been docketed, the appeal may be dismissed by the bankruptcy judge on the filing of a stipulation for dismissal signed by all the parties, or on motion and notice by the appellant.

(2) *After Docketing.* If an appeal has been docketed and the parties to the appeal sign and file with the clerk of the district court or the clerk of the bankruptcy appellate panel an agreement that the appeal be dismissed and pay any court costs or fees that may be due, the clerk of the district court or the clerk of the bankruptcy appellate panel shall enter an order dismissing the appeal. An appeal may also be dismissed on motion of the appellant on terms and conditions fixed by the district court or bankruptcy appellate panel.

[(d) EFFECT OF TAKING A DIRECT APPEAL TO THE COURT OF APPEALS] (Abrogated Mar. 30, 1987, eff. Aug. 1, 1987)

(e) ELECTION TO HAVE APPEAL HEARD BY DISTRICT COURT INSTEAD OF BANKRUPTCY APPELLATE PANEL; WITHDRAWAL OF ELECTION.

(1) *Separate Writing for Election.* An election to have an appeal heard by the district court under 28 U.S.C. §158(c)(1) may be made only by a statement of election contained in a separate writing filed within the time prescribed by 28 U.S.C. §158(c)(1).

(2) *Withdrawal of Election.* A request to withdraw the election may be filed only by written stipulation of all the parties to the appeal or their attorneys of record. Upon such a stipulation, the district court may either transfer the appeal to the bankruptcy appellate panel or retain the appeal in the district court.

(f) CERTIFICATION FOR DIRECT APPEAL TO COURT OF APPEALS.

(1) *Timely Appeal Required.* A certification of a judgment, order, or decree of a bankruptcy court to a court of appeals under 28 U.S.C. §158(d)(2) shall not be effective until a timely appeal has been taken in the manner required by subdivisions (a) or (b) of this rule and the notice of appeal has become effective under Rule 8002.

(2) *Court Where Certification Made and Filed.* A certification that a circumstance specified in 28 U.S.C. §158(d)(2)(A)(i)–(iii) exists shall be filed in the court in which a matter is pending for purposes of 28 U.S.C. §158(d)(2) and this rule. A matter is pending in a bankruptcy court until the docketing, in accordance with Rule 8007(b), of an appeal taken under 28 U.S.C. §158(a)(1) or (2), or the grant of leave to appeal under 28 U.S.C. §158(a)(3). A matter is pending in a district court or bankruptcy appellate panel after the docketing, in accordance with Rule 8007(b), of an appeal taken under 28 U.S.C. §158(a)(1) or (2), or the grant of leave to appeal under 28 U.S.C. §158(a)(3).

(A) *Certification by Court on Request or Court's Own Initiative.*

(i) Before Docketing or Grant of Leave to Appeal. Only a bankruptcy court may make a certification on request or on its own initiative while the matter is pending in the bankruptcy court.

(ii) After Docketing or Grant of Leave to Appeal. Only the district court or bankruptcy appellate panel involved may make a certification on request of the parties or on its own initiative while the matter is pending in the district court or bankruptcy appellate panel.

(B) *Certification by All Appellants and Appellees Acting Jointly.* A certification by all the appellants and appellees, if any, acting jointly may be made by filing the appropriate Official Form with the clerk of the court in which the matter is pending. The certification may be accompanied by a short statement of the basis for the certification, which may include the information listed in subdivision (f)(3)(C) of this rule.

(3) *Request for Certification; Filing; Service; Contents.*

(A) A request for certification shall be filed, within the time specified by 28 U.S.C. §158(d)(2), with the clerk of the court in which the matter is pending.

(B) Notice of the filing of a request for certification shall be served in the manner required for service of a notice of appeal under Rule 8004.

(C) A request for certification shall include the following:

(i) the facts necessary to understand the question presented;

(ii)the question itself;

(iii) the relief sought;

(iv) the reasons why the appeal should be allowed and is authorized by statute or rule, including why a circumstance specified in 28 U.S.C. §158(d)(2)(A)(i)–(iii) exists; and

(v) an attached copy of the judgment, order, or decree complained of and any related opinion or memorandum.

(D) A party may file a response to a request for certification or a cross request within 14 days after the notice of the request is served, or another time fixed by the court.

(E) Rule 9014 does not govern a request, cross request, or any response. The matter shall be submitted without oral argument unless the court otherwise directs.

(F) A certification of an appeal under 28 U.S.C. §158(d)(2) shall be made in a separate document served on the parties.

(4) *Certification on Court's Own Initiative.*

(A) A certification of an appeal on the court's own initiative under 28 U.S.C. §158(d)(2) shall be made in a separate document served on the parties in the manner required for service of a notice of appeal under Rule 8004. The certification shall be accompanied by an opinion or memorandum that contains the information required by subdivision (f)(3)(C)(i)–(iv) of this rule.

(B) A party may file a supplementary short statement of the basis for certification within 14 days after the certification.

(5) *Duties of Parties After Certification.* A petition for permission to appeal in accordance with F.R.App.P. 5 shall be filed no later than 30 days after a certification has become effective as provided in subdivision (f)(1).

(As amended Mar. 30, 1987, eff. Aug. 1, 1987; Apr. 30, 1991, eff. Aug. 1, 1991; Apr. 11, 1997, eff. Dec. 1, 1997; Apr. 23, 2008, eff. Dec. 1, 2008; Mar. 26, 2009, eff. Dec. 1, 2009.)

NOTES OF ADVISORY COMMITTEE ON RULES—1983

These rules in Part VIII apply only to appeals to the district courts or bankruptcy appellate panels. Subsequent appeals to the courts of appeals, or direct appeals by agreement of the parties under 28 U.S.C. §1293(b), are governed by the Federal Rules of Appellate Procedure.

Subdivisions (a) and (b) require that a notice of appeal be filed whenever a litigant seeks to secure appellate review by the district court or bankruptcy appellate panel. An appeal from an interlocutory order which will be heard only if leave is granted under 28 U.S.C. §§1334(b) or 1482(b) is taken by filing a notice of appeal accompanied by a motion for leave to appeal which complies with the requirements set forth in Rule 8003. Rule 8003 also governs other aspects of interlocutory appeals.

Subdivision (c) is an adaptation of Rule 42 F.R.App.P.

Subdivision (d) deals with the situation in which an appellant perfects an appeal to the district court or a bankruptcy appellate panel and also a direct appeal pursuant to 28 U.S.C. §1293(b) to the court of appeals. This subdivision provides that once the appeal to the court of appeals is taken, a notice of appeal to the district court or bankruptcy appellate panel shall be dismissed and, if the first appeal is to the district court or bankruptcy appellate panel, the first appeal shall be dismissed. Paragraph (3) gives an appellant or cross appellant an opportunity to file an appeal to the district court or bankruptcy appellate panel if the court of appeals dismisses the direct appeal because the judgment, order, or decree appealed from is not final. Since the court of appeals has determined the judgment, order, or decree is not final, the new appeal is an appeal for which leave is necessary.

NOTES OF ADVISORY COMMITTEE ON RULES—1987 AMENDMENT

Subdivisions (a) and (b) are amended to conform to the 1984 amendments.

Subdivision (d) is abrogated because there is no direct appeal to the court of appeals under 28 U.S.C. §158, as enacted by the 1984 amendments.

Subdivision (e) is new. Section 158(b)(1) of title 28 authorizes the circuit councils to establish bankruptcy appellate panels. Appeals may not be heard by these panels unless the district court authorizes the referral and all parties to the appeal consent. This rule requires that the parties consent to such an appeal; however, the method of consenting to an appeal may be the subject of a rule promulgated by a circuit council under Rule 8018.

NOTES OF ADVISORY COMMITTEE ON RULES—1991 AMENDMENT

Reference to the Official Form number is deleted in anticipation of future revision and renumbering of the Official Forms.

NOTES OF ADVISORY COMMITTEE ON RULES—1997 AMENDMENT

This rule is amended to conform to the Bankruptcy Reform Act of 1994 which amended 28 U.S.C. §158. As amended, a party may—without obtaining leave of the court—appeal from an interlocutory order or decree of the bankruptcy court issued under §1121(d) of the Code increasing or reducing the time periods referred to in §1121.

Subdivision (e) is amended to provide the procedure for electing under 28 U.S.C. §158(c)(1) to have an appeal heard by the district court instead of the bankruptcy appellate panel service. This subdivision is applicable only if a bankruptcy appellate panel service is authorized under 28 U.S.C. §158(b) to hear the appeal.

GAP Report on Rule 8001. The heading of subdivision (e) is amended to clarify that it applies to the election to have an appeal heard by the district court instead of the BAP. The final paragraph of the Committee Note is revised to clarify that subdivision (e) is applicable only if a BAP is authorized to hear the appeal.

COMMITTEE NOTES ON RULES—2008 AMENDMENT

Subdivision (e) is amended by redesignating the subdivision as (e)(1) and adding new subdivision (e)(2). Subdivision (e)(2) explicitly recognizes the district court's authority to transfer an appeal to the bankruptcy appellate panel on two conditions: first, all of the parties to the appeal must have agreed to request the withdrawal of the election to have the district court hear the appeal; and, second, the district court must decide whether to grant the request for withdrawal. The district court has discretion either to keep the case or transfer it to the bankruptcy appellate panel, which will prevent strategic behavior by parties and avoid the wasting of judicial resources.

Subdivision (f) is added to the rule to implement the 2005 amendments to 28 U.S.C. §158(d). That section authorizes appeals directly to the court of appeals, with that court's consent, upon certification that a ground for the appeal exists under §158(d)(2)(A)(i)–(iii). Certification can be made by the court on its own initiative under subdivision (f)(4), or in response to a request of a party or a majority of the appellants and appellees (if any) under subdivision (f)(3). Certification also can be made by all of the appellants and appellees under subdivision (f)(2)(B). Under subdivision (f)(1), certification is effective only when a timely appeal is commenced under subdivision (a) or (b), and a notice of appeal has been timely filed under Rule 8002. These actions will provide sufficient notice of the appeal to the circuit clerk, so the rule dispenses with the uncodified temporary procedural requirements set out in §1233(b)(4) of the Bankruptcy Abuse Prevention and Consumer Protection Act of 2005, Pub. L. No. 109–8.

The rule adopts a bright-line test for identifying the court in which a matter is pending. Under subdivision (f)(2), the bright-line chosen is the "docketing" under Rule 8007(b) of an appeal of an interlocutory order or decree under 28 U.S.C. §158(a)(2) or a final judgment, order or decree under 28 U.S.C. §158(a)(1), or the granting of leave to appeal any other interlocutory judgment, order or decree under 28 U.S.C. §158(a)(3), whichever is earlier.

To ensure that parties are aware of a certification, the rule requires either that it be made on the Official

Form (if being made by all of the parties to the appeal) or on a separate document (whether the certification is made on the court's own initiative or in response to a request by a party). This is particularly important because the rule adopts the bankruptcy practice established by Rule 8001(a) and (b) of requiring a notice of appeal in every instance, including interlocutory orders, of appeals from bankruptcy court orders, judgments, and decrees. Because this requirement is satisfied by filing the notice of appeal that takes the appeal to the district court or bankruptcy appellate panel in the first instance, the rule does not require a separate notice of appeal if a certification occurs after a district court or bankruptcy appellate panel decision.

A certification under subdivision (f)(1) does not place the appeal in the circuit court. Rather, the court of appeals must first authorize the direct appeal. Subdivision (f)(5) therefore provides that any party intending to pursue the appeal in the court of appeals must seek that permission under Rule 5 of the Federal Rules of Appellate Procedure. Subdivision (f)(5) requires that the petition for permission to appeal be filed within 30 days after an effective certification.

Changes Made After Publication. The second paragraph of the Committee Note was amended to identify more specifically the different ways in which the certification of a direct appeal to the court of appeals.

COMMITTEE NOTES ON RULES—2009 AMENDMENT

The rule is amended to implement changes in connection with the amendment to Rule 9006(a) and the manner by which time is computed under the rules. The deadlines in the rule are amended to substitute a deadline that is a multiple of seven days. Throughout the rules, deadlines are amended in the following manner:

- 5-day periods become 7-day periods
- 10-day periods become 14-day periods
- 15-day periods become 14-day periods
- 20-day periods become 21-day periods
- 25-day periods become 28-day periods

REFERENCES IN TEXT

The Federal Rules of Appellate Procedure, referred to in subd. (f)(5), are set out in the Appendix to Title 28, Judiciary and Judicial Procedure.

Rule 8002. Time for Filing Notice of Appeal

(a) FOURTEEN-DAY PERIOD. The notice of appeal shall be filed with the clerk within 14 days of the date of the entry of the judgment, order, or decree appealed from. If a timely notice of appeal is filed by a party, any other party may file a notice of appeal within 14 days of the date on which the first notice of appeal was filed, or within the time otherwise prescribed by this rule, whichever period last expires. A notice of appeal filed after the announcement of a decision or order but before entry of the judgment, order, or decree shall be treated as filed after such entry and on the day thereof. If a notice of appeal is mistakenly filed with the district court or the bankruptcy appellate panel, the clerk of the district court or the clerk of the bankruptcy appellate panel shall note thereon the date on which it was received and transmit it to the clerk and it shall be deemed filed with the clerk on the date so noted.

(b) EFFECT OF MOTION ON TIME FOR APPEAL. If any party makes a timely motion of a type specified immediately below, the time for appeal for all parties runs from the entry of the order disposing of the last such motion outstanding. This provision applies to a timely motion:

(1) to amend or make additional findings of fact under Rule 7052, whether or not granting the motion would alter the judgment;

(2) to alter or amend the judgment under Rule 9023;

(3) for a new trial under Rule 9023; or

(4) for relief under Rule 9024 if the motion is filed no later than 14 days after the entry of judgment. A notice of appeal filed after announcement or entry of the judgment, order, or decree but before disposition of any of the above motions is ineffective to appeal from the judgment, order, or decree, or part thereof, specified in the notice of appeal, until the entry of the order disposing of the last such motion outstanding. Appellate review of an order disposing of any of the above motions requires the party, in compliance with Rule 8001, to amend a previously filed notice of appeal. A party intending to challenge an alteration or amendment of the judgment, order, or decree shall file a notice, or an amended notice, of appeal within the time prescribed by this Rule 8002 measured from the entry of the order disposing of the last such motion outstanding. No additional fees will be required for filing an amended notice.

(c) EXTENSION OF TIME FOR APPEAL.

(1) The bankruptcy judge may extend the time for filing the notice of appeal by any party, unless the judgment, order, or decree appealed from:

(A) grants relief from an automatic stay under § 362, § 922, § 1201, or § 1301;

(B) authorizes the sale or lease of property or the use of cash collateral under § 363;

(C) authorizes the obtaining of credit under § 364;

(D) authorizes the assumption or assignment of an executory contract or unexpired lease under § 365;

(E) approves a disclosure statement under § 1125; or

(F) confirms a plan under § 943, § 1129, § 1225, or § 1325 of the Code.

(2) A request to extend the time for filing a notice of appeal must be made by written motion filed before the time for filing a notice of appeal has expired, except that such a motion filed not later than 21 days after the expiration of the time for filing a notice of appeal may be granted upon a showing of excusable neglect. An extension of time for filing a notice of appeal may not exceed 21 days from the expiration of the time for filing a notice of appeal otherwise prescribed by this rule or 14 days from the date of entry of the order granting the motion, whichever is later.

(As amended Mar. 30, 1987, eff. Aug. 1, 1987; Apr. 30, 1991, eff. Aug. 1, 1991; Apr. 29, 1994, eff. Aug. 1, 1994; Apr. 11, 1997, eff. Dec. 1, 1997; Mar. 26, 2009, eff. Dec. 1, 2009.)

NOTES OF ADVISORY COMMITTEE ON RULES—1983

This rule is an adaptation of Rule 4(a) F.R.App.P. The time to appeal from a judgment, order, or decree of a bankruptcy judge is 10 days, rather than the 30 days provided for in the civil practice. The shortened time is specified in order to obtain prompt appellate review, often important to the administration of a case under the Code. If a timely notice of appeal is filed, other parties have an additional 10 days within which to file a notice of appeal. A notice of appeal filed within the additional 10 day period by an appellee is a cross appeal.

but there is a separate appeal if a non-appellee files a notice of appeal within that 10 day period. The district courts and bankruptcy appellate panels have inherent authority to consolidate appeals.

Subdivision (b) is essentially the same as Rule 4(a)(4) of the F.R.App.P.

Subdivision (c) is similar to former Bankruptcy Rule 802(c). To expedite the disposition of appeals the maximum extension of time is 20 days instead of the 30 days provided by Rule 4(a)(5) of the F.R.App.P. Subject to the exceptions set forth in subdivision (c), the court may extend the time for taking an appeal when a motion for extension is filed after the expiration of the original 10 day period but no later than 20 days after the expiration of the original 10 day period. Orders of the bankruptcy court relating to the sale of property, extension of credit, confirmation of a plan, dismissal or conversion of the case, and approval of the disclosure statement are of such significance to the administration of the case, the parties in interest, and third parties that this subdivision requires that either an appeal or a motion for extension be filed within the original 10 day period.

If a timely notice of appeal is not filed, no appeal may be taken later. Former Bankruptcy Rule 803, which provided that a referee's judgment became final when the appeal period expired, has been omitted as unnecessary.

NOTES OF ADVISORY COMMITTEE ON RULES—1991 AMENDMENT

Subdivision (a) is amended to conform to F.R.App.P. 4(a)(2) which is designed to avoid the loss of the right to appeal when a notice of appeal is filed prematurely.

Subdivision (b)(1) is deleted because Rule 9015 was abrogated in 1987.

NOTES OF ADVISORY COMMITTEE ON RULES—1994 AMENDMENT

These amendments are intended to conform to the 1993 amendments to F.R.App.P. 4(a)(4) and 6(b)(2)(i).

This rule as amended provides that a notice of appeal filed before the disposition of a specified postjudgment motion will become effective upon disposition of the motion. A notice filed before the filing of one of the specified motions or after the filing of a motion but before disposition of the motion is, in effect, suspended until the motion is disposed of, whereupon, the previously filed notice effectively places jurisdiction in the district court or bankruptcy appellate panel.

Because a notice of appeal will ripen into an effective appeal upon disposition of a postjudgment motion, in some instances there will be an appeal from a judgment that has been altered substantially because the motion was granted in whole or in part. The appeal may be dismissed for want of prosecution when the appellant fails to meet the briefing schedule. But, the appellee may also move to strike the appeal. When responding to such a motion, the appellant would have an opportunity to state that, even though some relief sought in a postjudgment motion was granted, the appellant still plans to pursue the appeal. Because the appellant's response would provide the appellee with sufficient notice of the appellant's intentions, the rule does not require an additional notice of appeal in that situation.

The amendment provides that a notice of appeal filed before the disposition of a postjudgment tolling motion is sufficient to bring the judgment, order, or decree specified in the original notice of appeal to the district court or bankruptcy appellate panel. If the judgment is altered upon disposition of a postjudgment motion, however, and if a party who has previously filed a notice of appeal wishes to appeal from the disposition of the motion, the party must amend the notice to so indicate. When a party files an amended notice, no additional fees are required because the notice is an amendment of the original and not a new notice of appeal.

Subdivision (b) is also amended to include, among motions that extend the time for filing a notice of appeal, a motion under Rule 9024 that is filed within 10 days after entry of judgment. The addition of this motion conforms to a similar amendment to F.R.App.P. 4(a)(4) made in 1993, except that a Rule 9024 motion does not toll the time to appeal unless it is filed within the 10-day period. The reason for providing that the motion extends the time to appeal only if it is *filed* within the 10-day period is to enable the court and the parties in interest to determine solely from the court records whether the time to appeal has been extended by a motion for relief under Rule 9024.

NOTES OF ADVISORY COMMITTEE ON RULES—1997 AMENDMENT

Subdivision (c) is amended to provide that a request for an extension of time to file a notice of appeal must be *filed* within the applicable time period. This amendment will avoid uncertainty as to whether the mailing of a motion or an oral request in court is sufficient to request an extension of time, and will enable the court and the parties in interest to determine solely from the court records whether a timely request for an extension has been made.

The amendments also give the court discretion to permit a party to file a notice of appeal more than 20 days after expiration of the time to appeal otherwise prescribed, but only if the motion was timely filed and the notice of appeal is filed within a period not exceeding 10 days after entry of the order extending the time. This amendment is designed to protect parties that file timely motions to extend the time to appeal from the harshness of the present rule as demonstrated in *In re Mouradick*, 13 F.3d 326 (9th Cir. 1994), where the court held that a notice of appeal filed within the 3-day period expressly prescribed by an order granting a timely motion for an extension of time did not confer jurisdiction on the appellate court because the notice of appeal was not filed within the 20-day period specified in subdivision (c).

The subdivision is amended further to prohibit any extension of time to file a notice of appeal—even if the motion for an extension is filed before the expiration of the original time to appeal—if the order appealed from grants relief from the automatic stay, authorizes the sale or lease of property, use of cash collateral, obtaining of credit, or assumption or assignment of an executory contract or unexpired lease under §365, or approves a disclosure statement or confirms a plan. These types of orders are often relied upon immediately after they are entered and should not be reviewable on appeal after the expiration of the original appeal period under Rule 8002(a) and (b).

GAP Report on Rule 8002. No changes to the published draft.

COMMITTEE NOTES ON RULES—2009 AMENDMENT

The rule is amended to implement changes in connection with the amendment to Rule 9006(a) and the manner by which time is computed under the rules. The deadlines in the rule are amended to substitute a deadline that is a multiple of seven days. Throughout the rules, deadlines are amended in the following manner:

- 5-day periods become 7-day periods
- 10-day periods become 14-day periods
- 15-day periods become 14-day periods
- 20-day periods become 21-day periods
- 25-day periods become 28-day periods

Rule 8003. Leave to Appeal

(a) CONTENT OF MOTION; ANSWER. A motion for leave to appeal under 28 U.S.C. §158(a) shall contain: (1) a statement of the facts necessary to an understanding of the questions to be presented by the appeal; (2) a statement of those questions and of the relief sought; (3) a statement of the reasons why an appeal should be granted; and (4) a copy of the judgment, order, or decree complained of and of any opinion or memorandum relating thereto. Within 14 days after service of the motion, an adverse party may file with the clerk an answer in opposition.

(b) TRANSMITTAL; DETERMINATION OF MOTION. The clerk shall transmit the notice of appeal, the motion for leave to appeal and any answer thereto to the clerk of the district court or the clerk of the bankruptcy appellate panel as soon as all parties have filed answers or the time for filing an answer has expired. The motion and answer shall be submitted without oral argument unless otherwise ordered.

(c) APPEAL IMPROPERLY TAKEN REGARDED AS A MOTION FOR LEAVE TO APPEAL. If a required motion for leave to appeal is not filed, but a notice of appeal is timely filed, the district court or bankruptcy appellate panel may grant leave to appeal or direct that a motion for leave to appeal be filed. The district court or the bankruptcy appellate panel may also deny leave to appeal but in so doing shall consider the notice of appeal as a motion for leave to appeal. Unless an order directing that a motion for leave to appeal be filed provides otherwise, the motion shall be filed within 14 days of entry of the order.

(d) REQUIREMENT OF LEAVE TO APPEAL. If leave to appeal is required by 28 U.S.C. §158(a) and has not earlier been granted, the authorization of a direct appeal by a court of appeals under 28 U.S.C. §158(d)(2) shall be deemed to satisfy the requirement for leave to appeal.

(As amended Mar. 30, 1987, eff. Aug. 1, 1987; Apr. 23, 2008, eff. Dec. 1, 2008; Mar. 26, 2009, eff. Dec. 1, 2009.)

NOTES OF ADVISORY COMMITTEE ON RULES—1983

Subdivisions (a) and (b) of this rule are derived from Rules 5 and 6 F.R.App.P. The motion for leave to appeal is addressed to the district court or the bankruptcy appellate panel, although filed with the clerk of the bankruptcy court.

Subdivision (c) provides that if a party mistakenly believes the order appealed from is final and files only a notice of appeal, the appeal is not automatically dismissed. The district court or bankruptcy appellate panel has the options to direct that a motion be filed, to decide exclusively on the papers already filed to grant leave to appeal, or to deny leave to appeal. Cf. 28 U.S.C. §2103.

COMMITTEE NOTES ON RULES—2008 AMENDMENT

The rule is amended to add subdivision (d) to solve the jurisdictional problem that could otherwise ensue when a district court or bankruptcy appellate panel has not granted leave to appeal under 28 U.S.C. §158(a)(3). If the court of appeals accepts the appeal, the requirement of leave to appeal is deemed satisfied. However, if the court of appeals does not authorize a direct appeal, the question of whether to grant leave to appeal remains a matter to be resolved by the district court or the bankruptcy appellate panel.

Changes Made After Publication. No changes were made after publication.

COMMITTEE NOTES ON RULES—2009 AMENDMENT

The rule is amended to implement changes in connection with the amendment to Rule 9006(a) and the manner by which time is computed under the rules. The deadlines in the rule are amended to substitute a deadline that is a multiple of seven days. Throughout the rules, deadlines are amended in the following manner:

- 5-day periods become 7-day periods
- 10-day periods become 14-day periods
- 15-day periods become 14-day periods
- 20-day periods become 21-day periods
- 25-day periods become 28-day periods

Rule 8004. Service of the Notice of Appeal

The clerk shall serve notice of the filing of a notice of appeal by mailing a copy thereof to counsel of record of each party other than the appellant or, if a party is not represented by counsel, to the party's last known address. Failure to serve notice shall not affect the validity of the appeal. The clerk shall note on each copy served the date of the filing of the notice of appeal and shall note in the docket the names of the parties to whom copies are mailed and the date of the mailing. The clerk shall forthwith transmit to the United States trustee a copy of the notice of appeal, but failure to transmit such notice shall not affect the validity of the appeal.

(As amended Mar. 30, 1987, eff. Aug. 1, 1987; Apr. 30, 1991, eff. Aug. 1, 1991.)

NOTES OF ADVISORY COMMITTEE ON RULES—1983

This rule is an adaptation of Rule 3(d) F.R.App.P.

NOTES OF ADVISORY COMMITTEE ON RULES—1991 AMENDMENT

This rule is amended to keep the United States trustee informed of the progress of the case.

Rule 8005. Stay Pending Appeal

A motion for a stay of the judgment, order, or decree of a bankruptcy judge, for approval of a supersedeas bond, or for other relief pending appeal must ordinarily be presented to the bankruptcy judge in the first instance. Notwithstanding Rule 7062 but subject to the power of the district court and the bankruptcy appellate panel reserved hereinafter, the bankruptcy judge may suspend or order the continuation of other proceedings in the case under the Code or make any other appropriate order during the pendency of an appeal on such terms as will protect the rights of all parties in interest. A motion for such relief, or for modification or termination of relief granted by a bankruptcy judge, may be made to the district court or the bankruptcy appellate panel, but the motion shall show why the relief, modification, or termination was not obtained from the bankruptcy judge. The district court or the bankruptcy appellate panel may condition the relief it grants under this rule on the filing of a bond or other appropriate security with the bankruptcy court. When an appeal is taken by a trustee, a bond or other appropriate security may be required, but when an appeal is taken by the United States or an officer or agency thereof or by direction of any department of the Government of the United States a bond or other security shall not be required.

(As amended Mar. 30, 1987, eff. Aug. 1, 1987.)

NOTES OF ADVISORY COMMITTEE ON RULES—1983

The first, third, and fourth sentences of this rule are adaptations of Rule 8(a) and (b) F.R.App.P. The second sentence of the rule is derived from §39(c) of the Bankruptcy Act and confers on the bankruptcy judge discretion respecting the stay or continuation of other proceedings in the case while an appeal is pending.

The last sentence of the rule, which specifically subjects a trustee to the same kind of security requirements as other litigants, is derived from former Bankruptcy Rule 805. The exemption of the United States from the bond or security requirements is the same as the exemption contained in Rule 62(e) F.R.Civ.P.

Sections 363(m) and 364(e) of the Code provide that unless an order approving a sale of property, or authorizing the obtaining of credit or the incurring of debt is stayed pending appeal, the sale of property to a good faith purchaser or a good faith extension of credit, with or without any priority or lien, shall not be affected by the reversal or modification of such order on appeal, whether or not the purchaser or creditor knows of the pendency of the appeal.

Rule 8006. Record and Issues on Appeal

Within 14 days after filing the notice of appeal as provided by Rule 8001(a), entry of an order granting leave to appeal, or entry of an order disposing of the last timely motion outstanding of a type specified in Rule 8002(b), whichever is later, the appellant shall file with the clerk and serve on the appellee a designation of the items to be included in the record on appeal and a statement of the issues to be presented. Within 14 days after the service of the appellant's statement the appellee may file and serve on the appellant a designation of additional items to be included in the record on appeal and, if the appellee has filed a cross appeal, the appellee as cross appellant shall file and serve a statement of the issues to be presented on the cross appeal and a designation of additional items to be included in the record. A cross appellee may, within 14 days of service of the cross appellant's statement, file and serve on the cross appellant a designation of additional items to be included in the record. The record on appeal shall include the items so designated by the parties, the notice of appeal, the judgment, order, or decree appealed from, and any opinion, findings of fact, and conclusions of law of the court. Any party filing a designation of the items to be included in the record shall provide to the clerk a copy of the items designated or, if the party fails to provide the copy, the clerk shall prepare the copy at the party's expense. If the record designated by any party includes a transcript of any proceeding or a part thereof, the party shall, immediately after filing the designation, deliver to the reporter and file with the clerk a written request for the transcript and make satisfactory arrangements for payment of its cost. All parties shall take any other action necessary to enable the clerk to assemble and transmit the record.

(As amended Mar. 30, 1987, eff. Aug. 1, 1987; Apr. 30, 1991, eff. Aug. 1, 1991; Apr. 29, 1994, eff. Aug. 1, 1994; Mar. 26, 2009, eff. Dec. 1, 2009.)

NOTES OF ADVISORY COMMITTEE ON RULES—1983

This rule is an adaptation of Rule 10(b) F.R.App.P. The last sentence of the rule is derived from Rule 11(a) F.R.App.P.

NOTES OF ADVISORY COMMITTEE ON RULES—1991 AMENDMENT

The seven-day time periods are changed to 10 days to conform to Rule 75(b)(2) F.R.Civ.P. and Rule 10(b)(3) F.R.App.P. The amendment requiring a party to provide a copy of the items designated for the record is to facilitate the amendments to Rule 8007 providing for retention by the bankruptcy clerk of the original record.

NOTES OF ADVISORY COMMITTEE ON RULES—1994 AMENDMENT

The amendment to the first sentence of this rule is made together with the amendment to Rule 8002(b), which provides, in essence, that certain specified postjudgment motions suspend a filed notice of appeal until the disposition of the last of such motions. The purpose of this amendment is to suspend the 10-day period for filing and serving a designation of the record and statement of the issues if a timely postjudgment motion is made and a notice of appeal is suspended under Rule 8002(b). The 10-day period set forth in the first sentence of this rule begins to run when the order disposing of the last of such postjudgment motions outstanding is entered. The other amendments to this rule are stylistic.

COMMITTEE NOTES ON RULES—2009 AMENDMENT

The rule is amended to implement changes in connection with the amendment to Rule 9006(a) and the manner by which time is computed under the rules. The deadlines in the rule are amended to substitute a deadline that is a multiple of seven days. Throughout the rules, deadlines are amended in the following manner:

- 5-day periods become 7-day periods
- 10-day periods become 14-day periods
- 15-day periods become 14-day periods
- 20-day periods become 21-day periods
- 25-day periods become 28-day periods

Rule 8007. Completion and Transmission of the Record; Docketing of the Appeal

(a) DUTY OF REPORTER TO PREPARE AND FILE TRANSCRIPT. On receipt of a request for a transcript, the reporter shall acknowledge on the request the date it was received and the date on which the reporter expects to have the transcript completed and shall transmit the request, so endorsed, to the clerk or the clerk of the bankruptcy appellate panel. On completion of the transcript the reporter shall file it with the clerk and, if appropriate, notify the clerk of the bankruptcy appellate panel. If the transcript cannot be completed within 30 days of receipt of the request the reporter shall seek an extension of time from the clerk or the clerk of the bankruptcy appellate panel and the action of the clerk shall be entered in the docket and the parties notified. If the reporter does not file the transcript within the time allowed, the clerk or the clerk of the bankruptcy appellate panel shall notify the bankruptcy judge.

(b) DUTY OF CLERK TO TRANSMIT COPY OF RECORD; DOCKETING OF APPEAL. When the record is complete for purposes of appeal, the clerk shall transmit a copy thereof forthwith to the clerk of the district court or the clerk of the bankruptcy appellate panel. On receipt of the transmission the clerk of the district court or the clerk of the bankruptcy appellate panel shall enter the appeal in the docket and give notice promptly to all parties to the judgment, order, or decree appealed from of the date on which the appeal was docketed. If the bankruptcy appellate panel directs that additional copies of the record be furnished, the clerk of the bankruptcy appellate panel shall notify the appellant and, if the appellant fails to provide the copies, the clerk shall prepare the copies at the expense of the appellant.

(c) RECORD FOR PRELIMINARY HEARING. If prior to the time the record is transmitted a party moves in the district court or before the bankruptcy appellate panel for dismissal, for a stay pending appeal, for additional security on the bond on appeal or on a supersedeas bond, or for any intermediate order, the clerk at the request of any party to the appeal shall transmit to the clerk of the district court or the clerk of the bankruptcy appellate panel a copy of the parts of the record as any party to the appeal shall designate.

(As amended Mar. 30, 1987, eff. Aug. 1, 1987; Apr. 30, 1991, eff. Aug. 1, 1991.)

NOTES OF ADVISORY COMMITTEE ON RULES—1983

Subdivision (a) is an adaptation of Rule 11(b) F.R.App.P.

Subdivision (b) is similar to former Bankruptcy Rule 807. The duty of the clerk of the bankruptcy court to transmit the record as soon as the record is complete is derived from the second paragraph of Rule 11(b) F.R.App.P. The last sentence of the subdivision applies to appeals to bankruptcy appellate panels. Additional copies of the record may be needed when the appendix to the brief required under Rule 8009(b) is not adequate in the judgment of the bankruptcy appellate panel for disposition of the appeal. If additional copies are required, the appellant will arrange for the production of the copies; if the appellant fails to do so, the clerk of the bankruptcy appellate panel shall prepare the copies at the expense of the appellant.

Subdivision (c) is derived from subdivisions (c), (e) and (f) of Rule 11 F.R.App.P. and subdivision (d) is essentially the same as Rule 11(b) F.R.App.P.

NOTES OF ADVISORY COMMITTEE ON RULES—1991 AMENDMENT

This rule is amended to require that the bankruptcy clerk retain the original record and transmit a copy of the record to the clerk of the district court or bankruptcy appellate panel. Transmission of the original documents may cause disruption in the continuing administration of the case in the bankruptcy court.

Rule 8008. Filing and Service

(a) FILING. Papers required or permitted to be filed with the clerk of the district court or the clerk of the bankruptcy appellate panel may be filed by mail addressed to the clerk, but filing is not timely unless the papers are received by the clerk within the time fixed for filing, except that briefs are deemed filed on the day of mailing. An original and one copy of all papers shall be filed when an appeal is to the district court; an original and three copies shall be filed when an appeal is to a bankruptcy appellate panel. The district court or bankruptcy appellate panel may require that additional copies be furnished. Rule 5005(a)(2) applies to papers filed with the clerk of the district court or the clerk of the bankruptcy appellate panel if filing by electronic means is authorized by local rule promulgated pursuant to Rule 8018.

(b) SERVICE OF ALL PAPERS REQUIRED. Copies of all papers filed by any party and not required by these rules to be served by the clerk of the district court or the clerk of the bankruptcy appellate panel shall, at or before the time of filing, be served by the party or a person acting for the party on all other parties to the appeal. Service on a party represented by counsel shall be made on counsel.

(c) MANNER OF SERVICE. Service may be personal or by mail. Personal service includes delivery of the copy to a clerk or other responsible person at the office of counsel. Service by mail is complete on mailing.

(d) PROOF OF SERVICE. Papers presented for filing shall contain an acknowledgment of service by the person served or proof of service in the form of a statement of the date and manner of service and of the names of the persons served, certified by the person who made service. The clerk of the district court or the clerk of the bankruptcy appellate panel may permit papers to be filed without acknowledgment or proof of service but shall require the acknowledgment or proof of service to be filed promptly thereafter.

(As amended Mar. 30, 1987, eff. Aug. 1, 1987; Apr. 23, 1996, eff. Dec. 1, 1996.)

NOTES OF ADVISORY COMMITTEE ON RULES—1983

This rule is an adaptation of Rule 25 F.R.App.P. Motions, briefs, appendices when required, statements, and any other filed paper must be accompanied by the specified number of copies. Rules 8001 and 8004 govern the number of copies of the notice of appeal which must be filed.

NOTES OF ADVISORY COMMITTEE ON RULES—1996 AMENDMENT

This rule is amended to permit, but not require, district courts and, where bankruptcy appellate panels have been authorized, circuit councils to adopt local rules that allow filing of documents by electronic means, subject to the limitations contained in Rule 5005(a)(2). See the committee note to the amendments to Rule 5005. Other amendments to this rule are stylistic.

GAP Report on Rule 8008. No changes since publication, except for stylistic changes.

Rule 8009. Briefs and Appendix; Filing and Service

(a) BRIEFS. Unless the district court or the bankruptcy appellate panel by local rule or by order excuses the filing of briefs or specifies different time limits:

(1) The appellant shall serve and file a brief within 14 days after entry of the appeal on the docket pursuant to Rule 8007.

(2) The appellee shall serve and file a brief within 14 days after service of the brief of appellant. If the appellee has filed a cross appeal, the brief of the appellee shall contain the issues and argument pertinent to the cross appeal, denominated as such, and the response to the brief of the appellant.

(3) The appellant may serve and file a reply brief within 14 days after service of the brief of the appellee, and if the appellee has cross-appealed, the appellee may file and serve a reply brief to the response of the appellant to the issues presented in the cross appeal within 14 days after service of the reply brief of the appellant. No further briefs may be filed except with leave of the district court or the bankruptcy appellate panel.

(b) APPENDIX TO BRIEF. If the appeal is to a bankruptcy appellate panel, the appellant shall serve and file with the appellant's brief excerpts of the record as an appendix, which shall include the following:

(1) The complaint and answer or other equivalent pleadings;

(2) Any pretrial order;

(3) The judgment, order, or decree from which the appeal is taken;

(4) Any other orders relevant to the appeal;

(5) The opinion, findings of fact, or conclusions of law filed or delivered orally by the court and citations of the opinion if published;

(6) Any motion and response on which the court rendered decision;

(7) The notice of appeal;

(8) The relevant entries in the bankruptcy docket; and

(9) The transcript or portion thereof, if so required by a rule of the bankruptcy appellate panel.

An appellee may also serve and file an appendix which contains material required to be included by the appellant but omitted by appellant.

(As amended Mar. 30, 1987, eff. Aug. 1, 1987; Mar. 26, 2009, eff. Dec. 1, 2009.)

NOTES OF ADVISORY COMMITTEE ON RULES—1983

Subdivision (a) of this rule is adapted from Rules 28(a) and 31(a) F.R.App.P. The introductory clause of the rule recognizes the desirability of allowing local and individual variation in the filing of briefs. The numbered paragraphs prescribe shorter periods than the corresponding periods allowed by Rule 31(a) F.R.App.P.

Subdivision (b), which is similar to an interim rule for bankruptcy appellate panels promulgated by the Ninth Circuit, applies only when an appeal is to an appellate panel. The appellant must prepare an appendix to the brief which contains the documents relevant to the appeal. With the appendix available to each member of the appellate panel, it is unlikely that multiple copies of the record will be necessary. The last sentence of the subdivision enables the appellee to correct an omission of the appellant.

Rule 30 F.R.App.P., which governs the preparation of the appendix in appeals taken to the courts of appeals, specifies fewer documents which must be included in the appendix but permits the parties to include any other material.

NOTES OF ADVISORY COMMITTEE ON RULES—1987 AMENDMENT

The amendment to Rule 8007(c) permits a rule of the bankruptcy appellate panel to provide that the record is to be retained rather than transmitted. The new paragraph (9) of subdivision (b) of this rule complements Rule 8007(c) by authorizing a rule of the panel to require inclusion of the transcript or a portion thereof in the appendix.

COMMITTEE NOTES ON RULES—2009 AMENDMENT

The rule is amended to implement changes in connection with the amendment to Rule 9006(a) and the manner by which time is computed under the rules. The deadlines in the rule are amended to substitute a deadline that is a multiple of seven days. Throughout the rules, deadlines are amended in the following manner:

- 5-day periods become 7-day periods
- 10-day periods become 14-day periods
- 15-day periods become 14-day periods
- 20-day periods become 21-day periods
- 25-day periods become 28-day periods

Rule 8010. Form of Briefs; Length

(a) FORM OF BRIEFS. Unless the district court or the bankruptcy appellate panel by local rule otherwise provides, the form of brief shall be as follows:

(1) *Brief of the Appellant.* The brief of the appellant shall contain under appropriate headings and in the order here indicated:

(A) A table of contents, with page references, and a table of cases alphabetically arranged, statutes and other authorities cited, with references to the pages of the brief where they are cited.

(B) A statement of the basis of appellate jurisdiction.

(C) A statement of the issues presented and the applicable standard of appellate review.

(D) A statement of the case. The statement shall first indicate briefly the nature of the case, the course of the proceedings, and the disposition in the court below. There shall follow a statement of the facts relevant to the issues presented for review, with appropriate references to the record.

(E) An argument. The argument may be preceded by a summary. The argument shall contain the contentions of the appellant with respect to the issues presented, and the reasons therefor, with citations to the authorities, statutes and parts of the record relied on.

(F) A short conclusion stating the precise relief sought.

(2) *Brief of the Appellee.* The brief of the appellee shall conform to the requirements of paragraph (1)(A)–(E) of this subdivision, except that a statement of the basis of appellate jurisdiction, of the issues, or of the case need not be made unless the appellee is dissatisfied with the statement of the appellant.

(b) REPRODUCTION OF STATUTES, RULES, REGULATIONS, OR SIMILAR MATERIAL. If determination of the issues presented requires reference to the Code or other statutes, rules, regulations, or similar material, relevant parts thereof shall be reproduced in the brief or in an addendum or they may be supplied to the court in pamphlet form.

(c) LENGTH OF BRIEFS. Unless the district court or the bankruptcy appellate panel by local rule or order otherwise provides, principal briefs shall not exceed 50 pages, and reply briefs shall not exceed 25 pages, exclusive of pages containing the table of contents, tables of citations and any addendum containing statutes, rules, regulations, or similar material.

NOTES OF ADVISORY COMMITTEE ON RULES—1983

This rule is derived from subdivisions (a), (b), (c), and (f) of Rule 28 F.R.App.P.

When an appeal is to a bankruptcy appellate panel and an appendix is filed pursuant to Rule 8009(b) and reference is made in a brief to parts of the record included in the appendix, the reference should be to the appropriate pages of the appendix at which those parts appear.

Rule 8011. Motions

(a) CONTENT OF MOTIONS; RESPONSE; REPLY. A request for an order or other relief shall be made by filing with the clerk of the district court or the clerk of the bankruptcy appellate panel a motion for such order or relief with proof of service on all other parties to the appeal. The motion shall contain or be accompanied by any matter required by a specific provision of these rules governing such a motion, shall state with particularity the grounds on which it is based, and shall set forth the order or relief sought. If a motion is supported by briefs, affidavits or other papers, they shall be served and filed with the motion. Any party may file a response in opposition to a motion other than one for a procedural order within seven days after service of the motion, but the district court or the bankruptcy appellate panel may shorten or extend the time for responding to any motion.

(b) DETERMINATION OF MOTIONS FOR PROCEDURAL ORDERS. Notwithstanding subdivision (a) of this rule, motions for procedural orders, including any motion under Rule 9006, may be acted on at any time, without awaiting a response thereto and without hearing. Any party adversely affected by such action may move for reconsideration, vacation, or modification of the action.

(c) DETERMINATION OF ALL MOTIONS. All motions will be decided without oral argument unless the court orders otherwise. A motion for a stay, or for other emergency relief may be denied if not presented promptly.

(d) EMERGENCY MOTIONS. Whenever a movant requests expedited action on a motion on the ground that, to avoid irreparable harm, relief is needed in less time than would normally be required for the district court or bankruptcy appellate panel to receive and consider a response, the word "Emergency" shall precede the title of the motion. The motion shall be accompanied by an affidavit setting forth the nature of the emergency. The motion shall state whether all grounds advanced in support thereof were submitted to the bankruptcy judge and, if any grounds relied on were not submitted, why the motion should not be remanded to the bankruptcy judge for reconsideration. The motion shall include the office addresses and telephone numbers of moving and opposing counsel and shall be served pursuant to Rule 8008. Prior to filing the motion, the movant shall make every practicable effort to notify opposing counsel in time for counsel to respond to the motion. The affidavit accompanying the motion shall also state when and how opposing counsel was notified or if opposing counsel was not notified why it was not practicable to do so.

(e) POWER OF A SINGLE JUDGE TO ENTERTAIN MOTIONS. A single judge of a bankruptcy appellate panel may grant or deny any request for relief which under these rules may properly be sought by motion, except that a single judge may not dismiss or otherwise decide an appeal or a motion for leave to appeal. The action of a single judge may be reviewed by the panel.

NOTES OF ADVISORY COMMITTEE ON RULES—1983

Subdivisions (a), (b) and (e) of this rule conform substantially to subdivisions (a), (b) and (c) of Rule 27 F.R.App.P. Subdivisions (c) and (d) are taken from Rule 13(c) and (d) of the Rules of the First Circuit governing appeals to bankruptcy appellate panels.

Rule 8012. Oral Argument

Oral argument shall be allowed in all cases unless the district judge or the judges of the bankruptcy appellate panel unanimously determine after examination of the briefs and record, or appendix to the brief, that oral argument is not needed. Any party shall have an opportunity to file a statement setting forth the reason why oral argument should be allowed.

Oral argument will not be allowed if (1) the appeal is frivolous; (2) the dispositive issue or set of issues has been recently authoritatively decided; or (3) the facts and legal arguments are adequately presented in the briefs and record and the decisional process would not be significantly aided by oral argument.

NOTES OF ADVISORY COMMITTEE ON RULES—1983

This rule is derived from Rule 34(a) F.R.App.P. The other details of oral argument which are covered by the remaining subdivisions of Rule 34 F.R.App.P are not in these rules and are left to local rule or order of the court.

Rule 8013. Disposition of Appeal; Weight Accorded Bankruptcy Judge's Findings of Fact

On an appeal the district court or bankruptcy appellate panel may affirm, modify, or reverse a bankruptcy judge's judgment, order, or decree or remand with instructions for further proceedings. Findings of fact, whether based on oral or documentary evidence, shall not be set aside unless clearly erroneous, and due regard shall be given to the opportunity of the bankruptcy court to judge the credibility of the witnesses.

(As amended Mar. 30, 1987, eff. Aug. 1, 1987.)

NOTES OF ADVISORY COMMITTEE ON RULES—1983

This rule accords to the findings of a bankruptcy judge the same weight given the findings of a district judge under Rule 52 F.R.Civ.P. See also Rules 7052(a) and 9014.

NOTES OF ADVISORY COMMITTEE ON RULES—1987 AMENDMENT

The amendment to this rule conforms the appellate review standard to Rule 52 F.R.Civ.P., as amended in August 1985.

Rule 8014. Costs

Except as otherwise provided by law, agreed to by the parties, or ordered by the district court or the bankruptcy appellate panel, costs shall be taxed against the losing party on an appeal. If a judgment is affirmed or reversed in part, or is vacated, costs shall be allowed only as ordered by the court. Costs incurred in the production of copies of briefs, the appendices, and the record and in the preparation and transmission of the record, the cost of the reporter's transcript, if necessary for the determination of the appeal, the premiums paid for cost of supersedeas bonds or other bonds to preserve rights pending appeal and the fee for filing the notice of appeal shall be taxed by the clerk as costs of the appeal in favor of the party entitled to costs under this rule.

(As amended Mar. 30, 1987, eff. Aug. 1, 1987.)

NOTES OF ADVISORY COMMITTEE ON RULES—1983

This rule is an adaptation of Rule 39(a), (c) and (e) of the F.R.App.P. Under this rule all costs are taxed by the clerk of the bankruptcy court.

Rule 8015. Motion for Rehearing

Unless the district court or the bankruptcy appellate panel by local rule or by court order otherwise provides, a motion for rehearing may be filed within 14 days after entry of the judgment of the district court or the bankruptcy appellate panel. If a timely motion for rehearing is filed, the time for appeal to the court of appeals for all parties shall run from the entry of the order denying rehearing or the entry of subsequent judgment.

(As amended Mar. 30, 1987, eff. Aug. 1, 1987; Mar. 26, 2009, eff. Dec. 1, 2009.)

NOTES OF ADVISORY COMMITTEE ON RULES—1983

This is an adaptation of the first sentence of Rule 40(a) F.R.App.P. The filing of a motion for rehearing does not toll the time for taking an appeal to the court of appeals from the district court or the bankruptcy appellate panel. Appeals from a district court or a bankruptcy appellate panel are to the appropriate court of appeals. Under Rule 4(a)(4) F.R.App.P. the filing of post-trial motions in the district court has the effect of vitiating any prior notice of appeal and, on the district court's disposition of those post-trial motions, a new appeal period starts. Rule 4 F.R.App.P. does not, however, contain any provision which stays or otherwise alters the time for taking an appeal to the court of appeals when a motion for rehearing is filed under Rule 8015 with the district court or bankruptcy appellate panel.

NOTES OF ADVISORY COMMITTEE ON RULES—1987 AMENDMENT

The amendment, which is derived from Rule 8002(b), Rule 4(a)(4) F.R.App.P., and Rule 11.1 Sup.Ct.R., clarifies the effect of the filing of a timely motion for rehearing. If a timely motion is filed, the appeal period to the court of appeals begins to run on the entry of an order denying the motion or the entry of a subsequent judgment.

COMMITTEE NOTES ON RULES—2009 AMENDMENT

The rule is amended to implement changes in connection with the amendment to Rule 9006(a) and the manner by which time is computed under the rules. The deadline in the rule is amended to substitute a deadline that is a multiple of seven days. Throughout the rules, deadlines are amended in the following manner:

- 5-day periods become 7-day periods
- 10-day periods become 14-day periods
- 15-day periods become 14-day periods
- 20-day periods become 21-day periods
- 25-day periods become 28-day periods

Rule 8016. Duties of Clerk of District Court and Bankruptcy Appellate Panel

(a) ENTRY OF JUDGMENT. The clerk of the district court or the clerk of the bankruptcy appellate panel shall prepare, sign and enter the judgment following receipt of the opinion of the court or the appellate panel or, if there is no opinion, following the instruction of the court or the appellate panel. The notation of a judgment in the docket constitutes entry of judgment.

(b) NOTICE OF ORDERS OR JUDGMENTS; RETURN OF RECORD. Immediately on the entry of a judgment or order the clerk of the district court or the clerk of the bankruptcy appellate panel shall transmit a notice of the entry to each party to the appeal, to the United States trustee, and to the clerk, together with a copy of any opinion respecting the judgment or order, and shall make a note of the transmission in the docket. Original papers transmitted as the record on appeal shall be returned to the clerk on disposition of the appeal.

(As amended Mar. 30, 1987, eff. Aug. 1, 1987; Apr. 30, 1991, eff. Aug. 1, 1991.)

NOTES OF ADVISORY COMMITTEE ON RULES—1983

Subdivision (a) of this rule is adapted from Rule 36 F.R.App.P. Subdivision (b) is similar to subdivisions (c) and (d) of Rule 45 F.R.App.P.

NOTES OF ADVISORY COMMITTEE ON RULES—1991 AMENDMENT

Subdivision (b) is amended to enable the United States trustee to monitor the progress of the case. The requirements of this subdivision apply to an order of the district court or bankruptcy appellate panel staying its judgment pending appeal to the court of appeals pursuant to Rule 8017(b).

Rule 8017. Stay of Judgment of District Court or Bankruptcy Appellate Panel

(a) AUTOMATIC STAY OF JUDGMENT ON APPEAL. Judgments of the district court or the bankruptcy appellate panel are stayed until the expiration of 14 days after entry, unless otherwise ordered by the district court or the bankruptcy appellate panel.

(b) STAY PENDING APPEAL TO THE COURT OF APPEALS. On motion and notice to the parties to the appeal, the district court or the bankruptcy appellate panel may stay its judgment pending an appeal to the court of appeals. The stay shall not extend beyond 30 days after the entry of the judgment of the district court or the bankruptcy appellate panel unless the period is extended for cause shown. If before the expiration of a stay entered pursuant to this subdivision there is an appeal to the court of appeals by the party who obtained the stay, the stay shall continue until final disposition by the court of appeals. A bond or other security may be required as a condition to the grant or continuation of a stay of the judgment. A bond or other security may be required if a trustee obtains a stay but a bond or security shall not be required if a stay is obtained by the United States or an officer or agency thereof or at the direction of any department of the Government of the United States.

(c) POWER OF COURT OF APPEALS NOT LIMITED. This rule does not limit the power of a court of appeals or any judge thereof to stay proceedings during the pendency of an appeal or to suspend, modify, restore, or grant an injunction during the pendency of an appeal or to make any order appropriate to preserve the status quo or the effectiveness of the judgment subsequently to be entered.

(As amended Mar. 26, 2009, eff. Dec. 1, 2009.)

NOTES OF ADVISORY COMMITTEE ON RULES—1983

This rule is derived from Rule 62 F.R.Civ.P. and Rule 41 F.R.App.P.

Subdivision (a) accords to the parties to an appeal 10 days within which to decide whether to pursue an appeal to the court of appeals. In ordinary civil litigation there is a similar opportunity. Rule 62(a) F.R.Civ.P. automatically stays enforcement of a district court's judgment in a civil action and Rule 41(a) F.R.App.P. provides that the mandate of the court of appeals shall not issue for 21 days, unless the court otherwise directs. The district court or bankruptcy appellate panel may reduce the 10 day period of this subdivision.

Subdivision (b) vests in the district courts and the bankruptcy appellate panels the same authority the courts of appeals have under Rule 41(b) F.R.App.P. to stay their judgments pending appeal. Perfection of an appeal to the court of appeals while a stay entered by the district court or bankruptcy appellate panel is in effect results in the automatic continuation of that stay during the course of the appeal in the court of appeals.

Subdivision (c) is the same as Rule 62(g) F.R.Civ.P.

COMMITTEE NOTES ON RULES—2009 AMENDMENT

The rule is amended to implement changes in connection with the amendment to Rule 9006(a) and the manner by which time is computed under the rules. The deadline in the rule is amended to substitute a deadline that is a multiple of seven days. Throughout the rules, deadlines are amended in the following manner:

- 5-day periods become 7-day periods
- 10-day periods become 14-day periods
- 15-day periods become 14-day periods
- 20-day periods become 21-day periods
- 25-day periods become 28-day periods

Rule 8018. Rules by Circuit Councils and District Courts; Procedure When There is No Controlling Law

(a) LOCAL RULES BY CIRCUIT COUNCILS AND DISTRICT COURTS.

(1) Circuit councils which have authorized bankruptcy appellate panels pursuant to 28 U.S.C. §158(b) and the district courts may, acting by a majority of the judges of the council or district court, make and amend rules governing practice and procedure for appeals from orders or judgments of bankruptcy judges to the respective bankruptcy appellate panel or district court consistent with—but not duplicative of—Acts of Congress and the rules of this Part VIII. Local rules shall conform to any uniform numbering system prescribed by the Judicial Conference of the United States. Rule 83 F.R.Civ.P. governs the procedure for making and amending rules to govern appeals.

(2) A local rule imposing a requirement of form shall not be enforced in a manner that causes a party to lose rights because of a nonwillful failure to comply with the requirement.

(b) PROCEDURE WHEN THERE IS NO CONTROLLING LAW. A bankruptcy appellate panel or district judge may regulate practice in any manner consistent with federal law, these rules, Official Forms, and local rules of the circuit council or district court. No sanction or other disadvantage may be imposed for noncompliance with any requirement not in federal law, federal rules, Official Forms, or the local rules of the circuit council or district court unless the alleged violator has been furnished in the particular case with actual notice of the requirement.

(As amended Mar. 30, 1987, eff. Aug. 1, 1987; Apr. 27, 1995, eff. Dec. 1, 1995.)

NOTES OF ADVISORY COMMITTEE ON RULES—1983

This rule is similar to Rule 47 F.R.App.P. and Rule 83 F.R.Civ.P. Local rules governing procedure before the bankruptcy courts may be promulgated under Rule 9028.

NOTES OF ADVISORY COMMITTEE ON RULES—1987 AMENDMENT

Rule 83 F.R.Civ.P. was amended in August 1985 to require greater participation by the public in the rule making process. The amendment to Rule 8018 incorporates Rule 83 F.R.Civ.P. Under 28 U.S.C. §158(b)(2), appeals may be taken to a bankruptcy appellate panel only if the district court so authorizes. If a district court does not authorize appeals to the bankruptcy appellate panel, appeals will be to the district court. This rule is amended to authorize district courts to promulgate rules for appeals.

NOTES OF ADVISORY COMMITTEE ON RULES—1995 AMENDMENT

The amendments to this rule conform to the amendments to Rule 9029. See Committee Note to the amendments to Rule 9029.

REFERENCES IN TEXT

The Federal Rules of Civil Procedure, referred to in subd. (a)(1), are set out in the Appendix to Title 28, Judiciary and Judicial Procedure.

Rule 8019. Suspension of Rules in Part VIII

In the interest of expediting decision or for other cause, the district court or the bankruptcy appellate panel may suspend the requirements or provisions of the rules in Part VIII, except Rules 8001, 8002 and 8013, and may order proceedings in accordance with the direction.

(As amended Mar. 30, 1987, eff. Aug. 1, 1987.)

NOTES OF ADVISORY COMMITTEE ON RULES—1983

This rule is derived from Rule 2 F.R.App.P.

Rule 8020. Damages and Costs for Frivolous Appeal

If a district court or bankruptcy appellate panel determines that an appeal from an order, judgment, or decree of a bankruptcy judge is frivolous, it may, after a separately filed motion or notice from the district court or bankruptcy appellate panel and reasonable opportunity to respond, award just damages and single or double costs to the appellee.

(Added Apr. 11, 1997, eff. Dec. 1, 1997.)

NOTES OF ADVISORY COMMITTEE ON RULES—1997

This rule is added to clarify that a district court hearing an appeal, or a bankruptcy appellate panel, has the authority to award damages and costs to an appellee if it finds that the appeal is frivolous. By conforming to the language of Rule 38 F.R.App.P., this rule recognizes that the authority to award damages and costs in connection with frivolous appeals is the same for district courts sitting as appellate courts, bankruptcy appellate panels, and courts of appeals.

GAP Report on Rule 8020. No changes to the published draft.

PART IX—GENERAL PROVISIONS

Rule 9001. General Definitions

The definitions of words and phrases in §101, §902 and §1101 and the rules of construction in §102 of the Code govern their use in these rules. In addition, the following words and phrases used in these rules have the meanings indicated:

(1) "Bankruptcy clerk" means a clerk appointed pursuant to 28 U.S.C. §156(b).

(2) "Bankruptcy Code" or "Code" means title 11 of the United States Code.

(3) "Clerk" means bankruptcy clerk, if one has been appointed, otherwise clerk of the district court.

(4) "Court" or "judge" means the judicial officer before whom a case or proceeding is pending.

(5) "Debtor." When any act is required by these rules to be performed by a debtor or

when it is necessary to compel attendance of a debtor for examination and the debtor is not a natural person: (A) if the debtor is a corporation, "debtor" includes, if designated by the court, any or all of its officers, members of its board of directors or trustees or of a similar controlling body, a controlling stockholder or member, or any other person in control; (B) if the debtor is a partnership, "debtor" includes any or all of its general partners or, if designated by the court, any other person in control.

(6) "Firm" includes a partnership or professional corporation of attorneys or accountants.

(7) "Judgment" means any appealable order.

(8) "Mail" means first class, postage prepaid.

(9) "Notice provider" means any entity approved by the Administrative Office of the United States Courts to give notice to creditors under Rule 2002(g)(4).

(10) "Regular associate" means any attorney regularly employed by, associated with, or counsel to an individual or firm.

(11) "Trustee" includes a debtor in possession in a chapter 11 case.

(12) "United States trustee" includes an assistant United States trustee and any designee of the United States trustee.

(As amended Mar. 30, 1987, eff. Aug. 1, 1987; Apr. 30, 1991, eff. Aug. 1, 1991; Apr. 25, 2005, eff. Dec. 1, 2005.)

NOTES OF ADVISORY COMMITTEE ON RULES—1987 AMENDMENT

The terms "bankruptcy clerk" and "clerk" have been defined to reflect that unless otherwise stated, for the purpose of these rules, the terms are meant to identify the court officer for the bankruptcy records. If a bankruptcy clerk is appointed, all filings are made with the bankruptcy clerk. If one has not been appointed, all filings are with the clerk of the district court. Rule 5005.

The rule is also amended to include a definition of "court or judge". Since a case or proceeding may be before a bankruptcy judge or a judge of the district court, "court or judge" is defined to mean the judicial officer before whom the case or proceeding is pending.

NOTES OF ADVISORY COMMITTEE ON RULES—1991 AMENDMENT

Section 582 of title 28 provides that the Attorney General may appoint one or more assistant United States trustees in any region when the public interest so requires. This rule is amended to clarify that an assistant United States trustee, as well as any designee of the United States trustee, is included within the meaning of "United States trustee" in the rules.

COMMITTEE NOTES ON RULES—2005 AMENDMENT

The rule is amended to add the definition of a notice provider and to renumber the final three definitions in the rule. A notice provider is an entity approved by the Administrative Office of the United States Courts to enter into agreements with entities to give notice to those entities in the form and manner agreed to by those parties. The new definition supports the amendment to Rule 2002(g)(4) that authorizes a notice provider to give notices under Rule 2002.

Many entities conduct business on a national scale and receive vast numbers of notices in bankruptcy cases throughout the country. Those entities can agree with a notice provider to receive their notices in a form and at an address or addresses that the creditor and notice provider agree upon. There are processes currently in use that provide substantial assurance that notices are not misdirected. Any notice provider would have to demonstrate to the Administrative Office of the United States Courts that it could provide the service in a manner that ensures the proper delivery of notice to creditors. Once the Administrative Office of the United States Courts approves the notice provider to enter into agreements with creditors, the notice provider and other entities can establish the relationship that will govern the delivery of notices in cases as provided in Rule 2002(g)(4).

Changes Made After Publication and Comment. No changes since publication.

REFERENCES IN TEXT

The Bankruptcy Act of 1898 as amended, referred to in pars. (1) and (2), is act July 1, 1898, ch. 541, 30 Stat. 544, as amended, which was classified generally to former Title 11, Bankruptcy. Sections 1(10) and 2a of this Act were classified to sections 1(10) and 11(a), respectively, of former Title 11. The Act was repealed effective Oct. 1, 1979, by Pub. L. 95–598, §§401(a), 402(a), Nov. 6, 1978, 92 Stat. 2682, section 101 of which enacted revised Title 11.

Rule 9002. Meanings of Words in the Federal Rules of Civil Procedure When Applicable to Cases Under the Code

The following words and phrases used in the Federal Rules of Civil Procedure made applicable to cases under the Code by these rules have the meanings indicated unless they are inconsistent with the context:

(1) "Action" or "civil action" means an adversary proceeding or, when appropriate, a contested petition, or proceedings to vacate an order for relief or to determine any other contested matter.

(2) "Appeal" means an appeal as provided by 28 U.S.C. §158.

(3) "Clerk" or "clerk of the district court" means the court officer responsible for the bankruptcy records in the district.

(4) "District Court," "trial court," "court," "district judge," or "judge" means bankruptcy judge if the case or proceeding is pending before a bankruptcy judge.

(5) "Judgment" includes any order appealable to an appellate court.

(As amended Mar. 30, 1987, eff. Aug. 1, 1987; Apr. 22, 1993, eff. Aug. 1, 1993.)

REFERENCES IN TEXT

The Federal Rules of Civil Procedure, referred to in text, are set out in the Appendix to Title 28, Judiciary and Judicial Procedure.

NOTES OF ADVISORY COMMITTEE ON RULES—1993 AMENDMENT

This rule is revised to include the words "district judge" in anticipation of amendments to the Federal Rules of Civil Procedure.

Rule 9003. Prohibition of Ex Parte Contacts

(a) GENERAL PROHIBITION. Except as otherwise permitted by applicable law, any examiner, any party in interest, and any attorney, accountant, or employee of a party in interest shall refrain from ex parte meetings and communications with the court concerning matters affecting a particular case or proceeding.

(b) UNITED STATES TRUSTEE. Except as otherwise permitted by applicable law, the United States trustee and assistants to and employees or agents of the United States trustee shall refrain from ex parte meetings and communications with the court concerning matters affecting a particular case or proceeding. This rule does not preclude communications with the court to discuss general problems of administration and improvement of bankruptcy administration, including the operation of the United States trustee system.

(As amended Mar. 30, 1987, eff. Aug. 1, 1987; Apr. 30, 1991, eff. Aug. 1, 1991.)

NOTES OF ADVISORY COMMITTEE ON RULES—1983

This rule regulates the actions of parties in interest and their attorneys or others employed by parties in interest. This regulation of the conduct of parties in interest and their representative is designed to insure that the bankruptcy system operates fairly and that no appearance of unfairness is created. See H. Rep. No. 95–595, 95th Cong., 1st Sess. 95 et seq. (1977).

This rule is not a substitute for or limitation of any applicable canon of professional responsibility or judicial conduct. See, *e.g.*, Canon 7, EC7–35, Disciplinary Rule 7–110(B) of the Code of Professional Responsibility: "Generally, in adversary proceedings a lawyer should not communicate with a judge relative to a matter pending before, or which is to be brought before, a tribunal over which he presides in circumstances which might have the effect or give the appearance of granting undue advantage to one party;" and Canon 3A(4) of the Code of Judicial Conduct: "A judge should . . . neither initiate nor consider ex parte or other communications concerning a pending or impending proceeding."

NOTES OF ADVISORY COMMITTEE ON RULES—1987 AMENDMENT

This rule is amended to apply to both the bankruptcy judges and the district judges of the district.

NOTES OF ADVISORY COMMITTEE ON RULES—1991 AMENDMENT

Subdivision (a) is amended to extend to examiners the prohibition on ex parte meetings and communications with the court.

Subdivision (b) is derived from Rule X–1010.

Rule 9004. General Requirements of Form

(a) LEGIBILITY; ABBREVIATIONS. All petitions, pleadings, schedules and other papers shall be clearly legible. Abbreviations in common use in the English language may be used.

(b) CAPTION. Each paper filed shall contain a caption setting forth the name of the court, the title of the case, the bankruptcy docket number, and a brief designation of the character of the paper.

NOTES OF ADVISORY COMMITTEE ON RULES—1983

Subdivision (b). Additional requirements applicable to the caption for a petition are found in Rule 1005, to the caption for notices to creditors in Rule 2002(m), and to the caption for a pleading or other paper filed in an adversary proceeding in Rule 7010. Failure to comply with this or any other rule imposing a merely formal requirement does not ordinarily result in the loss of rights. See Rule 9005.

Rule 9005. Harmless Error

Rule 61 F.R.Civ.P. applies in cases under the Code. When appropriate, the court may order the correction of any error or defect or the cure of any omission which does not affect substantial rights.

REFERENCES IN TEXT

The Federal Rules of Civil Procedure, referred to in text, are set out in the Appendix to Title 28, Judiciary and Judicial Procedure.

Rule 9005.1. Constitutional Challenge to a Statute—Notice, Certification, and Intervention

Rule 5.1 F.R.Civ.P. applies in cases under the Code.

(Added Apr. 30, 2007, eff. Dec. 1, 2007.)

COMMITTEE NOTES ON RULES—2007

The rule is added to adopt the new rule added to the Federal Rules of Civil Procedure. The new Civil Rule replaces Rule 24(c) F. R. Civ. P., so the cross reference to Civil Rule 24 contained in Rule 7024 is no longer sufficient to bring the provisions of new Civil Rule 5.1 into adversary proceedings. This rule also makes Civil Rule 5.1 applicable to all contested matters and other proceedings within the bankruptcy case.

Changes After Publication. No changes were made after publication.

REFERENCES IN TEXT

The Federal Rules of Civil Procedure, referred to in text, are set out in the Appendix to Title 28, Judiciary and Judicial Procedure.

Rule 9006. Computing and Extending Time

(a) COMPUTING TIME. The following rules apply in computing any time period specified in these rules, in the Federal Rules of Civil Procedure, in any local rule or court order, or in any statute that does not specify a method of computing time.

(1) *Period Stated in Days or a Longer Unit.* When the period is stated in days or a longer unit of time:

(A) exclude the day of the event that triggers the period;

(B) count every day, including intermediate Saturdays, Sundays, and legal holidays; and

(C) include the last day of the period, but if the last day is a Saturday, Sunday, or legal holiday, the period continues to run until the end of the next day that is not a Saturday, Sunday, or legal holiday.

(2) *Period Stated in Hours.* When the period is stated in hours:

(A) begin counting immediately on the occurrence of the event that triggers the period;

(B) count every hour, including hours during intermediate Saturdays, Sundays, and legal holidays; and

(C) if the period would end on a Saturday, Sunday, or legal holiday, then continue the period until the same time on the next day that is not a Saturday, Sunday, or legal holiday.

(3) *Inaccessibility of Clerk's Office.* Unless the court orders otherwise, if the clerk's office is inaccessible:

(A) on the last day for filing under Rule 9006(a)(1), then the time for filing is extended to the first accessible day that is not a Saturday, Sunday, or legal holiday; or

(B) during the last hour for filing under Rule 9006(a)(2), then the time for filing is extended to the same time on the first accessible day that is not a Saturday, Sunday, or legal holiday.

(4) *"Last Day" Defined.* Unless a different time is set by a statute, local rule, or order in the case, the last day ends:

(A) for electronic filing, at midnight in the court's time zone; and

(B) for filing by other means, when the clerk's office is scheduled to close.

(5) *"Next Day" Defined.* The "next day" is determined by continuing to count forward when the period is measured after an event and backward when measured before an event.

(6) *"Legal Holiday" Defined.* "Legal holiday" means:

(A) the day set aside by statute for observing New Year's Day, Martin Luther King Jr.'s Birthday, Washington's Birthday, Memorial Day, Independence Day, Labor Day, Columbus Day, Veterans' Day, Thanksgiving Day, or Christmas Day;

(B) any day declared a holiday by the President or Congress; and

(C) for periods that are measured after an event, any other day declared a holiday by the state where the district court is located. (In this rule, "state" includes the District of Columbia and any United States commonwealth or territory.)

(b) ENLARGEMENT.

(1) *In General.* Except as provided in paragraphs (2) and (3) of this subdivision, when an act is required or allowed to be done at or within a specified period by these rules or by a notice given thereunder or by order of court, the court for cause shown may at any time in its discretion (1) with or without motion or notice order the period enlarged if the request therefor is made before the expiration of the period originally prescribed or as extended by a previous order or (2) on motion made after the expiration of the specified period permit the act to be done where the failure to act was the result of excusable neglect.

(2) *Enlargement Not Permitted.* The court may not enlarge the time for taking action under Rules 1007(d), 2003(a) and (d), 7052, 9023, and 9024.

(3) *Enlargement Governed By Other Rules.* The court may enlarge the time for taking action under Rules 1006(b)(2), 1017(e), 3002(c), 4003(b), 4004(a), 4007(c), 4008(a), 8002, and 9033, only to the extent and under the conditions stated in those rules. In addition, the court may enlarge the time to file the statement required under Rule 1007(b)(7), and to file schedules and statements in a small business case under § 1116(3) of the Code, only to the extent and under the conditions stated in Rule 1007(c)

(c) REDUCTION.

(1) *In General.* Except as provided in paragraph (2) of this subdivision, when an act is required or allowed to be done at or within a specified time by these rules or by a notice given thereunder or by order of court, the court for cause shown may in its discretion with or without motion or notice order the period reduced.

(2) *Reduction Not Permitted.* The court may not reduce the time for taking action under Rules 2002(a)(7), 2003(a), 3002(c), 3014, 3015, 4001(b)(2), (c)(2), 4003(a), 4004(a), 4007(c), 4008(a), 8002, and 9033(b). In addition, the court may not reduce the time under Rule 1007(c) to file the statement required by Rule 1007(b)(7).

(d) FOR MOTIONS—AFFIDAVITS. A written motion, other than one which may be heard ex parte, and notice of any hearing shall be served not later than seven days before the time specified for such hearing, unless a different period is fixed by these rules or by order of the court. Such an order may for cause shown be made on ex parte application. When a motion is supported by affidavit, the affidavit shall be served with the motion; and, except as otherwise provided in Rule 9023, opposing affidavits may be served not later than one day before the hearing, unless the court permits them to be served at some other time.

(e) TIME OF SERVICE. Service of process and service of any paper other than process or of notice by mail is complete on mailing.

(f) ADDITIONAL TIME AFTER SERVICE BY MAIL OR UNDER RULE 5(b)(2)(D), (E), OR (F) F.R.CIV.P. When there is a right or requirement to act or undertake some proceedings within a prescribed period after service and that service is by mail or under Rule 5(b)(2)(D), (E), or (F) F.R.Civ.P., three days are added after the prescribed period would otherwise expire under Rule 9006(a).

(g) GRAIN STORAGE FACILITY CASES. This rule shall not limit the court's authority under § 557 of the Code to enter orders governing procedures in cases in which the debtor is an owner or operator of a grain storage facility.

(As amended Mar. 30, 1987, eff. Aug. 1, 1987; Apr. 25, 1989, eff. Aug. 1, 1989; Apr. 30, 1991, eff. Aug. 1, 1991; Apr. 23, 1996, eff. Dec. 1, 1996; Apr. 26, 1999, eff. Dec. 1, 1999; Apr. 23, 2001, eff. Dec. 1, 2001; Apr. 25, 2005, eff. Dec. 1, 2005; Apr. 23, 2008, eff. Dec. 1, 2008; Mar. 26, 2009, eff. Dec. 1, 2009.)

NOTES OF ADVISORY COMMITTEE ON RULES—1983

Subdivision (a). This rule is an adaptation of Rule 6 F.R.Civ.P. It governs the time for acts to be done and proceedings to be had in cases under the Code and any litigation arising therein.

Subdivision (b) is patterned after Rule 6(b) F.R.Civ.P. and Rule 26(b) F.R.App.P.

Paragraph (1) of this subdivision confers on the court discretion generally to authorize extensions of time for doing acts required or allowed by these rules or orders of court. The exceptions to this general authority to extend the time are contained in paragraphs (2) and (3).

In the interest of prompt administration of bankruptcy cases certain time periods may not be extended. Paragraph (2) lists the rules which establish time periods which may not be extended: Rule 1007(d), time for filing a list of 20 largest creditors; Rule 1017(b)(3), 30 day period for sending notice of dismissal for failure to pay the filing fee; Rule 1019(2), 20 day period for notice of conversion to a chapter 7 case; Rule 2003(a), meeting of creditors not more than 40 days after order for relief; Rule 2003(d), 10 days for filing a motion for resolution of an election dispute; Rule 3014, time for the § 1111(b)(2) election; Rule 4001(b), expiration of stay 30 days following the commencement of final hearing; Rule 7052(b), 10 day period to move to amend findings of fact; Rule 9015(f), 20 day period to move for judgment notwithstanding the verdict; Rule 9023, 10 day period to move for a new trial; and Rule 9024, time to move for relief from judgment.

Many rules which establish a time for doing an act also contain a specific authorization and standard for granting an extension of time and, in some cases, limit the length of an extension. In some instances it would be inconsistent with the objective of the rule and sound administration of the case to permit extension under Rule 9006(b)(1), but with respect to the other rules it is appropriate that the power to extend time be supplemented by Rule 9006(b)(1). Unless a rule which contains a specific authorization to extend time is listed in paragraph (3) of this subdivision, an extension of the time may be granted under paragraph (1) of this subdivision. If a rule is included in paragraph (3) an extension may not be granted under paragraph (1). The following rules are listed in paragraph (3): Rule 1006(b)(2), time for paying the filing fee in installments; Rule 3002(c), 90 day period for filing a claim in a chapter 7 or 13 case; Rule 4003(b), 30 days for filing objections to a claim of exemptions; Rule 4004(a), 60 day period to object to a discharge; Rule 4007(b), 60 day period to file a dischargeability complaint; and Rule 8002, 10 days for filing a notice of appeal.

Subdivision (c). Paragraph (1) of this subdivision authorizes the reduction of the time periods established by these rules or an order of the court. Excluded from this general authority are the time periods established by the rules referred to in paragraph (2) of the subdivision: Rule 2002 (a) and (b), 20 day and 25 day notices of certain hearings and actions in the case; Rule 2003(a), meeting of creditors to be not less than 20 days after the order for relief; Rule 3002(c), 90 days for filing a claim in a chapter 7 or 13 case; Rule 3014, time for §1111(b)(2) election; Rule 3015, 10 day period after filing of petition to file a chapter 13 plan; Rule 4003(a), 15 days for a dependent to claim exemptions; Rule 4004(a), 60 day period to object to a discharge; Rule 4007(c), 60 day period to file a dischargeability complaint; and Rule 8002, 10 days for filing a notice of appeal. Reduction of the time periods fixed in the rules referred to in this subdivision would be inconsistent with the purposes of those rules and would cause harmful uncertainty.

Subdivision (d) is derived from Rule 6(d) F.R.Civ.P. The reference is to Rule 9023 instead of to Rule 59(c) F.R.Civ.P. because Rule 9023 incorporates Rule 59 F.R.Civ.P. but excepts therefrom motions to reconsider orders allowing and disallowing claims.

Subdivision (f) is new and is the same as Rule 6(e) F.R.Civ.P.

NOTES OF ADVISORY COMMITTEE ON RULES—1987 AMENDMENT

Subdivision (a) is amended to conform to the 1984 amendments to Rule 6 F.R.Civ.P.

Subdivision (b). The reference to Rule 4001(b) in paragraph (3) is deleted because of the amendments made to Rule 4001. Rule 9033, which is new, contains specific provisions governing the extension of time to file objections to proposed findings of fact and conclusions of law. Rule 9033 is added to the rules referred to in paragraph (3).

Subdivision (c). Rule 4001(b)(2) and (c)(2) provide that a final hearing on a motion to use cash collateral or a motion for authority to obtain credit may be held no earlier than 15 days after the filing of the motion. These two rules are added to paragraph (2) to make it clear that the 15 day period may not be reduced. Rule 9033 is also added to paragraph (2).

Subdivision (g) is new. Under §557 of the Code, as enacted by the 1984 amendments, the court is directed to expedite grain storage facility cases. This subdivision makes it clear this rule does not limit the court's authority under §557.

The original Advisory Committee Note to this rule included the 25 day notice period of Rule 2002(b) as a time period which may not be reduced under Rule 9006(c)(2). This was an error.

NOTES OF ADVISORY COMMITTEE ON RULES—1989 AMENDMENT

Prior to 1987, subdivision (a) provided that intermediate weekends and legal holidays would not be counted in the computation of a time period if the prescribed or allowed time was less than 7 days. This rule was amended in 1987 to conform to Fed. R. Civ. P. 6(a) which provides for the exclusion of intermediate weekends and legal holidays if the time prescribed or allowed is less than 11 days. An undesirable result of the 1987 amendment was that 10-day time periods prescribed in the interest of prompt administration of bankruptcy cases were extended to at least 14 calendar days.

As a result of the present amendment, 10-day time periods prescribed or allowed will no longer be extended to at least 14 calendar days because of intermediate weekends and legal holidays.

NOTES OF ADVISORY COMMITTEE ON RULES—1991 AMENDMENT

As a result of the 1989 amendment to this rule, the method of computing time under subdivision (a) is not the same as the method of computing time under Rule 6(a) F.R.Civ.P. Subdivision (a) is amended to provide that it governs the computation of time periods prescribed by the Federal Rules of Civil Procedure when the Bankruptcy Rules make a civil rule applicable to a bankruptcy case or proceeding.

Subdivision (b)(2) is amended because of the deletion of Rule 1019(2). Reference to Rule 9015(f) is deleted because of the abrogation of Rule 9015 in 1987.

Subdivision (b)(3) is amended to limit the enlargement of time regarding dismissal of a chapter 7 case for substantial abuse in accordance with Rule 1017(e).

NOTES OF ADVISORY COMMITTEE ON RULES—1996 AMENDMENT

Subdivision (c)(2) is amended to conform to the abrogation of Rule 2002(a)(4) and the renumbering of Rule 2002(a)(8) to Rule 2002(a)(7).

GAP Report on Rule 9006. No changes since publication, except for a stylistic change.

COMMITTEE NOTES ON RULES—1999 AMENDMENT

Rule 9006(b)(2) is amended to conform to the abrogation of Rule 1017(b)(3).

GAP Report on Rule 9006. The proposed amendment to Rule 9006(b)(2) has been added as a technical change to conform to the abrogation of Rule 1017(b)(3). The proposed amendment to Rule 9006(c)(2), providing that the time under Rule 1019(6) to file a request for payment of an administrative expense after a case is converted to chapter 7 could not be reduced by the court, was deleted. The proposed amendments to Rule 1019(6) have been changed so that the court will fix the time for filing the request for payment. Since the court will fix the time limit, the court should have the power to reduce it. *See* GAP Report to Rule 1019(6).

COMMITTEE NOTES ON RULES—2001 AMENDMENT

Rule 5(b) F. R. Civ. P., which is made applicable in adversary proceedings by Rule 7005, is being restyled and amended to authorize service by electronic means—or any other means not otherwise authorized under Rule 5(b)—if consent is obtained from the person served. The amendment to Rule 9006(f) is intended to extend the three-day "mail rule" to service under Rule 5(b)(2)(D), including service by electronic means. The three-day rule also will apply to service under Rule 5(b)(2)(C) F. R. Civ. P. when the person served has no known address and the paper is served by leaving a copy with the clerk of the court.

Changes Made After Publication and Comments. No changes were made.

COMMITTEE NOTES ON RULES—2005 AMENDMENT

Rule 9006(f) is amended, consistent with a corresponding amendment to Rule 6(e) of the F.R. Civ. P., to clarify the method of counting the number of days to respond after service either by mail or under Civil Rule 5(b)(2)(C) or (D). Three days are added after the prescribed period expires. If, before the application of Rule 9006(f), the prescribed period is less than 8 days, intervening Saturdays, Sundays, and legal holidays are excluded from the calculation under Rule 9006(a). Some illustrations may be helpful.

Under existing Rule 9006(a), assuming that there are no legal holidays and that a response is due in seven days, if a paper is filed on a Monday, the seven day response period commences on Tuesday and concludes on Wednesday of the next week. Adding three days to the end of the period would extend it to Saturday, but because the response period ends on a weekend, the response day would be the following Monday, two weeks after the filing of the initial paper. If the paper is filed on a Tuesday, the seven-day response period would end on the following Thursday, and the response time would also be the following Monday. If the paper is mailed on a Wednesday, the initial seven-day period would expire nine days later on a Friday, but the response would again be due on the following Monday because of Rule 9006(f). If the paper is mailed on a Thursday, however, the seven day period ends on Monday, eleven days after the mailing of the service because of the exclusion of the two intervening Saturdays and Sundays. The response is due three days later on the following Thursday. If the paper is mailed on a Friday, the seven day period would conclude on a Tuesday, and the response is due three days later on a Friday.

No other change in the system of counting time is intended.

Other changes are stylistic.

Changes Made After Publication and Comment. The phrase "would otherwise expire under Rule 9006(a)" was added to the end of the rule to clarify further that the three day extension is to be added to the end of the period that is established under the counting provisions of Rule 9006(a). This also maintains a parallel construction with Civil Rule 6(e) in which the same addition to the rule was made after the public comment period.

COMMITTEE NOTES ON RULES—2008 AMENDMENT

Subdivision (b)(3) is amended to implement §1116(3) of the Code, as amended by the 2005 amendments, which places specific limits on the extension of time for filing schedules and statements of financial affairs in a small business case.

Subdivisions (b)(3) and (c)(2) are amended to provide that enlargement or reduction of the time to file the statement of completion of a personal financial management course required by Rule 1007(b)(7) are governed by Rule 1007(c). Likewise, the amendments to subdivisions (b)(3) and (c)(2) recognize that the enlargement of time to file a reaffirmation agreement is governed by Rule 4008(a), and that reduction of the time provided under that rule is not permitted.

Other amendments are stylistic.

Changes Made After Publication. Subdivision (b)(3) was amended to provide that Rule 9006 does not govern the enlargement of time to file a reaffirmation agreement, the statement required under Rule 1007(b)(7), or the time to file schedules and statements of financial affairs in small business cases. The title of subdivision (b)(3) was also amended to more accurately describe the operation of the provision. Subdivision (c)(2) was amended to recognize that the court may not reduce the time under Rule 1007(c) to file the statement required by Rule 1007(b)(7).

COMMITTEE NOTES ON RULES—2009 AMENDMENT

Subdivision (a). Subdivision (a) has been amended to simplify and clarify the provisions that describe how deadlines are computed. Subdivision (a) governs the computation of any time period found in a Federal Rule of Bankruptcy Procedure, a Federal Rule of Civil Procedure, a statute, a local rule, or a court order. In accordance with Bankruptcy Rule 9029(a), a local rule may not direct that a deadline be computed in a manner inconsistent with subdivision (a).

The time-computation provisions of subdivision (a) apply only when a time period must be computed. They do not apply when a fixed time to act is set. The amendments thus carry forward the approach taken in *Violette v. P.A. Days, Inc.*, 427 F.3d 1015, 1016 (6th Cir. 2005) (holding that Civil Rule 6(a) "does not apply to situations where the court has established a specific calendar day as a deadline"), and reject the contrary holding of *In re American Healthcare Management, Inc.*, 900 F.2d 827, 832 (5th Cir. 1990) (holding that Bankruptcy Rule 9006(a) governs treatment of date-certain deadline set by court order). If, for example, the date for filing is "no later than November 1, 2007," subdivision (a) does not govern. But if a filing is required to be made "within 10 days" or "within 72 hours," subdivision (a) describes how that deadline is computed.

Subdivision (a) does not apply when computing a time period set by a statute if the statute specifies a method of computing time. *See, e.g.*, 11 U.S.C. §527(a)(2) (debt relief agencies must provide a written notice to an assisted person "not later than 3 business days" after providing bankruptcy assistance services).

Subdivision (a)(1). New subdivision (a)(1) addresses the computation of time periods that are stated in days. It also applies to time periods that are stated in weeks, months, or years. *See, e.g.*, Federal Rule of Civil Procedure 60(c)(1) made applicable to bankruptcy cases under Rule 9024. Subdivision (a)(1)(B)'s directive to "count every day" is relevant only if the period is stated in days (not weeks, months, or years).

Under former Rule 9006(a), a period of eight days or more was computed differently than a period of less than eight days. Intermediate Saturdays, Sundays, and legal holidays were included in computing the longer periods, but excluded in computing the shorter periods. Former Rule 9006(a) thus made computing deadlines unnecessarily complicated and led to counterintuitive results.

Under new subdivision (a)(1), all deadlines stated in days (no matter the length) are computed in the same way. The day of the event that triggers the deadline is not counted. All other days—including intermediate Saturdays, Sundays, and legal holidays—are counted, with only one exception: if the period ends on a Saturday, Sunday, or legal holiday, then the deadline falls on the next day that is not a Saturday, Sunday, or legal holiday. An illustration is provided below in the discussion of subdivision (a)(5). Subdivision (a)(3) addresses filing deadlines that expire on a day when the clerk's office is inaccessible.

Where subdivision (a) formerly referred to the "act, event, or default" that triggers the deadline, new subdivision (a) refers simply to the "event" that triggers the deadline; this change in terminology is adopted for brevity and simplicity, and is not intended to change meaning.

Periods previously expressed as less than eight days will be shortened as a practical matter by the decision to count intermediate Saturdays, Sundays, and legal holidays in computing all periods. Many of those periods have been lengthened to compensate for the change. *See, e.g.*, Rules 2008 (trustee's duty to notify court of acceptance of the appointment within five days is extended to seven days); 6004(b) (time for filing and service of objection to proposed use, sale or lease of property extended from five days prior to the hearing to seven days prior to the hearing); and 9006(d) (time for giving notice of a hearing extended from five days prior to the hearing to seven days).

Most of the 10-day periods were adjusted to meet the change in computation method by setting 14 days as the new period. *See, e.g.*, Rules 1007(h) (10-day period to file supplemental schedule for property debtor becomes entitled to acquire after the commencement of the case is extended to 14 days); 3020(e) (10-day stay of order confirming a chapter 11 plan extended to 14 days); 8002(a) (10-day period in which to file notice of appeal extended to 14 days). A 14-day period also has the advantage that the final day falls on the same day of the week as the event that triggered the period—the14th day after a Monday, for example, is a Monday. This advantage of using week-long periods led to adopting seven-day periods to replace some of the periods set at less than 10 days, 21-day periods to replace 20-day periods, and 28-day periods to replace 25-day periods.Thirty-day and longer periods, however, were generally retained without change.

Subdivision (a)(2). New subdivision (a)(2) addresses the computation of time periods that are stated in hours. No such deadline currently appears in the Federal Rules of Bankruptcy Procedure. But some statutes contain deadlines stated in hours, as do some court orders issued in expedited proceedings.

Under subdivision (a)(2), a deadline stated in hours starts to run immediately on the occurrence of the event that triggers the deadline. The deadline generally ends when the time expires. If, however, the time period expires at a specific time (say, 2:17 p.m.) on a Saturday, Sunday, or legal holiday, then the deadline is extended to the same time (2:17 p.m.) on the next day that is not a Saturday, Sunday, or legal holiday. Periods stated in hours are not to be "rounded up" to the next whole hour. Subdivision (a)(3) addresses situations when the clerk's office is inaccessible during the last hour before a filing deadline expires.

Subdivision (a)(2)(B) directs that every hour be counted. Thus, for example, a 72-hour period that commences at 10:23 a.m. on Friday, November 2, 2007, will run until 9:23 a.m. on Monday, November 5; the discrepancy in start and end times in this example results from the intervening shift from daylight saving time to standard time.

Subdivision (a)(3). When determining the last day of a filing period stated in days or a longer unit of time, a day on which the clerk's office is not accessible because of the weather or another reason is treated like a Saturday, Sunday, or legal holiday. When determining the end of a filing period stated in hours, if the clerk's office is inaccessible during the last hour of the filing period computed under subdivision (a)(2) then the period is extended to the same time on the next day that is not a weekend, holiday, or day when the clerk's office is inaccessible.

Subdivision (a)(3)'s extensions apply "[u]nless the court orders otherwise." In some circumstances, the court might not wish a period of inaccessibility to trigger a full 24-hour extension; in those instances, the court can specify a briefer extension.

The text of the rule no longer refers to "weather or other conditions" as the reason for the inaccessibility of the clerk's office. The reference to "weather" was deleted from the text to underscore that inaccessibility can occur for reasons unrelated to weather, such as an outage of the electronic filing system. Weather can still be a reason for inaccessibility of the clerk's office. The rule does not attempt to define inaccessibility. Rather, the concept will continue to develop through caselaw. *See, e.g.*, William G. Phelps, *When Is Office of Clerk of Court Inaccessible Due to Weather or Other Conditions for Purpose of Computing Time Period for Filing Papers under Rule 6(a) of Federal Rules of Civil Procedure*, 135 A.L.R. Fed. 259 (1996) (collecting cases). In addition, many local provisions address inaccessibility for purposes of electronic filing. *See, e.g.*, D. Kan. Rule 5.4.11 ("A Filing User whose filing is made untimely as the result of a technical failure may seek appropriate relief from the court.").

Subdivision (a)(4). New subdivision (a)(4) defines the end of the last day of a period for purposes of subdivision (a)(1). Subdivision (a)(4) does not apply in computing periods stated in hours under subdivision (a)(2), and does not apply if a different time is set by a statute, local rule, or order in the case. A local rule may provide, for example, that papers filed in a drop box after the normal hours of the clerk's office are filed as of the day that is date-stamped on the papers by a device in the drop box.

28 U.S.C. §452 provides that "[a]ll courts of the United States shall be deemed always open for the purpose of filing proper papers, issuing and returning process, and making motions and orders." A corresponding provision exists in Rule 5001(a). Some courts have held that these provisions permit an after-hours filing by handing the papers to an appropriate official. *See, e.g.*, *Casalduc v. Diaz*, 117 F.2d 915, 917 (1st Cir. 1941). Subdivision (a)(4) does not address the effect of the statute on the question of after-hours filing; instead, the rule is designed to deal with filings in the ordinary course without regard to Section 452.

Subdivision (a)(5). New subdivision (a)(5) defines the "next" day for purposes of subdivisions (a)(1)(C) and (a)(2)(C). The Federal Rules of Bankruptcy Procedure contain both forward-looking time periods and backward-looking time periods. A forward-looking time period requires something to be done within a period of time *after* an event. *See, e.g.*, Rules 1007(c) ("[t]he schedules, statements, and other documents shall be filed by the debtor within 14 days of the entry of the order for relief"); 1019(5)(B)(ii) ("the trustee, not later than 30 days after conversion of the case, shall file and transmit to the United States trustee a final report and account"); and 7012(a) ("If a complaint is duly served, the defendant shall serve an answer within 30 days after the issuance of the summons, except when a different time is prescribed by the court.").

A backward-looking time period requires something to be done within a period of time *before* an event. *See, e.g.*, Rules 6004(b) ("an objection to a proposed use, sale, or lease of property shall be filed and served not less than seven days before the date set for the proposed action"); 9006(d) ("A written motion, other than one which may be heard ex parte, and notice of any hearing shall be served not later than seven days before the time specified for such hearing"). In determining what is the "next" day for purposes of subdivisions (a)(1)(C) and (a)(2)(C), one should continue counting in the same direction—that is, forward when computing a forward-looking period and backward when computing a backward-looking period. If, for example, a filing is due within 10 days *after* an event, and the tenth day falls on Saturday, September 1, 2007, then the filing is due on Tuesday, September 4, 2007 (Monday, September 3, is Labor Day). But if a filing is due 10 days *before* an event, and the tenth day falls on Saturday, September 1, then the filing is due on Friday, August 31.

Subdivision (a)(6). New subdivision (a)(6) defines "legal holiday" for purposes of the Federal Rules of Bankruptcy Procedure, including the time-computation provisions of subdivision (a). Subdivision (a)(6) continues to include within the definition of "legal holiday" days that are declared a holiday by the President or Congress.

For forward-counted periods—*i.e.*, periods that are measured after an event—subdivision (a)(6)(C) includes certain state holidays within the definition of legal holidays, and defines the term "state"—for purposes of subdivision (a)(6)—to include the District of Columbia and any commonwealth or territory of the United States. Thus, for purposes of subdivision (a)(6)'s definition of "legal holiday," "state" includes the District of Columbia, Guam, American Samoa, the U.S. Virgin Islands, the Commonwealth of Puerto Rico, and the Commonwealth of the Northern Mariana Islands.

However, state legal holidays are not recognized in computing backward-counted periods. For both forward- and backward-counted periods, the rule thus protects those who may be unsure of the effect of state holidays. For forward-counted deadlines, treating state holidays the same as federal holidays extends the deadline. Thus, someone who thought that the federal courts might be closed on a state holiday would be safeguarded against an inadvertent late filing. In contrast, for backward-counted deadlines, not giving state holidays the treatment of federal holidays allows filing on the state holiday itself rather than the day before. Take, for example, Monday, April 21, 2008 (Patriot's Day, a legal holiday in the relevant state). If a filing is due 14 days after an event, and the fourteenth day is April 21, then the filing is due on Tuesday, April 22 because Monday, April 21 counts as a legal holiday. But if a filing is due 14 days before an event, and the fourteenth day is April 21, the filing is due on Monday, April 21; the fact that April 21 is a state holiday does not make April 21 a legal holiday for purposes of computing this backward-counted deadline. But note that if the clerk's office is inaccessible on Monday, April 21, then subdivision (a)(3) extends the April 21 filing deadline forward to the next accessible day that is not a Saturday, Sunday or legal holiday—no earlier than Tuesday, April 22.

Changes Made After Publication. The reference to Rule 6(a)(1) in subdivision (a)(3)(A) at line 50 of the rule as it was published was corrected by referring instead to Rule 9006(a)(1).

The Standing Committee changed Rule 9006(a)(6) to exclude state holidays from the definition of "legal holiday" for purposes of computing backward-counted periods; conforming changes were made to the Committee Note to subdivision (a)(6). In addition, the term "possession" was deleted from the definition of "state" in subdivision (a)(6), and a conforming change was made to the Committee Note.

[*Subdivision (d).*] The rule is amended to implement changes in connection with the amendment to Rule 9006(a) and the manner by which time is computed under the rules. The deadline in the rule is amended to substitute a deadline that is a multiple of seven days. Throughout the rules, deadlines are amended in the following manner:

- 5-day periods become 7-day periods
- 10-day periods become 14-day periods
- 15-day periods become 14-day periods
- 20-day periods become 21-day periods
- 25-day periods become 28-day periods

Subdivision (f) is amended to conform to the changes made to Rule 5(b)(2) of the Federal Rules of Civil Procedure as a part of the Civil Rules Restyling Project. As a part of that project, subparagraphs (b)(2)(C) and (D) of that rule were rewritten as subparagraphs (b)(2)(D), (E), and (F). The cross reference to those rules contained in subdivision (f) of this rule is corrected by this amendment.

REFERENCES IN TEXT

The Federal Rules of Civil Procedure, referred to in subds. (a) and (f), are set out in the Appendix to Title 28, Judiciary and Judicial Procedure.

Rule 9007. General Authority to Regulate Notices

When notice is to be given under these rules, the court shall designate, if not otherwise specified herein, the time within which, the entities to whom, and the form and manner in which the notice shall be given. When feasible, the court may order any notices under these rules to be combined.

(As amended Mar. 30, 1987, eff. Aug. 1, 1987.)

Rule 9008. Service or Notice by Publication

Whenever these rules require or authorize service or notice by publication, the court shall, to the extent not otherwise specified in these rules, determine the form and manner thereof, including the newspaper or other medium to be used and the number of publications.

Rule 9009. Forms

Except as otherwise provided in Rule 3016(d), the Official Forms prescribed by the Judicial Conference of the United States shall be observed and used with alterations as may be appropriate. Forms may be combined and their contents rearranged to permit economies in their use. The Director of the Administrative Office of the United States Courts may issue additional forms for use under the Code. The forms shall be construed to be consistent with these rules and the Code.

(As amended Apr. 30, 1991, eff. Aug. 1, 1991; Apr. 23, 2008, eff. Dec. 1, 2008.)

NOTES OF ADVISORY COMMITTEE ON RULES—1983

The rule continues the obligatory character of the Official Forms in the interest of facilitating the processing of the paperwork of bankruptcy administration, but provides that Official Forms will be prescribed by the Judicial Conference of the United States. The Supreme Court and the Congress will thus be relieved of the burden of considering the large number of complex forms used in bankruptcy practice. The use of the Official Forms has generally been held subject to a "rule of substantial compliance" and some of these rules, for example Rule 1002, specifically state that the filed document need only "conform substantially" to the Official Form. See also Rule 9005. The second sentence recognizes the propriety of combining and rearranging Official Forms to take advantage of technological developments and resulting economies.

The Director of the Administrative Office is authorized to issue additional forms for the guidance of the bar.

NOTES OF ADVISORY COMMITTEE ON RULES—1991 AMENDMENT

Rule 9029 [9009] is amended to clarify that local court rules may not prohibit or limit the use of the Official Forms.

COMMITTEE NOTES ON RULES—2008 AMENDMENT

The rule is amended to provide that a plan proponent in a small business chapter 11 case need not use an Official Form of a plan of reorganization and disclosure statement. The use of those forms is optional, and under Rule 3016(d) the proponent may submit a plan and disclosure statement in those cases that does not conform to the Official Forms.

Changes Made After Publication. No changes were made after publication.

Rule 9010. Representation and Appearances; Powers of Attorney

(a) AUTHORITY TO ACT PERSONALLY OR BY ATTORNEY. A debtor, creditor, equity security holder, indenture trustee, committee or other party may (1) appear in a case under the Code and act either in the entity's own behalf or by an attorney authorized to practice in the court, and (2) perform any act not constituting the practice of law, by an authorized agent, attorney in fact, or proxy.

(b) NOTICE OF APPEARANCE. An attorney appearing for a party in a case under the Code shall file a notice of appearance with the attorney's name, office address and telephone number, unless the attorney's appearance is otherwise noted in the record.

(c) POWER OF ATTORNEY. The authority of any agent, attorney in fact, or proxy to represent a creditor for any purpose other than the execution and filing of a proof of claim or the acceptance or rejection of a plan shall be evidenced by a power of attorney conforming substantially to the appropriate Official Form. The execution of any such power of attorney shall be acknowledged before one of the officers enumerated in 28 U.S.C. §459, §953, Rule 9012, or a person authorized to administer oaths under the laws of the state where the oath is administered.

(As amended Mar. 30, 1987, eff. Aug. 1, 1987; Apr. 30, 1991, eff. Aug. 1, 1991.)

NOTES OF ADVISORY COMMITTEE ON RULES—1983

This rule is substantially the same as former Bankruptcy Rule 910 and does not purport to change prior holdings prohibiting a corporation from appearing *pro se*. See *In re Las Colinas Development Corp.*, 585 F.2d 7 (1st Cir. 1978).

NOTES OF ADVISORY COMMITTEE ON RULES—1987 AMENDMENT

Subdivision (c) is amended to include a reference to Rule 9012 which is amended to authorize a bankruptcy judge or clerk to administer oaths.

NOTES OF ADVISORY COMMITTEE ON RULES—1991 AMENDMENT

References to Official Form numbers in subdivision (c) are deleted in anticipation of future revision and renumbering of the Official Forms.

Rule 9011. Signing of Papers; Representations to the Court; Sanctions; Verification and Copies of Papers

(a) SIGNATURE. Every petition, pleading, written motion, and other paper, except a list, schedule, or statement, or amendments thereto, shall be signed by at least one attorney of record in the attorney's individual name. A party who is not represented by an attorney shall sign all papers. Each paper shall state the signer's address and telephone number, if any. An unsigned paper shall be stricken unless omission of the signature is corrected promptly after being called to the attention of the attorney or party.

(b) REPRESENTATIONS TO THE COURT. By presenting to the court (whether by signing, filing, submitting, or later advocating) a petition, pleading, written motion, or other paper, an attorney or unrepresented party is certifying that to the best of the person's knowledge, information, and belief, formed after an inquiry reasonable under the circumstances,—[1]

(1) it is not being presented for any improper purpose, such as to harass or to cause unnecessary delay or needless increase in the cost of litigation;

(2) the claims, defenses, and other legal contentions therein are warranted by existing law or by a nonfrivolous argument for the extension, modification, or reversal of existing law or the establishment of new law;

(3) the allegations and other factual contentions have evidentiary support or, if specifically so identified, are likely to have evidentiary support after a reasonable opportunity for further investigation or discovery; and

(4) the denials of factual contentions are warranted on the evidence or, if specifically so identified, are reasonably based on a lack of information or belief.

(c) SANCTIONS. If, after notice and a reasonable opportunity to respond, the court determines that subdivision (b) has been violated, the court may, subject to the conditions stated below, impose an appropriate sanction upon the attorneys, law firms, or parties that have violated subdivision (b) or are responsible for the violation.

(1) *How Initiated.*

(A) *By Motion.* A motion for sanctions under this rule shall be made separately from other motions or requests and shall describe the specific conduct alleged to violate subdivision (b). It shall be served as provided in Rule 7004. The motion for sanctions may not be filed with or presented to the court unless, within 21 days after service of the motion (or such other period as the court may prescribe), the challenged paper, claim, defense, contention, allegation, or denial is not withdrawn or appropriately corrected, except that this limitation shall not apply if the conduct alleged is the filing of a petition in violation of subdivision (b). If warranted, the court may award to the party prevailing on the motion the reasonable expenses and attorney's fees incurred in presenting or opposing the motion. Absent exceptional circumstances, a law firm shall be held jointly responsible for violations committed by its partners, associates, and employees.

(B) *On Court's Initiative.* On its own initiative, the court may enter an order describing the specific conduct that appears to violate subdivision (b) and directing an attorney, law firm, or party to show cause why it has not violated subdivision (b) with respect thereto.

(2) *Nature of Sanction; Limitations.* A sanction imposed for violation of this rule shall be limited to what is sufficient to deter repetition of such conduct or comparable conduct by others similarly situated. Subject to the limitations in subparagraphs (A) and (B), the sanction may consist of, or include, directives of a nonmonetary nature, an order to pay a penalty into court, or, if imposed on motion and warranted for effective deterrence, an order directing payment to the movant of some or all of the reasonable attorneys' fees and other expenses incurred as a direct result of the violation.

(A) Monetary sanctions may not be awarded against a represented party for a violation of subdivision (b)(2).

(B) Monetary sanctions may not be awarded on the court's initiative unless the court issues its order to show cause before a voluntary dismissal or settlement of the claims made by or against the party which is, or whose attorneys are, to be sanctioned.

(3) *Order.* When imposing sanctions, the court shall describe the conduct determined to constitute a violation of this rule and explain the basis for the sanction imposed.

(d) INAPPLICABILITY TO DISCOVERY. Subdivisions (a) through (c) of this rule do not apply to disclosures and discovery requests, responses, objections, and motions that are subject to the provisions of Rules 7026 through 7037.

(e) VERIFICATION. Except as otherwise specifically provided by these rules, papers filed in a case under the Code need not be verified. Whenever verification is required by these rules, an unsworn declaration as provided in 28 U.S.C. § 1746 satisfies the requirement of verification.

[1] So in original. The comma probably should not appear.

(f) COPIES OF SIGNED OR VERIFIED PAPERS. When these rules require copies of a signed or verified paper, it shall suffice if the original is signed or verified and the copies are conformed to the original.

(As amended Mar. 30, 1987, eff. Aug. 1, 1987; Apr. 30, 1991, eff. Aug. 1, 1991; Apr. 11, 1997, eff. Dec. 1, 1997.)

NOTES OF ADVISORY COMMITTEE ON RULES—1983

Subdivision (a). Excepted from the papers which an attorney for a debtor must sign are lists, schedules, statements of financial affairs, statements of executory contracts, Chapter 13 Statements and amendments thereto. Rule 1008 requires that these documents be verified by the debtor. Although the petition must also be verified, counsel for the debtor must sign the petition. See Official Form No. 1. An unrepresented party must sign all papers.

The last sentence of this subdivision authorizes a broad range of sanctions.

The word "document" is used in this subdivision to refer to all papers which the attorney or party is required to sign.

Subdivision (b) extends to all papers filed in cases under the Code the policy of minimizing reliance on the formalities of verification which is reflected in the third sentence of Rule 11 F.R.Civ.P. The second sentence of subdivision (b) permits the substitution of an unsworn declaration for the verification. See 28 U.S.C. §1746. Rules requiring verification or an affidavit are as follows: Rule 1008, petitions, schedules, statements of financial affairs, Chapter 13 Statements and amendments; Rule 2006(e), list of multiple proxies and statement of facts and circumstances regarding their acquisition; Rule 4001(c), motion for ex parte relief from stay; Rule 7065, incorporating Rule 65(b) F.R.Civ.P. governing issuance of temporary restraining order; Rule 8011(d), affidavit in support of emergency motion on appeal.

NOTES OF ADVISORY COMMITTEE ON RULES—1987 AMENDMENT

The statement of intention of the debtor under §521(2) of the Code is added to the documents which counsel is not required to sign.

NOTES OF ADVISORY COMMITTEE ON RULES—1991 AMENDMENT

Subdivision (a) is amended to conform to Rule 11 F.R.Civ.P. where appropriate, but also to clarify that it applies to the unnecessary delay or needless increase in the cost of the administration of the case. Deletion of the references to specific statements that are excluded from the scope of this subdivision is stylistic. As used in subdivision (a) of this rule, "statement" is limited to the statement of financial affairs and the statement of intention required to be filed under Rule 1007. Deletion of the reference to the Chapter 13 Statement is consistent with the amendment to Rule 1007(b).

NOTES OF ADVISORY COMMITTEE ON RULES—1997 AMENDMENT

This rule is amended to conform to the 1993 changes to F.R.Civ.P. 11. For an explanation of these amendments, see the advisory committee note to the 1993 amendments to F.R.Civ.P. 11.

The "safe harbor" provision contained in subdivision (c)(1)(A), which prohibits the filing of a motion for sanctions unless the challenged paper is not withdrawn or corrected within a prescribed time after service of the motion, does not apply if the challenged paper is a petition. The filing of a petition has immediate serious consequences, including the imposition of the automatic stay under §362 of the Code, which may not be avoided by the subsequent withdrawal of the petition. In addition, a petition for relief under chapter 7 or chapter 11 may not be withdrawn unless the court orders dismissal of the case for cause after notice and a hearing.

GAP Report on Rule 9011. The proposed amendments to subdivision (a) were revised to clarify that a party not represented by an attorney must sign lists, schedules, and statements, as well as other papers that are filed.

Rule 9012. Oaths and Affirmations

(a) PERSONS AUTHORIZED TO ADMINISTER OATHS. The following persons may administer oaths and affirmations and take acknowledgments: a bankruptcy judge, clerk, deputy clerk, United States trustee, officer authorized to administer oaths in proceedings before the courts of the United States or under the laws of the state where the oath is to be taken, or a diplomatic or consular officer of the United States in any foreign country.

(b) AFFIRMATION IN LIEU OF OATH. When in a case under the Code an oath is required to be taken a solemn affirmation may be accepted in lieu thereof.

(As amended Mar. 30, 1987, eff. Aug. 1, 1987; Apr. 30, 1991, eff. Aug. 1, 1991.)

NOTES OF ADVISORY COMMITTEE ON RULES—1983

This rule is derived from Rule 43(d) F.R.Civ.P.

The provisions of former Bankruptcy Rule 912(a) relating to who may administer oaths have been deleted as unnecessary. Bankruptcy judges and the clerks and deputy clerks of bankruptcy courts are authorized by statute to administer oaths and affirmations and to take acknowledgments. 28 U.S.C. §§459, 953. A person designated to preside at the meeting of creditors has authority under Rule 2003(b)(1) to administer the oath. Administration of the oath at a deposition is governed by Rule 7028.

NOTES OF ADVISORY COMMITTEE ON RULES—1987 AMENDMENT

Subdivision (a) has been added to the rule to authorize bankruptcy judges and clerks to administer oaths.

NOTES OF ADVISORY COMMITTEE ON RULES—1991 AMENDMENT

This rule is amended to conform to the 1986 amendment to §343 which provides that the United States trustee may administer the oath to the debtor at the §341 meeting. This rule also allows the United States trustee to administer oaths and affirmations and to take acknowledgments in other situations. This amendment also affects Rule 9010(c) relating to the acknowledgment of a power of attorney. The words "United States trustee" include a designee of the United States trustee pursuant to Rule 9001 and §102(9) of the Code.

Rule 9013. Motions: Form and Service

A request for an order, except when an application is authorized by these rules, shall be by written motion, unless made during a hearing. The motion shall state with particularity the grounds therefor, and shall set forth the relief or order sought. Every written motion other than one which may be considered ex parte shall be served by the moving party on the trustee or debtor in possession and on those entities specified by these rules or, if service is not required or the entities to be served are not specified by these rules, the moving party shall serve the entities the court directs.

(As amended Mar. 30, 1987, eff. Aug. 1, 1987.)

NOTES OF ADVISORY COMMITTEE ON RULES—1983

This rule is derived from Rule 5(a) and Rule 7(b)(1) F.R.Civ.P. Except when an application is specifically authorized by these rules, for example an application under Rule 2014 for approval of the employment of a professional, all requests for court action must be made by motion.

Rule 9014. Contested Matters

(a) MOTION. In a contested matter not otherwise governed by these rules, relief shall be requested by motion, and reasonable notice and opportunity for hearing shall be afforded the party against whom relief is sought. No response is required under this rule unless the court directs otherwise.

(b) SERVICE. The motion shall be served in the manner provided for service of a summons and complaint by Rule 7004. Any paper served after the motion shall be served in the manner provided by Rule 5(b) F. R. Civ. P.

(c) APPLICATION OF PART VII RULES. Except as otherwise provided in this rule, and unless the court directs otherwise, the following rules shall apply: 7009, 7017, 7021, 7025, 7026, 7028-7037, 7041, 7042, 7052, 7054-7056, 7064, 7069, and 7071. The following subdivisions of Fed. R. Civ. P. 26, as incorporated by Rule 7026, shall not apply in a contested matter unless the court directs otherwise: 26(a)(1) (mandatory disclosure), 26(a)(2) (disclosures regarding expert testimony) and 26(a)(3) (additional pre-trial disclosure), and 26(f) (mandatory meeting before scheduling conference/discovery plan). An entity that desires to perpetuate testimony may proceed in the same manner as provided in Rule 7027 for the taking of a deposition before an adversary proceeding. The court may at any stage in a particular matter direct that one or more of the other rules in Part VII shall apply. The court shall give the parties notice of any order issued under this paragraph to afford them a reasonable opportunity to comply with the procedures prescribed by the order.

(d) TESTIMONY OF WITNESSES. Testimony of witnesses with respect to disputed material factual issues shall be taken in the same manner as testimony in an adversary proceeding.

(e) ATTENDANCE OF WITNESSES. The court shall provide procedures that enable parties to ascertain at a reasonable time before any scheduled hearing whether the hearing will be an evidentiary hearing at which witnesses may testify.

(As amended Mar. 30, 1987, eff. Aug. 1, 1987; Apr. 26, 1999, eff. Dec. 1, 1999; Apr. 29, 2002, eff. Dec. 1, 2002; Apr. 26, 2004, eff. Dec. 1, 2004.)

NOTES OF ADVISORY COMMITTEE ON RULES—1983

Rules 1017(d), 3020(b)(1), 4001(a), 4003(d), and 6006(a), which govern respectively dismissal or conversion of a case, objections to confirmation of a plan, relief from the automatic stay and the use of cash collateral, avoidance of a lien under §552(f) of the Code, and the assumption or rejection of executory contracts or unexpired leases, specifically provide that litigation under those rules shall be as provided in Rule 9014. This rule also governs litigation in other contested matters.

Whenever there is an actual dispute, other than an adversary proceeding, before the bankruptcy court, the litigation to resolve that dispute is a contested matter. For example, the filing of an objection to a proof of claim, to a claim of exemption, or to a disclosure statement creates a dispute which is a contested matter. Even when an objection is not formally required, there may be a dispute. If a party in interest opposes the amount of compensation sought by a professional, there is a dispute which is a contested matter.

When the rules of Part VII are applicable to a contested matter, reference in the Part VII rules to adversary proceedings is to be read as a reference to a contested matter. See Rule 9002(1).

COMMITTEE NOTES ON RULES—1999 AMENDMENT

This rule is amended to delete Rule 7062 from the list of Part VII rules that automatically apply in a contested matter.

Rule 7062 provides that Rule 62 F.R.Civ.P., which governs stays of proceedings to enforce a judgment, is applicable in adversary proceedings. The provisions of Rule 62, including the ten-day automatic stay of the enforcement of a judgment provided by Rule 62(a) and the stay as a matter of right by posting a supersedeas bond provided in Rule 62(d), are not appropriate for most orders granting or denying motions governed by Rule 9014.

Although Rule 7062 will not apply automatically in contested matters, the amended rule permits the court, in its discretion, to order that Rule 7062 apply in a particular matter, and Rule 8005 gives the court discretion to issue a stay or any other appropriate order during the pendency of an appeal on such terms as will protect the rights of all parties in interest. In addition, amendments to Rules 3020, 4001, 6004, and 6006 automatically stay certain types of orders for a period of ten days, unless the court orders otherwise.

GAP Report on Rule 9014. No changes since publication.

COMMITTEE NOTES ON RULES—2002 AMENDMENT

The list of Part VII rules that are applicable in a contested matter is extended to include Rule 7009 on pleading special matters, and Rule 7017 on real parties in interest, infants and incompetent persons, and capacity. The discovery rules made applicable in adversary proceedings apply in contested matters unless the court directs otherwise.

Subdivision (b) is amended to permit parties to serve papers, other than the original motion, in the manner provided in Rule 5(b) F.R. Civ.P. When the court requires a response to the motion, this amendment will permit service of the response in the same manner as an answer is served in an adversary proceeding.

Subdivision (d) is added to clarify that if the motion cannot be decided without resolving a disputed material issue of fact, an evidentiary hearing must be held at which testimony of witnesses is taken in the same manner as testimony is taken in an adversary proceeding or at a trial in a district court civil case. Rule 43(a), rather than Rule 43(e), F.R. Civ.P. would govern the evidentiary hearing on the factual dispute. Under Rule 9017, the Federal Rules of Evidence also apply in a contested matter. Nothing in the rule prohibits a court from resolving any matter that is submitted on affidavits by agreement of the parties.

Subdivision (e). Local procedures for hearings and other court appearances in a contested matter vary from district to district. In some bankruptcy courts, an evidentiary hearing at which witnesses may testify usually is held at the first court appearance in the contested matter. In other courts, it is customary for the court to delay the evidentiary hearing on disputed factual issues until some time after the initial hearing date. In order to avoid unnecessary expense and inconvenience, it is important for attorneys to know whether they should bring witnesses to a court appearance. The purpose of the final sentence of this rule is to require that the court provide a mechanism that will enable attorneys to know at a reasonable time before a scheduled hearing whether it will be necessary for witnesses to appear in court on that particular date.

Other amendments to this rule are stylistic.

Changes Made After Publication and Comments:

The Advisory Committee made two changes to subdivision (d) after considering the comments received addressing the proposed rule. First, the word "material" is inserted to make explicit that which was implied in the published version of the proposed rule. Second, the reference to F.R.Civ.P. 43(a) was removed. The purpose of proposed subdivision (d) was to recognize that testimony should be taken in the same manner in both contested matters and adversary proceedings. The revision to the published rule states this more directly.

The Committee Note was amended to reflect the changes made in the text of the rule.

COMMITTEE NOTES ON RULES—2004 AMENDMENT

The rule is amended to provide that the mandatory disclosure requirements of Fed. R. Civ. P. 26, as incorporated by Rule 7026, do not apply in contested matters. The typically short time between the commencement and resolution of most contested matters makes the mandatory disclosure provisions of Rule 26 ineffective. Nevertheless, the court may by local rule or by order in a particular case provide that these provisions of the rule apply in a contested matter.

Changes Made After Publication. No changes since publication.

REFERENCES IN TEXT

The Federal Rules of Civil Procedure, referred to in subds. (b) and (c), are set out in the Appendix to Title 28, Judiciary and Judicial Procedure.

Rule 9015. Jury Trials

(a) APPLICABILITY OF CERTAIN FEDERAL RULES OF CIVIL PROCEDURE. Rules 38, 39, 47–49, and 51, F.R.Civ.P., and Rule 81(c) F.R.Civ.P. insofar as it applies to jury trials, apply in cases and proceedings, except that a demand made under Rule 38(b) F.R.Civ.P. shall be filed in accordance with Rule 5005.

(b) CONSENT TO HAVE TRIAL CONDUCTED BY BANKRUPTCY JUDGE. If the right to a jury trial applies, a timely demand has been filed pursuant to Rule 38(b) F.R.Civ.P., and the bankruptcy judge has been specially designated to conduct the jury trial, the parties may consent to have a jury trial conducted by a bankruptcy judge under 28 U.S.C. §157(e) by jointly or separately filing a statement of consent within any applicable time limits specified by local rule.

(c) APPLICABILITY OF RULE 50 F.R.CIV.P. Rule 50 F.R.Civ.P. applies in cases and proceedings, except that any renewed motion for judgment or request for a new trial shall be filed no later than 14 days after the entry of judgment.

(Added Apr. 11, 1997, eff. Dec. 1, 1997; amended Mar. 26, 2009, eff. Dec. 1, 2009.)

NOTES OF ADVISORY COMMITTEE ON RULES—1997

This rule provides procedures relating to jury trials. This rule is not intended to expand or create any right to trial by jury where such right does not otherwise exist.

GAP Report on Rule 9015. No changes to the published draft.

COMMITTEE NOTES ON RULES—2009 AMENDMENT

The rule is amended by deleting Rule 50 F.R.Civ.P. from the list in subdivision (a) of rules made applicable in cases and proceedings. However, subdivision (c) is added to make Rule 50 applicable in cases and proceedings, but it limits the time for filing certain post judgment motions to 14 days after the entry of judgment. The amendment is necessary because Rule 50 F.R.Civ.P. was amended in 2009 to extend the deadline for the filing of these post judgment motions to 28 days. That deadline corresponds to the 30-day deadline for filing a notice of appeal in a civil case under Rule 4(a)(1)(A) F.R.App.P. In a bankruptcy case, the deadline for filing a notice of appeal is 14 days. Therefore, the 28-day deadline for filing these post judgment motions would effectively override the notice of appeal deadline under Rule 8002(a) but for this amendment.

Other amendments are stylistic.

REFERENCES IN TEXT

The Federal Rules of Civil Procedure, referred to in text, are set out in the Appendix to Title 28, Judiciary and Judicial Procedure.

Rule 9016. Subpoena

Rule 45 F.R.Civ.P. applies in cases under the Code.

(As amended Mar. 30, 1987, eff. Aug. 1, 1987.)

NOTES OF ADVISORY COMMITTEE ON RULES—1983

Although Rule 7004(d) authorizes nationwide service of process, Rule 45 F.R.Civ.P. limits the subpoena power to the judicial district and places outside the district which are within 100 miles of the place of trial or hearing.

REFERENCES IN TEXT

The Federal Rules of Civil Procedure, referred to in text, are set out in the Appendix to Title 28, Judiciary and Judicial Procedure.

Rule 9017. Evidence

The Federal Rules of Evidence and Rules 43, 44 and 44.1 F.R.Civ.P. apply in cases under the Code.

NOTES OF ADVISORY COMMITTEE ON RULES—1983

Sections 251 and 252 of Public Law 95–598, amended Rule 1101 of the Federal Rules of Evidence to provide that the Federal Rules of Evidence apply in bankruptcy courts and to any case or proceeding under the Code. Rules 43, 44 and 44.1 of the F.R.Civ.P., which supplement the Federal Rules of Evidence, are by this rule made applicable to cases under the Code.

Examples of bankruptcy rules containing matters of an evidentiary nature are: Rule 2011, evidence of debtor retained in possession; Rule 3001(f), proof of claim constitutes prima facie evidence of the amount and validity of a claim; and Rule 5007(c), sound recording of court proceedings constitutes the record of the proceedings.

REFERENCES IN TEXT

The Federal Rules of Evidence and the Federal Rules of Civil Procedure, referred to in text, are set out in the Appendix to Title 28, Judiciary and Judicial Procedure.

Rule 9018. Secret, Confidential, Scandalous, or Defamatory Matter

On motion or on its own initiative, with or without notice, the court may make any order which justice requires (1) to protect the estate or any entity in respect of a trade secret or other confidential research, development, or commercial information, (2) to protect any entity against scandalous or defamatory matter contained in any paper filed in a case under the Code, or (3) to protect governmental matters that are made confidential by statute or regulation. If an order is entered under this rule without notice, any entity affected thereby may move to vacate or modify the order, and after a hearing on notice the court shall determine the motion.

(As amended Mar. 30, 1987, eff. Aug. 1, 1987.)

NOTES OF ADVISORY COMMITTEE ON RULES—1983

This rule provides the procedure for invoking the court's power under § 107 of the Code.

Rule 9019. Compromise and Arbitration

(a) COMPROMISE. On motion by the trustee and after notice and a hearing, the court may approve a compromise or settlement. Notice shall be given to creditors, the United States trustee, the debtor, and indenture trustees as provided in Rule 2002 and to any other entity as the court may direct.

(b) AUTHORITY TO COMPROMISE OR SETTLE CONTROVERSIES WITHIN CLASSES. After a hearing on such notice as the court may direct, the court may fix a class or classes of controversies and authorize the trustee to compromise or settle controversies within such class or classes without further hearing or notice.

(c) ARBITRATION. On stipulation of the parties to any controversy affecting the estate the court may authorize the matter to be submitted to final and binding arbitration.

(As amended Mar. 30, 1987, eff. Aug. 1, 1987; Apr. 30, 1991, eff. Aug. 1, 1991; Apr. 22, 1993, eff. Aug. 1, 1993.)

NOTES OF ADVISORY COMMITTEE ON RULES—1983

Subdivisions (a) and (c) of this rule are essentially the same as the provisions of former Bankruptcy Rule 919 and subdivision (b) is the same as former Rule 8–514(b), which was applicable to railroad reorganizations. Subdivision (b) permits the court to deal efficiently with a case in which there may be a large number of settlements.

NOTES OF ADVISORY COMMITTEE ON RULES—1991 AMENDMENT

This rule is amended to enable the United States trustee to object or otherwise be heard in connection with a proposed compromise or settlement and otherwise to monitor the progress of the case.

NOTES OF ADVISORY COMMITTEE ON RULES—1993 AMENDMENT

Subdivision (a) is amended to conform to the language of § 102(1) of the Code. Other amendments are stylistic and make no substantive change.

Rule 9020. Contempt Proceedings

Rule 9014 governs a motion for an order of contempt made by the United States trustee or a party in interest.

(As amended Mar. 30, 1987, eff. Aug. 1, 1987; Apr. 30, 1991, eff. Aug. 1, 1991; Apr. 23, 2001, eff. Dec. 1, 2001.)

NOTES OF ADVISORY COMMITTEE ON RULES—1983

Section 1481 of Title 28 provides that a bankruptcy court "may not . . . punish a criminal contempt not committed in the presence of the judge of the court or warranting a punishment of imprisonment." Rule 9020 does not enlarge the power of bankruptcy courts.

Subdivision (a) is adapted from former Bankruptcy Rule 920 and Rule 42 F.R.Crim.P. Paragraph (1) of the subdivision permits summary imposition of punishment for contempt if the conduct is in the presence of the court and is of such nature that the conduct "obstruct[s] the administration of justice." See 18 U.S.C. § 401(a). Cases interpreting Rule 42(a) F.R.Crim.P. have held that when criminal contempt is in question summary disposition should be the exception: summary disposition should be reserved for situations where it is necessary to protect the judicial institution. 3 Wright, *Federal Practice & Procedure—Criminal* § 707 (1969). Those cases are equally pertinent to the application of this rule and, therefore, contemptuous conduct in the presence of the judge may often be punished only after the notice and hearing requirements of subdivision (b) are satisfied.

If the bankruptcy court concludes it is without power to punish or to impose the proper punishment for conduct which constitutes contempt, subdivision (a)(3) authorizes the bankruptcy court to certify the matter to the district court.

Subdivision (b) makes clear that when a person has a constitutional or statutory right to a jury trial in a criminal contempt matter this rule in no way affects that right. See *Frank v. United States*, 395 U.S. 147 (1969).

The Federal Rules of Civil Procedure do not specifically provide the procedure for the imposition of civil contempt sanctions. The decisional law governing the procedure for imposition of civil sanctions by the district courts will be equally applicable to the bankruptcy courts.

NOTES OF ADVISORY COMMITTEE ON RULES—1987 AMENDMENT

The United States Bankruptcy Courts, as constituted under the Bankruptcy Reform Act of 1978, were courts of law, equity, and admiralty with an inherent contempt power, but former 28 U.S.C. § 1481 restricted the criminal contempt power of bankruptcy judges. Under the 1984 amendments, bankruptcy judges are judicial officers of the district court, 28 U.S.C. §§ 151, 152(a)(1). There are no decisions by the courts of appeals concerning the authority of bankruptcy judges to punish for either civil or criminal contempt under the 1984 amendments. This rule, as amended, recognizes that bankruptcy judges may not have the power to punish for contempt.

Sound judicial administration requires that the initial determination of whether contempt has been committed should be made by the bankruptcy judge. If timely objections are not filed to the bankruptcy judge's order, the order has the same force and effect as an order of the district court. If objections are filed within 10 days of service of the order, the district court conducts a de novo review pursuant to Rule 9033 and any order of contempt is entered by the district court on completion of the court's review of the bankruptcy judge's order.

NOTES OF ADVISORY COMMITTEE ON RULES—1991 AMENDMENT

The words "with the clerk" in subdivision (c) are deleted as unnecessary. See Rules 5005(a) and 9001(3).

COMMITTEE NOTES ON RULES—2001 AMENDMENT

The amendments to this rule cover a motion for an order of contempt filed by the United States trustee or a party in interest. This rule, as amended, does not address a contempt proceeding initiated by the court sua sponte.

Whether the court is acting on motion under this rule or is acting sua sponte, these amendments are not intended to extend, limit, or otherwise affect either the contempt power of a bankruptcy judge or the role of the district judge regarding contempt orders. Issues relating to the contempt power of bankruptcy judges are substantive and are left to statutory and judicial development, rather than procedural rules.

This rule, as amended in 1987, delayed for ten days from service the effectiveness of a bankruptcy judge's order of contempt and rendered the order subject to de novo review by the district court. These limitations on contempt orders were added to the rule in response to the Bankruptcy Amendments and Federal Judgeship Act of 1984, Pub. L. No. 98-353, 98 Stat. 333, which provides that bankruptcy judges are judicial officers of the district court, but does not specifically mention contempt power. *See* 28 U.S.C. §151. As explained in the committee note to the 1987 amendments to this rule, no decisions of the courts of appeals existed concerning the authority of a bankruptcy judge to punish for either civil or criminal contempt under the 1984 Act and, therefore, the rule as amended in 1987 "recognizes that bankruptcy judges may not have the power to punish for contempt." Committee Note to 1987 Amendments to Rule 9020.

Since 1987, several courts of appeals have held that bankruptcy judges have the power to issue civil contempt orders. *See, e.g., Matter of Terrebonne Fuel and Lube, Inc.*, 108 F.3d 609 (5th Cir. 1997); *In re Rainbow Magazine, Inc.*, 77 F.3d 278 (9th Cir. 1996). Several courts have distinguished between a bankruptcy judge's civil contempt power and criminal contempt power. *See, e.g., Matter of Terrebonne Fuel and Lube, Inc.*, 108 F.3d at 613, n. 3 ("[a]lthough we find that bankruptcy judge's [sic] can find a party in civil contempt, we must point out that bankruptcy courts lack the power to hold persons in criminal contempt."). For other decisions regarding criminal contempt power, *see, e.g., In re Ragar*, 3 F.3d 1174 (8th Cir. 1993); *Matter of Hipp, Inc.*, 895 F.2d 1503 (5th Cir. 1990). To the extent that Rule 9020, as amended in 1987, delayed the effectiveness of civil contempt orders and required de novo review by the district court, the rule may have been unnecessarily restrictive in view of judicial decisions recognizing that bankruptcy judges have the power to hold parties in civil contempt.

Subdivision (d), which provides that the rule shall not be construed to impair the right to trial by jury, is deleted as unnecessary and is not intended to deprive any party of the right to a jury trial when it otherwise exists.

Changes Made After Publication and Comments. No changes were made in the text of the proposed amendments. Stylistic changes were made to the Committee Note.

Rule 9021. Entry of Judgment

A judgment or order is effective when entered under Rule 5003.

(As amended Mar. 30, 1987, eff. Aug. 1, 1987; Mar. 26, 2009, eff. Dec. 1, 2009.)

NOTES OF ADVISORY COMMITTEE ON RULES—1983

Subdivision (a). This rule is derived from Rule 58 F.R.Civ.P. The requirement that a judgment entered in an adversary proceeding or contested matter be set forth on a separate document is to eliminate uncertainty as to whether an opinion or memorandum of the court is a judgment. There is no sound reason to require that every order in a case under the Code be evidenced by a separate document.

Subdivision (b) establishes a procedure for entering a judgment of a bankruptcy court for the recovery of money or property in an index of judgments kept by the clerk of the district court. It clarifies the availability of the same remedies for the enforcement of a bankruptcy court judgment as those provided for the enforcement of a district court judgment. See 28 U.S.C. §§1961–63. When indexed in accordance with subdivision (b) of this rule a judgment of the bankruptcy court may be found by anyone searching for liens of record in the judgment records of the district court. Certification of a copy of the judgment to the clerk of the district court provides a basis for registration of the judgment pursuant to 28 U.S.C. §1963 in any other district. When so registered, the judgment may be enforced by issuance of execution and orders for supplementary proceedings that may be served anywhere within the state where the registering court sits. See 7 Moore, *Federal Practice* 2409–11 (2d ed. 1971). The procedures available in the district court are not exclusive, however, and the holder of a judgment entered by the bankruptcy court may use the remedies under Rules 7069 and 7070 even if the judgment is indexed by the clerk of the district court.

Subdivision (c) makes it clear that when a district court hears a matter reserved to it by 28 U.S.C. §§1471, 1481, its judgments are entered in the district court's civil docket and in the docket of the bankruptcy court. When the district court acts as an appellate court, Rule 8016(a) governs the entry of judgments on appeal.

NOTES OF ADVISORY COMMITTEE ON RULES—1987 AMENDMENT

Former subdivision (a) was derived from Rule 58 F.R.Civ.P. As amended, Rule 9021 adopts Rule 58. The reference in Rule 58 to Rule 79(a) F.R.Civ.P. is to be read as a reference to Rule 5003.

COMMITTEE NOTES ON RULES—2009 AMENDMENT

The rule is amended in connection with the amendment that adds Rule 7058. The entry of judgment in adversary proceedings is governed by Rule 7058, and the entry of a judgment or order in all other proceedings is governed by this rule.

Changes Made After Publication. No changes since publication.

REFERENCES IN TEXT

The Federal Rules of Civil Procedure, referred to in text, are set out in the Appendix to Title 28, Judiciary and Judicial Procedure.

Rule 9022. Notice of Judgment or Order

(a) JUDGMENT OR ORDER OF BANKRUPTCY JUDGE. Immediately on the entry of a judgment or order the clerk shall serve a notice of entry in the manner provided in Rule 5(b) F.R.Civ.P. on the contesting parties and on other entities as the court directs. Unless the case is a chapter 9 municipality case, the clerk shall forthwith transmit to the United States trustee a copy of the judgment or order. Service of the notice shall be noted in the docket. Lack of notice of the entry does not affect the time to appeal or relieve or authorize the court to relieve a party for failure to appeal within the time allowed, except as permitted in Rule 8002.

(b) JUDGMENT OR ORDER OF DISTRICT JUDGE. Notice of a judgment or order entered by a district judge is governed by Rule 77(d) F.R.Civ.P. Unless the case is a chapter 9 municipality case, the clerk shall forthwith transmit to the United States trustee a copy of a judgment or order entered by a district judge.

(As amended Mar. 30, 1987, eff. Aug. 1, 1987; Apr. 30, 1991, eff. Aug. 1, 1991; Apr. 23, 2001, eff. Dec. 1, 2001.)

NOTES OF ADVISORY COMMITTEE ON RULES—1983

Subdivision (a) of this rule is an adaptation of Rule 77(d) F.R.Civ.P.

Subdivision (b) complements Rule 9021(b). When a district court acts as an appellate court, Rule 8016(b) requires the clerk to give notice of the judgment on appeal

NOTES OF ADVISORY COMMITTEE ON RULES—1991 AMENDMENT

This rule is amended to enable the United States trustee to be informed of all developments in the case so that administrative and supervisory functions provided in 28 U.S.C. §586(a) may be performed.

COMMITTEE NOTES ON RULES—2001 AMENDMENT

Rule 5(b) F.R.Civ.P., which is made applicable in adversary proceedings by Rule 7005, is being restyled and amended to authorize service by electronic means—or any other means not otherwise authorized under Rule 5(b)—if consent is obtained from the person served. The amendment to Rule 9022(a) authorizes the clerk to serve notice of entry of a judgment or order by electronic means if the person served consents, or to use any other means of service authorized under Rule 5(b), including service by mail. This amendment conforms to the amendments made to Rule 77(d) F.R.Civ.P.

Changes Made After Publication and Comments. No changes were made.

REFERENCES IN TEXT

The Federal Rules of Civil Procedure, referred to in subd. (b), are set out in the Appendix to Title 28, Judiciary and Judicial Procedure.

Rule 9023. New Trials; Amendment of Judgments

Except as provided in this rule and Rule 3008, Rule 59 F.R.Civ.P. applies in cases under the Code. A motion for a new trial or to alter or amend a judgment shall be filed, and a court may on its own order a new trial, no later than 14 days after entry of judgment.

(As amended Mar. 26, 2009, eff. Dec. 1, 2009.)

NOTES OF ADVISORY COMMITTEE ON RULES—1983

Rule 59 F.R.Civ.P. regulates motions for a new trial and amendment of judgment. Those motions must be served within 10 days of the entry of judgment. No similar time limit is contained in Rule 3008 which governs reconsideration of claims.

COMMITTEE NOTES ON RULES—2009 AMENDMENT

The rule is amended to limit to 14 days the time for a party to file a post judgment motion for a new trial and for the court to order sua sponte a new trial. In 2009, Rule 59 F. R. Civ. P. was amended to extend the deadline for these actions to 28 days after the entry of judgment. That deadline corresponds to the 30-day deadline for filing a notice of appeal in a civil case under Rule 4(a)(1)(A) F.R.App.P. In a bankruptcy case, however, the deadline for filing a notice of appeal is 14 days. Therefore, the 28-day deadline for filing a motion for a new trial or a motion to alter or amend a judgment would effectively override the notice of appeal deadline under Rule 8002(a) but for this amendment.

REFERENCES IN TEXT

The Federal Rules of Civil Procedure, referred to in text, are set out in the Appendix to Title 28, Judiciary and Judicial Procedure.

Rule 9024. Relief from Judgment or Order

Rule 60 F.R.Civ.P. applies in cases under the Code except that (1) a motion to reopen a case under the Code or for the reconsideration of an order allowing or disallowing a claim against the estate entered without a contest is not subject to the one year limitation prescribed in Rule 60(c), (2) a complaint to revoke a discharge in a chapter 7 liquidation case may be filed only within the time allowed by §727(e) of the Code, and (3) a complaint to revoke an order confirming a plan may be filed only within the time allowed by §1144, §1230, or §1330.

(As amended Apr. 30, 1991, eff. Aug. 1, 1991; Apr. 23, 2008, eff. Dec. 1, 2008.)

NOTES OF ADVISORY COMMITTEE ON RULES—1983

Motions to reopen cases are governed by Rule 5010. Reconsideration of orders allowing and disallowing claims is governed by Rule 3008. For the purpose of this rule all orders of the bankruptcy court are subject to Rule 60 F.R.Civ.P.

Pursuant to §727(e) of the Code a complaint to revoke a discharge must be filed within one year of the entry of the discharge or, when certain grounds of revocation are asserted, the later of one year after the entry of the discharge or the date the case is closed. Under §1144 and §1330 of the Code a party must file a complaint to revoke an order confirming a chapter 11 or 13 plan within 180 days of its entry. Clauses (2) and (3) of this rule make it clear that the time periods established by §§727(e), 1144 and 1330 of the Code may not be circumvented by the invocation of F.R.Civ.P. 60(b).

NOTES OF ADVISORY COMMITTEE ON RULES—1991 AMENDMENT

Clause (3) is amended to include a reference to §1230 of the Code which contains time limitations relating to revocation of confirmation of a chapter 12 plan. The time periods prescribed by §1230 may not be circumvented by the invocation of F.R.Civ.P. 60(b).

COMMITTEE NOTES ON RULES—2008 AMENDMENT

The rule is amended to conform to the changes made to the Federal Rules of Civil Procedure through the restyling of those rules effective on December 1, 2007.

REFERENCES IN TEXT

The Federal Rules of Civil Procedure, referred to in text, are set out in the Appendix to Title 28, Judiciary and Judicial Procedure.

Rule 9025. Security: Proceedings Against Sureties

Whenever the Code or these rules require or permit the giving of security by a party, and security is given in the form of a bond or stipulation or other undertaking with one or more sureties, each surety submits to the jurisdiction of the court, and liability may be determined in an adversary proceeding governed by the rules in Part VII.

NOTES OF ADVISORY COMMITTEE ON RULES—1983

This rule is an adaptation of Rule 65.1 F.R.Civ.P. and applies to any surety on a bond given pursuant to §303(e) of the Code, Rules 2001, 2010, 5008, 7062, 7065, 8005, or any other rule authorizing the giving of such security.

Rule 9026. Exceptions Unnecessary

Rule 46 F.R.Civ.P. applies in cases under the Code.

REFERENCES IN TEXT

The Federal Rules of Civil Procedure, referred to in text, are set out in the Appendix to Title 28, Judiciary and Judicial Procedure.

Rule 9027. Removal

(a) NOTICE OF REMOVAL.

(1) *Where Filed; Form and Content.* A notice of removal shall be filed with the clerk for the district and division within which is located the state or federal court where the civil action is pending. The notice shall be signed pursuant to Rule 9011 and contain a short and plain statement of the facts which entitle the party filing the notice to remove, contain a statement that upon removal of the claim or cause of action the proceeding is core or non-core and, if non-core, that the party filing the notice does or does not consent to entry of final orders or judgment by the bankruptcy judge, and be accompanied by a copy of all process and pleadings.

(2) *Time for Filing; Civil Action Initiated Before Commencement of the Case Under the Code.* If the claim or cause of action in a civil action is pending when a case under the Code is commenced, a notice of removal may be filed only within the longest of (A) 90 days after the order for relief in the case under the Code, (B) 30 days after entry of an order terminating a stay, if the claim or cause of action in a civil action has been stayed under §362 of the Code, or (C) 30 days after a trustee qualifies in a chapter 11 reorganization case but not later than 180 days after the order for relief.

(3) *Time for filing; civil action initiated after commencement of the case under the Code.* If a claim or cause of action is asserted in another court after the commencement of a case under the Code, a notice of removal may be filed with the clerk only within the shorter of (A) 30 days after receipt, through service or otherwise, of a copy of the initial pleading setting forth the claim or cause of action sought to be removed, or (B) 30 days after receipt of the summons if the initial pleading has been filed with the court but not served with the summons.

(b) NOTICE. Promptly after filing the notice of removal, the party filing the notice shall serve a copy of it on all parties to the removed claim or cause of action.

(c) FILING IN NON-BANKRUPTCY COURT. Promptly after filing the notice of removal, the party filing the notice shall file a copy of it with the clerk of the court from which the claim or cause of action is removed. Removal of the claim or cause of action is effected on such filing of a copy of the notice of removal. The parties shall proceed no further in that court unless and until the claim or cause of action is remanded.

(d) REMAND. A motion for remand of the removed claim or cause of action shall be governed by Rule 9014 and served on the parties to the removed claim or cause of action.

(e) PROCEDURE AFTER REMOVAL.

(1) After removal of a claim or cause of action to a district court the district court or, if the case under the Code has been referred to a bankruptcy judge of the district, the bankruptcy judge, may issue all necessary orders and process to bring before it all proper parties whether served by process issued by the court from which the claim or cause of action was removed or otherwise.

(2) The district court or, if the case under the Code has been referred to a bankruptcy judge of the district, the bankruptcy judge, may require the party filing the notice of removal to file with the clerk copies of all records and proceedings relating to the claim or cause of action in the court from which the claim or cause of action was removed.

(3) Any party who has filed a pleading in connection with the removed claim or cause of action, other than the party filing the notice of removal, shall file a statement admitting or denying any allegation in the notice of removal that upon removal of the claim or cause of action the proceeding is core or non-core. If the statement alleges that the proceeding is non-core, it shall state that the party does or does not consent to entry of final orders or judgment by the bankruptcy judge. A statement required by this paragraph shall be signed pursuant to Rule 9011 and shall be filed not later than 14 days after the filing of the notice of removal. Any party who files a statement pursuant to this paragraph shall mail a copy to every other party to the removed claim or cause of action.

(f) PROCESS AFTER REMOVAL. If one or more of the defendants has not been served with process, the service has not been perfected prior to removal, or the process served proves to be defective, such process or service may be completed or new process issued pursuant to Part VII of these rules. This subdivision shall not deprive any defendant on whom process is served after removal of the defendant's right to move to remand the case.

(g) APPLICABILITY OF PART VII. The rules of Part VII apply to a claim or cause of action removed to a district court from a federal or state court and govern procedure after removal. Repleading is not necessary unless the court so orders. In a removed action in which the defendant has not answered, the defendant shall answer or present the other defenses or objections available under the rules of Part VII within 21 days following the receipt through service or otherwise of a copy of the initial pleading setting forth the claim for relief on which the action or proceeding is based, or within 21 days following the service of summons on such initial pleading, or within seven days following the filing of the notice of removal, whichever period is longest.

(h) RECORD SUPPLIED. When a party is entitled to copies of the records and proceedings in any civil action or proceeding in a federal or a state court, to be used in the removed civil action or proceeding, and the clerk of the federal or state court, on demand accompanied by payment or tender of the lawful fees, fails to deliver certified copies, the court may, on affidavit reciting the facts, direct such record to be supplied by affidavit or otherwise. Thereupon the proceedings, trial and judgment may be had in the court, and all process awarded, as if certified copies had been filed.

(i) ATTACHMENT OR SEQUESTRATION; SECURITIES. When a claim or cause of action is removed to a district court, any attachment or sequestration of property in the court from which the claim or cause of action was removed shall hold the property to answer the final judgment or decree in the same manner as the property would have been held to answer final judgment or decree had it been rendered by the court from which the claim or cause of action was removed. All bonds, undertakings, or security given by either party to the claim or cause of action prior to its removal shall remain valid and effectual notwithstanding such removal. All injunctions issued, orders entered and other proceedings had prior to removal shall remain in full force and effect until dissolved or modified by the court.

(As amended Mar. 30, 1987, eff. Aug. 1, 1987; Apr. 30, 1991, eff. Aug. 1, 1991; Apr. 29, 2002, eff. Dec. 1, 2002; Mar. 26, 2009, eff. Dec. 1, 2009.)

NOTES OF ADVISORY COMMITTEE ON RULES—1983

Under 28 U.S.C. §1478(a) "any claim or cause of action in a civil action, other than a proceeding before the

United States Tax Court or a civil action by a Government unit to enforce [a] . . . regulatory or police power" may be removed "if the bankruptcy courts have jurisdiction over such claim or cause of action." This rule specifies how removal is accomplished, the procedure thereafter, and the procedure to request remand of the removed claim or cause of action. If the claim or cause of action which is removed to the bankruptcy court is subject to the automatic stay of §362 of the Code, the litigation may not proceed in the bankruptcy court until relief from the stay is granted.

The subdivisions of this rule conform substantially to 28 U.S.C. §§1446–1450 and Rule 81(a) F.R.Civ.P. pertaining to removal to the district courts.

Subdivision (a)(1) is derived from 28 U.S.C. §1446(a).

Subdivisions (a)(2) and (a)(3) are derived from paragraphs one and two of 28 U.S.C. §1446(b). Timely exercise of the right to remove is as important in bankruptcy cases as in removals from a state court to a district court.

Subdivision (a)(2) governs the situation in which there is litigation pending and a party to the litigation becomes a debtor under the Code. Frequently, removal would be of little utility in such cases because the pending litigation will be stayed by §362(a) on commencement of the case under the Code. As long as the stay remains in effect there is no reason to impose a time limit for removal to the bankruptcy court and, therefore, clause (B) of subdivision (a)(2) provides that a removal application may be filed within 30 days of entry of an order terminating the stay. Parties to stayed litigation will not be required to act immediately on commencement of a case under the Code to protect their right to remove. If the pending litigation is not stayed by §362(a) of the Code, the removal application must ordinarily be filed within 90 days of the order for relief. Clause (C) contains an alternative period for a chapter 11 case. If a trustee is appointed, the removal application may be filed within 30 days of the trustee's qualification, provided that the removal application is filed not more than 180 days after the order for relief.

The removal application must be filed within the longest of the three possible periods. For example, in a chapter 11 case if the 90 day period expires but a trustee is appointed shortly thereafter, the removal application may be filed within 30 days of the trustee's qualification but not later than 180 days after the order for relief. Nevertheless, if the claim or cause of action in the civil action is stayed under §362, the application may be filed after the 180 day period expires, provided the application is filed within 30 days of an order terminating the stay.

Subdivision (a)(3) applies to the situation in which the case under the Code is pending when the removable claim or cause of action is asserted in a civil action initiated in other than the bankruptcy court. The time for filing the application for removal begins to run on receipt of the first pleading containing the removable claim or cause of action. Only litigation not stayed by the Code or by court order may properly be initiated after the case under the Code is commenced. See *e.g.*, §362(a).

Subdivision (b). With one exception, this subdivision is the same as 28 U.S.C. §1446(d). The exemption from the bond requirement is enlarged to include a trustee or debtor in possession. Complete exemption from the bond requirement for removal is appropriate because of the limited resources which may be available at the beginning of a case and the small probability that an action will be improperly removed.

Recovery on the bond is permitted only when the removal was improper. If the removal is proper but the bankruptcy court orders the action remanded on equitable grounds, 28 U.S.C. §1478(b), there is no recovery on the bond.

Subdivisions (c) and (d) are patterned on 28 U.S.C. §1446(e).

Subdivision (e). There is no provision in the Federal Rules of Civil Procedure for seeking remand. The first sentence of this subdivision requires that a request for remand be by motion and that the moving party serve all other parties; however, no hearing is required. In recognition of the intrusion of the removal practice on the state and federal courts from which claims or causes of action are removed, the subdivision directs the bankruptcy court to decide remand motions as soon as practicable. The last sentence of this subdivision is derived from 28 U.S.C. §1446(c)

Subdivisions (f) and (g), with appropriate changes to conform them to the bankruptcy context, are the same as 28 U.S.C. §1447(a) and (b) and 28 U.S.C. §1448, respectively.

Subdivisions (h) and (i) are taken from Rule 81(c) F.R.Civ.P.

Subdivisions (j) and (k) are derived from 28 U.S.C. §1449 and §1450, respectively.

Remand orders of bankruptcy judges are not appealable. 28 U.S.C. §1478(b).

This rule does not deal with the question whether a single plaintiff or defendant may remove a claim or cause of action if there are two or more plaintiffs or defendants. See 28 U.S.C. §1478.

NOTES OF ADVISORY COMMITTEE ON RULES—1987 AMENDMENT

Section 1452 of title 28, with certain exceptions, provides for removal of claims or causes of action in civil actions pending in state or federal courts when the claim or cause of action is within the jurisdiction conferred by 28 U.S.C. §1334. An order granting or denying a motion for remand is not appealable. 28 U.S.C. §1452(b). Under subdivision (e), as amended, the district court must enter the order on the remand motion; however, the bankruptcy judge conducts the initial hearing on the motion and files a report and recommendation. The parties may file objections. Review of the report and recommendation is pursuant to Rule 9033.

Subdivision (f) has been amended to provide that if there has been a referral pursuant to 28 U.S.C. §157(a) the bankruptcy judge will preside over the removed civil action.

Subdivision (i) has been abrogated consistent with the abrogation of Rule 9015.

NOTES OF ADVISORY COMMITTEE ON RULES—1991 AMENDMENT

The abrogation of subdivision (b) is consistent with the repeal of 28 U.S.C. §1446(d). The changes substituting the notice of removal for the application for removal conform to the 1988 amendments to 28 U.S.C. §1446.

Rules 7008(a) and 7012(b) were amended in 1987 to require parties to allege in pleadings whether a proceeding is core or non-core and, if non-core, whether the parties consent to the entry of final orders or judgment by the bankruptcy judge. Subdivision (a)(1) is amended and subdivision (f)(3) is added to require parties to a removed claim or cause of action to make the same allegations. The party filing the notice of removal must include the allegation in the notice and the other parties who have filed pleadings must respond to the allegation in a separate statement filed within 10 days after removal. However, if a party to the removed claim or cause of action has not filed a pleading prior to removal, there is no need to file a separate statement under subdivision (f)(3) because the allegation must be included in the responsive pleading filed pursuant to Rule 7012(b).

Subdivision (e), redesignated as subdivision (d), is amended to delete the restriction that limits the role of the bankruptcy court to the filing of a report and recommendation for disposition of a motion for remand under 28 U.S.C. §1452(b). This amendment is consistent with §309(c) of the Judicial Improvements Act of 1990, which amended §1452(b) so that it allows an appeal to the district court of a bankruptcy court's order determining a motion for remand. This subdivision is also amended to clarify that the motion is a contested matter governed by Rule 9014. The words "filed with the clerk" are deleted as unnecessary. See Rules 5005(a) and 9001(3).

COMMITTEE NOTES ON RULES—2002 AMENDMENT

Subdivision (a)(3) is amended to clarify that if a claim or cause of action is initiated after the commencement of a bankruptcy case, the time limits for filing a notice of removal of the claim or cause of action apply whether the case is still pending or has been suspended, dismissed, or closed.

Changes Made After Publication and Comments. No changes were made.

COMMITTEE NOTES ON RULES—2009 AMENDMENT

The rule is amended to implement changes in connection with the amendment to Rule 9006(a) and the manner by which time is computed under the rules. The deadlines in the rule are amended to substitute a deadline that is a multiple of seven days. Throughout the rules, deadlines are amended in the following manner:

- 5-day periods become 7-day periods
- 10-day periods become 14-day periods
- 15-day periods become 14-day periods
- 20-day periods become 21-day periods
- 25-day periods become 28-day periods

Rule 9028. Disability of a Judge

Rule 63 F.R.Civ.P. applies in cases under the Code.

(As amended Mar. 30, 1987, eff. Aug. 1, 1987.)

NOTES OF ADVISORY COMMITTEE ON RULES—1983

This rule is an adaptation of Rule 63 F.R.Civ.P.

NOTES OF ADVISORY COMMITTEE ON RULES—1987 AMENDMENT

Rule 9028 has been changed to adopt the procedures contained in Rule 63 of the Federal Rules of Civil Procedure for substituting a judge in the event of disability.

REFERENCES IN TEXT

The Federal Rules of Civil Procedure, referred to in text, are set out in the Appendix to Title 28, Judiciary and Judicial Procedure.

Rule 9029. Local Bankruptcy Rules; Procedure When There is No Controlling Law

(a) LOCAL BANKRUPTCY RULES.

(1) Each district court acting by a majority of its district judges may make and amend rules governing practice and procedure in all cases and proceedings within the district court's bankruptcy jurisdiction which are consistent with—but not duplicative of—Acts of Congress and these rules and which do not prohibit or limit the use of the Official Forms. Rule 83 F.R.Civ.P. governs the procedure for making local rules. A district court may authorize the bankruptcy judges of the district, subject to any limitation or condition it may prescribe and the requirements of 83 F.R.Civ.P., to make and amend rules of practice and procedure which are consistent with—but not duplicative of—Acts of Congress and these rules and which do not prohibit or limit the use of the Official Forms. Local rules shall conform to any uniform numbering system prescribed by the Judicial Conference of the United States.

(2) A local rule imposing a requirement of form shall not be enforced in a manner that causes a party to lose rights because of a nonwillful failure to comply with the requirement.

(b) PROCEDURE WHEN THERE IS NO CONTROLLING LAW. A judge may regulate practice in any manner consistent with federal law, these rules, Official Forms, and local rules of the district. No sanction or other disadvantage may be imposed for noncompliance with any requirement not in federal law, federal rules, Official Forms, or the local rules of the district unless the alleged violator has been furnished in the particular case with actual notice of the requirement.

(As amended Mar. 30, 1987, eff. Aug. 1, 1987; Apr. 30, 1991, eff. Aug. 1, 1991; Apr. 27, 1995, eff. Dec. 1, 1995.)

NOTES OF ADVISORY COMMITTEE ON RULES—1983

This rule is an adaptation of Rule 83 F.R.Civ.P. and Rule 57(a) F.R.Crim.P. Under this rule bankruptcy courts may make local rules which govern practice before those courts. Circuit councils and district courts are authorized by Rule 8018 to make local rules governing appellate practice.

NOTES OF ADVISORY COMMITTEE ON RULES—1987 AMENDMENT

Rule 9029 is amended to authorize the district court to promulgate local rules governing bankruptcy practice. This rule, as amended, permits the district court to authorize the bankruptcy judges to promulgate or recommend local rules for adoption by the district court.

Effective August 1, 1985, Rule 83 F.R.Civ.P., governing adoption of local rules, was amended to achieve greater participation by the bar, scholars, and the public in the rule making process; to authorize the judicial council to abrogate local rules; and to make certain that single-judge standing orders are not inconsistent with these rules or local rules. Rule 9029 has been amended to incorporate Rule 83. The term "court" in the last sentence of the rule includes the judges of the district court and the bankruptcy judges of the district. Rule 9001(4).

NOTES OF ADVISORY COMMITTEE ON RULES—1991 AMENDMENT

This rule is amended to make it clear that the Official Forms must be accepted in every bankruptcy court.

NOTES OF ADVISORY COMMITTEE ON RULES—1995 AMENDMENT

Subdivision (a). This rule is amended to reflect the requirement that local rules be consistent not only with applicable national rules but also with Acts of Congress. The amendment also states that local rules should not repeat applicable national rules and Acts of Congress.

The amendment also requires that the numbering of local rules conform with any uniform numbering system that may be prescribed by the Judicial Conference. Lack of uniform numbering might create unnecessary traps for counsel and litigants. A uniform numbering system would make it easier for an increasingly national bar and for litigants to locate a local rule that applies to a particular procedural issue.

Paragraph (2) of subdivision (a) is new. Its aim is to protect against loss of rights in the enforcement of local rules relating to matters of form. For example, a party should not be deprived of a right to a jury trial because its attorney, unaware of—or forgetting—a local rule directing that jury demands be noted in the caption of the case, includes a jury demand only in the body of the pleading. The proscription of paragraph (2) is narrowly drawn—covering only violations that are not willful and only those involving local rules directed to matters of form. It does not limit the court's power to impose substantive penalties upon a party if it or its attorney stubbornly or repeatedly violates a local rule, even one involving merely a matter of form. Nor does it affect the court's power to enforce local rules that involve more than mere matters of form—for example, a local rule requiring that a party demand a jury trial within a specified time period to avoid waiver of the right to a trial by jury.

Subdivision (b). This rule provides flexibility to the court in regulating practice when there is no controlling law. Specifically, it permits the court to regulate practice in any manner consistent with federal law, with rules adopted under 28 U.S.C. §2075, with Official Forms, and with the district's local rules.

This rule recognizes that courts rely on multiple directives to control practice. Some courts regulate practice through the published Federal Rules and the local rules of the court. Some courts also have used internal operating procedures, standing orders, and other internal directives. Although such directives continue to be authorized, they can lead to problems. Counsel or litigants may be unaware of various directives. In addition, the sheer volume of directives may impose an unreasonable barrier. For example, it may be difficult to obtain copies of the directives. Finally, counsel or litigants may be unfairly sanctioned for failing to comply with a directive. For these reasons, the amendment to this rule disapproves imposing any sanction or other disadvantage on a person for noncompliance with such an internal directive, unless the alleged violator has been furnished in a particular case with actual notice of the requirement.

There should be no adverse consequence to a party or attorney for violating special requirements relating to practice before a particular judge unless the party or attorney has actual notice of those requirements. Furnishing litigants with a copy outlining the judge's practices—or attaching instructions to a notice setting a case for conference or trial—would suffice to give actual notice, as would an order in a case specifically adopting by reference a judge's standing order and indicating how copies can be obtained.

REFERENCES IN TEXT

The Federal Rules of Civil Procedure, referred to in subd. (a)(1), are set out in the Appendix to Title 28, Judiciary and Judicial Procedure.

Rule 9030. Jurisdiction and Venue Unaffected

These rules shall not be construed to extend or limit the jurisdiction of the courts or the venue of any matters therein.

(As amended Mar. 30, 1987, eff. Aug. 1, 1987.)

NOTES OF ADVISORY COMMITTEE ON RULES—1983

The rule is an adaptation of Rule 82 F.R.Civ.P.

Rule 9031. Masters Not Authorized

Rule 53 F.R.Civ.P. does not apply in cases under the Code.

NOTES OF ADVISORY COMMITTEE ON RULES—1983

This rule precludes the appointment of masters in cases and proceedings under the Code.

REFERENCES IN TEXT

The Federal Rules of Civil Procedure, referred to in text, are set out in the Appendix to Title 28, Judiciary and Judicial Procedure.

Rule 9032. Effect of Amendment of Federal Rules of Civil Procedure

The Federal Rules of Civil Procedure which are incorporated by reference and made applicable by these rules shall be the Federal Rules of Civil Procedure in effect on the effective date of these rules and as thereafter amended, unless otherwise provided by such amendment or by these rules.

(As amended Apr. 30, 1991, eff. Aug. 1, 1991.)

NOTES OF ADVISORY COMMITTEE ON RULES—1991 AMENDMENT

This rule is amended to provide flexibility so that the Bankruptcy Rules may provide that subsequent amendments to a Federal Rule of Civil Procedure made applicable by these rules are not effective with regard to Bankruptcy Code cases or proceedings. For example, in view of the anticipated amendments to, and restructuring of, Rule 4 F.R.Civ.P., Rule 7004(g) will prevent such changes from affecting Bankruptcy Code cases until the Advisory Committee on Bankruptcy Rules has an opportunity to consider such amendments and to make appropriate recommendations for incorporating such amendments into the Bankruptcy Rules.

REFERENCES IN TEXT

The Federal Rules of Civil Procedure, referred to in text, are set out in the Appendix to Title 28, Judiciary and Judicial Procedure.

The effective date of these rules, referred to in text, is Aug. 1, 1983. See Effective Date note set out prec. Rule 1001 of this Appendix.

Rule 9033. Review of Proposed Findings of Fact and Conclusions of Law in Non-Core Proceedings

(a) SERVICE. In non-core proceedings heard pursuant to 28 U.S.C. §157(c)(1), the bankruptcy judge shall file proposed findings of fact and conclusions of law. The clerk shall serve forthwith copies on all parties by mail and note the date of mailing on the docket.

(b) OBJECTIONS: TIME FOR FILING. Within 14 days after being served with a copy of the proposed findings of fact and conclusions of law a party may serve and file with the clerk written objections which identify the specific proposed findings or conclusions objected to and state the grounds for such objection. A party may respond to another party's objections within 14 days after being served with a copy thereof. A party objecting to the bankruptcy judge's proposed findings or conclusions shall arrange promptly for the transcription of the record, or such portions of it as all parties may agree upon or the bankruptcy judge deems sufficient, unless the district judge otherwise directs.

(c) EXTENSION OF TIME. The bankruptcy judge may for cause extend the time for filing objections by any party for a period not to exceed 21 days from the expiration of the time otherwise prescribed by this rule. A request to extend the time for filing objections must be made before the time for filing objections has expired, except that a request made no more than 21 days after the expiration of the time for filing objections may be granted upon a showing of excusable neglect.

(d) STANDARD OF REVIEW. The district judge shall make a de novo review upon the record or, after additional evidence, of any portion of the bankruptcy judge's findings of fact or conclusions of law to which specific written objection has been made in accordance with this rule. The district judge may accept, reject, or modify the proposed findings of fact or conclusions of law, receive further evidence, or recommit the matter to the bankruptcy judge with instructions.

(Added Mar. 30, 1987, eff. Aug. 1, 1987; amended Mar. 26, 2009, eff. Dec. 1, 2009.)

NOTES OF ADVISORY COMMITTEE ON RULES—1987

Section 157(c)(1) of title 28 requires a bankruptcy judge to submit proposed findings of fact and conclusions of law to the district court when the bankruptcy judge has heard a non-core proceeding. This rule, which is modeled on Rule 72 F.R.Civ.P., provides the procedure for objecting to, and for review by, the district court of specific findings and conclusions.

Subdivision (a) requires the clerk to serve a copy of the proposed findings and conclusions on the parties. The bankruptcy clerk, or the district court clerk if there is no bankruptcy clerk in the district, shall serve a copy of the proposed findings and conclusions on all parties.

Subdivision (b) is derived from Rule 72(b) F.R.Civ.P. which governs objections to a recommended disposition by a magistrate.

Subdivision (c) is similar to Rule 8002(c) of the Bankruptcy Rules and provides for granting of extensions of time to file objections to proposed findings and conclusions.

Subdivision (d) adopts the de novo review provisions of Rule 72(b) F.R.Civ.P.

COMMITTEE NOTES ON RULES—2009 AMENDMENT

The rule is amended to implement changes in connection with the amendment to Rule 9006(a) and the manner by which time is computed under the rules. The deadlines in the rule are amended to substitute a deadline that is a multiple of seven days. Throughout the rules, deadlines are amended in the following manner:

- 5-day periods become 7-day periods
- 10-day periods become 14-day periods
- 15-day periods become 14-day periods
- 20-day periods become 21-day periods
- 25-day periods become 28-day periods

Rule 9034. Transmittal of Pleadings, Motion Papers, Objections, and Other Papers to the United States Trustee

Unless the United States trustee requests otherwise or the case is a chapter 9 municipality case, any entity that files a pleading, motion, objection, or similar paper relating to any of the following matters shall transmit a copy thereof to the United States trustee within the time required by these rules for service of the paper:

(a) a proposed use, sale, or lease of property of the estate other than in the ordinary course of business;

(b) the approval of a compromise or settlement of a controversy;

(c) the dismissal or conversion of a case to another chapter;

(d) the employment of professional persons;

(e) an application for compensation or reimbursement of expenses;

(f) a motion for, or approval of an agreement relating to, the use of cash collateral or authority to obtain credit;

(g) the appointment of a trustee or examiner in a chapter 11 reorganization case;

(h) the approval of a disclosure statement;

(i) the confirmation of a plan;

(j) an objection to, or waiver or revocation of, the debtor's discharge;

(k) any other matter in which the United States trustee requests copies of filed papers or the court orders copies transmitted to the United States trustee.

(Added Apr. 30, 1991, eff. Aug. 1, 1991.)

NOTES OF ADVISORY COMMITTEE ON RULES—1991

Section 307 of the Code gives the United States trustee the right to appear and be heard on issues in cases and proceedings under the Code. This rule is intended to keep the United States trustee informed of certain developments and disputes in which the United States trustee may wish to be heard. This rule, which derives from Rule X-1008, also enables the United States trustee to monitor the progress of the case in accordance with 28 U.S.C. §586(a). The requirement to transmit copies of certain pleadings, motion papers and other documents is intended to be flexible in that the United States trustee in a particular judicial district may request copies of papers in certain categories, and may request not to receive copies of documents in other categories, when the practice in that district makes that desirable. When the rules require that a paper be served on particular parties, the time period in which service is required is also applicable to transmittal to the United States trustee.

Although other rules require that certain notices be transmitted to the United States trustee, this rule goes further in that it requires the transmittal to the United States trustee of other papers filed in connection with these matters. This rule is not an exhaustive list of the matters of which the United States trustee may be entitled to receive notice.

Rule 9035. Applicability of Rules in Judicial Districts in Alabama and North Carolina

In any case under the Code that is filed in or transferred to a district in the State of Alabama or the State of North Carolina and in which a United States trustee is not authorized to act, these rules apply to the extent that they are not inconsistent with any federal statute effective in the case.

(Added Apr. 30, 1991, eff. Aug. 1, 1991; amended Apr. 11, 1997, eff. Dec. 1, 1997.)

NOTES OF ADVISORY COMMITTEE ON RULES—1991

Section 302(d)(3) of the Bankruptcy Judges, United States Trustees, and Family Farmer Bankruptcy Act of 1986 provides that amendments to the Code relating to United States trustees and quarterly fees required under 28 U.S.C. §1930(a)(6) do not become effective in any judicial district in the States of Alabama and North Carolina until the district elects to be included in the United States trustee system, or October 1, 1992, whichever occurs first, unless Congress extends the deadline. If the United States trustee system becomes effective in these districts, the transition provisions in the 1986 Act will govern the application of the United States trustee amendments to cases that are pending at that time. See §302(d)(3)(F). The statute, and not the bankruptcy court, determines whether a United States trustee is authorized to act in a particular case.

Section 302(d)(3)(I) of the 1986 Act authorizes the Judicial Conference of the United States to promulgate regulations governing the appointment of bankruptcy administrators to supervise the administration of estates and trustees in cases in the districts in Alabama and North Carolina until the provisions of the Act relating to the United States trustee take effect in these districts. Pursuant to this authority, in September 1987, the Judicial Conference promulgated regulations governing the selection and appointment of bankruptcy administrators and regulations governing the establishment, duties, and functions of bankruptcy administrators. Guidelines relating to the bankruptcy administrator program have been prescribed by the Director of the Administrative Office of the United States Courts.

Many of these rules were amended to implement the United States trustee system in accordance with the 1986 Act. Since the provisions of the 1986 Act relating to the United States trustee system are not effective in cases in Alabama and North Carolina in which a bankruptcy administrator is serving, rules referring to United States trustees are at least partially inconsistent with the provisions of the Bankruptcy Code and title 28 of the United States Code effective in such cases.

In determining the applicability of these rules in cases in Alabama and North Carolina in which a United States trustee is not authorized to act, the following guidelines should be followed:

(1) The following rules do not apply because they are inconsistent with the provisions of the Code or title 28 in these cases: 1002(b), 1007(1), 1009(c), 2002(k), 2007.1(b), 2015(a)(6), 2020, 3015(b), 5005(b), 7004(b)(10), 9003(b), and 9034.

(2) The following rules are partially inconsistent with the provisions of the Code effective in these cases and, therefore, are applicable with the following modifications:

(a) *Rule 2001(a) and (c)*—The court, rather than the United States trustee, appoints the interim trustee.

(b) *Rule 2003*—The duties of the United States trustee relating to the meeting of creditors or equity security holders are performed by the officer determined in accordance with regulations of the Judicial Conference, guidelines of the Director of the Administrative Office, local rules or court orders.

(c) *Rule 2007*—The court, rather than the United States trustee, appoints committees in chapter 9 and chapter 11 cases.

(d) *Rule 2008*—The bankruptcy administrator, rather than the United States trustee, informs the trustee of how to qualify.

(e) *Rule 2009(c) and (d)*—The court, rather than the United States trustee, appoints interim trustees in chapter 7 cases and trustees in chapter 11, 12 and 13 cases.

(f) *Rule 2010*—The court, rather than the United States trustee, determines the amount and sufficiency of the trustee's bond.

(g) *Rule 5010*—The court, rather than the United States trustee, appoints the trustee when a case is reopened.

(3) All other rules are applicable because they are consistent with the provisions of the Code and title 28 effective in these cases, except that any reference to the United States trustee is not applicable and should be disregarded.

Many of the amendments to the rules are designed to give the United States trustee, a member of the Executive Branch, notice of certain developments and copies of petitions, schedules, pleadings, and other papers. In contrast, the bankruptcy administrator is an officer in the Judicial Branch and matters relating to notice of developments and access to documents filed in the clerk's office are governed by regulations of the Judicial Conference of the United States, guidelines of the Administrative Office of the United States Courts, local rules, and court orders. Also, requirements for disclosure of connections with the bankruptcy administrator in applications for employment of professional persons, restrictions on appointments of relatives of bankruptcy administrators, effects of erroneously filing papers with the bankruptcy administrator, and other matters not covered by these rules may be governed by regulations of the Judicial Conference, guidelines of the Director of the Administrative Office, local rules, and court orders.

This rule will cease to have effect if a United States trustee is authorized in every case in the districts in Alabama and North Carolina.

NOTES OF ADVISORY COMMITTEE ON RULES—1997 AMENDMENT

Certain statutes that are not codified in title 11 or title 28 of the United States Code, such as §105 of the Bankruptcy Reform Act of 1994, Pub. L. 103–394, 108 Stat. 4106, relate to bankruptcy administrators in the judicial districts of North Carolina and Alabama. This amendment makes it clear that the Bankruptcy Rules do not apply to the extent that they are inconsistent with these federal statutes.

GAP Report on Rule 9035. No changes to the published draft.

Rule 9036. Notice by Electronic Transmission

Whenever the clerk or some other person as directed by the court is required to send notice by mail and the entity entitled to receive the notice requests in writing that, instead of notice by mail, all or part of the information required to be contained in the notice be sent by a specified type of electronic transmission, the court may direct the clerk or other person to send the information by such electronic transmission. Notice by electronic means is complete on transmission.

(Added Apr. 22, 1993, eff. Aug. 1, 1993; amended Apr. 25, 2005, eff. Dec. 1, 2005.)

NOTES OF ADVISORY COMMITTEE ON RULES—1993

This rule is added to provide flexibility for banks, credit card companies, taxing authorities, and other entities that ordinarily receive notices by mail in a large volume of bankruptcy cases, to arrange to receive by electronic transmission all or part of the information required to be contained in such notices.

The use of electronic technology instead of mail to send information to creditors and interested parties will be more convenient and less costly for the sender and the receiver. For example, a bank that receives by mail, at different locations, notices of meetings of creditors pursuant to Rule 2002(a) in thousands of cases each year may prefer to receive only the vital information ordinarily contained in such notices by electronic transmission to one computer terminal.

The specific means of transmission must be compatible with technology available to the sender and the receiver. Therefore, electronic transmission of notices is permitted only upon request of the entity entitled to receive the notice, specifying the type of electronic transmission, and only if approved by the court.

Electronic transmission pursuant to this rule completes the notice requirements. The creditor or interested party is not thereafter entitled to receive the relevant notice by mail.

COMMITTEE NOTES ON RULES—2005 AMENDMENT

The rule is amended to delete the requirement that the sender of an electronic notice must obtain electronic confirmation that the notice was received. The amendment provides that notice is complete upon transmission. When the rule was first promulgated, confirmation of receipt of electronic notices was commonplace. In the current electronic environment, very few internet service providers offer the confirmation of receipt service. Consequently, compliance with the rule may be impossible, and the rule could discourage the use of electronic noticing.

Confidence in the delivery of email text messages now rivals or exceeds confidence in the delivery of printed materials. Therefore, there is no need for confirmation of receipt of electronic messages just as there is no such requirement for paper notices.

Changes Made After Publication and Comment. No changes since publication.

Rule 9037. Privacy Protection For Filings Made with the Court

(a) REDACTED FILINGS. Unless the court orders otherwise, in an electronic or paper filing made with the court that contains an individual's social-security number, taxpayer-identification number, or birth date, the name of an individual, other than the debtor, known to be and identified as a minor, or a financial-account number, a party or nonparty making the filing may include only:

(1) the last four digits of the social-security number and taxpayer-identification number;

(2) the year of the individual's birth;

(3) the minor's initials; and

(4) the last four digits of the financial-account number.

(b) EXEMPTIONS FROM THE REDACTION REQUIREMENT. The redaction requirement does not apply to the following:

(1) a financial-account number that identifies the property allegedly subject to forfeiture in a forfeiture proceeding;

(2) the record of an administrative or agency proceeding unless filed with a proof of claim;

(3) the official record of a state-court proceeding;

(4) the record of a court or tribunal, if that record was not subject to the redaction requirement when originally filed;

(5) a filing covered by subdivision (c) of this rule; and

(6) a filing that is subject to § 110 of the Code.

(c) FILINGS MADE UNDER SEAL. The court may order that a filing be made under seal without redaction. The court may later unseal the filing or order the entity that made the filing to file a redacted version for the public record.

(d) PROTECTIVE ORDERS. For cause, the court may by order in a case under the Code:

(1) require redaction of additional information; or

(2) limit or prohibit a nonparty's remote electronic access to a document filed with the court.

(e) OPTION FOR ADDITIONAL UNREDACTED FILING UNDER SEAL. An entity making a redacted filing may also file an unredacted copy under seal. The court must retain the unredacted copy as part of the record.

(f) OPTION FOR FILING A REFERENCE LIST. A filing that contains redacted information may be filed together with a reference list that identifies each item of redacted information and specifies an appropriate identifier that uniquely corresponds to each item listed. The list must be filed under seal and may be amended as of right. Any reference in the case to a listed identifier will be construed to refer to the corresponding item of information.

(g) WAIVER OF PROTECTION OF IDENTIFIERS. An entity waives the protection of subdivision (a) as to the entity's own information by filing it without redaction and not under seal.

(Added Apr. 30, 2007, eff. Dec. 1, 2007.)

COMMITTEE NOTES ON RULES—2007

The rule is adopted in compliance with section 205(c)(3) of the E-Government Act of 2002, Public Law No. 107-347. Section 205(c)(3) requires the Supreme Court to prescribe rules "to protect privacy and security concerns relating to electronic filing of documents and the public availability . . . of documents filed electronically." The rule goes further than the E-Government Act in regulating paper filings even when they are not converted to electronic form, but the number of filings that remain in paper form is certain to diminish over time. Most districts scan paper filings into the electronic case file, where they become available to the public in the same way as documents initially filed in electronic form. It is electronic availability, not the form of the initial filing, that raises the privacy and security concerns addressed in the E-Government Act.

The rule is derived from and implements the policy adopted by the Judicial Conference in September 2001 to address the privacy concerns resulting from public access to electronic case files. *See* http://www.privacy.uscourts.gov/Policy.htm. The Judicial Conference policy is that documents in case files generally should be made available electronically to the same extent they are available at the courthouse, provided that certain "personal data identifiers" are not included in the public file.

While providing for the public filing of some information, such as the last four digits of an account number, the rule does not intend to establish a presumption that this information never could or should be protected. For example, it may well be necessary in individual cases to prevent remote access by nonparties to any part of an account number or social-security number. It may also be necessary to protect information not covered by the redaction requirement—such as driver's license numbers and alien registration numbers—in a particular case. In such cases, protection may be sought under subdivision (c) or (d). Moreover, the rule does not affect the protection available under other rules, such as Rules 16 and 26(c) of the Federal Rules of Civil Procedure, or under other sources of protective authority.

Any personal information not otherwise protected by sealing or redaction will be made available over the internet. Counsel should therefore notify clients of this fact so that an informed decision may be made on what information is to be included in a document filed with the court.

An individual debtor's full social-security number or taxpayer-identification number is included on the notice of the § 341 meeting of creditors sent to creditors. Of course, that is not filed with the court, see Rule 1007(f) (the debtor "submits" this information), and the copy of the notice that is filed with the court does not include the full social-security number or taxpayer-identification number. Thus, since the full social-security number or taxpayer-identification number is not filed with the court, it is not available to a person searching that record.

The clerk is not required to review documents filed with the court for compliance with this rule. As subdivision (a) recognizes, the responsibility to redact filings rests with counsel, parties, and others who make filings with the court.

Subdivision (d) recognizes the court's inherent authority to issue a protective order to prevent remote access to private or sensitive information and to require redaction of material in addition to that which would be redacted under subdivision (a) of the rule. These orders may be issued whenever necessary either by the court on its own motion, or on motion of a party in interest.

Subdivision (e) allows an entity that makes a redacted filing to file an unredacted document under seal. This provision is derived from section 205(c)(3)(iv) of the E-Government Act. Subdivision (f) allows the option to file a reference list of redacted information. This provision is derived from section 205(c)(3)(v) of the E-Government Act, as amended in 2004.

In accordance with the E-Government Act, subdivision (f) of the rule refers to "redacted" information. The term "redacted" is intended to govern a filing that is prepared with abbreviated identifiers in the first instance, as well as a filing in which a personal identifier is edited after its preparation.

Subdivision (g) allows an entity to waive the protections of the rule as to that entity's own information by filing it in unredacted form. An entity may elect to waive the protection if, for example, it is determined that the costs of redaction outweigh the benefits to privacy. As to financial account numbers, the instructions to Schedules E and F of Official Form 6 note that the debtor may elect to include the complete account number on those schedules rather than limit the number to the final four digits. Including the complete number would operate as a waiver by the debtor under subdivision (g) as to the full information that the debtor set out on those schedules. The waiver operates only to the extent of the information that the entity filed without redaction. If an entity files an unredacted identifier by mistake, it may seek relief from the court.

Trial exhibits are subject to the redaction requirements of Rule 9037 to the extent they are filed with the court. Trial exhibits that are not initially filed with the court must be redacted in accordance with this rule if and when they are filed as part of an appeal or for other reasons.

Changes After Publication. Rule 9037 is intended to parallel as closely as possible Civil Rule 5.2 and Criminal Rule 49.1. The Advisory Committees have worked together to maintain as much consistency as possible in the three versions of the rule. The rule has been revised to implement the several style revisions suggested by the Style Subcommittee of the Standing Committee. Subdivision (b) was reorganized and renumbered. Subdivisions (b)(1) and (b)(3) were added in response to suggestions by the Department of Justice. Subdivision (b)(4), formerly subdivision (b)(2), was amended in response to the suggestion of the Committee on Court Administration and Case Management so that the subdivision now refers to court records that become a part of the record in the pending matter. The term "entity" has been substituted for "person" in subdivision (c) and for "party" in subdivisions (e) and (f) to conform the rule to the definitions provided in the Bankruptcy Code.

[PART X—UNITED STATES TRUSTEES]
(Abrogated Apr. 30, 1991, eff. Aug. 1, 1991)

OFFICIAL FORMS

[NOTE: *These official forms should be observed and used with such alterations as may be appropriate to suit the circumstances. See Rule 9009.*]

INTRODUCTION AND GENERAL INSTRUCTIONS

Rule 9009 of the Federal Rules of Bankruptcy Procedure states that the Official Forms prescribed by the Judicial Conference of the United States "shall be observed and used." The Official Forms, accordingly, are obligatory in character.

Rule 9009 expressly permits the user of the Official Forms to make such "alterations as may be appropriate," and the use of the Official Forms has been held to be subject to a "rule of substantial compliance." Some rules, for example Fed.R.Bankr.P. 3001(a), specifically state that the filed document need only "conform substantially" to the Official Form. A document for which an Official Form is prescribed generally will meet the standard of substantial compliance if the document contains the complete substance, that is, all of the information required by the Official Form.

Rule 9009 also expressly permits the contents of Official Forms to be rearranged, and the format of the Official Forms traditionally has been quite flexible. The forms of the voluntary petition, the schedules, and the statement of financial affairs are printed and sold by private publishers. Design features such as type face, type size, layout, and side and top margins were not prescribed by the Judicial Conference, but rather left to the professional judgment of each publisher.

A great deal of variation, accordingly, has developed. Some publishers also add forms that are not official but which have been drafted by the publisher. A form for a chapter 13 plan, for example, frequently is included with commercially printed packages of forms for filing cases under chapter 13, although there is no Official Form for this purpose. The variety of formats has accelerated since the introduction of computer software for generating the petitions, schedules, and statements of affairs. It is the policy of the Judicial Conference that such diversity is desirable and should be encouraged.

The sheer volume of bankruptcy cases, however, has compelled the Judicial Conference, for the first time, to prescribe the format of certain Official Forms. In particular, the format of Form 1, the Voluntary Petition, now is prescribed. This format is designed to assist the clerk of the bankruptcy court to enter the case in the court's computer database and ensures that all required information is available to both the clerk and the United States trustee at the inception of the case. The rule of substantial compliance continues to apply, however. Accordingly, publishers may vary the size and style of the type and may alter the size and shape of the boxes on the form, within the bounds of that rule.

The Official Forms of the petitions, schedules, and statement of financial affairs, (Forms 1, 5, 6, and 7), are to be printed on one side of the paper only. Each page is to be prepunched with two holes at the top, and sufficient top margin allowed so that neither caption nor text is destroyed or obscured. Compliance with these standards will facilitate both the securing of the papers in the case file and review of the file by the public.

Although Rule 9009 permits alteration, for most of the Official Forms, alteration will be appropriate only in rare circumstances. The special forms for chapter 11 cases, on the other hand, seldom will be used without alterations. Forms 12 through 15, while legally sufficient in any chapter 11 case, are intended by the Judicial Conference, and most often will be used, as a framework for drafting a document specially tailored to the particular case. These alterations generally will take the form of additions to the prescribed elements.

Rule 9009 provides for a balance of prescribed substance, to which full adherence is expected in all but the most unusual cases, and flexible formatting, under which requirements are kept to the minimum necessary for proper operation of the courts and the bankruptcy system. While Rule 9009 recognizes the overall need for flexibility, Rule 9029 makes it clear that the Official Forms must be accepted in every bankruptcy court.

Under Rule 9029, courts may not reject documents presented for filing in novel or unfamiliar formats if those documents contain the substance prescribed by the Official Form and meet the requirements for one-sided printing, pre-punched holes, and adequate top margins. Nor are courts authorized to impose local forms which vary in substance from the Official Forms or reject papers presented for filing on Official Forms on the basis that the proffered documents differ from a locally preferred version.

SPECIAL INSTRUCTIONS FOR COMPUTER-GENERATED FORMS

In Form 1, the Voluntary Petition, if a box contains multiple choices, a computer-generated petition that shows only the choice made is acceptable for filing. All sections of the petition must be shown and completed, however, unless instructions on the Official Form of the petition state that the box is applicable only to cases filed under a chapter other than the one selected by the debtor. If the debtor has no information to provide for a particular box, for example if the debtor has no prior bankruptcies to report, a computer-generated petition should so indicate by stating "None."

Form 6, the Schedules, on which the debtor reports all of the debtor's assets and liabilities, has been prescribed in a columnar format. Columns help to organize the information which the debtor is required to report and should be used when the printed schedules are completed on a typewriter. In a computerized law office, however, the organizational structure of the schedules can be built into the computer program, and a rigid columnar format may be a hindrance rather than a help.

Schedules generated by computer which provide all of the information requested by the prescribed form are fully acceptable, regardless of the format of the printed page. The information must be appropriately labeled, however. In Schedule B, for example, all of the categories of personal property must be printed on the filed document together with the debtor's response to each. The space occupied by each category may be expanded, however, so that attachments are not needed. Instructions provided on the printed forms can simply be built into the computer program; they need not be reprinted on the filed document.

Form 7, the Statement of Financial Affairs, contains a series of questions which direct the debtor to answer by furnishing information. If the answer to a question is "None," or the question is not applicable, an affirmative statement to that effect is required. To assure that the trustee and the creditors can review the debtor's statement properly, the complete text of each question must be printed on the filed document.

Form 9, the Notice of Filing under the Bankruptcy Code, Meeting of Creditors, and Fixing of Dates, will be prepared by the clerk of the bankruptcy court in most cases. The form is designed for use with automated printing and mailing equipment. Two free lines, which do not appear on the printed blank form, have been programmed into the form. Courts may use this space to add local information, such as directions for obtaining copies of the debtor's schedules.

[Introduction and General Instructions provided by the Advisory Committee on Bankruptcy Rules of the Judicial Conference, June 28, 1990, H. Doc. 102-80, pp. 507, 534, 102d Congress, 1st Session.]

B 1 (Official Form 1) (1/08)

United States Bankruptcy Court | **Voluntary Petition**

Name of Debtor (if individual, enter Last, First, Middle):	Name of Joint Debtor (Spouse) (Last, First, Middle):
All Other Names used by the Debtor in the last 8 years (include married, maiden, and trade names):	All Other Names used by the Joint Debtor in the last 8 years (include married, maiden, and trade names):
Last four digits of Soc. Sec. or Individual-Taxpayer I.D. (ITIN) No./Complete EIN (if more than one, state all):	Last four digits of Soc. Sec. or Individual-Taxpayer I.D. (ITIN) No./Complete EIN (if more than one, state all):
Street Address of Debtor (No. and Street, City, and State): ZIP CODE	Street Address of Joint Debtor (No. and Street, City, and State): ZIP CODE
County of Residence or of the Principal Place of Business:	County of Residence or of the Principal Place of Business:
Mailing Address of Debtor (if different from street address): ZIP CODE	Mailing Address of Joint Debtor (if different from street address): ZIP CODE

Location of Principal Assets of Business Debtor (if different from street address above): ZIP CODE

Type of Debtor
(Form of Organization)
(Check **one** box.)

☐ Individual (includes Joint Debtors)
See Exhibit D on page 2 of this form.
☐ Corporation (includes LLC and LLP)
☐ Partnership
☐ Other (If debtor is not one of the above entities, check this box and state type of entity below.)

Nature of Business
(Check **one** box.)

☐ Health Care Business
☐ Single Asset Real Estate as defined in 11 U.S.C. § 101(51B)
☐ Railroad
☐ Stockbroker
☐ Commodity Broker
☐ Clearing Bank
☐ Other

Tax-Exempt Entity
(Check box, if applicable.)

☐ Debtor is a tax-exempt organization under Title 26 of the United States Code (the Internal Revenue Code).

Chapter of Bankruptcy Code Under Which the Petition is Filed (Check **one** box.)

☐ Chapter 7
☐ Chapter 9
☐ Chapter 11
☐ Chapter 12
☐ Chapter 13
☐ Chapter 15 Petition for Recognition of a Foreign Main Proceeding
☐ Chapter 15 Petition for Recognition of a Foreign Nonmain Proceeding

Nature of Debts
(Check one box.)

☐ Debts are primarily consumer debts, defined in 11 U.S.C. § 101(8) as "incurred by an individual primarily for a personal, family, or house-hold purpose."
☐ Debts are primarily business debts.

Filing Fee (Check one box.)

☐ Full Filing Fee attached.

☐ Filing Fee to be paid in installments (applicable to individuals only). Must attach signed application for the court's consideration certifying that the debtor is unable to pay fee except in installments. Rule 1006(b). See Official Form 3A.

☐ Filing Fee waiver requested (applicable to chapter 7 individuals only). Must attach signed application for the court's consideration. See Official Form 3B.

Chapter 11 Debtors

Check one box:
☐ Debtor is a small business debtor as defined in 11 U.S.C. § 101(51D).
☐ Debtor is not a small business debtor as defined in 11 U.S.C. § 101(51D).

Check if:
☐ Debtor's aggregate noncontingent liquidated debts (excluding debts owed to insiders or affiliates) are less than $2,190,000.

- -

Check all applicable boxes:
☐ A plan is being filed with this petition.
☐ Acceptances of the plan were solicited prepetition from one or more classes of creditors, in accordance with 11 U.S.C. § 1126(b).

Statistical/Administrative Information

☐ Debtor estimates that funds will be available for distribution to unsecured creditors.
☐ Debtor estimates that, after any exempt property is excluded and administrative expenses paid, there will be no funds available for distribution to unsecured creditors.

THIS SPACE IS FOR COURT USE ONLY

Estimated Number of Creditors

☐	☐	☐	☐	☐	☐	☐	☐	☐	☐
1-49	50-99	100-199	200-999	1,000-5,000	5,001-10,000	10,001-25,000	25,001-50,000	50,001-100,000	Over 100,000

Estimated Assets

☐	☐	☐	☐	☐	☐	☐	☐	☐	☐
$0 to $50,000	$50,001 to $100,000	$100,001 to $500,000	$500,001 to $1 million	$1,000,001 to $10 million	$10,000,001 to $50 million	$50,000,001 to $100 million	$100,000,001 to $500 million	$500,000,001 to $1 billion	More than $1 billion

Estimated Liabilities

☐	☐	☐	☐	☐	☐	☐	☐	☐	☐
$0 to $50,000	$50,001 to $100,000	$100,001 to $500,000	$500,001 to $1 million	$1,000,001 to $10 million	$10,000,001 to $50 million	$50,000,001 to $100 million	$100,000,001 to $500 million	$500,000,001 to $1 billion	More than $1 billion

B 1 (Official Form 1) (1/08) Page 2

Voluntary Petition *(This page must be completed and filed in every case.)*	Name of Debtor(s):	
All Prior Bankruptcy Cases Filed Within Last 8 Years (If more than two, attach additional sheet.)		
Location Where Filed:	Case Number:	Date Filed:
Location Where Filed:	Case Number:	Date Filed:
Pending Bankruptcy Case Filed by any Spouse, Partner, or Affiliate of this Debtor (If more than one, attach additional sheet.)		
Name of Debtor:	Case Number:	Date Filed:
District:	Relationship:	Judge:

Exhibit A

(To be completed if debtor is required to file periodic reports (e.g., forms 10K and 10Q) with the Securities and Exchange Commission pursuant to Section 13 or 15(d) of the Securities Exchange Act of 1934 and is requesting relief under chapter 11.)

☐ Exhibit A is attached and made a part of this petition.

Exhibit B

(To be completed if debtor is an individual whose debts are primarily consumer debts.)

I, the attorney for the petitioner named in the foregoing petition, declare that I have informed the petitioner that [he or she] may proceed under chapter 7, 11, 12, or 13 of title 11, United States Code, and have explained the relief available under each such chapter. I further certify that I have delivered to the debtor the notice required by 11 U.S.C. § 342(b).

X ______________________________

Signature of Attorney for Debtor(s) (Date)

Exhibit C

Does the debtor own or have possession of any property that poses or is alleged to pose a threat of imminent and identifiable harm to public health or safety?

☐ Yes, and Exhibit C is attached and made a part of this petition.

☐ No.

Exhibit D

(To be completed by every individual debtor. If a joint petition is filed, each spouse must complete and attach a separate Exhibit D.)

☐ Exhibit D completed and signed by the debtor is attached and made a part of this petition.

If this is a joint petition:

☐ Exhibit D also completed and signed by the joint debtor is attached and made a part of this petition.

Information Regarding the Debtor - Venue
(Check any applicable box.)

☐ Debtor has been domiciled or has had a residence, principal place of business, or principal assets in this District for 180 days immediately preceding the date of this petition or for a longer part of such 180 days than in any other District.

☐ There is a bankruptcy case concerning debtor's affiliate, general partner, or partnership pending in this District.

☐ Debtor is a debtor in a foreign proceeding and has its principal place of business or principal assets in the United States in this District, or has no principal place of business or assets in the United States but is a defendant in an action or proceeding [in a federal or state court] in this District, or the interests of the parties will be served in regard to the relief sought in this District.

Certification by a Debtor Who Resides as a Tenant of Residential Property
(Check all applicable boxes.)

☐ Landlord has a judgment against the debtor for possession of debtor's residence. (If box checked, complete the following.)

____
(Name of landlord that obtained judgment)

____
(Address of landlord)

☐ Debtor claims that under applicable nonbankruptcy law, there are circumstances under which the debtor would be permitted to cure the entire monetary default that gave rise to the judgment for possession, after the judgment for possession was entered, and

☐ Debtor has included with this petition the deposit with the court of any rent that would become due during the 30-day period after the filing of the petition.

☐ Debtor certifies that he/she has served the Landlord with this certification. (11 U.S.C. § 362(l)).

B 1 (Official Form) 1 (1/08) Page 3

Voluntary Petition
(This page must be completed and filed in every case.)

Name of Debtor(s):

Signatures

Signature(s) of Debtor(s) (Individual/Joint)

I declare under penalty of perjury that the information provided in this petition is true and correct.
[If petitioner is an individual whose debts are primarily consumer debts and has chosen to file under chapter 7] I am aware that I may proceed under chapter 7, 11, 12 or 13 of title 11, United States Code, understand the relief available under each such chapter, and choose to proceed under chapter 7.
[If no attorney represents me and no bankruptcy petition preparer signs the petition] I have obtained and read the notice required by 11 U.S.C. § 342(b).

I request relief in accordance with the chapter of title 11, United States Code, specified in this petition.

X ______________________________
Signature of Debtor

X ______________________________
Signature of Joint Debtor

____
Telephone Number (if not represented by attorney)

____
Date

Signature of a Foreign Representative

I declare under penalty of perjury that the information provided in this petition is true and correct, that I am the foreign representative of a debtor in a foreign proceeding, and that I am authorized to file this petition.

(Check only **one** box.)

☐ I request relief in accordance with chapter 15 of title 11, United States Code. Certified copies of the documents required by 11 U.S.C. § 1515 are attached.

☐ Pursuant to 11 U.S.C. § 1511, I request relief in accordance with the chapter of title 11 specified in this petition. A certified copy of the order granting recognition of the foreign main proceeding is attached.

X ______________________________
(Signature of Foreign Representative)

____
(Printed Name of Foreign Representative)

____
Date

Signature of Attorney*

X ______________________________
Signature of Attorney for Debtor(s)

____
Printed Name of Attorney for Debtor(s)

____
Firm Name

____
Address

____
____
____
Telephone Number

____
Date

*In a case in which § 707(b)(4)(D) applies, this signature also constitutes a certification that the attorney has no knowledge after an inquiry that the information in the schedules is incorrect.

Signature of Non-Attorney Bankruptcy Petition Preparer

I declare under penalty of perjury that: (1) I am a bankruptcy petition preparer as defined in 11 U.S.C. § 110; (2) I prepared this document for compensation and have provided the debtor with a copy of this document and the notices and information required under 11 U.S.C. §§ 110(b), 110(h), and 342(b); and, (3) if rules or guidelines have been promulgated pursuant to 11 U.S.C. § 110(h) setting a maximum fee for services chargeable by bankruptcy petition preparers, I have given the debtor notice of the maximum amount before preparing any document for filing for a debtor or accepting any fee from the debtor, as required in that section. Official Form 19 is attached.

____
Printed Name and title, if any, of Bankruptcy Petition Preparer

____
Social-Security number (If the bankruptcy petition preparer is not an individual, state the Social-Security number of the officer, principal, responsible person or partner of the bankruptcy petition preparer.) (Required by 11 U.S.C. § 110.)

____
Address

____

X ______________________________

____
Date

Signature of bankruptcy petition preparer or officer, principal, responsible person, or partner whose Social-Security number is provided above.

Names and Social-Security numbers of all other individuals who prepared or assisted in preparing this document unless the bankruptcy petition preparer is not an individual.

If more than one person prepared this document, attach additional sheets conforming to the appropriate official form for each person.

A bankruptcy petition preparer's failure to comply with the provisions of title 11 and the Federal Rules of Bankruptcy Procedure may result in fines or imprisonment or both. 11 U.S.C. § 110; 18 U.S.C. § 156.

Signature of Debtor (Corporation/Partnership)

I declare under penalty of perjury that the information provided in this petition is true and correct, and that I have been authorized to file this petition on behalf of the debtor.

The debtor requests the relief in accordance with the chapter of title 11, United States Code, specified in this petition.

X ______________________________
Signature of Authorized Individual

____
Printed Name of Authorized Individual

____
Title of Authorized Individual

____
Date

B 1A (Official Form 1, Exhibit A) (9/97)

[If debtor is required to file periodic reports (e.g., forms 10K and 10Q) with the Securities and Exchange Commission pursuant to Section 13 or 15(d) of the Securities Exchange Act of 1934 and is requesting relief under chapter 11 of the Bankruptcy Code, this Exhibit "A" shall be completed and attached to the petition.]

UNITED STATES BANKRUPTCY COURT

In re ____________________________,	)	Case No. __________
Debtor	)	
	)	
	)	Chapter 11

EXHIBIT "A" TO VOLUNTARY PETITION

1. If any of the debtor's securities are registered under Section 12 of the Securities Exchange Act of 1934, the SEC file number is ________________.

2. The following financial data is the latest available information and refers to the debtor's condition on ________________.

a. Total assets $ ____________

b. Total debts (including debts listed in 2.c., below) $ ____________

c. Debt securities held by more than 500 holders:				Approximate number of holders:
secured ❐	unsecured ❐	subordinated ❐	$ __________	__________
secured ❐	unsecured ❐	subordinated ❐	$ __________	__________
secured ❐	unsecured ❐	subordinated ❐	$ __________	__________
secured ❐	unsecured ❐	subordinated ❐	$ __________	__________
secured ❐	unsecured ❐	subordinated ❐	$ __________	__________
d. Number of shares of preferred stock			__________	__________
e. Number of shares common stock			__________	__________

Comments, if any:

3. Brief description of debtor's business:

4. List the names of any person who directly or indirectly owns, controls, or holds, with power to vote, 5% or more of the voting securities of debtor:

B 1C (Official Form 1, Exhibit C) (9/01)

[If, to the best of the debtor's knowledge, the debtor owns or has possession of property that poses or is alleged to pose a threat of imminent and identifiable harm to the public health or safety, attach this Exhibit "C" to the petition.]

UNITED STATES BANKRUPTCY COURT

In re ______________________________,	)	Case No. ______________
Debtor	)	
	)	
	)	Chapter ______________

EXHIBIT "C" TO VOLUNTARY PETITION

1. Identify and briefly describe all real or personal property owned by or in possession of the debtor that, to the best of the debtor's knowledge, poses or is alleged to pose a threat of imminent and identifiable harm to the public health or safety (attach additional sheets if necessary):

2. With respect to each parcel of real property or item of personal property identified in question 1, describe the nature and location of the dangerous condition, whether environmental or otherwise, that poses or is alleged to pose a threat of imminent and identifiable harm to the public health or safety (attach additional sheets if necessary):

B 1D (Official Form 1, Exhibit D) (12/09)

UNITED STATES BANKRUPTCY COURT

__________ District of __________

In re____________________________ Case No._____________
Debtor (if known)

EXHIBIT D - INDIVIDUAL DEBTOR'S STATEMENT OF COMPLIANCE WITH CREDIT COUNSELING REQUIREMENT

Warning: You must be able to check truthfully one of the five statements regarding credit counseling listed below. If you cannot do so, you are not eligible to file a bankruptcy case, and the court can dismiss any case you do file. If that happens, you will lose whatever filing fee you paid, and your creditors will be able to resume collection activities against you. If your case is dismissed and you file another bankruptcy case later, you may be required to pay a second filing fee and you may have to take extra steps to stop creditors' collection activities.

Every individual debtor must file this Exhibit D. If a joint petition is filed, each spouse must complete and file a separate Exhibit D. Check one of the five statements below and attach any documents as directed.

❒ 1. Within the 180 days **before the filing of my bankruptcy case,** I received a briefing from a credit counseling agency approved by the United States trustee or bankruptcy administrator that outlined the opportunities for available credit counseling and assisted me in performing a related budget analysis, and I have a certificate from the agency describing the services provided to me. *Attach a copy of the certificate and a copy of any debt repayment plan developed through the agency.*

❒ 2. Within the 180 days **before the filing of my bankruptcy case,** I received a briefing from a credit counseling agency approved by the United States trustee or bankruptcy administrator that outlined the opportunities for available credit counseling and assisted me in performing a related budget analysis, but I do not have a certificate from the agency describing the services provided to me. *You must file a copy of a certificate from the agency describing the services provided to you and a copy of any debt repayment plan developed through the agency no later than 14 days after your bankruptcy case is filed.*

B 1D (Official Form 1, Exh. D) (12/09) – Cont. Page 2

☐ 3. I certify that I requested credit counseling services from an approved agency but was unable to obtain the services during the seven days from the time I made my request, and the following exigent circumstances merit a temporary waiver of the credit counseling requirement so I can file my bankruptcy case now. *[Summarize exigent circumstances here.]*

____

____

____

____

If your certification is satisfactory to the court, you must still obtain the credit counseling briefing within the first 30 days after you file your bankruptcy petition and promptly file a certificate from the agency that provided the counseling, together with a copy of any debt management plan developed through the agency. Failure to fulfill these requirements may result in dismissal of your case. Any extension of the 30-day deadline can be granted only for cause and is limited to a maximum of 15 days. Your case may also be dismissed if the court is not satisfied with your reasons for filing your bankruptcy case without first receiving a credit counseling briefing.

☐ 4. I am not required to receive a credit counseling briefing because of: *[Check the applicable statement.] [Must be accompanied by a motion for determination by the court.]*

☐ Incapacity. (Defined in 11 U.S.C. § 109(h)(4) as impaired by reason of mental illness or mental deficiency so as to be incapable of realizing and making rational decisions with respect to financial responsibilities.);

☐ Disability. (Defined in 11 U.S.C. § 109(h)(4) as physically impaired to the extent of being unable, after reasonable effort, to participate in a credit counseling briefing in person, by telephone, or through the Internet.);

☐ Active military duty in a military combat zone.

☐ 5. The United States trustee or bankruptcy administrator has determined that the credit counseling requirement of 11 U.S.C. § 109(h) does not apply in this district.

I certify under penalty of perjury that the information provided above is true and correct.

Signature of Debtor: ________________________

Date: ________________

(Added Aug. 1, 1991; amended Mar. 16, 1993; Mar. 14, 1995; Oct. 1, 1997; Dec. 1, 2001; Dec. 1, 2002; Dec. 1, 2003; Oct. 17, 2005; Oct. 1, 2006; Dec. 1, 2007; Jan. 1, 2008; Dec. 1, 2008; Dec. 1, 2009.)

NOTES OF ADVISORY COMMITTEE ON RULES—1991

Form 1, the Voluntary Petition, is to be used to commence a voluntary case under chapter 7, 11, 12, or 13 of the Bankruptcy Code. A chapter 9 petition requires other allegations, (see § 109(c) of the Code), but this form may be adapted for such use. The form also may be adapted for use in filing a petition ancillary to a foreign proceeding under § 304 of the Code.

The form departs from the traditional format of a captioned pleading. All of the elements of the caption prescribed in Rule 1005 have been retained. Their placement on the page, however, has been changed to make the form compatible with electronic data processing by the clerk. The form of the caption of the case for use in other documents, formerly incorporated in Official Form No. 1, has been made a separate Form 16A.

All names used by the debtor, including trade names, names used in doing business, married names, and maiden names should be furnished in the spaces provided. If there is not sufficient room for all such names on the form itself, the list should be continued on an additional sheet attached to the petition. A complete list will enable creditors to identify the debtor properly when they receive notices and orders.

Redesign of this form into a box format also is intended to provide the court, the United States trustee, and other interested parties with as much information as possible during the 15-day period provided by Rule 1007(c), when schedules and statements may not have been filed. The box format separates into categories the data provided by the debtor, and enables the form to be used by all voluntary debtors in all chapters.

For the first time, the form requires both a street address and any separate mailing address, as well as any separate addresses used by a joint debtor. Disclosure of prior bankruptcies is new to the petition but formerly was required in the statement of financial affairs; its inclusion in the petition is intended to alert the trustee to cases in which an objection to discharge pursuant to §727(a)(8) or (a)(9) or a motion to dismiss under §109(g) may be appropriate. The information about pending related cases, also new to the petition, signals the clerk to assign the case to the judge to whom any related case has been assigned.

Rule 1008 requires all petitions to be verified or contain an unsworn declaration as provided in 28 U.S.C. §1746. The unsworn declaration on page two of the petition conforms with 28 U.S.C. §1746, which permits the declaration to be made in the manner indicated with the same force and effect as a sworn statement. The form may be adapted for use outside the United States by adding the words "under the laws of the United States" after the word "perjury."

Exhibit "A," to be attached to the petition of a corporate debtor, is for the purpose of supplying the Securities and Exchange Commission with information it needs at the beginning stages of a chapter 11 case in order to determine how actively to monitor the proceedings. Exhibit "B" was added by §322 of Pub. L. No. 98-353, the Bankruptcy Amendments and Federal Judgeship Act of 1984. The references to chapters 11 and 12 of the Code found in Exhibit "B" and its related allegations were added by §283(aa) of the 1986 amendments, (Pub. L. No. 99-554). This exhibit has been included in the form of the petition.

The form effects a merger of the petition and the bankruptcy cover sheet to assist the clerk in providing the statistical information required by the Director of the Administrative Office of the United States Courts pursuant to the Congressional reporting mandates of 28 U.S.C. §604. The Director is authorized to change the particulars of the statistical portion of the form as needed in the performance of these statutory duties.

NOTES OF ADVISORY COMMITTEE ON RULES—1993 AMENDMENT

The form has been amended to require a debtor not represented by an attorney to provide a telephone number so that court personnel, the trustee, other parties in the case, and their attorneys can contact the debtor concerning matters in the case.

NOTES OF ADVISORY COMMITTEE ON RULES—1995 AMENDMENT

The form is amended to provide space for signing by a "bankruptcy petition preparer," as required under section 110 of the Code, which was added by the Bankruptcy Reform Act of 1994. In addition to signing, a bankruptcy petition preparer is required by section 110 to disclose the information requested. All signatories of Form 1 are requested to provide the clerk's office with a telephone number.

A chapter 11 debtor that qualifies as a "small business" under section 101 of the Code, as amended by the 1994 Act, may elect special, expedited treatment under amendments made to chapter 11 by the 1994 Act. The court may order that a creditors committee not be appointed in a small business case. Accordingly, the first page of the petition is amended to require a small business filing under chapter 11 to identify itself. The petition also is amended to offer a small business chapter 11 debtor an opportunity to exercise its right to elect to be considered a small business at the commencement of the case.

Several clarifying and technical amendments also have been made to indicate that a debtor is to check only one box with respect to "Type of Debtor" and "Nature of Debt," to clarify the intent that the individual signing on behalf of a corporation or partnership is authorized to file the petition, and to require a debtor to represent that it is eligible for relief under the chapter of title 11 specified in the petition.

NOTES OF ADVISORY COMMITTEE ON RULES—1997 AMENDMENT

The form has been substantially amended to simplify its format and make the form easier to complete correctly. The Latin phrase "In re" has been deleted as unnecessary. The amount of information requested in the boxes labeled "Type of Debtor" and "Nature of Debt" has been reduced, and the reporting by a corporation of whether it is a publicly held entity has been moved to Exhibit "A" of the petition. The box labeled "Representation by Attorney" has been deleted; the information it contained is requested in the signature boxes on the second page of the form.

In the statistical information section, the labels on the ranges of estimated assets and liabilities have been rewritten to improve the accuracy of reporting. The asset/liability range of $10 million to $100 million has been divided into two categories to promote better statistical reporting of business cases. Requests for information in chapter 11 and chapter 12 cases concerning the number of the debtor's employees and equity security holders have been deleted.

The second page of the form has been simplified so that a debtor need only sign the petition once. The request for information concerning the filing of a plan has been deleted.

Exhibit "A" has been simplified. In addition, the category of chapter 11 debtors required to file Exhibit "A" is modified to include a corporation, partnership, or other entity, but only if the debtor has issued publicly-traded equity securities or debt instruments. Most small corporations will not be required to file Exhibit "A."

COMMITTEE NOTES ON RULES—2001 AMENDMENT

The form has been amended to require the debtor to disclose whether the debtor owns or has possession of any property that poses or is alleged to pose a threat of imminent and identifiable harm to public health or safety. If any such property exists, the debtor must complete and attach Exhibit "C" describing the property, its location, and the potential danger it poses. Exhibit "C" will alert the United States trustee and any person selected as trustee that immediate precautionary action may be necessary.

COMMITTEE NOTES ON RULES—2002 AMENDMENT

The form has been amended to provide a checkbox for designating a clearing bank case filed under subchapter V of chapter 7 of the Code enacted by §112 of Pub. L. No. 106-554 (December 21, 2000).

COMMITTEE NOTES ON RULES—2003 AMENDMENT

The form is amended to require the debtor to disclose only the last four digits of the debtor's social security number to afford greater privacy to the individual debtor, whose bankruptcy case records may be available on the Internet. Pursuant to §110(c) of the Bankruptcy Code, the certification by a non-attorney bankruptcy petition preparer requires a petition preparer to provide the full social security number of the individual who actually prepares the document.

COMMITTEE NOTES ON RULES—2005 AMENDMENT

The form is amended to implement amendments to the Bankruptcy Code contained in the Bankruptcy Abuse Prevention and Consumer Protection Act of 2005, Pub. L. No. 109-8, 119 Stat. 23 (April 20, 2005). The period for which the debtor must provide all names used and information about any prior bankruptcy cases is now eight years to match the required time between the granting of discharges to the same debtor in §727(a)(8) of the Code as amended in 2005. The box indicating the debtor's selection of a chapter under which to file the case has been amended to delete "Sec. 304 - Case ancillary to foreign proceeding" and replace it with "Chapter 15 Petition for Recognition of a Foreign Main Proceeding" and "Chapter 15 Petition for Recognition of a Foreign Nonmain Proceeding" reflecting the 2005 repeal of §304 and enactment of chapter 15 of the Code. A statement of venue to be used in a chapter 15 case also has been added.

The section of the form labeled "Type of Debtor" has been revised and subtitled "Form of Organization." This section is revised to make it clear that a limited liability corporation ("LLC") and limited liability partnership ("LLP") should identify itself as a "corporation." A new section titled "Nature of Business" has been created that includes both existing check boxes that identify certain types of debtors for which the Bankruptcy Code provides special treatment, such as stockbrokers and railroads, and a new checkbox for a "health care business" for which the 2005 amendments to the Code include specific requirements. This section of the form also contains checkboxes for single asset real estate debtors and nonprofit organizations which will be used by trustees and creditors and by the Director of the Administrative Office of the United States Courts in preparing statistical reports and analyses. The statistical section of the form also is amended to provide more detail concerning the number of creditors in a case. A check box also has been added for a debtor to indicate that the debtor is applying for a waiver of the filing fee, to implement the 2005 enactment of 28 U.S.C. §1930(f) authorizing the bankruptcy court to waive the filing fee in certain circumstances.

Although the 2005 Act eliminated an eligible debtor's option to elect to be treated as a "small business" in a chapter 11 case, new provisions for such debtors added to the Code in 2005 make it desirable to identify eligible debtors at the outset of the case. Accordingly, the section of the form labeled "Chapter 11 Small Business" has been revised and renamed "Chapter 11 Debtors" for this purpose. Chapter 11 debtors that meet the definition of "small business debtor" in §101 of the Code are directed to identify themselves in this section of the form. In addition, chapter 11 debtors whose aggregate noncontingent debts owed to non-insiders or affiliates are less than $2 million are directed to identify themselves in this section.

A space is provided for individuals to certify that they have received budget and credit counseling prior to filing, as required by §109(h) which was added to the Code in 2005, or to request a waiver of the requirement. Space also is provided for a debtor who is a tenant of residential real property to state whether the debtor's landlord has a judgment against the debtor for possession of the premises, whether under applicable nonbankruptcy law the debtor would be permitted to cure the monetary default, and whether the debtor has made the appropriate deposit with the court. This addition to the form implements §362(l) which was added to the Code in 2005.

The signature sections and the declaration under penalty of perjury by an individual debtor concerning the notice received about bankruptcy relief, the declaration under penalty of perjury by a bankruptcy petition preparer, and the declaration and certification by an attorney all are amended to include new material mandated by the 2005 Act. A signature section also is provided for a representative of a foreign proceeding.

COMMITTEE NOTES ON RULES—2006 AMENDMENT

Page one of the form is amended in several ways to assist the courts in evaluating their workload and fulfilling the statistical reporting requirements of 28 U.S.C. §159. Section 159 was enacted as part of the Bankruptcy Abuse Prevention and Consumer Protection Act of 2005 (BAPCPA), Pub. L. No. 109-8 and takes effect October 17, 2006. Accordingly, in the section of the form labeled "Nature of Business," the instruction is amended to specify that only one box should be checked and only if the debtor is any of the entities listed. The "nonprofit" choice is separated into a discrete section and the language amended to the more precise "tax-exempt."

In addition, the section labeled "Type of Debtor" is amended to include, below the checkbox for "Individual or Joint," a direction to "See Exhibit D on page 2 of this form." Exhibit D replaces the certification concerning prepetition credit counseling and is described below. The section labeled "Nature of Debts" is amended to state the statutory definition of a "consumer debt" and to modify both the consumer and business categories by adding the word "primarily" to both make it clearer to individual debtors that "business" may be the more appropriate choice if personal debts have been incurred to finance a business venture.

In the section labeled "Chapter 11 Debtors," the language concerning whether the debtor owes less than $2 million is re-styled for clarity. This section also is augmented to provide the court with notice when a case if [sic] filed as a "pre-packaged" chapter 11 reorganization case. Two checkboxes are offered, using language adapted from §1126(b) of the Code. Lastly, the information requested concerning estimated assets and liabilities is abbreviated, with the number of ranges reduced and the scope of each range amended. Statistical reports now will be derived from actual dollar amounts of assets and liabilities as shown on the debtor's schedules. The information on the petition, accordingly, is for case management and public information purposes only.

Exhibit D replaces the section formerly labeled "Certification Concerning Debt Counseling by Individual/Joint Debtor(s)." Early cases decided under the 2005 amendments to the Bankruptcy Code indicate that individual debtors may not be aware of the requirement to obtain prepetition credit counseling, the few and very narrow exceptions to that requirement, or the potentially dire consequences to their efforts to obtain bankruptcy relief if they fail to complete the requirement. Accordingly, page 2 of the petition instructs individual debtors to attach a completed Exhibit D and makes it clear that each spouse in a joint case must complete and attach a separate Exhibit D. Exhibit D itself includes a warning about the requirement to obtain counseling and the consequences of failing to fulfill this requirement. It further provides checkboxes and instructions concerning the additional documents that are required in particular circumstances, in order to minimize the number of cases which the court must dismiss for ineligibility.

COMMITTEE NOTES ON RULES—2005-2007 AMENDMENT

[The 2005-2007 Committee Note incorporates Committee Notes previously published in 2005 and 2006.]

The form is amended to implement amendments to the Bankruptcy Code contained in the Bankruptcy Abuse Prevention and Consumer Protection Act of 2005, Pub. L. No. 109-8, 119 Stat. 23 (April 20, 2005) ("BAPCPA"). The period for which the debtor must provide all names used and information about any prior bankruptcy cases is now eight years to match the required time between the granting of discharges to the same debtor in §727(a)(8) of the Code as amended in 2005. In conformity with Rule 9037, the debtor is directed to provide only the last four digits of any individual's tax-identification number.

The box indicating the debtor's selection of a chapter under which to file the case is amended to delete "Sec. 304—Case ancillary to foreign proceeding" and replace it with "Chapter 15 Petition for Recognition of a Foreign Main Proceeding" and "Chapter 15 Petition for Recognition of a Foreign Nonmain Proceeding" reflecting the 2005 repeal of §304 and enactment of chapter 15 of the Code. A statement of venue to be used in a chapter 15 case also is added on page 2 of the form.

The section labeled "Type of Debtor" is amended to include, below the checkbox for "Individual or Joint," a direction to "See Exhibit D on page 2 of this form." This addition alerts individual debtors that Exhibit D on page 2 of the form applies to them. Exhibit D, more fully described below, addresses the prepetition credit counseling requirements added to the Code by BAPCPA. The subtitle, "Form of Organization," is added, and this section also is revised to make clear that a limited liability corporation ("LLC") or limited liability partnership ("LLP") should identify itself as a "corporation."

The form also is amended in several ways to assist the courts in evaluating their workload and fulfilling the statistical reporting requirements of 28 U.S.C. §159, enacted as part of BAPCPA. Accordingly, a new section of the form labeled "Nature of Business," is added that contains both existing checkboxes that identify certain types of debtors for which the Bankruptcy Code provides special treatment, such as stockbrokers and railroads, and a new checkbox for a "health care business" for which the 2005 amendments to the Code include specific requirements. This section of the form also contains a checkbox for single asset real estate debtors, so they can be identified at the time of filing. All other businesses will mark the checkbox labeled "Other." Another new section titled "Tax-Exempt Entity" contains a checkbox to be used by qualified organizations. The Judicial Conference of the United States and the Administrative Office of the United States Courts will use this information in preparing statistical reports and analyses for Congress.

A checkbox also is added for an individual debtor to indicate that the debtor is applying for a waiver of the filing fee, to implement the 2005 enactment of 28 U.S.C. §1930(f) authorizing the bankruptcy court to waive the filing fee in certain circumstances. The description directs the debtor to the Official Form for the application that must be filed for the court's consideration.

The section labeled "Nature of Debts" is amended to state the statutory definition of a "consumer debt" and to modify both the consumer and business categories by adding the word "primarily" to both choices to make it clearer to individual debtors that "business" may be the appropriate choice if personal debts have been incurred to finance a business venture.

Although the 2005 Act eliminated from the Code any option to elect to be treated as a "small business" in a chapter 11 case, new provisions for "small business" debtors added by BAPCPA make it desirable to identify eligible debtors at the outset of the case. Accordingly, the section of the form labeled "Chapter 11 Small Business" is revised and renamed "Chapter 11 Debtors" for this purpose. Chapter 11 debtors that meet the definition of "small business debtor" in §101 of the Code are directed to identify themselves in this section of the form. Chapter 11 debtors whose aggregate noncontingent debts owed to non-insiders or affiliates are less than $2,190,000 are directed to identify themselves in this section. A third part of this section attempts to identify chapter 11 cases that are filed as pre-packaged cases, using criteria taken from §1126(b) of the Code. Identifying "pre-packs" at filing will assist judges and court staff to manage these cases appropriately.

The statistical information concerning the number of creditors and estimated assets and liabilities is revised to provide more detail.

BAPCPA also added a new §109(h) to the Code. To implement this provision, a section labeled "Exhibit D" is inserted on page 2 of the form, and a separate Exhibit D is added. These additions will enable individual debtors to certify that they have received budget and credit counseling prior to filing, as required by §109(h), or request a temporary waiver of, or exemption from, the requirement, if they meet the statutory requirements for such relief. Exhibit D includes directions to attach required documentation or, if the debtor requests a temporary waiver or an exemption, a motion for a determination by the court. Exhibit D also states the requirement that all individual debtors must obtain a briefing from an approved credit counseling agency before filing a bankruptcy case, unless one of the very limited exceptions applies, and further states the consequences that may be faced by any debtor who fails to comply.

Space is provided on page 2 for a debtor who is a tenant of residential real property to certify whether the debtor's landlord has a judgment against the debtor for possession of the premises, whether under applicable nonbankruptcy law the debtor would be permitted to cure the monetary default, and whether the debtor has made the appropriate deposit with the court. This addition to the form implements §362(l) which was added to the Code in 2005. And a box is provided that allows the debtor to certify that s/he has served the landlord with the certification as required by §362(l)(1).

The signature sections and the declaration under penalty of perjury by an individual debtor concerning the notice received about bankruptcy relief, the declaration under penalty of perjury by a bankruptcy petition preparer, and the attorney signature box are amended to include new material mandated by the 2005 Act. The attorney signature box is also amended to remind the attorney that in a case in which §707(b)(4)(D) applies, that the signature constitutes a certification that the attorney has no knowledge after an inquiry that the information in the schedules filed with the petition is incorrect. A signature section is also provided for a representative of a foreign proceeding.

Committee Notes on Rules—2008 Amendment

Paragraph 3 of Exhibit D is amended to delete any reference to a requirement that a debtor file a motion with the court to obtain an order approving a request for the postponement of the debtor's obligation to obtain a credit counseling briefing prior to the commencement of the case. The paragraph immediately following numbered paragraph 3 is also amended to reflect the deletion of the need for a separate motion beyond the completion of the certification itself. That paragraph continues to warn the debtor that the case may be dismissed if the court does not find that a postponement is warranted. It also advises the debtor that, even if the court concludes that postponement of the obligation is appropriate, the debtor still must complete the briefing within the time allowed under the Code.

Official Form 2
6/90

DECLARATION UNDER PENALTY OF PERJURY ON BEHALF OF A CORPORATION OR PARTNERSHIP

I, [the president *or* other officer *or* an authorized agent of the corporation] [*or* a member *or* an authorized agent of the partnership] named as the debtor in this case, declare under penalty of perjury that I have read the foregoing [list *or* schedule *or* amendment *or* other document (describe)] and that it is true and correct to the best of my information and belief.

Date ________________________

Signature __________________________________

____
(Print Name and Title)

(Added Aug. 1, 1991.)

NOTES OF ADVISORY COMMITTEE ON RULES—1991

This form is derived from former Official Form No. 4. Rule 1008 requires that all petitions, lists, schedules, statements, and amendments thereto be verified or contain an unsworn declaration conforming with 28 U.S.C. §1746. This form or adaptations of the form have been incorporated into the official forms of the petitions, schedules, and statement of financial affairs. See Official Forms 1, 5, 6, and 7. The form has been amended for use in connection with other papers required by these rules to be verified or contain an unsworn declaration.

B 3A (Official Form 3A) (12/07)

UNITED STATES BANKRUPTCY COURT

In re ______________________________________,
Debtor

Case No. ____________________

Chapter ____________

APPLICATION TO PAY FILING FEE IN INSTALLMENTS

1. In accordance with Fed. R. Bankr. P. 1006, I apply for permission to pay the filing fee amounting to $__________ in installments.

2. I am unable to pay the filing fee except in installments.

3. Until the filing fee is paid in full, I will not make any additional payment or transfer any additional property to an attorney or any other person for services in connection with this case.

4. I propose the following terms for the payment of the Filing Fee.*

$ _______________ Check one ☐ With the filing of the petition, or
☐ On or before ___________

$ _______________ on or before ______________________________

$ _______________ on or before ______________________________

$ _______________ on or before ______________________________

* The number of installments proposed shall not exceed four (4), and the final installment shall be payable not later than 120 days after filing the petition. For cause shown, the court may extend the time of any installment, provided the last installment is paid not later than 180 days after filing the petition. Fed. R. Bankr. P. 1006(b)(2).

5. I understand that if I fail to pay any installment when due, my bankruptcy case may be dismissed and I may not receive a discharge of my debts.

____
Signature of Attorney Date

____
Name of Attorney

____
Signature of Debtor Date
(In a joint case, both spouses must sign.)

____
Signature of Joint Debtor (if any) Date

DECLARATION AND SIGNATURE OF NON-ATTORNEY BANKRUPTCY PETITION PREPARER (See 11 U.S.C. § 110)

I declare under penalty of perjury that: (1) I am a bankruptcy petition preparer as defined in 11 U.S.C. § 110; (2) I prepared this document for compensation and have provided the debtor with a copy of this document and the notices and information required under 11 U.S.C. §§ 110(b), 110(h), and 342(b); (3) if rules or guidelines have been promulgated pursuant to 11 U.S.C. § 110(h) setting a maximum fee for services chargeable by bankruptcy petition preparers, I have given the debtor notice of the maximum amount before preparing any document for filing for a debtor or accepting any fee from the debtor, as required under that section; and (4) I will not accept any additional money or other property from the debtor before the filing fee is paid in full.

____
Printed or Typed Name and Title, if any, of Bankruptcy Petition Preparer

____
Social-Security No. (Required by 11 U.S.C. § 110.)

If the bankruptcy petition preparer is not an individual, state the name, title (if any), address, and social-security number of the officer, principal, responsible person, or partner who signs the document.

____

____
Address

x_______________________________
Signature of Bankruptcy Petition Preparer

____
Date

Names and Social-Security numbers of all other individuals who prepared or assisted in preparing this document, unless the bankruptcy petition preparer is not an individual:

If more than one person prepared this document, attach additional signed sheets conforming to the appropriate Official Form for each person.
A bankruptcy petition preparer's failure to comply with the provisions of title 11 and the Federal Rules of Bankruptcy Procedure may result in fines or imprisonment or both. 11 U.S.C. § 110; 18 U.S.C. § 156.

B 3A (Official Form 3A) (12/07) - Cont.

UNITED STATES BANKRUPTCY COURT

In re ______________________________________,
Debtor

Case No. ____________________

Chapter ___________

ORDER APPROVING PAYMENT OF FILING FEE IN INSTALLMENTS

☐ IT IS ORDERED that the debtor(s) may pay the filing fee in installments on the terms proposed in the foregoing application.

☐ IT IS ORDERED that the debtor(s) shall pay the filing fee according to the following terms:

$ ____________________ Check one ☐ With the filing of the petition, or
☐ On or before ______________

$ ____________________ on or before ____

$ ____________________ on or before ____

$ ____________________ on or before ____

☐ IT IS FURTHER ORDERED that until the filing fee is paid in full the debtor(s) shall not make any additional payment or transfer any additional property to an attorney or any other person for services in connection with this case.

BY THE COURT

Date: ____________________

____
United States Bankruptcy Judge

(Added Aug. 1, 1991; amended Mar. 14, 1995; Oct. 1, 1997; Dec. 1, 2003; Oct. 17, 2005; Dec. 1, 2007.)

NOTES OF ADVISORY COMMITTEE ON RULES—1991

This form is derived from former Official Form No. 2. A statement that the applicant is unable to pay the filing fee except in installments has been added as required by Rule 1006(b).

NOTES OF ADVISORY COMMITTEE ON RULES—1995 AMENDMENT

This form is a "document for filing" that may be prepared by a "bankruptcy petition preparer" as defined in 11 U.S.C. §110, which was added to the Code by the Bankruptcy Reform Act of 1994; accordingly, a signature line is provided for such preparer. In addition to signing, a bankruptcy petition preparer is required by section 110 to disclose the information requested. A signature line for a debtor's attorney also is added, as required by Rule 9011.

NOTES OF ADVISORY COMMITTEE ON RULES—1997 AMENDMENT

The form has been reorganized and the paragraphs numbered. The debtor's certification concerning payment for services in the case has been placed ahead of the statement of proposed terms for installment payment of court fees. Acknowledgement by the debtor of the potential consequences of failure to pay any installment when due has been added. (See 11 U.S.C. §707(a)(2).) The language of the form also has been changed to conform to Rule 1006 and to clarify that a debtor is not disqualified from paying the filing fee in installments because the debtor has paid money to a bankruptcy petition preparer.

COMMITTEE NOTES ON RULES—2003 AMENDMENT

Pursuant to §110(c) of the Bankruptcy Code, the certification by a non-attorney bankruptcy petition preparer requires a petition preparer to provide the full social security number of the individual who actually prepares the document pursuant to §110(c) of the Code.

COMMITTEE NOTES ON RULES—2005 AMENDMENT

The form is amended to direct the debtor to state that, until the filing fee is paid in full, the debtor will not make any additional payment or transfer any additional property to an attorney or any other person for services in connection with the case. The declaration and certification by a non-attorney bankruptcy petition preparer in the form are amended to include material mandated by §110 of the Code as amended by the Bankruptcy Abuse Prevention and Consumer Protection Act of 2005, Pub. L. No. 109–8, 119 Stat. 23 (April 20, 2005). The certification by a non-attorney bankruptcy petition preparer is re-named a declaration and also is revised to include material mandated by §110 of the Code as amended in 2005. The order is amended to provide space for the court to set forth a payment schedule other than the one proposed by the debtor.

COMMITTEE NOTES ON RULES—2005–2007 AMENDMENT

[The 2005–2007 Committee Note incorporates the Committee Note previously published in 2005.]

The form is amended to direct the debtor to state that, until the filing fee is paid in full, the debtor will not make any additional payment or transfer any additional property to an attorney or any other person for services in connection with the case. The declaration and certification by a non-attorney bankruptcy petition preparer in the form are amended to include material mandated by §110 of the Code as amended by the Bankruptcy Abuse Prevention and Consumer Protection Act of 2005, Pub. L. No. 109–8, 119 Stat. 23 (April 20, 2005). The certification by a non-attorney bankruptcy petition preparer is re-named a declaration and also is revised to include material mandated by §110 of the Code as amended in 2005. The order is amended to provide space for the court to set forth a payment schedule other than the one proposed by the debtor.

B 3B (Official Form 3B) (12/07)

APPLICATION FOR WAIVER OF THE CHAPTER 7 FILING FEE FOR INDIVIDUALS WHO CANNOT PAY THE FILING FEE IN FULL OR IN INSTALLMENTS

The court fee for filing a case under chapter 7 of the Bankruptcy Code is $299.

If you cannot afford to pay the full fee at the time of filing, you may apply to pay the fee in installments. A form, which is available from the bankruptcy clerk's office, must be completed to make that application. If your application to pay in installments is approved, you will be permitted to file your petition, generally completing payment of the fee over the course of four to six months.

If you cannot afford to pay the fee either in full at the time of filing or in installments, you may request a waiver of the filing fee by completing this application and filing it with the Clerk of Court. A judge will decide whether you have to pay the fee. By law, the judge may waive the fee only if your income is less than 150 percent of the official poverty line applicable to your family size and you are unable to pay the fee in installments. You may obtain information about the poverty guidelines at www.uscourts.gov or in the bankruptcy clerk's office.

Required information. Complete all items in the application, and attach requested schedules. Then sign the application on the last page. If you and your spouse are filing a joint bankruptcy petition, you both must provide information as requested and sign the application.

B 3B (Official Form 3B) (12/07) – Cont.

UNITED STATES BANKRUPTCY COURT

In re: ____________________ Case No. ____________________
Debtor(s) (if known)

APPLICATION FOR WAIVER OF THE CHAPTER 7 FILING FEE FOR INDIVIDUALS WHO CANNOT PAY THE FILING FEE IN FULL OR IN INSTALLMENTS

Part A. Family Size and Income

1. Including yourself, your spouse, and dependents you have listed or will list on Schedule I (Current Income of Individual Debtors(s)), how many people are in your family? (Do not include your spouse if you are separated AND are not filing a joint petition.) _________

2. Restate the following information that you provided, or will provide, on Line 16 of Schedule I. Attach a completed copy of Schedule I, if it is available.

   Total Combined Monthly Income (Line 16 of Schedule I): $____________

3. State the monthly net income, if any, of dependents included in Question 1 above. Do not include any income already reported in Item 2. If none, enter $0.

   $____________

4. Add the "Total Combined Monthly Income" reported in Question 2 to your dependents' monthly net income from Question 3.

   $____________

5. Do you expect the amount in Question 4 to increase or decrease by more than 10% during the next 6 months? Yes ___ No ___

   If yes, explain.

Part B. Monthly Expenses

6. EITHER (a) attach a completed copy of Schedule J (Schedule of Monthly Expenses), and state your total monthly expenses reported on Line 18 of that Schedule, OR (b) if you have not yet completed Schedule J, provide an estimate of your total monthly expenses.

   $____________

7. Do you expect the amount in Question 6 to increase or decrease by more than 10% during the next 6 months? Yes ___ No ___
   If yes, explain.

Part C. Real and Personal Property

EITHER (1) attach completed copies of Schedule A (Real Property) and Schedule B (Personal Property), OR (2) if you have not yet completed those schedules, answer the following questions.

8. State the amount of cash you have on hand. $____________

9. State below any money you have in savings, checking, or other accounts in a bank or other financial institution.

Bank or Other Financial Institution:	Type of Account such as savings, checking, CD:	Amount:
____________	____________	$__________
____________	____________	$__________

B 3B (Official Form 3B) (12/07) – Cont.

10. State below the assets owned by you. **Do not list ordinary household furnishings and clothing.**

Home — Address: ______________ ______________ — Value: $ ______________ Amount owed on mortgages and liens: $ ______________

Other real estate — Address: ______________ ______________ — Value: $ ______________ Amount owed on mortgages and liens: $ ______________

Motor vehicle — Model/Year: ______________ ______________ — Value: $ ______________ Amount owed: $ ______________

Motor vehicle — Model/Year: ______________ ______________ — Value: $ ______________ Amount owed: $ ______________

Other — Description ______________ ______________ — Value: $ ______________ Amount owed: $ ______________

11. State below any person, business, organization, or governmental unit that owes you money and the amount that is owed.

Name of Person, Business, or Organization that Owes You Money	Amount Owed
______________	$ ______________
______________	$ ______________

Part D. Additional Information.

12. Have you paid an **attorney** any money for services in connection with this case, including the completion of this form, the bankruptcy petition, or schedules? Yes ___ No ___
If yes, how much have you paid? $ ______________

13. Have you promised to pay or do you anticipate paying an **attorney** in connection with your bankruptcy case? Yes ___ No ___
If yes, how much have you promised to pay or do you anticipate paying? $ ______________

14. Have you paid **anyone other than an attorney** (such as a bankruptcy petition preparer, paralegal, typing service, or another person) any money for services in connection with this case, including the completion of this form, the bankruptcy petition, or schedules? Yes ___ No ___
If yes, how much have you paid? $ ______________

15. Have you promised to pay or do you anticipate paying **anyone other than an attorney** (such as a bankruptcy petition preparer, paralegal, typing service, or another person) any money for services in connection with this case, including the completion of this form, the bankruptcy petition, or schedules? Yes ___ No ___
If yes, how much have you promised to pay or do you anticipate paying? $ ______________

16. Has anyone paid an attorney or other person or service in connection with this case, on your behalf? Yes ___ No ___

If yes, explain.

B 3B (Official Form 3B) (12/07) -- Cont.

17. Have you previously filed for bankruptcy relief during the past eight years? Yes ___ No ___

Case Number (if known)	Year filed	Location of filing	Did you obtain a discharge? (if known)
________	____	________	Yes ___ No ___ Don't know ___
________	____	________	Yes ___ No ___ Don't know ___

18. Please provide any other information that helps to explain why you are unable to pay the filing fee in installments.

19. I (we) declare under penalty of perjury that I (we) cannot currently afford to pay the filing fee in full or in installments and that the foregoing information is true and correct.

Executed on: ________________ ________________________
Date Signature of Debtor

________________ ________________________
Date Signature of Codebtor

DECLARATION AND SIGNATURE OF BANKRUPTCY PETITION PREPARER (See 11 U.S.C. § 110)

I declare under penalty of perjury that: (1) I am a bankruptcy petition preparer as defined in 11 U.S.C. § 110; (2) I prepared this document for compensation and have provided the debtor with a copy of this document and the notices and information required under 11 U.S.C. §§ 110(b), 110(h), and 342(b); and (3) if rules or guidelines have been promulgated pursuant to 11 U.S.C. § 110(h) setting a maximum fee for services chargeable by bankruptcy petition preparers, I have given the debtor notice of the maximum amount before preparing any document for filing for a debtor or accepting any fee from the debtor, as required under that section.

____ ____________________
Printed or Typed Name and Title, if any, of Bankruptcy Petition Preparer Social-Security No. (Required by 11 U.S.C. §110.)

If the bankruptcy petition preparer is not an individual, state the name, title (if any), address, and social-security number of the officer, principal, responsible person, or partner who signs the document.

____

____
Address

x________________________________ ____________________
Signature of Bankruptcy Petition Preparer Date

Names and Social-Security numbers of all other individuals who prepared or assisted in preparing this document, unless the bankruptcy petition preparer is not an individual:

If more than one person prepared this document, attach additional signed sheets conforming to the appropriate Official Form for each person.

A bankruptcy petition preparer's failure to comply with the provisions of title 11 and the Federal Rules of Bankruptcy Procedure may result in fines or imprisonment or both. 11 U.S.C. § 110; 18 U.S.C. § 156.

B 3B (Official Form 3B) (12/07) -- Cont.

UNITED STATES BANKRUPTCY COURT

In re: ____________________ Case No. ____________________
Debtor(s)

ORDER ON DEBTOR'S APPLICATION FOR WAIVER OF THE CHAPTER 7 FILING FEE

Upon consideration of the debtor's "Application for Waiver of the Chapter 7 Filing Fee," the court orders that the application be:

[ ] GRANTED.

This order is subject to being vacated at a later time if developments in the administration of the bankruptcy case demonstrate that the waiver was unwarranted.

[ ] DENIED.

The debtor shall pay the chapter 7 filing fee according to the following terms:

$ __________ on or before __________

$ __________ on or before __________

$ __________ on or before __________

$ __________ on or before __________

Until the filing fee is paid in full, the debtor shall not make any additional payment or transfer any additional property to an attorney or any other person for services in connection with this case.

IF THE DEBTOR FAILS TO TIMELY PAY THE FILING FEE IN FULL OR TO TIMELY MAKE INSTALLMENT PAYMENTS, THE COURT MAY DISMISS THE DEBTOR'S CASE.

[ ] SCHEDULED FOR HEARING.

A hearing to consider the debtor's "Application for Waiver of the Chapter 7 Filing Fee" shall be held on ____________________ at ________ am/pm at ____.
(address of courthouse)

IF THE DEBTOR FAILS TO APPEAR AT THE SCHEDULED HEARING, THE COURT MAY DEEM SUCH FAILURE TO BE THE DEBTOR'S CONSENT TO THE ENTRY OF AN ORDER DENYING THE FEE WAIVER APPLICATION BY DEFAULT.

BY THE COURT:

DATE: __________

____
United States Bankruptcy Judge

(Added Oct. 17, 2005; amended Apr. 9, 2006; Dec. 1, 2007.)

COMMITTEE NOTES ON RULES—2005

This form is new. 28 U.S.C. §1930(f), enacted as part of the Bankruptcy Abuse [Prevention] and Consumer Protection Act of 2005, Pub. L. No. 109–8, 119 Stat. 23 (April 20, 2005), provides that "under procedures prescribed by the Judicial Conference of the United States, the district court or the bankruptcy court may waive the filing fee in a case under chapter 7 of title 11 for an individual if the court determines that such individual has income less than 150 percent of the income official poverty line . . . applicable to a family of the size involved and is unable to pay that fee in installments." To implement this provision, Interim Rule 1006 adds a new subdivision (c). Official Form 3B is the form referenced in that subdivision, and is to be used by individual chapter 7 debtors when applying for a waiver of the filing fee. A corresponding standard order also is included.

COMMITTEE NOTES ON RULES—2005-2007 AMENDMENT

[The 2005–2007 Committee Note incorporates the Committee Note previously published in 2005.]

This form is new. 28 U.S.C. §1930(f), enacted as part of the Bankruptcy Abuse and Consumer Protection Act of 2005, Pub. L. No. 109–8, 119 Stat. 23 (April 20, 2005), provides that "under procedures prescribed by the Judicial Conference of the United States, the district court or the bankruptcy court may waive the filing fee in a case under chapter 7 of title 11 for an individual if the court determines that such individual has income less than 150 percent of the income official poverty line . . . applicable to a family of the size involved and is unable to pay that fee in installments." To implement this provision, Fed. R. Bankr. P.1006 adds a new subdivision (c). Official Form 3B is the form referenced in that subdivision, and is to be used by individual chapter 7 debtors when applying for a waiver of the filing fee. A corresponding standard order also is included.

B4 (Official Form 4) (12/07)

United States Bankruptcy Court

_______________ District Of _______________

In re ________________________________, Case No. ________________
Debtor

Chapter ___________

LIST OF CREDITORS HOLDING 20 LARGEST UNSECURED CLAIMS

Following is the list of the debtor's creditors holding the 20 largest unsecured claims. The list is prepared in accordance with Fed. R. Bankr. P. 1007(d) for filing in this chapter 11 [*or* chapter 9] case. The list does not include (1) persons who come within the definition of "insider" set forth in 11 U.S.C. § 101, or (2) secured creditors unless the value of the collateral is such that the unsecured deficiency places the creditor among the holders of the 20 largest unsecured claims. If a minor child is one of the creditors holding the 20 largest unsecured claims, state the child's initials and the name and address of the child's parent or guardian, such as "A.B., a minor child, by John Doe, guardian." Do not disclose the child's name. See, 11 U.S.C. §112 and Fed. R. Bankr. P. 1007(m).

(1)	(2)	(3)	(4)	(5)
Name of creditor and complete mailing address, including zip code	*Name, telephone number and complete mailing address, including zip code, of employee, agent, or department of creditor familiar with claim who may be contacted*	*Nature of claim (trade debt, bank loan, government contract, etc.)*	*Indicate if claim is contingent, unliquidated, disputed or subject to setoff*	*Amount of claim [if secured also state value of security]*

Date: ____________________

____
Debtor

[Declaration as in Form 2]

(Added Aug. 1, 1991; amended Mar. 16, 1993; Oct. 17, 2005; Dec. 1, 2007.)

NOTES OF ADVISORY COMMITTEE ON RULES—1991

This form is derived from former Official Form No. 9. In conformity with Rule 1007(d) and in recognition of the notice function served by this list under Rule 4001, governmental units must be listed if they are among the creditors holding the 20 largest claims.

Rule 1008 requires all lists to be verified or contain an unsworn declaration conforming with 28 U.S.C. §1746.

NOTES OF ADVISORY COMMITTEE ON RULES—1993 AMENDMENT

The form has been amended to delete reference to the specific subsection of 11 U.S.C. §101 in connection with the definition of the term "insider." Section 101 of the Bankruptcy Code contains numerous definitions, and statutory amendments from time to time have resulted in the renumbering of many of its subsections. The more general reference will avoid the necessity to amend the form further in the event of future amendments to §101.

COMMITTEE NOTES ON RULES—2005 AMENDMENT

The form is amended to direct that the name of any minor child not be disclosed. The amendment implements §112 of the Code, which was added by the Bankruptcy Abuse Prevention and Consumer Protection Act of 2005, Pub. L. No. 109–8, 119 Stat. 23 (April 20, 2005).

COMMITTEE NOTES ON RULES—2005-2007 AMENDMENT

[The 2005-2007 Committee Note incorporates Committee Notes previously published in 2005 and 2006.]

The form is amended to direct that the name of any minor child not be disclosed. The amendment implements §112 of the Code, which was added by the Bankruptcy Abuse Prevention and Consumer Protection Act of 2005, Pub. L. No. 109-8, 119 Stat. 23 (April 20, 2005). In addition, the form is amended to add to the reference to Rule 1007(m) a direction to include for noticing purposes the name, address, and legal relationship to the child of "a person described" in that rule. Rule 1007(m) requires the person named to be someone on whom process would be served in an adversary proceeding against the child.

B 5 (Official Form 5) (12/07)

UNITED STATES BANKRUPTCY COURT

INVOLUNTARY PETITION

IN RE (Name of Debtor – If Individual: Last, First, Middle)	ALL OTHER NAMES used by debtor in the last 8 years (Include married, maiden, and trade names.)
Last four digits of Social-Security or other Individual's Tax-I.D. No./Complete EIN (If more than one, state all.)	
STREET ADDRESS OF DEBTOR (No. and street, city, state, and zip code) COUNTY OF RESIDENCE OR PRINCIPAL PLACE OF BUSINESS ZIP CODE	MAILING ADDRESS OF DEBTOR (If different from street address) ZIP CODE

LOCATION OF PRINCIPAL ASSETS OF BUSINESS DEBTOR (If different from previously listed addresses)

CHAPTER OF BANKRUPTCY CODE UNDER WHICH PETITION IS FILED

☐ Chapter 7 ☐ Chapter 11

INFORMATION REGARDING DEBTOR (Check applicable boxes)

Nature of Debts (Check **one** box.)	**Type of Debtor** (Form of Organization)	**Nature of Business** (Check **one** box.)
Petitioners believe ☐ Debts are primarily consumer debts ☐ Debts are primarily business debts	☐ Individual (Includes Joint Debtor) ☐ Corporation (Includes LLC and LLP) ☐ Partnership ☐ Other (If debtor is not one of the above entities, check this box and state type of entity below.) ____________________	☐ Health Care Business ☐ Single Asset Real Estate as defined in 11 U.S.C. § 101(51)(B) ☐ Railroad ☐ Stockbroker ☐ Commodity Broker ☐ Clearing Bank ☐ Other

VENUE	**FILING FEE** (Check one box)
☐ Debtor has been domiciled or has had a residence, principal place of business, or principal assets in the District for 180 days immediately preceding the date of this petition or for a longer part of such 180 days than in any other District. ☐ A bankruptcy case concerning debtor's affiliate, general partner or partnership is pending in this District.	☐ Full Filing Fee attached ☐ Petitioner is a child support creditor or its representative, and the form specified in § 304(g) of the Bankruptcy Reform Act of 1994 is attached. *[If a child support creditor or its representative is a petitioner, and if the petitioner files the form specified in § 304(g) of the Bankruptcy Reform Act of 1994, no fee is required.]*

PENDING BANKRUPTCY CASE FILED BY OR AGAINST ANY PARTNER OR AFFILIATE OF THIS DEBTOR (Report information for any additional cases on attached sheets.)

Name of Debtor	Case Number	Date
Relationship	District	Judge

ALLEGATIONS (Check applicable boxes)	COURT USE ONLY
1. ☐ Petitioner (s) are eligible to file this petition pursuant to 11 U.S.C. § 303 (b). 2. ☐ The debtor is a person against whom an order for relief may be entered under title 11 of the United States Code. 3.a. ☐ The debtor is generally not paying such debtor's debts as they become due, unless such debts are the subject of a bona fide dispute as to liability or amount; or b. ☐ Within 120 days preceding the filing of this petition, a custodian, other than a trustee, receiver, or agent appointed or authorized to take charge of less than substantially all of the property of the debtor for the purpose of enforcing a lien against such property, was appointed or took possession.	

B 5 (Official Form 5) (12/07) – Page 2

Name of Debtor____________________

Case No.________________________

TRANSFER OF CLAIM

☐ Check this box if there has been a transfer of any claim against the debtor by or to any petitioner. Attach all documents that evidence the transfer and any statements that are required under Bankruptcy Rule 1003(a).

REQUEST FOR RELIEF

Petitioner(s) request that an order for relief be entered against the debtor under the chapter of title 11, United States Code, specified in this petition. If any petitioner is a foreign representative appointed in a foreign proceeding, a certified copy of the order of the court granting recognition is attached.

Petitioner(s) declare under penalty of perjury that the foregoing is true and correct according to the best of their knowledge, information, and belief.

x_______________________ Signature of Petitioner or Representative (State title) _______________________ Name of Petitioner Date Signed Name & Mailing Address of Individual ____________ Signing in Representative Capacity ____________	x_______________________ Signature of Attorney Date _______________________ Name of Attorney Firm (If any) _______________________ Address _______________________ Telephone No.
x_______________________ Signature of Petitioner or Representative (State title) _______________________ Name of Petitioner Date Signed Name & Mailing Address of Individual ____________ Signing in Representative Capacity ____________	x_______________________ Signature of Attorney Date _______________________ Name of Attorney Firm (If any) _______________________ Address _______________________ Telephone No.
x_______________________ Signature of Petitioner or Representative (State title) _______________________ Name of Petitioner Date Signed Name & Mailing Address of Individual ____________ Signing in Representative Capacity ____________	x_______________________ Signature of Attorney Date _______________________ Name of Attorney Firm (If any) _______________________ Address _______________________ Telephone No.

PETITIONING CREDITORS

Name and Address of Petitioner	Nature of Claim	Amount of Claim
Name and Address of Petitioner	Nature of Claim	Amount of Claim
Name and Address of Petitioner	Nature of Claim	Amount of Claim
Note: If there are more than three petitioners, attach additional sheets with the statement under penalty of perjury, each petitioner's signature under the statement and the name of attorney and petitioning creditor information in the format above.		Total Amount of Petitioners' Claims

_____continuation sheets attached

(Added Aug. 1, 1991; amended Sept. 22, 1992; Dec. 1, 2002; Dec. 1, 2003; Oct. 17, 2005; Oct. 1, 2006; Dec. 1, 2007.)

NOTES OF ADVISORY COMMITTEE ON RULES—1991

This form has been redesigned in a box format similar to that of Form 1. See Advisory Committee Note to Form 1.

The allegations required under §303 are grouped together, and a separate section has been provided for additional allegations based upon the prohibitions and requirements set forth in Rule 1003(a) concerning transfer of claims by petitioning creditors. Petitioners may wish to supplement the allegations set forth in the form with a further statement of facts. Additional information concerning any allegation can be requested by the debtor as part of the discovery process.

Each petitioning creditor, by signing on the line provided, signs both the petition and the unsworn declaration which 28 U.S.C. §1746 permits instead of verification. The addresses as well as the names of individuals signing the petition in a representative capacity are required, together with disclosure of which petitioner is represented by each signatory.

This form is intended to be used in every involuntary case, including that of a partnership. The separate form for a petition by a partner has been abrogated. Pursuant to §303(b)(3)(A) of the Code, a petition by fewer than all of the general partners seeking an order for relief with respect to the partnership is treated as an involuntary petition. Such a petition is adversarial in character because not all of the partners are joining in the petition.

Section 303(b)(3)(B) permits a petition against the partnership if relief has been ordered under the Code with respect to all of the general partners. In that event, the petition may be filed by a general partner, a trustee of a general partner's estate, or a creditor of the partnership. This form may be adapted for use in that type of case.

28 U.S.C. §1408(1) specifies the proper venue alternatives for all persons, including partnerships, as domicile, residence, principal place of business, or location of principal assets. Venue also may be based on a pending case commenced by an affiliate, general partner, or partnership pursuant to 28 U.S.C. §1408(2). Both options are set forth in the block labeled "Venue."

28 U.S.C. §1746 permits the unsworn declaration instead of a verification. See Committee Note to Form 2.

NOTES OF ADVISORY COMMITTEE ON RULES—1992 AMENDMENT

The form has been amended to require the dating of signatures.

COMMITTEE NOTES ON RULES—2002 AMENDMENT

The form is amended to give notice that no filing fee is required if a child support creditor or its representative is a petitioner, and if the petitioner also files a form detailing the child support debt, its status, and other characteristics, as specified in §304(g) of the Bankruptcy Reform Act of 1994, Pub. L. No. 103–394, 108 Stat. 4106 (Oct. 22, 1994).

COMMITTEE NOTES ON RULES—2003 AMENDMENT

The form is amended to require the petitioner to disclose the debtor's employer identification number, if any, and only the last four digits of the debtor's social security number to afford greater privacy to the individual debtor, whose bankruptcy case records may be available on the Internet. The form also is amended to delete the request for information concerning the "Type of Business," as this data no longer is collected for statistical purposes.

COMMITTEE NOTES ON RULES—2005 AMENDMENT

The form has been amended to delete statistical information no longer required and to add "as to liability or amount" to the language concerning debts that are the subject of a bona fide dispute, in conformity with §303 of the Code as amended by the Bankruptcy Abuse Prevention and Consumer Protection Act of 2005, Pub. L. No. 109–8, 119 Stat. 23 (April 20, 2005). The petitioning creditors must now provide, to the extent known to them, all other names used by the debtor during the 8 years, rather than 6 years, before the filing of the petition. A new check box is provided for the petitioning creditors to identify the debtor that is a "health care business" as defined in §101 of the Code, thereby alerting the court and the United States trustee of the necessity under §333 to appoint an ombudsman to represent the interests of the patients of the health care business. These amendments also implement the 2005 amendments to the Code. A new checkbox also is provided for a "clearing bank," which may become a debtor upon the filing of a petition at the direction of the Board of Governors of the Federal Reserve System; this addition conforms to an amendment to §109(b)(2) of the Code which was enacted in 2000.

COMMITTEE NOTES ON RULES—2006 AMENDMENT

The section of the form labeled "Information Regarding Debtor" is amended to facilitate, to the extent available in an involuntary case, the collection of the same statistical information that is requested in a voluntary case. Accordingly, information about whether the debtor is an individual, a corporation, or some other type of entity is separated from the checklist of types of debtors, such as health care businesses and railroads, concerning which the Code provides for specialized treatment.

COMMITTEE NOTES ON RULES—2005–2007 AMENDMENT

[The 2005–2007 Committee Note incorporates Committee Notes previously published in 2005 and 2006.]

The form has been amended to delete statistical information about the debtor that no longer is required, and to substitute checkboxes similar to those on the voluntary petition form. The form also is amended to add "as to liability or amount" to the language concerning debts that are the subject of a bona fide dispute, in conformity with §303 of the Code as amended by the Bankruptcy Abuse Prevention and Consumer Protection Act of 2005, Pub. L. No. 109–8, 119 Stat. 23 (April 20, 2005). The petitioning creditors must now provide, to the extent known to them, all other names used by the debtor during the 8 years, rather than 6 years, before the filing of the petition. In conformity with Rule 9037, the petitioning creditors are directed to provide only the last four digits of any individual's tax-identification number. A new checkbox is provided for the petitioning creditors to identify the debtor that is a "health care business" as defined in §101 of the Code, thereby alerting the court and the United States trustee of the necessity under §333 of the Code to appoint an ombudsman to represent the interests of the patients of the health care business. These amendments also implement the 2005 amendments to the Code. A new checkbox also is provided for a "clearing bank," which may become a debtor upon the filing of a petition at the direction of the Board of Governors of the Federal Reserve System; this addition conforms to an amendment to §109(b)(2) of the Code, which was enacted in 2000.

B6 Cover (Form 6 Cover) (12/07)

FORM 6. SCHEDULES

Summary of Schedules
Statistical Summary of Certain Liabilities and Related Data (28 U.S.C. § 159)

Schedule A - Real Property
Schedule B - Personal Property
Schedule C - Property Claimed as Exempt
Schedule D - Creditors Holding Secured Claims
Schedule E - Creditors Holding Unsecured Priority Claims
Schedule F - Creditors Holding Unsecured Nonpriority Claims
Schedule G - Executory Contracts and Unexpired Leases
Schedule H - Codebtors
Schedule I - Current Income of Individual Debtor(s)
Schedule J - Current Expenditures of Individual Debtors(s)

Unsworn Declaration Under Penalty of Perjury

GENERAL INSTRUCTIONS: The first page of the debtor's schedules and the first page of any amendments thereto must contain a caption as in Form 16B. Subsequent pages should be identified with the debtor's name and case number. If the schedules are filed with the petition, the case number should be left blank.

Schedules D, E, and F have been designed for the listing of each claim only once. Even when a claim is secured only in part or entitled to priority only in part, it still should be listed only once. A claim which is secured in whole or in part should be listed on Schedule D only, and a claim which is entitled to priority in whole or in part should be listed on Schedule E only. Do not list the same claim twice. If a creditor has more than one claim, such as claims arising from separate transactions, each claim should be scheduled separately.

Review the specific instructions for each schedule before completing the schedule.

B6 Summary (Official Form 6 - Summary) (12/07)

United States Bankruptcy Court

In re ______________________________, Case No. ________________
Debtor
Chapter __________

SUMMARY OF SCHEDULES

Indicate as to each schedule whether that schedule is attached and state the number of pages in each. Report the totals from Schedules A, B, D, E, F, I, and J in the boxes provided. Add the amounts from Schedules A and B to determine the total amount of the debtor's assets. Add the amounts of all claims from Schedules D, E, and F to determine the total amount of the debtor's liabilities. Individual debtors also must complete the "Statistical Summary of Certain Liabilities and Related Data" if they file a case under chapter 7, 11, or 13.

NAME OF SCHEDULE	ATTACHED (YES/NO)	NO. OF SHEETS	ASSETS	LIABILITIES	OTHER
A - Real Property			$		
B - Personal Property			$		
C - Property Claimed as Exempt					
D - Creditors Holding Secured Claims				$	
E - Creditors Holding Unsecured Priority Claims (Total of Claims on Schedule E)				$	
F - Creditors Holding Unsecured Nonpriority Claims				$	
G - Executory Contracts and Unexpired Leases					
H - Codebtors					
I - Current Income of Individual Debtor(s)					$
J - Current Expenditures of Individual Debtors(s)					$
TOTAL			$	$	

B 6 Summary (Official Form 6 - Summary) (12/07)

United States Bankruptcy Court

In re ____,
Debtor

Case No. ______________________

Chapter ______________

STATISTICAL SUMMARY OF CERTAIN LIABILITIES AND RELATED DATA (28 U.S.C. § 159)

If you are an individual debtor whose debts are primarily consumer debts, as defined in § 101(8) of the Bankruptcy Code (11 U.S.C. § 101(8)), filing a case under chapter 7, 11 or 13, you must report all information requested below.

☐ Check this box if you are an individual debtor whose debts are NOT primarily consumer debts. You are not required to report any information here.

This information is for statistical purposes only under 28 U.S.C. § 159.

Summarize the following types of liabilities, as reported in the Schedules, and total them.

Type of Liability	**Amount**
Domestic Support Obligations (from Schedule E)	$
Taxes and Certain Other Debts Owed to Governmental Units (from Schedule E)	$
Claims for Death or Personal Injury While Debtor Was Intoxicated (from Schedule E) (whether disputed or undisputed)	$
Student Loan Obligations (from Schedule F)	$
Domestic Support, Separation Agreement, and Divorce Decree Obligations Not Reported on Schedule E	$
Obligations to Pension or Profit-Sharing, and Other Similar Obligations (from Schedule F)	$
TOTAL	$

State the following:

Average Income (from Schedule I, Line 16)	$
Average Expenses (from Schedule J, Line 18)	$
Current Monthly Income (from Form 22A Line 12; **OR**, Form 22B Line 11; **OR**, Form 22C Line 20)	$

State the following:

1. Total from Schedule D, "UNSECURED PORTION, IF ANY" column		$
2. Total from Schedule E, "AMOUNT ENTITLED TO PRIORITY" column.	$	
3. Total from Schedule E, "AMOUNT NOT ENTITLED TO PRIORITY, IF ANY" column		$
4. Total from Schedule F		$
5. Total of non-priority unsecured debt (sum of 1, 3, and 4)		$

B6A (Official Form 6A) (12/07)

In re ______________________________, Case No. ______________________
Debtor (If known)

SCHEDULE A - REAL PROPERTY

Except as directed below, list all real property in which the debtor has any legal, equitable, or future interest, including all property owned as a co-tenant, community property, or in which the debtor has a life estate. Include any property in which the debtor holds rights and powers exercisable for the debtor's own benefit. If the debtor is married, state whether the husband, wife, both, or the marital community own the property by placing an "H," "W," "J," or "C" in the column labeled "Husband, Wife, Joint, or Community." If the debtor holds no interest in real property, write "None" under "Description and Location of Property."

Do not include interests in executory contracts and unexpired leases on this schedule. List them in Schedule G - Executory Contracts and Unexpired Leases.

If an entity claims to have a lien or hold a secured interest in any property, state the amount of the secured claim. See Schedule D. If no entity claims to hold a secured interest in the property, write "None" in the column labeled "Amount of Secured Claim."

If the debtor is an individual or if a joint petition is filed, state the amount of any exemption claimed in the property only in Schedule C - Property Claimed as Exempt.

DESCRIPTION AND LOCATION OF PROPERTY	NATURE OF DEBTOR'S INTEREST IN PROPERTY	HUSBAND, WIFE, JOINT, OR COMMUNITY	CURRENT VALUE OF DEBTOR'S INTEREST IN PROPERTY, WITHOUT DEDUCTING ANY SECURED CLAIM OR EXEMPTION	AMOUNT OF SECURED CLAIM
		Total➤		

(Report also on Summary of Schedules.)

B 6B (Official Form 6B) (12/07)

In re ______________________________, Case No. ____________________
Debtor (If known)

SCHEDULE B - PERSONAL PROPERTY

Except as directed below, list all personal property of the debtor of whatever kind. If the debtor has no property in one or more of the categories, place an "x" in the appropriate position in the column labeled "None." If additional space is needed in any category, attach a separate sheet properly identified with the case name, case number, and the number of the category. If the debtor is married, state whether the husband, wife, both, or the marital community own the property by placing an "H," "W," "J," or "C" in the column labeled "Husband, Wife, Joint, or Community." If the debtor is an individual or a joint petition is filed, state the amount of any exemptions claimed only in Schedule C - Property Claimed as Exempt.

Do not list interests in executory contracts and unexpired leases on this schedule. List them in Schedule G - Executory Contracts and Unexpired Leases.

If the property is being held for the debtor by someone else, state that person's name and address under "Description and Location of Property."
If the property is being held for a minor child, simply state the child's initials and the name and address of the child's parent or guardian, such as "A.B., a minor child, by John Doe, guardian." Do not disclose the child's name. See, 11 U.S.C. §112 and Fed. R. Bankr. P. 1007(m).

TYPE OF PROPERTY	NONE	DESCRIPTION AND LOCATION OF PROPERTY	HUSBAND, WIFE, JOINT, OR COMMUNITY	CURRENT VALUE OF DEBTOR'S INTEREST IN PROPERTY, WITH-OUT DEDUCTING ANY SECURED CLAIM OR EXEMPTION
1. Cash on hand.				
2. Checking, savings or other financial accounts, certificates of deposit or shares in banks, savings and loan, thrift, building and loan, and homestead associations, or credit unions, brokerage houses, or cooperatives.				
3. Security deposits with public utilities, telephone companies, landlords, and others.				
4. Household goods and furnishings, including audio, video, and computer equipment.				
5. Books; pictures and other art objects; antiques; stamp, coin, record, tape, compact disc, and other collections or collectibles.				
6. Wearing apparel.				
7. Furs and jewelry.				
8. Firearms and sports, photographic, and other hobby equipment.				
9. Interests in insurance policies. Name insurance company of each policy and itemize surrender or refund value of each.				
10. Annuities. Itemize and name each issuer.				
11. Interests in an education IRA as defined in 26 U.S.C. § 530(b)(1) or under a qualified State tuition plan as defined in 26 U.S.C. § 529(b)(1). Give particulars. (File separately the record(s) of any such interest(s). 11 U.S.C. § 521(c).)				

B 6B (Official Form 6B) (12/07) – Cont.

In re ______________________________, Case No. ____________________
Debtor (If known)

SCHEDULE B - PERSONAL PROPERTY
(Continuation Sheet)

TYPE OF PROPERTY	NONE	DESCRIPTION AND LOCATION OF PROPERTY	HUSBAND, WIFE, JOINT, OR COMMUNITY	CURRENT VALUE OF DEBTOR'S INTEREST IN PROPERTY, WITH-OUT DEDUCTING ANY SECURED CLAIM OR EXEMPTION
12. Interests in IRA, ERISA, Keogh, or other pension or profit sharing plans. Give particulars.				
13. Stock and interests in incorporated and unincorporated businesses. Itemize.				
14. Interests in partnerships or joint ventures. Itemize.				
15. Government and corporate bonds and other negotiable and non-negotiable instruments.				
16. Accounts receivable.				
17. Alimony, maintenance, support, and property settlements to which the debtor is or may be entitled. Give particulars.				
18. Other liquidated debts owed to debtor including tax refunds. Give particulars.				
19. Equitable or future interests, life estates, and rights or powers exercisable for the benefit of the debtor other than those listed in Schedule A – Real Property.				
20. Contingent and noncontingent interests in estate of a decedent, death benefit plan, life insurance policy, or trust.				
21. Other contingent and unliquidated claims of every nature, including tax refunds, counterclaims of the debtor, and rights to setoff claims. Give estimated value of each.				

B 6B (Official Form 6B) (12/07) – Cont.

In re ______________________________, Case No. ____________________
Debtor (If known)

SCHEDULE B - PERSONAL PROPERTY

(Continuation Sheet)

TYPE OF PROPERTY	NONE	DESCRIPTION AND LOCATION OF PROPERTY	HUSBAND, WIFE, JOINT, OR COMMUNITY	CURRENT VALUE OF DEBTOR'S INTEREST IN PROPERTY, WITH-OUT DEDUCTING ANY SECURED CLAIM OR EXEMPTION
22. Patents, copyrights, and other intellectual property. Give particulars.				
23. Licenses, franchises, and other general intangibles. Give particulars.				
24. Customer lists or other compilations containing personally identifiable information (as defined in 11 U.S.C. § 101(41A)) provided to the debtor by individuals in connection with obtaining a product or service from the debtor primarily for personal, family, or household purposes.				
25. Automobiles, trucks, trailers, and other vehicles and accessories.				
26. Boats, motors, and accessories.				
27. Aircraft and accessories.				
28. Office equipment, furnishings, and supplies.				
29. Machinery, fixtures, equipment, and supplies used in business.				
30. Inventory.				
31. Animals.				
32. Crops - growing or harvested. Give particulars.				
33. Farming equipment and implements.				
34. Farm supplies, chemicals, and feed.				
35. Other personal property of any kind not already listed. Itemize.				

________ continuation sheets attached Total➤ $

(Include amounts from any continuation sheets attached. Report total also on Summary of Schedules.)

B 6C (Official Form 6C) (12/07)

In re ______________________________________, Case No. ______________________
Debtor (If known)

SCHEDULE C - PROPERTY CLAIMED AS EXEMPT

Debtor claims the exemptions to which debtor is entitled under:
(Check one box)
☐ 11 U.S.C. § 522(b)(2)
☐ 11 U.S.C. § 522(b)(3)

☐ Check if debtor claims a homestead exemption that exceeds $136,875.

DESCRIPTION OF PROPERTY	SPECIFY LAW PROVIDING EACH EXEMPTION	VALUE OF CLAIMED EXEMPTION	CURRENT VALUE OF PROPERTY WITHOUT DEDUCTING EXEMPTION

B 6D (Official Form 6D) (12/07)

In re ______________________, Case No. ______________________
Debtor (If known)

SCHEDULE D - CREDITORS HOLDING SECURED CLAIMS

State the name, mailing address, including zip code, and last four digits of any account number of all entities holding claims secured by property of the debtor as of the date of filing of the petition. The complete account number of any account the debtor has with the creditor is useful to the trustee and the creditor and may be provided if the debtor chooses to do so. List creditors holding all types of secured interests such as judgment liens, garnishments, statutory liens, mortgages, deeds of trust, and other security interests.

List creditors in alphabetical order to the extent practicable. If a minor child is the creditor, state the child's initials and the name and address of the child's parent or guardian, such as "A.B., a minor child, by John Doe, guardian." Do not disclose the child's name. See, 11 U.S.C. §112 and Fed. R. Bankr. P. 1007(m). If all secured creditors will not fit on this page, use the continuation sheet provided.

If any entity other than a spouse in a joint case may be jointly liable on a claim, place an "X" in the column labeled "Codebtor," include the entity on the appropriate schedule of creditors, and complete Schedule H – Codebtors. If a joint petition is filed, state whether the husband, wife, both of them, or the marital community may be liable on each claim by placing an "H," "W," "J," or "C" in the column labeled "Husband, Wife, Joint, or Community."

If the claim is contingent, place an "X" in the column labeled "Contingent." If the claim is unliquidated, place an "X" in the column labeled "Unliquidated." If the claim is disputed, place an "X" in the column labeled "Disputed." (You may need to place an "X" in more than one of these three columns.)

Total the columns labeled "Amount of Claim Without Deducting Value of Collateral" and "Unsecured Portion, if Any" in the boxes labeled "Total(s)" on the last sheet of the completed schedule. Report the total from the column labeled "Amount of Claim Without Deducting Value of Collateral" also on the Summary of Schedules and, if the debtor is an individual with primarily consumer debts, report the total from the column labeled "Unsecured Portion, if Any" on the Statistical Summary of Certain Liabilities and Related Data.

☐ Check this box if debtor has no creditors holding secured claims to report on this Schedule D.

CREDITOR'S NAME AND MAILING ADDRESS INCLUDING ZIP CODE AND AN ACCOUNT NUMBER *(See Instructions Above.)*	CODEBTOR	HUSBAND, WIFE, JOINT, OR COMMUNITY	DATE CLAIM WAS INCURRED, NATURE OF LIEN, AND DESCRIPTION AND VALUE OF PROPERTY SUBJECT TO LIEN	CONTINGENT	UNLIQUIDATED	DISPUTED	AMOUNT OF CLAIM WITHOUT DEDUCTING VALUE OF COLLATERAL	UNSECURED PORTION, IF ANY
ACCOUNT NO.			VALUE $					
ACCOUNT NO.			VALUE $					
ACCOUNT NO.			VALUE $					
____ continuation sheets attached			Subtotal ► (Total of this page)				$	$
			Total ► (Use only on last page)				$	$
							(Report also on Summary of Schedules.)	(If applicable, report also on Statistical Summary of Certain Liabilities and Related Data.)

B 6D (Official Form 6D) (12/07) – Cont. 2

In re ______________________________, **Case No.** __________________________

Debtor **(if known)**

SCHEDULE D - CREDITORS HOLDING SECURED CLAIMS

(Continuation Sheet)

CREDITOR'S NAME AND MAILING ADDRESS INCLUDING ZIP CODE AND AN ACCOUNT NUMBER (*See Instructions Above.*)	CODEBTOR	HUSBAND, WIFE, JOINT, OR COMMUNITY	DATE CLAIM WAS INCURRED, NATURE OF LIEN , AND DESCRIPTION AND VALUE OF PROPERTY SUBJECT TO LIEN	CONTINGENT	UNLIQUIDATED	DISPUTED	AMOUNT OF CLAIM WITHOUT DEDUCTING VALUE OF COLLATERAL	UNSECURED PORTION, IF ANY
ACCOUNT NO.			VALUE $					
ACCOUNT NO.			VALUE $					
ACCOUNT NO.			VALUE $					
ACCOUNT NO.			VALUE $					
ACCOUNT NO.			VALUE $					
Sheet no.____of____continuation sheets attached to Schedule of Creditors Holding Secured Claims			Subtotal (s)► (Total(s) of this page)				$	$
			Total(s) ► (Use only on last page)				$	$
							(Report also on Summary of Schedules.)	(If applicable, report also on Statistical Summary of Certain Liabilities and Related Data.)

B 6E (Official Form 6E) (12/07)

In re ______________________________, **Case No.**______________________
Debtor **(if known)**

SCHEDULE E - CREDITORS HOLDING UNSECURED PRIORITY CLAIMS

A complete list of claims entitled to priority, listed separately by type of priority, is to be set forth on the sheets provided. Only holders of unsecured claims entitled to priority should be listed in this schedule. In the boxes provided on the attached sheets, state the name, mailing address, including zip code, and last four digits of the account number, if any, of all entities holding priority claims against the debtor or the property of the debtor, as of the date of the filing of the petition. Use a separate continuation sheet for each type of priority and label each with the type of priority.

The complete account number of any account the debtor has with the creditor is useful to the trustee and the creditor and may be provided if the debtor chooses to do so. If a minor child is a creditor, state the child's initials and the name and address of the child's parent or guardian, such as "A.B., a minor child, by John Doe, guardian." Do not disclose the child's name. See, 11 U.S.C. §112 and Fed. R. Bankr. P. 1007(m).

If any entity other than a spouse in a joint case may be jointly liable on a claim, place an "X" in the column labeled "Codebtor," include the entity on the appropriate schedule of creditors, and complete Schedule H-Codebtors. If a joint petition is filed, state whether the husband, wife, both of them, or the marital community may be liable on each claim by placing an "H," "W," "J," or "C" in the column labeled "Husband, Wife, Joint, or Community." If the claim is contingent, place an "X" in the column labeled "Contingent." If the claim is unliquidated, place an "X" in the column labeled "Unliquidated." If the claim is disputed, place an "X" in the column labeled "Disputed." (You may need to place an "X" in more than one of these three columns.)

Report the total of claims listed on each sheet in the box labeled "Subtotals" on each sheet. Report the total of all claims listed on this Schedule E in the box labeled "Total" on the last sheet of the completed schedule. Report this total also on the Summary of Schedules.

Report the total of amounts entitled to priority listed on each sheet in the box labeled "Subtotals" on each sheet. Report the total of all amounts entitled to priority listed on this Schedule E in the box labeled "Totals" on the last sheet of the completed schedule. Individual debtors with primarily consumer debts report this total also on the Statistical Summary of Certain Liabilities and Related Data.

Report the total of amounts not entitled to priority listed on each sheet in the box labeled "Subtotals" on each sheet. Report the total of all amounts not entitled to priority listed on this Schedule E in the box labeled "Totals" on the last sheet of the completed schedule. Individual debtors with primarily consumer debts report this total also on the Statistical Summary of Certain Liabilities and Related Data.

☐ Check this box if debtor has no creditors holding unsecured priority claims to report on this Schedule E.

TYPES OF PRIORITY CLAIMS (Check the appropriate box(es) below if claims in that category are listed on the attached sheets.)

☐ **Domestic Support Obligations**

Claims for domestic support that are owed to or recoverable by a spouse, former spouse, or child of the debtor, or the parent, legal guardian, or responsible relative of such a child, or a governmental unit to whom such a domestic support claim has been assigned to the extent provided in 11 U.S.C. § 507(a)(1).

☐ **Extensions of credit in an involuntary case**

Claims arising in the ordinary course of the debtor's business or financial affairs after the commencement of the case but before the earlier of the appointment of a trustee or the order for relief. 11 U.S.C. § 507(a)(3).

☐ **Wages, salaries, and commissions**

Wages, salaries, and commissions, including vacation, severance, and sick leave pay owing to employees and commissions owing to qualifying independent sales representatives up to $10,950* per person earned within 180 days immediately preceding the filing of the original petition, or the cessation of business, whichever occurred first, to the extent provided in 11 U.S.C. § 507(a)(4).

☐ **Contributions to employee benefit plans**

Money owed to employee benefit plans for services rendered within 180 days immediately preceding the filing of the original petition, or the cessation of business, whichever occurred first, to the extent provided in 11 U.S.C. § 507(a)(5).

B 6E (Official Form 6E) (12/07) – Cont.

In re ____, **Case No.**________________________
Debtor **(if known)**

☐ **Certain farmers and fishermen**

Claims of certain farmers and fishermen, up to $5,400* per farmer or fisherman, against the debtor, as provided in 11 U.S.C. § 507(a)(6).

☐ **Deposits by individuals**

Claims of individuals up to $2,425* for deposits for the purchase, lease, or rental of property or services for personal, family, or household use, that were not delivered or provided. 11 U.S.C. § 507(a)(7).

☐ **Taxes and Certain Other Debts Owed to Governmental Units**

Taxes, customs duties, and penalties owing to federal, state, and local governmental units as set forth in 11 U.S.C. § 507(a)(8).

☐ **Commitments to Maintain the Capital of an Insured Depository Institution**

Claims based on commitments to the FDIC, RTC, Director of the Office of Thrift Supervision, Comptroller of the Currency, or Board of Governors of the Federal Reserve System, or their predecessors or successors, to maintain the capital of an insured depository institution. 11 U.S.C. § 507 (a)(9).

☐ **Claims for Death or Personal Injury While Debtor Was Intoxicated**

Claims for death or personal injury resulting from the operation of a motor vehicle or vessel while the debtor was intoxicated from using alcohol, a drug, or another substance. 11 U.S.C. § 507(a)(10).

* Amounts are subject to adjustment on April 1, 2010, and every three years thereafter with respect to cases commenced on or after the date of adjustment.

____ continuation sheets attached

B 6E (Official Form 6E) (12/07) – Cont.

In re ________________________________, Case No. ____________________________
Debtor (if known)

SCHEDULE E - CREDITORS HOLDING UNSECURED PRIORITY CLAIMS

(Continuation Sheet)

Type of Priority for Claims Listed on This Sheet

CREDITOR'S NAME, MAILING ADDRESS INCLUDING ZIP CODE, AND ACCOUNT NUMBER *(See instructions above.)*	CODEBTOR	HUSBAND, WIFE, JOINT, OR COMMUNITY	DATE CLAIM WAS INCURRED AND CONSIDERATION FOR CLAIM	CONTINGENT	UNLIQUIDATED	DISPUTED	AMOUNT OF CLAIM	AMOUNT ENTITLED TO PRIORITY	AMOUNT NOT ENTITLED TO PRIORITY, IF ANY
Account No.									
Account No.									
Account No.									
Account No.									
Sheet no. ___ of ___ continuation sheets attached to Schedule of Creditors Holding Priority Claims						Subtotals➤ (Totals of this page)	$	$	
						Total➤ (Use only on last page of the completed Schedule E. Report also on the Summary of Schedules.)	$		
						Totals➤ (Use only on last page of the completed Schedule E. If applicable, report also on the Statistical Summary of Certain Liabilities and Related Data.)		$	$

B 6F (Official Form 6F) (12/07)

In re ______________________________, **Case No.** ______________________________
Debtor **(if known)**

SCHEDULE F - CREDITORS HOLDING UNSECURED NONPRIORITY CLAIMS

State the name, mailing address, including zip code, and last four digits of any account number, of all entities holding unsecured claims without priority against the debtor or the property of the debtor, as of the date of filing of the petition. The complete account number of any account the debtor has with the creditor is useful to the trustee and the creditor and may be provided if the debtor chooses to do so. If a minor child is a creditor, state the child's initials and the name and address of the child's parent or guardian, such as "A.B., a minor child, by John Doe, guardian." Do not disclose the child's name. See, 11 U.S.C. §112 and Fed. R. Bankr. P. 1007(m). Do not include claims listed in Schedules D and E. If all creditors will not fit on this page, use the continuation sheet provided.

If any entity other than a spouse in a joint case may be jointly liable on a claim, place an "X" in the column labeled "Codebtor," include the entity on the appropriate schedule of creditors, and complete Schedule H - Codebtors. If a joint petition is filed, state whether the husband, wife, both of them, or the marital community may be liable on each claim by placing an "H," "W," "J," or "C" in the column labeled "Husband, Wife, Joint, or Community."

If the claim is contingent, place an "X" in the column labeled "Contingent." If the claim is unliquidated, place an "X" in the column labeled "Unliquidated." If the claim is disputed, place an "X" in the column labeled "Disputed." (You may need to place an "X" in more than one of these three columns.)

Report the total of all claims listed on this schedule in the box labeled "Total" on the last sheet of the completed schedule. Report this total also on the Summary of Schedules and, if the debtor is an individual with primarily consumer debts, report this total also on the Statistical Summary of Certain Liabilities and Related Data..

☐ Check this box if debtor has no creditors holding unsecured claims to report on this Schedule F.

CREDITOR'S NAME, MAILING ADDRESS INCLUDING ZIP CODE, AND ACCOUNT NUMBER *(See instructions above.)*	CODEBTOR	HUSBAND, WIFE, JOINT, OR COMMUNITY	DATE CLAIM WAS INCURRED AND CONSIDERATION FOR CLAIM. IF CLAIM IS SUBJECT TO SETOFF, SO STATE.	CONTINGENT	UNLIQUIDATED	DISPUTED	AMOUNT OF CLAIM
ACCOUNT NO.							
ACCOUNT NO.							
ACCOUNT NO.							
ACCOUNT NO.							
						Subtotal➤	$
____continuation sheets attached						Total➤ (Use only on last page of the completed Schedule F.) (Report also on Summary of Schedules and, if applicable, on the Statistical Summary of Certain Liabilities and Related Data.)	$

B 6F (Official Form 6F) (12/07) - Cont.

In re ______________________________, Case No. ______________________
Debtor (if known)

SCHEDULE F - CREDITORS HOLDING UNSECURED NONPRIORITY CLAIMS

(Continuation Sheet)

CREDITOR'S NAME, MAILING ADDRESS INCLUDING ZIP CODE, AND ACCOUNT NUMBER (See instructions above.)	CODEBTOR	HUSBAND, WIFE, JOINT, OR COMMUNITY	DATE CLAIM WAS INCURRED AND CONSIDERATION FOR CLAIM. IF CLAIM IS SUBJECT TO SETOFF, SO STATE.	CONTINGENT	UNLIQUIDATED	DISPUTED	AMOUNT OF CLAIM
ACCOUNT NO.							
ACCOUNT NO.							
ACCOUNT NO.							
ACCOUNT NO.							
ACCOUNT NO.							

Sheet no._____ of_____ continuation sheets attached to Schedule of Creditors Holding Unsecured Nonpriority Claims

Subtotal➤ $

Total➤ $
(Use only on last page of the completed Schedule F.)
(Report also on Summary of Schedules and, if applicable on the Statistical Summary of Certain Liabilities and Related Data.)

B 6G (Official Form 6G) (12/07)

In re ______________________________, Case No.____________________
Debtor (if known)

SCHEDULE G - EXECUTORY CONTRACTS AND UNEXPIRED LEASES

Describe all executory contracts of any nature and all unexpired leases of real or personal property. Include any timeshare interests. State nature of debtor's interest in contract, i.e., "Purchaser," "Agent," etc. State whether debtor is the lessor or lessee of a lease. Provide the names and complete mailing addresses of all other parties to each lease or contract described. If a minor child is a party to one of the leases or contracts, state the child's initials and the name and address of the child's parent or guardian, such as "A.B., a minor child, by John Doe, guardian." Do not disclose the child's name. See, 11 U.S.C. §112 and Fed. R. Bankr. P. 1007(m).

☐ Check this box if debtor has no executory contracts or unexpired leases.

NAME AND MAILING ADDRESS, INCLUDING ZIP CODE, OF OTHER PARTIES TO LEASE OR CONTRACT.	DESCRIPTION OF CONTRACT OR LEASE AND NATURE OF DEBTOR'S INTEREST. STATE WHETHER LEASE IS FOR NONRESIDENTIAL REAL PROPERTY. STATE CONTRACT NUMBER OF ANY GOVERNMENT CONTRACT.

B 6H (Official Form 6H) (12/07)

In re ______________________________,
Debtor

Case No. ______________________
(if known)

SCHEDULE H - CODEBTORS

Provide the information requested concerning any person or entity, other than a spouse in a joint case, that is also liable on any debts listed by the debtor in the schedules of creditors. Include all guarantors and co-signers. If the debtor resides or resided in a community property state, commonwealth, or territory (including Alaska, Arizona, California, Idaho, Louisiana, Nevada, New Mexico, Puerto Rico, Texas, Washington, or Wisconsin) within the eight-year period immediately preceding the commencement of the case, identify the name of the debtor's spouse and of any former spouse who resides or resided with the debtor in the community property state, commonwealth, or territory. Include all names used by the nondebtor spouse during the eight years immediately preceding the commencement of this case. If a minor child is a codebtor or a creditor, state the child's initials and the name and address of the child's parent or guardian, such as "A.B., a minor child, by John Doe, guardian." Do not disclose the child's name. See, 11 U.S.C. §112 and Fed. R. Bankr. P. 1007(m).

☐ Check this box if debtor has no codebtors.

NAME AND ADDRESS OF CODEBTOR	NAME AND ADDRESS OF CREDITOR

B6I (Official Form 6I) (12/07)

In re ______________________________, Case No. ______________________
Debtor (if known)

SCHEDULE I - CURRENT INCOME OF INDIVIDUAL DEBTOR(S)

The column labeled "Spouse" must be completed in all cases filed by joint debtors and by every married debtor, whether or not a joint petition is filed, unless the spouses are separated and a joint petition is not filed. Do not state the name of any minor child. The average monthly income calculated on this form may differ from the current monthly income calculated on Form 22A, 22B, or 22C.

Debtor's Marital Status:	DEPENDENTS OF DEBTOR AND SPOUSE	
	RELATIONSHIP(S):	AGE(S):

Employment:	DEBTOR	SPOUSE
Occupation		
Name of Employer		
How long employed		
Address of Employer		

INCOME: (Estimate of average or projected monthly income at time case filed)	DEBTOR	SPOUSE
1. Monthly gross wages, salary, and commissions (Prorate if not paid monthly)	$	$
2. Estimate monthly overtime	$	$
3. SUBTOTAL	$	$
4. LESS PAYROLL DEDUCTIONS		
a. Payroll taxes and social security	$	$
b. Insurance	$	$
c. Union dues	$	$
d. Other (Specify): ____________	$	$
5. SUBTOTAL OF PAYROLL DEDUCTIONS	$	$
6. TOTAL NET MONTHLY TAKE HOME PAY	$	$
7. Regular income from operation of business or profession or farm (Attach detailed statement)	$	$
8. Income from real property	$	$
9. Interest and dividends	$	$
10. Alimony, maintenance or support payments payable to the debtor for the debtor's use or that of dependents listed above	$	$
11. Social security or government assistance (Specify): ____________	$	$
12. Pension or retirement income	$	$
13. Other monthly income (Specify): ____________	$	$
14. SUBTOTAL OF LINES 7 THROUGH 13	$	$
15. AVERAGE MONTHLY INCOME (Add amounts on lines 6 and 14)	$	$
16. COMBINED AVERAGE MONTHLY INCOME: (Combine column totals from line 15)	$	

(Report also on Summary of Schedules and, if applicable, on Statistical Summary of Certain Liabilities and Related Data)

17. Describe any increase or decrease in income reasonably anticipated to occur within the year following the filing of this document:

B6J (Official Form 6J) (12/07)

In re ________________________________, Debtor

Case No. ________________________ (if known)

SCHEDULE J - CURRENT EXPENDITURES OF INDIVIDUAL DEBTOR(S)

Complete this schedule by estimating the average or projected monthly expenses of the debtor and the debtor's family at time case filed. Prorate any payments made bi-weekly, quarterly, semi-annually, or annually to show monthly rate. The average monthly expenses calculated on this form may differ from the deductions from income allowed on Form22A or 22C.

☐ Check this box if a joint petition is filed and debtor's spouse maintains a separate household. Complete a separate schedule of expenditures labeled "Spouse."

1. Rent or home mortgage payment (include lot rented for mobile home) $______
   - a. Are real estate taxes included? Yes ______ No ______
   - b. Is property insurance included? Yes ______ No ______
2. Utilities: a. Electricity and heating fuel $______
   - b. Water and sewer $______
   - c. Telephone $______
   - d. Other ______________________ $______
3. Home maintenance (repairs and upkeep) $______
4. Food $______
5. Clothing $______
6. Laundry and dry cleaning $______
7. Medical and dental expenses $______
8. Transportation (not including car payments) $______
9. Recreation, clubs and entertainment, newspapers, magazines, etc. $______
10. Charitable contributions $______
11. Insurance (not deducted from wages or included in home mortgage payments)
    - a. Homeowner's or renter's $______
    - b. Life $______
    - c. Health $______
    - d. Auto $______
    - e. Other ______________________ $______
12. Taxes (not deducted from wages or included in home mortgage payments)
    (Specify) ______________________ $______
13. Installment payments: (In chapter 11, 12, and 13 cases, do not list payments to be included in the plan)
    - a. Auto $______
    - b. Other ______________________ $______
    - c. Other ______________________ $______
14. Alimony, maintenance, and support paid to others $______
15. Payments for support of additional dependents not living at your home $______
16. Regular expenses from operation of business, profession, or farm (attach detailed statement) $______
17. Other ______________________ $______
18. AVERAGE MONTHLY EXPENSES (Total lines 1-17. Report also on Summary of Schedules and, if applicable, on the Statistical Summary of Certain Liabilities and Related Data.) $______
19. Describe any increase or decrease in expenditures reasonably anticipated to occur within the year following the filing of this document:
20. STATEMENT OF MONTHLY NET INCOME
    - a. Average monthly income from Line 15 of Schedule I $______
    - b. Average monthly expenses from Line 18 above $______
    - c. Monthly net income (a. minus b.) $______

B6 Declaration (Official Form 6 - Declaration) (12/07)

In re ______________________________, **Case No.** ______________________
Debtor **(If known)**

DECLARATION CONCERNING DEBTOR'S SCHEDULES

DECLARATION UNDER PENALTY OF PERJURY BY INDIVIDUAL DEBTOR

I declare under penalty of perjury that I have read the foregoing summary and schedules, consisting of _____ sheets, and that they are true and correct to the best of my knowledge, information, and belief.

Date ______________________ Signature: ______________________________
Debtor

Date ______________________ Signature: ______________________________
(Joint Debtor, if any)

[If joint case, both spouses must sign.]

DECLARATION AND SIGNATURE OF NON-ATTORNEY BANKRUPTCY PETITION PREPARER (See 11 U.S.C. § 110)

I declare under penalty of perjury that: (1) I am a bankruptcy petition preparer as defined in 11 U.S.C. § 110; (2) I prepared this document for compensation and have provided the debtor with a copy of this document and the notices and information required under 11 U.S.C. §§ 110(b), 110(h) and 342(b); and, (3) if rules or guidelines have been promulgated pursuant to 11 U.S.C § 110(h) setting a maximum fee for services chargeable by bankruptcy petition preparers, I have given the debtor notice of the maximum amount before preparing any document for filing for a debtor or accepting any fee from the debtor, as required by that section.

______________________________ ______________________
Printed or Typed Name and Title, if any, of Bankruptcy Petition Preparer
Social Security No. *(Required by 11 U.S.C. § 110.)*

If the bankruptcy petition preparer is not an individual, state the name, title (if any), address, and social security number of the officer, principal, responsible person, or partner who signs this document.

____
____
____
Address

X ______________________________ ______________________
Signature of Bankruptcy Petition Preparer Date

Names and Social Security numbers of all other individuals who prepared or assisted in preparing this document, unless the bankruptcy petition preparer is not an individual:

If more than one person prepared this document, attach additional signed sheets conforming to the appropriate Official Form for each person.

A bankruptcy petition preparer's failure to comply with the provisions of title 11 and the Federal Rules of Bankruptcy Procedure may result in fines or imprisonment or both. 11 U.S.C. § 110; 18 U.S.C. § 156.

DECLARATION UNDER PENALTY OF PERJURY ON BEHALF OF A CORPORATION OR PARTNERSHIP

I, the ______________________ [the president or other officer or an authorized agent of the corporation or a member or an authorized agent of the partnership] of the ______________________ [corporation or partnership] named as debtor in this case, declare under penalty of perjury that I have read the foregoing summary and schedules, consisting of _____ sheets (*Total shown on summary page plus 1*), and that they are true and correct to the best of my knowledge, information, and belief.

Date ______________________
Signature: ______________________________

____
[Print or type name of individual signing on behalf of debtor.]

[An individual signing on behalf of a partnership or corporation must indicate position or relationship to debtor.]

Penalty for making a false statement or concealing property: Fine of up to $500,000 or imprisonment for up to 5 years or both. 18 U.S.C. §§ 152 and 3571.

(Added Aug. 1, 1991; amended Mar. 16, 1993; Mar. 14, 1995; Oct. 1, 1997; Dec. 1, 2003; Oct. 17, 2005; Oct. 1, 2006; Dec. 1, 2007.)

NOTES OF ADVISORY COMMITTEE ON RULES—1991

These schedules shall be used to comply with §521(1) of the Code and Rule 1007(b). Schedules A, B, D, E, and F constitute the schedule of assets and liabilities. Schedules I and J constitute a schedule of current income and current expenditures for individual and joint debtors. Two new schedules have been created, Schedule G—Executory Contracts and Unexpired Leases, and Schedule H—Codebtors.

The order of the schedules has been arranged with the summary sheet in front and with the schedules of assets appearing first, followed by the schedules of liabilities. This structure corresponds to the customary pattern by which trustees and creditors review these documents and to the format of the accounting profession for balance sheets.

The schedules require a complete listing of assets and liabilities but leave many of the details to investigation by the trustee. Instructions in the former schedules to provide details concerning "written instruments" relating to the debtor's property or debts have been deleted. Section 521(3) of the Code requires the debtor to cooperate with the trustee, who can administer the estate more effectively by requesting any documents from the debtor rather than relying on descriptions in the schedules which may prove to be inaccurate.

Leasehold interests in both real and personal property are to be reported in Schedule G—Executory Contracts and Unexpired Leases. This information should not be repeated in the schedules of assets.

Generally in these schedules, a creditor's claim will be listed only once, even if the claim is secured only in part, or is entitled only in part to priority under §507(a) of the Code, with the remainder of the claim to be treated as a general unsecured claim. For example, a partially secured creditor whose claim is reported in Schedule D—Creditors Holding Secured Claims will be listed together with the value of the property securing the claim and a notation of the amount of any unsecured portion of the claim. Information concerning the unsecured portion should not be repeated in Schedule F—Creditors Holding Nonpriority Unsecured Claims. Any resulting overstatement of the amounts owed on secured and priority claims as reported on the summary sheet is offset by a corresponding understatement of the amount owed on unsecured claims.

If a debtor has no property or no creditors in a particular category, an affirmative statement to that effect is required. Married debtors should indicate whether property is jointly or separately owned and whether spouses are jointly or separately liable for debts, using the columns provided in the schedules.

Former "Schedule B-3. Property not otherwise scheduled," has been deleted and its two questions moved. Schedule B—Personal Property now includes at item 33, "Other personal property of any kind not already listed." The only other question on former Schedule B-3 concerned assignments for the benefit of creditors; it has been moved to the Statement of Financial Affairs.

Schedule A—Real Property. Instructions at the top of the form indicate the scope of the interests in property to be reported on the schedule. Leasehold interests of the debtor are not reported here but on the Schedule of Executory Contracts and Unexpired Leases. The trustee will request copies of deeds or other instruments necessary to the administration of the estate.

Schedule B—Personal Property. This schedule is to be used for reporting all of the debtor's interests in personal property except leases and executory contracts, which are to be listed on the Schedule of Executory Contracts and Unexpired Leases. Several new categories of property have been added to the schedule, *i.e.*, aircraft, and interests in IRA, ERISA, Keogh, or other pension or profit-sharing plans. To minimize the potential for concealment of assets, the debtor must declare whether the debtor has any property in each category on the schedule. The trustee can request copies of any documents concerning the debtor's property necessary to the administration of the estate.

Schedule C—Property Claimed as Exempt. The form of the schedule has been modified to eliminate duplication of information provided elsewhere. The location of property, for example, which formerly was required here, is disclosed in the schedules of real and personal property. The requirement that the debtor state the present use of the property also has been eliminated as best left to inquiry by the trustee. Exemptions in some states are granted by constitutional provisions: accordingly, the requirement that the debtor state the "statute" creating an exemption has been changed to request a statement of the relevant "law."

This schedule adds a new requirement that the debtor state the market value of the property in addition to the amount claimed as exempt.

Schedule D—Creditors Holding Secured Claims. Schedules D, E, and F have been redesigned with address boxes sized to match the number of characters which can be accommodated on the computerized noticing systems used by the courts. The size also closely approximates that of standard mailing labels. Space is designated at the top of the box for the debtor's account number with the creditor. The design of the form is intended to reduce the volume of misdirected creditor mail.

The form requires the debtor to state affirmatively that a claim is disputed, unliquidated, or contingent. The existence of any type of codebtor is to be disclosed, but details are to be provided in Schedule H, as they are not needed here. Duplication of information also has been kept to a minimum by deleting requests that the debtor indicate on this schedule whether a debt has been reduced to judgment and the date on which a creditor repossessed any collateral. Requests for details concerning negotiable instruments and the consideration for a claim, formerly part of the schedule, are left to the trustee's inquiries.

Schedule E—Creditors Holding Unsecured Priority Claims. The schedule lists all of the types of claims entitled to priority and requires the debtor to indicate the existence of claims in each category. Continuation sheets are provided. The type of priority claim is to be noted at the top of the continuation sheet, and each type must be reported on a separate sheet. This schedule also requires the debtor to indicate the existence of any codebtors. As in Schedule D—Creditors Holding Secured Claims, requests for information concerning judgments and negotiable instruments have been deleted.

Schedule F—Creditors Holding Unsecured Nonpriority Claims. This schedule has been revised generally in conformity with the other schedules of creditors. If a claim is subject to setoff, the debtor is required to so state.

Schedule G—Executory Contracts and Unexpired Leases. Rule 1007(b) requires the debtor to file a schedule of executory contracts and unexpired leases, unless the court orders otherwise. All unexpired leases of either real or personal property are to be reported on this schedule. The schedule also requires the debtor to disclose specific information to assist the trustee in identifying leases which must be assumed within 60 days after the order for relief or be deemed rejected under §365(d) of the Code.

Schedule H—Schedule of Codebtors. This schedule is designed to provide the trustee and creditors with information about codebtors of all types other than spouses in joint cases. The completed schedule provides information concerning non-debtor parties, such as guarantors and non-debtor spouses having an interest in property as tenants by the entirety. In chapter 12 and chapter 13 cases, the completed schedule also indicates those persons who may be entitled to certain protections from creditor action under §§1201 and 1301 of the Code.

Schedule I—Schedule of Current Income of Individual Debtor(s) and Schedule J—Schedule of Current Expenditures of Individual Debtor(s). Former Official Form No. 6A has been divided into a schedule of current income and a separate schedule of current expenditures. The language is substantially the same as in former Official Form No. 6A. In light of the abrogation of Official Form No. 10, the Chapter 13 Statement, style changes have been made so that these schedules can be used by individual and joint debtors in all chapters.

NOTES OF ADVISORY COMMITTEE ON RULES—1993 AMENDMENT

Schedule E (Creditors Holding Unsecured Priority Claims) has been changed to conform to the statutory amendment that added subsection (a)(8) to §507 of the Code. Pub. L. No. 101–647, (Crime Control Act of 1990), added the new subsection, which had the effect of creating an eighth priority for claims of certain governmental units based on commitments to maintain the capital of an insured depository institution.

NOTES OF ADVISORY COMMITTEE ON RULES—1995 AMENDMENT

Schedule E—Creditors Holding Unsecured Priority Claims is amended to add the new seventh priority afforded to debts for alimony, maintenance, or support of a spouse, former spouse, or child of the debtor by the Bankruptcy Reform Act of 1994. Statutory references are amended to conform to the paragraph numbers of section 507(a) of the Code as renumbered by the 1994 Act. Schedule E also is amended to add commissions owed to certain independent sales representatives and to raise the maximum dollar amounts for certain priorities in accordance with amendments made by the 1994 Act to section 507(a) of the Code. The 1994 Act also amended section 104 of the Code to provide for future adjustment of the maximum dollar amounts specified in section 507(a) to be made by administrative action at three-year intervals to reflect changes in the consumer price index. Schedule E is amended to give notice that these dollar amounts are subject to change without formal amendment to the official form.

The Schedules are a "document for filing" that may be prepared by a "bankruptcy petition preparer" as defined in 11 U.S.C. §110, which was added to the Code by the 1994 Act; accordingly, a signature line for such preparer is added. In addition to signing, a bankruptcy petition preparer is required by section 110 to disclose the information requested.

NOTES OF ADVISORY COMMITTEE ON RULES—1997 AMENDMENT

The form is amended to add to the column labels a reference to community liability for claims. The amendment is technical and corrects an editorial oversight.

COMMITTEE NOTES ON RULES—2003 AMENDMENT

The instructions to Schedule D (Creditors Holding Secured Claims), Schedule E (Creditors Holding Unsecured Priority Claims), and Schedule F (Creditors Holding Unsecured Nonpriority Claims) are amended to inform the debtor that the debtor must list the last four digits of any account number with the listed creditor, and that the debtor may, in its discretion, include the entire account number in the schedules. Schedule I (Current Income of Individual Debtor(s)) is amended to provide greater privacy to minors and other dependents of the debtor by deleting the requirement that the debtor disclose their names. Pursuant to §110(c) of the Bankruptcy Code, the certification by a non-attorney bankruptcy petition preparer requires a petition preparer to provide the full social security number of the individual who actually prepares the document.

COMMITTEE NOTES ON RULES—2005 AMENDMENT

The forms of the Schedules of Assets and Liabilities are amended to implement the provisions of the Bankruptcy Abuse Prevention and Consumer Protection Act of 2005, Pub. L. No. 109–8, 119 Stat. 23, (April 20, 2005). An amendment that directs the debtor to avoid disclosing the name of any minor child occurs in several of the schedules in conformity with §112 which was added to the Code in 2005. Section 112 provides for the debtor to provide the name of any minor child confidentially to the court, should the trustee need the information to evaluate properly the information filed by the debtor.

The "Statistical Summary of Certain Liabilities" is added to collect information needed to prepare statistical reports required under 28 U.S.C. §159, which was enacted as part of the 2005 Act.

Schedules A, B, C, and D are amended to delete the word "market" from the columns in which the debtor reports the value of various kinds of property. Amendments to §506 of the Code enacted in 2005 specify that "replacement value" must be used in connection with certain property. The schedules no longer specify "market" value and permit the debtor to choose the appropriate one, whether that be replacement, market, or some other value. Valuation of property, generally, is the subject of extensive provisions in the Code, and the deletion of the word "market" from the determinations of value to be made by the debtor on the schedules is intended to remove any inference about choice of valuation standard. This deletion simply indicates that the form takes no position on which Code provision or valuation standard may be applicable in any instance.

The following paragraphs describe changes that are specific to each schedule.

Schedule B—Personal Property is amended to require the debtor to list any interests in an education IRA, as §541(b)(5), added to the Code in 2005, makes special provision for them. The schedule also is amended to require the debtor to disclose the existence of any customer lists or other compilations containing personally identifiable information provided by an individual to the debtor in connection with obtaining a product or service from the debtor for personal, family, or household purposes. This amendment implements §332, which was added to the Code in 2005.

Schedule C—Property Claimed as Exempt is amended to delete descriptive information concerning the length of domicile required for the debtor to qualify to claim certain exemptions. Any summary of the amendments enacted in 2005 to §522 of the Code concerning these requirements might inadvertently cause the debtor to lose important rights. Accordingly, the form now directs the debtor to indicate whether exemptions are being claimed under §522(b)(2) or §522(b)(3) and whether the debtor claims a homestead exemption that exceeds $125,000.

Schedule E—Creditors Holding Unsecured Priority Claims is amended to implement the changes in priority to which a claim may be entitled under 11 U.S.C. §507 as amended by the 2005 Act and to add the new priority included in the Reform Act for claims for death or personal injury while the debtor was intoxicated. "Subtotal" and "Total" boxes have been added to the column labeled "Amount Entitled to Priority" to assist the individual debtor to complete the Current Monthly Income ("CMI" or "Means Test") form.

Schedule G—Executory Contracts and Unexpired Leases is amended by deleting the note to the debtor advising that parties listed on this schedule may not receive notice of the filing of the bankruptcy case unless they also are listed on one of the schedules of liabilities. The better practice is for all parties to transactions with the debtor to receive notice of the filing of the case, and an amendment to Rule 1007 requiring the debtor to provide a mailing list that includes these parties is scheduled to take effect December 1, 2005.

Schedule H—Codebtors is amended to add specifics about community property jurisdictions in connection with the requirement to provide the name of any spouse of a debtor who resides or resided in a community property jurisdiction. This amendment also mirrors amendments made in 1997 to Official Form 7, the Statement of Financial Affairs, and will assure that these codebtors receive notice of the filing of the bankruptcy case. The form also is amended to extend from six years to eight years the time period for which this information is reported pursuant to the 2005 amendments to §727(a)(8) of the Code.

Schedule I—Current Income of Individual Debtor(s) is amended to require the income of a nondebtor spouse to be reported in cases filed under chapters 7 and 11. Line numbers have been added to assist the debtor in calculating and reporting totals. A new subtotal line for income from sources other than as an employee and a new "total monthly income" line provide for this form to be used in conjunction with Schedule J to satisfy the requirements of §521(a)(1)(B)(v), which was added to the Code in 2005. The form also has been revised to provide the statement concerning any anticipated increase or decrease in income required in §521(a)(1)(B)(vi), which also was added to the Code in 2005.

Schedule J—Current Expenditures of Individual Debtor(s). A direction has been added to require the debtor to report any increase or decrease in expenses anticipated to occur within the year following the filing of the document, as required by §521(a)(1)(B)(vi), which was added to the Code in 2005. The form also is amended to provide, in conjunction with Schedule I, a statement of monthly net income, itemized to show how the amount is calculated, as required by §522(a)(1)(B)(v), which was added to the Code in 2005.

Declaration Concerning Debtor's Schedules. The declaration by a non-attorney bankruptcy petition preparer is amended to include material mandated by §110 of the Code as amended in 2005.

COMMITTEE NOTES ON RULES—2006 AMENDMENT

In order to comply fully with the statistical reporting requirements of 28 U.S.C. §159, which was enacted as part of the 2005 Act [Bankruptcy Abuse Prevention and Consumer Protection Act of 2005, Pub. L. 109–8, Apr. 20, 2005, 119 Stat. 23] and takes effect in October 2006, the "Statistical Summary of Certain Liabilities" is renamed "Statistical Summary of Certain Liabilities and Related Data," and additional information is required to be stated there. Collecting in one place the bulk of the information to be used in the reports required under 28 U.S.C. §159 will assist the courts and the Director of the Administrative Office of the United States Courts to fulfill their statutory responsibilities.

Schedule D is amended to provide for creating a total of any unsecured amounts (amounts that exceed the value of the collateral) owed to creditors holding secured claims, and for stating this amount on the Statistical Summary of Certain Liabilities and Related Data. Schedule E is amended to provide for creating totals of the amounts entitled to priority and of any amounts that exceed the statutory limits on certain priorities and to direct the debtor to report these amounts on the Statistical Summary of Certain Liabilities and Related Data. Schedule F is amended to direct the debtor to report the total of this schedule both on the Summary of Schedules and on the Statistical Summary of Certain Liabilities.

The statistical reports required under 28 U.S.C. §159 must include "the current monthly income, average income, and average expenses" of individual debtors with primarily consumer debts as reported on the schedules filed by those debtors. Accordingly, Schedules I and J, on which debtors already are directed to report average income and average expenses are amended to label the totals arrived at by completing the schedules as "average monthly income" and "average monthly expenses." These amendments make no substantive changes, simply conforming the terminology on these schedules to that used in §159.

The amount of the debtor's current monthly income, which also is required by §159, is derived from Official Forms 22A, 22B, or 22C, depending on the chapter under which the debtor files. This amount is included on the Statistical Summary of Certain Liabilities and Related Data as a convenience to make reports under §159 easier to compile.

The Declaration Concerning Debtor's Schedules is amended in the section designated for signing and verifying by an individual or joint debtor. The amendment accommodates the requirement that individual debtors must complete both the Summary of Schedules and the Statistical Summary of Certain Liabilities and Related Data by directing the debtor to state number of pages being verified as the number of sheets in the completed schedules "plus 2."

COMMITTEE NOTES ON RULES—2005–2007 AMENDMENT

[The 2005–2007 Committee Note incorporates Committee Notes previously published in 2005 and 2006.]

The forms of the Schedules of Assets and Liabilities are amended to implement the provisions of the Bankruptcy Abuse Prevention and Consumer Protection Act of 2005, Pub. L. No. 109–8, 119 Stat. 23, (April 20, 2005) ("BAPCPA"). An amendment that directs the debtor to avoid disclosing the name and address of any minor child occurs in Schedules B, D, E, F, G, and H in conformity with §112 which was added to the Code in 2005. Section 112 provides for the debtor to furnish the name of any minor child confidentially to the court, should the trustee need the information to evaluate properly the information filed by the debtor. In addition, those schedules are amended to add to the reference to Rule 1007(m), with respect to a minor child, a direction to include for noticing purposes the name, address, and legal relationship to the child of "a person described" in that rule. Rule 1007(m) requires the person named to be someone on whom process would be served in an adversary proceeding against the child.

The "Statistical Summary of Certain Liabilities and Related Data" is added to collect from individual debtors with primarily consumer debts the information needed to prepare statistical reports required under 28 U.S.C. §159, which was enacted as part of BAPCPA. Collecting the bulk of the information to be used in these statistical reports in the Summary of Schedules and the statistical summary will assist the courts and the Director of the Administrative Office to fulfill their statutory responsibilities. Schedules D and E are amended to provide additional totals and, together with Schedule F, to direct debtors who must complete the statistical summary to report total amounts there. Similarly, Schedules I and J are amended to conform their terminology to that used in 28 U.S.C. §159 and direct debtors who must complete the statistical summary to report the specified amounts there.

Schedules A, B, C, and D are amended to delete the word "market" from the columns in which the debtor reports the value of various kinds of property. Amendments to §506 of the Code enacted in 2005 specify that "replacement value" must be used in connection with certain property. The schedules no longer specify "market" value and permit the debtor to choose the appropriate one, whether that be replacement, market, or some other value. Valuation of property, generally, is the subject of extensive provisions in the Code, and the deletion of the word "market" from the determinations of value to be made by the debtor on the schedules is intended to remove any inference about choice of valuation standard. This deletion simply indicates that the form takes no position on which Code provision or valuation standard may be applicable in any particular instance.

The following paragraphs describe changes that are specific to each schedule:

Schedule B—Personal Property is amended to require the debtor to list any interests in an education IRA, because §541(b)(5), added to the Code in 2005, makes special provision for them. The schedule is also amended to require the debtor to disclose the existence of any customer lists or other compilations containing personally identifiable information provided by an individual to the debtor in connection with obtaining a product or service from the debtor for personal, family, or household purposes. This amendment implements §332, which was added to the Code by BAPCPA in 2005.

Schedule C—Property Claimed as Exempt is amended to delete descriptive information concerning the length of domicile required for the debtor to qualify to claim certain exemptions. Any summary of the BAPCPA amendments to § 522 of the Code concerning these requirements might inadvertently cause the debtor to lose important rights. Accordingly, the form now directs the debtor to indicate whether exemptions are being claimed under § 522(b)(2) or § 522(b)(3) and whether the debtor claims a homestead exemption that exceeds $136,875.

Schedule D—Creditors Holding Secured Claims is amended to provide for creating a total of any unsecured amounts (amounts that exceed the value of the collateral) owed to creditors holding secured claims. In addition to facilitating statistical reporting, providing a breakdown of the amounts owed to creditors listed on this schedule will assist the individual debtor in completing the means test calculation under § 707(b)(2)(A)(i) of the Code.

Schedule E—Creditors Holding Unsecured Priority Claims is amended to implement the changes in priority to which a claim may be entitled under 11 U.S.C. § 507 as amended by BAPCPA and to add the new priority included in the 2005 Act for claims for death or personal injury while the debtor was intoxicated. "Subtotal" and "Total" boxes have been added to the columns labeled "Amount Entitled to Priority" and "Amount Not Entitled to Priority" for statistical reporting purposes and to assist the individual debtor in completing the means test calculation under § 707(b)(2)(A)(i) of the Code.

Schedule H—Codebtors is amended to add specifics about community property jurisdictions in connection with the requirement to provide the name of any spouse of a debtor who resides or resided in a community property jurisdiction. This amendment also mirrors amendments made in 1997 to Official Form 7, the Statement of Financial Affairs, and will assure that these codebtors receive notice of the filing of the bankruptcy case. The form also is amended to extend from six years to eight years the time period for which this information is reported pursuant to the 2005 amendments to § 727(a)(8) of the Code.

Schedule I—Current Income of Individual Debtor(s) is amended to make it clear that "every" married debtor must provide income information for both spouses, unless the spouses are separated and a joint petition is not filed. The description of the income to be reported is revised to clarify that the purpose of this schedule is to obtain information about actual income on the date the bankruptcy case is filed and which a debtor reasonably expects in the future in contrast to the debtor's "current monthly income" as defined in § 101(10A) and reported on Form 22A, 22B, or 22C. And a statement included at the top of the form also explains that the income calculated [sic] this form may be different than the current monthly income. Line numbers have been added to assist the debtor in calculating and reporting totals. A new subtotal line for income from sources other than as an employee and a new "average monthly income" line will enable this form to be used in conjunction with Schedule J to satisfy the requirements of § 521(a)(1)(B)(v), which was added to the Code by BAPCPA. New statistical reporting requirements in 28 U.S.C. § 159 also require "average monthly income." In addition, the form is revised to provide the statement concerning any anticipated increase or decrease in income required in § 521(a)(1)(B)(vi), also added to the Code in 2005.

Schedule J—Current Expenditures of Individual Debtor(s). In conjunction with amendments to Schedule I, the form is amended to provide for reporting the debtor's actual "average monthly expenses," as required by 28 U.S.C. § 159 and a statement of monthly net income, itemized to show how the amount is calculated, as required by § 522(a)(1)(B)(v), which was added to the Code by BAPCPA in 2005. In addition, line numbers have been inserted and the description of expenses revised to make it clear than [sic] the purpose of this schedule is to obtain information about a debtor's actual and reasonably foreseeable expenses on the date the bankruptcy case is filed. And a statement similar to the statement at the top of Schedule I explains that the expenses calculated on the form may differ from the expenses calculated on Forms [sic] 22A or 22C. A direction has been added to require the debtor to report any increase or decrease in expenses anticipated to occur within the year following the filing of the document, as required by § 521(a)(1)(B)(vi), which also was added to the Code in 2005.

Declaration Concerning Debtor's Schedules. The declaration by individual or joint debtors is amended to require the debtor to merely state the total number of pages being verified. The declaration and signature of any non-attorney bankruptcy petition preparer is amended to include material mandated by § 110 of the Code as amended in 2005.

B 7 (Official Form 7) (12/07)

UNITED STATES BANKRUPTCY COURT

In re:____________________________________, Case No. ______________________________
Debtor (if known)

STATEMENT OF FINANCIAL AFFAIRS

This statement is to be completed by every debtor. Spouses filing a joint petition may file a single statement on which the information for both spouses is combined. If the case is filed under chapter 12 or chapter 13, a married debtor must furnish information for both spouses whether or not a joint petition is filed, unless the spouses are separated and a joint petition is not filed. An individual debtor engaged in business as a sole proprietor, partner, family farmer, or self-employed professional, should provide the information requested on this statement concerning all such activities as well as the individual's personal affairs. To indicate payments, transfers and the like to minor children, state the child's initials and the name and address of the child's parent or guardian, such as "A.B., a minor child, by John Doe, guardian." Do not disclose the child's name. See, 11 U.S.C. §112 and Fed. R. Bankr. P. 1007(m).

Questions 1 - 18 are to be completed by all debtors. Debtors that are or have been in business, as defined below, also must complete Questions 19 - 25. **If the answer to an applicable question is "None," mark the box labeled "None."** If additional space is needed for the answer to any question, use and attach a separate sheet properly identified with the case name, case number (if known), and the number of the question.

DEFINITIONS

"In business." A debtor is "in business" for the purpose of this form if the debtor is a corporation or partnership. An individual debtor is "in business" for the purpose of this form if the debtor is or has been, within six years immediately preceding the filing of this bankruptcy case, any of the following: an officer, director, managing executive, or owner of 5 percent or more of the voting or equity securities of a corporation; a partner, other than a limited partner, of a partnership; a sole proprietor or self-employed full-time or part-time. An individual debtor also may be "in business" for the purpose of this form if the debtor engages in a trade, business, or other activity, other than as an employee, to supplement income from the debtor's primary employment.

"Insider." The term "insider" includes but is not limited to: relatives of the debtor; general partners of the debtor and their relatives; corporations of which the debtor is an officer, director, or person in control; officers, directors, and any owner of 5 percent or more of the voting or equity securities of a corporate debtor and their relatives; affiliates of the debtor and insiders of such affiliates; any managing agent of the debtor. 11 U.S.C. § 101.

---

1. Income from employment or operation of business

None ☐

State the gross amount of income the debtor has received from employment, trade, or profession, or from operation of the debtor's business, including part-time activities either as an employee or in independent trade or business, from the beginning of this calendar year to the date this case was commenced. State also the gross amounts received during the **two years** immediately preceding this calendar year. (A debtor that maintains, or has maintained, financial records on the basis of a fiscal rather than a calendar year may report fiscal year income. Identify the beginning and ending dates of the debtor's fiscal year.) If a joint petition is filed, state income for each spouse separately. (Married debtors filing under chapter 12 or chapter 13 must state income of both spouses whether or not a joint petition is filed, unless the spouses are separated and a joint petition is not filed.)

AMOUNT SOURCE

2

2. Income other than from employment or operation of business

None ☐

State the amount of income received by the debtor other than from employment, trade, profession, operation of the debtor's business during the **two years** immediately preceding the commencement of this case. Give particulars. If a joint petition is filed, state income for each spouse separately. (Married debtors filing under chapter 12 or chapter 13 must state income for each spouse whether or not a joint petition is filed, unless the spouses are separated and a joint petition is not filed.)

AMOUNT	SOURCE

3. Payments to creditors

Complete a. or b., as appropriate, and c.

None ☐

a. *Individual or joint debtor(s) with primarily consumer debts:* List all payments on loans, installment purchases of goods or services, and other debts to any creditor made within **90 days** immediately preceding the commencement of this case unless the aggregate value of all property that constitutes or is affected by such transfer is less than $600. Indicate with an asterisk (*) any payments that were made to a creditor on account of a domestic support obligation or as part of an alternative repayment schedule under a plan by an approved nonprofit budgeting and credit counseling agency. (Married debtors filing under chapter 12 or chapter 13 must include payments by either or both spouses whether or not a joint petition is filed, unless the spouses are separated and a joint petition is not filed.)

NAME AND ADDRESS OF CREDITOR	DATES OF PAYMENTS	AMOUNT PAID	AMOUNT STILL OWING

None ☐

b. Debtor whose debts are not primarily consumer debts: List each payment or other transfer to any creditor made within **90 days** immediately preceding the commencement of the case unless the aggregate value of all property that constitutes or is affected by such transfer is less than $5,475. If the debtor is an individual, indicate with an asterisk (*) any payments that were made to a creditor on account of a domestic support obligation or as part of an alternative repayment schedule under a plan by an approved nonprofit budgeting and credit counseling agency. (Married debtors filing under chapter 12 or chapter 13 must include payments and other transfers by either or both spouses whether or not a joint petition is filed, unless the spouses are separated and a joint petition is not filed.)

NAME AND ADDRESS OF CREDITOR	DATES OF PAYMENTS/ TRANSFERS	AMOUNT PAID OR VALUE OF TRANSFERS	AMOUNT STILL OWING

None ☐

c. *All debtors:* List all payments made within **one year** immediately preceding the commencement of this case to or for the benefit of creditors who are or were insiders. (Married debtors filing under chapter 12 or chapter 13 must include payments by either or both spouses whether or not a joint petition is filed, unless the spouses are separated and a joint petition is not filed.)

NAME AND ADDRESS OF CREDITOR AND RELATIONSHIP TO DEBTOR	DATE OF PAYMENT	AMOUNT PAID	AMOUNT STILL OWING

4. Suits and administrative proceedings, executions, garnishments and attachments

None ☐

a. List all suits and administrative proceedings to which the debtor is or was a party within **one year** immediately preceding the filing of this bankruptcy case. (Married debtors filing under chapter 12 or chapter 13 must include information concerning either or both spouses whether or not a joint petition is filed, unless the spouses are separated and a joint petition is not filed.)

CAPTION OF SUIT AND CASE NUMBER	NATURE OF PROCEEDING	COURT OR AGENCY AND LOCATION	STATUS OR DISPOSITION

None ☐

b. Describe all property that has been attached, garnished or seized under any legal or equitable process within **one year** immediately preceding the commencement of this case. (Married debtors filing under chapter 12 or chapter 13 must include information concerning property of either or both spouses whether or not a joint petition is filed, unless the spouses are separated and a joint petition is not filed.)

NAME AND ADDRESS OF PERSON FOR WHOSE BENEFIT PROPERTY WAS SEIZED	DATE OF SEIZURE	DESCRIPTION AND VALUE OF PROPERTY

5. Repossessions, foreclosures and returns

None ☐

List all property that has been repossessed by a creditor, sold at a foreclosure sale, transferred through a deed in lieu of foreclosure or returned to the seller, within **one year** immediately preceding the commencement of this case. (Married debtors filing under chapter 12 or chapter 13 must include information concerning property of either or both spouses whether or not a joint petition is filed, unless the spouses are separated and a joint petition is not filed.)

NAME AND ADDRESS OF CREDITOR OR SELLER	DATE OF REPOSSESSION, FORECLOSURE SALE, TRANSFER OR RETURN	DESCRIPTION AND VALUE OF PROPERTY

6. Assignments and receiverships

None ☐ a. Describe any assignment of property for the benefit of creditors made within **120 days** immediately preceding the commencement of this case. (Married debtors filing under chapter 12 or chapter 13 must include any assignment by either or both spouses whether or not a joint petition is filed, unless the spouses are separated and a joint petition is not filed.)

NAME AND ADDRESS OF ASSIGNEE	DATE OF ASSIGNMENT	TERMS OF ASSIGNMENT OR SETTLEMENT

None ☐ b. List all property which has been in the hands of a custodian, receiver, or court-appointed official within **one year** immediately preceding the commencement of this case. (Married debtors filing under chapter 12 or chapter 13 must include information concerning property of either or both spouses whether or not a joint petition is filed, unless the spouses are separated and a joint petition is not filed.)

NAME AND ADDRESS OF CUSTODIAN	NAME AND LOCATION OF COURT CASE TITLE & NUMBER	DATE OF ORDER	DESCRIPTION AND VALUE Of PROPERTY

7. Gifts

None ☐ List all gifts or charitable contributions made within **one year** immediately preceding the commencement of this case except ordinary and usual gifts to family members aggregating less than $200 in value per individual family member and charitable contributions aggregating less than $100 per recipient. (Married debtors filing under chapter 12 or chapter 13 must include gifts or contributions by either or both spouses whether or not a joint petition is filed, unless the spouses are separated and a joint petition is not filed.)

NAME AND ADDRESS OF PERSON OR ORGANIZATION	RELATIONSHIP TO DEBTOR, IF ANY	DATE OF GIFT	DESCRIPTION AND VALUE OF GIFT

8. Losses

None ☐ List all losses from fire, theft, other casualty or gambling within **one year** immediately preceding the commencement of this case **or since the commencement of this case.** (Married debtors filing under chapter 12 or chapter 13 must include losses by either or both spouses whether or not a joint petition is filed, unless the spouses are separated and a joint petition is not filed.)

DESCRIPTION AND VALUE OF PROPERTY	DESCRIPTION OF CIRCUMSTANCES AND, IF LOSS WAS COVERED IN WHOLE OR IN PART BY INSURANCE, GIVE PARTICULARS	DATE OF LOSS

9. Payments related to debt counseling or bankruptcy

None ☐

List all payments made or property transferred by or on behalf of the debtor to any persons, including attorneys, for consultation concerning debt consolidation, relief under the bankruptcy law or preparation of a petition in bankruptcy within **one year** immediately preceding the commencement of this case.

NAME AND ADDRESS OF PAYEE	DATE OF PAYMENT, NAME OF PAYER IF OTHER THAN DEBTOR	AMOUNT OF MONEY OR DESCRIPTION AND VALUE OF PROPERTY

10. Other transfers

None ☐

a. List all other property, other than property transferred in the ordinary course of the business or financial affairs of the debtor, transferred either absolutely or as security within **two years** immediately preceding the commencement of this case. (Married debtors filing under chapter 12 or chapter 13 must include transfers by either or both spouses whether or not a joint petition is filed, unless the spouses are separated and a joint petition is not filed.)

NAME AND ADDRESS OF TRANSFEREE, RELATIONSHIP TO DEBTOR	DATE	DESCRIBE PROPERTY TRANSFERRED AND VALUE RECEIVED

None ☐

b. List all property transferred by the debtor within **ten years** immediately preceding the commencement of this case to a self-settled trust or similar device of which the debtor is a beneficiary.

NAME OF TRUST OR OTHER DEVICE	DATE(S) OF TRANSFER(S)	AMOUNT OF MONEY OR DESCRIPTION AND VALUE OF PROPERTY OR DEBTOR'S INTEREST IN PROPERTY

11. Closed financial accounts

None ☐

List all financial accounts and instruments held in the name of the debtor or for the benefit of the debtor which were closed, sold, or otherwise transferred within **one year** immediately preceding the commencement of this case. Include checking, savings, or other financial accounts, certificates of deposit, or other instruments; shares and share accounts held in banks, credit unions, pension funds, cooperatives, associations, brokerage houses and other financial institutions. (Married debtors filing under chapter 12 or chapter 13 must include information concerning accounts or instruments held by or for either or both spouses whether or not a joint petition is filed, unless the spouses are separated and a joint petition is not filed.)

NAME AND ADDRESS OF INSTITUTION	TYPE OF ACCOUNT, LAST FOUR DIGITS OF ACCOUNT NUMBER, AND AMOUNT OF FINAL BALANCE	AMOUNT AND DATE OF SALE OR CLOSING

12. Safe deposit boxes

None ☐

List each safe deposit or other box or depository in which the debtor has or had securities, cash, or other valuables within **one year** immediately preceding the commencement of this case. (Married debtors filing under chapter 12 or chapter 13 must include boxes or depositories of either or both spouses whether or not a joint petition is filed, unless the spouses are separated and a joint petition is not filed.)

NAME AND ADDRESS OF BANK OR OTHER DEPOSITORY	NAMES AND ADDRESSES OF THOSE WITH ACCESS TO BOX OR DEPOSITORY	DESCRIPTION OF CONTENTS	DATE OF TRANSFER OR SURRENDER, IF ANY

13. Setoffs

None ☐

List all setoffs made by any creditor, including a bank, against a debt or deposit of the debtor within **90 days** preceding the commencement of this case. (Married debtors filing under chapter 12 or chapter 13 must include information concerning either or both spouses whether or not a joint petition is filed, unless the spouses are separated and a joint petition is not filed.)

NAME AND ADDRESS OF CREDITOR	DATE OF SETOFF	AMOUNT OF SETOFF

14. Property held for another person

None ☐

List all property owned by another person that the debtor holds or controls.

NAME AND ADDRESS OF OWNER	DESCRIPTION AND VALUE OF PROPERTY	LOCATION OF PROPERTY

15. Prior address of debtor

None ☐

If debtor has moved within **three years** immediately preceding the commencement of this case, list all premises which the debtor occupied during that period and vacated prior to the commencement of this case. If a joint petition is filed, report also any separate address of either spouse.

ADDRESS	NAME USED	DATES OF OCCUPANCY

16. Spouses and Former Spouses

None ☐ If the debtor resides or resided in a community property state, commonwealth, or territory (including Alaska, Arizona, California, Idaho, Louisiana, Nevada, New Mexico, Puerto Rico, Texas, Washington, or Wisconsin) within **eight years** immediately preceding the commencement of the case, identify the name of the debtor's spouse and of any former spouse who resides or resided with the debtor in the community property state.

NAME

17. Environmental Information.

For the purpose of this question, the following definitions apply:

"Environmental Law" means any federal, state, or local statute or regulation regulating pollution, contamination, releases of hazardous or toxic substances, wastes or material into the air, land, soil, surface water, groundwater, or other medium, including, but not limited to, statutes or regulations regulating the cleanup of these substances, wastes, or material.

"Site" means any location, facility, or property as defined under any Environmental Law, whether or not presently or formerly owned or operated by the debtor, including, but not limited to, disposal sites.

"Hazardous Material" means anything defined as a hazardous waste, hazardous substance, toxic substance, hazardous material, pollutant, or contaminant or similar term under an Environmental Law.

None ☐ a. List the name and address of every site for which the debtor has received notice in writing by a governmental unit that it may be liable or potentially liable under or in violation of an Environmental Law. Indicate the governmental unit, the date of the notice, and, if known, the Environmental Law:

SITE NAME AND ADDRESS	NAME AND ADDRESS OF GOVERNMENTAL UNIT	DATE OF NOTICE	ENVIRONMENTAL LAW

None ☐ b. List the name and address of every site for which the debtor provided notice to a governmental unit of a release of Hazardous Material. Indicate the governmental unit to which the notice was sent and the date of the notice.

SITE NAME AND ADDRESS	NAME AND ADDRESS OF GOVERNMENTAL UNIT	DATE OF NOTICE	ENVIRONMENTAL LAW

None ☐ c. List all judicial or administrative proceedings, including settlements or orders, under any Environmental Law with respect to which the debtor is or was a party. Indicate the name and address of the governmental unit that is or was a party to the proceeding, and the docket number.

NAME AND ADDRESS OF GOVERNMENTAL UNIT	DOCKET NUMBER	STATUS OR DISPOSITION

18 . Nature, location and name of business

None ☐ a. *If the debtor is an individual*, list the names, addresses, taxpayer-identification numbers, nature of the businesses, and beginning and ending dates of all businesses in which the debtor was an officer, director, partner, or managing executive of a corporation, partner in a partnership, sole proprietor, or was self-employed in a trade, profession, or other activity either full- or part-time within **six years** immediately preceding the commencement of this case, or in which the debtor owned 5 percent or more of the voting or equity securities within **six years** immediately preceding the commencement of this case.

If the debtor is a partnership, list the names, addresses, taxpayer-identification numbers, nature of the businesses, and beginning and ending dates of all businesses in which the debtor was a partner or owned 5 percent or more of the voting or equity securities, within **six years** immediately preceding the commencement of this case.

If the debtor is a corporation, list the names, addresses, taxpayer-identification numbers, nature of the businesses, and beginning and ending dates of all businesses in which the debtor was a partner or owned 5 percent or more of the voting or equity securities within **six years** immediately preceding the commencement of this case.

NAME	LAST FOUR DIGITS OF SOCIAL-SECURITY OR OTHER INDIVIDUAL TAXPAYER-I.D. NO. (ITIN)/ COMPLETE EIN	ADDRESS	NATURE OF BUSINESS	BEGINNING AND ENDING DATES

None ☐ b. Identify any business listed in response to subdivision a., above, that is "single asset real estate" as defined in 11 U.S.C. § 101.

NAME	ADDRESS

The following questions are to be completed by every debtor that is a corporation or partnership and by any individual debtor who is or has been, within **six years** immediately preceding the commencement of this case, any of the following: an officer, director, managing executive, or owner of more than 5 percent of the voting or equity securities of a corporation; a partner, other than a limited partner, of a partnership, a sole proprietor, or self-employed in a trade, profession, or other activity, either full- or part-time.

*(An individual or joint debtor should complete this portion of the statement **only** if the debtor is or has been in business, as defined above, within six years immediately preceding the commencement of this case. A debtor who has not been in business within those six years should go directly to the signature page.)*

---

19. Books, records and financial statements

None ☐ a. List all bookkeepers and accountants who within **two years** immediately preceding the filing of this bankruptcy case kept or supervised the keeping of books of account and records of the debtor.

NAME AND ADDRESS	DATES SERVICES RENDERED

None ☐ b. List all firms or individuals who within **two years** immediately preceding the filing of this bankruptcy case have audited the books of account and records, or prepared a financial statement of the debtor.

NAME	ADDRESS	DATES SERVICES RENDERED

None ☐ c. List all firms or individuals who at the time of the commencement of this case were in possession of the books of account and records of the debtor. If any of the books of account and records are not available, explain.

NAME	ADDRESS

None ☐ d. List all financial institutions, creditors and other parties, including mercantile and trade agencies, to whom a financial statement was issued by the debtor within **two years** immediately preceding the commencement of this case.

NAME AND ADDRESS	DATE ISSUED

20. Inventories

None ☐ a. List the dates of the last two inventories taken of your property, the name of the person who supervised the taking of each inventory, and the dollar amount and basis of each inventory.

DATE OF INVENTORY	INVENTORY SUPERVISOR	DOLLAR AMOUNT OF INVENTORY (Specify cost, market or other basis)

None ☐ b. List the name and address of the person having possession of the records of each of the inventories reported in a., above.

DATE OF INVENTORY	NAME AND ADDRESSES OF CUSTODIAN OF INVENTORY RECORDS

21 . Current Partners, Officers, Directors and Shareholders

None ☐ a. If the debtor is a partnership, list the nature and percentage of partnership interest of each member of the partnership.

NAME AND ADDRESS	NATURE OF INTEREST	PERCENTAGE OF INTEREST

None ☐ b. If the debtor is a corporation, list all officers and directors of the corporation, and each stockholder who directly or indirectly owns, controls, or holds 5 percent or more of the voting or equity securities of the corporation.

NAME AND ADDRESS	TITLE	NATURE AND PERCENTAGE OF STOCK OWNERSHIP

22 . Former partners, officers, directors and shareholders

None ☐ a. If the debtor is a partnership, list each member who withdrew from the partnership within **one year** immediately preceding the commencement of this case.

NAME	ADDRESS	DATE OF WITHDRAWAL

None ☐ b. If the debtor is a corporation, list all officers or directors whose relationship with the corporation terminated within **one year** immediately preceding the commencement of this case.

NAME AND ADDRESS	TITLE	DATE OF TERMINATION

---

23 . Withdrawals from a partnership or distributions by a corporation

None ☐ If the debtor is a partnership or corporation, list all withdrawals or distributions credited or given to an insider, including compensation in any form, bonuses, loans, stock redemptions, options exercised and any other perquisite during **one year** immediately preceding the commencement of this case.

NAME & ADDRESS OF RECIPIENT, RELATIONSHIP TO DEBTOR	DATE AND PURPOSE OF WITHDRAWAL	AMOUNT OF MONEY OR DESCRIPTION AND VALUE OF PROPERTY

---

24. Tax Consolidation Group.

None ☐ If the debtor is a corporation, list the name and federal taxpayer-identification number of the parent corporation of any consolidated group for tax purposes of which the debtor has been a member at any time within **six years** immediately preceding the commencement of the case.

NAME OF PARENT CORPORATION	TAXPAYER-IDENTIFICATION NUMBER (EIN)

---

25. Pension Funds.

None ☐ If the debtor is not an individual, list the name and federal taxpayer-identification number of any pension fund to which the debtor, as an employer, has been responsible for contributing at any time within **six years** immediately preceding the commencement of the case.

NAME OF PENSION FUND	TAXPAYER-IDENTIFICATION NUMBER (EIN)

* * * * * *

[If completed by an individual or individual and spouse]

I declare under penalty of perjury that I have read the answers contained in the foregoing statement of financial affairs and any attachments thereto and that they are true and correct.

Date ______________________ Signature of Debtor ______________________

Date ______________________ Signature of Joint Debtor (if any) ______________________

[If completed on behalf of a partnership or corporation]

I declare under penalty of perjury that I have read the answers contained in the foregoing statement of financial affairs and any attachments thereto and that they are true and correct to the best of my knowledge, information and belief.

Date ______________________ Signature ______________________

Print Name and Title ______________________

[An individual signing on behalf of a partnership or corporation must indicate position or relationship to debtor.]

__continuation sheets attached

Penalty for making a false statement: Fine of up to $500,000 or imprisonment for up to 5 years, or both. 18 U.S.C. §§ 152 and 3571

DECLARATION AND SIGNATURE OF NON-ATTORNEY BANKRUPTCY PETITION PREPARER (See 11 U.S.C. § 110)

I declare under penalty of perjury that: (1) I am a bankruptcy petition preparer as defined in 11 U.S.C. § 110; (2) I prepared this document for compensation and have provided the debtor with a copy of this document and the notices and information required under 11 U.S.C. §§ 110(b), 110(h), and 342(b); and, (3) if rules or guidelines have been promulgated pursuant to 11 U.S.C. § 110(h) setting a maximum fee for services chargeable by bankruptcy petition preparers, I have given the debtor notice of the maximum amount before preparing any document for filing for a debtor or accepting any fee from the debtor, as required by that section.

______________________ ______________________

Printed or Typed Name and Title, if any, of Bankruptcy Petition Preparer — Social-Security No. (Required by 11 U.S.C. § 110.)

If the bankruptcy petition preparer is not an individual, state the name, title (if any), address, and social-security number of the officer, principal, responsible person, or partner who signs this document.

____

Address

______________________ ______________________

Signature of Bankruptcy Petition Preparer — Date

Names and Social-Security numbers of all other individuals who prepared or assisted in preparing this document unless the bankruptcy petition preparer is not an individual:

If more than one person prepared this document, attach additional signed sheets conforming to the appropriate Official Form for each person

A bankruptcy petition preparer's failure to comply with the provisions of title 11 and the Federal Rules of Bankruptcy Procedure may result in fines or imprisonment or both. 18 U.S.C. § 156.

(Added Aug. 1, 1991; amended Mar. 16, 1993; Mar. 14, 1995; Sept. 19, 2000; Dec. 1, 2003; Oct. 17, 2005; Dec. 1, 2007.)

NOTES OF ADVISORY COMMITTEE ON RULES—1991

This form consolidates questions from former Official Forms No. 7, No. 8, and No. 10. This form is to be completed by all debtors. An individual debtor engaged in business as a sole proprietor, partner, family farmer, or self-employed professional should provide the information requested on this statement concerning all such activities as well as the individual's personal affairs.

The Chapter 13 Statement, former Official Form No. 10, has been abrogated. Chapter 13 debtors are to complete this statement and the schedules prescribed in Official Form 6.

All questions have been converted to affirmative directions to furnish information, and each question must be answered. If the answer is "none," or the question is not applicable, the debtor is required to so state by marking the box labeled "None" provided at each question.

See Committee Note to Form 2 for a discussion of the unsworn declaration at the end of this form.

NOTES OF ADVISORY COMMITTEE ON RULES—1993 AMENDMENT

The form has been amended in two ways. In the second paragraph of the instructions, the third sentence has been deleted to clarify that only a debtor that is or has been in business as defined in the form should answer Questions 16–21. In addition, administrative proceedings have been added to the types of legal actions to be disclosed in Question 4.a.

NOTES OF ADVISORY COMMITTEE ON RULES—1995 AMENDMENT

This form is a "document for filing" that may be prepared by a "bankruptcy petition preparer" as defined in 11 U.S.C. §110, which was added to the Code by the Bankruptcy Reform Act of 1994; accordingly, a signature line for such preparer is added. In addition to signing, a bankruptcy petition preparer is required by section 110 to disclose the information requested.

NOTES OF ADVISORY COMMITTEE ON RULES—2000 AMENDMENT

The form has been amended to provide more information to taxing authorities, pension fund supervisors, and governmental units charged with environmental protection and regulation. Four new questions have been added to the form, covering community property owned by a debtor and the debtor's non-filing spouse or former spouse (Question 16), environmental information (Question 17), any consolidated tax group of a corporate debtor (Question 24), and the debtor's contributions to any employee pension fund (Question 25). In addition, every debtor will be required to state on the form whether the debtor has been in business within six years before filing the petition and, if so, must answer the remaining questions on the form (Questions 19–25). This is an enlargement of the two-year period previously specified. One reason for the longer "reach back" period is that business debtors often owe taxes that have been owed for more than two years. Another is that some of the questions already addressed to business debtors request information for the six-year period before the commencement of the case. Application of a six-year period to this section of the form will assure disclosure of all relevant information.

COMMITTEE NOTES ON RULES—2003 AMENDMENT

Pursuant to §110(c) of the Bankruptcy Code, the certification by a non-attorney bankruptcy petition preparer requires a petition preparer to provide the full social security number of the individual who actually prepares the document.

COMMITTEE NOTES ON RULES—2005 AMENDMENT

The form is amended in several ways to reflect changes in the Bankruptcy Code made by the Bankruptcy Abuse Prevention and Consumer Protection Act of 2005, Pub. L. No. 109–8, 119 Stat. 23 (April 20, 2005). A new sentence in the introduction advises the debtor not to disclose the name and address of any minor child.

The definition of "in business" is amended in the introductory section and in Question 1 and Question 18 to clarify that various part-time activities can result in the debtor being "in business" for purposes of the form.

Question 1 is amended to specify that, in addition to the income from the debtor's primary employment, the debtor must include income from part-time activities either as an employee or from self-employment. The debtor now also will report the source of all income from employment or operation of a business, even if there is only one source, in order to assist the trustee in reviewing the pay stubs, etc., filed by the debtor in the case.

Question 3 is amended to accommodate amendments to §547(c) of the Code enacted in 2005 which exempt from recovery by the trustee payments by a debtor for a domestic support obligation or as part of an alternative repayment schedule negotiated by an approved nonprofit budgeting and credit counseling agency. In addition, Question 3 now requires a debtor with primarily non-consumer debts to report only those transfers that aggregate more than $5,000 to any creditor in the 90-day period prior to the filing of the petition, as a result of the addition of §547(c)(9) to the Code in 2005.

In Question 10, the extension of the reachback period for transfers from one year to two years reflects the 2005 amendment to §548(a)(1) of the Code to permit a trustee to avoid a fraudulent transfer made by the debtor within two years of the date of the filing of the petition. Question 10 also is amended to implement new §548(e) added to the Code in 2005 to require the debtor to disclose all transfers to any self-settled asset protection trust within the ten years before the filing of the petition.

Question 15 is amended to extend from two years to three years the preterition time period for which the debtor must disclose the addresses of all premises occupied by the debtor. This information will assist the trustee, the United States trustee, and the court to ascertain whether any homestead exemption asserted by the debtor is properly claimed under §522(v)(3)(A) as amended, and §§522(p) and (q) as added to the Code in 2005.

The form also is amended to extend from six years to eight years the period before the filing of the petition concerning which the debtor is required to disclose the name of the debtor's spouse or of any former spouse who resides or resided with the debtor in a community property state. In addition, the certification by a non-attorney bankruptcy petition preparer is renamed a "declaration" and is amended to include material mandated by 11 U.S.C. §110 as amended by the 2005 Act.

COMMITTEE NOTES ON RULES—2005-2007 AMENDMENT

[The 2005–2007 Committee Note incorporates the Committee Note previously published in 2005.]

The form is amended in several ways to reflect changes in the Bankruptcy Code made by the Bankruptcy Abuse Prevention and Consumer Protection Act of 2005, Pub. L. No. 109–8, 119 Stat. 23 (April 20, 2005). A new sentence in the introduction advises the debtor not to disclose the name and address of any minor child in conformity with §112, which was added to the Code by the 2005 Act. In addition, the form is amended to add to the reference to Rule 1007(m) with respect to a minor child a direction to include for noticing purposes the name, address, and legal relationship to the child of "a person described" in that rule. Rule 1007(m) requires the person named to be someone on whom process would be served in an adversary proceeding against the child.

The definition of "in business" is amended in the introductory section and in Question 1 and Question 18 to clarify that various part-time activities can result in the debtor being "in business" for purposes of the form.

Question 1 is amended to specify that, in addition to the income from the debtor's primary employment, the debtor must include income from part-time activities either as an employee or from self-employment. The debtor now also will report the source of all income from employment or operation of a business, even if there is only one source, in order to assist the trustee in reviewing the pay stubs, etc., filed by the debtor in the case.

Question 3 is amended to accommodate amendments to § 547(c) of the Code enacted in 2005 which exempt from recovery by the trustee payments by a debtor for a domestic support obligation or as part of an alternative repayment schedule negotiated by an approved nonprofit budgeting and credit counseling agency. In addition, Question 3 now requires a debtor with primarily non-consumer debts to report only those transfers that aggregate more than $5,475 to any creditor in the 90-day period prior to the filing of the petition, as a result of the addition of § 547(c)(9) to the Code in 2005. In addition, the language of the question is revised for clarity.

In Question 10, the extension of the reach-back period for transfers from one year to two years reflects the 2005 amendment to § 548(a)(1) of the Code to permit a trustee to avoid a fraudulent transfer made by the debtor within two years before the date of the filing of the petition. Question 10 also is amended to implement new § 548(e) added to the Code in 2005 to require the debtor to disclose all transfers to any self-settled asset protection trust within the ten years before the filing of the petition.

Question 15 is amended to extend from two years to three years the prepetition time period for which the debtor must disclose the addresses of all premises occupied by the debtor. This information will assist the trustee, the United States trustee, and the court to ascertain whether any homestead exemption asserted by the debtor is properly claimed under § 522(b)(3)(A) as amended, and §§ 522(p) [sic] and (q) as added to the Code in 2005.

The form also is amended to extend from six years to eight years the period before the filing of the petition concerning which the debtor is required to disclose the name of the debtor's spouse or of any former spouse who resides or resided with the debtor in a community property state. In addition, the certification by a non-attorney bankruptcy petition preparer is renamed a "declaration" and is amended to include material mandated by 11 U.S.C. § 110 as amended by the 2005 Act.

B 8 (Official Form 8) (12/08)

UNITED STATES BANKRUPTCY COURT

In re ______________________________, Case No. ____________________
Debtor Chapter 7

CHAPTER 7 INDIVIDUAL DEBTOR'S STATEMENT OF INTENTION

PART A – Debts secured by property of the estate. *(Part A must be fully completed for **EACH** debt which is secured by property of the estate. Attach additional pages if necessary.)*

Property No. 1

Creditor's Name:	**Describe Property Securing Debt:**

Property will be *(check one)*:
❒ Surrendered ❒ Retained

If retaining the property, I intend to *(check at least one)*:
❒ Redeem the property
❒ Reaffirm the debt
❒ Other. Explain ______________________________ (for example, avoid lien using 11 U.S.C. § 522(f)).

Property is *(check one)*:
❒ Claimed as exempt ❒ Not claimed as exempt

Property No. 2 *(if necessary)*

Creditor's Name:	**Describe Property Securing Debt:**

Property will be *(check one)*:
❒ Surrendered ❒ Retained

If retaining the property, I intend to *(check at least one)*:
❒ Redeem the property
❒ Reaffirm the debt
❒ Other. Explain ______________________________ (for example, avoid lien using 11 U.S.C. § 522(f)).

Property is *(check one)*:
❒ Claimed as exempt ❒ Not claimed as exempt

PART B – Personal property subject to unexpired leases. *(All three columns of Part B must be completed for each unexpired lease. Attach additional pages if necessary.)*

Property No. 1		
Lessor's Name:	**Describe Leased Property:**	Lease will be Assumed pursuant to 11 U.S.C. § 365(p)(2): ❒ YES ❒ NO

Property No. 2 *(if necessary)*		
Lessor's Name:	**Describe Leased Property:**	Lease will be Assumed pursuant to 11 U.S.C. § 365(p)(2): ❒ YES ❒ NO

Property No. 3 *(if necessary)*		
Lessor's Name:	**Describe Leased Property:**	Lease will be Assumed pursuant to 11 U.S.C. § 365(p)(2): ❒ YES ❒ NO

_____ continuation sheets attached *(if any)*

I declare under penalty of perjury that the above indicates my intention as to any property of my estate securing a debt and/or personal property subject to an unexpired lease.

Date: ______________________________
Signature of Debtor

____
Signature of Joint Debtor

B 8 (Official Form 8) (12/08) Page 3

CHAPTER 7 INDIVIDUAL DEBTOR'S STATEMENT OF INTENTION

(Continuation Sheet)

PART A - Continuation

Property No.	
Creditor's Name:	**Describe Property Securing Debt:**

Property will be *(check one)*:
❒ Surrendered ❒ Retained

If retaining the property, I intend to *(check at least one)*:
❒ Redeem the property
❒ Reaffirm the debt
❒ Other. Explain ______________________________ (for example, avoid lien using 11 U.S.C. § 522(f)).

Property is *(check one)*:
❒ Claimed as exempt ❒ Not claimed as exempt

PART B - Continuation

Property No.		
Lessor's Name:	**Describe Leased Property:**	Lease will be Assumed pursuant to 11 U.S.C. § 365(p)(2): ❒ YES ❒ NO

Property No.		
Lessor's Name:	**Describe Leased Property:**	Lease will be Assumed pursuant to 11 U.S.C. § 365(p)(2): ❒ YES ❒ NO

(Added Aug. 1, 1991; amended Mar. 14, 1995; Oct. 1, 1997; Dec. 1, 2003; Oct. 17, 2005; Dec. 1, 2008.)

NOTES OF ADVISORY COMMITTEE ON RULES—1991

This form is derived from former Official Form No. 8A. Rule 1007(b)(2) requires the debtor to serve a copy of this statement on the trustee and all creditors named in the statement. In a joint case, if the property and debts of both debtors are the same, the form may be adapted for joint use. If joint debtors have separate debts, however, each debtor must use a separate form.

NOTES OF ADVISORY COMMITTEE ON RULES—1995 AMENDMENT

This form is a "document for filing" that may be prepared by a "bankruptcy petition preparer" as defined in 11 U.S.C. §110, which was added to the Code by the Bankruptcy Reform Act of 1994; accordingly, a signature line for such preparer is added. In addition to signing, a bankruptcy petition preparer is required by section 110 to disclose the information requested.

NOTES OF ADVISORY COMMITTEE ON RULES—1997 AMENDMENT

The form is amended to conform more closely to the language of the Bankruptcy Code. The amendments also make clear that the form is not intended to take a position regarding whether the options stated on the form are the only choices available to the debtor. Compare *Lowry Federal Credit Union v. West*, 882 F.2d 1543 (10th Cir. 1989), with *In re Taylor*, 3 F.3d 1512 (11th Cir. 1993).

COMMITTEE NOTES ON RULES—2003 AMENDMENT

Pursuant to §110(c) of the Bankruptcy Code, the certification by a non-attorney bankruptcy petition preparer requires a petition preparer to provide the full social security number of the individual who actually prepares the document.

COMMITTEE NOTES ON RULES—2005 AMENDMENT

The form is amended to conform to §521(a)(6), which was added to the Code by the Bankruptcy Abuse Prevention and Consumer Protection Act of 2005, Pub. L. No. 109-8, 119 Stat. 23 (April 20, 2005), by adding a section covering personal property subject to an unexpired lease and an option labeled "lease will be assumed pursuant to 11 U.S.C. §362(h)(1)(A)" to the choices a debtor may make. The certification by a non-attorney bankruptcy petition preparer in the form is renamed a "declaration" and is amended to include material mandated by the 2005 amendments to §110 of the Code.

COMMITTEE NOTES ON RULES—2008 AMENDMENT

The form is amended to conform to §362(h), which was added to the Code, and §521(a)(2), which was amended, by the Bankruptcy Abuse Prevention and Consumer Protection Act of 2005, Pub. L. No. 109-8, 119 Stat. 23 (April 20, 2005), by expanding the questions directed to the debtor regarding leased personal property and property subject to security interests. The form is also amended and reformatted to require the debtor to complete a series of statements describing the property and setting out what actions the debtor intends to take for each listed asset. The amended form is intended to elicit more complete information about the debtor's intentions with regard to property subject to security interests and personal property leases than has been obtained under the current version of the form.

In addition, the form is amended to specify that the debtor's signature is a declaration under penalty of perjury, as required by Rule 1008, and to provide space for the co-debtor's signature. A continuation page has been provided for use if necessary. The Declaration of Non-Attorney Bankruptcy Petition Preparer has been deleted from the form as duplicative of Form 19, Declaration and Signature of Non-Attorney Bankruptcy Petition Preparer. Form 19 contains both the petition preparer's declaration and signature and the notice the petition preparer is required to give to the debtor under §110 of the Code.

Official Form 9
(9/97)

FORM 9. NOTICE OF COMMENCEMENT OF CASE UNDER THE BANKRUPTCY CODE, MEETING OF CREDITORS, AND DEADLINES

9A..........Chapter	7, Individual/Joint, No-Asset Case
9B..........Chapter	7, Corporation/Partnership, No-Asset Case
9C..........Chapter	7, Individual/Joint, Asset Case
9D..........Chapter	7, Corporation/Partnership, Asset Case
9E..........Chapter	11, Individual/Joint Case
9E(Alt.)..Chapter	11, Individual/Joint Case
9F..........Chapter	11, Corporation/Partnership Case
9F(Alt.)..Chapter	11, Corporation/Partnership Case
9G..........Chapter	12, Individual/Joint Case
9H..........Chapter	12, Corporation/Partnership Case
9I..........Chapter	13, Individual/Joint Case

B9A (Official Form 9A) (Chapter 7 Individual or Joint Debtor No Asset Case) (12/07)

UNITED STATES BANKRUPTCY COURT______________ **District of** ______________________

Notice of
Chapter 7 Bankruptcy Case, Meeting of Creditors, & Deadlines

[A chapter 7 bankruptcy case concerning the debtor(s) listed below was filed on ____________________(date).]
or [A bankruptcy case concerning the debtor(s) listed below was originally filed under chapter______________on
______________________(date) and was converted to a case under chapter 7 on____________________(date).]

You may be a creditor of the debtor. **This notice lists important deadlines.** You may want to consult an attorney to protect your Rights. All documents filed in the case may be inspected at the bankruptcy clerk's office at the address listed below. NOTE: The staff of the bankruptcy clerk's office cannot give legal advice.

See Reverse Side for Important Explanations

Debtor(s) (name(s) and address):	Case Number:
	Last four digits of Social-Security or Individual Taxpayer-ID (ITIN) No(s)./Complete EIN:
All other names used by the Debtor(s) in the last 8 years (include married, maiden, and trade names):	Bankruptcy Trustee (name and address):
Attorney for Debtor(s) (name and address): Telephone number:	Telephone number:

Meeting of Creditors

Date: / / Time: ( ) A. M. ( ) P. M. Location:

Presumption of Abuse under 11 U.S.C. § 707(b)

See "Presumption of Abuse" on the reverse side.

Depending on the documents filed with the petition, one of the following statements will appear.

The presumption of abuse does not arise.
Or
The presumption of abuse arises.
Or
Insufficient information has been filed to date to permit the clerk to make any determination concerning the presumption of abuse. If more complete information, when filed, shows that the presumption has arisen, creditors will be notified.

Deadlines:

Papers must be *received* by the bankruptcy clerk's office by the following deadlines:

Deadline to File a Complaint Objecting to Discharge of the Debtor or to Determine Dischargeability of Certain Debts:

Deadline to Object to Exemptions:
Thirty (30) days after the *conclusion* of the meeting of creditors.

Creditors May Not Take Certain Actions:

In most instances, the filing of the bankruptcy case automatically stays certain collection and other actions against the debtor and the debtor's property. Under certain circumstances, the stay may be limited to 30 days or not exist at all, although the debtor can request the court to extend or impose a stay. If you attempt to collect a debt or take other action in violation of the Bankruptcy Code, you may be penalized. Consult a lawyer to determine your rights in this case.

Please Do Not File A Proof of Claim Unless You Receive a Notice To Do So.

Creditor with a Foreign Address:

A creditor to whom this notice is sent at a foreign address should read the information under "Do Not File a Proof of Claim at This Time" on the reverse side.

Address of the Bankruptcy Clerk's Office: Telephone number:	**For the Court:** Clerk of the Bankruptcy Court:
Hours Open:	Date:

EXPLANATIONS	B9A (Official Form 9A) (12/07)
Filing of Chapter 7 Bankruptcy Case	A bankruptcy case under Chapter 7 of the Bankruptcy Code (title 11, United States Code) has been filed in this court by or against the debtor(s) listed on the front side, and an order for relief has been entered.
Legal Advice	The staff of the bankruptcy clerk's office cannot give legal advice. Consult a lawyer to determine your rights in this case.
Creditors Generally May Not Take Certain Actions	Prohibited collection actions are listed in Bankruptcy Code § 362. Common examples of prohibited actions include contacting the debtor by telephone, mail, or otherwise to demand repayment; taking actions to collect money or obtain property from the debtor; repossessing the debtor's property; starting or continuing lawsuits or foreclosures; and garnishing or deducting from the debtor's wages. Under certain circumstances, the stay may be limited to 30 days or not exist at all, although the debtor can request the court to extend or impose a stay.
Presumption of Abuse	If the presumption of abuse arises, creditors may have the right to file a motion to dismiss the case under § 707(b) of the Bankruptcy Code. The debtor may rebut the presumption by showing special circumstances.
Meeting of Creditors	A meeting of creditors is scheduled for the date, time, and location listed on the front side. *The debtor (both spouses in a joint case) must be present at the meeting to be questioned under oath by the trustee and by creditors.* Creditors are welcome to attend, but are not required to do so. The meeting may be continued and concluded at a later date without further notice.
Do Not File a Proof of Claim at This Time	There does not appear to be any property available to the trustee to pay creditors. *You therefore should not file a proof of claim at this time.* If it later appears that assets are available to pay creditors, you will be sent another notice telling you that you may file a proof of claim, and telling you the deadline for filing your proof of claim. If this notice is mailed to a creditor at a foreign address, the creditor may file a motion requesting the court to extend the deadline.
Discharge of Debts	The debtor is seeking a discharge of most debts, which may include your debt. A discharge means that you may never try to collect the debt from the debtor. If you believe that the debtor is not entitled to receive a discharge under Bankruptcy Code § 727 (a) *or* that a debt owed to you is not dischargeable under Bankruptcy Code § 523 (a) (2), (4), or (6), you must start a lawsuit by filing a complaint in the bankruptcy clerk's office by the "Deadline to File a Complaint Objecting to Discharge of the Debtor or to Determine Dischargeability of Certain Debts" listed on the front side. The bankruptcy clerk's office must receive the complaint and any required filing fee by that Deadline.
Exempt Property	The debtor is permitted by law to keep certain property as exempt. Exempt property will not be sold and distributed to creditors. The debtor must file a list of all property claimed as exempt. You may inspect that list at the bankruptcy clerk's office. If you believe that an exemption claimed by the debtor is not authorized by law, you may file an objection to that exemption. The bankruptcy clerk's office must receive the objections by the "Deadline to Object to Exemptions" listed on the front side.
Bankruptcy Clerk's Office	Any paper that you file in this bankruptcy case should be filed at the bankruptcy clerk's office at the address listed on the front side. You may inspect all papers filed, including the list of the debtor's property and debts and the list of the property claimed as exempt, at the bankruptcy clerk's office.
Creditor with a Foreign Address	Consult a lawyer familiar with United States bankruptcy law if you have any questions regarding your rights in this case.
Refer To Other Side For Important Deadlines and Notices	

B9B (Official Form 9B) (Chapter 7 Corporation/Partnership No Asset Case) (12/07)

UNITED STATES BANKRUPTCY COURT______________ **District of**________________________

Notice of
Chapter 7 Bankruptcy Case, Meeting of Creditors, & Deadlines

[A chapter 7 bankruptcy case concerning the debtor(s) listed below was filed on ____________________(date).]
or [A bankruptcy case concerning the debtor(s) listed below was originally filed under chapter________________on
____________________(date) and was converted to a case under chapter 7 on________________(date).]

You may be a creditor of the debtor. **This notice lists important deadlines.** You may want to consult an attorney to protect your Rights. All documents filed in the case may be inspected at the bankruptcy clerk's office at the address listed below. NOTE: The staff of the bankruptcy clerk's office cannot give legal advice.

See Reverse Side for Important Explanations

Debtor(s) (name(s) and address):	Case Number:
	Last four digits of Social-Security or Individual Taxpayer-ID (ITIN) No(s)./Complete EIN:
All other names used by the debtor(s) in the last 8 years (include trade names):	Bankruptcy Trustee (name and address):
Attorney for Debtor(s) (name and address):	
Telephone number:	Telephone number:

Meeting of Creditors

Date: / / Time: ( ) A. M. ( ) P. M. Location:

Creditors May Not Take Certain Actions:

In most instances, the filing of the bankruptcy case automatically stays certain collection and other actions against the debtor and the debtor's property. Under certain circumstances, the stay may be limited to 30 days or not exist at all, although the debtor can request the court to extend or impose a stay. If you attempt to collect a debt or take other action in violation of the Bankruptcy Code, you may be penalized. Consult a lawyer to determine your rights in this case.

Please Do Not File A Proof of Claim Unless You Receive a Notice To Do So.

Creditor with a Foreign Address:

A creditor to whom this notice is sent at a foreign address should read the information under "Do Not File a Proof of Claim at This Time" on the reverse side.

Address of the Bankruptcy Clerk's Office:	**For the Court:**
	Clerk of the Bankruptcy Court:
Telephone number:	
Hours Open:	Date:

EXPLANATIONS	B9B (Official Form 9B) (12/07)
Filing of Chapter 7 Bankruptcy Case	A bankruptcy case under Chapter 7 of the Bankruptcy Code (title 11, United States Code) has been filed in this court by or against the debtor(s) listed on the front side, and an order for relief has been entered.
Legal Advice	The staff of the bankruptcy clerk's office cannot give legal advice. Consult a lawyer to determine your rights in this case.
Creditors Generally May Not Take Certain Actions	Prohibited collection actions are listed in Bankruptcy Code § 362. Common examples of prohibited actions include contacting the debtor by telephone, mail, or otherwise to demand repayment; taking actions to collect money or obtain property from the debtor; repossessing the debtor's property; and starting or continuing lawsuits or foreclosures. Under certain circumstances, the stay may be limited to 30 days or not exist at all, although the debtor can request the court to extend or impose a stay.
Meeting of Creditors	A meeting of creditors is scheduled for the date, time, and location listed on the front side. *The debtor's representative must be present at the meeting to be questioned under oath by the trustee and by creditors.* Creditors are welcome to attend, but are not required to do so. The meeting may be continued and concluded at a later date without further notice.
Do Not File a Proof of Claim at This Time	There does not appear to be any property available to the trustee to pay creditors. *You therefore should not file a proof of claim at this time.* If it later appears that assets are available to pay creditors, you will be sent another notice telling you that you may file a proof of claim, and telling you the deadline for filing your proof of claim. If this notice is mailed to a creditor at a foreign address, the creditor may file a motion requesting the court to extend the deadline.
Bankruptcy Clerk's Office	Any paper that you file in this bankruptcy case should be filed at the bankruptcy clerk's office at the address listed on the front side. You may inspect all papers filed, including the list of the debtor's property and debts and the list of the property claimed as exempt, at the bankruptcy clerk's office.
Creditor with a Foreign Address	Consult a lawyer familiar with United States bankruptcy law if you have any questions regarding your rights in this case.
Refer To Other Side For Important Deadlines and Notices	

B9C (Official Form 9C) (Chapter 7 Individual or Joint Debtor Asset Case) (12/07)

UNITED STATES BANKRUPTCY COURT_____________ District of_______________________

Notice of
Chapter 7 Bankruptcy Case, Meeting of Creditors, & Deadlines

[A chapter 7 bankruptcy case concerning the debtor(s) listed below was filed on ____________________(date).]
or [A bankruptcy case concerning the debtor(s) listed below was originally filed under chapter________________on ________________________(date) and was converted to a case under chapter 7 on________________(date).]

You may be a creditor of the debtor. **This notice lists important deadlines.** You may want to consult an attorney to protect your Rights. All documents filed in the case may be inspected at the bankruptcy clerk's office at the address listed below. NOTE: The staff of the bankruptcy clerk's office cannot give legal advice.

See Reverse Side for Important Explanations

Debtor(s) (name(s) and address):	Case Number:
	Last four digits of Social-Security or Individual Taxpayer-ID (ITIN) No(s)./Complete EIN:
All other names used by the Debtor(s) in the last 8 years (include married, maiden, and trade names):	Bankruptcy Trustee (name and address):
Attorney for Debtor(s) (name and address):	
Telephone number:	Telephone number:

Meeting of Creditors

Date: / / Time: ( ) A. M. ( ) P. M. Location:

Presumption of Abuse under 11 U.S.C. § 707(b)
See "Presumption of Abuse" on the reverse side.

Depending on the documents filed with the petition, one of the following statements will appear.

The presumption of abuse does not arise.
Or
The presumption of abuse arises.
Or
Insufficient information has been filed to date to permit the clerk to make any determination concerning the presumption of abuse. If more complete information, when filed, shows that the presumption has arisen, creditors will be notified.

Deadlines:
Papers must be *received* by the bankruptcy clerk's office by the following deadlines:

Deadline to File a Proof of Claim:
For all creditors (except a governmental unit): For a governmental unit:

Creditor with a Foreign Address:
A creditor to whom this notice is sent at a foreign address should read the information under "Claims" on the reverse side.

Deadline to File a Complaint Objecting to Discharge of the Debtor or to Determine Dischargeability of Certain Debts:

Deadline to Object to Exemptions:
Thirty (30) days after the *conclusion* of the meeting of creditors.

Creditors May Not Take Certain Actions:
In most instances, the filing of the bankruptcy case automatically stays certain collection and other actions against the debtor and the debtor's property. Under certain circumstances, the stay may be limited to 30 days or not exist at all, although the debtor can request the court to extend or impose a stay. If you attempt to collect a debt or take other action in violation of the Bankruptcy Code, you may be penalized. Consult a lawyer to determine your rights in this case.

Address of the Bankruptcy Clerk's Office:	**For the Court:**
	Clerk of the Bankruptcy Court:
Telephone number:	
Hours Open:	Date:

EXPLANATIONS	B9C (Official Form 9C) (12/07)
Filing of Chapter 7 Bankruptcy Case	A bankruptcy case under Chapter 7 of the Bankruptcy Code (title 11, United States Code) has been filed in this court by or against the debtor(s) listed on the front side, and an order for relief has been entered.
Legal Advice	The staff of the bankruptcy clerk's office cannot give legal advice. Consult a lawyer to determine your rights in this case.
Creditors Generally May Not Take Certain Actions	Prohibited collection actions are listed in Bankruptcy Code § 362. Common examples of prohibited actions include contacting the debtor by telephone, mail, or otherwise to demand repayment; taking actions to collect money or obtain property from the debtor; repossessing the debtor's property; starting or continuing lawsuits or foreclosures; and garnishing or deducting from the debtor's wages. Under certain circumstances, the stay may be limited to 30 days or not exist at all, although the debtor can request the court to extend or impose a stay.
Meeting of Creditors	A meeting of creditors is scheduled for the date, time, and location listed on the front side. *The debtor (both spouses in a joint case) must be present at the meeting to be questioned under oath by the trustee and by creditors.* Creditors are welcome to attend, but are not required to do so. The meeting may be continued and concluded at a later date without further notice.
Claims	A Proof of Claim is a signed statement describing a creditor's claim. If a Proof of Claim form is not included with this notice, you can obtain one at any bankruptcy clerk's office. A secured creditor retains rights in its collateral regardless of whether that creditor files a Proof of Claim. If you do not file a Proof of Claim by the "Deadline to File a Proof of Claim" listed on the front side, you might not be paid any money on your claim from other assets in the bankruptcy case. To be paid you must file a Proof of Claim even if your claim is listed in the schedules filed by the debtor. Filing a Proof of Claim submits the creditor to the jurisdiction of the bankruptcy court, with consequences a lawyer can explain. For example, a secured creditor who files a Proof of Claim may surrender important nonmonetary rights, including the right to a jury trial. **Filing Deadline for a Creditor with a Foreign Address:** The deadlines for filing claims set forth on the front of this notice apply to all creditors. If this notice has been mailed to a creditor at a foreign address, the creditor may file a motion requesting the court to extend the deadline.
Discharge of Debts	The debtor is seeking a discharge of most debts, which may include your debt. A discharge means that you may never try to collect the debt from the debtor. If you believe that the debtor is not entitled to receive a discharge under Bankruptcy Code § 727 (a) *or* that a debt owed to you is not dischargeable under Bankruptcy Code § 523 (a) (2), (4), or (6), you must start a lawsuit by filing a complaint in the bankruptcy clerk's office by the "Deadline to File a Complaint Objecting to Discharge of the Debtor or to Determine Dischargeability of Certain Debts" listed on the front side. The bankruptcy clerk's office must receive the complaint and any required filing fee by that Deadline.
Exempt Property	The debtor is permitted by law to keep certain property as exempt. Exempt property will not be sold and distributed to creditors. The debtor must file a list of all property claimed as exempt. You may inspect that list at the bankruptcy clerk's office. If you believe that an exemption claimed by the debtor is not authorized by law, you may file an objection to that exemption. The bankruptcy clerk's office must receive the objections by the "Deadline to Object to Exemptions" listed on the front side.
Presumption of Abuse	If the presumption of abuse arises, creditors may have the right to file a motion to dismiss the case under § 707(b) of the Bankruptcy Code. The debtor may rebut the presumption by showing special circumstances.
Bankruptcy Clerk's Office	Any paper that you file in this bankruptcy case should be filed at the bankruptcy clerk's office at the address listed on the front side. You may inspect all papers filed, including the list of the debtor's property and debts and the list of the property claimed as exempt, at the bankruptcy clerk's office.
Liquidation of the Debtor's Property and Payment of Creditors' Claims	The bankruptcy trustee listed on the front of this notice will collect and sell the debtor's property that is not exempt. If the trustee can collect enough money, creditors may be paid some or all of the debts owed to them, in the order specified by the Bankruptcy Code. To make sure you receive any share of that money, you must file a Proof of Claim, as described above.
Creditor with a Foreign Address	Consult a lawyer familiar with United States bankruptcy law if you have any questions regarding your rights in this case.
Refer To Other Side For Important Deadlines and Notices	

B9D (Official Form 9D) (Chapter 7 Corporation/Partnership Asset Case) (12/07)

UNITED STATES BANKRUPTCY COURT______________ **District of**______________________

Notice of
Chapter 7 Bankruptcy Case, Meeting of Creditors, & Deadlines

[A chapter 7 bankruptcy case concerning the debtor(s) listed below was filed on ____________________(date).]
or [A bankruptcy case concerning the debtor(s) listed below was originally filed under chapter______________ on ______________________(date) and was converted to a case under chapter 7 on________________(date).]

You may be a creditor of the debtor. **This notice lists important deadlines.** You may want to consult an attorney to protect your Rights. All documents filed in the case may be inspected at the bankruptcy clerk's office at the address listed below. NOTE: The staff of the bankruptcy clerk's office cannot give legal advice.

See Reverse Side for Important Explanations

Debtor(s) (name(s) and address):	Case Number:
	Last four digits of Social-Security or Individual Taxpayer-ID (ITIN) No(s)./Complete EIN:
All other names used by the Debtor(s) in the last 8 years (include trade names):	Bankruptcy Trustee (name and address):
Attorney for Debtor(s) (name and address): Telephone number:	Telephone number:

Meeting of Creditors

Date: / / Time: ( ) A. M. ( ) P. M. Location:

Deadline to File a Proof of Claim

Papers must be *received* by the bankruptcy clerk's office by the following deadlines:

For all creditors (except a governmental unit): For a governmental unit:

Creditor with a Foreign Address:
A creditor to whom this notice is sent at a foreign address should read the information under "Claims" on the reverse side.

Creditors May Not Take Certain Actions:

In most instances, the filing of the bankruptcy case automatically stays certain collection and other actions against the debtor and the debtor's property. Under certain circumstances, the stay may be limited to 30 days or not exist at all, although the debtor can request the court to extend or impose a stay. If you attempt to collect a debt or take other action in violation of the Bankruptcy Code, you may be penalized. Consult a lawyer to determine your rights in this case.

Address of the Bankruptcy Clerk's Office:	**For the Court:**
Telephone number:	Clerk of the Bankruptcy Court:
Hours Open:	Date:

EXPLANATIONS	B9D (Official Form 9D) (12/07)
Filing of Chapter 7 Bankruptcy Case	A bankruptcy case under Chapter 7 of the Bankruptcy Code (title 11, United States Code) has been filed in this court by or against the debtor(s) listed on the front side, and an order for relief has been entered.
Legal Advice	The staff of the bankruptcy clerk's office cannot give legal advice. Consult a lawyer to determine your rights in this case.
Creditors Generally May Not Take Certain Actions	Prohibited collection actions are listed in Bankruptcy Code § 362. Common examples of prohibited actions include contacting the debtor by telephone, mail, or otherwise to demand repayment; taking actions to collect money or obtain property from the debtor; repossessing the debtor's property; and starting or continuing lawsuits or foreclosures. Under certain circumstances, the stay may be limited to 30 days or not exist at all, although the debtor can request the court to extend or impose a stay.
Meeting of Creditors	A meeting of creditors is scheduled for the date, time, and location listed on the front side. *The debtor's representative must be present at the meeting to be questioned under oath by the trustee and by creditors.* Creditors are welcome to attend, but are not required to do so. The meeting may be continued and concluded at a later date without further notice.
Claims	A Proof of Claim is a signed statement describing a creditor's claim. If a Proof of Claim form is not included with this notice, you can obtain one at any bankruptcy clerk's office. A secured creditor retains rights in its collateral regardless of whether that creditor files a Proof of Claim. If you do not file a Proof of Claim by the "Deadline to File a Proof of Claim" listed on the front side, you might not be paid any money on your claim from other assets in the bankruptcy case. To be paid, you must file a Proof of Claim even if your claim is listed in the schedules filed by the debtor. Filing a Proof of Claim submits the creditor to the jurisdiction of the bankruptcy court, with consequences a lawyer can explain. For example, a secured creditor who files a Proof of Claim may surrender important nonmonetary rights, including the right to a jury trial. **Filing Deadline for a Creditor with a Foreign Address:** The deadlines for filing claims set forth on the front of this notice apply to all creditors. If this notice has been mailed to a creditor at a foreign address, the creditor may file a motion requesting the court to extend the deadline.
Liquidation of the Debtor's Property and Payment of Creditors' Claims	The bankruptcy trustee listed on the front of this notice will collect and sell the debtor's property that is not exempt. If the trustee can collect enough money, creditors may be paid some or all of the debts owed to them, in the order specified by the Bankruptcy Code. To make sure you receive any share of that money, you must file a Proof of Claim, as described above.
Bankruptcy Clerk's Office	Any paper that you file in this bankruptcy case should be filed at the bankruptcy clerk's office at the address listed on the front side. You may inspect all papers filed, including the list of the debtor's property and debts and the list of the property claimed as exempt, at the bankruptcy clerk's office.
Creditor with a Foreign Address	Consult a lawyer familiar with United States bankruptcy law if you have any questions regarding your rights in this case.
Refer To Other Side For Important Deadlines and Notices	

B9E (Official Form 9E) (Chapter 11 Individual or Joint Debtor Case) (12/07)

UNITED STATES BANKRUPTCY COURT______________ **District of**______________________

Notice of
Chapter 11 Bankruptcy Case, Meeting of Creditors, & Deadlines

[A chapter 11 bankruptcy case concerning the debtor(s) listed below was filed on __________________ (date).]
or [A bankruptcy case concerning the debtor(s) listed below was originally filed under chapter______________ on
____________________ (date) and was converted to a case under chapter 11 on______________(date).]

You may be a creditor of the debtor. **This notice lists important deadlines.** You may want to consult an attorney to protect your rights. All documents filed in the case may be inspected at the bankruptcy clerk's office at the address listed below.
NOTE: The staff of the bankruptcy clerk's office cannot give legal advice.

See Reverse Side for Important Explanations

Debtor(s) (name(s) and address):	Case Number:
	Last four digits of Social-Security or Individual Taxpayer-ID (ITIN) No(s)./Complete EIN:
All other names used by the Debtor(s) in the last 8 years (include married, maiden, and trade names):	Attorney for Debtor(s) (name and address): Telephone number:

Meeting of Creditors

Date: / / Time: ( ) A. M. ( ) P. M. Location:

Deadlines:

Papers must be *received* by the bankruptcy clerk's office by the following deadlines:

Deadline to File a Proof of Claim:
Notice of deadline will be sent at a later time.

Creditor with a Foreign Address:
A creditor to whom this notice is sent at a foreign address should read the information under "Claims" on the reverse side

Deadline to File a Complaint to Determine Dischargeability of Certain Debts:

Deadline to File a Complaint Objecting to Discharge of the Debtor:

First date set for hearing on confirmation of plan
Notice of that date will be sent at a later time.

Deadline to Object to Exemptions:

Thirty (30) days after the *conclusion* of the meeting of creditors.

Creditors May Not Take Certain Actions:

In most instances, the filing of the bankruptcy case automatically stays certain collection and other actions against the debtor and the debtor's property. Under certain circumstances, the stay may be limited to 30 days or not exist at all, although the debtor can request the court to extend or impose a stay. If you attempt to collect a debt or take other action in violation of the Bankruptcy Code, you may be penalized. Consult a lawyer to determine your rights in this case.

Address of the Bankruptcy Clerk's Office: **Telephone number:**	**For the Court:** Clerk of the Bankruptcy Court:
Hours Open:	Date:

EXPLANATIONS	B9E (Official Form 9E) (12/07)
Filing of Chapter 11 Bankruptcy Case	A bankruptcy case under Chapter 11 of the Bankruptcy Code (title 11, United States Code) has been filed in this court by or against the debtor(s) listed on the front side, and an order for relief has been entered. Chapter 11 allows a debtor to reorganize or liquidate pursuant to a plan. A plan is not effective unless confirmed by the court. You may be sent a copy of the plan and a disclosure statement telling you about the plan, and you might have the opportunity to vote on the plan. You will be sent notice of the date of the confirmation hearing, and you may object to confirmation of the plan and attend the confirmation hearing. Unless a trustee is serving, the debtor will remain in possession of the debtor's property and may continue to operate any business.
Legal Advice	The staff of the bankruptcy clerk's office cannot give legal advice. Consult a lawyer to determine your rights in this case.
Creditors Generally May Not Take Certain Actions	Prohibited collection actions are listed in Bankruptcy Code § 362. Common examples of prohibited actions include contacting the debtor by telephone, mail, or otherwise to demand repayment; taking actions to collect money or obtain property from the debtor; repossessing the debtor's property; starting or continuing lawsuits or foreclosures; and garnishing or deducting from the debtor's wages. Under certain circumstances, the stay may be limited to 30 days or not exist at all, although the debtor can request the court to extend or impose a stay.
Meeting of Creditors	A meeting of creditors is scheduled for the date, time, and location listed on the front side. *The debtor (both spouses in a joint case) must be present at the meeting to be questioned under oath by the trustee and by creditors.* Creditors are welcome to attend, but are not required to do so. The meeting may be continued and concluded at a later date without further notice. The court, after notice and a hearing, may order that the United States trustee not convene the meeting if the debtor has filed a plan for which the debtor solicited acceptances before filing the case.
Claims	A Proof of Claim is a signed statement describing a creditor's claim. If a Proof of Claim form is not included with this notice, you can obtain one at any bankruptcy clerk's office. You may look at the schedules that have been or will be filed at the bankruptcy clerk's office. If your claim is scheduled and is *not* listed as disputed, contingent, or unliquidated, it will be allowed in the amount scheduled unless you filed a Proof of Claim or you are sent further notice about the claim. Whether or not your claim is scheduled, you are permitted to file a Proof of Claim. If your claim is not listed at all *or* if your claim is listed as disputed, contingent, or unliquidated, then you must file a Proof of Claim or you might not be paid any money on your claim and may be unable to vote on a plan. The court has not yet set a deadline to file a Proof of Claim. If a deadline is set, you will be sent another notice. A secured creditor retains rights in its collateral regardless of whether that creditor files a Proof of Claim. Filing a Proof of Claim submits the creditor to the jurisdiction of the bankruptcy court, with consequences a lawyer can explain. For example, a secured creditor who files a Proof of Claim may surrender important nonmonetary rights, including the right to a jury trial. **Filing Deadline for a Creditor with a Foreign Address:** The deadline for filing claims will be set in a later court order and will apply to all creditors unless the order provides otherwise. If notice of the order setting the deadline is sent to a creditor at a foreign address, the creditor may file a motion requesting the court to extend the deadline.
Discharge of Debts	Confirmation of a chapter 11 plan may result in a discharge of debts, which may include all or part of your debt. *See* Bankruptcy Code § 1141 (d). Unless the court orders otherwise, however, the discharge will not be effective until completion of all payments under the plan. A discharge means that you may never try to collect the debt from the debtor except as provided in the plan. If you believe that a debt owed to you is not dischargeable under Bankruptcy Code § 523 (a) (2), (4), or (6), you must start a lawsuit by filing a complaint in the bankruptcy clerk's office by the "Deadline to File a Complaint to Determine Dischargeability of Certain Debts" listed on the front side. The bankruptcy clerk's office must receive the complaint and any required filing fee by that Deadline. If you believe that the debtor is not entitled to receive a discharge under Bankruptcy Code § 1141 (d) (3), you must file a complaint with the required filing fee in the bankruptcy clerk's office not later than the first date set for the hearing on confirmation of the plan. You will be sent another notice informing you of that date.
Exempt Property	The debtor is permitted by law to keep certain property as exempt. Exempt property will not be sold and distributed to creditors, even if the debtor's case is converted to chapter 7. The debtor must file a list of property claimed as exempt. You may inspect that list at the bankruptcy clerk's office. If you believe that an exemption claimed by the debtor is not authorized by law, you may file an objection to that exemption. The bankruptcy clerk's office must receive the objection by the "Deadline to Object to Exemptions" listed on the front side.
Bankruptcy Clerk's Office	Any paper that you file in this bankruptcy case should be filed at the bankruptcy clerk's office at the address listed on the front side. You may inspect all papers filed, including the list of the debtor's property and debts and the list of the property claimed as exempt, at the bankruptcy clerk's office.
Creditor with a Foreign Address	Consult a lawyer familiar with United States bankruptcy law if you have any questions regarding your rights in this case.
Refer To Other Side For Important Deadlines and Notices	

B9E ALT (Official Form 9E ALT) (Chapter 11 Individual or Joint Debtor Case) (12/07)

UNITED STATES BANKRUPTCY COURT ____________ **District of** ____________________

Notice of
Chapter 11 Bankruptcy Case, Meeting of Creditors, & Deadlines

[A chapter 11 bankruptcy case concerning the debtor(s) listed below was filed on ______________(date).]
or [A bankruptcy case concerning the debtor(s) listed below was originally filed under chapter ____________ on ______________(date) and was converted to a case under chapter 11 on ____________(date).]

You may be a creditor of the debtor. **This notice lists important deadlines.** You may want to consult an attorney to protect your rights. All documents filed in the case may be inspected at the bankruptcy clerk's office at the address listed below.
NOTE: The staff of the bankruptcy clerk's office cannot give legal advice.

See Reverse Side for Important Explanations

Debtor(s) (name(s) and address):	Case Number:
	Last four digits of Social-Security or Individual Taxpayer-ID (ITIN) No(s)./Complete EIN:
All other names used by the Debtor(s) in the last 8 years (include married, maiden, and trade names):	Attorney for Debtor(s) (name and address): Telephone number:

Meeting of Creditors

Date: / / Time: ( ) A. M. ( ) P. M. Location:

Deadlines:

Papers must be *received* by the bankruptcy clerk's office by the following deadlines:

Deadline to File a Proof of Claim:

For all creditors (except a governmental unit): For a governmental unit:

Creditor with a Foreign Address:
A creditor to whom this notice is sent at a foreign address should read the information under "Claims" on the reverse side.

Deadline to File a Complaint to Determine Dischargeability of Certain Debts:

Deadline to File a Complaint Objecting to Discharge of the Debtor:

First date set for hearing on confirmation of plan
Notice of that date will be sent at a later time.

Deadline to Object to Exemptions:

Thirty (30) days after the *conclusion* of the meeting of creditors.

Creditors May Not Take Certain Actions:
In most instances, the filing of the bankruptcy case automatically stays certain collection and other actions against the debtor and the debtor's property. Under certain circumstances, the stay may be limited to 30 days or not exist at all, although the debtor can request the court to extend or impose a stay. If you attempt to collect a debt or take other action in violation of the Bankruptcy Code, you may be penalized. Consult a lawyer to determine your rights in this case.

Address of the Bankruptcy Clerk's Office:	For the Court:
Telephone number:	Clerk of the Bankruptcy Court:
Hours Open:	Date:

	EXPLANATIONS B9E ALT (Official Form 9E ALT) (12/07)
Filing of Chapter 11 Bankruptcy Case	A bankruptcy case under Chapter 11 of the Bankruptcy Code (title 11, United States Code) has been filed in this court by or against the debtor(s) listed on the front side, and an order for relief has been entered. Chapter 11 allows a debtor to reorganize or liquidate pursuant to a plan. A plan is not effective unless confirmed by the court. You may be sent a copy of the plan and a disclosure statement telling you about the plan, and you might have the opportunity to vote on the plan. You will be sent notice of the date of the confirmation hearing, and you may object to confirmation of the plan and attend the confirmation hearing. Unless a trustee is serving, the debtor will remain in possession of the debtor's property and may continue to operate any business.
Legal Advice	The staff of the bankruptcy clerk's office cannot give legal advice. Consult a lawyer to determine your rights in this case.
Creditors Generally May Not Take Certain Actions	Prohibited collection actions are listed in Bankruptcy Code § 362. Common examples of prohibited actions include contacting the debtor by telephone, mail, or otherwise to demand repayment; taking actions to collect money or obtain property from the debtor; repossessing the debtor's property; starting or continuing lawsuits or foreclosures; and garnishing or deducting from the debtor's wages. Under certain circumstances, the stay may be limited to 30 days or not exist at all, although the debtor can request the court to extend or impose a stay.
Meeting of Creditors	A meeting of creditors is scheduled for the date, time, and location listed on the front side. *The debtor (both spouses in a joint case) must be present at the meeting to be questioned under oath by the trustee and by creditors.* Creditors are welcome to attend, but are not required to do so. The meeting may be continued and concluded at a later date without further notice. The court, after notice and a hearing, may order that the United States trustee not convene the meeting if the debtor has filed a plan for which the debtor solicited acceptances before filing the case.
Claims	A Proof of Claim is a signed statement describing a creditor's claim. If a Proof of Claim form is not included with this notice, you can obtain one at any bankruptcy clerk's office. You may look at the schedules that have been or will be filed at the bankruptcy clerk's office. If your claim is scheduled and is *not* listed as disputed, contingent, or unliquidated, it will be allowed in the amount scheduled unless you filed a Proof of Claim or you are sent further notice about the claim. Whether or not your claim is scheduled, you are permitted to file a Proof of Claim. If your claim is not listed at all *or* if your claim is listed as disputed, contingent, or unliquidated, then you must file a Proof of Claim by the "Deadline to File a Proof of Claim" listed on the front side or you might not be paid any money on your claim and may be unable to vote on a plan. A secured creditor retains rights in its collateral regardless of whether that creditor files a Proof of Claim. Filing a Proof of Claim submits the creditor to the jurisdiction of the bankruptcy court, with consequences a lawyer can explain. For example, a secured creditor who files a Proof of Claim may surrender important nonmonetary rights, including the right to a jury trial. **Filing Deadline for a Creditor with a Foreign Address:** The deadlines for filing claims set forth on the front of this notice apply to all creditors. If this notice has been mailed to a creditor at a foreign address, the creditor may file a motion requesting the court to extend the deadline.
Discharge of Debts	Confirmation of a chapter 11 plan may result in a discharge of debts, which may include all or part of your debt. *See* Bankruptcy Code § 1141 (d). Unless the court orders otherwise, however, the discharge will not be effective until completion of all payments under the plan. A discharge means that you may never try to collect the debt from the debtor except as provided in the plan. If you believe that a debt owed to you is not dischargeable under Bankruptcy Code § 523 (a) (2), (4), or (6), you must start a lawsuit by filing a complaint in the bankruptcy clerk's office by the "Deadline to File a Complaint to Determine Dischargeability of Certain Debts" listed on the front side. The bankruptcy clerk's office must receive the complaint and any required filing fee by that Deadline. If you believe that the debtor is not entitled to receive a discharge under Bankruptcy Code § 1141 (d) (3), you must file a complaint with the required filing fee in the bankruptcy clerk's office not later than the first date set for the hearing on confirmation of the plan. You will be sent another notice informing you of that date.
Exempt Property	The debtor is permitted by law to keep certain property as exempt. Exempt property will not be sold and distributed to creditors, even if the debtor's case is converted to chapter 7. The debtor must file a list of property claimed as exempt. You may inspect that list at the bankruptcy clerk's office. If you believe that an exemption claimed by the debtor is not authorized by law, you may file an objection to that exemption. The bankruptcy clerk's office must receive the objection by the "Deadline to Object to Exemptions" listed on the front side.
Bankruptcy Clerk's Office	Any paper that you file in this bankruptcy case should be filed at the bankruptcy clerk's office at the address listed on the front side. You may inspect all papers filed, including the list of the debtor's property and debts and the list of the property claimed as exempt, at the bankruptcy clerk's office.
Creditor with a Foreign Address	Consult a lawyer familiar with United States bankruptcy law if you have any questions regarding your rights in this case.
Refer To Other Side For Important Deadlines and Notices	

B9F (Official Form 9F) (Chapter 11 Corporation/Partnership Case) (12/08)

UNITED STATES BANKRUPTCY COURT ______________ **District of** ______________________

Notice of
Chapter 11 Bankruptcy Case, Meeting of Creditors, & Deadlines

[A chapter 11 bankruptcy case concerning the debtor(s) listed below was filed on ________________(date).]
or [A bankruptcy case concerning the debtor(s) listed below was originally filed under chapter ______________ on ____________________(date) and was converted to a case under chapter 11 on______________(date).]

You may be a creditor of the debtor. **This notice lists important deadlines.** You may want to consult an attorney to protect your rights. All documents filed in the case may be inspected at the bankruptcy clerk's office at the address listed below.
NOTE: The staff of the bankruptcy clerk's office cannot give legal advice.

See Reverse Side for Important Explanations

Debtor(s) (name(s) and address):	Case Number: Last four digits of Social-Security or Individual Taxpayer-ID (ITIN) No(s)./Complete EIN:
All other names used by the Debtor(s) in the last 8 years (include trade names):	Attorney for Debtor(s) (name and address): Telephone number:

Meeting of Creditors

Date: / / Time: ( ) A. M. ( ) P. M. Location:

Deadline to File a Proof of Claim

Proof of Claim must be *received* by the bankruptcy clerk's office by the following deadline:

Notice of deadline will be sent at a later time.

Creditor with a Foreign Address:
A creditor to whom this notice is sent at a foreign address should read the information under "Claims" on the reverse side.

Deadline to File a Complaint to Determine Dischargeability of Certain Debts:

Creditors May Not Take Certain Actions:
In most instances, the filing of the bankruptcy case automatically stays certain collection and other actions against the debtor and the debtor's property. Under certain circumstances, the stay may be limited to 30 days or not exist at all, although the debtor can request the court to extend or impose a stay. If you attempt to collect a debt or take other action in violation of the Bankruptcy Code, you may be penalized. Consult a lawyer to determine your rights in this case.

Address of the Bankruptcy Clerk's Office: **Telephone number:**	**For the Court:** Clerk of the Bankruptcy Court:
Hours Open:	Date:

EXPLANATIONS	B9F (Official Form 9F) (12/08)
Filing of Chapter 11 Bankruptcy Case	A bankruptcy case under Chapter 11 of the Bankruptcy Code (title 11, United States Code) has been filed in this court by or against the debtor(s) listed on the front side, and an order for relief has been entered. Chapter 11 allows a debtor to reorganize or liquidate pursuant to a plan. A plan is not effective unless confirmed by the court. You may be sent a copy of the plan and a disclosure statement telling you about the plan, and you might have the opportunity to vote on the plan. You will be sent notice of the date of the confirmation hearing, and you may object to confirmation of the plan and attend the confirmation hearing. Unless a trustee is serving, the debtor will remain in possession of the debtor's property and may continue to operate any business.
Legal Advice	The staff of the bankruptcy clerk's office cannot give legal advice. Consult a lawyer to determine your rights in this case.
Creditors Generally May Not Take Certain Actions	Prohibited collection actions are listed in Bankruptcy Code § 362. Common examples of prohibited actions include contacting the debtor by telephone, mail, or otherwise to demand repayment; taking actions to collect money or obtain property from the debtor; repossessing the debtor's property; and starting or continuing lawsuits or foreclosures. Under certain circumstances, the stay may be limited to 30 days or not exist at all, although the debtor can request the court to extend or impose a stay.
Meeting of Creditors	A meeting of creditors is scheduled for the date, time, and location listed on the front side. *The debtor's representative must be present at the meeting to be questioned under oath by the trustee and by creditors.* Creditors are welcome to attend, but are not required to do so. The meeting may be continued and concluded at a later date without further notice. The court, after notice and a hearing, may order that the United States trustee not convene the meeting if the debtor has filed a plan for which the debtor solicited acceptances before filing the case.
Claims	A Proof of Claim is a signed statement describing a creditor's claim. If a Proof of Claim form is not included with this notice, you can obtain one at any bankruptcy clerk's office. You may look at the schedules that have been or will be filed at the bankruptcy clerk's office. If your claim is scheduled and is *not* listed as disputed, contingent, or unliquidated, it will be allowed in the amount scheduled unless you filed a Proof of Claim or you are sent further notice about the claim. Whether or not your claim is scheduled, you are permitted to file a Proof of Claim. If your claim is not listed at all *or* if your claim is listed as disputed, contingent, or unliquidated, then you must file a Proof of Claim or you might not be paid any money on your claim and may be unable to vote on a plan. The court has not yet set a deadline to file a Proof of Claim. If a deadline is set, you will be sent another notice. A secured creditor retains rights in its collateral regardless of whether that creditor files a Proof of Claim. Filing a Proof of Claim submits the creditor to the jurisdiction of the bankruptcy court, with consequences a lawyer can explain. For example, a secured creditor who files a Proof of Claim may surrender important nonmonetary rights, including the right to a jury trial. **Filing Deadline for a Creditor with a Foreign Address:** The deadline for filing claims will be set in a later court order and will apply to all creditors unless the order provides otherwise. If notice of the order setting the deadline is sent to a creditor at a foreign address, the creditor may file a motion requesting the court to extend the deadline.
Discharge of Debts	Confirmation of a chapter 11 plan may result in a discharge of debts, which may include all or part of your debt. *See* Bankruptcy Code § 1141 (d). A discharge means that you may never try to collect the debt from the debtor, except as provided in the plan. If you believe that a debt owed to you is not dischargeable under Bankruptcy Code § 1141 (d) (6) (A), you must start a lawsuit by filing a complaint in the bankruptcy clerk's office by the "Deadline to File a Complaint to Determine Dischargeability of Certain Debts" listed on the front side. The bankruptcy clerk's office must receive the complaint and any required filing fee by that deadline.
Bankruptcy Clerk's Office	Any paper that you file in this bankruptcy case should be filed at the bankruptcy clerk's office at the address listed on the front side. You may inspect all papers filed, including the list of the debtor's property and debts and the list of the property claimed as exempt, at the bankruptcy clerk's office.
Creditor with a Foreign Address	Consult a lawyer familiar with United States bankruptcy law if you have any questions regarding your rights in this case.
Refer To Other Side For Important Deadlines and Notices	

B9F ALT (Official Form 9F ALT) (Chapter 11 Corporation/Partnership Case) (12/07)

UNITED STATES BANKRUPTCY COURT ______________ **District of** ______________________________

Notice of
Chapter 11 Bankruptcy Case, Meeting of Creditors, & Deadlines

[A chapter 11 bankruptcy case concerning the debtor(s) listed below was filed on _____________________(date).]
or [A bankruptcy case concerning the debtor(s) listed below was originally filed under chapter________________on
_______________________(date) and was converted to a case under chapter 11 on______________(date).]

You may be a creditor of the debtor. **This notice lists important deadlines.** You may want to consult an attorney to protect your rights. All documents filed in the case may be inspected at the bankruptcy clerk's office at the address listed below.
NOTE: The staff of the bankruptcy clerk's office cannot give legal advice.

See Reverse Side for Important Explanations

Debtor(s) (name(s) and address):	Case Number: Last four digits of Social-Security or Individual Taxpayer-ID (ITIN) No(s)./Complete EIN:
All other names used by the Debtor(s) in the last 8 years (include trade names):	Attorney for Debtor(s) (name and address): Telephone number:

Meeting of Creditors

Date: / / Time: ( ) A. M. ( ) P. M. Location:

Deadline to File a Proof of Claim

Proof of Claim must be *received* by the bankruptcy clerk's office by the following deadline:

For all creditors (except a governmental unit): For a governmental unit:

Creditor with a Foreign Address:
A creditor to whom this notice is sent at a foreign address should read the information under "Claims" on the reverse side.

Deadline to File a Complaint to Determine Dischargeability of Certain Debts:

Creditors May Not Take Certain Actions:
In most instances, the filing of the bankruptcy case automatically stays certain collection and other actions against the debtor and the debtor's property. Under certain circumstances, the stay may be limited to 30 days or not exist at all, although the debtor can request the court to extend or impose a stay. If you attempt to collect a debt or take other action in violation of the Bankruptcy Code, you may be penalized. Consult a lawyer to determine your rights in this case.

Address of the Bankruptcy Clerk's Office: **Telephone number:**	**For the Court:** Clerk of the Bankruptcy Court:
Hours Open:	Date:

EXPLANATIONS	B9F ALT (Official Form 9F ALT) (12/07)
Filing of Chapter 11 Bankruptcy Case	A bankruptcy case under Chapter 11 of the Bankruptcy Code (title 11, United States Code) has been filed in this court by or against the debtor(s) listed on the front side, and an order for relief has been entered. Chapter 11 allows a debtor to reorganize or liquidate pursuant to a plan. A plan is not effective unless confirmed by the court. You may be sent a copy of the plan and a disclosure statement telling you about the plan, and you might have the opportunity to vote on the plan. You will be sent notice of the date of the confirmation hearing, and you may object to confirmation of the plan and attend the confirmation hearing. Unless a trustee is serving, the debtor will remain in possession of the debtor's property and may continue to operate any business.
Legal Advice	The staff of the bankruptcy clerk's office cannot give legal advice. Consult a lawyer to determine your rights in this case.
Creditors Generally May Not Take Certain Actions	Prohibited collection actions are listed in Bankruptcy Code § 362. Common examples of prohibited actions include contacting the debtor by telephone, mail, or otherwise to demand repayment; taking actions to collect money or obtain property from the debtor; repossessing the debtor's property; and starting or continuing lawsuits or foreclosures. Under certain circumstances, the stay may be limited to 30 days or not exist at all, although the debtor can request the court to extend or impose a stay.
Meeting of Creditors	A meeting of creditors is scheduled for the date, time, and location listed on the front side. *The debtor's representative must be present at the meeting to be questioned under oath by the trustee and by creditors.* Creditors are welcome to attend, but are not required to do so. The meeting may be continued and concluded at a later date without further notice. The court, after notice and a hearing, may order that the United States trustee not convene the meeting if the debtor has filed a plan for which the debtor solicited acceptances before filing the case.
Claims	A Proof of Claim is a signed statement describing a creditor's claim. If a Proof of Claim form is not included with this notice, you can obtain one at any bankruptcy clerk's office. You may look at the schedules that have been or will be filed at the bankruptcy clerk's office. If your claim is scheduled and is *not* listed as disputed, contingent, or unliquidated, it will be allowed in the amount scheduled unless you filed a Proof of Claim or you are sent further notice about the claim. Whether or not your claim is scheduled, you are permitted to file a Proof of Claim. If your claim is not listed at all *or* if your claim is listed as disputed, contingent, or unliquidated, then you must file a Proof of Claim by the "Deadline to File Proof of Claim" listed on the front side, or you might not be paid any money on your claim and may be unable to vote on a plan. A secured creditor retains rights in its collateral regardless of whether that creditor files a Proof of Claim. Filing a Proof of Claim submits the creditor to the jurisdiction of the bankruptcy court, with consequences a lawyer can explain. For example, a secured creditor who files a Proof of Claim may surrender important nonmonetary rights, including the right to a jury trial. **Filing Deadline for a Creditor with a Foreign Address:** The deadlines for filing claims set forth on the front of this notice apply to all creditors. If this notice has been mailed to a creditor at a foreign address, the creditor may file a motion requesting the court to extend the deadline.
Discharge of Debts	Confirmation of a chapter 11 plan may result in a discharge of debts, which may include all or part of your debt. *See* Bankruptcy Code § 1141 (d). A discharge means that you may never try to collect the debt from the debtor, except as provided in the plan. If you believe that a debt owed to you is not dischargeable under Bankruptcy Code § 1141 (d) (6) (A), you must start a lawsuit by filing a complaint in the bankruptcy clerk's office by the "Deadline to File a Complaint to Determine Dischargeability of Certain Debts" listed on the front side. The bankruptcy clerk's office must receive the complaint and any required filing fee by that deadline.
Bankruptcy Clerk's Office	Any paper that you file in this bankruptcy case should be filed at the bankruptcy clerk's office at the address listed on the front side. You may inspect all papers filed, including the list of the debtor's property and debts and the list of the property claimed as exempt, at the bankruptcy clerk's office.
Creditor with a Foreign Address	Consult a lawyer familiar with United States bankruptcy law if you have any questions regarding your rights in this case.
Refer To Other Side For Important Deadlines and Notices	

B9G (Official Form 9G) (Chapter 12 Individual or Joint Debtor Family Farmer or Family Fisherman) (12/07)

UNITED STATES BANKRUPTCY COURT_____________ **District of**_________________________

Notice of
Chapter 12 Bankruptcy Case, Meeting of Creditors, & Deadlines

[The debtor(s) listed below filed a chapter 12 bankruptcy case on _________________(date).]
or [A bankruptcy case concerning the debtor(s) listed below was originally filed under chapter______________on
___________________(date) and was converted to a case under chapter 12 on______________(date).]

You may be a creditor of the debtor. **This notice lists important deadlines.** You may want to consult an attorney to protect your rights. All documents filed in the case may be inspected at the bankruptcy clerk's office at the address listed below.
NOTE: The staff of the bankruptcy clerk's office cannot give legal advice.

See Reverse Side for Important Explanations

Debtor(s) (name(s) and address):	Case Number:
	Last four digits of Social-Security or Individual Taxpayer-ID (ITIN) No(s)./Complete EIN:
All other names used by the Debtor(s) in the last 8 years (include married, maiden, and trade names):	Bankruptcy Trustee (name and address):
Attorney for Debtor(s) (name and address): Telephone number:	Telephone number:

Meeting of Creditors

Date: / / Time: ( ) A. M. ( ) P. M. Location:

Deadlines:

Papers must be *received* by the bankruptcy clerk's office by the following deadlines:

Deadline to File a Proof of Claim:

For all creditors(except a governmental unit): For a governmental unit:

Creditor with a Foreign Address:

A creditor to whom this notice is sent at a foreign address should read the information under "Claims" on the reverse side.

Deadline to File a Complaint to Determine Dischargeability of Certain Debts:

Deadline to Object to Exemptions:

Thirty (30) days after the *conclusion* of the meeting of creditors.

Filing of Plan, Hearing on Confirmation of Plan

[The debtor has filed a plan. The plan or a summary of the plan is enclosed. The hearing on confirmation will be held:
Date:__________________Time:_______________Location:______________________]
or [The debtor has filed a plan. The plan or a summary of the plan and notice of confirmation hearing will be sent separately.]
or [The debtor has not filed a plan as of this date. You will be sent separate notice of the hearing on confirmation of the plan.]

Creditors May Not Take Certain Actions:

In most instances, the filing of the bankruptcy case automatically stays certain collection and other actions against the debtor, the debtor's property, and certain codebtors. Under certain circumstances, the stay may be limited to 30 days or not exist at all, although the debtor can request the court to extend or impose a stay. If you attempt to collect a debt or take other action in violation of the Bankruptcy Code, you may be penalized. Consult a lawyer to determine your rights in this case.

Address of the Bankruptcy Clerk's Office:	**For the Court:**
Telephone number:	Clerk of the Bankruptcy Court:
Hours Open:	Date:

EXPLANATIONS	B9G (Official Form 9G) (12/07)
Filing of Chapter 12 Bankruptcy Case	A bankruptcy case under Chapter 12 of the Bankruptcy Code (title 11, United States Code) has been filed in this court by the debtor(s) listed on the front side, and an order for relief has been entered. Chapter 12 allows family farmers and family fishermen to adjust their debts pursuant to a plan. A plan is not effective unless confirmed by the court. You may object to confirmation of the plan and appear at the confirmation hearing. A copy or summary of the plan [is included with this notice] *or* [will be sent to you later], and [the confirmation hearing will be held on the date indicated on the front of this notice] *or* [you will be sent notice of the confirmation hearing]. The debtor will remain in possession of the debtor's property and may continue to operate the debtor's business unless the court orders otherwise.
Legal Advice	The staff of the bankruptcy clerk's office cannot give legal advice. Consult a lawyer to determine your rights in this case.
Creditors Generally May Not Take Certain Actions	Prohibited collection actions against the debtor and certain codebtors are listed in Bankruptcy Code § 362 and § 1201. Common examples of prohibited actions include contacting the debtor by telephone, mail, or otherwise to demand repayment; taking actions to collect money or obtain property from the debtor; repossessing the debtor's property; starting or continuing lawsuits or foreclosures; and garnishing or deducting from the debtor's wages. Under certain circumstances, the stay may be limited in duration or not exist at all, although the debtor may have the right to request the court to extend or impose a stay.
Meeting of Creditors	A meeting of creditors is scheduled for the date, time, and location listed on the front side. *The debtor (both spouses in a joint case) must be present at the meeting to be questioned under oath by the trustee and by creditors.* Creditors are welcome to attend, but are not required to do so. The meeting may be continued and concluded at a later date without further notice.
Claims	A Proof of Claim is a signed statement describing a creditor's claim. If a Proof of Claim form is not included with this notice, you can obtain one at any bankruptcy clerk's office. A secured creditor retains rights in its collateral regardless of whether that creditor files a Proof of Claim. If you do not file a Proof of Claim by the "Deadline to File a Proof of Claim" listed on the front side, you might not be paid any money on your claim from other assets in the bankruptcy case. To be paid you must file a Proof of Claim even if your claim is listed in the schedules filed by the debtor. Filing a Proof of Claim submits the creditor to the jurisdiction of the bankruptcy court, with consequences a lawyer can explain. For example, a secured creditor who files a Proof of Claim may surrender important nonmonetary rights, including the right to a jury trial. **Filing Deadline for a Creditor with a Foreign Address:** The deadlines for filing claims set forth on the front of this notice apply to all creditors. If this notice has been mailed to a creditor at a foreign address, the creditor may file a motion requesting the court to extend the deadline.
Discharge of Debts	The debtor is seeking a discharge of most debts, which may include your debt. A discharge means that you may never try to collect the debt from the debtor. If you believe that a debt owed to you is not dischargeable under Bankruptcy Code § 523 (a) (2), (4), or (6), you must start a lawsuit by filing a complaint in the bankruptcy clerk's office by the "Deadline to File a Complaint to Determine Dischargeability of Certain Debts" listed on the front side. The bankruptcy clerk's office must receive the complaint and any required filing fee by that Deadline.
Exempt Property	The debtor is permitted by law to keep certain property as exempt. Exempt property will not be sold and distributed to creditors, even if the debtor's case is converted to chapter 7. The debtor must file a list of all property claimed as exempt. You may inspect that list at the bankruptcy clerk's office. If you believe that an exemption claimed by the debtor is not authorized by law, you may file an objection to that exemption. The bankruptcy clerk's office must receive the objection by the "Deadline to Object to Exemptions" listed on the front side.
Bankruptcy Clerk's Office	Any paper that you file in this bankruptcy case should be filed at the bankruptcy clerk's office at the address listed on the front side. You may inspect all papers filed, including the list of the debtor's property and debts and the list of the property claimed as exempt, at the bankruptcy clerk's office.
Creditor with a Foreign Address	Consult a lawyer familiar with United States bankruptcy law if you have any questions regarding your rights in this case.
Refer To Other Side For Important Deadlines and Notices	

B9H (Official Form 9H) (Chapter 12 Corporation/Partnership Family Farmer or Family Fisherman) (12/07)

UNITED STATES BANKRUPTCY COURT______________ **District of** ______________

Notice of
Chapter 12 Bankruptcy Case, Meeting of Creditors, & Deadlines

[The debtor [corporation] *or* [partnership] listed below filed a chapter 12 bankruptcy case on ______________ (date).]
or [A bankruptcy case concerning the debtor [corporation] *or* [partnership] listed below was originally filed under chapter ______________
on ______________ (date) and was converted to a case under chapter 12 on ______________(date).]

You may be a creditor of the debtor. **This notice lists important deadlines.** You may want to consult an attorney to protect your rights. All documents filed in the case may be inspected at the bankruptcy clerk's office at the address listed below.
NOTE: The staff of the bankruptcy clerk's office cannot give legal advice.

See Reverse Side for Important Explanations

Debtor(s) (name(s) and address):	Case Number:
	Last four digits of Social-Security or Individual Taxpayer-ID (ITIN) No(s)./Complete EIN:
All other names used by the Debtor(s) in the last 8 years (include trade names):	Bankruptcy Trustee (name and address):
Attorney for Debtor(s) (name and address): Telephone number:	Telephone number:

Meeting of Creditors

Date: / / Time: ( ) A. M. ( ) P. M. Location:

Deadlines:

Papers must be *received* by the bankruptcy clerk's office by the following deadlines:

Deadline to File a Proof of Claim:

For all creditors(except a governmental unit): For a governmental unit:

Creditor with a Foreign Address:

A creditor to whom this notice is sent at a foreign address should read the information under "Claims" on the reverse side.

Deadline to File a Complaint to Determine Dischargeability of Certain Debts:

Filing of Plan, Hearing on Confirmation of Plan

[The debtor has filed a plan. The plan or a summary of the plan is enclosed. The hearing on confirmation will be held:
Date:______________Time:______________Location:______________]
or [The debtor has filed a plan. The plan or a summary of the plan and notice of confirmation hearing will be sent separately.]
or [The debtor has not filed a plan as of this date. You will be sent separate notice of the hearing on confirmation of the plan.]

Creditors May Not Take Certain Actions:

In most instances, the filing of the bankruptcy case automatically stays certain collection and other actions against the debtor and the debtor's property. Under certain circumstances, the stay may be limited to 30 days or not exist at all, although the debtor can request the court to extend or impose a stay. If you attempt to collect a debt or take other action in violation of the Bankruptcy Code, you may be penalized. Consult a lawyer to determine your rights in this case.

Address of the Bankruptcy Clerk's Office: **Telephone number:**	**For the Court:** Clerk of the Bankruptcy Court:
Hours Open:	Date:

EXPLANATIONS	B9H (Official Form 9H) (12/07)
Filing of Chapter 12 Bankruptcy Case	A bankruptcy case under Chapter 12 of the Bankruptcy Code (title 11, United States Code) has been filed in this court by the debtor listed on the front side, and an order for relief has been entered. Chapter 12 allows family farmers and family fishermen to adjust their debts pursuant to a plan. A plan is not effective unless confirmed by the court. You may object to confirmation of the plan and appear at the confirmation hearing. A copy or summary of the plan [is included with this notice] *or* [will be sent to you later], and [the confirmation hearing will be held on the date indicated on the front of this notice] *or* [you will be sent notice of the confirmation hearing]. The debtor will remain in possession of the debtor's property and may continue to operate the debtor's business unless the court orders otherwise.
Legal Advice	The staff of the bankruptcy clerk's office cannot give legal advice. Consult a lawyer to determine your rights in this case.
Creditors Generally May Not Take Certain Actions	Prohibited collection actions against the debtor and certain codebtors are listed in Bankruptcy Code § 362 and § 1201. Common examples of prohibited actions include contacting the debtor by telephone, mail, or otherwise to demand repayment; taking actions to collect money or obtain property from the debtor; repossessing the debtor's property; and starting or continuing lawsuits or foreclosures. Under certain circumstances, the stay may be limited in duration or not exist at all, although the debtor may have the right to request the court to extend or impose a stay.
Meeting of Creditors	A meeting of creditors is scheduled for the date, time, and location listed on the front side. *The debtor's representative must be present at the meeting to be questioned under oath by the trustee and by creditors.* Creditors are welcome to attend, but are not required to do so. The meeting may be continued and concluded at a later date without further notice.
Claims	A Proof of Claim is a signed statement describing a creditor's claim. If a Proof of Claim form is not included with this notice, you can obtain one at any bankruptcy clerk's office. A secured creditor retains rights in its collateral regardless of whether that creditor files a Proof of Claim. If you do not file a Proof of Claim by the "Deadline to File a Proof of Claim" listed on the front side, you might not be paid any money on your claim from other assets in the bankruptcy case. To be paid you must file a Proof of Claim even if your claim is listed in the schedules filed by the debtor. Filing a Proof of Claim submits the creditor to the jurisdiction of the bankruptcy court, with consequences a lawyer can explain. For example, a secured creditor who files a Proof of Claim may surrender important nonmonetary rights, including the right to a jury trial. **Filing Deadline for a Creditor with a Foreign Address:** The deadlines for filing claims set forth on the front of this notice apply to all creditors. If this notice has been mailed to a creditor at a foreign address, the creditor may file a motion requesting the court to extend the deadline.
Discharge of Debts	The debtor is seeking a discharge of most debts, which may include your debt. A discharge means that you may never try to collect the debt from the debtor. If you believe that a debt owed to you is not dischargeable under Bankruptcy Code § 523 (a) (2), (4), or (6), you must start a lawsuit by filing a complaint in the bankruptcy clerk's office by the "Deadline to File a Complaint to Determine Dischargeability of Certain Debts" listed on the front side. The bankruptcy clerk's office must receive the complaint and any required filing fee by that Deadline.
Bankruptcy Clerk's Office	Any paper that you file in this bankruptcy case should be filed at the bankruptcy clerk's office at the address listed on the front side. You may inspect all papers filed, including the list of the debtor's property and debts and the list of the property claimed as exempt, at the bankruptcy clerk's office.
Creditor with a Foreign Address	Consult a lawyer familiar with United States bankruptcy law if you have any questions regarding your rights in this case.
Refer To Other Side For Important Deadlines and Notices	

B9I (Official Form 9I) (Chapter 13 Case) (12/07)

UNITED STATES BANKRUPTCY COURT____________ **District of**____________________

Notice of
Chapter 13 Bankruptcy Case, Meeting of Creditors, & Deadlines

[The debtor(s) listed below filed a chapter 13 bankruptcy case on __________________ (date).]
or [A bankruptcy case concerning the debtor(s) listed below was originally filed under chapter____________
on ______________________ (date) and was converted to a case under chapter 13 on____________(date).]

You may be a creditor of the debtor. **This notice lists important deadlines.** You may want to consult an attorney to protect your rights. All documents filed in the case may be inspected at the bankruptcy clerk's office at the address listed below.
NOTE: The staff of the bankruptcy clerk's office cannot give legal advice.

See Reverse Side for Important Explanations

Debtor(s) (name(s) and address):	Case Number:
	Last four digits of Social-Security or Individual Taxpayer-ID (ITIN) No(s)./Complete EIN:
All other names used by the Debtor(s) in the last 8 years (include married, maiden, and trade names):	Bankruptcy Trustee (name and address):
Attorney for Debtor(s) (name and address): Telephone number:	Telephone number:

Meeting of Creditors
Date: / / Time: ( ) A. M. ( ) P. M. Location:

Deadlines:
Papers must be *received* by the bankruptcy clerk's office by the following deadlines:
Deadline to File a Proof of Claim:
For all creditors (except a governmental unit):
For a governmental unit (except as otherwise provided in Fed . R. Bankr. P. 3002(c)(1)):

Creditor with a Foreign Address:
A creditor to whom this notice is sent at a foreign address should read the information under "Claims" on the reverse side

Deadline to File a Complaint to Determine Dischargeability of Certain Debts:

Deadline to Object to Exemptions:
Thirty (30) days after the *conclusion* of the meeting of creditors.

Filing of Plan, Hearing on Confirmation of Plan
[The debtor has filed a plan. The plan or a summary of the plan is enclosed. The hearing on confirmation will be held:
Date:______________ Time:______________ Location:______________________________]
or [The debtor has filed a plan. The plan or a summary of the plan and notice of confirmation hearing will be sent separately.]
or [The debtor has not filed a plan as of this date. You will be sent separate notice of the hearing on confirmation of the plan.]

Creditors May Not Take Certain Actions:
In most instances, the filing of the bankruptcy case automatically stays certain collection and other actions against the debtor, the debtor's property, and certain codebtors. Under certain circumstances, the stay may be limited to 30 days or not exist at all, although the debtor can request the court to extend or impose a stay. If you attempt to collect a debt or take other action in violation of the Bankruptcy Code, you may be penalized. Consult a lawyer to determine your rights in this case.

Address of the Bankruptcy Clerk's Office:	**For the Court:**
Telephone number:	Clerk of the Bankruptcy Court:
Hours Open:	Date:

EXPLANATIONS	B9I (Official Form 9I) (12/07)
Filing of Chapter 13 Bankruptcy Case	A bankruptcy case under Chapter 13 of the Bankruptcy Code (title 11, United States Code) has been filed in this court by the debtor(s) listed on the front side, and an order for relief has been entered. Chapter 13 allows an individual with regular income and debts below a specified amount to adjust debts pursuant to a plan. A plan is not effective unless confirmed by the bankruptcy court. You may object to confirmation of the plan and appear at the confirmation hearing. A copy or summary of the plan [is included with this notice] *or* [will be sent to you later], and [the confirmation hearing will be held on the date indicated on the front of this notice] *or* [you will be sent notice of the confirmation hearing]. The debtor will remain in possession of the debtor's property and may continue to operate the debtor's business, if any, unless the court orders otherwise.
Legal Advice	The staff of the bankruptcy clerk's office cannot give legal advice. Consult a lawyer to determine your rights in this case.
Creditors Generally May Not Take Certain Actions	Prohibited collection actions against the debtor and certain codebtors are listed in Bankruptcy Code § 362 and § 1301. Common examples of prohibited actions include contacting the debtor by telephone, mail, or otherwise to demand repayment; taking actions to collect money or obtain property from the debtor; repossessing the debtor's property; starting or continuing lawsuits or foreclosures; and garnishing or deducting from the debtor's wages. Under certain circumstances, the stay may be limited to 30 days or not exist at all, although the debtor can request the court to exceed or impose a stay.
Meeting of Creditors	A meeting of creditors is scheduled for the date, time, and location listed on the front side. *The debtor (both spouses in a joint case) must be present at the meeting to be questioned under oath by the trustee and by creditors.* Creditors are welcome to attend, but are not required to do so. The meeting may be continued and concluded at a later date without further notice
Claims	A Proof of Claim is a signed statement describing a creditor's claim. If a Proof of Claim form is not included with this notice, you can obtain one at any bankruptcy clerk's office. A secured creditor retains rights in its collateral regardless of whether that creditor files a Proof of Claim. If you do not file a Proof of Claim by the "Deadline to File a Proof of Claim" listed on the front side, you might not be paid any money on your claim from other assets in the bankruptcy case. To be paid you must file a Proof of Claim even if your claim is listed in the schedules filed by the debtor. Filing a Proof of Claim submits the creditor to the jurisdiction of the bankruptcy court, with consequences a lawyer can explain. For example, a secured creditor who files a Proof of Claim may surrender important nonmonetary rights, including the right to a jury trial. **Filing Deadline for a Creditor with a Foreign Address:** The deadlines for filing claims set forth on the front of this notice apply to all creditors. If this notice has been mailed to a creditor at a foreign address, the creditor may file a motion requesting the court to extend the deadline.
Discharge of Debts	The debtor is seeking a discharge of most debts, which may include your debt. A discharge means that you may never try to collect the debt from the debtor. If you believe that a debt owed to you is not dischargeable under Bankruptcy Code § 523 (a) (2) or (4), you must start a lawsuit by filing a complaint in the bankruptcy clerk's office by the "Deadline to File a Complaint to Determine Dischargeability of Certain Debts" listed on the front side. The bankruptcy clerk's office must receive the complaint and any required filing fee by that deadline.
Exempt Property	The debtor is permitted by law to keep certain property as exempt. Exempt property will not be sold and distributed to creditors, even if the debtor's case is converted to chapter 7. The debtor must file a list of all property claimed as exempt. You may inspect that list at the bankruptcy clerk's office. If you believe that an exemption claimed by the debtor is not authorized by law, you may file an objection to that exemption. The bankruptcy clerk's office must receive the objection by the "Deadline to Object to Exemptions" listed on the front side.
Bankruptcy Clerk's Office	Any paper that you file in this bankruptcy case should be filed at the bankruptcy clerk's office at the address listed on the front side. You may inspect all papers filed, including the list of the debtor's property and debts and the list of the property claimed as exempt, at the bankruptcy clerk's office.
Creditor with a Foreign Address	Consult a lawyer familiar with United States bankruptcy law if you have any questions regarding your rights in this case.
Refer To Other Side For Important Deadlines and Notices	

(Added Aug. 1, 1991; amended Sept. 22, 1992; Mar. 16, 1993; Mar. 14, 1995; Oct. 1, 1997; Dec. 1, 2003; Oct. 17, 2005; Oct. 1, 2006; Dec. 1, 2007; Dec. 1, 2008.)

NOTES OF ADVISORY COMMITTEE ON RULES—1991

The form has been redesigned to facilitate electronic generation of notice to creditors concerning the filing of the petition, the meeting of creditors, and important deadlines in the case. Adoption of a box format, with significant dates highlighted, is intended to assist creditors who may be unfamiliar with bankruptcy cases to understand the data provided. Nine variations of the form, designated 9A through 9I, have been created to meet the specialized notice requirements for chapters 7, 11, 12, and 13, asset and no-asset cases, and the various types of debtors.

NOTES OF ADVISORY COMMITTEE ON RULES—1992 AMENDMENT

Forms 9B, 9D, 9F, and 9H are amended to make a technical correction in the reference to Rule 9001(5). Form 9H also contains a technical correction deleting the reference to a complaint object to discharge of the debtor.

NOTES OF ADVISORY COMMITTEE ON RULES—1993 AMENDMENT

The title page of the form has been amended to conform to the headings used on Forms 9A–9I. Alternate versions of Form 9E and Form 9F have been added for the convenience of districts that routinely set a deadline for filing claims in a chapter 11 case. When a creditor receives the alternate form in a case, the box labeled "Filing Claims" will contain information about the bar date as follows: "Deadline for filing a claim: (date)." If no deadline is set in a particular case, either the court will use Form 9E or Form 9F, as appropriate, or the alternate form will be used with the following sentence appearing in the box labeled "Filing Claims": "When the court sets a deadline for filing claims, creditors will be notified."

NOTES OF ADVISORY COMMITTEE ON RULES—1995 AMENDMENT

The form is amended to provide notice of the claims filing period provided to "a governmental unit" by section 502(b)(9) of the Code as amended by the Bankruptcy Reform Act of 1994. A court that routinely sets a deadline for filing proofs of claim at the outset of chapter 11 cases and, accordingly, uses Form 9E(Alt.) or Form 9F(Alt.) retains the option in any case in which no deadlines actually are set to substitute a message stating that creditors will be notified if the court fixes a deadline.

The form also is amended to add, in the paragraph labeled "Discharge of Debts," a reference to dischargeability actions under section 523(a)(15) of the Code, which was added by the 1994 Act.

NOTES OF ADVISORY COMMITTEE ON RULES—1997 AMENDMENT

Forms 9A, 9I (and the alternate versions of Forms 9E and 9F) have been amended, redesigned, and rewritten. Minor conforming changes have been made to respond to amendments made in the Bankruptcy Reform Act of 1994: the longer claims filing period for governmental units in section 502(b)(9) of the Code (see Forms 9C, 9D, 9E(Alt.), 9F(Alt.), 9G, 9H, and 9I); and a reference to dischargeability actions under section 523(a)(15) (see Forms 9A, 9C, 9E, and 9E(Alt.), 9G, and 9H). All of the forms have been substantially revised to make them easier to read and understand. The titles have been simplified. Recipients are told why they are receiving the notice. Explanations are provided on the back of the form and are set in larger type. Plain English is used. Deadlines are highlighted on the front of the form. Recipients are told that papers must be received by the bankruptcy clerk's office by the applicable deadline. The box for the trustee has been deleted from the chapter 11 notices (Forms 9E and 9F and the alternates). Various alternatives are set out in brackets in many of the forms, permitting each bankruptcy clerk's office to tailor the forms even more precisely to fit the needs of a particular case. The court may use blank spaces on the form to include additional information applicable to the particular district.

COMMITTEE NOTES ON RULES—2003 AMENDMENT

The form is amended to add to the information provided to creditors, the trustee and the United States trustee, all the names used by the debtor during the six years prior to the filing of the petition. The form includes the debtor's full employer identification number, if any, as well as the last four digits of the debtor's social security number. Rule 2002(a)(1) also is amended to direct the clerk to include the debtor's full social security number and employer identification number on the notices served on the United States trustee, the trustee, and creditors. This will enable creditors to identify the debtor accurately. The copy of Official Form 9 included in the case file, however, will show only the last four digits of the debtor's social security number. This should afford greater privacy to the individual debtor, whose bankruptcy case records may be available on the Internet.

COMMITTEE NOTES ON RULES—2005 AMENDMENT

The form is amended in a variety of way [sic] to implement the provisions of the Bankruptcy Abuse Prevention and Consumer Protection Act of 2005, Pub. L. No. 109–8, 119 Stat. 23 (April 20, 2005). All versions of the form are amended to advise creditors to consult an attorney concerning what rights they may have in the specific case. All versions of the form are also amended to provide information about filing claims to creditors with foreign addresses and to advise those creditors to consult a lawyer familiar with United States bankruptcy law regarding any questions they may have about their rights in a particular case. These amendments implement §1514, which was added to the Code in 2005.

Forms 9A and 9C are amended to include a box in which the clerk can notify creditors in a chapter 7 case filed by an individual with primarily consumer debts whether the presumption of abuse has arisen under §707(b) of the Code as amended in 2005. Under §342(d) of the Code, the clerk has a duty to notify creditors concerning the presumption within ten days of the filing of the petition. If [sic] cases in which the debtor does not file Official Form 22A with the petition, the forms provide for the clerk to state that insufficient information has been filed, and to inform creditors that if later-filed information indicates that the presumption arises, creditors will be sent another notice.

In cases involving serial filers (debtors who have filed more than one case within a specified period), the automatic stay provided by §362(a) of the Code as amended in 2005 may not apply or may be limited in duration, unless the stay is extended or imposed by court order. The form contains a general statement alerting debtors to this possibility.

Section 1514, added to the Code in 2005, also requires that a secured creditor with a foreign address be advised whether the creditor is required to file a proof of claim, and Forms 9B, 9D, 9E, 9E (Alt.), 9F, 9F (Alt.), 9G, 9H, and 9I are amended to include general information addressing that question. Forms 9E, 9E (Alt.), 9F, and 9F (Alt.) also are amended to inform creditors that in a case in which the debtor has filed a plan for which it has solicited acceptances before filing the case, the court may, after notice and a hearing, order that the United States trustee not convene a meeting of creditors.

Forms 9E and 9E Alt. are amended to state that, unless the court orders otherwise, an individual chapter 11 debtor's discharge is not effective until completion of all payments under the plan, as provided in §1141(d)(5) which was added to the Code in 2005. Forms 9F and 9F (Alt.) are amended to include a deadline to file a complaint to determine the discharge ability of a debt, in conformity with §1141(d)(6) which was added to the Code in 2005.

Form 9I is amended to include a deadline to file a complaint to determine the discharge ability of certain debts. This amendment implements 2005 amendment [sic] to §1328(a)(1) of the Code.

COMMITTEE NOTES ON RULES—2006 AMENDMENT

Forms 9G and 9H are amended to add "family fisherman" to the title and to the description of chapter 12. The 2005 amendments to the Code added a "family fisherman," as defined in §101(19A), to the persons eligible to file a bankruptcy case under chapter 12. Form 9I is amended to provide general notice to parties in interest of the potential for a claim to be filed late in the case.

COMMITTEE NOTES ON RULES—2005-2007 AMENDMENT

[The 2005-2007 Committee Note incorporates Committee Notes previously published in 2005 and 2006.]

The form is amended in a variety of ways to implement the provisions of the Bankruptcy Abuse Prevention and Consumer Protection Act of 2005, Pub. L. No. 109-8, 119 Stat. 23 (April 20, 2005). All versions of the form are amended to advise creditors to consult an attorney concerning what rights they may have in the specific case. All versions of the form also are amended to provide to creditors with foreign addresses information about filing claims and to advise those creditors to consult a lawyer familiar with United States bankruptcy law regarding any questions they may have about their rights in a particular case. These amendments implement §1514, which was added to the Code in 2005.

Forms 9A and 9C are amended to include a box in which the clerk can notify creditors in a chapter 7 case filed by an individual with primarily consumer debts if the presumption of abuse has arisen under §707(b) of the Code as amended in 2005. Under §342(d) of the Code, the clerk has a duty to notify creditors concerning the presumption within ten days of the filing of the petition. In cases in which the debtor does not file Official Form 22A with the petition, the forms provide for the clerk to state that insufficient information has been filed, and to inform creditors that if later-filed information indicates that the presumption arises, creditors will be sent another notice. Forms 9G and 9H are amended to add "family fishermen" to the notices used in chapter 12 cases, in conformity with the 2005 amendments to the Code extending the provisions of chapter 12 to family fishermen.

In cases involving serial filers (debtors who have filed more than one case within a specified period), the automatic stay provided by §362(a) of the Code as amended in 2005 may not apply or may be limited in duration, unless the stay is extended or imposed by court order. The form contains a general statement alerting debtors to this possibility.

Section 1514, added to the Code in 2005, also requires that a secured creditor with a foreign address be advised whether the creditor is required to file a proof of claim, and Forms 9B, 9D, 9E, 9E (Alt.), 9F, 9F (Alt.), 9G, 9H, and 9I are amended to include general information addressing that question. Forms 9E, 9E (Alt.), 9F, and 9F (Alt.) also are amended to inform creditors that in a case in which the debtor has filed a plan for which it has solicited acceptances before filing the case, the court may, after notice and a hearing, order that the United States trustee not convene a meeting of creditors.

Forms 9E and 9E (Alt.) are amended to state that, unless the court orders otherwise, an individual chapter 11 debtor's discharge is not effective until completion of all payments under the plan, as provided in §1141(d)(5) which was added to the Code in 2005. Forms 9F and 9F (Alt.) are amended to include a deadline to file a complaint to determine the dischargeability of a debt, in conformity with §1141(d)(6), which also was added to the Code in 2005.

Form 9I is amended to include a deadline to file a complaint to determine the dischargeability of certain debts. This amendment implements a 2005 amendment to §1328(a) of the Code.

In addition, all versions of the form are amended to provide to the public only the last four digits of any individual debtor's taxpayer-identification number. This amendment implements Rule 9037.

B 10 (Official Form 10) (12/08)

UNITED STATES BANKRUPTCY COURT | **PROOF OF CLAIM**

Name of Debtor: | Case Number:

NOTE: *This form should not be used to make a claim for an administrative expense arising after the commencement of the case. A request for payment of an administrative expense may be filed pursuant to 11 U.S.C. § 503.*

Name of Creditor (the person or other entity to whom the debtor owes money or property):

Name and address where notices should be sent:

Telephone number:

☐ Check this box to indicate that this claim amends a previously filed claim.

Court Claim Number:__________
(If known)

Filed on:__________

Name and address where payment should be sent (if different from above):

Telephone number:

☐ Check this box if you are aware that anyone else has filed a proof of claim relating to your claim. Attach copy of statement giving particulars.

☐ Check this box if you are the debtor or trustee in this case.

1. Amount of Claim as of Date Case Filed: $__________

If all or part of your claim is secured, complete item 4 below; however, if all of your claim is unsecured, do not complete item 4.

If all or part of your claim is entitled to priority, complete item 5.

☐ Check this box if claim includes interest or other charges in addition to the principal amount of claim. Attach itemized statement of interest or charges.

2. Basis for Claim: __________
(See instruction #2 on reverse side.)

3. Last four digits of any number by which creditor identifies debtor: __________

3a. Debtor may have scheduled account as: __________
(See instruction #3a on reverse side.)

4. Secured Claim (See instruction #4 on reverse side.)
Check the appropriate box if your claim is secured by a lien on property or a right of setoff and provide the requested information.

Nature of property or right of setoff: ☐Real Estate ☐Motor Vehicle ☐Other
Describe:

Value of Property:$__________ **Annual Interest Rate**_____%

Amount of arrearage and other charges as of time case filed included in secured claim,

if any: $__________ **Basis for perfection:** __________

Amount of Secured Claim: $__________ **Amount Unsecured: $**__________

5. Amount of Claim Entitled to Priority under 11 U.S.C. §507(a). If any portion of your claim falls in one of the following categories, check the box and state the amount.

Specify the priority of the claim.

☐ Domestic support obligations under 11 U.S.C. §507(a)(1)(A) or (a)(1)(B).

☐ Wages, salaries, or commissions (up to $10,950*) earned within 180 days before filing of the bankruptcy petition or cessation of the debtor's business, whichever is earlier – 11 U.S.C. §507 (a)(4).

☐ Contributions to an employee benefit plan – 11 U.S.C. §507 (a)(5).

☐ Up to $2,425* of deposits toward purchase, lease, or rental of property or services for personal, family, or household use – 11 U.S.C. §507 (a)(7).

☐ Taxes or penalties owed to governmental units – 11 U.S.C. §507 (a)(8).

☐ Other – Specify applicable paragraph of 11 U.S.C. §507 (a)(__).

Amount entitled to priority:

$__________

**Amounts are subject to adjustment on 4/1/10 and every 3 years thereafter with respect to cases commenced on or after the date of adjustment.*

6. Credits: The amount of all payments on this claim has been credited for the purpose of making this proof of claim.

7. Documents: Attach redacted copies of any documents that support the claim, such as promissory notes, purchase orders, invoices, itemized statements of running accounts, contracts, judgments, mortgages, and security agreements. You may also attach a summary. Attach redacted copies of documents providing evidence of perfection of a security interest. You may also attach a summary. *(See instruction 7 and definition of "redacted" on reverse side.)*

DO NOT SEND ORIGINAL DOCUMENTS. ATTACHED DOCUMENTS MAY BE DESTROYED AFTER SCANNING.

If the documents are not available, please explain:

Date:

Signature: The person filing this claim must sign it. Sign and print name and title, if any, of the creditor or other person authorized to file this claim and state address and telephone number if different from the notice address above. Attach copy of power of attorney, if any.

FOR COURT USE ONLY

Penalty for presenting fraudulent claim: Fine of up to $500,000 or imprisonment for up to 5 years, or both. 18 U.S.C. §§ 152 and 3571.

B 10 (Official Form 10) (12/08) – Cont.

INSTRUCTIONS FOR PROOF OF CLAIM FORM

The instructions and definitions below are general explanations of the law. In certain circumstances, such as bankruptcy cases not filed voluntarily by the debtor, there may be exceptions to these general rules.

Items to be completed in Proof of Claim form

Court, Name of Debtor, and Case Number:
Fill in the federal judicial district where the bankruptcy case was filed (for example, Central District of California), the bankruptcy debtor's name, and the bankruptcy case number. If the creditor received a notice of the case from the bankruptcy court, all of this information is located at the top of the notice.

Creditor's Name and Address:
Fill in the name of the person or entity asserting a claim and the name and address of the person who should receive notices issued during the bankruptcy case. A separate space is provided for the payment address if it differs from the notice address. The creditor has a continuing obligation to keep the court informed of its current address. See Federal Rule of Bankruptcy Procedure (FRBP) 2002(g).

1. Amount of Claim as of Date Case Filed:
State the total amount owed to the creditor on the date of the Bankruptcy filing. Follow the instructions concerning whether to complete items 4 and 5. Check the box if interest or other charges are included in the claim.

2. Basis for Claim:
State the type of debt or how it was incurred. Examples include goods sold, money loaned, services performed, personal injury/wrongful death, car loan, mortgage note, and credit card. If the claim is based on the delivery of health care goods or services, limit the disclosure of the goods or services so as to avoid embarrassment or the disclosure of confidential health care information. You may be required to provide additional disclosure if the trustee or another party in interest files an objection to your claim.

3. Last Four Digits of Any Number by Which Creditor Identifies Debtor:
State only the last four digits of the debtor's account or other number used by the creditor to identify the debtor.

3a. Debtor May Have Scheduled Account As:
Use this space to report a change in the creditor's name, a transferred claim, or any other information that clarifies a difference between this proof of claim and the claim as scheduled by the debtor.

4. Secured Claim:
Check the appropriate box and provide the requested information if the claim is fully or partially secured. Skip this section if the claim is entirely unsecured. (See DEFINITIONS, below.) State the type and the value of property that secures the claim, attach copies of lien documentation, and state annual interest rate and the amount past due on the claim as of the date of the bankruptcy filing.

5. Amount of Claim Entitled to Priority Under 11 U.S.C. §507(a).
If any portion of your claim falls in one or more of the listed categories, check the appropriate box(es) and state the amount entitled to priority. (See DEFINITIONS, below.) A claim may be partly priority and partly non-priority. For example, in some of the categories, the law limits the amount entitled to priority.

6. Credits:
An authorized signature on this proof of claim serves as an acknowledgment that when calculating the amount of the claim, the creditor gave the debtor credit for any payments received toward the debt.

7. Documents:
Attach to this proof of claim form redacted copies documenting the existence of the debt and of any lien securing the debt. You may also attach a summary. You must also attach copies of documents that evidence perfection of any security interest. You may also attach a summary. FRBP 3001(c) and (d). If the claim is based on the delivery of health care goods or services, see instruction 2. Do not send original documents, as attachments may be destroyed after scanning.

Date and Signature:
The person filing this proof of claim must sign and date it. FRBP 9011. If the claim is filed electronically, FRBP 5005(a)(2), authorizes courts to establish local rules specifying what constitutes a signature. Print the name and title, if any, of the creditor or other person authorized to file this claim. State the filer's address and telephone number if it differs from the address given on the top of the form for purposes of receiving notices. Attach a complete copy of any power of attorney. Criminal penalties apply for making a false statement on a proof of claim.

DEFINITIONS

Debtor
A debtor is the person, corporation, or other entity that has filed a bankruptcy case.

Creditor
A creditor is a person, corporation, or other entity owed a debt by the debtor that arose on or before the date of the bankruptcy filing. See 11 U.S.C. §101 (10)

Claim
A claim is the creditor's right to receive payment on a debt owed by the debtor that arose on the date of the bankruptcy filing. See 11 U.S.C. §101 (5). A claim may be secured or unsecured.

Proof of Claim
A proof of claim is a form used by the creditor to indicate the amount of the debt owed by the debtor on the date of the bankruptcy filing. The creditor must file the form with the clerk of the same bankruptcy court in which the bankruptcy case was filed.

Secured Claim Under 11 U.S.C. §506(a)
A secured claim is one backed by a lien on property of the debtor. The claim is secured so long as the creditor has the right to be paid from the property prior to other creditors. The amount of the secured claim cannot exceed the value of the property. Any amount owed to the creditor in excess of the value of the property is an unsecured claim. Examples of liens on property include a mortgage on real estate or a security interest in a car. A lien may be voluntarily granted by a debtor or may be obtained through a court proceeding. In some states, a court judgment is a lien. A claim also may be secured if the creditor owes the debtor money (has a right to setoff).

Unsecured Claim
An unsecured claim is one that does not meet the requirements of a secured claim. A claim may be partly unsecured if the amount of the claim exceeds the value of the property on which the creditor has a lien.

Claim Entitled to Priority Under 11 U.S.C. §507(a)
Priority claims are certain categories of unsecured claims that are paid from the available money or property in a bankruptcy case before other unsecured claims.

Redacted
A document has been redacted when the person filing it has masked, edited out, or otherwise deleted, certain information. A creditor should redact and use only the last four digits of any social-security, individual's tax-identification, or financial-account number, all but the initials of a minor's name and only the year of any person's date of birth.

Evidence of Perfection
Evidence of perfection may include a mortgage, lien, certificate of title, financing statement, or other document showing that the lien has been filed or recorded.

INFORMATION

Acknowledgment of Filing of Claim
To receive acknowledgment of your filing, you may either enclose a stamped self-addressed envelope and a copy of this proof of claim or you may access the court's PACER system (www.pacer.psc.uscourts.gov) for a small fee to view your filed proof of claim.

Offers to Purchase a Claim
Certain entities are in the business of purchasing claims for an amount less than the face value of the claims. One or more of these entities may contact the creditor and offer to purchase the claim. Some of the written communications from these entities may easily be confused with official court documentation or communications from the debtor. These entities do not represent the bankruptcy court or the debtor. The creditor has no obligation to sell its claim. However, if the creditor decides to sell its claim, any transfer of such claim is subject to FRBP 3001(e), any applicable provisions of the Bankruptcy Code (11 U.S.C. § 101 *et seq.*), and any applicable orders of the bankruptcy court.

(Added Aug. 1, 1991; amended Mar. 16, 1993; Mar. 14, 1995; Oct. 1, 1997; Dec. 1, 2003; Oct. 17, 2005; Dec. 1, 2007; Dec. 1, 2008.)

NOTES OF ADVISORY COMMITTEE ON RULES—1991

This form replaces former Official Forms No. 19, No. 20, and No. 21. The box format and simplified language are intended to facilitate completion of the form.

The form directs the claimant to attach documents to support the claim or, if voluminous, a summary of such documents. These include any security agreement (if not included in the writing on which the claim is founded), and evidence of perfection of any security interest. See Committee Note to Rule 3001(d) concerning satisfactory evidence of perfection. If the claim includes prepetition interest or other charges such as attorney fees, a statement giving a detailed breakdown of the elements of the claim is required.

Rule 2002(g) requires the clerk to update the mailing list in the case by substituting the address provided by a creditor on a proof of claim, if that address is different from the one supplied by the debtor. The form contains checkboxes to assist the clerk in performing this duty. The form also alerts the trustee when the claim is an amendment to or replacement for an earlier claim.

NOTES OF ADVISORY COMMITTEE ON RULES—1993 AMENDMENT

The form has been amended to accommodate inclusion of the priority afforded in §507(a)(8) of the Code, which was added by Pub. L. No. 101-647, (Crime Control Act of 1990), and to avoid the necessity of further amendment to the form if other priorities are added to §507(a) in the future. In addition, sections 4 and 5 of the form have been amended to clarify that only prepetition arrearages and charges are to be included in the amount of the claim.

NOTES OF ADVISORY COMMITTEE ON RULES—1995 AMENDMENT

The form is amended to add the seventh priority granted by the Bankruptcy Reform Act of 1994 to debts for alimony, maintenance, or support of a spouse, former spouse, or child of the debtor. The form also amends the Code reference to the priority afforded to tax debts and the dollar maximums for the priorities granted to wages and customer deposits in conformity with amendments made by the 1994 Act to section 507(a) of the Code. The 1994 Act also amended section 104 of the Code to provide for future adjustment of the dollar amounts specified in section 507(a) to be made by administrative action at three-year intervals to reflect changes in the consumer price index. The form is amended to include notice that these dollar amounts are subject to change without formal amendment to the official form.

NOTES OF ADVISORY COMMITTEE ON RULES—1997 AMENDMENT

Numbered sections 4. and 5. of the form have been reformatted to eliminate redundant information and make it easier to complete the form correctly. A creditor will report the total amount of the claim first, and will report only that amount unless the claim is secured by collateral or entitled to a priority under §507 of the Code.

Explanatory definitions and instructions for completing the form also have been added.

COMMITTEE NOTES ON RULES—2003 AMENDMENT

The form is amended to require a wage, salary, or other compensation creditor to disclose only the last four digits of the creditor's social security number to afford greater privacy to the creditor. A trustee can request the full information necessary for tax withholding and reporting at the time the trustee makes a distribution to creditors.

COMMITTEE NOTES ON RULES—2005 AMENDMENT

The form is amended to conform to changes in the priority afforded the claims of certain creditors in §507(a) of the Code as amended by the Bankruptcy Abuse Prevention and Consumer Protection Act of 2005, Pub. L. No. 109-8, 119 Stat. 23 (April 20, 2005).

COMMITTEE NOTES ON RULES—2005-2007 AMENDMENT

[The 2005-2007 Committee Note incorporates the Committee Note previously published in 2005.]

The form is amended to conform to changes in the priority afforded the claims of certain creditors in §507(a) of the Code as amended by the Bankruptcy Abuse Prevention and Consumer Protection Act of 2005, Pub. L. No. 109-8, 119 Stat. 23 (April 20, 2005).

In addition, the form and its instructions are amended in several respects based on the experiences of creditors and trustees in using it and on the technological changes that have occurred in the courts' processing of claims. A definition of the word "redacted" has been added in conformity with Rule 9037.

The creditor now has a space in which to provide a separate payment address if different from the creditor's address for receiving notices in the case. The checkboxes for indicating that the creditor's address provided on the proof of claim is a new address, and that the creditor never received any notices from the court in the case have been deleted. The computer systems now used by the courts make it unnecessary for a creditor to "flag" a new address or call attention to the fact that the creditor is making its first appearance in the case. In place of the deleted items is a new checkbox to be used when a debtor or a trustee files a proof of claim for a creditor; it will alert the clerk to send the notice required by Rule 3004. The box for indicating whether the claim replaces a previously filed claim also has been deleted as no longer necessary in light of the 2005 amendments to Rules 3004 and 3005. The creditor simply will amend the claim filed by the other party.

Requests for the creditor to state the date on which the debt was incurred and the date on which any court judgment concerning the debt was obtained have been deleted, based on reports from trustees that they rely on the documents supporting the claim for this information. The checkboxes for stating the basis for the creditor's claim have been replaced with a blank in which the creditor is to provide this information. Examples of the most common categories, based on the former checkboxes, can be found in the instructions on the form. The request to state the account number by which the creditor identifies the debtor has been moved to paragraph 3 of the form and has been revised to request only the last four digits of the number, in conformity with Rule 9037. In addition, a new paragraph 3a gives the creditor a place to notify the trustee and the court of any change in the creditor's name, or that the claim has been transferred, or to provide any other information to clarify a difference between the proof of claim and the creditor's claim as scheduled by the debtor.

The adjective "total" is deleted from the sections of the form where the creditor states the amount of the claim and the creditor now simply reports the amount of the claim. If the claim is a general unsecured claim, no further details are stated on the form, although a creditor still must attach a copy of any writing on which the claim is based, as required by Rule 3001(c), and must attach a statement itemizing any interest or other charges (in addition to the principal) that are included in the claim. If the claim or any part of it is secured or entitled to priority under §507(a) of the Code the creditor is directed to provide details in the appropriate sections of the form. The creditor now states the amount to be afforded priority only once, in the section of the form designated for describing the specific priority being asserted. The introductory language in the section where the creditor describes any priority to which it is entitled has been revised for clarity. The word "collateral" has been replaced with the less colloquial and more accurate phrase "lien on property" throughout the form.

Information about obtaining acknowledgment from the court of the filing of the proof of claim is revised and moved to a new section on the reverse side called "Information." This new section also alerts a creditor to the possibility that it may be approached about selling its claim, advises that the court has no role in any such solicitations, and states that a creditor is under no obligation to accept any offer to purchase its claim. A new instruction is added about signing a proof of claim. This instruction includes citations to Rules 9011 and 5005(a)(2) concerning signature requirements in an electronic filing environment.

Finally, all of the definitions and instructions on the reverse side of the form are amended generally to reflect the deletions, additions, and other changes made on page 1. These include a reminder to the creditor to keep the court informed of any changes in its address. The instructions now appear at the top of the page, and the text is revised both to reflect the substantive changes to the form and to improve the clarity and style of this explanatory material.

COMMITTEE NOTES ON RULES—2008 AMENDMENT

The form is amended at box seven on page one, and instructions two and seven on page two, to instruct the claimant that the information contained in or attached to a claim based on the delivery of health care goods or services should be limited so as to avoid embarrassment or the unnecessary disclosure of confidential information. The claimant is informed that additional disclosure may be required if the trustee or another party in interest objects to the claim.

Page two of the form is also amended to revise slightly the definitions of "creditor" and "claim" to conform more closely to the definitions of those terms in the Code.

Official Form 11A
6/90

United States Bankruptcy Court

_______________ District Of _______________

In re _______________________,
Debtor

Case No. ___________

Chapter __________

GENERAL POWER OF ATTORNEY

To ______________________________ of * ______________________________, and
______________________________ of * ______________________________.

The undersigned claimant hereby authorizes you, or any one of you, as attorney in fact for the undersigned and with full power of substitution, to vote on any question that may be lawfully submitted to creditors of the debtor in the above-entitled case; [*if appropriate*] to vote for a trustee of the estate of the debtor and for a committee of creditors; to receive dividends; and in general to perform any act not constituting the practice of law for the undersigned in all matters arising in this case.

Dated: ______________________

Signed: ______________________

By ______________________

as ______________________

Address: ______________________

____

[*If executed by an individual*] Acknowledged before me on ______________________.

[*If executed on behalf of a partnership*] Acknowledged before me on ______________________, by ______________________, who says that he [*or* she] is a member of the partnership named above and is authorized to execute this power of attorney in its behalf.

[*If executed on behalf of a corporation*] Acknowledged before me on ______________________, by ______________________, who says that he [*or* she] is ______________________ of the corporation named above and is authorized to execute this power of attorney in its behalf.

____

____
[*Official character.*]

* State mailing address.

(Added Aug. 1, 1991.)

NOTES OF ADVISORY COMMITTEE ON RULES—1991

This form previously was numbered Official Form No. 17.

Official Form 11B
6/90

United States Bankruptcy Court

________________ District Of ________________

In re ______________________,
Debtor

Case No. ____________

Chapter __________

SPECIAL POWER OF ATTORNEY

To ____________________________________ of * ____________________________________, and
____________________________________ of * ____________________________________.

The undersigned claimant hereby authorizes you, or any one of you, as attorney in fact for the undersigned [*if desired*: and with full power of substitution,] to attend the meeting of creditors of the debtor or any adjournment thereof, and to vote in my behalf on any question that may be lawfully submitted to creditors at such meeting or adjourned meeting, and for a trustee or trustees of the estate of the debtor.

Dated: ____________________

Signed: ______________________________

By ______________________________

as ______________________________

Address: ______________________________

____

[*If executed by an individual*] Acknowledged before me on ____________________.

[*If executed on behalf of a partnership*] Acknowledged before me ______________________________, by ________________________, who says that he [*or* she] is a member of the partnership named above and is authorized to execute this power of attorney in its behalf.

[*If executed on behalf of a corporation*] Acknowledged before me on ______________________________, by ________________________, who says that he [*or* she] is __________________________ of the corporation named above and is authorized to execute this power of attorney in its behalf.

____

____
[*Official character.*]

* State mailing address.

(Added Aug. 1, 1991.)

NOTES OF ADVISORY COMMITTEE ON RULES—1991

This form previously was numbered Official Form No. 18.

Official Form 12
(12/03)

Form 12. ORDER AND NOTICE FOR HEARING ON DISCLOSURE STATEMENT

[Caption as in Form 16A]

ORDER AND NOTICE FOR HEARING ON DISCLOSURE STATEMENT

To the debtor, its creditors, and other parties in interest:

A disclosure statement and a plan under chapter 11 [*or* chapter 9] of the Bankruptcy Code having been filed by ______________________________ on ______________________________,

IT IS ORDERED and notice is hereby given, that:

1. The hearing to consider the approval of the disclosure statement shall be held at: ____________________, on ____________________, at ____________ o'clock __.m.

2. ____________________ is fixed as the last day for filing and serving in accordance with Fed. R. Bankr. P. 3017(a) written objections to the disclosure statement.

3. Within __________ days after entry of this order, the disclosure statement and plan shall be distributed in accordance with Fed. R. Bankr. P. 3017(a).

4. Requests for copies of the disclosure statement and plan shall be mailed to the debtor in possession [*or* trustee *or* debtor *or* ____________________] at * ____________________.

Dated: ____________________

BY THE COURT

____
United States Bankruptcy Judge

* State mailing address

(Added Aug. 1, 1991.)

NOTES OF ADVISORY COMMITTEE ON RULES—1991

This form previously was numbered Official Form No. 28. The form is related to Rule 3017(a). Section 1125 of the Code requires court approval of a disclosure statement before votes may be solicited for or against a plan in either chapter 11 reorganization or chapter 9 municipality cases.

Objections to the disclosure statement may be filed. Rule 3017(a) specifies that the court may fix a time for the filing of objections or they can be filed at any time prior to approval of the statement.

Rule 3017(a) also specifies the persons who are to receive copies of the statement and plan prior to the hearing. These documents will not be sent to all parties in interest because at this stage of the case it could be unnecessarily expensive and confusing. However, any party in interest may request copies. The request should be made in writing (Rule 3017(a)), and sent to the person mailing the statement and plan which, as the form indicates, would usually be the proponent of the plan.

This form may be adapted for use if more than one disclosure statement is to be considered by the court.

Official Form 13
(12/03)

Form 13. ORDER APPROVING DISCLOSURE STATEMENT AND FIXING TIME FOR FILING ACCEPTANCES OR REJECTIONS OF PLAN, COMBINED WITH NOTICE THEREOF

[Caption as in Form 16A]

ORDER APPROVING DISCLOSURE STATEMENT AND FIXING TIME FOR FILING ACCEPTANCES OR REJECTIONS OF PLAN, COMBINED WITH NOTICE THEREOF

A disclosure statement under chapter 11 of the Bankruptcy Code having been filed by ______________________________, on ____________________ [*if appropriate*, and by ______________________________, on ____________________], referring to a plan under chapter 11 of the Code filed by __________________________, on ________________ [*if appropriate*, and by __________________________, on _________________ respectively] [*if appropriate*, as modified by a modification filed on ________________]; and

It having been determined after hearing on notice that the disclosure statement [*or* statements] contain[s] adequate information:

IT IS ORDERED, and notice is hereby given, that:

A. The disclosure statement filed by _________________________ dated ______________ [*if appropriate*, and by ___________________________, dated ________________ is [are] approved.

B. ________________________ is fixed as the last day for filing written acceptances or rejections of the plan [*or* plans] referred to above.

C. Within ____________ days after the entry of this order, the plan [*or* plans] *or* a summary *or* summaries thereof approved by the court, [and [*if appropriate*] a summary approved by the court of its opinion, if any, dated _____________, approving the disclosure statement [*or* statements]], the disclosure statement [*or* statements], and a ballot conforming to Official Form 14 shall be mailed to creditors, equity security holders, and other parties in interest, and shall be transmitted to the United States trustee, as provided in Fed. R. Bankr. P. 3017(d).

D. If acceptances are filed for more than one plan, preferences among the plans so accepted may be indicated.

E. *[If appropriate]* ______________ is fixed for the hearing on confirmation of the plan [*or* plans].

F. *[If appropriate]* _______________ is fixed as the last day for filing and serving pursuant to Fed. R. Bankr. P. 3020(b)(1) written objections to confirmation of the plan.

Dated: ______________________

BY THE COURT

____
United States Bankruptcy Judge

[If the court directs that a copy of the opinion should be transmitted in lieu of or in addition to the summary thereof, the appropriate change should be made in paragraph C of this order.]

(Added Aug. 1, 1991.)

NOTES OF ADVISORY COMMITTEE ON RULES—1991

This form is derived from former Official Form No. 29. The form may be adapted for use if more than one disclosure statement is approved by the court.

Official Form 14
(12/03)

Form 14. CLASS [ ] BALLOT FOR ACCEPTING OR REJECTING PLAN OF REORGANIZATION

[Caption as in Form 16A]

CLASS [ ] BALLOT FOR ACCEPTING OR REJECTING PLAN OF REORGANIZATION

[Proponent] filed a plan of reorganization dated *[Date]* (the "Plan") for the Debtor in this case. The Court has *[conditionally]* approved a disclosure statement with respect to the Plan (the "Disclosure Statement"). The Disclosure Statement provides information to assist you in deciding how to vote your ballot. If you do not have a Disclosure Statement, you may obtain a copy from *[name, address, telephone number and telecopy number of proponent/proponent's attorney.]* Court approval of the disclosure statement does not indicate approval of the Plan by the Court.

You should review the Disclosure Statement and the Plan before you vote. You may wish to seek legal advice concerning the Plan and your classification and treatment under the Plan. Your *[claim] [equity interest]* has been placed in class [ ] under the Plan. If you hold claims or equity interests in more than one class, you will receive a ballot for each class in which you are entitled to vote.

If your ballot is not received by *[name and address of proponent's attorney or other appropriate address]* on or before *[date]*, and such deadline is not extended, your vote will not count as either an acceptance or rejection of the Plan.

If the Plan is confirmed by the Bankruptcy Court it will be binding on you whether or not you vote.

ACCEPTANCE OR REJECTION OF THE PLAN

[At this point the ballot should provide for voting by the particular class of creditors or equity holders receiving the ballot using one of the following alternatives;]

[If the voter is the holder of a secured, priority, or unsecured nonpriority claim:]

The undersigned, the holder of a Class [ ] claim against the Debtor in the unpaid amount of Dollars ($)

[or, if the voter is the holder of a bond, debenture, or other debt security:]

The undersigned, the holder of a Class [ ] claim against the Debtor, consisting of Dollars ($) principal amount of *[describe bond, debenture, or other debt security]* of the Debtor (For purposes of this Ballot, it is not necessary and you should not adjust the principal amount for any accrued or unmatured interest.)

[or, if the voter is the holder of an equity interest:]

The undersigned, the holder of Class [ ] equity interest in the Debtor, consisting of ______ shares or other interests of *[describe equity interest]* in the Debtor

Official Form 14 continued
(12/03)

[In each case, the following language should be included:]

(Check one box only)

[ ] ACCEPTS THE PLAN [ ] REJECTS THE PLAN

Dated: ____________________

Print or type name: ____________________________

Signature: ____________________________________

Title (if corporation or partnership) ______________

Address: ______________________________

____

RETURN THIS BALLOT TO:

[Name and address of proponent's attorney or other appropriate address]

(Added Aug. 1, 1991; amended Oct. 1, 1997.)

NOTES OF ADVISORY COMMITTEE ON RULES—1991

This form is derived from former Official Form No. 30. The form has been amended to facilitate the voting of a debtor's shares held in "street name." The form may be adapted to designate the class in which each ballot is to be tabulated. It is intended that a separate ballot will be provided for each class in which a holder may vote.

NOTES OF ADVISORY COMMITTEE ON RULES—1997 AMENDMENT

The form has been substantially amended to simplify its format and make it easier to complete correctly.

Directions or blanks for proponent to complete the text of the ballot are in italics and enclosed within brackets. A ballot should include only the applicable language from the alternatives shown on this form and should be adapted to the particular requirements of the case.

If the plan provides for creditors in a class to have the right to reduce their claims so as to qualify for treatment given to creditors whose claims do not exceed a specified amount, the ballot should make provisions for the exercise of that right. See section 1122(b) of the Code.

If debt or equity securities are held in the name of a broker/dealer or nominee, the ballot should require the furnishing of sufficient information to assure that duplicate ballots are not submitted and counted and that ballots submitted by a broker/dealer or nominee reflect the votes of the beneficial holders of such securities. See Rule 3017(e).

In the event that more than one plan of reorganization is to be voted upon, the form of ballot will need to be adapted to permit holders of claims or equity interests (a) to accept or reject each plan being proposed, and (b) to indicate preferences among the competing plans. See section 1129(c) of the Code.

Form B15
(Rev. 12/01)

Form 15. ORDER CONFIRMING PLAN

[Caption as in Form 16A]

ORDER CONFIRMING PLAN

The plan under chapter 11 of the Bankruptcy Code filed by ____________________, on __________ *[if applicable*, as modified by a modification filed on __________] or a summary thereof, having been transmitted to creditors and equity security holders; and

It having been determined after hearing on notice that the requirements for confirmation set forth in 11 U.S.C. § 1129(a) *[or, if appropriate,* 11 U.S.C. § 1129(b)] have been satisfied;

IT IS ORDERED that:

The plan filed by ____________________, on __________, *[If appropriate, include dates and any other pertinent details of modifications to the plan]* is confirmed. *[If the plan provides for an injunction against conduct not otherwise enjoined under the Code, include the information required by Rule 3020.]*

A copy of the confirmed plan is attached.

Dated: __________

BY THE COURT

____
United States Bankruptcy Judge.

(Added Aug. 1, 1991; amended Dec. 1, 2001.)

NOTES OF ADVISORY COMMITTEE ON RULES—1991

This form is derived from former Official Form No. 31. The form has been simplified to avoid the necessity of repeating the statutory requirements of 11 U.S.C. §1129(a). In the case of an individual chapter 11 debtor, Form 18 may be adapted for use together with this form.

COMMITTEE NOTES ON RULES—2001 AMENDMENT

The form is amended to conform to the December 1, 2001, amendments to Rule 3020.

B16A (Official Form 16A) (12/07)

Form 16A. CAPTION (FULL)

United States Bankruptcy Court

________________ District Of ________________

In re ____________________________________,)
[Set forth here all names including married, maiden, and trade names used by debtor within last 8 years.])
Debtor) Case No. ______________
)
Address ____________________________________)
)
____________________________________) Chapter __________
)
Last four digits of Social-Security or Individual Tax-Payer-Identification (ITIN) No(s).,(if any): ___________)
____________________________________)
Employer Tax-Identification (EIN) No(s).(if any): _____)
____________________________________)

[Designation of Character of Paper]

(Added Aug. 1, 1991; amended Mar. 14, 1995; Dec. 1, 2003; Oct. 17, 2005; Dec. 1, 2007.)

NOTES OF ADVISORY COMMITTEE ON RULES—1991

This form has been transferred from former Official Form No. 1, which included the form of caption for the case. Rule 9004(b) requires a caption to set forth the title of the case. Rule 1005 provides that the title of the case shall include the debtor's name, all other names used by the debtor within six years before the commencement of the case, and the debtor's social security and tax identification numbers. This form of caption is prescribed for use on the petition, the notice of the meeting of creditors, the order of discharge, and the documents relating to a chapter 11 plan, (Official Forms 1, 9, 12, 13, 14, 15, and 18). See Rule 2002(m). In the petition (Official Form 1), and the notice of the meeting of creditors, (Official Form 9), the information required by Rule 1005 appears in a block format. A notation of the chapter of the Bankruptcy Code under which the case is proceeding has been added to the form.

NOTES OF ADVISORY COMMITTEE ON RULES—1995 AMENDMENT

The form is amended to provide for the debtor's address to appear in the caption in furtherance of the duty of the debtor to include this information on every notice given by the debtor. The Bankruptcy Reform Act of 1994 amended section 342 of the Code to add this requirement.

COMMITTEE NOTES ON RULES—2003 AMENDMENT

The form is amended to require disclosure of only the last four digits of the debtor's social security number to afford greater privacy to the individual debtor, whose bankruptcy case records may be available over the Internet.

COMMITTEE NOTES ON RULES—2005 AMENDMENT

The form is amended to require that the title of the case include all names used by the debtor within the last eight years in conformity with §727(a)(8) as amended by the Bankruptcy Abuse Prevention and Consumer Protection Act of 2005, Pub. L. No. 109-8, 119 Stat. 23

(April 20, 2005), extending from six years to eight years the period during which a debtor is barred from receiving successive discharges.

COMMITTEE NOTES ON RULES—2005-2007 AMENDMENT

[The 2005-2007 Committee Note incorporates the Committee Note previously published in 2005.]

The form is amended to require that the title of the case include all names used by the debtor within the last eight years in conformity with §727(a)(8) as amended by the Bankruptcy Abuse Prevention and Consumer Protection Act of 2005, Pub. L. No. 109-8, 119 Stat. 23 (April 20, 2005), extending from six years to eight years the period during which a debtor is barred from receiving successive discharges. In conformity with Rule 9037, the filer is directed to provide only the last four digits of any individual debtor's taxpayer-identification number.

Official Form 16B
12/94

FORM 16B. CAPTION (SHORT TITLE)

(May be used if 11 U.S.C. § 342(c) is not applicable)

United States Bankruptcy Court

________________ District Of ________________

In re ________________________,
Debtor

Case No. ________________

Chapter ____________

[Designation of Character of Paper]

(Added Aug. 1, 1991; amended Mar. 14, 1995.)

NOTES OF ADVISORY COMMITTEE ON RULES—1991

This form of caption is prescribed for general use in filing papers in a case under the Bankruptcy Code. Rule 9004(b) requires a caption to set forth the title of the case, and Rule 1005 specifies that the title must include all names used by the debtor within six years before the commencement of the case and the debtor's social security and tax identification numbers. This information is necessary in the petition, the notice of the meeting of creditors, the order of discharge, and the documents relating to the plan in a chapter 11 case. See Rule 2002(m) and Official Form 16A. In other notices, motions, applications, and papers filed in a case, however, a short title containing simply the names of the debtor or joint debtors may be used. Additional names, such as any under which the debtor has engaged in business, may be included in the short title as needed.

NOTES OF ADVISORY COMMITTEE ON RULES—1995 AMENDMENT

The title of this form is amended to specify that it can be used when section 342(c) of the Code, as added by the Bankruptcy Reform Act of 1994, is not applicable.

Official Form 16C
(12/03)

FORM 16C. CAPTION OF COMPLAINT IN ADVERSARY PROCEEDING FILED BY A DEBTOR

[Abrogated]

(Added Aug. 1, 1991; amended Mar. 14, 1995; Dec. 1, 2003.)

NOTES OF ADVISORY COMMITTEE ON RULES—1991

This form previously was numbered Official Form No. 34. A notation of the chapter of the Bankruptcy Code under which the case is proceeding has been added to the form. Rule 7010 refers to this form as providing the caption of a pleading in an adversary proceeding.

NOTES OF ADVISORY COMMITTEE ON RULES—1995 AMENDMENT

The form is amended to conform to the amendments made to section 342 of the Code by the Bankruptcy Reform Act of 1994.

COMMITTEE NOTES ON RULES—2003 AMENDMENT

The form is abrogated. An amendment to Official Form 16A directs that only the last four digits of the debtor's social security number should appear in a caption. Section 342(c) of the Bankruptcy Code continues to require the debtor to provide a creditor with the debtor's name, address, and taxpayer identification number on any notice the debtor is required to give to the creditor. An individual debtor can fulfill this requirement by including the debtor's social security account number on only the creditor's copy of any notice or summons the debtor may serve on the creditor.

Official Form 16D
(12/04)

Form 16D. CAPTION FOR USE IN ADVERSARY PROCEEDING

United States Bankruptcy Court

_______________ District Of _______________

In re ______________________, *Debtor*	)	Case No. ______________
	)	Chapter __________
______________________, *Plaintiff*	)	
______________________, *Defendant*	)	Adv. Proc. No. ______________

COMPLAINT [*or* other Designation]

[If in a Notice of Appeal (see Form 17) or other notice filed and served by a debtor, this caption must be altered to include the debtor's address and Employer's Tax Identification Number(s) or last four digits of Social Security Number(s) as in Form 16A.]

(Added Mar. 14, 1995; amended Dec. 1, 2004.)

NOTES OF ADVISORY COMMITTEE ON RULES—1995

This form of caption may be used in an adversary proceeding when section 342(c) of the Code, as added by the Bankruptcy Reform Act of 1994, is not applicable.

COMMITTEE NOTES ON RULES—2004 AMENDMENT

This form is amended to reflect the 2003 abrogation of Form 16C. As a complaint initiating an adversary proceeding serves as a notice to the defendant of the filing of an action, a debtor filing an adversary proceeding must follow the notice requirements of §342(c) of the Code. To protect individual privacy a debtor should use the defendant's copy of the summons to be served with the complaint to provide the information required by §342(c) to any creditor named as a defendant.

Official Form 17
(12/04)

United States Bankruptcy Court

______________ District Of ______________

In re ______________________,
Debtor

Case No. ____________________

Chapter ______________

[Caption as in Form 16A, 16B, or 16D, as appropriate]

NOTICE OF APPEAL

______________________________, the plaintiff [*or* defendant *or* other party] appeals under 28 U.S.C. § 158(a) or (b) from the judgment, order, or decree of the bankruptcy judge (describe) entered in this adversary proceeding [*or other proceeding, describe type*] on the __________ day of ______________, _____.
(month) (year)

The names of all parties to the judgment, order, or decree appealed from and the names, addresses, and telephone numbers of their respective attorneys are as follows:

Dated: ________________________

Signed: ____
Attorney for Appellant (or Appellant, if not represented by an Attorney)

Attorney Name: ________________________________

Address: ______________________________________

____

Telephone No: ______________________________________

If a Bankruptcy Appellate Panel Service is authorized to hear this appeal, each party has a right to have the appeal heard by the district court. The appellant may exercise this right only by filing a separate statement of election at the time of the filing of this notice of appeal. Any other party may elect, within the time provided in 28 U.S.C. § 158(c), to have the appeal heard by the district court.

If a child support creditor or its representative is the appellant, and if the child support creditor or its representative files the form specified in § 304(g) of the Bankruptcy Reform Act of 1994, no fee is required.

(Added Aug. 1, 1991; amended Mar. 14, 1995; Oct. 1, 1997; Dec. 1, 2002; Dec. 1, 2004.)

NOTES OF ADVISORY COMMITTEE ON RULES—1991 AMENDMENT

This form is derived from former Official Form No. 35. The form has been amended to indicate that a final order may be entered other than in an adversary proceeding.

NOTES OF ADVISORY COMMITTEE ON RULES—1995 AMENDMENT

The form is amended to reflect the amendments to 28 U.S.C. §158 concerning bankruptcy appellate panels made by the Bankruptcy Reform Act of 1994. Section 158(d) requires an appellant who elects to appeal to a district court rather than a bankruptcy appellate panel to do so "at the time of filing the appeal."

The 1994 Act also amended 28 U.S.C. §158(a) to permit immediate appeal of interlocutory orders increasing or reducing a chapter 11 debtor's exclusive period to file a plan under section 1121 of the Code. The form is amended to provide appropriate flexibility.

NOTES OF ADVISORY COMMITTEE ON RULES—1997 AMENDMENT

The form has been amended to conform to Rule 8001(a), which requires the notice to contain the names of all parties to the judgment, order, or decree appealed from and the names, addresses, and telephone numbers of their respective attorneys. A party filing a notice of appeal pro se should provide equivalent information.

COMMITTEE NOTES ON RULES—2002 AMENDMENT

The form is amended to give notice that no filing fee is required if a child support creditor or its representative is the appellant, and if the child support creditor or its representative files a form detailing the child support debt, its status, and other characteristics, as specified in §304(g) of the Bankruptcy Reform Act of 1994, Pub. L. No. 103-396[394], 108 Stat. 4106 (Oct. 22, 1994).

COMMITTEE NOTES ON RULES—2004 AMENDMENT

The form is amended to reflect the 2003 abrogation of Form 16C.

B18 (Official Form 18) (12/07)

United States Bankruptcy Court

______________ District Of ______________

In re ______________________________________,)
[Set forth here all names including married, maiden, and trade names used by debtor within last 8 years.])
Debtor) Case No. ______________

Address ______________________________)

______________________________) Chapter 7

Last four digits of Social-Security or other Individual Taxpayer-Identification No(s)(if any).: ______________________)

Employer Tax-Identification No(s).(EIN) [if any]: ______________)

DISCHARGE OF DEBTOR

It appearing that the debtor is entitled to a discharge, **IT IS ORDERED:** The debtor is granted a discharge under section 727 of title 11, United States Code, (the Bankruptcy Code).

Dated: ____________________

BY THE COURT

____

United States Bankruptcy Judge

SEE THE BACK OF THIS ORDER FOR IMPORTANT INFORMATION.

B18 (Official Form 18) (12/07) - Cont.

EXPLANATION OF BANKRUPTCY DISCHARGE
IN A CHAPTER 7 CASE

This court order grants a discharge to the person named as the debtor. It is not a dismissal of the case and it does not determine how much money, if any, the trustee will pay to creditors.

Collection of Discharged Debts Prohibited

The discharge prohibits any attempt to collect from the debtor a debt that has been discharged. For example, a creditor is not permitted to contact a debtor by mail, phone, or otherwise, to file or continue a lawsuit, to attach wages or other property, or to take any other action to collect a discharged debt from the debtor. *[In a case involving community property:* There are also special rules that protect certain community property owned by the debtor's spouse, even if that spouse did not file a bankruptcy case.] A creditor who violates this order can be required to pay damages and attorney's fees to the debtor.

However, a creditor may have the right to enforce a valid lien, such as a mortgage or security interest, against the debtor's property after the bankruptcy, if that lien was not avoided or eliminated in the bankruptcy case. Also, a debtor may voluntarily pay any debt that has been discharged.

Debts that are Discharged

The chapter 7 discharge order eliminates a debtor's legal obligation to pay a debt that is discharged. Most, but not all, types of debts are discharged if the debt existed on the date the bankruptcy case was filed. (If this case was begun under a different chapter of the Bankruptcy Code and converted to chapter 7, the discharge applies to debts owed when the bankruptcy case was converted.)

Debts that are Not Discharged.

Some of the common types of debts which are not discharged in a chapter 7 bankruptcy case are:

a. Debts for most taxes;

b. Debts incurred to pay nondischargeable taxes;

c. Debts that are domestic support obligations;

d. Debts for most student loans;

e. Debts for most fines, penalties, forfeitures, or criminal restitution obligations;

f. Debts for personal injuries or death caused by the debtor's operation of a motor vehicle, vessel, or aircraft while intoxicated;

g. Some debts which were not properly listed by the debtor;

h. Debts that the bankruptcy court specifically has decided or will decide in this bankruptcy case are not discharged;

i. Debts for which the debtor has given up the discharge protections by signing a reaffirmation agreement in compliance with the Bankruptcy Code requirements for reaffirmation of debts; and

j. Debts owed to certain pension, profit sharing, stock bonus, other retirement plans, or to the Thrift Savings Plan for federal employees for certain types of loans from these plans.

This information is only a general summary of the bankruptcy discharge. There are exceptions to these general rules. Because the law is complicated, you may want to consult an attorney to determine the exact effect of the discharge in this case.

(Added Aug. 1, 1991; amended Mar. 14, 1995; Oct. 1, 1997; Oct. 17, 2005; Dec. 1, 2007.)

NOTES OF ADVISORY COMMITTEE ON RULES—1991

This form previously was numbered Official Form No. 27. The form has been revised to accommodate cases commenced by the filing of either a voluntary or an involuntary petition.

NOTES OF ADVISORY COMMITTEE ON RULES—1995 AMENDMENT

The form is amended to include debts described in section 523(a)(15) of the Code, which was added by the Bankruptcy Reform Act of 1994, in the list of debts discharged unless determined by the court to be nondischargeable.

NOTES OF ADVISORY COMMITTEE ON RULES—1997 AMENDMENT

The discharge order has been simplified by deleting paragraphs which had detailed some, but not all, of the effects of the discharge. These paragraphs have been replaced with a plain English explanation of the discharge. This explanation is to be printed on the reverse of the order, to increase understanding of the bankruptcy discharge among creditors and debtors. The bracketed sentence in the second paragraph should be included when the case involves community property.

COMMITTEE NOTES ON RULES—2005 AMENDMENT

The form is amended to require that the title of the case include all names used by the debtor within the eight years prior to the filing of the petition in the case in conformity with §727(a)(8) as amended by the Bankruptcy Abuse Prevention and Consumer Protection Act of 2005, Pub. L. No. 109-8, 119 Stat. 23 (April 20, 2005), extending from six years to eight years the period during which a debtor is barred from receiving successive discharges. The explanation part of the form is amended to include additional types of debts that are not discharged under §523(a) as amended in 2005 and to revise certain terminology in conformity with provisions of the 2005 Act.

COMMITTEE NOTES ON RULES—2005-2007 AMENDMENT

[The 2005-2007 Committee Note incorporates the Committee Note previously published in 2005.]

The form is amended to require that the title of the case include all names used by the debtor within the eight years prior to the filing of the petition in the case in conformity with §727(a)(8) as amended by the Bankruptcy Abuse Prevention and Consumer Protection Act of 2005, Pub. L. No. 109-8, 119 Stat. 23 (April 20, 2005), extending from six years to eight years the period during which a debtor is barred from receiving successive discharges. The explanation part of the form is amended to include additional types of debts that are not discharged under §523(a), as amended in 2005, and to revise certain terminology in conformity with provisions of the 2005 Act. In conformity with Rule 9037 and Official Form 16A, the caption also is amended to provide only the last four digits of any individual debtor's taxpayer-identification number.

B19 (Official Form 19) (12/07)

United States Bankruptcy Court

In re ______________________________, Debtor

Case No. ________________

Chapter ____________

DECLARATION AND SIGNATURE OF NON-ATTORNEY BANKRUPTCY PETITION PREPARER (*See* 11 U.S.C. § 110)

I declare under penalty of perjury that: (1) I am a bankruptcy petition preparer as defined in 11 U.S.C. § 110; (2) I prepared the accompanying document(s) listed below for compensation and have provided the debtor with a copy of the document(s) and the attached notice as required by 11 U.S.C. §§ 110(b), 110(h), and 342(b); and (3) if rules or guidelines have been promulgated pursuant to 11 U.S.C. § 110(h) setting a maximum fee for services chargeable by bankruptcy petition preparers, I have given the debtor notice of the maximum amount before preparing any document for filing for a debtor or accepting any fee from the debtor, as required by that section.

Accompanying documents:

____

____

____

____

____

Printed or Typed Name and Title, if any, of Bankruptcy Petition Preparer:

____

Social-Security No. of Bankruptcy Petition Preparer (Required by 11 U.S.C. § 110):

____

If the bankruptcy petition preparer is not an individual, state the name, title (if any), address, and social-security number of the officer, principal, responsible person, or partner who signs this document.

____

____

Address

X_________________________________ ____________________

Signature of Bankruptcy Petition Preparer Date

Names and social-security numbers of all other individuals who prepared or assisted in preparing this document, unless the bankruptcy petition preparer is not an individual:

If more than one person prepared this document, attach additional signed sheets conforming to the appropriate Official Form for each person.

A bankruptcy petition preparer's failure to comply with the provisions of title 11 and the Federal Rules of Bankruptcy Procedure may result in fines or imprisonment or both. 11 U.S.C. § 110; 18 U.S.C. § 156.

B19 (Official Form 19) (12/07) - Cont. 2

NOTICE TO DEBTOR BY NON-ATTORNEY BANKRUPTCY PETITION PREPARER

[Must be filed with any document(s) prepared by a bankruptcy petition preparer.]

I am a bankruptcy petition preparer. I am not an attorney and may not practice law or give legal advice. Before preparing any document for filing as defined in § 110(a)(2) of the Bankruptcy Code or accepting any fees, I am required by law to provide you with this notice concerning bankruptcy petition preparers. Under the law, § 110 of the Bankruptcy Code (11 U.S.C. § 110), I am forbidden to offer you any legal advice, including advice about any of the following:

- whether to file a petition under the Bankruptcy Code (11 U.S.C. § 101 et seq.);
- whether commencing a case under chapter 7, 11, 12, or 13 is appropriate;
- whether your debts will be eliminated or discharged in a case under the Bankruptcy Code;
- whether you will be able to retain your home, car, or other property after commencing a case under the Bankruptcy Code;
- the tax consequences of a case brought under the Bankruptcy Code;
- the dischargeability of tax claims;
- whether you may or should promise to repay debts to a creditor or enter into a reaffirmation agreement with a creditor to reaffirm a debt;
- how to characterize the nature of your interests in property or your debts; or
- bankruptcy procedures and rights.

[The notice may provide additional examples of legal advice that a bankruptcy petition preparer is not authorized to give.]

In addition, under 11 U.S.C. § 110(h), the Supreme Court or the Judicial Conference of the United States may promulgate rules or guidelines setting a maximum allowable fee chargeable by a bankruptcy petition preparer. As required by law, I have notified you of this maximum allowable fee, if any, before preparing any document for filing or accepting any fee from you.

______________________________ ______________________________

Signature of Debtor Date Joint Debtor (if any) Date

[In a joint case, both spouses must sign.]

(Added Dec. 1, 2007.)

COMMITTEE NOTES ON RULES—2005–2007

[The 2005–2007 Committee Note incorporates the Committee Notes to Forms 19A and 19B previously published in 2005.]

This form is new. It is derived from form 19B and replaces forms 19A and 19B (which forms are abrogated). The form contains the notice a bankruptcy petition preparer is required to give to a debtor under §110 of the Code as amended by the Bankruptcy Abuse Prevention and Consumer Protection Act of 2005, Pub. L. No. 109-8, 119 Stat. 23 (April 20, 2005), and the bankruptcy petition preparer's signed declaration (also required by §110 of the Code) that the notice was given to the debtor.

The notice states, in language mandated in the 2005 Act, that the bankruptcy petition preparer is not an attorney and must not give legal advice. The notice also includes examples of advice a bankruptcy petition preparer may not give that are taken from §110(e)(2) of the Code.

Although space is provided in the declaration to list multiple documents prepared for a single filing, a new form 19 must be completed and accompany subsequent filings. For example, one form 19 listing all forms prepared by the bankruptcy petition preparer would be filed with the debtor's petition package. Another form 19 would be required if the debtor files amended schedules later in the case that were prepared by the bankruptcy petition preparer.

The form must be signed by the debtor and the bankruptcy petition preparer where indicated, and must be filed with each document for filing prepared by the bankruptcy petition preparer.

[Form 19A. Abrogated Dec. 1, 2007]

(Added Mar. 14, 1995; amended Dec. 1, 2003; Oct. 17, 2005.)

NOTES OF ADVISORY COMMITTEE ON RULES—1995

This form is new. The Bankruptcy Reform Act of 1994 requires a "bankruptcy petition preparer," as defined in 11 U.S.C. §110, to sign any "document for filing" that the bankruptcy petition preparer prepares for compensation on behalf of a debtor, to disclose on the document certain information, and to provide the debtor with a copy of the document. This form or adaptations of this form have been incorporated into the official forms of the voluntary petition, the schedules, the statement of financial affairs, and other official forms that typically would be prepared for a debtor by a bankruptcy petition preparer. This form is to be used in connection with any other document that a bankruptcy petition preparer prepares for filing by a debtor in a bankruptcy case.

COMMITTEE NOTES ON RULES—2003 AMENDMENT

Pursuant to §110(c) of the Bankruptcy Code, the certification by a non-attorney bankruptcy petition preparer requires a petition preparer to provide the full social security number of the individual who actually prepares the document.

COMMITTEE NOTES ON RULES—2005 AMENDMENT

The certification by a non-attorney bankruptcy petition preparer in this form is renamed a "declaration" and is amended to include material mandated by amendments to §110 of the Code in the Bankruptcy Abuse Prevention and Consumer Protection Act of 2005, Pub. L. No. 109–8, 119 Stat. 23 (April 20, 2005).

[Form 19B. Abrogated Dec. 1, 2007]

(Added Oct. 17, 2005.)

COMMITTEE NOTES ON RULES—2005

This form is new. It contains the notice a non-attorney bankruptcy petition preparer is required to give to a debtor under §110 of the Code as amended by the Bankruptcy Abuse Prevention and Consumer Protection Act of 2005, Pub. L. No. 109–8, 119 Stat. 23 (April 20, 2005). The notice states, in language mandated in the 2005 Act, that the bankruptcy petition preparer is not an attorney and must not give legal advice. The form includes examples of advice a bankruptcy petition preparer may not give that are take [sic] from §110(e)(2), which also was added to the Code in 2005. The notice must be signed by the debtor and by the bankruptcy petition preparer and filed with any document for filing prepared by the bankruptcy petition preparer.

Official Form 20A
(12/03)

United States Bankruptcy Court

_______________ District Of _______________

In re ________________________________, *Set forth here all names including married, maiden, and trade names used by debtor within last 6 years.]* Debtor	)	Case No. ____________
Address ______________________________ ______________________________	)	Chapter ________
Employer's Tax Identification (EIN) No(s). *[if any]:* ________ ______________________________	)	
Last four digits of Social Security No(s).: ____________	)	

NOTICE OF [MOTION TO] [OBJECTION TO]

_____________ has filed papers with the court to [relief sought in motion or objection].

<u>Your rights may be affected.</u> You should read these papers carefully and discuss them with your attorney, if you have one in this bankruptcy case. (If you do not have an attorney, you may wish to consult one.)

If you do not want the court to [relief sought in motion or objection], or if you want the court to consider your views on the [motion] [objection], then on or before <u>(date)</u>, you or your attorney must:

[File with the court a written request for a hearing {*or, if the court requires a written response*, an answer, explaining your position} at:

{address of the bankruptcy clerk's office}

If you mail your {request}{response} to the court for filing, you must mail it early enough so the court will **receive** it on or before the date stated above.

You must also mail a copy to:

{movant's attorney's name and address}

{names and addresses of others to be served}]

[Attend the hearing scheduled to be held on <u>(date)</u>, <u>(year)</u>, at ____a.m./p.m. in Courtroom ____, United States Bankruptcy Court, {address}.]

[Other steps required to oppose a motion or objection under local rule or court order.]

If you or your attorney do not take these steps, the court may decide that you do not oppose the relief sought in the motion or objection and may enter an order granting that relief.

Date: ____________________

Signature: ____________________
Name:
Address:

(Added Oct. 1, 1997.)

NOTES OF ADVISORY COMMITTEE ON RULES—1997

These forms [20A and 20B] are new. They are intended to provide uniform, plain English explanations to parties regarding what they must do to respond in certain contested matters which occur frequently in bankruptcy cases. Such explanations have been given better in some courts than in others. The forms are intended to make bankruptcy proceedings more fair, equitable, and efficient, by aiding parties, who sometimes do not have counsel, in understanding the applicable rules. It is hoped that use of these forms also will decrease the number of inquiries to bankruptcy clerks' offices.

These notices will be sent by the movant unless local rules provide for some other entity to give notice.

These forms are not intended to dictate the specific procedures to be used by different bankruptcy courts. The forms contain optional language that can be used or adapted, depending on local procedures. Similarly, the signature line will be adapted to identify the actual sender of the notice in each circumstance. All adaptations of the form should carry out the intent to give notice of applicable procedures in easily understood language.

Official Form 20B
(12/03)

United States Bankruptcy Court

______________ District Of ______________

In re ______________________________, *Set forth here all names including married, maiden, and trade names used by debtor within last 6 years.]* Debtor	)	Case No. ____________
Address ______________________________ ______________________________	)	Chapter ________
Employer's Tax Identification (EIN) No(s). *[if any]:* ________ ______________________________	)	
Last four digits of Social Security No(s).: __________	)	

NOTICE OF OBJECTION TO CLAIM

______________ has filed an objection to your claim in this bankruptcy case.

Your claim may be reduced, modified, or eliminated. You should read these papers carefully and discuss them with your attorney, if you have one.

If you do not want the court to eliminate or change your claim, then on or before __(date)__, you or your lawyer must:

{If required by local rule or court order.}

[File with the court a written response to the objection, explaining your position, at:

{address of the bankruptcy clerk's office}

If you mail your response to the court for filing, you must mail it early enough so that the court will **receive** it on or before the date stated above.

You must also mail a copy to:

{objector's attorney's name and address}

{names and addresses of others to be served}]

Attend the hearing on the objection, scheduled to be held on (date), (year) , at _____a.m./p.m. in Courtroom ____, United States Bankruptcy Court, {address}

If you or your attorney do not take these steps, the court may decide that you do not oppose the objection to your claim.

Date: ______________

Signature: ______________________
Name:
Address:

(Added Oct. 1, 1997.)

NOTES OF ADVISORY COMMITTEE ON RULES—1997

These forms [20A and 20B] are new. They are intended to provide uniform, plain English explanations to parties regarding what they must do to respond in certain contested matters which occur frequently in bankruptcy cases. Such explanations have been given better in some courts than in others. The forms are intended to make bankruptcy proceedings more fair, equitable, and efficient, by aiding parties, who sometimes do not have counsel, in understanding the applicable rules. It is hoped that use of these forms also will decrease the number of inquiries to bankruptcy clerks' offices.

These notices will be sent by the movant unless local rules provide for some other entity to give notice.

These forms are not intended to dictate the specific procedures to be used by different bankruptcy courts. The forms contain optional language that can be used or adapted, depending on local procedures. Similarly, the signature line will be adapted to identify the actual sender of the notice in each circumstance. All adaptations of the form should carry out the intent to give notice of applicable procedures in easily understood language.

B 21 (Official Form 21) (12/07)

UNITED STATES BANKRUPTCY COURT

In re ______________________________,	)
[Set forth here all names including married, maiden,	)
and trade names used by debtor within last 8 years]	)
	)
Debtor	) Case No. ____________
Address	)
	) Chapter ____________
	)
Last four digits of Social-Security or Individual Taxpayer-	)
Identification (ITIN) No(s).,(if any):	)
	)
Employer Tax-Identification (EIN) No(s).(if any):	)
	)

STATEMENT OF SOCIAL-SECURITY NUMBER(S)
*(or other Individual Taxpayer-Identification Number(s) (ITIN(s)))**

1.Name of Debtor (Last, First, Middle):______________________________
(Check the appropriate box and, if applicable, provide the required information.)

☐ Debtor has a Social-Security Number and it is: ____________
(If more than one, state all.)

☐ Debtor does not have a Social-Security Number but has an Individual Taxpayer-Identification Number (ITIN), and it is: ____________
(If more than one, state all.)

☐ Debtor does not have either a Social-Security Number or an Individual Taxpayer-Identification Number (ITIN).

2.Name of Joint Debtor (Last, First, Middle):______________________________
(Check the appropriate box and, if applicable, provide the required information.)

☐ Joint Debtor has a Social-Security Number and it is: ____________
(If more than one, state all.)

☐ Joint Debtor does not have a Social-Security Number but has an Individual Taxpayer-Identification Number (ITIN) and it is: ____________
(If more than one, state all.)

☐ Joint Debtor does not have either a Social-Security Number or an Individual Taxpayer-Identification Number (ITIN).

I declare under penalty of perjury that the foregoing is true and correct.

X ____
Signature of Debtor Date

X ____
Signature of Joint Debtor Date

---

* *Joint debtors must provide information for both spouses.*

Penalty for making a false statement: Fine of up to $250,000 or up to 5 years imprisonment or both. 18 U.S.C. §§ 152 and 3571.

(Added Dec. 1, 2003; amended Dec. 1, 2007.)

COMMITTEE NOTES ON RULES—2003

The form implements Rule 1007(f), which requires a debtor to submit a statement under penalty of perjury setting out the debtor's Social Security number. The form is necessary because Rule 1005 provides that the caption of the petition includes only the final four digits of the debtor's Social Security number. The statement provides the information necessary for the clerk to include the debtor's full Social Security number on the notice of the meeting of creditors, as required under Rule 2002(a)(1). Creditors in a case, along with the trustee and United States trustee or bankruptcy administrator, will receive the full Social Security number on their copy of the notice of the meeting of creditors. The copy of that notice which goes into the court file will show only the last four digits of the number.

COMMITTEE NOTES ON RULES—2007 AMENDMENT

The form is amended to direct an individual debtor who does not have a social-security number but has another government-issued individual taxpayer-identification number to furnish that number to the court. In light of the new Rule 9037 which limits public disclosure to all but the last four digits of any individual taxpayer-identification number, the amendment to this form will ensure that the court and creditors can properly identify a debtor who does not have a social-security number.

B22A (Official Form 22A) (Chapter 7) (12/08)

In re ______________________
Debtor(s)

Case Number: ________________
(If known)

According to the information required to be entered on this statement (check one box as directed in Part I, III, or VI of this statement):

☐ **The presumption arises.**
☐ **The presumption does not arise.**
☐ **The presumption is temporarily inapplicable.**

CHAPTER 7 STATEMENT OF CURRENT MONTHLY INCOME AND MEANS-TEST CALCULATION

In addition to Schedules I and J, this statement must be completed by every individual chapter 7 debtor, whether or not filing jointly. Unless the exclusion in Line 1C applies, joint debtors may complete a single statement. If the exclusion in Line 1C applies, each joint filer must complete a separate statement.

	Part I. MILITARY AND NON-CONSUMER DEBTORS
1A	**Disabled Veterans.** If you are a disabled veteran described in the Declaration in this Part IA, (1) check the box at the beginning of the Declaration, (2) check the box for "The presumption does not arise" at the top of this statement, and (3) complete the verification in Part VIII. Do not complete any of the remaining parts of this statement. ☐ **Declaration of Disabled Veteran.** By checking this box, I declare under penalty of perjury that I am a disabled veteran (as defined in 38 U.S.C. § 3741(1)) whose indebtedness occurred primarily during a period in which I was on active duty (as defined in 10 U.S.C. § 101(d)(1)) or while I was performing a homeland defense activity (as defined in 32 U.S.C. §901(1)).
1B	**Non-consumer Debtors.** If your debts are not primarily consumer debts, check the box below and complete the verification in Part VIII. Do not complete any of the remaining parts of this statement. ☐ **Declaration of non-consumer debts.** By checking this box, I declare that my debts are not primarily consumer debts.
1C	**Reservists and National Guard Members; active duty or homeland defense activity.** Members of a reserve component of the Armed Forces and members of the National Guard who were called to active duty (as defined in 10 U.S.C. § 101(d)(1)) after September 11, 2001, for a period of at least 90 days, or who have performed homeland defense activity (as defined in 32 U.S.C. § 901(1)) for a period of at least 90 days, are excluded from all forms of means testing during the time of active duty or homeland defense activity and for 540 days thereafter (the "exclusion period"). If you qualify for this temporary exclusion, (1) check the appropriate boxes and complete any required information in the Declaration of Reservists and National Guard Members below, (2) check the box for "The presumption is temporarily inapplicable" at the top of this statement, and (3) complete the verification in Part VIII. **During your exclusion period you are not required to complete the balance of this form, but you must complete the form no later than 14 days after the date on which your exclusion period ends, unless the time for filing a motion raising the means test presumption expires in your case before your exclusion period ends.** ☐ **Declaration of Reservists and National Guard Members.** By checking this box and making the appropriate entries below, I declare that I am eligible for a temporary exclusion from means testing because, as a member of a reserve component of the Armed Forces or the National Guard a. ☐ I was called to active duty after September 11, 2001, for a period of at least 90 days and ☐ I remain on active duty /or/ ☐ I was released from active duty on ______________, which is less than 540 days before this bankruptcy case was filed; OR b. ☐ I am performing homeland defense activity for a period of at least 90 days /or/ ☐ I performed homeland defense activity for a period of at least 90 days, terminating on ______________, which is less than 540 days before this bankruptcy case was filed.

B22A (Official Form 22A) (Chapter 7) (12/08) 2

Part II. CALCULATION OF MONTHLY INCOME FOR § 707(b)(7) EXCLUSION

2	**Marital/filing status.** Check the box that applies and complete the balance of this part of this statement as directed. a. ☐ Unmarried. **Complete only Column A ("Debtor's Income") for Lines 3-11.** b. ☐ Married, not filing jointly, with declaration of separate households. By checking this box, debtor declares under penalty of perjury: "My spouse and I are legally separated under applicable non-bankruptcy law or my spouse and I are living apart other than for the purpose of evading the requirements of § 707(b)(2)(A) of the Bankruptcy Code." **Complete only Column A ("Debtor's Income") for Lines 3-11.** c. ☐ Married, not filing jointly, without the declaration of separate households set out in Line 2.b above. **Complete both Column A ("Debtor's Income") and Column B ("Spouse's Income") for Lines 3-11.** d. ☐ Married, filing jointly. **Complete both Column A ("Debtor's Income") and Column B ("Spouse's Income") for Lines 3-11.**		
	All figures must reflect average monthly income received from all sources, derived during the six calendar months prior to filing the bankruptcy case, ending on the last day of the month before the filing. If the amount of monthly income varied during the six months, you must divide the six-month total by six, and enter the result on the appropriate line.	**Column A Debtor's Income**	**Column B Spouse's Income**
3	**Gross wages, salary, tips, bonuses, overtime, commissions.**	$	$
4	**Income from the operation of a business, profession or farm.** Subtract Line b from Line a and enter the difference in the appropriate column(s) of Line 4. If you operate more than one business, profession or farm, enter aggregate numbers and provide details on an attachment. Do not enter a number less than zero. **Do not include any part of the business expenses entered on Line b as a deduction in Part V.** a. Gross receipts — $ b. Ordinary and necessary business expenses — $ c. Business income — Subtract Line b from Line a	$	$
5	**Rent and other real property income.** Subtract Line b from Line a and enter the difference in the appropriate column(s) of Line 5. Do not enter a number less than zero. **Do not include any part of the operating expenses entered on Line b as a deduction in Part V.** a. Gross receipts — $ b. Ordinary and necessary operating expenses — $ c. Rent and other real property income — Subtract Line b from Line a	$	$
6	**Interest, dividends and royalties.**	$	$
7	**Pension and retirement income.**	$	$
8	**Any amounts paid by another person or entity, on a regular basis, for the household expenses of the debtor or the debtor's dependents, including child support paid for that purpose.** Do not include alimony or separate maintenance payments or amounts paid by your spouse if Column B is completed.	$	$
9	**Unemployment compensation.** Enter the amount in the appropriate column(s) of Line 9. However, if you contend that unemployment compensation received by you or your spouse was a benefit under the Social Security Act, do not list the amount of such compensation in Column A or B, but instead state the amount in the space below: Unemployment compensation claimed to be a benefit under the Social Security Act — Debtor $ ________ — Spouse $ ________	$	$

10	**Income from all other sources.** Specify source and amount. If necessary, list additional sources on a separate page. **Do not include alimony or separate maintenance payments paid by your spouse if Column B is completed, but include all other payments of alimony or separate maintenance.** Do not include any benefits received under the Social Security Act or payments received as a victim of a war crime, crime against humanity, or as a victim of international or domestic terrorism. a. ____ $ b. ____ $ Total and enter on Line 10	$	$
11	**Subtotal of Current Monthly Income for § 707(b)(7).** Add Lines 3 thru 10 in Column A, and, if Column B is completed, add Lines 3 through 10 in Column B. Enter the total(s).	$	$
12	**Total Current Monthly Income for § 707(b)(7).** If Column B has been completed, add Line 11, Column A to Line 11, Column B, and enter the total. If Column B has not been completed, enter the amount from Line 11, Column A.	$	

Part III. APPLICATION OF § 707(b)(7) EXCLUSION

13	**Annualized Current Monthly Income for § 707(b)(7).** Multiply the amount from Line 12 by the number 12 and enter the result.	$
14	**Applicable median family income.** Enter the median family income for the applicable state and household size. (This information is available by family size at www.usdoj.gov/ust/ or from the clerk of the bankruptcy court.) a. Enter debtor's state of residence: ______ b. Enter debtor's household size: ______	$
15	**Application of Section 707(b)(7).** Check the applicable box and proceed as directed. ☐ **The amount on Line 13 is less than or equal to the amount on Line 14.** Check the box for "The presumption does not arise" at the top of page 1 of this statement, and complete Part VIII; do not complete Parts IV, V, VI or VII. ☐ **The amount on Line 13 is more than the amount on Line 14.** Complete the remaining parts of this statement.	

Complete Parts IV, V, VI, and VII of this statement only if required. (See Line 15.)

Part IV. CALCULATION OF CURRENT MONTHLY INCOME FOR § 707(b)(2)

16	**Enter the amount from Line 12.**	$
17	**Marital adjustment.** If you checked the box at Line 2.c, enter on Line 17 the total of any income listed in Line 11, Column B that was NOT paid on a regular basis for the household expenses of the debtor or the debtor's dependents. Specify in the lines below the basis for excluding the Column B income (such as payment of the spouse's tax liability or the spouse's support of persons other than the debtor or the debtor's dependents) and the amount of income devoted to each purpose. If necessary, list additional adjustments on a separate page. If you did not check box at Line 2.c, enter zero. a. ____ $ b. ____ $ c. ____ $ Total and enter on Line 17.	$
18	**Current monthly income for § 707(b)(2).** Subtract Line 17 from Line 16 and enter the result.	$

Part V. CALCULATION OF DEDUCTIONS FROM INCOME

Subpart A: Deductions under Standards of the Internal Revenue Service (IRS)

19A	**National Standards: food, clothing and other items.** Enter in Line 19A the "Total" amount from IRS National Standards for Food, Clothing and Other Items for the applicable household size. (This information is available at www.usdoj.gov/ust/ or from the clerk of the bankruptcy court.)	$

19B	**National Standards: health care.** Enter in Line a1 below the amount from IRS National Standards for Out-of-Pocket Health Care for persons under 65 years of age, and in Line a2 the IRS National Standards for Out-of-Pocket Health Care for persons 65 years of age or older. (This information is available at www.usdoj.gov/ust/ or from the clerk of the bankruptcy court.) Enter in Line b1 the number of members of your household who are under 65 years of age, and enter in Line b2 the number of members of your household who are 65 years of age or older. (The total number of household members must be the same as the number stated in Line 14b.) Multiply Line a1 by Line b1 to obtain a total amount for household members under 65, and enter the result in Line c1. Multiply Line a2 by Line b2 to obtain a total amount for household members 65 and older, and enter the result in Line c2. Add Lines c1 and c2 to obtain a total health care amount, and enter the result in Line 19B. **Household members under 65 years of age** / **Household members 65 years of age or older** a1. Allowance per member ___ / a2. Allowance per member ___ b1. Number of members ___ / b2. Number of members ___ c1. Subtotal ___ / c2. Subtotal ___	$
20A	**Local Standards: housing and utilities; non-mortgage expenses.** Enter the amount of the IRS Housing and Utilities Standards; non-mortgage expenses for the applicable county and household size. (This information is available at www.usdoj.gov/ust/ or from the clerk of the bankruptcy court).	$
20B	**Local Standards: housing and utilities; mortgage/rent expense.** Enter, in Line a below, the amount of the IRS Housing and Utilities Standards; mortgage/rent expense for your county and household size (this information is available at www.usdoj.gov/ust/ or from the clerk of the bankruptcy court); enter on Line b the total of the Average Monthly Payments for any debts secured by your home, as stated in Line 42; subtract Line b from Line a and enter the result in Line 20B. **Do not enter an amount less than zero.** a. IRS Housing and Utilities Standards; mortgage/rental expense — $ b. Average Monthly Payment for any debts secured by your home, if any, as stated in Line 42 — $ c. Net mortgage/rental expense — Subtract Line b from Line a.	$
21	**Local Standards: housing and utilities; adjustment.** If you contend that the process set out in Lines 20A and 20B does not accurately compute the allowance to which you are entitled under the IRS Housing and Utilities Standards, enter any additional amount to which you contend you are entitled, and state the basis for your contention in the space below:	$
22A	**Local Standards: transportation; vehicle operation/public transportation expense.** You are entitled to an expense allowance in this category regardless of whether you pay the expenses of operating a vehicle and regardless of whether you use public transportation. Check the number of vehicles for which you pay the operating expenses or for which the operating expenses are included as a contribution to your household expenses in Line 8. ☐ 0 ☐ 1 ☐ 2 or more. If you checked 0, enter on Line 22A the "Public Transportation" amount from IRS Local Standards: Transportation. If you checked 1 or 2 or more, enter on Line 22A the "Operating Costs" amount from IRS Local Standards: Transportation for the applicable number of vehicles in the applicable Metropolitan Statistical Area or Census Region. (These amounts are available at www.usdoj.gov/ust/ or from the clerk of the bankruptcy court.)	$
22B	**Local Standards: transportation; additional public transportation expense.** If you pay the operating expenses for a vehicle and also use public transportation, and you contend that you are entitled to an additional deduction for your public transportation expenses, enter on Line 22B the "Public Transportation" amount from IRS Local Standards: Transportation. (This amount is available at www.usdoj.gov/ust/ or from the clerk of the bankruptcy court.)	$

23	**Local Standards: transportation ownership/lease expense; Vehicle 1.** Check the number of vehicles for which you claim an ownership/lease expense. (You may not claim an ownership/lease expense for more than two vehicles.) ☐ 1 ☐ 2 or more. Enter, in Line a below, the "Ownership Costs" for "One Car" from the IRS Local Standards: Transportation (available at www.usdoj.gov/ust/ or from the clerk of the bankruptcy court); enter in Line b the total of the Average Monthly Payments for any debts secured by Vehicle 1, as stated in Line 42; subtract Line b from Line a and enter the result in Line 23. **Do not enter an amount less than zero.** a. IRS Transportation Standards, Ownership Costs — $ b. Average Monthly Payment for any debts secured by Vehicle 1, as stated in Line 42 — $ c. Net ownership/lease expense for Vehicle 1 — Subtract Line b from Line a.	$
24	**Local Standards: transportation ownership/lease expense; Vehicle 2.** Complete this Line only if you checked the "2 or more" Box in Line 23. Enter, in Line a below, the "Ownership Costs" for "One Car" from the IRS Local Standards: Transportation (available at www.usdoj.gov/ust/ or from the clerk of the bankruptcy court); enter in Line b the total of the Average Monthly Payments for any debts secured by Vehicle 2, as stated in Line 42; subtract Line b from Line a and enter the result in Line 24. **Do not enter an amount less than zero.** a. IRS Transportation Standards, Ownership Costs — $ b. Average Monthly Payment for any debts secured by Vehicle 2, as stated in Line 42 — $ c. Net ownership/lease expense for Vehicle 2 — Subtract Line b from Line a.	$
25	**Other Necessary Expenses: taxes.** Enter the total average monthly expense that you actually incur for all federal, state and local taxes, other than real estate and sales taxes, such as income taxes, self-employment taxes, social-security taxes, and Medicare taxes. **Do not include real estate or sales taxes.**	$
26	**Other Necessary Expenses: involuntary deductions for employment.** Enter the total average monthly payroll deductions that are required for your employment, such as retirement contributions, union dues, and uniform costs. **Do not include discretionary amounts, such as voluntary 401(k) contributions.**	$
27	**Other Necessary Expenses: life insurance.** Enter total average monthly premiums that you actually pay for term life insurance for yourself. **Do not include premiums for insurance on your dependents, for whole life or for any other form of insurance.**	$
28	**Other Necessary Expenses: court-ordered payments.** Enter the total monthly amount that you are required to pay pursuant to the order of a court or administrative agency, such as spousal or child support payments. **Do not include payments on past due obligations included in Line 44.**	$
29	**Other Necessary Expenses: education for employment or for a physically or mentally challenged child.** Enter the total average monthly amount that you actually expend for education that is a condition of employment and for education that is required for a physically or mentally challenged dependent child for whom no public education providing similar services is available.	$
30	**Other Necessary Expenses: childcare.** Enter the total average monthly amount that you actually expend on childcare—such as baby-sitting, day care, nursery and preschool. **Do not include other educational payments.**	$
31	**Other Necessary Expenses: health care.** Enter the total average monthly amount that you actually expend on health care that is required for the health and welfare of yourself or your dependents, that is not reimbursed by insurance or paid by a health savings account, and that is in excess of the amount entered in Line 19B. **Do not include payments for health insurance or health savings accounts listed in Line 34.**	$
32	**Other Necessary Expenses: telecommunication services.** Enter the total average monthly amount that you actually pay for telecommunication services other than your basic home telephone and cell phone service—such as pagers, call waiting, caller id, special long distance, or internet service—to the extent necessary for your health and welfare or that of your dependents. **Do not include any amount previously deducted.**	$
33	**Total Expenses Allowed under IRS Standards.** Enter the total of Lines 19 through 32.	$

B22A (Official Form 22A) (Chapter 7) (12/08) 6

	Subpart B: Additional Living Expense Deductions **Note: Do not include any expenses that you have listed in Lines 19-32**	
34	**Health Insurance, Disability Insurance, and Health Savings Account Expenses.** List the monthly expenses in the categories set out in lines a-c below that are reasonably necessary for yourself, your spouse, or your dependents. a. Health Insurance $ b. Disability Insurance $ c. Health Savings Account $ Total and enter on Line 34	$
	If you do not actually expend this total amount, state your actual total average monthly expenditures in the space below: $ ________	
35	**Continued contributions to the care of household or family members.** Enter the total average actual monthly expenses that you will continue to pay for the reasonable and necessary care and support of an elderly, chronically ill, or disabled member of your household or member of your immediate family who is unable to pay for such expenses.	$
36	**Protection against family violence.** Enter the total average reasonably necessary monthly expenses that you actually incurred to maintain the safety of your family under the Family Violence Prevention and Services Act or other applicable federal law. The nature of these expenses is required to be kept confidential by the court.	$
37	**Home energy costs.** Enter the total average monthly amount, in excess of the allowance specified by IRS Local Standards for Housing and Utilities, that you actually expend for home energy costs. **You must provide your case trustee with documentation of your actual expenses, and you must demonstrate that the additional amount claimed is reasonable and necessary.**	$
38	**Education expenses for dependent children less than 18.** Enter the total average monthly expenses that you actually incur, not to exceed $137.50 per child, for attendance at a private or public elementary or secondary school by your dependent children less than 18 years of age. **You must provide your case trustee with documentation of your actual expenses, and you must explain why the amount claimed is reasonable and necessary and not already accounted for in the IRS Standards.**	$
39	**Additional food and clothing expense.** Enter the total average monthly amount by which your food and clothing expenses exceed the combined allowances for food and clothing (apparel and services) in the IRS National Standards, not to exceed 5% of those combined allowances. (This information is available at www.usdoj.gov/ust/ or from the clerk of the bankruptcy court.) **You must demonstrate that the additional amount claimed is reasonable and necessary.**	$
40	**Continued charitable contributions.** Enter the amount that you will continue to contribute in the form of cash or financial instruments to a charitable organization as defined in 26 U.S.C. § 170(c)(1)-(2).	$
41	**Total Additional Expense Deductions under § 707(b).** Enter the total of Lines 34 through 40	$

Subpart C: Deductions for Debt Payment

42 **Future payments on secured claims.** For each of your debts that is secured by an interest in property that you own, list the name of the creditor, identify the property securing the debt, state the Average Monthly Payment, and check whether the payment includes taxes or insurance. The Average Monthly Payment is the total of all amounts scheduled as contractually due to each Secured Creditor in the 60 months following the filing of the bankruptcy case, divided by 60. If necessary, list additional entries on a separate page. Enter the total of the Average Monthly Payments on Line 42.

	Name of Creditor	Property Securing the Debt	Average Monthly Payment	Does payment include taxes or insurance?
a.			$	☐ yes ☐ no
b.			$	☐ yes ☐ no
c.			$	☐ yes ☐ no
			Total: Add Lines a, b and c.	

$

43 **Other payments on secured claims.** If any of debts listed in Line 42 are secured by your primary residence, a motor vehicle, or other property necessary for your support or the support of your dependents, you may include in your deduction 1/60th of any amount (the "cure amount") that you must pay the creditor in addition to the payments listed in Line 42, in order to maintain possession of the property. The cure amount would include any sums in default that must be paid in order to avoid repossession or foreclosure. List and total any such amounts in the following chart. If necessary, list additional entries on a separate page.

	Name of Creditor	Property Securing the Debt	1/60th of the Cure Amount
a.			$
b.			$
c.			$
			Total: Add Lines a, b and c

$

44 **Payments on prepetition priority claims.** Enter the total amount, divided by 60, of all priority claims, such as priority tax, child support and alimony claims, for which you were liable at the time of your bankruptcy filing. **Do not include current obligations, such as those set out in Line 28.** $

45 **Chapter 13 administrative expenses.** If you are eligible to file a case under chapter 13, complete the following chart, multiply the amount in line a by the amount in line b, and enter the resulting administrative expense.

a.	Projected average monthly chapter 13 plan payment.	$
b.	Current multiplier for your district as determined under schedules issued by the Executive Office for United States Trustees. (This information is available at www.usdoj.gov/ust/ or from the clerk of the bankruptcy court.)	x
c.	Average monthly administrative expense of chapter 13 case	Total: Multiply Lines a and b

$

46 **Total Deductions for Debt Payment.** Enter the total of Lines 42 through 45. $

Subpart D: Total Deductions from Income

47 **Total of all deductions allowed under § 707(b)(2).** Enter the total of Lines 33, 41, and 46. $

B22A (Official Form 22A) (Chapter 7) (12/08) 8

	Part VI. DETERMINATION OF § 707(b)(2) PRESUMPTION	
48	**Enter the amount from Line 18 (Current monthly income for § 707(b)(2))**	$
49	**Enter the amount from Line 47 (Total of all deductions allowed under § 707(b)(2))**	$
50	**Monthly disposable income under § 707(b)(2).** Subtract Line 49 from Line 48 and enter the result	$
51	**60-month disposable income under § 707(b)(2).** Multiply the amount in Line 50 by the number 60 and enter the result.	$
52	**Initial presumption determination.** Check the applicable box and proceed as directed. ☐ **The amount on Line 51 is less than $6,575** Check the box for "The presumption does not arise" at the top of page 1 of this statement, and complete the verification in Part VIII. Do not complete the remainder of Part VI. ☐ **The amount set forth on Line 51 is more than $10,950.** Check the box for "The presumption arises" at the top of page 1 of this statement, and complete the verification in Part VIII. You may also complete Part VII. Do not complete the remainder of Part VI. ☐ **The amount on Line 51 is at least $6,575, but not more than $10,950.** Complete the remainder of Part VI (Lines 53 through 55).	
53	**Enter the amount of your total non-priority unsecured debt**	$
54	**Threshold debt payment amount.** Multiply the amount in Line 53 by the number 0.25 and enter the result.	$
55	**Secondary presumption determination.** Check the applicable box and proceed as directed. ☐ **The amount on Line 51 is less than the amount on Line 54.** Check the box for "The presumption does not arise" at the top of page 1 of this statement, and complete the verification in Part VIII. ☐ **The amount on Line 51 is equal to or greater than the amount on Line 54.** Check the box for "The presumption arises" at the top of page 1 of this statement, and complete the verification in Part VIII. You may also complete Part VII.	
	Part VII: ADDITIONAL EXPENSE CLAIMS	
56	**Other Expenses.** List and describe any monthly expenses, not otherwise stated in this form, that are required for the health and welfare of you and your family and that you contend should be an additional deduction from your current monthly income under § 707(b)(2)(A)(ii)(I). If necessary, list additional sources on a separate page. All figures should reflect your average monthly expense for each item. Total the expenses.	

	Expense Description	Monthly Amount
a.		$
b.		$
c.		$
	Total: Add Lines a, b and c	$

	Part VIII: VERIFICATION	
57	I declare under penalty of perjury that the information provided in this statement is true and correct. *(If this is a joint case, both debtors must sign.)* Date: ________________ Signature: ________________ *(Debtor)* Date: ________________ Signature: ________________ *(Joint Debtor, if any)*	

(Added Oct. 17, 2005; amended Oct. 1, 2006; Jan. 1, 2008; Dec. 19, 2008.)

COMMITTEE NOTES ON RULES—2005

A. Overview

Among the changes introduced by the Bankruptcy Abuse Prevention and Consumer Protection Act of 2005 [Pub. L. 109–8, Apr. 20, 2005, 119 Stat. 23] are interlocking provisions defining "current monthly income" and establishing a means test to determine whether relief under Chapter 7 should be presumed abusive. Current monthly income ("CMI") is defined in §101(10A) of the Code, and the means test is set out in §707(b)(2). These provisions have a variety of applications. In Chapter 7, if the debtor's CMI exceeds a defined level the debtor is subject to the means test, and §707(b)(2)(C) specifically requires debtors to file a statement of CMI and calculations to determine the applicability of the means test presumption. In Chapters 11 and 13, CMI provides the starting point for determining the disposable income that must be contributed to payment of unsecured creditors. Moreover, Chapter 13 debtors with CMI above defined levels are required by §1325(b)(3) to complete the means test in order to determine the amount of their monthly disposable income, and pursuant to §1325(b)(4), the level of CMI determines the "applicable commitment period" over which projected disposable income must be paid to unsecured creditors.

To provide for the reporting and calculation of CMI and for the completion of the means test where required, three separate official forms have been created—one for Chapter 7, one for Chapter 11, and one for Chapter 13. This note first describes the calculation of CMI that is common to all three of the forms, next describes the means test as set out in the Chapter 7 and 13 forms, and finally addresses particular issues that are unique to each of the separate forms.

B. Calculation of CMI

Although Chapters 7, 11, and 13 use CMI for different purposes, the basic computation is the same in each. As defined in §101(10A), CMI is the monthly average of certain income that the debtor (and in a joint case, the debtor's spouse) received in the six calendar months before the bankruptcy filing. The definition includes in this average (1) income from all sources, whether or not taxable, and (2) any amount paid by an entity other than the debtor (or the debtor's spouse in a joint case) on a regular basis for the household expenses of the debtor, the debtor's dependents, and (in a joint case) the debtor's spouse if not otherwise a dependent. At the same time, the definition excludes from the averaged income "benefits received under the Social Security Act" and certain payments to victims of terrorism, war crimes, and crimes against humanity.

Each of the forms provides for reporting income items constituting CMI. The items are reported in a set of entry lines—Part II of the Chapter 7 form and Part I of the forms for Chapter 11 and Chapter 13—that include separate columns for reporting income of the debtor and of the debtor's spouse. The first of these entry lines includes a set of instructions and check boxes indicating when the "debtor's spouse" column must be completed. The instructions also direct the required averaging of reported income.

The subsequent entry lines specify several common types of income and are followed by a "catch-all" line for other income. The specific entry lines address (a) gross wages; (b) business income; (c) rental income; (d) interest, dividends, and royalties; (e) pension and retirement income; (f) regular contributions to the debtor's household expenses; and (g) unemployment compensation. Gross wages (before taxes) are required to be entered. Consistent with usage in the Internal Revenue Manual and the American Community Survey of the Census Bureau, business and rental income is defined as gross receipts less ordinary and necessary expenses. Unemployment compensation is given special treatment. Because the federal government provides funding for state unemployment compensation under the Social Security Act, there may be a dispute about whether unemployment compensation is a "benefit received under the Social Security Act." The forms take no position on the merits of this argument, but give debtors the option of reporting unemployment compensation separately from the CMI calculation. This separate reporting allows parties in interest to determine the materiality of an exclusion of unemployment compensation and to challenge it. The forms provide for totaling the income lines.

C. The means test: deductions from current monthly income (CMI)

The means test operates by deducting from CMI defined allowances for living expenses and payment of secured and priority debt, leaving disposable income presumptively available to pay unsecured non-priority debt. These deductions from CMI under are set out in the Code at §707(b)(2)(A)(ii)-(iv). The forms for Chapter 7 and Chapter 13 have identical sections (Parts V and III, respectively) for calculating these deductions. The calculations are divided into subparts reflecting three different kinds of allowed deductions.

1. Deductions under IRS standards

Subpart A deals with deductions from CMI, set out in §707(b)(2)(A)(ii), for "the debtor's applicable monthly expense amounts specified under the National Standards and Local Standards, and the debtor's actual monthly expenses for the categories specified as Other Necessary Expenses issued by the Internal Revenue Service for the area in which the debtor resides." The forms provide entry lines for each of the specified expense deductions under the IRS standards, and instructions on the entry lines identify the website of the U.S. Trustee Program, where the relevant IRS allowances can be found. As with all of the deductions in §707(b)(2)(A)(ii), deductions under the IRS standards are subject to the proviso that they not include "any payments for debts."

The IRS National Standards provide a single allowance for food, clothing, household supplies, personal care, and miscellany, depending on income and household size. The forms contain an entry line for the applicable allowance.

The IRS Local Standards provide one set of deductions for housing and utilities and another set for transportation expenses, with different amounts for different areas of the country, depending on the size of the debtor's family and the number of the debtor's vehicles. Each of the amounts specified in the Local Standards are treated by the IRS as a cap on actual expenses, but because §707(b)(2)(A)(ii) provides for deductions in the "amounts specified under the . . . Local Standards," the forms treat these amounts as allowed deductions. The forms again direct debtors to the website of the U.S. Trustee Program to obtain the appropriate allowances.

The Local Standards for housing and utilities, as published by the IRS for its internal purposes, present single amounts covering all housing expenses; however, for bankruptcy purposes, the IRS has separated these amounts into a non-mortgage component and a mortgage/rent component. The non-mortgage component covers a variety of expenses involved in maintaining a residence, such as utilities, repairs and maintenance. The mortgage/rent component covers the cost of acquiring the residence. For homeowners with mortgages, the mortgage/rent component involves debt payment, since the cost of a mortgage is part of the allowance. Accordingly, the forms require debtors to deduct from the mortgage/rent component their average monthly mortgage payment (including required payments for taxes and insurance), up to the full amount of the IRS mortgage/rent component, and instruct debtors that this average monthly payment is the one reported on the separate line of the forms for deductions of secured debt under §707(b)(2)(a)(iii). The forms allow debtors to challenge the appropriateness of this method of computing the Local Standards allowance for housing and utilities and to claim any additional housing allowance to which they contend they are entitled, but the forms require specification of the basis for such a contention.

The IRS issues Local Standards for transportation in two components for its internal purposes as well as for bankruptcy: one component covers vehicle operation/public transportation expense and the other ownership/lease expense. The amount of the vehicle operation/public transportation allowance depends on the number of vehicles the debtor operates, with debtors who do not operate vehicles being given a public transportation allowance. The instruction for this line item makes it clear that every debtor is thus entitled to some transportation expense allowance. No debt payment is involved in this allowance. The ownership/lease component, on the other hand, may involve debt payment. Accordingly, the forms require debtors to reduce the allowance for ownership/lease expense by the average monthly loan payment amount (principal and interest), up to the full amount of the IRS ownership/lease expense amount. This average payment is as reported on the separate line of the forms for deductions of secured debt under §707(b)(2)(a)(iii).

The IRS does not set out specific dollar allowances for "Other Necessary Expenses." Rather, it specifies a number of categories for such expenses, and describes the nature of the expenses that may be deducted in each of these categories. Section 707(b)(2)(a)(ii) allows a deduction for the debtor's actual expenses in these specified categories, subject to its requirement that payment of debt not be included. Several of the IRS categories deal with debt repayment and so are not included in the forms. Several other categories deal with expense items that are more expansively addressed by specific statutory allowances. Subpart A sets out the remaining categories of "Other Necessary Expenses" in individual entry lines. Instructions in these entry lines reflect limitations imposed by the IRS and the need to avoid inclusion of items deducted elsewhere on the forms.

Subpart A concludes with a subtotal of the deductions allowed under the IRS standards.

2. Additional statutory expense deductions

In addition to the expense deductions allowed under the IRS standards, the means test makes provision—in subclauses (I), (II), (IV), and (V) of §707(b)(2)(A)(ii)—for six special expense deductions. Each of these additional expense items is set out on a separate entry line in Subpart B, introduced by an instruction that there should not be double counting of any expense already included in the IRS deductions. Contributions to tax-exempt charities provide another statutory expense deduction. Section 1325(b)(2)(A)(ii) expressly allows a deduction from CMI for such contributions (up to 15% of the debtor's gross income), and §707(b)(1) provides that in considering whether a Chapter 7 filing is an abuse, the court may not take into consideration "whether a debtor . . . continues to make [tax-exempt] charitable contributions." Accordingly, Subpart B also includes an entry line for charitable contributions. The subpart concludes with a subtotal of the additional statutory expense deductions.

3. Deductions for payment of debt

Subpart C of the forms deals with the means test's deductions from CMI for payment of secured and priority debt, as well as a deduction for administrative fees that would be incurred if the debtor paid debts through a Chapter 13 plan. In accord with §707(b)(2)(A)(iii), the deduction for secured debt is divided into two entry lines—one for payments that are contractually due during the 60 months following the bankruptcy filing, the other for amounts needed to retain necessary collateral securing debts in default. In each situation, the instructions for the entry lines require dividing the total payment amount by 60, as the statute directs. Priority debt, deductible pursuant to §707(b)(2)(A)(iv), is treated on a single entry line, also requiring division by 60. The defined deduction for the expenses of administering a Chapter 13 plan is allowed by §707(b)(2)(A)(ii)(III) only for debtors eligible for Chapter 13. The forms treat this deduction in an entry line requiring the eligible debtor to state the amount of the prospective Chapter 13 plan payment and multiply that payment amount by the percentage fee established for the debtor's district by the Executive Office for United States Trustees. The forms refer debtors to the website of the U.S. Trustee Program to obtain this percentage fee. The subpart concludes with a subtotal of debt payment deductions.

4. Total deductions

Finally, the forms direct that the subtotals from Subparts A, B, and C be added together to arrive at the total of allowed deductions from CMI under the means test.

5. Additional claimed deductions

The forms do not provide for means test deductions from CMI for expenses in categories that are not specifically identified as "Other Necessary Expenses" in the Internal Revenue Manual. However, debtors may wish to claim expenses that do not fall within the categories listed as "Other Necessary Expenses" in the forms. Part VII of the Chapter 7 form and Part VI of the Chapter 13 form provide for such expenses to be identified and totaled. Although expenses listed in these sections are not deducted from CMI for purposes of the means test calculation, the listing provides a basis for debtors to assert that these expenses should be deducted from CMI under §707(b)(2)(A)(ii)(I), and that the results of the forms' calculation, therefore, should be modified.

D. The chapter-specific forms

1. Chapter 7

The Chapter 7 form has several unique aspects. The form includes, in the upper right corner of the first page, a check box directing the debtor to state whether or not the calculations required by the form result in a presumption of abuse. The debtor is not bound by this statement and may argue, in response to a motion brought under §707(b)(1), that there should be no presumption despite the calculations required by the form. The check box is intended to give clerks of court a conspicuous indication of the cases for which they are required to provide notice of a presumption of abuse pursuant to §342(d).

Part I of the form implements the provision of §707(b)(2)(D) that excludes certain disabled veterans from all means testing, making it unnecessary to compute the CMI of such veterans. Debtors who declare under penalty of perjury that they are disabled veterans within the statutory definition are directed to verify their declaration in Part VII, to check the "no presumption" box at the beginning of the form, and to disregard the remaining parts of the form.

Part II of the form is the computation of CMI. Section 707(b)(7) eliminates standing to assert the means test's presumption of abuse if the debtor's annualized CMI does not exceed a defined median state income. For this purpose, the statute directs that CMI of the debtor's spouse be combined with the debtor's CMI even if the debtor's spouse is not a joint debtor, unless the debtor declares under penalty of perjury that the spouses are legally separated or living separately other than for purposes of evading the means test. Accordingly, the calculation of CMI in Part II directs a computation of the CMI of the debtor's spouse not only in joint cases, but also in cases of married debtors who do not make the specified declaration, and the CMI of both spouses in these cases is combined for purposes of determining standing under §707(b)(7).

Part III of the form provides for the comparison of the debtor's CMI to the applicable state median income for purposes of §707(b)(7). It then directs debtors whose income does not exceed the applicable median to verify the form, to check the "no presumption" box at the beginning of the form, and not to complete the remaining parts of the form. Debtors whose CMI does exceed the applicable state median are required to complete the remaining parts of the form.

Part IV of the form provides for an adjustment to the CMI of a married debtor, not filing jointly, whose spouse's CMI was combined with the debtor's for purposes of determining standing to assert the means test presumption. The means test itself does not charge a married debtor in a non-joint case with the income of the non-filing spouse, but rather only with contributions made by that spouse to the household expenses of the debtor or the debtor's dependents, as provided in the definition of CMI in §101(10A). Accordingly, Part IV calls for the combined CMI of Part II to be reduced by the amount of the non-filing spouse's income that was not contributed to the household expenses of the debtor or the debtor's dependents.

Part V of the form provides for a calculation of the means test's deductions from the debtor's CMI, as described above.

Part VI provides for a determination of whether the debtor's CMI, less the allowed deductions, gives rise to a presumption of abuse under §707(b)(2)(A). Depending on the outcome of this determination, the debtor is directed to check the appropriate box at the beginning of the form and to sign the verification in Part VIII. Part VII allows the debtor to claim additional deductions, as discussed above.

2. Chapter 11

The Chapter 11 form is the simplest of the three, since the means-test deductions of §707(b)(2) are not employed in determining the extent of an individual Chapter 11 debtor's disposable income. Section 1129(a)(15) requires payments of disposable income "as defined in section 1325(b)(2)," and that paragraph allows calculation of disposable income under judicially-determined standards, rather than pursuant to the means test deductions, specified for higher income Chapter 13 debtors by §1325(b)(3). However, §1325(b)(2) does require that CMI be used as the starting point in the judicial determination of disposable income, and so the Chapter 11 form requires this calculation (in Part I of the form), as described above, together with a verification (in Part II).

3. Chapter 13

Like the Chapter 7 form, the form for Chapter 13 debtors contains a number of special provisions. The upper right corner of the first page includes check boxes requiring the debtor to state whether, under the calculations required by the statement, the applicable commitment period under §1325(b)(4) is three years or five years and whether the means test deductions are required by §1325(b)(3) to be used in determining the debtor's disposable income. The check box is intended to inform standing trustees and other interested parties about these items, but does not prevent the debtor from arguing that the calculations required by the form do not accurately reflect the debtor's disposable income.

Part I of the form is a report of income to be used for determining CMI. Section 1325(b)(4) imposes a five-year applicable commitment period—rather than a three-year period—if the debtor's annualized CMI is not less than a defined median state income. For this purpose, as under §707(b)(4), the CMI of the debtor's spouse is required by the statute to be combined with the debtor's CMI, and there is no exception for spouses who are legally separated or living separately. Accordingly, the report of income in Part I directs a combined reporting of the income of both spouses in all cases of married debtors.

Part II of the form computes the applicable commitment period by annualizing the income calculated in Part I and comparing it to the applicable state median. The form allows debtors to contend that the income of a non-filing spouse should not be treated as CMI and permits debtors to claim a deduction for any income of a non-filing spouse to the extent that this income was not contributed to the household expenses of the debtor or the debtor's dependents. The debtor is directed to check the appropriate box at the beginning of the form, stating the applicable commitment period.

Part III of the form compares the debtor's CMI to the applicable state median, allowing a determination of whether the means-test deductions must be used, pursuant to §1325(b)(3), in calculating disposable income. For this purpose, since §1325(b)(3) does not provide for including the income of the debtor's spouse, the form directs a deduction of the income of a non-filing spouse that is not contributed to the household expenses of the debtor or the debtor's dependents. Again, the debtor is directed to check the appropriate box at the beginning of the form, indicating whether the means test deductions are applicable. If so, the debtor is directed to complete the remainder of the form. If not, the debtor is directed to complete the verification in Part VII but not complete the other parts of the form.

Part IV provides for calculation of the means-test deductions provided in §707(b)(2), described above, as incorporated by §1325(b)(3) for debtors with CMI above the applicable state median.

Part V provides for three adjustments required by special provisions affecting disposable income in Chapter 13. First, §1325(b)(2) itself excludes from the CMI used in determining disposable income certain "child support payments, foster care payments, [and] disability payments for a dependent child." Because payments of this kind are included in the definition of CMI in §101(10A), a line entry for deduction of these payments is provided. Second, a line entry is provided for deduction of contributions by the debtor to certain retirement plans, listed in §541(b)(7)(B), since that provision states that such contributions "shall not constitute disposable income, as defined in section 1325(b)." Third, the same line entry also allows a deduction from disposable income for payments on loans from retirement accounts that are excepted from the automatic stay by §362(b)(19), since §1322(f) provides that for a "loan described in section 362(b)(19) . . . any amounts required to repay such loan shall not constitute 'disposable income' under section 1325."

The Chapter 13 form does not provide a deduction from disposable income for the Chapter 13 debtor's anticipated attorney fees. There is no specific statutory allowance for such a deduction, and none appears necessary. Section 1325(b)(1)(B) requires that disposable income contributed to a Chapter 13 plan be used to pay "unsecured creditors." A debtor's attorney who has not taken a security interest in the debtor's property is an unsecured creditor who may be paid from disposable income.

Part VI of the form allows the debtor to claim additional deductions, as described above, and Part VII is the verification.

Committee Notes on Rules—2006 Amendment

Forms [sic] 22A, Line 43, and Form 22C, Line 48, are amended to delete the phrase "in default" with respect to "Other payments on secured claims." A debtor may be required to make other payments to the creditor even when the debt is not in default, such as to retain collateral. Form 22C, Line 17, also is amended to require all chapter 13 debtors, including those whose income falls below the applicable median income, to determine their disposable income under §1325(b)(3) of the Code by completing Part III of the form. Both forms contain stylistic amendments to conform the wording more closely to that used in the 2005 Act [Bankruptcy Abuse Prevention and Consumer Protection Act of 2005, Pub. L. 109–8, Apr. 20, 2005, 119 Stat. 23].

Committee Notes on Rules—2005–2008 Amendment

[The 2005–2007 [sic] Committee Note incorporates Committee Notes previously published in 2005 and 2006.]

A. Overview

Among the changes introduced by the Bankruptcy Abuse Prevention and Consumer Protection Act of 2005 was a set of interlocking provisions defining "current monthly income" and establishing a means test to determine whether relief under Chapter 7 should be presumed abusive. Current monthly income ("CMI") is defined in §101(10A) of the Code, and the means test is set out in §707(b)(2). These provisions have a variety of applications. In Chapter 7, if the debtor's CMI exceeds a defined level the debtor is subject to the means test, and §707(b)(2)(C) specifically requires debtors to file a statement of CMI and calculations to determine the applicability of the means test presumption. In Chapters 11 and 13, CMI provides the starting point for determining the disposable income that debtors may be required to pay to unsecured creditors. Moreover, Chapter 13 debtors with CMI above defined median income levels are required by §1325(b)(3) to use the deductions from income prescribed by the means test in order to determine what part of their income is "disposable," and pursuant to §1325(b)(4), the level of CMI determines the "applicable commitment period" over which projected disposable income must be paid to unsecured creditors.

To provide for the reporting and calculation of CMI and for the completion of the means test where required, three separate official forms have been created—one for Chapter 7, one for Chapter 11, and one for Chapter 13. This note first describes the calculation of CMI that is common to all three of the forms, next describes the means test deductions set out in the Chapter 7 and 13 forms, and finally addresses particular issues that are unique to each of the separate forms.

B. Calculation of CMI

Although Chapters 7, 11, and 13 use CMI for different purposes, the basic computation is the same in each. As defined in §101(10A), CMI is the monthly average of certain income that the debtor (and in a joint case, the debtor's spouse) received in the six calendar months before the bankruptcy filing. The definition includes in this average (1) income from all sources, whether or not taxable, and (2) any amount paid by an entity other than the debtor (or the debtor's spouse in a joint case) on a regular basis for the household expenses of the debtor, the debtor's dependents, and (in a joint case) the debtor's spouse if not otherwise a dependent. At the same time, the definition excludes from the averaged income "benefits received under the Social Security Act" and certain payments to victims of terrorism, war crimes, and crimes against humanity.

Each of the three forms provides for reporting income items constituting CMI. The items are reported in a set of entry lines—Part II of the form for Chapter 7 and Part I of the forms for Chapter 11 and Chapter 13—that include separate columns for reporting income of the debtor and of the debtor's spouse. The first of these entry lines includes a set of instructions and check boxes indicating when the "debtor's spouse" column must be completed. The instructions also direct the required averaging of reported income.

The subsequent entry lines for income reporting specify several common types of income and are followed by a "catch-all" line for other income. The entry lines address (a) gross wages; (b) business income; (c) rental income; (d) interest, dividends, and royalties; (e) pension and retirement income; (f) regular payments of the household expenses of the debtor or the debtor's dependents; (g) unemployment compensation, and (h) all other forms of income (the "catch-all" line).

Gross wages (before taxes) are required to be entered. However, consistent with usage in the Internal Revenue Manual and the American Community Survey of the Census Bureau, business and rental income are defined as gross receipts less ordinary and necessary expenses.

Unemployment compensation is given special treatment. Because the federal government provides funding for state unemployment compensation under the Social Security Act, there may be a dispute about whether unemployment compensation is a "benefit received under the Social Security Act." The forms take no position on the merits of this argument, but give debtors the option of reporting unemployment compensation separately from the CMI calculation. This separate reporting allows parties in interest to determine the materiality of an exclusion of unemployment compensation and to challenge it.

Alimony and child support are also given special treatment. Child support is not generally considered "income" to the recipient. See 26 U.S.C. §71(c). Thus, child support is only part of CMI if it is paid on a regular basis for the household expenses of the debtor or the debtor's dependents. On the other hand, alimony and other forms of spousal support are considered income to the recipient, and thus are within CMI regardless of the regularity and use of the payments. To address this distinction, the instruction in the entry line for regular payments of household expenses directs that the entry include regular child support payments used for household expenses of the debtor or the debtor's dependents, and the instruction for the "catch-all" line directs inclusion of all spousal support payments that are not otherwise reported as spousal income.

The forms provide for totaling the income reporting lines.

C. The means test: deductions from current monthly income

The means test operates by deducting from CMI defined allowances for living expenses and payment of secured and priority debt, leaving disposable income presumptively available to pay unsecured non-priority debt. These deductions from CMI are set out in the Code at §707(b)(2)(A)(ii)–(iv). The forms for Chapter 7 and Chapter 13 have similar sections (Parts V and IV, respectively) for calculating these deductions. The calculations are divided into subparts reflecting three different kinds of allowed deductions.

1. Deductions under IRS standards

Subpart A deals with deductions from CMI, set out in §707(b)(2)(A)(ii), for "the debtor's applicable monthly expense amounts specified under the National Standards and Local Standards, and the debtor's actual monthly expenses for the categories specified as Other Necessary Expenses issued by the Internal Revenue Service for the area in which the debtor resides." The forms provide entry lines for each of the specified expense deductions under the IRS standards, and instructions on the entry lines identify the website of the U.S. Trustee Program, where the relevant IRS allowances can be found. As with all of the deductions in §707(b)(2)(A)(ii), deductions under the IRS standards are subject to the proviso that they not include "any payments for debts."

National Standards. The IRS National Standards provide a single allowance for food, clothing, household supplies, personal care, and miscellany, depending on household size, which can be entered directly from a table supplied by the IRS. There is also a National Standard for out-of-pocket health care expenses, which provides two different per-person allowances, depending on age group: the allowance for persons 65 or older is greater than the allowance for those under 65. Accordingly, the forms direct debtors to compute the National Standard allowance for health care by first multiplying each of the two age-group allowances by the number of household members within that age group and then adding subtotals for the two age groups to obtain the total allowance.

Local Standards. The IRS Local Standards provide one set of deductions for housing and utilities and another set for transportation expenses, with different amounts for different areas of the country, depending on the size of the debtor's household and the number of the debtor's vehicles. Each of the amounts specified in the Local Standards are treated by the IRS as a cap on actual expenses, but because §707(b)(2)(A)(ii) provides for deductions in the "amounts specified under the . . . Local Standards," the forms treat these amounts as allowed deductions.

The Local Standards for housing and utilities, as published by the IRS for its internal purposes, present single amounts covering all housing expenses; however, for bankruptcy purposes, the IRS has provided the Executive Office for United States Trustees with information allowing a division of these amounts into a non-mortgage component and a mortgage/rent component. The non-mortgage component covers a variety of expenses involved in maintaining a residence, such as utilities, repairs and maintenance. The mortgage/rent component covers the cost of acquiring the residence. The forms take no position on the question of whether the debtor must actually be making payments on a home in order to claim a mortgage/rent allowance. For homeowners with mortgages, the mortgage/rent allowance involves debt payment, since the cost of a mortgage is the basis for the allowance. Accordingly, the forms require debtors to deduct from the mortgage/rent allowance their average monthly mortgage payment, up to the full amount of the IRS mortgage/rent allowance, and instruct debtors that this average monthly payment is the one reported on the separate line of the forms for deductions of secured debt under §707(b)(2)(a)(iii). The forms allow debtors to challenge the appropriateness of this method of computing the Local Standards allowance for housing and utilities and to claim any additional housing allowance to which they contend they are entitled, but the forms require specification of the basis for such a contention.

The IRS issues Local Standards for transportation in two components for its internal purposes as well as for bankruptcy: one component covers vehicle operation/public transportation expense and the other ownership/lease expense. The amount of the vehicle operation/public transportation allowance depends on the number of vehicles the debtor operates; debtors who do not operate vehicles are given a public transportation allowance, regardless of whether they actually use public transportation. It is not clear whether the public transportation allowance may also be claimed by debtors who do make use of public transportation but also operate vehicles. The forms permit debtors to claim both a public transportation and vehicle operating allowance, but take no position as to whether it is appropriate to claim both allowances. No debt payment is involved in the vehicle operation/public transportation component of the Local Standards for transportation.

The ownership/lease component, on the other hand, may involve debt payment. Accordingly, the forms require debtors to reduce the allowance for ownership/lease expense by the average monthly loan payment amount (principal and interest), up to the full amount of the IRS ownership/lease expense amount. This average payment is as reported on the separate line of the forms for deductions of secured debt under §707(b)(2)(a)(iii). The forms take no position on the question of whether the debtor must actually be making payments on a vehicle in order to claim the ownership/lease allowance.

Other Necessary Expenses. The IRS does not set out specific dollar allowances for "Other Necessary Expenses." Rather, it specifies a number of categories for such expenses, and describes the nature of the expenses that may be deducted in each of these categories. Section 707(b)(2)(a)(ii) allows a deduction for the debtor's actual expenses in these specified categories, subject to its requirement that payment of debt not be included. Several of the IRS categories deal with debt repayment and so are not included in the forms. Several other categories deal with expense items that are more expansively addressed by specific statutory allowances. Subpart A sets out the remaining categories of "Other Necessary Expenses" in individual entry lines. Instructions in these entry lines reflect limitations imposed by the IRS and the need to avoid inclusion of items deducted elsewhere on the forms.

Subpart A concludes with a subtotal of the deductions allowed under the IRS standards.

2. Additional statutory expense deductions

In addition to the expense deductions allowed under the IRS standards, the means test makes provision—in subclauses (I), (II), (IV), and (V) of §707(b)(2)(A)(ii)—for six special expense deductions. Each of these additional expense items is set out on a separate entry line in Subpart B, introduced by an instruction that tracks the statutory language and provides that there should not be double counting of any expense already included in the IRS deductions.

One of these special expense deductions presents a problem of statutory construction. Section 707(b)(2)A)(ii)(I) [sic], after directing the calculation of the debtor's monthly expenses under the IRS standards, states, "Such expenses shall include reasonably necessary health insurance, disability insurance, and health saving account expenses . . . ." There is no express statutory limitation to expenses actually incurred by the debtor, and so the provision appears to allow a reasonable "monthly expense" deduction for health and disability insurance or a health savings account even if the debtor does not make such payments, similar to the way in which the National Standards give an allowance for food, clothing and personal care expenses without regard to the debtor's actual expenditures. However, the statutory language might also be read as providing that the debtor's "Other Necessary Expenses" should include reasonable insurance and health savings account payments. Since "Other Necessary Expenses" are limited to actual expenditures, such a limitation could be implied here. The forms deal with this ambiguity by allowing the debtor to claim a deduction for reasonable insurance and health savings account expenses even if not made, but also require a statement of the amount actually expended in these categories, thus allowing a challenge by any party who believes that only actual expenditures are properly deductible.

Contributions to tax-exempt charities provide another statutory expense deduction. Section 707(b)(1) provides that in considering whether a Chapter 7 filing is an abuse, the court may not take into consideration "whether a debtor . . . continues to make [tax-exempt] charitable contributions." Section 1325(b)(2)(A)(ii) expressly allows a deduction from CMI for such contributions that are "reasonably necessary" (up to 15% of the debtor's gross income), and the Religious Liberty and Charitable Donation Clarification Act of 2005 [2006] added language to §1325(b)(3) to provide the same deduction for above-median income debtors whose disposable income is determined using means test deductions. Accordingly, Subpart B of both the Chapter 7 and Chapter 13 forms includes an entry line for charitable contributions, employing the different statutory deductions allowed in each context.

The Subpart B concludes with a subtotal of the additional statutory expense deductions.

3. Deductions for payment of debt

Subpart C deals with the means test's deductions from CMI for payment of secured and priority debt, as well as a deduction for administrative fees that would be incurred if the debtor paid debts through a Chapter 13 plan.

In accord with §707(b)(2)(A)(iii), the deduction for secured debt is divided into two entry lines—one for payments that are contractually due during the 60 months following the bankruptcy filing, the other for amounts needed to retain necessary collateral securing debts in default. In each situation, the instructions for the entry lines require dividing the total payment amount by 60, as the statute directs. The forms recognize another ambiguity in this connection: "payments contractually due" might either be understood as limited to payments of principal and interest (payable to secured creditor) or, in the context of a mortgage with an escrow, might be understood as including payments of property taxes and insurance (ultimately paid to taxing bodies and insurers, but initially payable to the mortgagee). The forms require the debtor to specify whether the amount deducted includes taxes and insurance, allowing a party in interest to inquire into the deduction and raise an objection.

Priority debt, deductible pursuant to §707(b)(2)(A)(iv), is treated on a single entry line, also requiring division by 60. The instruction for this line makes clear that only past due priority debt—not anticipated debts—should be included. Thus, future support or tax obligations, and future fees that might be payable to a Chapter 13 debtor's attorney, are not included.

The defined deduction for the expenses of administering a Chapter 13 plan is allowed by §707(b)(2)(A)(ii)(III) only for debtors eligible for Chapter 13. The forms treat this deduction in an entry line requiring the eligible debtor to state the amount of the prospective Chapter 13 plan payment and multiply that payment amount by the percentage fee established for the debtor's district by the Executive Office for United States Trustees. The forms refer debtors to the website of the U.S. Trustee Program to obtain this percentage fee.

The subpart concludes with a subtotal of debt payment deductions.

4. Total deductions

Finally, the forms direct that the subtotals from Subparts A, B, and C be added together to arrive at the total of allowed deductions from CMI under the means test.

5. Additional claimed deductions

The forms do not provide for means test deductions from CMI for expenses in categories that are not specifically identified as "Other Necessary Expenses" in the Internal Revenue Manual. However, debtors may wish to claim expenses that do not fall within the categories listed as "Other Necessary Expenses" in the forms. Part VII of the Chapter 7 form and Part VI of the Chapter 13 form provide for such expenses to be identified and totaled. Although expenses listed in these sections are not deducted from CMI for purposes of the means test calculation, the listing provides a basis for debtors to assert that these expenses should be deducted from CMI under §707(b)(2)(A)(ii)(I), and that the results of the forms' calculation should therefore be modified.

D. The chapter-specific forms

1. Chapter 7

The Chapter 7 form has several unique aspects. The form includes, in the upper right corner of the first page, a check box directing the debtor to state whether or not the calculations required by the form result in a presumption of abuse. The debtor is not bound by this statement and may argue, in response to a motion brought under §707(b)(1), that there should be no presumption despite the calculations required by the form. The check box is intended to give clerks of court a conspicuous indication of the cases for which they are required to provide notice of a presumption of abuse pursuant to §342(d).

Part I implements the provision of §707(b)(2)(D) that excludes certain disabled veterans from all means testing, making it unnecessary to compute the CMI of such veterans. Debtors who declare under penalty of perjury that they are disabled veterans within the statutory definition are directed to verify their declaration in Part VII, to check the "no presumption" box at the beginning of the form, and to disregard the remaining parts of the form.

Part I also provides an exclusion for debtors who do not have primarily consumer debts. These debtors are not subject to any of the provisions of §707(b)—including the requirement of §707(b)(2)(C) for filing a CMI statement—since §707(b) applies, by its terms, only to "an individual debtor . . . whose debts are primarily consumer debts." However, a debtor may be found to have asserted non-consumer status incorrectly. Unless such a debtor has filed the CMI form within the 45 days after filing the case, the case could be subject to automatic dismissal under §521(i). To avoid this possibility, debtors asserting principally non-consumer status may complete the appropriate portions of Part I, claim an exclusion from the balance of the form, and promptly file the form. If it is subsequently determined that the debtor does have primarily consumer debts, the form will have been filed within the deadline established by §521(i), and can be amended to include the necessary CMI and means test information.

Part II computes CMI for purposes of the safe harbor of §707(b)(7). Section 707(b)(7) prohibits a motion to dismiss based on the means test's presumption of abuse if the debtor's annualized CMI does not exceed a defined median state income. For this purpose, the statute directs that CMI of the debtor's spouse be combined with the debtor's CMI even if the debtor's spouse is not a joint debtor, unless the debtor declares under penalty of perjury that the spouses are legally separated or living separately other than for purposes of evading the means test.Accordingly, the calculation of CMI in Part II directs a computation of the CMI of the debtor's spouse not only in joint cases, but also in cases of married debtors who do not make the specified declaration, and the CMI of both spouses in these cases is combined for purposes of determining standing under §707(b)(7).

Part III compares the debtor's CMI to the applicable state median income for purposes of §707(b)(7). It then directs debtors whose income does not exceed the applicable median to verify the form, to check the "no presumption" box at the beginning of the form, and not to complete the remaining parts of the form. Debtors whose CMI does exceed the applicable state median are required to complete the remaining parts of the form.

Part IV adjusts the CMI of a married debtor, not filing jointly, whose spouse's CMI was combined with the debtor's in Part II. The means test itself does not charge a married debtor in a non-joint case with the income of the non-filing spouse, but only with payments regularly made by that spouse for the household expenses of the debtor or the debtor's dependents, as provided in the definition of CMI in §101(10A). Accordingly, Part IV calls for the combined CMI of Part II to be reduced by the amount of the non-filing spouse's income that was not regularly paid for the household expenses of the debtor or the debtor's dependents. The form requires that the alternative uses of the spouse's income be specified.

Part V of the form provides for a calculation of the means test's deductions from the debtor's CMI, as described above in §C.

Part VI provides for a determination of whether the debtor's CMI, less the allowed deductions, gives rise to a presumption of abuse under §707(b)(2)(A). Depending on the outcome of this determination, the debtor is directed to check the appropriate box at the beginning of the form and to sign the verification in Part VIII. Part VII allows the debtor to claim additional deductions, as discussed above in §C.5.

2. Chapter 11

The Chapter 11 form is the simplest of the three, since the means-test deductions of §707(b)(2) are not employed in determining the extent of an individual Chapter 11 debtor's disposable income. Section 1129(a)(15) requires payments of disposable income "as defined in section 1325(b)(2)," and that paragraph allows calculation of disposable income under judicially-determined standards, rather than pursuant to the means test deductions, specified for higher income Chapter 13 debtors by §1325(b)(3). However, §1325(b)(2) does require that CMI be used as the starting point in the judicial determination of disposable income, and so the Chapter 11 form requires this calculation (in Part I of the form), as described above, together with a verification (in Part II).

3. Chapter 13

Like the Chapter 7 form, the form for Chapter 13 debtors contains a number of special provisions. The upper right corner of the first page includes check boxes requiring the debtor to state whether, under the calculations required by the statement, the applicable commitment period under §1325(b)(4) is three years or five years and whether §1325(b)(3) requires the means-test deductions to be used in determining the debtor's disposable income. The check box is intended to inform standing trustees and other interested parties about these items, but does not prevent the debtor from arguing that the calculations required by the form do not accurately reflect the debtor's disposable income.

Part I is a report of income to be used for determining CMI. In the absence of full payment of allowed unsecured claims, §1325(b)(4) imposes a five-year applicable commitment period—rather than a three-year period—if the debtor's annualized CMI is not less than a defined median state income. For this purpose, as under §707(b)(7), §1325(b)(4) requires that the CMI of the debtor's spouse be combined with the debtor's CMI, but, unlike §707(b)(7), no exception is made for spouses who are legally separated or living separately. Accordingly, the report of income in Part I directs a combined reporting of the income of both spouses in all cases of married debtors.

Part II computes the applicable commitment period by annualizing the income calculated in Part I and comparing it to the applicable state median. The form allows debtors to contend that the income of a non-filing spouse should not be treated as CMI and permits debtors to claim a deduction for any income of a non-filing spouse to the extent that this income was not regularly paid for the household expenses of the debtor or the debtor's dependents (with the alternative uses specified). The debtor is directed to check the appropriate box at the beginning of the form, stating the applicable commitment period. The check box does not prevent a debtor from proposing an applicable commitment period of less than three or five years in conjunction with a plan that pays all allowed unsecured claims in full.

Part III compares the debtor's CMI to the applicable state median, allowing a determination of whether the means-test deductions must be used, pursuant to §1325(b)(3), in calculating disposable income. For this purpose, since §1325(b)(3) does not provide for including the income of the debtor's spouse, the form directs a deduction of the income of a nonfiling spouse that was not contributed to the household expenses of the debtor or the debtor's dependents. Again, the debtor is directed to check the appropriate box at the beginning of the form, indicating whether the means test deductions are applicable. If so, the debtor is directed to complete the remainder of the form. If not, the debtor is directed to complete the verification in Part VII but not complete the other parts of the form.

Part IV provides for calculation of the means-test deductions provided in §707(b)(2), described above in §C, as incorporated by §1325(b)(3) for debtors with CMI above the applicable state median.

Part V provides for four adjustments required by special provisions affecting disposable income in Chapter 13. First, §1325(b)(2) itself excludes from the CMI used in determining disposable income certain "child support payments, foster care payments, [and] disability payments for a dependent child." Because payments of this kind are included in the definition of CMI in §101(10A), a line entry for deduction of these payments is provided. Second, a line entry is provided for deduction of contributions by the debtor to certain retirement plans, listed in §541(b)(7)(B), since that provision states that such contributions "shall not constitute disposable income, as defined in section 1325(b)." Third, the same line entry also allows a deduction from disposable income for payments on loans from retirement accounts that are excepted from the automatic stay by §362(b)(19), since §1322(f) provides that for a "loan described in section 362(b)(19) . . . any amounts required to repay such loan shall not constitute 'disposable income' under section 1325." Finally, §1325(b)(3) requires that deductions from income for above-median income debtors be determined not only in accordance with the means test deductions, set out in subparagraph (A) of §707(b)(2), but also in accordance with subparagraph (B), which sets out the grounds for rebutting a presumption of abuse based on a demonstration of additional expenses justified by special circumstances. Part V includes an entry line for such additional expenses, with a warning that the debtor will be required (as provided by §707(b)(2)(B)) to document the expenses and provide a detailed explanation of the special circumstances that make them reasonable and necessary.

The Chapter 13 form does not provide a deduction from disposable income for the Chapter 13 debtor's anticipated attorney fees. No specific statutory allowance for such a deduction exists, and none appears necessary. Section 1325(b)(1)(B) requires that disposable income contributed to a Chapter 13 plan be used to pay "unsecured creditors." A debtor's attorney who has not taken a security interest in the debtor's property is an unsecured creditor who may be paid from disposable income.

Part VI allows the debtor to declare expenses not allowed under the form without deducting them from CMI, as described above in §C.5.

Committee Notes on Rules—2008 Amendment

The chapter 7 form is amended to implement the temporary exclusion from means testing created by the National Guard and Reservists Debt Relief Act of 2008. That law amended §707(b)(2)(D) for a period of three years by adding a new subsection (ii) to provide a temporary exclusion from the application of the means test for certain members of the National Guard and reserve components of the Armed Forces. The new temporary exclusion would last for the period that the qualifying debtor is on active duty or is performing a homeland defense activity, and for 540 days thereafter.

Because the exclusion for Reservists and National Guard members applies only for a defined period of time, it may expire during the course of the chapter 7 case filed by a debtor initially entitled to the exclusion. For that reason, a new check box is added to the top of the form that states that the "presumption is temporarily inapplicable." A debtor who is entitled to claim the Reservists and National Guard exclusion at the commencement of the chapter 7 case may check that box.

The new exclusion applies only to a debtor who satisfies all of the requirements of §707(b)(2)(D)(ii), and its expiration date depends on facts specific to each debtor. Therefore, in a joint case in which the exclusion in part 1C is claimed by either or both filers, each joint filer must complete a separate statement. If only one joint debtor qualifies for the exclusion in part IC [sic], the other joint debtor must complete the form.

Part 1C is added to the form to allow qualifying debtors to claim the temporary exclusion under §707(b)(2)(D)(ii). Debtors who declare under penalty of perjury that they satisfy all of the requirements of that provision are directed to verify their declaration in Part VIII and to check the "temporary presumption" box at the beginning of the form. They are not required to complete the remaining parts of the form for so long as the exclusion remains applicable.

A debtor who is or has been a Reservist or a National Guard member may qualify for the exclusion described in part 1C by being called to active duty service after September 11, 2001, for a period of at least 90 days, or while performing homeland defense activity for a period of at least 90 days. After the debtor has been released from active duty or has ceased performing homeland defense activity, the exclusion applies for a period of 540 days after the release date or cessation of homeland defense activity. Under those circumstances the debtor must state the date of release from active duty or the date on which the performance of homeland defense activity terminated.

If the Reservist and National Guard exclusion terminates during the course of a chapter 7 case—because of the expiration of the 540 day period following the release from active duty or the cessation of homeland defense activity—then the debtor may be required to complete the remaining parts of the form that are applicable to the debtor. If the exclusion terminates while a timely motion to dismiss under §707(b)(2) may still be filed, Interim Rule 1007-I(n) requires that the debtor complete the remaining parts of the form no later than 14 days after the termination. If the obligation to complete the form arises in these circumstances and the debtor has not previously completed the form, the clerk is required to give the debtor notice of the obligation.

B 22B (Official Form 22B) (Chapter 11) (01/08)

In re ______________________
Debtor(s)

Case Number: ______________
(If known)

CHAPTER 11 STATEMENT OF CURRENT MONTHLY INCOME

In addition to Schedules I and J, this statement must be completed by every individual chapter 11 debtor, whether or not filing jointly. Joint debtors may complete one statement only.

Part I. CALCULATION OF CURRENT MONTHLY INCOME

1	**Marital/filing status.** Check the box that applies and complete the balance of this part of this statement as directed. a. ☐ Unmarried. **Complete only Column A ("Debtor's Income") for Lines 2-10.** b. ☐ Married, not filing jointly. **Complete only Column A ("Debtor's Income") for Lines 2-10.** c. ☐ Married, filing jointly. **Complete both Column A ("Debtor's Income") and Column B ("Spouse's Income") for Lines 2-10.**		
	All figures must reflect average monthly income received from all sources, derived during the six calendar months prior to filing the bankruptcy case, ending on the last day of the month before the filing. If the amount of monthly income varied during the six months, you must divide the six-month total by six, and enter the result on the appropriate line.	**Column A Debtor's Income**	**Column B Spouse's Income**
2	**Gross wages, salary, tips, bonuses, overtime, commissions.**	$	$
3	**Net income from the operation of a business, profession, or farm.** Subtract Line b from Line a and enter the difference in the appropriate column(s) of Line 3. If more than one business, profession or farm, enter aggregate numbers and provide details on an attachment. Do not enter a number less than zero. a. Gross receipts — $ b. Ordinary and necessary business expenses — $ c. Business income — Subtract Line b from Line a.	$	$
4	**Net rental and other real property income.** Subtract Line b from Line a and enter the difference in the appropriate column(s) of Line 4. Do not enter a number less than zero. a. Gross receipts — $ b. Ordinary and necessary operating expenses — $ c. Rent and other real property income — Subtract Line b from Line a.	$	$
5	**Interest, dividends, and royalties.**	$	$
6	**Pension and retirement income.**	$	$
7	**Any amounts paid by another person or entity, on a regular basis, for the household expenses of the debtor or the debtor's dependents, including child support paid for that purpose.** Do not include alimony or separate maintenance payments or amounts paid by the debtor's spouse if Column B is completed.	$	$
8	**Unemployment compensation.** Enter the amount in the appropriate column(s) of Line 8. However, if you contend that unemployment compensation received by you or your spouse was a benefit under the Social Security Act, do not list the amount of such compensation in Column A or B, but instead state the amount in the space below: Unemployment compensation claimed to be a benefit under the Social Security Act — Debtor $ ______ — Spouse $ ______	$	$

B 22B (Official Form 22B) (Chapter 11) (01/08) 2

9	**Income from all other sources.** Specify source and amount. If necessary, list additional sources on a separate page. Total and enter on Line 9. **Do not include alimony or separate maintenance payments paid by your spouse if Column B is completed, but include all other payments of alimony or separate maintenance. Do not include** any benefits received under the Social Security Act or payments received as a victim of a war crime, crime against humanity, or as a victim of international or domestic terrorism. a. ____ $ b. ____ $	$	$
10	**Subtotal of current monthly income.** Add Lines 2 thru 9 in Column A, and, if Column B is completed, add Lines 2 through 9 in Column B. Enter the total(s).	$	$
11	**Total current monthly income.** If Column B has been completed, add Line 10, Column A to Line 10, Column B, and enter the total. If Column B has not been completed, enter the amount from Line 10, Column A.	$	

Part II: VERIFICATION

12	I declare under penalty of perjury that the information provided in this statement is true and correct. *(If this a joint case, both debtors must sign.)* Date: ________ Signature: ________ (Debtor) Date: ________ Signature: ________ (Joint Debtor, if any)

(Added Oct. 17, 2005; amended Jan. 1, 2008.)

COMMITTEE NOTES ON RULES—2005

For Committee Notes on Rules—2005 for form 22B, see note set out under form 22A.

COMMITTEE NOTES ON RULES—2005–2008 AMENDMENT

For Committee Notes on Rules—2005–2008 for form 22B, see note set out under form 22A.

B 22C (Official Form 22C) (Chapter 13) (01/08)

In re ______________________
Debtor(s)

Case Number: ______________
(If known)

According to the calculations required by this statement:
☐ **The applicable commitment period is 3 years.**
☐ **The applicable commitment period is 5 years.**
☐ **Disposable income is determined under § 1325(b)(3).**
☐ **Disposable income is not determined under § 1325(b)(3).**
(Check the boxes as directed in Lines 17 and 23 of this statement.)

CHAPTER 13 STATEMENT OF CURRENT MONTHLY INCOME AND CALCULATION OF COMMITMENT PERIOD AND DISPOSABLE INCOME

In addition to Schedules I and J, this statement must be completed by every individual chapter 13 debtor, whether or not filing jointly. Joint debtors may complete one statement only.

Part I. REPORT OF INCOME

1	**Marital/filing status.** Check the box that applies and complete the balance of this part of this statement as directed. a. ☐ Unmarried. **Complete only Column A ("Debtor's Income") for Lines 2-10.** b. ☐ Married. **Complete both Column A ("Debtor's Income") and Column B ("Spouse's Income") for Lines 2-10.**		
	All figures must reflect average monthly income received from all sources, derived during the six calendar months prior to filing the bankruptcy case, ending on the last day of the month before the filing. If the amount of monthly income varied during the six months, you must divide the six-month total by six, and enter the result on the appropriate line.	**Column A Debtor's Income**	**Column B Spouse's Income**
2	**Gross wages, salary, tips, bonuses, overtime, commissions.**	$	$
3	**Income from the operation of a business, profession, or farm.** Subtract Line b from Line a and enter the difference in the appropriate column(s) of Line 3. If you operate more than one business, profession or farm, enter aggregate numbers and provide details on an attachment. Do not enter a number less than zero. **Do not include any part of the business expenses entered on Line b as a deduction in Part IV.** a. Gross receipts — $ b. Ordinary and necessary business expenses — $ c. Business income — Subtract Line b from Line a	$	$
4	**Rent and other real property income.** Subtract Line b from Line a and enter the difference in the appropriate column(s) of Line 4. Do not enter a number less than zero. **Do not include any part of the operating expenses entered on Line b as a deduction in Part IV.** a. Gross receipts — $ b. Ordinary and necessary operating expenses — $ c. Rent and other real property income — Subtract Line b from Line a	$	$
5	**Interest, dividends, and royalties.**	$	$
6	**Pension and retirement income.**	$	$
7	**Any amounts paid by another person or entity, on a regular basis, for the household expenses of the debtor or the debtor's dependents, including child support paid for that purpose.** Do not include alimony or separate maintenance payments or amounts paid by the debtor's spouse.	$	$
8	**Unemployment compensation.** Enter the amount in the appropriate column(s) of Line 8. However, if you contend that unemployment compensation received by you or your spouse was a benefit under the Social Security Act, do not list the amount of such compensation in Column A or B, but instead state the amount in the space below: Unemployment compensation claimed to be a benefit under the Social Security Act — Debtor $ ______ — Spouse $ ______	$	$

9	**Income from all other sources.** Specify source and amount. If necessary, list additional sources on a separate page. Total and enter on Line 9. **Do not include alimony or separate maintenance payments paid by your spouse, but include all other payments of alimony or separate maintenance. Do not include** any benefits received under the Social Security Act or payments received as a victim of a war crime, crime against humanity, or as a victim of international or domestic terrorism. a. ____ $ b. ____ $	$	$
10	**Subtotal.** Add Lines 2 thru 9 in Column A, and, if Column B is completed, add Lines 2 through 9 in Column B. Enter the total(s).	$	$
11	**Total.** If Column B has been completed, add Line 10, Column A to Line 10, Column B, and enter the total. If Column B has not been completed, enter the amount from Line 10, Column A.	$	

Part II. CALCULATION OF § 1325(b)(4) COMMITMENT PERIOD

12	**Enter the amount from Line 11.**	$
13	**Marital adjustment.** If you are married, but are not filing jointly with your spouse, AND if you contend that calculation of the commitment period under § 1325(b)(4) does not require inclusion of the income of your spouse, enter on Line 13 the amount of the income listed in Line 10, Column B that was NOT paid on a regular basis for the household expenses of you or your dependents and specify, in the lines below, the basis for excluding this income (such as payment of the spouse's tax liability or the spouse's support of persons other than the debtor or the debtor's dependents) and the amount of income devoted to each purpose. If necessary, list additional adjustments on a separate page. If the conditions for entering this adjustment do not apply, enter zero. a. ____ $ b. ____ $ c. ____ $ Total and enter on Line 13.	$
14	**Subtract Line 13 from Line 12 and enter the result.**	$
15	**Annualized current monthly income for § 1325(b)(4).** Multiply the amount from Line 14 by the number 12 and enter the result.	$
16	**Applicable median family income.** Enter the median family income for applicable state and household size. (This information is available by family size at www.usdoj.gov/ust/ or from the clerk of the bankruptcy court.) a. Enter debtor's state of residence: ________ b. Enter debtor's household size: ______	$
17	**Application of § 1325(b)(4).** Check the applicable box and proceed as directed. ☐ **The amount on Line 15 is less than the amount on Line 16.** Check the box for "The applicable commitment period is 3 years" at the top of page 1 of this statement and continue with this statement. ☐ **The amount on Line 15 is not less than the amount on Line 16.** Check the box for "The applicable commitment period is 5 years" at the top of page 1 of this statement and continue with this statement.	

Part III. APPLICATION OF § 1325(b)(3) FOR DETERMINING DISPOSABLE INCOME

18	**Enter the amount from Line 11.**	$

B 22C (Official Form 22C) (Chapter 13) (01/08) 3

19	**Marital adjustment.** If you are married, but are not filing jointly with your spouse, enter on Line 19 the total of any income listed in Line 10, Column B that was NOT paid on a regular basis for the household expenses of the debtor or the debtor's dependents. Specify in the lines below the basis for excluding the Column B income (such as payment of the spouse's tax liability or the spouse's support of persons other than the debtor or the debtor's dependents) and the amount of income devoted to each purpose. If necessary, list additional adjustments on a separate page. If the conditions for entering this adjustment do not apply, enter zero. a. ___ $ b. ___ $ c. ___ $ Total and enter on Line 19.	$
20	**Current monthly income for § 1325(b)(3).** Subtract Line 19 from Line 18 and enter the result.	
21	**Annualized current monthly income for § 1325(b)(3).** Multiply the amount from Line 20 by the number 12 and enter the result.	$
22	**Applicable median family income.** Enter the amount from Line 16.	$
23	**Application of § 1325(b)(3).** Check the applicable box and proceed as directed. ☐ **The amount on Line 21 is more than the amount on Line 22.** Check the box for "Disposable income is determined under § 1325(b)(3)" at the top of page 1 of this statement and complete the remaining parts of this statement. ☐ **The amount on Line 21 is not more than the amount on Line 22.** Check the box for "Disposable income is not determined under § 1325(b)(3)" at the top of page 1 of this statement and complete Part VII of this statement. **Do not complete Parts IV, V, or VI.**	

Part IV. CALCULATION OF DEDUCTIONS FROM INCOME

Subpart A: Deductions under Standards of the Internal Revenue Service (IRS)

24A	**National Standards: food, apparel and services, housekeeping supplies, personal care, and miscellaneous.** Enter in Line 24A the "Total" amount from IRS National Standards for Allowable Living Expenses for the applicable household size. (This information is available at www.usdoj.gov/ust/ or from the clerk of the bankruptcy court.)	$
24B	**National Standards: health care.** Enter in Line a1 below the amount from IRS National Standards for Out-of-Pocket Health Care for persons under 65 years of age, and in Line a2 the IRS National Standards for Out-of-Pocket Health Care for persons 65 years of age or older. (This information is available at www.usdoj.gov/ust/ or from the clerk of the bankruptcy court.) Enter in Line b1 the number of members of your household who are under 65 years of age, and enter in Line b2 the number of members of your household who are 65 years of age or older. (The total number of household members must be the same as the number stated in Line 16b.) Multiply Line a1 by Line b1 to obtain a total amount for household members under 65, and enter the result in Line c1. Multiply Line a2 by Line b2 to obtain a total amount for household members 65 and older, and enter the result in Line c2. Add Lines c1 and c2 to obtain a total health care amount, and enter the result in Line 24B.	$
25A	**Local Standards: housing and utilities; non-mortgage expenses.** Enter the amount of the IRS Housing and Utilities Standards; non-mortgage expenses for the applicable county and household size. (This information is available at www.usdoj.gov/ust/ or from the clerk of the bankruptcy court).	$

Line 24B worksheet:

Household members under 65 years of age			Household members 65 years of age or older		
a1.	Allowance per member		a2.	Allowance per member	
b1.	Number of members		b2.	Number of members	
c1.	Subtotal		c2.	Subtotal	

25B	**Local Standards: housing and utilities; mortgage/rent expense.** Enter, in Line a below, the amount of the IRS Housing and Utilities Standards; mortgage/rent expense for your county and household size (this information is available at www.usdoj.gov/ust/ or from the clerk of the bankruptcy court); enter on Line b the total of the Average Monthly Payments for any debts secured by your home, as stated in Line 47; subtract Line b from Line a and enter the result in Line 25B. **Do not enter an amount less than zero.** a. IRS Housing and Utilities Standards; mortgage/rent expense — $ b. Average Monthly Payment for any debts secured by your home, if any, as stated in Line 47 — $ c. Net mortgage/rental expense — Subtract Line b from Line a.	$
26	**Local Standards: housing and utilities; adjustment.** If you contend that the process set out in Lines 25A and 25B does not accurately compute the allowance to which you are entitled under the IRS Housing and Utilities Standards, enter any additional amount to which you contend you are entitled, and state the basis for your contention in the space below:	$
27A	**Local Standards: transportation; vehicle operation/public transportation expense.** You are entitled to an expense allowance in this category regardless of whether you pay the expenses of operating a vehicle and regardless of whether you use public transportation. Check the number of vehicles for which you pay the operating expenses or for which the operating expenses are included as a contribution to your household expenses in Line 7. ☐ 0 ☐ 1 ☐ 2 or more. If you checked 0, enter on Line 27A the "Public Transportation" amount from IRS Local Standards: Transportation. If you checked 1 or 2 or more, enter on Line 27A the "Operating Costs" amount from IRS Local Standards: Transportation for the applicable number of vehicles in the applicable Metropolitan Statistical Area or Census Region. (These amounts are available at www.usdoj.gov/ust/ or from the clerk of the bankruptcy court.)	$
27B	**Local Standards: transportation; additional public transportation expense.** If you pay the operating expenses for a vehicle and also use public transportation, and you contend that you are entitled to an additional deduction for your public transportation expenses, enter on Line 27B the "Public Transportation" amount from IRS Local Standards: Transportation. (This amount is available at www.usdoj.gov/ust/ or from the clerk of the bankruptcy court.)	$
28	**Local Standards: transportation ownership/lease expense; Vehicle 1.** Check the number of vehicles for which you claim an ownership/lease expense. (You may not claim an ownership/lease expense for more than two vehicles.) ☐ 1 ☐ 2 or more. Enter, in Line a below, the "Ownership Costs" for "One Car" from the IRS Local Standards: Transportation (available at www.usdoj.gov/ust/ or from the clerk of the bankruptcy court); enter in Line b the total of the Average Monthly Payments for any debts secured by Vehicle 1, as stated in Line 47; subtract Line b from Line a and enter the result in Line 28. **Do not enter an amount less than zero.** a. IRS Transportation Standards, Ownership Costs — $ b. Average Monthly Payment for any debts secured by Vehicle 1, as stated in Line 47 — $ c. Net ownership/lease expense for Vehicle 1 — Subtract Line b from Line a.	$

B 22C (Official Form 22C) (Chapter 13) (01/08) 5

29	**Local Standards: transportation ownership/lease expense; Vehicle 2.** Complete this Line only if you checked the "2 or more" Box in Line 28. Enter, in Line a below, the "Ownership Costs" for "One Car" from the IRS Local Standards: Transportation (available at www.usdoj.gov/ust/ or from the clerk of the bankruptcy court); enter in Line b the total of the Average Monthly Payments for any debts secured by Vehicle 2, as stated in Line 47; subtract Line b from Line a and enter the result in Line 29. **Do not enter an amount less than zero.** a. IRS Transportation Standards, Ownership Costs — $ b. Average Monthly Payment for any debts secured by Vehicle 2, as stated in Line 47 — $ c. Net ownership/lease expense for Vehicle 2 — Subtract Line b from Line a.	$
30	**Other Necessary Expenses: taxes.** Enter the total average monthly expense that you actually incur for all federal, state, and local taxes, other than real estate and sales taxes, such as income taxes, self-employment taxes, social-security taxes, and Medicare taxes. **Do not include real estate or sales taxes.**	$
31	**Other Necessary Expenses: involuntary deductions for employment.** Enter the total average monthly deductions that are required for your employment, such as mandatory retirement contributions, union dues, and uniform costs. **Do not include discretionary amounts, such as voluntary 401(k) contributions.**	$
32	**Other Necessary Expenses: life insurance.** Enter total average monthly premiums that you actually pay for term life insurance for yourself. **Do not include premiums for insurance on your dependents, for whole life or for any other form of insurance.**	$
33	**Other Necessary Expenses: court-ordered payments.** Enter the total monthly amount that you are required to pay pursuant to the order of a court or administrative agency, such as spousal or child support payments. **Do not include payments on past due obligations included in Line 49.**	$
34	**Other Necessary Expenses: education for employment or for a physically or mentally challenged child.** Enter the total average monthly amount that you actually expend for education that is a condition of employment and for education that is required for a physically or mentally challenged dependent child for whom no public education providing similar services is available.	$
35	**Other Necessary Expenses: childcare.** Enter the total average monthly amount that you actually expend on childcare—such as baby-sitting, day care, nursery and preschool. **Do not include other educational payments.**	$
36	**Other Necessary Expenses: health care.** Enter the total average monthly amount that you actually expend on health care that is required for the health and welfare of yourself or your dependents, that is not reimbursed by insurance or paid by a health savings account, and that is in excess of the amount entered in Line 24B. **Do not include payments for health insurance or health savings accounts listed in Line 39.**	$
37	**Other Necessary Expenses: telecommunication services.** Enter the total average monthly amount that you actually pay for telecommunication services other than your basic home telephone and cell phone service—such as pagers, call waiting, caller id, special long distance, or internet service—to the extent necessary for your health and welfare or that of your dependents. **Do not include any amount previously deducted.**	$
38	**Total Expenses Allowed under IRS Standards.** Enter the total of Lines 24 through 37.	$

Subpart B: Additional Living Expense Deductions
Note: Do not include any expenses that you have listed in Lines 24-37

39	**Health Insurance, Disability Insurance, and Health Savings Account Expenses.** List the monthly expenses in the categories set out in lines a-c below that are reasonably necessary for yourself, your spouse, or your dependents. a. Health Insurance $ b. Disability Insurance $ c. Health Savings Account $ Total and enter on Line 39 **If you do not actually expend this total amount,** state your actual total average monthly expenditures in the space below: $ ________	$
40	**Continued contributions to the care of household or family members.** Enter the total average actual monthly expenses that you will continue to pay for the reasonable and necessary care and support of an elderly, chronically ill, or disabled member of your household or member of your immediate family who is unable to pay for such expenses. **Do not include payments listed in Line 34.**	$
41	**Protection against family violence.** Enter the total average reasonably necessary monthly expenses that you actually incur to maintain the safety of your family under the Family Violence Prevention and Services Act or other applicable federal law. The nature of these expenses is required to be kept confidential by the court.	$
42	**Home energy costs.** Enter the total average monthly amount, in excess of the allowance specified by IRS Local Standards for Housing and Utilities, that you actually expend for home energy costs. **You must provide your case trustee with documentation of your actual expenses, and you must demonstrate that the additional amount claimed is reasonable and necessary.**	$
43	**Education expenses for dependent children under 18.** Enter the total average monthly expenses that you actually incur, not to exceed $137.50 per child, for attendance at a private or public elementary or secondary school by your dependent children less than 18 years of age. **You must provide your case trustee with documentation of your actual expenses, and you must explain why the amount claimed is reasonable and necessary and not already accounted for in the IRS Standards.**	$
44	**Additional food and clothing expense.** Enter the total average monthly amount by which your food and clothing expenses exceed the combined allowances for food and clothing (apparel and services) in the IRS National Standards, not to exceed 5% of those combined allowances. (This information is available at www.usdoj.gov/ust/ or from the clerk of the bankruptcy court.) **You must demonstrate that the additional amount claimed is reasonable and necessary.**	$
45	**Charitable contributions.** Enter the amount reasonably necessary for you to expend each month on charitable contributions in the form of cash or financial instruments to a charitable organization as defined in 26 U.S.C. § 170(c)(1)-(2). **Do not include any amount in excess of 15% of your gross monthly income.**	$
46	**Total Additional Expense Deductions under § 707(b).** Enter the total of Lines 39 through 45.	$

Subpart C: Deductions for Debt Payment

47 **Future payments on secured claims.** For each of your debts that is secured by an interest in property that you own, list the name of the creditor, identify the property securing the debt, state the Average Monthly Payment, and check whether the payment includes taxes or insurance. The Average Monthly Payment is the total of all amounts scheduled as contractually due to each Secured Creditor in the 60 months following the filing of the bankruptcy case, divided by 60. If necessary, list additional entries on a separate page. Enter the total of the Average Monthly Payments on Line 47.

	Name of Creditor	Property Securing the Debt	Average Monthly Payment	Does payment include taxes or insurance?
a.			$	☐ yes ☐ no
b.			$	☐ yes ☐ no
c.			$	☐ yes ☐ no
			Total: Add Lines a, b, and c	

$

B 22C (Official Form 22C) (Chapter 13) (01/08) 7

48	**Other payments on secured claims.** If any of debts listed in Line 47 are secured by your primary residence, a motor vehicle, or other property necessary for your support or the support of your dependents, you may include in your deduction 1/60th of any amount (the "cure amount") that you must pay the creditor in addition to the payments listed in Line 47, in order to maintain possession of the property. The cure amount would include any sums in default that must be paid in order to avoid repossession or foreclosure. List and total any such amounts in the following chart. If necessary, list additional entries on a separate page.	

	Name of Creditor	Property Securing the Debt	1/60th of the Cure Amount
a.			$
b.			$
c.			$
			Total: Add Lines a, b, and c

48	(Total)	$
49	**Payments on prepetition priority claims.** Enter the total amount, divided by 60, of all priority claims, such as priority tax, child support and alimony claims, for which you were liable at the time of your bankruptcy filing. **Do not include current obligations, such as those set out in Line 33.**	$
50	**Chapter 13 administrative expenses.** Multiply the amount in Line a by the amount in Line b, and enter the resulting administrative expense.	

a.	Projected average monthly chapter 13 plan payment.	$
b.	Current multiplier for your district as determined under schedules issued by the Executive Office for United States Trustees. (This information is available at www.usdoj.gov/ust/ or from the clerk of the bankruptcy court.)	x
c.	Average monthly administrative expense of chapter 13 case	Total: Multiply Lines a and b

50	(Total)	$
51	**Total Deductions for Debt Payment.** Enter the total of Lines 47 through 50.	$

Subpart D: Total Deductions from Income

52	**Total of all deductions from income.** Enter the total of Lines 38, 46, and 51.	$

Part V. DETERMINATION OF DISPOSABLE INCOME UNDER § 1325(b)(2)

53	**Total current monthly income.** Enter the amount from Line 20.	$
54	**Support income.** Enter the monthly average of any child support payments, foster care payments, or disability payments for a dependent child, reported in Part I, that you received in accordance with applicable nonbankruptcy law, to the extent reasonably necessary to be expended for such child.	$
55	**Qualified retirement deductions.** Enter the monthly total of (a) all amounts withheld by your employer from wages as contributions for qualified retirement plans, as specified in § 541(b)(7) and (b) all required repayments of loans from retirement plans, as specified in § 362(b)(19).	$
56	**Total of all deductions allowed under § 707(b)(2).** Enter the amount from Line 52.	$

B 22C (Official Form 22C) (Chapter 13) (01/08) 8

57	**Deduction for special circumstances.** If there are special circumstances that justify additional expenses for which there is no reasonable alternative, describe the special circumstances and the resulting expenses in lines a-c below. If necessary, list additional entries on a separate page. Total the expenses and enter the total in Line 57. **You must provide your case trustee with documentation of these expenses and you must provide a detailed explanation of the special circumstances that make such expenses necessary and reasonable.**	

	Nature of special circumstances	Amount of expense
a.		$
b.		$
c.		$
		Total: Add Lines a, b, and c

57	(Total)	$
58	**Total adjustments to determine disposable income.** Add the amounts on Lines 54, 55, 56, and 57 and enter the result.	$
59	**Monthly Disposable Income Under § 1325(b)(2).** Subtract Line 58 from Line 53 and enter the result.	$

Part VI: ADDITIONAL EXPENSE CLAIMS

60 **Other Expenses.** List and describe any monthly expenses, not otherwise stated in this form, that are required for the health and welfare of you and your family and that you contend should be an additional deduction from your current monthly income under § 707(b)(2)(A)(ii)(I). If necessary, list additional sources on a separate page. All figures should reflect your average monthly expense for each item. Total the expenses.

	Expense Description	Monthly Amount
a.		$
b.		$
c.		$
	Total: Add Lines a, b, and c	$

Part VII: VERIFICATION

61 I declare under penalty of perjury that the information provided in this statement is true and correct. *(If this is a joint case, both debtors must sign.)*

Date: ____________________ Signature: ____________________ (Debtor)

Date: ____________________ Signature: ____________________ (Joint Debtor, if any)

(Added Oct. 17, 2005; amended Oct. 1, 2006; Jan. 1, 2008.)

Committee Notes on Rules—2005

For Committee Notes on Rules—2005 for form 22C, see note set out under form 22A.

Committee Notes on Rules—2006 Amendment

For Committee Notes on Rules—2006 Amendment for form 22C, see note set out under form 22A.

Committee Notes on Rules—2005-2008 Amendment

For Committee Notes on Rules—2005-2008 Amendment for form 22C, see note set out under form 22A.

B 23 (Official Form 23) (12/08)

UNITED STATES BANKRUPTCY COURT

In re ______________________________, Case No. ______________
Debtor

Chapter __________

DEBTOR'S CERTIFICATION OF COMPLETION OF POSTPETITION INSTRUCTIONAL COURSE CONCERNING PERSONAL FINANCIAL MANAGEMENT

Every individual debtor in a chapter 7, chapter 11 in which § 1141(d)(3) applies, or chapter 13 case must file this certification. If a joint petition is filed, each spouse must complete and file a separate certification. Complete one of the following statements and file by the deadline stated below:

❒ I, ______________________________, the debtor in the above-styled case, hereby
(Printed Name of Debtor)
certify that on ______________ *(Date)*, I completed an instructional course in personal financial management provided by ______________________________, an approved personal financial
(Name of Provider)
management provider.

Certificate No. *(if any)*: ______________________.

❒ I, ______________________________, the debtor in the above-styled case, hereby
(Printed Name of Debtor)
certify that no personal financial management course is required because of *[Check the appropriate box.]*:

❒ Incapacity or disability, as defined in 11 U.S.C. § 109(h);

❒ Active military duty in a military combat zone; or

❒ Residence in a district in which the United States trustee *(or bankruptcy administrator)* has determined that the approved instructional courses are not adequate at this time to serve the additional individuals who would otherwise be required to complete such courses.

Signature of Debtor: ______________________________

Date: __________

Instructions: Use this form only to certify whether you completed a course in personal financial management. (Fed. R. Bankr. P. 1007(b)(7).) Do NOT use this form to file the certificate given to you by your prepetition credit counseling provider and do NOT include with the petition when filing your case.

Filing Deadlines: In a chapter 7 case, file within 45 days of the first date set for the meeting of creditors under § 341 of the Bankruptcy Code. In a chapter 11 or 13 case, file no later than the last payment made by the debtor as required by the plan or the filing of a motion for a discharge under § 1141(d)(5)(B) or § 1328(b) of the Code. (See Fed. R. Bankr. P. 1007(c).)

(Added Oct. 17, 2005; amended Oct. 1, 2006; Dec. 1, 2007; Dec. 1, 2008.)

COMMITTEE NOTES ON RULES—2005

The form is new. Sections 727(a)(11) and 1328(g)(1), which were added to the Code by the Bankruptcy Abuse Prevention and Consumer Protection Act of 2005, Pub. L. No. 109–8, 119 Stat. 23 (April 20, 2005), require the debtor to complete an instructional course concerning personal financial management as a condition for receiving a discharge. The completed form, when filed by the debtor, will signal the clerk that this condition has been satisfied.

COMMITTEE NOTES ON RULES—2006 AMENDMENT

The form is amended to direct each individual debtor, including both spouses in a joint case, to file a separate certification and to provide the certificate number of the certificate of completion issued to the debtor by the approved personal financial management counselor. The form also is amended to include the deadlines for filing the certification in cases under chapters 7 and 13 and to instruct the debtor that the form is not to be used to file the certificate provided by the debtor's prepetition credit counselor.

COMMITTEE NOTES ON RULES—2005–2007 AMENDMENT

[The 2005–2007 Committee Note incorporates Committee Notes previously published in 2005 and 2006.]

The form was issued in 2005. Sections 727(a)(11), 1141(d)(3) and 1328(g)(1), which were added to the Code by the Bankruptcy Abuse Prevention and Consumer Protection Act of 2005, Pub. L. No. 109–8, 119 Stat. 23 (April 20, 2005), require individual debtors to complete an instructional course concerning personal financial management as a condition for receiving a discharge. The completed form will signal the clerk that this condition has been satisfied. Each individual debtor, including both spouses in a joint case, must file a separate certification and provide the certificate number of the certificate of completion issued to the debtor by the approved personal financial management counselor. Instructions are included that state the deadlines for filing the certification in chapter 7, chapter 11 in which § 1141(d)(3) applies, and chapter 13 cases, and remind the debtor that the form is not to be used for filing a certification of prepetition credit counseling.

B 24 (Official Form 24) (12/07)

[Caption as described in Fed. R. Bankr. P. 7010 or 9004(b), as applicable.]

CERTIFICATION TO COURT OF APPEALS BY ALL PARTIES

A notice of appeal having been filed in the above-styled matter on _________ *[Date]*, ___________________, _________________________, and _______________________, [*Names of all the appellants and all the appellees, if any]*, who are all the appellants [and all the appellees] hereby certify to the court under 28 U.S.C. § 158(d)(2)(A) that a circumstance specified in 28 U.S.C. § 158(d)(2) exists as stated below.

Leave to appeal in this matter ☐ is ☐ is not required under 28 U.S.C. § 158(a).

[If from a final judgment, order, or decree] This certification arises in an appeal from a final judgment, order, or decree of the United States Bankruptcy Court for the _________ District of _______________ entered on ____________ *[Date]*.

[If from an interlocutory order or decree] This certification arises in an appeal from an interlocutory order or decree, and the parties hereby request leave to appeal as required by 28 U.S.C. § 158(a).

[The certification shall contain one or more of the following statements, as is appropriate to the circumstances.]

The judgment, order, or decree involves a question of law as to which there is no controlling decision of the court of appeals for this circuit or of the Supreme Court of the United States, or involves a matter of public importance.

Or

The judgment, order, or decree involves a question of law requiring resolution of conflicting decisions.

Or

An immediate appeal from the judgment, order, or decree may materially advance the progress of the case or proceeding in which the appeal is taken.

B 24 (Official Form 24) (12/07) - Cont. Page 2

[The parties may include or attach the information specified in Rule 8001(f)(3)(C).]

Signed: *[If there are more than two signatories, all must sign and provide the information requested below. Attach additional signed sheets if needed.]*

Attorney for Appellant (or Appellant, if not represented by an attorney)	Attorney for Appellee (or Appellee if not represented by an attorney)
Printed Name of Signer	Printed Name of Signer
Address	Address
Telephone No.	Telephone No.
Date	Date

(Added Oct. 17, 2005; amended Dec. 1, 2007.)

COMMITTEE NOTES ON RULES—2005

This form is new. Rule 8001, as amended in 2005, requires that any certification of an appeal, bankruptcy court judgment, order, or decree directly to the United States Court of Appeals by all the appellants and appellees (if any) acting jointly be filed on this form.

COMMITTEE NOTES ON RULES—2005-2007 AMENDMENT

[The 2005-2007 Committee Note incorporates the Committee Note previously published in 2005.]

This form was issued in 2005. Rule 8001 requires that any certification of an appeal, bankruptcy court judgment, order, or decree directly to the United States Court of Appeals by all the appellants and appellees (if any) acting jointly be filed on this form.

B25A (Official Form 25A) (12/08)

United States Bankruptcy Court
____________________ District of ______________

In re______________________,
Debtor

Case No. ____________________

Small Business Case under Chapter 11

[NAME OF PROPONENT]'S PLAN OF REORGANIZATION, DATED [INSERT DATE]

ARTICLE I
SUMMARY

This Plan of Reorganization (the "Plan") under chapter 11 of the Bankruptcy Code (the "Code") proposes to pay creditors of [insert the name of the debtor] (the "Debtor") from [specify sources of payment, such as an infusion of capital, loan proceeds, sale of assets, cash flow from operations, or future income].

This Plan provides for __________ classes of secured claims; _____ classes of unsecured claims; and ______ classes of equity security holders. Unsecured creditors holding allowed claims will receive distributions, which the proponent of this Plan has valued at approximately __ cents on the dollar. This Plan also provides for the payment of administrative and priority claims [if payment is not in full on the effective date of this Plan with respect to any such claim (to the extent permitted by the Code or the claimant's agreement), identify such claim and briefly summarize the proposed treatment.]

All creditors and equity security holders should refer to Articles III through VI of this Plan for information regarding the precise treatment of their claim. A disclosure statement that provides more detailed information regarding this Plan and the rights of creditors and equity security holders has been circulated with this Plan. **Your rights may be affected. You should read these papers carefully and discuss them with your attorney, if you have one. (If you do not have an attorney, you may wish to consult one.)**

ARTICLE II
CLASSIFICATION OF CLAIMS AND INTERESTS

2.01 Class 1. All allowed claims entitled to priority under § 507 of the Code (except administrative expense claims under § 507(a)(2), ["gap" period claims in an involuntary case under § 507(a)(3),] and priority tax claims under § 507(a)(8)).

2.02 Class 2. The claim of ________________________, to the extent allowed as a secured claim under § 506 of the Code.

[Add other classes of secured creditors, if any. Note: Section 1129(a)(9)(D) of the Code provides that a secured tax claim which would otherwise meet the description of a priority tax claim under § 507(a)(8) of the Code is to be paid in the same manner and over the same period as prescribed in § 507(a)(8).]

2.03 Class 3. All unsecured claims allowed under § 502 of the Code.

[Add other classes of unsecured claims, if any.]

2.04 Class 4 . Equity interests of the Debtor. [If the Debtor is an individual, change this heading to "The interests of the individual Debtor in property of the estate."]

ARTICLE III
TREATMENT OF ADMINISTRATIVE EXPENSE CLAIMS, U.S. TRUSTEES FEES, AND PRIORITY TAX CLAIMS

3.01 Unclassified Claims. Under section §1123(a)(1), administrative expense claims, ["gap" period claims in an involuntary case allowed under § 502(f) of the Code,] and priority tax claims are not in classes.

3.02 Administrative Expense Claims. Each holder of an administrative expense claim allowed under § 503 of the Code [, and a "gap" claim in an involuntary case allowed under § 502(f) of the Code,] will be paid in full on the effective date of this Plan (as defined in Article VII), in cash, or upon such other terms as may be agreed upon by the holder of the claim and the Debtor.

3.03 Priority Tax Claims. Each holder of a priority tax claim will be paid [specify terms of treatment consistent with § 1129(a)(9)(C) of the Code].

3.04 United States Trustee Fees. All fees required to be paid by 28 U.S.C. §1930(a)(6) (U.S. Trustee Fees) will accrue and be timely paid until the case is closed, dismissed, or converted to another chapter of the Code. Any U.S. Trustee Fees owed on or before the effective date of this Plan will be paid on the effective date.

ARTICLE IV
TREATMENT OF CLAIMS AND INTERESTS UNDER THE PLAN

4.01 Claims and interests shall be treated as follows under this Plan:

B25A (Official Form 25A) (12/08) - Cont. 3

Class	Impairment	Treatment
Class 1 - Priority Claims	[State whether impaired or unimpaired.]	[Insert treatment of priority claims in this Class, including the form, amount and timing of distribution, if any. For example: "Class 1 is unimpaired by this Plan, and each holder of a Class 1 Priority Claim will be paid in full, in cash, upon the later of the effective date of this Plan as defined in Article VII, or the date on which such claim is allowed by a final non-appealable order. Except: ________."]
Class 2 – Secured Claim of [Insert name of secured creditor.]	[State whether impaired or unimpaired.]	[Insert treatment of secured claim in this Class, including the form, amount and timing of distribution, if any.] [Add class[es] of secured claims if applicable]
Class 3 - General Unsecured Creditors	[State whether impaired or unimpaired.]	[Insert treatment of unsecured creditors in this Class, including the form, amount and timing of distribution, if any.] [Add administrative convenience class if applicable]
Class 4 - Equity Security Holders of the Debtor	[State whether impaired or unimpaired.]	[Insert treatment of equity security holders in this Class, including the form, amount and timing of distribution, if any.]

ARTICLE V
ALLOWANCE AND DISALLOWANCE OF CLAIMS

5.01 Disputed Claim. A disputed claim is a claim that has not been allowed or disallowed [by a final non-appealable order], and as to which either: (i) a proof of claim has been filed or deemed filed, and the Debtor or another party in interest has filed an objection; or (ii) no proof of claim has been filed, and the Debtor has scheduled such claim as disputed, contingent, or unliquidated.

5.02 Delay of Distribution on a Disputed Claim. No distribution will be made on account of a disputed claim unless such claim is allowed [by a final non-appealable order].

5.03 Settlement of Disputed Claims. The Debtor will have the power and authority to settle and compromise a disputed claim with court approval and compliance with Rule 9019 of the Federal Rules of Bankruptcy Procedure.

ARTICLE VI
PROVISIONS FOR EXECUTORY CONTRACTS AND UNEXPIRED LEASES

6.01 Assumed Executory Contracts and Unexpired Leases.

(a) The Debtor assumes the following executory contracts and/or unexpired leases effective upon the [Insert "effective date of this Plan as provided in Article VII," "the date of the entry of the order confirming this Plan," or other applicable date]:

[List assumed executory contracts and/or unexpired leases.]

(b) The Debtor will be conclusively deemed to have rejected all executory contracts and/or unexpired leases not expressly assumed under section 6.01(a) above, or before the date of the order confirming this Plan, upon the [Insert "effective date of this Plan," "the date of the entry of the order confirming this Plan," or other applicable date]. A proof of a claim arising from the rejection of an executory contract or unexpired lease under this section must be filed no later than __________ (___) days after the date of the order confirming this Plan.

ARTICLE VII
MEANS FOR IMPLEMENTATION OF THE PLAN

[Insert here provisions regarding how the plan will be implemented as required under §1123(a)(5) of the Code. For example, provisions may include those that set out how the plan will be funded, as well as who will be serving as directors, officers or voting trustees of the reorganized debtor.]

ARTICLE VIII
GENERAL PROVISIONS

8.01 Definitions and Rules of Construction. The definitions and rules of construction set forth in §§ 101 and 102 of the Code shall apply when terms defined or construed in the Code are used in this Plan, and they are supplemented by the following definitions: [Insert additional definitions if necessary].

8.02 Effective Date of Plan. The effective date of this Plan is the eleventh business day following the date of the entry of the order of confirmation. But if a stay of the confirmation order is in effect on that date, the effective date will be the first business day after that date on which no stay of the confirmation order is in effect, provided that the confirmation order has not been vacated.

8.03 Severability. If any provision in this Plan is determined to be unenforceable, the determination will in no way limit or affect the enforceability and operative effect of any other provision of this Plan.

8.04 Binding Effect. The rights and obligations of any entity named or referred to in this Plan will be binding upon, and will inure to the benefit of the successors or assigns of such entity.

8.05 Captions. The headings contained in this Plan are for convenience of reference only and do not affect the meaning or interpretation of this Plan.

[8.06 Controlling Effect. Unless a rule of law or procedure is supplied by federal law (including the Code or the Federal Rules of Bankruptcy Procedure), the laws of the State of ____________ govern this Plan and any agreements, documents, and instruments executed in connection with this Plan, except as otherwise provided in this Plan.]

[8.07 Corporate Governance. [If the Debtor is a corporation include provisions required by § 1123(a)(6) of the Code.]]

ARTICLE IX
DISCHARGE

[If the Debtor is not entitled to discharge under 11 U.S.C. § 1141(d)(3) change this heading to **"NO DISCHARGE OF DEBTOR."**]

9.01. **[Option 1 – If Debtor is an individual and § 1141(d)(3) is not applicable]**
Discharge. Confirmation of this Plan does not discharge any debt provided for in this Plan until the court grants a discharge on completion of all payments under this Plan, or as otherwise provided in § 1141(d)(5) of the Code. The Debtor will not be discharged from any debt excepted from discharge under § 523 of the Code, except as provided in Rule 4007(c) of the Federal Rules of Bankruptcy Procedure.

[Option 2 – If the Debtor is a partnership and section 1141(d)(3) of the Code is not applicable]
Discharge. On the confirmation date of this Plan, the debtor will be discharged from any debt that arose before confirmation of this Plan, subject to the occurrence of the effective date, to the extent specified in § 1141(d)(1)(A) of the Code. The Debtor will not be discharged from any debt imposed by this Plan.

[Option 3 – If the Debtor is a corporation and § 1141(d)(3) is not applicable]

B25A (Official Form 25A) (12/08) - Cont. 6

Discharge. On the confirmation date of this Plan, the debtor will be discharged from any debt that arose before confirmation of this Plan, subject to the occurrence of the effective date, to the extent specified in § 1141(d)(1)(A) of the Code, except that the Debtor will not be discharged of any debt: (i) imposed by this Plan; (ii) of a kind specified in § 1141(d)(6)(A) if a timely complaint was filed in accordance with Rule 4007(c) of the Federal Rules of Bankruptcy Procedure; or (iii) of a kind specified in § 1141(d)(6)(B).

[Option 4 – If § 1141(d)(3) is applicable]

No Discharge. In accordance with § 1141(d)(3) of the Code, the Debtor will not receive any discharge of debt in this bankruptcy case.

ARTICLE X
OTHER PROVISIONS

[Insert other provisions, as applicable.]

Respectfully submitted,

By: ______________________________
The Plan Proponent

By: ______________________________
Attorney for the Plan Proponent

(Added Dec. 1, 2008.)

COMMITTEE NOTES ON RULES—2008

This form is new. It implements §433 of the Bankruptcy Abuse Prevention and Consumer Protection Act of 2005, Pub. L. No. 109-8, 119 Stat. 23 (April 20, 2005). This form for a small business chapter 11 plan of reorganization may be used in cases where the debtor (whether an individual or an artificial entity) is a small business debtor under §101(51D) of the Code. The form is intended to be used in conjunction with the small business chapter 11 disclosure statement form (Official Form 25B).

Because the type of debtor and the details of the proposed plan of reorganization may vary, the form is intended to provide an illustrative format, rather than a specific prescription for the language or content of a plan in any particular case. The form includes instructions and examples of the types of information needed to complete it.

B25B (Official Form 25B) (12/08)

United States Bankruptcy Court

__________________ District of ______________

In re____________________,
Debtor

Case No. ____________________

Small Business Case under Chapter 11

[NAME OF PLAN PROPONENT]'S DISCLOSURE STATEMENT, DATED [INSERT DATE]

Table of Contents

[Insert when text is finalized]

I. INTRODUCTION

This is the disclosure statement (the "Disclosure Statement") in the small business chapter 11 case of ____________ (the "Debtor"). This Disclosure Statement contains information about the Debtor and describes the [insert name of plan] (the "Plan") filed by [the Debtor] on [insert date]. A full copy of the Plan is attached to this Disclosure Statement as Exhibit A. ***Your rights may be affected. You should read the Plan and this Disclosure Statement carefully and discuss them with your attorney. If you do not have an attorney, you may wish to consult one.***

The proposed distributions under the Plan are discussed at pages __-__ of this Disclosure Statement. [General unsecured creditors are classified in Class __, and will receive a distribution of ___% of their allowed claims, to be distributed as follows _________.]

A. Purpose of This Document

This Disclosure Statement describes:

- The Debtor and significant events during the bankruptcy case,
- How the Plan proposes to treat claims or equity interests of the type you hold (*i.e.*, what you will receive on your claim or equity interest if the plan is confirmed),
- Who can vote on or object to the Plan,
- What factors the Bankruptcy Court (the "Court") will consider when deciding whether to confirm the Plan,
- Why [the Proponent] believes the Plan is feasible, and how the treatment of your claim or equity interest under the Plan compares to what you would receive on your claim or equity interest in liquidation, and
- The effect of confirmation of the Plan.

Be sure to read the Plan as well as the Disclosure Statement. This Disclosure Statement describes the Plan, but it is the Plan itself that will, if confirmed, establish your rights.

B. Deadlines for Voting and Objecting; Date of Plan Confirmation Hearing

The Court has not yet confirmed the Plan described in this Disclosure Statement. This section describes the procedures pursuant to which the Plan will or will not be confirmed.

1. *Time and Place of the Hearing to [Finally Approve This Disclosure Statement and] Confirm the Plan*

The hearing at which the Court will determine whether to [finally approve this Disclosure Statement and] confirm the Plan will take place on [insert date], at [insert time], in Courtroom _____, at the [Insert Courthouse Name, and Full Court Address, City, State, Zip Code].

2. *Deadline For Voting to Accept or Reject the Plan*

If you are entitled to vote to accept or reject the plan, vote on the enclosed ballot and return the ballot in the enclosed envelope to [insert address]. See section IV.A. below for a discussion of voting eligibility requirements.

Your ballot must be received by [insert date] or it will not be counted.

3. *Deadline For Objecting to the [Adequacy of Disclosure and] Confirmation of the Plan*

Objections to [this Disclosure Statement or to] the confirmation of the Plan must be filed with the Court and served upon [insert entities] by [insert date].

4. *Identity of Person to Contact for More Information*

If you want additional information about the Plan, you should contact [insert name and address of representative of plan proponent].

C. **Disclaimer**

The Court has [conditionally] approved this Disclosure Statement as containing adequate information to enable parties affected by the Plan to make an informed judgment about its terms. The Court has not yet determined whether the Plan meets the legal requirements for confirmation, and the fact that the Court has approved this Disclosure Statement does not constitute an endorsement of the Plan by the Court, or a recommendation that it be accepted. [The Court's approval of this Disclosure Statement is subject to final approval at the hearing on confirmation of the Plan. Objections to the adequacy of this Disclosure Statement may be filed until ______.]

II. **BACKGROUND**

A. **Description and History of the Debtor's Business**

The Debtor is a [corporation, partnership, etc.]. Since [insert year operations commenced], the Debtor has been in the business of _________. [Describe the Debtor's business].

B. **Insiders of the Debtor**

[Insert a detailed list of the names of Debtor's insiders as defined in §101(31) of the United States Bankruptcy Code (the "Code") and their relationship to the Debtor. For each insider, list all compensation paid by the Debtor or its affiliates to that person or entity during the two years prior to the commencement of the Debtor's bankruptcy case, as well as compensation paid during the pendency of this chapter 11 case.]

C. **Management of the Debtor Before and During the Bankruptcy**

During the two years prior to the date on which the bankruptcy petition was filed, the officers, directors, managers or other persons in control of the Debtor (collectively the "Managers") were [List the Managers of the Debtor prior to the petition date].

The Managers of the Debtor during the Debtor's chapter 11 case have been: [List Managers of the Debtor during the Debtor's chapter 11 case.]

After the effective date of the order confirming the Plan, the directors, officers, and voting trustees of the Debtor, any affiliate of the Debtor participating in a joint Plan with the Debtor, or successor of the Debtor under the Plan (collectively the "Post Confirmation Managers"), will be: [List Post Confirmation Managers of the Debtor.] The responsibilities and compensation of these Post Confirmation Managers are described in section __ of this Disclosure Statement.

D. **Events Leading to Chapter 11 Filing**

[Describe the events that led to the commencement of the Debtor's bankruptcy case.]

E. **Significant Events During the Bankruptcy Case**

[Describe significant events during the Debtor's bankruptcy case:

- Describe any asset sales outside the ordinary course of business, debtor in possession financing, or cash collateral orders.
- Identify the professionals approved by the court.
- Describe any adversary proceedings that have been filed or other significant litigation that has occurred (including contested claim disallowance proceedings), and any other significant legal or administrative proceedings that are pending or have been pending during the case in a forum other than the Court.
- Describe any steps taken to improve operations and profitability of the Debtor.
- Describe other events as appropriate.]

F. **Projected Recovery of Avoidable Transfers [Choose the option that applies]**

[Option 1 – If the Debtor does not intend to pursue avoidance actions]

The Debtor does not intend to pursue preference, fraudulent conveyance, or other avoidance actions.

[Option 2 – If the Debtor intends to pursue avoidance actions]

The Debtor estimates that up to $___________ may be realized from the recovery of fraudulent, preferential or other avoidable transfers. While the results of litigation cannot be predicted with certainty and it is possible that other causes of action may be identified, the following is a summary of the preference, fraudulent conveyance and other avoidance actions filed or expected to be filed in this case:

Transaction	Defendant	Amount Claimed

[Option 3 – If the Debtor does not yet know whether it intends to pursue avoidance actions]

The Debtor has not yet completed its investigation with regard to prepetition transactions. If you received a payment or other transfer within 90 days of the bankruptcy, or other transfer avoidable under the Code, the Debtor may seek to avoid such transfer.

G. **Claims Objections**

Except to the extent that a claim is already allowed pursuant to a final non-appealable order, the Debtor reserves the right to object to claims. Therefore, even if your claim is allowed for voting purposes, you may not be entitled to a distribution if an objection to your claim is later upheld. The procedures for resolving disputed claims are set forth in Article V of the Plan.

H. **Current and Historical Financial Conditions**

The identity and fair market value of the estate's assets are listed in Exhibit B. [Identify source and basis of valuation.]

The Debtor's most recent financial statements [if any] issued before bankruptcy, each of which was filed with the Court, are set forth in Exhibit C.

[The most recent post-petition operating report filed since the commencement of the Debtor's bankruptcy case are set forth in Exhibit D.] [A summary of the Debtor's periodic operating reports filed since the commencement of the Debtor's bankruptcy case is set forth in Exhibit D.]

III. **SUMMARY OF THE PLAN OF REORGANIZATION AND TREATMENT OF CLAIMS AND EQUITY INTERESTS**

A. **What is the Purpose of the Plan of Reorganization?**

As required by the Code, the Plan places claims and equity interests in various classes and describes the treatment each class will receive. The Plan also states whether each class of claims or equity interests is impaired or unimpaired. If the Plan is confirmed, your recovery will be limited to the amount provided by the Plan.

B. **Unclassified Claims**

Certain types of claims are automatically entitled to specific treatment under the Code. They are not considered impaired, and holders of such claims do not vote on the Plan. They may, however, object if, in their view, their treatment under the Plan does not comply with that required by the Code. As such, the Plan Proponent has *not* placed the following claims in any class:

1. *Administrative Expenses*

Administrative expenses are costs or expenses of administering the Debtor's chapter 11 case which are allowed under § 507(a)(2) of the Code. Administrative expenses also include the value of any goods sold to the Debtor in the ordinary course of business and received within 20 days before the date of the bankruptcy petition. The Code requires that all administrative expenses be paid on the effective date of the Plan, unless a particular claimant agrees to a different treatment.

The following chart lists the Debtor's estimated administrative expenses, and their proposed treatment under the Plan:

Type	Estimated Amount Owed	Proposed Treatment
Expenses Arising in the Ordinary Course of Business After the Petition Date		Paid in full on the effective date of the Plan, or according to terms of obligation if later
The Value of Goods Received in the Ordinary Course of Business Within 20 Days Before the Petition Date		Paid in full on the effective date of the Plan, or according to terms of obligation if later
Professional Fees, as approved by the Court.		Paid in full on the effective date of the Plan, or according to separate written agreement, or according to court order if such fees have not been approved by the Court on the effective date of the Plan
Clerk's Office Fees		Paid in full on the effective date of the Plan
Other administrative expenses		Paid in full on the effective date of the Plan or according to separate written agreement
Office of the U.S. Trustee Fees		Paid in full on the effective date of the Plan
TOTAL		

2. *Priority Tax Claims*

Priority tax claims are unsecured income, employment, and other taxes described by § 507(a)(8) of the Code. Unless the holder of such a § 507(a)(8) priority tax claim agrees otherwise, it must receive the present value of such claim, in regular installments paid over a period not exceeding 5 years from the order of relief.

B25B (Official Form 25B) (12/08) – Cont. 7

The following chart lists the Debtor's estimated § 507(a)(8) priority tax claims and their proposed treatment under the Plan:

Description (name and type of tax)	Estimated Amount Owed	Date of Assessment	Treatment
			Pmt interval = [Monthly] payment = Begin date = End date = Interest Rate % = Total Payout Amount = $
			Pmt interval = [Monthly] payment = Begin date = End date = Interest Rate % = Total Payout Amount = $

C. **Classes of Claims and Equity Interests**

The following are the classes set forth in the Plan, and the proposed treatment that they will receive under the Plan:

1. *Classes of Secured Claims*

Allowed Secured Claims are claims secured by property of the Debtor's bankruptcy estate (or that are subject to setoff) to the extent allowed as secured claims under § 506 of the Code. If the value of the collateral or setoffs securing the creditor's claim is less than the amount of the creditor's allowed claim, the deficiency will [be classified as a general unsecured claim].

The following chart lists all classes containing Debtor's secured prepetition claims and their proposed treatment under the Plan:

Class #	Description	Insider? (Yes or No)	Impairment	Treatment
	Secured claim of: Name = Collateral description = Allowed Secured Amount = $__________ Priority of lien = Principal owed = $__________ Pre-pet. arrearage = $__________ Total claim = $__________		[State whether impaired or unimpaired]	[Monthly] Pmt = Pmts Begin = Pmts End = [Balloon pmt] = Interest rate % = Treatment of Lien = [Additional payment required to cure defaults] =
	Secured claim of: Name = Collateral description = Allowed Secured Amount = $__________ Priority of lien = Principal owed = $__________ Pre-pet. arrearage = $__________ Total claim = $__________		[State whether impaired or unimpaired]	Monthly Pmt = Pmts Begin = Pmts End = [Balloon pmt] = Interest rate % = Treatment of Lien = [Additional payment required to cure defaults] =

2. *Classes of Priority Unsecured Claims*

Certain priority claims that are referred to in §§ 507(a)(1), (4), (5), (6), and (7) of the Code are required to be placed in classes. The Code requires that each holder of such a claim receive cash on the effective date of the Plan equal to the allowed amount of such claim. However, a class of holders of such claims may vote to accept different treatment.

The following chart lists all classes containing claims under §§ 507(a)(1), (4), (5), (6), and (a)(7) of the Code and their proposed treatment under the Plan:

Class #	Description	Impairment	Treatment
	Priority unsecured claim pursuant to Section [insert] Total amt of claims = $	[State whether impaired or unimpaired]	
	Priority unsecured claim pursuant to Section [insert] Total amt of claims = $	[State whether impaired or unimpaired]	

3. *Class[es] of General Unsecured Claims*

General unsecured claims are not secured by property of the estate and are not entitled to priority under § 507(a) of the Code. [Insert description of §1122(b) convenience class if applicable.]

The following chart identifies the Plan's proposed treatment of Class[es] __ through __, which contain general unsecured claims against the Debtor:

Class #	Description	Impairment	Treatment
	[1122(b) Convenience Class]	[State whether impaired or unimpaired]	[Insert proposed treatment, such as "Paid in full in cash on effective date of the Plan or when due under contract or applicable nonbankruptcy law"]
	General Unsecured Class	[State whether impaired or unimpaired]	Monthly Pmt = Pmts Begin = Pmts End = [Balloon pmt] = Interest rate % from [date] = Estimated percent of claim paid =

4. *Class[es] of Equity Interest Holders*

Equity interest holders are parties who hold an ownership interest (*i.e.*, equity interest) in the Debtor. In a corporation, entities holding preferred or common stock are equity interest holders. In a partnership, equity interest holders include both general and limited partners. In a limited liability company ("LLC"), the equity interest holders are the members. Finally, with respect to an individual who is a debtor, the Debtor is the equity interest holder.

The following chart sets forth the Plan's proposed treatment of the class[es] of equity interest holders: [There may be more than one class of equity interests in, for example, a partnership case, or a case where the prepetition debtor had issued multiple classes of stock.]

Class #	Description	Impairment	Treatment
	Equity interest holders	[State whether impaired or unimpaired]	

D. **Means of Implementing the Plan**

1. *Source of Payments*

Payments and distributions under the Plan will be funded by the following:

[Describe the source of funds for payments under the Plan.]

2. *Post-confirmation Management*

The Post-Confirmation Managers of the Debtor, and their compensation, shall be as follows:

Name	Affiliations	Insider (yes or no)?	Position	Compensation

E. **Risk Factors**

The proposed Plan has the following risks:

[List all risk factors that might affect the Debtor's ability to make payments and other distributions required under the Plan.]

F. **Executory Contracts and Unexpired Leases**

The Plan, in Exhibit 5.1, lists all executory contracts and unexpired leases that the Debtor will assume under the Plan. Assumption means that the Debtor has elected to continue to perform the obligations under such contracts and unexpired leases, and to cure defaults of the type that must be cured under the Code, if any. Exhibit 5.1 also lists how the Debtor will cure and compensate the other party to such contract or lease for any such defaults.

If you object to the assumption of your unexpired lease or executory contract, the proposed cure of any defaults, or the adequacy of assurance of performance, you must file and serve your objection to the Plan within the deadline for objecting to the confirmation of the Plan, unless the Court has set an earlier time.

All executory contracts and unexpired leases that are not listed in Exhibit 5.1 will be rejected under the Plan. Consult your adviser or attorney for more specific information about particular contracts or leases.

If you object to the rejection of your contract or lease, you must file and serve your objection to the Plan within the deadline for objecting to the confirmation of the Plan.

[***The Deadline for Filing a Proof of Claim Based on a Claim Arising from the Rejection of a Lease or Contract Is ______.*** Any claim based on the rejection of a contract or lease will be barred if the proof of claim is not timely filed, unless the Court orders otherwise.]

G. Tax Consequences of Plan

Creditors and Equity Interest Holders Concerned with How the Plan May Affect Their Tax Liability Should Consult with Their Own Accountants, Attorneys, And/Or Advisors.

The following are the anticipated tax consequences of the Plan: [List the following general consequences as a minimum: (1)Tax consequences to the Debtor of the Plan; (2) General tax consequences on creditors of any discharge, and the general tax consequences of receipt of plan consideration after confirmation.]

IV. CONFIRMATION REQUIREMENTS AND PROCEDURES

To be confirmable, the Plan must meet the requirements listed in §§ 1129(a) or (b) of the Code. These include the requirements that: the Plan must be proposed in good faith; at least one impaired class of claims must accept the plan, without counting votes of insiders; the Plan must distribute to each creditor and equity interest holder at least as much as the creditor or equity interest holder would receive in a chapter 7 liquidation case, unless the creditor or equity interest holder votes to accept the Plan; and the Plan must be feasible. These requirements are not the only requirements listed in § 1129, and they are not the only requirements for confirmation.

A. Who May Vote or Object

Any party in interest may object to the confirmation of the Plan if the party believes that the requirements for confirmation are not met.

Many parties in interest, however, are not entitled to vote to accept or reject the Plan. A creditor or equity interest holder has a right to vote for or against the Plan only if that creditor or equity interest holder has a claim or equity interest that is both (1) allowed or allowed for voting purposes and (2) impaired.

In this case, the Plan Proponent believes that classes _____ are impaired and that holders of claims in each of these classes are therefore entitled to vote to accept or reject the Plan. The Plan Proponent believes that classes _____ are unimpaired and that holders of claims in each of these classes, therefore, do not have the right to vote to accept or reject the Plan.

1. *What Is an Allowed Claim or an Allowed Equity Interest?*

Only a creditor or equity interest holder with an allowed claim or an allowed equity interest has the right to vote on the Plan. Generally, a claim or equity interest is allowed if either (1) the Debtor has scheduled the claim on the Debtor's schedules, unless the claim has been scheduled as disputed, contingent, or unliquidated, or (2) the creditor has filed a proof of claim or equity interest, unless an objection has been filed to such proof of claim or equity interest. When a claim or equity interest is not allowed, the creditor or equity interest holder holding the claim or equity interest cannot vote unless the Court, after notice and hearing, either overrules the objection or allows the claim or equity interest for voting purposes pursuant to Rule 3018(a) of the Federal Rules of Bankruptcy Procedure.

The deadline for filing a proof of claim in this case was _____.
[If applicable – The deadline for filing objections to claims is_____.]

2. *What Is an Impaired Claim or Impaired Equity Interest?*

As noted above, the holder of an allowed claim or equity interest has the right to vote only if it is in a class that is *impaired* under the Plan. As provided in § 1124 of the Code, a class is considered impaired if the Plan alters the legal, equitable, or contractual rights of the members of that class.

3. *Who is **Not** Entitled to Vote*

The holders of the following five types of claims and equity interests are *not* entitled to vote:

- holders of claims and equity interests that have been disallowed by an order of the Court;

- holders of other claims or equity interests that are not "allowed claims" or "allowed equity interests" (as discussed above), unless they have been "allowed" for voting purposes.

- holders of claims or equity interests in unimpaired classes;

- holders of claims entitled to priority pursuant to §§ 507(a)(2), (a)(3), and (a)(8) of the Code; and
- holders of claims or equity interests in classes that do not receive or retain any value under the Plan;
- administrative expenses.

Even If You Are Not Entitled to Vote on the Plan, You Have a Right to Object to the Confirmation of the Plan [and to the Adequacy of the Disclosure Statement].

4. *Who Can Vote in More Than One Class*

A creditor whose claim has been allowed in part as a secured claim and in part as an unsecured claim, or who otherwise hold claims in multiple classes, is entitled to accept or reject a Plan in each capacity, and should cast one ballot for each claim.

B. **Votes Necessary to Confirm the Plan**

If impaired classes exist, the Court cannot confirm the Plan unless (1) at least one impaired class of creditors has accepted the Plan without counting the votes of any insiders within that class, and (2) all impaired classes have voted to accept the Plan, unless the Plan is eligible to be confirmed by "cram down" on non-accepting classes, as discussed later in Section [B.2.].

1. *Votes Necessary for a Class to Accept the Plan*

A class of claims accepts the Plan if both of the following occur: (1) the holders of more than one-half (1/2) of the allowed claims in the class, who vote, cast their votes to accept the Plan, and (2) the holders of at least two-thirds (2/3) in dollar amount of the allowed claims in the class, who vote, cast their votes to accept the Plan.

A class of equity interests accepts the Plan if the holders of at least two-thirds (2/3) in amount of the allowed equity interests in the class, who vote, cast their votes to accept the Plan.

2. *Treatment of Nonaccepting Classes*

Even if one or more impaired classes reject the Plan, the Court may nonetheless confirm the Plan if the nonaccepting classes are treated in the manner prescribed by § 1129(b) of the Code. A plan that binds nonaccepting classes is commonly referred to as a "cram down" plan. The Code allows the Plan to bind nonaccepting classes of claims or equity interests if it meets all the requirements for consensual confirmation except the voting requirements of § 1129(a)(8) of the Code, does not "discriminate unfairly," and is "fair and equitable" toward each impaired class that has not voted to accept the Plan.

You should consult your own attorney if a "cramdown" confirmation will affect your claim or equity interest, as the variations on this general rule are numerous and complex.

C. **Liquidation Analysis**

To confirm the Plan, the Court must find that all creditors and equity interest holders who do not accept the Plan will receive at least as much under the Plan as such claim and equity interest holders would receive in a chapter 7 liquidation. A liquidation analysis is attached to this Disclosure Statement as Exhibit E.

D. **Feasibility**

The Court must find that confirmation of the Plan is not likely to be followed by the liquidation, or the need for further financial reorganization, of the Debtor or any successor to the Debtor, unless such liquidation or reorganization is proposed in the Plan.

1. *Ability to Initially Fund Plan*

The Plan Proponent believes that the Debtor will have enough cash on hand on the effective date of the Plan to pay all the claims and expenses that are entitled to be paid on that date. Tables showing the amount of cash on hand on the effective date of the Plan, and the sources of that cash are attached to this disclosure statement as Exhibit F.

2. *Ability to Make Future Plan Payments And Operate Without Further Reorganization*

The Plan Proponent must also show that it will have enough cash over the life of the Plan to make the required Plan payments.

The Plan Proponent has provided projected financial information. Those projections are listed in Exhibit G.

The Plan Proponent's financial projections show that the Debtor will have an aggregate annual average cash flow, after paying operating expenses and post-confirmation taxes, of $_–_. The final Plan payment is expected to be paid on _____.

[Summarize the numerical projections, and highlight any assumptions that are not in accord with past experience. Explain why such assumptions should now be made.]

You Should Consult with Your Accountant or other Financial Advisor If You Have Any Questions Pertaining to These Projections.

V. **EFFECT OF CONFIRMATION OF PLAN**

A. **DISCHARGE OF DEBTOR** [If the Debtor is not entitled to discharge pursuant to 11 U.S.C. § 1141(d)(3) change this heading to "**NO DISCHARGE OF DEBTOR**."]

[Option 1 – If Debtor is an individual and § 1141(d)(3) is not applicable]

Discharge. Confirmation of the Plan does not discharge any debt provided for in the Plan until the court grants a discharge on completion of all payments under the Plan, or as otherwise provided in § 1141(d)(5) of the Code. Debtor will not be discharged from any debt excepted from discharge under § 523 of the Code, except as provided in Rule 4007(c) of the Federal Rules of Bankruptcy Procedure.

[Option 2 – If the Debtor is a partnership and § 1141(d)(3) of the Code is not applicable]

Discharge. On the effective date of the Plan, the Debtor shall be discharged from any debt that arose before confirmation of the Plan, subject to the occurrence of the effective date, to the extent specified in § 1141(d)(1)(A) of the Code. However, the Debtor shall not be discharged from any debt imposed by the Plan. After the effective date of the Plan your claims against the Debtor will be limited to the debts imposed by the Plan.

[Option 3 – If the Debtor is a corporation and § 1141(d)(3) is not applicable]

Discharge. On the effective date of the Plan, the Debtor shall be discharged from any debt that arose before confirmation of the Plan, subject to the occurrence of the effective date, to the extent specified in § 1141(d)(1)(A) of the Code, except that the Debtor shall not be discharged of any debt (i) imposed by the Plan, (ii) of a kind specified in § 1141(d)(6)(A) if a timely complaint was filed in accordance with Rule 4007(c) of the Federal Rules of Bankruptcy Procedure, or (iii) of a kind specified in § 1141(d)(6)(B). After the effective date of the Plan your claims against the Debtor will be limited to the debts described in clauses (i) through (iii) of the preceding sentence.

[Option 4 – If § 1141(d)(3) is applicable]

No Discharge. In accordance with § 1141(d)(3) of the Code, the Debtor will not receive any discharge of debt in this bankruptcy case.

B. **Modification of Plan**

The Plan Proponent may modify the Plan at any time before confirmation of the Plan. However, the Court may require a new disclosure statement and/or revoting on the Plan.

[If the Debtor is not an individual, add the following: "The Plan Proponent may also seek to modify the Plan at any time after confirmation only if (1) the Plan has not been substantially consummated *and* (2) the Court authorizes the proposed modifications after notice and a hearing."]

[If the Debtor is an individual, add the following: "Upon request of the Debtor, the United States trustee, or the holder of an allowed unsecured claim, the Plan may be modified at any time after confirmation of the Plan but before the completion of payments under the Plan, to (1) increase or reduce the amount of payments under the Plan on claims of a particular class, (2) extend or reduce the time period for such payments, or (3) alter the amount of distribution to a creditor whose claim is provided for by the Plan to the extent necessary to take account of any payment of the claim made other than under the Plan."]

C. **Final Decree**

Once the estate has been fully administered, as provided in Rule 3022 of the Federal Rules of Bankruptcy Procedure, the Plan Proponent, or such other party as the Court shall designate in the Plan Confirmation Order, shall file a motion with the Court to obtain a final decree to close the case. Alternatively, the Court may enter such a final decree on its own motion.

VI. OTHER PLAN PROVISIONS

[Insert other provisions here, as necessary and appropriate.]

____
[Signature of the Plan Proponent]

____
[Signature of the Attorney for the Plan Proponent]

EXHIBITS

Exhibit A – Copy of Proposed Plan of Reorganization

Exhibit B – Identity and Value of Material Assets of Debtor

Exhibit C – Prepetition Financial Statements
(to be taken from those filed with the court)

Exhibit D – [Most Recently Filed Postpetition Operating Report][Summary of Postpetition Operating Reports]

B25B (Official Form 25B) (12/08) – Cont. 22

Exhibit E – Liquidation Analysis

Plan Proponent's Estimated Liquidation Value of Assets

Assets	
a. Cash on hand	$
b. Accounts receivable	$
c. Inventory	$
d. Office furniture & equipment	$
e. Machinery & equipment	$
f. Automobiles	$
g. Building & Land	$
h. Customer list	$
i. Investment property (such as stocks, bonds or other financial assets)	$
j. Lawsuits or other claims against third-parties	$
k. Other intangibles (such as avoiding powers actions)	$
Total Assets at Liquidation Value	$
Less: Secured creditors' recoveries	$
Less: Chapter 7 trustee fees and expenses	$
Less: Chapter 11 administrative expenses	$
Less: Priority claims, excluding administrative expense claims	$
[Less: Debtor's claimed exemptions]	$
(1) Balance for unsecured claims	$
(2) Total dollar amount of unsecured claims	$
Percentage of Claims Which Unsecured Creditors Would Receive Or Retain in a Chapter 7 Liquidation:	$
Percentage of Claims Which Unsecured Creditors Will Receive or Retain under the Plan:	____% [Divide (1) by (2)]
	____%

Exhibit F – Cash on hand on the effective date of the Plan

Cash on hand on effective date of the Plan:	$
Less –	
Amount of administrative expenses payable on effective date of the Plan	-
Amount of statutory costs and charges	-
Amount of cure payments for executory contracts	-
Other Plan Payments due on effective date of the Plan	-
Balance after paying these amounts..............	$

The sources of the cash Debtor will have on hand by the effective date of the Plan are estimated as follows:

$	Cash in Debtor's bank account now
+	Additional cash Debtor will accumulate from net earnings between now and effective date of the Plan [state the basis for such projections]
+	Borrowing [separately state terms of repayment]
+	Capital Contributions
+	Other
$	Total [This number should match "cash on hand" figure noted above

Exhibit G – Projections of Cash Flow and Earnings for Post-Confirmation Period

(Added Dec. 1, 2008.)

COMMITTEE NOTES ON RULES—2008

This form is new. It implements §433 of the Bankruptcy Abuse Prevention and Consumer Protection Act of 2005, Pub. L. No. 109–8, 119 Stat. 23 (April 20, 2005), which provides for an official form for a disclosure statement that may be used in cases where the debtor (whether an individual or an artificial entity) is a small business debtor under §101(51D) of the Code. The form provides a format for disseminating information to parties in interest about the plan of reorganization in a small business debtor's chapter 11 case, so that a party can make a reasonably informed judgment whether to accept, reject, or object to a proposed plan of reorganization or liquidation.

The form is intended to be used in conjunction with the form small business chapter 11 plan (Official Form 25A). As required by §433 of the 2005 Act, the form seeks to strike a practical balance between the reasonable needs of the courts, the United States trustee, creditors, and other parties in interest for reasonably complete information, on the one hand, and economy and simplicity for debtors, on the other. The form includes instructions and examples of the types of information needed to complete it.

Because the relevant legal requirements for, and effect of, a plan's confirmation may vary depending on the nature of the debtor and the details of the proposed plan, this form is intended to provide an illustrative format for disclosure, rather than a specific prescription for the language or content of a particular disclosure statement. The form highlights the factual and legal disclosures required for adequate disclosure under §1125 of the Code. The form is not intended to restrict a plan proponent from providing additional information where that would be useful. Plan proponents are encouraged to present material information in as clear a manner as possible, including, where feasible, by providing an accompanying executive summary, approved by the court, that highlights particular creditors' or interest holders' voting status and treatment under the plan.

Rule 3016 specifies the manner in which the disclosure statement is to be filed. Rule 3017 specifies the manner in which the court will consider it. Rule 3017.1 specifies special procedures for the court's conditional approval of a disclosure statement in a small business case.

B 25C (Official Form 25C) (12/08)

UNITED STATES BANKRUPTCY COURT

In re ______________________________ , Case No. ______________

Debtor

Small Business Case under Chapter 11

SMALL BUSINESS MONTHLY OPERATING REPORT

Month: ________________ Date filed: ________________

Line of Business: ________________ NAISC Code: ________________

IN ACCORDANCE WITH TITLE 28, SECTION 1746, OF THE UNITED STATES CODE, I DECLARE UNDER PENALTY OF PERJURY THAT I HAVE EXAMINED THE FOLLOWING SMALL BUSINESS MONTHLY OPERATING REPORT AND THE ACCOMPANYING ATTACHMENTS AND, TO THE BEST OF MY KNOWLEDGE, THESE DOCUMENTS ARE TRUE, CORRECT AND COMPLETE.

RESPONSIBLE PARTY:

____

Original Signature of Responsible Party

____

Printed Name of Responsible Party

Questionnaire: *(All questions to be answered on behalf of the debtor.)*	Yes	No
1. IS THE BUSINESS STILL OPERATING?	❒	❒
2. HAVE YOU PAID ALL YOUR BILLS ON TIME THIS MONTH?	❒	❒
3. DID YOU PAY YOUR EMPLOYEES ON TIME?	❒	❒
4. HAVE YOU DEPOSITED ALL THE RECEIPTS FOR YOUR BUSINESS INTO THE DIP ACCOUNT THIS MONTH?	❒	❒
5. HAVE YOU FILED ALL OF YOUR TAX RETURNS AND PAID ALL OF YOUR TAXES THIS MONTH	❒	❒
6. HAVE YOU TIMELY FILED ALL OTHER REQUIRED GOVERNMENT FILINGS?	❒	❒
7. HAVE YOU PAID ALL OF YOUR INSURANCE PREMIUMS THIS MONTH?	❒	❒
8. DO YOU PLAN TO CONTINUE TO OPERATE THE BUSINESS NEXT MONTH?	❒	❒
9. ARE YOU CURRENT ON YOUR QUARTERLY FEE PAYMENT TO THE U.S. TRUSTEE?	❒	❒
10. HAVE YOU PAID ANYTHING TO YOUR ATTORNEY OR OTHER PROFESSIONALS THIS MONTH?	❒	❒
11. DID YOU HAVE ANY UNUSUAL OR SIGNIFICANT UNANTICIPATED EXPENSES THIS MONTH?	❒	❒
12. HAS THE BUSINESS SOLD ANY GOODS OR PROVIDED SERVICES OR TRANSFERRED ANY ASSETS TO ANY BUSINESS RELATED TO THE DIP IN ANY WAY?	❒	❒
13. DO YOU HAVE ANY BANK ACCOUNTS OPEN OTHER THAN THE DIP ACCOUNT?	❒	❒

14. HAVE YOU SOLD ANY ASSETS OTHER THAN INVENTORY THIS MONTH?	❐	❐
15. DID ANY INSURANCE COMPANY CANCEL YOUR POLICY THIS MONTH?	❐	❐
16. HAVE YOU BORROWED MONEY FROM ANYONE THIS MONTH?	❐	❐
17. HAS ANYONE MADE AN INVESTMENT IN YOUR BUSINESS THIS MONTH?	❐	❐
18. HAVE YOU PAID ANY BILLS YOU OWED BEFORE YOU FILED BANKRUPTCY?	❐	❐

TAXES

DO YOU HAVE ANY PAST DUE TAX RETURNS OR PAST DUE POST-PETITION TAX OBLIGATIONS? ❐ ❐

IF YES, PLEASE PROVIDE A WRITTEN EXPLANATION INCLUDING WHEN SUCH RETURNS WILL BE FILED, OR WHEN SUCH PAYMENTS WILL BE MADE AND THE SOURCE OF THE FUNDS FOR THE PAYMENT.

(Exhibit A)

INCOME

PLEASE SEPARATELY LIST ALL OF THE INCOME YOU RECEIVED FOR THE MONTH. THE LIST SHOULD INCLUDE ALL INCOME FROM CASH AND CREDIT TRANSACTIONS. *(THE U.S. TRUSTEE MAY WAIVE THIS REQUIREMENT.)*

TOTAL INCOME $ ________

SUMMARY OF CASH ON HAND

Cash on Hand at Start of Month $ ________

Cash on Hand at End of Month $ ________

PLEASE PROVIDE THE TOTAL AMOUNT OF CASH CURRENTLY AVAILABLE TO YOU **TOTAL** $ ________

(Exhibit B)

EXPENSES

PLEASE SEPARATELY LIST ALL EXPENSES PAID BY CASH OR BY CHECK FROM YOUR BANK ACCOUNTS THIS MONTH. INCLUDE THE DATE PAID, WHO WAS PAID THE MONEY, THE PURPOSE AND THE AMOUNT. *(THE U.S. TRUSTEE MAY WAIVE THIS REQUIREMENT.)*

TOTAL EXPENSES $ ________

(Exhibit C)

CASH PROFIT

INCOME FOR THE MONTH *(TOTAL FROM EXHIBIT B)* $ ________

EXPENSES FOR THE MONTH *(TOTAL FROM EXHIBIT C)* $ ________

(Subtract Line C from Line B) **CASH PROFIT FOR THE MONTH** $ ________

UNPAID BILLS

PLEASE ATTACH A LIST OF ALL DEBTS (INCLUDING TAXES) WHICH YOU HAVE INCURRED SINCE THE DATE YOU FILED BANKRUPTCY BUT HAVE NOT PAID. THE LIST MUST INCLUDE THE DATE THE DEBT WAS INCURRED, WHO IS OWED THE MONEY, THE PURPOSE OF THE DEBT AND WHEN THE DEBT IS DUE. *(THE U.S. TRUSTEE MAY WAIVE THIS REQUIREMENT.)*

TOTAL PAYABLES $ ____________

(Exhibit D)

MONEY OWED TO YOU

PLEASE ATTACH A LIST OF ALL AMOUNTS OWED TO YOU BY YOUR CUSTOMERS FOR WORK YOU HAVE DONE OR THE MERCHANDISE YOU HAVE SOLD. YOU SHOULD INCLUDE WHO OWES YOU MONEY, HOW MUCH IS OWED AND WHEN IS PAYMENT DUE. *(THE U.S. TRUSTEE MAY WAIVE THIS REQUIREMENT.)*

TOTAL RECEIVABLES $ ____________

(Exhibit E)

BANKING INFORMATION

PLEASE ATTACH A COPY OF YOUR LATEST BANK STATEMENT FOR EVERY ACCOUNT YOU HAVE AS OF THE DATE OF THIS FINANCIAL REPORT OR HAD DURING THE PERIOD COVERED BY THIS REPORT.

(Exhibit F)

EMPLOYEES

NUMBER OF EMPLOYEES WHEN THE CASE WAS FILED? ____________

NUMBER OF EMPLOYEES AS OF THE DATE OF THIS MONTHLY REPORT? ____________

PROFESSIONAL FEES

BANKRUPTCY RELATED:

PROFESSIONAL FEES RELATING TO THE BANKRUPTCY CASE PAID DURING THIS REPORTING PERIOD? $ ____________

TOTAL PROFESSIONAL FEES RELATING TO THE BANKRUPTCY CASE PAID SINCE THE FILING OF THE CASE? $ ____________

NON-BANKRUPTCY RELATED:

PROFESSIONAL FEES NOT RELATING TO THE BANKRUPTCY CASE PAID DURING THIS REPORTING PERIOD? $ ____________

TOTAL PROFESSIONAL FEES NOT RELATING TO THE BANKRUPTCY CASE PAID SINCE THE FILING OF THE CASE? $ ____________

Page 4

B 25C (Official Form 25C) (12/08)

PROJECTIONS

COMPARE YOUR ACTUAL INCOME AND EXPENSES TO THE PROJECTIONS FOR THE FIRST 180 DAYS OF YOUR CASE PROVIDED AT THE INITIAL DEBTOR INTERVIEW.

	Projected	Actual	Difference
INCOME	$ ______	$ ______	$ ______
EXPENSES	$ ______	$ ______	$ ______
CASH PROFIT	$ ______	$ ______	$ ______

TOTAL PROJECTED INCOME FOR THE NEXT MONTH: $ ______

TOTAL PROJECTED EXPENSES FOR THE NEXT MONTH: $ ______

TOTAL PROJECTED CASH PROFIT FOR THE NEXT MONTH: $ ______

ADDITIONAL INFORMATION

PLEASE ATTACH ALL FINANCIAL REPORTS INCLUDING AN INCOME STATEMENT AND BALANCE SHEET WHICH YOU PREPARE INTERNALLY.

(Added Dec. 1, 2008.)

COMMITTEE NOTES ON RULES—2008

This form is new. It implements §§434 and 435 of the Bankruptcy Abuse Prevention and Consumer Protection Act of 2005, Pub. L. No. 109-8, 119 Stat. 23 (April 20, 2005), which provided for rules and an official form to assist small business debtors in chapter 11 cases to fulfill their responsibilities under §308 of the Code, a provision added by the 2005 Act. The form directs the debtor to disclose the information required under §308 and resembles those developed earlier by the United States trustees for use in supervising debtors in possession in chapter 11 cases.

Official Form 26 (12/08)

United States Bankruptcy Court
__________________ District of ______________

In re____________________, Case No. ____________________

Debtor Chapter 11

PERIODIC REPORT REGARDING VALUE, OPERATIONS AND PROFITABILITY OF ENTITIES IN WHICH THE ESTATE OF [NAME OF DEBTOR] HOLDS A SUBSTANTIAL OR CONTROLLING INTEREST

This is the report as of _________on the value, operations and profitability of those entities in which the estate holds a substantial or controlling interest, as required by Bankruptcy Rule 2015.3. The estate of [Name of Debtor] holds a substantial or controlling interest in the following entities:

Name of Entity	Interest of the Estate	Tab #

This periodic report (the "Periodic Report") contains separate reports ("Entity Reports") on the value, operations, and profitability of each entity listed above.

Each Entity Report shall consist of three exhibits. Exhibit A contains a valuation estimate for the entity as of a date not more than two years prior to the date of this report. It also contains a description of the valuation method used. Exhibit B contains a balance sheet, a statement of income (loss), a statement of cash flows, and a statement of changes in shareholders' or partners' equity (deficit) for the period covered by the Entity Report, along with summarized footnotes. Exhibit C contains a description of the entity's business operations.

THIS REPORT MUST BE SIGNED BY A REPRESENTATIVE OF THE TRUSTEE OR DEBTOR IN POSSESSION.

The undersigned, having reviewed the above listing of entities in which the estate of [Debtor] holds a substantial or controlling interest, and being familiar with the Debtor's financial affairs, verifies under the penalty of perjury that the listing is complete, accurate and truthful to the best of his/her knowledge.

Official Form 26 (12/08) – Cont. 2

Date: __________

____
Signature of Authorized Individual

____
Name of Authorized Individual

____
Title of Authorized Individual

[If the Debtor is an individual or in a joint case]

Signature(s) of Debtor(s) (Individual/Joint)

____
Signature of Debtor

____
Signature of Joint Debtor

Official Form 26 (12/08) – Cont. 3

Exhibit A
Valuation Estimate for [Name of Entity]

[Provide a statement of the entity's value and the value of the estate's interest in the entity, including a description of the basis for the valuation, the date of the valuation and the valuation method used. This valuation must be no more than two years old. Indicate the source of this information.]

Official Form 26 (12/08) – Cont. 4

Exhibit B
Financial Statements for [Insert Name of Entity]

Official Form 26 (12/08) – Cont. 5

Exhibit B-1
Balance Sheet for [Name of Entity]
As of [date]

[Provide a balance sheet dated as of the end of the most recent six-month period of the current fiscal year and as of the end of the preceding fiscal year. Indicate the source of this information.]

Official Form 26 (12/08) – Cont. 6

Exhibit B-2

Statement of Income (Loss) for [Name of Entity]

Period ending [date]

[Provide a statement of income (loss) for the following periods:

(i) For the initial report:
a. the period between the end of the preceding fiscal year and the end of the most recent six-month period of the current fiscal year; and
b. the prior fiscal year.
(ii) For subsequent reports, since the closing date of the last report.

Indicate the source of this information.]

Official Form 26 (12/08) – Cont. 7

Exhibit B-3

Statement of Cash Flows for [Name of Entity]

For the period ending [date]

[Provide a statement of changes in cash flows for the following periods:

(i) For the initial report:
a. the period between the end of the preceding fiscal year and the end of the most recent six-month period of the current fiscal year; and
b. the prior fiscal year.
(ii) For subsequent reports, since the closing date of the last report.

Indicate the source of this information.]

Official Form 26 (12/08) – Cont. 8

Exhibit B-4

Statement of Changes in Shareholders'/Partners' Equity (Deficit) for [Name of Entity]

period ending [date]

[Provide a statement of changes in shareholders'/partners equity (deficit) for the following periods:

(i) For the initial report:
a. the period between the end of the preceding fiscal year and the end of the most recent six-month period of the current fiscal year; and
b. the prior fiscal year.
(ii) For subsequent reports, since the closing date of the last report.

Indicate the source of this information.]

Official Form 26 (12/08) – Cont. 9

Exhibit C
Description of Operations for [name of entity]

[Describe the nature and extent of the estate's interest in the entity.

Describe the business conducted and intended to be conducted by the entity, focusing on the entity's dominant business segment(s). Indicate the source of this information.]

(Added Dec. 1, 2008.)

COMMITTEE NOTES ON RULES—2008

This form is new. It implements §419 of the Bankruptcy Abuse Prevention and Consumer Protection Act of 2005, Pub. L. No. 109-8, 119 Stat. 23 (April 20, 2005), which requires a chapter 11 debtor to file periodic reports on the profitability of any entities in which the estate holds a substantial or controlling interest. The form is to be used when required by Bankruptcy Rule 2015.3, with such variations as may be approved by the court pursuant to subdivisions (d) and (e) of that rule. The form includes instructions and examples of the types of information needed to complete it.

B27 (Official Form27) (12/09)

United States Bankruptcy Court

______________ District Of ______________

In re ______________________,
Debtor

Case No. ______________
Chapter ___

REAFFIRMATION AGREEMENT COVER SHEET

This form must be completed in its entirety and filed, with the reaffirmation agreement attached, within the time set under Rule 4008. It may be filed by any party to the reaffirmation agreement.

1. Creditor's Name:______________________

2. Amount of the debt subject to this reaffirmation agreement:
$_____ on the date of bankruptcy $_____ to be paid under reaffirmation agreement

3. Annual percentage rate of interest: ______% prior to bankruptcy
______% under reaffirmation agreement (____ Fixed Rate ____ Adjustable Rate)

4. Repayment terms (if fixed rate): $______ per month for _______ months

5. Collateral, if any, securing the debt: Current market value: $________
Description: ______________________________________

6. Does the creditor assert that the debt is nondischargeable? ___Yes ___ No
(If yes, attach a declaration setting forth the nature of the debt and basis for the contention that the debt is nondischargeable.)

Debtor's Schedule I and J Entries	Debtor's Income and Expenses as Stated on Reaffirmation Agreement
7A. Total monthly income from Schedule I, line 16 $_______	7B. Monthly income from all sources after payroll deductions $_______
8A. Total monthly expenses from Schedule J, line 18 $_______	8B. Monthly expenses $_______
9A. Total monthly payments on reaffirmed debts not listed on Schedule J $_______	9B. Total monthly payments on reaffirmed debts not included in monthly expenses $_______
	10B. Net monthly income $_______ (Subtract sum of lines 8B and 9B from line 7B. If total is less than zero, put the number in brackets.)

B27 (Official Form27) (12/09) Page 2

11. Explain with specificity any difference between the income amounts (7A and 7B):

____

____

12. Explain with specificity any difference between the expense amounts (8A and 8B):

____

____

If line 11 or12 is completed, the undersigned debtor, and joint debtor if applicable, certifies that any explanation contained on those lines is true and correct.

____________________	____________________
Signature of Debtor (only required if line 11 or 12 is completed)	Signature of Joint Debtor (if applicable, and only required if line 11 or 12 is completed)

Other Information

☐ Check this box if the total on line 10B is less than zero. If that number is less than zero, a presumption of undue hardship arises (unless the creditor is a credit union) and you must explain with specificity the sources of funds available to the Debtor to make the monthly payments on the reaffirmed debt: ____

____

Was debtor represented by counsel during the course of negotiating this reaffirmation agreement?
_____Yes ______No

If debtor was represented by counsel during the course of negotiating this reaffirmation agreement, has counsel executed a certification (affidavit or declaration) in support of the reaffirmation agreement?
_____Yes ______No

FILER'S CERTIFICATION

I hereby certify that the attached agreement is a true and correct copy of the reaffirmation agreement between the parties identified on this Reaffirmation Agreement Cover Sheet.

____
Signature

____
Print/Type Name & Signer's Relation to Case

(Added Dec. 1, 2009.)

COMMITTEE NOTES ON RULES—2009

This form is new. It gathers certain financial information, including information necessary for the court to determine whether a reaffirmation agreement creates a presumption of undue hardship under §524(m) of the Code, and it allows the debtor to provide additional information that may rebut such a presumption.

To implement the requirements of Bankruptcy Rule 4008(b), the form also provides for a disclosure of any differences between the income and expenses reported on schedules I and J and the income and expenses reported in the debtor's statement in support of the reaffirmation agreement, together with an explanation of any such differences.

Finally, the form requires a certification that the information supplied is true and correct.

Made in United States
Orlando, FL
05 November 2026

90231409R00350